Crossfire

Crossfire

An Argument Rhetoric and Reader

Second Edition

Gary Goshgarian
Northeastern University

Kathleen Krueger

 LONGMAN

An imprint of Addison Wesley Longman, Inc.

New York • Reading, Massachusetts • Menlo Park, California • Harlow, England
Don Mills, Ontario • Sydney • Mexico City • Madrid • Amsterdam

Executive Editor: Anne Elizabeth Smith
Developmental Editor: Leslie Taggart
Project Coordination and Text Design: Ruttle, Shaw & Wetherill, Inc.
Cover Design: Kay Petronio
Electronic Production Manager: Angel Gonzalez Jr.
Manufacturing Manager: Willie Lane
Printer and Binder: R. R. Donnelley & Sons Company
Cover Printer: The Lehigh Press, Inc.

For permission to use copyrighted material, grateful acknowledgment is made to the copyright holders on pp. 682–685, which are hereby made part of this copyright page.

Library of Congress Cataloging-in-Publication Data
Crossfire: an argument rhetoric and reader / [edited by] Gary Goshgarian,
   Kathleen Krueger. —2nd ed.
     p.   cm.
   Includes index.
   ISBN 0–673–98006–5. — ISBN 0–673–98007–3 (instructor's manual)
   1. English language—Rhetoric.   2. Persuasion (Rhetoric).
3. College readers.   I. Goshgarian, Gary.   II. Krueger, Kathleen.
PE1431.C76   1996
808' .0427—dc20   96–1365
                                                     CIP

2345678910—DOC—999897

BRIEF CONTENTS

CONTENTS

PREFACE

Crossfire: An Argument Rhetoric and Reader is about arguments: how to read them and how to write them. As indicated by the title, the book has two parts. The "rhetoric" section consists of eight chapters explaining the strategies of writing persuasively. The "reader" section, consists of eight thematic units containing 78 arguments in action—an assortment of provocative contemporary debates. As you will see, the two parts are interrelated. The rhetoric chapters illustrate how to argue effectively by analyzing sample arguments from professional writers and students. Each of the essays contained in the reader section has prereading and postreading exercises that ask students to apply what they have learned about argumentation in the rhetoric chapters. The efforts to link the reading and writing processes reflect our fundamental belief that the two skills are bound and that students learn how to write persuasively by reading critically.

Why the focus on arguments? There are two good reasons. First, skillful argumentation draws on highly developed thought processes. It requires clear thinking, a strong grasp of an issue, awareness of opposing points of view, the ability to distinguish between opinion and fact, the use of solid supporting evidence, a clear sense of one's audience, logical organization, and a well-reasoned conclusion. Second, most pieces of writing produced by college students will be exercises in persuasion—efforts to demonstrate the validity of an opinion, observation, or idea. This is true whether one is discussing tragic irony in *Oedipus Rex*, analyzing the causes of World War I, explaining the strengths of a favorite movie, or writing a letter to a school newspaper protesting next year's tuition increase. Even in a lab report on the refraction of light, a writer needs to convince the instructor of the validity of the findings. Furthermore, the need for these skills doesn't end with graduation. The demands for persuasive writing will extend into professional life every time one is required to write a business letter, proposal, project report, or memorandum.

Organization of the Book

The Rhetoric

Since our overall goal is to stimulate student's thinking about how issues are argued, we organized the rhetoric chapters so that they emphasize the actual process of writing arguments, moving from prewriting "brainstorming" exercises to shaping the final product. Each of the eight chapters focuses on a particular facet or principle of argumentation. The hierarchical nature of these chapters allows students to build on the knowledge of the previous chapter to work through the next. At the end of each chapter, there are exercises keyed to the particular feature of argument addressed therein, thus allowing students to test themselves immediately on those features.

Chapter 1 offers an overview of argumentation, clarifying arguable topics from those that are not. Chapter 2 discusses how to begin writing arguments. Here we have emphasized brainstorming techniques to develop argumentative topics as well as provided suggestions on refining topics and anticipating opposing views. Chapter 3 focuses on ways to organize the material the writer has gathered. Here we distinguish two basic kinds of arguments—positions and proposals—with some advice on how to outline each. Chapter 4 moves outward to readers, encouraging students to think about the different kinds of audiences they may have to address. This chapter stresses the importance of appreciating the views and needs of others (that there are more sides to an argument than one's own) and of establishing the arguer's credibility. Chapter 5 is concerned with evidence. How writers create persuasive arguments or "prove" their claims largely depends on how well they marshal evidence supporting what they argue—that is, facts, testimony, statistics, and observations—without which their assertions are simply weak generalizations. Chapter 6 introduces the socially constructed Toulmin model of logic. Chapter 7 summarizes how to read arguments and test them for logical fallacies.

Chapter 8, "Documenting Arguments," is a handbook on writing argumentation research papers. Here we discuss how to find sources in the library, how to provide readers with documentation of supporting evidence in both MLA and APA styles, and the proper format of research papers, including the importance and use of endnotes, references, bibliographies, quotations, and so on. As in most of the preceding chapters, we include here samples of student writing, one of which is a fully documented research paper written in MLA style.

The Readings

The 69 contemporary and 9 classical essays that constitute the readings cover a wide range of provocative issues that we think will interest students and instructors alike. Our hope is that the selections will get students thinking about the various debates going on in their world, acquainting them with current controversial issues and diverse points of view. But more than that, we hope the readings will generate lively class discussions, inviting students into the debates so as to broaden their thinking and inspire their writing. In short, we hope to make students part of the "crossfire" exchange of views that charge our age.

The 69 contemporary essays are organized according to 7 broad thematic chapters: "Gender Identity," "Race and Ethnicity," "Social Issues," "Ethical and Moral Issues," "Freedom of Expression," "Education," and "Advertising." Each chapter is subdivided into three or four specific topical categories containing two or more essays that take different argumentative slants on a particular issue. Our intention is to demonstrate that most controversial subjects have multiple facets and cannot be reduced to an either-or stand. For instance, of the 8 essays in Chapter 13, "Freedom of Expression," three clustered under "Racial Slurs" question what to do about racist language, each pressing for a different solution. While Charles R. Lawrence III argues for censorship and Nat Hentoff argues for freedom of expression, Garry Wills offers a solution that falls midway between the two. Even such hotly controversial issues as abortion don't always draw clear battle lines. Anna Quindlen's essay, "Some Thoughts About Abortion" (in Chapter 12, "Social Issues"), for example, reveals the anguishing ambivalence of many people torn between the legal and moral aspects of a woman's right to terminate a pregnancy.

Although it is true that many arguments cannot be reduced to simple pro-or-con stances—that there are shades of gray—some issues tend to invite strong oppositions. Consider capital punishment. Most people are either for it or against it. Thus, Chapters 9–15 end with a section called "Oppositions," which pit head-to-head two essays taking opposite stands on a particular issue—for example, capital punishment, immigration policy, sex in advertising, and feminism. We hope that these "Oppositions" pieces inspire students to defend or attack either position while providing the shades of gray. It is our belief that beginning writers need to appreciate a dichotomy on issues before branching out to finer distinctions.

All of the essays in Chapters 9–15 represent not only a wide range of provocative topics but different kinds of argumentative strategies. Some pieces persuade with iron-clad logic. Others are strong emotional appeals. Still others base their cases on ethical or moral grounds. Some are quiet, subtle pieces. And some are impassioned pleas.

The final unit of essays, "Arguments That Shaped History," includes nine classical pieces ranging from Plato to Martin Luther King, Jr. Besides reflecting a diversity of argumentation strategies, these selections are powerful examples of persuasion that have proven their timeless value in the classroom. Their words are as relevant today as when they were composed.

Study Apparatus

In order to help students get the most out of the readings, we have included a variety of apparatus. First, each of the reading chapters opens with an introduction underscoring the importance of the essays and the rationale behind their selection. Second, each essay is preceded by an introduction containing thematic and biographic information as well as questions to consider before and during the actual reading process. Third, each essay is followed by a set of review questions. "Topical Considerations" focus on important matters of content, with an emphasis on the student's own experience, beliefs, and values. "Rhetorical Considerations" include a number of questions about the different motives and writing strategies of the authors—questions intended to stimulate analytical thinking about the logic, organization, and quality of supporting evidence as well as the adequate representation of opposing views. Because all of the arguments are clustered in groups of two or more, we have tried to frame questions of comparison and contrast. "Writing Assignments" contain suggested expository and research paper topics in response to the issues covered in the essays. Finally, at the end of the book is a glossary of rhetorical terms used throughout the text.

New to This Edition

The wide acceptance of our first edition of *Crossfire: An Argument Rhetoric and Reader* is more than gratifying. It clearly suggests that our original efforts at making an accessible argumentation text were not lost. Nonetheless, this second edition is, we think, even better as it reflects the insights and suggestions of many of the instructors and students who used the first edition. Those particular features that people found most useful we left unchanged; we made careful revisions where improvement was needed. We have also been guided by some of the exciting research being done in composition studies in the past few years.

Although our principles and approach have remained the same in the Rhetoric chapters (1–8), we have made a number of changes. In Chapter 1, "Understanding Persuasion," we have added a detailed discussion of critical reading. We demonstrate the vital connection between critical reading and critical writing: The more adept one becomes at analyzing and reacting to another's written work, the better one is at analyzing and reacting to one's own. In this chapter we offer some clear tips on how to read critically, demonstrating each in detail with a critical analysis of a sample essay. In the Exercises, we ask students to critically read a sample essay, applying the strategies outlined in the chapter.

Chapter 2, "Finding Arguments," contains new graphics and some helpful exercises. In Chapter 3, "Shaping Arguments," the discussion of outlines has been expanded with more samples. As with all the rhetoric chapters, the presentation has been enhanced with boxes of tips and important points.

Chapter 4, "Addressing Audiences," has been significantly expanded. Although instructors liked the discussion of different audiences, they requested more detailed discussion of language. In response, we added a new section, "Choosing Your Words," in which we discuss the importance of using language that is appropriate and accurate. We begin with a detailed explanation of the difference between denotation and connotation. With the aid of charts and boxes, we then discuss the importance of replacing abstract and vague language with concrete and specific words. Toward the end of the chapter is a section on figurative language and a discussion of metaphors, similes, personification, euphemisms and clichés. The chapter closes on the importance of defining technical terms and creating stipulative definitions of familiar ones. Reflecting the expansion of the chapter are the new exercises that ask students to apply what they have learned to a variety of samples, including writing a full essay.

Chapter 5, "Using Evidence," has been reorganized and expanded. The discussion of supporting evidence now includes a discussion of the values of drawing on one's own experience as evidence. We also explain, with examples, how arguments can manipulate audience response by use of slanted evidence. And as in other chapters, boxes and charts enhance the opportunities for quick reference and review.

Chapter 6, "Establishing Claims: Thinking Like a Skeptic," has been completely revised; it now focuses on the Toulmin model of argument and provides analyses of two sample essays, one written by a student. Chapter 7, which examines logical fallacies, has been expanded with more examples and exercises.

Chapter 8, "Documenting Arguments," keeps the user-friendly, step-by-step process which so many instructors and students found useful. The revised chapter adds coverage of primary and secondary research sources and much specific information on finding information in the library, in the community, and on-line. A new student research paper prepared in MLA (4th edition) style has been added, and new entries in the MLA and APA style guide cover how to document electronic sources.

Part Two, Current Debates, contains 69 essays, over a third of which are new to this edition, and most written since the last. Those essays from the first edition that proved dated or no longer useful to students and instructors were dropped. We have retained those essays that were popular, while adding essays that reflect some recent public controversies and which we feel would have special appeal to students: teenage pregnancy, euthanasia, legalization of drugs, movie and television violence, and the classroom experience.

Acknowledgments

There are many people who at the very least deserve our acknowledgment and gratitude. Although it is impossible to thank all of them, there are some for whose help we are particularly grateful. First we would like to thank many colleagues and friends who supported us in this project and whose suggestions proved most useful: Stuart Peterfreund, Becky Mallaghan, Tricia O'Neill, and Janet Carr of the Department of English at Northeastern University. We would also like to thank those instructors who answered lenghty questionnaires on the first edition and who supplied many helpful comments and suggestions for the second. They are:

Nancy Blattner, Southeast Missouri State University
Robert Canter, Virginia Polytechnic University
Mark Christensen, Bemedji State University
Mary Lou Cutrera, Louisiana State University
James Hissom, West Virginia Institute of Technology
Susan Injejikian, Glendale Community College
Rebecca Innocent, Southern Methodist University
Susan D. Irvin, Indiana University
Ausra Kubilius, New Hampshire College
Lee McKnight, Stillman College
Vicki Mudry, University of Michigan
Paul H. Schmidt, Georgia State University
Diane Scott, Mesa College
Becky Stamm, Columbus State Community College

Al Young, University of Wisconsin, Stevens Point
Karen Waters, Marymount College
Charles Wilbert, New Hampshire College

A special thanks goes out to Robert Canter who helped in revising some of the rhetorical chapters, and to Virginia Tiefel, who updated our research information. For their assistance in putting together the study apparatus for the essays, we would like to thank Jeanne Phoenix Laurel, Phebe Jensen, and Elizabeth Swanson. Their lively and imaginative questions and writing assignments will no doubt provide some stimulating responses from students in the classroom and on paper.

We would also like to express our gratitude to several people at Harper-Collins, especially our editor Patricia Rossi, on whose good cheer and wisdom we could always count; our developmental editor, Leslie Taggart, who helped clarify our thoughts and who contributed some fine words and ideas of her own; Lynn Cattafi, Ms. Rossi's ever-efficient assistant, and Thomas J. Conville, III, our project manager.

Finally, our fond appreciation to Jean Hagan, Jane Graham, Larry Rosenblum, Tweedy Watkins, and Robert and Alice Krueger for their endless support, and to Nathan and David Goshgarian for their patience.

Gary Goshgarian
Kathleen Krueger

PART ONE

STRATEGIES FOR WRITING ARGUMENTS

CHAPTER

1

UNDERSTANDING PERSUASION

Thinking Like a Critic

Think of the times in the course of a single day someone tries to convince you of something. Your roommate wants to borrow your hair dryer, a friend tries to persuade you to see this movie instead of that movie next weekend, or your English instructor urges you to get your next paper in on time. When you pick up a magazine or turn on the radio or television, you are relentlessly barraged by advertisements, all calculated to separate you from your money.

You are also confronted with the more weighty issues of our world—issues that require serious deliberation or demand decisions. A campus debate rages over attempts to regulate "hurtful" kinds of expression. Heated political ads vie to persuade you to vote for Candidate Lopez instead of Candidate Gallagher. A religious evangelist appears on your doorstep to convince you to alter your lifestyle and embrace salvation. A homeless person asks for a handout. A news report on the bombing of an abortion clinic sets off a debate between you and friends on what's right and wrong.

In fact, nearly everywhere you turn, you'll find some issue being contested. And, if you watch closely, you may discover something else. The people who are most successful in these debates—those whose points of view end up getting the most exposure and who have the most influence on decisions—are the people who understand how to *persuade* others. They have mastered the power of *argument* in order to shape their worlds. Access to those powers of persuasion aren't governed solely by one's age or background or income; anyone can learn the techniques needed to create successful arguments.

This book is designed to help you achieve two goals: (1) to think critically about the power of other people's arguments; (2) to achieve persuasive results in your own arguments.

Argument

Broadly speaking, *persuasion* means influencing someone to do something. It takes many forms: fast-paced glittering ads, high-flying promises from salespeople, emotional or ethical appeals from charity groups, even physical threats. What will concern us in this book is **argument**—the form of persuasion that relies on reasoning and thoughtful appeal to convince people to do what the arguer wants. Rhetorical arguments may contain glitter, promises, emotional appeals, and even veiled threats; but their chief power comes from the arguer's ability to convince people through language.

For most of us, the word *argument* summons an image of people having a noisy confrontation, as you frequently see on televised "debate" shows. As negative as that image may be, it contains the essential elements of argument: Somebody with a strong opinion tries to demonstrate the effectiveness of that view, hoping to persuade others to change positions or take a particular course of action. What our image of argument may not include, however, are some of the underlying keys to argumentative success: respecting opposing points of view, recognizing points of agreement, and appealing to people's desire to associate with the accepted point of view on any topic.

Because this is a book about writing, we'll be concentrating on the aspects of persuasion that most apply in writing, as opposed to those that work best in other forms (advertisements or oral appeals, for instance). Although a written argument can be passionate, emotional, or even hurtful, a good one will demonstrate a rhetorical foundation of clear thinking, logical development, and solid supporting evidence to persuade a reader that one's view is worth hearing. The ultimate object might be to convince readers to change their thinking on an issue. But that does not always happen. However, if you can construct a well-fashioned argument, at least you will win the consideration and respect of your audience. You can get your consumers to listen to your "pitch."

One misconception some people have is that all arguments are *won* or *lost*. That may be true in debates, but in real life few arguments are decided so clearly. A reasonable goal for written argument is to get your readers to give your point of view a thoughtful hearing. If you are obsessed with "winning" every argument, you will end up frustrated and disappointed. If you concentrate, instead, on learning how to get readers to pay careful attention to what you say, you will become more persuasive—and get better results. It's important at the outset to put aside the winners/losers mindset if you want to become more persuasive.

Most of what you write in college and beyond will attempt to persuade someone that what you have to say is worthy of consideration, whether it's a paper stating your views on immigration laws, an analysis of "madness" in *King Lear*, a letter to the editor of your school newspaper regarding women's varsity basketball, or a lab report on the solubility of salt. The same demands of persuasion and argument will carry over into your professional life. Such writing might be in the form of progress reports on students or colleagues, legal briefs, business reports, medical evaluations, memos to colleagues, results of a technical study or scientific experiment, proposals, maybe even a sales speech. In searching for a job or career, you might have to sell yourself in letters of inquiry.

The success or failure of those attempts will strongly depend on how well you argue your case. Therefore, it's important that as a college student you learn the skills of writing persuasive arguments. Even if you never write another argument, you will read and hear them the rest of your life.

What Makes an Argument?

Arguments, in a sense, underlie nearly all forms of writing. Whenever you express ideas, you are attempting to persuade somebody to agree with you. However, not every matter can be formally argued. Nor are some things worth the effort. So, before we go on to discuss the different strategies, we should make clear what subjects do and do not lend themselves to argument.

Facts Are Not Arguable

Because **facts** are readily verifiable, they can't be argued. Of course, people might dispute a fact. For instance, you might disagree with a friend's claim that Thomas Jefferson was the second president of the United States. But to settle your dispute, all you have to do is consult an encyclopedia. What makes a fact a fact and, thus, inarguable, is that it has only one answer. It occurs in time and space and cannot be disputed. A fact either *is* or *is not* something. Thomas Jefferson was the third president of the United States, not the second. John Adams was the second. Those are facts. So are the following statements:

- The distance between Boston and New York City is 214 miles.
- Martin Luther King, Jr.'s Birthday is not celebrated in all 50 states.
- I got a 91 on my math test.
- The Washington Monument is 555 feet high.
- The Japanese smoke more cigarettes per capita than any other people on earth.
- My dog Fred died a year ago.
- Canada borders the United States to the North.

All that is required to prove or disprove any of these statements is to check with some authority for the right answer. Sometimes facts are not easily verifiable. For instance, "Yesterday, 1,212,031 babies were born in the world." Or, "More people have black hair than any other color." These statements may be true, but it would be a daunting, if not impossible, challenge to prove them. And what would be the point?

Opinions Based on Personal Taste or Preference Are Not Arguable

Conflicting opinions are the basis of all argument. However, you must be careful to distinguish between opinions based on personal taste and opinions based on judgments. Someone who asks your "opinion" about which color shoes to buy is simply seeking your color preference—black versus brown, say. If someone asks your "opinion" of a certain movie, the matter could be more complicated.

Beyond whether or not you liked it, what might be sought is your aesthetic evaluation of the film: a judgment about the quality of acting, directing, cinematography, set design—all measured by critical standards you've developed over years of moviegoing. Should you be asked your "opinion" of voluntary euthanasia, your response would probably focus on moral and ethical questions: Is the quality of life more important than the duration of life? What, if any, circumstances justify the taking of a life? Who should make so weighty a decision—the patient, the patient's family, the attending physician, a health team?

The word *opinion* is commonly used to mean different things. As just illustrated, depending on the context, opinion can refer to personal preference, a reaction to or analysis of something, or an evaluation, belief, or judgment, all of which are different. In this text, we will categorize all these different possibilities as either opinions of taste or opinions of judgment.

Opinions of taste come down to personal preferences, based on subjective and, ultimately, unverifiable judgments. Each of the following statements is an opinion of taste:

- George looks good in blue.
- Pizza is my favorite food.
- Brian May of the group Queen is the greatest living rock guitarist.
- Video games are a waste of time.

Each of these statements is inarguable. Let's consider the first: "George looks good in blue." Is it a fact? Not really, since there is no objective way to measure its validity. You might like George in blue, whereas someone else might prefer him in red. Is the statement then debatable? No. Even if someone retorts, "George does *not* look good in blue," what would be the basis of argument but personal preference? And where would the counterargument go? Nowhere.

Even if a particular preference were backed by strong feelings, it would not be worth debating, nor might you sway someone to your opinion. For instance, let's say you make the statement that you never eat hamburger. You offer the following as reasons:

1. You're disgusted by the sight of ground-up red meat.
2. When the meat is cooked, its smell disgusts you.
3. Hamburgers remind you of the terrible argument that broke out at a family barbecue some years ago.

4. You once got very sick after eating meat loaf.
5. You think beef cattle are the dirtiest of farm animals.

Even with all these "reasons" to support your point of view, you have not constructed an argument that goes beyond your own personal preference. In fact, the
"reasons" you cite are themselves grounded in personal preferences. They amount
to explanations rather than an argument. The same is true of the statements about
pizza, musicians, and video games.

Opinions Based on Judgments Are Arguable

An *opinion of judgment* is one that weighs the pros and cons of an issue and determines their relative worth. That "something" might be a book, a song, or public issue, such as capital punishment. Such an opinion represents a position on an issue
that is measured against standards other than those of personal taste—standards
that are rooted in values and beliefs of our culture: what's true and false, right and
wrong, good and bad, better and worse. Consequently, such an opinion is arguable.

In other words, personal opinions or personal preferences can be transformed into bona fide arguments. Let's return to the example of hamburger. Suppose you want to turn your own dislike for ground meat into a paper persuading
others to give up eating beef. There are several approaches you can take to make a
convincing argument. For one, you can take a health slant, arguing that vegetarians
have lower mortality rates than people whose diets are high in animal fat and cholesterol; or that the ingestion of all the hormones in beef increase the risks of cancer.
You might even take an environmental approach, pointing out that the more beef
we eat, the more we encourage the conversion of woodlands and rain forests into
grazing land, thus destroying countless animals and their habitats. You can even
take an ethical stand, arguing from an animal-rights point of view that intensive
farming practices create inhumane treatment of animals—that is, crowding, force-
feeding, and force-breeding. You might also argue that the killing of animals is
morally wrong.

The point is that personal opinions can be starting points for viable arguments. But those opinions must be developed according to recognizable standards
of values and beliefs.

Critical Reading

Reading through these chapters you will notice that we stress the need for you to
empathize with your readers: to put yourself in their place, figure out what their
concerns and values are, and strategically present information that will best persuade them. In return, you hope that they will be empathetic readers, willing to
keep open minds and give you, the writer, the benefit of the doubt.

When you read the arguments of others, it's very tempting to read *only* in
this empathic manner, rather than questioning what the writer tells you. It's easier

to read empathically than any other way. But empathic reading only encourages a surface reading and, therefore, won't help you dissect a writer's ideas. Critical reading does.

But what is **critical reading**? If you've ever read a magazine article, newspaper editorial or a piece of advertising and found yourself questioning the claims of the authors, you have already exercised the basics of critical reading: You looked beneath the surface of words and thought about their meaning and significance. You asked the authors questions such as:

- What did you mean by that?
- Can you back up that statement?
- How do you define that term?
- So what?
- How did you draw that conclusion?
- Do all experts agree?
- Isn't this evidence dated?

You made such statements as:

- Other experts would disagree.
- What's not true.
- You're contradicting yourself.
- I see your point, but I don't agree.
- That's not a good choice of words.
- You're jumping to conclusions.
- Good point. I never thought of that.
- This is an extreme view.

Whether conscious or unconscious, such responses indicated that you were thinking *critically* about what you read. You were weighing claims, asking for definitions, evaluating information, looking for proofs, questioning assumptions, and making judgments. In short, you were processing another's words, not just taking them in.

Why Read Critically?

When you read critically you think critically. And that means instead of blindly accepting what's written on a page, you separate yourself from the text and decide for yourself what is or is not important or logical or right. And you do so because you bring to your reading your own perspective, experience, education, and personal values, as well as your powers of comprehension and analysis.

Critical reading is an active process of discovery. You discover where an author stands on an issue; you discover the strengths and weaknesses of the author's argument; and you decide which side outweighs the other. The end result is that you have a better understanding of the issue. By asking questions of the author, by analyzing where the author stands with respect to other views of the issue, including your own, you actively enter the debate. This way, reading becomes an active and reactive process. Not only does critical reading sharpen your focus on an issue, but it heightens your ability to absorb arguments. And ultimately this will lead to being a better writer, because critical reading is the first step to critical writing. Good writers look at the written word the way a carpenter looks at a house—they study the fine details and the way details connect and create the whole. It's the same with critical reading. The better you become at analyzing and reacting to another's written work, the better you become at analyzing and reacting to your own: Is it logical? Do my points come across clearly? Are my examples solid enough? Is this the best wording? Is my conclusion persuasive? In other words, critical reading will help you to train the same critical eye to evaluate your own writing, thereby making you both a better reader and a better writer.

Even though you already employ many strategies of critical reading, we'd like to offer you some techniques to make you an even better critical reader.

Preview: To Read Critically . . .

- Summarize what you read
- Outline what you read
- Analyze what you read
- Argue with what you read
- Annotate what you read

SAMPLE ARGUMENT FOR ANALYSIS

Perils of Prohibition
Elizabeth M. Whelan

1   My colleagues at the Harvard School of Public Health, where I studied preventive medicine, deserve high praise for their recent study on teenage drinking. What they found in their survey of college students was that they drink "early and . . . often," frequently to the point of getting ill.

2   As a public-health scientist with a daughter, Christine, heading to college this fall, I have professional and personal concerns about teen binge drinking. It is imperative that we explore *why* so many young people abuse alcohol. From my own study of the effects of alcohol restrictions and my observations of Christine and her friends' predicament about drinking, I believe that today's laws are unrealistic. Prohibiting the sale of liquor to responsible young adults creates an atmosphere where binge drinking and alcohol abuse have

become a problem. American teens, unlike their European peers, don't learn how to drink gradually, safely, and in moderation.

3   Alcohol is widely accepted and enjoyed in our culture. Studies show that moderate drinking can be good for you. But we legally proscribe alcohol until the age of 21 (why not 30 or 45?). Christine and her classmates can drive cars, fly planes, marry, vote, pay taxes, take out loans and risk their lives as members of the U.S. armed forces. But laws in all 50 states say that no alcoholic beverages may be sold to anyone until that magic 21st birthday. We didn't always have a national "21" rule. When I was in college, in the mid-'60s, the drinking age varied from state to state. This posed its own risks, with underage students crossing state lines to get a legal drink.

4   In parts of the Western world, moderate drinking by teenagers and even children under their parents' supervision is a given. Though the per capita consumption of alcohol in France, Spain and Portugal is higher than in the United States, the rate of alcoholism and alcohol abuse is lower. A glass of wine at dinner is normal practice. Kids learn to regard moderate drinking as an enjoyable family activity rather than as something they have to sneak away to do. Banning drinking by young people makes it a badge of adulthood—a tantalizing forbidden fruit.

5   Christine and her teenage friends like to go out with a group to a club, comedy show or sports bar to watch the game. But teens today have to go on the sly with fake IDs and the fear of getting caught. Otherwise, they're denied admittance to most places and left to hang out on the street. That's hardly a safer alternative. Christine and her classmates now find themselves in a legal no man's land. At 18, they're considered adults. Yet when they want to enjoy a drink like other adults, they are, as they put it, "disenfranchised."

6   Comparing my daughter's dilemma with my own as an "underage" college student, I see a difference—and one that I think has exacerbated the current dilemma. Today's teens are far more sophisticated than we were. They're treated less like children and have more responsibilities than we did. This makes the 21 restriction seem anachronistic.

7   For the past few years, my husband and I have been preparing Christine for college life and the inevitable partying—read keg of beer—that goes with it. Last year, a young friend with no drinking experience was violently ill for days after he was introduced to "clear liquids in small glasses" during freshman orientation. We want our daughter to learn how to drink sensibly and avoid this pitfall. Starting at the age of 14, we invited her to join us for a glass of champagne with dinner. She'd tried it once before, thought it was "yucky" and declined. A year later, she enjoyed sampling wine at family meals.

8   When, at 16, she asked for a Mudslide (a bottled chocolate-milk-and-rum concoction), we used the opportunity to discuss it with her. We explained the alcohol content, told her the alcohol level is lower when the drink is blended with ice and compared it with a glass of wine. Since the drink of choice on campus is beer, we contrasted its potency with wine and hard liquor and stressed the importance of not drinking on an empty stomach.

9   Our purpose was to encourage her to know the alcohol content of what she is served. We want her to experience the effects of liquor in her own home, not on the highway and not for the first time during a college orientation week with free-flowing suds. Although Christine doesn't drive yet, we regularly reinforce the concept of choosing a designated driver. Happily, that already seems a widely accepted practice among our daughter's friends who drink.

10   We recently visited the Ivy League school Christine will attend in the fall. While we were there, we read a story in the college paper about a student who was nearly electrocuted when, in a drunken state, he climbed on top of a moving train at a railroad station near the campus. The student survived, but three of his limbs were later amputated. This incident reminded me of a tragic death on another campus. An intoxicated student maneuvered himself into a chimney. He was found three days later when frat brothers tried to light a fire in the fireplace. By then he was dead.

11   These tragedies are just two examples of our failure to teach young people how to use alcohol prudently. If 18-year-olds don't have legal access to even a beer at a public place, they have no experience handling liquor on their own. They feel "liberated" when they arrive on campus. With no parents to stop them, they have a "let's make up for lost time" attitude. The result: binge drinking.

12   We should make access to alcohol legal at 18. At the same time, we should come down much harder on alcohol abusers and drunk drivers of all ages. We should intensify our efforts at alcohol education for adolescents. We want them to understand that it is perfectly OK not to drink. But if they do, alcohol should be consumed in moderation.

13   After all, we choose to teach our children about safe sex, including the benefits of teen abstinence. Why, then, can't we—schools and parents alike—teach them about safe drinking?

Summarize What You Read

Perhaps the most important technique for understanding and evaluating what you read is to summarize it. This means boiling the essay down to its main points. In your journal or notebook, try to write a brief (about 100 words) synopsis of the writer's arguments, using your own words. Note the claim or thesis of the argument and the chief supporting points. It's important actually to write these points, rather than to highlight them passively with a pen or pencil, since the act of jotting down a summary helps you absorb the argument.

To demonstrate, we will apply the above techniques for critical reading to the essay, "Perils of Prohibition," which originally appeared in *Newsweek* (May 29, 1995) and which was written by Elizabeth M. Whelan, president of the American Council on Science and Health.

In the brief paragraph below, we offer a summary of Whelan's essay, being careful to use our own words rather than the author's so as to avoid plagiarism. At times, it may be impossible to avoid using the author's own words in a summary; therefore, be certain to use quotation marks.

> One reason American youths drink alcohol to excess is because of the law. Because they are prohibited from drinking alcohol until age 21, young people abuse alcohol when on their own. By contrast Europeans drink at an earlier age, yet alcohol abuse is lower than in the United States. Ironically, our eighteen-year olds can vote, marry, and serve in the military like other adults, and they are more sophisticated than their counterparts from a generation ago. Yet regarding alcohol they are treated like children. The drinking age should be lowered, and parents should, like Whelan, educate their children on moderation. Likewise, those who abuse alcohol or drive while drunk should be punished severely.

Although this paragraph seems to do a fairly good job of summarizing Whelan's essay, it took us a few tries to get it down, to reduce it to the essential points. So don't be too discouraged when trying to summarize a reading on your own.

Outline What You Read

Brief outlining of an essay is another good way to see how a writer has structured ideas. When you physically diagram the claims and the supporting evidence, you can better assess the quality of the argument and decide how persuasive it is. Chapter 3 gives a more detailed discussion of outlining an essay; but for the moment we suggest a brief and concise breakdown of an essay's components. This is done by simply jotting down a one-sentence summary of each paragraph. Sometimes brief paragraphs elaborating the same point can be lumped together:

- Point 1
- Point 2
- Point 3
- Point 4
- Point 5
- Point 6, etc.

Even though such outlines are rather primitive, they are useful because they demonstrate at a glance how the various parts of an essay are connected—that is, the organization and the sequence of ideas. Later, in Chapter 3, we show how full formal outlines are valuable at determining how the various parts of an essay are connected, whether the organization is logical and complete, if the evidence is sequenced properly, and whether or not there are any omissions or lack of proportion.

Below is a sentence outline of "Perils of Prohibition:"

- **Point 1**: Studies show that teenagers drink too much.

- **Point 2**: The author, a public-health scientist and mother, thinks that the 21 law encourages alcohol abuse and binge drinking not found in European peers.
- **Point 3**: Eighteen-year-olds can vote, drive cars, take out loans, and serve in the military like other adults, but they aren't allowed to drink like other adults.
- **Point 4**: European kids learn moderate drinking and have lower abuse problems.
- **Point 5**: The author's underage daughter and peers must sneak around the law to be allowed into "adult" bars and clubs.
- **Point 6**: The author and her husband have explained to their daughter how to drink sensibly and avoid abuse and accidents.
- **Point 7**: Some young people meet tragic ends because they never learned how to drink safely.
- **Point 8**: The drinking age should be lowered to prevent kids from binge-drinking when on their own so as to " 'make up for lost time.' "
- **Point 9**: Like safe sex, we should teach young people about safe alcohol consumption while punishing any who abuse it.

At this point you should have a fairly good grasp of the author's stand on the issue. It is now time to analyze the argument in its parts and as a whole.

Analyze What You Read

To analyze something means breaking it down into its components, examining those components up close, and evaluating their significance and how they relate as a whole. In part you already did this above by making a brief outline of an argument. But there is more, since analyzing what you read involves interpreting and evaluating the points of an argument as well as its presentation—that is, its language and structure. Ultimately, analyzing an essay after you've established the gist of the author's argument will help you understand what may not be evident at first. A close examination of the author's words will take you beneath the surface and sharpen your understanding of the issue at hand.

While there is no set procedure for analyzing an argument, we offer some specific questions you should raise when reading an essay that is trying to sway you to its view:

- What are the author's assumptions?
- What kind of audience is the author addressing?
- What are the author's purpose and intentions?
- How well does the author accomplish those purposes?
- How convincing is the evidence presented? Is it pertinent? Is it reliable? Is it specific enough? Is it sufficient? Is the evidence slanted or dated?
- How good are the sources of the evidence enlisted? Were they based on personal experience or scientific data or outside authorities?
- Did the author address opposing views on the issue?

- Is the author persuasive in his or her perspective?

Later chapters review the kinds of audiences one might address and the different types of evidence available. But for the sake of illustration, let's apply these questions to Elizabeth M. Whelan's essay.

- What are the author's assumptions?

Assumes the audience would be concerned about adolescent drinking and might be concerned about lowering the drinking age.

Assumes today's teens are more sophisticated than they were years ago.

Assumes the family should take primary responsibility to teach kids about drinking.

Assumes certain degree of reasonableness on part of kids—that is, that once they learn the dangers of alcohol they will use that information rationally and safely.

- What kind of audience is the author addressing?

Parents concerned about adolescent drinking and adolescents concerned about the high drinking age.

Members of the educated upper middle class (she attended Harvard; daughter going to Ivy League college; drinking champagne at dinner; sampling different wines).

People who take a rational approach to problems.

- What are the author's purpose and intentions?

To convince audience that inexperience and lack of education regarding alcohol can have deadly consequences.

To convince audience that the 21 law should be changed.

- How well does the author accomplish those purposes?

Offers appropriate, credible, and accessible examples of her points.

Keeps a good focus. She does not get side-tracked by issues that would cloud her argument, for example, kids who are irresponsible or who drink because they are insecure, depressed, or alcoholic.

- How convincing is the evidence presented? Is it pertinent? Is it reliable? Is it specific enough? Is it sufficient? Is the evidence slanted or dated?

In paragraph 1, author establishes her credibility by announcing her prestigious medical background. Though she never directly draws on it, this reference instantly suggests that Whelan has scientific data at hand and understands the facts and studies. In other words, she's more than just a concerned mother.

Her evidence of alcohol-related tragedies underscores the seriousness of the issue and supports her assertion that abuse has lethal consequences.

However, her evidence is projected—that is, it's based on what could happen if certain measures were taken. Instead of drawing on research studies, she assumes that tragedies would be reduced if young people were properly educated. She does not address alcohol abuse based on depression, peer pressure, addiction, and youthful indiscretion.

- Did the author address opposing views on the issue?

  Author does not address opposing views on the issue. She does not directly entertain the view that lowering the drinking age will only increase the problem since more adolescents will be able to drink legally.

  Author goes with the positive power of her own recommendations.

- Is the author persuasive in her perspective?

  The author is persuasive if the reader buys the view that proper family education regarding alcohol will result in rational and responsible behavior on the part of teens.

Argue with What You Read

While we break down critical reading into discrete steps, these steps will, of course, overlap in the actual process. That is, while reading this essay you were at once summarizing and evaluating Whelan's points in your head, perhaps even counterarguing them. If something strikes you as true or well said, you'll make a mental note of it. If something rubs you wrong, you'll also make mental note. You argue back as you're going along. For beginning writers, a good strategy is to convert that automatic mental response into actual notetaking.

In your journal or notebook (or, as suggested below, in the margins of the text), question and challenge the writer. Jot down any points in the essay that do not measure up to your expectations or personal views. Note anything you are skeptical about. Scratch down any questions you have about the claims, views, or evidence. If some point or conclusion seems forced or unfounded, record it and briefly explain why. The more skeptical and questioning you are, the better reader you are. Likewise, make note of what features of the essay impressed you—outstanding points, interesting wording, clever or amusing phrases or allusions, particular references, the general structure of the piece. Also record what you learned from the reading and what aspects about the issue you would like to learn more about.

Of course, you may not feel qualified to pass judgment on an author's views, especially if the author is a professional writer or expert on a particular subject.

Sometimes the issue being argued might be too technical, or you may not feel as informed as you'd like to be to make critical evaluations. Nonetheless, you are an intelligent person with an instinct to determine if an argument is sound, logical, and convincing. What you can do in such instances—and another good habit to get into—is think of other views on the issue. If you've read or heard opposing views, jot them down. Even if you haven't, the essay should contain some reference to the opposition from which you could draw a counterposition.

Let's return to Whelan's essay. While it's theoretically possible to argue with every sentence in the piece, let's select a couple of key points that may have struck you as presumptuous, overstated, or inconsistent with your own experience.

In paragraph 3, for example, Whelan makes the point that kids have to wait until they are 21 years old to drink legally although they're considered adults in many other important ways:

> Christine and her classmates can drive cars, fly planes, marry, vote, pay taxes, take out loans and risk their lives as members of the U.S. armed forces.

While these potentials are true, you might wonder what percentage of your own classmates fly planes, pay taxes, are married, and currently risk their lives in the military. In other words, just how realistic are her claims regarding the adult responsibilities of today's 18-year-olds? In fact, from what Whelan says about Christine and her friends, some readers might think that today's kids are more indulged and, thus, less responsible.

Or, in paragraph 5 look at Whelan's assumption that Christine and her friends are reasonable—that they will be able "to enjoy a drink" like an adult. This statement implies moderation and restraint and that drinking is an exercise in taste analysis as opposed to simply getting high and excited. Do you seriously think that experience and reason will make adolescents drink safely? Or that ignorance and inexperience are the only reasons behind alcohol abuse? If you don't agree with the author's assumptions here, you should jot down why. You can make notes in your notebook or journal, as well as on the essay as you read, as explained below.

Annotate What You Read

A good habit to form when reading an essay is underlining (or highlighting) key passages and making marginal notes. (If you do not own the publication the essay appears in, or choose not to mark it up, make a photocopy of the piece.) We recommend doing this on the second or third reading, once you've gotten a handle on the essay's general ideas.

We don't have any specific guidelines for annotation except whatever suits you best. You can write full sentences of response, or some shorthand codes. Sometimes "Why?" or "True" or "NO!" will be enough to help you respond to a writer's claims and position. If you come across a word or reference that is unfamiliar to you, underline or circle it. Once you've located the main thesis or claim, highlight or underline it and jot "CLAIM" in the margin. Notice the annotations on Figure 1.1.

3   Alcohol is widely accepted and enjoyed in our culture. Studies show that moderate drinking can be good for you. But we legally proscribe alcohol until the age of 21 (why not 30 or 45?). Christine and her classmates can drive cars, fly planes, marry, vote, pay taxes, take out loans and risk their lives as members of the U.S. armed forces. But laws in all 50 states say that no alcoholic beverages may be sold to anyone until that magic 21st birthday. We didn't always have a national "21" rule. When I was in college, in the mid-'60s, the drinking age varied from state to state. This posed its own risks, with underage students crossing state lines to get a legal drink.

— How? Such as?

} Typical teenages?

} Is this relevant?

4   In parts of the Western world, moderate drinking by teenagers and even children under their parents' supervision is a given. Though the per capita consumption of alcohol in France, Spain and Portugal is higher than in the United States, the rate of alcoholism and alcohol abuse is lower. A glass of wine at dinner is normal practice. Kids learn to regard moderate drinking as an enjoyable family activity rather than as something they have to sneak away to do. Banning drinking by young people makes it a badge for adulthood—a tantalizing forbidden fruit.

— How much lower?

Key Point

5   Christine and her teenage friends like to go out with a group to a club, comedy show or sports bar to watch the game. But teens today have to go on the sly with fake IDs and the fear of getting caught. Otherwise, they're denied admittance to most places and left to hang out on the street. That's hardly a safer alternative. Christine and her classmates now find themselves in a legal no man's land. At 18, they're considered adults. Yet when they want to enjoy a drink like other adults, they are, as they put it, "disenfranchised."

> True!

— meaning?

6   Comparing my daughter's dilemma with my own as an "underage" college student, I see a difference—and one that I think has exacerbated the current dilemma. Today's teens are far more sophisticated than we were. They're treated less like children and have more responsibilities than we did. This makes the 21 restriction seem anachronistic.

— How so?

— meaning?

Figure 1.1

The Slants of Argument

We've already talked about how arguments are produced by people for various reasons and audiences. As this book develops, we will look at argument and persuasion from a series of "slants": as matters for writers, architects, readers, advocates, skeptics, cross-examiners, and researchers. The truth is, people who write and read arguments (i.e., just about everybody) wear all of these "hats" in the persuasive process—sometimes more than one at a time. But to make things easier for you as students of argument and persuasion, we have separated each slant so that you can consider it in more detail. As you work through the chapters, think carefully about what "hat" you're wearing—but don't forget the others are important too!

EXERCISES

1. Make a census of some of the arguments you are exposed to in the course of a day. List these in a notebook that you'll be keeping throughout this term. If you are working in groups in your classroom, compare results with your group members.

2. Classify the results of the census in exercise 1 into those that are arguable versus those that are nonarguable. Which kinds of argument do you face most often? Which least often? Based on your census, what assumptions can you make about the roles persuasion plays in your community?

3. Pick an argument from your census—perhaps an editorial from your local newspaper. Now apply the strategies we listed above for critical reading. That is:

   - Summarize what you read
   - Outline what you read
   - Analyze what you read
   - Argue with what you read
   - Annotate what you read

4. The following editorial was written by *Boston Globe* columnist Jeff Jacoby. Read it carefully, making notes or annotations. Then follow the directions and answer the questions that follow.

SAMPLE ARGUMENT FOR ANALYSIS

Why So Much Aid for AIDS?
Jeff Jacoby

1   Jesse Helms could have done without the vitriol. Even if he shares a common view that homosexual acts are distasteful and unnatural, it wasn't necessary or

gentlemanly to say so, at least not in a newspaper interview, and particularly not when talking about people who have AIDS. The senator from North Caroline (annual tobacco crop: 595 million pounds) would never describe lung cancer patients as the victims of their own "deliberate, disgusting, revolting conduct," even though, as a rule, they are. He should have resisted his temptation to say it about AIDS patients.

2   Predictably, Helms' execration of homosexuals obscured the real point he had set out to make. Which was: The government is spending too much money on AIDS.

3   According to the US Public Health Service, the government will spend $2 billion this year on AIDS research and prevention ($2.7 billion, if you include funds earmarked for treatment). That compares with just $800 million allocated to heart disease. Yet AIDS will kill less than 2 percent of Americans who die this year, while heart disease will kill more than 33 percent.

4   In 15 years, AIDS has killed 270,000 Americans. Heart disease kills that many every 19 weeks. The disproportion is staggering. Is it logical—or fair—to be spending $2\frac{1}{2}$ times more money on AIDS than on heart disease, which kills 18 times as many people?

5   Last year, 40,000 people died of AIDS in the United States. That is fewer than the number who died of diabetes. Fewer than the number who died of pneumonia and flu. Fewer than the number who died of cancer—fewer, in fact, than the number who die of cancer *every month*. Yet more federal money is spent to fight AIDS than to fight any of these other diseases. Is that good public policy? Is it good science?

6   Would that there were ample funds to combat every illness to which human beings are prone. But the federal debt is severe, the demands for cures are many, and the government's dollars are limited. It is hard to see a justification for raising AIDS to a privileged status, as though it poses a graver threat than diseases that kill far more victims, and kill them just as dead.

7   This issue isn't new. In 1992, the Associated Press calculated that the US government was spending about $79,000 for every American who died of AIDS—as against only $7,300 for every death from cervical cancer, $6,300 for diabetes, $2,800 for breast cancer, $800 for prostate cancer, and $600 for stroke. "There is more money going into AIDS," the AP was told by Dr. David Denhardt, chairman of biological sciences at Rutgers University, "than any rational distribution would come up with."

8   Now Helms is fixing his attention on the matter just as Congress prepares to reauthorize the Ryan White Care Act of 1990. At stake is not only $3.6 billion (over the next five years) for the treatment of people with AIDS, but the principle that one—and only one—class of sufferers is entitled to such a subsidy. Politically, the Ryan White Act is popular. Morally, it is problematic.

9   Ryan White funds do not go for research; they save no lives. The money is used wholly for care—drugs, meals, inpatient treatment, at-home nursing. It's a blessing for those sick with AIDS, of course, but such largesse is not offered to the victims of other illnesses. "For anybody with any disease besides

AIDS, the sign on the door reads, 'Go Away!' " notes AIDS scholar Michael Fumento.   "There is no Gilda Radner Act for victims of ovarian cancer, no Ronald Reagan Act for Alzheimer's Disease patients."

10   To take care of sick people who are aged or poor, Americans created Medicare and Medicaid. Those programs do not discriminate among diseases. But Ryan White funds are reserved exclusively for AIDS patients. And the argument for creating this unique, $3.6 billion benefit for a tiny fraction of the population is—what, exactly?

11   Maybe it was possible to rationalize the enormous funding disparity in favor of AIDS back when some scientists believed that AIDS was going to "break out" into the public at large. But there has been no heterosexual breakout. Long after the point by which many alarmists expected the plague to be widespread, AIDS in America remains a disease confined almost exclusively to homosexuals, drug abusers, and their sexual partners.

12   That does not minimize the horror of AIDS, a cruel, wasting disease that cuts down victims in the prime of life. But unlike most cancers, unlike muscular dystrophy, unlike Lou Gehrig's disease, unlike schizophrenia, unlike Alzheimer's—horrors all—AIDS is a disease whose cause is not a mystery. We all know how AIDS is spread. It is hard to justify preferential treatment for a disease that can usually be prevented.

13   The life of an AIDS patient is no less precious than that of someone with any other disease. But it isn't more precious, either. What Helms ought to have said is that every AIDS patient deserves compassion and help. Then he might have added that those who claim that people with AIDS are entitled to special compassion and special help bear the burden of explaining why.

Briefly summarize Jacoby's argument here. Next make a rough outline of the piece. Reread the piece and answer the following:

- What are Jacoby's assumptions?
- What kind of audience is he addressing? Does he assume his readers are neutral toward the topic? Sympathetic? Hostile? Does he play into any prejudices of his audience?
- What are his purpose and intentions in the essay?
- How well does he accomplish those purposes?
- How convincing is the evidence he presents? Is it pertinent? Reliable? Is it specific enough? Is it sufficient? Is any of the evidence slanted or dated?
- How good are the sources of the evidence enlisted? Were they based on personal experience or scientific data or outside authorities?
- Did Jacoby address opposing views on the issue? Where, for instance?
- Is he persuasive in his perspective?

Discuss your responses in small groups to hear the range of answers your classmates have given.

CHAPTER 2

FINDING ARGUMENTS

Thinking Like a Writer

Whereas most of us have no trouble coming up with a contentious statement, or offering our opinions on some matter, somehow when we're asked to *write* an argument we feel paralyzed. Writing is such a *permanent* thing, it seems. To write something down means we have to commit ourselves to some position or proposal. We have to take a risk and let other people know what we think and feel and believe. This makes us vulnerable, and nobody likes being vulnerable. But it also makes us human.

Perhaps it will help if you think of writing not as a way of freezing what you think or believe in words but as *a way to know* what your positions and proposals may be. As such, you can see writing as a means of growth, of discovery, of exploration. It's scary being an explorer, but it's also fun and challenging. Who secretly doesn't want to be Indiana Jones, at least once in a while? So this chapter will help you see the slant of arguments that writers see. Or, as novelist E. M. Forster explained, "How will I know what I think until I've seen what I've said?"

Exploration, of course, takes time. We're not recommending a writing process that you can begin an hour before a paper is due and succeed at; rather, we're recommending what real writers do: Take time to think your writing through. (One of our collaborators has a sign over her desk: "You don't finish your writing, you just hit your deadline.") This means starting assignments early, working through all the stages, and allowing time to revise and polish your work before you submit it. Learning to write well is the same as learning to perform any other skilled activity: You have to practice your strokes or your scales to be a good tennis player or pianist, and you have to practice your craft to be a good writer. As you gain more experience, some of the stages of the writing process will go more quickly for you, on most projects. But even when you get to be a polished logician, you may find yourself writing about a topic that requires you to work out the assumptions in your argument slowly and painstakingly. That's okay. All writers do that. Welcome to the club.

The Writing Process

Many rhetorical theorists have tried to describe the writing process, but it's a little like describing snowflakes: Everyone is different. Each person has different ways of writing, especially for different jobs. Think about it for a minute. You can dash off a note to your roommate in a second, but if you're writing a job application letter, you'll probably take a great deal more time. If you only have 20 minutes to answer an essay question on a history exam, you'll get it done somehow; but give you an entire semester to write a history term paper on the same subject, and you'll probably spend several weeks (if not months) doing the same job. The length really isn't that much greater, but the assignment and your response to it dictate a different writing process.

What most people studying the writing process agree on is that almost everyone goes through four distinct stages when writing.

Incubating

When something prompts you to write (your boss tells you to do it, you get an assignment, a letter has to be answered), you spend some time either mentally or physically getting yourself ready to respond. You may make notes, gather old documents, go to the library, or stare out the window: You're *incubating* the ideas you'll use to respond to this writing stimulus.

Framing

In this stage you begin, however haltingly, to put words to paper. Some people make an outline; others leap into a draft in an attempt to get some ideas down on paper. Many people like to start by sketching out their conclusions so that they can see where their writing must take them. Others prefer the linear, start-with-the-introduction system that moves them through a task. The first goal in the framing stage, as in building a house, is to get a skeleton of the writing together so that you can start adding material to fill it out. At some point in the framing process, you also take your potential readers into account in order to get some idea of what they're expecting you to say and prepare to deliver what they want.

Reshaping

Once you have a draft framed, you're ready to do the hard work of writing: *rewriting*. At this stage, you may start moving chunks of your paper around, or making a new outline, or adding or cutting material to fill in gaps or eliminate imbalances. You'll have your readers much more clearly in mind because your goal is to please and persuade them: what you know about their wants, needs, and standards will help you decide on a final shape for your paper, even if it means throwing away nearly everything you have framed. (A bad paper that's finished is still a bad paper; that's why you need to allow time for flexibility. Writers who are pressed for time sometimes have to polish up something that's not good and hope their readers won't notice. This technique doesn't usually work.) At the reshaping stage, most good writers like to get feedback from other writers so that they get a sense of what their eventual readers will think of their writing: in a classroom situation, this usually involves exchanging drafts with classmates or having conferences with your instructor.

Polishing

To have the greatest chance of persuading your readers, your work needs to be as readable as possible. That's why, after you've reshaped it, you need to go back and smooth out the creases and bumps in your text. You may need to work on your sentence structure so that words "flow" for your readers. Or you may want to change words here and there to heighten their impact. If other people have read your paper, you may wish to act on some of their suggestions for improvement. You always need to *edit* and *proofread* what you've written so that no unnecessary "static" distracts your readers from getting the message you're trying to convey. And you have to produce a copy: either by hand writing it, typing it, or convincing your balky computer printer to spit it out.

In a nutshell, that's the writing process. Now, let's look at how you might exploit the features of that process when you start writing arguments.

Finding Topics to Argue

Every writer knows the experience of being blocked. Or of having a topic but not knowing what to say about it. Or having only one point to make about an issue. To help generate more ideas, writers need to tap both internal and external resources.

In Your Immediate Vicinity

The world around you is full of arguments; you just need to take a moment to look for them. Look at the front page and editorial pages of your campus newspaper, for instance. What's going on? Look on billboards and bulletin boards. What are people having meetings about? What changes are coming up? Listen to the conversations of people on the bus, or waiting in line at the bookstore, or in the library. What's up? Look through the magazines in your room, or at the ads on television, or even at the junk mail that fills your mailbox. What claims are people making? What are people asking you to do, or think, or wear, or look like, or feel? These are sources of potential arguments; all you have to do is become aware of them. As Thoreau once put it, "Only that day dawns to which we are awake."

In Your Larger Worlds

Don't limit yourself to campus. Often there are debates and discussions going on in your workplace, in your place of worship, on your block, in your town. You belong to a number of communities; each has its issues of interest, and in those issues you can find plenty to write about. And these environments aren't the only places you'll find sources for arguments; the world turns on proposals, positions, and controversies. It's almost impossible to turn on the radio or television today without seeing someone presenting an opinion. Make a list of the issues that interest you. What are the headlines in the newspaper? What's Congress voting on? Where are the hot spots around the globe (or in the larger universe)? Novelist Mercedes Lackey once said, when asked where she got the plots for her science fiction novels, "I just walk down the street in Oklahoma City." She is right: All a writer needs is curiosity. A sequence of questions such as "Why is that person frowning? What happened to him? Has he been unfairly treated?" can lead to a topic that's interesting to you, if you're willing to use your imagination. Don't stick to the familiar: this is all experimental territory just waiting to be explored.

Developing Argumentative Topics

Ideas alone aren't arguments, and many inexperienced writers have trouble making the jump from subject to argument. For example, you may be interested in rock and roll. That's a subject—a big one. What can you argue about it? You could ask yourself, "What are the facts about rock and roll? When did it start? How can it be defined? What differentiates, say, heavy metal from slam rock or thrash rock or grunge rock? Why are there so few well-known female rockers?" You can ask functional questions, such as "Who is the most influential figure in rock? Is rock more relevant than, say hip-hop?" You might ask aesthetic questions about the importance of melody or lyrics or harmony, or ethical questions such as whether the industry should put parental advisory labels on albums. You could even consider moral questions such as whether rock videos encourage sexism or violence.

In recognizing the multiple possibilities of issues, you may find you have more to say on a topic than you think.

Brainstorming Topics

Now that you have some idea of the kind of matters that are and are not arguable, you next have to come up with a topic to argue. If your instructor has already given you a specific assignment, then that task is behind you. But if you have no specific assignment, and you're on your own, you may find it difficult to come up with something. And you're not alone. Students often complain that the hardest thing about writing is deciding what to write about.

To ease the selection task, we suggest a brainstorming strategy. Take out a piece of paper and jot down whatever comes to your head in response to these questions:

What issues in print or TV news interest you?

What issues make you angry?

What problems in your dorm/on campus/in your town/in your country concern you?

What political issue concerns you most?

What aspects about the environment worry you?

If you were your professor/dean/college president/mayor/governor/senator/president, what would be the first thing you'd do?

What policies/practices/regulations/laws would you like to see changed?

What do you talk about or argue over with friends or classmates?

What ideas from books or articles have challenged your thinking?

What books/movies/music/fashions/art do you love, and why?

What books/movies/music/fashions/art do you hate, and why?

What personalities in politics/show business/the media/academia do you have strong feelings about?

Here's a quick brainstorming list one student developed.

Issues That Make Me Angry
1. People who live off welfare.
2. Excessive salaries for athletes.
3. People who protest movie violence but who oppose bans on assault rifles.
4. Teachers who don't know how to teach.
5. All the foul language in movies and on TV.

Once you have brainstormed a list, organize the issues according to categories—for example, political, social, environmental, educational issues, and so on. Then transfer the list to your notebook. Now, whenever an assignment comes up, you'll have a database of ideas to consult.

Reading

The material you read is full of fruitful sources for arguments. You might find materials in your casual reading, such as magazines and newspapers. Or perhaps you are reading something for a class that gets you thinking. You might want to know how a theory was derived, or what some results are based on, or even why two different experts draw different conclusions from the same evidence. Reading a science fiction novel may make you wonder about the plausibility of alien languages, or reading a murder mystery may get you interested in forensic anthropology. Get in the habit of making brief notes on what you read, again in your notebook, so that you'll increase that database of possible ideas for arguments.

Discussion

As already suggested, talking to other people is a great source of ideas, and so is listening. Brainstorming doesn't always have to be a lonely activity; you and other writers can toss ideas around, or simply take inventory of the things you talk about over lunch or on coffee breaks. As Larry King and other talk show hosts prove every day, America loves to talk. Take advantage of it—and take notes.

Keeping a Notebook

You've probably noticed that we encourage recording ideas and observations in a notebook. This is a technique used by many professional writers. The notebook doesn't have to be fancy; the cheap supermarket variety works just as well as the $4000 portable color computer. (If you're comfortable at a keyboard, a computer disk makes a great notebook and fits in your shirt pocket too.)

Writers use notebooks as portable file cabinets of ideas. In it we record anything in language that interests us, not just materials for a current project. We may copy down a word or phrase or sentence we hear that we like, or photocopy and staple in a piece by a writer we admire, or even add in things that infuriate or amuse us. (One of our collaborators tries to add "aggravation of the week" to her notebook.) Not only does a notebook become a supermarket of ideas and strategies, but there's something very positive about the simple act of *copying* words. Somehow, physically writing or typing them makes them yours; you learn something about technique in doing the physical work. (That's why we don't recommend making too many photocopies; you don't psychically store the information in the same way you do when you copy out a passage.)

For the beginning argument writer, a notebook is invaluable. You can use yours to include notes on possible topics; examples of good introductions and conclusions; catchy words, phrases, and titles; examples of logical fallacies—just about anything a writer might need. When you begin keeping the notebook, set yourself some formal goal: adding 100 words a day, or writing five days out of the week. Then *stick to it*. Notebooks don't fill themselves. It takes discipline to keep a notebook, and discipline is a characteristic of good writers. If you don't do the work, your creativity won't ever break through. Throughout this text, we've scattered suggestions and exercises for using notebooks; if you want to master fully the power of argument, we encourage you to *do* these. Don't just read them; write!

Review: To Develop Argumentative Topics . . .

Brainstorm to find multiple possibilities

Read and take notes

Discuss ideas with others

Keep an argument notebook

Refining Topics

Once you have found—through reading, discussing, or keeping notebooks—some subjects that strike you as interesting, you have to begin winnowing out manageable chunks about which you can write. So the next step is to look over your list and reduce it to those topics that are legitimately arguable. (See Chapter 1 for a refresher.)

Reducing Your Options

You can't write about everything at once, so you'll have to choose a handful you can consider at one time from your initial group of subjects. After reducing your list to, say, five topics, your next step is to determine if your subjects are manageable. You don't want a subject that is too broad or unwieldy or which would require prohibitive amounts of research. You would not want to argue that "Women have always been discriminated against in sports." You could write a book about that if you had the time to do all the research. To write a short paper, you have to narrow your subject down. "The women's basketball team at State U should get more television coverage" is a manageable reduction of your first idea, and one that you can handle in an average-length paper (see Figure 2.1). The more narrow you make your topic, the more you restrict your research and tighten the focus of your argument.

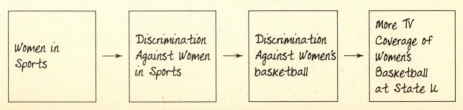

Figure 2.1

Avoiding Overspecialized Topics

Likewise, don't pick a topic that requires extensive specialized knowledge, such as how to reduce the trade deficit or the problems inherent in thermonuclear fusion. The issue you choose should be one you know a little something about and, to keep you interested, about which you have strong convictions. Also, it should be an issue you are willing to spend a reasonable amount of time exploring on your own or perhaps in the library. Aside from writing a convincing argument, a parallel goal of any project you research is to become better informed and more appreciative of the complexity of the issue. Therefore, select a topic on which you wish to be well informed and that you are willing to investigate and reflect upon.

Formulating Claims

After you've settled on a topic to argue, the next step is to formulate your **claim**. The claim is the heart of your argument. Whether you hope to demonstrate a truth, change your readers' minds, or inspire your audience to take action, someplace in your argument must be the assertion that you will prove. In argument papers, this assertion or claim functions as the **thesis** of the paper, and it's vital to the argument. The claim says precisely what you believe. It is the position or opinion you want your readers to accept or the action you want them to take. So it's important to make it clear in your mind. Many writers, in fact, write their claims on a notecard or Post-it note and place it where they can see it. (This was the famous strategy Bill Clinton's campaign team used to great effect in the 1992 elections: They had a sign reading "It's the economy, stupid" posted over their desks so that they'd keep focused on their claim.)

Although at times the claim might not be directly stated, in most arguments it takes the form of a single declarative sentence stated clearly. Because the claim often serves as the conclusion that you want to "prove" in your argument, it will often be signaled by certain words: *in conclusion, therefore, consequently, the real question is, the point is, it follows that, my suggestion is.* Here's an example:

> Therefore, I don't believe doctors should be punished for helping terminally ill patients end their lives.

Since many arguments are proposals (see Chapter 3 for more discussion) or recommendations for solving certain problems, it may be useful to frame your claim as a conditional statement that reflects both the problem and the solution. This can be accomplished with split phrases like *either . . . or, neither . . . nor, if . . . then.* For instance:

> Either we remove the huge profit incentive by legalizing drugs, or we continue to allow our cities to degenerate into bloody battlefields where gangs of youths kill themselves and others.

And:

If the city's schools are to survive, then the superintendent must get rid of the troublemakers so that the other 95 percent who want to learn can do so.

Many claims that recommend a solution to a problem will contain a "should" word—for example, *should, must, ought to be, needs to be, must be, is imperative that,* and *has to be.* In this text we'll call these *obligation verbs* because they talk about what people are obliged to do. And since claims must have support to convince a reader, they are often followed by "because" statements—that is, statements that justify a claim by explaining why something is true or recommended or beneficial:

Sport hunting is immoral because it reduces the sanctity of all life.

Other words function as "because" words signaling statements of support: *since, for, as indicated by, for the (simple) reason that, assuming the fact that:*

I am opposed to gun legislation for the simple reason that I don't think it works.

Later in this chapter, we will demonstrate how "because reasoning" can be helpful in formulating support for your argument claim.

Formulating your claim in an argument paper is very important for three basic reasons. First, it establishes the subject of your argument. Second, it solidifies your own stand or attitude on the issue. Third, it sets up the kind of reasoning strategy your argument may be structured on.

As for the placement of your claim, there is no rigid rule. It can appear anywhere in your paper. Your opening sentence could be your claim; or it might be the statement on which you conclude your argument. Or it could come in the middle. Where it is positioned is determined by the kind of reasoning process you follow. But more about this in Chapters 3 and 6.

Anticipating Opposition

Once you have selected a topic that is legitimately arguable and one you'd like to pursue, your next step is coming up with some key points you want to make in your paper. Because your topic is an issue with more than one side, you should expect that some of your readers will not agree with you. Unlike other kinds of expository writing, argument implies opposition: pros and cons for every topic. Not to anticipate potential counterpoints at the onset might leave you fashioning an argument that will be wide open for counterattack.

For instance, on the issue of discrimination in collegiate sports, you might underscore the fact that the operating budget of the women's varsity basketball team is a fraction of that for the men's team. As evidence, you might point to the comparative lack of advertising, lower attendance at games, and poorer coverage than with men's teams. Unless you anticipate views from the other side, your argument, when written, may fall apart should an opponent inform you that women's basketball teams have lower budgets simply because they attract smaller paying audiences. Although that counterpoint may strike you as unethical, even subtly sexist, not having prepared for it leaves you somewhat defenseless. Had you been better prepared, you could have acknowledged that opposing point and then countered it with the reasoning that the low budget is the cause of the problem, not the result of it. Putting more money into advertising and coverage could only boost attendance and, thus, revenue.

In short, we recommend that even before you write a word of your argument that you identify your key points and at the same time anticipate counterpoints. Otherwise you leave yourself open to damaging counterarguments as well as claims of naïveté and lack of information. On some highly controversial issues, you may find it necessary to familiarize yourself with arguments from both sides. While much more will be offered in Chapter 8 on researching your topics, you could check your library for books on the topic or magazine articles topically listed in one of the many indexing sources in your college library.

To make your case as effective as possible, you must be fair and thorough in what you present as opposing points. You should include what opponents would consider their strongest and most convincing arguments. To list only their weakest points or to present them in a poor light would only slant the issue and work against you in the long run. A winning argument greatly depends upon demonstrating your knowledge of the issue and your responsibility as a representative of your side.

"Yes, but . . ." Dialogues

Imagine you were in a face-to-face debate with an opponent and you ran down your list and to each of your points the response was "Yes, but . . . [something]." What might that something be? Consider for a moment how a debate about controlling the use of animals in medical testing might go. You begin:

> Animal testing is categorically inhumane.

From what you've heard and read of the other side, one response might be the following:

> Yes, but without animal testing otherwise fatal diseases would have no cures. That would be even more inhumane.

Another point you might consider preparing for could go like this:

> Since humans will benefit from testing, human subjects would yield more reliable results than animals.

If you've read up on the issue, you might have come upon the counterargument:

> Yes, but using humans in tests of toxic drugs or chemicals would be unethical.

Imagining your discussion as a "Yes, but . . ." situation enables you to work through a number of possibilities. It also requires you to get your imagination involved, a crucial role in persuasive success.

Review: To Anticipate the Opposition . . .

Research opposing points
Create "yes, but . . ." dialogues
Develop pro/con checklists

Pro/Con Checklists

To sharpen the points of opposition and, ultimately, your own case, we recommend framing this point/counterpoint ("Yes, but . . .") dialogue in two parallel columns, one pro (in this case, your points), the other con (the opposition's counterpoints). Of course, not all points on all issues will have the equal and opposite counterpoints, although most will. You may also find that on some issues, one side has more entries than the other. If your side has more items than the opposition, you may have a good chance at persuasive success: if it has fewer, you probably have your work cut out. The pro/con list gives you an initial sense of how strong the various sides of the case are; it's a good early checkpoint.

Making a pro/con checklist is useful for several reasons. First, it helps you solidify your own stand on the issue. It puts you in the position of having to formulate points on which to construct an argument. Second, by anticipating counterpoints, you can better test the validity and strength of your points. This is very important because vital to any successful argument is the refutation of the opposition. You cannot win over an audience unless you acknowledge and overturn their potential opposition. By listing anticipated resistance, you can determine the weak spots in the opposition. Third, by tabulating your own points of argument, you can determine which are your strongest and which are your weakest. In this way you can determine how to organize your arguments—which points to put at the beginning of your paper and which to put in the conclusion. Depending on the issue, you may decide, for the sake of impact, to begin with the strongest and proceed to the weakest. This is a strategy of most advertisers—hitting the potential customer right off with the biggest sales pitch. Or, you may decide on the more climactic effect—beginning with the weakest point and building to the strongest and most dramatic, thereby signing off with a punch. Fourth, by ordering your key points, you can create a potential framework on which to construct your argument. Each of the five points listed could be a separate part of the essay—either a separate paragraph or cluster of paragraphs.

In Chapter 3 we will offer more on the structuring of your argument paper. But for the moment, let it suffice to say that making a point/counterpoint checklist will prove very handy in organizing your thoughts and planning your reasoning strategies. The box on page 32 shows two sample pro/con checklists.

Sample Pro/Con Checklists

CLAIM: "The medical establishment should put an end to the inhumane practice of using animals in experimentation."

Pro ("Because . . .")	Con ("Yes, but . . .")
Animal testing is categorically inhumane.	It's more inhumane not to find cures to fatal diseases.
All living creatures have inherent rights.	Humans have greater rights.
Animals cannot reason but they can experience pain.	Researchers do not let animals suffer needlessly.
Millions of animals each year are left to suffer.	Suffering is exaggerated.
Since humans will benefit from testing, human subjects would yield more reliable results than animals.	Using humans in tests of toxic chemicals or drugs is unethical.

CLAIM: "America should legalize drugs since the war against them is costly and unwinnable."

Pro	Con
Too many officials are corrupted by all the money to be made.	Most officials are still dedicated.
Foreign governments don't cooperate enough.	We could step up the incentives for cooperation.
The 1980s' "Just Say No" campaign failed.	Decriminalization will tell young people that drugs are okay.
Billions spent on stopping drugs drains us.	No cost is too great to end the scourge of drugs.
Cheaper drugs will end much street crime.	Cheaper drugs will just create more addicts and more criminals.
Only addicts will be allowed to buy drugs.	Legalization ignores the root causes of addiction: despair and helplessness.

EXERCISES

1. Try to determine from the following list which subjects are arguable and which are not.
   a. Letter grades in all college courses should be replaced by pass/fail grades.
   b. Capital punishment is no deterrent to crime.
   c. Lobster is my favorite seafood.
   d. Professor Greene is one of the best professors on campus.
   e. The university should install condom machines in all dormitories.
   f. Pornography poses a threat to women.
   g. Minorities make up only 9 percent of the upper management positions in corporate America.
   h. The earth's population will be 7 billion by the year 2000.
   i. The production and sale of cigarettes must be outlawed for the health of the American public.
   j. Last night's sunset over the mountains was spectacular.
   k. The swelling in her leg could indicate a blood clot has formed.
   l. Advertisers will stop at nothing to make useless products seem wonderful.
   m. AIDS testing for health care workers should be mandatory.
   n. Bilingual education programs fail to help non-English-speaking children become part of mainstream society.
   o. Abortion is a decision that should be left up to women, not the courts.
   p. I think women are better drivers than men.
   q. You sometimes have no choice but to break a law, especially when that law is a bad one.
   r. There are too many divorces in this country.
   s. Given all the billions of galaxies and billions of stars in each galaxy, there must be life elsewhere.
   t. Broccoli prevents cancer.

2. In your argument notebook, create a pro/con checklist for the following topics. Make two columns: pro on one side, con on the other. If possible, team up with other students to brainstorm opposing points on each issue. Try to come up with five or six solid points and counterpoints.
   a. I think women are better drivers than men.
   b. Capital punishment is no deterrent to crime.
   c. "Hard" sciences like math are more difficult than "soft" sciences like sociology.
   d. The production and sale of cigarettes must be outlawed for the health of the American public.
   e. The university should reduce tuition for those students who maintained an A average during the previous year.

CHAPTER

3

Shaping Arguments

Thinking Like an Architect

Just as there is no best way to build a house, there is no best structure for an argument. Some essays will take an inductive approach (discussed in Chapter 6) and begin with a specific circumstance, then present arguments and evidence in support or opposition to that circumstance. Others will adopt a deductive approach (see Chapter 6) and begin with an idea or philosophical principle, move to a specific circumstance, then conclude with why that circumstance is right and should be maintained, or wrong and should be changed. Some essays express their conclusions in the opening paragraphs. Others build up to them in the last paragraph. As an architect will tell you, the structure that gets built will depend on the site, the people doing the building, and the people who are going to buy the house. Arguments are no different. Depending on you, your goals, and your readers, you'll write very different kinds of arguments.

Although no two arguments look alike, they all have three basic structural parts: a beginning, a middle, and an end. And each part performs certain basic functions. This isn't a simplistic definition. As in architecture, each part is there for a purpose; leave out one of the parts, and the whole collapses. So let's look at those parts and the jobs they do.

Components of an Argument

Following is an organizational pattern for argument papers—a pattern to which, with some variations, most of the essays in this book conform. We offer it to help you plan your own argument papers. Although this model contains most of the components of arguments, it is not a recipe written in stone. You should not feel bound to follow it when constructing every argument. In fact, you might find it more effective to move blocks of writing around, or omit material. For instance, on issues unfamiliar to readers, it might make sense to begin with background infor-

34

mation so that the context of your discussion will be understood. With familiar issues, it might be more persuasive to open with refutations of opposing views. On especially controversial topics, you might wish to reserve your refutations for the main body of the paper. Or, for dramatic effect, you might decide to save your refutations to the very end, thereby creating a kind of persuasive last punch. As a writer, you're free to modify this model any way you like; often you may want to try different models in different drafts of your paper to see which arrangement works best in each case. As with houses, your choices in building arguments are numerous.

The Beginning

The beginning of your argument accomplishes in a small space three important goals:

1. It introduces you, the writer. Here your audience meets you—senses your tone, your attitude toward your subject, and the general style of the piece.
2. It appeals to your readers' reason, emotions, and/or sense of ethics. This can be done in a simple value statement, an anecdote, or some bald but high-impact statistics intended to raise your readers' anger or pity.
3. It identifies the topic and, perhaps, indicates your stand.

Depending on the issue and the audience, the beginning can run a paragraph or two. In most arguments, the beginning will end with a clear statement of the claim you are making—your thesis. Although "Once upon a time . . ." is probably the most remembered introduction, it's not always the most effective; more ingenuity on your point is needed to "hook" your readers.

In *The Village Voice*, columnist Nat Hentoff recently began a column calling for eliminating duplication in the U.S. military by saying that he had telephoned the Pentagon press office for a comment on the subject. "Oh," said the officer with whom he spoke, "You want the *other* press office." As Hentoff remarked, he could have ended the column at that point; instead, he went on to develop his idea, confident that this introductory example would make his readers sympathetic to his point.

Composing good beginnings requires hard work. That's why many writers keep a journal or notebook in which they copy the strategies of writers they admire; that's how we happened to have a copy of Hentoff's introduction. As beginning arguers, you may want to develop your own repertoire of start-up strategies by copying strategies you admire into your own argument notebook.

The Middle

The middle portion of your argument is where you do the argumentative work: presenting your information, handling the opposition, making your case. If you think of it in terms of building construction, here's where you pour a foundation and lay the framework; put in all the walls, floors, and systems; and have the building inspector examine your work. There are a number of substages.

Background Information

After indicating the topic or problem and your position on it, you might analyze the problem's causes and effects. You might cite how the problem developed and how it has affected others or society at large. Here you would pursue in some depth the impact and the consequences should the situation not be altered for the better. If handled correctly, this can be the most persuasive and convincing part of your argument. You might also offer your own personal experience as testimony to the seriousness of the problem. For instance, in "Which Way Black America?— Anti-Abortion" (page 374), Pamela Carr begins with her own experience as a pregnant teenager to argue that abortion is no solution for the black community. This sets the stage for working out the rest of the essay.

Survey of Alternate Points of View

Here you review opposing viewpoints, thereby showing your grasp of the issue. You might even acknowledge the sincerity of those holding contrary views while citing the merits of their alternative solutions. This demonstrates how sincere and open-minded you are to your reader. Such acknowledgments also help establish your authority as a writer. Shelby Steele exploits this strategy quite effectively in "Affirmative Action: The Price of Preference" (page 258).

Arguments in Support of Claim

These arguments comprise the thrust of your main argument and, therefore, the major portion of your essay. Here you present your proposal, claim, or statement of position on the particular issue, followed by your reasons and supporting evidence—evidence based on facts, statistics, other data, testimony of authorities, or examples. Depending on the issue, this section usually takes several paragraphs. Most of the essays in this reader use this method; Susan Jacoby's "I Am a First Amendment Junkie" (page 468) is a good example.

Refutation of Possible Objections

Good writers know that readers aren't neutral on controversial topics. Somebody out there holds contrary opinions. It's always wise, therefore, to anticipate possible objections so that you can offer rebuttals and refutations. The kinds of objections you anticipate, of course, depend on your familiarity with your audience—their interests, values, needs, standards, and so on. (More will be said on addressing opposing views in Chapter 4.) Raising opinions to be refuted not only demonstrates your awareness of the issue, but it also strengthens your own case while raising your credibility. One good example of careful refutation is Garry Wills' "In Praise of Censure" (page 458).

The End

The end is usually a short paragraph or two where you conclude your argument. Essentially, your ending summarizes your main arguments by reaffirming your stand on the issue, maybe even suggesting what actions should be taken. Or it might make an appeal to your readers to take action. It can contain another anecdote, a passionate summation, or even a quiet but resonant sentence. Lincoln's "Gettysburg Address," for example, ends with the quiet "government of the people, by the people, and for the people," which is one of the most memorable phrases in American political theory. Looking over the essays in this book, it seems to us that no two end quite alike. As a writer, you have a lot of choices; experimentation is usually the best way of deciding what will work for you. Many writers copy effective conclusions into their journals or working notebooks so that they can refresh their memories when writing their own arguments.

To illustrate this three-part argument pattern, Clara Spotted Elk's essay "Indian Bone" appears on pages 38–39 followed by an analysis of its key structural features.

Review: The Structure of an Argument

The Beginning . . .

Introduces you as a writer

States the problem

Establishes your position and appeal

The Middle . . .

Gives background information

Surveys alternate points of view

Offers arguments supporting the claim

Refutes possible objections

The End . . .

Summarizes your position and implications

Invites readers to share your conclusion

and/or take action

SAMPLE ARGUMENT FOR ANALYSIS

Indian Bones
Clara Spotted Elk

1   Millions of American Indians lived in this country when Columbus first landed on our shores. After the western expansion, only about 250,000 Indians survived. What happened to the remains of those people who were decimated by the advance of the white man? Many are gathering dust in American museums.

2   In 1985, I and some Northern Cheyenne chiefs visited the attic of the Smithsonian's Natural History Museum in Washington to review the inventory of their Cheyenne collection. After a chance inquiry, a curator pulled out a drawer in one of the scores of cabinets that line the attic. There were the jumbled bones of an Indian. "A Kiowa," he said.

3   Subsequently, we found that 18,500 Indian remains—some consisting of a handful of bones, but mostly full skeletons—are unceremoniously stored in the Smithsonian's nooks and crannies. Other museums, individuals and Federal agencies such as the National Park Service also collect the bones of Indian warriors, women, and children. Some are on display as roadside tourist attractions. It is estimated that another 600,000 Indian remains are secreted away in locations across the country.

4   The museum community and forensic scientists vigorously defend these grisly collections. With few exceptions, they refuse to return remains to the tribes that wish to rebury them, even when grave robbing has been documented. They want to maintain adequate numbers of "specimens" for analysis and say they are dedicated to "the permanent curation of Indian skeletal remains."

5   Indian people are tired of being "specimens." The Northern Cheyenne word for ourselves is "tsistsistas"—human beings. Like people the world over, one of our greatest responsibilities is the proper care of the dead.

6   We are outraged that our religious views are not accepted by the scientific community and that the graves of our ancestors are desecrated. Many tribes are willing to accommodate some degree of study for a limited period of time—provided that it would help Indian people or mankind in general. But how many "specimens" are needed? We will not accept grave robbing and the continued hoarding of our ancestors' remains.

7   Would this nefarious collecting be tolerated if it were discovered that it affected other ethnic groups? (Incidentally, the Smithsonian also collects skeletons of blacks.) What would happen if the Smithsonian had 18,500 Holocaust victims in the attic? There would be a tremendous outcry in this country. Why is there no outcry about the Indian collection?

8   Indians are not exotic creatures for study. We are human beings who practice living religions. Our religion should be placed not only on a par with science when it comes to determining the disposition of our ancestors but on a par with every other religion practiced in this country.

9   To that end, Sen. Daniel K. Inouye will soon reintroduce the "Bones Bill" to aid Indians in retrieving the remains of their ancestors from museums. As in the past, the "Bones Bill" will most likely be staunchly resisted by the collectors of Indian skeletons—armed with slick lobbyists, lots of money and cloaked in the mystique of science.

10   Scientists have attempted to defuse this issue by characterizing their opponents as radical Indians, out of touch with the culture and with little appreciation of science. Armed only with a moral obligation to our ancestors, the Indians who support the bill have few resources and little money.

11   But, in my view, the issue should concern all Americans—for it raises very disturbing questions. American Indians want only to reclaim and rebury their dead. Is this too much to ask?

Analyzing the Structure

Now let's examine this essay according to the organizational features discussed so far.

The Beginning

Paragraph 1 clearly introduces the nature of the problem: The remains of the Indians "decimated by the advance of the white man" have wrongfully ended up "gathering dust in American museums." It isn't until paragraph 6 that Spotted Elk spells out her position: "We are outraged that our religious views are not accepted by the scientific community and that the graves of our ancestors are desecrated." (Since this essay was written for newspaper publication, the paragraphs are shorter than they might be in a formal essay; you may not want to delay your thesis until the sixth paragraph in that kind of structure.) Notice, too, that in the introduction the author's persona begins to assert itself in the brief and pointed summation of the American Indian's fate. When Spotted Elk mentions the staggering decline in the population of her ancestors, we sense a note of controlled but righteous anger in her voice. Citation of the gruesome facts of history also appeals to the reader's ethical sense by prompting reflection on the Indians' demise.

The Middle

- **Background Information**   Paragraphs 2 and 3 establish the context of the author's complaint. Paragraph 2 is personal testimony to the problem—how she and other Native Americans viewed an unceremonious "jumble of bones" in the museum drawer and were stunned by the representative insensitivity of their host curator, who treated the human remains as if they were a fossil. Paragraph 3 projects the problem to progressively larger contexts and magnitudes—from the single Kiowa in a drawer to the 18,500 in the Smithsonian at large; from that institution's collection to the estimated 600,000 remains in other museums, federal agencies and institutions, and "roadside tourist attractions." The broader scope of the problem is underscored here.

- **Survey of Alternate Points of View**   In paragraph 4, Spotted Elk tersely sums up the opposing position of the "museum community and forensic scientists": " . . . they refuse to return remains to the tribes." She also states their reasoning: "They want to maintain adequate numbers of "specimens" for analysis and say they are dedicated to 'the permanent curation of Indian skeletal remains.' "

- **Arguments in Support of the Claim**   Paragraphs 5 through 9 constitute the heart of Spotted Elk's argument. Here she most forcefully argues her objections and offers her reasons with supporting details: Indians resent being treated as specimens and want to bury their dead as do other religious people (paragraphs 5 and 6). She follows that with a concession that many Indians would accommodate some degree of anthropological study for a period of time, but do not approve of the huge permanent collections that now fill museums.

    In paragraph 7 the author continues to support her claim that American Indians have been discriminated against with regard to the disposition of ancestral remains. She writes that there would be a public outcry if the remains of other ethnic groups such as Holocaust victims were hoarded. Her proposal for change appears in paragraph 8: "Our religion should be placed not only on a par with science when it comes to determining the disposition of our ancestors but on a par with every other religion practiced in this country." This is the logical consequence of the problem she has addressed to this point. That proposal logically leads into paragraph 9, where she mentions efforts by Senator Daniel Inouye to see the "Bones Bill" passed into law. Throughout, Spotted Elk uses emotional words and phrases—*grisly, unceremoniously, slick lobbyists, cloaked in mystique*—to reinforce her points.

- **Refutation of Possible Objections**   In paragraph 10, the author addresses objections of the opposition, in this case those "[s]cientists [who] have attempted to defuse this issue by characterizing their opponents as radical Indians, out of touch with their culture and with little appreciation of science." She refutes all three charges (of being "radical," as well as out of touch with Indian culture and science) with the phrase "[a]rmed only with a moral obligation to our ancestors"—a phrase that reaffirms her strong connection with her culture. On the contrary, it is science that is out of touch with the "living religion" of Native Americans.

The End

The final paragraph brings closure to the argument. Briefly the author reaffirms her argument that Native Americans "want only to reclaim and rebury their dead." The question that makes up the final line of the essay is more than rhetorical, for it reminds us of the point introduced back in paragraph 5—that American Indians are no different than any other religious people with regard to the disposition of their ancestors. A powerful question brings the essay's conclusion into sharp focus.

Blueprints for Arguments

This pattern gives some idea of the general organization of an essay, but it does not reflect fine subdivisions or the way the various parts of the essay are logically connected. This can be done by making an outline. Think of an outline as a blueprint of the argument you're building: It reveals structure and framework but leaves out the materials that cover the frame.

Opinions differ as to the value of making outlines before writing an essay. Some writers need to make formal outlines to organize their thoughts. Others simply scratch down a few key ideas. Others write essays spontaneously without any preliminary writing. For the beginning writers, outlines are valuable aids because they demonstrate at a glance how the various parts of an essay are connected, whether the organization is logical and complete, if the evidence is sequenced properly, and whether or not there are any omissions or lack of proportion. Your outline need not be elaborate. You might simply jot down your key arguments in a hierarchy from strongest to weakest:

Introduction

Argument 1

Argument 2

Argument 3

Argument 4

Conclusion

This blueprint might be useful if you want to capture your readers' attention immediately with your most powerful appeal. Or, you might use a reverse hierarchy, beginning with your weakest argument and proceeding to your strongest, in order to achieve a climactic effect for an audience sympathetic to your cause. As a writer, the outline will help you build your case.

You might prefer, as do some writers, to construct an outline after writing a rough draft instead of before. This lets you create a draft without restricting the free flow of ideas and helps you rewrite by determining where you need to fill in, cut out, or reorganize. You may discover where your line of reasoning was not logical; you may also reconsider whether you should arrange your reasons from the most important to the least or vice versa in order to create a more persuasive effect. Ultimately, outlining after the first draft could prove to be useful in producing subsequent drafts and a polished final effort.

Outlines are also useful when evaluating somebody else's writing. Reducing the argument of the opposition to the bare bones exposes holes in the reasoning process, scanty evidence, and lack of emphasis. In writing this book, we used all three processes: We developed an outline to write the first draft and sway a publisher to accept it. Then experienced teachers read the draft and suggested changes to the outline to make it more effective. Finally, one of our collaborators took all the suggestions and her own ideas, and created a new outline to help us revise the text. In our case, all three strategies were equally valuable.

The Formal Outline

Some teachers like students to submit a *formal outline* with their papers to show that students have checked their structure carefully. This kind of outlining includes several rules to follow:

- Identify main ideas with capital Roman numerals.
- Identify subsections of main ideas with capital letters, indented one set of spaces from the main ideas.
- Identify support for subsections with Arabic numerals indented two sets of spaces from the main ideas.
- Identify the parts of the support with lowercase Roman numerals, indented three sets of spaces from the main ideas.
- Identify further subdivisions with lowercase letters and then italic numbers, each indented one set of spaces to the right of the previous subdivision.
- Make sure all items have at least two points; it's considered improper in formal outlining to have only one point under any subdivision.

Here's what a formal outline can look like. If you are using a commercial word processing program, check its documentation; it may have an outlining feature, including setting the correct spacing and lettering or numbering.

    I. Main idea
       A. Sub-idea
          1. Supporting detail
             i. evidence
                a. subdivision
                b. subdivision
                   1. item
                   2. item
             ii. evidence
          2. Supporting detail
             i. evidence
             ii. evidence
       B. Sub-idea
          1. Supporting detail
          2. Supporting detail
             i. evidence
             ii. evidence

    II. Main idea
        A. Sub-idea
            1. Supporting detail
                i. evidence
                ii. evidence
            2. Supporting detail
                i. evidence
                ii. evidence
        B. Sub-idea
            1. Supporting detail
                i. evidence
                ii. evidence
            2. Supporting detail
                i. evidence
                ii. evidence

    You'll notice that there are no designations of "beginning," "middle," or "end" in the outline above. The reason is that these are organizational parts of an essay, while the above divisions and subdivisions are topical parts of an essay. Of course, the arrangement of ideas usually correlates with the organization of the essay. That is, the sequence of topics or main ideas move from the beginning to the end of an argument. It should be pointed out that opposing arguments usually fall under the second or third "Main idea" heading as you will see below.

    What follows is a formal topical outline of Clara Spotted Elk's essay, "Indian Bones" from pages 38–39:

    I. Hoarding of Indian remains
        A. At Smithsonian
            1. Single Kiowa at Smithsonian
            2. 18,500 others
        B. In other locations
    II. Authorities' defense of collections
        A. Refusal to return grave-robbed remains
        B. Maintainence of "specimens"
    III. Indians' response
        A. Outrage
            1. Desire to be seen as humans
            2. Desire to have religion accepted by science
            3. Nonacceptance of desecration of graves
            4. Resentment of lack of outcry by public
        B. Accommodation
            1. Limitation in time
            2. Service to Indians and mankind
        C. Demand equality with other religions
    IV. "Bones Bill" legislation

A. Resistance from scientific community
1. Slick lobbyists
2. Money
3. Scientific mystique
4. Characterization of Indians
   i. Radicals
   ii. Out of touch with culture
   iii. Little appreciation of science
B. Indian counter-resistance
1. Few resources
2. Little money
3. Moral obligation to ancestors

You should keep in mind that an outline should not force your writing to conform to a rigid pattern and, thus, turn your essay into something stilted and uninspired. Follow the model as a map, taking detours when necessary or inspired.

Two Basic Shapes for Arguments

Consider the following claims for arguments (several, in fact, with minor rewording, have come from essays in this book):

1. Watching television helps to eliminate some traditional family rituals.
2. Pornography poses a threat to women.
3. *Bridges of Madison County* is an intelligent, sensitive movie.
4. Bilingual education programs fail to help non-English-speaking children become part of mainstream society.
5. Affirmative action is intended to reverse the long-standing tradition of unjust racial exclusion.
6. Cigarette advertising should be banned from billboards everywhere.
7. Medical doctors should not advertise.
8. Americans by law should be required to vote.
9. The production and sale of cigarettes ought to be outlawed.
10. Pass/fail grades have to be eliminated across the board if standards are to be maintained.

Looking over these statements, you might notice some patterns. The verbs in the first five are all in the present tense: *helps, poses, is, fail, is intended to.* However, each of the last five statements includes "should" words: *should, should not, ought to be, have to be.* These **obligation verbs** are found in almost all claims proposing solutions to a problem.

What distinguishes the first group from the second is more than the form of the verb. The first five claims are statements of the writer's stand on a controversial issue as it currently exists. The second group are proposals for what *should* be. Essentially, all the arguments in this book—and the ones you'll most likely write and read in your careers—fall into one of these two categories or a combination of each, for often a writer states his or her position on an issue, then follows it with proposals for changes. Later in this chapter we will discuss proposals. But for the moment, let's take a look at position arguments.

Position Arguments

A *position argument* scrutinizes one side of a controversial issue. In such an argument, the writer not only establishes his or her stand, but argues vigorously in defense of it. Position arguments are less likely to point to a solution to a problem. Instead, they are philosophical in nature—the kinds of arguments on which political and social principles are founded, laws are written, and business and governmental policies are established. Position papers also tend to address themselves to the ethical and moral aspects of a controversy. If, for instance, you were opposed to the university's policy of mandatory testing for the AIDS virus, you might write a position paper protesting your school's infringement of individual rights and invasion of privacy.

As indicated by the present tense of the verbs in the first five claims, the position argument deals with the **status quo**—the way things are, the current state of affairs. Such an argument reminds the audience that something *currently* is good or bad, better or worse, right or wrong. Like all arguments, they tend to be aimed at changing the audience's feelings about an issue—euthanasia, abortion, capital punishment, and so on. That is why many position papers tend to direct their appeals to the reader's sense of ethics rather than reason.

By contrast, proposal arguments identify a problem and recommend a likely solution. That's why their claims contain verbs that *obligate* the readers to take some action. In this sense, they are practical rather than philosophical. For instance, if you were concerned about the spread of AIDS among college students, you might write a paper proposing that condom machines be installed in all dormitories. When you offer a proposal, you're trying to affect the future.

What to Look for in Position Arguments

Following are some key features of position arguments. These can be used to help you evaluate someone's stand on an issue. As a checklist, they can also help guide you in writing your own position papers.

The Writer Deals with a Controversial Issue. The best kind of position paper is one that focuses on a debatable issue, one in which there is clear disagreement: abortion, capital punishment, euthanasia, affirmative action, sex in advertising, freedom of speech, gay rights, homelessness, gun control. These are the issues that our society debates, that offer many "sides," and that make up a good part of the readings in this book.

The Writer Clearly States the Position. Readers should not be confused about where an author stands on an issue. Although the actual issue may be complex, the claim should be stated emphatically and straightforwardly. Don't waffle with, "Using the death penalty in some situations and with some rights of appeal probably doesn't do much to lower crime anyway"; far better is an emphatic "Capital punishment is no deterrent to crime."

In formulating your claim, be certain that your word choice is not ambiguous. Otherwise, the argument will be muddled and, ultimately, unconvincing. Ambiguity, however, should not be confused with ambivalence. Ambiguity is vagueness or lack of clarity; ambivalence means having simultaneously conflicting feelings. On particularly complex or difficult issues, you can feel legitimate ambivalence. If you feel ambivalent about a position, you have two options: Choose another issue that you can argue more emphatically, or write a claim that clearly spells out your ambivalence and the conditions that determine your taking one side or the other on the issue. In her essay, "Some Thoughts on Abortion" (see page 366), Anna Quindlen argues that for "thoughtful people" abortion offers no easy answers, no absolutes. For her thesis statement she writes, " . . . I know it [abortion] is the right thing in some times and places. That is where I find myself now, in the middle, hating the idea of abortions, but hating the idea of having them outlawed."

The Writer Cites Opposing Positions and Potential Objections. For every argument there is bound to be a counterargument, and sometimes more than one. Such is the nature of controversy. As a writer representing a position, you cannot assume that your readers are fully aware of or understand all the disagreement surrounding the issue you're arguing. Nor can you make a persuasive case without anticipating challenges. So in your argument you must spell out accurately and fairly the main points of the opposition and objections that might arise. We offer six reasons for doing this and doing it early in your paper:

1. *You reduce your own vulnerability.* You don't want to appear ill-informed or naive on an issue. Therefore, it makes sense to acknowledge opposing points of view to show how well you've investigated the topic and how sensitive you are to it. Suppose, for instance, you are writing a paper arguing that "anyone who commits suicide is insane." To avoid criticism, you would have to be prepared to answer objections that fully rational people with terminal illnesses often choose to take their own lives so as to avoid a painful demise and curtail the suffering of loved ones. Even if you strongly disagree with your opposition, recognizing views from the other side demonstrates that you are a person of responsibility and tolerance—two qualities for which most writers of argument strive.

2. *You distinguish your own position.* By citing opposing views, you distinguish your own position from that of others. This not only helps clarify the differences, but lays out the specific points of the opposition to be refuted or discredited. Some writers do this at the outset of their arguments as a setup for their counterarguments. Look, for instance, at how David Bruck sums up the views of the opposition in the opening sentences of his attack on capital punishment, "No Death Penalty":

   Mayor Edward Koch contends that the death penalty "affirms life." By failing to execute murderers, he says, we "signal a lessened regard for the value of the victim's life." Koch suggests that people who oppose the death penalty are like Kitty Genovese's neighbors, who heard her cries for help but did nothing while an attacker stabbed her to death.

Not only does Bruck summarize the main thrust of Edward Koch's argument (that we trivialize murder unless we execute murderers), but he defines where he needs to stage his counterattack—such as on the question of retribution. In fact, he spends the rest of his essay trying to demolish each of Koch's points by demonstrating how capital punishment is ironically irreverent in its view of human life and reckless in practice.

3. *You can refute opposing views.* A good refutation can challenge an opponent's ideas and examine the basis for the opposition arguments—whether personal, ideological, or moral. For instance, if you were refuting Michael Levin's "The Case for Torture" (page 110), you might point out that few methods of torture would force a terrorist to confess in under two hours, and that those methods might leave the terrorist unable to communicate information accurately, thus weakening Levin's argument that torture is a desirable tool in handling crises.

4. *You might also challenge an opponent's logic, demonstrating where the reasoning suffers from flaws in logic.* For instance, the argument that Ms. Shazadi must be a wonderful mother because she's a great manager does not logically follow. While some qualities of a good manager might bear on successful motherhood, not all do. In fact, it can be argued that the very qualities that make a good manager—leadership, drive, ruthlessness, determination— might damage a parent-child relationship. (For more on logical fallacies, see Chapter 7.)

5. *You might challenge the evidence supporting an argument.* If possible, try to point out unreliable, unrealistic, or irrelevant evidence offered by the opposition; question the truth of counterarguments; or point to distortions. The Realtor who boasts of oceanside property is vulnerable to challenge if the house in question is actually half a mile from the beach.

6. *You can gain strength through concessions.* Admitting weaknesses in your own stand demonstrates that you are realistic, that you don't suffer from an inflated view of the virtues of your position. It also lends credibility to your argument while helping project yourself as fair-minded. (See Chapter 4 for discussion of different strategies for anticipating opposing points of view.)

The Writer Offers a Well-Reasoned Argument to Support the Position. A position paper must do more than simply state your stand on an issue. It must try to persuade readers to accept your position as credible and convince them to adjust their thinking about the issue. Toward those ends, you should make every effort to demonstrate the best reasons for your beliefs and support the positions you hold. That means presenting honest and logically sound arguments.

Persuaders use three kinds of appeal: to *reason,* to *emotions,* and to readers' sense of *ethics.* You may have heard these described as the appeals of *logos, pathos,* and *ethos.* Although it is difficult to separate the emotional and ethical components from the rational or logical structure of an argument, the persuasive powers of a position argument may mean the proper combination of these three appeals. Not all arguments will cover all three appeals. Some will target logic alone and offer as support statistics and facts. Others centering around moral, religious, or personal values will appeal to a reader's emotions as well as reason. (These arguments are most successful for a readership that need not be convinced by force of reason alone.) Arguments based on emotion aim to reinforce and inspire followers to stand by their convictions. The most successful arguments are those that use multiple strategies to appeal to readers' hearts and minds.

When the issue centers on right-or-wrong or good-or-bad issues, position arguments make their appeals to the audience's ethical sense. In such papers your strategy has two intentions: one, to convince the reader that you are a person of goodwill and moral character and, thus, enhance your credibility; and, two, to suggest that any decent and moral readers will share your position.

The Writer's Supporting Evidence is Convincing. A position paper does not end with an incontrovertible proof such as in a demonstration of a scientific law or mathematical theorem. No amount of logic can prove conclusively that your functional judgment is right or wrong; if that were the case, there would be few arguments. It is also impossible to prove that your aesthetic judgments are superior to another's or that a particular song, movie, or book is better than another. But your arguments have a greater chance of being persuasive if you can present evidence that convinces your readers that your argument is valid.

We'll say more on this in Chapter 5, but for now remember that a strong argument needs convincing evidence: facts, figures, personal observations, testimony of outside authorities, and specific examples. In general, the more facts supporting a position, the more reason there is for the reader to accept that position as valid. The same is true when refuting another position. An author needs to supply sound reasons and evidence to disprove or discredit an opponent's stand.

The Writer Projects a Reasonable Persona. Whenever we read an argument, we cannot help but be aware of the person behind the works. Whether it's in the choice of expressions, the tenacity of opinion, the kinds of examples, the force of the argument, the nature of the appeal, or the humor or sarcasm, we hear the author's voice and form an impression of the person. That impression, which is projected by the voice and tone of the writing, is the writer's *persona.*

Persona is communicated in a variety of ways: diction or the choice of words (formal, colloquial, slang, jargon, charged terms); the sentence style (long or short, simple or complex); and the kinds of evidence offered (from cool scientific data to inflammatory examples). As in face-to-face debates, a full range of feelings can be projected by the tone of a written argument: anger, irony, jest, sarcasm, seriousness.

Persona is the vital bond linking the writer to the reader. In fact, the success or failure of an argument might be measured by the extent to which the reader accepts the persona in an argument. If you like the voice you hear, then you have already begun to identify with the writer and are more likely to share in the writer's assumptions and opinions. If, however, that persona strikes you as harsh, distant, or arrogant, you might have difficulty subscribing to the author's argument even if it makes sense logically.

A good position argument projects a reasonable persona, one that is sincere and willing to consider opposing points of view. Although readers may not be convinced enough to change their stand or behavior, a writer with a reasonable persona can at least capture their respect and consideration. In Chapter 4, we'll discuss ways for you to create such a persona based on the identity of your readers.

A word of warning, though. Not every persona has to be reasonable or pleasant, although for a beginner this works best. If an arrogant persona is fortified by wit and intelligence, you may find it stimulating, even charming. A persona—whether outrageous, humorous, biting, or sarcastic—can be successful if it is executed with style and assurance. Some of the best arguments in Part 2 of this book have biting edges. When you read an argument with a memorable persona, jot down in your argument notebook the details of how the writer created it; that way, you can turn back to this information when you're trying to create personas for the arguments you write.

Review: Features of Position Arguments

- Controversial issue
- Position clearly stated
- Opposing positions cited
- Well-reasoned appeals
- Good supporting evidence
- Reasonable persona projected

Here's an example of a brief position argument written by Michele Fields, a journalism student, on the question of giving handouts to panhandlers. As you read it, consider how she has incorporated the six key points of position arguments in it. (You may wish to make a rough outline in your argument notebook, as well as take notes on her techniques.)

SAMPLE ARGUMENT FOR ANALYSIS

A Cup of Conscience
Michele Fields

1   The sing-song begging chants and almost subvocal mumbles for spare change ring in the evening air over Newbury Street. Instead of merely asking for a dollar, the queries represent a collective question of social responsibility. When

my evening stroll was interrupted by a series of panhandlers last weekend, I ran through the whole gamut of emotions: On one hand I truly felt pity that my fellow citizens were reduced to begging for survival, but on a baser level I was annoyed that my evening out with friends was constantly being interrupted (the retort "Why don't you get a job?" kept leaping to mind). I felt guilty passing these unlucky people by when my friends and I were on our way to a nice restaurant. At the same time, I was unreasonably angry at them for making *me* feel guilty. What was I supposed to do?

2   I'm no Mother Teresa. I am a student. I have responsibilities to myself, my family, and my friends—but where does social responsibility fit into the life of a young adult? Sure, I could give a dollar to a panhandler for food, but who's to say he won't spend it on cheap wine or crack? If I put a dollar in a beggar's cup, I could be sending her, and others like her, the message that doing nothing is profitable. I might only be encouraging the trend.

3   On my way home for Christmas at the end of my first semester of college, I met a young panhandler in New York's Port Authority bus station. She couldn't have been much older than I was, and I listened while she told me she needed five dollars to make bus fare to Ohio. She said in earnest that she needed to get home and that she would send me the money later. The spirit of Christmas, together with my over-romanticized idea of the noble and honest poor that I got from reading too many Jack Kerouac novels, inspired me to lend her the money. Since it was only five dollars, I told myself, I can prove that the poor can be trusted if given a chance and that my generosity will be rewarded. I never saw the money again, but I did learn a valuable lesson: The only purpose that five dollars served was to stroke my own ego. Maybe she did go to Ohio, but I doubt it. I don't think I made a difference in that girl's life, except to make her a panhandler who was five dollars richer.

4   Giving change to panhandlers can ease one's conscience but doesn't necessarily do any permanent good. Guilty conscience and social conscience are completely separate motives for charity: Guilty conscience is what motivates you to throw your spare change in a cup. Social conscience is a commitment to change. From here on, when I decide to donate my time or money, I'll make sure it is making a real difference. As the saying goes, "Give a man a fish and he'll eat for a day; teach a man to fish and he'll eat for a lifetime." The next time I walk down Newbury Street, I won't give in to emotional manipulation. I may not be able to change the world, but at least I'll be working on the cure—not just treating the symptoms.

Analysis of a Position Argument

Let's look at how Fields incorporated the six features of a position argument to construct this brief position argument.

- **The Writer Deals with a Controversial Issue**   Fields has chosen how one might react to panhandling as her issue. It's controversial because the growing problems of homelessness and begging are challenges facing many communities.

- **The Writer Clearly States the Position**   In paragraph 1, Fields lays out her position by relating a series of incidents and describing her reaction to them. To invite her readers' engagement with the topic, she phrases the position statement as a pair of questions: "What was I supposed to do?" and " . . . where does social responsibility fit into the life of a young adult?"

- **The Writer Cites Opposing Positions and Potential Objections**   In paragraph 2, Fields weaves the opposing points of view into an internal dialogue. On the one hand there's the imperative to give charity directly; on the other hand, there's the cynical view that panhandlers will use the money to buy liquor or drugs, or see it as an excuse to continue their begging ways. In paragraph 3, she allows for the possibility that the money she gave was well used, but regrets that she never found out about it: "Maybe she did go to Ohio."

- **The Writer Offers a Well-Reasoned Argument to Support the Position**   Because her paper is so short (it was designed as an editorial), Fields doesn't spend a great deal of time constructing an elaborate argument. But she does set up an inductive structure, using two actual incidents to support her conclusion that giving time and money to charitable organizations designed to help the homeless change their lives is better than throwing handouts into a cup.

- **The Writer's Supporting Evidence Is Convincing**   Anecdotes aren't always the best kinds of evidence, but here Fields puts them to good effect. She cites two different cases—the street beggars and the sympathetic young girl in the bus station—to demonstrate her point that giving money to panhandlers has no long-term effect. It sustains the problem. She also uses her evidence to build to a careful distinction: the difference between guilt and social consciousness. These set up her final statement of position—that she's going to try to solve the real problems causing begging instead of treating the symptoms.

- **The Writer Projects a Reasonable Persona**   The persona Fields creates is one with which other students can identify. She pokes a bit of fun at herself ("no Mother Teresa" and "over-romanticized ideal of the noble poor I got from reading too many Jack Kerouac novels") to show her readers that she's not playing holier-than-thou. In recreating her inner dialogues, she also reveals the conflicts that have led her to this position, assuming (probably correctly) that many of her readers have felt the same ambivalence. Because her readers are likely to identify with her self-mockery and confusion, she has a good chance of persuading them to adopt her position.

Proposal Arguments

Position arguments examine existing conditions. *Proposal arguments*, however, look to the future. They make recommendations for changes in the status quo—namely, changes in a policy, practice, or attitude. Essentially, what every proposal writer says is this: "Here is the problem, and this is what I think should be done about it." The hoped-for result, of course, is a new course of action or way of thinking.

Proposals are the most common kind of argument. We hear them all the time: "There ought to be a law against that"; "The government should do something about these conditions." And we're always making proposals of some kind: "Van should work out more"; "You ought to see that movie"; "We should recycle more of our trash." As pointed out earlier in this chapter, because proposals are aimed at correcting problems, they almost always make their claims in obligation verbs such as *must, ought to, needs to be,* and *must.*

Sometimes proposal arguments take up local problems and make very practical recommendations for immediate solutions. For instance, to reduce the long lines at the photocopy machines in your campus library, you might propose that the school invests in more copiers and puts them throughout the building. Proposal arguments also seek to correct or improve conditions with more far-reaching consequences. If, for example, too many of your classmates smoke, you might write a proposal to your school's administration to remove all cigarette machines from campus buildings or to designate nonsmoking areas on campus.

Still other proposals address perennial social issues in an effort to change public behavior and governmental policy. A group of physicians might recommend that all American cars be equipped with air bags. Or an organization of concerned parents might ask that the federal government put a ban on toys that contain toxic or flammable materials. Everyone has ideas about things that should be changed; proposals are the means we use to make those changes happen.

What to Look for in Proposal Arguments

Proposals have two basic functions: (1) They inform the readers that there is a problem; and (2) they make recommendations about how to correct those problems. Most of the essays in this book are proposal arguments. In fact, most of the arguments you'll probably write will be proposals. Therefore, to help you sharpen your own critical ability to build and analyze proposal arguments, here are some guidelines.

The Writer States the Problem Clearly. Because a proposal argument seeks to change the reader's mind and/or behavior, you first must demonstrate that a problem exists. You do this for several reasons. Your audience may not be aware that the problem exists or they may have forgotten it or think that it has already been solved. Sympathetic audiences may need to be reinspired to take action. It is crucial, therefore, that proposals clearly define the problem and the undesirable or dangerous consequences if matters are not corrected.

For both uninformed or sympathetic audiences, writers often try to demonstrate how the problem personally affects the reader. An argument for greater measures against shoplifting can be more convincing when you illustrate how petty thefts inevitably lead to higher prices. Or a paper proposing the elimination of pesticides might interest the everyday gardener by demonstrating how such carcinogenic chemicals can contaminate local drinking water. To make the problem even more convincing, the claim should be supported by solid evidence—statistics, historical data, examples, testimony of witnesses and experts, maybe even personal experience. (For more discussion of these matters, see Chapter 4.)

The Writer Clearly Proposes How to Solve the Problem. After stating just what the problem is, you then need to tell your readers how to solve it. This is the heart of the proposal, the writer's plan of action. Besides a detailed explanation of what should be done and how, the proposal should supply reliable supporting evidence for the plan: testimony of others, ideas from authorities, statistics from studies.

The Writer Argues Convincingly That This Proposal Will Solve the Problem. Perhaps the first question readers ask is "Can this solution work?" Writers usually address this question by examining the forces behind the problem and demonstrating how their plan will counter those forces. Suppose, for instance, you propose putting condom machines in all college dorms as a means of combating the spread of AIDS. To build a convincing case, you would have to summon evidence documenting how condoms significantly reduce the spread of AIDS.

The Writer Convincingly Explains How the Solution Will Work. Usually, readers next ask how will the plan be put into action, how will it solve the problem? Writers usually answer by detailing their plan's advantages, how efficiently (or cheaply, safely, conveniently, etc.) their proposals can be carried out. For the condom machine proposal, that might mean explaining how readily available machines leave students little excuse for unsafe sex. Students cannot complain that they jeopardized their health because they never made it to the local pharmacy. To add to the argument, you might cite other advantages of the proposal—that is, the easy installation of machines and the low prices of the contents.

The Writer Anticipates Objections to the Proposed Solution. Writers expect disagreement and objections to proposal arguments: Proposals are aimed at changing the status quo, and many people are opposed to or are fearful of change. If you want to persuade readers, especially hostile ones, you must show that you respect their sides of the argument too. Most proposal writers anticipate audience response to fortify their case and establish credibility. (See Chapters 2 and 4 for more discussion of anticipating opposing points of view.)

The Writer Explains Why This Solution Is Better Than Other Alternatives. Although you may believe that your solution to a problem is best, you cannot expect readers automatically to share that sentiment. Nor can you expect readers not to wonder about other solutions. A good proposal writer will almost always weigh alternative possibilities and attempt to demonstrate the superiority of his or her plan and the disadvantages of the opposition's. (See Chapter 4 for more discussion.) In the condom machine proposal, you might argue that availability is better than unavailability; that protection is better than no protection; and that while not completely safe, condoms reduce the risk of contracting the AIDS virus by 85 percent.

The Writer Projects a Reasonable Persona. As in position arguments, your persona is an important factor in proposals, for it conveys your attitude toward the subject and the audience. Because a proposal is intended to win readers to your side, the best strategy is to project a persona that is fair-minded. Even if you dislike or are angry about somebody else's views on an issue, projecting a reasonable and knowledgeable tone will have a more persuasive effect than a tone of belligerence.

Review: Features of Proposal Arguments

- Problem clearly stated
- Solution clearly proposed
- Why solution will work
- How solution will work
- Objections addressed
- Why proposal is better than alternatives
- Reasonable persona projected

If you are arguing for condom machines in dormitories, you would be wise to recognize that some people might object to the proposal because availability might be interpreted as encouragement of sexual behavior. So as not to offend or antagonize such readers, adopting a serious, straightforward tone might be the best mode of presenting the case.

The following essay is an example of a proposal argument that centers around a highly charged topic in our society—capital punishment. Because of the rising crime rate in America, it is a topic that is frequently debated, and one that may continue to be. This essay was written by John O'Sullivan, the editor of *The National Review,* where this article appeared. Before you read, think about the issue and the different arguments that might be offered for and against capital punishment. You might even make a pro/con checklist of opposing points in your argument notebook. As you read the essay, keep in mind the guidelines we've discussed so far.

SAMPLE ARGUMENT FOR ANALYSIS

Simply Killing
John O'Sullivan

1   Murder is becoming so commonplace in New York as to be hardly worth noticing. At least the authorities seem to take that view. *Saturday Night Live* parodied official attitudes only slightly when it had a police spokesman assure viewers that "for every victim of violent crime, four people visit the Metropolitan Museum of Art."

2   Still, some murders have a pointless fiendishness about them that makes one doubt the very humanity of the killers. Last month, for instance, a young woman store manager was surprised by an intruder, tied up, and was

stabbed and shot while helpless. The same day a city official was mugged on the subway, handed over his money, and was shot anyway.

3   Maybe the murderers in these cases killed for fun. We have no reason to think the only serial killers are those like Jeffrey Dahmer who obligingly keep the corpses in refrigerators for easy checking. On any one day, New York's subways probably contain a dozen or so muggers who have come to enjoy the momentary feeling of total power that murdering a helpless stranger gives them.

4   They may also be "rational" murderers who have worked out that by killing a victim they are also killing a witness—and at little or no additional cost. For the penalty for murder, once it has been plea-bargained downward by hard-pressed courts, differs only slightly from that for robbery.

5   The answer is to raise the cost of murder. Murderers of both kinds will pause before killing if the punishment they risk rises from a short prison sentence to the death penalty. Murder in the course of robbery should therefore carry a mandatory death sentence.

6   Mandatory? Yes, death must be certain on conviction. There cannot be any exceptions which, by reducing the likelihood of execution, persuade the potential murderer that the odds still favor killing the victim. That would, in my view, reduce the murder rate.

7   But even if it could be shown that the death penalty has no unique power to deter, I would still favor it. It satisfies our sense of justice that people guilty of especially violent crimes should face especially severe punishment.

8   Is this outlook "uncivilized"? Opponents of the death penalty use the word to signify merely something they don't like, the opposite of a visit to the Metropolitan Museum. But John Sparrow, the Tory[1] wit and Warden of All Souls[2] (who died last month), used to tell the story of two castaways who reach an island where the first sight that greets them is a gallows from which a corpse dangles.

9   "Thank God," says one of them. "It's a civilized country." Sparrow was not being ironic. He realized that only a civilized country restrains crime by the formal process of legal execution.

10   In an uncivilized country, the citizens rely upon private force to defend themselves against the lawlessness, daylight robbery, and casual murders fostered by the absence of effective lawful punishments. Although a country may dispense with capital punishment once it considers civilized habits to be so firmly entrenched as not to require such drastic support, a premature move in that direction will be rewarded by a resurgence of barbarity.

11   New York today makes his point.

---

[1]**Tory:** British conservative party

[2]**Warden:** British academic title roughly equivalent to our college presidents. **All Souls:** a constituent college of Oxford University.

12   Britain had its own Jeffrey Dahmer a decade ago in Denis Nielsen, a minor civil servant who picked up young men, took them home, strangled them, propped them up at the table, and chatted to the corpses at meal times.

13   Was this insanity? Or an extreme way of overcoming British reserve? Nielsen himself was sure he was sane.

14   When Brian Masters, the author of *Killing for Company*, told him that he was distantly related to Virginia Woolf, the news unsettled him.

15   "She went mad, you know," said the serial murderer uneasily.

Analysis of a Proposal Argument

Now that you've read O'Sullivan's essay, let's test it against our guidelines.

- **The Writer States the Problem Clearly**   The general problem is expressed in the title of O'Sullivan's essay. The particular problem is the rampant murder rate in New York City. O'Sullivan wastes no time in raising this, for he dramatically states it in the opening sentence: "Murder is becoming so commonplace in New York as to be hardly worth noticing." Immediately this assertion advises the uninformed of the severity of New York's violent crime while it reminds others of how pervasive the problem is.

- **The Writer Clearly Proposes How to Solve the Problem**   O'Sullivan's solution to the murder problem is to eliminate murderers. His recommendation forms the lead sentence of paragraph 5: "The answer is to raise the cost of murder." Not only is this proposal statement the topic sentence of the paragraph, but it is also the claim on which he continues to build throughout the rest of his argument.

- **The Writer Argues Convincingly That This Proposal Will Solve the Problem**   One question readers might raise is "Will the mandatory death penalty solve the rising crime problem?" O'Sullivan does not offer any solid evidence to support his claim. Nonetheless, he argues that a mandatory death sentence "would . . . reduce the murder rate." He picks up on this in paragraph 10 when he says that without capital punishment, a country will suffer "a resurgence of barbarity."

    Of course, without hard data, these suppositions add little solid support to his proposal. Clearly realizing that, and anticipating potential objections, O'Sullivan adds that even if execution does not deter a potential killer, he would still favor the death penalty because it "satisfies our sense of justice that people guilty of especially violent crimes should face especially severe punishment." Therefore, to compensate for the lack of hard evidence, the author introduces another point to his argument: retribution. O'Sullivan also particularizes the problem by citing two specific examples of particularly brutal and senseless killings. To help bring home the threat to the average New York citizen or potential visitor, he speculates in the third paragraph how "[o]n any one day, New York's subways probably contain a dozen or so" potential murderers. In any argument, personalizing the problem is a useful strategy in winning over even the most unsympathetic reader. Here the reminder that the reader may be the next victim is particularly persuasive.

- **The Writer Convincingly Explains How the Solution Will Work**   O'Sullivan doesn't explore this, although he could have made the argument often heard from proponents of the death penalty that execution is cheaper than keeping a prisoner alive for the remainder of his or her life.

- **The Writer Anticipates Objections to the Proposed Solution**   O'Sullivan anticipates two key convictions held by capital punishment opponents: (1) On the practical level, capital punishment does not clearly deter murderers. He acknowledges this point, then dismisses it to defend his proposal: "It satisfies our sense of justice that people guilty of especially violent crimes should face especially severe punishment." (2) Capital punishment is "uncivilized." To this objection he argues that unless a country is so civilized in its habits as to not need capital punishment, "a premature move" to dispense with it would result in "a resurgence of barbarity." To add credibility to his case, O'Sullivan shares an anecdote told by a highly respected conservative, John Sparrow. Since *The National Review* is written for a conservative audience, this witty story might carry extra weight with O'Sullivan's readers.

- **The Writer Explains Why This Solution Is Better Than Other Alternatives**   The alternative solution to mandatory capital punishment is imprisonment. To O'Sullivan, this alternative is unacceptable, since plea-bargaining in "hard-pressed" New York courts results in murder sentences that differ "only slightly from that for robbery." Mandatory execution, he argues, is the only way to persuade potential murderers, especially the "rational" ones, that killing a victim will cost them their own lives.

- **The Writer Projects a Reasonable Persona**   Throughout the essay, O'Sullivan maintains a reasonable and sincere persona. His concern for victims of senseless brutality comes through early in his references to the store manager and city official. In spite of a charged subject, O'Sullivan shows measured control in his discussion of both victims and killers. Each subject naturally invites charged language to arouse either anger or sympathy. And, yet, he manages some of each without casting his argument in emotional or slanted terms. On the contrary, "helpless" is the only subjective term used to describe victims, whereas "pointless fiendishness" is used to characterize some murders. Instead of tough talk, O'Sullivan's strategy is to present his case in cool and practical terms. Note, too, that his reference to the *Saturday Night Live* parody and John Sparrow's anecdote enliven his persona with wit and urbanity though the subject is gruesome.

EXERCISES

1. In your argument notebook, make a list of as many ways of beginning an argument as possible. Then find an example of each method that you think is effective and copy it into your notebook. If you are working in a group,

share your lists with each other; you may want to photocopy your lists so that each member has a "catalogue" of good beginnings to consider.

2. Repeat exercise 1, but this time collect endings for arguments. Again, your goal is to compile a catalogue of endings to consult when you are "stuck."

3. Think about the times when an outline is helpful. What circumstances seem to require outlines? When *don't* you need an outline? Compare your answers with those of other group members. Does everyone need to outline in the same circumstances? What do your results tell you about how writers organize material?

4. Construct a formal outline for John O'Sullivan's essay in this chapter, then compare it with another student's. If there are places where your outlines disagree, analyze why your readings are different.

5. Go back to the list of persuasive encounters you compiled for exercise 1 in Chapter 1. Now subdivide that list into position and proposal arguments. Which kind of argument are you most subjected to in a day? Why do you think this is so?

6. In your argument notebook, outline an argument that will refute either Clara Spotted Elk's or John O'Sullivan's argument. Sketch out what components you will want to include in your beginning, middle, and end, and identify how you will handle the key features of your argument. If your instructor asks you to do so, write a first draft of your essay from the notes you compile.

ADDRESSING AUDIENCES

Thinking Like a Reader

As we've already pointed out, the purpose in writing an argument is to shape opinions and to change minds. Knowing something about your readers will make it easier to achieve these goals. This may seem obvious, but a little reflection will probably give you a better appreciation of the situation. Look at your classmates, for instance. Are you all the same race? gender? age? ethnicity? Do you all listen to the same music? vote for the same candidate? attend the same church? dress alike? Unless you attend a very unusual school, the answer to most of these questions will be a resounding "no." People are different; what moves you may bore the person sitting behind you, whereas what puts you to sleep may inspire someone else to passionate activism. And what you see on the surface isn't the whole story about each of your classmates either. That rough-looking guy who works as a carpenter may write poems in his spare time; that middle-aged homemaker may have Metallica, Pearl Jam, or Queen Latifah tapes in her car. If you want to persuade any of these people, you're going to have to assess them carefully: That's a requirement for successful argument.

Knowing your audience will help you determine almost every aspect of the presentation of your case: the kind of language you use, the writing style (casual or formal, humorous or serious, technical or philosophical); the particular slant you take (appealing to the reader's reason, emotions, or ethics, or a combination of these); what emphasis to give the argument; the type of evidence you offer; and the kinds of authorities you cite. Also, this knowledge will let you better anticipate any objections to your position. In short, knowing your audience lets you adjust the shape of your argument the way you would refocus a camera after each photo you shoot.

If, for instance, you're writing for your economics professor, you would use technical vocabulary you would not use with your English professor. Likewise, in a newspaper article condemning alcohol abusers, you would have to keep in mind that some of your readers or their family members may be recovering alcoholics; they may take exception to your opinions. A travel piece for an upscale international magazine would need to have a completely different slant and voice than that of the travel section of a small local newspaper.

Knowing your audience might make the difference between a convincing argument and one that fails. Suppose, for instance, you decide to write an editorial for the student newspaper opposing a recently announced tuition hike. Chances are you would have a sympathetic audience in the student body because you share age, educational status, and interests. Most students do not like the idea of a higher tuition bill. That commonality might justify the blunt language and emotional slant of your appeal. It might even allow a few sarcastic comments directed at the administration. That same argument addressed to your school's board of trustees, however, would probably not win a round of applause. To them it would be wiser to adopt a more formal tone in painting a sympathetic picture of your financial strain; it's always smart to demonstrate an understanding of the opposition's needs, maybe even a compromise solution. In this case, your appeal to the trustees would be more credible were you to acknowledge the university's plight, while recommending alternative money-saving measures such as a new fund-raising program.

Or suppose you wrote an article with a religious thrust arguing against capital punishment. You argue that even in the case of confessed murderers, state execution is an immoral practice running counter to Christian doctrine; and for supporting evidence you offer direct quotations from the New Testament. Were you to submit your article to a religious publication, your reliance upon the authority of the scriptures would probably appeal to the editors. However, were you to submit that same article to the "My Turn" column for *Newsweek*, chances are it would be turned down, no matter how well written. The editors aren't necessarily an ungodly lot, but *Newsweek*, like most other large-circulation magazines, is published for an audience made up of people of every religious persuasion, as well as agnostics and atheists. *Newsweek* editors are not in the business of publishing material that excludes so large a segment of its audience. Knowing your readers works in two ways: It helps you decide what materials to put into your argument, and it helps you decide where to publish your argument (whether it be an electronic bulletin board, a local paper, or the op-ed page of *The Wall Street Journal*).

The Target Audience

The articles in this book come from a variety of publications, many of them magazines addressed to the "general" American readership. Others, however, come from publications directed to men or women, the political right or left, or from publications for people of particular ethnic, racial, and cultural identities. They're written for *target audiences*. When writers have a "target" audience in mind, particularly readers who share the same interests, opinions, and prejudices, they can take shortcuts with little risk of alienating anybody, because writer and readers have so many things in common. Consider the following excerpts concerning the use of animal testing in scientific research.

Contrary to a prevailing misperception, in vitro tests need not replace existing in vivo test procedures in order to be useful. They can contribute to chemical-safety evaluation right now. In vitro tests, for example, can be incorporated into the earliest stages of the risk-assessment process; they can be used to identify chemicals having the lowest probability of toxicity so that animals need be exposed only to less noxious chemicals.

It is clear from the technical terminology (e.g., *in vitro, in vivo, toxicity*), professional jargon (*test procedures, chemical-safety evaluation, risk-assessment process*), and the formal, detached tone, that the piece was intended for a scientifically educated readership. Not surprisingly, the article, "Alternatives to Animals in Toxicity Testing," was authored by two research scientists, Alan M. Goldberg and John M. Frazier, and published in *Scientific American* (August 1989). Contrast it with another approach to the topic:

> Almost 30 years ago, Queen had been a child herself, not quite two years old, living in Thailand under the care of her mother and another female elephant, the two who had tended to her needs every day since her birth. They taught her how to use her trunk, in work and play, and had given her a sense of family loyalty. But then Queen was captured, and her life was changed irrevocably by men with whips and guns. One man herded Queen by whipping and shouting at her while another shot her mother, who struggled after her baby until more bullets pulled her down forever.

What distinguishes this excerpt is the emotional appeal. This is not the kind of article one would find in *Scientific American* or most other scientific journals. Nor would you expect to see this kind of emotional appeal in a news magazine such as *Newsweek* or *Time*, or a general interest publication such as the Sunday magazine of many newspapers. The excerpt comes from an animal rights newsletter published by PETA, People for the Ethical Treatment of Animals. Given that particular audience, the writer safely assumes immediate audience sympathy with the plight of elephants. There is no need for the author to qualify or apologize for such sentimentalizing statements as "Queen had been a child herself" and "They taught her how to use her trunk, in work and play, and had given her a sense of family loyalty." In fact, given the context, the author is probably more interested in reminding readers of a shared cause than winning converts.

About That General Audience

Unless you're convinced that your readers are in total agreement with you or share your philosophical or professional interests, you may have some trouble picturing just whom you are persuading. It's tempting to say you're writing for a "general" audience; but, as we said at the beginning of this chapter, general audiences may contain very different people with different backgrounds, expectations, and standards. Writing for such audiences, then, may put additional pressure on you.

In reality, of course, most of your college writing will be for your professors. This can be a little confusing because you may find yourself trying to determine just what audience role your professor will take. You may even wonder why professors expect you to explain material with which they are familiar. You may feel that defining technical terms to your psychology instructor who covered them in class the week before, or summarizing a poem that you know your English professor can probably recite, is a waste of time. But they have a good reason: They assume the role of uninformed audience to let you show how much *you* know.

Of course, if you are arguing controversial issues you may find yourself in the awkward position of trying to second-guess your instructor's stand on an issue. You may even be tempted to tone down your presentation so as not to risk offense and, thus, an undesirable grade. Most instructors try not to let their biases affect their evaluation of a student's work. Their main concern is how well a student argues a position.

For some assignments, your instructor may specify an audience for you: members of the city council, the readers of the campus newspaper, Rush Limbaugh's radio listeners, and so on. But if no audience is specified, one of your earliest decisions about writing should be in choosing an audience. If you pick "readers of *The National Review,*" for instance, you'll know you're writing for mostly male, conservative, middle-aged, middle-class whites; the expectations of these readers are very different than for readers of *Jet* or *Stereophile*. If you are constrained to (or want the challenge of) writing for the so-called general audience construct a mental picture of who those people are so that you'll be able to shape your argument accordingly. Here are some of the characteristics we think you might include in your definition.

The "general" audience includes those people who read *Newsweek, Time,* and your local newspaper. That means people whose average age is about 30, whose educational level is high school plus two years of college, who make up the vast middle class of America, who politically stand in the middle of the road, and whose racial and ethnic origins span the world. You can assume that they read the daily newspaper and watch the evening news and are generally informed about what is going on in the country. You can assume a good comprehension of language nuances and a sense of humor. They are people who recognize who Shakespeare was, though they may not be able to quote passages or name ten of his plays. Nor will they necessarily be an expert in the latest theory of black holes or be able to explain how photo emulsions work. However, you can expect them to be open to technical explanations and willing to listen to arguments on birth control, gun control, weight control, and the issue of women in the military. More important, you can look upon your audience as people willing to hear what you have to say.

Guidelines for Knowing Your Audience

Before sitting down to write, think about your audience. Ask yourself the following questions: Will I be addressing other college students, or people of my parents' generation? Will my audience be of a particular political persuasion, or strongly identified with a specific cultural background? Will the age of my readers and their educational background influence the way they think about a given issue? On what criteria will they make their decisions about this issue? A good example of profiling your audience is evident in the 1992 presidential election. The Republicans gambled that "family values" and "leadership experience" were the chief criteria for voters. The Democrats, in a famous slogan, made the criterion, "The economy, stupid." As the election results showed, the Democrats assessed their audience more accurately than the Republicans did.

If you know your audience, you can determine what you have in common with them—what values, beliefs, interests, and life-style you share. And these insights will advise you if your readers will be sympathetic or hostile to your point of view. You may want to use the following checklist to help you assess your audience. If you like visual prompts, write the answers to these questions on a card or a slip of paper that you can hang over your desk, or display in a window on your computer screen, while you're working on your argument. Looking at these questions and answers occasionally will remind you to focus your writing for these particular people.

Audience Checklist

1. Who are the readers I will be addressing?
   a. What age group?
   b. Are they male, female, or both?
   c. What educational background?
   d. What socioeconomic status?
   e. What values, prejudices, assumptions do they have toward life?
   f. Whom might they have voted for in the last presidential race? How might they vote in the next one?
2. Where do my readers stand on the issue?
   a. Do they know anything about it?
   b. If so, how might they have learned about it?
   c. Are they hostile to my stand on the issue?
   d. Is there anything I have in common with my readers on the issue?
3. How do I want my readers to view the issue?
   a. If they are hostile to my view, can I persuade them to see the issue my way?
   b. If they are neutral, how can I convince them to take my side in the controversy?
   c. If they are sympathetic to my views, what new light can I shed on the issue? How can I reinspire them to take action?

Adapting to Your Readers' Attitudes

Writing for a general audience is a challenge because in that faceless mass are three kinds of readers you'll be addressing:

1. people who agree with you
2. people who are neutral—those who are unconvinced or uninformed on the issue
3. people who don't share your views, who might even be hostile to them

Each of these different subgroups will have different expectations of you and give you different obligations to meet if you are to present a convincing argument. Even readers sympathetic to your cause might not be familiar with special vocabulary, the latest developments around the issue, or some of the more subtle arguments from the opposition. Those hostile to your cause might be so committed to their own viewpoints that they might not take the time to think about the more subtle features of your position. And those neutral to the cause might simply need to be filled in on the issue and its background. If you're going to persuade your readers, you'll have to tailor your approach to suit their attitudes.

When addressing an audience, whether general or one of a particular persuasion, you must try to put yourself in their place. You must try to imagine the different needs and expectations these readers bring to your writing, always asking yourself what new information you can pass on and what new ways of viewing you can find for addressing the issue you're arguing. Let's look at some of the strategies you, as a writer, might use, depending on whether you anticipate a neutral, friendly, or unfriendly group of readers.

Addressing a Neutral Audience

Some writers think a neutral audience is easiest to write for, but many others find this the most challenging group of readers. After all, they're *neutral*; you don't know which way they're leaning, or what may make them commit to your position. Your best role is the conveyor of knowledge: The information you bring, and the ways in which you present it, are the means by which you hope to persuade a neutral audience. Here are some of the ways to convey that information.

Fill in the Background

There are some issues on which few people are neutral: abortion, capital punishment, drug legalization, gays in the military, gun control. Although you may feel passionate about these issues, some readers may never have given them a thought or made up their minds yet about them; or they may simply be uninformed. For instance, if you're part of a farming community, your concern about agricultural production might make you feel some urgency about preventing the loss of topsoil. To make a convincing case for readers from, say, Chicago or New York City, you first would have to tell them a little about what topsoil is and why it is crucial to agriculture. Similarly, as a resident of a large town, you might need to explain to readers from rural Vermont and Iowa why you think your community must institute mandatory recycling. In both cases it's important to fill your readers in on the issue; relate some of the history and background of the controversy. And all the while encourage them to weigh with an open mind the evidence you present.

Present the Pros and Cons of the Issue

Part of educating a neutral audience on your position is presenting a balanced picture of the issue—the pros and cons. Even though you are trying vigorously to sway readers to your side, you will be more persuasive if you treat opposing views fairly. You should clearly lay out the key arguments of the opposition, then demonstrate why your view is superior. Let your readers make their decisions based on comparisons. Not representing the other side leaves you open to criticism of distortion, and it may make your readers feel that you're patronizing them.

Personalize the Issues

One sure way of gaining readers' attention is to speak their language—that is, address their personal needs, hopes, and fears. (It's what skillful politicians do all the time on the campaign trail.) If you want to engage your readers' attention, demonstrate how the problem will affect them personally. On the matter of topsoil, explain how if nothing is done to prevent its erosion, the price of corn and beans will triple over the next three years. On the recycling issue, explain how unrestricted trash dumping will mean that city dwellers will try to dump more trash in rural areas.

Show Respect

When you're an informed person talking about an issue to people with less knowledge than you, there's a dangerous tendency to speak down to them. Think how you feel when someone "talks down" to you. Do you like it? How persuasive do you think you can be if your readers think you're talking down to them? Don't condescend to or patronize them. On the contrary, treat your readers as people who want to know what you know about the issue and who want you to demonstrate to them clearly and accurately why you think they should agree with you. Invite them into the debate, encouraging them with sound reasons and strong evidence to consider the merits of your side. Although your audience may not be as informed as you, they are willing to listen and deserve respect.

Addressing a Friendly Audience

Writing an argument for the already converted is a lot easier than writing for a neutral audience or one that is hostile. In a sense, half the battle is won because no minds have to be changed. You need not brace yourself for opposing views or refutations. Nor must you spend time filling your readers in on the history of the issue. Your role is simply to provide readers with new information and to renew enthusiasm for your shared position. Nonetheless, there are still some steps you should take.

Avoid Playing to Prejudices

One of the risks of addressing a sympathetic audience is appealing to prejudices rather than reason and facts. Although it might be tempting to mock those who don't agree with you or to demean their views, don't. Stooping to that level only diminishes your own authority and undermines your credibility. When referring to the opposition's arguments, use reason and hard evidence instead of insults and ridicule to underscore the weakness of their arguments. Encourage your readers to respect the opposition, maybe even recognize some merits of their arguments, even though you ultimately disagree. It's simply a classier approach, one that makes your readers feel somehow superior to your opponents. And it will win respect from friends and foes alike.

Offer New Information on the Opposition

Even though your readers may agree with you, remind them of the opposition's arguments. Recall what the other side considers its strongest counterpoints. Such a reminder serves important purposes. First, your audience might need to have their memories refreshed regarding the history of the issue. Second, you provide readers with important new information on the issue. Third, you keep readers open-minded.

Foster the Inoculation Effect

A fair and clear review of opposing arguments also provides like-minded readers with material to better defend your shared views on the issue. Some people might feel this undercuts the certainty of one's stand or makes readers wishy-washy, but the opposite is true. A balanced view of the issue ultimately strengthens the stand of a sympathetic audience. Just as your metabolism builds resistance to the flu when inoculated with a small amount of the offending microbes, so readers on your side can better fortify their own arguments when well-versed on the other side.

Addressing an Unfriendly Audience

As difficult as it may be to accept, some readers will be totally at odds with your views, even hostile to them. Writing for such a readership, of course, is especially challenging—far more than for neutral readers. So, how do you present your argument to people you have little chance of winning over?

Seek Common Ground and Remind Your Opponents of It

In this argumentative strategy, recommended by psychologist Carl Rogers, you try to empathize with your readers. Remind them of beliefs and standards you have in common; appreciate their concerns and anxieties. By empathizing with their position, especially at the beginning of an argument, you present yourself as a reasonable person, one whose views they should respect. You also lessen their fears and hostility toward you and your position, making it more possible for them to regard your case with an open mind. This provides you with an opportunity to show the advantages of your position to your readers.

Don't Antagonize Your Readers

Although conversion may be out of the question, your audience might benefit from seeing the issue from another side. In other words, approach a hostile audience as someone who can shed a different light on the problem. View them as people who are potentially interested in learning something new. Without being defensive, arrogant, or apologetic, make your claim, enumerate your reasons, and lay out the evidence for your readers to evaluate on their own. Regard them as intelligent people capable of drawing their own conclusions. You may not win converts, but you might at least lead some to recognize the merits of your side. You might even convince a few people to reconsider their views.

Remember the Golden Rule

Even though they may not agree with you, treat the opposition with respect. Look upon them as intelligent people who just happen to disagree with you. Demonstrate your understanding of their side of the issue. Show that you have made the effort to research the opposition. Give credit where credit is due. If some of their counterpoints make sense, say so. In short, treat those from the other side and their views as you would want to be treated. You may just win a few converts.

Choosing Your Words

Whether addressing friends, foes, or the undecided, you must take care that your readers fully understand your case. In part, this is accomplished by choosing your words carefully and by accurately defining any technical, unfamiliar, foreign, or abstract terms. A few specific tips follow about how to inform your readers without turning them off.

Distinguishing Denotation and Connotation

Many words, even the most common, carry special suggestions or associations called **connotations** that differ from the precise dictionary definitions, called **denotations.** For example, if you looked up the word *house* in the dictionary, one of the synonyms you'd find is *shelter*. Yet if you told people you lived in a shelter, they would think you were joking or that you live in a facility for the homeless or some kind of animal sanctuary. This is because *shelter* implies a covering or structure that protects those within from the elements or from danger. In other words, the term is not neutral as is the word *house*. Likewise, dictionary synonyms for *horse* include *steed* and *nag*, but the former implies an elegant and high-spirited riding animal, while the latter suggests one that is old and worn out.

Review: Addressing Audiences

A Neutral Audience

- Fill in the background
- Present the pros and cons of the issue
- Personalize the issues
- Show respect for your readers

A Friendly Audience

- Avoid playing to prejudices
- Offer new information on the opposition
- Foster the inoculation effect

An Unfriendly Audience

- Seek common ground
- Don't antagonize your readers
- Remember the Golden Rule

The denotations of words may be the same, but their connotations will almost always differ. And the reason is that dictionary denotations are essentially neutral, emotion-free, and generally approved by everybody, while connotations are most often associated with unfavorable attitudes or charged feelings that can influence readers' responses. Therefore, it is important to be aware of the shades of differences when choosing your words. Consider the different meanings the connotations of the bracketed choices lend these statements:

> By the time I got home I was _____ [sleepy, exhausted, weary, beat, dead].
>
> My boyfriend drives around in a red _____ [car, vehicle, buggy, clunker, jalopy].
>
> Even from the attic I could hear him _____ [shout, yell, bellow, scream, shriek].

Connotations can also be personal and, thus, powerful tools for shaping readers' responses to what you say. Consider the word *pig*. The dictionary definition, or denotation, would read something like this: "A domestic farm animal with a long, broad snout and a thick, fat body covered with coarse bristles." However, the connotation of *pig* is far more provocative, for it suggests someone who looks or acts like a pig; someone who is greedy or filthy; someone who is sexually immoral. (Most dictionaries list the connotations of words, although some connotations might only be found in a dictionary of slang—e.g., *The New Dictionary of American Slang,* edited by Robert L. Chapman, or *Slang!* by Paul Dickson.)

There is nothing wrong with using a word because of its connotations; but you must be aware that connotations will have an emotional impact on readers. You don't want to say something unplanned. You don't want to offend readers by using words loaded with unintentional associations. For instance, you wouldn't suggest to advertisers that they "should be more creative when hawking their products" unless you intended to insult them. Although the term *hawking* refers to selling, it is un-flattering and misleading because it connotes somebody moving up and down the streets peddling goods by shouting. Linguistically, the word comes from the same root as the word *huckster*, which refers to an aggressive merchant known for hag-gling and questionable practices.

Connotatively loaded language can be used to create favorable as well as un-favorable reactions. If you are arguing against the use of animals in medical re-search, you will get a stronger response if you decry the sacrifice of "puppies and kittens" rather than the cooler, scientific, and less charged "laboratory animals."

You can understand why politicians, newspaper columnists, and anyone ad-vocating a cause use connotative language. The loaded word is like a bullet for a writer making a strong argument. Consider the connotative impact of the italicized terms in the following excerpts taken from essays in this text:

> Black conservatives like Shelby Steele . . . are ready *to trash* affirmative ac-tion. . . (Adams, Charles G. "It's Past Time to Speak Out." p. 264.)

> Its author is longtime advertising *Bigfoot* Ed McCabe, whose claim to fame mostly resides in recognizing Frank Purdue's uncanny resemblance to his product. (Carroll, John. "Sex Is Still Doing the Selling." p. 594.)

> This year's list of would-be censors trying to *shoulder their way to the trough of celebrity* is hardly worth enumerating: Their 15 minutes might be up by the time I'm done. (Klavan, Andrew. "In Praise of Gore." p. 436.)

Each of the italicized words was selected not for its denotations but its nega-tive connotations. In the first example, Charles G. Adams could have easily selected the neutral verb *to abandon*, except that *to trash* suggests recklessly destroying some-thing in protest or disgust—an image that helps damn Steele as a turncoat to his race. Similarly, John Carroll might have referred to Ed McCabe in an objective term such as *executive* or *CEO*, but he opted for *Bigfoot* and its humorously unfa-vorable designations of Sasquatch, the huge and hairy humanoid creature thought by some to inhabit the forests of the Pacific Northwest—an image that also suggests McCabe's stature, power, and menace in his profession. The final example could have read as follows: "This year's list of would-be censors trying to *gain notoriety* is hardly worth enumerating: Their 15 minutes might be up by the time I'm done." However, Andrew Klavan clearly wanted to convey his disapproval of movie censors and, thus, selected words that create an image of them as aggressive and piglike, fighting their way to feed at fame.

Being Specific

To help readers better understand your argument, you need to use words that are precise enough to convey your exact meaning. If you simply say, "The weather last weekend was *terrible*," your readers are left to come up with their own interpretations of what the weather was like. Was it hot and muggy? cold and rainy? overcast and very windy? some of each? Chances are your readers won't come up with the same weather conditions you had in mind. However, if you said, "Last weekend it rained day and night and never got above forty degrees," readers will have a more precise idea of the weekend's weather. And you will have accomplished your purpose of saying just what you meant.

The terms **general** and **specific** are opposites just as **abstract** and **concrete** are opposites. General words do not name individual things but classes or groups of things: animals, trees, women. Specific words refer to individuals in a group: your pet canary, the oak tree outside your bedroom window, the first lady. Of course, general and specific are themselves relative terms. Depending on the context or your frame of reference, a word that is specific in one context may be general in another. For instance, there is no need to warn a vegetarian that a restaurant serves veal Oscar and beef Wellington when simply *meat* will do. In other words, there are degrees of specificity. The following list illustrates just such a sliding scale, moving downward from the more general to the more specific.

General	Animal	Person	Book	Clothing	Food	Machine
	feline	female	novel	footwear	seafood	vehicle
	cat	singer	American	shoes	fish	fighter jet
Specific	Daisy, my pet	Sheryl Crowe	*The Great Gatsby*	her Nikes	tuna	F-117

General words are useful in ordinary conversation where the people you're addressing understand your meaning and usually don't ask for clarification. The same is true in writing when you are addressing an audience familiar with your subject. In such instances, you can get away with occasional broad statements. For example, if you are running for class president, your campaign speeches would not require a great number of specifics as much as general statements of promise and principles:

> If elected, I intend to do what I can to ensure a comfortable classroom environment for each student at this college.

But when your audience is unfamiliar with your subject or when the context requires concrete details, generalities and abstract terms fall flat, leaving people wondering just exactly what you are trying to communicate. Let's say, for instance, you write a note to your dean explaining why you'd like to change the room where your English class meets. You wouldn't get very far on this appeal:

Room 107 Richards is too small and uncomfortable for our class.

However, if you offered some specifics evoking a sense of the room's unpleasantness, you'd make a more persuasive case for changing the room:

> Room 107 Richards has 20 fixed seats for 27 students, leaving those who come in late to sit on windowsills or the floor. Worse still is the air quality. The radiators are fixed on high and the windows don't open. By the end of the hour it must be 90 degrees in there, leaving everybody sweaty and wilted including Prof. Hazzard.

What distinguishes this paragraph is the use of concrete details: "20 fixed seats for 27 students"; late comers having to "sit on windowsills or on the floor"; "radiators fixed on high"; "the windows don't open"; "90 degrees"; and "everybody was left sweaty and wilted including Prof. Hazzard." But more than simply conjuring up a vivid impression of the room's shortcomings, these specifics add substance to your argument for a room change.

Concrete language is specific language—words that have definite meaning. Concrete language names persons, places and things: *Mother Teresa, Jose Canseco, New Zealand, Hartford, book, toothpaste.* Concrete terms conjure up vivid pictures in the minds of readers since they refer to particular things or qualities that can be perceived by your five senses—that is, they can be seen, smelled, tasted, felt, and heard. Abstract words, on the other hand, refer to qualities that do not have a definite concrete meaning. They denote intangible qualities that cannot be perceived directly by the senses but that are inferred from the senses—*powerful, foolish, talented, responsible, worthy.* Abstract words also denote concepts and ideas—*patriotism, beauty, victory, sorrow.* Although abstract terms can be useful depending on the context, writing that relies heavily on abstractions will fail to communicate clear meaning. Notice in the pairs below how concrete and specific details convert vague statements into vivid ones:

Abstract: He was very nicely dressed.

Concrete: He wore a dark gray Armani suit, white pinstriped shirt, and red paisley tie.

Abstract: Jim felt uncomfortable at Jean's celebration party.

Concrete: Jim's envy over Jean's promotion made him feel guilty.

Abstract: That was an incredible accident.

Concrete: A trailer truck jackknifed in the fog causing seven cars to plow into each other, killing two, injuring eight, and leaving debris for a quarter mile along Route 17.

Abstract language is also relative. It depends on circumstances and the experience of the person using them. A *cold* December morning to someone living in

Florida might mean temperatures in the forties or fifties. To residents of North Dakota, *cold* would designate air at subzero temperatures. It all depends on one's point of view. A *fair trial* might mean one thing to the prosecutor of a case, yet something completely different to the defense attorney. Likewise, what might be *offensive* language to your grandmother would probably not faze a hardened convict.

When employing abstract language you need to be aware that readers may not share your point of view. Consequently, you should be careful to clarify your terms or simply select concrete alternatives. Below is an excerpt from a student paper as it appeared in the first draft. As you can see, it is lacking in details and specifics and has a rather dull impact.

> **Vague:** Last year my mother nearly died from medicine when she went to the hospital. The bad reaction sent her into a coma for weeks, requiring life-support systems around the clock. Thankfully, she came out of the coma and was released, but somebody should have at least asked what, if any, allergies she had.

Although the paragraph reads smoothly, it communicates very little of the dramatic crisis being described. Without specific details and concrete words, the reader misses both the trauma and the seriousness of the hospital staff's neglect, thus dulling the argument for stronger safeguards. What follows is the same paragraph revised with the intent of making it more concrete.

> **Revised:** Last year my mother nearly died from a codeine-based painkiller when she was rushed to the emergency room at Emerson Hospital. The severe allergic reaction sent her into a coma for six weeks, requiring daily blood transfusions, thrice weekly kidney dialysis, continuous intravenous medicines, a tracheostomy, and round-the-clock intensive care. Thankfully, she came out of the coma and was released, but the ER staff was negligent in not determining from her or her medical records that she was allergic to codeine.

Using Figurative Language

Words have their literal meaning, but they also can mean something beyond dictionary definitions, as we have seen. The sentence "Mrs. Jones is an angel" does not mean that Mrs. Jones is literally a supernatural winged creature, but a very kind and pleasant woman. What makes the literally impossible meaningful here is figurative language.

Figurative language (or a **figure of speech**) is comparative language. It is language that represents something in terms of something else—in figures, symbols, or likeness (Mrs. Jones and an angel). It functions to make the ordinary appear extraordinary and the unfamiliar appear familiar. It also adds richness and complexity to abstractions. Here, for instance, is a rather bland literal statement: "Yesterday it was 96 degrees and very humid." Here's that same sentence rendered in figurative language: "Yesterday the air was like warm glue." What this version does is equate yesterday's humid air to glue on a feature shared by each—stickiness. And the result is more interesting than the original statement.

The comparison of humid air to glue is linked by the words *like*. This example represents one of the most common figures of speech, the **simile**. Derived from the Latin *similis*, the term means similar. A simile makes an explicit comparison between dissimilar things (humid air and glue). It says that A is like B. The connectives used in similes are most often the words *like, as,* and *than*:

- A school of minnows shot by me like pelting rain.
- His arms are as big as hams.
- They're meaner than junkyard dogs.

When the connectives *like, as,* or *than* are omitted, then we have another common figure of speech, the **metaphor**. The term is from the Greek meta (over) + *pherin* ("to carry or ferry") meaning to carry over meaning from one thing to another. Instead of saying that A is like B, a metaphor equates them—A *is* B. For example, Mrs. Jones and an angel are said to be one and the same, although we all know that literally the two are separate entities.

- This calculus problem is a real pain in the neck.
- The crime in this city is a cancer out of control.
- She's cool.

Sometimes writers will carelessly combine metaphors that don't go with each other. Known as **mixed metaphors,** these often produce ludicrous results. For example:

- The heat of his expression froze them in their tracks.
- The experience left a bad taste in her eyes.
- The arm of the law has two strikes against it.

When a metaphor has lost it figurative value, it is called a **dead metaphor:** the *mouth* of a river, the *eye* of a needle, the *face* of a clock. Originally, these expressions functioned as figures of speech, but their usage has become so common in our language that many have become **clichés** ("golden opportunity," "dirt cheap," "a clinging vine"). More will be said about clichés below, but our best advice is to avoid them. Because they have lost their freshness, they're unimaginative and they dull your writing.

Another common figure of speech is **personification**, in which human or animal characteristics or qualities are attributed to inanimate things or ideas. We hear it all the time: trees *bow* in the wind; fear *grips* the heart; high pressure areas *sit* on the northeast. Such language is effective in making abstract concepts concrete and vivid and possibly more interesting:

- Graft and corruption walk hand in hand in this town.
- The state's new tax law threatens to gobble up our savings.
- Nature will give a sigh of relief the day they close down that factory.

As with other figures of speech, personification must be used appropriately and with restraint. If it's overdone it ends up calling undue attention to itself while leaving readers baffled:

> Drugs have slouched their way into our schoolyards and playgrounds, laughing up their sleeves at the law and whispering vicious lies to innocent children.

For the sake of sounding literary, drugs here are personified as pushers slouching, laughing, and whispering. But such an exaggeration runs the risk of being rejected by readers as pretentious. If this happens, the vital message may well be lost. One must also be careful not to take shortcuts. Like dead metaphors, many once-imaginative personifications have become clichés: "justice is blind," "virtue triumphed," "walking death." While such may be handy catch phrases, they are trite and would probably be dismissed by critical readers as lazy writing.

Another figure of speech worth mentioning is the **euphemism**, which is a polite way of saying something blunt or offensive. Instead of toilets, restaurants have *restrooms.* Instead of a sales person, furniture stores send us *mattress technicians.* Instead of false teeth, people in advertising wear *dentures.* The problem with euphemisms is that they conceal the true meaning of something. The result can be a kind of doubletalk—language inflated for the sake of deceiving the listener. Business and government are notorious for such practices. When workers are laid off, corporations talk about *restructuring* or *downsizing.* A few years ago the federal government announced *a revenue enhancement* when it really meant that taxes were going up; likewise, the Environmental Protection Agency referred to acid rain as *poorly buffered precipitation;* and when the CIA ordered a *nondiscernible microbionoculator* it got a poison dart. Not only are such concoctions pretentious, but they are dishonest. Fancy-sounding language is a camouflage to hard truths.

Fancy-sounding language also has no place in good writing. When euphemisms are overdone, the result is a lot of verbiage and little meaning. Consider the example below before the euphemisms and pretentious language were reduced:

- **Overdone:** In the event that gaming industry establishments be rendered legal, law enforcement official spokespersons have identified a potential crisis situation as the result of influence exerted by the regional career-offender cartel.

Readers may have to review this a few times before they understand what's being said. Even if they don't give up, a reader's job is not to rewrite your words. Writing with clarity and brevity shows respect for your audience. Here is the same paragraph with its pretentious wordiness and euphemisms edited down:

Revised: Should casino gambling be legalized, police fear organized crime may take over.

Of course, not all euphemisms are double-talk concoctions. Some may be necessary to avoid sounding insensitive or causing pain. To show respect in a sympathy card to bereaved survivors, it might be more appropriate to use the expression *passed away* instead of the blunt *died.* Recently terms such as *handicapped* or *cripple* have given way to less derogatory replacements such as *a person with disabilities*. Likewise we hear *a person with AIDS* instead of "AIDS victim," which reduces the person to a disease or a label.

As with metaphors and personification, some euphemism have passed into the language and become artifacts, making their usage potentially stale. People over age 65 are no longer "old" or "elderly," they're *senior citizens;* slums are *substandard housing;* the poor are *socially disadvantaged*. Although such euphemism grew out of noble intentions, they tend to abstract reality. A Jules Feiffer cartoon from a few years ago captured the problem well. It showed a man talking to himself:

> I used to think I was poor. Then they told me I wasn't poor, I was needy. They told me it was self-defeating to think of myself as needy, I was deprived. Then they told me underprivileged was overused. I was disadvantaged. I still don't have a dime. But I have a great vocabulary.

Although euphemisms were created to take the bite off reality, they can also take the bite out of your writing if not used appropriately. As Feiffer implies, sometimes it's better to say it like it is; depending on the context, "poor" simply might have more bite than some sanitized cliché. Similarly, some old people resent being called "seniors" not just because the term is an overused label, but because it abstracts the condition of old age. Our advice regarding euphemisms is to know when they are appropriate and to use them sparingly. Good writing simply means knowing when the right expression will get the response you want.

Avoiding Clichés

A cliché (or trite expression) is a phrase that is old and overused to the point of being unoriginal and stale. At one time clichés were fresh and potent, yet overuse has left them flat. In speech we may resort to clichés for quick meaning. However, clichés can dull your writing and make you seem lazy for choosing a phrase on tap rather than trying to think of more original and colorful wording. Consider these familiar examples:

apple of his eye

bigger than both of us

climbing the walls

dead as a doornail

head over heels

last but not least

mind over matter

ripe old age

short but sweet

white as a ghost

The problem with clichés is that they fail to communicate anything unique. To say you were "climbing the walls," for example, is an expression that could fit a wide variety of contradictory meanings. Out of context, it could mean that you were in a state of high anxiety, anger, frustration, excitement, fear, happiness, or unhappiness. Even in context, the expression is dull. Furthermore, because such clichés are ready made and instantly handy, they blot out the exact detail you intended to convey to your reader.

Clichés are the refuge of writers who don't make the effort to come up with fresh and original expressions. To avoid them, we recommend being alert for any phrases that you have heard many times before and coming up with fresh substitutes. Consider the brief paragraph below, which is full of clichés marked in italics, and its revision:

> **Trite:** *In this day and age* a university ought to be concerned with ensuring that its women students take courses that will strengthen their understanding of their own past achievements and future *hopes and dreams*. At the same time any school *worth its salt* should be *ready and able* to provide *hands-on experience*, activities, and courses that reflect a commitment to diversity and inclusiveness. Education must *seize the opportunity* of leading us *onward and upward* so that we don't slide back to the male-only curriculum emphasis of the *days of old*.

> **Revised:** A university today ought to be concerned with ensuring that its women students take courses that will strengthen their understanding of their own past achievements and future possibilities. At the same time any decent school should provide experience, activities, and courses that reflect a commitment to diversity and inclusiveness. Education must lead us forward so that we don't revert to the male-only curriculum emphasis of the past.

Defining Technical Terms

Special or technical vocabulary that is not clear from the context can function as instant roadblocks to freely flowing communication between you and your readers— sympathetic to your views or not. You cannot expect a novice in political science to know the meaning of *hegemony* or a nonmedical person to know exactly what you mean by *nephrological necrosis*. To avoid alienating nonexpert readers, you'll have to define such uncommon terms.

And you can do so without being obtrusive and without disrupting the flow of your writing with "time-outs" here and there to define terms. Notice how smoothly definitions have been slipped into the following passages.

1. "Before going to Everest we must go to the Thyangboche Monastery for a Pujah, or blessing ceremony, for safety on the climb." (Tabin, Geoffrey. "1988 on Chomolungma: New Records and Deathly Stunts Atop the World." *Trilogy* [1992]:16.)

2. "Animal rights thinkers accuse trappers of 'speciesism,' a vile sin that gives human life higher priority than the lives of animals." (Hall, Pat, Judy Hall, and Larry Amkraut. "Fur Trapping: Forget Bambi; Face Reality." *Trilogy* [1992]:89.)

3. "The basic theory of the greenhouse effect is quite simple. The earth's atmosphere consists mainly of oxygen and nitrogen, but there are small concentrations of various 'greenhouse' gases—notably carbon dioxide (CO_2), water vapour, methane, and chlorofluorocarbons (CFCs)—which play a very important role in maintaining the planet's 'heat balance.'" (Tyler, Charles. "Toward a Warmer World." *Geographical* April [1990].)

4. "Photokeratosis, the scientific name for what is more commonly known as snow blindness, is like a sunburn of the eye." (McKibben, Bill. *The End of Nature* [1989]:195.)

Clarifying Familiar Terms

Even some familiar terms can lead to misunderstanding because they are used in so many different ways with so many different meanings: *liberal, Native American, lifestyle, decent, active*. It all depends on who is using the word. For instance, to an environmentalist the expression *big business* might connote profit-hungry and sinister industrial conglomerates that pollute the elements; to a conservative, however, the phrase might mean the commercial and industrial establishment that drives our economy. Likewise, a *liberal* does not mean the same thing to a Democrat as it does to a Republican. Even if you're writing for a sympathetic audience, be as precise as you can about familiar terms. Remember the advice of novelist George Eliot: "We have all got to remain calm, and call things by the same names other people call them by."

Stipulating Definitions

For words that don't have a fixed or standard meaning, writers often offer a *stipulative* definition that explains what they mean by the term. For instance, in his essay "Regulating Racist Speech on Campus" (page 445), Charles R. Lawrence defines *racist language* as "injurious speech" aimed at making people feel inferior because of their race: "Assaultive racist speech functions as a preemptive strike. The invective is experienced as a blow, not as a proffered idea, and once the blow is struck, it is unlikely that a dialogue will follow." By stipulating language with the power to injure as opposed to language that simply insults, the author justifies his claim that such language does not deserve the protection of the First Amendment, since it falls under the category of "fighting words"—words exempt from such protection because "'their very utterance inflicts injury or intends to incite an immediate breach of the peace.'"

Similarly, although we have all heard about the controversy surrounding attempts to fight crime through "gun control," a writer making a case for or against such legislation will need to supply a precise definition of *gun control*. In order to give the argument focus, the author will have to stipulate which kinds of guns and what kinds of control. In her essay, "A Case Against Firearms" (page 287), Sarah Brady clearly does this: "Two pieces of federal legislation can make a difference right now. First, we must require a national waiting period [of seven days] before the purchase of a handgun, to allow for a criminal-records check. . . . We must also stop the sale and domestic production of semiautomatic assault weapons." Such stipulations focus her argument and eliminate any misunderstanding by the audience.

Because we live in a multicultural society of shifting definitions and blurring categories, at times you may find it necessary to stipulate the ethnic and racial makeup of certain people. Suppose you are writing about *Hispanic people*. This term has been used to encompass millions of people of different countries, races, religions, and cultures—Cuban expatriots, Quiche Indians of Guatemala, Puerto Ricans of African blood, Mexican Americans, Jewish immigrants from Spain, and residents of Colombia. So as not to conflate disparate cultures and therefore cause misunderstanding and possible offense, it is necessary to offer a stipulative definition of the term. Depending on your purposes, it is reasonable to stipulate Hispanics as people with one or more Spanish parents. Or, you might write that you are referring to people raised in countries where Spanish is the primary language. Or you might stipulate people who simply have linguistic roots in Spanish-speaking Latin America. Some people might dispute your definition (or suggest you use a different term, such as *Latino*), but at least you will have clarified the people about whom you are writing.

Similarly, it would be wise to supply stipulative definitions when defending an unpopular position. In his essay "Brother, Don't Spare a Dime" (page 307), Christopher Awalt argues that "the homeless themselves must bear the blame for their manifold troubles." Realizing how callous such an attitude might sound, Awalt wisely steps back to stipulate what he means by homeless: not those temporarily homeless and "eager to reorganize their lives," but "those who are chronically so. Whether because of mental illness, alcoholism, poor education, drug addiction or simple laziness, these homeless are content to remain as they are . . . (and) prefer a life of no responsibility at all."

Stipulating your terms is like making a contract with your reader: You set down in black and white the important terms and their limits. The result is that you eliminate any misunderstanding and reduce your own vulnerability. And that can make the difference between a weak and a potent argument.

Avoiding Overdefinition

Where do you stop explaining and begin assuming your reader knows what you mean? What terms are "technical" or "specialized" or "important" enough to warrant definition? You certainly don't want to define terms unnecessarily or to oversimplify. In so doing, you run the risk of dulling the thrust of your claims while insulting the intelligence of your readers. Just how to strike a balance is a matter of good judgment about the needs and capabilities of your audience.

A good rule of thumb is to assume that your readers are almost as knowledgeable as you. This way, you minimize the risk of patronizing them. Another rule

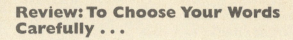

Review: To Choose Your Words Carefully . . .

Consider both denotative and connotative meanings

Be as specific and concrete as your context requires

Use figurative language to add richness and complexity

Check figurative language for precision and clarity

Be alert for clichés and unnecessary euphemisms

Define technical terms that are not clear from the context

Define familiar terms and terms with multiple meanings

of thumb is the synonym test. If you can think of a word or short phrase that is an exact synonym for some specialized or important term in your argument, you probably don't need to define it. On the other hand, if you need a long phrase or sentence to paraphrase the term, you may want to work in a definition; it could be needed. And don't introduce your definitions with clauses like "As I'm sure you know" or "You don't need to be told that . . ." If the audience didn't need to know this, you wouldn't be telling them, and if they do know what the terms mean, you may insult their intelligence with such condescending introductions.

Using Sarcasm and Humor Sparingly

Although we caution you against using sarcasm or humor too often, there are times when they can be very effective techniques of persuasion. Writers will often bring out their barbs for the sake of drawing blood from the opposition and snickers from the sympathetic. But artful sarcasm must be done with care. Too strong, and you run the risk of trivializing the issue or alienating your audience with a bad joke. Too vague or esoteric, and nobody will catch the joke. It's probably safest to use these touches when you are writing for a sympathetic audience; they're most likely to appreciate your wit. There is no rule of thumb here. Like any writer, you'll have to decide when to use these techniques and how to artfully work them in.

EXERCISES

1. Let's say you were assigned to write a position paper defending the construction of a nuclear power plant in your state. What special appeals would you make were you to address your paper to the governor? To residents living next to the site where the proposed plant is to be built? To prospective construction workers and general contractors? To local environmentalists?

2. Choose one of the following claims, then list in sentence form three reasons supporting the argument. When you've finished, list in sentence form three reasons in opposition to the claim:
   a. Snowboarders are a menace to skiers.
   b. To save lives, all passenger vehicles in this country, including vans, should be equipped with driver's side airbags.
   c. Condoms should be advertised on television.
   d. Men as well as women should have parental leaves from their jobs.
3. Let's assume you have made up your mind on gun control. Write a brief letter to the editor of your local newspaper stating your views on the issue. In your letter, fairly and accurately represent arguments of the opposition while pointing out any logical weaknesses, flaws, impracticalities, and other problems you see. What different emphasis would your letter have were it to appear in a gun owner's newsletter? In a pro–gun control newsletter?
4. Write a letter to your parents explaining why you need an extra hundred dollars of spending money this month.
5. Each of the sentences below will take on a different meaning depending on the connotations of the words in brackets. Explain how each choice colors the writer's attitude and the reader's reaction to the statement.
   a. Sally's style of dress is really _____ [weird, exotic, unusual].
   b. If a factory is _____ [polluting, stinking up, fouling] the air over your house, you have a right to sue.
   c. Anyone who thinks that such words have no effect is _____ [unaware, ignorant, unconscious] of political history.
   d. The anti-immigration passion being stirred up in this country has become _____ [popular, trendy, common].
   e. It was clear from the way she _____ [stomped, marched, stepped] out of the room how she felt about the decision.
6. Identify the figures of speech used in the following sentences from essays in this book. In each example note the two things being compared and explain why you think the comparisons are appropriate or not:
   a. "I must say that the emphasis on publication is a juggernaut that is running without guidance, without vision, without direction, without principle." (Patricia Nelson Limerick)
   b. "This goes beyond using Madonna for target practice. It even goes beyond lowering the sexual thermostat of the culture." (Ellen Goodman)
   c. "Which does not mean smoking pot is a free ride: Some people have severe, though short-term, anxiety reactions to it." (Peter Gorman)
   d. "Fiction lives or dies not on its messages, but on the depth and power of the emotional experience it provides." (Andrew Klavan)
   e. "Strutting up to grand brownstones, a couple of young men relieve themselves in the bushes." (Madeline Drexler)
   f. "It is absurd to suggest that the government step in to censor viewing that parents have acquiesced in." (Robert Scheer)
   g. "Fighting commercialism, of course, is like wrestling your way out of a spider web" (Deborah Baldwin)

7. Rewrite the following paragraph to eliminate the clichés and trite expressions.

It is not that we don't care about what goes on up in space, it's that the vast majority of red-blooded Americans are hard put to see what these untold billions of dollars can do. While great strides have been made in space research, we ask ourselves: Is life any safer? Are material goods all the more abundant? Are we living to a ripe old age because of these vast expenditures? Beyond the shadow of a doubt the answer is a resounding no. Those in Congress with a vested interest need to be brought back to reality, for the nation's pressing problems of crime, homelessness, and unemployment are right here on Mother Earth. Nothing is sacred including the budget for NASA which should follow the footsteps of other programs and be slashed across the board. Yes, that will be a rude awakening to some who will have to bite the bullet, but there are just so many tax dollars to go around. And in the total scheme of things, wasting it on exploring the depths of outer space is not the way it should be.

8. The following essay was written by animal activist Barbara Drews. Read it carefully, making notes or annotating it. Then answer the questions that follow.

SAMPLE FOR ANALYSIS/ARGUMENT

Dream of a Long Fur Coat
Barbara Drews

1 There's a chill in the air as the sun drops below the horizon on this clear December evening.

2 All is quiet in the desert except for the first tentative rustlings of those animals who hunt or forage for food under the safe cover of darkness.

3 Suddenly a loud "*crack*" shatters the still twilight as a steel leghold trap slams shut on the leg of a young Grey Fox. In the shocked silence of the desert, her screams can be heard for miles. Overwhelmed by agonizing pain and terror, and with no thought save that of escape, the fox frantically struggles and bites at the steel monster that has crushed her leg in its jaws.

4 She is fighting for her very life, and in her pain she may even chew off her own leg. The trappers call this "wring off," and though she is free again, in her weakened condition, she is probably doomed to death by predation or gangrene.

5 It's just as likely that because of pain, shock and exhaustion, she'll withdraw into a sleep-like trance to await her fate. After many hours, even days of suffering she'll die, probably from exposure, attack by other animals, starvation or blood loss. If she's still alive when the trapper finally returns, he

will stomp her to death or stand on her throat and chest until she stops fighting for breath. He may just stun her with a blow to the head and skin her while she's still alive. What is left of her pitiful body is tossed aside and left to rot.

6   In the U.S. as many as 17 million wild animals are trapped and killed every year for their fur. For every animal that is wanted at least two more are what the trappers call "trash" animals, such as eagles, songbirds, deer, domestic animals and even children. Some records show that as high as 95 percent of the animals trapped are "non-target" animals. Therefore, a conservative estimate of the total number of animals maimed and killed by leghold traps exceeds 35 million.

7   Frank Conibear, who retired after 32 years of trapping, wrote that "as great as the sufferings are of the animals who die a natural death, the sufferings occasioned by the common steel trap are incomparably greater."

8   According to internationally known author and animal rights activist, Cleveland Amory, "until the leghold trap is outlawed, any woman who wears a wild fur has on her back at least 150 hours of torture." The leghold trap has been banned in more than 65 countries, yet this diabolical device is still commonly used throughout the United States.

9   December is pelting season at most fur ranches. The word "ranch" is a cruel euphemism for a concentration camp of animals stuffed into tiny cages. Like the factory farming of animals we use for food, fur ranches are designed for maximum profit with no thought given to the physical or psychological well-being of the animals. Intense stress and suffering exacerbated by overcrowding, excessive in-breeding and an unnatural diet of industrial waste, chicken manure and fish offal cause a sad variety of diseases and genetic defects. Premature death is common, but as long as the fur is not marred the cause of death is not considered important enough to warrant changes.

10   On killing day, the young animals will cease their habitual neurotic pacing to watch in dread as the men make their way down the rows of cages. As their turn comes, each lashes out in terror at the gloved hand that grabs him behind his neck.

11   Killing techniques vary, but the cheapest, and therefore the preferred method is spinal dislocation. Other techniques include poison, gassing with hot carbon monoxide and anal electrocution. All killing methods have one thing in common; minimal damage to the fur rather than a quick and humane death for the animal.

12   The fur industry's massive advertising campaign tell us that every little girl dreams of one day owning a fur coat. Ignoring the fact that every fur coat represents the prolonged and unnecessary suffering of as many as 80 animals, wearing fur is touted as a luxurious sign of success and affluence. With the skillful use of colorful euphemisms, the consumer is spared the blood and gore, the terror and pain.

13   Animals are exploited and oppressed because they have no recourse. Throughout the world there are countless prisons where billions of innocent animals are forced to live unnatural lives of misery and deprivation.

14   These prisons are called research labs, farms, zoos, ranches or rodeos, but they are prisons just the same. No crime is necessary to become an inmate, and death is the only escape. Mankind has found innumerable ways to justify its role in the carnage, but surely the torture and murder of another animal just to satisfy our greed and vanity is nothing less than obscene.

EXERCISES

1. Locate Drew's claim or thesis statement and briefly summarize her argument. Next make a rough outline of the piece.
2. What kind of audience is Drew addressing? Are they sympathetic, hostile, or neutral? Did she play to any prejudices of her audience? Did she sound antagonistic anywhere? Did she seek common ground with her audience?
3. What specifically is Drew's purpose in the essay? How well does she accomplish that purpose? How convincing is the evidence presented? Is it pertinent? reliable? Is it specific enough? Is it sufficient? Does any of the evidence seem slanted? exaggerated? dated? How good are the sources of the evidence enlisted? Would you have liked substantiation of any claims?
4. Did Drew address opposing views on the issue? Is Drew persuasive in her perspective?
5. Go through the essay again and underline the concrete words that add vividness and interest. Do these terms strike you as effective in bolstering her argument? Are there any places you would have substituted more specific, concrete language? If so, where?
6. Identify any figures of speech in Drew's essay—metaphors, similes, personification. In each case, note what different things are being compared and explain why the comparison is appropriate or not. Can you find any examples of clichés or euphemism?
7. Did Drew define any technical terms or stipulate any definitions? If not, should she have?

CHAPTER 5

USING EVIDENCE

Thinking Like an Advocate

Because this is a democracy, there's a widespread conviction in our society that having opinions is our responsibility as citizens—a conviction supported by our fast-forward, multi-media culture. You see it on the nightly news every time a reporter sticks a microphone in the face of somebody on the street, or whenever Oprah Winfrey or Phil Donahue moves into the studio audience. It's the heart of talk radio and television programs. In the newspapers and magazines it comes in the form of "opinion polls" that tally up our positions on all sorts of weighty issues:

"Should condoms be distributed in high schools?"

"Is the economy this year in better shape than it was last year at this time?"

"Do you think the American judicial system is just?"

"Can the government do more to prevent domestic terrorism?"

"Is capital punishment a deterrent to crime?"

"Is the president doing a good job running the country?"

All this on-the-spot opinion making encourages people to take an immediate stand on an issue, whether or not they have sufficient understanding and information about it. Holding an opinion on a matter does not necessarily mean you have investigated the issue, that you've carefully considered the view of others (including the opposition), or that you've gathered enough information to defend your position. If you want to make successful arguments, you'll need more than a gut reaction or simple reliance on yourself for "truth."

This means thinking of yourself as an *advocate*—a prosecutor or defense attorney, if you like. You're going to need a case to present to the jury of your readers, one that will convince them that your interpretation is plausible. Like an advocate, when you're constructing an argument, you look for ammunition to put before your readers: facts, statistics, people's experiences—or, in one word, *evidence*. The jury will judge your argument jointly on the evidence you bring forth and the interpretation you present of that evidence. So, like an advocate, to write successful arguments you'll need to be able to understand and weigh the value of the *supporting evidence* for your case.

How Much Evidence Is Enough?

Like any advocate, you'll need to decide *how much* evidence to present to your readers. Your decision will vary from case to case, although with more practice you'll find it easier to judge. Common sense is a good predictor: If the evidence was enough to persuade you, it's probably enough to persuade like-minded readers. Unsympathetic readers may need more proof. The more unexpected or unorthodox your claim, the more evidence you'll need to convince skeptical readers. And it's often as much a case of the *right* evidence as the *right amount* of evidence. One fact or statistic, if it touches on your readers' most valued standards and principles, may be enough to swing an argument for a particular group. Here's where **outlining** (recall Chapter 3) can help; an outline will help you make sure you present evidence for every assertion you make.

It's easier to gather too much evidence and winnow out the least effective than to have too little and try to expand it. One of our teachers used to call this the "Cecil B. DeMille strategy," after the great Hollywood producer. DeMille's theory was that if audiences were impressed by five dancers, they'd really be overwhelmed by five hundred—but just to be sure, he'd hire a thousand. That's a good spirit to have when writing arguments; you can always use a sentence like "Of the 116 explosions in GMC trucks with side-mounted fuel tanks, four cases are most frequently cited" and then go on to discuss those four. You've let your readers know that another 112 are on record so that they can weigh this fact when considering the four you examine in particular. You may never need a thousand pieces of evidence, or dancers, in an argument, but there's no harm in thinking big!

Why Arguments Need Supporting Evidence

Evidence is composed of facts and their interpretations. As we said in Chapter 1, facts are pieces of information that can be verified—that is, statistics, examples, testimony, historical details. For instance, it is a fact that SAT verbal scores across the nation have gone up for the last three years. One interpretation might be that students today are spending more time reading and less time watching television than students in the 1980s. Another interpretation might be that secondary schools are putting more emphasis on language skills. A third might be that changes in the test or the prevalence of test-preparation courses have contributed to the higher scores.

In everyday conversation we make claims without offering supporting evidence: "Poverty is the reason why there is so much crime"; "The president is doing a lousy job handling the economy"; "Foreign cars are better than American cars." Although we may have good reasons to back up such statements, we're not often called upon to do so, at least not in casual conversation. In written arguments, however, presenting evidence is critical, and the failure to do so is glaring. Without supporting data and examples, an argument is hollow. It will bore the reader, fail to convince, and collapse under criticism. Consider the following:

> Video games are a danger to the mental well-being of children. Some children play video games for hours on end, and the result is that their behavior and concentration is greatly affected. Many of them display bad behavior. Others have difficulty doing other more important things. Parents with young children should be more strict as to what video games their kids play and how long they play them.

Chances are this paragraph has not convinced you that video games are a threat to kids. The sample lacks the details that might persuade you. For instance, exactly what kind of bad behavior do children display? And what specific video games out of the hundreds on the market are the real culprits? How is concentration actually affected? What "more important things" does the author mean? And how many hours of video consumption need occur before signs of dangerous behavior begin to manifest themselves?

Consider how much sharper and more persuasive the following rewrite is with the addition of some specific details, facts, and examples:

> Video games may be fun for kids, but they can have detrimental effects on their behavior. They encourage violent behavior. A steady dosage of some of the more violent games clearly results in more aggressive behavior. One study by the Department of Psychology at State University has shown that after two hours of "Urban Guerrilla," 60 percent of the 12 boys and 20 percent of the 12 girls tested began to mimic the street fighting gestures—punching, kicking, karate-chopping each other. It was also shown that such games negatively affect concentration. Even after half an hour had lapsed from the conclusion of their game playing, the boys had difficulty settling down to read or draw. Since my parents restricted my little brother's game playing to weekends, he concentrates when completing his homework and has fewer fights with his best friend.

By citing the academic study as well as the concrete case of your own brother, you give readers something substantial to consider. (Of course, readers might object, saying that the essay only suggests that video games affect boys negatively, so you'd have to prepare to refute that assertion. And they might object to the small size of these studies, but you could handle that too.) Presenting supporting evidence puts meat on the bones of your argument. (In Chapter 8 we will go into greater depth about how to gather research evidence, particularly from the library.)

Forms of Evidence

When you begin to develop an argument, we hope you make a list of your points and the opposition's and develop a pro/con list, as we suggested in Chapter 2. But you may still need to expand and deepen your understanding of the issue by collecting useful evidence from both sides of the issue. Don't neglect this critical step: Remember, the bulk of your argument is composed of material supporting your claim.

Writers enlist four basic kinds of evidence to support their arguments: personal experience (theirs and others'), outside authorities, factual references and examples, and statistics. We'll examine each separately, but you'll probably want to use combinations of these kinds of evidence when building your arguments in order to convince a wide range of readers.

Personal Experience—Yours and Others'

The power of *personal testimony* cannot be underestimated. Think of the number of movies that have failed at the box office in spite of huge and expensive ad campaigns. Think of the number of times you've read a book on the recommendation of friends—or taken a certain course or shopped at a particular store. You might even be attending the college you're at on the recommendation of someone you know. Many people find the word-of-mouth judgments that make up personal testimony the most persuasive kind of evidence.

In written arguments, the personal testimony of other people is used to affirm facts and support your claim. Essentially, their experiences provide you with eyewitness accounts of events that are not available to you. And such accounts may prove crucial in winning over an audience. Suppose you are writing about the rising abuse of alcohol among college students. In addition to statistics and hard facts, your argument can gain strength from quoting the experience of a first-year student who nearly died one night from alcoholic poisoning. Or in a local paper decrying the discrimination against minorities in hiring, consider the authenticity provided by an interview of neighborhood residents who felt they were passed over for a job because of race or ethnic identity.

Your own eyewitness testimony can also be a powerful tool of persuasion. Suppose, for example, that you are writing a paper in which you argue that the big teaching hospital in the city provides far better care and has a lower death rate than the small rural hospital in your town. The hard facts and statistics on the quality of care and comparative mortality rates that you provide will certainly have a stark persuasiveness. But consider the dramatic impact on those figures were you to re-count how your own trip to the rural emergency room nearly cost you your life be-cause of understaffing or the lack of critical but expensive diagnostic equipment.

Personal observation and that of others you may know is useful and valuable in arguments. However, you should be careful not to draw hasty conclusions from such testimony. The fact that you and three of your friends are staunchly in favor of replacing letter grades with a pass/fail system does not support the claim that the student body at your school is in favor of the conversion. You need a much greater sample. Likewise, the dislike most people in your class feel for a certain professor is not justification for the claim that the university tenure system should be abolished. On such complex issues, you need more than a personal testimony to make a case.

You also have to remember the "multiple-perspective" rule. As any police officer can tell you, there are as many versions of the "truth" of an incident as peo-ple who saw it. The people involved in a car accident see it one way (or more), and witnesses in a car heading in the other direction may interpret events differently, as will people in an apartment six stories above the street where the accident took place. Your job is to sort out the different testimonies and make sense of them. Per-sonal experience—yours and that of people you know—is valuable. However, on bigger issues you need statistics and data, as well as the evidence provided by out-side authorities.

Outside Authorities

Think of the number of times you've heard statements such as these:

"Scientists have found that . . . "

"Scholars inform us that . . ."

"According to his biographer, President Lincoln decided that . . . "

What these statements have in common is the appeal to outside authori-ties—people recognized as experts in a given field, people who can speak knowl-edgeably about a subject. Because authoritative opinions are such powerful tools of persuasion, you hear them all the time in advertisements. Automobile manufactur-ers will quote the opinions of professional race car drivers; the makers of toothpaste will cite dentists' claims; and famous basketball players push namebrand sneakers all the time. Similarly, a good trial lawyer will almost always rely upon forensic ex-perts or other such authorities to help sway a jury.

For the most part, experts usually try to be objective and fair-minded when asked for opinions. But like everyone else, their testimony can't always be without bias or personal interest. An expert with a vested interest in an issue might slant the testimony in his or her favor; it's human nature to want to be right. The dentist who has just purchased a huge number of shares in a new toothpaste company would not be an unbiased expert. You wouldn't turn for unbiased opinion on lung cancer to scientists working for tobacco companies, or ask an employee facing the loss of his or her job to comment on the advisability of layoffs. When you cite authorities, you should be careful to note any possibility of bias so that your readers can fairly weigh the contributions. (This is often done through *attribution;* see Chapter 8.) Knowing that Professor Brown's research will benefit from construction of the supercollider doesn't make her enthusiasm for its other potential benefits less credible, but it does help your readers see her contributions to your argument in their proper context.

If you are going to cite authorities, you must also make sure that your experts are competent, that they have expertise in their fields. You wouldn't turn to a professional beekeeper for opinions on laser surgery any more than you would quote a civil engineer on macroeconomic theory. And yet, this is done all the time in advertising. Although it makes better sense to ask a veterinarian for a professional opinion about what to feed your pet, advertisers hire known actors to push dog food (as well as yogurt and skin cream). Of course, in advertising, celebrity sells. But that's not the case in most written arguments. It would not impress a critical reader to cite Michael Jackson's views on the use of fetal tissue or the greenhouse effect. Again, think about the criteria your readers have. Whom would they respect on this topic? Those are the experts to cite.

Factual References and Examples

Facts do as much to inform as they do to persuade, as we mentioned in Chapter 1. If somebody wants to sell you something, they'll pour on the details. For instance, ask the used car salesperson about that red 1993 Ford Explorer in the lot and the salesperson will hold forth about what a "creampuff" it is: only 18,400 original miles, mint condition, five-speed transmission with overdrive, all black leather interior, and loaded—AC, power brakes, cruise control, premium sound system, captain's chair, and so on. Or listen to how the cereal manufacturers inform you that their toasted Os now contain "all-natural oat bran, which has been found to prevent cancer." Information is not always neutral. The very selection process implies intent. By offering specific facts or examples about your claim, you can make a persuasive argument.

The strategy in using facts and examples is to get readers so absorbed in all the information that they nearly forget they are being persuaded to buy or do something. So common is this strategy in television ads that some have been given the name "infomercials"—ads that give the impression of being a documentary on the benefits of a product. For instance, you might be familiar with the margarine commercial narrated by a man who announces that at 33 years old he had a heart attack. He then recounts the advice of his doctor for avoiding coronary disease, beginning with the need for exercise and climaxing with the warning about cutting down on cholesterol. Not until the very end of the ad does the narrator inform us that, taking advantage of his second chance, the speaker has switched to a particular brand of margarine, which, of course, is cholesterol free.

In less blatant form, this "informational" strategy can be found in newspaper columns and editorials, where the authors give the impression that they are simply presenting the facts surrounding particular issues, when, in reality, they may be attempting to persuade readers to see things their way. For instance, suppose in an apparently objective commentary a writer discusses how history is replete with people wrongfully executed for first-degree murder. Throughout the piece the author cites several specific cases where it was learned too late that the defendant had been framed or that the real killer had confessed. On the surface the piece may appear to be simply presenting historical facts, but the more subtle intention may be to convince people that capital punishment is morally wrong. The old tagline from *Dragnet*, "I just want the facts," isn't quite the whole picture. How those facts are used is also part of their persuasive impact.

Often facts and examples are used to establish cause/effect relationships. It's very important, both when writing and reading arguments, to test the links that the facts forge. For instance, it may rain the day after every launch of the space shuttle, but does that fact prove that shuttle launches influence the atmosphere of Florida? It may be true that China severely restrained the pro-democracy movement in mainland cities, but does this example mean the government will try to eliminate democracy in Hong Kong when China reclaims the island in 1999? And sometimes experts disagree; one might see the rise in prostate cancer rates for vasectomy patients as reason to abolish the surgery; another might point to other contributing causes (diet, lack of exercise, shortage of a particular hormone). If you don't have the expertise to determine which of the conflicting experts is correct, you'll probably decide based on the *weight of the evidence*—whichever side has the most people or the most plausible arguments supporting it. This, in fact, is how most juries judge cases.

Statistics

People are impressed by numbers. Saying that 77 percent of the student body at your school supports a woman's right to have an abortion is far more persuasive than saying that a lot of people on campus are pro-choice. **Statistics** have a special no-nonsense authority. Batting averages, medical statistics, polling results (election and otherwise), economic indicators, the stock market index, unemployment figures, scientific ratings, FBI statistics, percentages, demographic data—they are all reported in numbers. And if they're accurate, they are difficult to argue, though a skillful manipulator can use statistics to mislead.

The demand for statistics has made market research a huge business in America. During an election year, weekly and daily results on voters' opinions of the candidates are released from various news organizations and TV networks as well as independent polling companies such as the Harris and Gallup organizations. Most of the brand-name products you buy, the TV shows and movies you watch, or the CDs you listen to were made available after somebody did test studies on sample populations in order to determine the potential success of these items. Those same statistics are then used in promotional ads. Think of the number of times you've heard claims such as these:

> "Nine out of ten doctors recommend Zappo aspirin."
>
> "Our new Speed King copier turns out 24 percent more copies per minute."
>
> "Sixty-eight percent of those polled approve of women in military combat roles."

Of course, these claims bear further examination. If you polled only ten doctors, nine of whom recommended Zappo, that's not a big enough sample to imply that 90 percent of *all* doctors do. (More information about **logical fallacies** like these will be found in Chapter 7.) As Mark Twain once observed, "There are lies, damned lies, and statistics."

Numbers don't lie; they can be bent. Sometimes to sway an audience, claim makers will cite figures that are inaccurate or dated, or they will sometimes intentionally misuse accurate figures to make their case. If, for instance, somebody claims that 139 students and professors protested the invitation of a certain controversial guest to your campus, it would be a distortion of the truth not to mention that another 1500 attended the talk and gave the speaker a standing ovation.

When reading statistics it is always wise to be skeptical. Likewise, when quoting numbers, try to be accurate and honest. Be certain that your sources are themselves accurate. In the 1996 presidential campaign, the Republican party claimed that Bill Clinton had raised taxes 128 times while governor of Arkansas, trying to impress upon voters the notion that Clinton frequently raised taxes. When this claim was investigated, voters discovered that the "tax increases" included raising fees on fishing licenses, imposing court costs on convicted criminals, and counting some increases several times. As the Democratic party pointed out in rebuttal, under the Republican means of calculating "tax increases," former President George Bush, a Republican, had raised taxes nearly 350 times!

Also, be on guard for the "bandwagon" use of statistics, a technique used all too frequently in advertising. The manufacturer who claims that its flaked corn cereal is 100 percent cholesterol free misleads the public because no breakfast cereal of any brand contains cholesterol (which is found only in animal fats). French fries prepared in pure vegetable oil are also cholesterol free, but that doesn't mean that they're the best things for your health. Manufacturers who use terms like *cholesterol free*, *light*, and *low fat* are trying to get you to jump on the bandwagon of healthy eating and buy their products without really examining the basis for their nutritional claims. Although it's tempting to use such crowd-pleasing statistics, it's a good idea to avoid them in your own arguments because they are deceptive. If your readers discover your deception, your chance of persuading them to accept your position or proposals becomes faint.

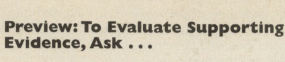

Preview: To Evaluate Supporting Evidence, Ask . . .

- Is the evidence sufficient?
- Is the evidence detailed enough?
- Is the evidence relevant?
- Does the evidence fit the claim?
- Is the evidence up to date and verifiable?
- Is the evidence biased?

Some Tips About Supporting Evidence

Because, as argument writers, you'll be using evidence on a routine basis, it will help you to develop a systematic approach to testing the evidence you want to use. Here are some questions to ask yourself about the evidence you enlist in an argument.

Do You Have a Sufficient Number of Examples to Support Your Claim?

You don't want to jump to conclusions based on too little evidence. Suppose you want to make the case that electric cars would be better for the environment than motor vehicles. If all you offer as evidence is the fact that electric vehicles don't pollute the air, your argument would be somewhat thin. Your argument would be much more convincing if you offered the following evidence: that in addition to zero emission at the tailpipe—which is good for the atmosphere—electric cars do not use engine fluids or internal combustion parts, all of which constitute wastes that contaminate our landfills and water supplies. Furthermore, because electric vehicles don't use gasoline or oil, the hazards associated with storage of such fluids are eliminated.

Likewise you should avoid making hasty generalizations based on your own experience as evidence. For instance, if your Acme Airlines flight to Chattanooga was delayed last week, you shouldn't conclude that Acme Airlines always leaves late. However, you would have a persuasive case were you to demonstrate how over the last six months 47 percent of the frequent flyers you interviewed complained that Acme flights left late.

Is Your Evidence Detailed Enough?

The more specific the details, the more persuasive your argument. Instead of generalizations, cite figures, dates, and facts; instead of paraphrases, offer quotations of experts. Remember that your readers are subconsciously saying, "Show me! Prove it!" If you want to tell people how to bake bread, you wouldn't write, "Mix some flour with some yeast and water"; you'd say, "Dissolve one packet of yeast in 1 cup of warm water and let it sit for ten minutes. Then slowly mix in 3 cups of sifted whole wheat flour." Or, as we did in our electric car example above, instead of simply asserting that there would be none of the fluid or solid wastes associated with internal combustion vehicles, specify that in electric vehicles there would be no motor oil, engine coolants, transmission fluid or filters, spark plugs, ignition wires, and gaskets to end up in landfills. What your readers want are specifics—and that's what you should give them.

Is Your Evidence Relevant to the Claim or Conclusion You Make?

Select evidence based on how well it supports the point you are arguing, not on how interesting, novel, or humorous it is or how hard you had to work to find it. For instance, if you are arguing about whether John Lennon is the most influential songwriter in rock and roll history, you wouldn't mention that he had two sons or that he owned dairy cattle; those are facts, but they have nothing to do with the influence of his lyrics. The historian Barbara Tuchman relates that in writing *The Guns of August,* she discovered that the kaiser bought his wife the same birthday present every year: 12 hats of his choosing, which he required her to wear. Tuchman tried to use this detail in chapter one, then chapter two, and so on, but was finally obligated to relegate the detail to a stack of notecards marked "Unused." It just didn't fit, even though for her it summarized his stubborn selfishness. (She did work it into a later essay, which is why we know about it.) Learn her lesson: Irrelevant evidence distracts an audience and weakens an argument's persuasive power.

Does Your Conclusion (or Claim) Exceed the Evidence?

Don't make generalizations about whole groups when your evidence points to select members. Baseball may be the national pastime, but it would be unwise to claim that *all* Americans love baseball. Experience tells you that some Americans prefer football or basketball, while others don't like any sports. Claims that are out of proportion to the evidence run the risk of stereotyping. A good way to avoid sweeping generalizations when you write is to avoid using superlatives such as *all, nobody, everyone, always, never.* Likewise, try to get in the habit of using qualifiers to limit your claims: *some, many, often.* These latter words will limit your vulnerability to rebuttal.

Is Your Evidence Up to Date and Verifiable?

You want to be sure that the evidence you enlist isn't so dated or vague that it fails to support your claim. For instance, it wouldn't be accurate to say that Candidate Oshawa fails to support the American worker because 15 years ago he purchased a foreign car. His recent and current actions are far more relevant. When you're citing evidence, your readers will expect you to be specific enough for them to verify what you say. A writer supporting animal rights may cite the cases of rabbits whose eyes were burned by pharmacological testing, but such tests have been outlawed in the United States for many years. Another may point to medical research that appears to abuse its human subjects, but not name the researchers, the place where the testing took place, or the year in which this happened. Your readers have no way of verifying the claim and may become suspicious of the entire argument because your factual claims are so hard to check.

Is Your Evidence Slanted?

Sometimes writers select evidence that supports their case while ignoring evidence that does not. Often referred to as "stacking the deck" (see Chapter 7), this practice makes for an unfair argument, and one that could be disastrous for the arguer. Even though some of your evidence has merit, your argument will be dismissed if your audience discovers that you slanted or suppressed evidence.

For example, suppose you heard an upperclassman make the following statement: "If I were you I'd avoid taking course with Professor Gorman at all costs. He gives surprise quizzes, he assigns fifty pages a night, and he refuses to grade on a curve." Even if these reasons are true, that may not be the whole truth. Suppose you learned that Professor Gorman was, in fact, a very dynamic and talented teacher whose classes successfully stimulate the learning process. To hold back on that information is to let possible drawbacks outweigh the benefits. But the risk is making your argument suspect.

Sometimes writers will take advantage of their readers' lack of information on a topic and offer evidence that really doesn't support their claims. Recently several newspapers reported that a study written up in the *Archives of Internal Medicine* proved that eating nuts prevents heart attacks. According to the study, some thirty thousand Seventh-Day Adventists were asked to rate the frequency with which they ate certain foods. Those claiming to eat nuts five times or more a week reported fewer heart attacks. What the newspapers failed to report was that all Seventh-Day Adventists are vegetarians, and that those who ate more nuts also ate fewer dairy products (which are high in cholesterol and saturated fat, both of which contribute to heart disease) and eggs (also high in cholesterol) than others in the study. Newspapers also failed to report that all the subsequent pro-nut publicity was distributed by a nut growers association.*

It is to your benefit that you present all relevant evidence, that you weigh both sides of an issue. Otherwise your argument might not be taken seriously. Let's return to the argument that electric cars are more beneficial to the environment than cars with internal combustion engines. Your key evidence is the fact that electric cars do not use petroleum products and various motor parts that contribute to the pollution of air, land, and waterways. If you left your argument at this, you

---

*Mirkin, Gabe and Diana Rich. *Fat Free Flavor Full*, Boston: Little, Brown, 1995: 51.

would be guilty of suppressing an important concern regarding electric vehicles: the disposal of the great amounts of lead in the huge electric vehicles batteries. Failure to acknowledge that opposing point reduces your credibility as a writer and leaves you open to counterattack. Readers would either wonder about your attempt at deception or about your ignorance. Either way they would dismiss your argument.

A much better strategy would be to confront this concern and then try to overcome it. While acknowledging that lead is a dangerous pollutant, you could point out that over 95 percent of battery lead is recycled. You could also point out that progress is being made to improve battery technology and create alternatives such as the kinds of fuel cells used in spacecraft.* The result is a balanced presentation that makes your own case stronger.

In summary, using evidence means putting yourself in an advocate's place. You'll probably do this while building your argument, and certainly when you revise; then you should see yourself as an advocate for the other side and scrutinize your evidence as if you were going to challenge it in court. As a reader, you need to keep that Missouri "show me!" attitude in mind at all times. A little healthy skepticism will help you test the information you're asked to believe. The next chapter will help you do so.

EXERCISES

Here is a paper written by a first-year student, Meg Kelley. Read it carefully and take notes about it in your argument notebook. Then, either individually or in your work group, answer the questions that follow.

SAMPLE ARGUMENT FOR ANALYSIS

RU 486: The French Abortion Pill and Its Benefits
Meg Kelley

1   For many years, abortion and women's rights have been heated issues in this country. The issue has always been which is more sacred, the right of Americans to choose, or the right of unborn human beings to live.

2   In 1980, a new side to the conflict was introduced when French scientists developed a pill called RU 486.

---

*May, Thomas J. "Electric Cars Will Benefit the Environment and the Economy," *The Boston Globe* 10 Aug. 1994: 15.

According to Susan Jacoby (1992), this new pill is a steroid drug containing antiprogestins which inhibit the naturally occurring progesterone, a hormone in the female body important to the implanting of a fertilized egg into the uterus wall. RU 486 can be used to abort a fetus if taken within nine weeks of conception, and can also be used to inhibit the implantation of a newly fertilized egg if taken within 72 hours of unprotected sexual intercourse. This "morning-after" pill has been available in many European countries, including France and Holland, since 1988; however, it is still illegal in the United States. This drug should be allowed into the country and made available to the women who need it, both for idealistic reasons like the "certain inalienable rights" granted under the U.S. Constitution, and for the practical reasons that it offers a safe alternative to surgical abortion, with few side effects, and may offer further, undiscovered advantages.

3   There are hundreds of thousand of unwanted pregnancies in the United States every year. The unwanted pregnancy may be due to rape, where the woman is helplessly victimized and left with the child of her attacker. A teenage girl who was never taught about effective contraception, or who was told myths about how to have "safe" sex ("You can't get pregnant the first time") may find herself in this situation. Contraceptives fail: a ripped condom, a wrongly used diaphragm. The birth control pill is only 99.9% safe; what about the other 0.1%?

Or what about the woman who forgets to take the pill? Everyone makes stupid mistakes. Should she have to pay for hers for the rest of her life? Sure, many people will say, "You play, you pay." But we're not talking about making a bad bet on a horse; we're talking about a normal, biological human behavior.

4   Abortions are performed every day in the U.S. on women who find themselves in an unplanned pregnancy. For young girls constrained by parental consent laws in some states, illegal abortions are the route to salvation. Many of these abortions are unsafe, performed by non-doctors using unsterile instruments and risky proce-dures, which lead to tremendous complications, infec-tion, illness, and sometimes death. Then there are the legal abortions. These are more sterile, performed by qualified medical professionals, and offer less danger to women's physical health. However, in these, as in any surgical procedure, there can be complications. The women are still scared, still have to "go under the knife" so to speak, and many have to fight their way through lines of people screaming "Don't kill your baby" in order even to get into the clinic. The women may have to travel long distances to gain access to the clinic, stay overnight because of legal waiting periods, take time off from work or school to have the surgery, and then recover afterwards.

5   However, for many, no amount of bed rest can heal the emotional pain in a situation like this. If you get

rid of a part of you, your own flesh and blood, you will suffer, regardless of how you do it. Surgical abortion often leaves women feeling psychologically violated as well, and often they lose confidence in their sexuality, simply due to the nature of the surgery.

6   With RU 486, as Jacoby points out, there are no incisions, no hospital stays or absences from work, just the pill, pure and simple. The abortion pill has been found to have few side effects: A few women suffer slight nausea and vomiting, no more than the birth control pill causes. Women can take it easily, and it is effective; moreover, it can be administered in a doctor's office, rather than involving an expensive clinic or hospital stay. Moreover, RU 486 is believed to have other helpful uses. One particularly promising one is as a treatment for breast cancer. Breast cancer depends on progesterone to survive; the antiprogestins of RU 486 kill the cancer by attacking what it lives on. And scientists are still testing the drug for other productive uses.

7   Although the practical reasons for approving RU 486 to be marketed in the United States are many, there is one important matter that should be the ultimate reason for its approval, and that is principle. The Declaration of Independence, the blueprint of American freedom, states that "All men [and women] are created equal" and that every person has "certain unalienable rights" including "life, liberty, and the pursuit of happiness,"

which cannot be denied them by any government. Women in the United States should have the right to choose their fates themselves. Basically, by denying the availability of RU 486, the government is limiting women's choices. Although abortion is now legal, our government for the past twelve years has opposed it, and has prevented making RU 486 available, because that would make abortion more readily accessible. The citizens of the United States have not asked for such restrictions; what we have is a small group of people whose ideology is dictating what the general population can do. Our government is made up mostly of men, who cannot know the complications of being physically pregnant, and who cannot possibly relate, no matter how vivid or sympathetic their imaginations are, to the chemical, emotional, and psychological changes pregnancy makes in a woman's life. This is truly an issue that should be decided by the people most affected by it.

8   Many people who oppose importing RU 486 will give you the basic pro-life reasons why the pill should not be available. First, they feel that the unborn fetus has the right to the "life" in that "life, liberty, and the pursuit of happiness." Certainly, any child should have the right to all these things, but bringing an unwanted child into a more-than-likely single parent home with a low income and poor opportunities is not guaranteeing these rights, but almost surely destroying them. As Henry David Thoreau in *Walden* states: "And not, when I

come to die, discover that I had not lived. I did not wish to live that what was not life, living is so dear" (257). "Life" in this case means more than heartbeats, breathing, walking, talking. It means being "alive," able to enjoy childhood without having to get a job at age ten to help support your family, or growing up in a bug-infested apartment where there is no heat or there are people being murdered outside your door, of continuing the vicious cycle of teen pregnancy by likely becoming a teen parent yourself. The life envisioned by the Founding Fathers [and Mothers] does not encompass being kicked out by your parents, dropping out of school, being forced to live on the streets, begging for change and scavenging food out of trash barrels. Isn't forcing a baby to live and make its way in the world under such miserable conditions much crueler than flushing a fertilized egg out of the body before it can be implanted in the uterus?

9   The people who oppose RU 486 will also say that the abortion pill, if allowed on the U.S. market, will also be used as a means of birth control, since women won't bother to use contraception if they have access to such an easy way to abort a fetus. I personally don't feel that the majority of sexually active women in the U.S. are so ignorant or lazy as to prefer any kind of abortion to safe precautions. Besides, most women know that contraception is also used to prevent the spread of some sexually transmitted diseases. They aren't going to be

more likely to expose themselves to infertility or death
just because RU 486 is available. The final reason opponents give for banning RU 486 is that there could be
yet-unknown side effects. Well, this is true of all
drugs. No one is ever sure that the side effects that
have already been discovered will be the only ones, for
any drug. We allow the use of many experimental drugs in
this country, including chemotherapy for cancer and AZT
for AIDS, without outlawing them because they may have
unknown side effects. As long as the women who take the
drug are informed of the known side effects and the possibility of more, they should be allowed to use the drug
under a physician's supervision.

10   I feel very strongly that the abortion pill should
be allowed into the United States and released onto the
market, in order to better the lives of many. We have so
many impoverished, hopeless families out there, trapped
in a cycle of poverty because of a mistake a man and
woman make in a moment of time. We should give these
women a chance to make something of their lives without
these unplanned pregnancies, thus sparing the children
as well. Why should we force these women to bear these
unwanted babies when they are not ready or able to care
for them, and consequently have two bitter, possibly impoverished people in the world, where there could have
been one (sadder but) wiser person making something of
her life and having children when she was prepared for
that responsibility? RU 486 provides a safe alternative

to all this misfortune, where everyone would benefit.
Certainly allowing the use of RU 486 will not solve all
the problems of poverty, homelessness, and inequality in
this country, but it would relieve one of the worst consequences of those problems. And the principle behind
the right to choose is much too great to be jeopardized
by a government that does not like the idea of abortion.
In his first week in office, President Clinton told the
government to review this policy; it's time to do more,
and overturn it.

Works Cited

Jacoby, Susan. "What You Thought: RU 486." *Glamour* (Dec.
    1992): 116.

Thoreau, Henry David. *Walden*. Cutchogue: Buccaneer, 1986.

1. What claim (Chapter 2) is Kelley arguing? What are the grounds for her claim? What do you think the pros and cons she listed in developing this argument might have been?
2. Who might Kelley's audience be? What clues does she give you? What do you think are the values and criteria the readership holds?
3. What different forms of evidence (personal, outside authorities, factual references, statistics) does Kelley provide? Which form(s) of evidence does she rely on most?
4. Evaluate the supporting evidence Kelley provides. Is it relevant? Is it detailed enough? Does it seem dated and verifiable? Does her claim exceed her evidence? Does her evidence strike you as slanted? If you were her readers, would you be persuaded by her argument? What changes (if any) in evidence would you recommend to help her make her argument more persuasive?
5. Outline in your notebook an argument responding to Kelley's. You may concur with, oppose, or modify her claim. Make a pro/con list and sketch the kinds of evidence you would need to make your argument persuasive. Who would your readers be? What would be an appropriate place to publish your essay? If you're working in groups, compare your answers with your peers, and comment on the effectiveness of each proposed response.

ESTABLISHING CLAIMS

Thinking Like a Skeptic

You have decided the issue you're going to argue. With the aid of a pro/con checklist, you've sharpened your ideas and prepared for possible objections. You've thought about your audience and determined what you have in common, where you might agree, and where you might disagree. You have also gathered some solid evidence to support your main arguments. And you have formulated a clear thesis statement or claim. Now it's time to establish the logical structure of your argument and decide how best to arrange this material to persuade your readers.

If you've ever tried handing in a paper made up of slapped-together evidence and first-draft organization, you probably discovered a blueprint for disaster. Perhaps you didn't test your work, didn't revise it, or didn't think about how it would "play" to a reader. You assumed that because *you* understood how the parts fit together, your readers would as well. To help you detect and correct these problems, this chapter is slanted toward thinking like a *skeptic*—a skeptical building inspector, to be exact—because a skeptical attitude works best.

To construct a persuasive argument, one that has a chance of convincing your readers to do or feel or believe what you want, you have to pay careful attention to the *logical structure* you are building. You can't take anything for granted; you have to question every step you take, every joist and joint. You have to ask yourself if you're using the right material for the right purpose, the right tool at the right time. In other words, you have to think like a building inspector examining a half-built split-level house—one whose builder is notoriously crafty at compromising quality. That's where a healthy skepticism—and a logical system—come in.

The Toulmin Model

Stephen Toulmin, a British philosopher and logician, analyzed hundreds of arguments from various fields of politics and law.* He concluded that nearly every argu-

*Toulmin, Stephen. *The Uses of Argument.* Cambridge: Cambridge University Press, 1958.

ment has certain patterns and parts. The best arguments, Toulmin found, are those addressed to a skeptical audience, one eager to question the reasoning where it seems faulty, to demand support for wobbly assumptions, and to raise counterarguments.

The slightly re-tooled version of the Toulmin model we describe below encourages you to become a skeptical audience. It provides archeological, everyday terms to help you unearth, weigh, and, if necessary, fix an argument's logical structures. It lets you verify that the major premises in your argument or those of your opposition are clear and accurate, helps you determine whether repairs to your claims are needed and whether counter arguments are addressed, shows you where supporting evidence may be needed, and helps you avoid logical fallacies. And since Toulmin's terms are designed to be broadly practical, they allow you to present your case to a wide variety of readers.

Toulmin's Terms

According to Toulmin, a fully developed argument has six parts. These parts are the *claim,* the *underlying claim,* the *grounds,* the *backing,* the *qualifier,* and the *rebuttal.*

The Claim

The *claim* is the assertion that you are trying to prove. It is the position you take in your argument, often as a proposal with which you are asking your reader to agree. In a well-constructed argument, everything makes its ultimate claim, its conclusion, seem inevitable.

The Underlying Claim

The claim is often an argument's surface claim. Such surface claims are based on a many-layered series of more foundational claims. These are an argument's *underlying claims.* A broad, often half-buried generalization that applies to a number of different situations, the underlying claim is the principle that connects the grounds to the claim and holds the argument together. It explains why the evidence (the grounds) supports the claim. Without it, your readers might not follow the reasoning in your argument. Underlying claims can take the form of legal and moral principles, laws of nature, or even common sense.

The Grounds

Just as every argument contains a claim, every claim needs supporting evidence— the *grounds* that bolster your claim and that your audience accepts without requiring further proof.

The word grounds conjures architectural, archeological, or geological images. Thinking in these figurative terms helps you visualize how arguments are built and work. Imagine, then, an Amish barn raising—or the way a lot of very un-Amish, suburban houses are constructed these days. After the foundation is dug and laid, prefabricated walls are put up. They're then stabilized by buttressing boards that are jammed into diagonal place between the walls and the ground. Think of the underlying claim as an argument's half-buried foundation. Everything is based on this foundation—including the argument's walls, its claims. The grounds are like those buttressing boards: they are lines of evidence that hold the walls up and together. The concluding claim or conclusion is the roof. The difference between arguments and buildings is that these buttressing boards, the grounds, aren't taken away when the argument's structure is complete.

The Backing

Because your underlying claim is an assumption, you cannot be certain that it will always be accepted by your readers. So you provide reasons to back it up. These reasons, called *backing*, indicate that the underlying claim is reliable in a particular argument, though it doesn't have to be true in all cases at all times.

The Qualifiers

Qualifiers provide a way to indicate when, why, and how your underlying claim *is* reliable. They're words or phrases such as *often, probably, possibly, almost always;* verbs like *may* and *might, can* and *could;* or adjectives and adverbs that yoke your claim to some condition. The subtlest kind of qualifier is an adjective that acknowledges that your claim is true to a degree: "Coming from a dysfunctional family *often* makes it *harder* to resist the angry lure of crime." Not always impossible, but *often harder.*

You need to consider a few qualifications about using qualifiers; like antibiotics, they're too powerful to use unwisely. Using too few qualifiers can indicate that you're exaggerating your argument's validity. As you'll see in Chapter 7, common fallacies are most potentially valid arguments that go astray by not qualifying their claims enough, if at all. Using *no* qualifiers can mean that you misunderstand the meaning of qualified claims. Although many students think a qualified claim is a weak claim, in fact the qualified claim is often the most persuasive. Few truths are *simply* true, few claims *always* right. A well-qualified claim, then, shows that the writer respects both the difficulty of the issue and the intelligence of the reader.

Nevertheless, qualifiers alone cannot substitute for reasoning your way to the tough, subtle distinctions on which the most persuasive arguments depend. For example, look at the claim that "Innocent people have an inviolable right to life." It's wisely qualified, since just saying "People have an inviolable right to life" wouldn't hold up. Hitler, after all, was a human. Did he too have "an inviolable right to life"? But even *innocent,* is not qualification enough. It raises too many tough, troubling questions. "Innocent" of what? "Innocent" by whose judgment, and why? What if killing a few innocent people were the only way to end a war that is killing *many* innocent people?

Using a lot of qualifiers, therefore, is no guarantee that your argument is carefully reasoned. In fact, strongly qualifying your argument's key claim may be a sign that you doubt your argument's validity. But such doubt can itself be encouraging. Misusing or overusing qualifiers can indicate that your instinct of anxiety is right—that you've discovered better reasons to doubt your initial argument than to defend it. In fact, acknowledging the appeal of a flawed claim—and describing how you only discovered its flaws once you tried trumpeting its strengths—is an effective way of earning the reader's respect. It shows you to be an honest arguer capable of learning from errors—and thus worth learning *from*.

Deciding what to state and what to imply is a large part of writing any good argument. Just as a building's cross-beams don't have to be visible to be working, not everything important in an argument has to be stated. For example, if someone were to claim that winters in Minnesota are "mostly long and cold," we probably wouldn't stop the flow of argument to ask him to define the qualifier *mostly*. We'd instead keep the qualifier in mind, and let the Minnesotan's definition of "mostly" emerge, implied, from the rest of the story. Similarly, it's sometimes wise to leave your argument's qualifiers implied.

Still, it's often better to risk belaboring the obvious. To minimize the chances that your reader will misunderstand (or altogether miss) your meaning, qualify your claims as clearly and explicitly as possible. "Reading" the argument you're writing like a skeptical reader will help you decide what qualifiers are needed where, and how explicitly they need to be stated.

The Rebuttals

Reading your argument skeptically also allows you to anticipate, answer, and even preempt *rebuttals*. Rebuttals represent the exceptions to the claim. There are many different kinds of rebuttals, and any persuasive argument ought to acknowledge and incorporate the most important rebuttals. Rebuttals are like large-scale qualifiers. They acknowledge and explain the conditions or situations where your claim would not be true—while still proving how your claim *is* true under other conditions. It's wise, then, to anticipate such rebuttals by regularly acknowledging all your argument's limits. Not just to beat your reader to the rebuttal, but to prompt yourself to craft your claims more carefully.

Let's say, for example, that a sportswriter argues that allowing big-market baseball teams to monopolize talent ruins competition by perpetuating dynasties. Your rebuttal might be to cite the overlooked grounds of ignored evidence—grounds that complicate, if not contradict, the writer's claim: "Then why have small-market teams won four of the last ten World Series?" Had the sportswriter anticipated and integrated this rebuttal, she would have improved the argument—from her underlying claim up. Her argument would have taken into account this rebuttal in the form of more careful qualifications. "While the rule of money doesn't guarantee that the richer teams will always win the World Series, it does make it more difficult for hard-pressed teams to compete for available talent." This is now, of course, a less sweeping claim—and therefore more precise and persuasive.

Review: Six Parts of an Argument

Claim	The assertion you are trying to prove
Underlying claim	A generalization that explains why the evidence supports the claim
Grounds	The supporting evidence for the claim
Backing	The reasons that show the underlying claim is reliable
Qualifiers	The words that show when, how, and why your underlying claim is reliable
Rebuttal	The exceptions to the claim

Of course, no writer can anticipate the readers' every rebuttal. Nor should you even try to. But you should test your argument by trying to rebut it yourself. You'll get more peace of mind about your papers if you argue more with yourself about your arguments. Then revise your arguments with those rebuttals in mind. Strive to make readers' rebuttals redundant by fixing all the flaws you can detect. Flatter your pride by being ruthless about your reasoning.

Field Work: Excavating Underlying Claims

Excavating your underlying claims in order to explicate your argument can help you in several ways: you persuade your reader more effectively, see where your own arguments may be flawed more clearly, and identify the crux of otherwise confusing debates more quickly.

For example, let's say that you wanted to prove that education is a universal right. There are a number of ways to do this. You could start by invoking another right that your reader is likely to believe in—the right to opportunity, say. Then you could move from that right toward the right to education and show how the two are related, reciprocal, or dependent on one another. Or you could start with common-sense observations that your reader is likely to share with you—that ignorance costs more than education, for example. And then you could show your reader how these observations provide grounds for proving that education is indeed a universal right.

No matter how you build your argument, it's usually best to start at the bottom and work up. Remember, any kind of sound argument, like any kind of sound building, must have a solid foundation. Base your argument on your deepest underlying claims—the first principles likely to have the broadest, even deepest, support among your readers. This will start your argument off on the right foot, putting you and your reader on firmly common ground. From there,

Underlying Claims

Notice how many layers of underlying claims are here as you practice deciding how deeply to dig.

Claim	Education is a universal right.
Underlying claim	Each person has an inherent, inalienable right to opportunity. Education fosters opportunity. Therefore education is part of the right to opportunity.
Underlying claim	Rights are codified respect for the human being and potential of innocent others. Justice requires us to facilitate innocent others' well-being, and universally available education does this. Therefore education is a universal right. To be just, we must honor and facilitate that right.
Underlying claim	Education is better than ignorance.
Underlying claim	Don't you believe that *you* have an inherent right to education just because you're human? Then grant to others what you would have granted to you.

it's easier to persuade your audience, step by step, that your argument is no house of cards built on sand.

It's not always necessary to dig so deeply. In fact, we could safely leave our second-to-last underlying claim implied. Ignorance being more costly than education is so widely shared a belief, such broadly common ground, that it can just as well be left half-buried in implication. And we *should* leave some of our last, deepest underlying claim unstated. Even though this argument, like many arguments, does implicitly appeal to the Golden Rule, that appeal is better left implicit. For making this appeal explicit might lead many readers to think that you're linking education and religion, or basing rights on religion, or extolling a particular religion. You can—and often should—challenge readers to ask themselves if *they* would like to be the beneficiaries of their own arguments—without digging so deeply that you hit the live wire of unnecessary problems.

Although we must be careful about moral arguments that raise religious questions, we must also be careful about shying away from stating underlying claims just because they're based on moral bedrock. Most arguments are implicitly moral—the *ought-to* element in most arguments is central. For example, take the scientific method. One of its chief maxims is, "You can't get a value from a fact." This means that the facts that science reveals can't tell us what's right and wrong. Science provides information, not ethics. Yet even this is a moral argument of sorts. It tells us how we ought to see the natural world (as amoral) and how we ought to see science (as morally neutral). It tells us that it's right to value facts for their own sake. So as long as you're honest about your argument's ought-to-aims, and as long as those aims are benevolent, you should not shy away from basing your argument on its naturally moral bedrock. That, in fact, is where the most fertile—and contentious—common ground will be. Most readers are interested in arguments because they're interested in justice, in moral good.

Moreover, it's often effective to highlight your argument's moral bedrock. Doing so allows your reader to see that even if she may disagree with you in practice, she may agree with you in principle. Or at least that you're arguing from a basis of sincere, well-meaning principles. This kind of honesty not only demonstrates your good intentions, but honors your reader's own interest in the issue. And admiring readers are more likely to see your argument more clearly—and thus judge it more fairly.

Digging down to this deeply moral common ground also helps both you and your reader see the specific step that your reader is unwilling to take, the point at which your shared aim splits into different, perhaps even colliding means. By arguing like an archeologist, you will be offering your reader a chance to retrace his own logical steps—all the way back to his own sense of justice.

And you'll save yourself a lot of time and trouble, for Toulmin's terms allow you to quickly discover what's driving our most deadlocked debates. Take, for example, the notoriously knotty issue of capital punishment. The pro side says, in essence, "When you deliberately take an innocent human life, you forfeit your own right to life." While the con side says, in effect, "No matter what you do, you cannot forfeit your own inviolable right to life." By digging down to where these opposing claims fundamentally clash, you can see why capital punishment is among our most divisive debates.

This digging is, of course, no guarantee that you can reconcile opponents. But it does more than clarify the debate: it can also cool the bad feelings that can so skew any argument. Comparing opposing arguments at their most fundamental level allows adversaries to see each other's motives—and this can civilize even the debates it can't resolve. In the capital punishment debate, for example, each side can see that the other guy is not necessarily a blood-thirsty brute or a lily-livered bleeding heart, but someone who also cares about justice.

Let's now turn to two sample arguments, testing our version of the Toulmin model in ways that can help you test your own arguments more effectively. The first of these was published in *Newsweek* in 1982. In it, Michael Levin, a philosopher at the City University of New York, argues that, under certain conditions, torture is "morally mandatory."

SAMPLE ARGUMENT FOR ANALYSIS

The Case for Torture

Michael Levin

1   It is generally assumed that torture is impermissible, a throwback to a more brutal age. Enlightened societies reject it outright, and regimes suspected of using it risk the wrath of the United States.

2   I believe this attitude is unwise. There are situations in which torture is not merely permissible but morally mandatory. Moreover, these situations are moving from the realm of imagination to fact.

3   Suppose a terrorist has hidden an atomic bomb on Manhattan Island, which will detonate at noon on July 4 unless . . . (here follow the usual demands for money and release of his friends from jail). Suppose, further, that he is caught at 10 A.M. on the fateful day, but—preferring death to failure—won't disclose where the bomb is. What do we do? If we follow due process—wait for his lawyer, arraign him—millions of people will die. If the only way to save those lives is to subject the terrorist to the most excruciating possible pain, what grounds can there be for not doing so? I suggest there are none. In any case, I ask you to face the question with an open mind.

4   Torturing the terrorist is unconstitutional? Probably. But millions of lives surely outweigh constitutionality. Torture is barbaric? Mass murder is far more barbaric. Indeed, letting millions of innocents die in deference to one who flaunts his guilt is moral cowardice, an unwillingness to dirty one's hands. If you caught the terrorist, could you sleep nights knowing that millions died because you couldn't bring yourself to apply the electrodes?

5   Once you concede that torture is justified in extreme cases, you have admitted that the decision to use torture is a matter of balancing innocent lives against the means needed to save them. You must now face more realistic cases involving more modest numbers. Someone plants a bomb on a jumbo jet. He alone can disarm it, and his demands cannot be met (or if they can, we refuse to set a precedent by yielding to his threats). Surely we can, we must, do anything to the extortionist to save the passengers. How can we tell 300, or 100, or 10 people who never asked to be put in danger, "I'm sorry, you'll have to die in agony, we just couldn't bring ourselves to . . ."

6   Here are the results of an informal poll about a third, hypothetical, case. Suppose a terrorist group kidnapped a newborn baby from a hospital. I asked four mothers if they would approve of torturing kidnappers if that were necessary to get their own newborns back. All said yes, the most "liberal" adding that she would like to administer it herself.

7   I am not advocating torture as punishment. Punishment is addressed to deeds irrevocably past. Rather, I am advocating torture as an acceptable measure for preventing future evils. So understood, it is far less objectionable than many extant punishment. Opponents of the death penalty, for example, are

forever insisting that executing a murderer will not bring back his victim (as if the purpose of capital punishment were supposed to be resurrection, not deterrence or retribution). But torture, in the cases described, is intended not to bring anyone back but to keep innocents from being dispatched. The most powerful argument against using torture as a punishment or to secure confessions is that such practices disregard the rights of the individual. Well, if the individual is all that important—and he is—it is correspondingly important to protect the rights of individuals threatened by terrorists. If life is so valuable that it must never be taken, the lives of the innocents must be saved even at the price of hurting the one who endangers them.

8   Better precedents for torture are assassination and preemptive attack. No Allied leader would have flinched at assassinating Hitler, had that been possible. (The Allies did assassinate Heydrich.) Americans would be angered to learn that Roosevelt could have had Hitler killed in 1943—thereby shortening the war and saving millions of lives—but refused on moral grounds. Similarly, if nation A learns that nation B is about to launch an unprovoked attack, A has a right to save itself by destroying B's military capability first. In the same way, if the police can by torture save those who would otherwise die at the hands of kidnappers or terrorists, they must.

9   There is an important difference between terrorists and their victims that should mute talk of the terrorist's "rights." The terrorist's victims are at risk unintentionally, not having asked to be endangered. But the terrorist knowingly initiated his actions. Unlike his victims, he volunteered for the risks of his deed. By threatening to kill for profit or idealism, he renounces civilized standards. And he can have no complaint if civilization tries to thwart him by whatever means necessary.

10   Just as torture is justified only to save lives (not extort confessions or recantations), it is justifiably administered only to those *known* to hold innocent lives in their hands. Ah, but how can the authorities ever be sure they have the right malefactor? Isn't there a danger of error and abuse? Won't We turn into Them?

11   Questions like these are disingenuous in a world in which terrorists proclaim themselves and perform for television. The name of their game is public recognition. After all, you can't very well intimidate a government into releasing your freedom fighters unless you announce that it is your group that has seized its embassy. "Clear guilt" is difficult to define, but when 40 million people see a group of masked gunmen seize an airplane on the evening news, there is not much question about who the perpetrators are. There will be hard cases where the situation is murkier. Nonetheless, a line demarcating the legitimate use of torture can be drawn. Torture only the obviously guilty, and only for the sake of saving innocents, and the line between Us and Them will remain clear.

12   There is little danger that the Western democracies will lose their way if they choose to inflict pain as one way of preserving order. Paralysis in the face of evil is the greatest danger. Some day soon a terrorist will threaten tens of

thousands of lives, and torture will be the only way to save them. We had better start thinking about this.

An Analysis Based on the Toulmin Model

Clearly, Levin takes a controversial stand on a provocative issue. In fact, his stand is one that most civilized people might find repulsive. It seems barbaric, if not bizarre. Tame terrorists with torture? Doesn't that reduce us to their lowest level? Moreover, since this is an essay written by a professional philosopher for a national audience, it's reasonable to wonder if Levin's argument is so eager for blood because it's so far removed from everyday life—too "academic," in the worst sense of the word.

Nonetheless, one must view Levin's proposal in light of the horrific acts of terrorism that have plagued the world for the last decade—and recently come so close to home in the 1993 bombing of New York's World Trade Center and the 1995 bombing of the Murrah Federal Building in Oklahoma City. Born out of frustration and anger, the essay challenges "enlightened societies" by arguing that there are circumstances in which torture is the right and proper means of saving innocent lives. In other words, it challenges *us* to be skeptical of our assumptions about Levin's aims and means, to wonder if Levin's argument really is as barbaric or as abstruse as it seems. Let's begin by seeing how Levin constructs his argument with a series of subarguments—all of which hinge together.

Levin opens the essay with assumptions that he hopes to prove "unwise": that "torture is impermissible," "a throwback to a more brutal age"; that "Enlightened societies reject it outright"; that the United States would be wrathful toward those regimes suspected of using torture. In the second paragraph Levin sets up the underlying claim that will recur throughout the rest of the essay, shaping his argument's logical pattern: "There are situations in which torture is not merely permissible but morally mandatory."

Then in the third paragraph, he introduces the first of three hypothetical examples—and, thus, his first patch of grounds. (In these fortunately still-hypothetical cases, Levin's "evidence" must remain examples.)

Subargument 1

Underlying claim	There are extreme situations in which torture is not merely possible but morally mandatory.
Grounds	A terrorist unwilling to disclose the location of an atomic bomb he planted in Manhattan is an extreme situation.
Conclusion	Therefore, it is not only permissible but morally mandatory to subject the terrorist who has planted an atomic bomb to torture.

Most people will support Levin's grounds here: The prospect of a terrorist atomic bomb in Manhattan can make us jump just about anywhere that seems even a little safer. It's Levin's broad underlying claim—that torture may be "morally mandatory"—that may cause a rift. Torture seems to violate the very spirit of Jeffersonian democracy: the rights of the individual, whether victim or victimizer, to be treated according to civilized standards. But Levin is quite aware of his audience's likely response. In fact, in many ways, his whole argument is a rebuttal to the commonplace (and therefore rarely voiced) belief that civilized societies should never resort to torture. Levin is careful, then, to reason from general principles to a conclusion that validly follows—a powerful way of leading readers to a conclusion that they might otherwise find, and leave, as uncomfortable.

To make it easier for his audience to accept torture as a way of saving innocent lives, Levin begins his reasoning process with his most extreme hypothetical case: the possible death of millions. His next step is toward narrower, but more familiar grounds. He downscales his example, personalizing them to eventually lead readers to accept torture as a measure of preventing the deaths of any number of innocents. He does this in the opening sentence of paragraph 5 by reminding us of the conclusion he has just led us to: "Once you concede that torture is justified in extreme cases, you have admitted that the decision to use torture is a matter of balancing innocent lives against the means needed to save them." If we've already been convinced by the first hypothetical case, then we can begin to warm up to less extreme cases—namely, a jet with 300, 100, or even 10 people aboard.

Subargument 2

Underlying claim	We must use torture in extreme cases to save innocent lives.
Grounds	An extortionist plotting to bomb a planeful of innocent passengers is an extreme case.
Conclusion	We must torture the extortionist plotting to bomb a planeful of innocent passengers.

Although Levin's grounds are still supportable, his underlying claim has become less problematic since the conclusion of the first subargument. In other words, if you've accepted the first hypothetical use of torture, it shouldn't be too difficult to accept the moral necessity of its use here.

Before we can even begin to imagine an enormous evil, we often need to see or imagine actual persons who have suffered that evil. In effect, any large leap of understanding needs a specifically scuffed pair of shoes into which our sympathy can step. In moving toward fewer, more specific examples of who can benefit from the civilized use of torture, Levin moves to provide these shoes. He increasingly narrows the scope of his examples to enlarge their emotional—and thus moral—force.

This tactic not only moves us, by our senses of sympathy and outrage, closer to Levin's conclusion, it also strengthens Levin's argument in other, even subtler ways. It allows Levin to vary his evidence with increasingly individual examples—to avoid redundancy as he repeats his claims. Presenting a series of imaginable, moving examples enables him to outmaneuver expected rebuttals. And by making his argument increasingly exact, its conditions of validity increasingly acute, Levin demonstrates that he's well aware of the limitations of his argument.

In fact, his argument not only acknowledges limits at every turn, it's intended *to* limit the excess that is evil. In other words, qualifiers are central to his argument. The same desire to minimize the suffering of innocents that compels him to advocate torture also compels him to describe the very limited, but very compelling, conditions under which torture is "morally mandatory." Accordingly, Levin carefully steps from millions to 300, 100, 10, and, finally, to the case of a single newborn baby. By implication the same reasoning would apply as much for the first two examples as it does with four real mothers Levin interviewed:

Subargument 3 (implied, not stated in the essay)

Underlying claim   We must use torture in extreme cases to save innocent lives.

Grounds   A kidnapped newborn baby is an extreme case.

Conclusion   We must torture the kidnapper of a newborn baby.

Once again, repetition has rendered Levin's underlying claim less problematic. We've seen this before. But what about Levin's grounds now? Have they become so narrow that they're now unsupportable? Is the kidnapping of a newborn baby extreme enough to justify torturing the kidnapper to save the baby's life? Since this would be the assumption that most readers would be least likely to accept, Levin appeals to four real mothers, the most "liberal" of whom says that "she would like to administer it herself." If a "liberal" mother would sanction torture, Levin resoundingly implies, what's wrong with the rest of us?

In paragraph 7, Levin picks up on and integrates anticipated objections—the rebuttals he touched upon in the opening paragraph and again in paragraph 4 (that torture is unconstitutional and barbaric). Here he offers a stipulative definition of torture as an underlying claim—one that constructs another subargument, which in turn supports the grounds of his three hypothetical cases.

Subargument 4

Underlying claim   A preemptive strike is an acceptable measure for preventing future evils.

Grounds   Torture is a preemptive strike.

Conclusion   Torture is an acceptable measure of preventing future evils.

Levin's underlying claim is surrounded, if not supported, by especially broad and sturdy grounds here—the historical precedents cited in paragraph 8 with the references to the Allies and Hitler and the hypothetical case of nation A and nation B. The support for the grounds themselves—that torture is a preemptive strike against terrorism—is an assumption that Levin finds no need to explicitly support. He instead chooses to leave it implied, presumably because it's as understandable as the case of the mothers in paragraph 6—that torturing the kidnapper might prevent the newborn from being harmed.

This third subargument is the logical link to the next. But what the subargument does not clearly explain is *who* finds it acceptable to use torture as a way of preventing future evils. And, yet Levin has very cleverly specified those who would in the previous subargument: the "300, or 100, or 10 people who never asked to be put in danger" (subargument 1); the four mothers in the implied subargument 3; the Allied leaders of World War II, including those Americans who "would be angered to learn that Roosevelt could have had Hitler killed in 1943"; and the hypothetical nations A and B of paragraph 8. Notice also how Levin increases both the number and level of authority as he progresses from one subargument to the next (from passengers on a plane to whole nations). All of this leads to the inevitable conclusion: "if the police can by torture save those who would otherwise die at the hands of kidnappers, they must."

Subargument 5

Underlying claim	Authorities have the right to make preemptive attacks on those who would destroy innocent lives.
Grounds	The use of torture is a preemptive attack.
Conclusion	Authorities have the right to make use of torture on those who would destroy innocent lives.

Finally, Levin turns his argument to the question of "civilized standards," which he introduced in the essay's opening paragraph. It is the one moral question he has not addressed—what he refers to as "the line between Us and Them." He offers as his underlying claim a big slab or moral bedrock: "By threatening to kill for profit or idealism, he [the terrorist] renounces civilized standards. And he can have no complaint if civilization tries to thwart him by whatever means necessary." That statement, supported by earlier assumptions that mass murder, for instance, "is more barbaric than torture," leads inevitably to the final subargument:

Subargument 6

Underlying claim	Somebody who kills for profit or idealism renounces his or her rights to civilized standards of treatment.
Grounds	Terrorists kill for profit.
Conclusion	Therefore, terrorists renounce their rights to civilized standards of treatment.

Levin makes a strong case for the civilized, even "moral," use of torture. Even so, Levin could have much improved his case had he dug a little deeper and presented what he found there a little differently. Levin's fundamental claim, however reasonable, however unsettling, still stops short of his deepest underlying claim. And it is unearthed a step too late: claims about one's wish to defend the innocent will suffer if they come after an advocacy of torture. Levin would have made an even better case for his advocacy of torture had he made it even more basic—that is, more openly based on the bedrock belief with which the greatest number of his readers are most likely to most emphatically agree: "It's wrong to make innocent people suffer." Or, less negatively, "Innocent people have the right to live free from violation and violence." And Levin could have put this more personally, more confessionally—and thus have earned himself an even more immediate, if not more intense measure of his reader's respect: "I want to keep innocent people from being made to suffer."

Indeed, acknowledging that most of his audience shares these sentiments would have been the best way to open the essay because it would have started his argument on the broadest available common ground with his reader: "Most of us want to protect innocent people from the threat of evil. Yet most of us also shudder at the idea of torture; it seems like exactly the kind of evil we despise. But to better protect innocent people from evil, we should rethink our automatic aversion to the idea of using torture under any circumstances."

Granted, this level of argument is, and only can be, a starting point. To elaborate on this consensual claim, you would have to take a further series of steps—at any one of which any number of readers might balk. But had Levin started his argument with its deepest underlying claim, he would have both put his argument in the best light and better enlightened readers about where and why their means may differ from Levin's.

Levin's essay addresses an enormously complex moral dilemma—and it was written by a professional philosopher for a national audience. But by digging down to Levin's underlying claims, our retooled Toulmin model allowed us to see that Levin's essay was neither as bizarre nor as abstract as it might otherwise have seemed. Can our Toulmin model be as useful to college students writing argumentative essays about less monumental matters for their instructors?

The following brief argument was written by a first-year student. It's followed by the responses of a small group of first- and second-year students who used the Toulmin model to understand Spokas' argument and reply with their own. Read Spokas' essay critically, making notes in your argument notebook. Try to notice if and how its different parts hinge together—and where some of these parts need to be reworked.

SAMPLE ARGUMENT FOR ANALYSIS

For the Love of the Game
Melissa Spokas

1   Picture this. You're an Olympic-caliber swimmer.
You're training hard every day. The Olympic Trials come
and go. Before you know it, you're a member of the U.S.
Olympic swim team. You're training longer and harder

than ever before, for the major goal of your life is in your grasp. The Olympics come and you are favored to do well; some even pick you as a potential winner.

2   You step onto the starting blocks; the gun is fired. You dive into the cold still water and swim the fastest time of your life, only to be touched out at the wall by another swimmer. She's a relative unknown who's never before medalled in world-class competition. But suddenly she's taller, heavier, more muscular than you've ever seen her.

3   You suspect that she's been taking drugs, probably anabolic steroids. Her changed, more masculine appearance, as well as her markedly improved time suggest this. But drug test results taken right after the race show no signs of drugs in her system. Somehow, you're convinced that she cheated and beat the testing system. Bitterly you ask the question, "Shouldn't there be mandatory drug testing for all competitors, not just a few, and not just at pre-announced times?"

4   The intent of the Olympic drug testing program is to eliminate any competitive edge that results from the use of synthetic aids (Hainline 197). Drug testing was introduced in 1968, but it wasn't until the 1976 Summer Games in Montreal that testing for anabolic steroids began. Since that time, nearly 100 athletes have tested positive for steroid use in Olympic competition.

5   Different athletic organizations have differing policies on drug testing. For example, the U.S. Olympic

Committee publishes a banned substance list, then tests its top finishers and also randomly samples other team members (Hainline 198). If an athlete tests positive, he or she is suspended for four years; in the realm of worldclass athletics, with its brief career length, this effectively ends an athlete's competitive career. The athletic federations of other countries have different policies; some, as in the former East Germany, devoted considerable ingenuity to helping their athletes "beat" the tests. Some other organizations use drug prevention education instead of mandatory drug testing; this is still primarily the case in high school athletics.

6   And who should be tested? That opinion varies; some say only the top finishers, while others argue for random testing of participants. There are four common options; the first is no testing at all. The second is "to test athletes for probable or reasonable cause" (Hainline 197). Such testing is done when there is suspicion of the athlete's using a substance on the banned list; however, sometimes prescribed or over-the-counter medications may cause positive tests. Female athletes taking birth control pills are particularly vulnerable to this trap. The third option is mandatory random testing of all participants, and the fourth is mandatory testing of top finishers at announced times, such as after a competition.

7   I believe that the third option is the only plausible one, and that it should be adopted by all countries

who send athletes to the Olympics. Testing should occur randomly: in training, at meets, or in the off-season. If athletes know when they are to be tested, they can "taper down" so that no trace of drugs will be found in their system on a particular date. Ben Johnson's famous disqualification from the 1988 summer Olympics was due to a miscalculation of when he should have started tapering down; this mathematical mistake stripped him of the title, "World's Fastest Human." Random testing will make it impossible for athletes and their trainers to cheat the intent of drug testing by tapering down. It will force them to reduce if not abandon taking anabolic steroids to enhance their performances, for the chance of losing their careers and potential earnings will be too great.

8   Drugs like anabolic steroids give an unfair advantage to athletes who use them; this isn't what sports, particularly Olympic sports, are supposed to be about. They're not supposed to be about winning at all costs, but about competition and love of the sport; these are the terms cited in the Olympic Creed each participant recites at the beginning of the Games. Anabolic steroids have also been proven physically harmful to human health, as victims like the late Lyle Alzado demonstrate. In the short term, steroids yield larger muscle mass and improved performance, but in the long term, steroid users face a number of debilitating, even potentially fatal, physical consequences from using the drug.

Sports are supposed to improve your health and fitness, not destroy them. Steroid use is contrary to what sports are all about.

9   The Olympic goal isn't about winning, but about taking part, about being part of the "youth of the world" called together every four years. That's why they're called the Olympic *Games*. If random drug testing were mandatory, then this "win-at-all-costs" attitude would disappear, and the real meaning of the Olympic Creed would have a chance to make a comeback.

Bibliography

Asken, Michael, *Dying to Win*. Washington, D.C.: Acropolis Books, LTD., 1988.

Hainline, Brian, and Gary Wadler, *Drugs and the Athlete*. Philadelphia: F.A. Davis, 1989.

Students' Analysis Based on the Toulmin Model

Note how the students quoted below responded to Spokas' argument impulsively at first, but then crafted their immediate responses into well-reasoned, well-organized arguments.

The students first noticed and began to debate Spokas' concluding claim, expressed in paragraph 7: Olympic athletes should submit to random drug testing. They then rushed to voice their own underlying claims: "Even Olympic athletes retain a right to privacy"; "Random drug-tests do not violate a right to privacy," and so on. But sensing that they needed something more concrete on which to base their own arguments, they returned to Spokas' argument to look for what "supported" Spokas' claim. They quickly uncovered her grounds: the evidence she had gathered and her interpretation of the Olympic ideal. The students here differed over whether Spokas' grounds were supportive.

"Ben Johnson's irrelevant," said one. "One guy with a lot of gall is too inflammatory an example. You can't base an argument about rules that will apply to everybody on what one person did."

"If they'd been randomly testing the East Germans all along, there wouldn't be Ben Johnsons. The Olympics would have showcased athletic competition instead of just steroid freaks."

"*Just* steroid freaks? Aren't you overgeneralizing a little?"

After this conversation the students became careful to make better qualified claims and soon dug down to Spokas' underlying claim. They identified it as explicitly stated at the beginning of paragraph 8: "Drugs like anabolic steroids give an unfair advantage to athletes who use them; this isn't what sports, particularly Olympic sports, are supposed to be about." The students then looked for this claim's backing and suspected that it wasn't strong enough, leaving Spokas' underlying claim "too wobbly."

Several students dug deeply enough to realize that Spokas, like Levin, had stopped a layer short in her argument. Recognizing that Spokas' argument was fundamentally about the relationship between "the Olympic spirit" and the right to privacy—and on the parameters of the right to privacy—they thought she had failed to signal her argument's deeper context and concerns. And for overlooking a related issue: "False-positive test results are common," one student wrote. "So if you're going to mandate random drug tests, it's only fair to provide some kind of appeals process."

Digging this deeply into Spokas' argument helped the students unearth and refine their own underlying claims:

- "Okay, so the Olympic Creed stresses participation, not winning [paragraph 8]. These are called *games*, not *meets* or *competitions* [paragraph 9]. But that doesn't tell us why the spirit of competition overrules the right to privacy. That's why Spokas is saying here, and that's what I disagree with."
- "But *you* haven't told us *why* the right to privacy means you should have the right to choose to do something but be exempt from its requirements."
- "And *you* haven't told us why the right to privacy can be an admission ticket."

One student dug especially deep. Although he wasn't sure of the answer, he realized that the question here was one of fairness, of justice, in its largest senses. "Clean competition," he wrote, "offers the spectacle of fairness. A pure fairness we don't often see outside of sports, where life is often rigged."

Only after the students had recognized that the issue revolved around a clash of rights—the right to privacy versus the Olympic audience's right to "the spectacle of fairness"—did they return to Spokas' argument to look for her qualifiers. They found two: that prescribed or over-the-counter medications like contraceptives *may* cause false results, and that even randomly tested athletes *might* find other ways to cheat. But despite their exceptional excavational skills, these students had trouble noting what's often the subtlest part of any argument: the rebuttals it attempts to answer. Only when they were revising their own written arguments—and trying to integrate the rebuttals they'd received from their peers—did the students notice that Spokas' whole argument is, in effect, a rebuttal. It argues against the argument that testing athletes at announced testing times is both as reliable and more proper than random testing, a rebuttal made explicit in paragraph 7.

The Toulmin model asks us to focus on what makes our arguments true: the evidence supporting them, and the circumstances under which the evidence is believable. It compels us to consider not only our case and our readers, but our standards of reason as well. Excavating Spokas' logic with the Toulmin model in hand allowed these students to see her arguments' strengths and flaws. And to build on them both.

TESTING ARGUMENTS

Thinking Like a Cross-Examiner

As you build and revise your arguments to make sure they are as effective as possible in persuading others that your point of view is sound, you need to critically question each link in your chain of reasoning, just as your readers will eventually do. When you read the arguments of others, you need to pay attention to the writer's strategies, assertions, and logic to decide if the argument is reasonable. In other words, you must read like the cross-examining attorney in a court case: You must look for the strengths and weaknesses of an argument and decide which side outweighs the other.

Sometimes writers make errors in logic. Such errors are called **logical fallacies**, a term derived from the Latin *fallere* meaning "to deceive." Used unintentionally, these fallacies deceive writers into feeling that their arguments are more persuasive than they are. Even though an argument might be emotionally persuasive and even sound valid, a fallacy creates a flaw in the logic of an argument, thereby weakening its structure and inviting counterattacks.

Not all logical fallacies are unintentional. Sometimes a fallacy is deliberately employed—for example, when the writer's goal has more to do with persuading than arriving at the truth. Every day we are confronted with fallacies in media commercials and advertisements. Likewise, every election year the airwaves are full of candidates' bloated claims and pronouncements rife with logical fallacies of all kinds.

Whether to strengthen your own writing or to resist fallacies in the arguments of others, it makes sense to be aware of such conscious or unconscious deceptions in reasoning. This chapter will help you examine some of the most common logical fallacies.

Preview: Logical Fallacies

- *Ad hominem* argument
- *Ad populum* argument
- *Ad misericordiam* argument
- *Post hoc, ergo propter hoc*
- Circular reasoning
- Begging the question
- False analogy
- Hasty generalization
- *Non sequitur*
- Stacking the deck
- False dilemmas
- The bandwagon appeal
- Slippery slope

Ad Hominem Argument

From the Latin "to the man," the **ad hominem** argument is a personal attack on an opponent rather than on the opponent's views. Certainly the integrity of a writer may be important to readers who are trying to decide if what the writer says is trustworthy. Nonetheless, it is usually more persuasive and honorable to focus on issues instead of character flaws. If, for instance, you are writing a paper against the use of animals in medical research and you refer to the opposition as "cold-hearted scientists only interested in fame and fortune," you will probably alienate the people you are trying to win over. The same is true if you remind your readers that your opponent, an advocate of the legalization of marijuana, once served time for drug abuse. It really doesn't matter that an advocate for a longer academic year once got caught cheating in college.

There may be, however, cases in which an *ad hominem* attack is a warranted and legitimate rhetorical tool. For instance, in his defense of capital punishment, Edward Koch begins his essay "The Death Penalty Is Justice" (page 338) with the deft use of an *ad hominem* attack to undercut the validity of statements opposing the death penalty by two killers just before their executions. He writes:

> It is a curiosity of modern life that we find ourselves being lectured on morality by cold-blooded killers. . . . I can't help wondering what prompted these murderers to speak out against killing as they entered the deathhouse door. Did their newfound reverence for life stem from the realization that they were about to lose their own?

Such a charged opening undermines the opposing point of view immediately.

Perhaps the most notorious practitioners of *ad hominem* strategies are politicians who resort to assaults on opponents' moral character instead of debating policies. We saw such tactics in the 1996 presidential campaigns with the attention given to claims of Bill Clinton's avoidance of military service during the Vietnam War. Critics outraged by Clinton's lack of military service often made the statement:

> The American people don't want a military draftdodger to be the next commander-in-chief.

Even though some voters saw Bill Clinton's protest against the Vietnam War a generation ago as laudable and heroic, critics viewed it as unpatriotic and a sign of moral weakness, even cowardice. Clearly, the moral integrity of a candidate for office is critical to voters trying to decide who they would like in the Oval Office or governor's mansion or mayor's seat. And, yet, such personal criticisms, even if true, can be overemphasized and, therefore, undercut the attacker's credibility. Overreliance on *ad hominem* arguments also makes the writer come across as mean-spirited and desperate. It is wise, therefore, to avoid the reckless use of *ad hominem* arguments and to focus on the substance of an opponent's claim.

Examples of *Ad Hominem* Arguments

- How could Tom accuse her of being careless. He's such a slob.
- Of course Helen claimed that O. J. Simpson was innocent. She is black after all.
- We cannot expect Ms. Lucas to know what it means to feel oppressed; she is president of a large bank.

Ad Populum Argument

From the Latin "to the people," an *ad populum* argument is just that—an argument aimed at appealing to the supposed prejudices and emotions of the masses. Writers attempt to manipulate readers by using emotional and provocative language to add appeal to their claims. The problem with the *ad populum* argument, however, is that such language sometimes functions as a smoke screen hiding the lack of ideas in the argument. You'll find examples of this fallacy on the editorial pages of your local newspaper—for example, the letter from parents raising a furor over the fact that they don't want their child or the children of their friends and neighbors taught by teachers with foreign accents; or the columnist who makes the *ad populum* case against capital punishment by inflating the number of innocent people wrongfully executed by the state; or the writer who argues that if gays and lesbians are allowed to serve in the military, our national defense will be jeopardized by "sex maniacs."

Writers who resort to *ad populum* arguments undermine their credibility in two major ways. First, they make assumptions (usually inaccurate) about their audience's shared beliefs based on socioeconomic class, political persuasion, religious identity, profession, education, and so on. Most of your arguments in college will be addressed to neutral audiences, not some special interest group. Even if you know the prejudices of your audience, such an appeal at best only persuades those already convinced. Second, emotional language cannot replace the force of logic and supporting evidence.

However, when expertly used, some of these fallacies can be witty and persuasive. In a recent essay, humorist P. J. O'Rourke resorts to the *ad populum* technique as a way of diminishing his opposition. Accusing the environmental movement of tyranny, he writes:

> Like abortion opponents and Iranian imams, the environmentalists have the right to tell the rest of us what to do because they are morally correct and we are not. Plus the tree squeezers care more, which makes them an elite—an aristocracy of mushiness.*

Even for those who view this comparison as exaggerated, it taps into the prejudices of readers who view antiabortionists as self-righteous and Iranian religious leaders as dangerously dictatorial. The tactic is a clever one, for O'Rourke, a political conservative, tries to provoke a knee-jerk reaction in liberals by likening one of their causes, the environmental movement, to the perennial foe of an even more emotional liberal cause, the pro-choice movement. Furthermore, O'Rourke's ironic breakdown of the world into two camps, the "morally correct" "elite" and the rest of us, leaves the unguarded reader little option but resentment at being viewed as unenlightened—especially by "tree squeezers." Whereas this example illustrates how *ad populum* fallacies may succeed in advancing a point, they can undercut an argument when employed awkwardly or by accident.

_____

*O'Rourke, P. J. "The Greenhouse Affect," *Rolling Stone,* June 1992: 403.

Examples of *Ad Populum* Arguments

- High school students don't learn anything these days. Teachers are at fault.
- Every red-blooded American male will love the latest Sylvester Stallone movie.
- If you want to see the crime rate drop, tell Hollywood to stop making movies that glorify violence.

Ad Misericordiam Argument

Also derived from Latin, the ***ad misericordiam*** argument is the appeal "to pity." This appeal to our emotions need not be fallacious or faulty. A writer, having argued several solid points logically, may make an emotional appeal for extra support. Your local humane society, for instance, might ask you to donate money so that it can expand it facilities for abandoned animals. To convince you, the society might point out how, over the last few years, the number of strays and unwanted pets has tripled. And because of budget constraints, the society has been forced to appeal to the public. It may claim that a donation of $25 would house and feed a stray animal for a month. Any amount you give, they explain, will ultimately aid the construction of a new pet "dormitory" wing. To bolster the appeal, the Humane Society literature might then describe how the adorable puppy and kitten in the enclosed photo would have to be put to death unless the overcrowding of the society's facilities is relieved by donations such as yours.

When an argument is based solely on the exploitation of the reader's pity, however, the issue gets lost. There's an old joke about a man who murdered his parents and appealed to the court for leniency because he was an orphan. It's a funny line because it ludicrously illustrates how pity has nothing to do with murder. Let's take a more realistic example. If you were a lawyer whose client was charged with bank embezzlement, you would not get very far basing your defense solely on the fact that the defendant was abused as a child. Yes, you may touch the hearts of the jurors, even move them to pity. Yet that would not exonerate your client. The abuse the defendant suffered as a child, as woeful as that is, has nothing to do with his or her crime as an adult. Any intelligent prosecutor would point out the attempt to manipulate the court with a sob story while distracting it from more important factors such as justice.

Writers who resort to *ad misericordiam* approaches lack strong arguments and relevant evidence. To avoid being misled yourself, be alert to arguments that singularly try to persuade you by wrenching your heart-strings when real facts and logic are dry.

Examples of *Ad Misericordiam* Arguments

- It makes no difference if he was guilty of Nazi war crimes. The man is eighty years old and in frail health, so he should not be made to stand trial.
- Paula is 14 years old and lives on welfare with her mother; she suffers serious depression and functions like a child half her age. She should not be sent to adult court where she will be tried for armed robbery so she can spend her formative years behind bars.

Post Hoc, Ergo Propter Hoc

The Latin **post hoc, ergo propter hoc** is translated as "after this, therefore because of this." A *post hoc, ergo propter hoc* argument is one that establishes a questionable cause-and-effect relationship between events. In other words, because event *X* follows event *Y*, event *X* causes event *Y*. For instance, you would be making a *post hoc* argument if you claimed, "Every time my brother Bill accompanies me to Fenway Park, the Red Sox lose." The reasoning here is fallacious because we all know that although the Red Sox lose whenever Bill joins you at Fenway Park, his presence does not cause the team to lose. Experience tells us that there simply is no link between the two events. The only explanation is coincidence.

Our conversations are littered with these dubious claims: "Every time I plan a pool party, it rains"; "Whenever I drive to Chicago, I get a flat tire." "Every movie that Harry recommends turns out to be a dud." What they underscore is our pessimism or dismay, rather than any belief in the truth of such statements.

It's not surprising that *post hoc* reasoning is often found in arguments made by people prone to superstition—people looking for big, simple explanations. You would be committing such a fallacy if, for instance, you claimed that you got a C on your math test because a black cat crossed your path that morning or because you broke a mirror the night before. *Post hoc* fallacies are also practiced by those bent on proving conspiracies. Following the assassination of President Kennedy in 1963, there was considerable effort by some to link the deaths of many people involved in the investigation to a government cover-up, even though the evidence was scanty. Today we hear Democrats protest that America goes to war every time Republicans are in office and Republicans protest that America gets poorer when Democrats are in office.

You might also have heard people argue that since the women's liberation movement, the number of latchkey children has risen sharply. The claim essentially says that the women's movement is directly responsible for the rise in working mothers over the last 25 years. While it is true that the women's movement has made it more acceptable for mothers to return to the job force, the prime reason is particular to the individual. For some it is simple economics; for others, personal fulfillment; for others still, a combination. The feminist movement is one among many factors linked with women in the work force and the consequent rise in latchkey children.

To avoid *post hoc* fallacies, be certain that a cause-and-effect relationship between events can be demonstrated. Be sure also that you have sufficient evidence.

Circular Reasoning

Circular reasoning is another common fallacy into which writers fall. In it, the conclusion of a deductive argument is hidden in the premise of that argument. Thus,

Examples of *Post Hoc, Ergo Propter Hoc* Arguments

- Just two weeks after they raised the speed limit, three people were killed on that road.
- I saw Ralph in the courthouse; he must have been arrested.
- It's no wonder the crime rate has shot up. The state legislature voted to lower the drinking age.

the argument goes around in a circle. For instance: "Steroids are dangerous because they ruin your health." This translates: Steroids are dangerous because they are dangerous. Sometimes the circularity gets camouflaged in a tangle of words: "The high cost of living in today's America is a direct consequence of the exorbitant prices manufacturers and retailers are placing on their products and services." Cut away the excess, and this translates: The high cost of living is due to the high cost of living. Repetition of key terms or ideas is not evidence. Nor does it prove anything. Instead of simply restating your premise, find solid evidence to support it.

Examples of Circular Reasoning

- People who are happy with their work are cheerful because they enjoy what they're doing.
- Only a welfare mother can appreciate the plight of welfare mothers.
- Bank robbers should be punished because they broke the law.

Begging the Question

Similar to circular reasoning, **begging the question** passes off as true an assumption that needs to be proven. For instance, to say that the defendant is innocent because he passed a polygraph test begs the question: Does passing a polygraph test mean somebody is innocent? Sometimes the begged question is itself loaded in a bigger question: "Are you ever going to act like you are equal and pay for one of our

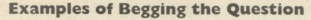

Examples of Begging the Question

- That foolish law should be repealed.
- She is compassionate because she's a woman.
- If you haven't written short stories, you shouldn't be criticizing them.

dates?" The begged question here is whether paying the costs of a date is a measure of sexual equality.

False Analogy

When you draw an analogy, you compare two things that are alike in one or more ways. In any form of writing analogies are very useful, as they expand meaning and demonstrate imagination. In arguments they can be wonderful tools for persuasion. Unfortunately, they can also lead the writer astray and make his or her argument vulnerable to attack.

The problem with **false analogies** arises when the two things compared do not match up feature for feature, and ideas being compared do not logically connect or are pressed beyond legitimacy. The result is a false analogy. For instance, a candidate for a high-powered job may ask us to employ him because of his extraordinary heroics during the Persian Gulf War. He may even claim that being CEO is like fighting a battle: You need to be brave, tough in mind and body, and willing to take punishment as well as deal out punishment. Although the argument might sound appealing, running a company involves more than combat skills. Certainly it is important for a corporate executive to be strong and tough-minded. However, an office full of five-star generals might not be expert at dealing with economic reces-

Examples of False Analogy

- The Ship of State is about to wreck on the rocks of recession; we need a new pilot.
- This whole gun control issue is polarizing the nation the way slavery did people living above and below the Mason-Dixon line. Do we want another Civil War?
- Letting emerging nations have nuclear weapons is like giving loaded guns to children.

sion or product liability. The fallacy is that the analogy is imperfect. Business and soldiering overlap minimally.

A sound analogy will clarify a difficult or unfamiliar concept by comparing it with something easily understood or familiar.

Hasty Generalization

As the name indicates, the **hasty generalization** occurs when you arrive at a conclusion based on too little evidence. It's one of the most frequently heard fallacies. If your scrambled eggs were undercooked at Buster's Diner last week, you would be making a hasty claim if you said that Buster's serves lousy food. Although this might be true, one incident does not a conclusion make. You need more evidence. If after three more visits you were still dissatisfied with your meals, then you would be entitled to your conclusion, and you might want to avoid Buster's. Likewise, getting a D on a French test does not warrant your claim that you lack what it takes to master a foreign language; you might not have studied effectively, been ill on the day of the test, or been the victim of vindictive grading.

A generalization can only be as sound as its supporting evidence. A good rule of thumb for avoiding hasty generalizations is to be certain you can cite factual evidence to support your points; if you have to go on hunches, or "I heard this once on the *Tonight Show*," you're probably being hasty. To avoid sweeping, uncritical statements, be careful when using words such as *always, all, none, nobody, never, only,* and *most.* Instead, consider qualifying your claims with words that are less limiting, such as *many, some, often, seldom,* to name a few.

Examples of Hasty Generalizations

- Homosexuals ought not to teach in public schools because they'll only encourage more students to behave like them.
- I'm failing organic chemistry because the teaching assistant doesn't speak English well.
- This book was written by a Harvard professor, so it must be good.

Non Sequitur

From the Latin for "does not follow," a *non sequitur* draws a conclusion that does not follow logically from the premise. For instance, suppose you make the following claim: "Ms. Marshall is such a good teacher, it's hard to believe she wears such ugly clothes." Your statement would be fallacious because the ability to teach has nothing to do with taste in clothing. Some of the worst teachers might be the best dressers. Although you might want to believe a good teacher would be a good dresser, there is no reason to think so. For the supposition to work, you would need to establish a clear connection between the premise and conclusion. And unless one is made through well-reasoned explanations, readers will not accept your cause-and-effect relationship.

Political campaigns are notorious for *non sequiturs*. During the 1992 presidential campaign people claimed, "Ross Perot would be a good president because he's so rich." As it turned out, despite all his media attention and money, Perot failed to carry a single state or win any electoral votes. American voters decided that his plain speaking and wealth didn't necessarily qualify him to manage the government or represent America to the world.

Examples of *Non Sequiturs*

- Mr. Thompson has such bad breath, it's a wonder he sings so well.
- She's so pretty, she must be smart.
- I supported his candidacy for president because his campaign was so efficiently run.

Stacking the Deck

When you give only the evidence that supports your premise, while disregarding or withholding contrary evidence, you are **stacking the deck**. (Science students may know this as "data beautification," the habit of recording only those results that match what an experiment is expected to predict.) A meat packing manufacturer may advertise that its all-beef hot dogs "now contain 10 percent less fat." Although that may sound like good news, what we are not being told is that the hot dogs still contain 30 percent fat.

This stacking-the-deck fallacy is common not only in advertising but also in debates of controversial matters. The faculty of a college, for instance, may petition the firing of its president for failing to grant needed raises while an expensive new football stadium is being built. The complaint would not be fair, however, if the faculty ignored mentioning that the stadium funds were specifically earmarked for athletic improvement by the billionaire benefactor. Also, if the complaint left un-recognized the many accomplishments of the president, such as the successful capital campaign, the plans for a new library, and the influx of notable scholars, it would be an example of stacking the deck.

To avoid stacking-the-deck fallacies, be certain that you consider all the evidence on both sides of an issue. In fact, that's one of the reasons why we have advised you to make a pro/con list when writing your own arguments. You may not want to promote interest in opposing ideas in your paper, but it is better and more honorable to give concessions to the opposition and to attempt to point out the weaknesses in those ideas so as to strengthen your own stand.

Examples of Stacking the Deck

- Parents should realize that private schools simply encourage elitism in young people.
- We cannot take four more years of her in office given the way she voted against the death penalty.
- Dickens' *Bleak House* is six hundred pages of boring prose.

False Dilemmas

An easy fallacy to yield to is the reduction of complex issues into a **false dilemma** involving two choices: **either** this **or** that. For example, "Either we legalize abortion or we send young women to back-alley butchers," "Love America or leave it," "Either we keep gun ownership legal or only criminals will have guns." Such sloganizing ultimatums, although full of dramatic impact, unfortunately appeal to people's ignorance and prejudices. For the susceptible audience, such false dilemmas preclude consideration of other, more thoughtful alternatives. Be careful not to reduce issues to black and white when there are many shades in between.

Examples of False Dilemmas

- English should be the official language of the United States, and anybody who doesn't like it can leave.
- Movies today are full of either violence or sex.
- Either we put warning labels on records and compact discs, or we'll see more and more teenagers committing suicide.

The Bandwagon Appeal

This familiar strategy makes the claim that everybody is doing this and thinking that. If we don't want to be left out, we better get on the **bandwagon** and do and think the same things. The basic appeal in this argument is that of belonging to the group, behaving like the majority. It plays on our fears of being different, of being excluded. Of course, the appeal is fallacious inasmuch as we are asked to "get with it" without weighing the evidence of what is being promoted: "Smart shoppers shop at Sears"; "America reads Danielle Steel."

To avoid being lured by the bandwagon appeal, ask what the hard evidence is behind the claims. To avoid the same fallacy in your own writing, rely on logic and solid support rather than the fears of your readership.

Examples of Bandwagon Appeals

- Everybody's going to the Smashing Pumpkins concert.
- Nobody will go along with that proposal.
- It's a fact that obesity is a sign of weakness.

Slippery Slope

The **slippery slope** presumes one event will inevitably lead to a chain of other events that end in a catastrophe—as one slip on a mountain top will cause a climber to tumble down and bring with him or her all those in tow. This domino-effect reasoning is fallacious because it depends more on presumption than hard evidence: "Censorship of obscene material will spell the end to freedom of the press"; "A ban on ethnic slurs will mean no more freedom of speech"; "If assault rifles are outlawed, handguns will be next." America's involvement in Vietnam was the result of a slippery slope argument: "If Vietnam falls to the Communists, all of Southeast Asia, and eventually India and its neighbors, will fall under the sway of

Examples of Slippery Slope Arguments

- Legalized abortion is a step toward creating an antilife society.
- A ban on ethnic slurs will mean no more freedom of speech.
- If we let them build those condos, the lake will end up polluted, the wildlife will die off, and the landscape will be scarred forever.

communism." Even though Vietnam did fall, the result has not been the widespread rise of communism in the region; on the contrary, communism has fallen on hard times.

To avoid the slippery slope of reasoning, consider the possible in-between steps—those between the initial event and disaster. Work out the stages carefully: What would really happen if a community censored obscene material? Who would be the censors? Would they want to expand their range? Would the press inevitably cave in to the censors' control? If you are working to refute a slippery slope argument, always ask for proof that the slide will occur as your opponents predict; if you can break the chain of events, you refute the entire argument.

EXERCISES

1. In your notebook, list examples of logical fallacies you find in essays, news articles, editorials, advertising, junk mail, and other persuasive materials that you confront on a daily basis. Based on the information you and other group members collect, draw some hypotheses about which fallacies are most prevalent today and why. If your instructor requests you to do so, convert those hypotheses into an outline of an argument essay for your campus newspaper.

2. Explain the faulty logic of the following statements. Of what fallacy (or fallacies) is each an example?

   a. When did you stop hiring other people to take your exams for you?
   b. He's too smart to play football; besides he broke his leg 10 years ago.
   c. If we don't put warning labels on record albums, we'll see more and more teenagers committing suicide.
   d. Karen must be depressed; she wore dark clothes all weekend.
   e. How can you accuse me of being late? You're such a slowpoke.
   f. Rap music isn't music because it's just noise and words.
   g. He's at least 6 feet 6 inches tall, so he must be a terrific basketball player.
   h. People who are happy with their work are cheerful because they enjoy what they're doing.
   i. Indians living on reservations get the necessities of life at government expense, so they have no worries.
   j. Take Tummy Tops laxative instead of Mellow Malt, because Tummy Tops contains calcium while Mellow Malt has aluminum and magnesium.
   k. Lite Cheese Popcorn contains 34 percent fewer calories!
   l. Any decent person will agree that Nazism has no place in modern society.

CHAPTER 8

DOCUMENTING ARGUMENTS

Thinking Like a Researcher

Most arguments derive their success from the evidence they contain, so good argumentative writers learn to find evidence from many sources and present the best evidence to support their claims. In the academic world, much of that evidence is gathered through *research*, either conducted in a lab or field, or through examination of the previously published work of other investigators and scholars. The research paper that you may be asked to write challenges you to learn how more experienced writers find and present evidence that meets the standards of the academic community.

When you walk through the library, you are surrounded with researched arguments. The book claiming that the Kennedy assassination was part of a CIA conspiracy is a researched argument. So is the journal article asserting that Shakespeare's plays were written by Sir Francis Bacon, and the research report that claims AZT is an effective treatment for some AIDS patients. The article in *Fortune* on the need for changes in the capital gains tax is one too, as is the review claiming that Nirvana is the most important band of the 1990s. All of these arguments have something in common: To back up their claims, their authors have brought in supporting evidence which they gathered through a focused research effort. That evidence gives you and readers like you grounds by which to decide whether or not you will agree with the authors' claims. Libraries, then, aren't just storehouses for history; they're arsenals for good writers.

In the previous chapters we've stressed the importance of finding evidence that will impress readers of your argument's merits. To review, researched evidence plays an important role in convincing readers of the following:

- Expert, unbiased authorities agree with your position in whole or in part, adding to your credibility.
- Your position or proposal is based on facts, statistics, and real-life examples, not mere personal opinion.
- You understand the opposing arguments as well as your own.
- Your sources of information are verifiable, since researched evidence is always accompanied by documentation.

A good analogy to use, once again, is that of the lawyer presenting a case to a jury. When you write a researched argument, you're making a case to a group of people who will make a decision about a subject. Not only do you present your arguments in the case, but you call on witnesses to offer evidence and expert opinion, which you then interpret and clarify for the jury. In a researched argument, your sources are your witnesses.

Writing an argumentative research paper isn't different from writing any other kind of argument, except in scale. You will need more time to write the paper in order to conduct and assimilate your research, the paper is usually longer than nonresearched papers, and the formal presentation (including documentation) must be addressed in more detail. The argumentative research paper is an extension and refinement of the essays you've been writing. It's not a different species of argument.

Finding a Topic

As in all arguments, researched argument topics can be generated from your immediate local concerns, or from more global concerns; neither is "better" as a source. Arguments of immediate or local concern might include topics such as a proposed tuition increase or curriculum revision, planned economic or architectural changes in your town, an election issue, a campus or local controversy, and so on. Arguments from the world at large can be gathered nearly everywhere. Is there a national controversy, such as parental warning labels on records and CDs, that interests you? What about an ethical issue such as doctor-assisted suicide? A political issue such as intervening in a civil war? A social issue such as dismantling affirmative action programs? If you have been keeping an argument journal this semester, you can page back through it to find inspirations. We say inspirations—plural—because it's always wise to have several possibilities in mind at the start.

David Perez, the student writer of the paper you'll see developed in this chapter, was assigned by his instructor to bring in a list of four possible topics for his researched argument. The professor also gave David and his classmates five suggestions to help them find topics:

1. Pick a topic you'd like to pursue for several weeks; there won't be time to pick another if in two weeks you tire of your first topic.
2. Pick a topic that's not so recent or so obscure that you can't find published sources on it.
3. Pick a topic that you and your readers can deal with objectively. There's plenty to argue about without getting bogged down in matters of belief, dogma, or prejudice.
4. Pick a topic about which you can find diverse sources. If all your evidence comes from one book or one interest group, you won't be able to present a balanced argument.
5. Limit your paper to 10 double-spaced pages. If you want to work with a broad topic such as abortion or education, pick a subdivision of it that you

can treat thoroughly in this space. Students who don't limit their topics write unfocused papers and get low grades.

In his argument journal, David listed 10 or 12 topics he found interesting; the partial list below includes some of the topics he had been investigating since the course began.

Are homeless shelters more dangerous than the streets?

Do owners of media conglomerates censor the news according to their own political leanings?

SAT scores—why are they more important than high school grades in getting admitted to the university?

Pornography on the Internet—how prevalent is it?

Shouldn't we spend more money and effort helping victims of crime, and less on housing criminals?

Did affirmative action work? How would we know if it did or didn't?

Should students be required to pay activity fees if they don't take part in campus activities?

Although David wanted to know more about all these topics and the others on his list, he finally narrowed the list to the four topics he later handed in to his instructor:

Pornography on the Internet is not as widely available as the media leads us to believe.

Even students who don't participate in campus activities should pay activity fees.

SAT scores are weighed too heavily in college admissions decisions.

Violence on TV affects children negatively, but it doesn't turn them into criminals.

David's instructor accepted three of his four topics; the one on activity fees, she believed, was too narrow to generate the amount of research that David would need to write his paper. David began his preliminary research in the college library.

Sources of Information

There are two basic kinds of research sources, and depending partly on the kind of issue you've picked to research, one may prove more helpful than the other. The first kind is *primary sources,* which include first-hand accounts of events (interviews, diaries, court records, letters, manuscripts). The second is *secondary sources,* which interpret, comment on, critique, explain, or evaluate events or primary sources.

Secondary sources include most reference works and any books or articles that expand on primary sources. Depending on whether you choose a local or more global issue to write about, you may decide to focus more on primary or more on secondary sources; but in most research, you'll want to consider both.

Primary Sources

If you choose a topic of local concern to write about, your chief challenge will be finding enough research material; very current controversies or issues won't yet be indexed (in newspaper indexes or *The Readers' Guide to Periodical Literature,* for example) or have books written about them, so you may have to rely more heavily on interviews and other primary research methods to find information. If you choose a local issue to argue, consider the following questions.

- Which experts on campus or in the community might you interview to find out the pros and cons of the debated issue? An administrator at your college? A professor? The town manager? Think of at least two local experts who could provide an overview of the issue, from different angles or perspectives.
- What local resources—such as a local newspaper, radio station, TV station, or political group—are available for gathering printed or broadcast information? If one of your topics is a campus issue, for example, the student newspaper, student committees or groups, university on-line discussion groups, or the student governmental body might be places to search for information.

Once you determine that you have several possible sources of information available locally, your next step is to set up interviews or make arrangements to read or view related materials. Most students find that experts are eager to talk about local issues and have little problem setting up interviews. However, you'll need to allow plenty of time in your research schedule to gather background information, phone for interviews, prepare your questions, and write up your notes afterward. If you're depending on primary research for the bulk of your information, get started as soon as the paper is assigned.

Preparing for Interviews

A few common courtesies apply when preparing for interviews. First, be prepared to discuss the purpose of your interview when setting up an appointment. Second, go into the interview with a list of questions that show you have already thought about the issue. Be on time, and be prepared with notebook and pen to record important points. If you think you may want to quote someone directly, ask their permission to do so and read the quotation back to them to check it for accuracy.

Conducting Interviews

Be prepared to jot down only key words or ideas during the interview, reserving time afterward to take more detailed notes. Keep the interview on track by asking

Preparing Interview Questions

Consider the following guidelines as you prepare questions for an interview.

- Find out as much information as you can about the issue and about the expert's stand on the issue before the interview. Then you won't waste interview time on general details you could have found in the newspaper or on the local TV news.
- Ask open-ended questions that allow the authority to respond freely, rather than questions requiring only a "yes" or "no" answer.
- Prepare more questions than you think you need, and rank them in order of priority according to your purpose. Using the most important points as a guide, sequence the list in a logical progression.

focused questions if the interviewee wanders in responding to your question. When you are leaving, ask if it would be okay to call if you find you have other questions later.

Writing up Interviews

As soon as possible after the interview, review the notes you jotted down and flesh out the details of the conversation. Think about what you learned. How does the information you gathered relate to your main topic or question? Did you gather any information that surprised or intrigued you? What questions remain? Record the date of your interview in your notes as you may need this information to document your source when you write the paper.

Secondary Sources

Although many primary sources—published interviews, public documents, results of experiments, and first-person accounts of historical events, for example—are available in the college library, the library is also a vast repository of secondary source material. If your topic is regional, national, or international in scope, you'll want to consider both of these kinds of sources. For example, if your topic is proposed changes to the Social Security System, you might find information in the Congressional Record on committee deliberations, a primary source, and also read editorials on the op-ed page of the *New York Times* for interpretive commentary, a secondary source.

A Search Strategy

Because the sheer amount of information in the library can be daunting, plan how you will find information before you start your search. And always consult a reference librarian if you get stuck in planning your search or if you can't find the information you need.

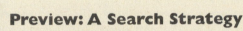

Preview: A Search Strategy

- Know what your topic is
- Get an overview of your topic
- Compile a working bibliography
- Locate sources
- Evaluate sources
- Take notes

Knowing What Your Topic Is

Your argument journal may remind you of potential topics, and Chapter 2 covered how to develop a topic. But what if you still can't think of a topic? You might try browsing through two books that contain information on current issues.

Facts on File (1940 to the present). A weekly digest of current news.

Editorials on File (1970 to the present). Selected editorials from U.S. and Canadian newspapers reprinted in their entirety.

Also, think about which subjects from Part 2 of this book you find interesting. These three sources should give you a wealth of ideas to draw on.

Getting an Overview of Your Topic

If you know little about your topic, encyclopedias can give you general background information. Just as important, encyclopedia articles often end with bibliographies on their subjects—bibliographies prepared by experts in the field. Using such bibliographies can save you hours in the library.

If your library houses specialized encyclopedias related to your topic, check them first. If not, go to the general encyclopedias. Following is a list of specialized and general encyclopedias you may find helpful.

General Encyclopedias

Academic American Encyclopedia. Print. CD-ROM. Written for high school and college students. Comprehensive index is volume 21.

New Encyclopedia Britannica. Scholarly articles. Will be available online and on CD-ROM–projected date is late 1995. *Micropaedia* is a ten-volume index of the *New Encyclopedia Britannica.*

Encyclopedia Americana. Extensive coverage of science and technology and excellent on American history. Index is volume 30.

Specialized Encyclopedias

Encyclopedia of American Economic History (1980). Overview of U.S. economic history and aspects of American social history related to economics.

Encyclopedia of Bioethics (1995). Covers life sciences and health care.

Encyclopedia of Philosophy (1972). Scholarly articles on philosophy and philosophers.

Encyclopedia of Religion (1987). Covers theoretical, practical, and sociological aspects of religion worldwide.

Encyclopedia of Social Work (1987). Covers social work issues including minorities and women.

Encyclopedia of World Art (1959–1967). Covers artists and art works and contains many reproductions of art works.

McGraw-Hill Encyclopedia of Science and Technology (1992). Print and CD-ROM. Covers physical, natural, and applied science.

Be sure to check the dates of encyclopedias to make sure you are finding the most current information available.

Compiling a Working Bibliography

Because you don't know at the beginning of your search which sources will prove most relevant to your narrowed topic, keep track of every source you consult. Record complete publication information about each source in your notebook, on 3" × 5" index cards, or on printouts of on-line sources. The list that follows describes the information you'll need for particular kinds of sources.

For a Book

Authors' and/or editors' names

Full title, including subtitle

Place of publication (city, state, country)

Date of publication (from the copyright page)

Name of publisher

Volume or edition numbers

Library call number

For an Article

Authors' names

Title and subtitle of article

Title of periodical (magazine, journal, newspaper)

Volume number and issue number, if any

Date of the issue

All page numbers on which the article appears

Library location

For an Electronic Source

Authors' names, if given

Title of material accessed

Date of material, if given

Title of the database

Publication medium (e.g., CD-ROM, diskette, microfiche, on-line)

Name of the vendor, if relevant

Electronic publication date

Date of access to the material, if relevant

Path specification, for on-line media (e.g., FTP information; directory; file name)

Note that for electronic sources, which come in many different formats, you should record all the information that would allow another researcher to retrieve the documents you used. This will vary from source to source, but the important point is to give as much information as you can.

Your instructor may ask you to prepare an **annotated bibliography**, in which you briefly note the potential usefulness of your sources and perhaps evaluate them for accuracy, currency, or bias. Sample entries from David Perez's annotated bibliography are reproduced below. The next section discusses how to evaluate sources.

Sample Entries for an Annotated Bibliography

Baron, Jonathan, and M. Frank Norman. "SAT's, Achievement Tests, and High School Class Rank as Predictors of College Performance." *Education and Psychological Measurement* Winter 1992: 1047-1055. This

study attempts to determine the validity of the SAT
test in combination with high school class rank and
achievement test scores as a predictor of college
success. The result of this study was basically
that the SAT test may not be the most effective
means at determining college achievement. In addition, the paper suggests that a greater reliance
should be placed on achievement tests in terms of
college acceptance. The study was not biased and
contained relevant information, but the statistics
were not easily understandable.

Bernstein, Douglas A., Edward J. Roy, Thomas K. Srull,
and Christoper D. Wickens. *Psychology*. 2nd ed.
Boston: Houghton Mifflin, 1991. The section on the
SAT test found in this book can prove to be quite
useful. The book is not biased and presents both
sides of the argument. First, it supports the validity of the test, but also points out to its
drawbacks. The test is seen as ineffective because
one is able to take special courses. Also it is
not an aptitude test, but rather an achievement
test. So by presenting both sides of the issue,
this book can definitely be used as a source for
the research paper.

Burns, Frances Ann. "SATs." *United Press International* 1
Sept. 1991: Section: Regional News. The importance
of this article to the research paper is the opinions of various individuals on the subject of SATs.

The article states that the SAT is not a reflection of school performance and is not a good predictor of college success. The information that I received from this paper was pretty relevant to my topic even though the main focus of the article did not exactly deal with my research question.

Dembner, Alice. "Revised PSAT Is Put to Test This Week." *The Boston Globe* 11 Oct. 1993, sec. Metro: 1+. This article first gives a general background on the format of the new SAT test. It goes into the specifics of the test, and claims that it still is a poor predictor of college success. It claims that the same biases that were present in the old test still remain in the new one. This article is useful for the research paper because it focuses on the future of the SAT test and not just on what has happened in the past.

D'Souza, Dinesh. "Standardized Tests Are Imperfect, but Necessary." *The Atlanta Journal and Constitution* 28 Aug. 1991: Sec A: 9. This article presents the opinion that the SAT test is a good predictor of college success. It attempts to refute the claim of the test being racially biased by saying that the test was originally used to prevent such problems. By instituting an objective test, colleges would not be able to subjectively reject minority students. The article was written fairly well, but still alludes to the obvious fact that minority

```
students do perform worse on the test and that it

is a biased examination.
```

A working bibliography (as opposed to an annotated bibliography) would include the complete publication information for each source, but not the evaluation of its usefulness to the paper.

Locating Sources

Your college library offers a range of methods and materials for finding the precise information you need. Here is a brief guide to locating periodicals, books, and electronic sources.

Finding Periodicals

Instead of going to the periodicals room and leafing page by page through magazines, journals, and newspapers to find information pertinent to your topic, use periodical indexes to locate the articles you need. Here is a list of some of the periodical indexes often available in college libraries. If your library does not house these indexes, ask the reference librarian the best way to find periodical articles in your library. When deciding whether to use the printed or electronic versions of these indexes, carefully note the dates of the material they reference. For example, you cannot use the CD-ROM version of *The Readers' Guide to Periodical Literature* to find a source from 1979. However, for a more current source (from 1983 to present), use the CD-ROM version since it provides abstracts of articles. These will allow you to decide whether locating the full article is worth your time and effort.

Periodical Indexes

General

Readers' Guide to Periodical Literature. 1915 to present. Print. Indexes popular journals and magazines and some reviews of movies, plays, books, and television.

Readers' Guide Abstracts. 1983 to present. CD-ROM. Same content as *Readers' Guide* but with abstracts.

Newspaper Abstracts Ondisc. 1985 to present. CD-ROM. Abstracts to articles in nine newspapers: *Boston Globe; Atlanta Constitution; Chicago Tribune; Christian Science Monitor; Los Angeles Times; New York Times* (1987 to present); *Wall Street Journal; Washington Post; USA Today.*

New York Times. 1851 to present. Print. 1990 to present. CD-ROM. Extensive coverage is national and international.

Periodical Abstracts. 1986 to present. CD-ROM. Index to over 950 general periodicals.

ABI/Inform. August 1971 to present. Online and CD-ROM. About eight hundred thousand citations to articles in 1400 periodicals. Good source for business-related topics. Complete text of articles from 500 publications since 1991.

Newspaper Abstracts. 1985 to present. Online. Indexes and abstracts articles in 27 major American newspapers.

Specialized

Applied Science and Technology Index. 1913 to present. Print. 1983 to present. CD-ROM. Covers all areas of science and technology.

Art Index. 1929 to present. Print. 1984 to present. CD-ROM. Wide coverage of art and allied fields.

Business Periodicals Index. 1958 to present. Print. 1982 to present. CD-ROM. Covers all areas of business.

Education Index. 1929 to present. June 1983 to present. CD-ROM. Covers elementary, secondary, and higher education.

PAIS International in Print (formerly *Public Affairs Information Service Bulletin*). 1915 to present. Print. 1972 to present. CD-ROM. Excellent index to journals, books, and reports in economics, social conditions, government, and law.

Ethnic News Watch. 1990 to present. CD-ROM. Indexes newspapers published by various ethnic groups. Includes full text of most articles.

Social Sciences Index. (*International Index* 1907–1965; *Social Sciences and Humanities* 1965–1974; *Social Sciences Index* 1974 to present). 1907 to present. Print. 1983 to present. CD-ROM. Indexes scholarly journals in political science, sociology, psychology, and related fields.

Humanities Index. (See *Social Sciences Index* for name changes.) 1907 to present. Print. 1984 to present. CD-ROM. Covers scholarly journals in literature, history, philosophy, folklore, and other fields in the humanities.

America: History and Life. 1964 to present. Print. 1982 to present. CD-ROM. Index and abstracts to articles in over 2,000 journals. Covers the history and culture of the United States and Canada from prehistory to the present.

SPORT Discus. 1975 to present. CD-ROM. Covers sports, physical education, physical fitness, and sports medicine.

Sociofile. 1974 to present. CD-ROM. Coverage includes family and socialization, culture, social differentiation, social problems, and social psychology.

Essay and General Literature Index. 1900 to present. Print. 1985 to present. CD-ROM. Indexes essays and chapters in collected works. Emphasis is on social sciences and humanities.

Finding Books

Your library catalog, whether available in printed (card), electronic, or microform format, indexes the books your library holds. (You may be able to access other kinds of sources using the catalog as well, for example, government documents, or maps.) Every catalog provides access to books in three basic ways: by author, title, and general subject. If the catalog is electronic, you can also use keyword searching to locate books. In a keyword search on a computer terminal, you type in a word related to your topic, and the catalog lists all the sources that include that word in the title.

To make keyword searching more efficient, you can often combine two or more search terms. For example, if you know that you want information on "violence," and can narrow that to "violence and music not rap music," the catalog will give you a much shorter list of sources than if you had typed only "violence," which is a very broad topic. This is called Boolean searching, and the typical ways you can combine terms are to use "and" to combine search terms; "or" to substitute search terms (for example, "violent crime" or "assault"); and "not" to exclude terms. For example, suppose you are looking for information on cigarette smoking by teenagers. In a Boolean search, you could use the search phrase: *teenager or youth and smoking not marijuana.*

If you are searching by subject rather than author or title, it's useful to know that libraries organize subject headings according to the *Library of Congress Subject Headings* (*LCSH*). These are large red books, usually located near the library's catalog. You will save time and be more successful if you look up your subject in the *LCSH*. For example, if you search the catalog using the term "movies," you won't find a single source. If you look up "movies" in the *LCSH*, it will tell you that the subject heading is "motion pictures." Type in "motion pictures," and you'll find the sources you need.

Listed below are other useful sources of information.

Biographies

There are so many different biographical sources that it is difficult to know which one has the information you need. The following title will save you a lot of time. *Biography and Genealogy Master Index, 1980–1990.* Print. 1993. CD-ROM. (spans from B.C. to the present).

Index to more than 350 biographical sources.

Biography Index. 1947 to present. Print. 1984 to present. CD-ROM. International and all occupations. Guide to sources in books, periodicals, letters, diaries, etc.

Contemporary Authors. 1962 to present. Print. 1960 to present. CD-ROM. Contains biographical information about authors and lists of their works.

Almanacs

World Almanac and Book of Facts. 1968 to present. Print. CD-ROM (Microsoft Bookshelf). Facts about government, business, society, etc. International in scope.

Statistical Abstract of the United States. 1879 to present. Print. Published by the U.S. Bureau of the Census. Good source for statistics about all aspects of the United States including economics, education, society, and politics.

Statistical Masterfile. 1984 to present. CD-ROM. State and national government statistics and private and international.

Reviews, Editorials

Book Review Digest. 1905 to present. Print. 1983 to present. CD-ROM. Index to book reviews with excerpts from the reviews.

Book Review Index. 1965 to present. Print. 1965 to date. CD-ROM. Indexes to more books than the above but doesn't have excerpts from reviews.

Bibliographies

Look for these in journal articles, books, encyclopedia articles, biographical sources, etc.

Finding Internet Sources

You may have access to the Internet through campus computer labs or your own computer, if you have one. The easiest way to access the Net is by using the World Wide Webb (WWW), a point-and-click system in which related documents are linked. Many colleges and universities have their own webs, through which you can access their library catalogs. Some universities have even organized WWW searches by subject; for example, Stanford University provides Web searchers called Yahoo that allow you to search for information by subject. You can also access the Internet via other search engines such as Archie and Veronica. A number of books that discuss Internet access and use are available; here are two that are popular.

Krol, Ed. *The Whole Internet: User's Guide and Catalog.* 2nd ed. Canada: O'Reilly & Associates, 1994.

Gilster, Paul. *The Internet Navigator.* 2nd ed. New York: John Wiley, 1994.

Remember that the Internet is constantly changing, so no book will be completely up to date on how to access its information. Check to see if your college has workshops or courses on using the Internet—it's an important research tool and it's worth your time to learn how to navigate in cyberspace.

Evaluating Sources

The first examination of your sources isn't intended to find the precise nuggets you'll use in your final paper; rather, it is a preliminary assessment to help you decide if the material is *relevant* and *reliable* for your purposes. You can often sense a source's relevance by skimming it's preface, introduction, table of contents, conclusion, and index (for books) or abstract and headings (for articles) to see whether your topic appears and how often. Many students mark their bibliography cards with numbers (1 = most relevant, 2 = somewhat relevant, 3 = not very relevant) to help them remember what sources they most want to examine. If a source contains no relevant material, mark the bibliography card "unusable" but don't discard it; if you refine your topic or claim later, you may want to go back to that source.

The reliability of a source is judged in a number of ways:

- Check the date: Is it recent?
- Look at the footnotes: Is the author's evidence recent?
- Is the author an expert in the field? To find out, use the biographical sources listed later in this chapter, or find book reviews in the reference section.
- Where does the author work? A source's credentials may influence your readers. You may also find out what biases the author may have; for example, if the author is the founder of Scientists Against Animal Research, you'll have a good idea about his or her personal beliefs on the subject.

Although you don't want to be overwhelmed by taking detailed notes yet, feel free to record your impressions or the connections you find between authors or ideas in your argument notebook; these may help you as you draft your paper.

When you have decided which sources look most promising, you may be ready to start gathering information from articles, books, and electronic sources; or you may want to reconsider your topic or approach to it.

Taking Notes

There are as many different styles of note taking as there are writers. Some people like to use 4" × 6" cards, recording one idea on each card. This is useful because you can easily shift cards around as you change your outline; you don't have to recopy material as often. Other students take their notes in their argument journals, or on sheets of wide computer paper so that they can make notes or copy bibliographic references in the margins. If you decide to use note cards, we offer two words of advice: First, mark every note card in some way to identify the source. You might want to use the author's name, a short abbreviation of the title, or some kind of numbering system tying your note cards and bibliography together. Don't neglect this or you'll find yourself desperately searching for a reference at 2 A.M. on the day your paper is due with no way to track it down. Second, on each note card indicate whether it's a summary, paraphrase, or direct quote; some people use different colored cards, pens, or highlighters to distinguish the three kinds of notes. Other people use the initials, *S, P,* and *Q* to make the cards. This designation proves useful when deciding on how and when to *document* your sources (see page 161).

Most research notes fall into three categories: summarizing, paraphrasing, and quoting.

Summary

Summary is most useful when you want to record the gist of an author's idea without the background or supporting evidence. To summarize accurately, you condense an extended idea into a sentence or more in your own words. Your goal is to record the *essence* of the idea without copying all the words.

Here's David's summary of a passage from one of his sources. The original reads:

> But critics say the exam remains a poor predictor of college achievement, retains a bias that hurts girls and minority students, and allows those who can afford coaching a distinct advantage. . . .
>
> Haney said he doesn't think the revised test will address many of the old test's problems. "Height is a better indicator of people's weight than this college admissions test is of how people will do in college," he said, referring to one problem.
>
> Cinthia Schuman, executive director of Fair Test, a Cambridge-based organization that monitors testing, said the "new test, like the old test, is a multiple-choice exam that places too much emphasis on speed and choosing the right answer."
>
> —From Alice Dembner, "Revised PSAT Is Put to Test This Week"

David summarized this passage on a notecard (see Figure 8.1 on page 152).

Paraphrase

Paraphrasing is useful when you want to preserve an author's line of reasoning, but don't want or need to use the original words. When you paraphrase, you restate the original in your own words and sentence structure. Here is another excerpt from Dembner's article, and David's paraphrase is shown in Figure 8.2 on page 152.

> "As far as humanly possible, the test has always been free of bias," he said. "There are inequities in educational systems and society, but the test can never correct for that."

Dembner / Summary

Critics of the standardized SAT and PSAT believe these tests are biased against women and minorities, give an unfair advantage to students who can pay to take prep courses, and rely too much on quick responses to multiple-choice questions.

Figure 8.1

While acknowledging that a student's high school record will always be the best predictor of college achievement, Montague said test revisers hoped to bring the exams closer to the mark. "But," he added, "no one had any grand hopes of it being dramatically different."

Dembner / Paraphrase of Montague, p. 3

Montague, a College Board member, believes that problems of bias reside in social organizations and institutions, rather than in the tests themselves. He agrees that students' grades in high school are the best indicator of how they will fare in college, but he notes that changes to the SAT and PSAT should make the tests more accurate at forecasting students' potential for success in college.

Figure 8.2

Quotation

Quoting directly should be used only when the author's words are particularly memorable or succinct, or when the author presents factual or numerical evidence that can't be easily paraphrased. You must copy the author's *exact* wording, spelling, capitalization, and punctuation *as you find it* (even if it contains an obvious mistake). Proofread every direct quotation at least twice; it's easier than you think to leave something out, change a verb tense, or add a word or two. If you want to add words for grammatical completeness or clarity, put them in square brackets such as these [ ]. If you want to eliminate words, mark the omission with three spaced periods, called *ellipsis points* (if the omission comes at the end of a sentence, the ellipsis is typed with four spaced periods). If you find a source you are certain to quote from, it might be worthwhile photocopying it to avoid errors when reading the words.

Here are examples of effective and ineffective quotation, based on another excerpt from Dembner's article.

Original

She is particularly incensed that the PSAT is still being used to determine National Merit scholarships. "More than 60 percent of scholarship recipients are males, despite the fact that females get higher grades in high school and college," she said. "Because of its form, content, and coachability, the test gives wealthy white students an advantage. This is not a level playing field for women or minorities."

Effective Quotation

Cinthia Schuman, executive director of Fair Test, says the PSAT's "form, content, and coachability" mean that women and minorities together get less than half as many National Merit scholarships as their white male peers.

Ineffective Quotation

Cinthia Schuman, executive director of Fair Test, says that National Merit scholarships should not be based on the PSAT because the test "gives wealthy white students an advantage."

Drafting Your Paper

Sometimes the sheer size of a researched argument paper can be intimidating. As a result, some writers suffer from "writer's block" when they start composing the paper. Here are several strategies for starting your draft.

1. **Write a Five-Minute Summary.** The five-minute summary asks you to write a quick, one- or two-paragraph description of what your final paper will say. Basically you're creating a thumbnail sketch of the paper in order to clarify in your own mind how the paper will come together. The summary doesn't have to be formal; some people don't even use complete sentences.

Almost always these summaries dispel writer's block and get your creativity flowing.

2. **Divide the Paper into Sections.** Dividing the paper into sections makes the task of writing a long paper more manageable. Most writers divide a paper, as we did in Chapter 3, into beginning, middle, and end, and further subdivide the middle.

3. **First Draft the Sections You're Confident About.** Drafting the sections you feel most confident about first builds momentum for drafting other parts of the paper. As reported by many students, this strategy might also lead you to alter the slant or emphasis of the final paper, thereby resulting in a better product.

4. **Use a Simple Code to Indicate Sources.** Using a simple code to indicate sources will save you a great deal of time in revising your paper. As you write your draft, you may not want to interrupt the flow of ideas to copy quotes or summaries from note cards; instead, you can insert into your draft the author's or source's name and a quick reference to the content so that you'll know on a later draft what you intended to include. Here's an example from David's first draft of how these coded references work:

> Students without a 1000 on their SAT will not be admitted to the University of Texas even if they have good grades in high school/Eberstein interview. For this reason students are obviously worried about their scores and understand the significance of this exam/Chi Q in Justin 9/NYT News 24.

Here you can see David's code at work as he refers to notes from an interview with Eberstein, a quotation by Chi from page 9 of a source written by Justin, and information from page 24 of the New York Times News Service source. Later he will have to incorporate these sources into the draft; but for the time being he simply lists in shorthand the evidence to support his general statements.

Incorporating Your Research

Because the effort in finding sources and taking notes is so time-consuming, some writers think that their work will be "wasted" if they don't somehow cram all the notes they've taken into their final papers. Unfortunately the results of such cramming often looks less like a paper and more like note cards stapled together in a long string with an occasional sentence wedged between to provide transitions. Every successful writer ends up gathering more research data than is needed for a paper. But isn't it better to have plenty of material to pick and choose from than not to have enough to make a persuasive case? The five tests we explained at the end of Chapter 5 (sufficiency, detail, relevance, avoidance of excess, and appropriateness) should determine which notes to incorporate into the final draft. Here, too, the flexibility of having one note per card may help you because you can shuffle and change the sequence of sources to see which order of presentation will have the most impact on your readers. If you're working with a computer, you may find yourself marking and moving blocks of text around as you judge the arrangement of your evidence. The first arrangement you come up with may not always be the best. Allow yourself some flexibility!

When incorporating sources into your paper, you don't want the "seams" to show between your own writing and the summaries, paraphrases, and quotations from your sources. So it's worth your effort to spend some time writing sentences and phrases that smoothly introduce sources into the text. Consider these two examples:

Awkward:	Imani Phillips of Kenwood Academy fears not being admitted to college and her SAT score will "boost her mediocre school record" (Justin 10).
Revised:	Imani Phillips, who fears not being admitted to college, hopes her SAT score will "boost her mediocre school record" (Justin 10).

Remember that while *you*, the writer, may understand how a particular source supports your points, your *readers* may miss the connections unless you provide them. "But I know what I meant!" isn't much of a defense when your readers can't follow your chain of thought. Again, we fall back on the analogy of making a case to a jury: A good attorney not only presents a witness's testimony but helps the jury understand what that testimony means.

Attribution

Many students fail to understand the importance of introducing their sources when they incorporate them into a paper. This introduction is called *attribution*, and it is an important part of the process of documentation. Attribution shows your readers that your evidence comes from identifiable, reliable sources. When the attribution contains the name of a book or the author's professional affiliation or other credentials, it also psychologically suggests to your readers how reliable the source may be. For instance, if you present a statistic on divorce and attribute it to the book *How to Pick Up Women*, your readers are less likely to respect that statistic's weight than if it came from the U.S. Census Bureau. Likewise, if you cite evidence that eating rutabagas prevents colon cancer, your readers will treat the evidence differently if it comes from an unbiased researcher at the Mayo Clinic rather than from one at the American Rutabaga Institute. In neither case is the evidence less likely to be true, but the attribution in both cases makes the difference.

Many students have only one phrase in their repertoires for attribution: "According to . . ." This works, but it is not very informative. By choosing a more connotative argumentative verb, as you do when you state a position or proposal (see Chapter 3), you can signal to your readers the source's attitude toward the statement. For instance, consider this sentence:

Attribution Verbs

Source Is Neutral

comments	observes	says
describes	points out	sees
explains	records	thinks
illustrates	reports	writes
notes		

Source Infers or Suggests, But Doesn't Actually Say So

analyzes	asks	assesses
concludes	considers	finds
predicts	proposes	reveals
shows	speculates	suggests
supposes	infers	implies

Source Argues

alleges	claims	contends
defends	disagrees	holds
insists	maintains	argues

Source Agrees with Someone/Something Else

admits	agrees	concedes
concurs	grants	allows

Source Is Uneasy or Disagrees

belittles	bemoans	complains
condemns	deplores	deprecates
derides	laments	warns

Senator Smith _____ that the change is needed.

Look how changing the verb can change the way your audience regards Smith's position (not all of these verbs will work in this sentence structure).

If you're not sure of the connotations of any of these verbs, or if you're not sure that the sentence you created works with a particular choice, consult an unabridged dictionary or your instructor. Clumsy attribution can distract readers in the same way typos and grammatical errors can, so you want to make your attributions as smooth as possible. (For placement of a bibliographic reference after attributed material, see page 161.)

Revising and Editing Your Paper

After you have worked your source material into a draft, it's time to look at your writing skeptically, as your readers will. Start by testing all the parts of your argument, then change, delete, add, or reorganize material to make your case more effectively. This may not be easy to do because you've been living with this topic for several weeks and may have lost your objectivity and ability to see the gaps. (If you're working in writing groups, ask another member to read your paper and offer you some feedback on it.)

To help you revise your argument, we recommend making an outline of the draft *as you've written it*—not as you intended to write it. This will serve as an x-ray of the paper, helping you detect any holes or imbalances. Moreover, it will show you the actual order in which points are presented so that you can consider reorganizing or changing your argumentative strategy. The strategies explained in Chapters 5 to 7 for assessing evidence, considering claims, and identifying logical fallacies ought to help you at this stage; apply them as stringently to your own writing as you would to an essay you're reading.

If you made notes in your argument notebook at an earlier date about connections you wanted to make in your final paper, now is the time to include those connections if, in fact, they fit into the paper's final shape. You might also consider other kinds of evidence to include. Can you think of personal experiences or those of other people to support the evidence of your outside authorities? Have you found facts and statistics to buttress the opinions you present? What are your readers' criteria for judging an issue? Have you presented claims that meet those criteria and phrased them in that manner? It's also time to make sure that all transitions between points are included and are accurate. For instance, if you switch points around, make sure that the point you call "second" is actually the second, not the third or fourth. Also check that you've included documentation for all your sources and that you have bibliography note cards or other records of documentation information to prepare the notes in your final copy. Then polish your prose so that your sentences are smooth, your paragraphs are complete, and your grammar and punctuation are precise. Many students "let down" their efforts when they sense their papers are nearing completion; as a result, their final grades suffered. The revising and editing stage requires sharp attention. Don't undercut all your hard research efforts by presenting your argument in anything but its best form.

Preparing and Proofreading Your Final Manuscript

Once you have polished the draft to your satisfaction, it is time to attend to the presentation of your paper. Flawless presentation is important in research, not only because of the appreciation it will win from your instructor and readers, but also because it will reinforce your credibility with your readers. A sloppy paper with typographic or grammatical errors, missing documentation, or illegible print makes your readers think that *you* are sloppy—and that your argument might be sloppy as well. A well-prepared paper suggests to your readers that you have taken extra care that everything is correct—not only the presentation, but the content as well. This good impression may make readers more inclined to accept your arguments.

Most instructors expect research papers to be neatly and legibly typed with clear titles, double spacing, standard margins (1-inch) and type sizes (10- or 12-point), and minimal handwritten corrections. Your last name and the page number should appear in the upper right-hand corner of every page after the title page. For English courses the standard guide to manuscript format is the *MLA Handbook for Writers of Research Papers*, 4th edition. MLA requirements are spelled out in most college composition handbooks and illustrated in David's final paper (see page 171). Before you submit your paper, proofread it carefully for typographical errors, misspellings, omitted words, and other minor errors. If possible, let several hours elapse before your final proofreading so you can see more clearly what you've typed instead of what you *think* you typed. Never let the pressure of a deadline keep you from proofreading your paper. Readers get annoyed by minor errors, and annoyed readers are less likely to be persuaded by the content of your argument.

Plagiarism

Plagiarism is a crime in the academic community. The scholarly world operates by exchanging information and acknowledging the sources of this information. If you fail to acknowledge your sources, or make it appear that someone else's work is actually your own, you are sabotaging the exchange of scholarly information. You're blocking the channels. Perhaps it doesn't seem important to you now, but you should know that plagiarism has very serious consequences. It can earn you a failing grade on an assignment or for a course, a suspension or even expulsion from school, and/or a permanent notation on the transcripts that future employers and graduate schools will see. Even if you are never caught, you've still stolen ideas and words from someone.

Plagiarism falls into two categories: intentional plagiarism and accidental plagiarism. International plagiarism includes copying a phrase, a sentence, or a longer passage from a source and passing it off as your own; summarizing or paraphrasing someone else's ideas without acknowledgment; and buying or borrowing a paper written by someone else and submitting it as your own. Accidental plagiarism includes forgetting to place quotation marks around someone else's words, and not acknowledging a source because you were ignorant of the need to document it. Carelessness and ignorance are not defenses against plagiarism.

Many questions about plagiarism involve the tricky subject of *common knowledge*—that is, standard information in a field of study, as well as common sense observations and proverbial wisdom. Standard information includes the major facts in a discipline—for example, the chemical formula for water is H_2O or the Seneca Falls Convention for Women's Rights took place in 1848. If most of your sources accept such a fact without acknowledgment, you can assume it is common knowledge to readers in that field. However, if you're dealing with lesser-known facts (the number of soldiers at the Battle of Hastings), interpretations of those facts (such as assessments of the importance of the Seneca Falls meeting), or a specialist's observation (a scholar's analysis of Susan B. Anthony's rhetoric), you'll need to provide documentation.

Common sense information, such as the notions that politicians are concerned with getting votes or that icy roads make driving dangerous, need not be documented. Proverbs and clichés don't need documentation either, although proverbs taken from recognized poems or literary works do. (Thus, "A stitch in time" needs no documentation, but "To be or not to be" should carry a reference to *Hamlet*).

Here are four simple rules to help you avoid plagiarism.

1. *Take your research notes carefully.* Write down (or print out) a full bibliographical reference for each source (the forms for these appear on pages 161–170). Also note whether you are quoting, paraphrasing, or summarizing what you find in your source (see earlier discussion in this chapter). If your notes are clear and thorough, you'll never have to worry about which words and ideas are yours and which are your sources'.

2. *Always introduce your source carefully so that your audience knows to whom they're listening.* Proper attribution is a signal to your readers that you're switching from your own work to someone else's. It also is a signal to you to check that a source is represented accurately (with no exaggeration) and that a bibliographic citation appears in your list of Works Cited or References.

3. *When in doubt, document.* While it is possible to overdocument, it is not an intellectual crime to do so. Rather, it reveals a lack of self-confidence in your own argument, or your determination to prove to your instructor and readers that you've seen every source ever published on your subject. However, overdocumenting is less serious an academic sin than plagiarizing!

4. *Enter the documentation right after the use of the source; it doesn't "carry over" between paragraphs or pages.* It is tempting, especially when using one source for an extended period, to leave all the documentation until the end of a large passage of text (which might be several paragraphs or several pages in length). But even if you weave attribution skillfully throughout the whole passage, the convention in academics is that you document a source in each paragraph in which you use it. And if another source intervenes, it is twice

as important that the main source is documented in every paragraph of use. So if you use the same article in four successive paragraphs, each of those paragraphs must have some parenthetical source reference. With skillful attribution that parenthetical reference can be reduced to a simple page number, which won't interrupt the "flow" of your text.

To understand how plagiarism works, let's look at some of the ways writers might handle, or mishandle, this passage from Dennis Baron's article "English in a Multicultural Society," which appeared in the Spring 1991 issue of *Social Policy,* pages 5–14. Here's the original passage, from page 8:

> The notion of a national language sometimes wears the disguise of inclusion: we must all speak English to participate meaningfully in the democratic process. Sometimes it argues unity: we must speak one language to understand one another and share both culture and country. Those who insist on English often equate bilingualism with lack of patriotism. Their intention to legislate official English often masks racism and certainly fails to appreciate cultural difference: it is a thinly veiled measure to disenfranchise anyone not like "us."

Plagiarized Use

> Supporters of U.S. English argue we must all speak one language to understand one another and share both culture and country. But Dennis Baron argues that "their intention to legislate official English often masks racism and certainly fails to appreciate cultural difference" ("English in a Multicultural Society," *Social Policy,* Spring, 1991, p. 8). English-only legislation really intends to exclude anyone who is not like "us."

This is plagiarism because the writer has copied Baron's words in the first sentence and paraphrased them in the last, but made it appear as though only the middle sentence were actually taken from Baron's article.

Plagiarized Use

> Calls for a national language sometimes wear the disguise of inclusion, according to linguist Dennis Baron. When U.S. English argues that we must all speak English to participate meaningfully in the democratic process, or that we must speak one language to understand one another and share both culture and country, Baron says they are masking racism and failing to appreciate cultural difference (Baron 8).

Here the plagiarism comes in presenting Baron's actual words without quotation marks, so it looks as if the writer is paraphrasing rather than quoting. Even with the attribution and the citation of the source, this paragraph is still an example of plagiarism because the direct quotes are disguised as the writer's paraphrase.

Acceptable Use

> Linguist Dennis Baron argues that supporters of official English legislation use the reasons of inclusion, unity, and patriotism to justify these laws, but that their efforts may hide racist and culturally intolerant positions. Baron says that

sometimes, English-only laws are "thinly-veiled measure[s] to disenfranchise anyone not like 'us'" (8).

Here the source is properly handled. The writer paraphrases most of the original text in the first sentence, then skillfully incorporates a direct quotation in the second (note the use of square brackets to make the noun agree in number with the verb, and the conversion of double quotation marks from the original into single quotation marks in the quote). The attribution clearly says that both points are taken from Baron, but the quotation marks show where Baron's actual words, rather than the writer's, are used.

Documentation

Almost every academic discipline has developed its own system of *documentation,* a sort of code for indicating where the writer's evidence may be found. A good way to think of the rules of documentation is by analogy to a sport like basketball: Academic readers expect you to play by the established rules (what to document, how to avoid plagiarism, how to attribute sources). If you want to play the game, you have to observe the rules. At the same time, as you probably know, there are accepted variations on the rules (e.g., 30- or 45-second shot clocks, the dimensions of the 3-point line) in certain basketball leagues. The various styles of documentation used in the humanities, social sciences, and natural sciences are the equivalent of these acceptable variations.

You must document any idea or words you *summarize, paraphrase,* or *quote directly* from a source. The two most common variations on documentation used in colleges and universities are the Modern Language Association (MLA) style used widely in the humanities, and the American Psychological Association (APA) style, used widely in the social sciences. We will explain them in detail later in this chapter. (Some of your courses may also require you to use CBE [Council of Biology Editors] style; *The Chicago Manual of Style,* which you might know as Turabian style; or a journalistic style guide like *The Associated Press Style Book.*) Think of these systems not as annoyances for you as a writer, but as rule books for playing the game of researched writing on different courts. Your instructor will tell you what set of rules you are to use.

Where Does the Documentation Go?

Fortunately, both MLA and APA styles have abandoned footnotes in favor of intext references, and a source list at the end of the paper, a much neater format to work with. In both styles, you put a brief reference or attribution to your source in parentheses within the body of the paper, and a full bibliographical citation in a list of *Works Cited* (MLA) or *References* (APA). (These are the equivalents of what you probably called a "Bibliography" in high school.) Documenting your sources, if performed properly, will help you avoid plagiarism. The shape that citations take in the two systems, however, is a little different, so make sure you observe the forms carefully.

Documentation Styles

Let's look at how both systems handle documentation for some of the most commonly used information sources. Suppose you want to quote from Charles Siebert's article, "The DNA We've Been Dealt," which appeared in the September 17, 1995, issue of the *New York Times Magazine.* Here's how it would appear in your list of sources:

MLA   Siebert, Charles. "The DNA We've Been Dealt." *New York Times Magazine* 17 Sept. 1995: 50-64.

APA   Siebert, C. (1995, September 17). The DNA we've been dealt. *New York Times Magazine,* pp. 50-64.

As you can see, each style orders information differently. Likewise, both styles put on a parenthetical reference in the paper to show where the evidence comes from, but again they do it differently.

MLA   One author reports that "the Genome Project is expected to leave us with a complete readout of our biological blueprint by the year 2005 (at an estimated cost of $3 billion)" (Siebert 53).

If the author's name appears in your attribution, only the page number needs to go in the parentheses:

MLA   Charles Siebert reports that "the Genome Project is expected to leave us with a complete readout of our biological blueprint by the year 2005 (at an estimated cost of $3 billion)" (53).

Both references tell your readers that they can find this source in your Works Cited list, alphabetized by the last name "Siebert." If you had more than one reference to Siebert in your Works Cited list, then you would add a shortened form of the title in the parentheses so readers would know to which Siebert article you are referring (Siebert, *DNA* 53).

The APA style references for the same situations would be

APA   One author reports that "the Genome Project is expected to leave us with a complete readout of our biological blueprint by the year 2005 (at an estimated cost of $3 billion)" (Siebert, 1995, p. 53).

or

APA   Charles Siebert (1995) reports that "the Genome Project
                                 is expected to leave us with a complete readout of our bi-
                                 ological blueprint by the year 2005 (at an estimated cost
                                 of $3 billion)" (p. 53).

When you use more than one work by an author in your paper, APA style distinguishes them by date of publication. For example, if you cited two Siebert articles
from 1995, the earlier one is designated 1995a, and the second is called 1995b.

A Brief Guide to MLA and APA Styles

The handbooks for MLA and APA documentation are available in most college libraries. If you don't find the information you need in the following brief guide,
look for these books in your library.

> Joseph Gibaldi, *MLA Handbook for Writers of Research Papers,* 4th ed. New
> York: MLA, 1995.
>
> *Publication Manual of the American Psychological Association,* 4th ed. Wash-
> ington, D.C.: APA, 1994.

General Format for Books

MLA   Author. Title. Edition. City of Publication: Publisher,
                                 Year.

APA   Author. (Year of Publication). Title. City of
                                 Publication, State: Publisher.

One Author

MLA   Kozol, Jonathan. Savage Inequalities: Children in Amer-
                                     ica's Schools. New York: Crown, 1991.

APA   Kozol, J. (1991). Savage inequalities: Children
                                 in America's schools. New York: Crown.

MLA uses the author's full first name plus middle initial, whereas APA uses
the initial of the first name (unless more initials are needed to distinguish among
people with the same initials). APA only capitalizes first words and proper nouns in
titles and subtitles; MLA capitalizes all words except prepositions, conjunctions,

and particles. Finally, MLA permits the abbreviation of certain publishers' names, whereas APA drops unnecessary words such as *Co., Inc.,* and *Publishers.*

Two or More Authors

MLA

Pyles, Thomas, and John Algeo. <u>History and Development of the English Language</u>. 4th ed. Fort Worth: Harcourt, 1993.

APA

Pyles, T., & Algeo, J. (1993). <u>History and development of the English language</u> (4th ed.). Fort Worth, TX: Harcourt, Brace, Jovanovich.

In MLA style, only the first author's name is given last name first. In APA style, the ampersand (&) is used to join authors' names. The ampersand is also used in parenthetical references (e.g., "[Pyles & Algeo 1993, p. 23]") but not in attributions (e.g., "According to Pyles and Algeo"). In MLA style, for works having four or more authors, you may replace all but the first author's name by the abbreviation *et al.* You may use that abbreviation in APA style if there are six or more authors.

More Than One Work by an Author

MLA

Baron, Dennis. <u>Grammar and Gender</u>. New Haven: Yale, 1986.

---. <u>Grammar and Good Taste</u>. New Haven: Yale, 1982.

In MLA style, if you cite more than one work by a particular author, the individual works are listed in alphabetical order. For the second and any additional entries, type three hyphens and a period instead of the author's name; then skip a space and type the title, underlined.

In APA style, when citing more than one work by an author, the author's name is repeated and the entries are listed chronologically (first published to most recent) rather than in alphabetical order. If two works by one author are published in the same year, then the works are listed alphabetically by title.

Anthology with an Editor

MLA

Shapiro, Michael, ed. <u>Language and Politics.</u> New York: New York UP, 1984.

APA

Shapiro, M. (Ed.). (1984). <u>Language and politics.</u> New York: New York University Press.

Essay in a Collection or Anthology

MLA

Davis, Vivian I. "Paranoia in Language Politics." <u>Not Only English: Reaffirming America's Multilin-</u>

gual Heritage. Ed. Harvey A. Daniels. Urbana, IL: NCTE, 1990. 71–76.

APA   Davis, V. (1990). Paranoia in language politics. In H. Daniels (Ed.), Not only English: Reaffirming America's multilingual heritage (pp. 71–76). Urbana, IL: NCTE.

Multivolume Work

MLA   Lincoln, Abraham. The Collected Works of Abraham Lincoln. Ed. Roy P. Basler. 5 vols. New Brunswick: Rutgers UP, 1953.

APA   Lincoln, A. (1953). The collected works of Abraham Lincoln (R. P. Basler, Ed.). (Vol. 5). New Brunswick, NJ: Rutgers University Press.

Book with a Group or Corporate Author

MLA   Committee on Classroom Practices, NCTE. Non-native and Nonstandard Dialect Students. Classroom Practices in Teaching English, 1982–1983. Urbana: NCTE, 1982.

APA   Committee on classroom practices, NCTE (1982). Non-native and nonstandard dialect students. Classroom practices in teaching English, 1982–1983. Urbana, IL: NCTE.

Begin the entry with the corporate or group name alphabetized by the first letter of the main word [not including *a, an,* or *the*].

Reference Works

MLA   "Language." The New Columbia Encyclopedia. 1975 ed.

APA   Risanowsky, A. (1975). Language. In New Columbia Encyclopedia (Vol. 11, pp. 143–148). New York: Columbia.

If the reference book is widely available (such as a major encyclopedia or bibliography), a short bibliography form as shown here is acceptable in MLA; APA recommends including more information rather than less. For a less widely known reference book, MLA recommends using the form for a book, multiple-authored book, or series, depending on what the book is.

Editor's Preparation of a Previous Work

MLA   Austen, Jane. <u>Pride and Prejudice.</u> Ed. R. W. Chapman. Oxford: Oxford UP, 1988.

APA   Austen, J. (1988). <u>Pride and prejudice</u> (R. W. Chapman, Ed.). Oxford: Oxford University Press. (Original work published 1813)

Anonymous Work

MLA   <u>Microsoft Windows Version 3.1</u>. Belleville: Microsoft, 1992.

APA   <u>Microsoft Windows Version 3.1</u>. (1992). Belleville: Microsoft.

Articles

MLA format and APA format for articles are similar to the formats for books. One of the few differences concerns the "volume number" of each issue. Volume numbers for any magazine or journal found in a library or acquired by subscription (these usually appear six times a year or less) should be included in your entry. If a journal appears monthly or more frequently, or can be acquired on newsstands, you can usually omit the volume number. If the journal has continuous pagination (i.e., if the January volume ends on page 88 and the February volume begins on page 89), you don't need to include the month or season of the issue in your citation. If the journal starts over with page 1 in each issue, then you must include the month or season in your citation.

Magazines and newspapers (unlike scholarly journals) often dispense articles over several pages (for instance pages 35–37, then continuing on 114–115). MLA and APA permit using the form "35+" instead of typing out all the pages on which such articles appear, except that in APA references to newspaper articles, all page numbers must be noted.

MLA   Author. "Article Title." <u>Journal or Magazine Title</u> volume number (Date): inclusive pages.

APA   Author. (Date). Article title. <u>Journal or Magazine Title, volume number,</u> inclusive pages.

Scholarly Journal with Continuous Pagination

MLA   Madrid, Arturo. "Official English: A False Policy Issue." <u>Annals of the American Association of Political and Social Sciences</u> 508 (1990): 62–65.

APA   Madrid, A. (1990). Official English: False policy issue. <u>Annals of the American Association of Political and Social Sciences, 508,</u> 62–65.

Scholarly Journal with Each Issue Paged Separately

MLA   Baron, Dennis. "English in a Multicultural America." <u>Social Policy</u> 31 (Spring 1991): 5–14. If this journal used issue numbers instead of seasons, the form would be <u>Social Policy</u> 31.1 (1991): 5–14.

APA   Baron, D. (1991). English in a multicultural America. <u>Social Policy, 31</u> (Spring), 5–14.

Magazine Article

MLA   Joelson, J. R. "English: The Language of Liberty." *The Humanist* July/Aug. 1989: 35.

APA   Joelson, J. R. (1989, July/August). English: The language of liberty. *The Humanist*, 35.

This is the form for a magazine that appears monthly. For a magazine that appears bimonthly or weekly, see the examples under "Anonymous Articles."

Anonymous Article

MLA   "Lessons from the U.S. Army." <u>Fortune</u> 22 Mar. 1993: 68.

APA   Lessons from the U.S. army. (1993, March 22). <u>Fortune</u>, 68.

Review

MLA   Estrada, Alfred J. "Divided Over a Common Language." Rev. of <u>Hold Your Tongue: Bilingualism and the Politics of "English Only"</u>, by James Crawford. <u>Washington Post</u> 4 Oct. 1992: WBK-4+.

APA   Estrada, A. (1992, October 4). Divided over a common language [Review of the book <u>Hold your tongue: Bilingualism and the politics of "English Only"</u>]. <u>The Washington Post</u>, pp. WBK-4, WBK-8.

When newspapers designate sections with identifying letters (e.g., A, B, or here WBK), that information is included in the reference. The "4+" indicates that the review begins on page 4 and continues on other, nonadjacent pages in the newspaper. APA includes initial particles such as "The" in a newspaper title; MLA omits them. If the reviewer's name does not appear, begin with "Rev. of *Title*" in the MLA system or [Review of the book *Title*]" in the APA system. If the reviewer's name does not appear, but the review has a title, begin with the title of the review in both systems.

Newspaper Article

MLA
> Maliconico, Joseph. "New Influx of Immigrants." <u>New Jersey News-Tribune</u> 17 Mar. 1991: A-1.

APA
> Maliconico, J. (1991, March 17). New influx of immigrants. <u>The New Jersey News-Tribune,</u> p. A-1.

Newspaper Editorial

MLA
> Gilmar, Sybil T. "Language Foreign to U.S. Schools." Editorial. <u>Philadelphia Inquirer</u> 25 Apr. 1990: 17-A.

APA
> Gilmar, S. (1990, April 25). Language foreign to U.S. schools [Editorial]. <u>The Philadelphia Inquirer,</u> p. 17-A.

Letter to the Editor of a Magazine or Newspaper

MLA
> Shumway, Norman D. "Make English the Official Language." Letter. <u>Chicago Tribune</u> 30 Aug. 1992, sec. 4: 2.

APA
> Shumway, N. (1992, August 30). Make English the official language [Letter to the editor]. <u>Chicago Tribune,</u> sec. 4, p. 2.

If the newspaper or magazine doesn't give a title to the letter, skip that information and use the rest of the citation form.

Electronic Sources

Information Service Such as ERIC (Educational Resources Information Center) or NTIS (National Technical Information Service)

MLA
> Curiel, Herman. <u>Legalizing the Status of English: A New Form of Oppression for Minority Groups</u> Paper presented at the 65th Annual Meeting of the Southwestern Social Science Association, 1987. ERIC ED 281 704.

APA   Curiel, H. (1987). <u>Legalizing the status of English: A new form of oppression for minority groups</u>. Paper presented at the 65th annual meeting of the Southwestern Social Science Association. (ERIC Document Reproduction Service No. ERIC ED 281 704)

Miscellaneous Sources

Film, Filmstrip, Slide Program, and Videotape

MLA   Lee, Spike, dir. <u>Do the Right Thing</u>. Perf. Lee, Danny Aiello, Ossie Davis, Ruby Dee, and Richard Edson. Paramount, 1989.

APA   Lee, S. (Director). (1989). <u>Do the right thing</u>. Hollywood, CA: Paramount

For a filmstrip, slide program, or videotape, include the name of the medium after the title, without underlining (italicizing) or using quotation marks, and add the running time to the end. If you are citing the work as a whole, rather than the work of one of the creative artists involved in the project, start with the title instead. For instance:

MLA   <u>Do the Right Thing</u>. Dir. Spike Lee. Videocassette. Paramount, 1989. 120 mins.

APA   Lee, S. (Director). (1989). <u>Do the right thing</u>. Videotape. Hollywood, CA: Paramount.

Television or Radio Program

MLA   <u>The Bilingual Battle</u>. Narr. Steve Adubato, Jr. WWOR, Secaucus. 25 March 1991.

APA   Adubato Jr., S. (Narrator). (1991, March 25). <u>The bilingual battle.</u> Secaucus: WWOR.

Interview

MLA   Pennington, Professor Linda Beth. Personal Interview. 20 April 1993.

APA*   Pennington, L. (1993, 20 April). [Personal interview.]

If the interview is conducted by telephone, teleconferencing, or electronic mail, you should indicate that in the citation.

*The APA doesn't offer formal forms for "unrecoverable" materials such as personal letters or e-mail messages, lectures, and speeches, and in professional practice these are not included in References listings. However, in collegiate writing assignments, most instructors will ask you to include them. Your may, therefore, have to design a hybrid citation form based on these more standard forms. Remember that the APA encourages you to provide more, rather than less, information in your citations. The MLA has forms for almost any kind of communication, even nonrecoverable ones. Consult the *MLA Handbook* to find additional forms.

Sample MLA Paper

The SAT: Is It an Effective Predictor of College Success?

David Perez

Professor Friend

English 306

21 November 1993

On seven Saturday mornings throughout the year, thousands of high school students go off to their local testing sites to take a single examination that could be their ticket to college. Each year over 1.2 million high school students take the Scholastic Aptitude Test (SAT), which is used by most U.S. colleges to measure potential students' academic ability. College hopefuls all over the country spend more than $100 million in preparation and testing for this one examination (Piccoli G7). This standardized test is probably the most emphasized college admissions exam in the United States today.

Established in 1926, the SAT was designed by the College Board, which claims that the test is a valid predictor of how well a student will do in college (Scripps Howard News Service 3A). It assists college administrators in selecting student applicants by assessing their verbal and mathematical skills. For example, students with a score of less than 1000 on their SAT are not admitted to the University of Texas even if they have good grades in high school. Obviously, students are

worried about their scores and understand the significance of this exam. Jang Chi of Currie High School says,
"this test will determine the rest of my life" (Justin
9). Therefore, a fair test that can actually predict
college performance is crucial.

The validity of the SAT as a predictor of college
performance has been disputed ever since its inception.
Test defenders point out that the test saves time and
money for college admission boards and is a tool that
colleges can use to directly compare one student with
another. Test critics claim that the test is biased
against minorities and women and that students can manipulate their scores through prep courses. Therefore,
the validity of the SAT is a controversy that cannot be
easily resolved—which is unfortunate because of the emphasis that colleges place on it.

The primary reason colleges use the SAT to assess
student performance is probably that most high school
students take this examination. This allows admission
boards to directly compare one student with another. In
some cases, grade point averages (GPA) do not reflect
the applicant's course load or the difficulty of his or
her high school. A student from a small rural high
school may achieve a better GPA than a student from a
tough private high school, but may be less likely to
succeed in college because of a lack of academic preparation. Rensselaer Polytechnic Institute in Troy, New
York, solves this problem by using the SAT because it

gives "some basis to compare everybody based on the same experience" (Ordovensky 4D). Timothy Light, president of Middlebury College, put it best when he said that the SAT was effective in "identifying subgroups within a group . . . it gives you a ballpark" (Flint A41). College admission boards use the SAT to avoid rejecting students who come from tougher high schools with harder course loads, who probably have a better chance of succeeding on the college scene.

Colleges also favor the SAT because it saves time and money. For example, the University of Texas, which relies heavily on the SAT, does not have to request essays and résumés from each student. The college thus spends less time on each application, which in turn saves money for the university. Maurice Salter, a private educational consultant in Los Angeles, points out that large schools do not always have the luxury of reviewing every individual case. People are transformed into numbers to make "quick, scientific decisions" (Justin 7). This keeps the costs of college admissions minimal, which leaves more money for educational purposes. Colleges are able to look only at a person's high school GPA and SAT scores and make a decision about whether to admit that individual.

The final argument in favor of the test is an interesting one offered by Dinesh D'Souza. He claims that before the implementation of the SAT, colleges could subjectively choose any student they wanted. This allowed for substantial racism in the selection process of many schools (D'Souza 9). The SAT was used as an instrument to help fight this discrimination against minorities, who had not been given a fair chance at college admission. This objective test was seen by many as a chance for minority students to provide their ability to succeed in college. Colleges, in theory, would no longer be able to subjectivly reject students because the SAT offered a way to directly compare minority students with children of "WASP privilege" (D'Souza 9).

D'Souza's argument is seen by opponents of the SAT as quite ironic, considering that they believe the examination is inherently biased against minorities. Many studies have verified the test-taking advantage that white, upper-class males have over women, minorities, and individuals who come from lower socioeconomic levels. Such bias could invalidate the SAT because the exam is supposed to directly compare every high school student; but if it gives an unfair advantage to white upper class males over other groups, these comparisons are not accurate.

Women are adversely affected by the SAT because they do not perform as well as men. Studies show that women score an average of 57 points less than their male counterparts on the SAT (Kleiman 8). Yet women tend to outperform men in college despite these lower SAT scores (Piccoli G8). Also, a study done by ETS researcher Gita Wilder shows that men are better at skills required in a multiple-choice test. Her reasoning is that women tend to think more deeply about each question while men jump to conclusions, which is better when taking a multiple-choice test (Piccoli G6). Sarah Stockwell of the University of Chicago agrees with Wilder's point because she believes that women are more likely to think that the exam measures intelligence and that "guessing on the test is cheating" (Kleiman 6). All these points invalidate the SAT because it underestimates the potential success of women students.

Women are not the only group at a disadvantage. Stockwell claims that a 200-point differential in test scores exists between blacks and whites (Kleiman 7). This figure was verified in a recent study by Rex Bolinger (Bolinger 5). This gap is very alarming because the purpose of the SAT was partly to prevent college admissions boards from subjectively rejecting minority students. However, if the test itself is biased against their groups, its whole intention is undermined. The National Center for Fair and Open Testing claims that many more SAT questions are set in the context of white males than minority cultures (Piccoli G6). For example, on one test, a question drew a parallel between "runner: marathon" and "oarsman: regatta." Research done by ETS shows that 53 percent of white males answered the question correctly, compared with only 22 percent of blacks, probably because more upper-class whites have a chance to be familiar with boating terminology. This is just a single example showing that the test fails to provide equal opportunity for minorities to score as well as whites.

Individuals from lower socioeconomic backgrounds are likewise disadvantaged. Wealthy and middle-income students consistently average 100 points higher than their poor counterparts (Hick 1C). Bolinger verified this fact, concluding that higher socioeconomic levels influence SAT scores positively. This statistic is unsurprising since students from inner cities are often deprived of quality education. Outdated books and less qualified teachers are the result of a lack of funds in poorer school districts. Higher income students have access to more learning opportunities and are thus better prepared to take the SAT, says the College Board (Hick 1C). However, these reasons alone do not invalidate the SAT. Rather, critics call for reform because the test questions are biased against lower income individuals. As with the regatta question, FairTest claims that the SAT favors "upper-class white males, who are taught from birth to respond to the kind of thinking that the test rewards" (Hick 1C). This suggests that the test does not measure scholastic aptitude, but rather an individual's upbringing.

The SAT discriminates against women and minorities because of the types of questions it asks. In addition, hard workers who do well in high school are sometimes rejected by colleges based solely on their SAT scores. Terry Weiner, an associate dean at Union College, claims that the most important variable for college success has to be the motivation to work hard. She believes that those who worked hard in high school are most likely to do well in college (Scripps Howard News Service 3A). Students may perform well in high school but poorly on the SAT because of various factors, such as stress, time management problems, test bias, and simple inability to perform well on this particular kind of test. The importance of doing well causes students to feel "a residual pang of anxiety" (New York Times News Service 24). This stress often causes a student not to work to his or her potential. The test's time limit sometimes intimidates students to hurry their work and does not allow them to score as well as they should. The test bias discussed previously also affects minorities who are hard workers. Finally, the simple inability to perform well on this specific examination is sometimes the basis for poor scores. John Katzman claims that the SAT is not a test of math or reading skills, but a test of "how well you take the SAT" (Piccoli G8). For all these reasons, the SAT may not favor hard workers who would succeed in college. For example, my roommate Marc Eberstein scored a 930 on his SAT, but was able through hard work to pass the provisional program at the University of Texas with a 3.75 GPA (Eberstein).

One of the most common criticisms against the SAT is the fact that some students can "cheat" by taking SAT prep courses in order to do well on the exam. Instead of focusing on learning the mathematical and verbal skills that the test was intended to measure, students learn tricks and shortcuts to solve the problems. Some schools, such as Bates College, realize this problem exists and don't use the test, because "frantic coaching" skews scores (Burns). Courses like the Princeton Review claim that they improve a student's score by an average of 150 points (Burns). But individuals from lower socioeconomic levels cannot afford the $525 cost of the Princeton Review. The fact that some students are able to raise their scores artificially through prep courses again invalidates the SAT.

Many arguments support or oppose the SAT as an indicator of college success. The exam is incredibly important to high school students because college admissions rely heavily on it. The truth is that colleges are the only beneficiaries of this test because it allows them to save time and money, and to compare students from widely different high schools. College boards' dependence on the SAT places many students at a disadvantage. For women, minorities, and students from lower socioeconomic backgrounds, the SAT can be a barrier to higher education. To ensure equal access to the opportunities that a college education makes available, we need a new selection process for college applicants that is convenient for colleges, yet fair to students.

Works Cited

Bolinger, Rex. "The Effect of Socioeconomic Levels and
     Similar Instruction on Scholastic Aptitude Test
     Scores of Asian, Black, Hispanic, and White Stu-
     dents." 1992: 19.

Burns, Frances Ann. "SATs." *United Press International* 1
     Sept. 1991: Regional News.

D'Souza, Dinesh. "Standardized Tests are Imperfect, but
     Necessary." *Atlanta Journal and Constitutional* 28
     Aug. 1991, sec A: 9+.

Eberstein, Marc. Personal Interview. 9 Nov. 1993.

Flint, Anthony. "Some Colleges Make SAT Optional."
     Boston Globe 2 Dec. 1990: A33+.

Hick, Virginia. "College Entrance Test Scores Reflect
     Students Income." *St Louis Post-Dispatch* 29 Aug.
     1991: 1C+.

Justin, Neal. "Stress Test." *Chicago Tribune* 17 Oct.
     1990, Style: 9+.

Kleiman, Carol. "SAT Fails Another Test on Fairness to
     Women." *Chicago Tribune* 27 July 1992, Business: 6+.

New York Times News Service. "Revised SAT Feeds Test-
     Taking Anxiety Among College-Bound." *Chicago Tri-
     bune* 10 June 1993, News: 24+.

Ordovensky, Pat. "Colleges Put Grade above SAT Scores."
     USA Today 12 Nov. 1991: 4D+.

Piccoli, Sean. "Charges Persist SAT's Biased Against
     Women and Minorities." *Washington Times* 5 Aug.
     1991: G6+.

Scripps Howard News Service. "Some Schools Drop Entry

Test." *St. Petersburg Times* 7 June 1993: 3A+.

As we hope this chapter has demonstrated, the researched argument is different from the other arguments you've written only in quantity and format, not in quality. You still must make a claim and find evidence to support it, tailor your presentation to your readers, and use a logical structure that considers the various sides of an issue. As you progress in your academic life and, later, professional careers, you will find that variations on the researched argument can become successful senior projects, theses, sales proposals, journal articles, grant proposals, even books—so mastering the skills of argumentative writing will serve you well.

PART TWO

CURRENT DEBATES

GENDER IDENTITY

The feminist movement was reborn, some thirty years ago, out of the recognition that women lacked the access to power and opportunity enjoyed by men. Over the decades, women have accomplished much in areas of equal pay, reproductive rights, and child care. Likewise, traditional roles of both women and men at home, in the workplace, and in society have been challenged and, to some extent, altered. The essays in this chapter explore the struggles and triumphs of men and women in the last decade of the twentieth century as they continue to redefine who they are.

In the wake of the feminist movement, interest in men's issues has exploded. More and more colleges offer courses in men's studies; male-bonding wilderness retreats have become big business; and books on the male psyche and the mythic dimensions of masculinity have appeared regularly on bestseller lists over the last ten years. In fact, some say that the 1990s might just turn out to be the decade of the men's movement. Driving the movement is a variety of forces: women's criticism of men's shortcomings as husbands, fathers, and lovers; the debilitating pressures of the economy; and men's confusion over what it means to be a man today.

The first three essays, subsumed under the heading "On Being Male," consider a key challenge for men of the 1990s: separating expectations from reality, myth from fact. Although women have long identified the oppressive effects of female stereotypes, it is only recently that men have realized how their own gender has suffered the demands of traditional roles. Each of the three selections examines different aspects of the "male mystique"—the presumptions, the limitations, and the harm they cause to both men and women. In the first essay, "The Men We Carry in Our Minds," Scott Russell Sanders challenges the widely held cultural assumption that being male comes with inalienable cachet: power, status, and privilege. He argues that many of these benefits automatically associated with manhood mask the pain and vulnerability of the ordinary man's life. In the second piece, "Men as Success Objects," psychologist and author Warren Farrell makes the case that just as females are unfairly valued for their beauty, males are measured by their wage-earning potential. Our third selection, "Conan and Me," by Bill Persky, humorously recounts the author's struggle with an intruder in his bedroom. This conflict sets into motion the incongruous strands of Persky's identity shaped by influences as disparate as Conan the Barbarian and mom.

The next five essays, clustered under "On Being Female," consider some of the victories and challenges facing the American woman. Because of the feminist movement, today's young women are free to make active choices instead of forced accommodations. From medical schools to welding unions, many of the old barriers are down. Yet appearances and stereotypical expectations of women still present barriers to full expression. In "Femininity," Susan Brownmiller reminds us that the pressures of being feminine can still be demeaning to women in that they create confusion, distraction, and a fear of being unattractive to men. Next, in "Wears Jump Suit. Sensible Shoes. Uses Husband's Last Name," Deborah Tannen examines the ways women are "marked" in American culture. From the way women do their hair to the title they take (Miss, Ms., Mrs.) messages go out. In fact, a woman can't get dressed in the morning without "inviting interpretations of her character," Tannen says. In "Just as Fierce," Katherine Dunn debunks the stereotype of woman as the meeker and weaker sex. Her account of a female boxer's aggression in the ring as well as other accounts of fierce females challenges commonly held notions of female strength.

In our "Oppositions," pieces, we see two radically different appraisals of the feminist movement. One writer, Anna Quindlen wants to regalvanize the movement while the other writer, Kay Ebeling, would like to eliminate the movement. What worries Anna Quindlen in "Feminist" is that 1990s women are taking for granted the hard-won victories of the past. To Kay Ebeling, however, the feminist movement has backfired on women. In "The Failure of Feminism," she vigorously contends that the women's movement has created just the opposite of liberation: a caste of overworked women abandoned by men free to live the good life.

BEING MALE

The Men We Carry in Our Minds
Scott Russell Sanders

Scott Russell Sanders grew up on the dirt-poor back roads of Tennessee and Ohio, where men aged early from lives of punishing physical labor or died young in military service. When he got to college, Sanders was baffled when the daughters of bankers, lawyers, and physicians accused him and his sex of "having cornered the world's pleasures." This essay, devoid of rancor, examines the presumptuousness of male stereotypes. This essay also appears in Sanders' book *Paradise of Bombs* (1987).

BEFORE YOU READ

Consider the stereotypical view that being male automatically grants one power, status, and privilege. Then think about two or three men you know well, such as a father, brother, or friend. Do their everyday life experiences bear out this generalization? How or how not?

AS YOU READ

As you read, list the occupations and obligations of the men mentioned. What socio economic segment of society is being described? What does this suggest about the relationship between gender and class?

1 "This must be a hard time for women," I say to my friend Anneke. "They have so many paths to choose from, and so many voices calling them."

2 "I think its' a lot harder for men," she replies.

3 "How do you figure that?"

4 "The women I know feel excited, innocent, like crusaders in a just cause. The men I know are eaten up with guilt."

5 "Women feel such pressure to be everything, do everything," I say. "Career, kids, art, politics. Have their babies and get back to the office a week later. It's as if they're trying to overcome a million years' worth of evolution in one lifetime."

6 "But we help one another. And we have this deep-down sense that we're in the *right*—we've been held back, passed over, used—while men feel they're in the wrong. Men are the ones who've been discredited, who have to search their souls."

7 I search my soul. I discover guilty feelings aplenty—toward the poor, the Vietnamese, Native Americans, the whales, an endless list of debts. But toward women I feel something more confused, a snarl of shame, envy, wary, tenderness, and amazement. This muddle troubles me. To hide my unease I say, "You're right, it's tough being a man these days."

8 "Don't laugh," Anneke frowns at me. "I wouldn't be a man for anything. It's much easier being the victim. All the victim has to do is break free. The persecutor has to live with his past."

9 How deep is that past? I find myself wondering. How much of an inheritance do I have to throw off?

10 When I was a boy growing up on the back road of Tennessee and Ohio, the men I knew labored with their bodies. They were marginal farmers, just scraping by, or welders, steelworkers, carpenters; they swept floors, dug ditches, mined coal, or drove trucks, their forearms ropy with muscle; they trained horses, stoked furnaces, made tires, stood on assembly lines wrestling parts onto cars and refrigerators. They got up before light, worked all day long

whatever the weather, and when they came home at night they looked as though somebody had been whipping them. In the evenings and on weekends they worked on their own places, tilling gardens that were lumpy with clay, fixing broken-down cars, hammering on houses that were always too drafty, too leaky, too small.

11   The bodies of the men I knew were twisted and maimed in ways visible and invisible. The nails of their hands were black and split, the hands tattooed with scars. Some had lost fingers. Heavy lifting had given many of them finicky backs and guts weak from hernias. Racing against conveyor belts had given them ulcers. Their ankles and knees ached from years of standing on concrete. Anyone who had worked for long around machines was hard of hearing. They squinted, and the skin of their faces was creased like the leather of old work gloves. There were times, studying them, when I dreaded growing up. Most of them coughed, from dust or cigarettes, and most of them drank cheap wine or whiskey, so their eyes looked bloodshot and bruised. The fathers of my friends always seemed older than the mothers. Men wore out sooner. Only women lived into old age.

12   As a boy I also knew another sort of men, who did not sweat and break down like mules. They were soldiers, and so far as I could tell they scarcely worked at all. But when the shooting started, many of them would die. This was what soldiers were *for,* just as a hammer was for driving nails.

13   Warriors and toilers: those seemed, in my boyhood vision, to be the chief destinies for men. They weren't the only destinies, as I learned from having a few male teachers, from reading books, and from watching television. But the men on television—the politicians, the astronauts, the generals, the savvy lawyers, the philosophical doctors, the bosses who gave orders to both soldiers and laborers—seemed as remote and unreal to me as the figures in Renaissance tapestries. I could no more imagine growing up to become one of these cool, potent creatures than I could imagine becoming a prince.

14   A nearer and more hopeful example was that of my father, who had escaped from a red-dirt farm to a tire factory, and from the assembly line to the front office. Eventually he dressed in a white shirt and tie. He carried himself as if he had been born to work with his mind. But his body, remembering the earlier years of slogging work, began to give out on him in his fifties, and it quit on him entirely before he turned 65.

15   A scholarship enabled me not only to attend college, a rare enough feat in my circle, but even to study in a university meant for the children of the rich. Here I met for the first time young men who had assumed from birth that they would lead lives of comfort and power. And for the first time I met women who told me that men were guilty of having kept all the joys and privileges of the earth for themselves. I was baffled. What privileges? What joys? I thought about the maimed, dismal lives of most of the men back home. What had they stolen from their wives and daughters? The right to go five days a week, 12 months a year, for 30 or 40 years to a steel mill or a coal mine? The

right to drop bombs and die in war? The right to feel every leak in the roof, every gap in the fence, every cough in the engine as a wound they must mend? The right to feel, when the layoff comes or the plant shuts down, not only afraid but ashamed?

16   I was slow to understand the deep grievances of women. This was because, as a boy, I had envied them. Before college, the only people I had ever known who were interested in art or music or literature, the only ones who read books, the only ones who ever seemed to enjoy a sense of ease and grace were the mothers and daughters. Like the menfolk, they fretted about money, they scrimped and made do. But, when the pay stopped coming in, they were not the ones who had failed. Nor did they have to go to war, and that seemed to me a blessed fact. By comparison with the narrow, ironclad days of fathers, there was an expansiveness, I thought, in the days of mothers. They went to see neighbors, to shop in town, to run errands at school, at the library, at church. No doubt, had I looked harder at their lives, I would have envied them less. It was not my fate to become a woman, so it was easier for me to see the graces. I didn't see, then, what a prison a house could be, since houses seemed to me brighter, handsomer places than any factory. I did not realize—because such things were never spoken of—how often women suffered from men's bullying. Even then I could see how exhausting it was for a mother to cater all day to the needs of young children. But if I had been asked, as a boy, to choose between tending a baby and tending a machine, I think I would have chosen the baby. (Having now tended both, I know I would choose the baby.)

17   So I was baffled when the women at college accused me and my sex of having cornered the world's pleasures. I think something like my bafflement has been felt by other boys (and by girls as well) who grew up in dirt-poor farm country, in mining country, in black ghettos, in Hispanic barrios, in the shadows of factories, in Third World nations—any place where the fate of men is just as grim and bleak as the fate of women.

18   When the women I met a college thought about the joys and privileges of men, they did not carry in their minds the sort of men I had known in my childhood. They thought of their fathers, who were bankers, physicians, architects, stockbrokers, the big wheels of the big cities. They were never laid off, never short of cash at month's end, never lined up for welfare. These fathers made decisions that mattered. They ran the world.

19   The daughters of such men wanted to share in this power, this glory. So did I. They yearned for a say over their future, for jobs worthy of their abilities, for the right to live at peace, unmolested, whole. Yes, I thought, yes yes. The difference between me and these daughters was that they saw me, because of my sex, as destined from birth to become like their fathers, and therefore as an enemy to their desires. But I knew better. I wasn't an enemy, in fact or in feeling. I was an ally. If I had known, then, how to tell them so, would they have believed me? Would they now?

Topical Considerations

1. Sanders first became aware of feminist issues when he went to college, and his past experiences did not prepare him for the "gender lesson" he was exposed to there. Have you had a similar experience upon coming to college or at other times in your life?

2. In paragraph 7, Sanders states that he has feelings of guilt toward a number of minority groups or social causes, but that his feelings toward women are more complicated. What do you think might be the reasons for his conclusion? Can you identify with his feelings?

3. Do you think that Sanders wants his readers to become more sympathetic toward men after reading this essay? Use examples in the test to explain your answer.

4. How might the people from Sanders' youth respond to this essay (i.e., lower-income, blue-collar men and women who stay at home)? How do you think the parents of Sanders' college classmates (i.e., upper-class, white-collar men and women who are also professionals) would respond?

5. Might Sanders be sympathetic to feminist issues? Or would he argue that women, not men, are the privileged class?

6. Sanders' friend Anneke says: "I wouldn't be a man for anything. It's much easier being the victim" (paragraph 8). Do you agree with this statement? Why or why not?

Rhetorical Considerations

1. Sanders begins his essay recounting a present-day discussion with a female friend. How does this help set up the argument that follows?

2. Sanders relates his argument entirely in the first-person, using personal anecdotes and narratives to illustrate his point. How might this essay differ if told from a more objective (third-person) point of view illustrated by statistics?

3. Sanders uses descriptive language throughout the essay. Does this language illustrate the issue of gender expectations and roles, or does it obscure Sanders' argument?

4. Who would be the most sympathetic reader of Sanders' essay? Explain your answer.

5. In paragraph 18, Sanders says that the fathers of his college classmates "were never laid off, never short of cash at month's end, never lined up for welfare." Do you think this statement is as factual as Sanders makes it sound? What is the effect of such a statement?

6. Sanders ends his essay with a question about women: "If I had known, then, how to tell them [women] so [that he was their ally], would they have be-

lieved me?" What is the effect of this question as a conclusion to the essay? Does it conclude Sanders' argument well?

Writing Assignments

1. Write a letter responding to Sanders as if you were one of his female college classmates. Make sure to describe in detail the personal experiences that have formed your perspective on male and female stereotypes.
2. Look over Sanders' conclusion and then write an essay answering his final two questions: If he had told his female classmates that he was an ally, would they have believed him? Do you think they would now?
3. Continue the dialogue between Sanders and his friend Anneke. Using the brief arguments begun in the few introductory sentences, construct a dialogue/debate between them, that has them remain true to their respective points of view.

Men as Success Objects
Warren Farrell

"With all the focus on the discrimination against women, few understand the sexism directed against men." Such is the argument of author Warren Farrell, who examines the roots of men's anxiety about themselves in this essay. Farrell's focus is on men's unequal responsibility to succeed in the workplace, to prove their worth by making money, to be, as the author puts it, "a wallet." Warren Farrell is a psychologist and author of the 1986 bestseller, *Why Men Are the Way They Are* as well as *The Myth of Male Power* (1993). The following article first appeared in the November/December 1988 issue of *Family Therapy Network*.

BEFORE YOU READ

Have you ever heard a man complain about being a "success object"—in other words, someone valued for the money he earns rather than for himself? If so, cite some of the comments. Have you heard women make comments about men as success objects? What might these comments reveal about men and women's attitudes toward the responsibility of earning money?

AS YOU READ

As you read this essay, list four generalizations Farrell makes about the way men and women view each other. Carefully compare each generalization against your own experience or observations. Do you agree or disagree with these generalizations?

Why or why not? In your opinion, do these generalizations weaken or reinforce Farrell's argument?

1   For thousands of years, marriages were about economic security and survival. Let's call this Stage I in our culture's conception of marriage. Beginning in the 1950s, marriages became focused on personal fulfillment and we entered into the era of the Stage II relationship. In Stage II, love was redefined to include listening to each other, joint parenting, sexual fulfillment, and shared decision-making. As a result, many traditional marriages consummated in Stage I failed under the new Stage II expectations. Thus we had the great surge of divorces beginning in the '60s.

2   The increasing incidence of divorce altered the fundamental relationship between women, men, and the workplace. Before divorce became common, most women's income came from men, so discrimination in favor of a woman's husband benefited her. But, as the divorce rate mushroomed, the same discrimination often hurt her. Before divorce became a common expectation, we had two types of inequality—women's experience of unequal rights in the workplace and men's experience of unequal responsibility for succeeding in the workplace. To find a woman to love him, a man had to "make his mark" in the world. As women increasingly had to provide for themselves economically, we confined our examination of inequality between the sexes to inequality in the workplace. What was ignored was the effect of inequality in the homeplace. Also ignored was a man's feeling that no woman would love him if he volunteered to be a full-time househusband instead of a full-time provider. As a result, we falsely assumed that the experience of inequality was confined to women.

3   Because divorces led to a change in the pressures on women (should she *become* a doctor, marry a doctor, or have a career and marry a doctor?), that change became "news" and her new juggling act got attention in the media. Because the underlying pressures on men did not change (women still married men who earned more than they did), the pressure on men to succeed did not change, and, therefore, received no attention. With all the focus on discrimination against women, few understood the sexism directed against men.

4   The feminist perspective on relationships has become like fluoride in water—we drink it without being aware of its presence. The complaints about men, the idea the "men are jerks," have become so integrated into our unconscious that even advertisers have caught on. After analyzing 1,000 commercials in 1987, researcher Fred Hayward found that when an ad called for a negative portrayal in a male-female interaction, an astonishing 100 percent of the time the "bad guy" was the man.

5   This anti-male bias isn't confined to TV commercials. A sampling of the cards in the "Love and Friendship" section of a greeting card store revealed these gems:

"If they can send one man to the moon, why can't they send them all?"

"When you unzip a man's pants . . . his brains fall out."

"If we can make penicillin out of moldy cheese . . . maybe we can make men out of the low-lifes in this town."

6   A visit to the bookstore turns up titles like *No Good Men*. Imagine *No Good Women* or *No Good Jews*. And what do the following titles have in common? *Men Who Can't Love; Men Who Hate Women and the Women Who Love Them; Smart Women/Foolish Choices; Successful Women, Angry Men; Peter Pan Syndrome.*

7   Feminism-as-fluoride has left us acknowledging the working mother ("Superwoman") without even being aware of the working father. It is by now well recognized that, even among men who do more housework or more childcare than their wives, almost never does the man truly share the 24-hour-a-day psychological responsibility of ministering to everyone's needs, egos, and schedules.

8   But it is not so widely recognized that, despite the impact feminism has had on the contemporary family, almost every father still remains 24-hour-a-day psychological responsibility for the family's financial well-being. Even women who earn more than their husbands tell me that they know their husbands would support their decision to earn as much or as little as they wish. If a woman marries a successful man, then she knows she will have an option to work or not, but not an obligation. Almost all men see bringing home a healthy salary as an obligation, not an option.

9   A woman today has three options.

Option 1: Full-time career.

Option 2: Full-time family.

Option 3: Some combination of career and family.

10   A man sees himself as having three "slightly different" options:

Option 1: Work full time.

Option 2: Work full time.

Option 3: Work full time.

11   The U.S. Bureau of the Census explains that full-time working males work an average of eight hours more per week on their jobs than full-time working females.

12   Since many women now earn substantial incomes, doesn't this relieve the pressure on men to be a wallet? No. Why? Because successful women do exactly what less-successful women do—"marry up," that is, marry a man

whose income is greater than her own. According to statistics, if a woman cannot marry up or marry someone with a high wage-earning potential, she does not marry at all. Therefore, a man often reflexively backs away from a woman he's attracted to when he discovers she's more successful than he is because he senses he's only setting himself up for rejection. Ultimately, she'll dump him for a more successful man. She may sleep with him, or live with him, but not marry him unless she spots "potential." Thus, of top female executives, 85 percent don't get married; the remaining 15 percent almost all marry up. Even successful women have not relaxed the pressure on men to succeed.

13   Ask a girl in junior high or high school about the boy whom she would "absolutely love" to ask her out to the prom and chances are almost 100 percent that she would tell you her fantasy boy is *both* good-looking *and* successful (a jock or student leader, or someone who "has potential"). Ask a boy whom he would absolutely love to ask out to the prom and chances are almost 100 percent his fantasy girl is good-looking. Only about 25 percent will also be interested in a girl's "strong career potential" (or her being a top female jock). His invisible curriculum, then, taught him that being good-looking is not enough to attract a good-looking girl—he must be successful *in addition* to being good-looking. This was his experience of inequality: "Good-looking boy does not equal good-looking girl." Why are boys willing to consider themselves unequal to girls' attention until they hit their heads against 21 other boys on a football field?

14   In part, the answer is because boys are addicted. In all cultures, boys are addicted to the images of beautiful women. And in American culture this is enormously magnified. Boys are exposed to the images of beautiful women about 10 million times per year via television, billboards, magazines, etc. In the process, the naturally beautiful girl becomes a *genetic celebrity*. Boys become addicted to the image of the quasi-anorexic female. To be the equal of this genetic celebrity, the adolescent boy must become an *earned celebrity* (by performing, paying on dates, etc.). Until he is an earned celebrity, he feels like a groupie trying to get a celebrity's attention.

15   Is there an invisible curriculum for girls and boys growing up? Yes. For girls, "If you want to have your choice among boys, you had better be beautiful." For boys, it's "You had better be handsome *and* successful." If a boy wants a romantic relationship with a girl he must not only be successful and perform, he must pay and pursue—risk sexual rejection. Girls think of the three Ps—performing, paying and pursuing—as male power. Boys see the three Ps as what they must do to earn their way to female love and sexuality. They see these not as power, but as compensations for powerlessness. This is the adolescent male's experience of inequality.

Topical Considerations

1. Who is Farrell's ideal reader? Do you think that his argument will win "opposing" readers to his side? Where and how?

2. In paragraph 4, Farrell discusses unfair depiction of men in advertising. Can you think of some examples to support his claim? Do you think that women are also depicted unfairly? What are some examples?
3. What are the differences between men's and women's options, according to Farrell? Looking back over your own experience and the experience of people you know, do Farrell's claims ring true to you? How so? If not, where does your experience differ?
4. Do you agree with Farrell's statement in paragraph 8 that "If a woman marries a successful man, then she knows she will have an option to work or not, but not an obligation"? Why or why not?
5. Has Farrell changed your way of thinking about gender issues? Are you more sympathetic to his cause? Why or why not?

Rhetorical Considerations

1. Farrell begins his argument with a discussion of divorce and its effects on men and women. How does he use this to introduce his argument? Do you think his introduction functions effectively?
2. How effective is the analogy that Farrell sets up in paragraph 4—that "the feminist perspective on relationships has become like fluoride in water"? Do you think this analogy might offend some readers?
3. What are the strengths and weaknesses of Farrell's use of statistics in his essay?
4. How would you describe Farrell's voice in this article? What kind of person do you think he is from his tone? Use passages from the text to support your answers.
5. Because Farrell does not use personal anecdotes as does Sanders, his essay might seem more objective. Is it? If yes, cite where and why. If no, describe why not.

Writing Assignments

1. More and more men are staying at home while their wives work. Pretend that you are one of those househusbands and respond to Farrell's argument in a letter.
2. Using Farrell's argument as your opposition, write a debate or a dialogue in which you refute Farrell's stance point by point.
3. Try to formulate your own lists of options for men and women today. Explain these options, and how and why they are similar to or different from Farrell's.
4. Write a response to Farrell's piece in which you defend his opinion. Then write a response in which you oppose it. Finally, write about Farrell's essay as if you were a "reporter"—that is, summarize the text in a neutral manner.

Conan And Me
Bill Persky

Today's idealized image of the male encompasses more than the stoic and tough John Waynesque stereotype of the past. Today's male must also be sensitive and emotionally accessible. That is, Arnold Schwarzenegger with feelings. What follows is an amusing but telling anecdote about such a man whose ideal of himself comes to the rescue at a dangerous moment. Mr. Persky's reflections on his behavior one fated night celebrate not just traditional male behavior but, ultimately, trust in one-self.

Bill Persky has been writing, directing, and producing television shows for the last four decades. He is the winner of five Emmy awards. With Sam Danoff, he wrote and produced "The Dick Van Dyke Show," "That Girl," and "Kate & Allie," among others. His considerable talent for eliciting dramatic meaning from an incident is evident in this essay, which originally appeared in *Esquire* magazine in May 1989.

BEFORE YOU READ

Imagine a burglar breaks into a home or apartment. Would a man and woman react in different or similar ways to this dangerous situation? Can such generalizations be made? Why or why not?

AS YOU READ

Note the strategies used to inject humor into this essay. List two forms of humor used and give examples of them.

1   Carl Reiner once said that he didn't believe Englishmen really had accents, they just all got together and agreed to talk that way to make the rest of us feel bad. The act was probably rooted in feelings of inadequacy dating back to their origin as druids who were still running around painted blue long after everyone else had moved on to cooked food and world conquest. Carl believed that if, at three in the morning, you crept into a room where an Englishman was sleeping and shouted *"Fire!"* he would wake in panic and say, *"Fire! Let's get the hell out of here!"* with no accent whatsoever.

2   Though I would gladly lose my New York accent under any circumstance, I have some images of myself that I'd like to think are real. And I have wondered how they would hold up if Carl crept into my room some night and sounded the alarm. I know who I would *like* to be in that rude awakening: I'd grab the kids and the cat and lead everyone in the building to safety, all with the calm, clear voice that I've already selected from several I've tried out in the shower. But I've always known that if that moment came, no matter what I

may have hoped or planned, there would be only me, the real me, the one I doubt, question, and hide from the world and, with less success, from myself.

3   My moment came one morning last summer. It wasn't 3:00 A.M. but sometime after 5:00, and it wasn't Carl's shout of "Fire!" but the muffled thumping of a man climbing through my bedroom window. Instantly I found out who I was: an unlikely combination of Arnold Schwarzenegger and my mother.

4   I am still not sure who was the most effective as I leapt naked from my bed, grabbing the first weapon at hand, my pillow, and went on the attack, screaming, *"Get out! Get out!"* in a high-pitched voice. I resented my mother speaking for me at a time like that, and I consciously tried to get into a lower register, but it was her moment, and I couldn't take it away from her.

5   Schwarzenegger was doing a lot better, and I was pleased with him. He was actually engaged in hand-to-hand combat with an intruder who was three quarters of the way into my room. The window opened only a foot and a half, being held in place by a dowel I had inserted between the top and the frame to prevent anyone from climbing in. I made a note to get a longer pole if I lived.

6   The struggle raged as my burglar (we'd known each other long enough at this point for some familiarity) was pushing against a flower box to come the rest of the way in, and I was pushing and swinging my pillow to get him out. I needed a more formidable weapon. Actually, it was right there on the night table, but in my initial panic I had missed it—*The Bonfire of the Vanities*. Hitting him with that would have done major damage *and* made some kind of social comment.

7   Since the narrow opening was preventing either of us from making any headway, we were at a stalemate. My warrior self suddenly perceived with Zen clarity that if I removed the pole, I could open the window fully and my chances of getting him all the way out would improve. The thought that it would improve his chance of getting all the way in didn't occur to me. That's the trouble with Zen, it's so self-involved. I emitted a fierce yell borrowed from a sushi chef and yanked the pole free. Suddenly the tide of battle turned in my favor, as he was now up against a naked maniac with a pole instead of a pillow, and my mother switched from "Get out! Get out!" to a more macho *"You son of a bitch!"*

8   The combination must have been awesome, because he started to plead in what I am sure was his mother's voice, *"Don't hurt me! Don't hurt me!"* Don't hurt him? The thought never entered my mind, but as long as he brought it up, I considered it as an option. I could use the new upper-body strength I'd developed at the Vertical Club to knock him senseless. Originally I'd planned on using it to improve my serve. The struggle intensified until somehow his mother and my mother got to talking, as mothers will, and "Don't hurt me, Don't hurt me" seemed like a good idea all around. So I gave him a shove that wasn't needed to get him out and covered his escape over the wall with a hail of four-letter words, finally finding the voice I'd practiced for the occasion.

9   I closed and locked the window, drew the drapes, and stood waiting. I wasn't sure for what, probably to go into shock or some other reaction that comes when danger is past. This was only the second real fight I ever had. The first was fifty years ago in the third grade when Jerry Matz challenged me to meet him after school for reasons I can't for the life of me recall, but I think it was about who was going to marry Nina Yanoff. What I do remember is that I was nauseated all day and cried throughout the fight and even after I had won. Now here I was, not crying, not even breathing hard. I settled for calling the police. I felt it was the responsible thing to do, and I was dying to tell somebody.

10   My burglar and I are now just another crime statistic along with the other apartment on Sixty-second Street that was burglarized that night while the occupants slept. The police are sure it was my burglar after he left me, so apparently our encounter had little impact on his life. But it's had a very profound effect on mine. I've made the obvious adjustments of sleeping in shorts, keeping the fireplace poker next to my bed, and getting bars for the windows. (That information is for my mother, whom I never told about the incident but who will probably read this, and I wouldn't want her to worry.)

11   On a less obvious but more meaningful level, the incident has changed the way I see myself in Carl's hypothesis. At the core I am tougher and braver than I knew. Even with the high-pitched voice, I really like the guy I turned out to be. I'd like to be that guy more often, and I think I know why I'm not. It isn't a question of courage but *clarity*, and the freedom that comes when you know you're right. In our daily lives things are never as clear-cut as someone coming through our bedroom window. They're vague or oblique, and our first instinct waits as we filter through too much information and conditioning. We lose that initial impulse that's pure us.

12   My burglar probably had a lousy childhood and was from a deprived racial or economic group. He might have been a terrific kid with all kinds of potential who never had a chance. In retrospect he might have been the real victim. But that night he was coming through my bedroom window, and one thing was crystal clear—he didn't belong there. So I was free to act as who I really am. It was a great feeling, one I would like to hold on to, trust, and go with. Every day there are less obvious intruders coming through the windows of my spirit and my soul, and they don't belong there either. So let them beware: Arnold and my mother are waiting.

Topical Considerations

1. Explain what Carl Reiner meant when he said that he "didn't believe Englishmen really had accents, they just all got together and agreed to talk that way to make the rest of us feel bad." How might a British accent make an American feel bad about him- or herself? Do you have different responses to

different kinds of accents? If so, do these responses reflect feelings you might have about yourself? Explain.

2. In paragraph 2, Persky says that if ever faced with an urgent situation "there would be only me, the real me, the one I doubt, question, and hide from the world and, with less success, from myself." What does this statement say about the kinds of behavior Persky attributes to "men" in dangerous situations? What kinds of demands and expectations are placed upon men by society? How are these expectations reinforced? Do these expectations—as well as those placed upon women—create the need for people to hide their real selves from the world? Explain.

3. When Persky describes his initial response to an intruder he calls himself "an unlikely combination of Arnold Schwarzenegger and my [Persky's] mother." What do you take these two referents, in combination, to signify about Persky? How does Persky's choice of models here correspond to the stereotypes he is exposing in the piece? Do you believe that sex-role differences are determined biologically or culturally? Explain. What would Persky say about this?

Rhetorical Considerations

1. How effective is the opening Reiner quote? In what way does this introductory paragraph set up the tone and content of the rest of the piece? Explain.

2. From the information provided, what do you know about the narrator? Is he reliable—one with whom you find yourself identifying? If so, point to specific places where you feel Persky has made his narrator particularly accessible. Do you feel that the perspective from which the essay is narrated is in keeping with the content of the piece? Explain.

3. Part of the point of this essay is that men are culturally conditioned to act in ways corresponding to sex-role stereotypes. What kind of clues—in the form of cultural artifacts—does Persky drop regarding his own cultural conditioning? What function do these clues have on reader response to Persky's argument?

4. Reread Persky's concluding paragraph. How would you summarize this conclusion in relation to the main thrust of the argument? In your opinion, does it work effectively to close the piece? Explain.

Writing Assignments

1. Write an essay in which you consider your own sense of cultural conditioning. How do you feel your behavior has been conditioned by sex-role expectations? Is there a gap between the "real" you and the affectations you take on as a means of survival in contemporary culture?

2. Write a first-person narrative of a situation where your actions were based upon the demands of sex-role conditioning—or a situation in which you were able to shed your cultural conditioning, as Persky did when confronted by an intruder.

3. Conduct interviews with at least five other students regarding the force of sex-role conditioning. You might ask them what role such conditioning plays in their lives and what are its sources in popular culture; also, what are their feelings as to the pros and cons derived from such conditioning? Then write a report of your findings.

4. Write an essay in which you explore the terms *masculine* and *feminine*. You might undertake library research as to the origins of the words—their derivations and original connotations—or research their changing implications over the years.

Being Female

Femininity
Susan Brownmiller

In this piece, Susan Brownmiller's analytical scalpel cuts into the notion of femininity and exposes standards of beauty and vulnerability that entice women into a fruitless and, ultimately, self-limiting quest. Femininity allowed Brownmiller as a child to feel "like a fairy princess"; but as an adolescent, she increasingly began to experience femininity as "bafflingly inconsistent at the same time that it was minutely, demandingly concrete, a rigid code of appearance and behavior defined by do's and don't-do's. . . ." An adult perspective reveals how femininity's quest for physical perfection, for a soft and gentle disposition in need of male protection, ultimately stunts a women's identity and sense of self.

Susan Brownmiller, a journalist and novelist, has written widely on women's issues. She has published *Against Our Will* (1975), a study of rape, and *Femininity* (1984), from which this essay comes. She is most recently the author of *Seeing Vietnam* (1994).

BEFORE YOU READ

Regardless of your gender, the concept of femininity is probably one you have been familiar with since childhood. In what ways (rituals, toys, clothing) was femininity conveyed to you? How did you react to the message of femininity? Did you try to emulate feminine qualities? Was there a time in your life when you rejected traditional femininity? Or redefined it? Has the notion of femininity had a positive or negative effect on you or those you know?

AS YOU READ

Cite a passage that conveys an experience or feeling about appearances you or someone you know has felt. What qualities of the passage make it powerful or convincing? How does the passage fit into Brownmiller's argument?

1 We had a game in our house called "setting the table" and I was Mother's helper. Forks to the left of the plate, knives and spoons to the right. Placing the cutlery neatly, as I recall, was one of my first duties, and the event was alive with meaning. When a knife or a fork dropped to the floor, that meant a man was unexpectedly coming to dinner. A falling spoon announced the surprise arrival of a female guest. No matter that these visitors never arrived on cue, I had learned a rule of gender identification. Men were straight-edged, sharply pronged and formidable, women were softly curved and held the food in a rounded well. It made perfect sense, like the division of pink and blue that I saw in babies, an orderly way of viewing the world. Daddy, who was gone all day at work and who loved to putter at home with his pipe, tobacco and tool chest, was knife and fork. Mommy and Grandma, with their ample proportions and pots and pans, were grownup soup spoons, large and capacious. And I was a teaspoon, small and slender, easy to hold and just right for pudding, my favorite dessert.

2   Being good at what was expected of me was one of my earliest projects, for not only was I rewarded, as most children are, for doing things right, but excellence gave pride and stability to my childhood existence. Girls were different from boys, and the expression of that difference seemed mine to make clear. Did my loving, anxious mother, who dressed me in white organdy pinafores and Mary Janes and who cried hot tears when I got them dirty, give me my first instruction? Of course. Did my doting aunts and uncles with their gifts of pretty dolls and miniature tea sets add to my education? Of course. But even without the appropriate toys and clothes, lessons in the art of being feminine lay all around me and I absorbed them all: the fairy tales that were read to me at night, the brightly colored advertisements I pored over in magazines before I learned to decipher the words, the movies I saw, the comic books I hoarded, the radio soap operas I happily followed whenever I had to stay in bed with a cold. I loved being a little girl, or rather I loved being a fairy princess, for that was who I thought I was.

3   As I passed through a stormy adolescence to a stormy maturity, femininity increasingly became an exasperation, a brilliant, subtle esthetic that was

bafflingly inconsistent at the same time that it was minutely, demandingly concrete, a rigid code of appearance and behavior defined by do's and don't-do's that went against my rebellious grain. Femininity was a challenge thrown down to the female sex, a challenge no proud, self-respecting young woman could afford to ignore, particularly one with enormous ambition that she nursed in secret, alternately feeding or starving its inchoate life in tremendous confusion.

4   "Don't lose your femininity" and "Isn't it remarkable how she manages to retain her femininity?" had terrifying implications. They spoke of a bottom-line failure so irreversible that nothing else mattered. The pinball machine had registered "tilt," the game had been called. Disqualification was marked on the forehead of a woman whose femininity was lost. No records would be entered in her name, for she had destroyed her birthright in her wretched, ungainly effort to imitate a man. She walked in limbo, this hapless creature, and it occurred to me that one day I might see her when I looked in the mirror. If the danger was so palpable that warning notices were freely posted, wasn't it possible that the small bundle of resentments I carried around in secret might spill out and place the mark on my own forehead? Whatever quarrels with femininity I had I kept to myself; whatever handicaps femininity imposed, they were mine to deal with alone, for there was no women's movement to ask the tough questions, or to brazenly disregard the rules.

5   Femininity, in essence, is a romantic sentiment, a nostalgic tradition of imposed limitations. Even as it hurries forward in the 1980s, putting on lipstick and high heels to appear well dressed, it trips on the ruffled petticoats and hoopskirts of an era gone by. Invariably and necessarily, femininity is something that a woman had more of in the past, not only in the historic past of prior generations, but in each woman's personal past as well—in the virginal innocence that is replaced by knowledge, in the dewy cheek that is coarsened by age, in the "inherent nature" that a woman seems to misplace so forgetfully whenever she steps out of bonds. Why should this be so? The XX chromosomal message has not been scrambled, the estrogen-dominated hormonal balance is generally as biology intended, the reproductive organs, whatever use one has made of them, are usually in place, the breasts of whatever size are most often where they should be. But clearly, biological femaleness is not enough.

6   Femininity always demands more. It must constantly reassure its audience by a willing demonstration of difference, even when one does not exist in nature, or it must seize and embrace a natural variation and compose a rhapsodic symphony upon the notes. Suppose one doesn't care to, has other things on her mind, is clumsy or tone-deaf despite the best instruction and training? To fail at the feminine difference is to appear not to care about men, and to risk the loss of their attention and approval. To be insufficiently feminine is viewed as a failure in core sexual identity, or as a failure to care sufficiently about oneself, for a woman found wanting will be appraised (and will appraise

herself) as mannish or neutered or simply unattractive, as men have defined these terms.

7   We are talking, admittedly, about an exquisite esthetic. Enormous pleasure can be extracted from feminine pursuits as a creative outlet or purely as relaxation; indeed, indulgence for the sake of fun, or art, or attention, is among femininity's great joys. But the chief attraction (and the central paradox, as well) is the competitive edge that femininity seems to promise in the unending struggle to survive, and perhaps to triumph. The world smiles favorably on the feminine woman: it extends little courtesies and minor privilege. Yet the nature of this competitive edge is ironic, at best, for one works at femininity by accepting restrictions, by limiting one's sights, by choosing an indirect route, by scattering concentration and not giving one's all as a man would to his own, certifiably masculine, interests. It does not require a great leap of imagination for a woman to understand the feminine principle as a grand collection of compromises, large and small, that she simply must make in order to render herself a successful woman. If she has difficulty in satisfying femininity's demands, if its illusions go against her grain, or if she is criticized for her shortcomings and imperfections, the more she will see femininity as a desperate strategy of appeasement, a strategy she may not have the wish or the courage to abandon, for failure looms in either direction.

8   It is fashionable in some quarters to describe the feminine and masculine principles as polar ends of the human continuum, and to sagely profess that both polarities exist in all people. Sun and moon, yin and yang, soft and hard, active and passive, etcetera, may indeed be opposites, but a linear continuum does not illuminate the problem. (Femininity, in all its contrivances, is a very active endeavor.) What, then, is the basic distinction? The masculine principle is better understood as a driving ethos of superiority designed to inspire straightforward, confident success, while the feminine principle is composed of vulnerability, the need for protection, the formalities of compliance and the avoidance of conflict—in short, an appeal of dependence and good will that gives the masculine principle its romantic validity and its admiring applause.

9   Femininity pleases men because it makes them appear more masculine by contrast; and, in truth, conferring an extra portion of unearned gender distinction on men, an unchallenged space in which to breathe freely and feel stronger, wiser, more competent, is femininity's special gift. One could say that masculinity is often an effort to please women, but masculinity is known to please by displays of mastery and competence while femininity pleases by suggesting that these concerns, except in small matters, are beyond its intent. Whimsy, unpredictability and patterns of thinking and behavior that are dominated by emotion, such as tearful expressions of sentiment and fear, are thought to be feminine precisely because they lie outside the established route to success.

10   If in the beginnings of history the feminine woman was defined by her physical dependency, her inability for reasons of reproductive biology to triumph over the forces of nature that were the tests of masculine strength and power, today she reflects both an economic and emotional dependency that is still considered "natural," romantic and attractive. After an unsettling fifteen years in which many basic assumptions about the sexes were challenged, the economic disparity did not disappear. Large numbers of women—those with small children, those left high and dry after a mid-life divorce—need financial support. But even those who earn their own living share a universal need for connectedness (call it love, if you wish). As unprecedented numbers of men abandon their sexual interest in women, others, sensing opportunity, choose to demonstrate their interest through variety and a change in partners. A sociological fact of the 1980s is that female competition for two scarce resources—men and jobs—is especially fierce.

11   So it is not surprising that we are currently witnessing a renewed interest in femininity and an unabashed indulgence in feminine pursuits. Femininity serves to reassure men that women need them and care about them enormously. By incorporating the decorative and the frivolous into its definition of style, femininity functions as an effective antidote to the unrelieved seriousness, the pressure of making one's way in a harsh, difficult world. In its mandate to avoid direct confrontation and to smooth over the fissures of conflict, femininity operates as a value system of niceness, a code of thoughtfulness and sensitivity that in modern society is sadly in short supply.

12   There is no reason to deny that indulgence in the art of feminine illusion can be reassuring to a woman, if she happens to be good at it. As sexuality undergoes some dizzying revisions, evidence that one is a woman "at heart" (the inquisitor's question) is not without worth. Since an answer of sorts may be furnished by piling on additional documentation, affirmation can arise from such identifiable but trivial feminine activities as buying a new eyeliner, experimenting with the latest shade of nail color, or bursting into tears at the outcome of a popular romance novel. Is there anything destructive in this? Time and cost factors, a deflection of energy and an absorption in fakery spring quickly to mind, and they need to be balanced, as in a ledger book, against the affirming advantage.

13   Throughout this book [*Femininity*] I have attempted to trace significant feminine principles to basic biology, for feminine expression is conventionally praised as an enhancement of femaleness, or the raw materials of femaleness shaped and colored to perfection. Sometimes I found that a biological connection did exist, and sometimes not, and sometimes I had to admit that many scientific assumptions about the nature of femaleness were unresolved and hotly debated, and that no sound conclusion was possible before all the evidence was in. It was more enlightening to explore the origins of femininity in borrowed affectations of upper-class status, and in the historic subjugation of women through sexual violence, religion and law, where certain myths about the nature of women were put forward as biological fact. It was also instructive to approach femininity from the angle of seductive glamour, which usually

does not fit smoothly with aristocratic refinement, accounting for some contradictory feminine messages that often appear as an unfathomable puzzle.

14   The competitive aspect of femininity, the female-against-female competition produced by the effort to attract and secure men, is one of the major themes I have tried to explore. Male-against-male competition for high rank and access to females is a popular subject in anthropology, in the study of animals as well as humans, but few scholars have thought to examine the pitched battle of females for ranking and access to males. Yet the struggle to approach the feminine ideal, to match the femininity of other women, and especially to outdo them, is the chief competitive arena (surely it is the only sanctioned arena) in which the American woman is wholeheartedly encouraged to contend. Whether or not this absorbing form of competition is a healthy or useful survival strategy is a critical question.

15   Hymns to femininity, combined with instruction, have never been lacking. Several generations of us are acquainted with sugar and spice, can recite the job description for "The Girl That I Marry" (doll-size, soft and pink, wears lace and nail polish, gardenia in the hair), or wail the payoff to "Just Like a Woman" ("She breaks like a little girl"). My contribution may be decidedly unmusical, but it is not a manual of how-not-to, nor a wholesale damnation. Femininity deserves some hard reckoning, and this is what I have tried to do.

Topical Considerations

1. In paragraph 2, Brownmiller discusses the "lessons in the art of being feminine" found in fairy tales, advertisements, and movies. Do you think children of both genders form social roles from similar lessons? Give examples.
2. How would Brownmiller react to Farrell's idea of the male as a "wallet"? To Sanders' notion of the male? Give examples from Brownmiller's text to support your reasoning.
3. What does Brownmiller mean by the "exquisite esthetic"? How important is this concept to the formation of her argument?
4. What, according to Brownmiller, are traditional definitions of masculinity and femininity. Do you agree with those definitions? Why or why not?
5. In paragraph 12, Brownmiller suggests that sexuality is undergoing "some dizzying revisions." What does she mean by this? Can you furnish some real-life examples?

Rhetorical Considerations

1. Brownmiller begins her essay with a personal anecdote depicting family superstitions. How effective is this paragraph in framing her argument? Are the analogies drawn between male/female traits and silverware clear? Why or why not?

2. Like Ebeling, Brownmiller discusses biological differences between men and women. Which author uses the concept better to support her argument? Why?

3. Brownmiller draws upon personal experience in paragraphs 1, 2, and 3. Do these paragraphs strengthen her argument? If so, how? In the section where she relies more on factual or philosophical evidence, is her argument more convincing? Why or why not?

4. This essay provides the introductory chapter to a book about femininity. Does the voice, tone, and style of this essay make you want to read the book? Is the introduction too general? Too specific? Where?

Writing Assignments

1. Imagine that you are writing the introduction for a book titled *Femininity*. Write an essay that will serve as the introduction. Your essay should (a) make readers want to read on, (b) explain what you mean by *femininity*, and (c) describe what you expect your book to "do."

2. Do the same as for number 1, but for a book titled *Masculinity*.

3. Interview people from three or more generations (grandparents, parents, older siblings, younger siblings, your peers) by asking them to define *femininity* and *masculinity*. Write an essay to report on your findings. Try to explain the differences and similarities between generations and between men and women.

Wears Jump Suit. Sensible Shoes. Uses Husband's Last Name.
Deborah Tannen

According to Deborah Tannen, women are disproportionately "marked" beings in our society. How they style their hair, what kinds of clothes or shoes they wear, the makeup they wear—or don't wear—these all signal certain messages. Messages that establish a certain identity. Messages that will be judged. By comparison, men have fewer options and, thus, are free to remain unmarked.

Deborah Tannen is a professor of linguistics at Georgetown University and the author of the bestsellers *You Just Don't Understand: Men and Women in Conversation* (1990) and *Talking Nine to Five* (1994). This essay originally appeared in *The New York Times Magazine* in June 1993.

BEFORE YOU READ

Take note of the different clothing styles of your male classmates. Then note the different styles worn by the females. Is there a greater range in how the women dress as opposed to the men? What statements about a person do the different styles make?

AS YOU READ

In your opinion, is the existence of "markers" in women's clothing and style positive, negative, or neutral? Would it be better if clothing and style did not send messages? Is it unfortunate that women's clothing has more markers than men's clothing?

1   Some years ago I was at a small working conference of four women and eight men. Instead of concentrating on the discussion I found myself looking at the three other women at the table, thinking how each had a different style and how each style was coherent.

2   One woman had dark brown hair in a classic style, a cross between Cleopatra and Plain Jane. The severity of her straight hair was softened by wavy bangs and ends that turned under. Because she was beautiful, the effect was more Cleopatra than plain.

3   The second woman was older, full of dignity and composure. Her hair was cut in a fashionable style that left her with only one eye, thanks to a side part that let a curtain of hair fall across half her face. As she looked down to read her prepared paper, the hair robbed her of bifocal vision and created a barrier between her and the listeners.

4   The third woman's hair was wild, a frosted blond avalanche falling over and beyond her shoulders. When she spoke she frequently tossed her head, calling attention to her hair and away from her lecture.

5   Then there was makeup. The first woman wore facial cover that made her skin smooth and pale, a black line under each eye and mascara that darkened already dark lashes. The second wore only a light gloss on her lips and a hint of shadow on her eyes. The third had blue bands under her eyes, dark blue shadow, mascara, bright red lipstick and rouge; her fingernails flashed red.

6   I considered the clothes each woman had worn during the three days of the conference: In the first case, man-tailored suits in primary colors with solid-color blouses. In the second, casual but stylish black T-shirts, a floppy collarless jacket and baggy slacks or a skirt in neutral colors. The third wore a sexy jump suit; tight sleeveless jersey and tight yellow slacks; a dress with gaping armholes and an indulged tendency to fall off one shoulder.

7   Shoes? No. 1 wore string sandals with medium heels; No. 2, sensible, comfortable walking shoes; No. 3, pumps with spike heels. You can fill in the jewelry, scarves, shawls, sweaters—or lack of them.

8   As I amused myself finding coherence in these styles, I suddenly wondered why I was scrutinizing only the women. I scanned the eight men at the table. And then I knew why I wasn't studying them. The men's styles were unmarked.

9   The term "marked" is a staple of linguistic theory. It refers to the way language alters the base meaning of a word by adding a linguistic particle that has no meaning on its own. The unmarked form of a word carries the meaning

that goes without saying—what you think of when you're not thinking anything special.

10   The unmarked tense of verbs in English is the present—for example, *visit*. To indicate past, you mark the verb by adding *ed* to yield *visited*. For future, you add a word: *will visit*. Nouns are presumed to be singular until marked for plural, typically by adding *s* or *es*, so *visit* becomes *visits* and *dish* becomes *dishes*.

11   The unmarked forms of most English words also convey "male." Being male is the unmarked case. Endings like *ess* and *ette* mark words as "female." Unfortunately, they also tend to mark them for frivolousness. Would you feel safe entrusting your life to a doctorette? Alfre Woodard, who was an Oscar nominee for best supporting actress, says she identifies herself as an actor because "actresses worry about eyelashes and cellulite, and women who are actors worry about the characters we are playing." Gender markers pick up extra meanings that reflect common associations with the female gender: not quite serious, often sexual.

12   Each of the women at the conference had to make decisions about hair, clothing, makeup and accessories, and each decision carried meaning. Every style available to us was marked. The men in the group had made decisions, too, but the range from which they chose was incomparably narrower. Men can choose styles that are marked, but they don't have to, and in this group none did. Unlike the women, they had the option of being unmarked.

13   Take the men's hair styles. There was no marine crew cut or oily longish hair falling into eyes, no asymmetrical, two-tiered construction to swirl over a bald top. One man was unabashedly bald; the others had hair of standard length, parted on one side, in natural shades of brown or gray or graying. Their hair obstructed no views, left little to toss or push back or run fingers through and, consequently, needed and attracted no attention. A few men had beards. In a business setting, beards might be marked. In this academic gathering, they weren't.

14   There could have been a cowboy shirt with string tie or a three-piece suit or a necklaced hippie in jeans. But there wasn't. All eight men wore brown or blue slacks and nondescript shirts of light colors. No man wore sandals or boots; their shoes were dark, closed, comfortable and flat. In short, unmarked.

15   Although no man wore makeup, you couldn't say the men didn't wear makeup in the sense that you could say a woman didn't wear makeup. For men, no makeup is unmarked.

16   I asked myself what style we women could have adopted that would have been unmarked, like the men's. The answer was none. There is no unmarked woman.

17   There is no woman's hair style that can be called standard, that says nothing about her. The range of women's hair styles is staggering, but a woman whose hair has no particular style is perceived as not caring about how she looks, which can disqualify her for many positions, and will subtly diminish her as a person in the eyes of some.

18   Women must choose between attractive shoes and comfortable shoes. When our group made an unexpected trek, the woman who wore flat, laced shoes arrived first. Last to arrive was the woman in spike heels, shoes in hand and a handful of men around her.

19   If a woman's clothing is tight or revealing (in other words, sexy), it sends a message—an intended one of wanting to be attractive, but also a possibly unintended one of availability. If her clothes are not sexy, that too sends a message, lent meaning by the knowledge that they could have been. There are thousands of cosmetic products from which women can choose and myriad ways of applying them. Yet no makeup at all is anything but unmarked. Some men see it as a hostile refusal to please them.

20   Women can't even fill out a form without telling stories about themselves. Most forms give four titles to choose from. "Mr." carries no meaning other than that the respondent is male. But a woman who checks "Mrs." or "Miss" communicates not only whether she has been married but also whether she has conservative tastes in forms of address—and probably other conservative values as well. Checking "Ms." declines to let on about marriage (checking "Mr." declines nothing since nothing was asked), but it also marks her as either liberated or rebellious, depending on the observer's attitudes and assumptions.

21   I sometimes try to duck these variously marked choices by giving my title as "Dr."—and in so doing risk marking myself as either uppity (hence sarcastic responses like "Excuse *me*!") or an overachiever (hence reactions of congratulatory surprise like "Good for you!").

22   All married women's surnames are marked. If a woman takes her husband's name, she announces to the world that she is married and has traditional values. To some it will indicate that she is less herself, more identified by her husband's identity. If she does not take her husband's name, this too is marked, seen as worthy of comment: she has *done* something; she has "kept her own name." A man is never said to have "kept his own name" because it never occurs to anyone that he might have given it up. For him using his own name is unmarked.

23   A married woman who wants to have her cake and eat it too may use her surname plus his, with or without a hyphen. But this too announces her marital status and often results in a tongue-tying string. In a list (Harvey O'Donovan, Jonathan Feldman, Stephanie Woodbury McGillicutty), the woman's multiple name stands out. It is marked.

24   I have never been inclined toward biological explanations of gender differences in language, but I was intrigued to see Ralph Fasold bring biological phenomena to bear on the question of linguistic marking in his book "The Sociolinguistics of Language." Fasold stresses that language and culture are particularly unfair in treating women as the marked case because biologically it is the male that is marked. While two X chromosomes make a female, two Y chromosomes make nothing. Like the linguistic markers *s, es* or *ess*, the Y chromosome doesn't "mean" anything unless it is attached to a root form—an X chromosome.

25   Developing this idea elsewhere, Fasold points out that girls are born with fully female bodies, while boys are born with modified female bodies. He invites men who doubt this to lift up their shirts and contemplate why they have nipples.

26   In his book, Fasold notes "a wide range of facts which demonstrates that female is the unmarked sex." For example, he observes that there are a few species that produce only females, like the whiptail lizard. Thanks to parthenogenesis, they have no trouble having as many daughters as they like. There are no species, however, that produce only males. This is no surprise, since any such species would become extinct in its first generation.

27   Fasold is also intrigued by species that produce individuals not involved in reproduction, like honeybees and leaf-cutter ants. Reproduction is handled by the queen and a relatively few males; the workers are sterile females. "Since they do not reproduce," Fasold says, "there is no reason for them to be one sex or the other, so they default, so to speak, to female."

28   Fasold ends his discussion of these matters by pointing out that if language reflected biology, grammar books would direct us to use "she" to include males and females and "he" only for specifically male referents. But they don't. They tell us that "he" means "he or she," and that "she" is used only if the referent is specifically female. This use of "he" as the sex-indefinite pronoun is an innovation introduced into English by grammarians in the 18th and 19th centuries, according to Peter Mühlhäusler and Rom Harré in "Pronouns and People." From at least about 1500, the correct sex-indefinite pronoun was "they," as it still is in casual spoken English. In other words, the female was declared by grammarians to be the marked case.

29   Writing this article may mark me not as a writer, not as a linguist, not as an analyst of human behavior, but as a feminist—which will have positive or negative, but in any case powerful, connotations for readers. Yet I doubt that anyone reading Ralph Fasold's book would put that label on him.

30   I discovered the markedness inherent in the very topic of gender after writing a book on differences in conversational style based on geographical region, ethnicity, class, age and gender. When I was interviewed, the vast majority of journalists wanted to talk about the differences between women and men. While I thought I was simply describing what I observed—something I had learned to do as a researcher—merely mentioning women and men marked me as a feminist for some.

31   When I wrote a book devoted to gender differences in ways of speaking, I sent the manuscript to five male colleagues, asking them to alert me to any interpretation, phrasing or wording that might seem unfairly negative toward men. Even so, when the book came out, I encountered responses like that of the television talk show host who, after interviewing me, turned to the audience and asked if they thought I was male-bashing.

32   Leaping upon a poor fellow who affably nodded in agreement, she made him stand and asked, "Did what she said accurately describe you?" "Oh, yes," he answered. "That's me exactly." 'And what she said about

women—does that sound like your wife?" "Oh yes," he responded. "That's her exactly." "Then why do you think she's male-bashing?" He answered, with disarming honesty, "Because she's a woman and she's saying things about men."

33   To say anything about women and men without marking oneself as either feminist or anti-feminist, male-basher or apologist for men seems as impossible for a woman as trying to get dressed in the morning without interpretations of her character.

34   Sitting at the conference table musing on these matters, I felt sad to think that we women didn't have the freedom to be unmarked that the men sitting next to us had. Some days you just want to get dressed and go about your business. But if you're a woman, you can't, because there is no unmarked woman.

Topical Considerations

1. In paragraphs 1–7, Tannen describes the styles of three different women, noting that each style was "coherent." At the end of paragraph 7, based upon the information provided by Tannen, what kinds of generalizations might you make about the three different women described? In your opinion, are such generalizations useful in thinking about your "impressions" of people? Explain.

2. According to Tannen, women's style choices are all marked in some way, whereas men have the option of "unmarked" styles. What does she mean by marked and unmarked styles? Do you experience the same difficulties with marking in your life? Explain.

3. According to Tannen, how might a woman's style choices affect her employment opportunities? Is the same true for men? How do you, regardless of your gender, make choices about your own appearance? What do these choices have to do with employment and other opportunities you might be interested in?

4. In paragraph 24, Tannen states that she has "never been inclined toward biological explanations of gender differences in language. . . ." Based on the information in Tannen's article, what is your understanding of such "biological" explanations? Do you buy into them as relevant to the issues of gender marking in language or fashion? Why or why not?

5. According to Tannen, what is the relationship between the marking of females linguistically and the marking of female style choices? In your opinion, what kind of effect does this marking have upon men and women in their daily lives?

6. Regarding her work on gender differences in language, Tannen says, "While I thought I was simply describing what I observed . . . merely mentioning women and men marked me as a feminist for some" (paragraph 30). What

is Tannen's complaint about being labeled as such? From this sample of her work, would you describe Tannen as a feminist? Why or why not?

Rhetorical Considerations

1. In her introduction (paragraphs 1–7), Tannen describes in detail the appearance of three women at a recent conference. What is Tannen's strategy in these paragraphs? In your opinion, is this an effective introduction to the piece? Explain.
2. Tannen's essay links gendered marking in terms of style with marking in linguistic theory. Reread the article, circling passages that serve as transitions or direct connections between these two ideas. Overall, has Tannen made smooth connections here? How so?
3. Is Tannen's use of the first-person perspective effective in this essay? Why or why not? What is the effect of her shift to the third person in certain parts of her essay?
4. What kind of evidence does Tannen provide for her argument that females are the "marked" case in contemporary culture? Has she provided enough evidence to convince you as a reader? Why or why not?

Writing Assignments

1. Write a detailed first-person description of the dress of women and men in a given situation—for example, your classroom, your table at dinner, your dormitory or apartment building. Draw conclusions that either support or refute Tannen's idea of gender marking in terms of fashion.
2. Imagine a society where neither men nor women were "marked" with regard to appearance. What would men and women look like? What would they wear? How would this "unmarked" society differ from the one we currently inhabit? In creating this new world, think of all the consequences of removing markings according to gender—socially, politically, economically, culturally. Be as creative as you can!
3. With three or four other classmates, conduct an examination of sources in popular culture of "marked" fashion choices. You might explore television, magazines, films, and advertisements for their fashion content. Then write a collaborative essay discussing the role of the media in the phenomenon of marking described by Tannen, including a consensus of your positions on the issue. Does the media play a positive role in the development of fashion trends? How does this role affect gender relationships and the marking of women, or both men? Your writing project might be supplemented with visuals illustrating your arguments.

Just as Fierce
Katherine Dunn

A woman hurling punches in the boxing ring jolts one's image of womanhood. Such a scene pits the stereotype of woman as gentle and meek against the taboo of woman as violent and brutal. Yet in this provocative essay, Katherine Dunn documents the story of a young woman boxer to argue that women are capable of violence and aggression on the same scale as men. Furthermore, she argues, society's refusal to recognize violence in women consigns them to a weak and dependent position. Whether you agree or disagree with these ideas, this essay will challenge your notion of female strength.

Katherine Dunn is a boxing reporter and novelist. Her most recent novel is *Geek Love* (1990), and her most recent non-fiction book is *Death Scenes* (1996). This article originally appeared in *Mother Jones* in 1994.

BEFORE YOU READ

Assuming from the title of the essay, "Just as Fierce," that the author is going to argue that women are aggressive, what might be the advantages or disadvantages for women in the acknowledgment that they are just as violent as men? Consider this from the point of view of roles they might hold in domestic, personal, and professional situations.

AS YOU READ

Consider Ms. Dunn's discussion of women as perpetrators of domestic violence. Does this discussion serve as evidence of women's aggression and strength? Do you find it convincing? Questionable? Is evidence being slanted? Manipulated? Why or why not?

1   The girl wanted to fight. She was young and blonde and she spoke good English and at first the guys in the boxing gym laughed.

2   But when Dallas Malloy stepped into an amateur boxing ring in Lynnwood, Wash., last year, she broached a barrier far more imposing than the crusty male bastion of the sport. She challenged an ancient and still powerful tradition of what it is to be female. She defied what may be our most pervasive notion of gender difference—the idea that men are physically aggressive and women are not.

3   Malloy was 16 years old, the youngest daughter of college professors. She was already an accomplished pianist, writer, and athlete when she drew international attention by suing U.S. Amateur Boxing for gender discrimination and won the right for American women to compete as amateur boxers. Reporters and television news crews from three continents jostled for space at

ringside to watch Malloy outpoint Heather Poyner in the first sanctioned women's match.

4   Asked why they wanted to fight, the young women said they enjoyed it, just as some men and boys do.

5   The more potent, unasked question is how society at large reacts to eager, voluntary violence by females, and to the growing evidence that women can be just as aggressive as men. A small part of that question was answered in the bleachers that October fight night, as packs of rowdy women lawyers waved manicured fists and cheered with tears streaming down their cheeks.

6   After 13 years as a boxing reporter, I was a little misty myself on that historic night. Much about Dallas Malloy seemed familiar. A certain steadiness in her eyes reminded me of the woman who raised me.

7   My mother, still a witty and gifted artist in her hale 80s, got a rifle a few years ago. I pity the burglar who gives her a chance to use it. When we kids were small, she never had a formal weapon but made do with whatever came to hand. Her broom, skillet, spoon, or shovel served to rein in pesky bill collectors, hostile relatives, rats, rattlesnakes, rambunctious drunks, or any other threat to the peace of her regime. Mom came from a line of frontier females who could drive four horses and the school bus, plow and shoot straight, slaughter beeves and negotiate a sale, reroof the barn, and then go home to embroider flowers on pillowcases while supervising the kids' math homework.

8   One of Mom's favorite relatives was her Aunt Myrtle, a gentle woman, revered by her farming clan. A classic Myrtle tale describes how she dashed into the subzero cold one winter night, clad only in boots and a nightie, to battle a pack of prairie wolves who were killing her prize turkeys. My mother, a child then, watched amazed from the kitchen window as Myrtle the dainty, the kind, danced with her kindling hatchet flashing into the skulls and spines of fanged and flickering beasts. Blood exploded in black sprays across the snow. "And that Christmas," the story always ends, "she gave us kids wolfskin mittens, with the fur side in, and stitched snowflakes on the cuffs."

9   More than 70 years have passed since Myrtle swung her hatchet. Our current era is downwind from the social upheaval of the Vietnam War, the pacifism of the civil rights movement, and the determined progress of feminism. American culture is torn between our long romance with violence and our terror of the devastation wrought by war and crime and environmental havoc. In our struggle to restrain the violence and contain the damage, we tend to forget that the human capacity for aggression is more than a monstrous defect, that it is also a crucial survival tool. The delicate task is to understand the nature, uses, and hazards of the tool. The first step is to recognize that it exists, and that we all possess it to one degree or another—even us women.

10   This is difficult because so many of us are convinced that women are incapable of aggression on the same scale as men—that women are physically too weak, or are inherently, biologically different in aggressive capacity, or are spiritually superior to the whole concept of violence. These beliefs are the

legacy of ancient, traditional definitions of the female role, inadvertently augmented by some recent efforts to combat the oppressive social factors that still assail women.

11   But most of us would not be here without a generous sprinkling of physically aggressive women in our bloodlines. Throughout most of human history, long before antibiotics and prepackaged foods, many women had to be strong or they didn't survive. They had to be fierce or their young did not survive. And these gifts have not declined in this upholstered age of air conditioning.

12   The regular cop on the night beat in my neighborhood is alone in her patrol car because of budget cuts. Some midnights I can see her parked across the street, doing paperwork by the dash lights. The clerks at the local 24-hour market say our cop calmly interrupted a mugging in the parking lot last week. The bad guy was big and wild, but she grabbed him and held him facedown on the pavement until her backup arrived. A thumbhold of some kind, the clerks think.

13   During the last few decades, American women have proven their efficacy in every law enforcement agency, earned the trust of those who fight forest fires beside them, and struggled for the right to demonstrate brains, resourcefulness, courage, and strength in a thousand venues from sports to the space shuttle. But the idea that women can't take care of themselves still permeates our culture.

14   The bouncer at many a college tavern will let a scrawny, pencil-necked male wander home alone at 2 A.M., but will insist on an escort for the captain of the women's soccer team. This kind of protectionist attitude, however grounded in good intentions, defines women as less than equal to men. It also reinforces the stereotype of the helpless female for both victim and assailant: Women believe they are helpless against male aggression; criminals see women as vulnerable.

15   The fact that women are subject to rape (and men, for the most part, aren't) is often used as the reason why females warrant special protection. While this distinction is not to be dismissed, the fact remains that the majority of rapes in the United States are committed behind closed doors by people known to the victims. Rape by strangers on the street is dramatically less frequent than muggings and assaults. Advocating protectionism for women based solely on their vulnerability to rape further reinforces their victimization, and discounts other vicious acts as serious crimes. Women's "rapability" seems small justification for the uncategorial separation of the sexes.

16   There is no denying that some women could use the protection of a stronger person—but so could some men. And when the soccer captain, a fit, fleet expert in the elbow, kick, and headbutt believes she needs a bodyguard to get to her dorm room, she has been robbed of part of her own identity.

17   Ironically, some of the most dedicated defenders of women have enhanced this mythology of weakness, rather than worked to combat it. The intense campaigns against domestic violence, rape, sexual harassment, and inequity in the schools all too often depend on an image of women as weak and

victimized. A few well-known feminist leaders, including Andrea Dworkin, Catherine MacKinnon, and Patricia Ireland, regularly portray women as help- less targets of male violence.

18   This idea that males are physically aggressive and females are not has distinct drawbacks for both sexes. Defining men as the perpetrators of all vio- lence is a viciously immoral judgment of an entire gender. And defining women as inherently nonviolent condemns us to the equally restrictive role of sweet, meek, and weak.

19   Most arguments for a difference in aggression between the sexes fluctu- ate somewhere between nature and nurture. But hard as it may be to believe, there is no known biological reason that women cannot be as physically ag- gressive as men. Geneticist Anne Fausto-Sterling and biologist Ruth Hubbard are two of the many women scholars who are critical of research that postu- lates a variety of biologically determined gender differences beyond the repro- ductive functions. Both scholars argue that the innumerable factors of nature and nurture affect each other in highly complex ways.

20   Anne Fausto-Sterling has examined many familiar theories of biological difference. Her work debunks claims that physiological differences exist in male and female brains, and that females have better verbal abilities, worse visual-spatial abilities, and less capacity for mathematics than males.

21   Fausto-Sterling also attacks the central idea that males are inherently, biologically more aggressive than females. She specifically deflates the myth of testosterone—often named as the root cause of war, riots, murder, bar brawls, corporate takeovers, wife beating, clear-cutting, and other forms of "male" aggression—demonstrating that no credible evidence indicates that testosterone causes aggression. In fact, studies of soldiers preparing for battle in Vietnam suggest that testosterone levels actually drop severely in anticipa- tion of stressful situations.

22   Gender differences in the form and context in which aggression is ex- pressed, concludes Fausto-Sterling, are more likely to be caused by learned and cultural factors than by biology. The broad spectrum of aggressive behav- ior in humans is far more complex than the mere squirting of a gland. Science is only beginning to grapple with the jungle of questions and concerns that surround it.

23   Even our understanding of physical differences between women and men is changing. In "The Politics of Women's Biology," Ruth Hubbard points out that many physical characteristics are extremely variable, depending on environmental and behavioral factors. We tend to assume, for example, that men are genetically endowed with greater upper-body strength. But this dis- parity (and others of size and strength) between the sexes is inflated by cultural strictures on exercise, variations in diet, and other factors.

24   Training of female athletes is so new that the limits of female possibility are still unknown. In 1963 the first female marathon runners were almost an hour and a half slower than the best male runners. Twenty years later the

fastest women were within 15 minutes of the winning male speed. Female sprinters are now within a fraction of a second of the top male speeds, and some experts predict that early in the next century women will match male runners.

25   Perhaps the strongest evidence that women have as broad and deep a capacity for physical aggression as men is anecdotal. And as with men, this capacity has expressed itself in acts from the brave to the brutal, the selfless to the senseless.

26   Historical examples of female aptitude for the organized violence of warfare, for instance, include the 19th-century tradition of African women warriors who formed the core legions of the kingdom of Dahomey and the 800,000 Russian women who fought in every combat position and flew as fighter pilots during World War II. The gradual movement of women into combat positions in the military forces of Canada, Britain, the Netherlands, Norway, the United States, and other nations is evidence of a growing contemporary understanding that women can be as dangerous as men.

27   And while national military forces have historically resisted the full participation of women soldiers, female talent has found plenty of scope in revolutionary and terrorist groups around the planet. According to criminologists Harold J. Vetter and Gary R. Perlstein, nearly a quarter of the original Russian revolutionary terrorists were women—mostly from the educated middle class. More recently, Ulrike Meinhof and the other women of the nihilist Baader-Meinhof Gang were only the most publicized of many female terrorists in Europe. There is also substantial female revolutionary involvement in the Irish Republican Army, the Basque Separatists, the Italian Red Brigades, and the Palestinian Intifada, as well as in revolutionary groups throughout Asia, Africa, and Central and South America.

28   In "Shoot the Women First," British journalist Eileen MacDonald published remarkable interviews with 20 female terrorists, including Leila Khalid, leader of the Popular Front for the Liberation of Palestine in the '70s. The book's title is taken from advice reportedly given by Interpol to anti-terrorist squads. Many experts, it seems, consider female terrorists more dangerous than males. They are reputed to endure more pain and to stay cooler in a crisis. The Basque women interviewed by MacDonald gleefully admitted to escaping severe punishment when caught by claiming that a boyfriend had fooled or forced them into robbing the bank, firing the gun, or planting the bomb. The women saw this as outwitting the authorities by turning their own antiquated macho mind-set against them.

29   Nonetheless, it is still popular to assert that all female criminals are driven by male threat or patriarchal pressure. (The characters in "Thelma & Louise" and the defense of serial killer Aileen Wuornos are good examples of this stereotype.) Although on the surface this presumption of female innocence corrupted by male aggression seems complimentary, in fact it is deeply patronizing. Columnist Amy Pagnozzi, writing for the New York Daily News on the

trial of Lorena Bobbitt, said, "A baby. That's what an American jury decided Lorena Bobbitt was yesterday, in deciding she was not responsible for her actions. It is a decision that infantilizes and imperils all women."

30   On the rare occasion when a woman has been held responsible for her actions, she's been branded a monster far more frightening than a male perpetrating the same acts. For years scholars believed female criminals were hormonally abnormal, with more body hair, low intelligence, even an identifiable bone structure. Freud thought all female criminals wanted to be men. The female criminal violates two laws—the legal and cultural structure against crime and the equally profound taboo against violent females.

31   As in the public sphere, there is ample evidence that women can be as physically aggressive behind closed doors as men. Here, too, a failure to acknowledge the bad that women can do is a failure to take women seriously.

32   We should not be surprised when women's aggression is expressed in the one place where they have traditionally held equal or superior status, the home. And it is in the home where that most frightening of crimes, child abuse, most often occurs. Studies of family violence and reports from state and national agencies are consistent in finding that while males commit the majority of sexual molestations of children, women commit more physical abuse of children than men. A Justice Department study released this July found that a full 55 percent of offspring murders are committed by women.

33   Considering how much more time women spend caring for children than men do, these figures shouldn't be surprising. Unless, of course, we fail to recognize that women are capable of violent reactions to stress just as men are. Yet female involvement is scarcely visible in the media's coverage of child abuse.

34   Spousal abuse is an area where research is questioning still more closely held beliefs about sex roles and violence. Historically, the campaign against wife battering has been a primary vehicle for the "men violent, women nonviolent" message. There is no question that a terrible number of women are brutalized, and even killed, by their male partners. Every effort should be made to punish the perpetrators, help the victims, and, most of all, prevent such crimes in the future. But this reality is only part of the complex and ugly domestic violence picture.

35   An increasing amount of research suggests that women are violent in domestic situations just as often as men. Studies based on large, random samples from the whole population have found domestic violence to be distributed more or less equally between the sexes. These include studies conducted by Dr. Suzanne Steinmetz, director of the Family Research Institute at Indiana University-Purdue University at Indianapolis, and by Murray Straus and Richard Gelles, who have conducted the large-scale National Family Violence Survey over a period of 17 years; and research by Anson Shupe, William A. Stacey, and Lonnie R. Hazlewood.

36   The overall pattern depicted by Straus and Gelles is that spousal violence falls into four categories of essentially equal size: male battery of an unresisting

female partner; female battery of an unresisting male partner; mutual battery usually initiated by the male; and mutual battery usually initiated by the female.

37   They found that when only the women's version of events was analyzed (that is, the men's version of events was omitted), the results were the same. When only the most severe forms of violence were analyzed, the results were the same. (In a fist-to-fist row, a bigger, stronger man is obviously far more likely to injure a smaller woman than the reverse. But a man's superior strength is often neutralized by a woman's use of weapons.)

38   The public has received a dramatically different picture of domestic violence. Other, more widely publicized studies do suggest that women assault their spouses much less frequently than men and rarely or never initiate mutual assaults. But these studies are based on small, self-selected "treatment group" samples or police records and are statistically less likely to measure accurately the overall rate and form of domestic violence.

39   The rhetoric and reality clash: Our mythic fantasies of a female ideal contradict and undermine the actual strength and multidimensionality of women. In cases where female aggression is destructive, our denial compounds the problem.

40   In boxing, they say it's the punch you don't see coming that knocks you out. In the wider world, the reality we ignore or deny is the one that weakens our most impassioned efforts toward improvement.

41   We live with a distinct double standard about male and female aggression. Women's aggression isn't considered real. It isn't dangerous, it's only cute. Or it's always self-defense or otherwise inspired by a man. In the rare case where a woman is seen as genuinely responsible, she is branded a monster—an "unnatural" woman.

42   But slowly these stereotypes are crumbling. We are starting to realize that, in the words of columnist Linda Ellerbee, "The truth is that women, like it or not, can be brutal, too. Brutality's not sexist."

43   I suspect that the mythology of females as essentially nonviolent grew out of a profound impulse to give special protection to the bearers of future generations—a sort of gender version of the non-combatant status of medics and Red Cross workers. But the problem is the same for all noncombatants, whether in wartime or danger-ridden peace: You can still get hurt, but you're not allowed to fight back.

44   Then, too, we humans don't respect victims, and the disrespect in the language of the nonviolent female nature is too familiar. It echoes the chauvinist romances of past male authorities who explained why women needed to be banned from vast sections of the workplace, prevented from learning to read, excluded from doing business or owning property, and relieved of the onerous responsibility of making fundamental decisions about their lives.

45   Such rhetoric is absurd in a time when millions of American women are shoulder to shoulder with male colleagues in every field of human endeavor. Women have fought for their achievements over decades, battling in

courtrooms, classrooms, legislatures, workshops, and the streets of the nation. It took the ferocious, unconquerable will of a great many women to win recognition for equal intelligence, invention, organization, and stamina.

46   In the boxing world, that kind of courage is known as heart. Now, with the possibility of genuine equality visible in the distance, it is self-destructive lunacy to deny the existence of women's enormous fighting heart.

47   It is time to recognize the variability of females, just as we do males. Women are real. Our reality covers the whole human megillah, from feeble to fierce, from bad to good, from endangered to dangerous. We don't just deserve power, we have it. And power in this and every other society is not just the capacity to benefit those around us. It includes, absolutely and necessarily, the ability to inflict damage and the willingness to accept responsibility.

Topical Considerations

1. What is Dunn's basic argument regarding women and physical aggression? Do you agree with this argument? Why or why not?

2. Much of Dunn's essay challenges traditional cultural ideas of gender difference, of "what it is to be female" (paragraph 2). Do you agree with Dunn's formulation of "what it is to be female" in this culture? To be male? Do you perceive a difference between cultural stereotypes and the reality of men's and women's lives? Explain.

3. In paragraph 19, Dunn invokes a debate which she calls "nature versus nurture." How does she define the terms of this debate? Do you agree with her position?

4. Dunn opens her essay with a description of the first sanctioned women's boxing match in the United States. In paragraphs 26–28, she addresses the issue of women in combat roles in the military, another issue that has been hotly contested recently. What is your opinion about the presence of women in these traditionally male arenas? Did your ideas about this issue change after reading Dunn's essay? Why or why not?

5. Dunn refers to the issue of women's *responsibility* throughout her essay (see paragraphs 29–30). What is her position on responsibility? Do you agree with her?

6. Dunn concludes in paragraph 41 that "we live with a distinct double standard about male and female aggression." How does Dunn define this double standard? According to her argument, what are its origins and consequences? What are her ideas about how to resolve this double standard?

7. Dunn ends her essay with a discussion of power, but one could argue that this is the subject of the entire piece. In your opinion, how is the issue of power relevant to Dunn's argument? What kind of power is she referring to? Do you agree with her ideas of how women must gain "equal" power to men?

Rhetorical Considerations

1. Think again about Dunn's basic arguments, then reread her first paragraph. How does this line set the tone for the entire essay? What information does Dunn provide the reader in the first line?

2. In paragraphs 7 and 8, Dunn gives two descriptive anecdotes about women in her family. Keeping in mind Dunn's larger arguments, what do these anecdotes *show* us about women without actually *telling* us? How do they work to support Dunn's revision of traditional notions of gender difference?

3. What personal experiences and relationships qualify Dunn to address the topic of women and aggression? How might her attitudes affect the response of different kinds of readers?

4. Much of the substance of Dunn's essay is evidence of women's capacity for violent aggression, and of traditional gender ideals which attempt to deny this capacity. What kinds of sources and authorities does Dunn use to back up her claims? Does she provide enough thorough documentation of her sources? Provide specific examples from the text in explaining your answer.

5. In paragraphs 34–38, Dunn attempts to cast a new light on common media representations of domestic violence. How does she deal specifically with conflicting sources? How does she explain the differences in evidence found in studies in the field, and how does the resolution of these conflicts affect the success or failure of her argument? Are you convinced by the explanations she offers her readers in this regard? Why or why not?

6. What tone does Dunn adopt in her essay? How does this tone affect your reception of her ideas? Explain.

Writing Assignments

1. Write a narrative essay relating an experience in your own life to the issue of women's capacity for physical aggression. For instance, have you known a woman—or do you have a legendary female ancestor—like Dunn's mother or Aunt Myrtle? Have you ever witnessed a conflict between men and women over the issue of women's aggression?

2. Imagine that you are a woman who has been denied access to a military education. Write a persuasive essay arguing for your admission to this training program. Or, write your essay from the perspective of the school's administration, arguing against allowing females to participate in military training.

3. Write an exploratory essay addressing the effects of traditional representations of women in the United States. Some areas of your exploration might be television, film, art, advertisements, and magazines. How do art and media representations of women either enforce or refute the perception of

women as inherently nonaggressive? Be sure to include analyses of specific cultural texts in your essay.

4. Write a position paper arguing your views about some aspects of gender equality in the late 20th century. Dunn claims that "the possibility of genuine equality [is] visible in the distance." Do you agree? Using specific examples to support your positions, be sure to address the issue of whether acknowledgment of women's aggression is an important part of achieving gender equality.

OPPOSITIONS: FEMINISM

Feminist
Anna Quindlen

Anna Quindlen remembers life before the feminist revolution. An ardent feminist, she joined the struggle for women's equality 20 years ago and now enjoys its benefits. But in this piece, she worries that today's women—beneficiaries of feminism but never foot soldiers in the cause—may let their sense of entitlement lure them into a false sense of security. She fears that old stereotypes and limitations may reemerge unless today's self-described "generation of individualists" works as a group for women's rights.

Anna Quindlen's nationally syndicated column, "Public and Private," appears in the *New York Times* and other newspapers around the country. She was a reporter and editor with the *Times* from 1977 to 1986 when she created the popular column, "Life in the 30s," where this essay first appeared in August 1988. Her essays have been published in the collections *Living Out Loud* (1990) and *Thinking Out Loud* (1993). Ms. Quindlen is a Pulitzer Prize recipient; her first novel, *Object Lessons,* was published in 1991 and her second novel, *One True Thing,* was published in 1994.

BEFORE YOU READ

What particular rights, fought for and won by the feminist movement, have enhanced your life? Have you played any role in the feminist movement? Do you feel any compulsion to take action to support the feminist cause? What are your reasons for your involvement or lack of involvement? Need one be a woman to be involved in the feminist movement?

AS YOU READ

As you read this essay, make a brief list of your own ideas about the way women's lives have improved in the past 20 years. What areas for improvement still exist?

1   I would like to say that I became a feminist to make the world better for women everywhere, but in truth it was to make the world better for me. This was almost twenty years ago, and altruism was not my strong suit; to paraphrase Rhett Butler, the only cause I believed in was me. Nor was I struck by the rank injustice of sex discrimination. It just seemed like men got all the good stuff.

2   I grew up in a city run by men, in a church run by men, in a household run by a man. Men had comfortable shoes, a life outside the home, and money in their wallets. Women had children, who are wonderful but not sufficient unto themselves, at least for me. The best job you could get as a woman then involved a lifetime vow of chastity, which was not my thing. I figured either life was going to be considerably different for me than it was for my mother, or I was going to be angry all the time. I jumped on the bandwagon. I've never gotten off.

3   As I watched the convention of the National Organization for Women on television the other night, I realized my only real political identification has been with women's rights. It is the only cause I have ever believed in that has improved the world. Life for many women is not the same as it was when I was young, and I do not believe it will ever be so again. I do not believe that ever again will there be a handful of token women in the graduating class at Harvard Law School. I do not believe that ever again will there be a handful of female New York City police officers.

4   Change is exceedingly slow, but somehow sure. My friend the female rabbi still meets up with the occasional father of the bride who will not pay for the wedding if she officiates. To write that sentence alone is a measure of the shock of the new, and the stubborn strength of the old. On the one hand, the father of the bride and his wallet. On the other, a rabbi who is a woman.

5   I went to a women's college. Not long ago I was asked what it was like. At the time I was speaking at a college that until 1969 had been all-male and fiercely proud to be so. I said it was a little like learning to swim while holding on to the side of the pool; I didn't learn the arm movements until after I graduated, but by that time I was one hell of a kicker.

6   When I began school there were still marks on the university buildings made by student demonstrators. Perhaps that was why some of us were happy to view our own feminism as a liberal and not a radical political movement. A liberal movement is precisely what we got. We were permitted limited access to the world of men provided that to some considerable extent we mimicked their behavior but did not totally alter our own.

7   I suppose we sometimes feel disappointed with our circumstances today because now that the liberal movement has taken place, now that women are performing cardiac surgery and becoming members of the welders' unions, it has become clearer than ever that what we really needed was a radical movement. We have given the word an ominous connotation, but in fact it means only a root change. We needed a root change in the way things work: in the way everyone approached work, in the way everyone approached the

care of children, in the way everyone, male and female, approached the balance of life and work and obligations and inclinations. I do not think this really came about.

8   Everyone now accepts that men, too, can cry, but women still often have more reason to. "We must fight for parental leaves for mothers and fathers," one feminist told me, and I knew she was right, except that I didn't know many men who were going to take paternity leaves if they were offered. I suppose we must fight to raise sons who will take them.

9   We still find ourselves dependent on the kindness of strangers, from Supreme Court justices to husbands and lovers. I do not believe that we are likely to go back to a time when patients refuse to be treated by female doctors, but I think we could go back to a time when doctors of both sexes are forbidden by law to perform abortions. I think that institutions run by men, with a sprinkling of women in high places, may begin to feel self-congratulatory and less enthusiastic about hiring and promotion efforts about which they have always been ambivalent.

10   It is difficult to communicate some of the terror of this to young women who have grown up with a sense of entitlement, who were born in the year in which a bin was filled with undergarments on the Atlantic City boardwalk in protest of the Miss America pageant, who grew up knowing that they could go to Princeton or rabbinical school or the moon if they worked at it hard enough, who have never been asked how fast they typed.

11   Some have told me that they do not think of themselves as feminists, that they are a generation of individualists who do not align themselves with a group cause, particularly one which represents battles they believe have been largely won.

12   Perhaps it was a particularly female thing about me, but I did not feel qualified, when I was young, to be an individualist. I felt that by birth I was part of a group, and that the single hallmark of that group was that they were denied access to money and power by virtue of biology. That seemed overwhelming to me at seventeen, and it seemed to present me with two choices. One was to distinguish myself from other women. The other was to stand up for the rights of women as a group. I wasn't capable of going it alone. Luckily, I didn't have to. I had my sisters.

Topical Considerations

1. Quindlen's argument includes a discussion of the difference between liberal feminism and radical feminism. Which does Quindlen seem to prefer and why?

2. Looking in the newspapers and to your own experience, discuss Quindlen's statement in paragraph 9: "We still find ourselves dependent on the kindness of strangers, from Supreme Court justices to husbands and lovers." What do you think Quindlen means by this statement? Explain why you agree or disagree with it.

3. What does Quindlen think of the "generation of individualists" that she describes in paragraph 11? Does her self-exclusion from that group exclude others from her argument?
4. Quindlen discusses, or uses in her examples, college-educated women. How would women without college educations respond to this piece?
5. Has this essay changed your views of feminism? If so, how? If not, why not?

Rhetorical Considerations

1. What is the effect of Quindlen's opening sentence? Does she seem authoritative? Credible? Honest? Does this make you want to keep reading the essay?
2. Quindlen's tone is somewhat informal throughout? Does this strengthen or weaken the force of her argument?
3. Quindlen writes with much focus on herself. How would the impact of the essay change were it written in a more objective third-person style?
4. How effective is the analogy that Quindlen sets up in paragraph 5 (likening going to a women's college to learning to swim while holding onto the side of the pool)? How do analogies in general affect persuasion?
5. Find examples of emotional appeals within Quindlen's essay, and comment on their effectiveness.
6. Did the title of this piece give you an initial sense of the essay's content? Do you think it is a good one? Can you come up with a more specific or more effective title?

Writing Assignments

1. Do you think it is easier to be a feminist if you are a woman, or do you think that men can understand and support feminist issues? In supporting your point of view, discuss your own experience as well as the experiences of people you know or famous people who exemplify your position.
2. Write a refutation of Quindlen's argument from the point of view of a male from a lower- to middle-class background. Examine all of the evidence given by Quindlen and demonstrate how she has misrepresented the situation.
3. Pretend that you have been asked to write a letter about feminism and male-female relationships in the 1990s for inclusion in a time capsule, which will be opened 50 years from now. What would you highlight as the most important contributions and consequences of feminism?

The Failure of Feminism
Kay Ebeling

Like Anna Quindlen, Kay Ebeling joined the feminist revolution as a young woman. Unlike Quindlen, Ebeling has little praise for what the feminist movement has accomplished in the past 25 years. Whereas others celebrate women's hard-won victories in education, employment, and reproduction, the author of this provocative essay calls feminism "The Great Experiment That Failed." Given the biological reality that women, not men, have babies, Ebeling says that all the movement has produced is "frenzied and overworked women dropping kids off at day-care centers." Only men have been liberated by feminism.

A single mother, Ebeling is a free-lance writer from Humboldt Country, California. This tough and spirited essay first appeared in *Newsweek* in November 1990.

BEFORE YOU READ

Jot down the various criticisms of the feminist movement you have heard people express. Which criticisms do you think are valid and why? Which are not valid?

AS YOU READ

Describe the tone the author established in the first paragraph. Is this tone maintained throughout the essay? Does the tone make you more or less sympathetic to the author's point of view?

1   The other day I had the world's fastest blind date. A Yuppie from Eureka penciled me in for 50 minutes on a Friday and met me at a watering hole in the rural northern California town of Arcata. He breezed in, threw his jammed daily planner on the table and shot questions at me, watching my reactions as if it were a job interview. He eyed how much I drank. Then he breezed out to his next appointment. He had given us 50 minutes to size each other up and see if there was any chance for romance. His exit was so fast that as we left he let the door slam back in my face. It was an interesting slam.

2   Most of our 50-minute conversation had covered the changing state of male-female relationships. My blind date was 40 years old, from the Experimental Generation. He is "actively pursuing new ways for men and women to interact now that old traditions no longer exist." That's a real quote. He really did say that, when I asked him what he like to do. This was a man who'd read Ms. Magazine and believed every word of it. He'd been single for 16 years but had lived with a few women during that time. He was off that evening for a ski weekend, meeting someone who was paying her own way for the trip.

3   I too am from the Experimental Generation, but I couldn't even pay for my own drink. To me, feminism has backfired against women. In 1973 I left what could have been a perfectly good marriage, taking with me a child in diapers, a 10-year-old Plymouth and Volume 1, Number One of Ms. Magazine. I was convinced I could make it on my own. In the last 15 years my ex has married or lived with a succession of women. As he gets older, his women stay in their 20s. Meanwhile, I've stayed unattached. He drives a BMW. I ride buses.

4   Today I see feminism as the Great Experiment That Failed, and women in my generation, its perpetrators, are the casualties. Many of us, myself included, are saddled with raising children alone. The resulting poverty makes us experts at cornmeal recipes and ways to find free recreation on weekends. At the same time, single men from our generation amass fortunes in CDs and real-estate ventures so they can breeze off on ski weekends. Feminism freed men, not women. Now men are spared the nuisance of a wife and family to support. After childbirth, if his wife's waist doesn't return to 20 inches, the husband can go out and get a more petite woman. It's far more difficult for the wife, now tied down with a baby, to find a new man. My blind date that Friday waved goodbye as he drove off in his RV. I walked home and paid the sitter with laundry quarters.

5   The main message of feminism was: woman, you don't need a man; remember, those of you around 40, the phrase: "A woman without a man is like a fish without a bicycle?" That joke circulated through "consciousness raising" groups across the country in the '70s. It was a philosophy that made divorce and cohabitation casual and routine. Feminism made women disposable. So today a lot of females are around 40 and single with a couple of kids to raise on their own. Child-support payments might pay for a few pairs of shoes, but in general, feminism gave men all the financial and personal advantages over women.

6   What's worse, we asked for it. Many women decided: you don't need a family structure to raise your children. We packed them off to day-care centers where they could get their nurturing from professionals. Then we put on our suits and ties, packed our briefcases and took off on this Great Experiment, convinced that there was no difference between ourselves and the guys in the other offices.

"Biological Thing"

7   How wrong we were. Because like it or not, women have babies. It's this biological thing that's just there, these organs we're born with. The truth is, a woman can't live the true feminist life unless she denies her childbearing biology. She has to live on the pill, or have her tubes tied at an early age. Then she can keep up with the guys with an uninterrupted career and then, when she's 30, she'll be paying her own way on ski weekends too.

8   The reality of feminism is a lot of frenzied and overworked women dropping kids off at day-care centers. If the child is sick, they just send along some children's Tylenol and then rush off to underpaid jobs that they don't even like. Two of my working-mother friends told me they were mopping floors and folding laundry after midnight last week. They live on five hours of sleep, and it shows in their faces. And they've got husbands! I'm not advocating that women retrogress to the brainless housewives of the '50s who spent afternoons baking macaroni sculptures and keeping Betty Crocker files. Post–World War II women were the first to be left with a lot of free time, and

they weren't too creative in filling it. Perhaps feminism was a reaction to that Brainless Betty, and in that respect, feminism has served a purpose.

9   Women should get educations so they can be brainy in the way they raise their children. Women can start small businesses, do consulting, write freelance out of the home. But women don't belong in 12-hour-a-day executive office positions, and I can't figure out today what ever made us think we would want to be there in the first place. As long as that biology is there, women can't compete equally with men. A ratio cannot be made using disproportionate parts. Women and men are not equal, we're different. The economy might even improve if women came home, opening up jobs for unemployed men, who could then support a wife and children, the way it was, pre-feminism.

10   Sometimes on Saturday nights I'll get dressed up and go out club-hopping or to the theater, but the sight of all those other women my age, dressed a little too young, made up to hide encroaching wrinkles, looking hopefully into the crowds, usually depresses me. I end up coming home, to spend my Saturday night with my daughter asleep in her room nearby. At least the NBC Saturday-night lineup is geared demographically to women at home alone.

Topical Considerations

1. Summarize Ebeling's argument. Which of her points influenced you most and why? Which influenced you least and why?
2. How do you think Quindlen would respond to Ebeling's claim that feminism has failed? How do you respond to that claim?
3. How does Ebeling portray men in this essay? Do you think that the picture she paints of men is a fair one? Does it strengthen her argument or weaken it?
4. How does Ebeling use the fact that "like it or not, women have babies" to further argue that feminism has failed women? Do you agree with her assertion? Why or why not?
5. Ebeling states: "Women don't belong in 12-hour-a-day executive office positions" (paragraph 9). How do you feel about this statement? Who does it exclude from her argument?
6. How do you think a househusband would respond to Ebeling's essay?

Rhetorical Considerations

1. Describe the effect of the first paragraph. Does it clue the reader into what the essay will be arguing? How?
2. In paragraph 5, Ebeling boils feminism down to one sentence: "Woman, you don't need a man." Do you think that statement is an accurate (or fair) reduction of feminism? How useful is it in supporting Ebeling's argument?

3. What is the effect of the boldface subheading "Biological thing" in paragraph 7? What does this tell you about this aspect of Ebeling's argument?
4. Does the ending of the essay work to conclude Ebeling's argument forcibly? Why or why not?
5. Throughout the essay, Ebeling uses short, terse sentences. ("He drives a BMW. I ride buses.") How effective is this device for you as a reader?

Writing Assignments

1. From your own experience, write an essay that explains if you think feminism has succeeded or failed. Use specific examples from your life (or from the lives of people you know) to support your argument.
2. Imagine a debate between Ebeling and Quindlen (or between Ebeling and another feminist who believes that the cause has succeeded). As you write the dialogue, make sure that you give equal support to both sides of the argument.
3. Write a response to Ebeling's essay as if you were a female executive who is also a mother. How might you refute Ebeling's argument? Or would you agree with it?

CHAPTER 10

RACE AND ETHNICITY

The United States is a union predicated on shared moral values, political and economic self-interest, and a common language. But least we forget, America is also a nation of immigrants—people of different races, ethnic identities, religions, and languages. It is a nation whose motto *e pluribus unum* ("one out of many") bespeaks the pride in its multicultural heritage. In this chapter, we explore some of the issues—the prejudice, the social conflicts, the search for roots—faced by people whose identity is torn between two cultures.

Although America has been a multi-ethnic and multiracial society since its founding, it was not until the last three decades that different groups of Americans began to reassert their ethnic and racial identity. In their search for roots, African Americans and Native Americans, Latinos and Latvians alike have looked with pride to their heritage to distinguish themselves from the mainstream. But not all people have rushed to proclaim their ethnic and religious heritage. In our opening essay, "Cultural Baggage," Barbara Ehrenreich explains that coming from a long line of white, Anglo-Irish atheists, she felt culturally nondistinct—like a woman from "a race of none." But instead of feeling deprived or un-American, she learned to enjoy her cultural nullity. In fact, she argues that the world would be a better place if people were not caught up in the different ethnic and religious rituals of their heritage.

By contrast, the next four essays collectively argue that the world would be a better place if people were more tolerant of those who are culturally different. For these authors, tolerance is the first step to eliminating the most ugly signs of prejudice—ethnic and racial stereotypes.

By definition, stereotypes are erroneous assumptions about individuals based on their race, ethnic descent, social class, gender and physical appearance. Forged by ignorance and fear, stereotypes damningly reduce whole groups of people to certain ascribed characteristics so as to justify their presumed faults. Jews are materialistic, blacks are lazy, Latinos are hot-tempered, Asians are mysterious, Native Americans are stoic, the French are oversexed, the Irish are drunks, Middle Easterners are terrorists. Not only are such caricatures foolishly simplistic impositions on others, they restrict and distort our expectations of the victims. Worse still, the victims sometimes adopt the same denigrating self-images so as to identify with the definitions. In "Cultural Etiquette: A Guide," Amoja Three Rivers attempts to shed some light—and levity—on the serious task of dispelling racial myths and stereotypes. Arguing that "race is an arbitrary and meaningless concept," she offers readers guidelines for relating to people who are different from them. In the past Asian/Pacific people have suffered from a variety of racist stereotypes which are rejected by most people today. However, according to Alexandra Tantranon-Saur, author of "What's Behind the 'Asian Mask?'" some seemingly innocuous assumptions denigrate Asian Americans depicting them as compliant rather than capable, obsequious rather than gracious. Even more crippling are the stereotypical expectations thrust on African Americans. Leonce Gaiter, an accomplished black professional raised in a middle-class home, often must confront the befuddled reaction of colleagues and associates who assume he couldn't really be black if he doesn't talk jive, have a prison record, and play basketball. And in "Presumed Guilty," Anton Shammas discusses the plight of a Middle Easterner detained for questioning in the Oklahoma City bombing of 1995, his detainment based largely on his Mid-Eastern appearance as opposed to hard evidence.

The next three essays, clustered under the topic of "Equal Opportunity," focus on our nation's largest minority. No other people are more painfully familiar with the sting of racial prejudice than African Americans. Although slavery and legalized oppression have receded into our nation's past, and although the Civil Rights movement of the 1960s put an end to state-enforced repression and institutional discrimination, many blacks still face daily reminders of the racism embedded in our society. They point to black-white income gaps, poor housing, inferior inner-city schools, and higher infant-mortality rates.

Of late, however, there has been a growing black debate on racism. When is it real, and when is it just an excuse for blacks' failure to solve their own problems? Some of the arguments have forced black Americans to re-examine what it means to be black in America today. In "Harping on Racism," Roger Wilkins answers the claim that activists spend too much time blaming the plight of African Americans on racism. As he explains, he "harps" on the subject because to solve a problem we first must admit it exists.

One of the most positive efforts to reverse 200 years of racism is affirmative action. In theory, such policies correct the past while empowering blacks; in practice, affirmative action has caused serious contention among blacks and cries of reverse discrimination by whites. The next two essays reflect the debate over affirmative action. In "Affirmative Action: The Price of Preference," black conservative Shelby Steele argues that after 20 years of implementation, affirmative action has produced more bad than good, especially for blacks. Black columnist Charles G. Adams could not disagree more. In "It's Past Time to Speak Out," Adams argues that affirmative action is a corrective device intended to reverse long-standing customs and procedures of unjust racial exclusion.

For our two "Oppositions" pieces we turn to American immigration policy. At the heart of this controversy is the impact that the 8.5 million people expected to immigrate to the United States in the 1990s will have on the culture, economy, and language of the nation. In "A Statue With Limitations," demographer B. Meredith Burke calls for limits on population growth and immigration in order to prevent depletion of the resources of our fastest-growing states. An opposing view is communicated by Renee Loth whose "The Big New Mix" argues that the flood of outsiders is good for the country because they stimulate the economy, improve living conditions, and reverse the current "birth dearth."

IDENTITY AND STEREOTYPES

Cultural Baggage
Barbara Ehrenreich

A society celebrating diversity encourages people to research their ethnic and racial roots and to revive family and cultural traditions practiced so ardently in the past. But when Barbara Ehrenreich is asked by a friend about her ethnic background, Ehrenreich is surprised to hear herself reply, "None." In her life ethnicity, religion, and family traditions had been eclipsed by "skepticism, curiosity and wide-eyed ecumenical tolerance"—attributes that she feels may serve humanity well. This piece, which first appeared in the *New York Times Sunday Magazine* in April 1992, argues that going on to find new identities may be more important than resurrecting the old.

Barbara Ehrenreich is a columnist for *Time* magazine and author of *The Worst Years of Our Lives: Irreverent Notes from a Decade of Greed* (1990) and the novel, *Kipper's Game* (1993).

BEFORE YOU READ

Do you have friends or family members who seem unaware or indifferent to their ethnic or religious identity? Does this lack of interest make them more or less interesting? More or less ethical? More or less certain of who they are?

AS YOU READ

As you read, think about how a person with a strong ethnic or religious identity might respond to this essay. Describe what such a person's reaction might be.

1 An acquaintance was telling me about the joys of rediscovering her ethnic and religious heritage. "I know exactly what my ancestors were doing 2,000 years ago," she said, eyes gleaming with enthusiasm, "and *I can do the same things*

now." Then she leaned forward and inquired politely, "And what is your ethnic background, if I may ask?"

2   "None," I said, that being the first word in line to get out of my mouth.
Well, not "none," I backtracked. Scottish, English, Irish—that was something, I
supposed. Too much Irish to qualify as a WASP; too much of the hated English
to warrant a "Kiss Me, I'm Irish" button; plus there are a number of dead ends
in the family tree due to adoptions, missing records, failing memories and the
like. I was blushing by this time. Did "none" mean I was rejecting my heritage
out of Anglo-Celtic self-hate? Or was I revealing a hidden ethnic chauvinism
in which the Britannically derived serve as a kind of neutral standard compared with the ethnic "others"?

3   Throughout the 60's and 70's, I watched one group after another—
African Americans, Latinos, Native Americans—stand up and proudly reclaim
their roots while I just sank back ever deeper into my seat. All this excitement
over ethnicity stemmed, I uneasily sensed, from a past in which *their* ancestors
had been trampled upon by *my* ancestors, or at least by people who looked
very much like them. In addition, it had begun to seem almost un-American
not to have some sort of hyphen at hand, linking one to more venerable times
and locales.

4   But the truth is, I was raised with none. We'd eaten ethnic foods in my
childhood home, but these were all borrowed, like the pasties, or Cornish
meat pies, my father had picked up from his fellow miners in Butte, Mont. If
my mother had one rule, it was militant ecumenism in all matters of food and
experience. "Try new things," she would say, meaning anything from sweet-
breads to clams, with an emphasis on the "new."

5   As a child, I briefly nourished a craving for tradition and roots. I immersed myself in the works of Sir Walter Scott. I pretended to believe that the
bagpipe was a musical instrument. I was fascinated to learn from a grandmother that we were descended from certain Highland clans and longed for a
pleated skirt in one of their distinctive tartans.

6   But in "Ivanhoe," it was the dark-eyed "Jewess" Rebecca I identified
with, not the flaxen-haired bimbo Rowena. As for clans: Why not call them
"tribes," those bands of half-clad peasants and warriors whose idea of cuisine
was stuffed sheep gut washed down with whisky? And then there was the sting
of Disraeli's remark—which I came across in my early teens—to the effect that
his ancestors had been leading orderly, literate lives when my ancestors were
still rampaging through the Highlands daubing themselves with blue paint.

7   Motherhood put the screws on me, ethnicitywise. I had hoped that by
marrying a man of Eastern European-Jewish ancestry I would acquire for my
descendants the ethnic genes that my own forebears so sadly lacked. At one
point, I even subjected the children to a seder of my own design, including a
little talk about the flight from Egypt and its relevance to modern social issues.
But the kids insisted on buttering their matzohs and snickering through my
talk. "Give me a break, Mom," the older one said. "You don't even believe in
God."

8   After the tiny pagans had been put to bed, I sat down to brood over Elijah's wine. What had I been thinking? The kids knew that their Jewish grandparents were secular folks who didn't hold seders themselves. And if ethnicity eluded me, how could I expect it to take root in my children, who are not only Scottish-English-Irish, but Hungarian-Polish-Russian to boot?

9   But, then, on the fumes of Manischewitz, a great insight took form in my mind. It was true, as the kids said, that I didn't "believe in God." But this could be taken as something very different from an accusation—a reminder of a genuine heritage. My parents had not believed in God either, nor had my grandparents or any other progenitors going back to the great-great level. They had become disillusioned with Christianity generations ago—just as, on the in-law side, my children's other ancestors had shaken off their Orthodox Judaism. This insight did not exactly furnish me with an "identity," but it was at least something to work with: we are the kind of people, I realized—whatever our distant ancestors' religions—who do *not* believe, who do not carry on traditions, who do not do things just because someone has done them before.

10   The epiphany went on: I recalled that my mother never introduced a procedure for cooking or cleaning by telling me, "Grandma did it this way." What did Grandma know, living in the days before vacuum cleaners and disposable toilet mops? In my parents' general view, new things were better than old, and the very fact that some ritual had been performed in the past was a good reason for abandoning it now. Because what was the past, as our forebears knew it? Nothing but poverty, superstition and grief. "Think for yourself," Dad used to say. "Always ask why."

11   In fact, this may have been the ideal cultural heritage for my particular ethnic strain—bounced as it was from the Highlands of Scotland across the sea, out to the Rockies, down into the mines and finally spewed out into high-tech, suburban America. What better philosophy, for a race of migrants, than "Think for yourself"? What better maxim, for a people whose whole world was rudely inverted every 30 years or so, than "Try new things"?

12   The more tradition-minded, the newly enthusiastic celebrants of Purim and Kwanzaa and Solstice, may see little point to survival if the survivors carry no cultural freight—religion, for example, or ethnic tradition. To which I would say that skepticism, curiosity and wide-eyed ecumenical tolerance are also worthy elements of the human tradition and are at least as old as such notions as "Serbian" or "Croatian," "Scottish" or "Jewish." I make no claims for my personal line of progenitors except that they remained loyal to the values that may have induced all of our ancestors, long, long ago, to climb down from the trees and make their way into the open plains.

13   A few weeks ago, I cleared my throat and asked the children, now mostly grown and fearsomely smart, whether they felt any stirrings of ethnic or religious identity, etc., which might have been, ahem, insufficiently nourished at home. "None," they said, adding firmly, "and the world would be a better place if nobody else did, either." My chest swelled with pride, as would my mother's, to know that the race of "none" marches on.

Topical Considerations

1. How does the author attempt to be "ethnic" by embracing her husband's Jewish heritage? What are the consequences of this attempt? Might her attitude toward Judaism be offensive to people of that culture?
2. What does Ehrenreich mean by the term *ethnic chauvinism* in the question posed in paragraph 2: "Or was I revealing a hidden ethnic chauvinism in which the Britannically derived serve as a kind of neutral standard compared with the ethnic 'others'"?
3. How has "Cultural Baggage" influenced your thinking about your own cultural heritage? Is your thinking more or less like Ehrenreich's?
4. What is Ehrenreich's attitude toward people who celebrate their cultural identity? Cite examples from the text.
5. Briefly summarize Ehrenreich's argument. How does her ultimate endorsement of the "race of none" shape her argument?

Rhetorical Considerations

1. How does the essay's title, "Cultural Baggage," foreshadow the tenor of the essay? Do you feel that the traditions of your heritage are like "baggage" or a burden?
2. Where in the essay can you find examples that support the premise that Ehrenreich is addressing an audience like herself—people of white, Anglo descent? If white Anglos are her intended audience, has she constructed an *ad populum* argument?
3. Consider paragraphs 3, 11, and 12. Using evidence from these paragraphs, show how Ehrenreich deduces the belief that her "race of none" is more progressive than other cultures.

Writing Assignments

1. Write a paper in which you support or refute the following statement: "In present day American society, only a white person can shed his or her cultural baggage." Use examples from Ehrenreich and your own personal experiences to support your position.
2. Ehrenreich writes that "in 'Ivanhoe' it was the dark-eyed 'Jewess' Rebecca I identified with, not the flaxen-haired bimbo Rowena" (paragraph 6). Write a paper that analyzes your childhood heroes. Did they always physically resemble you? If not, what qualities attracted you to them? How has your view of these heroes changed with the rise of cultural and multicultural awareness?

3. Consider the essay's title, "Cultural Baggage." Interview one or more persons who have strong roots in a foreign culture. Do these people feel that their native culture is "baggage" to be shed as they acclimate to American life?

Cultural Etiquette: A Guide
Amoja Three Rivers

Proclaiming that "no one living in Western society is exempt from the influences of racism, racial stereotypes, race and cultural prejudices, and anti-Semitism," Amoja Three Rivers exposes the racist and ethnocentric terms in which we often think. In a piece that combines chiding lecture, stern reprimand, and spirited reminders, Three Rivers challenges the reader to reexamine complacently held cultural notions. Ironically "etiquette" is put aside so that we might treat one another more kindly.

Amoja Three Rivers is a cofounder of the Accessible African Heritage Project. This piece originally appeared in *Ms.* in 1991.

BEFORE YOU READ

What would be your reaction if someone were to claim that you made a racist, sexist, or otherwise insensitive remark? Are you defensive? apologetic? irritated? grateful? Can you explain your reaction?

AS YOU READ

Three Rivers concludes her piece asking, "Does reading this guide make you uncomfortable?" Answer her question candidly and explain your answer. Do you feel attacked by the author? How would you describe her persona? How does this persona add to or detract from the author's persuasiveness?

1   Cultural Etiquette is intended for people of all "races," nationalities, and creeds, not necessarily just "white" people, because no one living in Western society is exempt from the influences of racism, racial stereotypes, race and cultural prejudices, and anti-Semitism. I include anti-Semitism in the discussion of racism because it is simply another manifestation of cultural and racial bigotry.

2   All people are people. It is ethnocentric to use a generic term such as "people" to refer only to white people and then racially label everyone else. This creates and reinforces the assumption that whites are the norm, the real people, and that all others are aberrations.

3   "Exotic," when applied to human beings, is ethnocentric and racist.

4   While it is true that most citizens of the U.S.A. are white, at least four fifths of the world's population consists of people of color. Therefore, it is sta-

tistically incorrect as well as ethnocentric to refer to us as minorities. The term "minority" is used to reinforce the idea of people of color as "other."

5   A cult is a particular system of religious worship. If the religious practices of the Yorubas constitute a cult, then so do those of the Methodists, Catholics, Episcopalians, and so forth.

6   A large radio/tape player is a boom-box, or a stereo or a box or a large metallic ham sandwich with speakers. It is not a "ghetto blaster."

7   Everybody can blush. Everybody can bruise. Everybody can tan and get sunburned. Everybody.

8   Judaism is no more patriarchal than any other patriarchal religion.

9   Koreans are not taking over. Neither are Jews. Neither are the Japanese. Neither are the West Indians. These are myths put out and maintained by the ones who really have.

10   All hair is "good" hair. Dreadlocks, locks, dreads, natty dreads, et cetera, is an ancient traditional way that African people sometimes wear their hair. It is not braided, it is "locked." Locking is the natural tendency of African hair to knit and bond to itself. It locks by itself, we don't have to do anything to it to make it lock. It is permanent; once locked, it cannot come undone. It gets washed just as regularly as anyone else's hair. No, you may not touch it, don't ask.

11   One of the most effective and insidious aspects of racism is cultural genocide. Not only have African Americans been cut off from our African tribal roots, but because of generations of whites pitting African against Indian, and Indian against African, we have been cut off from our Native American roots as well. Consequently, most African Native Americans no longer have tribal affiliations, or know for certain what people they are from.

12   Columbus didn't discover diddly-squat.

13   Slavery is not a condition unique to African people. In fact, the word "slave" comes from the Slav people of Eastern Europe. Because so many Slavs were enslaved by other people (including Africans), their very name came to be synonymous with the condition.

14   Native Americans were also enslaved by Europeans. Because it is almost impossible to successfully enslave large numbers of people in their own land, most enslaved Native Americans from the continental U.S. were shipped to Bermuda, and the West Indies, where many inter-married with the Africans.

15   People do not have a hard time because of their race or cultural background. No one is attacked, abused, oppressed, pogromed, or enslaved because of their race, creed, or cultural background. People are attacked, abused, oppressed, pogromed, or enslaved because of racism and anti-Semitism. There is a subtle but important difference in the focus here. The first implies some inherent fault or shortcoming within the oppressed person or group. The second redirects the responsibility back to the real source of the problem.

16   Asians are not "mysterious," "fatalistic," or "inscrutable."

17   Native Americans are not stoic, mystical, or vanishing.

18   Latin people are not more hot-tempered, hot-blooded, or emotional than anyone else. We do not have flashing eyes, teeth, or daggers. We are lovers pretty much like other people. Very few of us deal with any kind of drugs.

19   Middle Easterners are not fanatics, terrorists, or all oil-rich.

20   Jewish people are not particularly rich, clannish, or expert in money matters.

21   Not all African Americans are poor, athletic, or ghetto-dwellers.

22   Most Asians in the U.S. are not scientists, mathematicians, geniuses, or wealthy.

23   Southerners are no less intelligent than anybody else.

24   It is not a compliment to tell someone: "I don't think of you as Jewish/Black/Asian/Latina/Middle Eastern/Native American." Or "I think of you as white."

25   Do not use a Jewish person or person of color to hear your confession of past racist transgressions. If you have offended a particular person, then apologize directly to that person.

26   Also don't assume that Jews and people of color necessarily want to hear about how prejudiced your Uncle Fred is, no matter how terrible you think he is.

27   If you are white and/or gentile, do not assume that the next Jewish person or person of color you see will feel like discussing this guide with you. Sometimes we get tired of teaching this subject.

28   If you are white, don't brag to a person of color about your overseas trip to our homeland. Especially when we cannot afford such a trip. Similarly, don't assume that we are overjoyed to see the expensive artifacts you bought.

29   Words like "gestapo," "concentration camp" and "Hitler" are only appropriate when used in reference to the Holocaust.

30   "Full-blood," "half-breed," "quarter-blood." Any inference that a person's "race" depends on blood is racist. Natives are singled out for this form of bigotry and are denied rights on that basis.

31   "Scalping": a custom also practiced by the French, the Dutch, and the English.

32   Do you have friends or acquaintances who are terrific except they're really racist? If you quietly accept that part of them, you are giving their racism tacit approval.

33   As an exercise, pretend you are from another planet and you want an example of a typical human being for your photo album. Having never heard of racism, you'd probably pick someone who represents the majority of the people on the planet—an Asian person.

34   How many is too many? We have heard well-meaning liberals say things like "This event is too white. We need more people of color." Well, how many do you need? Fifty? A hundred? Just what is your standard for personal racial comfort?

35   People of color and Jewish people have been so all their lives. Further, if we have been raised in a place where white gentiles predominate, then we have been subjected to racism/anti-Semitism all our lives. We are therefore experts on our own lives and conditions. If you do not understand or believe or agree with what someone is saying about their own oppression, do not automatically assume that they are wrong or paranoid or oversensitive.

36   It is not "racism in reverse" or "segregation" for Jews or people of color to come together in affinity groups for mutual support. Sometimes we need some time and space apart from the dominant group just to relax and be ourselves. If people coming together for group support makes you feel excluded, perhaps there's something missing in your own life or cultural connections.

37   The various cultures of people of color often seem very attractive to white people. (Yes, we are wonderful, we can't deny it.) But white people should not make a playground out of other people's cultures. We are not quaint. We are not exotic. We are not cool.

38   Don't forget that every white person alive today is also descended from tribal peoples. If you are white, don't neglect your own ancient traditions. They are as valid as anybody else's, and the ways of your own ancestors need to be honored and remembered.

39   "Race" is an arbitrary and meaningless concept. Races among humans don't exist. If there ever was any such thing as race, there has been so much constant crisscrossing of genes for the last 500,000 years that it would have lost all meaning anyway. There are no real divisions between us, only a continuum of variations that constantly change, as we come together and separate according to the movement of human populations.

40   Anyone who functions in what is referred to as the "civilized" world is a carrier of the disease of racism.

41   Does reading this guide make you uncomfortable? Angry? Confused? Are you taking it personally? Well, not to fret. Racism has created a big horrible mess, and racial healing can sometimes be painful. Just remember that Jews and people of color do not want or need anybody's guilt. We just want people to accept responsibility when it is appropriate, and actively work for change.

Topical Considerations

1. Three Rivers discusses several different cultures in her essay. Which cultural insensitivities mentioned by Three Rivers are new to you? Will you follow Three Rivers' advice regarding these? Do you disagree with any of her rules?
2. In the final paragraph Three Rivers asks, "Does reading this guide make you uncomfortable?" What parts of the essay could make a reader uncomfortable, and why? Did you feel any discomfort?

3. Paragraph 15 begins, "People do not have a hard time because of their race or cultural background." Does the reference to "People" here mean all people? If not, who?
4. In this discussion of racial etiquette is there room for the physically challenged? Considering the injustices Three Rivers cites, how would she include this group in her guide?

Rhetorical Considerations

1. Three Rivers writes in the first person plural. Who is the "we" in this essay? Does Three Rivers ever abandon this strategy? Do you feel the author can speak credibly for all the cultures implied in her use of "we"?
2. Three Rivers claims her guide "is intended for people of all 'races,' nationalities, and creeds, not necessarily just 'white' people" (paragraph 1). Do you believe her guide is for everyone, or does she have a specific audience in mind? If so, for whom is the guide intended?
3. Consider how Three Rivers addresses her audience in paragraphs 30–34. Describe what kind of person you think Three Rivers is. Explain how her style has led you to your conclusion.
4. Three Rivers easily moves between colloquial ("Columbus didn't discover diddly-squat.") and academic (". . . it is statistically incorrect as well as ethnocentric . . .") use of language. What is her purpose in doing this? Is it an effective strategy?
5. Why do you think Three Rivers has called her essay "Cultural Etiquette"? Why might she have used this format to discuss her subject?
6. Do you think Three Rivers has constructed an *ad populum* argument? If so, what are her assumptions regarding her audience?

Writing Assignments

1. Consider these statements: "Race is an arbitrary and meaningless concept. Races among humans don't exist." Drawing evidence from this essay, others in the chapter, and your own experience, write an essay in which you agree or disagree with these statements.
2. Write your own version of cultural etiquette. Try to dispel stereotypes that have affected you or your thinking.
3. Three Rivers says "Columbus didn't discover diddly-squat." Considering the controversy surrounding the 500th anniversary of the "discovery" of America, write a paper explaining your opinion of Columbus's impact on the early peoples of the Americas. Consult your library for recent reassessments of Columbus's "discovery" and its consequences.
4. Do you agree that in our culture "the assumption [is] that whites are the norm, the real people, and that all others are aberrations." Write a paper in

which you explore your feelings about this assumption, citing specific evidence as support. You might, for instance, consider current literature, advertising, music, or movies.

What's Behind the "Asian Mask"?
Alexandra Tantranon-Saur

The term *yellow peril*, reminiscent of the detention centers endured by thousands of Japanese during World War II, was clearly hurtful in intent and damning in effect. But since that time, other seemingly innocuous terms such as *model minority* have emerged to label Asian/Pacific Americans. In this essay, Tantranon-Saur argues that traits of passivity and compliance, implicit in terms like *model minority*, are also damaging.

Alexandra Tantranon-Saur is a computer consultant and a builder of musical instruments. This article originally appeared in the journal *Our Asian Inheritance* in 1986.

BEFORE YOU READ

Assuming you are aquainted with people from a variety of cultural backgrounds, have language patterns, communication cues, or communication styles ever made it difficult for you to converse with a member of that group? Did they ever lead to a misunderstanding? If so, how?

AS YOU READ

After reading Tantranon-Saur's argument, are you convinced that Asian/Pacific Americans are stereotyped in a seemingly innocuous way? If so, in what way is the stereotyping a handicap?

1   First the "yellow peril," now the "model minority"—most of you know enough to scoff at these racist stereotypes. Some are beginning to know the violence and sorrow visited upon the Asian and Pacific peoples in this country by ordinary white people blinded by stereotypes, and mourn and rage with us as we demand justice.

2   But there is yet another layer to penetrate, a layer of seemingly innocuous assumptions, that clouds your vision of us, and confuses your attempt to find, work with, experience us. You see us wearing masks; we see you imagining we should prefer your cultures to ours! Let's take a look at this "Asian mask."

3   *Asian/Pacific people are quiet.* Asian/Pacific people are not quiet! Certainly in this area[1] most of us have had a chance to visit one Chinatown or another; is it quiet? Lots of Chinese, especially the older immigrants, walking on

[1] The San Francisco Bay area.

the streets having loud and musical conversations with each other. Chinese working-class women waiting tables and shouting to each other and the cooks. Pushing their carts of dim sum through the aisles, tempting the weekend brunch crowd with *"Ha gow! Shui mei! Cha-shu bow!"*[2] For the Chinese, as for many other peoples, the issue of speaking quietly versus loudly is a class issue.

4   And as for the volume of spoken words—no one can tell me Asian/Pacific people don't say much. My mother, sister and I outtalk my non-Asian father hands down. My Asian/Pacific friends can outtalk me. Go into the Thai Buddhist temple during service. The monks have to chant over the microphone; everyone else is talking. In language class, the children talk and the teachers talk louder.

5   Don't get me wrong; I'm sure there are some quiet Asian/Pacific people. I've heard there are. (Even I occasionally like to be quiet.) I just don't know any.

6   So why does it appear to non-Asian/Pacific people (and in fact to many Asian/Pacific Americans as well) that we are quiet? A closer look at some common Asian/Pacific American conversational habits may surprise you.

7   The *pause*. I learned the proper way to speak was to leave pauses in between thoughts and even sentences. We sculpt the flow of our words with silences; spaces for thinking, reflecting, relaxing. Get together with people who talk like this, hold your tongue, and you'll see how comfortably a conversation goes. You can think with pauses! You can see that, from a purely mechanical point of view, most people who speak without pauses will be constantly interrupting us; and while we wait for the longer pause which signals that the speaker has finished a thought and that the next speaker may start, the non-Asian/Pacific people will talk on and on, marveling that they have found such a good listener who seems to have nothing to say.

8   But this is more than just a mechanical speech pattern. I was taught, and I observe this in other Asian/Pacific Americans, to be constantly aware of the attention level of my listener, in fact to monitor and nurture it. The *pause* is part of this. If someone else immediately grabs the moment of silence, then that person must not have been listening with much attention, right? In fact, they may have been waiting desperately to get a chance to unload. So of course they should get the attention if they're that desperate.

9   The pause is also often lengthened into the *question pause*. That is: from time to time it is good to stop in the middle and see if a listener asks, "What else? Say more!" This is a useful check to see if they are listening and interested. If they don't ask, why continue to talk?

10   In addition to monitoring the attention level in our listener, the *start-off question* is the most clear example of actively building our listener's attention level. You all know this one. I want to tell you what I think about the World Bank (we have been talking about canoeing), so I ask you what *you* think

---

2 Different types of Chinese hors d'oeuvres. (Ed.)

about the World Bank. Why don't I just start out on the World Bank? Well, why should I assume that you'll be able to listen to that? First I check, and I listen to you, and by the time you have gotten whatever you need to off your chest, you will probably realize that you want to know what *I* think about the World Bank.

11   You may notice another attention-maintaining technique we use in conversations. It is the frequent *sorry's* you hear. If you find this irritating, it's no wonder—you probably think we are apologizing! Many people were apparently raised to think that "I'm sorry" is an admission of guilt or statement of contriteness or self-denigration. I'm sorry, it's not true. It simply means, "no offense intended by what I have to say to you." It means, "listen to me knowing that you are not being personally attacked"; it means, "listen attentively with an open mind."

12   You will notice that my behavior is based on the assumption that I pay better attention to others than do non-Asian/Pacific people. Can this be true? In the sense of having the habit of thinking about others in uncomfortable situations, it is true. How can this happen, that we pay better attention?

13   Part of this is a survival technique, not unique to Asian/Pacific Americans: the experience of an oppressed people is that we have to pay more attention to the feelings of our oppressors than vice versa. Everyone knows this one—how much time do we spend talking about the boss? We know the boss's habits, preferences, moods, irrationalities—we have to! But the boss is unlikely to know ours. The same thing happens between people of color and white people.

14   But the primary reason that Asian/Pacific people pay more attention to others has to do with the principles of cooperation and exchange, which form the basis of our societies and cultures. Consider typical Asian/Pacific group behavior:

15   *Asian/Pacific people have a pattern of going last ("invisibility").* If you could be a fly on my shoulder in an Asian/Pacific group, you would notice the conversational customs I mentioned above. If you look also at how the group attention flows from subject to subject, you would see that our number one priority is to take care of the group as a whole. You will notice us attending to business matters first. We will rarely risk the integrity of the group by presenting "personal" needs or demands before all the group needs are taken care of. This cooperative behavior functions quite well in the Asian/Pacific context.

16   Let me tell you a story illustrating what often happens in the mixed context. In a group dealing with issues of internalized racism, we first separated into our "racial" groups (Asian/Pacific, African, European, Latino/a[3, 4]) with a list of questions to answer and two lists to make and present to the larger group. The schedule allowed forty-five minutes total for presentations. Back in

---

[3]We unfortunately had no Native American group.

[4]These terms are not inclusive or descriptive enough. African Americans, Latinos, and Latinas are working hard to find names that define themselves accurately and respectfully.

the larger group, we Asians made our presentation first, and for the most part simply read through the two lists. That took about five minutes. The African group was next. They had decided not to do the assigned questions and lists, and instead made up four different lists, and presented them, each member of the group speaking several times. That took about twenty minutes. It was important for the African group to make the exercise useful by changing it as needed, and to express to the group the feelings that had come up for them. The schedule would just have to give. It was important to us to make sure things moved along as planned (i.e., time-wise and assignment-wise); instead of changing the assignment and schedule, we would wait with our feelings.

17   Both fine approaches. But again, simply the mechanics of mixing the two approaches mean that, without thoughtful intervention, our personal needs will come last, if at all. If others are unaware of our approach, and are carrying around "quiet/unemotional Asian" stereotypes of us, it may never occur to them to ask us, after everything else is done, "Well, what about *your* feelings?"

18   *Asian/Pacific people are "nice" and "polite."* These so-called Asian traits are praised by those who would like to keep us in line (teachers and employers, for example) and damned by our loving supporters who wish we would assimilate to Western-style bumper-car social interactions. I'm sorry, folks (see above), but I just have to complain about labeling being "nice" and "polite" as a problem. Why don't we use the right words? Gracious and hospitable. Cultural strengths which help us maintain the functioning and integrity of our families and groups. It sure never stopped us from making war on each other, exploiting each other, defending ourselves, or making revolution! The problem is not the behavior itself; it is the inability to choose another behavior when more appropriate. Obviously *that* has nothing to do with being Asian or Pacific, but rather with the experience of being immigrant minorities and being murdered in large numbers.

19   A variation on this is *Asian/Pacific people don't show their feelings.* Just like anyone else, we will laugh, cry, rage, shiver, and melt with love, as soon as we get enough loving attention. And, just like anyone else, our feelings are written all over our faces and bodies. Not seeing how we express it is part of the "they all look the same to me" syndrome. "But what if someone always has the same look on their face?" you say. Put on your thinking cap! What does it mean if your friend has the same feelings frozen into her face all the time she's around you? That's a rather eloquent message, I would say. "But she can't/won't tell me what she's feeling!" Nope, we sure do resist translating for you, don't we?

20   *Asian/Pacific people need assertiveness training.* It sure might look like that to someone accustomed to bumper-car social interactions. But welcome, ye weary bumper cars, to another cultural setting. Interactions between Asian/Pacific people are based to a great extent upon cooperation and exchange. Consider the group behavior—cooperation before individualism. Consider the *start-off question*—I give you attention first, then you offer it back

to me. Exchange is an important cultural principle. A non-Asian/Pacific American was counseling an Indian woman on a decision she needed to make. The conversation went something like this:

"After all, who's the most important?"

"My mother."

"Wrong!"

"My father?"

"No!"

"My sister?"

"*You* are!"

"? ? ?"

21   In the Indian social system, you make someone else the most important; watch out for their welfare, make decisions based on their needs. *You* get to be the most important for someone else; you have someone thinking about *your* needs. You give and you get, and it all evens out.

22   Several Japanese and Japanese American customs also illustrate this exchange principle. You don't split up the bill at a restaurant; you treat your friends, knowing that the next time they will treat you back. People pay attention to each other through *exchange of appreciations*. The woman who has spent three days preparing a feast offers it to her guests with "This isn't much, but please help yourselves." This is a signal for the guests to express their appreciation of her. They respond without rancor, because they, too, will get validated by the same mechanism. This extends to speaking about the children— "My daughter, she isn't very good at that." "But she's so good at these other things. You have a fine daughter!" Of course, sometimes it is important that you let someone know what you can do. In that case, your friend speaks for you. You never have to toot your own horn.

23   This is not to say that people don't get squished by these rules. The Japanese have a saying, "The nail that stands above the others will get hammered down to the same level." The historical lack of natural resources required cooperation and discouraged individualism, there having been no excess to cover the risks of individual mistakes. Now the Japanese are far beyond survival level, and the cultural survival techniques have not been discarded. But within the cultural context, the exchange principle functions well.

24   *What's a friend to do?* How can you put your new-found insights into action? These suggestions and exercises will not only bring you closer to us, but will also challenge you to act clearly and decisively in groups and one-to-one relationships.

1. Take responsibility for equal time-sharing, especially in mixed groups.
2. Notice and deal with the feelings that come up for you when there is silence in a conversation. There is often desperation behind the habit of filling every second with words. An appreciation of silence will allow you to awarely encourage us to break the silence when we choose.

3. Notice when Asian/Pacific people are not talking. Assume that when we are not talking, you are interrupting us. It will become obvious what to do. Also, don't assume we are finished when we stop talking. It may be a *thinking pause* or a *question pause*, instead of an *end-of-thought pause*. It is perfectly acceptable to simply ask if we are finished.

4. Don't try to assist us by taking the perspective that we should change our behavior, but rather that we need to have more choices. Remember the exchange principle. We need to deal with the hurt we experience when other people don't come through on the exchange, but instead simply take from us. Encourage us to have the highest expectations of our allies, to require your attention, in fact to demand it, instead of always giving if first and waiting for it to be offered back.

5. Talk and listen Asian/Pacific-style with us. Practice recognizing and using the various *pauses.*

6. Remember that our "politeness," "apologies," etcetera, are not necessarily forms of self-invalidation. In European American culture, these habits are often also considered to be signs of the weakness of the female. In this way, acting out sexism/internalized sexism by wishing us to give up our "weak" habits can turn out to be racist. Don't buy it! These are women's cultural strengths as well as Asian/Pacific cultural strengths.

7. Remember that, just like anyone else, we will express and release the full range of emotions as soon as we get enough caring attention. And, just like anyone else, our feelings are written all over our faces and bodies. We will do you the favor of not translating. Trust your thinking, make lots of mistakes, and pretty soon you'll be able not only to translate, but to think and see Asian/Pacific-style, too.

Topical Considerations

1. Tantranon-Saur spends much of her essay deflating American stereotypes of Asian/Pacific people. In paragraph 3 she writes, "Asian/Pacific people are not quiet!" Is the author replacing one stereotype about Asian/Pacific people with another?

2. Using specific references, answer Tantranon-Saur's question, "What's behind the 'Asian Mask'?"

3. In paragraph 20 the author refers to "bumper-car social interactions." Could she be accused of stereotyping non-Asians? Explain your answer.

4. Explain how the seemingly "innocuous" description *model minority* (paragraph 1) can be construed as derogatory. Come up with three other "seemingly innocuous" descriptions from other cultures and explain how they are not complimentary.

5. The author dismisses the description of Asian/Pacific people as "nice and polite" and asks, "Why don't we use the right words? Gracious and hos-

pitable" (paragraph 18). Explain why "nice and polite" are unacceptable to Tantranon-Saur.

Rhetorical Considerations

1. In the first paragraph, Tantranon-Saur sets up an effective "we" versus "you" strategy that is carried through the essay. Who are "we" and "you"? How does this strategy affect you, the reader?
2. How does the analogy to the boss-employee relationship in paragraph 13 help you to better understand what it means to be oppressed and/or misunderstood?
3. What comments in Tantranon-Saur's essay help to create a friendly and inviting tone? How does her strategy compare with that of Three Rivers? Which is more effective in persuading the audience? Explain using examples from each essay.
4. Tantranon-Saur concludes her essay with a list of "suggestions and exercises" (paragraph 24) toward cultural understanding and tolerance. What purpose does this list serve? How many of her suggestions can be applied to people of other cultural backgrounds?
5. How does Tantranon-Saur make an *ad populum* argument in her claim that "the issue of people speaking quietly versus loudly is a class issue" (paragraph 3)? Based on your experience, do you agree or disagree with this?

Writing Assignments

1. What other cultures wear masks in America? Using Tantranon-Saur's essay as a model, write a paper that removes the mask of another culture and explains how the mask came to be worn.
2. Tantranon-Saur says that the so-called weak habits like politeness and a tendency to apologize are "women's cultural strength as well as Asian/Pacific cultural strengths." Write a paper in which you discuss how women's "'weak' habits" could be their strength.

The Revolt of the Black Bourgeoisie
Leonce Gaiter

To create and shape one's identity is a supremely difficult task. Battling against negative stereotypes makes the job even more difficult. The author of this piece, a middle-class, educated, and professionally accomplished black man, constantly battled the expectation that a real black person was a "semiliterate, hoop-shooting former prison inmate." In this essay he examines why one segment of the black community, namely the underclass, has been selected to represent the whole. He exhorts African Americans not to "perpetuate the notion that African Americans are invariably doomed to the lower class."

Leonce Gaiter lives in Los Angeles and frequently writes about social issues. This article originally appeared in the *New York Times Magazine* in 1994.

BEFORE YOU READ

What forms of popular culture create and reinforce racial stereotypes most forcefully? Literature? Music? Visual Arts? Dance? Film? Television? Are negative stereotypes more likely to be embedded in one form of popular culture rather than another? Why might this be so?

AS YOU READ

Do you agree with Gaiter that one segment of black society, the underclass, characterizes the pervasive view of blacks? Or do you think views are more multidimensional?

1   At a television network where I once worked, one of my bosses told me I almost didn't get hired because his superior had "reservations" about me. The job had been offered under the network's Minority Advancement Program. I applied for the position because I knew I was exceptionally qualified. I would have applied for the position regardless of how it was advertised.

2   After my interview, the head of the department told my boss I wasn't really what he had in mind for a Minority Advancement Program job. To the department head, hiring a minority applicant meant hiring someone unqualified. He wanted to hire some semiliterate, hoop-shooting former prison inmate. That, in his view, was a "real" black person. That was someone worthy of the program.

3   I had previously been confronted by questions of black authenticity. At Harvard, where I graduated in 1980, a white classmate once said to me, "Oh, you're not really a black person." I asked her to explain. She could not. She had known few black people before college, but a lifetime of seeing black people depicted in the American media had taught her that real black people talked a certain way and were raised in certain places. In her world, black people did not attend elite colleges. They could not stand as her intellectual equals or superiors. Any African-American who shared her knowledge of Austen and Balzac—while having to explain to her who Douglass and DuBois

were—had to be *willed* away for her to salvage her sense of superiority as a white person. Hence the accusation that I was "not really black."

4   But worse than the white majority harboring a one-dimensional vision of blackness are the many blacks who embrace this stereotype as our true nature. At the junior high school I attended in the mostly white Washington suburb of Silver Spring, Md., a black girl once stopped me in the hallway and asked belligerently, "How come you talk so proper?" Astonished, I could only reply, "It's proper*ly*," and walk on. This girl was asking why I spoke without the so-called black accent pervasive in the lower socioeconomic strata of black society, where exposure to mainstream society is limited. This girl was asking, Why wasn't I impoverished and alienated? In her world view, a black male like me couldn't exist.

5   Within the past year, however, there have been signs that blacks are openly beginning to acknowledge the complex nature of our culture. Cornel West, a professor of religion and the director of Afro-American Studies at Princeton University, discusses the growing gulf between the black underclass and the rest of black society in his book "Race Matters"; black voices have finally been raised against the violence, misogyny and vulgarity marketed to black youth in the form of gangsta rap; Ellis Cose's book "The Rage of a Privileged Class," which concentrates on the problems of middle- and upper-income blacks, was excerpted as part of a Newsweek magazine cover story; Bill Cosby has become a vocal crusader against the insulting depiction of African-Americans in "hip-hop generation" TV shows.

6   Yes, there are the beginnings of a new candor about our culture, but the question remains, How did one segment of the African-American community come to represent the whole? First, black society itself placed emphasis on that lower caste. This made sense because historically that's where the vast majority of us were placed; it's where American society and its laws were designed to keep us. Yet although doors have opened to us over the past 20 years, it is still commonplace for black leaders to insist on our community's uniform need for social welfare programs, inner-city services, job skills training, etc. Through such calls, what has passed for a black political agenda has been furthered only superficially; while affirmative action measures have forced an otherwise unwilling majority to open some doors for the black middle class, social welfare and Great Society-style programs aimed at the black lower class have shown few positive results.

7   According to 1990 census figures, between 1970 and 1990 the number of black families with incomes under $15,000 rose from 34.6 percent of the black population to 37 percent, while the number of black families with incomes of $35,000 to $50,000 rose from 13.9 percent to 15 percent of the population, and those with incomes of more than $50,000 rose from 9.9 percent to 14.5 percent of the black population.

8   Another reason the myth of an all-encompassing black underclass survives—despite the higher number of upper-income black families—is that it

fits with a prevalent form of white liberalism, which is just as informed by racism as white conservatism. Since the early 70's, good guilt-liberal journalists and others warmed to the picture of black downtrodden masses in need of their help. Through the agency of good white people, blacks would rise. This image of African-Americans maintained the lifeline of white superiority that whites in this culture cling to, and therefore this image of blacks stuck. A strange tango was begun. Blacks seeking advancement opportunities allied themselves with whites eager to "help" them. However, those whites continued to see blacks as inferiors, victims, cases, and not as equals, individuals or, heaven forbid, competitors.

9   It was hammered into the African-American psyche by media-appointed black leaders and the white media that it was essential to our political progress to stay economically and socially deprived. To be recognized and recognize oneself as middle or upper class was to threaten the political progress of black people. That girl who asked why I spoke so "proper" was accusing me of political sins—of thwarting the progress of our race.

10   Despite progress toward a more balanced picture of black America, the image of black society as an underclass remains strong. Look at local news coverage of the trial of Damian Williams and Henry Watson, charged with beating the white truck driver Reginald Denny during the 1992 South-Central L.A. riots. The press showed us an African-print-wearing cadre of Williams and Watson supporters trailing Edi M. O. Faal, William's defense attorney, like a Greek chorus. This chorus made a point of standing in the camera's range. They presented themselves as the voice of South-Central L.A., the voice of the oppressed, the voice of the downtrodden, the voice of the city's black people.

11   To anyone watching TV coverage of the trial, all blacks agreed with Faal's contention that his clients were prosecuted so aggressively because they are black. Period. Reporters made no effort to show opposing black viewpoints. (In fact, the media portrait of the Los Angeles riot as blacks vs. whites and Koreans was a misrepresentation. According to the Rand Corporation, a research institute in Santa Monica, blacks made up 36 percent of those arrested during the riot; Latinos made up 51 percent). The black bourgeoisie and intelligentsia remained largely silent. We had too long believed that to express disagreement with the "official line" was to be a traitor.

12   TV networks and cable companies gain media raves for programs like "Laurel Avenue," an HBO melodrama about a working-class black family lauded for its realism, a real black family complete with drug dealers, drug users, gun toters and basketball players. It is akin to the media presenting "Valley of the Dolls" as a realistic portrayal of the ways of white women.

13   The Fox network offers a differing but equally misleading portrait of black Americans, with "Martin." While blue humor has long been a staple of black audiences, it was relegated to clubs and records for *mature* black audiences. It was not peddled to kids or to the masses.

14   Now the blue humor tradition is piped to principally white audiences. If TV was as black as it is white—if there was a fair share of black love stories,

black dramas, black detective heroes—these blue humor images would not be a problem. Right now, however, they stand as images to which whites can condescend.

15   Imagine being told by your peers, the records you hear, the programs you watch, the "leaders" you see on TV, classmates, prospective employers— imagine being told by virtually everyone that in order to be your true self you must be ignorant and poor, or at least seem so.

16   Blacks must now see to it that our children face no such burden. We must see to it that the white majority, along with vocal minorities within the black community (generally those with a self-serving political agenda), do not perpetuate the notion that African-Americans are invariably doomed to the underclass.

17   African-Americans are moving toward seeing ourselves—and demanding that others see us—as individuals, not as shards of a degraded monolith. The American ideal places primacy on the rights of the individual, yet historically African-Americans have been denied those rights. We blacks can effectively demand those rights, effectively demand justice only when each of us sees him or herself as an individual with the right to any of the opinions, idiosyncrasies and talents accorded any other American.

Topical Considerations

1. Analyze the story Gaiter tells in the first two paragraphs about his experience applying for a job in a television network. How does this anecdote introduce the major themes of Gaiter's argument? Explain how the hiring program's title—the Minority Advancement program—contributes to the expectations of Gaiter's department head.

2. Consider the other two anecdotes with which Gaiter opens his essay: the conversations with a white female student at Harvard (paragraph 3) and a black female student in junior high school (paragraph 4). Why does Gaiter describe his college experience first? How do the settings for each anecdote add to the persuasiveness of this portion of his argument? How do all three anecdotes raise what Gaiter calls "questions of black authenticity"? (paragraph 3).

3. Analyze Gaiter's attitude toward the "black political agenda" described in paragraph 6. Who precisely in the black community was that agenda designed to serve? How successful has it been, according to Gaiter?

4. How, according to Gaiter, have white liberals helped to sustain the "myth of all-encompassing black underclass" (paragraph 8)? What is Gaiter's personal opinion of these liberals; how can you tell? Explain how the perpetuation of this myth caused Gaiter and other middle-class blacks to be accused of "thwarting the progress of our race" (paragraph 9).

5. In paragraphs 10–15, Gaiter gives examples of the way television portrays African-Americans. Is there a particular logic behind Gaiter's move from

news coverage to the blue humor of "Martin"? What is the relationship Gaiter implies here between fact and fiction?

Rhetorical Considerations

1. Consider Gaiter's choice of the term "bourgeoisie" instead of "middle class" to define his constituency. What are the usual connotations of this word? How does Gaiter's use of this word indicate his political bias?

2. Consider the effect of Gaiter's second reference to the junior high school student's question about his speech, in paragraph 9. What purpose does it serve to allude to this incident a second time? In what ways does altering the context for the student's words contribute to Gaiter's point?

3. Notice that in paragraph 5, Gaiter shifts from anecdotes related to anonymous black and white women to a list of prominent black males. What is the effect of this shift? What does it tell us about the way Gaiter views these men and their influence on the future of black America?

4. Consider paragraph 7, a portion of the essay dedicated exclusively to the citation of statistics. What do these statistics show? How effective is their use at this particular moment in the essay? What is the significance of the fact that Gaiter allows the numbers to speak for themselves, with relatively little interpretation?

5. In paragraphs 16 and 17 Gaiter addresses black readers directly, using words like "we," "our children" and "ourselves." To what extent does this language represent a shift in Gaiter's sense of audience? What is the rhetorical effect of using this particular language at this point is his essay?

Writing Assignments

1. Write an essay analyzing Gaiter's political bias. Use your discussion to consider the value of openly acknowledging one's political assumptions in an argument.

2. Should soap operas and sitcoms be treated as serious registers of America's racial consciousness? Write an essay arguing for or against Gaiter's conclusions about the influence such programs have on public opinion, supporting your argument with secondary articles as well as primary observations.

3. To what extent do African Americans subscribe to the view of " 'real' black people" described in paragraph 3? Research this question with one or two other students. Based on personal observation, discussions with friends and acquaintances, and secondary research, analyze and critique Gaiter's assumption that most African Americans subscribe to the vision of " 'real' " black people described in paragraph 2. Try to locate opinions from social groups not represented by Gaiter, including low-income African Americans.

Write either one group or several individual essays on this topic, in either case supporting your argument with the group's research.

4. Write an essay exploring Gaiter's claim that most white liberals conceal racism beneath their dedication to achieving racial equality. Your research should include interviews with faculty and staff who have been hired to perform affirmative action or equal opportunity initiatives. Also, determine to what extent programs designed to "advance" minorities are doomed to failure because, by definition, they reinforce the stereotype of racial inferiority.

Presumed Guilty
Anton Shammas

In the aftermath of the Oklahoma City bombing, many news reports quickly targeted "Islamic militants" as prime suspects. This immediately qualified Ibrahim Ahmad as a potential terrorist. Because Mr. Ahmad is Middle Eastern in appearance, was wearing a jogging suit similar to that worn by a man leaving the bombing site, and was catching a plane to Amman, Jordan, he was detained and questioned for two days. As Anton Shammas writes, it was only the apprehension of Timothy McVeigh that liberated Mr. Ahmad. Clearly the racist stereotyping assumed that a Middle Eastern terrorist was responsible for the bombing.

Anton Shammas is a Palestinian novelist currently residing in Ann Arbor, Michigan.

BEFORE YOU READ

Recalling early news reports immediately following the 1995 Oklahoma City bombing, did you accept the then-prevalent theories that Middle Eastern terrorists were responsible for the bombing? Did you question these theories? Why or why not?

AS YOU READ

Clearly, author Anton Shammas identifies with Ibrahim Ahmad, the victim of a stereotype. Does this identification slant or cloud the perspective of Shammas? Does it make him a more or less reliable narrator?

1   Two weeks after the Oklahoma City bombing, Americans who are "Middle Eastern in appearance" still wait to be absolved of a crime they did not commit—a statement of some sort from their countrymen that would wipe out that

media-conjured collective composite sketch of the "Islamic militants" who at first were suspected of destroying the Federal Building.

2   But with so many victims still under the rubble and so many bodies haunting the American memory, and with so many urgent questions yet to be answered, why would white America turn its attention to the sense of injury felt by one of its ethnic minorities?

3   President Clinton said the day after the bombing that "this is not a question of anybody's country of origin" and "we should not stereotype anybody," but news organizations, including CNN, kept reporting for two days afterward that "several men of Middle Eastern origin" had driven away from the Federal Building shortly before the blast.

4   Oklahoma television stations added appropriate touches of color: the men were seen speeding away in a brown Chevrolet pickup truck with tinted windows. And the anchorman of Detroit's "Eyewitness News" said the night after the explosion that the Federal Building "had the Middle East written all over it." (This in a city that is home to 280,000 Arab-Americans.)

5   Timothy McVeigh, the Government's prime suspect, was already in custody on speeding charges. But all the attention was focused on Ibrahim Ahmad of Oklahoma City, a frequent flyer between stereotypes. He was wearing a jogging suit similar to one supposedly worn by a man leaving the site of the explosion, and since he was headed to Amman, Jordan, and he looked totally un-American, Mr. Ahmad was interrogated over the course of two days.

6   I left Jerusalem, and the Middle East, eight years ago and came to the University of Michigan at Ann Arbor thinking that I'd take time off from the danger zone and leave the unsettled dust of the Israeli-Palestinian conflict behind me for a while. Ann Arbor, a charming town, seemed the perfect refuge.

7   And now I learn that Michigan, which I'd thought was the soul of tranquillity, is home of the Michigan Militia, a name whose mere sound strums a kind of terrifying Lebanese tune inside my head; that Decker, Mich., may be more explosive than Armageddon and Jerusalem combined; that Mark ("Death to the New World Order!") Koernke, one of Mr. McVeigh's ideological mentors, and a short-wave prophet of doom, works as a custodian on the Ann Arbor campus, which I had foolishly thought was the most peaceful place on earth.

8   In short, I feel totally taken in. The media retracted their initial finger-pointing and—hoping for short memory spans—are now backing away from their early reports. It's no longer Middle Eastern but "foreign" terrorism that was at first suspected. One can't help but think, though, that all parties concerned would have been better off if it had been a Middle Eastern terrorist act. All the self-appointed experts on "Islamic militants" would have recycled their arguments, reminding Americans that Muslims are the world's only fanatic extremists and their true post-cold-war enemies.

9   Words have come home to roost: bloody, violent, terrifying words. Home has become an uncertain, uncharted, shifting ground. The black-and-

white world picture of "them" versus "us" has been blurred beyond recognition and buried under the rubble.

10   The Middle East will be greatly missed.

Topical Considerations

1. In paragraph 4, Shammas quotes a Detroit news anchorman's comment that the Oklahoma City bombing " 'had the Middle East written all over it.' " Explain what the anchorman understands as the signature of the Middle East. Would the statement have been more or less offensive if it had been made by someone from a city with a smaller Arab American population?
2. What does Shammas mean when he describes Ibrahim Ahmad as "a frequent flyer between stereotypes" (paragraph 5)? Consider what this statement suggests about attitudes toward Arabs throughout the West. If Ahmad was wearing "a jogging suit," what were the distinguishing features that made him appear "totally un-American" (paragraph 5)?
3. Why does Shammas draw attention to the fact that he is writing from the University of Michigan? How does he strengthen his argument by contrasting Ann Arbor with Jerusalem?
4. Who is Mark Koernke, and why does Shammas mention him in paragraph 7? Does this reference to Koernke add to or detract from Shammas' argument that all of America is divided by racial stereotypes?
5. Analyze Shammas' description of his reasons for coming to America in paragraph 6. What unspoken assumption about Middle Eastern terrorism does he suggest here?
6. Shammas opens paragraph 8 by stating that he feels "totally taken in," but he does not state precisely what it is that he mistakenly trusted. What does the balance of the paragraph tell you about the nature of his trust? Why does Shammas feel so betrayed?

Rhetorical Considerations

1. Notice that many of Shammas' paragraphs are made up of single sentences. Consider Shammas' motives for wanting to connect so much material as a single unbroken thought. Does this use of sentence structure add to or detract from the emotional content of the essay?
2. Look at Shammas' use of the term "absolved" in his opening paragraph. What are its connotations? Analyze what Shammas implies with the prominent use of this word.
3. What is the tone of this argument? Describe the specific rhetorical strategies Shammas uses to create this tone. Does his tone evoke sympathy from his

audience, or does it magnify the "us-them" division implicit in the stereotype he finds so offensive?

4. What is the rhetorical function of the word "home" in paragraph 9? Notice that even though this is a short paragraph, Shammas builds it out of several short sentences. Why does he do this?

Writing Assignments

1. Analyze the news accounts published in the immediate wake of the Oklahoma City bombing in April 1995. Based on your research, do you think Shammas' sense of "injury" in this article is justified? Write an essay that either attacks or substantiates Shammas' charge that early news reports relied on racist stereotypes of Middle Easterners.

2. Think about the ways in which the political or social history of a nation shape ethnic or national stereotypes. Focusing on a specific country, region, or nationality—Palestine, Ireland, Australia, South America, Germany, etc.—write an essay that analyzes the origins of such pernicious generalizations in political or social terms.

AFFIRMATIVE ACTION

Harping on Racism
Roger Wilkins

Who is responsible for the plight of disadvantaged blacks in America today? Should whites who imposed slavery and segregation accept responsibility for centuries of oppression? What role does racism play in the perpetuation of the poverty, drug abuse, and unemployment that plague segments of the black community? To the discomfort of some, these are a few of the provocative questions raised by author Roger Wilkins in this article, which first appeared in *Mother Jones* in December of 1989.

BEFORE YOU READ

Most of us will probably agree that racism is a problem in our society. Before you read this essay, try to decide with whom the responsibility lies to dispel racism and make up for past oppression. Individuals? Society collectively? Historical figures who perpetuated slavery and segregation? Where does responsibility begin and end?

AS YOU READ

As you read, try to decide if Wilkins is "harping on racism" or if he's making a valid point about accepting responsibility for the scourge of racism.

1   Not a month goes by without some reminder of the explosive power of the word *racism*.

2   The most recent reminder for me came at a library in Washington, after an informal talk in which I traced inner-city drug savagery back to its roots in slavery. I emphasized the harsh oppression suffered by black persons who remained largely in the South until the 1950s, mentioned their sudden displacement by the mechanization of southern agriculture and forced migration to cities, and concluded with a picture of their descendants today—feared, despised, and economically irrelevant in postindustrial society. I observed that some of these people manage to keep their balance and fight on up to decent lives.

3   I tried to demonstrate that the problems associated with their condition arise from the sweep of history in the United States. I mentioned, as well, that affluent blacks should make efforts to help disadvantaged blacks, and sketched a plan of federal educational, therapeutic, and counseling programs that might make a difference.

4   But after the talk, a slight, elderly white woman took me to task, telling me sternly that if people like me would only stop "harping" on racism and would instead teach morality in the ghetto, we might make some progress. She had heard nothing beyond the word *racism*. I can understand her reaction. I'm prepared to have to explain, and defend, my views to an elderly white woman. But I have no patience for blacks who ought to know better.

5   William Raspberry, the distinguished black columnist for the *Washington Post*, recently addressed an article to "members of the civil rights establishment" that resembled the white woman's mini-lecture to me. "I don't underestimate either the persistence of racism or its effects. But it does seem to me that you spend too much time thinking about racism," Raspberry wrote.

6   The column was occasioned by a letter from a nice white man who had written that he liked black people, sympathized with the plight of the black poor, and wanted to know what he could do to help. In addition to advising black leaders to come up with an answer to the man's question, Raspberry really unloaded on civil rights advocates.

7   "You cite statistics on everything and black-white income gaps and test scores to differential infant mortality and longevity rates as proof of racism. You publish reports on the plight of black America, implying that racism, almost alone, explains that plight. You hold rallies in Queens, and you march through Forsyth County, Georgia, to expose racism.

8   "It is as though your whole aim is to get white people to acknowledge their racism and accept their guilt. Well, suppose they did: What would that change?"

9   Well, quite a lot, as a matter of fact. The issue isn't guilt. It's responsibility. Any fair reading of history will find that since the mid-seventeenth century, whites have oppressed some blacks so completely as to disfigure their humanity. Too many whites point to the debased state of black culture and institutions as proof of the inferiority of the blacks they have mangled.

10   Such is the essence of the ideological onslaught deployed against poor blacks throughout the 1980s. Ronald Reagan's famous "welfare queen" was his way of locating the nub of black problems in the souls of the black poor. The logical implication of the war on poor blacks is simple: black people simply need to pull up their socks. That idea is wrong and must be resisted. Black people who use powerful voices to give credence to this attack are seriously injuring the weakest Americans.

11   The people who govern and spend as if there is no tomorrow argue as though yesterday doesn't count. But current problems consist of more than the sum of fleeting impressions. Like it or not, slavery, the damage from legalized oppression during the century that followed emancipation, and the racism that still infects the entire nation follow a direct line to ghetto life today.

12   As ecologist Murray Bookchin wrote in another context in the *Progressive* recently: "To trace a chain of events from its cause to its consequence is an unfamiliar task for people who have been conditioned to see life as a television sitcom or talk show composed of discrete, self-contained, anecdotal segments. We live, in effect, on a diet of short takes devoid of logic or long-range effect."

13   If we are ever to solve the awful problem of racism, we need to define it accurately by tracing it from "its cause to its consequence." That's the first step in attempting to contain racism's continued virulence in national life.

14   I don't write and talk about racism to make whites feel guilty, but because I believe that to solve a problem, we must first admit it exists. Like an individual who cannot solve a cancer problem, an alcohol problem, or a drug problem by denying it, a nation cannot deal fundamentally with racism by denying its existence. White people don't like to talk about racism because it is ugly. Denial is a central element of racism, and feel-good, do-nothing denial was elevated to a high art form over the last eight years.

15   Civil rights advocates use statistics and reports and descriptions of the racism in our culture to help Americans understand that the weight of our history shapes the way we act, think, and organize both our economy and our governmental priorities. And we blacks talk about racism to demonstrate that it is not just our problem, though God knows we'd solve it by ourselves if we could.

16   As Raspberry should know, over the past twenty-five years we have produced by the truckload the program proposals for which he asks. And they've been ignored, largely because of the racism he doesn't want us to mention. If Raspberry, or anybody else, has an idea about how to get the country to accept responsibility for its history, those of us whom he admonishes for making white people feel uncomfortable would be glad to hear it.

Topical Considerations

1. According to Wilkins, how is affirmative action a demonstration of white people's responsibility to black Americans?
2. In paragraph 14 Wilkins says, "White people don't like to talk about racism because it is ugly." Do you agree or disagree with this statement? What other reasons can you offer?
3. In paragraph 9 Wilkins writes, "Any fair reading of history will find that since the mid-seventeenth century, whites have oppressed some blacks so completely as to disfigure their humanity." According to Wilkins, what is the purpose of revealing past racial injustice?
4. Whose criticism does Wilkins feel is more important to address, the elderly white woman's or Raspberry's? Why?
5. Consider paragraph 10. Do you agree with Wilkins' assessment of the racial climate in America in the 1980s? In the Democratic Clinton administration, do you see a brighter future for race relations?

Rhetorical Considerations

1. Wilkins' essay is constructed as a defense. What does the author feel is being attacked, and who is the attacker?
2. In paragraph 16 Wilkins attacks the position of William Raspberry. Would you say this is an *ad hominem* attack, or is it justified?
3. How convincing is the evidence supporting Wilkins' case for civil rights advocates and the documenting of past racial injustices? Did his argument change your thinking about this issue?
4. How effective is the title of this essay? What tone and attitude does it convey?

Writing Assignments

1. According to Wilkins, white society must stop denying the existence of racism. If this is ever realized, what might be the next step in eradicating the effects of past injustices? Write a paper in which you outline your plan.
2. Try to determine the affirmative action policy of your school's admissions department. Are there numerical quotas? Write a paper in which you defend or criticize the policy.
3. Apply the previous assignment to some business in your community or to a local government office.

Affirmative Action: The Price of Preference
Shelby Steele

Affirmative action is an outgrowth of the 1964 Civil Rights Act and, later, the establishment of the Equal Employment Opportunity Commission (EEOC). Its policies were developed to guarantee equal opportunity to all regardless of race, color, gender, religion, or national origin. In particular, its aim was to compensate African Americans for a long and woeful tradition of discrimination in employment. When first established some two decades ago, black Americans unanimously applauded the new opportunities. But over the years unanimity has fallen away. In fact, some blacks, including Shelby Steele, are highly critical of affirmative action. In this essay Steele argues that under affirmative action blacks stand to lose more than they gain. He contends that preferential treatment in employment fosters an inferiority complex in the people it is designed to benefit.

Steele, a professor of English at San José State University, is a leading figure in a national debate regarding black issues. In 1990, he gained national prominence with the publication of his book *The Content of Our Character: A New Vision of Race in America*, from which this essay comes. He has also written articles for *Harper's, Commentary*, and the *New York Times Magazine*.

BEFORE YOU READ

Do you associate affirmative action with "equal opportunity" or "preferential treatment"? Explain your answer with reference to a specific case, if you can.

AS YOU READ

Steele says that for his children to indicate their race on a college application is "something of a Faustian bargain." What does he mean by this comparison? How, according to Steele, might the term *Faustian bargain* apply to any black benefiting from affirmative action?

1   In a few short years, when my two children will be applying to college, the affirmative action policies by which most universities offer black students some form of preferential treatment will present me with a dilemma. I am a middle-class black, a college professor, far from wealthy, but also well-removed from the kind of deprivation that would qualify my children for the label "disadvantaged." Both of them have endured racial insensitivity from whites. They have been called names, have suffered slights, and have experienced firsthand the peculiar malevolence that racism brings out in people. Yet, they have never experienced racial discrimination, have never been stopped by their race on any path they have chosen to follow. Still, their society now tells them that if they will only designate themselves as black on their college applications, they

will likely do better in the college lottery than if they conceal this fact. I think there is something of a Faustian bargain in this.

2   Of course, many blacks and a considerable number of whites would say that I was sanctimoniously making affirmative action into a test of character. They would say that this small preference is the meagerest recompense for centuries of unrelieved oppression. And to these arguments other very obvious facts must be added. In America, many marginally competent or flatly incompetent whites are hired everyday—some because their white skin suits the conscious or unconscious racial preference of their employer. The white children of alumni are often grandfathered into elite universities in what can only be seen as a residual benefit of historic white privilege. Worse, white incompetence is always an individual matter, while for blacks it is often confirmation of ugly stereotypes. The Peter Principle was not conceived with only blacks in mind. Given that unfairness cuts both ways, doesn't it only balance the scales of history that my children now receive a slight preference over whites? Doesn't this repay, in a small way, the systematic denial under which their grandfather lived out his days?

3   So, in theory, affirmative action certainly has all the moral symmetry that fairness requires—the injustice of historical and even contemporary white advantage is offset with black advantage; preference replaces prejudice, inclusion answers exclusion. It is reformist and corrective, even repentant and redemptive. And I would never sneer at these good intentions. Born in the late forties in Chicago, I started my education (a charitable term in this case) in a segregated school and suffered all the indignities that come to blacks in a segregated society. My father, born in the South, only made it to the third grade before the white man's fields took permanent priority over his formal education. And though he educated himself into an advanced reader with an almost professorial authority, he could only drive a truck for a living and never earned more than ninety dollars a week in his entire life. So yes, it is crucial to my sense of citizenship, to my ability to identify with the spirit and the interests of America, to know that this country, however imperfectly, recognizes its past sins and wishes to correct them.

4   Yet good intentions, because of the opportunity for innocence they offer us, are very seductive and can blind us to the effects they generate when implemented. In our society, affirmative action is, among other things, a testament to white goodwill and to black power, and in the midst of these heavy investments, its effects can be hard to see. But after twenty years of implementation, I think affirmative action has shown itself to be more bad than good and that blacks—whom I will focus on in this essay—now stand to lose more from it than they gain.

5   In talking with affirmative action administrators and with blacks and whites in general, it is clear that supporters of affirmative action focus on its good intentions while detractors emphasize its negative effects. Proponents talk about "diversity" and "pluralism"; opponents speak of "reverse discrimination," the unfairness of quotas and set-asides. It was virtually impossible to

find people outside either camp. The closest I came was a white male manager at a large computer company who said, "I think it amounts to reverse discrimination, but I'll put up with a little of that for a little more diversity." I'll live with a little of the effect to gain a little of the intention, he seemed to be saying. But this only makes him a halfhearted supporter of affirmative action. I think many people who don't really like affirmative action support it to one degree or another anyway.

6   I believe they do this because of what happened to white and black Americans in the crucible of the sixties when whites were confronted with their racial guilt and blacks tasted their first real power. In this stormy time white absolution and black power coalesced into virtual mandates for society. Affirmative action became a meeting ground for these mandates in the law, and in the late sixties and early seventies it underwent a remarkable escalation of its mission from simple anti-discrimination enforcement to social engineering by means of quotas, goals, timetables, set-asides and other forms of preferential treatment.

7   Legally, this was achieved through a series of executive orders and EEOC guidelines that allowed racial imbalances in the workplace to stand as proof of racial discrimination. Once it could be assumed that discrimination explained racial imbalances, it became easy to justify group remedies to presumed discrimination, rather than the normal case-by-case redress for proven discrimination. Preferential treatment through quotas, goals, and so on is designed to correct imbalances based on the assumption that they always indicate discrimination. This expansion of what constitutes discrimination allowed affirmative action to escalate into the business of social engineering in the name of anti-discrimination, to push society toward statistically proportionate racial representation, without any obligation of proving actual discrimination.

8   What accounted for this shift, I believe, was the white mandate to achieve a new racial innocence and the black mandate to gain power. Even though blacks had made great advances during the sixties without quotas, these mandates, which came to head in the very late sixties, could no longer be satisfied by anything less than racial preferences. I don't think these mandates in themselves were wrong, since whites clearly needed to do better by blacks and blacks needed more real power in society. But, as they came together in affirmative action, their effect was to distort our understanding of racial discrimination in a way that allowed us to offer the remediation of preference on the basis of mere color rather than actual injury. By making black the color of preference, these mandates have reburdened society with the very marriage of color and preference (in reverse) that we set out to eradicate. The old sin is reaffirmed in a new guise.

9   But the essential problem with this form of affirmative action is the way it leaps over the hard business of developing a formerly oppressed people to the point where they can achieve proportionate representation on their own (given equal opportunity) and goes straight for the proportionate representation. This may satisfy some whites of their innocence and some blacks of their power, but it does very little to truly uplift blacks. . . .

10   Racial representation is not the same thing as racial development, yet affirmative action fosters a confusion of these very different needs. Representation can be manufactured; development is always hard-earned. However, it is the music of innocence and power that we hear in affirmative action that causes us to cling to it and to its distracting emphasis on representation. The fact is that after twenty years of racial preferences, the gap between white and black median income is greater than it was in the seventies. None of this is to say that blacks don't need policies that ensure our right to equal opportunity, but what we need more is the development that will let us take advantage of society's efforts to include us.

11   I think that one of the most troubling effects of racial preferences for blacks is a kind of demoralization, or put another way, an enlargement of self-doubt. Under affirmative action the quality that earns us preferential treatment is an implied inferiority. However this inferiority is explained—and it is easily enough explained by the myriad deprivations that grew out of our oppression—it is still inferiority. There are explanations, and then there is the fact. And the fact must be borne by the individual as a condition apart from the explanation, apart even from the fact that others like himself also bear this condition. In integrated situations where blacks must compete with whites who may be better prepared, these explanations may quickly wear thin and expose the individual to racial as well as personal self-doubt.

12   All of this is compounded by the cultural myth of black inferiority that blacks have always lived with. What this means in practical terms is that when blacks deliver themselves into integrated situations, they encounter a nasty little reflex in whites, a mindless, atavistic reflex that responds to the color black with alarm. Attributions may follow this alarm if the white cares to indulge them, and if they do, they will most likely be negative—one such attribution is intellectual ineptness. I think this reflex and the attributions that may follow it embarrass most whites today, therefore, it is usually quickly repressed. Nevertheless, on an equally atavistic level, the black will be aware of the reflex his color triggers and will feel a stab of horror at seeing himself reflected in this way. He, too, will do a quick repression, but a lifetime of such stabbings is what constitutes his inner realm of racial doubt.

13   The effects of this may be a subject for another essay. The point here is that the implication of inferiority that racial preferences engender in both the white and black mind expands rather than contracts this doubt. Even when the black sees no implication of inferiority in racial preferences, he knows that whites do, so that—consciously or unconsciously—the result is virtually the same. The effect of preferential treatment—the lowering of normal standards to increase black presentation—puts blacks at war with an expanded realm of debilitating doubt, so that the doubt itself becomes an unrecognized preoccupation that undermines their ability to perform, especially in integrated situations. On largely white campuses, blacks are five times more likely to drop out than whites. Preferential treatment, no matter how it is justified in the light of day, subjects blacks to a midnight of self-doubt, and so often transforms their advantage into a revolving door.

14   Another liability of affirmative action comes from the fact that it indirectly encourages blacks to exploit their own past victimization as a source of power and privilege. Victimization, like implied inferiority, is what justifies preference, so that to receive the benefits of preferential treatment one must, to some extent, become invested in the view of one's self as a victim. In this way, affirmative action nurtures a victim-focused identity in blacks. The obvious irony here is that we become inadvertently invested in the very condition we are trying to overcome. Racial preferences send us the message that there is more power in our past suffering than our present achievements—none of which could bring us a *preference* over others.

15   When power itself grows out of suffering, then blacks are encouraged to expand the boundaries of what qualifies as racial oppression, a situation that can lead us to paint our victimization in vivid colors, even as we receive the benefits of preference. The same corporations and institutions that give us preference are also seen as our oppressors. At Stanford University minority students—some of whom enjoy as much as $15,000 a year in financial aid—recently took over the president's office demanding, among other things, more financial aid. The power to be found in victimization, like any power, is intoxicating and can lend itself to the creation of a new class of super-victims who can feel the pea of victimization under twenty mattresses. Preferential treatment rewards us for being underdogs rather than for moving beyond that status—a misplacement of incentives that, along with its deepening of our doubt, is more than a yoke than a spur.

16   But, I think, one of the worst prices that blacks pay for preference has to do with an illusion. I saw this illusion at work recently in the mother of a middle-class black student who was going off to his first semester of college. "They owe us this, so don't think for a minute that you don't belong there." This is the logic by which many blacks, and some whites, justify affirmative action—it is something "owed," a form of reparation. But this logic overlooks a much harder and less digestible reality, that it is impossible to repay blacks living today for the historic suffering of the race. If all blacks were given a million dollars tomorrow morning it would not amount to a dime on the dollar of three centuries of oppression, nor would it obviate the residues of that oppression that we still carry today. The concept of historic reparation grows out of man's need to impose a degree of justice on the world that simply does not exist. Suffering can be endured and overcome, it cannot be repaid. Blacks cannot be repaid for the injustice done to the race, but we can be corrupted by society's guilty gestures of repayment.

17   Affirmative action is such a gesture. It tells us that racial preferences can do for us what we cannot do for ourselves. The corruption here is in the hidden incentive *not* to do what we believe preferences will do. This is an incentive to be reliant on others just as we are struggling for self-reliance. And it keeps alive the illusion that we can find some deliverance in repayment. The hardest thing for any sufferer to accept is that his suffering excuses him from very little and never has enough currency to restore him. To think otherwise is to prolong the suffering.

18   But if not preferences, then what? I think we need social policies that are committed to two goals: the educational and economic development of disadvantaged people, regardless of race, and the eradication from our society—through close monitoring and severe sanctions—of racial, ethnic, or gender discrimination. Preferences will not deliver us to either of these goals, since they tend to benefit those who are not disadvantaged—middle-class white women and middle-class blacks—and attack one form of discrimination with another. Preferences are inexpensive and carry the glamour of good intentions—change the numbers and the good deed is done. To be against them is to be unkind. But I think the unkindest cut is to bestow on children like my own an undeserved advantage while neglecting the development of those disadvantaged children on the East Side of my city who will likely never be in a position to benefit from a preference. Give my children fairness; give disadvantaged children a better shot at development—better elementary and secondary schools, job training, safer neighborhoods, better financial assistance for college, and so on. Fewer blacks go to college today than ten years ago; more black males of college are in prison or under the control of the criminal justice system than in college. This despite racial preferences.

19   The mandates of black power and white absolution out of which preferences emerged were not wrong in themselves. What was wrong was that both races focused more on the goals of these mandates than on the means to the goals. Blacks can have no real power without taking responsibility for their own educational and economic development. Whites can have no racial innocence without earning it by eradicating discrimination and helping the disadvantaged to develop. Because we ignored the means, the goals have not been reached, and the real work remains to be done.

Topical Considerations

1. In paragraph 1 Steele mentions a Faustian bargain. What is a Faustian bargain? What is the nature of Steele's own Faustian bargain?
2. In paragraph 2 Steele poses two questions and then proceeds to answer them throughout the essay. Summarize his answers to these questions using specific references from the essay.
3. At several points in his essay, Steele likens affirmative action to social engineering. Why does Steele feel the two are similar?
4. Steele spends much of the essay pointing to problems associated with affirmative action and racial preference. In place of affirmative action, what does Steele feel blacks need to enable them to take advantage of opportunity?
5. Describe all the problems associated with affirmative action according to Steele. Do you think these problems are serious enough to abandon affirmative action programs?
6. Do you believe, as Steele suggests, that preferential treatment can lead to "a new class of super-victims who can feel the pea of victimization under

twenty mattresses" (paragraph 15)? (To what work in children's literature is Steele alluding?)

7. In paragraph 17 Steele writes, "The hardest thing for any sufferer to accept is that his suffering excuses him from very little and never has enough currency to restore him. To think otherwise is to prolong the suffering." Do you agree or disagree, and why?

Rhetorical Considerations

1. What rhetorical purpose does Steele's anecdote about his own children in paragraph 1 serve for this essay?
2. How does Steele use statistical data to bolster his argument (cite specific references from the essay)? Is this strategy effective?
3. How does Steele make his point without wholly rejecting affirmative action? Is this an effective strategy?
4. In paragraph 2 Steele writes of "many blacks and a considerable number of whites." How do words such as "many" and "considerable" help Steele create a balanced argument? Find other examples that make a similar impact.
5. Show through at least three examples how Steele presents the opposition's argument. Why is this a particularly strong rhetorical device? Does he convince you?
6. What would Roger Wilkins perceive as the main flaw in Steele's argument? What would Steele perceive as the main flaw in Wilkin's argument?

Writing Assignments

1. Steele is a persuasive essayist. Examine his strategies and try to be equally persuasive in refuting his argument.
2. Write an essay using Steele's statement as your theme: "In education, a revolving door; in employment, a glass ceiling."
3. Some critics would accuse Steele of "blaming the victim." Explain why you agree or disagree with their position.
4. Write an essay illuminating the differences and possible points of convergence in Wilkins' and Steele's essays.

It's Past Time to Speak Out
Charles G. Adams

This piece offers a classical defense of affirmative action, a policy designed to guarantee equality of opportunity to all regardless of race, color, gender, religion, or national origin. In this essay, Charles G. Adams is incensed at interpretations of affirmative action as discrimination in reverse and at the failure of some prominent black leaders and scholars to defend it. He offers an impassioned defense of affirmative action as a "corrective device intended to reverse long-standing customs and procedures of unjust racial exclusion."

Charles G. Adams is a columnist for *The Michigan Chronicle*, where this article first appeared in January of 1991.

BEFORE YOU READ

Do you feel you have ever been excluded from fair consideration for employment, school admission, membership in a group, an athletic event, or a school office because of your gender, race, color, or religious or sexual orientation? What were the circumstances? Were you able to fight what may have been unfair exclusion from consideration? What, if anything, do you feel should have been done to ensure fair consideration for you?

AS YOU READ

As you read think about the author's voice. Do you find it neutral, impassioned, strident, or something else? Does this tone engage you or alienate you?

1   The writer of the Book of Ecclesiastes says that there is a time to be silent and a time to speak. I hold that it is past time to speak out on affirmative action. Either it will be vigorously defended or it will be totally destroyed.

2   I am in my 21st year as a columnist for the Michigan Chronicle and for more than half of that time I have been pleading that Black scholars, lawyers, leaders and speakers stand up and speak out in promotion and defense of the principle, policy and practice of affirmative action. It just hasn't happened. There has been too much silence, apathy and indifference on the part of Blacks with regard to affirmative action which is as crucial for the survival of Blacks as the State of Israel and semitic sensitivity are vital for Jews.

3   Whenever the interests of Jews and Israel are attacked, Jewish journalists, lawyers, rabbis and leaders rise quickly and vociferously to the defense. But when affirmative action is under attack, as it has been for more than 12 years, there is no reply, refutation or repudiation from the Black community of leaders and speakers.

4   That is criminal indifference and neglect. Our race is being destroyed not so much by the vicious attacks of our enemies as by the appalling silence and location of our friends and fellows. Again let me call on all Blacks of intelligence, influence and commitment to use the Black journals, newspapers, books, lecture halls and pulpits to widely explain the position, principle, policy and practice of affirmative action to our own race. Too many Blacks do not understand what it means or why it is necessary.

5   Affirmative action is a corrective device intended to reverse long-standing customs and procedures of unjust racial exclusion. It is not discrimination

in reverse. It is discrimination to reverse a racially discriminatory system of power distribution.

6   Corrective justice demands that government, institutions and corporations that have been "color struck" for generations must not all of a sudden pretend to be so "color blind" that they fail to make special provisions in order to help the historically racially excluded segment of the population catch up to an equal position at the starting line of competition.

7   Civil rights laws that require that institutions no longer segregate or discriminate against Blacks as they once did are necessary but not sufficient measures to correct long-entrenched wrongs against Blacks. Since institutions have discriminated against Blacks for hundreds of years, they must now discriminate in favor of Blacks for at least the next 25 years in order to give them a chance to make it to the starting line.

8   Equal opportunity is not the mere absence of discrimination but the presence of special inducements and provisions designed to close the gap between Blacks and Whites. The concrete reality of equal opportunity depends not only upon an open road but also upon an equal start. If a race has been historically locked out of parts of the labor pool by deliberate denials of opportunities for training and experience, how in the world can that race ever get the requisite training or accumulate sufficient experience to compete for jobs and positions?

9   The late Whitney Young argued with passionate pen and skilled tongue that those who had been systematically and habitually excluded by race alone would require special inducements of inclusion and redoubled encouragements in order to narrow the gap in economics between Blacks and White. I heard him give a graphic illustration to score the point.

10   He called upon his audience to visualize two men running the mile in a track meet. One is well equipped, wears track shoes and runs on cinders. The other is barefoot and runs in the sand. Also, his legs are scarred, having been broken by vicious, racist attacks.

11   It is no surprise that one runner is far behind the other and seemingly has no chance to catch up. The fellow who is behind is given track shoes and placed on the cinder track. Naturally it takes time to get his feet on the track. Seconds later it should surprise no one that the newly equipped and admitted runner is still yards behind and will never catch up unless something special is done to help him by virtue of his previous condition. That "something special" is "affirmative action" or remedial justice.

12   Those who now pretend to be Reaganistically color-blind are those who are denying necessary remedies for wounded Black competitors. They call affirmative action "reverse discrimination" or "racism in reverse." Nothing could be farther from the truth.

13   Knaves have taken a good term and twisted it to make a trap for fools. Black conservatives like Shelby Steele, Thomas Sewell, Glen Lourey and Michael Williams are ready to trash affirmative action now that they themselves have made it through school and into positions of privilege and power. But until the few who are blessed look back and reach down to assist the

masses who are still held down and locked out, there will be no security, survival or success for anybody.

14   We are all bound together in a single garment of destiny, as Martin Luther King said, and we will either overcome as one nation or we will each be destroyed separately.

Topical Considerations

1. How do Adams and Steele differ in their opinion about civil rights laws? Give specific examples from the essays.
2. Consider Adams' statement: "The concrete reality of equal opportunity depends not only upon an open road but also upon an equal start" (paragraph 8). Do you believe affirmative action provides an equal start? What are its strengths; its weaknesses? Support your responses with examples from the essay.
3. In paragraph 11 Adams says that the "newly equipped" runner of the parable "will never catch up unless something special is done to help him by virtue of his previous condition." What does Adams believe is that "something special"? Would Steele agree with the first part of Adams' statement? What does Steele believe is the "something special"?
4. In paragraph 12 Adams uses the phrase "Reaganistically color-blind." What does he mean by it? Do you agree with the premise underlying this phrase? Explain your answer.
5. Has Adams' essay changed or reinforced your thinking about affirmative action? If so, in what ways? Which points of his essay do you find particularly convincing?

Rhetorical Considerations

1. In paragraph 9 what rhetorical purpose does Adams' citing of the late Whitney Young serve? Do you feel the reference to Young is effective?
2. What logical fallacy is Adams guilty of in paragraphs 1, 2, and 14? What is his purpose in using this fallacy?
3. In paragraph 9 Adams makes use of a parable told to him by Whitney Young. Do you feel it is an effective reference here?
4. What are the rhetorical reasons for Adams' quoting the Bible in the first paragraph of his essay?

Writing Assignments

1. Pretend you are the moderator of a debate between Charles Adams and Shelby Steele. What questions would you pose and how would each respond? (Pose at least three questions.)

2. Adams states in paragraph 7, "Since institutions have discriminated against Blacks for hundreds of years, they must now discriminate in favor of Blacks for at least the next 25 years in order to give them a chance to make it to the starting line." Do you agree with this statement? If so, do you feel affirmative action is effective in giving blacks a chance to "make it to the starting line"? If not, propose your own solution to the problem.

3. Objectively summarize Adams' and Steele's positions with regard to affirmative action. Then rewrite your essay, slanting it in favor of one side.

OPPOSITIONS:
IMMIGRATION POLICY

A Statue With Limitations
B. Meredith Burke

In a sense, a demographer can look into a crystal ball and predict concentrations of population specific to a time and place. B. Meredith Burke does this and is deeply concerned about the implications of population growth, particularly for states such as California, Florida, and New York. Burke argues that if projections are correct, these states, which absorb large numbers of immigrants, will soon experience unsustainable population growth compounding already existing environmental and social problems. Now is the time, she says, to take action and limit immigration. B. Meredith Burke, a demographer and economist from Cupertino, California, has written articles on immigration and other social policy issues for the *New York Times, The Wall Street Journal,* and *Newsweek* where this essay first appeared in February 1992.

BEFORE YOU READ

The United States is a nation of immigrants, but are there areas of the nation where immigrants are more or less welcome than others? Why do you think this is so? What are you own feelings about the continuing influx of immigrants? In your view should immigration be further restricted than it is, or should we have an open-door policy? How do you feel about U.S. policy regarding Haitians and others wanting to leave their homelands?

AS YOU READ

Some of Burke's argument is based on demographic projections—for example, the population of the United States will reach 611 million by the year 2080. As you read these projections, ask yourself whether it makes sense to make immigration policy decisions now based on such distant projections? What unanticipated events might radically alter such predictions?

1   Imagine if 25 years ago someone had identified lung cancer as a major problem, had pinpointed smoking as a major contributory factor, and even quantified its effects—and then had assumed that people's smoking behavior was a timeless "given." What would you call the failure to ask two questions: is smoking a changeable behavior—and if yes, how do we get people to quit? In nonacademic terms, I would call it a cop-out.

2   Politicians, planners and concerned citizens in my state of California keep debating how to solve such worsening problems as urban sprawl, environmental degradation (including the paving over of prime agricultural land), traffic congestion and bulging school enrollments. They correctly identify the growth of population from 10.6 million in 1950 to 20 million in 1970 to 30 million today as the major underlying factor. But the debate never rises above "managing growth" to the more global questions: is population growth an eternal "given" and, if not, what is needed to stop it?

3   California Gov. Pete Wilson has said that "we will have to minimize the magnetic effect of the generosity of this state." But when asked if our state can support not only 30 million but 40 million or 50 million people, he could only point out that freedom of residence is constitutionally guaranteed. In other words, states do not control their population size. The federal government does. Immigration and refugee policies are federal responsibilities.

4   But both the executive and the legislative branches are fashioning policy with barely a nod to the resultant American demographic future. In 1965, when Congress overhauled the Northern European-biased country-of-origins policy that had ruled immigration quotas since 1921, it was unclear what the effects would be. No one asked then: by how much will immigration increase? Where will the new pool of immigrants settle? Should we set a date to evaluate the effects of the new immigration and survey citizen and local-area response?

No "Tolerable" Growth

5   When Congress expanded the immigration quota from 500,000 to 700,000 in November 1990, the effects of America's future again went unexamined. Alan Simpson, who led the Senate's action, represents Wyoming, the state that ranks 51st in population among the 50 states plus the District of Columbia. His state is not among the six whose home population will be appreciably affected. California, New York and Florida absorb more than 50 percent of immigrants; Texas, New Jersey and Illinois absorb an additional 20 percent.

6   A demographic rule of thumb is that the doubling time of a population can be calculated by dividing 70 by the annual percentage growth rate. Between 1950 and 1990 we grew from 150 million to 250 million people. Today

a 1 percent growth rate adds 2.5 million people annually; in 70 years it may well add 5 million people—every year and primarily in the same few locations. There is no "tolerable" growth rate. Either all growth stops, or the size expands until our natural resources run out.

7   Last winter demographers Dennis Ahlburg and James Vaupel published U.S. population projections that differed sharply from those of the Census Bureau. Based on what I consider much more realistic assumptions about future mortality, fertility and immigration, their three most reasonable estimates for the year 2080 are 487 million, 539 million and 611 million Americans. Projections should be viewed as blueprints offering a still-modifiable future. On the heels of Earth Day 1970, after Congress commissioned the National Academy of Sciences report "Population and the American Future," both activists and legislators failed to enlist the public in debating the alternative scenarios presented. Californians, city dwellers and farmers alike, missed the chance to tell policymakers that they did not want a state congested with 10 million more people within 20 years. Floridians lost the chance to keep remnants of the Everglades free from further encroachment and drainage.

8   Our physical habitat is being threatened by an immigrant flow that represents only 1 percent of Third World annual population growth. Curtailing immigration while voting generous family planning and nonmilitary aid packages can far better benefit citizens of the developing countries than the status quo. Americans must trade a national vision of a beckoning Statue of Liberty and a vision of wide-open spaces for a more realistic one of a world of limits and constraints.

9   Our demographic future is in our hands. Several routes could lead to a stationary population, including one-child families and moderate, continuous immigration; or two-child families and no immigration. If these models seem unappealing, we can go on with unchanging policies and end up with 550 million Americans, primarily in 20 urban areas in seven or eight states, in 2070—and a billion Americans 70 years after that.

National Consensus

10   In short, demographic reality will not permit us to evade hard choices. We need a national consensus that those cities and states most affected by growth should have a decisive vote in shaping immigration policy. This may require a 27th constitutional amendment that will allocate immigration-setting power to the electorates. A lot of effort? Yes—but less than that required to support and govern a population of 1 billion Americans.

Topical Considerations

1. Before reading Burke's essay, did you have any opinions on immigration? If so, has this essay influenced your view of the matter? How? If not, has she raised your awareness of the importance of this issue?

2. Of all of Burke's examples, choose the one that would most likely convince you to vote for strict immigration quotas. Explain your choice.

3. Comment on the line, "Our demographic future is in our hands," (paragraph 9). According to the author, who has the ability to curb population? Do you feel that she is realistic?

4. Trace the essay's chain of immigration from 1965 to the present (paragraphs 3 to 5). What do the circumstances that surround each new immigration statistic say about America's view of immigration?

5. In seven of the ten paragraphs in this essay, Burke lists statistics. What role do statistics play in the essay? How do these facts lead you to either support or disagree with Burke?

Rhetorical Considerations

1. Burke begins with an analogy to smoking. Is this analogy an effective comparison to the population problem? Offer an alternative analogy.

2. In paragraph 9 Burke offers "[s]everal routes . . . to a stationary population." By beginning the paragraph stating that the future is in "our hands," does Burke allow the reader room to develop his or her own solutions? Is her strategy rhetorically effective, or alienating?

3. Burke couches most of her argument in large numbers. But between the numbers are emotionally charged words and phrases that are meant to sway the reader. Choose four strong words or phrases and show how they further Burke's fear of the spread of immigration.

4. How does Burke "stack the deck" in her essay? Does this technique make her essay less believable, or does she have sufficient evidence to make a sound argument?

5. What are three possible meanings of the title of the essay?

6. Is Burke's rhetorical strategy of using just numbers effective enough to win over those not schooled in demography? Substitute three of the statistics with your own persuasive statements.

Writing Assignments

1. Consider Burke's essay and rewrite the inscription on the Statue of Liberty to explain that the United States is now a "world of limits and constraints" (paragraph 8). Use your library to look up the original inscription.

2. Write a paper in which you explore what the world would be like if, as Burke suggests, the United States became a country that mandated "two-child families and no immigration" (paragraph 9). Consider America's philosophical foundation as well as its technological, cultural, environmental, and political future.

3. In the next essay, "The Big New Mix," Renee Loth argues that "immigrants adjust to America more than the country adjusts to them." Consider Burke's

predictions for the future. How do you feel about the continuing influx of immigrants? Do you believe the United States should honor its Statue of Liberty pledge? Write an essay in which you answer these questions using specific examples.

The Big New Mix
Renee Loth

Eight and a half million immigrants are expected in the United States in the 1990s. Although some demographers such as B. Meredith Burke (author of the previous essay) greet this trend with trepidation, others have hopeful anticipation. Some analysts see immigrants as usurpers of jobs; others see them as necessary to spur the economy. Some fear that immigrants will maintain separate ethnic identities, whereas others argue that immigrants will blend with the dominant culture.

In this piece Renee Loth, a writer for the *Boston Globe*, where this article first appeared in October 1991, gives an overview of how immigration might affect the United States in the twenty-first century.

BEFORE YOU READ

What is the prevailing attitude toward immigrants and immigration in your home community, and on what is it based? Why, in your community, might a particular immigrant group be admired or feared?

AS YOU READ

Loth cites a number of demographic statistics throughout her essay. Is her handling of the statistics dry and wooden or natural and smooth? Can you explain her approach to using statistics?

1   Given the implacable surge of Asian and Hispanic immigrants over the past decade, it might seem that we'll soon be celebrating Tet instead of Columbus Day and eating tacos on the Fourth of July—er, *Cinco de Mayo*. The ascendancy of English-only movements, the backlash against political correctness, and the dismantling of hiring quotas are all symptoms of a growing anxiety on the part of some "natives" that the 8.5 million immigrants expected in the 1990s will render the United States unrecognizable.

2   But demographers, who limit their study to just the statistics, are remarkably sanguine about the effect of massive in-migration on the dominant American culture. To these number crunchers, the past is prologue, and the past suggests that immigrants adjust to America more than the country adjusts to them.

3   The annealing powers of the melting pot are stronger than the will to retain separate ethnic identities, they say. With few exceptions, immigrants tend to intermarry, become fluent in English, and have smaller families with each succeeding generation. They leave the ghetto and move to the suburbs, leave the labor unions and strive to become managers, and drop their ethnic customs except on holidays. In the dry terminology of demographic science, they "regress toward the mean."

4   "The overwhelming number of people who emigrate want an American passport, not just the green card," says Christopher Jencks, professor of sociology and urban affairs at Northwestern University. Julian L. Simon, an economist at the University of Maryland, concurs: "They want to play baseball, not pachinko."

5   This is not to say that demographers don't anticipate stress and dislocation as the immigrant waves continue to wash over America. Although newcomers may be beneficial to the US economy as a whole, try telling that to the individual who loses his job to an immigrant willing to work for lower pay. As American blacks can attest, assimilation gets progressively harder as it moves through the barriers of ethnicity, religion, and race. Asians and Hispanics, who now account for 74 percent of all US immigration, must breach all three levels to join mainstream America.

6   Moreover, some believe that the trend toward multiculturalism could itself retard assimilation, as immigrants realize there is a benefit to retaining their ethnic distinctions. "To the extent that we have codified some of these groups, we may be preserving them," says Jeffrey Passel, director of the program for research on immigration policy at the Urban Institute, in Washington, D.C. Passel and others think that second-generation ethnics may resist assimilation because certain rights and privileges have been attached to the "new tribalism." Ironically, the very people who promote ethnic and racial separateness are often the fiercest opponents of discrimination.

7   The numbers suggest that the current flood of immigrants, as overwhelming as it may sometimes seem, will be easier to absorb than the so-called European migration that every right-thinking American now celebrates. Although the 656,000 legal immigrants who arrived in 1990 represent the largest single wave since 1924, it is but a fraction of the European migration when taken as a percentage of the US population. Although today's immigrants may seem uniquely "foreign," they are probably no more strange to us now than the Southern and Eastern Europeans were to the prevailing American culture at the turn of the century. And though the US Census does predict that Hispanics, blacks, and Asians eventually will outnumber whites in America, one widely used demographic model developed by the Urban Institute—which adjusts for falling fertility rates—doesn't show that occurring until 2090, a century away.

8   Leon Bouvier, a demographer at Tulane University, is a dissenting voice. He projects that America will become "a majority minority" nation by 2050, and within just 20 years in New York, California, and Texas. "It's a mo-

mentous shift, and to close your eyes to it can lead to enormous problems between groups," he says. Bouvier, who served on the US Select Commission on
Immigration and Refugee Policy in 1980, advocates reducing immigration
quotas to 450,000 a year, almost half the present level.

9   All of these projections come with the caveat that demography is an inexact science, its predictive purity corrupted by politics, human behavior, and
other imponderables. Birth rates are dropping for all immigrant groups, but
new child-friendly government tax breaks could interfere with the neat models. Congress periodically votes to "diversify" immigration quotas, correcting
trends toward over-representation of one nationality or another. (Indeed, in
1986 Congress legalized 3 million mostly Hispanic immigrants in one sweeping amnesty period.)

10   Demographic definitions are quirky and ever-changing. Until 1980 the
US Census considered people of Pakistani or Indian descent "white" but now
counts them as Asian. World events can and probably will change the nature
of the 120,000 political refugees admitted annually under current immigration
laws. "If we believed the projections of 1914 for 1990," says Charles Keely,
professor of international migration at Georgetown University, "we would be
a country overrun by pizza parlors and delicatessens by now." No one predicted spring rolls.

11   We asked demographers, historians, and social scientists to envision
America in the 21st century along social, economic, and political lines. Will
English lose its unifying power to a Babel of foreign tongues? Will the growing
numbers of Asians and Hispanics be reflected in political clout? Will the country resemble more a stew, with each ingredient melting into the whole; a parfait, with a clear hierarchy of distinct ingredients; or a salad, with all the elements tossed together but retaining their individual character?

12   Observers as diverse as historian Arthur Schlesinger and economist
Robert J. Samuelson worry that the currently fashionable ethic of "celebrating
differences" will atomize America, elevating the special interest above the national interest. Nowhere is that concern more acute than in the debate over
bilingualism. Although it is not a new issue—in 1919 Theodore Roosevelt
warned against becoming "dwellers in a polyglot boarding house"—the US
Census does record an increase over the past 20 years in households in which
English is not the dominant language spoken. Some Americans find this a
threat, and English-only laws were passed in 17 states during the 1980s. Former US Sen. S. I. Hayakawa (R-California) has been pushing a constitutional
amendment restricting bilingual education lest the United States become "another Quebec."

13   Most of our prognosticators doubt that America will become bilingual
in the next century. "Speaking English will still be really important to success
as an American concept," says Jencks. A kind of Canadian or Swiss-style pluralism, he says, is difficult to obtain in a country as large and media-sensitive
as the United States. Not entirely in jest, Jencks adds: "Historically, the tradi-

tion is that people of low status have to learn the language of the high, so we may all have to learn Japanese."

14   One key difference between the European migrations and the current waves gives our experts pause, however. The migrations of the 1920s were interrupted, first by restrictive legislation, then by the Great Depression and World War II. That gave immigrants a "breather" in which to adapt to American culture. Today, by contrast, there is a continuous stream of fresh immigrants keeping the old-country customs, and language, alive.

15   Raul Yzaguirre is president of the National Council of la Raza, a Hispanic-rights group in Washington. He notes that his ancestors came to America in 1721, yet he still speaks Spanish. "History has shown that you cannot outlaw a language," he says. "You can't artificially impose a culture or try to oppress a culture. That's what's happening in the [former] Soviet Union right now."

16   Yzaguirre envisions a multilingual, multicultural America in the 21st century, with more Latin influence on music, art, politics, and popular culture. Hispanics will learn English, but the English language itself will "learn Spanish." More and more Spanish words will be incorporated into *Webster's,* he says, "just like 'pizza' and 'chutzpah.' "

17   Whether such piquancy is a good thing is largely a matter of taste. "For some people, one immigrant is too many," says Keely. "Dade County [Florida] goes ape when 40,000 Haitians show up. In New York City, that's a block party."

18   Julian Simon, author of *The Economic Consequences of Immigration*, thinks the new immigrants are a nearly unalloyed good: They'll stimulate the economy, improve the American standard of living, reverse the birth dearth, and provide for baby boomers in their old age.

19   "The more immigrants that come, the brighter our economic future is across the board," he says. "They mean a higher standard of living, greater productivity, better international competitiveness, and the only painless solution to the deficit. It's an extraordinary opportunity to achieve every one of our economic national goals at once."

20   More profound than the "browning of America," Simon notes, is its graying. The US Census projects that the over-65 population, currently around 26 million, will be 39 million by the year 2010 and 51 million by 2020. The Urban Institute model projects an average life expectancy in the year 2090 of 90.2 years, which is 14 more years of Social Security than the current average. Since most immigrants arrive when they are young and healthy, Simon believes they could be the needed relief to the burden of an aging US population.

21   Congress has helped out by passing an immigration law, which became effective October 1, that increases the quotas for managerial and high-tech workers from 58,000 year to 140,000. Michael Hoefer, chief demographer for the US Immigration and Naturalization Service, explains that the new law also

tries to address a pent-up demand for visas for the children and spouses of permanent residents, especially those from Mexico, the Phillipines, and the Dominican Republic. In addition, it lowers barriers erected in 1965 to immigrants from Northern European countries, such as Ireland (thanks to congressmen Joseph Kennedy and Brian Donnolly).

22   Capitalism is one of the strongest assimilators known in the United States. Many women striving to climb the corporate ladder have found pressure to adopt "male" management styles to fit in comfortably. Similarly, most experts believe the corporate culture will subsume individual ethnic cultures, especially in white-collar jobs. "You have to be more traditional than traditional to be the first one through any of these doors," says Jencks, predicting relatively little diversity at the top. "It's part of the nature of corporate America to be homogenous."

23   Three crucial economic programs that eased assimilation for the children of European immigrants are missing today, however. Nothing worked better to assimilate second-generation immigrants in the 1940s than the FHA loan, the GI Bill, and the federal interstate highways program that helped create suburbia. "Those government programs had a great absorption impact," says Keely. "They allowed mixing of people, allowed access to education, and a great deal of economic prosperity."

24   For generations, politics served as a social escalator for Irish and Italian immigrants locked out of traditional avenues to wealth and power. In his cultural history of Massachusetts, *Bibles, Brahmins and Bosses*, Thomas O'Connor describes the practical value of political patronage in the early years of this century. "For many an Irish ward boss," he writes, "politics was an invaluable opportunity to provide effective help and assistance to his own people when they could not obtain what they needed from any other source." The needs were basic, he writes, but often unattainable: food, eyeglasses, pardons, jobs.

25   Today, the spoils system of politics is largely out of favor, or at least out of money, and the offspring of Irish and Italian machine pols have assimilated to WASPy suburbs and taken careers in banking. The new immigrants, especially Asians, have been somewhat slower to become politically active. For those who come from countries with little or no tradition in democracy, there is cultural resistance to political activism. It is difficult to imagine survivors of Pol Pot's killing fields having much enthusiasm for politics.

26   "It will be a long process for that refugee movement . . . to become savvy to the white political structure," says Andrew Buni, a history professor at Boston College who specializes in issues of immigration and ethnicity. Moreover, according to Hoefer, at the US Immigration Service, even though Asians have the highest naturalization rates of any immigrants, few of the post-Vietnam-era immigrants have been here for the seven years required to become citizens.

27   Like most ethnic groups, Asians are not monolithic. A Sony executive and a Vietnamese boat person may both be considered of Asian descent, but there the similarity ends. Cambodians, Vietnamese, Koreans, Hmong, and

Laotians all speak different languages. "It's hard enough to get a coalition of Democrats together on something, let alone people whose languages and customs and political alliances in their own worlds are vastly different from each other," says Professor Buni.

28   Nor can Hispanics be expected to vote in a singular way. Cuban-Americans tend to be very conservative and Mexicans rather liberal. George Bush won the "Hispanic" vote in Miami in 1988, but Michael Dukakis won the "Hispanic" vote in Texas. "It would be disingenuous to argue that we think exactly alike on the same issues," says Lisa Navarette, of the National Council of la Raza.

29   Ironically, one key to better political representation for minorities—legislative redistricting—argues against assimilation, since the new immigrants need to cluster together in a single district to elect one of their own successfully. Hispanic leaders say the fact that they are more assimilated than most blacks puts them at a disadvantage in the redistricting sweepstakes. "There is more mobility within the Hispanic community, and that has prevented Hispanic clout," says Navarette.

30   Mexico sent the greatest number of immigrants to America in the 1980s, accounting for 12 percent of the nation's newcomers, not counting undocumented aliens. All of our demographic models predict that the number of Hispanics will soon overtake that of blacks in America. But it takes more than demographics to win elections. Unless Hispanics improve their naturalization rates and start to vote—just 13 percent of Mexicans who entered the country in 1977 had become citizens by 1989, compared with 50 percent of Asian immigrants and 44 percent of Eastern Europeans—their political muscle will not be proportionate to their numbers.

31   Most of our demographers agree that nativist fears about the "wretched refuse" at our shores could be cooled significantly by a quick course in American history. Like many of his colleagues, the Urban Institute's Passel is struck by similarities between reactions to the current wave of immigration and the xenophobia prevalent at the turn of the century.

32   "Eighty years ago, at the peak of the last great wave of immigration, people were concerned that the new immigrants would never fit in, that they were bringing alien ideas, that they would never learn English," Passel says. "It's the grandchildren of those people who are saying those same things now."

Topical Considerations

1. Loth writes, "For generations, politics served as a social escalator for Irish and Italian immigrants locked out of traditional avenues to wealth and power" (paragraph 24). Explain how, according to the essay, politics and politicians were able to help the Irish and Italian immigrants. Are today's immigrants able to use politics to their advantage?

2. In paragraphs 2 and 3, Loth explains her view of the role of a demographer. Compare how Loth and Burke view demographers and their science.
3. Paragraphs 7 and 14 examine the immigrant waves of the 1920s. Compare the experience of European immigrants with the experience of Middle Easterners, Asians, and Latinos today? How does Loth's explanation compare with the stories of your classmates, friends, or relatives?
4. In paragraph 22 Loth writes, "Capitalism is one of the strongest assimilators known in the United States." What does she mean by this? Aside from her reference to corporate America, how does she demonstrate the validity of this statement?
5. How does the essay's title reflect its theme? Do you believe "the big new mix" is an appropriate metaphor, or do you prefer one of the alternate names in paragraph 11 (or one of your own)?
6. In paragraph 12, Arthur Schlesinger and Robert J. Samuelson "worry that the currently fashionable ethic of 'celebrating differences' will atomize America, elevating the special interest above the national interest." How might this occur? Why is elevating one's special interest cause for worry?

Rhetorical Considerations

1. Loth is one of the only writers in this chapter who writes predominantly in the third person. Can a person who doesn't reveal his or her race write an effective paper about multiculturalism?
2. Is there an argument in this essay, or is this piece simply an informative article?
3. What makes Loth's essay inductive? Does she use an emotional appeal?
4. Can you read between the lines and the third person perspective to determine the political bent of the author? Cite specific examples to show whether she is liberal or conservative.
5. What is the rhetorical purpose in citing Thomas O'Connor, Leon Bouvier, Christopher Jencks, Raul Yzaguirre, and Julian Simon? Is the author's own voice present in this essay?

Writing Assignments

1. Project what America will be like in 2050 if, as Leon Bouvier predicts, America becomes "a majority minority." How might American politics, business, entertainment, and education change? Consider some of the projections in the essay.
2. In paragraph 6 Loth writes, "Ironically, the very people who promote ethnic and racial separateness are often the fiercest opponents of discrimination."

Using the essays in this chapter, write a paper in which you explore why Loth's statement is "ironic," and show the two elements can be reconciled.

3. Write an essay in which you show how aspects of other cultures have influenced your daily life. Give examples such as food, vocabulary, and clothing.

4. Refute or support Loth's assertion that there is currently a "backlash against political correctness" (paragraph 1). Cite evidence from this essay, other essays in the chapter, and recent periodicals.

CHAPTER 11

SOCIAL ISSUES

Gun control. Poverty and homelessness. Teenage pregnancy. Capital punishment. These are some of the most hotly debated issues in contemporary America. They are also issues that never seem to go away, that rumble from year to year in the media, in the courts of justice, in the halls of academe, and on Capitol Hill. Whether or not you've taken a firm stand on these issues, you may not be aware of their complexities—the emotional as well as ethical, moral, political, and legal aspects. As with so many of the arguments in this text, we have presented a variety of different views on each issue with the hope of offering points of view you may not have considered.

Perhaps the most disturbing social issue is the soaring rate of violent crime. Americans are killing, raping, and robbing one another at a rate greatly surpassing every other country that keeps crime statistics. In 1995 there were 25,000 murders committed in the United States, or nearly three an hour, as well as 18,000 reported rapes, 280,000 robberies, and 500,000 assaults. As public fear increases, so does the talk about crime prevention. And, inevitably, the talk turns to the subject of handguns—75 million of which are in the possession of private citizens. Is there a way to prevent guns from falling into the hands of the criminally minded or mentally unbalanced? This question is debated in the next four pieces. In "The Right to Bear Arms," the late Chief Justice Warren E. Burger takes a historical perspective in arguing that the Second Amendment of the Constitution of the United States does not guarantee the right of individuals to "bear arms." The next piece, "An Argument for Gun Control," by Sarah Brady, argues for a mandatory waiting period for handgun purchases. Warren Cassidy represents the opposite side in his essay "Gun Owners Are Not Bad People" in which he insists that a mandatory waiting period will penalize law-abiding buyers. In "Handguns in Our Homes Put Children at Risk," Derrick Jackson compellingly sketches one consequence of handguns' now ubiquitous nature: 5356 killings of children and teenagers by gunfire in a single year.

In another issue, America does not suffer from the abject poverty and homelessness that plagues parts of Africa, India, and Latin America; however, 33 million Americans live below the poverty line, and countless millions go home-less. Politicians and social activists debate over the causes and cures of poverty. Is government to blame, or is the individual ultimately responsible for his or her economic failures? What is the responsibility of society? Is the solution more welfare programs, or more jobs? The next four essays reflect the various debates over what to do about the twin plights of poverty and homelessness in this, the richest and scientifically most advanced nation on earth. In "Helping and Hating the Homeless," Peter Marin argues that society has specific obligations to those who have been "marginalized" against their wills. Taking an admittedly unpopular point of view, Christopher Awalt contends in "Brother, Don't Spare a Dime" that the homeless themselves must bear much of the blame for their trou-bles. Tackling the issue of welfare, political conservative Mickey Kaus states in "Yes, Something Will Work: Work" that welfare is to blame for the nation's swelling poverty class. In direct response to Kaus, Ruth Conniff criticizes Kaus's solution, calling it prejudicial, punitive, illogical, and inhuman. In "Culture of Cruelty," Conniff argues that Kaus discards the notion of economic justice and replaces it with blame and punishment.

Another issue of concern is that approximately 31 percent of babies are born out of wedlock every year to teenage parents. Recent rhetoric on the part of President Clinton and Health and Human Services Secretary Donna Shalala, has brought this issue to public debate. One view is that out-of-wedlock births to teenage mothers are responsible for our major social ills: poverty, crime, in-fant mortality, and low achievement—and that welfare benefits encourage teenage pregnancy. The opposing view sees teenage pregnancy not as the cause, but as the result of poverty, domestic violence, and poor education. In this view, welfare's role is to protect and nurture the victims of a neglectful society. The following four essays deal with the many questions and issues raised by teenage pregnancies. In the first essay, "Countering the Culture of Sex," social critic Ellen Goodman analyzes the role of Hollywood, the cultural message maker, in creating a social climate saturated with sex. In "The Name of the Game is Shame," Jonathan Alter advocates the stigma of shame as a tool to deter teenage pregnancy. In the third piece, "In Defense: Teenaged Mothers," Mike Males de-picts the teenage mother as a survivor who needs and deserves welfare benefits. And in the fourth piece, "Menace to Society?," Stephanie Coontz, herself a sin-gle mother, attacks the stereotypical notions of a single mother as feckless and selfish.

Finally at issue, is the death penalty the ultimate deterrent and a fitting punishment for crime? Or is it a cruel eye-for-an-eye retribution that our society should reject? The questions are raised in our "Oppositions" pair that closes this chapter. Edward I. Koch, former mayor of New York City, is in favor of capital punishment. He argues that execution helps affirm life while deterring crime. Attorney David Bruck, representing the opposing point of view, contends that capital punishment is a desperate symbol of the government's helplessness in fighting crimes of violence.

GUN CONTROL

The Right to Bear Arms
Warren E. Burger

While the crime rate in the United States grows to epidemic proportions, the debate over what to do about it continues. On one side are progun groups, such as the National Rifle Association who argue that American citizens have the constitutional right to bear arms. As the popular slogan goes, they contend that "Guns don't kill people—criminals do." On the other side are antigun groups, such as Handgun Control Inc., who argue for tighter restrictions on handguns and the outlawing of assault rifles.

We open the gun control debate with an essay by the late Chief Justice of the U.S. Supreme Court, Warren E. Burger. Taking a historical viewpoint in this article, which first appeared in *Parade* magazine in 1990, Burger contends that the main purpose of the Second Amendment was not to guarantee individuals the right to bear arms. Despite that widely held interpretation, Burger says the amendment was intended to ensure a more fundamental right, and he goes on to propose measures for reducing the "mindless homicidal carnage."

Appointed by President Nixon in 1969, Burger served as Chief Justice for seventeen years. He often voted in favor of decisions that led to major social changes. He died in 1995 at the age of 87.

BEFORE YOU READ

Consider the title of this essay. What does the "right to bear arms" mean to you? Why do you suppose Burger used such a title even though he argues for gun control? What do you anticipate his stand will be regarding hunting and target shooting? What about a person's right of self-protection?

AS YOU READ

Why does Burger spend so much time reviewing the history of the Second Amendment? Does his strategy create the persuasive effect he intends?

1   Our metropolitan centers, and some suburban communities of America, are setting new records for homicides by handguns. Many of our large centers have up to ten time the murder rate of all of Western Europe. In 1988, there were 9,000 handgun murders in America. Last year, Washington, D.C., alone had more than 400 homicides—setting a new record for our capital.

2   The Constitution of the United States, in its Second Amendment, guarantees a "right of the people to keep and bear arms." However, the meaning of this clause cannot be understood except by looking to the purpose, the setting, and the objectives of the draftsmen. The first ten amendments—the Bill of Rights—were not drafted at Philadelphia in 1787; that document came two years later than the Constitution. Most of the states already had bills of rights, but the Constitution might not have been ratified in 1788 if the states had not had assurances that a national Bill of Rights would soon be added.

3   People of that day were apprehensive about the new "monster" national government presented to them, and this helps explain the language and purpose of the Second Amendment. A few lines after the First Amendment's guarantees—against "establishment of religion," "free exercise" of religion, free speech and free press—came a guarantee that grew out of the deep-seated fear of a "national" or "standing" army. The same First Congress that approved the right to keep and bear arms also limited the national army to 840 men; Congress in the Second Amendment then provided:

> A well regulated Militia, being necessary to the security of a free State, the right of the people to keep and bear Arms, shall not be infringed.

4   In the 1789 debate in Congress on James Madison's proposed Bill of Rights, Elbridge Gerry argued that a state militia was necessary:

> . . . to prevent the establishment of a standing army, the bane of liberty . . . Whenever governments mean to invade the rights and liberties of the people, they always attempt to destroy the militia in order to raise an army upon their ruins.

5   We see that the need for a state militia was the predicate of the "right" guaranteed; in short, it was declared "necessary" in order to have a state military force to protect the security of the state. That Second Amendment clause must be read as though the word "because" was the opening word of the guarantee. Today, of course, the "state militia" serves a very different purpose. A huge national defense establishment has taken over the role of the militia of 200 years ago.

6   Some have exploited these ancient concerns, blurring sporting guns— rifles, shotguns, and even machine pistols—with all firearms, including what are now called "Saturday night specials." There is, of course, a great difference between sporting guns and handguns. Some regulation of handguns has long been accepted as imperative; laws relating to "concealed weapons" are common. That we may be "overregulated" in some areas of life has never held us back from more regulation of automobiles, airplanes, motorboats, and "concealed weapons."

7   Let's look at the history.

8   First, many of the 3.5 million people living in the thirteen original Colonies depended on wild game for food, and a good many of them required firearms for their defense from marauding Indians—and later from the French and English. Underlying all these needs was an important concept that each able-bodied man in each of the thirteen independent states had to help or defend his state.

9   The early opposition to the idea of national or standing armies was maintained under the Articles of Confederation; that confederation had no standing army and wanted none. The state militia—essentially a part-time citizen army, as in Switzerland today—was the only kind of "army" they wanted. From the time of the Declaration of Independence through the victory at Yorktown in 1781, George Washington, as the commander in chief of these volunteer-militia armies, had to depend upon the states to send those volunteers.

10   When a company of New Jersey militia volunteers reported for duty to Washington at Valley Forge, the men initially declined to take an oath to "the United States," maintaining, "Our country is New Jersey." Massachusetts Bay men, Virginians, and others felt the same way. To the American of the eighteenth century, his state was his country, and his freedom was defended by his militia.

11   The victory at Yorktown—and the ratification of the Bill of Rights a decade later—did not change people's attitudes about a national army. They had lived for years under the notion that each state would maintain its own military establishment, and the seaboard states had their own navies as well. These people, and their fathers and grandfathers before them, remembered how monarchs had used standing armies to oppress their ancestors in Europe. Americans wanted no part of this. A state militia, like a rifle and powder horn, was as much a part of life as the automobile is today; pistols were largely for officers, aristocrats—and dueling.

12   Against this background, it was not surprising that the provision concerning firearms emerged in very simple terms with the significant predicate—basing the right on the *necessity* for a "well regulated militia," a state army.

13   In the two centuries since then—with two world wars and some lesser ones—it has become clear, sadly, that we have no choice but to maintain a standing national army while still maintaining a "militia" by way of the National Guard, which can be swiftly integrated into the national defense forces.

14   Americans also have a right to defend their homes, and we need not challenge that. Nor does anyone seriously question that the Constitution protects the right of hunters to own and keep sporting guns for hunting game any more than anyone would challenge the right to own and keep fishing rods and other equipment for fishing—or to own automobiles. To "keep and bear arms" for hunting today is essentially a recreational activity and not an imperative of survival, as it was 200 years ago; "Saturday night specials" and machine guns are not recreational weapons and surely are as much in need of regulation as motor vehicles.

15   Americans should ask themselves a few questions. The Constitution does not mention automobiles or motorboats, but the right to keep and own an automobile is beyond question; equally beyond question is the power of the state to regulate the purchase or the transfer of such a vehicle and the right to license the vehicle and the driver with reasonable standards. In some places, even a bicycle must be registered, as must some household dogs.

16   If we are to stop this mindless homicidal carnage, is it unreasonable:

1. to provide that, to acquire a firearm, an application be made reciting age, residence, employment, and any prior criminal convictions?
2. to require that this application lie on the table for ten days (absent a showing for urgent need) before the license would be issued?
3. that the transfer of a firearm be made essentially as that of a motor vehicle?
4. to have a "ballistic fingerprint" of the firearm made by the manufacturer and filed with the license record so that, if a bullet is found in a victim's body, law enforcement might be helped in finding the culprit?

17   These are the kinds of questions the American people must answer if we are to preserve the "domestic tranquility" promised in the Constitution.

Topical Considerations

1. Given some of the more shocking instances of handgun misuse in the news (i.e., children and adolescents carrying guns to school, or disgruntled citizens opening fire on innocent bystanders in restaurants), do you feel that handgun laws need general revision? If so, what sorts of changes do you feel would be effective?
2. After reading Burger's history of the Second Amendment, do you feel that the "right to bear arms" should be protected by the Constitution? Why or why not? Did you feel the same way before reading the history?
3. Discuss the differences between a "standing army" and a "militia" as presented in Burger's article. How does the distinction between these terms relate to the issue of gun control?
4. How do you feel about having a handgun in your home? Would it make you feel uncomfortable or afraid, or would it make you feel secure? What are some of the dangers involved? Do the benefits or protections outweigh those dangers? Explain your answer.
5. Burger states in paragraph 14 that "Americans also have a right to defend their homes, and we need not challenge that." How far do you think this right goes in the law's eyes? If someone was threatening your home in some

way, would you feel justified in shooting, and perhaps killing, that person? Explain your answer.

6. In paragraph 16 Burger sets forth certain suggestions that he believes might help solve the problem of handgun homicides. Do you feel that these solutions would be effective? Why or why not? Should there be even more regulation by the government than Burger suggests? Or do you feel that any government intervention violates a basic constitutional right? Explain your answer.

Rhetorical Considerations

1. Examine the opening of Burger's article. Do you find the use of statistics in this introduction effective? Why or why not?
2. Burger spends a good portion of his article outlining the history and context of the Second Amendment to the Constitution. Do you find this much history necessary to Burger's article and useful in proving his argument? Why or why not?
3. Do you think Burger's analogy between registration of handguns and registration of motor vehicles is effective in his argument? Explain your answer.
4. In paragraph 16 Burger sets forth a series of proposals for revision to current handgun registration laws. These proposals take the form of questions. How effective do you find this strategy, rhetorically? Explain.
5. Burger's argument addressed only a very specific aspect of the issue of gun control. Do you find this narrowness of focus helpful or harmful to the overall effectiveness of his argument? Explain your answer.

Writing Assignments

1. Write an essay summarizing the views of two other authors in this section on the issue of gun control, comparing and contrasting their views with Burger's. Make you own position clear in your thesis statement and conclusion.
2. Burger's proposals outline policy changes for the registration of handguns that he hopes would help stop the "mindless homicidal carnage" associated with handgun ownership. However, it has often been noted by experts that most guns used in criminal activity have been obtained illegally and are not registered. Write an essay in which you make an argument that revision of registration laws is basically ineffective in solving the problem of handgun homicide.
3. Write an essay from the point of view of an antihunting activist regarding Burger's views about the legitimacy of owning sporting guns for hunting. (Hint: You might focus on the issue of constitutional rights.)

4. In paragraph 6 Burger brings up the issue of Americans being "overregu-lated" in some areas of life. Write an essay examining and evaluating ways in which our life is "overregulated" by government, state, church, or other "power institutions."

A Case Against Firearms
Sarah Brady

Sarah Brady, head of Handgun Control Inc., knows firsthand about gun violence. Her own future was partly destroyed on March 30, 1981, when would-be assassin John W. Hinckley, Jr. shot and wounded President Ronald Reagan and perma-nently disabled her husband James Brady, then White House press secretary. Seek-ing to reduce gun violence in America, gun control advocates have lobbied for pas-sage of the so-called Brady Bill, which calls for a mandatory waiting period on handgun purchases. Supported by Ronald Reagan, this bill, which is tied to a larger anticrime package including the ban on the sale and domestic production of semi-automatic weapons, is the first attempt by the federal government to restrict hand-gun sales since the 1960s. At the time of this printing, this anticrime package had not yet become law.

This article first appeared in *Time* magazine in January 1990.

BEFORE YOU READ

To convince her audience to support the Brady Bill, Sarah Brady must demonstrate that firearm violence has reached epidemic proportions in this country. Before you read her argument, think of which recent firearm incidents either locally or nation-ally would persuade her audience that such violence is a problem.

AS YOU READ

As you read this essay make note of Sarah Brady's examples of firearm violence. Are they effective? Too sensational? Not complete enough? Think how her opponents might respond to her examples. Also, notice that although Sarah Brady cites her own husband as a victim of handgun violence, she does not go into detail regarding his injuries. What do you think her reasoning is? Did this choice make her piece more or less effective?

1   As America enters the next decade, it does so with an appalling legacy of gun violence. The 1980s were tragic years that saw nearly a quarter of a million Americans die from handguns—four times as many as were killed in the Viet

Nam War. We began the decade by witnessing yet another President, Ronald Reagan, become a victim of a would-be assassin's bullet. That day my husband Jim, his press secretary, also became a statistic in America's handgun war.

2   Gun violence is an epidemic in this country. In too many cities, the news each night reports another death by a gun. As dealers push out in search of new addicts, Smalltown, U.S.A., is introduced to the mindless gun violence fostered by the drug trade.

3   And we are killing our future. Every day a child in this country loses his or her life to a handgun. Hundreds more are permanently injured, often because a careless adult left within easy reach a loaded handgun purchased for self-defense.

4   Despite the carnage, America stands poised to face an even greater escalation of bloodshed. The growing popularity of military-style assault weapons could turn our streets into combat zones. Assault weapons, designed solely to mow down human beings, are turning up at an alarming rate in the hands of those most prone to violence—drug dealers, gang members, hate groups and the mentally ill.

5   The Stockton, Calif., massacre of little children was a warning to our policy-makers. But Congress lacked the courage to do anything. During the year of inaction on Capital Hill, we have seen too many other tragedies brought about by assault weapons. In Louisville an ex-employee of a printing plant went on a shooting spree with a Chinese-made semiautomatic version of the AK–47, gunning down 21 people, killing eight and himself. Two Colorado women were murdered and several others injured by a junkie using a stolen MAC–11 semiautomatic pistol. And Congress votes itself a pay raise.

6   The National Rifle Association, meanwhile, breathes a sigh of relief, gratified that your attention is now elsewhere. The only cooling-off period the N.R.A. favors is a postponement of legislative action. It counts on public anger to fade before such outrage can be directed at legislators. The N.R.A. runs feel-good ads saying guns are not the problem and there is nothing we can do to prevent criminals from getting guns. In fact, it has said that guns in the wrong hands are the "price we pay for freedom." I guess I'm just not willing to hand the next John Hinckley a deadly handgun. Neither is the nation's law-enforcement community, the men and women who put their lives on the line for the rest of us every day.

7   Two pieces of federal legislation can make a difference right now. First, we must require a national waiting period before the purchase of a handgun, to allow for a criminal-records check. Police know that waiting periods work. In the 20 years that New Jersey has required a background check, authorities have stopped more than 10,000 convicted felons from purchasing handguns.

8   We must also stop the sale and domestic production of semiautomatic assault weapons. These killing machines clearly have no legitimate sporting purpose, as President Bush recognized when he permanently banned their importation.

9   These public-safety measures are supported by the vast majority of Americans—including gun owners. In fact, these measures are so sensible that I never realized the campaign to pass them into law would be such an uphill battle. But it can be done.

10   Jim Brady knows the importance of a waiting period. He knows the living hell of a gunshot wound. Jim and I are not afraid to take on the N.R.A. leaders, and we will fight them everywhere we can. As Jim said in his congressional testimony, "I don't question the rights of responsible gun owners. That's not the issue. The issue is whether the John Hinckleys of the world should be able to walk into gun stores and purchase handguns instantly. Are you willing and ready to cast a vote for a commonsense public-safety bill endorsed by experts—law enforcement?"

11   Are we as a nation going to accept America's bloodshed, or are we ready to stand up and do what is right? When are we going to say "Enough"? We can change the direction in which America is headed. We can prevent the 1990s from being bloodier than the past ten years. If each of you picks up a pen and writes to your Senators and Representatives tonight, you would be surprised at how quickly we could collect the votes we need to win the war for a safer America.

12   Let us enter a new decade committed to finding solutions to the problem of gun violence. Let your legislators know that voting with the gun lobby—and against public safety—is no longer acceptable. Let us send a signal to lawmakers that we demand action, not excuses.

Topical Considerations

1. What argument does Brady introduce in the opening paragraph and carry through the entire essay? Is this a strong and convincing argument? Do you agree with Brady?

2. In the first paragraph, Brady cites "yet another" presidential attack by "a would-be-assassin's bullet." Do you think that political assassinations or such attempts should impel us to take a firmer stand against handguns? Why or why not?

3. For what specific legislations is Sarah Brady asking? What evidence does she give that such measures will make a difference in the violence in this country? Do you agree with her reasoning? Do you find her appeals convincing? Enough to change peoples' attitudes?

4. Brady points out that the National Rifle Association is part of the reason our country has no effective national gun control legislation. Why is this? What is your opinion of the N.R.A. campaign against gun control? Why do you think it has so much influence?

5. If the author of this piece were not the wife of Jim Brady, would the article be as effective an appeal for gun control? Why or why not?

Rhetorical Considerations

1. In the opening paragraph, Brady says that the decade of the 1980s left us an "appalling legacy of gun violence." How does she communicate this idea?
2. What do you remember best about the writing in this essay? How was it effective in presenting the arguments? How was it convincing and persuasive?
3. How would you characterize the tone of this essay—reasoned and objective? Angry and bitter? Resigned and frustrated? Explain your answer.
4. Consider the last sentence in paragraph 5: "And Congress votes itself a pay raise." Does this sentence effectively resolve any points of the paragraph? What point does it make? What is the tone here?

Writing Assignments

1. If all the laws on the books prohibiting theft of property and drug abuse haven't aided enforcement, what is the likelihood that one or two more gun control laws will curb violence? Write an essay in which you offer a rebuttal to Sarah Brady's arguments for gun control legislation.
2. Write a paper in which you argue that requiring a national waiting period before purchasing a handgun does not compromise N.R.A. members' right to own and use guns. Nor does it violate the Bill of Rights or Americans' freedom to hunt, target shoot, or protect themselves.
3. Do you own a gun? If so, and if you do not use it for hunting or target-shooting, explain why you own it.
4. If you are not a gun owner, do you think you ever could be? Can you imagine circumstances in which you might feel compelled to purchase a gun?

Gun Owners Are Not Bad People
Warren Cassidy

Warren Cassidy argues that gun control will not reduce crime because criminals can always get guns illegally. Furthermore, any gun control laws will only deny law-abiding citizens their constitutional right to bear arms. Guns, he argues, help keep decent Americans free.

Cassidy is the executive vice president of the National Rifle Association, which has vigorously fought both the Brady Bill and other gun control legislation. This article first appeared in *Time* magazine in January 1990.

BEFORE YOU READ

Because Cassidy bases much of his argument on the Second Amendment of the Constitution of the United States, take the time to read and reflect on that amendment before you read this piece. Think about your interpretation of that amendment and about how it applies to the idea of gun control.

AS YOU READ

You will learn in paragraph 5 that 70 million Americans own firearms. Does this statement alarm you or comfort you? How does Cassidy present this information in a positive light and thus use it to support his argument that gun control laws are not desirable?

1   The American people have a right "to keep and bear arms." This right is protected by the Second Amendment to the Constitution, just as the right to publish editorial comment in this magazine is protected by the First Amendment. Americans remain committed to the constitutional right to free speech even when their most powerful oracles have, at time, abused the First Amendment's inherent powers. Obviously the American people believe no democracy can survive without a free voice.

2   In the same light, the authors of the Bill of Rights knew that a democratic republic has a right—indeed, a need—to keep and bear arms. Millions of American citizens just as adamantly believe the Second Amendment is crucial to the maintenance of the democratic process. Many express this belief through membership in the National Rifle Association of America.

3   Our cause is neither trendy nor fashionable, but a basic American belief that spans generations. The N.R.A.'s strength has never originated in Washington but instead has reached outward and upward from Biloxi, Albuquerque, Concord, Tampa, Topeka—from every point on the compass and from communities large and small. Those who fail to grasp this widespread commitment will never understand the depth of political and philosophical dedication symbolized by the letters N.R.A.

4   Scholars who have devoted careers to the study of the Second Amendment agree in principle that the right to keep and bear arms is fundamental to our concept of democracy. No high-court decision has yet found grounds to challenge this basic freedom. Yet some who oppose this freedom want to waive the constitutionality of the "gun control" question for the sake of their particular—and sometimes peculiar—brand of social reform.

5   In doing so they seem ready, even eager, to disregard a constitutional right exercised by at least 70 million Americans who own firearms. Contrary to current antigun evangelism, these gun owners are not bad people. They are hardworking, law abiding, tax paying. They are safe, sane and courteous in their use of guns. They have never been, nor will they ever be, a threat to law-and-order.

6   History repeatedly warns us that human character cannot be scrubbed free of its defects through vain attempts to regulate inanimate objects such as guns. What has worked in the past, and what we see working now, are tough, N.R.A.-supported measures that punish the incorrigible minority who place themselves outside the law.

7   As a result of such measures, violent crimes with firearms, like assault and robbery, have stabilized or are actually declining. We see proof that levels

of firearm ownership cannot be associated with levels of criminal violence, except for their deterrent value. On the other hand, tough laws designed to incarcerate violent offenders offer something gun control cannot: swift, sure justice meted out with no accompanying erosion of individual liberty.

8   Violent crime continues to rise in cities like New York and Washington even after severe firearm-control statutes were rushed into place. Criminals, understandably, have illegal ways of obtaining guns. Antigun laws—the waiting period, background checks, handgun bans, et al.—only harass those who obey them. Why should an honest citizen be deprived of a firearm for sport or self-defense when, for a gangster, obtaining a gun is just a matter of showing up on the right street corner with enough money?

9   Antigun opinion steadfastly ignores these realities known to rank-and-file police officers—men and women who face crime firsthand, not police administrators who face mayors and editors. These law-enforcement professionals tell us that expecting firearm restrictions to act as crime-prevention measures is wishful thinking. They point out that proposed gun laws would not have stopped heinous crimes committed by the likes of John Hinckley, Jr., Patrick Purdy, Laurie Dann or mentally disturbed, usually addicted killers. How can such crimes be used as examples of what gun control could prevent?

10   There are better ways to advance our society than to excuse criminal behavior. The N.R.A. initiated the first hunter-safety program, which has trained millions of young hunters. We are the shooting sports' leading safety organization, with more than 26,000 certified instructors training 750,000 students and trainees last year alone. Through 1989 there were 9,818 N.R.A.-certified law-enforcement instructors teaching marksmanship to thousands of peace officers.

11   Frankly, we would rather keep investing N.R.A. resources in such worthwhile efforts instead of spending our time and members' money debunking the failed and flawed promises of gun prohibitionists.

12   If you agree, I invite you to join the N.R.A.

Topical Considerations

1. Do you own a gun? If so, what are your reasons? If not, what circumstances would make you consider buying one? Explain your answer.
2. What does Cassidy see as the motives behind those who call for gun control? Is this a fair characterization of their motives? Can you think of others?
3. Citing scholarly interpretations of the Second Amendment, Cassidy argues that in a democracy the individual has the constitutional right to bear arms. Why does he believe gun control is unconstitutional? Does he make a valid point? Do you agree with him, or not? Do you know the original intention of the Second Amendment? If not, it might be a good idea to investigate this before you answer.

4. In the battle against crime, what does Cassidy offer as an alternative to gun control legislation? What evidence does he give that such alternatives work? What evidence is there that they are not working?

5. According to Cassidy, how will anti-gun measures prove useless in preventing crime? How will such measures "harass" law-abiding gun owners? Do you agree with his arguments here? Explain your answer.

6. Cassidy is clearly opposed to any legislation that will prevent gun owners from owning guns. What do you think he would say about legislation against the import and sale of assault rifles? What are your feelings about such legislation?

7. If you were judging a debate between Cassidy and Brady, who would you decide had won? Consider how well each of them addresses the issues and whether either one successfully argues a point that the other fails to note.

Rhetorical Considerations

1. How would you characterize the tone of this essay—reasoned and objective? Emotional and flag-waving? Angry and bitter? Resigned and frustrated?

2. What do you think was the intention (or intentions) of the author in this article? Was he trying to make a case against gun control, for firearms, or for joining the N.R.A.? Or, all three?

3. In paragraph 11, Cassidy refers to wasting N.R.A. resources and time "debunking the failed and flawed promises of gun prohibitionists." Do you think he successfully debunked the arguments of gun prohibitionists in his essay? Did he convince you their promises have "failed" or were "flawed?" Explain.

Writing Assignments

1. Write a letter to Warren Cassidy telling him what you thought of his case for firearms. Cite his specific points of argument.

2. Write a paper in which you argue for or against gun control measures such as waiting periods, background checks, handgun bans, and so forth. Use the arguments you find in either Cassidy's essay or Sarah Brady's that you believe are most convincing.

3. Have you ever witnessed a gun-related crime? If so, write a narrative description of the incident. Comment on how it influenced your views (if at all) on gun control.

4. Cassidy argues that the N.R.A.'s hunter-safety programs and civilian and police training along with its support for mandatory sentences for criminal

use of firearms do more for society than the gun prohibitionists. Write a paper in which you support or counter this claim.

Handguns in Our Homes Put Children at Risk
Derrick Z. Jackson

In 1991, 5356 children and teenagers were killed by gunfire. In ten years guns will replace cars as the nation's most deadly product. In view of these facts, Derrick Z. Jackson argues that measures must be taken to get handguns out of the reach of children. He builds his case on two points: First, he sketches several disturbing accounts of the accidental deaths of children by handgun, most perpetrated by 11-, 14-, and 15-year-old children with access to handguns; second, he scornfully reviews the measures politicians and public health figures did **not** take to get handguns out of homes. Without measures to control handguns, he argues, the carnage in our homes will continue.

Derrick Z. Jackson is a columnist for *The Boston Globe* and frequently writes about social and political issues.

BEFORE YOU READ

Do you personally feel that your safety is threatened by the 216 million firearms floating around our nation today? Explain why or why not.

AS YOU READ

Notice the language, level of diction, and selection of detail Derrick uses to describe deaths among children by handgun. Why did Derrick choose this language and this level of detail? Is it effective? Flat? Incendiary?

1   Nothing will come of last week's killings of children by children unless the grownups have had enough of guns.

2   In Chicago last week, an 11-year-old boy murdered a 14-year-old girl to impress his gang. The 11-year-old was then killed by two brothers in the gang, aged 14 and 16. Chicago Police Superintendent Matt Rodriguez said: "It goes back as far as the proliferation of firearms. We have immature, impressionable children armed with some of the most sophisticated weapons."

3   In rural High Bridge, N.J., a 13-year-old boy apparently killed an 11-year-old boy in the latter's bedroom with a gun found in the younger boy's house. The reason? He refused to apologize to a friend of the 13-year-old. After meeting with the accused killer, High Bridge's mayor, Alfred Schweikert, said, "He couldn't believe it happened. . . . They don't understand mortality."

4   Or morality. No one should call these murders senseless. They make sense in our United States of Arms. In 1970 there were about 100 million firearms floating around our nation. Today there are 216 million. With that kind of permissiveness, it is surprise that children are tempted by the trigger.

5   Politicians agonize over a crime bill that bans only the most hideous of assault weapons, while children pop away with the pistols owned by their parents or stolen from other adults. With a sapling sense of judgment that is often stunted by bloody movies in which guns solve all problems, by hopelessness or boredom in the streets and by child abuse, more than 100,000 teen-agers bring guns to school every day. In 1991, 5,356 children and teen-agers were killed by gunfire. The US teen-age murder rate is seven times higher than any nation in Western Europe.

6   After adults kill adults, you often hear calls for the death penalty. Children killing children exposes this as a cheap thrill. Are we really going to start dropping cyanide pellets underneath 11-year-olds? Even friends and relatives of the 14-year-old girl killed in Chicago had sympathy for the 11-year-old killer, who was abused as a toddler.

7   Some relatively bold politicians have suggested taxing handgun bullets. Almost none are willing to take on handguns themselves, even though the Centers for Disease Control has just announced that gun deaths are rising faster than any other kind of death except AIDS. In 1991, 1.1 million years of potential life, assuming death at the age of 65, were eliminated by guns.

8   President Clinton and Surgeon General Joycelyn Elders have proclaimed guns a public health disaster, yet there is no tax proposed on handguns, as there is on cigarettes, to help fund health care reform. While our government conducts surprise inspections to stop smoking in coal mines, no one has suggested a national plan to buy back guns.

9   We have massive public education campaigns against cigarettes. But since fear and the image of being tough on crime wins elections, almost no politician risks telling the voters that most Americans are not at a major risk of being murdered. We have allowed people to believe they can protect themselves with guns even as most major studies show that handgun ownership is a good way to significantly increase your chances of being killed in your own home.

10   With such poor aim as a society, it was only a matter of time before the very young started dropping. Young, low-income African-American males are doing a lot of the dying, but the carnage this year defies any stereotype. In Wenatchee, Wash., two 12-year-olds pumped 18 bullets into a migrant worker. In Prince George's County, after the first day of school last week, a 14-year-old was apparently accidentally killed when he and his 13-year-old friend played with a shotgun in the home of the younger child's grandfather.

11   In Nashville, Tenn., a 14-year-old boy confined to a wheelchair because of muscular dystrophy brought a gun to middle school. He let a classmate hold the gun in music class. The gun went off and killed a 13-year-old student. In Maple Grove, Minn., outside Minneapolis, a 15-year-old boy play-

ing with his father's gun killed a 14-year-old friend. In Sayreville, N.J., two boys, 14 and 15, killed themselves copying the suicide of rock star Kurt Cobain.

12   At the current pace of destruction, guns will replace cars as the nation's most deadly product within 10 years. We have banned smoking from most public indoor spaces because of secondhand smoke. We must now get handguns out of our homes so our children stop becoming victims of secondhand possession. On Sunday, again in Chicago, a 5-year-old accidentally killed his 3-year-old brother in gun play. What are we waiting for? A newborn to come firing out of its mother's womb?

Topical Considerations

1. Describe what Jackson believes has caused the current epidemic of "killings of children by children" (paragraph 1) in America. Are you convinced by this claim? Why or why not?

2. Explain Jackson's attitude toward the death penalty. Do you believe this issue is relevant to a discussion of children's use of handguns? Why or why not?

3. Analyze the comparison Jackson makes between gun control and antismoking regulations (paragraph 6–7; 12). What does Jackson imply is the parallel between these two issues? Has he convinced you that this is a reasonable analogy; why or why not?

4. How would Jackson respond to Warren Cassidy's claim that it is "wishful thinking" to imagine gun control will "act as crime prevention" ("Gun Owners are Not Bad People," paragraph 9)? Cite specific passages from Jackson's essay that address this claim. After reading both articles, which position, Jackson's or Cassidy's, do you endorse, and why?

Rhetorical Considerations

1. Consider Jackson's use of statistics to support his argument. Do you think he uses them effectively? Why or why not?

2. To support his argument, Jackson relies heavily on stories of murders by and of children. How effective do you find this strategy? What does Jackson gain by reciting so many different anecdotes? Where do you find the link between example and argument to be weak?

3. Consider Jackson's tone. What words or phrases convey this tone? Does the tone undercut or strengthen the force of his argument?

4. Evaluate Jackson's organizational strategy in this essay. Where does he state his thesis? How does he organize the different kinds of support offered here?

Writing Assignments

1. Consider Jackson's implication that children killing children is a serious problem in American society. Start by doing further research on this issue, trying especially to confirm or undercut Jackson's statistics about the number of guns in schools; the number of children killed by guns; and the number of accidental deaths per year. Your paper should either support or attack Jackson's depiction of the problem.
2. Write a letter to Warren Cassidy trying to convince him that the problem posed by children's ready access to handguns should make him rethink his position on gun control. Make sure you take into account Cassidy's beliefs, as expressed in his argument, as you decide how to approach him as an audience.
3. As a group, using the date of Jackson's article as a guide, gather together as many different newspaper accounts as possible of one of the murders mentioned in this essay. Try to get both local and national newspaper articles and determine any bias on the issue of gun control revealed by the newspaper accounts. Though two articles report the same event, there may be differences in organization, use of evidence, citations from authorities, tone, and accompanying photography which give a variety of slants to the incident. Write a group essay reporting your findings.

POVERTY AND HOMELESSNESS

Helping and Hating the Homeless
Peter Marin

The streets of America, once thought to be paved with gold, are now leaden mattresses for society's newest class: the homeless. This marginalized and disenfranchised group, made up of veterans, the mentally ill, the physically handicapped, the poverty-stricken, children, and alcoholics, now numbers 2 million by some estimates. In this essay Peter Marin asks the question, "What does society owe the homeless?" Marin reminds us that homelessness is usually the result of an ordinary life struck with trauma and catastrophe; and that we have a moral obligation to help homeless people regain their place in the social order by providing affordable housing and good wages. But he goes further and tackles the question of the voluntary homeless—street people, rebels, derelicts, those who choose to live "at the pale," on society's margins. To those, too, he says we have a moral obligation to offer a place to live, a way to exist.

Peter Marin is a contributing editor of *Harper's Magazine*, where this essay first appeared in longer form in 1987. He is the author of *Freedom and Its Discontents: Reflections on Four Decades of American Moral Experience* (1994), a study of homelessness in America.

BEFORE YOU READ

Most likely you've encountered a homeless person on the streets. What was your reaction when personally confronting the homeless? Did you feel pity? Fear? Anger? Disgust? Empathy? Try to describe your reaction.

AS YOU READ

As you read, compare your own reactions to the homeless with those of Peter Marin. Do you share his views? Explain.

1   When I was a child, I had a recurring vision of how I would end as an old man: alone, in a sparsely furnished second-story room I could picture quite precisely, in a walk-up on Fourth Avenue in New York, where the secondhand bookstores then were. It was not a picture which frightened me. I liked it. The idea of anonymity and solitude and marginality must have seemed to me, back then . . . both inviting and inevitable. Later, out of college, I took to the road, hitchhiking and traveling on freights, doing odd jobs here and there, criss-crossing the country. I liked that too: the anonymity and the absence of constraint and the rough community I sometimes found. I felt at home on the road, perhaps because I felt at home nowhere else, and periodically, for years, I would return to that world, always with a sense of relief and release.

2   I have been thinking a lot about that these days, now that transience and homelessness have made their way into the national consciousness, and especially since the town I live in, Santa Barbara, has become well known because of the recent successful campaign to do away with the meanest aspects of its "sleeping ordinances"—a set of foolish laws making it illegal for the homeless to sleep at night in public places. During that campaign I got to know many of the homeless men and women in Santa Barbara, who tend to gather, night and day, in a small park at the lower end of town, not far from the tracks and the harbor, under the rooflike, overarching branches of a gigantic fig tree, said to be the oldest on the continent. There one enters much the same world I thought, as a child, I would die in, and the one in which I traveled as a young man: a "marginal" world inhabited by all those unable to find a place in "our" world. . . .

3   Late last summer, at a city council meeting here in Santa Barbara, I saw, close up, the consequences of that strange combination of proximity and distance. The council was meeting to vote on the repeal of the sleeping ordi-

nances, though not out of any sudden sense of compassion or justice. Council members had been pressured into it by the threat of massive demonstrations—''The Selma of the Eighties'' was the slogan one heard among the homeless. But this threat that frightened the council enraged the town's citizens. Hundreds of them turned out for the meeting. One by one they filed to the microphone to curse the council and castigate the homeless. Drinking, doping, loitering, panhandling, defecating, urinating, molesting, stealing—the litany went on and on, was repeated over and over, accompanied by fantasies of disaster: the barbarian hordes at the gates, civilization ended.

4   What astonished me about the meeting was not what was said; one could have predicted that. It was the power and depth of the emotion revealed: the mindlessness of the fear, the vengefulness of the fury. Also, almost none of what was said had anything to do with the homeless people I know—not the ones I once traveled with, not the ones in town. They, the actual homeless men and women, might not have existed at all.

5   If I write about Santa Barbara, it is not because I think the attitudes at work here are unique. They are not. You find them everywhere in America. In the last few months I have visited several cities around the country, and in each of them I have found the same thing: more and more people in the streets, more and more suffering. (There are at least 350,000 homeless people in the country, perhaps as many as 3 million.) And, in talking to the good citizens of these cities, I found, almost always, the same thing: confusion and ignorance, or simple indifference, but anger too, and fear.

6   What follows here is an attempt to explain at least some of that anger and fear, to clear up some of the confusion, to chip away at the indifference. . . .

7   Homelessness, in itself, is nothing more than a condition visited upon men and women (and, increasingly, children) as the final stage of a variety of problems about which the word ''homelessness'' tells us almost nothing. Or, to put it another way, it is a catch basin into which pour all of the people disenfranchised or marginalized or scared off by processes beyond their control, those which lie close to the heart of American life. Here are the groups packed into the single category of ''the homeless'':

- Veterans, mainly from the war in Vietnam. In many American cities, vets make up close to 50 percent of all homeless males.
- The mentally ill. In some parts of the country, roughly a quarter of the homeless would, a couple of decades ago, have been institutionalized.
- The physically disabled or chronically ill, who do not receive any benefits or whose benefits do not enable them to afford permanent shelter.
- The elderly on fixed incomes whose funds are no longer sufficient for their needs.
- Men, women, and whole families pauperized by the loss of a job.
- Single parents, usually women, without the resources or skills to establish new lives.

- Runaway children, many of whom have been abused.
- Alcoholics and those in trouble with drugs (whose troubles often begin with one of the other conditions listed here).
- Immigrants, both legal and illegal, who often are not counted among the homeless because they constitute a "problem" in their own right.
- Traditional tramps, hobos, and transients, who have taken to the road or the streets for a variety of reasons and who prefer to be there.

8   You can quickly learn two things about the homeless from this list. First, you can learn that many of the homeless, before they were homeless, were people more or less like ourselves: members of the working or middle class. And you can learn that the world of the homeless has its roots in various policies, events, and ways of life for which some of us are responsible and from which some of us actually prosper.

9   We decide, as a people, to go to war, we ask our children to kill and to die, and the result, years later, is grown men homeless on the street.

10   We change, with the best intentions, the laws pertaining to the mentally ill, and then, without intention, neglect to provide them with services; and the result, in our streets, drives some of us crazy with rage.

11   We cut taxes and prune budgets, we modernize industry and shift the balance of trade, and the result of all these actions and errors can be read, sleeping form by sleeping form, on our city streets.

12   The liberals cannot blame the conservatives. The conservatives cannot blame the liberals. Homelessness is the *sum total* of our dreams, policies, intentions, errors, omissions, cruelties, kindnesses, all of it recorded, in flesh, in the life of the streets.

13   You can also learn from this list one of the most important things there is to know about the homeless—that they can be roughly divided into two groups: those who have had homelessness forced upon them and want nothing more than to escape it; and those who have at least in part *chosen* it for themselves, and now accept, or in some cases, embrace it.

14   I understand how dangerous it is to introduce the idea of choice into a discussion of homelessness. It can all too easily be used to justify indifference or brutality toward the homeless, or to argue that they are only getting what they "deserve." And yet it seems to me that it is only by taking choice into account, in all of the intricacies of its various forms and expressions, that one can really understand certain kinds of homelessness.

15   The fact is, many of the homeless are not only hapless victims but voluntary exiles, "domestic refugees," people who have turned not against life itself but against *us,* our life, American life. Look for a moment at the vets. The price of returning to America was to forget what they had seen or learned in Vietnam, to "put it behind them." But some could not do that, and the stress of trying showed up as alcoholism, broken marriages, drug addiction, crime. And it showed up too as life on the street, which was for some vets a desperate choice made in the name of life—the best they could manage. It was a way of

avoiding what might have occurred had they stayed where they were: suicide, or violence done to others.

16   We must learn to accept that there may indeed be people, and not only vets, who have seen so much of our world, or seen it so clearly, that to live in it becomes impossible. Here, for example, is the story of Alice, a homeless middle-aged woman in Los Angeles, where there are, perhaps, 50,000 homeless people. It was set down a few months ago by one of my students at the University of California, Santa Barbara, where I taught for a semester. I had encouraged them to go find the homeless and listen to their stories. And so, one day, when this student saw Alice foraging in a dumpster outside a McDonald's, he stopped and talked to her:

> She told me she had led a pretty normal life as she grew up and eventually went to college. From there she went on the Chicago to teach school. She was single and lived in a small apartment.
>
> One night, after she got off the train after school, a man began to follow her to her apartment building. When she got to her door she saw a knife and the man hovering behind her. She had no choice but to let him in. The man raped her.
>
> After that, things got steadily worse. She had a nervous breakdown. She went to a mental institution for three months, and when she went back to her apartment she found her belongings gone. The landlord had sold them to cover the rent she hadn't paid.
>
> She had no place to go and no job because the school had terminated her employment. She slipped into depression. She lived with friends until she could muster enough money for a ticket to Los Angeles. She said she no longer wanted to burden her friends, and that if she had to live outside, at least Los Angeles was warmer than Chicago.
>
> It is as if she began back then to take on the mentality of a street person. She resolved herself to homelessness. She's been out West since 1980, without a home or job. She seems happy, with her best friend being her cat. But the scars of memories still haunt her, and she is running from them, or should I say *him*.

17   This is, in essence, the same story one hears over and over again on the street. You begin with an ordinary life; then an event occurs—traumatic, catastrophic; smaller events follow, each one deepening the original wound; finally, homelessness becomes inevitable, or begins to *seem* inevitable to the person involved—the only way out of an intolerable situation. You are struck continually, hearing these stories, by something seemingly unique in American life, the absolute isolation involved. . . .

18   We like to think, in America, that everything is redeemable, that everything broken can be magically made whole again, and that what has been "dirtied" can be cleansed. . . .

19   Yes, many of those on the streets could be transformed, rehabilitated. But there are others whose lives have been irrevocably changed, damaged beyond repair, and who no longer want help, who no longer recognize the *need*

for help, and whose experience in our world has made them want only to be left alone. How, for instance, would one restore Alice's life, or reshape it in a way that would satisfy *our* notion of what a life should be? What would it take to return her to the fold? How to erase the four years of homelessness, which have become as familiar to her, and as much a home, as her "normal" life once was? . . .

20   The homeless, simply because they are homeless, are strangers, alien—and therefore a threat. Their presence, in itself, comes to constitute a kind of violence; it deprives us of our sense of safety. Let me use myself as an example. I know, and respect, many of those now homeless on the streets of Santa Barbara. Twenty years ago, some of them would have been my companions and friends. And yet, these days, if I walk through the park near my home and see strangers bedding down for the night, my first reaction, if not fear, is a sense of annoyance and intrusion, or worry and alarm. I think of my teenage daughter, who often walks through the park, and then of my house, a hundred yards away, and I am tempted—only tempted, but tempted, still—to call the "proper" authorities to have the strangers moved on. Out of sight, out of mind.

21   Notice: I do not bring them food. I do not offer them shelter or a shower in the morning. I do not even stop to talk. Instead, I think: my daughter, my house, my privacy. What moves me is not the threat of *danger*—nothing as animal as that. Instead there pops up inside of me, neatly in a row, a set of anxieties, ones you might arrange in a dollhouse living room and label: Family of bourgeois fears. The point is this: our response to the homeless is fed by a complex set of cultural attitudes, habits of thought, and fantasies and fears so familiar to us, so common, that they have become a *second* nature and might as well be instinctive, for all the control we have over them. And it is by no means easy to untangle this snarl of responses. What does seem clear is that the homeless embody all that bourgeois culture has for centuries tried to eradicate and destroy.

22   It is in the nineteenth century, in the Victorian era, that you can find the beginnings of our modern strategies for dealing with the homeless: the notion that they should be controlled and perhaps eliminated through "help." With the Victorians we begin to see the entangling of self-protection with social obligation, the strategy of masking self-interest and the urge to control as *moral duty*. Michel Foucault has spelled this out in his books on madness and punishment: the zeal with which the overseers of early bourgeois culture tried to purge, improve, and purify all of urban civilization—whether through schools and prisons, or, quite literally, with public baths and massive new water and sewage systems. Order, ordure—this is, in essence, the tension at the heart of bourgeois culture, and it was the singular genius of the Victorians to make it the main component of their medical, aesthetic, *and* moral systems. It was not a sense of justice or even empathy which called for charity or new attitudes toward the poor; it was *hygiene*. . . .

23   All of this is still true in America. . . . Here, for instance, is part of a paper a student of mine wrote about her first visit to a Rescue Mission on skid row.

The sermon began. The room was stuffy and smelly. The mixture of body odors and cooking was nauseating. I remember thinking: how can these people share this facility? They must be repulsed by each other. They had strange habits and dispositions. They were a group of dirty, dishonored, weird people to me.

When it was over I ran to my car, went home, and took a shower. I felt extremely dirty. Through the day I would get flashes of that disgusting smell.

24   To put it as bluntly as I can, for many of us the homeless are *shit*. And our policies toward them, our spontaneous sense of disgust and horror, our wish to be rid of them—all of this has hidden in it, close to its heart, our feelings about excrement . . .

25   What I am getting at here is the *nature* of the desire to help the homeless—what is hidden behind it and why it so often does harm. Every government program, almost every private project, is geared as much to the needs of those giving help as it is to the needs of the homeless. . . .

26   Santa Barbara, where I live, is as good an example as any. There are three main shelters in the city—all of them private. Between them they provide fewer than a hundred beds a night for the homeless. Two of the three shelters are religious in nature: the Rescue Mission and the Salvation Army. In the mission, as in most places in the country, there are elaborate and stringent rules. Beds go first to those who have not been there for two months, and you can stay for only two nights in any two-month period. No shelter is given to those who are not sober. Even if you go to the mission only for a meal, you are required to listen to sermons and participate in prayer, and you are regularly proselytized—sometimes overtly, sometimes subtly. There are obligatory, regimented showers. You go to bed precisely at ten: lights out, no reading, no talking. After the lights go out you will find fifteen men in a room with double-decker bunks. As the night progresses the room grows stuffier and hotter. Men toss, turn, cough, and moan, In the morning you are awakened precisely at five forty-five. Then breakfast. At seven-thirty you are back on the street.

27   The town's newest shelter was opened almost a year ago by a consortium of local churches. Families and those who are employed have first call on the beds—a policy which excludes the congenitally homeless. Alcohol is not simply forbidden *in* the shelter; those with a history of alcoholism must sign a "contract" pledging to remain sober and chemical-free. Finally, in a paroxysm of therapeutic bullying, the shelter has added a new wrinkle: if you stay more than two days you are required to fill out and then discuss with a social worker a complex form listing what you perceive as your personal failings, goals, and strategies—all of this for men and women who simply want a place to lie down out of the rain!

28   It is these attitudes, in various forms and permutations, that you find repeated endlessly in America. We are moved either to "redeem" the homeless or to punish them. Perhaps there is nothing consciously hostile about it. Perhaps it is simply that as the machinery of bureaucracy cranks itself up to deal with these problems, attitudes assert themselves automatically. But whatever

the case, the fact remains that almost every one of our strategies for helping the homeless is simply an attempt to rearrange the world *cosmetically*, in terms of how it looks and smells to *us*. Compassion is little more than the passion for control.

29   The central question emerging from all this is, What does a society owe to its members in trouble, and *how* is that debt to be paid? It is a question which must be answered in two parts: first, in relation to the men and women who have been marginalized against their will, and then, in a slightly different way, in relation to those who have chosen (or accept or even prize) their marginality.

30   As for those who have been marginalized against their wills, I think the general answer is obvious: A society owes its members whatever it takes for them to regain their places in the social order. And when it comes to specific remedies, one need only read backward the various processes which have created homelessness and then figure out where help is likely to do the most good. But the real point here is not the specific remedies required—affordable housing, say—but the basis upon which they must be offered, the necessary underlying ethical notion we seem in this nation unable to grasp: that those who are the inevitable casualties of modern industrial capitalism and the free-market system are entitled, by *right*, and by the simple virtue of their participation in that system, to whatever help they need. They are entitled to help to find and hold their places in the society whose social contract they have, in effect, signed and observed.

31   Look at that for just a moment: the notion of a contract. The majority of homeless Americans have kept, insofar as they could, to the terms of that contract. In any shelter these days you can find men and women who have worked ten, twenty, forty years, and whose lives have nonetheless come to nothing. These are people who cannot afford a place in the world they helped create. And in return? Is it life on the street they have earned? Or the cruel charity we so grudgingly grant them?

32   But those marginalized against their will are only half the problem. There remains, still, the question of whether we owe anything to those who are voluntarily marginal. What about them: the street people, the rebels, and the recalcitrants, those who have torn up their social contracts or returned them unsigned?

33   I was in Las Vegas last fall, and I went out to the Rescue Mission at the lower end of town, on the edge of the black ghetto, where I first stayed years ago on my way west. It was twilight, still hot; in the vacant lot next-door to the mission 200 men were lining up for supper. . . . There were elderly alcoholics in line, and derelicts, but mainly the men were the same sort I had seen here years ago: youngish, out of work, restless and talkative, and drifters and wanderers for whom the word "wanderlust" was invented.

34   At supper—long communal tables, thin gruel, stale sweet rolls, ice water—a huge black man in his twenties, fierce and muscular, sat across from me. "I'm from the Coast, man," he said. "Never been away from home before. Ain't sure I like it. Sure don't like *this* place. But I lost my job back home a

couple of weeks ago and figured, why wait around for another. I thought I'd come out here, see something of the world."

35   After supper, a squat Portuguese man in his mid-thirties, hunkered down against the mission wall, offered me a smoke and told me: "Been sleeping in my car, up the street, for a week. Had my own business back in Omaha. But I got bored, man. Sold everything, got a little dough, came out here. Thought I'd work construction. Let me tell you, this is one tough town."

36   In a world better than ours, I suppose, men (or women) like this might not exist. Conservatives seem to have no trouble imagining a society so well disciplined and moral that deviance of this kind would disappear. And leftists envision a world so just, so generous, that deviance would vanish along with inequity. But I suspect that there will always be something at work in some men and women to make them restless with the systems others devise for them, and to move them outward toward the edges of the world, where life is always riskier, less organized, and easier going.

37   Do we owe anything to these men and women, who reject our company and what we offer and yet nonetheless seem to demand *something* from us?

38   We owe them, I think, at least a place to exist, a way to exist. That may not be a *moral* obligation, in the sense that our obligation to the involuntarily marginal is clearly a moral one, but it is an obligation nevertheless, one you might call an existential obligation.

39   Of course, it may be that I think we owe these men something because I have liked men like them, and because I want their world to be there always, as a place to hide or rest. But there is more to it than that. I think we as a society need men like these. A society needs its margins as much as it needs art and literature. It needs holes and gaps, *breathing spaces,* let us say, into which men and women can escape and live, when necessary, in ways otherwise denied them. Margins guarantee to society a flexibility, an elasticity, and allow it to accommodate itself to the natures and needs of its members. When margins vanish, society becomes too rigid, too oppressive by far, and therefore inimical to life.

40   It is for such reasons that, in cultures like our own, marginal men and women take on a special significance. They are all we have left to remind us of the narrowness of the received truths we take for granted. "Beyond the pale," they somehow redefine the pale, or remind us, at least, that *something* is still out there, beyond the pale. They preserve, perhaps unconsciously, a dream that would otherwise cease to exist, the dream of having a place in the world, and of being *left alone.* . . .

41   Let me put it as simply as I can: what we see on the streets of our cities are two dramas, both of which cut to the troubled heart of the culture and demand from us a response we may not be able to make. There is the drama of those struggling to survive by regaining their place in the social order. And there is the drama of those struggling to survive outside of it.

42   The resolution of both struggles depends on a third drama occurring at the heart of the culture: the tension and contention between the magnanimity

we owe to life and the darker tendings of the human psyche: our fear of strangeness, our hatred of deviance, our love of order and control. How we mediate by default or design between those contrary forces will determine not only the destinies of the homeless but also something crucial about the nation, and perhaps—let me say it—about our own souls.

Topical Considerations

1. In paragraph 21, Marin says that his feelings toward homelessness are "*second* nature and might as well be instinctive." Compare paragraphs 20 and 21 to paragraph 1. How does Marin's view of the homeless change as he grows older? Have your views toward the homeless changed as you've grown older?

2. Consider paragraph 7. According to Marin, what is the problem with lumping all homeless people into one category? Do you think there is an alternative to a "catch basin" label for the homeless?

3. Who does Marin believe is responsible for the homeless problem—conservatives or liberals? If neither is to blame, what does Marin believe is the cause of the problem?

4. Marin contends in paragraph 39: "When margins vanish, society becomes too rigid, too oppressive by far, and therefore inimical to life." Look at paragraphs 2, 7, 30, 32, and 39: What are the "margins"? Who exists there? What are their contributions to society? Do you agree with Marin's vision of a society without margins?

5. Explain the reference to "The Selma of the Eighties" (paragraph 3). How is this incident in Selma similar to the homeless crisis in Santa Barbara?

6. How does the author perceive homeless shelters with religious affiliations? Do you believe he is portraying a balanced picture of these shelters?

7. Explain how, according to Marin, the Victorian era paved the way toward contemporary attitudes toward homelessness. Do you agree with his theory?

Rhetorical Considerations

1. Marin's title is "Helping and Hating the Homeless." How does this title set the reader up for the conflicting feelings that the homelessness issue triggers? Can you empathize with the conflicting emotions surrounding homelessness?

2. Marin states that the homeless issue unfolds into three different dramas (paragraph 41 and 42). Explain this metaphor. Do you believe that the essay supports this metaphor, or is the metaphor far-fetched?

3. Note the wording in Marin's claim: "Homelessness, in itself, is nothing more than a condition visited upon men and women (and, increasingly, children) . . ." (paragraph 7). Who does Marin imply is responsible for the homeless? Later in the essay Marin divides the homeless into the "active"

and "passive." Are the homeless who "actively" choose their life-style responsible? Are both types of homeless people victims?

4. Marin mentions Santa Barbara, a place with homeless people; Alice, a homeless person; and a skid row Rescue Mission. What does the author gain by using these three specific examples: How are these anecdotes relevant to the homeless issue in general?

5. Marin has not only felt "at home on the road" among the homeless, but he has also felt "a sense of annoyance and intrusion, of worry and alarm" among them. Does he use both experiences to create a cohesive argument, or is his argument lost in his own confusion? Use specific examples to either support or refute Marin's argument.

Writing Assignments

1. The title of the next essay is "Brother, Don't Spare a Dime," by Christopher Awalt. In paragraph 21 or Marin's essay, the author explains: "Notice: I do not bring them food. I do not offer them shelter or a shower in the morning. I do not even stop to talk." In short, he doesn't spare a dime. Write a paper in which you explore each author's refusal to give to the homeless. Are the authors sincere or hypocritical?

2. Paragraph 18 reads, "We like to think, in America, that everything is redeemable, that everything broken can be magically made whole again, and that what has been 'dirtied' can be cleansed." Write an essay in which you defend or refute this statement. Use examples from this essay and from at least three other contemporary issues.

Brother, Don't Spare a Dime
Christopher Awalt

In this piece, which first appeared in *Newsweek* in September 1991, Christopher Awalt asks "Who is to blame for the homeless?" To answer this question, he divides the homeless into two categories: the temporarily homeless and the chronically homeless. And in an argument that sharply differs from Peter Marin's in the previous essay, Awalt asserts that the chronically homeless must "bear the blame for their manifold troubles." Using personal experience and anecdotes, Awalt demonstrates that a lack of self-reliance and individual responsibility accounts for the plight of the chronically homeless.

BEFORE YOU READ

If you were formulating a policy outlining ways to help the homeless regain their place in society, what would be some of its key points? What would you be willing to provide to the homeless in ways of services, education, food, shelter, and funding, if anything? What services do you feel would be inappropriate to provide? Why?

AS YOU READ

Recall Peter Marin's view of those who choose homelessness and of the obligations society at large has to this population. How do the views of Marin and Awalt differ on this matter?

1   Homeless people are everywhere—on the street, in public buildings, on the evening news and at the corner parking lot. You can hardly step out of your house these days without meeting some haggard character who asks you for a cigarette or begs for "a little change." The homeless are not just constant symbols of wasted lives and failed social programs—they have become a danger to public safety.

2   What's the root of the homeless problem? Everyone seems to have a scapegoat: advocates of the homeless blame government policy; politicians blame the legal system; the courts blame the bureaucratic infrastructure; the Democrats blame the Republicans; the Republicans, the Democrats. The public blames the economy, drugs, the "poverty cycle" and "the breakdown of society." With all this finger-pointing, the group most responsible for the homeless being the way they are receives the least blame. That group is the homeless themselves.

3   How can I say this? For the past two years I have worked with the homeless, volunteering at the Salvation Army and at a soup kitchen in Austin, Texas. I have led a weekly chapel service, served food, listened, counseled, given time and money and shared in their struggles. I have seen their response to troubles, and though I'd rather report otherwise, many of them seem to have chosen the lifestyles they lead. They are unwilling to do the things necessary to overcome their circumstances. They must bear the greater part of the blame for their manifold troubles.

4   Let me qualify what I just said. Not everyone who finds himself out of a job and in the street is there because he wants to be. Some are victims of tragic circumstances. I met many dignified, capable people during my time working with Austin's homeless: the single father struggling to earn his high-school equivalency and to be a role model for his children; the woman who fled a good job in another city to escape an abusive husband; the well-educated young man who had his world turned upside down by divorce and a layoff. These people deserve every effort to help them back on their feet.

5   But they're not the real problem. They are usually off the streets and resuming normal lives within a period of weeks or months. Even while "down on their luck," they are responsible citizens, working in the shelters and applying for jobs. They are homeless, true, but only temporarily, because they are eager to reorganize their lives.

6   For every person temporarily homeless, though, there are many who are chronically so. Whether because of mental illness, alcoholism, poor education, drug addiction or simple laziness, these homeless are content to re-

main as they are. In many cases they choose the streets. They enjoy the freedom and consider begging a minor inconvenience. They know they can always get a job for a day or two for food, cigarettes and alcohol. The sophisticated among them have learned to use the system for what it's worth and figure that a trip through the welfare line is less trouble than a steady job. In a society that has mastered dodging responsibility, these homeless prefer a life of no responsibility at all.

Waste of Time

7   One person I worked with is a good example. He is an older man who has been on the streets for about 10 years. The story of his decline from respectability to alcoholism sounded believable and I wanted to help. After buying him toiletries and giving him clothes, I drove him one night to a Veterans Administration hospital, an hour and a half away, and put him into a detoxification program. I wrote him monthly to check on his progress and attempted to line up a job for him when he got out. Four months into his program, he was thinking and speaking clearly and talking about plans he wanted to make. At five months, he expressed concern over the life he was about to lead. During the sixth month, I called and was told that he had checked himself out and returned home. A month later I found him drunk again, back on the streets.

8   Was "society" to blame for this man? Hardly. It had provided free medical care, counseling and honest effort. Was it the fault of the economy? No. This man never gave the economy a chance to solve his problems. The only person who can be blamed for his failure to get off the streets is the man himself. To argue otherwise is a waste of time and compassion.

9   Those who disagree will claim that my experience is merely anecdotal and that one case does not a policy make. Please don't take my word for it. The next time you see someone advertising that he'll work for food, take him up on it. Offer him a hard day's work for an honest wage, and see if he accepts. If he does, tell him you'll pay weekly, so that he will have to work for an entire week before he sees any money. If he still accepts, offer a permanent job, with taxes withheld and the whole shebang. If he accepts again, hire him. You'll have a fine employee and society will have one less homeless person. My guess is that you won't find many takers. The truly homeless won't stay around past the second question.

10 So what are the solutions? I will not pretend to give ultimate answers. But whatever policy we decide upon must include some notion of self-reliance and individual responsibility. Simply giving over our parks, our airports and our streets to those who cannot and will not take care of themselves is nothing but a retreat from the problem and allows the public property that we designate for their "use" to fall into disarray. Education, drug and alcohol rehabilitation, treatment for the mentally ill and job training programs are all worthwhile projects, but without requiring some effort and accountability on the

part of the homeless for whom these programs are implemented, all these efforts do is break the taxpayer. Unless the homeless are willing to help themselves, there is nothing anyone else can do. Not you. Not me. Not the government. Not anyone.

Topical Considerations

1. Briefly summarize Awalt's argument. On what points do you agree with him? In what ways do you disagree? Has his argument changed your attitude toward homeless people? Explain.
2. Why does Awalt believe that the "root of the homeless problem" is the homeless themselves (paragraph 2)? Do you agree or disagree?
3. In paragraph 5 Awalt mentions the temporary homeless who are "usually off the streets and resuming normal lives within a period of weeks or months." What is Awalt's definition of *normal lives*? Does Awalt see any place in society for marginalized people? How is Awalt's view of marginalized people different from Marin's in the previous essay?
4. Who does Awalt consider to be the "chronically homeless?" Do you agree with his assumption?
5. What has Awalt's experiences with the homeless taught him? Do you think that his experience is unique or typical of those who work with the homeless?
6. In paragraph 10, Awalt asks, "So, what are the solutions [to the homeless problem]?" What is his answer? Do you agree that this is a realistic solution?

Rhetorical Considerations

1. What words in paragraph 1 convey to the reader Awalt's perception of the homeless? Do you think this forceful lead is a good rhetorical device, swaying the reader at the onset?
2. Would you say that Awalt makes an *ad populum* argument in the conclusion to convince his readers that the homeless themselves have caused the homeless crisis? If so, is it effective?
3. The title of the essay is a play on "Brother, Can You Spare a Dime?"—a question many homeless ask. Who is the "Brother" in Awalt's essay? Find examples from the text that show Awalt's use of familiar, friendly language to sway *his* "Brothers"?
4. Consider the perspective from which Awalt writes. How does he convince his readers that he is an authority on the homeless? Do you think his credentials make him a viable critic?
5. Does Awalt characterize homelessness as a matter of choice or necessity? Does he ever allow for an in-between area? Cite specific passages to support your point of view.

Writing Assignments

1. Interview people who have worked with the homeless. Write an essay that compares their experiences with that of Awalt. Include your own experience, if any, with the homeless.
2. Construct a dialogue between Awalt and a homeless person that begins, "Brother, can you spare a dime?" Describe where the dialogue took place, and have the homeless character explain the reason for his or her homelessness.
3. Create a campaign for the homeless that would satisfy Awalt. Show how those who can help themselves could do so. Propose creative solutions to help the "chronically homeless." Gauge when this could happen in America.

Yes, Something Will Work: Work
Mickey Kaus

How can one break the cycle of poverty? What can one do about growing welfare roles? Are welfare recipients "freeloaders" or worthy recipients of public assistance? What is the best way to help the poor and unemployed? In this piece Mickey Kaus offers his interpretation of how the underclass developed and argues that "if welfare is what enabled the underclass to form, might not altering welfare somehow 'de-enable' the underclass?" Moving from this premise, Kaus proposes a no-frills program linking mandatory work with any benefits. "In this regime," he writes, "young women contemplating motherhood would think twice about putting themselves in a position where they would have to juggle mothering with working."

Mickey Kaus is senior editor at *The New Republic* and the author of *The End of Equality*, an analysis of social welfare policy published in 1992. Kaus's essay first appeared in *Newsweek* in May 1992.

BEFORE YOU READ

What associations does the term *welfare recipient* evoke for you? Why might a person be on welfare? Do you feel the system serves a good purpose? Can you describe anyone you know who has been on welfare?

AS YOU READ

As you read note the language Kaus uses to describe the poor on welfare. Do any of his terms for welfare recipients seem slanted? If so, how does this affect the development of his argument? How does it affect your view of those recipients?

1 Call it the "solutions gap." What distinguishes the L.A. riots of 1992 from the L.A. riots of 1965 seems to be that in 1992 few Americans retain much confidence that the problems of the "ghetto poor" underclass can be overcome. Jack Kemp gets great press touting urban "enterprise zones," but does anybody but Kemp really think tax breaks will make businessmen flock to bombed-out South-Central Los Angeles?

2   What *would* solve the underclass problem? Start with the consensus explanation for how the mainly black underclass was formed in the first place. As told by University of Chicago sociologist William Julius Wilson, the story goes like this: When Southern blacks migrated North, they settled, thanks to segregation, in urban ghettos. Then, beginning in the 1960s, two things happened. First, well-paying, unskilled jobs started to leave the cities for the suburbs. Second, middle-class blacks, aided by civil-rights laws, began to leave as well. This out-migration left the poorest elements of black society behind—now isolated and freed from the restraints the black middle class had imposed. Without jobs and role models, those left in the ghettos drifted out of the labor market.

3   But this story leaves a crucial question hanging—a question asked by John Kasarda of the University of North Carolina: How were "economically displaced inner-city residents able to survive?" Kasarda's answer: "welfare programs." He notes that by 1982, in the central cities, there were more black single mothers who weren't working than who were. And 80 percent of these nonworking single mothers were getting some form of welfare, mainly Aid to Families with Dependent Children. AFDC not only provided an "economic substitute" for jobs, it provided that substitute in a form available, by and large, *only* to mothers in broken homes.

4   Bush spokesman Marlin Fitzwater had a point, then, when he blamed ghetto poverty on welfare programs. Welfare may not have been the main cause of the underclass, but it *enabled* the underclass to form. Without welfare, those left behind in the ghetto would have had to move to where the jobs were. Without welfare, it would have been hard for single mothers to survive without forming working families. Instead, between 1965 and 1974, the welfare rolls exploded—from 4.3 million recipients to 10.8 million. Simultaneously, the proportion of black children in single-mother homes jumped from 33 to over 50 percent.

5   So if welfare is what enabled the underclass to form, might not altering welfare somehow "de-enable" the underclass? Certainly, if we're looking for a handle on the culture of poverty, there is none bigger than the cash welfare programs that constitute 65 percent of the legal income of single mothers in the bottom fifth of the income distribution. Changing welfare to break the culture of poverty will take something much more radical, however, than the mild welfare reform Congress enacted in 1988. The 1988 law—which basically requires 10 percent of the welfare caseload to attend training classes or work part-time—is expected, at best, to reduce welfare rolls by a few percentage points.

6   But what if cash welfare (mainly AFDC and food stamps) were replaced with the offer of a useful government job paying just below the minimum wage? Single mothers (and anyone else) who needed money would not be given a check. They would be given free day care for their children. And they would be given the location of a government job site. If they showed up and worked, they'd be paid for their work. To make working worthwhile, the incomes of all low-wage workers would be boosted to the poverty line by expanding the Earned Income Tax Credit.

FDR's Idea

7   In this regime, young women contemplating single motherhood would think twice about putting themselves in a position where they would have to juggle mothering with working. Life as it is too often lived in the ghetto—in broken homes with no workers—would simply become impossible. The natural incentives to form two-parent families would reassert themselves. But even children of single mothers would grow up in homes structured by the rhythms and discipline of work.

8   This is not a new idea. It's an obvious idea, even. It's basically the approach Franklin D. Roosevelt took in 1935 when he replaced cash welfare with government jobs in the Works Progress Administration (WPA). Recently, a group of congressmen, led by Sen. David Boren of Oklahoma, proposed reviving the WPA, with about 75 percent of the jobs reserved for welfare mothers.

9   The objections to this idea are obvious, too. Replacing welfare with a neo-WPA would be very expensive—a reasonable estimate is around $50 billion a year. There would be ample potential for boondoggles. And the transition from the current welfare system would be harsh. Many who now support themselves on AFDC would simply fail to work. For those who wind up destitute, there would have to be a beefed-up system of in-kind support (soup kitchens, shelters, and the like).

10   Nevertheless, for all these pitfalls, the WPA approach has a virtue not shared by any of the other remedies offered up in the wake of the L.A. riots: it would work. Not within one generation, necessarily, or even two. But it would work eventually. Welfare is how the underclass (unhappily, unintentionally) survives. Change welfare, and the underclass will have to change as well.

Topical Considerations

1. Briefly summarize Kaus's solution to "the underclass problem." Do you agree with Kaus? Why or why not?
2. In paragraph 2, Kaus summarizes sociologist William Julius Wilson's explanation of how the black underclass was formed. As part of his explication,

Kaus writes, "This out-migration left the poorest elements of black society behind—now isolated and freed from the restraints the black middle class had imposed." What are the "restraints the black middle class had imposed" according to Kaus? Do you agree with this explanation? Why or why not?

3. In paragraph 4, Kaus claims that although welfare might not have been the main cause of poverty, it enabled the underclass to form. According to Kaus, how did welfare do this? Do you agree with his interpretation? Why or why not?

4. In paragraph 4, Kaus says, "Without welfare, it would have been hard for single mothers to survive without forming working families." What does Kaus mean by "working families"? According to Kaus, how would single mothers form working families. Do you feel this is a realistic assumption? Explain your answer.

5. What specific group of people does Kaus single out for the majority of his criticism in this essay? Do you feel this is an example of bias, or is his criticism justified? Explain your answer.

6. In paragraph 7, Kaus implies that economics is the main incentive for the formation of two-parent families. Do you agree with this implication? What other factors might influence formation of two-parent families?

Rhetorical Considerations

1. Consider the question in the first paragraph of this essay. Does Kaus pose this as a rhetorical question? Why or why not?

2. What rhetorical purposes does Kaus's citing of individuals such as John Kasarda and Marlin Fitzwater serve in his essay?

3. Identify the *post hoc, ergo propter hoc* argument in paragraph 4, and explain what makes it a *post hoc* argument. Does Kaus imply any other cause-and-effect relationships that may be unjustified?

Writing Assignments

1. Write an essay explaining your solution to the problem of poverty in this country.

2. Imagine that Kaus's idea has become the law of the land. You are a poor, single mother with two children ages three and five. Describe your day.

The Culture of Cruelty
Ruth Conniff

In this essay Ruth Conniff both describes and indicts the welfare reform proposals of analysts such as Mickey Kaus, the author of the previous essay. With stiletto-like jabs, Conniff argues that Kaus's work program is built on negative stereotypes of the poor and designed to punish the poor for their predicament. The title of her essay "The Culture of Cruelty," labels an attitude she deems callous, immoral, and punitive.

Conniff is associate editor of *The Progressive*, which published this piece in 1992.

BEFORE YOU READ

Conniff points out that in Wisconsin the average family of three on welfare receives about $500 a month in Aid to Families with Dependent Children (AFDC). Imagine that you are supporting yourself and two other people on this amount of money per month. What kind of life-style could you afford? How, if at all, does this exercise influence the way you view people living on welfare?

AS YOU READ

As you read this article, try to evaluate how carefully Conniff represents Kaus's position as she attempts to dismantle it. Where does she use reason and logic, and where does she make emotional and ethical appeals?

1 Not long ago I was on a morning radio show talking about welfare, when an irate caller from Milwaukee got on the line and introduced himself as "that most hated and reviled creature, the American taxpayer." He went on to vent his spleen, complaining about freeloading welfare mothers living high on the hog while he goes to work each day. "A whiff of starvation is what they need," he said.

2 I was chilled by the hatred in his voice, thinking about the mothers I know on welfare, imagining what it would be like for them to hear this.

3 One young woman I've met, Karetha Mims, recently moved to Wisconsin, fleeing the projects in Chicago after her little boy saw a seven-year-old playmate shot in the head. Mims is doing her best to make a better life for her son, a shy third-grader named Jermain. She volunteers at his elementary school, and worries about how he will fit in. The Mimses have received a cold welcome in Wisconsin, where the governor warns citizens that welfare families spilling across the border from Illinois will erode the tax base and ruin the "quality of life."

4 Of course, even in Wisconsin, life on welfare is no free ride. The average family of three receives about $500 a month in Aid to Families with Dependent Children—barely enough to pay the rent. Such figures are widely known. So is the fact that each state spends a small amount—about 3.4 per cent of our taxes, or a national total of $22.9 billion annually—on welfare. In contrast, we have now spent $87 billion—about $1,000 per taxpaying family—to bail out bank presidents at failed savings-and-loans.

5   But neither the enraged taxpayer nor my host on the radio program wanted to hear these dry facts. "What ever happened to the work ethic in this country?" the host demanded. "What about the immigrants who came over and worked their way up?"

6   I had the feeling I was losing my grasp on the conversation. I could see my host getting impatient, and the more I said the more I failed to answer her central question: *What's wrong with those people on welfare?*

7   The people on welfare whom I know have nothing wrong with them. They live in bad neighborhoods; they can't find safe, affordable child care; often, they are caught In an endless cycle of unemployment and low-wage work—quitting their jobs when a child gets sick, losing medical insurance when they go back to their minimum-wage jobs. They don't have enough money to cover such emergencies as dental work or car repairs. In short, they are poor. They are struggling hard just to make it, in the face of extreme hardship and in an increasingly hostile environment.

8   Meanwhile, rhetoric about lazy welfare bums is taking the country by storm. Policy experts keep coming up with new theories on the "culture of poverty" and its nameless perpetrators, members of a socially and morally deformed "underclass." Street hustlers, welfare families, drug addicts, and former mental patients," political scientist Lawrence Mead calls them.

9   "It's simply stupid to pretend the underclass is not mainly black," adds Mickey Kaus in his much-acclaimed new book *The End of Equality.* Kaus and fellow pundit Christopher Jencks, who wrote his own book this year—*Rethinking Social Policy: Race, Poverty, and the Underclass*—are two of the most recent riders on the underclass bandwagon. But the essence of their work is uncomfortably familiar. Both writers start by asking the question: *What's wrong with the underclass?,* and both proceed to talk about the depravity of poor black people, devoting large though inconclusive sections to such ideas as genetic inferiority and "Heredity, Inequality, and Crime."

10   Kaus paints a lurid picture of young black men who sneer at the idea of working for the minimum wage, which he says they deride as "chump change." (It's not clear where Kaus gets this information, since he doesn't cite any interviews with actual poor blacks.)

11   Why don't poor black people just get jobs and join the mainstream of society? Kaus asks rhetorically. While many African-Americans have moved up to the middle class, he writes, the important question is "what enabled some of them, a lower-class remnant, to stay behind in the ghetto? And what then allowed them to survive in the absence of legitimate sources of income?"

12   The answer, of course, is welfare. Kaus compares black people's attachment to poverty with a junkie's addiction to a drug. Welfare is the "enabling" force that indulges ghetto residents' propensity for living in squalor. When they stopped working hard and learned they could collect welfare while living in the ghetto, Kaus theorizes, poor black people's values eroded and they became a blight on society.

13   Kaus's solution to the "underclass problem," then, relies largely on such motivational initiatives as instilling a work ethic in lazy black youth

through hard labor and "military-style discipline." Likewise, he proposes cutting benefits to mothers who have more than one child, creating an example for their neighbors, who, he says, would "think twice" before becoming pregnant. . . .

14   . . . As more and more states treat poverty as an attitude problem, legislatures justify slashing the safety net and cutting back social programs that help poor people survive. The situation is particularly dire for the "extra" children of women on welfare, who are punished just for being born.

15   But in Kaus's estimation, the suffering of children is nothing next to the social benefits he thinks will accrue from causing pain to their mothers. "If we want to end the underclass, remember, the issue is not so much whether working or getting two years of cash will best help Betsy Smith, teenage high-school dropout, acquire the skills to get a good private sector job *after* she's become a single mother. It is whether the prospect of having to work will deter Betsy Smith from having an out-of-wedlock child in the first place. . . . The way to make the true costs of bearing a child out of wedlock clear is to let them be felt when they are incurred—namely, at the child's birth."

16   The callousness and immorality of such thinking, I believe, are part of a pathology that is spreading throughout our society. We might call it a "culture of cruelty."

17   Such theorists as Kaus and Jencks build the rational foundation beneath our national contempt for the poor. They lend legitimacy to the racist and misogynist stereotypes so popular with conservative politicians and disgruntled taxpayers who feel an economic crunch and are looking for someone to blame. Understanding the roots of the culture of cruelty, and trying to determine how, through the adoption of decent social values, we might overcome it, would be far more useful than any number of volumes of speculation by upper-class white experts on the attitudes and pathologies of the "underclass."

18   Underclass theory as promoted by Kaus and Jencks has four main characteristics:

- It is extremely punitive, appealing to a desire to put poor black people, especially women, in their place.
- It is based on prejudice rather than fact, full of stereotypical characters and flippant, unsupported assertions about their motivations and psychology.
- It is inconsistent in its treatment of rich and poor. While poor people need sternness and "military-style discipline," to use Kaus's words, the rich are coddled and protected. This third characteristic is particularly important, since treating the "underclass" as alien and inhuman permits the prescription of draconian belt-tightening that one would never impose on one's own family or friends.
- Finally, there is the persistent, faulty logic involved in claims that we can "end the cycle of poverty" by refusing aid to an entire generation of children. These children are thus punished for their mothers' sins in producing them, and, if such programs persist, they will soon have no

hope of getting out from under the weight of belonging to a despised lower caste. . . .

19   Kaus and Jencks remind me of nothing so much as precocious sophomores, dominating the class discussion, eager to sound off about the lives and motivations of people they have never met. . . .

20   Kaus wants to create a massive "neo-WPA" program, with guaranteed jobs for everyone. But the jobs, he says, should be "authoritarian, even a little militaristic," and they should pay less than the minimum wage. The program would not raise anyone out of poverty, since there would be no opportunity for advancement within it. We can't have a class of workers dependent on the state for permanent employment, Kaus reasons. Instead, once people have gained work "skills" through his jobs program, Kaus says, the transition to a job in the private sector will "take care of itself." Never mind the recession, the thousands of former middle-class workers who are now out of work, or the fact that even in the best of times we do not have a full-employment economy.

21   Anyway, Kaus never explains why the poor black men he talks about would abandon employment in the illegal economy to work in labor gangs, for even less than "chump change." Nor does he note that there is already an extensive discipline-dispensing institution for black men: our ever-expanding prison system. . . .

22   When Kaus turns to his plans for poor women and children, he reaches the absolute shallow end of his thinking. Mothers should be forced out of the home to do a job—any job—rather than be allowed to stay home with their children, Kaus says. The state should be prepared to invest a great deal of money in creating such jobs. "Even a leaf-raking job rakes leaves," he reasons. "If that's all someone's capable of doing, does that mean she shouldn't be paid for doing it? The alternative, remember, is to pay her to stay home and raise children."

23   Kaus takes his contempt for child-rearing to its logical extreme. First, the state must deny benefits to women who have more than one child, and insist that mothers go to work. Then, we must be on the lookout for signs of neglect when poor parents fail to provide a proper home for their children. "The long answer, then, is that society will also have to construct new institutions, such as orphanages. . . ."

24   So much for family values.

25   While Kaus deplores the "female-headed household" and the breakdown of the family as a central problem of the "underclass," his grand solution is to warehouse the children of the poor in vast institutions, away from love and nurturing care. Perhaps the state could also hire appropriate role models to come in and deliver speeches to the kids on the value of work. Kaus seems to think that's all they need.

26   Work, in Kaus's book, is supposed to become the value that binds society together. Work—at menial tasks for poverty-level wages—is supposed to give poor people a sense of citizenship and social equality. Work is even sup-

posed to bring the family back together, since, without AFDC, "soon enough ghetto women will be demanding and expecting that the men in their lives offer them stable economic support." And children will want to work "because they will have grown up in a home where the rhythms and discipline of obligation pervade daily life."

27   You would think Kaus was talking about a group of people who had it too easy. He fails to consider the fact that AFDC already does not pay enough to live on. And he ignores the fact—a fact even Jencks points out—that most people on welfare *already* work. Because AFDC payments are not enough to support a family, almost everyone who receives AFDC does some sort of labor. Many do not report it, since the Government docks a dollar of benefits for every dollar a welfare recipient earns. . . .

28   *The End of Equality* is a particularly scary piece of work because it drags bigotry into the daylight and presents it as egalitarianism, making disdain for the poor safe for liberals. In a way, Kaus brings the hidden agenda of underclass theory to fruition. He shifts the blame for a range of social ills—from crime to poverty and unemployment to segregation—onto the disenfranchised. This is the very heart of the culture of cruelty: Blame and punishment replace compassion and justice. Unburdened of the archaic principles of civil rights, Kaus says it proudly: The underclass means black people, and what blacks need is to be brought to heel.

29   Rather than addressing the inequities in our society—segregated schools, unjust wages, inadequate health care, things that social policy could actually fix—Kaus throws away the whole idea of economic injustice. He replaces it with a new villain—the "underclass," whom he blames not only for the problems of poor people on welfare, but for the problems of our society as a whole. Suddenly, the middle-class taxpayer, the politician, and the wealthy upper class are all victims. United in having been wounded by the "underclass," they are all innocent of any responsibility in society. Ominously, Kaus declares that it is only by gathering together and dealing with the "underclass problem" that we can make America a good place to live. . . .

30   There is a lively market these days for political theories that defend the rich and disparage the poor. The poor are a perfect scapegoat. After all, as Kaus points out, it is the suburbanites who vote. "Throwing money at the problem won't solve anything," is the old conservative mantra, chanted in exclusive clubs and suburban living rooms all over America.

31   Meanwhile, the cities seethe.

Topical Considerations

1. In paragraph 6, Conniff acknowledges her failure to answer the host's central question, "*What's wrong with those people on welfare?*" Why can't Conniff answer this question?

2. In paragraph 7 Conniff explains the reasons why people are on welfare. Summarize her explanation. Does this adequately answer the questions and criticisms of opponents of the welfare system? Why or why not?

3. In paragraph 8 Conniff cites political scientist Lawrence Mead's labels for members of the underclass: "[s]treet hustlers, welfare families, drug addicts, and former mental patients." Why might this grouping be considered offensive?

4. What does Conniff feel would be more useful than "any number of volumes of speculation by upper-class white experts" (paragraph 17) on the attitudes and pathologies of the "underclass"?

5. Conniff provides the four main characteristics of underclass theory proposed by Jencks and Kaus. How does Conniff arrive at this summary? Why might her interpretation be inaccurate?

Rhetorical Considerations

1. In the first paragraph, a caller irate about the welfare system says, "A whiff of starvation is what they need." How does this echo the title of the essay?

2. In paragraph 3 Conniff offers an anecdote about a welfare mother she knows. In the following paragraph, she includes statistical information about the welfare system. Do you feel the paragraphs are equally persuasive, or is one more persuasive than the other in terms of Conniff's argument? Explain your answer.

3. Conniff spends much of the essay interpreting the writing and positions of individuals such as Kaus who are opposed to the current welfare system. Identify any problems you see with this rhetorical strategy, and explain whether or not they detract from Conniff's argument.

4. Identify the bias Conniff displays in paragraph 17.

5. Identify and explain the rhetorical fallacy in paragraph 19.

6. In paragraphs 20 and 21, Conniff describes an idea of Kaus's more fully than in the preceding paragraph. Explain why this account strengthens Conniff's argument.

7. How might Kaus interpret the second to last statement in Conniff's essay as strengthening his own argument against welfare?

Writing Assignments

1. Create a logical dialogue about welfare reform between Conniff and Kaus using sentences from each essay.

2. If possible, write an essay describing a realistic solution to the problem of poverty that both Conniff and Kaus could support.

3. Write an essay defending or opposing the current welfare system. Take the opposing position to your true beliefs.

TEENAGE PREGNANCY

Countering the Culture of Sex
Ellen Goodman

With unmarried teenage mothers accounting for nearly one-third of the births in America in 1995, social commentators, health officials, and educators search for a campaign to deter unwanted and unplanned pregnancies. It is not uncommon to look to the entertainment industry for both the cause and the cure for our sex-saturated culture. In this essay, Ellen Goodman challenges the entertainment industry to acknowledge its role as "cultural message maker" and to balance its depiction of sex with some realism. If sex is going to be depicted, she argues, its consequences should be revealed as well.

Ellen Goodman is a widely syndicated, Pulitzer Prize–winning columnist. Collections of her columns have been published in several books including *Keeping in Touch* (1985), *Making Sense* (1989), and *Value Judgments* (1993). This article first appeared in *The Boston Globe* in 1995.

BEFORE YOU READ

List the factors you believe are responsible for the large numbers of unplanned pregnancies among teens. What change in policy, attitude, or practice would be the most effective way to reduce these numbers?

AS YOU READ

Make a list of current films, recordings, dramas, or videos that depict sexual activity. Do they, in your own opinion, contribute to irresponsible sexual behavior? Is Goodman's recommendation that the industry participate in an ad campaign regarding responsible sex reasonable or appropriate? Does this call for censorship?

1   When Kathleen Sylvester began researching welfare reform for the Progressive Policy Institute, she asked a Baltimore school principal the one thing she'd do to reduce the number of teen-age pregnancies.

2   The principal had an immediate two-word answer for her: "Shoot Madonna."

3   This was not a serious attempt on this educator's part to cure sex with violence. The principal was not a character assassin.

4   She was probably thinking of the Madonna of the 1980s, the one who wrote the classic paean to teen-age motherhood: "Papa Don't Preach." The Madonna of the '90s has a line in "Bedtime Stories" that sounds more like paean to Joycelyn Elders: "Happiness lies in your own hand."

5   But the principal was speaking in a familiar vocabulary. It's a language shared by parents, teachers, policy makers—the whole range of frustrated adults whose voices of reason are drowned out by a culture that sells kids sex as successfully as it sells them sneakers. Just Do It.

6   These messages that kids actually listen to ought to be piped into the hearing rooms where Congress is busy concocting a new welfare policy. The plan the House Ways and Means Committee is contemplating for teen-age mothers is called euphemistically "tough love." But our culture offers something else. Sex without consequences.

7   "How many times do kids see sex on TV," says Sylvester, "in which no one gets pregnant, no one gets AIDS and no one has to get up in the middle of the night to feed a baby?"

8   In the face of the onslaught, the true counterculture in America is not the "McGovernik elite" or, for heaven's sakes, PBS. It's parents and reasonable adults who are left to literally counter the culture, to do combat with the incessant messages of mainstream films, music, television—the conglomerate known as Hollywood—as best we can.

9   Hollywood may not *cause* teen pregnancy. But Sylvester and others are convinced that any national campaign that goes to the heart and hard core of the problem is going to have to engage these cultural message makers.

10   We're going to have to do more than label them as villains. We need them as allies.

11   It will take all their creativity to make a successful pitch against irresponsible sex and teen pregnancy. "Just say no" won't do it. Teen-agers are the most risk-taking part of the population. They're still being seduced by cigarette ads.

12   It will be harder to fashion a stand against sex than against smoking. After all, smoking is always bad for you; sex isn't. And hormones are even more powerful than nicotine addiction.

13   It will also be harder to campaign against unwed parenthood than against drunken driving. The campaign against drunken driving was successful in curbing dangerous behavior by creating a new social role: the designated driver. But a baby is a different sort of accident than a head-on collision.

14   If we can't preach, however much papa (and mama) may want to, we can say unequivocally in rhythm, rap or reel what Sylvester says in plain words: "It's wrong to bring a child into the world that you can't take care of." It's not cool, it's not manly, it's not womanly. It's wrong.

15   This goes beyond using Madonna for target practice. It even goes beyond lowering the sexual thermostat of the culture.

16   Entertainment executives like to say, on the one hand, that they are just reflecting reality and, on the other hand, that they're in the business of fantasy. With both hands they wave furious charges of censorship at any critic.

17   But how about more reality? In an ad campaign, in soap operas, movies, music.

18   Not long ago an outraged producer complained to Jay Winston, the public health guru who created the designated driver campaign: "Can you imagine that people are lobbying to have Tom Cruise use a condom? Tom Cruise?" Why is that so hard to imagine?

19   At Harvard's Kennedy School of Government, a nervous Barbra Streisand recently offered a spirited defense of the artist as citizen. But the problem isn't that this "cultural elite" is too political, it's that it isn't political enough. As Winston says, "They ought to be powerful players in this process. They need to come to the table."

20   Let's begin with some sexual truth-in-advertising: one part passion to two parts diapers. Sex and consequences. Try humming a few bars.

Topical Considerations

1. Describe the "new welfare policy" being "concocted" in Congress at the time of Goodman's essay. If you are not familiar with this plan, research it, using the date of Goodman's article (February 16th, 1995) as a guide. What is Goodman's attitude toward this plan? How does her article hope to shift the terms of the congressional debate?
2. What, for Goodman, is "wrong" about teen-age pregnancy (paragraph 14)? Do you agree with her? What other moral issues does teenage pregnancy raise for you, your friends, or adults you know?
3. Based on your own experience, do you agree with Goodman's claim that mass culture irresponsibly "sells kids sex as successfully as it sells them sneakers" (paragraph 5)? Give other examples of more responsible representations of sexuality in popular movies, music, or television.
4. Describe the strategies Goodman proposes in the fight against teenage pregnancy. Evaluate the strengths and weaknesses of this proposal.
5. Summarize Goodman's attitude toward censorship.

Rhetorical Considerations

1. Explain the importance of the term "counterculture" in this essay. How does Goodman redefine this word, and to what argumentative effect?
2. Consider the essay's references to Madonna, assessing the symbolic, rhetorical, or argumentative roles the media star plays in Goodman's work.

3. Closely analyze paragraphs 11–13. What function does this passage serve in Goodman's argument as a whole? How does the sentence structure contribute to the effectiveness of this portion of the essay?

Writing Assignments

1. Assign each member of your group one Madonna album and ask them to study the sexual attitude represented in the work. Then write a group report that analyzes how the treatment of sexuality in Madonna's work has changed in the course of her career.
2. Using the on-line catalogue, *Reader's Guide*, and newspaper indexes, research Ellen Goodman's past writings on teenage behavior, sexuality, and censorship. Write an essay that defines Goodman's characteristic stance on these topics. If you can, describe any progression in Goodman's attitude over the years.
3. Write a letter to a Hollywood star, such as Tom Cruise, Madonna, or Barbra Streisand, urging them to help implement Goodman's proposal. Be sure to anticipate and address objections this audience might have to Goodman's project.
4. Write an essay exploring the extent to which "Hollywood" does or does not influence the attitudes about sexuality held by you or your peers. Are other influences such as parents, religion, or school more or less important?

The Name of the Game Is Shame
Jonathan Alter

A familiar title in the high school English curriculum, Nathaniel Hawthorne's *The Scarlet Letter* is a testimonial to the power and pain of shame. In this novel, the scarlet letter A worn by Hester Prynne signifies an adulterous relationship and marks her as an offender and an outcast. Her very existence is a warning of the consequences of sexual transgression. In this essay, Jonathan Alters discusses the contemporary application of shame. In view of the alarming rates of teenage pregnancies, some twentieth century think tanks, White House Aides, and journalists feel a reapplication of the concept of shame might be an effective means of curbing teenage pregnancy. Jonathan Alter is a senior editor for *Newsweek*. This article appeared in his "Between the Lines" column in *Newsweek* in 1994.

BEFORE YOU READ

Do you share the view of Alter and others that shame should be a consequence of teenage pregnancy? Before reading Alter's piece, what forms might you imagine the application of shame to take?

AS YOU READ

At one point Alter writes, "The fact remains: every threat to the fabric of this country—from poverty to crime to homelessness—is connected to out-of-wedlock teen pregnancy." As you read, do you find evidence or support for this statement? Can this statement, as Alter asserts, properly be called a "fact?"

1   Tupac Shakur notwithstanding, the notion of shame is beginning to make a comeback in this country. Hallelujah, Hester Prynne. A moderate Democrat think tank, the Progressive Policy Institute, issued an important report last week arguing that President Clinton's anti-teen-pregnancy campaign (slated to begin early next year) must unequivocally state that it is "morally wrong" for unmarried teens to bear children, "must cast single motherhood as a selfish act" and "must resurrect the notion that it is dishonorable for a man to father a child he does not support." This might sound to many Americans like saying the sky is blue. *Of course* that behavior is wrong. But if, as expected, Clinton adopts this view as policy, it represents nothing short of an armistice. The war is over. The libertines lost. Anything goes doesn't go anymore.

2   Or does it? Listen to the voices of the coming backlash, the New Reactionaries. *You're making them feel guilty. You're blaming the victim. Who are you to judge someone else's choices?* As the welfare debate heats up, a certain segment of liberal thinking, still kicking, will try to turn back the clock and win just one more for the old moral relativism. Their targets will be not just Gingrich Republicans but also Clinton Democrats, who long before the recent election offered a series of value judgments about out-of-wedlock birth. In defending the status quo, the New Reactionaries derive their authority from the bone-chilling statistics of modern America: 30.5 percent of babies born out of wedlock, the highest in the world (22 percent for whites, 68 percent for blacks). Look, they say. This is the real America. And besides, it's not their fault.

3   Fair enough. The author of the PPI report, Kathleen Sylvester, argues that moral relativism must be ended without "castigating" the teen mothers themselves. Many have in fact been coerced into sex. That takes care of not hating the sinner. But how about the sin itself? The fact remains: every threat to the fabric of this country—from poverty to crime to homelessness—is connected to out-of-wedlock teen pregnancy. This scourge was not caused by economics; Calcutta's families are wretched but largely intact. It was caused by American cultural changes in the last two decades—aided by an irresponsible entertainment industry—that have lifted the stigma off both black and white communities. When the moral judgment of society is restored—in law and in everyday life—the numbers can be reduced over time. This will be worse for the "self-esteem" of the young mothers and fathers, but better for the younger siblings and friends who might learn from their shame.

4   It's easy to feel guilty about making others feel guilty, especially when so many single mothers heroically raise fine kids. But the temptation must be

resisted. "We've gotten to the point where to be "compassionate" is to refrain from judgment," says David Blankenhorn of the Institute for American Values in New York. "That's antithetical to our whole moral tradition." Blankenhorn is puzzled by the unevenness of society's reluctance to judge. Not all deviancy has been defined down, to use Pat Moynihan's formulation. "We are a society that doesn't mind making people feel bad about certain behavior: smoking, drugs, racially denigrating language," Blankenhorn notes. "But on sexuality and procreation—the heart of the social crisis—there's a reluctance to judge."

5   Some black leaders have given up on shame in favor of more radical ideas. Mayor-elect Marion Barry told The Washington Post recently that he now favors offering teenage mothers this choice: if they want welfare benefits, they must have Norplant to keep them from having another baby for the next five years. As White House aide Bruce Reed says, "Norplant is a debate on what you do in the *absence* of shame."

6   Reed wants to try shame first. It's there somewhere—in every community. Shame doesn't mean someone calling your baby a bastard. It means being forced to live with your parents instead of using welfare to get your own apartment. Instead of the young mother getting to leave school after getting pregnant, she should have to go to *more* school. Shame means beefing up enforcement of the often-ignored requirement that every birth certificate contain the social-security number of the father. Instead of the unwed father being seen in the neighborhood as a big man for spreading his seed, he should become a figure of pity, watching his wages withheld for child support. Like the threat of a shotgun marriage in years past, this might not shrink the libido, but it does concentrate the mind.

7   Amitai Etzioni, founder of the important "communitarian" movement, recommends the use of shame in many realms: publishing the names of men who solicit prostitutes; requiring drunk drivers to have labels on their license plates; even dunce caps for serious troublemakers: "Like any other tool, it can be abused, but that doesn't make it wrong in principle," says Etzioni. "Compared to jail, shame is a very benign tool."

8   The Constitution bars punishment that is "cruel *and* unusual." It says nothing about punishment that is merely unusual. The search for creative shame may sound sadistic or silly, but is it really worse than watching silently as boys are shipped to prison and girls to lives of poverty? The challenge is to combine shame and empathy, to shape the parents without rendering the babies "illegitimate," to draw a line between right and wrong so bright it can be seen forever. Risk ridicule. Think anew.

Topical Considerations

1. Compare Alter's assessment of what is "wrong" with teenage pregnancy with Goodman's. On what points do they agree? Where do they disagree?

2. Who does Alter mean by the "New Reactionaries" (paragraph 2)? What segment of the political population does the term "reactionary" usually refer to? Why do you suppose Alter uses this term? Do you find his use of it effective?
3. What negative impact does "out-of-wedlock teen pregnancy" (paragraph 3) have on American society, according to Alter? Does Alter convince you that teenage motherhood causes these problems? Why or why not?
4. Consider Alter's use of the word "shame." In what precise sense is he using this word? Be sure to analyze the examples of shame he provides in paragraph 6.
5. What strategy does Alter propose for coping with the problem of teenage pregnancy? Has he convinced you that his is a reasonable and potentially effective approach? Why or why not?

Rhetorical Considerations

1. Examine Alter's allusions to "Tupac Shakur" and "Hester Prynne" (paragraph 1). Who are they? What does Alter's use of these names add to the essay? What, if anything, did you find odd or misleading about Alter's references to Shakur and Prynne?
2. What assumptions does Alter make about his audience (paragraph 1)? How can you tell? Do these assumptions strengthen or weaken the effectiveness of his argument?
3. Consider the connotations of Alter's language in paragraphs 3 and 4. Which words or phrases are particularly charged, and why? Do you find his use of language here effective or detrimental?
4. Analyze Alter's use of expert opinion to support his argument. What kind of experts does he cite? Do these citations strengthen Alter's argument? Why or why not?
5. Characterize the kind of support Alter offers for his argument. What would you say is the main type of support? Where did you feel he needed more support?

Writing Assignments

1. Research Kathleen Sylvester's report on teen pregnancy for the Progressive Policy Institute (paragraph 3). Then write a paper comparing and contrasting Sylvester's and Alter's approaches to the problem.
2. Write a letter to Alter arguing that his essay does not account for the experience, problems, and concerns affecting the behavior of most teenagers.
3. Putting yourself in the place of a child born out of wedlock, write a letter to Alter supporting or attacking his argument.

4. Have each member of your group ask his or her family members to discuss the statements Alter lists in his first paragraph: "that it is 'morally wrong' for unmarried teens to bear children"; that "single motherhood is a selfish act"; and that "it is dishonorable for a man to father a child he does not support." Then analyze the responses together and write a report on your results which either supports or attacks Alter's assumption that most Americans support these statements.

In Defense of Teenaged Mothers
Mike Males

In the previous essay Jonathan Alter lays our nation's most pressing problems (poverty, crime, and homelessness) at the feet of pregnant teenagers. In this piece Mike Males presents a very different picture of the teenage mother. Instead of the willfully irresponsible welfare recipient Alter depicts, Males draws a picture of the teenage mother as, in many cases, a victim of emotional and physical abuse. In Males's view, her pregnancy may, ironically, give shape and meaning to her life. Males argues that the current attacks on teenage mothers have never been "angrier, more illogical, or more potentially devastating to a generation of young mothers and their babies. . . ."

Mike Males is a graduate student in the University of California-Irvine's School of Social Ecology. He reports on youth issues for *In These Times*. This article originally appeared in *The Progressive* in 1994.

BEFORE YOU READ

Create a sketch of the typical teenage mother. Include background details including socioeconomic level, home life, education, age, partner, motive for pregnancy, means of financial support. After reading this essay compare your sketch to that of Males. How do they compare? In your opinion which is more accurate?

AS YOU READ

Take the case of LaSalla Jackson described in the opening paragraph of this essay. What might be the benefit or consequence of the experience of shame recommended by Alter in her case? Is shame a "tool" you would recommend?

1   At the Crittenton Center for Young Women near downtown Los Angeles, seventeen-year-old LaSalla Jackson sets down her tiny infant and shows the scars on her calves where her drug-addicted mother beat her with an extension cord. Jackson left home when she had her baby to live at the Crittenton Center. After she graduates from the Center's high school, she plans to marry her child's twenty-three-year-old father, who visits twice a week. "I was watching

five little brothers, sisters, cousins at home," she says. "Here it's one, and I'm not getting hit around."

2   Almonica, another Crittenton resident, saw her mother set on fire and murdered by her stepfather during a drunken fight. At age sixteen, she got pregnant by a twenty-one-year-old man. "It was a way out," she says.

3   To President Clinton, these unwed teenaged mothers represent an assault on family integrity and public coffers. "Can you believe that a child who has a child gets more money from the Government for leaving home than for staying home with a parent or grandparent? That's not just bad policy, it's wrong," the President declared in his State of the Union address. "We will say to teenagers: If you have a child out of wedlock, we'll no longer give you a check to set up a separate household." Clinton has won praise from liberals and conservatives alike for his "family values" campaign, which includes welfare sanctions to force unwed teen mothers back into their parents' homes. Some Congressional Republicans have proposed cutting off welfare to all teen mothers to achieve the same end. "We want families to stay together," Clinton says.

4   But the supervising social worker at the Crittenton Center, Yale Gancherov, takes a different view. "The parents of these young women were violent, were drug abusers, were sexually abusive, were absent or neglectful. While privileged people may see a detriment in a teenager becoming a mother, these girls see it as a realistic improvement in their lives."

5   Current rhetoric about sex, values, and teenaged parenthood in the United States ignores several crucial realities. Contrary to welfare reformers' contention, many teenaged mothers cannot return home. Washington researchers Debra Boyer and David Fine's detailed 1992 study of pregnant teens and teenaged mothers showed that two-thirds had been raped or sexually abused, nearly always by parents, other guardians, or relatives.

6   Six in ten teen mothers' childhoods also included severe physical violence: being beaten with a stick, strap, or fist, thrown against walls, deprived of food, locked in closets, or burned with cigarettes or hot water.

7   Most teen mothers stay with their families even under difficult conditions. More than 60 per cent of the young mothers in Boyer and Fine's study lived with their parents, foster parents, or in institutions. Nearly all the rest lived with adult relatives, husbands, or friends, often with combinations of the above. "Very few live apart from adults," says Fine. Those who did, Fine says, are often escaping intolerable situations at home. "Young mothers who live away from home are significantly more likely to have been physically or sexually abused at home than those who live with parents."

8   Despite all the talk of "children having children" the large majority of births—as well as sexually transmitted disease, including AIDS—among teenaged girls is caused by adults. The most recent National Center for Health Statistics data show that only one-third of births among teenaged mothers involved teenaged fathers. Most were caused by adult men over the age of twenty.

9   In order to mold teenaged pregnancy into a safe, expedient issue, some uncomfortable facts have been suppressed—even by groups that know better.

10   Child advocates such as the Children's Defense Fund might be expected to speak out against official distortions of "teen" parenthood. Not so. Despite its excellent research papers, which show the complexity of the problems teenaged mothers face, a popular poster campaign by the Children's Defense Fund promotes a two-dimensional—and misleading—picture of the issue. **It's like being grounded for eighteen years,** says one poster, depicting teenaged mothers as naughty airheads. **Wait'll you see how fast he can run when you tell him you're pregnant,** says another, showing a stereotypical picture of a callous varsity jock.

11   "Teen-adult sex is not being dealt with," says Angie Karwan of Michigan's Planned Parenthood. Part of the reason, Karwan theorizes, is that the Federal preoccupation with teenaged sex influences programs that receive grant funding. "That's how the money is awarded," she told a reporter from Michigan's *Oakland Press.*

12   The spin put on teen pregnancy, in turn, has some serious consequences for social policy. Present policy blames teenaged mothers for causing a multi-billion-dollar social problem. Says Health and Human Services Secretary Donna Shalala, "We will never successfully deal with welfare reform until we reduce the amount of teenaged pregnancy."

13   In fact, the opposite seems to hold: Poverty causes early childbearing. The rapid increase in child and youth poverty, from 14 per cent in 1973 to 21 per cent in 1991, was followed—after a ten-year lag—by today's rise in teenaged childbearing. Like Ronald Reagan's anecdotes about "welfare Cadillac" black mothers, the allegation by Clinton's welfare-reform task force and members of Congress that teens have babies to collect the "incentive" of $150 a month in AFDC benefits has been repeatedly disproven.

14   Recent studies show that, rather than "risking the future" (the title of a 1987 National Research Council report), most adolescent mothers may be exercising their best option in bleak circumstances when they latch onto older men who promise them a "way out" of homes characterized by poverty, violence, and rape.

15   "Troubled, abused girls who have babies become more centered emotionally," says social worker Gancherov.

16   "They often gain the attention of professionals and social services. Such girls are more likely to stay in school with a baby than without. Their behavioral health improves."

17   A 1990 study of 2,000 youths found that teenaged mothers show significantly lower rates of substance abuse, stress, depression, and suicide than their peers.

18   "Becoming a mother is not the ideal way to accomplish these goals," Gancherov emphasizes. But impoverished girls who get pregnant may not be the heedless, self-destructive figures politicians and the media portray.

19   To decrease the incidence of teen pregnancy, we must improve environments for teens, Gancherov argues. Girls who see a brighter future ahead

have reason to delay childbearing. Dramatically lower rates of teenaged pregnancy in the suburbs, as opposed to the inner city, bear this out.

20   The Clinton Administration's budget and its rhetoric offer little to millions of youth subjected to poverty and physical, emotional, and sexual violence—conditions many girls form liaisons with older men to escape. Instead, the myth Clinton and those around him continue to foster is that of reckless teenaged mothers guilty of abusing adult moral values and welfare generosity. Female "survival strategies," in the words of sociologist Meda Chesney-Lind, are what the Government seeks to punish.

21   In an Administration led by the most knowledgeable child advocates ever, the concerted attack on adolescents has never been angrier, more illogical, or more potentially devastating to a generation of young mothers and their babies, who cannot fight back.

Topical Considerations

1. What, according to Males, are the "crucial realities" being ignored in contemporary debates about "sex, values, and teenaged parenthood" (paragraph 5)? Do you now think Alter and Goodman ignored these "realities"?
2. Why do teenage girls become pregnant, according to Males? Based on your own knowledge of teenage sexual practices, are you convinced by this analysis? Why or why not?
3. Explain why Males believes that the posters put out by the Children's Defense Fund promote "a two-dimensional—and misleading—picture of the issue" of teen pregnancy (paragraph 9). Explain why you agree or disagree that the posters are misleading.
4. Compare the different accounts of the relationship between poverty and teenage pregnancy offered by Alter and Males. Which account do you find more compelling, and why?
5. Has Males' argument changed your thinking about this issue? If so, in what ways? How would you reassess the arguments of Alter and Goodman in light of Males' claims?

Rhetorical Considerations

1. Evaluate this essay's use of authorities. Which experts are most important in supporting Males' claims? Has he provided an appropriate range of experts?
2. Describe where and how Males relies on appeals to readers' emotions. To what extent did you find these emotional appeals to be an effective argumentative strategy? In what ways might they weaken his argument?
3. Analyze the way Males appeals to his readers' sense of morality in the essay's last two paragraphs. What moral principles does Males believe are being

transgressed in current rhetoric about teenage mothers? Compare the way Males and Alter strike moral poses in their arguments.

Writing Assignments

1. Research Males' claim "Poverty causes early childbearing" (paragraph 12). If the evidence convinces you this statement is wrong, write a letter trying to convince Males to change his position; if you find corroborating evidence for this claim, write a letter trying to convince Alter to change his position.

2. If you are not now a parent, imagine how your life would change if you suddenly became a parent. Make sure to consider the impact on all areas of your life: school, work, social life, home life, etc. Then write an essay that imagines what your life would be like in five years if you had a child, comparing it to your imagined future without a child.

3. Why do American teenagers become pregnant? Interview three people in your community who work with young people to further explore this question. Interviewees could include school psychologists, clergy, youth counselors at your local Y.M.C.A. or Girl's Club, or other social work professionals. Using these interviews as evidence, write an essay that either supports or attacks Males' claim that pregnancy is a " 'survival strategy' " for many teenagers (paragraph 19).

Menaces to Society?
Stephanie Coontz

In this essay, author Stephanie Coontz objects to the stigmatization of single mothers. As a single mother as well as a professional family historian, Coontz points out that the castigation of welfare mothers provides a scapegoat for society's problems. She also argues that the attack on single motherhood is an attack on career mothers, divorced mothers, and women's independence itself.

Stephanie Coontz is a professor of History and Family Studies at The Evergreen State College in Olympia, Washington and author of *The Way We Never Were: American Families and the Nostalgia Trap* (1992).

BEFORE YOU READ

What is your definition of a family unit? Is there only one acceptable definition? Or does a variety of configurations make up a family? Is one type of family the ideal? Does the acceptance of anything other than the traditional nuclear family weaken the family unit?

AS YOU READ

Does Coontz's analysis of a family unit with a single mother have universal application? Or are her remarks directed to a particular social, economic, or professional level or class? How does this influence the applicability of her observations?

1   Every time I open the paper or turn on the news, it seems as if some politician or pundit is going on about the dire consequences of single parenthood. And it's not just conservatives who are leading the way. Today, politicians and columnists of every stripe are proudly trumpeting a new "bipartisan consensus"—single mothers are a menace, both to society and to their children. After a brief period when people stopped calling babies illegitimate simply because the father was not married to the mother, the term has come back in favor, often attached to invective so mean-spirited and cynical that it takes my breath away.

2   A *Newsweek* column called illegitimacy "the smoking gun in a sickening array of pathologies—crime, drug abuse, physical and mental illness, welfare dependency." The children of unwed mothers have been labeled a "social scourge," a "catastrophe," and a "plague." Senator Daniel Patrick Moynihan, a Democrat, believes that women who have children out of wedlock are engaging in "speciation." *Washington Post* columnist David Broder describes kids of single mothers as a whole new "breed" of human, a fearsome "species of fatherless children." Even President Clinton, himself the son of a single mother, now declares that single parenthood "is simply not right. . . . You shouldn't have a baby when you're not married. You just have to stop it."

3   Well, it's a little too late for me to just stop it. I am a never-married mother with a thirteen-year-old son. That's my boy—wrestling with all the dilemmas adolescents face in contemporary America—they're talking about: Kristopher, the social scourge. The catastrophe. The plague.

4   "You obviously didn't inherit a normal set of eardrums," I tease him, over the blare of his electric guitar, "but I don't really think you're a new species." He grins when I joke about it like this, but he reads the papers, and I can tell it hurts. Teenagers take labels very seriously. All too often they try to live up to them. Or down, as the case may be.

5   Actually, I'm luckier than most unwed mothers. Because I'm white, middle class, and an older, well-established professional, my son is sometimes afforded a sort of honorary "legitimacy." Last year, for instance, when Kris objected to a particularly cruel remark a health teacher made about single mothers, the teacher hastened to explain that she knew his mom was educated, financially secure, and clearly loving. "I'm sure your mom had good reasons for what she did."

6   In other words, I could tell Kris not to worry; he's different from those other bastards. For most of the attacks are directed at the unwed welfare mom, the teenager supposedly popping out new babies each year to get a hike of

about $65 in her monthly check. These are the families that former secretary of education Bill Bennett is referring to when he proposes cutting off economic assistance to single mothers and sending their children to orphanages. That's not me and my son. If I sit back and keep my mouth shut, no one would guess that my creative, compassionate youngster is one of "those" kids. Why, then, does this rhetoric make me so angry?

7   For one thing, as a family historian I know that unwed motherhood is not the major cause of our society's problems, and eliminating one-parent families won't fix our inner cities or end the need for welfare. In fact, a recent study shows that even if we reunited every single child in America with his or her bio-logical father, two-thirds of the children who are poor today would still be poor.

8   For another, while most of the cant about the dangers of illegitimacy is aimed at welfare mothers, I am struck by how quickly the rhetoric broadens into a more general attack on women's independence, sexual or otherwise. On television talk shows, the new family-values crusaders usually begin by castigating welfare mothers but move easily to "careerist" mothers who sup-posedly "rationalize material benefits in the name of children"; divorced women who put "individual self-actualization" before their kids' needs; women who remarry and expose their daughters to the "severe risk" of sexual abuse by men who lack a biological "investment" in the child. One *Fortune* magazine writer even blames our social ills on modern women's rejection of "the idea that women must be 'cared for' by men." It's time, they agree, to "restigmatize" both divorced and unwed mothers.

9   Yet I know from personal experience as well as sociological research that there are hundreds of paths leading to single motherhood. Some of the stories I hear would seem irresponsible to even the most ardent proponent of women's rights; others stem from complicated accidents or miscalculations that even the most radical right-winger would probably forgive.

10   At one recent workshop that I taught on family history, I met three other never-married mothers. One was a young girl who had gotten pregnant "by accident/on purpose" in the hope that her unfaithful boyfriend would marry her. It hadn't worked, and in the ensuing year she had sometimes left her baby unattended when she went out on dates. Jarred into self-examination after be-ing reported for neglect, she realized that going back to school and developing job skills was a more promising way of escaping her abusive parents than chasing boys. Another, now 25, had been 15 when she became pregnant. She considered abortion, but she would have had to drive 600 miles, by herself, to the nearest provider, and she didn't even have the money for a hotel room. Both these mothers had relied on welfare assistance to get by in their early days, and one was still on food stamps as she attended school. The third was an older, well-paid professional woman who had had three wedding plans fall through. She attributed her failures with men to being caught between two value systems: She was old-fashioned enough in her romantic fantasies to be attracted to powerful, take-charge men, but modern enough in her accom-plishments that such men generally found her threatening. Her last fiancé had

left her pregnant at age 35. With her biological clock ticking "now or never" in her ear, she decided to have the child.

11   What government agency or morals committee should decide which of us single mothers to stigmatize and which to excuse, or which of our children should be packed off to orphanages? And what about the harmful effects of such pronouncements and penalties on the children of all single parents?

12   Most single parents don't need politicians to heap more guilt and self-doubt on our heads. We're doing that just fine on our own. Everywhere we turn we see the statistics: Children of single-parent families are more likely to drop out of school, exhibit emotional distress, get in trouble with the law, and abuse drugs or alcohol than children who grow up with two biological parents. Most single parents I talk to are consumed with guilt and fear. What they really need to hear is that single parenthood is not an inevitable sentence of doom for their children.

13   And that is just what the latest research confirms. Yes, there are disadvantages for kids of single parents, but they are often exaggerated: Most kids, from every kind of family, turn out fine, so long as their mothers are not overly stressed by poverty, ongoing conflict with the child's father, or the very stigmatization that the family-values crusaders want to magnify.

14   Of course there are significant hardships in raising a child alone, but even a "traditional" family structure does not guarantee that the two parents are responsible, involved, or stable. Every family configuration offers certain challenges and benefits. My son, for example, has always been more candid with me about what's happening at school than most of his friends from two-parent families are with their parents. But I have more trouble than those parents finding opportunities to meet with Kris's teachers or scheduling a consistent time each day to be around while he does his homework. This turns out to be a common theme for most single parents. We typically spend less time supervising our child's schoolwork or talking to teachers than to adults in two-parent families, drawbacks that may lead to lower grades for our children. But we also spend more time talking with our kids, which might explain why children from one-parent households are often more articulate and experience themselves as more effective in the world than their two-parent peers. Single parents tend to praise good grades more than adults in two-parent families, providing an impetus for their children to do well in school. But single parents also tend to get angrier when grades fall, a reaction that may lead the child to be defiant—often lowering grades even more.

15   There are other trade-offs as well. While children of single mothers often grow up to be closer to their mothers and have more respect for working women than do kids from two-parent homes, the adolescent years can be particularly trying. When a teenager begins to demand more freedom, a single mother has no ally to take over the nay-saying when her voice gives out or to help her withstand a youth's insistence that "everybody else's parents let them. . . ." Like many single parents who have close relationships with their

children, I sometimes have trouble setting firm limits, even though I've studied the problems that result when adults allow their youngsters too much say in decision-making. I worry that my son's self-confidence, and his sense that he is entitled to negotiate limits with others the way he has always negotiated them with me, might lead him to do risky things or to question authority once too often.

16   Surely it's more helpful for single parents to learn how to build on their strengths and compensate for their weaknesses than to be demonized by politicians and pundits. But taking a stand against "immoral" mothers is easier and less politically risky than tackling the problems of our inner cities or addressing middle-class concerns. Our government will spend $25 billion on Aid to Families with Dependent Children this year, compared with roughly $51 billion in direct giveaways to business and another $53 billion in corporate tax breaks. But debates over subsidies only get posed in moral terms when women's sexuality is involved. After savings-and-loan corporations failed to "just say no" to risky loans and promiscuous spending on salaries, Uncle Sam handed them $150 billion of the taxpayers' money. "Underwriting tragedy is one thing," *Washington Post* columnist Charles Krauthammer has explained. "Underwriting wantonness is quite another."

17   The new family-values crusade also appeals to those uncomfortable with the changing role of women by emphatically reestablishing men as the "heads of the household." Consult your dictionary to discover the distinction between a legitimate and an illegitimate child. According to the traditional definition, any child brought into the world without a man's name on the birth certificate is not real, not authentic, not genuine, not rightful. No matter how much love, care, and effort a woman devotes to raising her children, she can never make them legitimate. But no matter how little effort a man puts into child rearing, his name on a piece of paper makes all the difference in the world to the status of his child.

18   The ancient Greeks believed that a woman contributed nothing to the production of a child except nine months' storage. In English common law, a child born out of wedlock was a *filius nullius*—the child of no one. We haven't come very far when President Clinton remarks that unwed mothers are "raising a whole generation of children who aren't sure they're the most important person in the world to anybody."

19   I don't want to use my personal and professional advantages to wheedle special dispensation for my son to be treated as a legitimate person. Legitimacy and respect should be the birthright of every child. Anyone needing appeal to tradition to stand up for that principle can look back more than 300 years, to the response of the Native Americans when the first family-values crusaders arrived on the shores of this continent. The Jesuit missionaries told the Montagnais-Naskapi Indians that men should take control of women's sexuality and parents should discipline their children more harshly. Otherwise, the good Fathers warned, your wives and daughters may give birth to babies that do not belong to you. The Native Americans were not persuaded. "You French people love only your own children," they replied, "but we love all the

children of the tribe." Wouldn't it be nice if America's politicians quit beating up on single parents and started operating from that set of family values?

Topical Considerations

1. What recently expressed attitudes about single motherhood provoked Coontz to write this essay? Do Alter and/or Goodman hold the attitudes attacked by Coontz?
2. Explain how Coontz supports her claim that "there are hundreds of paths leading to single motherhood" (paragraph 9). Does Coontz persuade you of this point? Why is it an important one for her argument?
3. Describe the impression you received from this essay of Coontz's 13-year-old son, Kristopher. Which details about Kristopher did you find most memorable? Why do you think Coontz included descriptions of her son? How does the portrait add to the effectiveness of her argument?
4. Analyze Coontz's skills as a mother. What are her strengths? What are her weaknesses? From reading this essay, how would you rate her parenting abilities, on a scale of one to ten?
5. Explain what Coontz means when she says that anti-illegitimacy rhetoric often "broadens into a more general attack on women's independence, sexual or otherwise" (paragraph 8). Does Coontz convince you of this point? Why or why not.
6. How does Coontz's defense of single motherhood differ from Mike Males'? Which defense do you find more compelling? Why?

Rhetorical Considerations

1. Explain how the word choice in the essay's first paragraph conveys Coontz's attitude toward her opposition.
2. How does Coontz establish credibility in this essay?
3. Where does Coontz refute challenges to her argument? How thorough and successful is her refutation? What potential opposition does she fail to consider?
4. Analyze the end of the essay. Why do you think Coontz includes the anecdote about Native Americans and European Jesuits? What makes this ending particularly powerful and appropriate to Coontz's article?

Writing Assignments

1. Write an essay attacking or defending Coontz's claim that "debates over subsidies only get posed in moral terms when women's sexuality is involved" (paragraph 16). To support your position, research public response to the

savings-and-loan bailout mentioned by Coontz, as well as congressional and public debate on social welfare programs.

2. Imagine you are Kristopher Coontz. Write a letter to the health teacher described in paragraph 5 and encourage her to rethink her attitude toward single mothers.

OPPOSITIONS: CAPITAL PUNISHMENT

The Death Penalty Is Justice
Edward I. Koch

There are more murders committed in New York City than in any other American city. From 1978 to 1990, Edward Koch, a long-active Democrat, served as mayor of New York City. During those years he established a reputation as a hard-driving, no-nonsense, and feisty leader. In the piece that follows, which was originally published in *The New Republic* in 1985, Koch argues that the death penalty is the only just recourse to "heinous crimes of murder." In building his case, he examines the arguments most frequently voiced by opponents to capital punishment.

Koch is the author of *Mayor: An Autobiography* (1984), written with William Rauch.

BEFORE YOU READ

Find the point in the introductory section of the essay where Koch states the intention and method of his argument. Does this establish confidence in the author? Does it inspire you to read on?

AS YOU READ

Koch tells the reader that he will examine and refute the seven arguments most frequently used to oppose capital punishment. As you read the essay, select the argument you think is most successfully refuted and select one that you think is weakly refuted.

1   Last December a man named Robert Lee Willie, who had been convicted of raping and murdering an 18-year-old woman, was executed in the Louisiana

state prison. In a statement issued several minutes before his death, Mr. Willie said: "Killing people is wrong. . . . It makes no difference whether it's citizens, countries, or governments. Killing is wrong." Two weeks later in South Carolina, an admitted killer named Joseph Carl Shaw was put to death for murdering two teenagers. In an appeal to the governor for clemency, Mr. Shaw wrote: "Killing is wrong when I did it. Killing is wrong when you do it. I hope you have the courage and moral strength to stop the killing."

2   It is a curiosity of modern life that we find ourselves being lectured on morality by cold-blooded killers. Mr. Willie previously had been convicted of aggravated rape, aggravated kidnapping, and the murders of a Louisiana deputy and a man from Missouri. Mr. Shaw committed another murder a week before the two for which he was executed, and admitted mutilating the body of the 14-year-old girl he killed. I can't help wondering what prompted these murderers to speak out against killing as they entered the deathhouse door. Did their newfound reverence for life stem from the realization that they were about to lose their own?

3   Life is indeed precious, and I believe the death penalty helps to affirm this fact. Had the death penalty been a real possibility in the minds of these murderers, they might well have stayed their hand. They might have shown moral awareness before their victims died, and not after. Consider the tragic death of Rosa Velez, who happened to be home when a man named Luis Vera burglarized her apartment in Brooklyn. "Yeah, I shot her," Vera admitted. "She knew me, and I knew I wouldn't go to the chair."

4   During my twenty-two years in public service, I have heard the pros and cons of capital punishment expressed with special intensity. As a district leader, councilman, congressman, and mayor, I have represented constituencies generally thought of as liberal. Because I support the death penalty for heinous crimes of murder, I have sometimes been the subject of emotional and outraged attacks by voters who find my position reprehensible or worse. I have listened to their ideas. I have weighed their objections carefully. I still support the death penalty. The reasons I maintain my position can be best understood by examining the arguments most frequently heard in opposition.

5   *1. The death penalty is "barbaric."* Sometimes opponents of capital punishment horrify with tales of lingering death on the gallows, of faulty electric chairs, or of agony in the gas chamber. Partly in response to such protests, several states such as North Carolina and Texas switched to execution by lethal injection. The condemned person is put to death painlessly, without ropes, voltage, bullets, or gas. Did this answer the objections of death penalty opponents? Of course not. On June 22, 1984, the *New York Times* published an editorial that sarcastically attacked the new "hygienic" method of death by injection, and stated that "execution can never be made humane through science." So it's not the method that really troubles opponents. It's the death itself they consider barbaric.

6   Admittedly, capital punishment is not a pleasant topic. However, one does not have to like the death penalty in order to support it any more than

one must like radical surgery, radiation, or chemotherapy in order to find necessary these attempts at curing cancer. Ultimately we may learn how to cure cancer with a simple pill. Unfortunately, that day has not yet arrived. Today we are faced with the choice of letting the cancer spread or trying to cure it with the methods available, methods that one day will almost certainly be considered barbaric. But to give up and do nothing would be far more barbaric and would certainly delay the discovery of an eventual cure. The analogy between cancer and murder is imperfect, because murder is not the "disease" we are trying to cure. The disease is injustice. We may not like the death penalty, but it must be available to punish crimes of cold-blooded murder, cases in which any other form of punishment would be inadequate and, therefore, unjust. If we create a society in which injustice is not tolerated, incidents of murder—the most flagrant form of injustice—will diminish.

7   *2. No other major democracy uses the death penalty.* No other major democracy—in fact, few other countries of any description—are plagued by a murder rate such as that in the United States. Fewer and fewer Americans can remember the days when unlocked doors were the norm and murder was a rare and terrible offense. In America the murder rate climbed 122 percent between 1963 and 1980. During that same period, the murder rate in New York City increased by almost 400 percent, and the statistics are even worse in many other cities. A study at M.I.T. showed that based on 1970 homicide rates a person who lived in a large American city ran a greater risk of being murdered than an American soldier in World War II ran of being killed in combat. It is not surprising that the laws of each country differ according to differing conditions and traditions. If other countries had our murder problem, the cry for capital punishment would be just as loud as it is here. And I daresay that any other major democracy where 75 percent of the people supported the death penalty would soon enact it into law.

8   *3. An innocent person might be executed by mistake.* Consider the work of Hugo Adam Bedau, one of the most implacable foes of capital punishment in this country. According to Mr. Bedau, it is "false sentimentality to argue that the death penalty should be abolished because of the abstract possibility that an innocent person might be executed." He cites a study of the 7,000 executions in this country from 1893 to 1971, and concludes that the record fails to show that such cases occur. The main point, however, is this. If government functioned only when the possibility of error didn't exist, government wouldn't function at all. Human life deserves special protection, and one of the best ways to guarantee that protection is to assure that convicted murderers do not kill again. Only the death penalty can accomplish this end. In a recent case in New Jersey, a man named Richard Biegenwald was freed from prison after serving 18 years for murder; since his release he has been convicted of committing four murders. A prisoner named Lemuel Smith, who, while serving four life sentences for murder (plus two life sentences for kidnapping and robbery) in New York's Green Haven Prison, lured a woman corrections officer into the chaplain's office and strangled her. He then mutilated and

dismembered her body. An additional life sentence for Smith is meaningless. Because New York has no death penalty statute, Smith has effectively been given a license to kill.

9   But the problem of multiple murder is not confined to the nation's penitentiaries. In 1981, 91 police officers were killed in the line of duty in this country. Seven percent of those arrested in the cases that have been solved had a previous arrest for murder. In New York City in 1976 and 1977, 85 persons arrested for homicide had a previous arrest for murder. Six of these individuals had two previous arrests for murder, and one had four previous murder arrests. During those two years the New York police were arresting for murder persons with a previous arrest for murder on the average of one every 8.5 days. This is not surprising when we learn that in 1975, for example, the median time served in Massachusetts for homicide was less than two and a half years. In 1976 a study sponsored by the Twentieth Century Fund found that the average time served in the United States for first-degree murder is ten years. The median time served may be considerably lower.

10   *4. Capital punishment cheapens the value of human life.* On the contrary, it can be easily demonstrated that the death penalty strengthens the value of human life. If the penalty for rape were lowered, clearly it would signal a lessened regard for the victims' suffering, humiliation, and personal integrity. It would cheapen their horrible experience, and expose them to an increased danger of recurrence. When we lower the penalty for murder, it signals a lessened regard for the value of the victim's life. Some critics of capital punishment, such as columnist Jimmy Breslin, have suggested that a life sentence is actually a harsher penalty for murder than death. This is sophistic nonsense. A few killers may decide not to appeal a death sentence, but the overwhelming majority make every effort to stay alive. It is by exacting the highest penalty for the taking of human life that we affirm the highest value of human life.

11   *5. The death penalty is applied in a discriminatory manner.* This factor no longer seems to be the problem it once was. The appeals process for a condemned prisoner is lengthy and painstaking. Every effort is made to see that the verdict and sentence were fairly arrived at. However, assertions of discrimination are not an argument for ending the death penalty but for extending it. It is not justice to exclude everyone from the penalty of the law if a few are found to be so favored. Justice requires that the law be applied equally to all.

12   *6. Thou Shalt Not Kill.* The Bible is our greatest source of moral inspiration. Opponents of the death penalty frequently cite the sixth of the Ten Commandments in an attempt to prove that capital punishment is divinely proscribed. In the original Hebrew, however, the Sixth Commandment reads ''Thou Shalt Not Commit Murder,'' and the Torah specifies capital punishment for a variety of offenses. The biblical viewpoint has been upheld by philosophers throughout history. The greatest thinkers of the 19th century—Kant, Locke, Hobbes, Rousseau, Montesquieu, and Mill—agreed that natural law properly authorizes the sovereign to take life in order to vindicate justice. Only

Jeremy Bentham was ambivalent. Washington, Jefferson, and Franklin endorsed it. Abraham Lincoln authorized executions for deserters in wartime. Alexis de Tocqueville, who expressed profound respect for American institutions, believed that the death penalty was indispensable to the support of social order. The United States Constitution, widely admired as one of the seminal achievements in the history of humanity, condemns cruel and inhuman punishment, but does not condemn capital punishment.

13   *7. The death penalty is state-sanctioned murder.* This is the defense with which Messrs. Willie and Shaw hoped to soften the resolve of those who sentenced them to death. By saying in effect, "You're no better than I am," the murderer seeks to bring his accusers down to his own level. It is also a popular argument among opponents of capital punishment, but a transparently false one. Simply put, the state has rights that the private individual does not. In a democracy, those rights are given to the state by the electorate. The execution of a lawfully condemned killer is no more an act of murder than is legal imprisonment an act of kidnapping. If an individual forces a neighbor to pay him money under threat of punishment, it's called extortion. If the state does it, it's called taxation. Rights and responsibilities surrendered by the individual are what give the state its power to govern. This contract is the foundation of civilization itself.

14   Everyone wants his or her rights, and will defend them jealously. Not everyone, however, wants responsibilities, especially the painful responsibilities that come with law enforcement. Twenty-one years ago a woman named Kitty Genovese was assaulted and murdered on a street in New York. Dozens of neighbors heard her cries for help but did nothing to assist her. They didn't even call the police. In such a climate the criminal understandably grows bolder. In the presence of moral cowardice, he lectures us on our supposed failings and tries to equate his crimes with our quest for justice.

15   The death of anyone—even a convicted killer—diminishes us all. But we are diminished even more by a justice system that fails to function. It is an illusion to let ourselves believe that doing away with capital punishment removes the murderer's deed from our conscience. The rights of society are paramount. When we protect guilty lives, we give up innocent lives in exchange. When opponents of capital punishment say to the state, "I will not let you kill in my name," they are also saying to murderers: "You can kill in your *own* name as long as I have an excuse for not getting involved."

16   It is hard to imagine anything worse than being murdered while neighbors do nothing. But something worse exists. When those same neighbors shrink back from justly punishing the murderer, the victim dies twice.

Topical Considerations

1. What would you say is Koch's key reason for supporting the death penalty? Does his argument seem convincing? Has it changed your attitude on the issue?

2. Koch distinguishes two issues: punishment and deterrence. Which of the arguments are rooted in punishment and which are rooted in deterrence?
3. What is Koch's argument against opponents' claim that the death penalty risks putting innocent people to death ? How sound is his stand?
4. In paragraph 4, Koch says that he supports capital punishment for "heinous crimes of murder." Do you think he is distinguishing different kinds of murder? In other words, do you think he is arguing capital punishment for special cases of murder? If so, what might be the criteria Koch suggests? Which criteria would you consider?
5. Can you think of any arguments against the death penalty that Koch fails to address? Can you think of any arguments for the death penalty that Koch may have missed?

Rhetorical Considerations

1. Where exactly does Koch make his thesis statement in this essay?
2. In paragraph 6, Koch likens murder to cancer and the death penalty to cancer treatment. How apt is this analogy?
3. Koch has built his case against the abolition of capital punishment by appeals to logic, emotion, and ethics. Reread the essay and find examples of each of these different appeals. Which were the most effective? Which were the least effective? Explain your answers.
4. How would you describe the tone of Koch's writing?

Writing Assignments

1. Suppose that your state legislature is considering a bill to abolish capital punishment. Write a letter to your state representative urging him or her to oppose the bill. Use the arguments from Koch's essay that you feel will be most convincing.
2. There are many opponents of capital punishment who say that the death penalty is "cruel and unusual punishment" and argue that the government should not be in the business of taking human lives. What is your feeling about this particular argument? Do you think the government has the right to take lives? Do you think that capital punishment reduces the government to the level of those who murder?

No Death Penalty
David Bruck

A month after *The New Republic* published Mayor Koch's defense of capital punishment in March 1985, it published the following response by David Bruck. Questioning the basis of Koch's defense argument and finding it morally dangerous, Bruck goes on to argue that Koch has made the electric chair a campaign platform. Frustrated and enraged by violent crime and the inability of government to stop it, the public, of course, supports the call for blood, says Bruck—even if the measure doesn't work.

Bruck is a lawyer in the South Carolina Office of Appellate Defense. A recent client of his was Susan Smith, accused and convicted of drowning her two young sons. Many of his defendants are prisoners under the death sentence.

BEFORE YOU READ

Since you know that David Bruck is a lawyer and that many of his clients await execution, what are two arguments you predict he might use to oppose the death penalty? If an argument is predictable, does that make it less convincing?

AS YOU READ

Both Edward Koch, author of the previous piece defending capital punishment, and David Bruck talk about whether or not an innocent person may be executed by mistake. Whose opinion do you agree with and why? Who do you think argues this specific point more successfully?

1   Mayor Ed Koch contends that the death penalty "affirms life." By failing to execute murderers, he says, we "signal a lessened regard for the value of the victim's life." Koch suggests that people who oppose the death penalty are like Kitty Genovese's neighbors, who heard her cries for help but did nothing while an attacker stabbed her to death.

2   This is the standard "moral" defense of death as punishment: even if executions don't deter violent crime any more effectively than imprisonment, they are still required as the only means we have of doing justice in response to the worst of crimes.

3   Until recently, this "moral" argument had to be considered in the abstract, since no one was being executed in the United States. But the death penalty is back now, at least in the southern states, where every one of the more than 30 executions carried out over the last two years have taken place. Those of us who live in those states are getting to see the difference between the death penalty in theory, and what happens when you actually try to use it.

4   South Carolina resumed executing prisoners in January with the electrocution of Joseph Carl Shaw. Shaw was condemned to death for helping to murder two teenagers while he was serving as a military policeman at Fort

Jackson, South Carolina. His crime, propelled by mental illness and PCP, was one of terrible brutality. It is Shaw's last words ("Killing was wrong when I did it. It is wrong when you do it. . . .") that so outraged Mayor Koch: he finds it "a curiosity of modern life that we are being lectured on morality by cold-blooded killers." And so it is.

5   But it was not "modern life" that brought this curiosity into being. It was capital punishment. The electric chair was J. C. Shaw's platform. (The mayor mistakenly writes that Shaw's statement came in the form of a plea to the governor for clemency: actually Shaw made it only seconds before his death, as he waited, shaved and strapped into the chair, for the switch to be thrown.) It was the chair that provided Shaw with celebrity and an opportunity to lecture us on right and wrong. What made this weird moral reversal even worse is that J. C. Shaw faced his own death with undeniable dignity and courage. And while Shaw died, the TV crews recorded another "curiosity" of the death penalty—the crowd gathered outside the deathhouse to cheer on the executioner. Whoops of elation greeted the announcement of Shaw's death. Waiting at the penitentiary gates for the appearance of the hearse bearing Shaw's remains, one demonstrator started yelling, "Where's the beef?"

6   For those who had to see the execution of J. C. Shaw, it wasn't easy to keep in mind that the purpose of the whole spectacle was to affirm life. It will be harder still when Florida executes a cop-killer named Alvin Ford. Ford has lost his mind during his years of death-row confinement, and now spends his days trembling, rocking back and forth, and muttering unintelligible prayers. This had led to litigation over whether Ford meets a centuries-old legal standard for mental competency. Since the Middle Ages, the Anglo-American legal system has generally prohibited the execution of anyone who is too mentally ill to understand what is about to be done to him and why. If Florida wins its case, it will have earned the right to electrocute Ford in his present condition. If it loses, he will not be executed until the state has first nursed him back to some semblance of mental health.

7   We can at least be thankful that this demoralizing spectacle involves a prisoner who is actually guilty of murder. But this may not always be so. The ordeal of Lenell Jeter—the young black engineer who recently served more than a year of a life sentence for a Texas armed robbery that he didn't commit—should remind us that the system is quite capable of making the very worst sort of mistake. That Jeter was eventually cleared is a fluke. If the robbery had occurred at 7 P.M. rather than 3 P.M., he'd have had no alibi, and would still be in prison today. And if someone had been killed in that robbery, Jeter probably would have been sentenced to death. We'd have seen the usual execution-day interviews with state officials and the victim's relatives, all complaining that Jeter's appeals took too long. And Jeter's last words from the gurney would have taken their place among the growing literature of death-house oration that so irrates the mayor.

8   Koch quotes Hugo Adam Bedau, a prominent abolitionist, to the effect that the record fails to establish that innocent defendants have been executed

in the past. But this doesn't mean, as Koch implies, that it hasn't happened. All Bedau was saying was that doubts concerning executed prisoners' guilt are almost never resolved. Bedau is at work now on an effort to determine how many wrongful death sentences may have been imposed: his list of murder convictions since 1900 in which the state eventually *admitted* error is some 400 cases long. Of course, very few of these cases involved actual executions: the mistakes that Bedau documents were uncovered precisely because the prisoner was alive and able to fight for his vindication. The cases where someone is executed are the very cases in which we're least likely to learn that we got the wrong man.

9   I don't claim that executions of entirely innocent people will occur very often. But they will occur. And other sorts of mistakes already have. Roosevelt Green was executed in Georgia two days before J. C. Shaw. Green and an accomplice kidnapped a young woman. Green swore that his companion shot her to death after Green had left, and that he knew nothing about the murder. Green's claim was supported by a statement that his accomplice made to a witness after the crime. The jury never resolved whether Green was telling the truth, and when he tried to take a polygraph examination a few days before his scheduled execution, the state of Georgia refused to allow the examiner into the prison. As the pressure for symbolic retribution mounts, the courts, like the public, are losing patience with such details. Green was electrocuted on January 9, while members of the Ku Klux Klan rallied outside the prison.

10   Then there is another sort of arbitrariness that happens all the time. Last October, Louisiana executed a man named Ernest Knighton. Knighton had killed a gas station owner during a robbery. Like any murder, this was a terrible crime. But it was not premeditated, and is the sort of crime that very rarely results in a death sentence. Why was Knighton electrocuted when almost everyone else who committed the same offense was not? Was it because he was black? Was it because his victim and all 12 members of the jury that sentenced him were white? Was it because Knighton's court-appointed lawyer presented no evidence on his behalf at his sentencing hearing? Or maybe there's no reason except bad luck. One thing is clear: Ernest Knighton was picked out to die the way a fisherman takes a cricket out of a bait jar. No one cares which cricket gets impaled on the hook.

11   Not every prisoner executed recently was chosen that randomly. But many were. And having selected these men so casually, so blindly, the death penalty system asks us to accept that the purpose of killing each of them is to affirm the sanctity of human life.

12   The death penalty states are also learning that the death penalty is easier to advocate than it is to administer. In Florida, where executions have become almost routine, the governor reports that nearly a third of his time is spent reviewing the clemency requests of condemned prisoners. The Florida Supreme Court is hopelessly backlogged with death cases. Some have taken five years to decide, and the rest of the Court's work waits in line behind the death appeals. Florida's death row currently holds more than 230 prisoners.

State officials are reportedly considering building a special "death prison" devoted entirely to the isolation and electrocution of the condemned. The state is also considering the creation of a special public defender unit that will do nothing else but handle death penalty appeals. The death penalty, in short, is spawning death agencies.

13   And what is Florida getting for all of this? The state went through almost all of 1983 without executing anyone: its rate of intentional homicide declined by 17 percent. Last year Florida executed eight people—the most of any state, and the sixth highest total for any year since Florida started electrocuting people back in 1924. Elsewhere in the U.S. last year, the homicide rate continued to decline. But in Florida, it actually rose by 5.1 percent.

14   But these are just the tiresome facts. The electric chair has been a center-piece of each of Koch's recent political campaigns, and he knows better than anyone how little the facts have to do with the public's support for capital punishment. What really fuels the death penalty is the justifiable frustration and rage of people who see that the government is not coping with violent crime. So what if the death penalty doesn't work? At least it gives us the satisfaction of knowing that we got one or two of the sons of bitches.

15   Perhaps we want retribution on the flesh and bone of a handful of convicted murderers so badly that we're willing to close our eyes to all of the demoralization and danger that come with it. A lot of politicians think so, and they may be right. But if they are, then let's at least look honestly at what we're doing. This lottery of death both comes from and encourages an attitude toward human life that is not reverent, but reckless.

16   And that is why the mayor is dead wrong when he confuses such fury with justice. He suggests that we trivialize murder unless we kill murderers. By that logic, we also trivialize rape unless we sodomize rapists. The sin of Kitty Genovese's neighbors wasn't that they failed to stab her attacker to death. Justice does demand that murderers be punished. And common sense demands that society be protected from them. But neither justice nor self-preservation demands that we kill men who we have already imprisoned.

17   The electric chair in which J. C. Shaw died earlier this year was built in 1912 at the suggestion of South Carolina's governor at the time, Cole Blease. Governor Blease's other criminal justice initiative was an impassioned crusade in favor of lynch law. Any lesser response, the governor insisted, trivialized the loathsome crimes of interracial rape and murder. In 1912 a lot of people agreed with Governor Blease that a proper regard for justice required both lynching and the electric chair. Eventually we are going to learn that justice requires neither.

Topical Considerations

1. Compare Bruck's account of J. C. Shaw's crime with that of Koch's account. Does knowing the circumstances—that is, the crime being "propelled by

mental illness and PCP"—strengthen Bruck's argument against capital punishment? Do these details weaken Koch's argument? How about the fact that Shaw's words, coming moments before his execution, were not, as Koch suggests, an appeal for clemency? Do these details change your stand on capital punishment?

2. What would you say forms the basis of Bruck's opposition to the death penalty? How does it compare with the basis of Koch's advocacy for the death penalty?

3. How does Bruck use the Lenell Jeter case? In your estimation, is this a convincing argument for the abolition of the death penalty? Why or why not?

4. How does Bruck make use of the research of abolitionist Hugo Adam Bedau, who is cited as support in Koch's essay? Do you think Bruck is successful in undermining Koch's own use of Bedau?

5. If not capital punishment, what form of justice do you think Bruck would see fit for "heinous crimes of murder"? What punishment(s) do you see fit?

6. In paragraph 10, Bruck brings up the case of Ernest Knighton, who was executed for a murder that was not premeditated. What do you think Koch would say about this case?

7. In paragraph 14, Bruck says that the public's support of capital punishment is fueled by the "frustration and rage of people who see that government is not coping with violent crime." Do you agree with this claim? Do you agree with the rationalization that even "if the death penalty doesn't work," at least "we got one or two of the sons of bitches."

Rhetorical Considerations

1. Where exactly does Bruck state his thesis?
2. What is the point of letting the reader know about the crowd's reaction to the execution of J. C. Shaw? How do these details add to the arguments the author is making?
3. In the previous essay, Koch says that the Bible, "our greatest source of moral inspiration" (paragraph 12), takes the eye-for-an-eye view of justice: The punishment for murder is death. How does Bruck counter this stand, and how effective is his argument against it?

Writing Assignments

1. Adopt the point of view of a supporter of capital punishment who has just read Bruck's essay. Write a letter to the author in which you offer a rebuttal to his argument. Include some emotional appeals and try to show some fallacies in Bruck's reasoning. You might make references to the Susan Smith case.

2. Suppose that your state legislature is considering a bill to abolish capital punishment. Write a letter to your state representative asking that he or she support the bill. Include the arguments in Bruck's essay that you feel will be most convincing.

3. Suppose you were on a panel of judges presiding over a debate between Edward I. Koch and David Bruck. Having heard their arguments in these essays, who would you decide had won the debate? Write an essay in which you defend your decision.

CHAPTER 12

ETHICAL AND MORAL ISSUES

Questions of right and wrong have challenged thinking people throughout history. From the dramas of Ancient Greece to the plays of Shakespeare to the novels of the nineteenth and twentieth century, literary works have tried to distinguish between what is right and what is wrong. Today moral issues infuse not only the lofty spheres of literature and philosophy but the daily life of every man and woman. One cannot leaf through a newspaper or turn on the news without confronting weighty issues such as euthanasia, abortion, animal rights, or drug use. Each of these subjects has created a firestorm of moral and ethical debate, and this chapter explores the various arguments.

Given the growing number of senior citizens in this country, health care issues such as care of the terminally ill pose moral dilemmas. At the heart of matters is not nature but new technology which can prolong life without regard to quality. Consequently, decisions arise about the right to take one's own life. In some states, in fact, attempts to legalize assisted suicide could, if successful, mean that laws against such could be declared unconstitutional. In "Scared to Die" Herbert Hendin protests such a policy change. Better, he says, to enhance and dignify the process of dying, than to obliterate this profound human experience. Ronald Dworkin, on the other hand, takes a different position in "When Is It Right to Die?" He refers to euthanasia as a decision so intimate and personal that it is among the moral liberties protected by the 14th Amendment of the Constitution. However, the final piece in this section, "Dead Complicated" by Elizabeth Rosenthal, reminds us how difficult it is to avoid ambiguities in a debate over mercy killing—in particular, the definition of "death."

It is the definition of "life" around which the debates of abortion rage. And it is a subject about which few people are neutral. The definition of life itself—with which scientists and lawmakers still grapple—is replete with moral, religious, political, and legal ramifications. On one side, pro-life supporters take the moral position that abortion is murder. On the other side, pro-choice advocates argue the moral stand that a woman has a right to control her own body. But as Anna Quindlen's essay demonstrates, the controversy of abortion has no easy answers. In "Some Thoughts About Abortion," she says that for all "thoughtful people" this subject invariably creates a conflict between heart and head, or between two moral positions. The next two essays represent contrary views of abortion from African American perspectives. In the first, "Which Way Black America?—Pro-Choice," Faye Wattleton argues that the erosion of a woman's rights to "reproductive privacy" will have a particularly devastating consequence for black women. By contrast, Pamela Carr in "Which Way Black America?—Anti-Abortion" contends that the systematic termination of nearly a half million black fetuses each year amounts to "a silent genocide." The last piece on the subject of abortion, "An Abortionist's Credo," is written by a physician who performs abortions. Elizabeth Karlin, M.D., argues that women have abortions because they place the highest values on motherhood—a role best not taken if not done well.

We move from the moral question of fetus rights to that of animal rights. Are we morally bound to protect animals against abuse as people are protected against sexism, racism, and homophobia? Is it permissible to experiment on animals for the sake of medical research? The individual most responsible for the surge in animal rights activism is Australian philosopher Peter Singer. We open this discussion with "Animal Liberation" where Singer argues that because animals can suffer they have a right not to be exploited or harmed for any reason, including medical research. Taking a contrary view, physician Ron Karpati, in "A Scientist: 'I Am the Enemy,'" justifies animal experimentation on the grounds that human life has higher value than animal life. Falling somewhere between these two extremes is the argument presented in "Why Worry About the Animals?" by Jean Bethke Elshtain. Although she neither believes that animals and humans have equal rights nor relentlessly defends the scientific research in the name of saving human lives, Elshtain says that reasoning, feeling people should be ethically disturbed by the toll taken on animals.

In our "Oppositions" section we explore the issue of drug use and the moral question of drug legalization. William J. Bennett, once the drug czar for President George Bush, sees drugs as so unequivocally dehumanizing—an influence that strips its users of simple decency, responsibility, and moral judgment—that he views even a discussion of the legalization of drugs as naive. Peter Gorman, on the other hand, views the legalization of marijuana and only marijuana as a sane, logical, and responsible choice.

EUTHANASIA

Scared to Death of Dying
Herbert Hendin

The debate over euthanasia continues to be unresolved. Does the person diagnosed with a terminal illness have the right to take his or her life? Is he or she entitled to a legal assisted suicide? Is suicide legitimized by the length of time left to live or the degree of pain and suffering anticipated? Or does the likelihood of a cure being found factor into this decision? Confronted with these issues individuals and legislatures in places such as Oregon are attempting to pass legislation that allows assisted suicide. In this essay, Herbert Hendin opposes these measures. Using a slippery slope argument, he demonstrates how in the Netherlands the legalization of assisted suicide, originally intended for terminally ill patients, now includes the chronically ill and psychologically distressed. The solution in Hendin's mind is to focus on humane care for the dying, on the relief of pain so that death can be a noble, not ignominious experience.

Herbert Hendin is executive director of the American Suicide Foundation and professor of psychiatry at New York Medical College.

BEFORE YOU READ

Imagine your reaction if confronted with the news you have a terminal illness. Would the option of assisted suicide be important to you? Why or why not?

AS YOU READ

Carefully note the slippery slope argument used in this piece. Is it convincing? Does it change your thinking?

1   The conflict over legalizing assisted suicide and euthanasia might well tear our society apart. Yet neither legalization nor opposition to it constitutes a public policy that addresses the much larger problem of how to care for the terminally ill.

2   The call for legalization is a symptom of our failure to develop a better response to death and the fear of intolerable pain or artificial prolongation of life.

3   The absence of such a policy permits doctors like Jack Kevorkian to be seen as the only champions of the terminally ill and legalization to be perceived as the cure for fear.

4   A law that Oregon voters approved in November would permit doctors to prescribe lethal drugs to patients judged to be in the last six months of life. The law, under a restraining order pending a hearing Monday on its constitutionality, is the latest example of how public frustration can lead to action that only compounds the problem.

5   It is not just that it is impossible to predict with certainty that a patient has only six months to live, making mistaken or falsified predictions inevitable. Any law that permits assisted suicide when patients are neither in pain nor imminently about to die will encourage people who fear death to take a quicker way out.

6   A few years ago, a young professional in his early 30's who had acute myelocytic leukemia was referred to me for consultation. With medical treatment, he was given a 25 percent chance of survival; without it, he was told, he would die in a few months.

7   His immediate reaction was a desperate preoccupation with suicide and a request for support in carrying it out. He was worried about becoming dependent and feared both the symptoms of his disease and the side effects of treatment. His anxieties about the painful circumstances that would surround his death were not irrational, but all his fears about dying amplified them.

8   Many patients and physicians displace anxieties about death onto the circumstances of dying—pain, dependence, loss of dignity, the unpleasant side effects resulting from medical treatment. Once the young man and I could talk about the possibility or likelihood of his dying—what separation from his family and the destruction of his body meant to him—his desperation subsided. He accepted medical treatment and used the remaining months of his life to become closer to his wife and parents. Two days before he died, he talked about what he would have missed without the opportunity for a loving parting.

9   Under the Oregon law, he probably would have asked a doctor's help in taking his own life. Because he was mentally competent and did not meet the clinical criteria for a diagnosis of depression, he would have qualified for assisted suicide and would surely have found a doctor who would agree to his request.

10   Since the Oregon law, using guidelines like those in effect in the Netherlands, does not require an independently referred doctor for a second opinion, he would have been referred by a physician supportive of assisted suicide to a colleague who was equally supportive. The evaluation would very likely have been pro forma. He could have been put to death in an unrecognized state of terror, unable to give himself the chance of getting well or of dying in the dignified way he did.

11   Many of us have known situations in which a doctor would have acted humanely by helping a terminally ill person die in the final weeks of an illness. Partly because of such experiences, when people are asked, "Are you in favor of euthanasia?" most answer yes.

12   But if people were asked, "If terminally ill, would you rather be given treatment to make you comfortable or have your life ended by a physician?" their responses might be different. Or consider this question: "If terminally ill, should it be your decision or your doctor's when you should die?"

13   My observations in the Netherlands persuade me that legalization of assisted suicide and euthanasia is not the answer to the problems of the terminally ill. The Netherlands has moved from assisted suicide to euthanasia, from euthanasia for the terminally ill to euthanasia for the chronically ill, from euthanasia for physical illness to euthanasia for psychological distress and from voluntary euthanasia to involuntary euthanasia (called "termination of the patient without explicit request"). The Dutch Government's own commissioned

research has documented that in more than 1,000 cases a year, doctors actively caused or hastened death without the patient's request.

14   Virtually every guideline established by the Dutch to regulate euthanasia has been modified or violated with impunity. A healthy but grief-stricken social worker mourning the death of her son two months earlier was assisted in suicide. A man in his 30's who is H.I.V.-positive but who has no symptoms and may not develop them for years was also helped to die, without any effort to address the terror behind his desire to end his life.

15   Euthanasia in the Netherlands—intended as an unfortunate necessity, in exceptional cases—has become almost a routine way of dealing with serious or terminal illness, and even with grief. A statute passed last year codifying guidelines provides added protection for doctors—but not for patients.

16   Yet the dangers threatened by legalization of assisted suicide can be avoided. They are being avoided elsewhere in Western Europe, where there is no great demand for legalizing assisted suicide or euthanasia.

17   Care for the terminally ill is better in the Scandinavian countries than in the United States and in the Netherlands. Scandinavian doctors do not accept excessive measures for prolonging life in people who are virtually dead, but neither do they encourage people to choose death prematurely.

18   There is a great deal of evidence that in the United States, as in the Netherlands, doctors are not sufficiently trained in the relief of pain and discomfort in terminally ill patients. We have not yet educated the public about their choices at the end of life. And we have not devoted enough time in medical schools to educating future physicians about the painful truth that there will be patients they will not be able to save but whose needs they must address.

19   Dr. Kevorkian and others are using the courts to test the law, and the Michigan Supreme Court ruled this week that the state may impose criminal penalties on those who assist in a suicide.

20   But we need more than a case-by-case testing or even a ruling by the United States Supreme Court if we are to address national concerns over how we die. We need a national commission to study the care of the terminally ill—one similar to the Presidential commission that in 1983 produced guidelines on when to withhold life-sustaining treatment from dying patients. Both euthanasia advocates and opponents would participate, but the panel would be primarily concerned with the larger question of the care of the terminally ill. Whatever its conclusions, a commission would educate the medical profession and the public and help us arrive at a consensus.

Topical Considerations

1. What laws and policies govern euthanasia and assisted suicide in the Netherlands? What evidence does Hendin offer in paragraphs 13 and 14 that these laws have created more problems than they solve?

2. Have you ever known someone who requested or received an assisted suicide? Or, have you ever considered it as an option you would like available to you? Has Hendin's article changed any of your perceptions or feelings about the issue?
3. When, according to Hendin, is assisted suicide an acceptable choice? What conditions must be met? What are unacceptable reasons?
4. What kinds of fears and anxieties can prompt a patient to request an inappropriate assisted suicide? Consider patients mentioned such as the leukemia patient, the grieving mother, or the HIV patient. Do you think that you might experience some of these emotions if you were one of these patients?
5. What does Hendin suggest as good individual responses to the kinds of fear and anxiety described in your answer to question 4 above? What must we do as a society to address such fears and anxieties?

Rhetorical Considerations

1. What seem to be Hendin's feelings about Jack Kevorkian? How can you tell? What function does the brief reference to Kevorkian in paragraph 3 play in Hendin's argument?
2. Why does Hendin stop his argument to describe a lengthy case study of a leukemia in paragraphs 6 through 10? What points about assisted suicide does this case allow him to make? How would Hendin's argument have had a different impact if he had been talking about terminally ill patients in general, rather than one specifically?
3. What would your answers be to the three questions at the end of paragraph 11 and in paragraph 12? Would you respond differently to one phrasing than to another? Why or why not? Why do you think Hendin does not supply the typical or "correct" answer to the last two questions?
4. Why does Hendin contrast policies in Scandinavian countries to those in the Netherlands? Do you think his comments about care for the terminally ill in paragraph 17 are an effective counterexample to the Oregon and Dutch laws?
5. Why do you think that Hendin does not provide any case studies or statistical information about euthanasia in the United States? Does this absence hurt his argument, since he does supply some information on the Netherlands?

Writing Assignments

1. This piece originally appeared in December 1994. Using your library's indexes to newspaper and other national news media, find out what has happened with the euthanasia issue in Oregon since then. Have any of the laws

changed? Have there been any cases of assisted suicide using (or circumventing) the laws? What kinds of public opinion responses have the laws and events prompted?

2. Choose one of Hendin's case studies: the leukemia patient (paragraph 6), the grief-stricken mother, or the man with HIV (both in paragraph 14). Assume that you are a close friend who has had an extensive long-distance telephone discussion with this person. He or she is considering suicide. Write a letter to this friend, enclosing and discussing a copy of this article. You may make whatever case you wish in the letter—for or against Hendin's article. However, you must address your friend's thoughts about suicide.

When Is It Right to Die?
Ronald Dworkin

This essay argues in favor of assisted suicide. Dworkin explains how the 14th Amendment of the Constitution with its protection of personal liberties is the touchstone for a recent decision in the state of Washington legalizing assisted suicide. Additionally, Dworkin rebuts the slippery slope logic that the previous piece is based on. Dworkin argues that legalizing assisted suicide would not lead to doctors callously taking the lives of sick elderly people whose care is expensive. Nor would it enable greedy or inconvenienced relatives to terminate a relative's life prematurely.

Ronald Dworkin is an author, most recently, of *Life's Dominion: An Argument about Abortion and Euthanasia* (1993). This essay first appeared in the *New York Times* in 1994.

BEFORE YOU READ

In your opinion does the practice of euthanasia show respect for the value of human life? Or does the practice of euthanasia degrade the intrinsic value of life?

AS YOU READ

Does Dworkin treat opposing views with respect or is he dismissive? How does this attitude affect his argument? Give an example.

1   A lawsuit decided in Seattle this month may well become the Roe v. Wade of euthanasia. Striking down a 140-year-old Washington State law, Federal District Court Judge Barbara Rothstein declared that as long as they are competent, terminally ill patients have a constitutional right to enlist a willing doctor's help in killing themselves. She decided, that is, that laws against assisted suicide, which exist in almost every state, are unconstitutional. Once again, the courts are at the center of a bitter moral and religious controversy.

2   Americans have been arguing about euthanasia for decades. Voters in two states, Washington and California, have rejected measures legalizing euthanasia in fairly close votes; another such measure is expected to be on the ballot in Oregon later this year. In Michigan, a special statute was passed to stop Dr. Jack Kevorkian from helping patients to die, but this month a jury refused to convict him of violating that statute even though he virtually admitted he had.

3   If Judge Rothstein's decision, or a similar one, is upheld in the Supreme Court, the constitution will pre-empt part of this sprawling debate: every state will have to recognize that though it can regulate doctor-assisted suicide, it can't prohibit it altogether. That result will outrage millions of conscientious citizens who think euthanasia an abomination in any form.

4   Judge Rothstein said her decision on euthanasia was "almost" compelled by the Supreme Court's 1992 decision in Planned Parenthood v. Casey, which reaffirmed Roe v. Wade. In Casey, the Court declared: "Matters involving the most intimate and personal choices a person may make in a lifetime . . . are central to the liberty protected by the 14th Amendment. At the heart of liberty is the right to define one's own concept of existence, of meaning, of the universe, and of the mystery of human life." Judge Rothstein observed, correctly, that the freedom of a competent dying person to hasten his or her own death falls under that description at least as clearly as does the right of a pregnant woman to choose abortion.

5   Many opponents of euthanasia try to distinguish the two issues by appealing to a "slippery slope" argument. They say, for example, that voluntary euthanasia will so habituate doctors to killing that they may begin executing sick, old, unwanted people whose care is expensive but who plainly want to live.

6   This contradicts common sense. Of course doctors know the moral difference between helping people who beg to die and killing those who want to live. If anything, ignoring the pain of terminal patients pleading for death rather than trying to help seems more likely to dull a doctor's humane instincts.

7   Some critics worry about the practice in the Netherlands, where doctors have given lethal injections to unconscious or incompetent terminal patients who did not explicitly ask to die. But Judge Rothstein's opinion applies only to assisted suicide, which demands an explicit request, and even if a legislature were to allow for such injection for patients incapable of taking pills or killing themselves in some other humane way, it could stipulate that an explicit request was still essential.

8   A more plausible version of the slippery-slope argument worries that if euthanasia is legalized, dying people whose treatment is expensive or burdensome may ask for help in committing suicide only because they feel guilty, and that family members may perhaps try to coax or shame them toward that decision. But states plainly have the power to guard against requests influenced by guilt, depression, poor care or financial worries. (The main plaintiff

in the Washington State case, the group Compassion in Dying, offers to assist only terminal patients who have repeated their request three times and have expressed no ambivalence or uncertainty.)

9   States also have the power to discourage distasteful, near assembly-line suicides like those arranged by Dr. Kevorkian. Patients go to him, and juries acquit him, only because there is no better alternative.

10   No set of regulations can be perfect. But it would be perverse to force competent people to die in great pain or in a drugged stupor for that reason, accepting a great and known evil to avoid the risk of a speculative one. In 1990 the Supreme Court held that states must respect some form of "living will" that allows people to specify in advance that certain procedures not be used to keep them alive, even though patients could be coaxed or shamed into signing such documents.

11   Some doctors already engage in a covert practice that is much more open to abuse than a scheme of voluntary euthanasia would be: they deliberately give dying patients fatal doses of painkilling drugs. But nobody thinks that this is a good reason to withhold all dangerous painkillers from terminal patients in torment.

12   These slippery-slope arguments, then, are very weak ones. They seem only disguises for the deeper convictions that actually move most opponents of euthanasia. Matthew Habiger, president of Human Life International, a "pro-life" organization, denounced the Compassion in Dying decision in terms that made those deeper convictions explicit. "The march toward a complete anti-life philosophy," he said, "can now be easily mapped: from contraception to abortion to euthanasia. Once life is no longer treated as a sacred gift from God, a society inevitably embraces death in all its forms."

13   In this view, all euthanasia—even when fully voluntary and rational—is wrong because human life has an objective, intrinsic value as well as subjective value for the person whose life it is, and euthanasia dishonors that intrinsic value. It is precisely this conviction that underlies most opposition to abortion as well. Many people, particularly those who agree with Mr. Habiger that human life is a divine gift, believe that ending it deliberately (except, perhaps, as punishment) is always the most profound insult to life's objective value.

14   But it would be wrong to think that those who are more permissive about abortion and euthanasia are indifferent to the value of life. Rather, they disagree about what respecting that value means. They think that in some circumstances—when a fetus is terribly deformed, for example—abortion may show more respect for life than childbirth would. And they think that dying with dignity shows more respect for their own life—better fits their sense of what is really important in and about human existence—than ending their life in long agony or senseless sedation.

15   Our Constitution takes no sides in these ancient disputes about life's "meaning." But it does protect people's right to die as well as to live, so far as possible, in the light of their own intensely personal convictions about "the mystery of human life." It insists that these values are too central to personal-

ity, too much at the core of liberty, to allow a majority to decide what everyone must believe.

16   Of course the law must protect people who think it would be appalling to be killed, even if they had only painful minutes to live. But the law must also protect those with the opposite conviction: that it would be appalling not to be offered an easier, calmer death with the help of doctors they trust. Making a person die in a way that others approve, but that affronts his own dignity, is a serious, unjustified, unnecessary form of tyranny.

Topical Considerations

1. According to paragraph 1, why is it significant that Judge Rothstein's position is stated in a federal court rather than in a state court? Why would a U.S. Supreme Court decision force all states to accept doctor-assisted suicide?

2. Passed in 1868, the 14th Amendment to the U.S. Constitution reads in part: "No State shall make or enforce any law which shall abridge the privileges or immunities of citizens of the United States; nor shall any State deprive any person of life, liberty, or property, without due process of law . . . " How do you think this amendment which asserts the rights of an individual relates to assisted suicide?

3. What is a "slippery slope" argument, first mentioned in paragraph 5? Describe one slippery slope argument that Dworkin considers, but rejects as not really damaging to his case for permitting assisted suicide.

4. Why does Dworkin dismiss Matthew Habiger's argument, which links euthanasia with abortion and contraception, as a slippery slope argument?

5. What role does shame play in Dworkin's argument and in the counterarguments he includes? Have you ever felt shame about something in your life? How can that experience help you understand why Dworkin wants to avoid shame in persuading people either for or against euthanasia?

Rhetorical Considerations

1. In paragraph 4, Dworkin agrees with Rothstein that "a competent dying person" must be allowed the constitutional freedom "to hasten his or her own death." How close to death must such a person be—days? months? years? Do you think that a competent person who is not dying should have this right? How do your answers to these questions leave gaps in his argument?

2. What do you think of Dworkin's decision to introduce a strong counterargument in paragraph 12, Matthew Habiger's opposition to euthanasia? Does this help or hinder Dworkin's own argument? Why or why not?

3. Why does Dworkin mention in paragraph 11 that some doctors are already, in effect, assisting in suicides by prescribing lethal doses of painkillers. How does he keep this detail from becoming a call to arms for stronger enforcement of existing laws, rather than part of his argument for greater leniency?
4. Dworkin refers several times to issues about abortion as he presents his argument on euthanasia. What is similar about abortion and euthanasia? What is different? Why does he include abortion in this discussion when it's not the central issue?
5. Did you find Dworkin's discussion of abortion distracting or confusing? Did it strengthen his case on euthanasia? Why or why not? Can you agree that one but not the other should be permissible, or do they come as a package deal?

Writing Assignments

1. Using information provided in the articles by Dworkin and by Hendin, draft a statute allowing doctor-assisted suicide. Be sure to include adequate safeguards against abuses and against the kinds of actions you find morally unacceptable. Your instructor may ask you to work in groups to come up with provisions for your law, or to set up debate teams on several of the provisions you select as a class.
2. Assume that you have been diagnosed with a fatal disease. You feel fine now, but within 6 months will be dead—and you know that your final weeks will be excruciatingly painful, with or without painkillers. Write a letter to your doctor and your loved ones explaining what services you do or do not want, under what conditions, and why.
3. Dr. Jack Kevorkian figures largely as a villain in both Dworkin's article and Hendin's. Using your library's news information services, sketch Kevorkian's career over the past decade. What has he done? What have people said about what he's done? Given the information you have located, do you agree that his actions have been morally repugnant, or do you think he's provided a good and necessary service for those whose suicides he has assisted?

Dead Complicated
Elisabeth Rosenthal

"Dead certain," "Wanted, dead or alive," "Till death do us part." These phrases, like so many in our language, attest to a certainty about death—what it is, when it happens, what it looks like. Yet when we read this essay it becomes clear that certainty about the definition of death eludes and confuses the doctors, ethicists, lawyers, and legislators trying so mightily to describe it. This confusion makes decisions regarding euthanasia doubly perplexing. The current elastic definition of death, based for most states on a nonfunctioning brain and brain stem and for others on the cessation of heart and lung activity, continues to complicate attitudes toward euthanasia.

Elisabeth Rosenthal, a physician, struggles to define what death is to her. This essay first appeared in *Discover* magazine in October 1992.

BEFORE YOU READ

An anencephalic infant is born with only a brain stem. Human awareness is utterly impossible. Nevertheless, the heart beats and the lungs breathe. In your opinion, is this infant dead or alive? Explain your answer.

AS YOU READ

How many different definitions of death can you find in this essay? Which makes the most sense to you?

1   In a recent test case a Florida couple sued a local hospital to have their doomed newborn child declared dead. Their daughter Theresa was an anencephalic infant, born with only a brain stem, a tiny stump of a brain. Since virtually all her brain was missing, she would never be aware of her existence. In addition, her faltering heart and lungs were bound to give out in a matter of days. If she was pronounced dead, her parents would at least be able to donate her organs to help other sick infants survive.

2   It was a reasonable request made by well-meaning parents. But a Florida circuit court rejected it on the grounds that the baby still had a brain stem. According to state law, she was therefore alive. Ten days later, while a fierce debate raged among doctors, ethicists, and lawyers, the infant's breathing stopped and her organs petered out for lack of oxygen, making them useless for transplantation.

3   As the sad case of baby Theresa demonstrates, the line between life and death is today often blurred. Once it was simple. A person was alive if his heart could beat and his lungs could breathe, and dead if they did not. It was an intuitive and satisfying definition. Who among us does not accept the *lub-dub* of a heart and the gentle rise and fall of a chest as reassuring signs of life? But now that machines can do the job of a heart or lung, these vital signs are no longer sufficient to define a living human being. Modern medicine has made the notion of heart-lung death increasingly inadequate, and we doctors must now rely on the much more abstract concept of brain death.

4   The idea was not immediately popular. Long after the first states adopted it in the early 1970s, others hung on to the traditional notion of heart-lung death, with absurd results. Ten years ago an intensive care patient being transferred from a hospital in Boston to one in Washington could have been alive in Massachusetts, dead in Connecticut, alive in New York and New Jersey, and dead again in D.C. These days, at least, there's greater consistency.

Most states, including Florida, use a "whole brain" concept of death: that is, the person is dead if the entire brain, including the brain stem, has ceased to function.

5   As in the case of baby Theresa, that has helped solve the legal dilemma of when to declare a patient dead, but it clearly hasn't resolved the question of when life ends in a way that satisfies the soul. Whole-brain death is diagnosed by an elaborate battery of neurological tests rather than by a gut instinct of what it means to be alive. And even doctors and nurses working in the twilight world of the intensive care unit may find it deeply disturbing that patients who are legally dead look from the outside just like patients who are legally alive.

6   A 1989 survey of doctors and nurses in Cleveland dramatically demonstrated the point. Most could define death as whole-brain death, all right. But in a written test many did not correctly identify whether the patients described were dead or alive. A quarter of the group identified a patient whose brain had ceased to function but whose heart was still pumping on life-support systems (legally dead) as alive! About an equal number declared dead a patient who was irreversibly unconscious but whose brain stem could still orchestrate basic functions like breathing (legally alive). That people who routinely witness death have trouble applying the definition of brain death to patients shows how poorly that definition fits with our intuitions and beliefs.

7   Indeed, in New York and New Jersey, lawmakers, under pressure from religious groups, have been forced to write an exemption to their statutes. A brain-dead practicing Catholic or Orthodox Jew can be treated as though alive, since his religious teachings hold that a beating heart is the benchmark of life.

8   The source of this subconscious resistance to brain death, I think, is clear. From an emotional standpoint it goes against the grain. And from a scientific standpoint, it's hard to define death at all when there's no well-defined minimum standard for membership in the club of human life. Is it having 23 chromosome pairs? A heartbeat? The ability to feel or think? Just as those involved in the abortion debate struggle to decide when life begins, doctors, ethicists, and legislators are struggling to decide when it ends. And as in the abortion debate, where they draw the line is often influenced by emotion, religious and moral beliefs, and politics.

9   Twenty-five years ago there was no such dilemma. Patients whose heart and lungs stopped quickly turned blue and pulseless and were declared dead. If their brain was destroyed by massive head injury, bleeding, or stroke, the heart and lungs succumbed as well since the lower part of the brain helps orchestrate their function. And then along came intensive care units, cardiopulmonary resuscitation, respirators, and heart-bypass pumps. I recall one 60-year-old patient who had emphysema and severe heart rhythm problems; she needed a respirator to breathe and had an electric-shock machine implanted in her heart to reset the rhythm when the organ stopped pumping. Although her lungs were shot and her heart stopped many times, she read, knitted, and entertained guests in her hospital room. Clearly alive.

10   With machines to breathe and pump blood, a breathing chest and beating heart could no longer be the hallmark of life. And so doctors turned toward a brain-oriented definition of death. The advent of organ transplantation also exerted a powerful influence, since hearts, livers, and lungs for transplant must be removed from bodies with blood and oxygen still coursing through their veins. Nevertheless, defining brain death continues to engender controversy.

11   Scientific conservatives argue that the entire brain must die for a person to be dead, and this whole-brain concept was enacted into law. But this definition allows babies like Theresa and patients in deep, irreversible comas with just a scrap of brain function to be counted as alive. To some people this makes no sense. Anencephalics and patients in a so-called persistent vegetative state have only a brain stem, a stalk of brain that allows their bodies to perform basic, reflexive functions like breathing. But they will never be conscious, never see, feel, or think in even the most rudimentary fashion. Such functions are controlled by the cortex, the furrowed outer layer of the higher brain. Consequently some doctors argue that the death of the cortex reduces a being to a state that's less than human—a state of death. Therefore people in persistent vegetative states and anencephalic infants should be counted as dead and their organs released for donation.

12   Another problem with whole-brain death is that it's tricky to ascertain. Often it takes the specialized knowledge of a neurologist to distinguish the person in an irreversible coma who is alive from the person in an irreversible coma who is dead—the key distinction being a functioning brain stem.

13   Many of the brain stem's duties involve extremely primitive reflexes: insuring that we breathe, move our eyes in a coordinated manner, blink when something grazes our eye. These simple maneuvers require great ingenuity to test in the intensive care unit. Patients who are unconscious and therefore unseeing do not look around to demonstrate eye coordination. And how do you tell if a patient's chest is moving air in a place where everyone is hooked up to breathing machines?

14   To test eye movements, neurologists resort to some bizarre tactics. For example, even in people who are deeply comatose, a good squirt of cold water in the ear causes the eyes to twitch uncontrollably toward the invaded ear. It is an extremely noxious stimulus (conscious patients will sense the world spinning and throw up), but it is a sure way to check that the brain stem is working.

15   To test breathing skill, doctors have devised an equally devious challenge called an apnea test. It is virtually impossible to tell if a person in a deep coma on a respirator can breathe just by turning off the machine. The centers in the brain stem that direct the lungs to take a breath sense high levels of carbon dioxide, a waste product of the body's metabolism, rather than low levels of oxygen, the essential gas that we all need.

16   When a comatose patient's respirator is turned off, the oxygen level begins to fall and the CO_2 level climbs. Since CO_2 is not terribly toxic to organs, the brain is programmed to allow high levels to build up before it panics and

directs the body to take a breath. And, unfortunately, the oxygen content of blood often dips to deadly levels before the CO_2 rises high enough to sound the brain-stem alarm. So—catch–22—if a doctor seeks to diagnose death by turning off a respirator, his search will become a self-fulfilling prophecy.

17   To avoid killing the patient in an attempt to determine if he is dead, doctors give comatose patients 100 percent oxygen to breathe through a ventilator for 10 to 20 minutes and then place a tube blowing a constant flow of oxygen into the airway leading to the lungs. They saturate the patient with oxygen, so that even if the body does not seek to breathe after the ventilator is turned off, the vital organs can survive. Under these conditions, the body is given 10 minutes to take a breath in response to the rising CO_2 after the ventilator is turned off. If it does, the patient is alive; if not, he is dead. It is a pretty elaborate subterfuge to figure out what should be obvious.

18   The point struck home during my training when I cared for a 50-year-old woman who had been sent into a persistent vegetative state by a ruptured aneurysm in her brain. She developed lung problems while on a ventilator and, after she came off the machine, remained prone to pneumonia. Each time a new infection imperiled oxygen flow to her brain, she came back to intensive care to be put on a respirator. And each time we called in a neurologist to determine if lack of oxygen had killed off the brain stem to render her dead. Although my patient looked exactly the same, the first three times the answer was no, but the fourth time it was yes.

19   Apart from the absurdity of situations like these, the insistence that every last brain cell must expire before a patient can be declared dead has also limited the supply of donor organs. A fragment of a brain stem can allow a patient to take some breaths, but (as was the case with baby Theresa) the breathing is often not sufficient to sustain vital organs.

20   That's another reason why a vocal minority of doctors have suggested that a patient needs some brain function above the primitive brain stem to qualify as a living human being—and that anything less makes him dead. Logic tells me they're right: If a beating heart does not suffice for us to be human beings, what is left but consciousness to link us all together?

21   Ethicists, of course, worry about a world in which a society chooses which parts of the brain are necessary to qualify an individual as human. If today we decide that a person in a persistent vegetative state is obviously not one of us, then tomorrow why not the woman who is severely retarded, or the man rendered speechless and immobile by a stroke? Having treated patients in all three states, it seems to me that there are clear distinctions. Even people who are severely retarded or paralyzed can experience something—can sense touch or taste food or feel pleasure. But in the endless coma of anencephaly or a persistent vegetative state, there is nothing.

22   So, were I to lapse into a persistent vegetative state or have a child born without a higher brain, I would desperately want the organs taken for donation in the hope that they might help others live. But, having said that, would I want society to allow me, as a practicing physician, to act on these instincts by declaring all patients with these conditions dead? Now I balk.

23   Although science and logic say these patients are dead, emotion shouts, no, they're alive! When I touch them, they're warm. When I place a stethoscope on their rising chests, I hear air moving and the vibrant beating of their hearts. George Annas, a lawyer at the Boston University School of Public Health, argues for a commonsense solution. "Dead is when you'd bury someone," he says. "To me the way to resolve the issue is to decide whether you'd bury someone with a beating heart. And the answer is no. In our society, being buried alive is the ultimate fear."

24   I have to agree. I just can't see putting people whose hearts are still beating and whose lungs are still breathing six feet under in a box—no matter how hopelessly comatose they may be. And with only a brain stem, those feats can in some fashion be performed.

25   So, reluctantly, I conclude that baby Theresa was alive and had to be allowed to die. Too bad we lost her organs.

Topical Considerations

1. What was the predominant legal definition of death in 1982, 10 years before Rosenthal published this article (1992)? What had it changed to in 1992? Why did this shift in definition occur?

2. According to the 1989 survey of doctors and nurses cited in this essay, how well do most healthcare providers understand the new legal and medical definitions of death? How well are they able to apply what they know to individual cases?

3. What two tests (see paragraphs 15 and 16) do neurologists perform on patients to determine a patient's status as alive or dead? What does Rosenthal find unpleasant or upsetting about these tests?

4. Why does Rosenthal call these two tests "devious"? What does "devious" mean in this context? Look the word up in a large or unabridged dictionary if you are not sure. Can you think of a test that you have found "devious"?

5. What is the "slippery slope" that Rosenthal fears in her hypothetical future described in paragraph 21? What concerns does she have about allowing "quality of life" to become the defining criterion for life or death?

6. Why does Rosenthal decide in the final paragraph of her article that baby Theresa "was alive," although she had so many medical problems that her death was imminent?

Rhetorical Considerations

1. In the first paragraph, Rosenthal describes baby Theresa as "doomed" What words and phrases in that paragraph reinforce the severity of the baby's problems?

2. Why does Rosenthal list this specific sequence of states in paragraph 4: Massachusetts, Connecticut, New York, New Jersey, and Washington,

D.C.? How does she use this sequence to build support for her agreement with the shift in legal definitions of death to "whole brain" function?

3. Where does Rosenthal identify her medical credentials? Does she present herself as an authority who knows better than her readers what decisions should be made? What effect does this voice (that is, the way she presents herself to readers) have on her argument?

4. Why does Rosenthal provide so much detail about the apnea test in paragraphs 16 and 17? Rewrite the information supplied in these two paragraphs in one concise sentence. Then explain how the wealth of material in the article helps support her argument.

5. Rosenthal mentions organ donation at three key points in her article: in paragraphs 1, 2, 10, and intermittently from paragraph 19 to the end of her article. How do these references each serve different purposes in her argument? What different emotional responses do they provoke?

Writing Assignments

1. Pretend that you are Dr. Elisabeth Rosenthal. Using the arguments in this article, write a letter to baby Theresa's parents explaining why you believe they are not legally or morally entitled to have Theresa declared dead. Make sure that your letter exhibits an appropriate level of compassion for these two distraught parents.

2. How comfortable do you feel about donating your organs in the event of your death? Have you considered the matter before now? Why or why not? Write a personal statement to your family, or to the people who would be contacted if you were to die suddenly, stating and explaining your wishes.

3. Using your library's news and scholarly journals resources, write a paper about organ donation. Depending on preliminary research and availability of material, you may want to focus on a single narrow issue, such as one of the following: reasons for organ donor shortages; ethical decisions about which patients are "first on line" to receive scarce organs; medical insurance or payment for organ transplants; animal-to-human transplants, where no donor can be found; specific cases that have received extensive media attention.

ABORTION

Some Thoughts About Abortion
Anna Quindlen

With the Supreme Court ruling on *Roe v. Wade* in 1973, every woman was granted the right to a legal abortion. However, the moral questions of whether or not a woman should have the choice to end a pregnancy and what considerations might justify such a termination still abound and speak to our most deeply held values and beliefs. In short, abortion may be a legal right, but is it moral to exercise this right? Like many people, Anna Quindlen grapples with these questions and finds herself in the ambivalent position of "hating the idea of abortions, hating the idea of having them outlawed."

Quindlen had a nationally syndicated column entitled "Public and Private," which appeared in the *New York Times* and other newspapers around the country. Many of her essays were published in *Living Out Loud* (1990) and *Thinking Out Loud* (1993), and she is the author of *Object Lessons,* a novel published in 1991, and *One True Thing,* published in 1994. This article first appeared in Quindlen's "Life in the 30's" column in 1986.

BEFORE YOU READ

Do you feel abortion should be legal? Illegal? Do you feel abortion is right in some situations, wrong in others? What are your two strongest arguments in support of your position?

AS YOU READ

Quindlen uses personal experiences with pregnancies—her own and that of young women—to help formulate her argument. As you read, consider whether these references provide strong evidence for Quindlen's point of view or whether they are too anecdotal, too personal.

1   It was always the look on their faces that told me first. I was the freshman dormitory counselor and they were the freshmen at a women's college where everyone was smart. One of them could come into my room, a golden girl, a valedictorian, an 800 verbal score on the SAT's, and her eyes would be empty, seeing only a busted future, the devastation of her life as she knew it. She had failed biology, messed up the math; she was pregnant.

2   That was when I became pro-choice.

3   It was the look in his eyes that I will always remember, too. They were as black as the bottom of a well, and in them for a few minutes I thought I saw myself the way I had always wished to be—clear, simple, elemental, at peace. My child looked at me and I looked back at him in the delivery room, and I realized that out of a sea of infinite possibilities it had come down to this: a specific person born on the hottest day of the year, conceived on a Christmas Eve, made by his father and me miraculously from scratch.

4   Once I believed that there was a little blob of formless protoplasm in there and a gynecologist went after it with a surgical instrument, and that was that. Then I got pregnant myself—eagerly, intentionally, by the right man, at

the right time—and I began to doubt. My abdomen still flat, my stomach roiling with morning sickness, I felt not that I had protoplasm inside but instead a complete human being in miniature to whom I could talk, sing, make promises. Neither of these views was accurate; instead, I think, the reality is something in the middle. And that is where I find myself now, in the middle, hating the idea of abortions, hating the idea of having them outlawed.

5   For I know it is the right thing in some times and places. I remember sitting in a shabby clinic far uptown with one of those freshmen, only three months after the Supreme Court had made what we were doing possible, and watching with wonder as the lovely first love she had had with a nice boy unraveled over the space of an hour as they waited for her to be called, degenerated into sniping and silences. I remember a year or two later seeing them pass on campus and not even acknowledge one another because their conjoining had caused them so much pain, and I shuddered to think of them married, with a small psyche in their unready and unwilling hands.

6   I've met 14-year-olds who were pregnant and said they could not have abortions because of their religion, and I see in their eyes the shadows of 22-year-olds I've talked to who lost their kids to foster care because they hit them or used drugs or simply had no money for food and shelter. I read not long ago about a teen-ager who said she meant to have an abortion but she spent the money on clothes instead; now she has a baby who turns out to be a lot more trouble than a toy. The people who hand out those execrable little pictures of dismembered fetuses at abortion clinics seem to forget the extraordinary pain children may endure after they are born when they are unwanted, even hated or simply tolerated.

7   I believe that in a contest between the living and the almost living, the latter must, if necessary, give way to the will of the former. That is what the fetus is to me, the almost living. Yet these questions began to plague me—and, I've discovered a good many other women—after I became pregnant. But they became even more acute after I had my second child, mainly because he is so different from his brother. On two random nights 18 months apart the same two people managed to conceive, and on one occasion the tumult within turned itself into a curly-haired brunet with merry black eyes who walked and talked late and loved the whole world, and on another it became a blond with hazel Asian eyes and a pug nose who tried the conquer the world almost as soon as he entered it.

8   If we were to have an abortion next time for some reason or another, which infinite possibility becomes, not a reality, but a nullity? The girl with the blue eyes? The improbable redhead? The natural athlete? The thinker? My husband, ever at the heart of the matter, put it another way. Knowing that he is finding two children somewhat more overwhelming than he expected, I asked if he would want me to have an abortion if I accidentally became pregnant again right away. "And waste a perfectly good human being?" he said.

9   Coming to this quandary has been difficult for me. In fact, I believe the issue of abortion is difficult for all thoughtful people. I don't know anyone who

has had an abortion who has not been haunted by it. If there is one thing I find intolerable about most of the so-called right-to-lifers, it is that they try to portray abortion rights as something that feminists thought up on a slow Saturday over a light lunch. That is nonsense. I also know that some people who support abortion rights are most comfortable with a monolithic position because it seems the strongest front against the smug and sometimes violent opposition.

10   But I don't feel all one way about abortion anymore, and I don't think it serves a just cause to pretend that many of us do. For years I believed that a woman's right to choose was absolute, but now I wonder. Do I, with a stable home and marriage and sufficient stamina and money, have the right to choose abortion because a pregnancy is inconvenient right now? Legally I do have that right; legally I want always to have that right. It is the morality of exercising it under those circumstances that makes me wonder.

11   Technology has foiled us. The second trimester has become a time of resurrection; a fetus at six months can be one woman's late abortion, another's premature, viable child. Photographers now have film of embryos the size of a grape, oddly human, flexing their fingers, sucking their thumbs. Women have amniocentesis to find out whether they are carrying a child with birth defects that they may choose to abort. Before the procedure, they must have a sonogram, one of those fuzzy black-and-white photos like a love song heard through static on the radio, which shows someone is in there.

12   I have taped on my VCR a public-television program in which somehow, inexplicably, a film is shown of a fetus in utero scratching its face, seemingly putting up a tiny hand to shield itself from the camera's eye. It would make a potent weapon in the arsenal of the antiabortionists. I grow sentimental about it as it floats in the salt water; part fish, part human being. It is almost living, but not quite. It has almost turned my heart around, but not quite turned my head.

Topical Considerations

1. Having read this essay, has your position on abortion changed? If so, how? What, if anything, in Quindlen's essay has shed a light on a side to the abortion controversy you may not have considered previously?

2. What is Quindlen's opinion on abortion at the beginning of the essay? At the end of the essay? What experiences have confirmed or changed Quindlen's position?

3. Refer to paragraph 10 and discuss Quindlen's dilemma regarding the legality and morality of abortion.

4. Have you had any experiences similar to Quindlen's regarding abortions for college students? Do you agree with Quindlen's contention in paragraph 5, ". . . I know it is the right thing in some times and places"? Why or why not?

5. In paragraph 8 Quindlen describes a possible third pregnancy and the aborted child's characteristics. Does this undercut her argument concerning the necessity of legal abortion? How do you react to her husband's comment, "And waste a perfectly good human being?"

6. What effect does Quindlen intend the descriptions of embryos in paragraphs 11 and 12 to have on her readers? On the validity of her argument?

Rhetorical Considerations

1. What is the form of this argument? Is it mostly an inductive argument or a deductive argument? Support your answer with evidence from the essay.

2. Explain Quindlen's abrupt change in tone in paragraph 3.

3. Would this essay be as powerful if Quindlen had not used first person narration? Do you find her description of very personal situations too revealing, or do they help illustrate the dilemma she and other thoughtful women face?

4. In paragraph 9 the author criticizes "so-called right-to-lifers." What does the term *so-called* reveal about her attitude? Does Quindlen criticize pro-choice advocates as well?

5. Where does Quindlen state the claim of her argument? Does it adequately summarize the argument?

6. In your opinion, what are the strongest points in Quindlen's argument? Do they come at the beginning of the article or the end, or are they scattered throughout?

Writing Assignments

1. Write a letter to a college freshman who is contemplating an abortion. Advise her by posing the questions you think she should consider when making this decision.

2. If possible, view a videotape or photographs that show the embryo as Quindlen describes it in paragraphs 11 and 12. Write an essay discussing how these images do or do not influence your opinion on abortion.

3. Gather literature from groups who are for and against abortion. Analyze the contents of the material from both sides for any logical fallacies. Then write an essay describing your findings.

Which Way Black America?— Pro-Choice
Faye Wattleton

In 1989 the Supreme Court passed a controversial ruling in the case of *Webster v. Reproductive Health Services* that allowed states to impose new restrictions on a woman's right to have an abortion. The decision set off renewed debates between pro-abortion supporters and those who wish to restrict or outlaw abortion. The legal and moral arguments are relevant to all Americans, but the two pieces that follow focus the debate on the black community. Representing the pro-choice stand is Faye Wattleton, past president of Planned Parenthood Federation of America. In this essay, which first appeared in the October 1989 issue of *Ebony*, Wattleton argues that legal restrictions on a woman's access to abortion services will have dangerous effects on all women. But, she argues, on black women the consequences will be devastating.

BEFORE YOU READ

If access to abortion services were restricted (by parental consent and notification requirements, for example), would all people regardless of race, economic status, and educational level be equally affected? Why or why not? What do your conclusions suggest about legislation designed to restrict abortion services?

AS YOU READ

As you read consider how Wattleton's invocation of "facts" (paragraph 4) influences how you see her argument. Do these "facts" validate the essay? Do they make her argument more or less persuasive?

1   It is ironic. As we celebrate the bicentennial of the Bill of Rights that guarantees Americans protection against the tyranny of the legislative process, we confront a serious threat to one of our most fundamental rights—our right to make independent reproductive decisions.

2   For eight years the Reagan administration wages a protracted war against both family planning programs and legal abortion. While the administration was unsuccessful in eliminating either, it was successful in shaping a federal court system that alarmingly reflects Mr. Reagan's vision of Americans' constitutional protections. Increasingly, decisions are being handed down by the federal courts that reflect a narrow and restricted interpretation of the Constitution and that threaten the future of many rights that Americans today take for granted.

3   Nowhere is this more explicitly demonstrated than in the Supreme Court's recent decision in *Webster v. Reproductive Health Services,* which allows states to impose severe restrictions on access to abortion services, particularly for poor women.

4   This decision has profound implications for the health and survival of the Black community. Black women are disproportionately poor, and poor Black women already have great difficulty in gaining access to reproductive health care information and services. Consider the following:

- Black women are twice as likely to experience unintended pregnancy and to seek abortions than White women.

- Black women are twice as likely to bear low birth-weight babies.
- The Black infant mortality rate is twice as high as that for White infants. 52% of all women with AIDS and 53% of all children with AIDS are Black.

5   The danger looms even larger when we consider the high incidence of pregnancy among Black teenagers. Clearly, we fail miserably in providing our children with the ways and means of preventing pregnancy. The rates of pregnancy, childbirth and pregnancy among Black teens in this country are double the rates for White teens. The impact of this tragedy is devastating. It threatens the lives and future of our children for generations to come and seriously undermines the structure of the family in our communities.

6   Any restrictions placed on the availability of family planning and abortion for young people will only exacerbate the problem. Young people need to be helped to seek the support and guidance of their loved ones when making sexual decisions. But when this is not possible, barriers such as parental consent and notification requirements must not be erected. They only force teenagers away from safe and reliable sources of reproductive health services and into the hands of unsafe and uncaring opportunists.

7   The affluent always have had the means to circumvent restrictions on contraceptive and abortion services. Poor Black women have not. Poor Black women have borne the brunt of the virtual cutoff of Medicaid funding for abortion and will certainly be the first to be forced to seek unsafe abortions if legal and safe abortions once again are restricted. Black women will be the first to be injured and the first to die.

8   There is strong support among key Black leaders and major Black and minority organizations for the rights to keep abortion safe and legal. These include the National Council of Negro Women and the National Urban League. In addition to my own organization, two other national organizations that were instrumental in organizing support for the April 9 pro-choice march in Washington, D.C., are headed by Black women—the Religious Coalition for Abortion Rights, headed by Patricia Tyson, and the YWCA, headed by Gwendolyn Calvert Baker.

9   It has been charged that few Black women actually marched in that massive demonstration in support of women's health and women's rights. The fact is that demonstrations requiring personal expense and travel have traditionally been made up largely of middle-class persons who have such means. Nevertheless, the number of Blacks among the marchers was reasonably close to the proportionate numbers of middle-class Blacks in America. Many who share our views simply could not be present.

10   Finally, when violent, extremist anti-abortion demonstrators had the audacity to compare their tactics of intimidation and harassment of women to the civil rights demonstrations of the 1960s, America's civil rights leaders stepped forward to condemn such notions. Among these leaders were Julian

Bond, James Farmer, Dorothy Height, the Rev. Jesse Jackson, John Jacob, Vernon Jordan, Barbara Jordan, Andrew Young, as well as several congressional representatives and leaders in law, business and education.

11   Black Americans, indeed *all* Americans, must realize that the courts can no longer be relied upon to protect our most precious rights to reproductive privacy, and the profile of Black women is being inalterably shaped by the erosion of these rights. We must refuse to be put off track in our efforts to make progress—socially, economically and privately. We must be *suspicious* when social problems are oversimplified or when quick fixes are proposed. We must remember: Without the right to take charge of our personal lives and our destinies, our other rights are virtually *meaningless.*

Topical Considerations

1. What is the connection between family planning and abortion? Why might Wattleton link the two? Do you see them as being related?
2. In your own words, describe the implications of the information Wattleton gives readers on health care for black women.
3. What is the "tragedy" (paragraph 5) to which Wattleton refers? Do you agree with her word choice?
4. Do you think that "parental consent" and "notification" laws are helpful or harmful for women? What do you think is a good age for a young woman to make up her own mind without the consent of her parents? How might your parents respond to your answer?
5. In paragraph 7, Wattleton writes, "Black women will be the first to be injured and the first to die." Why might this be the case? Is her argument contingent solely upon race? Consider other issues such as gender, class, and age.
6. Do you find Wattleton's argument persuasive? Why or why not?

Rhetorical Considerations

1. What is the difference between calling Wattleton's stance *pro-choice* or *pro-abortion?* How is this difference significant to how you read the article?
2. Consider the final sentence of the essay. How does this line relate to the issues Wattleton addresses? Can you think of specific rights that might become "meaningless"?
3. How does Wattleton make the transition from a discussion of poor women to a discussion of black women? Do you follow her logic?
4. How does Wattleton's shift from "Black Americans" to "*all* Americans" (paragraph 11) affect how you think about the issue? In the same paragraph,

Wattleton moves toward the use of "we." Do you feel a part of this "we"? Why or why not?

Writing Assignments

1. You are on a committee in charge of funding for Planned Parenthood. How do you respond to Wattleton's argument? What questions would you like to ask her before you grant or deny funding?
2. Write an essay agreeing or disagreeing with Wattleton's analysis. Consider issues of race, gender, and class in your analysis. Does Wattleton speak to "*all* Americans" (paragraph 11) as she claims to do?
3. Consider the role of audience in Wattleton's essay. How would you change her essay to convince a different audience of her argument?

Which Way Black America?— Anti-Abortion
Pamela Carr

Representing the anti-abortion position is Pamela Carr, spokesperson for Black Americans for Life. As Faye Wattleton did in the previous piece, Carr presents in this article, which first appeared in the October 1989 issue of *Ebony,* some sobering statistics in her argument. She also cites key black leaders in an effort to bolster her position. But unlike Wattleton, Carr draws a personal element into her debate: the experience of her own abortion, which, she says, taught her firsthand that abortion is no solution to the problems that plague black America.

BEFORE YOU READ

Carr's opening statement is "I am often asked why I, a young professional woman, am pro-life." To what stereotypical notion does this statement allude? Is it a stereotypical notion you hold? Does this statement make you curious about the essay, or does it deflate your interest? Why?

AS YOU READ

As you read this essay notice how Carr's thoughts about abortion in the black community relate to the ideals and goals of the civil rights movement. What are her observations and ideas on this subject? Do you agree or disagree with her?

1   I am often asked why I, a young professional woman, am pro-life. I am pro-life because of my knowledge, both personal and scientific, that every abortion in-

volves the taking of a human life. For the Black community, that means 1,000 African-Americans killed every day by abortion—more than 400,000 each year. The future of Black America is being threatened, our hope—through our children—destroyed in the name of convenience.

2   Is abortion a solution to break the poverty cycle? Will it enable young women and men to overcome unplanned obstacles to their education and career successes, and thus the success of the whole Black community?

3   No, abortion is not a solution, because it undermines the very ideals previous Black leaders stood for—the belief that each life is valuable and has something to contribute; whether Black or White, born or unborn.

4   Through my own abortion experience, I learned firsthand that abortion is no solution to the problems of the Black community.

5   On the verge of entering college, with a bright hope of educational and career success before me, I was horrified to learn my life plans were threatened by a small group of multiplying cells within me. I was pregnant. I panicked! I couldn't believe that it happened to me. How would I face my family and friends? I reluctantly asked my boyfriend to give me the money to get an abortion. He was hesitant because he wanted the baby.

6   It is important to know that I epitomized what was good and right in my community as a young Black woman. I was headed for success, allowing nothing from the past to hinder me. No obstacle would stop me from achieving my goals.

7   I had it all together. I was 17 and in my junior year of high school in Queens, New York. I believed in myself, my ability to make my own decisions, and my right to do so. I was an enterprising young woman ready to make my mark on the world. I had plans to graduate the following year with the hopes of attending one of the top Black colleges in the country. Nothing or no one could interfere with the plans I had made for my life.

8   I had been dating my boyfriend for about a year. We were well informed about sex education and the necessity of birth control. We were considered decent, intelligent and good students among our peers. We decided to become sexually active several months prior to the pregnancy.

9   Eventually, I contacted an older family friend in whom I confided. She informed my family about my pregnancy. My parents were hurt, but never ceased to remain concerned about me.

10   I had the "procedure" the following morning.

11   With my fears of a lost future and destroyed reputation behind me, I immediately faced a worse fear that I knew instinctively to be true. I had removed more than a "blob of tissue" or "the products of conception." I had killed my baby.

12   The anguish and the guilt I felt were unbelievable. I became deeply depressed. I no longer felt like that confident, jubilant young woman everyone knew me to be. Extreme feelings of insecurity followed me daily. My life took on new burdens. I could not have cared less about graduating from high school, or for that matter, attending college.

13   Over time, I was able to forgive myself and go on with my life, but always with the knowledge that I had swept away a part of my future which could never be recovered.

14   Abortion is offered as a solution to help young Blacks to forge forward to overcome present hindrances and to strive for brighter tomorrows. Yet, abortion only darkened my future. It took me many years to rise above the tide of confusion and guilt that flooded my life.

15   By allowing 400,000 Black babies to be systematically killed every year, we as African-Americans have strayed from the path of the leaders who fought so hard for our freedom. They would be alarmed today at how we forfeit the lives of our children, and, as a result, our future.

16   In the United States today, Black people only make up 12 percent of the population. Yet Black women have 25 percent of the abortions performed in our nation every year. For every three Black babies born, two die from abortion. It seems a silent genocide is taking place.

17   Teenage pregnancies, drugs, poverty and a lack of quality education are some of the problems that plague Black America. Abortion eliminates children, not these complex social problems. We shortchange ourselves when we buy the lie that we can improve the quality of our lives by terminating the lives of our children. How many more of them have to die before we realize that abortion is not a solution but another, more troubling, problem plaguing our community?

18   The solutions for the problems faced by the Black community will not be easy—they will require the effort of all of us working together. Let's take the first step by giving our children life because our children are our future.

19   Brave, positive leaders such as Harriet Tubman, Frederick Douglass, Martin Luther King Jr. and others have paved the way for the freedoms we possess today as Black Americans.

20   We cannot accept something so deeply wrong and unjust as abortion as a solution to the problems that still plague us. We cannot gain our freedom and our rights by taking away the lives of other members of the Black community. If we do, we have cheated ourselves of a future and betrayed the leaders who came before us and struggled so hard for our lives.

21   In the words of the great leader Martin Luther King Jr.: "Injustice anywhere is a threat to justice everywhere."

Topical Considerations

1. In paragraph 6, Carr writes, "It is important to know that I epitomized what was good and right in my community." Why is this "important"? How does Carr's own experience with abortion convince you or fail to convince you of her point? What was your stand on the issue before you read this essay?

2. When does Carr begin to focus her discussion on the African American community? How is this approach different from Wattleton's? Why might she have chosen this approach?

3. Carr insists that she and her boyfriend were well educated on birth control, but Wattleton in the preceding essay writes, "we fail miserably in providing our children with the ways and means of preventing pregnancy" (paragraph 5). Discuss the ways in which these contradictory statements might coexist.

4. Carr suggests that abortion is a betrayal of "the leaders who came before us and struggled so hard for our lives" (paragraph 20). What does she mean by this? Can you think of leaders outside the black community who would also feel this "betrayal"?

5. In your own words, describe what Carr means by "a silent genocide is taking place" (paragraph 16)? Do you agree with this analysis? What connotations can you think of for a word like *genocide*?

6. What is "the lie" (paragraph 17) to which Carr refers?

7. Do you think Carr wants all women to stop having abortions? Does she want to outlaw abortion? Why do you answer the way you do?

8. How might someone who is not an African American respond to this essay? What other positions might affect a reader's understanding of Carr's argument? For example, does gender, age, socioeconomic class, religion, or ethnic background make a difference in engaging Carr's essay?

Rhetorical Considerations

1. Carr begins her essay in the first person, but in paragraph 15, she moves her narrative to the third person. Why? Is this an effective strategy for convincing you of her argument? Consider her shift from specific/subjective to general/objective. Would you consider using this strategy to write a persuasive essay? Look at Faye Wattleton's essay—how is it different?

2. Pay specific attention to the way that language constructs an issue such as abortion. What is the difference between calling Carr's stance *anti-abortion* or *pro-life*? How does she describe pregnancy? Abortion? What purpose might these words serve in the context of Carr's argument?

3. Why does Carr mention famous leaders such as Harriet Tubman, Frederick Douglass, and Martin Luther King Jr.? How do these references add to or detract from the essay's effectiveness? Can you think of other instances when naming famous people is a persuasive strategy?

4. Consider the final sentence. In your own words, put this sentence in the context of Carr's argument. Compare it to Wattleton's conclusion.

5. How did Carr catch your attention? What was your initial reaction to the essay? Explain why you think you reacted the way you did. Does your prior opinion about the abortion issue affect the way you read the essay?

Writing Assignments

1. Abortion is one of the most controversial issues facing the United States to-day. It has been debated on many levels—personally and politically. Imagine that you are a Supreme Court Justice, and Carr has given this testimony to the Court. Write an essay responding to her argument. What questions would you like to ask her?
2. Write an essay agreeing or disagreeing with Carr's analysis of the effect of abortion on the African American community. Is the "procedure" unique to African Americans? Consider issues of race, gender, and class in your analysis. How might a poor Asian woman respond to Carr's argument? A rich white man?
3. Carr writes that "abortion is no solution to the problems of the Black community" (paragraph 4). She also says that the solutions "will not be easy" (paragraph 18). Imagine that you are a leader in the black community. Draft a proposal indicating some "solutions" to the "problems." How does abortion fit into your proposal?
4. Imagine yourself in a conversation with Carr and Wattleton. Set the scene, and create a dialogue between the two women and yourself.

An Abortionist's Credo
Elizabeth Karlin

A credo is a statement of principles or beliefs. In this essay, Elizabeth Karlin, a physician who performs abortions, states her deeply held professional convictions about abortion. She sees abortion as a medical procedure which, like coronary artery surgery, is a "response to things gone wrong." Further, she declares that women should have abortions out of "the desire to be a good mother." The statement of beliefs supports Karlin's argument that being an abortion provider is not a "filthy job" that "somebody has to do." Rather it is "the most challenging medicine I can think of."

Elizabeth Karlin, M.D., is the director of the Women's Medical Center of Madison, Wisconsin. This essay first appeared in the *New York Times* in March 1995.

BEFORE YOU READ

Why, in your opinion, might one choose to become a provider of abortions? What professional goals or beliefs might make one choose this field? Make a list of reasons to compare with Karlin's reasons.

AS YOU READ

What are the obstacles Dr. Karlin faces in her field? Which are the most difficult to overcome and why?

1   I don't do abortions because it's a filthy job and somebody has to do it. I do them because it is the most challenging medicine I can think of. I provide women with nurturing, preventive care to counteract a violent religious and political environment. I hope to do it well enough to prevent repeat abortions. Like coronary artery surgery, an abortion is a response to things gone wrong. It is not the underlying disease. Ignoring the disease is bad medicine.

2   There is only one reason I've ever heard for having an abortion: the desire to be a good mother. Women know when we don't have the resources to be the mother we expect to be. Those resources may be lacking because of rape, incest, alcohol, youth, poverty or an abusive relationship, but the resulting despair is the same. Women have abortions because they are aware of the overwhelming responsibility of motherhood. Of course, the punishers will have to continue escalating the penalty for abortion. Violence, or even the thought of an eternity in hell, is nothing compared to a woman's own despair over an unwanted pregnancy.

3   I don't know what the punishers will do when they read this, but it will be something. They've invaded my block carrying grisly pictures of full-term stillbirths with decapitated heads. They've jumped out at me when I walk my dogs at night. Once they invited extremists from around the country to march around my house seven times praying, in the hope that the house would fall down—a Jericho march. They plagued my mother, who was then 86 years old, with hang-up calls every three minutes for two days. (She finally said: "Thank you for your calls. You know how lonely we old ladies get. I'll expect your call in exactly three minutes." That was the end of that.) They sent hundreds of postcards to medical facilities in Wisconsin, proclaiming that I am an abortionist, with both my home and office addresses and phone numbers. They've invaded my office, repeatedly glued my locks shut and vandalized my office building. In some places now, they shoot to kill.

4   These people are very frightening, so I can't be too surprised when President Clinton and his candidate for Surgeon General, Dr. Henry W. Foster Jr., try to protect themselves with statements akin to "I think abortion is bad, but . . ." or, "I only did it a few times, for the best of reasons."

5   His reasons are between him and his patients. To invite a religious minority to participate in decisions affecting one medical procedure—one that involves only women, and frequently, suffering women—is appalling. It is like inviting Christian Scientists into a discussion of whether to use balloon angioplasty or medication to treat coronary artery disease. Requiring the approval of people who neither believe in nor understand the medicine involved is neither medically indicated nor wise.

6   Paradoxically, many of my patients come from among those groups who scream loudest against abortion. The counselor in our office often opens her interview by asking, "So, how long have you been pro-choice?" Laughter and the answer, "About 10 minutes," is the healthiest response. "I still don't believe in abortion," some women say, unaware that refusal to take responsibility for the decision means that I won't do the procedure.

7   From our questionnaire, we know that Catholic women are significantly overrepresented among those seeking abortions. Every Catholic woman who comes to my offices believes she is the unique, shameful exception. About 6 percent of my patients come from actively protesting, anti-abortion families, and 90 percent have said, "I would never have an abortion." Such a statement has two meanings: "I would never let my life or relationship be such a mess that I would need an abortion." And, "I am not like those *bad* women having abortions." What they are telling me is, "This abortion is different." My response is: "I'm sorry, but I only know how to do one kind of abortion—the kind that results when your heart sinks when you discover you are pregnant and the despair won't go away. If that's not the kind you want, leave now."

8   My patients believe the punishers: that if they die they will go straight to hell; that if they survive they will be infertile; that abortion causes breast cancer. Women still risk all this to be better mothers. They deserve medals for bravery.

9   Most doctors don't know much about abortion. This is not only because they have little or no exposure in medical school or residency, but also because 75 percent of women who see us don't tell their doctors they are having abortions—even when the doctor's ignorance about birth control was directly responsible for the unwanted pregnancy. Women who come to this abortion provider are expected to discuss their predisposition to unwanted pregnancy. We offer a soothing and safe environment to women who have come to expect humiliation. When we provide a full range of medical care and respect, we see a lower than expected repeat abortion rate.

10   Even when I was a strongly pro-choice general physician, testifying before our state legislature on reproductive issues, I—like many of you—thought an abortionist was a filthy man with dirty fingernails, dropping cigar ashes between a woman's legs as he worked. Now I find that an abortion provider is me—an honors medical graduate, a respected doctor in the community. I am blessed to be a feisty, increasingly radical middle-aged mother, providing important medical care, who travels the country to describe the joys and agonies of my job to medical students the age of my children.

11   Despite the Brookline murders, the first two months of 1995 have been the busiest since the gulf war call-up (the Bush abortions, we call them). But with Dr. Foster minimizing his association with abortion, legitimizing only a mere few, my patients—though no fewer—are more frantic.

12   My job is to stop the next abortion. To do this we expect our patients to leave us empowered, more informed, healthier and, yes, happier than when they came in. Last June, we received a clipping from a local newspaper featur-

ing one of our patients, the first of her extended family to finish college. She was bound for graduate school. She talked of emerging from a life of near slavery and constant childbearing and her plans for helping her sisters and nieces. She neglected to thank her local abortion provider for making this all possible. But it's O.K. I'm doing exactly what I want to be doing.

Topical Considerations

1. In her first paragraph, Karlin says that abortion is "a response to things gone wrong." What kinds of "things" does she list in this article?
2. Who are "the punishers"? Whom do they punish, and how?
3. How do Karlin and her mother respond to harassing telephone calls in paragraph 3? How would you and your mother respond if someone called your mom with similar news about your life? What kind of news would that be?
4. How does Karlin feel about Clinton's and Foster's comments about abortion in paragraph 4? Do you think that Karlin would ever use these statements herself? Why or why not?
5. What analogy does Karlin use in paragraph 5 to show why she believes "punishers" should not be allowed to prohibit abortion? Does she treat abortion as a medical or a psychological event in this analogy?
6. Why does Karlin believe that women who seek abortions should be awarded "medals for bravery"? What kinds of bravery have they shown?

Rhetorical Considerations

1. Does Karlin see the service she provides as medical, psychological, or both? Support your response with specific evidence from her article. How does her perspective affect her argument?
2. Where does Karlin reveal her own beliefs about the morality or moral issues which should govern abortion? How does her lack of direct discussion of her own moral beliefs help or hinder her argument?
3. Why does Karlin mention her own children in paragraph 10? How appropriate do you find this personal detail? How does it support her argument?
4. What is the rhetorical effect of calling people opposed to abortion "punishers" rather than "pro-life"? How fair is Karlin's term? How does it help or hinder her argument?
5. Why do you think Karlin entitled this article "An Abortionist's Credo"? What is a credo? Do you think the word's connotations are appropriate for this article? (Look the term up in a large or unabridged dictionary to find the word's connotations.)

Writing Assignments

1. From the point of view of someone Karlin would call a "punisher," write a letter responding to this article. What do you think of her term "punisher"? What do you think about her beliefs that you should not participate in decisions regarding abortion?
2. Look again at your list of "things gone wrong" to which abortion is a response (topical question 1). Discuss the effects of one of these factors on a woman's ability to be a good mother.
3. Using your library's new indexes, research the defeated nomination in the spring of 1995 of Dr. Henry W. Foster, Jr., mentioned in paragraph 4, for Surgeon General of the United States. What controversies surrounded Clinton's efforts to appoint him? Do you agree or disagree with Clinton's selection—for moral reasons? political reasons?

ANIMALS IN RESEARCH

Animal Liberation
Peter Singer

Peter Singer's book *Animal Liberation,* originally published in 1977 and re-issued in a second edition in 1990, is credited with igniting the animal rights movement in the United States. In this excerpt from that book, Singer introduces the concept of "speciesism"—what he defines as the toleration of unspeakable "cruelties inflicted on members of other species that would outrage us if performed on members of our own species." He argues that the perpetrators of speciesism—scientists and academics performing painful, redundant, and useless experiments on animals—should be subjected to strict and enforceable standards that protect and respect the rights of animals. Finally, he furnishes strategies and methods of protest designed to bring these issues to the public's attention.

Peter Singer, a prime catalyst of the modern animal rights movement, is director of the Centre for Human Bioethics at Monash University in Melbourne, Australia. He is also the author of *Practical Ethics* (1980) and *The Expanding Circle* (1981), and coauthor of *Embryo Experimentation* (1990).

BEFORE YOU READ

It would be interesting to know what, if any, animal experimentation is taking place at your school or university. Try to obtain this information and inquire as to what guidelines researchers must follow regarding animal experimentation. Does the research seem justified to you? Is it conducted in a humane way?

AS YOU READ

Clearly every experiment cited in this essay is a flagrant example of animal abuse, of what Singer sees as speciesism. There are no borderline cases. Does the use of such evidence work in Singer's favor? Does it, or can it, backfire by leading the reader to accept circumstances where animal suffering is justified or necessary?

1   How can these things happen? How can a man who is not a sadist spend his working day heating an unanesthetized dog to death, or driving a monkey into a lifelong depression, and then remove his white coat, wash his hands, and go home to dinner with his wife and children? How can taxpayers allow their money to be used to support experiments of this kind? And how can students go through a turbulent era of protest against injustice, discrimination, and oppression of all kinds, no matter how far from home, while ignoring the cruelties that are being carried out on their own campuses?

2   The answers to these questions stem from the unquestioned acceptance of speciesism. We tolerate cruelties inflicted on members of other species that would outrage us if performed on members of our own species. Speciesism allows researchers to regard the animals they experiment on as items of equipment, laboratory tools rather than living, suffering creatures. Sometimes they even refer to the animals in this way. Robert White of the Cleveland Metropolitan General Hospital, who has performed numerous experiments involving the transplanting of heads of monkeys, and the keeping alive of monkey brains in fluid, outside the body, has said in an interview that:

> Our main purpose here is to offer a living laboratory tool: a monkey "model" in which and by which we can design new operative techniques for the brain.

And the reporter who conducted the interview and observed White's experiments found his experience

> a rare and chilling glimpse into the cold, clinical world of the scientist, where the life of an animal has no meaning beyond the immediate purpose of experimentation.[1]

3   This "scientific" attitude to animals was exhibited to a large audience in December 1974 when the American public television network brought together Harvard philosopher Robert Nozick and three scientists whose work involves animals. The program was a follow-up to Fred Wiseman's controversial film *Primate,* which had taken viewers inside the Yerkes Primate Center, a research center in Atlanta, Georgia. Nozick asked the scientists whether the fact that an experiment will kill hundreds of animals is ever regarded, by scientists, as a reason for not performing it. One of the scientists answered: "Not that I know of." Nozick pressed his question: "Don't the animals count at all?" Dr. A.

Perachio, of the Yerkes Center, replied: "Why should they?" while Dr. D. Baltimore, of the Massachusetts Institute of Technology, added that he did not think that experimenting on animals raised a moral issue at all.[2]

4   As well as the general attitude of speciesism which researchers share with other citizens there are some special factors operating to make possible the experiments I have described. Foremost among these is the immense respect that we still have for scientists. Although the advent of nuclear weapons and environmental pollution have made us realize that science and technology need to be controlled to some extent, we still tend to be in awe of anyone who wears a white coat and has a PhD. In a well-known series of experiments Stanley Milgram, a Harvard psychologist, has demonstrated that ordinary people will obey the direction of a white-coated research worker to administer what appears to be (but in fact is not) electric shock to a human subject as "punishment" for failing to answer questions correctly; and they will continue to do this even when the human subject cries out and pretends to be in great pain.[3] If this can happen when the participant believes he is inflicting pain on a human, how much easier is it for a student to push aside his initial qualms when his professor instructs him to perform experiments on animals? What Alice Heim has rightly called the "indoctrination" of the student is a gradual process, beginning with the dissection of frogs in school biology classes. When the budding medical student, or psychology student, or veterinarian, reaches the university and finds that to complete the course of studies on which he has set his heart he must experiment on living animals, it is difficult for him to refuse to do so, especially since he knows that what he is being asked to do is standard practice in the field.

5   Individual students will often admit feeling uneasy about what they are asked to do, but public protests are very rare. An organized protest did occur in Britain recently, however, when students at the Welsh National School of Medicine in Cardiff complained publicly that a dog was unnecessarily injected with drugs more than 30 times to demonstrate a point during a lecture. The dog was then killed. One student said: "We learned nothing new. It could all have been looked up in textbooks. A film could be made so that only one dog dies and all this unnecessary suffering is stopped."[4] The student's comment was true; but such things happen routinely in every medical school. Why are protests so rare?

6   The pressure to conform does not let up when the student receives his degree. If he goes on to a graduate degree in fields in which experiments on animals are unusual, he will be encouraged to devise his own experiments and write them up for his PhD dissertation. We have already seen examples of work by PhD students—one student was a member of the team that irradiated beagles at the University of Rochester, [a study involving] the electric shocking of ducklings was work toward a PhD; and so was [an] experiment involving thirst and electric shock. . . . Naturally, if this is how students are educated they will tend to continue in the same manner when they become professors, and they will, in turn, train their own students in the same manner.

7   It is not always easy for people outside the universities to understand the rationale for the research carried out under university auspices. Originally, perhaps, scholars and researchers just set out to solve the most important problems and did not allow themselves to be influenced by other considerations. Perhaps some are still motivated by these concerns. Too often, though, academic research gets bogged down in petty and insignificant details because the big questions have been studied already, and have either been solved or proven too difficult. So the researcher turns away from the well-ploughed fertile fields in search of virgin territory where whatever he learns will be new, although the connection with a major problem may be more remote. So we find articles in the scientific journals with introductions like the following:

> Although swelling from trauma and inflammatory agents has been the subject of investigation for years, meager information exists on the quantitative changes that occur over a period of time. . . . In the present study a simple method was developed for measuring the volume of the rodent tail, and the changes which occur after standardized trauma have been reported.[5]

The "simple method" involves severely injuring the tails of seventy-three unanesthetized mice; and it is difficult to see how measuring the swelling of the tail of a mouse can tell us much about anything—except the amount a mouse's tail swells. Here is another example: While "the effects of controlled hemorrhage resulting in reversible and irreversible shock have been studied in detail" there are "relatively few articles concerned with the controlled study of exsanguinating hemorrhage"—that is, hemorrhage that drains the body of all its blood, or at least until death occurs. Noting that patterns of dying from suffocation, drowning, and other causes have been studied in detail but that studies of the general pattern of death from exsanguinating hemorrhage have been "based on experiments performed on very few animals," experimenters gave sixty-five dogs an anesthetic that permitted "quick recovery . . . and study of the dying process without the influence of deep anesthesia." They then opened the aortic cannula in each dog and watched them go through a period they termed "the agonal state" which took up to ten minutes and was terminated by death. The experimenters describe their report as "merely a description of observations" and not an attempt to elucidate the mechanisms of the changes observed.[6]

8   When we read reports of experiments that cause pain and are apparently not even intended to produce results of real significance we are at first inclined to think that there must be more to what is being done than we can understand—that the scientist must have some better reason for doing what he is doing than his report indicates. Yet as we go more deeply into the subject we find that what appears trivial on the surface very often really *is* trivial. Experimenters themselves often unofficially admit this. H. F. Harlow, whose experiments on monkeys I described earlier, was for twelve years editor of the

Journal of Comparative and Physiological Psychology, a journal which publishes more reports of painful experiments on animals than almost any other. At the end of this period, in which Harlow estimates he reviewed about 2,500 manuscripts submitted for publication, he wrote, in a semihumourous farewell note, that "most experiments are not worth doing and the data attained are not worth publishing."

9   On reflection, perhaps this is not so surprising. Researchers, even those in psychology, medicine, and the biological sciences, are human beings and are susceptible to the same influences as any other human beings. They like to get on in their careers, to be promoted, and to have their work read and discussed by their colleagues. Publishing papers in the appropriate journals is an important element in the rise up the ladder of promotion and increased prestige. This happens in every field, in philosophy or history as much as in psychology or medicine, and it is entirely understandable and in itself hardly worth criticizing. The philosopher or historian who publishes to improve his career prospect does little harm beyond wasting paper and boring his colleagues; the psychologist or medical researcher, or anyone else whose work involves experimenting on animals, however, can cause severe pain or prolonged suffering. His work should therefore be subject to much stricter standards of necessity. . . .

10   In the United States the only federal law on the matter is the Animal Welfare Act of 1970, which amended a 1966 act. The law set standards for the transportation, housing, and handling of animals sold as pets, exhibited, or intended for use in research. So far as actual experimentation is concerned, however, it effectively allows the researcher to do exactly as he pleases. One section of the law requires that those facilities which register under the act (and neither government agencies doing research nor many small facilities have to register) must lodge a report stating that when painful experiments were performed without the use of pain-relieving drugs this was necessary to achieve the objectives of the research project. No attempt is made to assess whether these "objectives" are sufficiently important to justify the infliction of pain. Under these circumstances the requirement does no more than make additional paperwork. You can't, of course, electric shock a dog into a state of helplessness if you anesthetize him at the same time; nor can you produce depression in a monkey while keeping him happy with drugs. So you can truthfully state that the objectives of the experiment cannot be achieved if pain-relieving drugs are used, and then go on with the experiment as you would have done before the act came into existence. . . .

11   When are experiments on animals justifiable? Upon learning of the nature of many contemporary experiments, many people react by saying that all experiments on animals should be prohibited immediately. But if we make our demands as absolute as this, the experimenters have a ready reply: Would we be prepared to let thousands of humans die if they could be saved by a single experiment on a single animal?

12   This question is, of course, purely hypothetical. There never has been and there never could be a single experiment that saves thousands of lives. The way to reply to this hypothetical question is to pose another: Would the experimenter be prepared to carry out his experiment on a human orphan under six months old if that were the only way to save thousands of lives?

13   If the experimenter would not be prepared to use a human infant then his readiness to use nonhuman animals reveals an unjustifiable form of discrimination on the basis of species, since adult apes, monkeys, dogs, cats, rats, and other mammals are more aware of what is happening to them, more self-directing, and, so far as we can tell, at least as sensitive to pain as a human infant. (I specified that the human infant be an orphan to avoid the complications of the feelings of parents, although in so doing I am being overfair to the experimenter, since the nonhuman animals used in experiments are not orphans and in many species the separation of mother and young clearly causes distress for both.)

14   There is no characteristic that human infants possess to a higher degree than adult nonhuman animals, unless we are to count the infant's potential as a characteristic that makes it wrong to experiment on him. Whether this characteristic should count is controversial—if we count it, we shall have to condemn abortion along with experiments on infants, since the potential of the infant and the fetus is the same. To avoid the complexities of this issue, however, we can alter our original question a little and assume that the infant is one with severe and irreversible brain damage that makes it impossible for him ever to develop beyond the level of a six-month-old infant. There are, unfortunately, many such human beings, locked away in special wards throughout the country, many of them long since abandoned by their parents. Despite their mental deficiencies, their anatomy and physiology is in nearly all respects identical with that of normal humans. If, therefore, we were to force-feed them with large quantities of floor polish, or drip concentrated solutions of cosmetics into their eyes, we would have a much more reliable indication of the safety of these products for other humans than we now get by attempting to extrapolate the results of tests on a variety of other species. The radiation experiments, the heatstroke experiments, and many other experiments described earlier in this chapter could also have told us more about human reactions to the experimental situation if they had been carried out on retarded humans instead of dogs and rabbits.

15   So whenever an experimenter claims that this experiment is important enough to justify the use of an animal, we should ask him whether he would be prepared to use a retarded human at a similar mental level to the animal he is planning to use. If his reply is negative, we can assume that he is willing to use a nonhuman animal only because he gives less consideration to the interests of members of other species than he gives to members of his own—and this bias is no more defensible than racism or any other form of arbitrary discrimination.

16   Of course, no one would seriously propose carrying out the experiments described in this chapter on retarded humans. Occasionally it has become known that some medical experiments have been performed on humans without their consent, and sometimes on retarded humans; but the consequences of these experiments for the human subjects are almost always trivial by comparison with what is standard practice for nonhuman animals. Still, these experiments on humans usually lead to an outcry against the experimenters, and rightly so. They are, very often, a further example of the arrogance of the research worker who justifies everything on the grounds of increasing knowledge. If experimenting on retarded, orphaned humans would be wrong, why isn't experimenting on nonhuman animals wrong? What difference is there between the two, except for the mere fact that, biologically, one is a member of our species and the other is not: But *that,* surely, is not a morally relevant difference, any more than the fact that a being is not a member of our race is a morally relevant difference. . . .

17   To return to the question of when an experiment might be justifiable. It will not do to say: "Never!" In extreme circumstances, absolutist answers always break down. Torturing a human being is almost always wrong, but it is not absolutely wrong. If torture were the only way in which we could discover the location of a nuclear time bomb hidden in a New York City basement, then torture would be justifiable. Similarly, if a single experiment could cure a major disease, that experiment would be justifiable. But in actual life the benefits are always much, much more remote, and more often than not they are nonexistent. So how do we decide when an experiment is justifiable?

18   We have seen that the experimenter reveals a bias in favor of his own species whenever he carries out an experiment on a nonhuman for a purpose that he would not think justified him in using a human being, even a retarded human being. This principle gives us a guide toward an answer to our question. Since a speciesist bias, like a racist bias, is unjustifiable, an experiment cannot be justifiable unless the experiment is so important that the use of a retarded human being would also be justifiable.

19   This is not an absolutist principle. I do not believe that it could *never* be justifiable to experiment on a retarded human. If it really were possible to save many lives by an experiment that would take just one life, and there were *no other way* those lives could be saved, it might be right to do the experiment. But this would be an extremely rare case. Not one tenth of one percent of the experiments now being performed on animals would fall into this category. Certainly none of the experiments described in this chapter could pass this test. . . .

20   At present scientists do not look for alternatives *simply because they do not care enough about the animals they are using.* I make this assertion on the best possible authority, since it has been more or less admitted by Britain's Research Defence Society, a group which exists to defend researchers from criticism by animal welfare organizations. A recent article in the *Bulletin* of the National Society for Medical Research (the American equivalent of the Re-

search Defence Society) described how the British group successfully fought off a proposed amendment to the British law regulating experiments that would have prohibited any experiment using live animals if the purpose of that experiment could be achieved by alternative means not involving animals. The main objections lodged by the Research Defence Society to this very mild attempt at reform were, first, that in some cases it may be cheaper to use animals than other methods, and secondly, that:

> in some cases alternatives may exist but they may be unknown to an investigator. With the vast amount of scientific literature coming out of even a very narrow field of study it is possible that an investigator may not know all that is now known about techniques or results in a particular area. . . .

(This ignorance would make the experimenter liable to prosecution under the proposed amendment.)

21   What do these objections amount to? The first can mean only one thing: that economic considerations are more important than the suffering of animals; as for the second, it is a strong argument for a total moratorium on animal experiments until every experimenter has had time to read up on the existing reports of alternatives available in his field and results already obtained. Is it not shocking that experimenters may be inflicting agony on animals only because they have not kept up with the literature in their field—literature that may contain reports of methods of achieving the same results without using animals? Or even reports of similar experiments that have been done already and are being endlessly repeated?

22   The objections of the Research Defence Society to the British amendment can be summed up in one sentence: the prevention of animal suffering is not worth the expenditure of extra money or of the time the experimenter would need to read the literature in his field. And of this "defense," incidentally, the National Society for Medical Research has said:

> The Research Defence Society of Great Britain deserves the plaudits of the world's scientific community for the manner in which it expressed its opposition to this sticky measure.[7] . . .

23   When all this has been said, there still remains the practical question: what can be done to change the widespread practice of experimenting on animals? Undoubtedly some action at the governmental level is needed, but what action precisely? And how can we succeed now when previous efforts failed? What can the ordinary citizen do to help bring about a change?

24   Unlike many other much needed reforms, this one does not lack popular support. We have already seen that in the United States a larger number of people wrote to the Defense Department about the beagle experiments than about the bombing of North Vietnam. In Britain, too, members of Parliament have reported receiving more mail from constituents concerned about the use of animals in laboratories than about the nation's entry into the European

Common Market.[8] A British opinion poll conducted in 1973 found that 73 percent of the electors disapproved of the use of animals in the testing of weapons, toiletries, and cosmetics. Barely one in ten actually approved of these practices; however, only about one in four knew that animals actually were being used to test weapons and cosmetics.[9]

25   Whatever reforms are proposed, . . . the most pressing need is that they include in a central, decision-making role a group of people totally free of any personal stake in the use of animals for research. Only in this way could effective control become a reality. United Action for Animals has proposed a "Public Science Council," consisting of nonanimal-using scientists, which would have authority to regulate the sums of public money that go into research in fields in which animals are used. By insisting on the replacement of animal-using methods by alternative methods not involving animals it would be possible for such a council to foster the growth of a new and more humane approach to scientific inquiry. This approach might not even require legislation, so far as the United States is concerned. All that would be necessary is that the research grants, public contracts, training grants, fellowships, and other awards now given to animal-using scientists be redirected toward other methods. A council of this sort might also contain representatives of the general public. The public provides the money for most scientific research; and the public has the right to direct the way in which its funds are used.

26   Until some major change in national policy has been effected, citizens can work on a more local level to make known what is happening all around the country, and quite possibly at universities and commercial laboratories in their own community. Students should refuse to carry out experiments required for their courses. Students and the animal welfare organizations should study the academic journals to find out where painful experiments are being carried out. They should then demonstrate against those university departments that abuse animals. Pressure should be put on universities to cut off funds to departments that have a bad record in this respect, and if the universities do not do so this should be publicized. Since universities are dependent on public good will for financial support, this method of protest should be effective. No doubt the cry will be raised that such demands are a restriction of "scientific freedom," but as there is no freedom to inflict agony on humans in the name of science, why should there be any freedom to inflict agony on other animals? Especially where public funds are involved, no one has a right to the freedom to use these funds to inflict pain.

27   The vital role played by public funds in the use of animals for experimentation suggests another political tactic. During the American involvement in Vietnam, opponents of that war withheld a portion of their taxes, roughly the proportion of the national revenues that went toward the war, as a way of emphasizing their opposition to the war. Such tactics should only be used in extreme cases; but perhaps this case is sufficiently extreme. Obviously experimenting on animals only uses a tiny fraction of the funds that went toward the war in Vietnam, although no figures are available to show how much is spent on animal experiments. A token tax withholding, say 1 percent of the tax

payable, would cover the amount actually spent, and serve as a symbolic form of protest that would enable every taxpayer to express his opposition to the use made of his taxes.

28   By publicly exposing what is happening behind closed laboratory doors, protesting against these things, writing letters to those legislators who provide the funds for them, withholding taxes, and publicizing the records of candidates for public office before elections, it may be possible to bring about a reform. But the problem is part of the larger problem of speciesism and it is unlikely to be eliminated altogether until speciesism itself is eliminated. Surely one day, though, our children's children, reading about what was done in laboratories in the twentieth century, will feel the same sense of horror and and incredulity at what otherwise civilized people can do that we now feel when we read about the atrocities of the Roman gladiatorial arenas or the eighteenth-century slave trade.

Notes

1. *Scope* (Durban, South Africa), 30 March 1973.
2. "The Price of Knowledge," broadcast in New York, 12 December 1974, WNET/13; transcript supplied courtesy WNET/13 and Henry Spira.
3. S. Milgram, *Obedience to Authority* (New York: Harper & Row, 1974). Incidentally, these experiments were widely criticized on ethical grounds because they involved human beings without their consent. It is indeed questionable whether Milgram should have deceived participants in his experiments as he did; but when we compare what was done to them with what is commonly done to nonhuman animals, we can appreciate the double standard with which critics of the experiment operate.
4. *South Wales Echo,* 21 January 1974.
5. S. Rosenthal, "Production and Measurement of Traumatic Swelling," *American Journal of Physiology,* 216 (3) p. 630 (March 1969).
6. R. Kirimli, S. Kampschulte, P. Safar, "Patterns of dying from exsanguinating hemorrhage in dogs." *Journal of Trauma,* 10 (5) p. 393 (May 1970).
7. *Bulletin of the National Society for Medical Research,* 24 (10) October 1973.
8. *Bulletin of the National Society for Medical Research,* 24 (10) October 1973.
9. From an address by Richard Ryder, reported in *RSPCA Today,* Summer 1974. The poll was conducted by N.O.P. Market Research Ltd.

Topical Considerations

1. Summarize, as best you can, the idea of "speciesism" as presented in Singer's article. Do you find the argument of speciesism to be a valid reason for opposition to animal testing? Why or why not?
2. In paragraph 4 Singer asserts that "we still tend to be in awe of anyone who wears a white coat and has a Ph.D." Do you agree with this statement? If

you were one of the "ordinary people" in Milgram's experiment (paragraph 4), how do you think you would have responded? Explain your answer.

3. What do you think about the term *indoctrination* as it is applied to medical and research students (paragraph 4)? Do you agree that such "indoctrination" begins with the dissection of frogs in biology class? Did you ever protest (or have the urge to protest) such lab activity, or, at least, refrain from participating?

4. Reread paragraph 7 of Singer's article. What is your opinion of the necessity of the experiments that Singer outlines? Do you agree that they seem irrelevant and useless? Why or why not? What implication does your response have in relation to the larger argument of animal rights?

5. In paragraph 9 Singer states that the work of researchers using animals "should . . . be subject to much stricter standards of necessity." He then goes on in paragraph 10 to discuss the federal laws that are in existence to regulate animal testing. What is your opinion of the laws? Do you agree that they need revision? Why or why not? What changes would you make in the laws?

6. Discuss Singer's contention that "whenever an experimenter claims that his experiment is important enough to justify the use of an animal, we should ask him whether he would be prepared to use a retarded human at a similar mental level to the animal he is planning to use" (paragraph 15). What is your response to this proposition? Keep in mind Singer's reasoning for his suggestion (paragraphs 13–15).

7. In paragraph 15 Singer compares discrimination on the basis of species to discrimination on the basis of race. What is your opinion of this comparison? Can such a comparison be made? Explain your answer.

8. Given the option of using products that have not been tested on animals, would you do so? Would your response change if those products were higher in cost than the ones tested on animals?

9. In paragraph 26 Singer calls upon students to "refuse to carry out experiments required for their courses." If you were in such a position, would you be willing to do this? What do you suppose your options would be in such a situation—and what might be the consequences? Explain your answer.

10. In this essay Singer focuses strictly on the rights of animals used in laboratory testing. Do you think that his arguments extend to the use of animals for meat and clothing as well? Why or why not? How do you think Singer feels about such issues? Explain.

Rhetorical Considerations

1. In general, do you find Singer's argument to be effective? Why or why not? What strategies does he use in arguing his point?

2. In paragraphs 6 and 7, Singer explicitly describes experiments performed upon laboratory animals. What is the effect of such graphic description? Is this an effective strategy in terms of his argument? Why or why not?

3. Reread Singer's article, looking for places where the author has appropriated quotations from the opposition and used them to support his own thesis. How do these quotations affect the reader's response to the opposition? To Singer's article? Explain your answer.

4. Analyze the logic in paragraphs 13–15. How does Singer support his idea that researchers should be as capable of justifying the use of a retarded human for research as they are of justifying the use of animals. What kind of proof does he give? Is he successful—that is, are you convinced? Why or why not?

5. In the last three paragraphs of his essay, Singer proposes solutions to the problems of animal rights in the laboratory. Is the presentation of these solutions effective? Why or why not?

6. In your opinion, does Singer have any special audience in mind? What assumptions about his audience does he make? Does he assume that the reader is on his side of the issue? Explain your answer with evidence from the essay.

Writing Assignments

1. Singer opens his essay with hypothetical questions that immediately reveal his position with regard to the animal rights issue. Rewrite this paragraph from the opposition's point of view; make your position just as immediately understood.

2. Imagine that you are taking a course in which you are asked to watch or participate in painful experiments using animals. Write a letter of protest to your professor outlining your reasons for refusing to participate in these activities.

3. Now imagine that you are outraged at Singer's insinuation that your animal experiments are inhumane. Write a letter to Singer defending your reasons for undertaking such study. Be sure to address Singer's arguments as they appear in his essay.

4. Singer's essay asks the reader to examine the difference between animals and humans. Keeping in mind the idea of speciesism, write an essay in which you explore such differences, leading to a conclusion about the issue of animals rights.

I Am the Enemy
Ron Karpati

Ron Karpati, a pediatrician and medical researcher, considers himself compassionate and caring. As a professional whose research aims to find cures for childhood illnesses, he bristles at allegations from animal rights activists claiming researchers pursue their own advancement by imposing needless suffering on animals. In this piece he defends the use of animals in medical research. He also raises disturbing questions about how medical research might be impaired if animal rights activists, "a vocal, but misdirected, minority," sway public opinion.

Ron Karpati is a graduate of UCLA Medical School. He trained in pediatrics at Children's Hospital of Los Angeles, specializing in pediatric oncology and bone marrow transplants at UCSF. This article first appeared in *Newsweek's* My Turn column in 1989.

BEFORE YOU READ

List some advances or cures in modern medicine made possible by animal research. Although animals may have suffered and died, is this research justifiable given the results? Should other methods have been used? Does human life take priority over animal life?

AS YOU READ

Karpati is reacting to criticisms directed against his own profession. How would you describe the tone of his essay? Defensive? Objective? Combative? Reasonable? How does the tone add to or detract from the force of the argument?

1   I am the enemy! One of those vilified, inhumane physician-scientists involved in animal research. How strange, for I have never thought of myself as an evil person. I became a pediatrician because of my love for children and my desire to keep them healthy. During medical school and residency, however, I saw many children die of leukemia, prematurity and traumatic injury—circumstances against which medicine has made tremendous progress, but still has far to go. More important, I also saw children, alive and healthy, thanks to advances in medical science such as infant respirators, potent antibiotics, new surgical techniques and the entire field of organ transplantation. My desire to tip the scales in favor of the healthy, happy children drew me to medical research.

2   My accusers claim that I inflict torture on animals for the sole purpose of career advancement. My experiments supposedly have no relevance to medicine and are easily replaced by computer simulation. Meanwhile, an apathetic public barely watches, convinced that the issue has no significance, and publicity-conscious politicians increasingly give way to the demands of the activists.

3   We in medical research have also been unconscionably apathetic. We have allowed the most extreme animal-rights protestors to seize the initiative and frame the issue as one of "animal fraud." We have been complacent in our belief that a knowledgeable public would sense the importance of animal research to the public health. Perhaps we have been mistaken in not responding to the emotional tone of the argument created by those sad posters of ani-

mals by waving equally sad posters of children dying of leukemia or cystic fibrosis.

4   Much is made of the pain inflicted on these animals in the name of medical science. The animal-rights activists contend that this is evidence of our malevolent and sadistic nature. A more reasonable argument, however, can be advanced in our defense. Life is often cruel, both to animals and human beings. Teenagers get thrown from the back of a pickup truck and suffer severe head injuries. Toddlers, barely able to walk, find themselves at the bottom of a swimming pool while a parent checks the mail. Physicians hoping to alleviate the pain and suffering these tragedies cause have but three choices: create an animal model of the injury or disease and use that model to understand the process and test new therapies; experiment on human beings—some experiments will succeed, most will fail—or finally, leave medical knowledge static, hoping that accidental discoveries will lead us to the advances.

5   Some animal-rights activists would suggest a fourth choice, claiming that computer models can simulate animal experiments, thus making the actual experiments unnecessary. Computers can simulate, reasonably well, the effects of well-understood principles on complex systems, as in the application of the laws of physics to airplane and automobile design. However, when the principles themselves are in question, as is the case with the complex biological systems under study, computer modeling alone is of little value.

6   One of the terrifying effects of the effort to restrict the use of animals in medical research is that the impact will not be felt for years and decades: drugs that might have been discovered will not be; surgical techniques that might have been developed will not be, and fundamental biological processes that might have been understood will remain mysteries. There is the danger that politically expedient solutions will be found to placate a vocal minority, while the consequences of those decisions will not be apparent until long after the decisions are made and the decision making forgotten.

7   Fortunately, most of us enjoy good health, and the trauma of watching one's child die has become a rare experience. Yet our good fortune should not make us unappreciative of the health we enjoy or the advances that make it possible. Vaccines, antibiotics, insulin and drugs to treat heart disease, hypertension and stroke are all based on animal research. Most complex surgical procedures, such as coronary-artery bypass and organ transplantation, are initially developed in animals. Presently undergoing animal studies are techniques to insert genes in humans in order to replace the defective ones found to be the cause of so much disease. These studies will effectively end if animal research is severely restricted.

8   In America today, death has become an event isolated from our daily existence—out of the sight and thoughts of most of us. As a doctor who has watched many children die, and their parents grieve, I am particularly angered by people capable of so much compassion for a dog or a cat, but with seemingly so little for a dying human being. These people seem so insulated from the reality of human life and death and what it means.

9   Make no mistake, however: I am not advocating the needlessly cruel treatment of animals. To the extent that the animal-rights movement has made us more aware of the needs of these animals, and made us search harder for suitable alternatives, they have made a significant contribution. But if the more radical members of this movement are successful in limiting further research, their efforts will bring about a tragedy that will cost many lives. The real question is whether an apathetic majority can be aroused to protect its future against a vocal, but misdirected, minority.

Topical Considerations

1. Do you agree with Karpati's representation of the public as "apathetic" with respect to the issue of animal rights? Why or why not? How do you view your own response to the issue?
2. In paragraph 3 Karpati wonders if the medical research profession has been "mistaken in not responding to the emotional tone of the argument created by those sad posters of animals by waving equally sad posters of children dying of leukemia or cystic fibrosis." What is your opinion of this kind of "campaigning," on either side of the issue? Does it work? Is it valid and responsible? Explain.
3. In his response to claims of animal rights activists that painful animal research is sadistic, Karpati simply says, "Life is often cruel" (paragraph 4). In your opinion, is this a reasonable response, or argument? Do you agree with Karpati? Why or why not?
4. Do you agree with Karpati's belief that "[i]n America today, death has become an event isolated from our daily existence" (paragraph 8)? What implications does this statement have for our lives, if it is true? Have we indeed begun to take medical progress for granted? Should we, as a society, attempt to isolate ourselves from the reality of death? What might be the consequences of such an isolation?
5. Karpati obviously believes that human life is of higher value than animal life, thereby justifying the use of animals in experimentation. Do you agree with his reasoning? Explain.
6. What do you suppose Karpati means by the term *animal fraud* (paragraph 3)? Do you agree that this term is at the heart of the issue?

Rhetorical Considerations

1. Karpati opens his essay with the statement, "I am the enemy!" and then goes on to refute that statement. How does this strategy work in terms of the reader's image of Karpati as a reliable authority? Is this an effective strategy? Why or why not?
2. Examine paragraph 4 of Karpati's essay. Do you think he gives adequate evidence to back up his claims? What about the last sentence where he outlines

the three methods available to research physicians looking for cures for human disease and suffering? What kind of evidence do you think might strengthen his argument?

3. Why do you suppose Karpati chose to write this essay in the first person? How is this style consistent or inconsistent with his method of proof? How does the point of view affect your response to the essay?
4. Is this article a statement of position or a statement of proposal? Explain your answer.
5. Reread Karpati's article, looking for places where Karpati directly or indirectly implicates the reader as part of the opposing view. How does this affect your response to the essay? Explain your answer.
6. If you were Karpati's editor, what changes would you ask Karpati to make in order to make his argument stronger?

Writing Assignments

1. Imagine that you are an animal rights activist who also happens to be the parent of a child with leukemia. How would you respond to Karpati's essay? How would you solve the conflicts inherent in this position?
2. Using the argument of "speciesism," write an essay in opposition to Karpati's piece. Respond to each of the arguments put forth in his article.
3. Write an essay to "both sides of the opposition" protesting the use of "sad posters" (paragraph 3) and explicit photographs to sway public opinion, arguing that such tactics are manipulative and deceptive.

Why Worry About the Animals?
Jean Bethke Elshtain

Are animal rights activists irrational, emotional, and sentimental? Are they violent fanatics willing to resort to civil disobedience including breaking and entering and damaging property? Or are they reasonable people giving careful thought to ethical issues raised by the suffering of animals in experimentation? Grappling with these questions, Jean Bethke Elshtain sketches the evolution of the animal rights movement. Intertwined in this discussion is the documentation of the agony and terror inflicted on animals in fields as varied as war research, the cosmetic industry, the fur industry, and hunting. What results is a powerful argument to reappraise one's obligation to the animal world and to take a position on animal rights that can be ethically justified.

Jean Bethke Elshtain holds the post of Centennial Professor of Political Science at Vanderbilt University. In addition to writing for periodicals such as *The Nation* and *The Progressive,* she has authored several books. Among them are *Public Man, Private Woman: Women in Social and Political Thought* (1981) and *Women and War* (1987). Recently she co-edited *Women, Militarism, and the Arms Race* (1990), and in 1995 her book *Democracy on Trial* was published. This article first appeared in *The Progressive* in March 1990.

BEFORE YOU READ

Do you have a preconceived opinion of animal rights activists as violent fanatics? Rational individuals committed to the humane/ethical treatment of animals? People with emotional problems looking for a cause? Other? What led you to this opinion?

AS YOU READ

Does Elshtain convince you that every thinking person has a moral, ethical stake in the way animals are treated? Did the essay have an impact on your thinking about the issue? Do you feel a moral obligation to take some type of action regarding the treatment of animals in experimentation and research, whether in the cosmetics, medical, or military industry? Or are animal rights issues irrelevant to you?

1   These things are happening or have happened recently:

- The wings of seventy-four mallard ducks are snapped to see whether crippled birds can survive in the wild. (They can't).
- Infant monkeys are deafened to study their social behavior, or turned into amphetamine addicts to see what happens to their stress level.
- Monkeys are separated from their mothers, kept in isolation, addicted to drugs, and induced to commit "aggressive" acts.
- Pigs are blowtorched and observed to see how they respond to third-degree burns. No painkillers are used.
- Monkeys are immersed in water and vibrated to cause damage.
- For thirteen years, baboons have their brains bashed at the University of Pennsylvania as research assistants laugh at signs of the animals' distress.
- Monkeys are dipped in boiling water; other animals are shot in the face with high-powered rifles.

2   The list of cruelties committed in the name of "science" or "research" could be expanded endlessly. "Fully 80 percent of the experiments involving rhesus monkeys are either unnecessary, represent useless duplication of previous work, or could utilize nonanimal alternatives," says John E. McArdle, a biologist and specialist in primates at Illinois Wesleyan University.

3   Growing awareness of animal abuse is helping to build an increasingly militant animal-welfare movement in this country and abroad—a movement that is beginning to have an impact on public policy. Secretary of Health and Human Services Frederick Goodwin complained recently that complying with

new federal regulations on the use—or abuse—of animals will drain off some 17 percent of the research funds appropriated to the National Institutes of Health. (It is cheaper to purchase, use, and destroy animals than to retool for alternative procedures.) One of the institutes, the National Institute of Mental Health, spends about thirty million dollars a year on research that involves pain and suffering for animals.

4   The new animal-welfare activists are drawing attention in part because of the tactics they espouse. Many preach and practice civil disobedience, violating laws against, say, breaking and entering. Some have been known to resort to violence against property and—on a few occasions—against humans.

5   Some individuals and groups have always fretted about human responsibility toward nonhuman creatures. In the ancient world, the historian Plutarch and the philosopher Porphyry were among those who insisted that human excellence embodied a refusal to inflict unnecessary suffering on all other creatures, human and nonhuman.

6   But with the emergence of the Western rationalist tradition, animals lost the philosophic struggle. Two of that tradition's great exponents, René Descartes and Immanuel Kant, dismissed out of hand the moral worth of animals. Descartes's view, which has brought comfort to every human who decides to confine, poison, cripple, infect, or dismember animals in the interest of human knowledge, was the more extreme: he held that animals are simply machines, devoid of consciousness or feeling. Kant, more sophisticated in his ethical reasoning, knew that animals could suffer but denied that they were self-conscious. Therefore, he argued, they could aptly serve as means to human ends.

7   To make sure that human sensibilities would not be troubled by the groans, cries, and yelps of suffering animals—which might led some to suspect that animals not only bleed but feel pain—researchers have for a century subjected dogs and other animals to an operation called a centriculocordectomy, which destroys their vocal cords.

8   Still, there have long been groups that placed the suffering of animals within the bounds of human concern. In the nineteenth and early twentieth centuries, such reform movements as women's suffrage and abolitionism made common cause with societies for the prevention of cruelty to animals. On one occasion in 1907, British suffragettes, trade-unionists, and their animal-welfare allies battled London University medical students in a riot triggered by the vivisection of a dog.

9   Traditionally, such concern has been charitable and, frequently, highly sentimental. Those who perpetrated the worst abuses against animals were denounced for their "beastly" behavior—the farmer who beat or starved his horse; the householder who chained and kicked his dog; the aristocratic hunter who, with his guests, slew birds by the thousands in a single day on his private game preserve.

10   For the most part, however, animals have been viewed, even by those with "humane" concerns, as means to human ends. The charitable impulse,

therefore, had a rather condescending, patronizing air: alas, the poor creatures deserve our pity.

11   The new animal-welfare movement incorporates those historic concerns but steers them in new directions. Philosophically, animal-rights activists seek to close the gap between "human" and "beast," challenging the entire Western rationalist tradition which holds that the ability to reason abstractly is *the* defining human attribute. (In that tradition, women were often located on a scale somewhere between "man" and "beast," being deemed human but not quite rational.)

12   Politically, the new abolitionists, as many animal-welfare activists call themselves, eschew sentimentalism in favor of a tough-minded, insistent claim that animals, too, have rights, and that violating those rights constitutes oppression. It follows that animals must be liberated—and since they cannot liberate themselves in the face of overwhelming human hegemony, they require the help of liberators much as slaves did in the last century.

13   Thus, the rise of vocal movements for animal well-being has strong historic antecedents. What is remarkable about the current proliferation of efforts is their scope and diversity. Some proclaim animal "rights." Others speak of animal "welfare" or "protection." Still others find the term "equality" most apt, arguing that we should have "equal concern" for the needs of all sentient creatures.

14   When so many issues clamor for our attention, when so many problems demand our best attempts at fair-minded solution, why animals, why now? There is no simple explanation for the explosion of concern, but it is clearly linked to themes of peace and justice. Perhaps it can be summed up this way: those who are troubled by the question of who is or is not within the circle of moral concern; those who are made queasy by our use and abuse of living beings for our own ends; those whose dreams of a better world are animated by some notion of a peaceable kingdom, *should* consider our relationship with the creatures that inhabit our planet with us—the creatures that have helped sustain us and that may share a similar fate with us unless we find ways to deflect if not altogether end the destruction of our earthly habitat.

15   Dozens of organizations have sprung up, operating alongside—and sometimes in conflict with—such older mainline outfits as the Humane Society, the Anti-Vivisection League, and the World Wildlife Fund. Among the new groups are People for the Ethical Treatment of Animals (PETA), Trans-Species Unlimited, In Defense of Animals, the Gorilla Foundation, Primarily Primates, Humane Farming Association, Farm Animal Reform, Alliance for Animals, Citizens to End Animal Suffering and Exploitation (CEASE), Whale Adoption Project, Digit Fund—the list goes on and on.

16   Some organizations focus on the plight of animals on factory farms, especially the condition of anemic, imprisoned veal calves kept in darkness and unable to turn around until they are killed at fourteen weeks. Others are primarily concerned with conditions in the wild, where the habitat of the panda,

among others, is being destroyed or where great and wonderful creatures like the black rhinoceros and the African elephant or magnificent cats like the snow leopard or the Siberian tiger are marching toward extinction, victims of greedy buyers of illegal tusks or pelts.

17   Another group of activists clusters around the use of animals in such profitable pursuits as greyhound racing, where dogs by the hundreds are destroyed once they cease "earning their keep," or in tourist attractions where such wonderfully intelligent social beings as the orca and the dolphin are turned into circus freaks for profit. In the wild, orcas can live for up to one hundred years; in captivity, the average, sadly misnamed "killer whale" lasts about five.

18   Those wonderful chimpanzees that have been taught to speak to us through sign-language also arouse concern. If the funding ends or a researcher loses interest, they are sometimes killed, sometimes turned over to the less-than-tender mercies of laboratory researchers to be addicted to cocaine, infected with a virus, or subjected to some other terrible fate. Eugene Linden describes, in his study *Silent Partners,* chimps desperately trying to convey their pain and fear and sadness to uncomprehending experimenters.

19   Use of animals in war research is an industry in itself, though one usually shielded from public view. Monkeys are the most likely subjects of experiments designed to measure the effects of neutron-bomb radiation and the toxicity of chemical-warfare agents. Beginning in 1957, monkeys were placed at varying distances from ground zero during atomic testing; those that didn't die immediately were encaged so that the "progress" of their various cancers might be noted.

20   Radiation experiments on primates continue. Monkeys' eyes are irradiated, and the animals are subjected to shocks of up to twelve hundred volts. Junior researchers are assigned the "death watch," and what they see are primates so distressed that they claw at themselves and even bite hunks from their own arms or legs in a futile attempt to stem the pain. At a government proving ground in Aberdeen, Maryland, monkeys are exposed to chemical-warfare agents.

21   Dolphins, animals of exquisite intelligence, have been trained by the military in such scenarios as injecting carbon dioxide cartridges into Vietnamese divers and planting and removing mines. The Navy announced in April 1989 that it would continue its thirty-million-dollar clandestine program, expanded in the Reagan years, to put dolphins to military use. The aim, the *New York Times* reported, is to use dolphins captured in the Gulf of Mexico to guard the Trident Nuclear Submarine Base at Bangor, Washington.

22   Several years ago, when I was writing a book on women and war, I came across references to the use of dogs in Vietnam. When I called the Pentagon and was put through to the chief of military history, Southeast Asia Branch, he told me that no books existed on the subject, but he did send me an excerpt from the *Vietnam War Almanac* that stated the U.S. military "made

extensive use of dogs for a variety of duties in Vietnam, including scouting, mine detecting, tracking, sentry duty, flushing out tunnels, and drug detecting." Evidently, many of these dogs were killed rather than returned home, since it was feared their military training ill-suited them for civilian life.

23   Much better known, because of an increasingly successful animal-rights campaign, is the use of animals to test such household products as furniture polish and such cosmetics as shampoo and lipstick.

24   For years, industry has determined the toxicity of floor wax and detergents by injecting various substances into the stomachs of beagles, rabbits, and calves, producing vomiting, convulsions, respiratory illness, and paralysis. The so-called LD (lethal dose) 50 test ends only when half the animals in a test group have died. No anesthesia or pain killers are administered.

25   Dr. Andrew Rowan, assistant dean of the Tufts University School of Medicine, has offered persuasive evidence that such testing methods are crude and inaccurate measures of a product's safety. For one thing, a number of potentially significant variables, including the stress of laboratory living, are not taken into account, thus tainting any comparison of the effect of a given substance on human consumers.

26   The LD50 is notoriously unreproducible; the method for rating irritation is extremely subjective; and interspecies variations make test results highly suspect when applied to the human organism.

27   Most notorious of the "tests" deployed by the multibillion-dollar cosmetics industry is the Draize, which has been used since the 1940s to measure the potential irritative effects of products. Rabbits—used because their eyes do not produce tears and, therefore, cannot cleanse themselves—are placed into stocks and their eyes are filled with foreign substances. When a rabbit's eyes ulcerate—again, no pain killers are used—the cosmetics testers (who are usually not trained laboratory researchers) report a result. To call this procedure "scientific" is to demean authentic science.

28   Curiously, neither the LD50 test nor the Draize is required by law. They continue in use because manufacturers want to avoid alarming consumers by placing warning labels on products. More accurate methods available include computer simulations to measure toxicity, cell-culture systems, and organ culture tests that use chicken-egg membranes.

29   The disdainful response by corporate America to animal-protection concerns seems, at least in this area, to be undergoing a slow shift toward new laboratory techniques that abandon wasteful, crude, and cruel animal testing. Several large cosmetics manufacturers, including Revlon, have only recently announced that they will phase out animal testing, confirming the claim of animal-welfare groups that the tests are unnecessary.

30   Among the nastier issues in the forefront of the "animal wars" is the controversy over hunting and trapping.

31   It's estimated that about seventeen million fur-bearing animals (plus "trash" animals—including pets—the trapper doesn't want) are mangled each

year in steel-jaw leg-hold traps that tear an animal's flesh and break its bones. Many die of shock or starvation before the trapper returns. Some animals chew off part of a limb in order to escape. More than sixty countries now ban the leg-hold trap, requiring the use of less painful and damaging devices.

32   Protests against the manufacture, sale, and wearing of fur coats have been aggressively—and successfully—mounted in Western Europe. In Holland, fur sales have dropped 80 percent in the last few years. Radical groups in Sweden have broken into fur farms to release minks and foxes. An effort to shame women who wear fur has had enormous impact in Great Britain.

33   Similar campaigns have been mounted in the United States, but the fur industry is waging a well-financed counterattack in this country. Curiously, the industry's efforts have been tacitly supported by some rights-absolutists within feminism who see wearing a fur coat as a woman's right. It's difficult to think of a greater reductio ad absurdum of the notion of "freedom of choice," but it seems to appeal to certain adherents of upwardly mobile, choice-obsessed political orthodoxy.

34   Hunting may be the final frontier for animal-welfare groups. Because hunting is tied to the right to bear arms, any criticism of hunting is construed as an attack on constitutional freedoms by hunting and gun organizations, including the powerful and effective National Rifle Association. A bumper sticker I saw on a pickup truck in Northampton, Massachusetts, may tell the tale: MY WIFE, YES. MY DOG, MAYBE. BUT MY GUN, NEVER.

35   For some animal protestionists, the case against hunting is open and shut. They argue that the vast majority of the estimated 170 million animals shot to death in any given year are killed for blood sport, not for food, and that the offspring of these slaughtered creatures are left to die of exposure or starvation. Defenders of blood sports see them as a skill and a tradition, a lingering relic of America's great frontier past. Others—from nineteenth century feminists to the Norman Mailer of *Why Are We in Vietnam?*—link the national mania for hunting with a deeper thirst for violence.

36   I am not convinced there is an inherent connection between animal killing and a more general lust for violence, but some disquieting evidence is beginning to accumulate. Battered and abused women in rural areas often testify, for example, that their spouses also abused animals, especially cows, by stabbing them with pitchforks, twisting their ears, kicking them, or, in one reported incident, using a board with a nail in it to beat a cow to death.

37   But even people who recoil from hunting and other abuses of animals often find it difficult to condemn such experiments as those cited at the beginning of this article, which are, after all, conducted to serve "science" and, perhaps, to alleviate human pain and suffering. Sorting out this issue is no easy task if one is neither an absolute prohibitionist nor a relentless defender of the scientific establishment. When gross abuses come to light, they are often reported in ways that allow and encourage us to distance ourselves from emotional and ethical involvement. Thus the case of the baboons whose brains

were bashed in at the University of Pennsylvania prompted the *New York Times* to editorialize, on July 31, 1985, that the animals "seemed" to be suffering. They *were* suffering, and thousands of animals suffer every day.

38   Reasonable people should be able to agree on this: that alternatives to research that involves animal suffering must be vigorously sought; that there is no excuse for such conditions as dogs lying with open incisions, their entrails exposed, or monkeys with untreated, protruding broken bones, exposed muscle tissue, and infected wounds, living in grossly unsanitary conditions amidst feces and rotting food; that quick euthanasia should be administered to a suffering animal after the conclusion of a pain-inducing procedure; that pre- and postsurgical care must be provided for animals; that research should not be needlessly duplicated, thereby wasting animal lives, desensitizing generations of researchers, and flushing tax dollars down the drain.

39   What stands in the way of change? Old habits, bad science, unreflective cruelty, profit, and, in some cases, a genuine fear that animal-welfare groups want to stop all research dead in its tracks. "Scientists fear shackles on research," intones one report. But why are scientists so reluctant to promote such research alternatives as modeling, in-vitro techniques, and the use of lower organisms? Because they fear that the public may gain wider knowledge of what goes on behind the laboratory door. Surely those using animals should be able to explain themselves and to justify their expenditure of the lives, bodies, and minds of other creatures.

40   There is, to be sure, no justification for the harassment and terror tactics used by some animal-welfare groups. But the scientist who is offended when an animal-welfare proponent asks, "How would you feel if someone treated your child the way you treat laboratory animals?" should ponder one of the great ironies in the continuing debate: research on animals is justified on grounds that they are "so like us."

41   I *do* appreciate the ethical dilemma here. As a former victim of polio, I have thought long and hard for years about animal research and human welfare. This is where I come down, at least for now:

42   First, most human suffering in this world cannot be ameliorated in any way by animal experimentation. Laboratory infliction of suffering on animals will not keep people healthy in Asia, Africa, and Latin America. As philosopher Peter Singer has argued, we already know how to cure what ails people in desperate poverty; they need "adequate nutrition, sanitation, and health care. It has been estimated that 250,000 children die each week around the world, and that one-quarter of these deaths are by dehydration due to diarrhea. A simple treatment, already known and needing no animal experimentation, could prevent the deaths of these children."

43   Second, it is not clear that a cure for terrible and thus far incurable diseases such as AIDS is best promoted with animal experimentation. Some American experts on AIDS admit that French scientists are making more rapid progress toward a vaccine because they are working directly with human volunteers, a course of action Larry Kramer, a gay activist, has urged upon Ameri-

can scientists. Americans have been trying since 1984 to infect chimpanzees with AIDS, but after the expenditure of millions of dollars, AIDS has not been induced in any nonhuman animal. Why continue down this obviously flawed route?

44   Third, we could surely agree that a new lipstick color, or an even more dazzling floor wax, should never be promoted for profit over the wounded bodies of animals. The vast majority of creatures tortured and killed each year suffer for *nonmedical* reasons. Once this abuse is eliminated, the really hard cases having to do with human medical advance and welfare can be debated, item by item.

45   Finally, what is at stake is the exhaustion of the eighteenth century model of humanity's relationship to nature, which had, in the words of philosopher Mary Midgley, "built into it a bold, contemptuous rejection of the nonhuman world."

46   Confronted as we are with genetic engineering and a new eugenics, with the transformation of farms where animals ranged freely into giant factories where animals are processed and produced like objects, with callous behavior on a scale never before imagined under the rubric of "science," we can and must do better than to dismiss those who care as irrational and emotional animal-lovers who are thinking with their hearts (not surprisingly, their ranks are heavily filled with women), and who are out to put a stop to the forward march of rationalism and science.

47   We humans do not deserve peace of mind on this issue. Our sleep should be troubled and our days riddled with ethical difficulties as we come to realize the terrible toll one definition of "progress" has taken on our fellow creatures.

48   We must consider our meat-eating habits as well. Meat-eating is one of the most volatile, because most personal, of all animal-welfare questions. Meat-eaters do not consider themselves immoral, though hard-core vegetarians find meat-eating repugnant—the consumption of corpses. Such feminist theorists as Carol Adams insist that there is a connection between the butchering of animals and the historic maltreatment of women. Certainly, there is a politics of meat that belongs on the agenda along with other animal-welfare issues.

49   I, for one, do not believe humans and animals have identical rights. But I do believe that creatures who can reason in their own ways, who can suffer, who are mortal beings like ourselves have a value and dignity we must take into account. Animals are not simply a means to our ends.

50   When I was sixteen years old, I journeyed on a yellow school bus from LaPorte, Colorado, to Fairbanks, Iowa, on a 4-H Club "exchange trip." On the itinerary was a visit to a meat-packing plant in Des Moines. As vivid as the day I witnessed it is the scene I replay of men in blood-drenched coats "bleeding" pigs strung up by their heels on a slowly moving conveyer belt. The pigs— bright and sensitive creatures, as any person who has ever met one knows— were screaming in terror before the sharp, thin blade entered their jugular veins. They continued to struggle and squeal until they writhed and fell silent.

51   The men in the slaughter room wore boots. The floor was awash in blood. I was horrified. But I told myself this was something I should remember. For a few months I refused to eat pork. But then I fell back into old habits—this was Colorado farm country in the late 1950s, after all.

52   But at one point, a few years ago, that scene and those cries of terror returned. This time I decided I would not forget, even though I knew my peace of mind would forever be disturbed.

Topical Considerations

1. Do you believe that the breaking of laws and/or the practice of violence in the name of animal rights work is justified? Why or why not, and with what kinds of qualifications? Explain your answer.

2. How would you describe "human responsibility toward nonhuman creatures" (paragraph 5)? What is the responsibility of humans toward animals? What kinds of limitations should our "responsibility" place upon our behavior?

3. Reread Elshtain's article, looking for places where she links the issues of animal rights and feminism. Do you agree that these two movements have points in common? How do you see the relationship between the two?

4. In paragraph 14 Elshtain examines the reasons for the rise in attention to the animal rights cause, citing "themes of peace and justice." Do you agree that the concepts of peace and justice should apply to members of the animal world? Explain your answer.

5. How do you feel about the use of animals in war research? Should the ultimate goal of the research dictate when animals may or may not be used? Do you see a difference between using animals for medical research and using animals for military research? Why or why not?

6. What is your opinion of the role of corporations in the animal rights debate? Do large companies that stand to profit from animal experimentation have a moral responsibility to find alternative means for testing their products? When does profit become a factor in the animal rights debate? Explain.

7. Elshtain brings up the possibility that animal killing by hunting and trapping is linked "with a deeper thirst for violence." Do you agree with this statement? What other aspects of our society reflect a need for or love of violence (paragraph 35)?

Rhetorical Considerations

1. How do you feel about Elshtain's introduction? What kind of tone does it set for the rest of the essay? Is this an effective way to open an essay? Why or why not?

2. Examine the organization of Elshtain's essay. Discuss the movement from informative history to statement of position to statement of proposal. What are the advantages and disadvantages of Elshtain's organizational choices? Explain your answer.

3. From a rhetorical standpoint, what is your view of the author's presentation of information? Do you think there is too much information to be adequately processed by the reader? If so, how might this essay be restructured to facilitate reader comprehension?

4. Elshtain's article changes from an informative tone to a statement of position to a statement of proposal. Locate where these changes occur, and discuss possible transition options. Should there be smoother transitions between sections? What strategies might you use to make the article flow better?

5. Examine Elshtain's conclusion. Is it as effective as it could be? Explain your answer.

6. Paragraph 38 begins with the statement "Reasonable people should be able to agree on this." What is Elshtain's strategy in using such an appeal? Do you find this statement effective? Why or why not?

Writing Assignments

1. In paragraph 6 Elshtain calls the "emergence of the Western rationalist tradition" a major cause of the current animal rights crisis. She cites two philosophers, Descartes and Kant, in her argument. Write a paper in which you examine the possible relationship between this philosophic position and the debate over animal rights. Do you feel that there is a philosophical basis for the mistreatment of animals?

2. In paragraphs 15–17 Elshtain describes the activities of many different animal rights groups. Choose one group and write an essay stating why you might join that particular group and how you propose to contribute to their cause.

3. Elshtain claims that one of the problems of animal use in research is the "[desensitization] of generations of researchers" (paragraph 38). Write an essay describing your thoughts about this claim. Do you feel that researchers in charge of painful animal experiments run the risk of becoming desensitized to the implications of such experiments? Do you see any dangers in such desensitization? Or do you feel that desensitization is a necessary part of research?

4. Write a letter responding to Elshtain's call that we consider our meat-eating habits. Take a clear stand on the issue, explaining with specific details why you feel the way you do. In the letter tell why you would be willing or unwilling to give up eating meat.

OPPOSITIONS: LEGALIZATION OF DRUGS

The American Nightmare
William J. Bennett

Serving as Director of the Office of National Drug Control Policy under President Bush from 1989 to 1992, William Bennett had the opportunity to hear and measure every imaginable argument both for and against the legalization of drugs. In this essay he dramatically presents his unequivocable opposition to the legalization of drugs. He deems arguments for legalization as "astoundingly naive and ridiculous." In prose sometimes fiery and always charged, he dispels the idea that legalization will reduce crime rates, chides liberal intellectuals willing to make drugs more easily accessible, and closes with an impassioned discussion of how drugs erode the human spirit of dignity and responsibility.

William J. Bennett was President Bush's "drug czar" and President Reagan's secretary of education. Presently he is a senior editor at *National Review* and a fellow at various conservative think tanks such as the Hudson Institute and the Heritage Foundation. This essay is from his book *The De-Valuing of America* (1992). His most recent book is *The Moral Compass* (1995).

BEFORE YOU READ

If found guilty, what sentencing should a drug dealer face? Consider different degrees of the crime: If he or she sold drugs to children? If he or she sold marijuana? Crack cocaine? Heroin? Was a drug kingpin?

AS YOU READ

This essay originally appeared in a book by William J. Bennett entitled *The De-Valuing of America*. How is the concept of the "de-valuing of America" expressed in this essay? Give two examples.

1 . . . The issue trailed me almost everywhere I went. "Why not legalize drugs?" became the familiar refrain. Given what I had seen after only three months on the job—given what drugs were doing to our cities, to our communities, and to our children—I thought it was an astoundingly naive and ridiculous question. How could anybody be in favor of making drugs *more* accessible, cheaper, and morally permissible? Here again was this incredible gap between a select but influential group in favor of legalization—and the great body of the American people. A foreigner visiting this country, listening to television

newscasts and reading press reports, editorials, and columns, would think that the American people were about evenly divided between those who favored legalization and those who did not. In fact, the overwhelming majority (88 percent) of the American people reject drug legalization. Nevertheless, a tremendous amount of ink was spilled, commentary offered, and talk show discussions held on the merits of legalization. Some of the more prominent voices in favor of (or leaning toward) legalization included Ethan A. Nadelmann, a professor at Princeton University; Kurt Schmoke, mayor of Baltimore; U.S. District Judge Robert Sweet; Representative George Crockett (D-Michigan); *New York Times* columnist Anthony Lewis; *The Nation; The Economist;* and some writers and editors of *National Review*.

2   The legalization debate presented me with a somewhat unusual situation. Throughout my public life, most of my battles had been against leading liberal voices. But on this issue, I drew criticism from the political right flank, including a number of prominent conservatives: William F. Buckley, free-market economist Milton Friedman, former Secretary of State George Shultz, and others. So legalization seemed respectable at both ends of the political spectrum.

3   At first, I resisted getting heavily involved in this debate. As I told a congressional committee, I was hired to wage the war, not to discuss whether it was worth fighting. That issue had already been resolved.

4   Some members of my staff and a few friends told me that the argument was impossible to ignore and that the more we engaged the debate, the more arguments we advanced against legalization, the more support we would get from the public. So I began to more directly and more publicly take on the issue of legalization in interviews, speeches, public forums, and even on national television.

5   Appearing on CNN's "Larry King Live," I found legalization getting a very sympathetic hearing. But after three or four phone calls in favor of legalization, a man in Villa Park, California, asked, "Why build prisons? Get tough like [Saudi] Arabia. Behead the damned drug dealers. We're just too damned soft." I sensed that King thought the guy was a bit of a crank.

6   In response I said, "One of the things that I think is a problem is that we are not doing enough that is morally proportional to the nature of the offense. I mean, what the caller suggests is morally plausible. Legally, it's difficult."

7   I could see King's eyes light up. He asked for a clarification. "Behead?"

8   "Yeah. Morally I don't have any problem with it," I said.

9   "You would behead . . ." King began again.

10   "Somebody selling drugs to a kid?" I said. "Morally I don't have any problem with that at all. I mean, ask most Americans if they saw somebody out on the streets selling drugs to their kid what they would feel morally justified in doing—tear them limb from limb."

11   King then asked what we should do.

12   "What we need to do is find some constitutional and legally permissible way to do what this caller suggests, not literally to behead, but to make the

punishment fit the crime. And the crime is horrible." During the program I strongly rejected the calls for drug legalization and endorsed capital punishment for major drug sellers.

13   The next morning *The Washington Post* ran extended excerpts from the show. Newspapers from around the country ran headlines saying "Drug Czar Bennett: Beheading Fitting." The political cartoonists had a field day. Massachusetts Governor Michael Dukakis ripped my "beheading" comments. Many newspaper editorial writers and columnists were critical. Even Dick Darman got into the act, sending me a "decision memo" comparing French technology (the guillotine) with Saudi Arabian/British technology (the scimitar or broadax).

14   The reaction was illustrative. Many of the elites ridiculed my opinion. But it resonated with the American people because they knew what drugs were doing, and they wanted a morally proportionate response. The late Lee Atwater, then chairman of the Republican National Committee, had been traveling in South Carolina when the story hit the wires. An assistant of mine asked Lee what the reaction beyond the Beltway was. "Hell, Bill," Lee told us, "the people are saying, 'We've finally got somebody in Washington who understands what's at stake.'"

15   I later used the incident in speeches to gauge the moral sentiments of my audiences. I would ask, "If you saw a drug dealer selling drugs to your children, what would your impulse be?" Most audiences responded that their impulse would be to do violence to the drug dealer. And that impulse is right; it is simply a matter of channeling that impulse into law, of civilizing our retribution into a proper sense of justice. "This war [on drugs] is not for delicate sensibilities," I said in a speech at the National Press Club. "This is tough stuff. We need to get tough, we need to get tough as hell, we need to do it right now." But many of the critics didn't agree, and they couldn't quite figure out why I wasn't brought down, or even harmed, by my "intemperate" comments to Larry King. What they didn't recognize is that the moral sense of the American people is sound. They had had it with drugs. They had seen the devastation. And they wanted us to fight.

16   In Alaska—where personal possession of marijuana was legal—Senator Murkowski and others implored me to weigh in on behalf of a new initiative seeking to recriminalize possession of marijuana. Not surprisingly, the percentage of high school students using dope in Alaska was much higher than in the rest of the nation.

17   When I accepted the invitation, the prolegalization forces went into action. The "pothead lobby," as I called it, distributed fliers in Anchorage and Fairbanks saying "Confront the Drug Bizarre." But when I arrived, there was very little opposition. A few bedraggled sixties types (including one woman who introduced herself as "the Dragon Lady") asked me mostly incomprehensible questions at an assembly in Anchorage. But there was no major confrontation. It later became apparent why. When the "pothead lobby" passed out fliers announcing my visit, they had put the wrong date on them. I had

been saying for a long time that marijuana makes people inattentive and stupid. I rested my case.

18   The legalization debate is for all intent and purposes over. But even to call it a "debate" suggests that the arguments in favor of drug legalization are rigorous, substantial and serious. At first glance some of the arguments sound appealing. But on further inspection one finds that at bottom they are nothing more than a series of unpersuasive and even disingenuous ideas that more sober minds recognize as a recipe for a public policy disaster.

19   Legalization removes the incentive to stay away from a life of drugs. Some people are going to smoke crack whether it's legal or illegal. But by keeping it illegal, we maintain the criminal sanctions that persuade most people that the good life cannot be reached by dealing drugs. And that's exactly why we have drug laws—to make drug use a wholly unattractive choice.

20   One of the clear lessons of Prohibition is that when we had laws against alcohol, there *was* less consumption of alcohol, less alcohol-related disease, fewer drunken brawls, and a lot less public drunkenness. And contrary to myth, there is no evidence that Prohibition caused big increases in crime.

21   I am not suggesting that we go back to Prohibition. Alcohol has a long, complicated history in this country, and unlike drugs, the American people accept alcohol. They have no interest in going back to Prohibition. But at least advocates of legalization should admit that legalized alcohol, which is responsible for some 100,000 deaths a year, is hardly a model for drug policy. As the columnist Charles Krauthammer has pointed out, the question is not which is worse, alcohol or drugs. The question is, should we accept both legalized alcohol *and* legalized drugs? The answer is no.

22   If drugs were legalized, use would surely soar. In fact, we have just undergone a kind of cruel national experiment in which drugs became cheap and widely available: that experiment is called the crack epidemic. It was only when cocaine was dumped into the country, and a three-dollar vial of crack could be bought on street corners, that we saw cocaine use skyrocket—mostly among the poor and disadvantaged.

23   The price that American society would have to pay for legalized drugs would be intolerably high: more drug-related accidents at work, on the highway, and in the airways; bigger losses in worker productivity; hospitals filled with drug emergencies; more students on drugs, meaning more dropouts; more pregnant women buying legal cocaine, meaning more abused babies *in utero*. Add to this the added cost of treatment, social welfare, and insurance, and welcome to the Brave New World of drug legalization.

24   To listen to legalization advocates, one might think that street crime would disappear with the repeal of our drug laws. But our best research indicates that most drug criminals were into crime well *before* they got into drugs. Making drugs legal would subsidize their habit. They would continue to rob and steal to pay for food, for clothes, for entertainment. And they would carry on with their drug trafficking by undercutting the legalized price of drugs and

catering to teenagers who (I assume) would be nominally restricted from buying drugs at the corner drugstore.

25   In my travels around the country I have seen nothing to support the legalizers' argument that lower drug prices would reduce crime. Virtually everywhere I have gone, police and DEA agents have told me that crime rates are highest where crack is cheapest.

26   If we did legalize drugs, we would no doubt have to reverse the policy, like those countries that had experimented with broad legalization and decided it was a failure. In 1975 Italy liberalized its drug law and now has one of the highest heroin-related death rates in Western Europe. One Italian government official told me that the citizens of Italy are eager to recriminalize the use of drugs. They had seen enough casualties.

27   And what about our children? If we make drugs more accessible, there will be more harm to children, direct and indirect. There will be more cocaine babies and more child abuse. Children after all are among the most frequent victims of violent, drug-related crimes—crimes that have nothing to do with the cost of acquiring the drugs. In Philadelphia in 1987 more than half the child-abuse fatalities involved at least one parent who was a heavy drug user. Seventy-three percent of the child-abuse cases in New York City in 1987 involved parental drug use.

28   And it would be disastrous suddenly to switch signals on our children in school, whom we have been teaching, with great effect, that drug use is wrong. Why, they will ask, have we changed our minds?

29   The whole legalization argument is based on the premise that progress is impossible. But there is now incontrovertible, unmistakable evidence of progress in the war on drugs. . . . Now would be exactly the wrong time to surrender and legalize.

30   The legalization argument also revealed something troubling about some intellectuals. I elaborated on this point at Harvard's John F. Kennedy School on December 11, 1989:

> America's intellectuals—and here I think particularly of liberal intellectuals—have spent much of the last nine years decrying the social programs of two Republican administrations in the name of the defenseless poor. But today, on the one outstanding issue that disproportionately hurts the poor—that is wiping out many of the poor—where are the liberal intellectuals to be found? They are on the editorial and op-ed pages, and in magazines, telling us with a sneer that our drug policy won't work. . . . One would think that a little more concern and serious thought would come from those who claim to care deeply about America's problems.

31   John Jacob, president of the Urban League, has said, "Drugs kill more blacks than the Klan ever did. They're destroying more children and more families than poverty ever did." But many of the same intellectuals who strongly supported a "war on poverty" were AWOL in the war on drugs. I talked about this the next day on "Good Morning America."

The intellectuals are way out of sync with the American people. The American people have seen the drug problem. They've seen it up close, unfortunately, and don't have any tolerance for the idea of legalization. The problem with intellectuals—the reason that it's worth making a speech and making a point—is that they do form a lot of opinion. What they say affects what gets said on the editorial pages, what's regarded as respectable and reliable views on this. And right now, by their objections or their intransigence or disagreement, they're keeping us from moving ahead. And again, the thing I don't understand is why those who say they speak for those worse off in society aren't just full-fledged in this effort. Nothing is destroying poor communities in this country so effectively as drugs and yet we have people balking at the idea of waging a full-scale effort.

32   Legalization is a fine position for those who wish to stand out from the crowd and who have the luxury of speaking from a safe distance. But instead of sophistication, advocates for legalization should seek out a clearer connection with reality. They should take a close look at the devastating effects of drugs.

33   James Q. Wilson, Collins Professor of Management and Political Science at UCLA, has written:

> . . . Even now, when the dangers of drug abuse are well understood, many educated people still discuss the drug problem in almost every way except the right way. They talk about the "costs" of drug use and the "socioeconomic factors" that shape that use. They rarely speak plainly—drug use is wrong because it is immoral and it is immoral because it enslaves the mind and destroys the soul. It is as if it were a mark of sophistication for us to shun the language of morality in discussing the problems of mankind.

34   In the end drug use is wrong because of what it does to human character. It degrades. It makes people less than they should be by burning away a sense of responsibility, subverting productivity, and making a mockery of virtue.

35   Using drugs is wrong not simply because drugs create medical problems; it is wrong because drugs destroy one's moral sense. People addicted to drugs neglect their duties. The lure can become so strong that soon people will do nothing else but take drugs. They will neglect God, family, children, friends, and jobs—everything in life that is important, noble, and worthwhile—for the sake of drugs. This is why from the very beginning we posed the drug problem as a moral issue. And it was the failure to recognize the moral consequences of drug use that led us into the drug epidemic in the first place. In the late 1960s, many people rejected the language of morality, of right and wrong. Since then we have paid dearly for the belief that drug use was harmless and even an enlightening, positive thing.

36   Drugs undermine the necessary virtues of a free society—autonomy, self-reliance, and individual responsibility. The inherent purpose of using drugs is secession from reality, from society, and from the moral obligations

individuals owe their family, their friends, and their fellow citizens. Drugs destroy the natural sentiments and duties that constitute our human nature and make our social life possible. As our founders would surely recognize, for a citizenry to be perpetually in a drug-induced haze doesn't bode well for the future of self-government.

37   When all is said and done, the most compelling case that can be made against drug use rests on moral grounds. No civilized society—especially a self-governing one—can be neutral regarding human character and personal responsibility.

Topical Considerations

1. What was public opinion about drug legalization just before Bennett appeared on CNN's "Larry King Live" talk show? How was the media misrepresenting public opinion? Why does Bennett list names at the end of paragraph 1 and mention the criticism he received "from the political right"?
2. Speaking on King's talk show, does Bennett actually call for beheading drug dealers as a realistic, practical solution to contemporary U.S. problems with drugs? What distinction does Bennett make between morally justifiable and constitutional actions?
3. What was the public response to Bennett's endorsement of beheading? Did the media represent his views accurately? Did the media represent the majority of citizens' opinions accurately?
4. Where does Bennett mention marijuana use? Does he satisfactorily address the issues that Gorman has raised in his article on drug legalization? What do you think Gorman would say about Bennett's discussion of marijuana?
5. According to Bennett, if drugs were legalized what would happen to (a) the amount of drug use, (b) crime and accident rates, and (c) child abuse?
6. Why does Bennett believe drug legalization is immoral? Why doesn't he believe that we should give in and legalize drugs, since so many people use them whether or not they are made legal? How does having a law on the books send a message to people about society's values?
7. Why does Bennett believe drug use is immoral? After all, isn't the user only harming himself or herself by using drugs?

Rhetorical Considerations

1. How is the media represented in Bennett's discussion of the "beheading" comment in the anecdote about the "Larry King Live" talk show? What does he imply about the media's control over public opinion?
2. Why do you think Bennett spends so much time and offers so much detail about the one-liner he made on the Larry King show? How effective is this

rather long story as part of his argument? Do you think it distracts reader attention from his argument?

3. In paragraphs 16 and 17, what images does Bennett use to show the dangers of marijuana? Does Bennett convince you that marijuana should continue to be classed along with other drugs, and therefore kept illegal? That is, do you find his argument effective?

4. In paragraph 22, Bennett compares the result of drug legalization to the effect of the recent crack cocaine epidemic. Is this analogy sound? Are there any features of the crack epidemic that don't exactly match drug legalization? Do you think Bennett makes reasonable inferences about what would happen if drugs were legalized?

5. Bennett claims in paragraph 29 that "there is now . . . evidence of progress in the war on drugs." What kind of progress does he cite; does he show that drug use is declining? Is this progress convincing or effective in his argument?

6. Examine Bennett's conclusion to this article, in paragraphs 34–37. What strategies does he use to get readers to agree with him? What emotional chords does he hope to strike here—what bandwagon does he invite people to jump on?

Writing Assignments

1. Working with classmates, design a survey to poll members of your school on their use of and attitudes about drugs, legalization, and effects of drug use. Make sure that your respondents feel comfortable giving truthful answers—that they are assured anonymity, and that your questions are not leading. How do your results compare with Bennett's claims? What, if any, differences are attributable to the age and life experience of people you have asked to participate in your survey?

2. Bennett argues that laws not only regulate behavior, but send messages to people about social values. Do other authors in this section on ethical and moral issues (euthanasia, abortion, animals in research) make this claim? If so, where? Do they agree with Bennett, that prohibiting some personal choices is necessary?

3. Using your school's library, look up the history and current activities of the Urban League, mentioned briefly in paragraph 31. What are its goals and aims? Why does the Urban League include drug use on its agenda of issues?

It's Time to Legalize Marijuana
Peter Gorman

William Bennett opposes the legalization of all drugs and makes no distinction in this argument among narcotics such as heroin, LSD, or marijuana. Peter Gorman, on the other hand, defends the legalization of a single drug—marijuana. He debunks a number of what he considers "myths" about marijuana and goes on to pose the question of whether our country is better served by "devoting our energies to searching out and criminalizing marijuana smokers and growers, or whether we would be better off legalizing and controlling the plant's use."

Peter Gorman is executive editor of *High Times* magazine.

BEFORE YOU READ

Which drugs do you consider more dangerous than others? More addictive than others? More conducive to criminal behavior than others? Do you believe that all, none, or some drugs should be legalized?

AS YOU READ

Are you convinced that marijuana is as harmless as Gorman implies it is? Why or why not? What would William Bennett think about Gorman's attitude toward marijuana?

1   In November 1894, the Indian Hemp Drugs Commission published the findings of an exhaustive research project devoted to discovering whether the use of cannabis, known in India as bhang, should be allowed to continue or be made illegal in that country. Among the things looked at by the British commission were the drug's effect on both the infrequent and frequent user, its cost to society and the potential problems related to its possible criminalization.

2   In its conclusion, the commission stated: "The moderate use of these [cannabis] drugs is the rule . . . excessive use is comparatively exceptional. The moderate use practically produces no ill effects. In all but the most exceptional cases the injury from habitual moderate use is not appreciable. The excessive use may certainly be accepted as very injurious, though it must be admitted that in many excessive consumers the injury is not clearly marked. The injury done by excessive use is, however, confined almost exclusively to the consumer himself; the effect on society is rarely appreciable."

3   The commission went on to suggest that prohibition of cultivation or use of cannabis was not warranted. Instead, it recommended that controls be put into place to assure adequate taxation and to limit the extent of legal possession.

4   One hundred years later and half a world away, between 300,000 and 400,000 Americans are being arrested each year for marijuana use, more than three-quarters of them for simple possession. Several thousand of those wind up serving mandatory sentences of five years or more.

5   On June 12, a poll taken by Parade magazine showed that 75 percent of respondents favored legalizing marijuana for general use, and nearly 90

percent favored the drug's availability for medical use. At nearly the same time, the US Department of Health and Human Services released its annual Household Survey of Drug Use in America, which indicated that at least 9 million people had smoked marijuana during the previous month.

6   Given that marijuana doesn't look as if it's going away, it may be time to broach the question of whether we as a country are better served by devoting our energies to searching and criminalizing marijuana smokers and growers, or whether we would be better off legalizing and controlling the plant's use.

7   The question is three-pronged because of the various uses of the hemp (cannabis) plant: industrial, medical and as an intoxicant.

8   Practically speaking, there are several reasons to allow hemp's cultivation for industrial uses. It can be made into fabric, paper, plastics and also used as fuel and food. Its cultivation on a large scale would allow us to slowly convert from a culture based on cotton and tree fiber—both of which use an enormous amount and array of environmentally harmful pesticides and chemicals in their processing—to a renewable resource that requires minimal chemical processing. Nearly two dozen countries, including England, France and Switzerland, have legalized hemp for such industrial uses, and find ready markets for their products.

9   Additionally, the hemp plant's use as an alternative medicine—currently outlawed for all but eight Americans, who receive their medical marijuana from the federal government—would be a potential boon to the thousands of glaucoma sufferers who go blind each year, to thousands with spasticity disorders, and to hundreds of thousands of cancer and AIDS patients who are dealing with the size effects of chemotherapy and AZT treatments.

10   But the primary question in the public mind concerning legalizing hemp is what damage will society sustain if people are allowed to go to the store and purchase marijuana? Reefer madness stereotypes, formed during the days preceding marijuana's prohibition in 1937, persist in many quarters, largely through a compliant media. The Partnership for a Drug Free America, financed primarily by cigarette, alcohol and pharmaceutical companies, has been given free full-page ads in almost every major newspaper in the United States—many of which have huge timber holdings that would suffer from the legalization of industrial hemp—and thousands of free radio and television spots. Little space in those same media outlets has ever been devoted to the number of ads the partnership was forced to pull because they were complete fabrications. But the partnership is not the only culprit in perpetuating the stereotype of the marijuana smoker. As recently as April 19, The Lassen County (Calif.) Times printed a story stating that marijuana smoking produces brain damage, nervous system damage, lung cancer, immune system dysfunction, male impotence, damages women's eggs and causes birth defects. Additionally, the paper reported that smoking marijuana produces breasts in male smokers and that female marijuana smokers grow hair on their chest, face and arms.

11   None of the above is true, at least according to several US government-financed studies that, for more than 50 years, have investigated marijuana's effects on humans. Many of those myths, however, simply refuse to die. But while we have been waiting for the millions of breasted men and bearded women to appear, there has not been a single case of either cancer or emphysema ever attributed to marijuana smoking, nor a single death.

12   Which does not mean smoking pot is a free ride: Some people have severe, though short-term, anxiety reactions to it. Those people should simply not smoke. And though marijuana is not physically addictive, some people become psychologically dependent on it. The same could be said about people who crave potato chips or eat too many chocolate chip cookies, though the marijuana smoker—unless he is also a chip or cookie addict—will not eventually as a result die from the complications of clogged arteries, obesity, or heart failure.

13   Another stereotype that persists is the connection between marijuana smoking and crime. However, the US Bureau of Justice Statistics has never linked marijuana to criminal activity, other than the criminal activity of buying, using, growing or smuggling marijuana. Again, this is not to say that there are not criminals who smoke marijuana and continue to commit criminal actions. It is to say that non-criminals who smoke do not commit criminal actions.

14   But if marijuana is not a physical threat to the user, and does not pose a threat to society from resulting criminal activity, why does it remain illegal? One of the arguments prohibitionists use is that it leads to harder drugs. And yet the National Institute of Drug Abuse suggests that alcohol and cigarettes are the gateway drugs, not marijuana. Of the 70 million to 100 million Americans who have smoked marijuana, fewer than 2 percent have ever used heroin. A second, and currently very popular, argument by prohibitionists is that marijuana is as much as 30 times stronger now than it used to be. Again, US government statistics don't back up that claim. The most recent National Institutes of Health statistics, through its Marijuana Potency Monitoring project, show that the average THC content (the psychoactive ingredient in cannabis) of marijuana seized by law enforcement during 1992 was 1.9 percent, the lowest figure for pot potency since 1980.

15   Which leaves many of us wondering exactly why marijuana remains illegal, and what would be the consequence of legalizing it? Is there a single person in America today who, on any given day, is unable to find a joint? Probably not. Would use surge if it were legalized? Probably for the short term, though if the history of alcohol prohibition and its relegalization are any model, that surge would level off.

16   On the positive side, the production of tax dollars and the savings to the criminal justice system would be in the tens of billions annually. Thousands of disenfranchised and criminalized marijuana smokers and their families would be reenfranchised into the system. The potential medical benefits could be judged by patients and their doctors, rather than by the Drug Enforcement Ad-

ministration. Additionally, the industrial use of hemp could fuel several leading industries while providing important environmental benefits.

17   That the single loudest voice against legalization during the past several years has been the Partnership for a Drug Free America, with its drug company backing, ought to tell us something.

18   And what it ought to tell us is the same thing the Indian Hemp Drugs Commission spelled out 100 years ago: Regulate, tax and let people who are not harming anyone do what they want, since they are going to anyway.

Topical Considerations

1. What did a British commission decide to do about the use of marijuana in India a century ago?
2. What lesson does Gorman think the U.S. government should learn from the British commission's findings? Why is he displeased that the U.S. government has taken so long learning this lesson?
3. What statistics does Gorman cite from other published sources about marijuana use, potency, and public opinion?
4. What information does Gorman supply as factual, relying on his own expertise or knowledge as executive editor of *High Times* magazine?
5. What analogy does Gorman use between the present ban on marijuana use and Prohibition (a ban on alcohol by constitutional amendment during the 1920s)? Where else does he use the word "prohibition"?
6. What does Gorman imply about the Partnership for a Drug Free America in paragraph 17? Where else does he refer to this organization, and in what context? Where is he hinting that the prohibition on marijuana use has come from within our government?

Rhetorical Considerations

1. How effective is Gorman's reliance on the recommendation of the Indian Hemp Drugs Commission? Consider, for example, differences in scientific knowledge and social patterns between the commission's audience, British imperial rulers of India, and the late 20th century United States.
2. Look again at the sources Gorman cites (other than the British commission). What kinds of information does he draw from published, reputable sources? from his own expertise? What is the effect of his choice to rely on one type of source or the other?
3. Gorman claims that there are three separate roles that marijuana or hemp can play in the United States today: industrial, medical, and intoxicant. Why does he spend so much time arguing for marijuana's use as an intoxicant? Is this an effective strategy?

4. Does an argument for one kind of use reinforce his arguments for the other kinds of uses? How effective is Gorman's strategy of presenting marijuana use as a package deal, including all three kinds of uses?

5. How does Gorman defuse the item printed in a California newspaper, described in paragraph 10?

6. Why does Gorman refer to Prohibition in paragraph 15? What connotations does this moment in U.S. history have, which Gorman could use to his advantage in his own argument?

Writing Assignments

1. Obtain some newspaper or magazine advertisements against marijuana use, such as the ones he has mentioned in paragraph 10. What do you think Gorman would say about these advertisements? What sources do you think Gorman would have to cite to show why these advertisements are unfair?

2. Compare and contrast William Bennett's beliefs about how people would respond to legalization with Gorman's beliefs about how people would respond to legalization. Remember that Bennett is writing about a broad spectrum of drugs, not just marijuana, while Gorman writes exclusively about marijuana—so draw your comparisons of their ideas carefully.

3. Using your school's library, find out more about Prohibition, the 18th Amendment to the U.S. Constitution. What were the rationales for enacting and for repealing this law? What were its effects on people's behavior and attitudes about alcohol? (Be sure to consult several different kinds of sources, such as encyclopedias, scholarly books and articles, public policy analyses, and newspaper archives.) Then compare Prohibition to the current ban on marijuana. Is Gorman's analogy sound?

4. Using your school's library, find out more about the medical or industrial uses of marijuana and hemp. Based on your findings, would you recommend legalizing marijuana for these specific uses, leaving its use as a recreational drug illegal? Why or why not?

CHAPTER

13

FREEDOM OF EXPRESSION

One of the pillars of Jeffersonian democracy is freedom of speech. It is a guarantee promised by the First Amendment of the U.S. Constitution—a guarantee designed to encourage the free exchange of ideas and beliefs and political debate. However, the fact that speech is protected by the First Amendment does not necessarily mean that it is always right, proper, or civil. What happens when the right of one person to express himself or herself conflicts with the rights of another to be free from verbal abuse? What happens when our television and movie screens are filled with violence? What happens when free expression runs up against community values? At what point does the degree of violence or offensiveness of expression warrant censorship? And, at what point does censorship begin to rock the pillars of democracy? These are some of the questions that are inevitably raised in an open society such as ours. Questions that clarify the issues are debated in this chapter.

Everyone agrees that violence dominates our movie and television screens. And many are convinced that viewing violence causes violent behavior. But no one agrees on a response. Is tolerance the answer? Or is outright censorship? Or something in between? The next three pieces represent the wide span of reactions. In "Honey, I Warped the Kids" Carl M. Cannon surveys the thousands of studies conducted since 1954 on the relationship between television violence and the real thing. In light of a preponderance of evidence linking the two, Cannon argues for restrictions on television mayhem. On the other hand, Robert Scheer looks at the same evidence and shares with Cannon the conviction that television violence and aggression are linked. But he argues passionately that government censorship is dangerous. In "In Praise of Gore," Andrew Klavan makes no apologies for violence on the screen. In fact he celebrates it. He opposes censorship of any kind and sees censorship as a "guilt-ridden slap at ourselves for taking pleasure in make believe acts."

One of the more difficult challenges to higher education has to do with First Amendment rights. Does the right to freedom of expression prevent universities from curbing certain forms of speech on campus—namely, racist, sexist and other offensive discourse? In "Regulating Racist Speech on Campus,"

Charles R. Lawrence argues that allowing people to demean other members of a college community violates student victims' rights to education. Taking the opposing side in "Free Speech on Campus," Nat Hentoff says that censorship of hate language threatens the very nature of a university and the spirit of academic freedom while making the forces of hate more dangerous. The next essay, "In Praise of Censure," responds to some of the same issues debated above: antifemale literature, obscene language, defamatory utterances against minority groups, homosexuals, and others. Yet, instead of a number of laws restricting offensive expression, Garry Wills calls for measures that fall between pained tolerance and outright suppression. He recommends censure, the free expression of moral disapproval.

We close with our two "opposition" pieces devoted to the debate on pornography—a matter which for years has tested the limits of the First Amendment and divided feminists. Although some people call for censorship laws protecting the civil rights of women, others fear a threat to the broad protection of free expression found in the Constitution. In our first "opposition" piece, "Let's Put Pornography Back in the Closet," Susan Brownmiller argues that the First Amendment should not protect obscene materials. In the opposing piece, "I Am a First Amendment Junkie," Susan Jacoby takes the position that the selective abolishment of First Amendment protection would weaken its democratic intent. She also points to the subjective nature of taste—the fact that what is obscene to one may be only mildly objectionable to another and even pleasant to a third.

MOVIE AND TELEVISION VIOLENCE

Honey, I Warped the Kids
Carl M. Cannon

The debate over the relationship between television violence and actual violence is not new. As early as 1954, the first congressional hearings examined this relationship. Since then as many as 3000 studies on television and violence have been completed. In this essay, Carl M. Cannon calls on that large body of research. He uses capsule summaries of the research to fuel his argument that, since almost all experts agree that television can cause aggressive behavior, it is reasonable to try to curb the amount of violence on television, especially programming directed at children. Carl M. Cannon is the White House correspondent for the *Baltimore Sun*. This article first appeared in *Mother Jones,* in 1993.

BEFORE YOU READ

Slasher films such as *The Texas Chainsaw Massacre, Friday the 13th, Part 2* and *Maniac* are seen as causes of insensitivity, aggression, and violence among the young viewers, particularly males, of these films. Is this an accurate judgment according to your experience? If so, would you argue that such films be censored?

AS YOU READ

Examine the author's comments on the studies he summarizes. Are these summaries adequate? In depth? Too sketchy? Evaluate the way the author uses this evidence to prove his case.

1   Tim Robbins and Susan Sarandon implore the nation to treat Haitians with AIDS more humanely. Robert Redford works for the environment. Harry Belafonte marches against the death penalty.

2   Actors and producers seem to be constantly speaking out for noble causes far removed from their lives. They seem even more vocal and visible now that there is a Democrat in the White House. But in the one area over which they have control—the excessive violence in the entertainment industry—Hollywood activists remain silent.

3   This summer, Washington was abuzz with talk about the movie *Dave,* in which Kevin Kline stars as the acting president. But every time I saw an ad featuring Kline, the movie I couldn't get out of my head as *Grand Canyon.* There are two scenes in it that explain much of what has gone wrong in America.

4   Kline's character has a friend, played by Steve Martin, who is a producer of the B-grade, violent movies that Hollywood euphemistically called "action" films. But after an armed robber shoots Martin's character in the leg, he has an epiphany.

5   "I can't make those movies any more," he decides. "I can't make another piece of art that glorifies violence and bloodshed and brutality. . . . No more exploding bodies, exploding buildings, exploding anything. I'm going to make the world a better place."

6   A month or two later, Kline calls on Martin at his Hollywood studio to congratulate him on the "new direction" his career has taken.

7   "What? Oh that," Martin says dismissively. "Fuck that. That's over. I must have been delirious for a few weeks there."

8   He then gins up every hoary excuse for Hollywood-generated violence you've ever heard, ending with: "My movies reflect what's going on; they don't make what's going on."

9   This is Hollywood's last line of defense for why it shows murder and mayhem on the big screen and the little one, in prime time and early in the morning, to children, adolescents, and adults:

10   We don't cause violence, we just report it.

11   Four years ago, I joined the legion of writers, researchers, and parents who have tried to force Hollywood to confront the more disturbing truth. I wrote a series of newspaper articles on the massive body of evidence that establishes a direct cause-and-effect relationship between violence on television and violence in society.

12   The orchestrated response from the industry—a series of letters seeking to discredit me—was something to behold.

13   Because the fact is, on the one issue over which they have power, the liberals in Hollywood don't act like progressive thinkers; they act like, say, the National Rifle Association:

14   Guns don't kill people, people kill people.

15   We don't cause violence in the world, we just reflect it.

16   The first congressional hearings into the effects of television violence took place in 1954. Although television was still relatively new, its extraordinary marketing power was already evident. The tube was teaching Americans what to buy and how to act, not only in advertisements, but in dramatic shows, too.

17   Everybody from Hollywood producers to Madison Avenue ad men would boast about this power—and seek to utilize it on dual tracks: to make money and to remake society along better lines.

18   Because it seemed ludicrous to assert that there was only one area—the depiction of violence—where television did not influence behavior, the television industry came up with this theory: Watching violence is cathartic. A violent person might be sated by watching a murder.

19   The notion intrigued social scientists, and by 1956 they were studying it in earnest. Unfortunately, watching violence turned out to be anything but cathartic.

20   In the 1956 study, one dozen four-year-olds watched a "Woody Woodpecker" cartoon that was full of violent images. Twelve other preschoolers watched "Little Red Hen," a peaceful cartoon. Then the children were observed. The children who watched "Woody Woodpecker" were more likely to hit other children, verbally accost their classmates, break toys, be disruptive, and engage in destructive behavior during free play.

21   For the next thirty years, researchers in all walks of the social sciences studied the question of whether television causes violence. The results have been stunningly conclusive.

22   "There is more published research on this topic than on almost any other social issue of our time," University of Kansas Professor Aletha C. Huston, chairwoman of the American Psychological Association's Task Force on Television and Society, told Congress in 1988. "Virtually all independent scholars agree that there is evidence that television can cause aggressive behavior."

23   There have been some three thousand studies of this issue—eighty-five of them major research efforts—and they all say the same thing. Of the eighty-

five major studies, the only one that failed to find a causal relationship between television violence and actual violence was paid for by NBC. When the study was subsequently reviewed by three independent social scientists, all three concluded that it actually did demonstrate a causal relationship.

24   Some highlights from the history of TV violence research:

25   • In 1973, when a town in mountainous western Canada was wired for television signals, University of British Columbia researchers observed first- and second-graders. Within two years, the incidence of hitting, biting, and shoving increased 160 percent in those classes.

26   • Two Chicago doctors, Leonard Eron and Rowell Huesmann, followed the viewing habits of a group of children for twenty-two years. They found that watching violence on television is the single best predictor of violent or aggressive behavior later in life, ahead of such commonly accepted factors as parents' behavior, poverty, and race.

27   "Television violence effects youngsters of all ages, of both genders, at all socioeconomic levels and all levels of intelligence," they told Congress in 1992. "The effect is not limited to children who are already disposed to being aggressive and is not restricted to this country."

28   • Fascinated by an explosion of murder rates in the United States and Canada that began in 1955, after a generation of North Americans had come of age on television violence, University of Washington Professor Brandon Centerwall decided to see if the same phenomenon could be observed in South Africa, where the Afrikaner-dominated regime had banned television until 1975.

29   He found that eight years after TV was introduced—showing mostly Hollywood-produced fare—South Africa's murder rate skyrocketed. His most telling finding was that the crime rate increased first in the white communities. This mirrors U.S. crime statistics in the 1950s and especially points the finger at television, because whites were the first to get it in both countries.

30   Bolder than most researchers, Centerwall argues flatly that without violent television programming, there might be as many as ten thousand fewer murders in the United States each year.

31   • In 1983, University of California, San Diego, researcher David P. Phillips wanted to see if there was a correlation between televised boxing matches and violence in the streets of America.

32   Looking at crime rates after every televised heavyweight championship fight from 1973 to 1978, Phillips found that the homicide rate in the United States rose by an average of 11 percent for approximately one week. Phillips also found that the killers were likely to focus their aggression on victims similar to the losing fighter: if he was white, the increased number of times were mostly white. The converse was true if the losing fighter was black.

33   • In 1988, researchers Daniel G. Linz and Edward Donnerstein of the University of California, Santa Barbara, and Steven Penrod of the University of Wisconsin studied the effects on young men of horror movies and "slasher" films.

34   They found that depictions of violence, not sex, are what desensitizes people.

35   They divided male students into four groups. One group watched no movies, a second watched nonviolent, X-rated movies, a third watched teenage sexual-innuendo movies, and a fourth watched the slasher films *Texas Chainsaw Massacre, Friday the 13th Part 2, Maniac,* and *Toolbox Murders.*

36   All the young men were placed on a mock jury panel and asked a series of questions designed to measure their empathy for an alleged female rape victim. Those in the fourth group measured lowest in empathy for the specific victim in the experiment—and for rape victims in general.

37   The anecdotal evidence is often more compelling than the scientific studies. Ask any homicide cop from London to Los Angeles to Bangkok if television violence induces real-life violence and listen carefully to the cynical, knowing laugh.

38   Ask David McCarthy, police chief in Greenfield, Massachusetts, why nineteen-year-old Mark Branch killed himself after stabbing an eighteen-year-old female college student to death. When cops searched his room they found ninety horror movies, as well as a machete and a goalie mask like those used by Jason, the grisly star of *Friday the 13th.*

39   Ask the families of thirty-five young men who committed suicide by playing Russian roulette after seeing the movie *The Deer Hunter.*

40   Ask George Gavito, a lieutenant in the Cameron County, Texas, sheriff's department, about a cult that sacrificed at least thirteen people on a ranch west of Matamoros, Mexico. The suspects kept mentioning a 1986 movie, *The Believers,* about rich families who engage in ritual sacrifice. "They talk about it like that had something to do with changing them," Gavito recalled later.

41   Ask LAPD lieutenant Mike Melton about Angel Regino of Los Angeles, who was picked up after a series of robberies and a murder in which he wore a blue bandanna and fedora identical to those worn by Freddy, the sadistic anti-hero of *Nightmare on Elm Street.* In case anybody missed the significance of his disguise, Regino told his victims that they would never forget him, because he was another Freddy Krueger.

42   Ask Britain Home Secretary Douglas Hurd, who called for further restrictions on U.S.-produced films after Michael Ryan of Hungerford committed Britain's worst mass murder in imitation of *Rambo,* massacring sixteen people while wearing a U.S. combat jacket and a bandoleer of ammunition.

43   Ask Sergeant John O'Malley of the New York Police Department about a nine-year-old boy who sprayed a Bronx office building with gunfire. The boy

explained to the astonished sergeant how he learned to load his Uzi-like firearm: "I watch a lot of TV."

44   Or ask Manteca, California, police detective Jeff Boyd about thirteen-year-old Juan Valdez, who, with another teenager, went to a man's home, kicked him, stabbed him, beat him with a fireplace poker, and then choked him to death with a dog chain.

45   Why, Boyd wanted to know, had the boys poured salt in the victim's wounds?

46   "Oh, I don't know," the youth replied with a shrug. "I just seen it on TV."

47   Numerous groups have called, over the years, for curbing television violence: the National Commission on the Causes and Prevention of Violence (1969), the U.S. Surgeon General (1972), the Canadian Royal Commission (1976), the National Institute of Mental Health (1982), the U.S. Attorney General's Task Force on Family Violence (1984), the National Parents Teachers Association (1987), and the American Psychological Association (1992).

48   During that time, cable television and movie rentals have made violence more readily available while at the same time pushing the envelope for network TV. But even leaving aside cable and movie rentals, a study of television programming from 1967 to 1989 showed only small ups and downs in violence, with the violent acts moving from one time slot to another but the overall violence rate remaining pretty steady—and pretty similar from network to network.

49   "The percent of prime-time programs using violence remains more than seven out of ten, as it has been for the entire twenty-two-year-period," researchers George Gerbner of the University of Pennsylvania Annenberg School for Communication and Nancy Signorielli of the University of Delaware wrote in 1990. For the past twenty-two years, they found, adults and children have been entertained by about sixteen violent acts, including two murders, in each evening's prime-time programming.

50   They also discovered that the rate of violence in children's programs is three times the rate in prime-time shows. By the age of eighteen, the average American child has witnessed at least eighteen thousand simulated murders on television.

51   By 1989, network executives were arguing that their violence was part of a larger context in which bad guys get their just desserts.

52   "We have never put any faith in mechanical measurements, such as counting punches or gunshots," said NBC's Alan Gerson. "Action and conflict must be evaluated within each specific dramatic context."

53   "Our policy," added Alfred R. Schneider of ABC, ". . . makes clear that when violence is portrayed [on TV], it must be reasonably related to plot development and character delineation."

54   Of course, what early-childhood experts could tell these executives is that children between the ages of four and seven simply make no connection between the murder at the beginning of a half-hour show and the man led

away in handcuffs at the end. In fact, psychologists know that very young children do not even understand death to be a permanent condition.

55   But all of the scientific studies and reports, all of the wisdom of cops and grief of parents have run up against Congress's quite proper fear of censorship. For years, Democratic Congressman Peter Rodino of New Jersey chaired the House Judiciary Committee and looked at calls for some form of censorship with a jaundiced eye. At a hearing five years ago, Rodino told witnesses that Congress must be a "protector of commerce."

56   "Well, we have children that we need to protect," replied Frank M. Palumbo, a pediatrician at Georgetown University Hospital and a consultant to the American Academy of Pediatrics. "What we have here is a toxic substance in the environment that is harmful to children."

57   Arnold Fege of the national PTA added, "Clearly, this committee would not protect teachers who taught violence to children. Yet why would we condone children being exposed to a steady diet of TV violence year after year?"

58   Finally there is a reason to hope for progress.

59   Early this summer, Massachusetts Democrat Edward Markey, chair of the House Energy and Commerce subcommittee on telecommunications, said that Congress may require manufacturers to build TV sets with a computer chip so that parents could block violent programs from those their children could select.

60   He joins the fight waged by Senator Paul Simon, a liberal Democrat from Illinois. Nine years ago, Simon flipped on a hotel television set hoping to catch the late news. "Instead," he has recalled many times, "I saw a man being sawed in half with a chainsaw, in living color."

61   Simon was unsettled by the image and even more unsettled when he wondered what repeatedly looking at such images would do to the mind of a fourteen-year-old.

62   When he found out, he called television executives, who told him that violence sells and that they would be at a competitive disadvantage if they acted responsibly.

63   Why not get together and adopt voluntary guidelines? Simon asked.

64   Oh, that would be a violation of antitrust law, they assured him.

65   Simon called their bluff in 1990 by pushing through Congress a law that allowed a three-year moratorium on antitrust considerations so that the industry could discuss ways to jointly reduce violence.

66   Halfway through that time, however, they had done nothing, and an angry Simon denounced the industry on the Senate floor. With a push from some prominent industry figures, a conference was set for this August 2 in Los Angeles.

67   This spring, CBS broadcast group president Howard Stringer said his network was looking for ways to cut back on violence in its entertainment, because he was troubled by the cost to society of continuing business-as-usual.

68   "We must admit we have a responsibility," he said.

69   Jack Valenti, the powerful head of the Motion Picture Association of America, wrote to producers urging them to participate in the August 2 conference. "I think it's more than a bunch of talk," Simon said. "I think this conference will produce some results. I think the industry will adopt some standards."

70   The federal government, of course, possesses the power to regulate the airwaves through the FCC, and Simon and others believe that this latent power to control violence—never used—has put the fear of God in the producers. He also thinks some of them are starting to feel guilty.

71   "We now have more people in jail and prison per capita than any country that keeps records, including South Africa," Simon says. "We've spent billions putting people behind bars, and it's had no effect on the crime rate. None. People realize there have to be other answers, and as they've looked around, they have settled on television as one of them."

72   Maybe Simon is right. Maybe Hollywood executives will get together and make a difference.

73   Or maybe, like Steven Martin's character in *Grand Canyon,* producers and directors from New York to Beverly Hills will wake up after Simon's antitrust exemption expires December 1, shake off the effects of their holiday hangovers, and when asked about their new commitment to responsible filmmaking, answer:

74   "What? Oh that. Fuck that. That's over. We must have been delirious for a few weeks there."

Topical Considerations

1. Does Cannon convince you that a relationship exists between televised and real violence? If he did, what was the most persuasive part of his argument? If he didn't, why not?

2. Explain why, for Cannon, the two scenes from the film *Grand Canyon* described in paragraphs 3–8 "explain much of what has gone wrong in America" (paragraph 3). Did you find Cannon's reference to the film effective? Why or why not?

3. Summarize the television industry's response to calls for a decrease in media violence over the past 25 years. How have the attitudes of network executives toward the problem changed? In what ways, if any, has violent television programming changed?

4. What solution to the problem of media violence does Cannon support? What proposed solutions to the problem does he reject? To what extent has he convinced you that his solution is right?

5. Cannon attributes the lack of congressional response to media violence to a "quite proper fear of censorship" (paragraph 55). Explain how Cannon ad-

dresses this fear. Do you find his discussion of censorship satisfying? Why or why not?

Rhetorical Considerations

1. Compare the evidence of the "scientific studies" Cannon cites in paragraphs 20–36 to the "anecdotal evidence" described in paragraphs 37–46. Which evidence, anecdotal or scientific, do you find more compelling, and why?
2. Analyze the analogy Cannon makes in paragraph 13 between "the liberals in Hollywood" and "the National Rifle Association." Do you find the comparison convincing? How are these two issues similar? How do they differ?
3. This relatively brief essay consists of 74 separate paragraphs. How did the existence of so many short paragraphs affect your response as a reader? What does the proliferation of short paragraphs tell you about the purpose, content, or method of Cannon's argument?
4. What assumptions does Cannon make about his audience; how can you tell? To what extent is Cannon effective in addressing this audience?
5. Describe the tone of Cannon's in his essay. Cite specific words, passages, and rhetorical strategies that create this particular tone.
6. Cannon ends his essay by returning to a line from the movie *Grand Canyon* which he had quoted in context at the beginning of his essay. Explain why you do or do not find Cannon's use of this anecdote effective as an ending.

Writing Assignments

1. Collect the "series of newspaper articles" (paragraph 11) in which Cannon wrote about television violence, as well as the "series of letters" written by the entertainment industry in rebuttal (paragraph 12). Then write an essay arguing that Cannon's credibility is either bolstered or damaged by knowledge of this controversy.
2. Write an essay arguing that *The Deer Hunter* (a film Cannon mentions in paragraph 39) does not glorify violence, and support your argument with detailed examples from the film.
3. Assign each member of your group one of the four major television networks to "cover" for an evening. Each student, with the help of program guides, should analyze the violent content of their network, tabulating each violent act and evaluating its context. Pool your observations in order to write a group report analyzing how responsibly networks depict violence during that one evening.

Violence Is Us

Robert Scheer

Like Carl M. Cannon in the previous essay, Robert Scheer agrees that viewing violence desensitizes people, particularly children, to the effects of violence. But he does not see censorship in the form of government intervention as the solution to this problem. Instead, he argues a very pragmatic solution rooted in a Hobsian view of human nature: Acknowledge that the baser human appetite for violence will generate a market in television or film. Withdraw your support of the market by "turning the damn thing off."

Robert Scheer is a contributing editor of the *Los Angeles Times*. The article originally appeared in *The Nation* in 1993.

BEFORE YOU READ

Can people's taste or predilection for viewing violence be altered or changed? Or is the viewing of violence an unalterable appetite? Is there any point in trying to make this change? Or is it best to allow a passive outlet for it?

AS YOU READ

Scheer's tone is matter-of-fact and cool. Find examples of cool dispassionate statements whose content some readers might find startling or objectionable.

1   Once again Congressional committees are holding hearings on TV violence, and network executives, sincere visages firmly in place, are promising to clean up their act. Attorney General Janet Reno testified that if they don't, "government should respond."

2   There is something so beside the point about this handwringing, which has gone on since 1952, when the first Congressional hearing on TV violence was held. In 1968 a national commission headed by Milton Eisenhower warned: "We are deeply troubled by the television's constant portrayal of violence . . . in pandering to a public preoccupation with violence that television itself has helped to generate."

3   Of course, violence and base stupidity on TV and in the movies is excessive and getting worse. With the proliferation of cable channels, the market has become much more competitive, and violence sells. Hardly a night of channel-flipping goes by when my cable service doesn't offer up several truly grotesque chainsaw massacre–type films complete with dismembered parts and spurting blood.

4   Then, too, there are the cleaner assassinations presented on the networks both in their entertainment and local news hours. Remember the orgy of voyeurism, with three separate network movies devoted to the Amy Fisher–Joey Buttafuoco story? So-called news shows featuring real-life crime represent a major segment of entertainment scheduling. The fatal graveside shooting of a woman by her ex-spouse, captured by a television news camera, was gratuitously "teased" during the evening in many markets to get people to watch the news that night.

5   Nor do I deny the claims of most experts that viewing violence desensitizes people, particularly children, to the actual effects of violence, leaving them more likely to act out in antisocial ways. As the American Psychological Association reported to Congress in 1988, "Virtually all independent scholars agree that there is evidence that television can cause aggressive behavior."

6   More than 200 major studies support the common-sense suspicion that watching endless hours of violence is a public health menace. Those same studies demonstrate, although the pro-censorship prudes will never accept it, that the violent R-rated movies—not the sexually explicit X-rated ones—desensitize men to sexual violence. (As an example of this weirdly skewed double standard, wannabe censor Rev. Donald Wildmon took out full-page ads attacking *NYPD Blue,* not for its explicit violence—six homicides in the first episode—but rather because of a nude lovemaking scene, calling it "soft-core pornography.")

7   Another thing those studies show is that the poorer a family is, meaning the more vulnerable and desperate, the more hours they will spend in front of the television set. Children in poverty are most often left alone with the TV as the only available babysitter.

8   It can hardly be a good thing that children's shows two years ago reached an all-time high of thirty-two violent incidents per hour and that nine in ten children's programs involve violence. An authoritative study by George Gerbner of the University of Pennsylvania indicated that the average 16-year-old has witnessed 200,000 violent acts on TV, including 33,000 murders. Given the ease with which children can get guns in this society, there has to be some connection between the ease with which citizens are blown away by teenagers on television and in what passes for real life. And when they do it in real life they can be assured of their fifteen minutes of fame with top billing on the nightly local news.

9   Wayne LaPierre, vice president of the National Rifle Association, had a good point when he complained recently, "It galls us that every night we get lectured by ABC, NBC and CBS News, and then they go to their entertainment programming and show all kinds of gratuitous violence." Hypocrites they are, and the voluntary labeling code that the network executives recently adopted in an effort to head off Congressional prohibitions on violent programing will change nothing. Although 72 percent of Americans polled by Times-Mirror say that we have too much violence on TV and it leads to higher crime rates,

many of them must be tuning in, or the television moguls wouldn't be scheduling such fare.

10   Maybe it is time to face the fact that we have all this mayhem in our art and our lives because we like violence. Or if we don't actually like it, we need it. Why else would we favor local news programs that stress ambulance-chasing "action news"? Whether it's local or foreign news, our attention is grabbed completely only when death and destruction are at hand. That's what the endless focus groups conducted by news organizations report. It is true, as Steven Bochco, creator of *NYPD Blue,* has stated, that the violence issue on prime time is a "bogus issue," because "there's more violence on the 5 o'clock news than anything you'll see on the networks during prime time."

11   Anyway, how can you control it without putting decision-making into the hands of small-minded censors? What are the guidelines? Some reasonable ones, to cut the harmful effects on children, were suggested by University of Michigan psychology professor Leonard Eron, who is the dean of research in this area. "Gratuitous violence that is not necessary to the plot should be reduced or eliminated," is one that the networks say they accept. Another we call agree on is that the "devastating effects of violence, the permanence of its consequences . . . should be made clear," meaning you hurt or die from gunshot wounds. So far so good, but what about when he tells us, "Perpetrators of violence should not be rewarded for their violent acts," and that "those who act aggressively should be punished"? Those last two, while admirable goals, would distort a reality in which many criminals do get away with their crimes. Do we want television writers to lie to us? Don't we adults need to face up to the truth that crime is out of control?

12   Maybe adults should watch what they want, but should children, who are by definition impressionable, be exposed to a steady diet of mind-numbing violence laced with general stupidity? No, they shouldn't, but is this an issue the government or other would-be censors ought to get involved with?

13   The answer is, They are already involved, but despite endless guidelines for children's television, the fare is nastier than ever. The reason is that every regulation produces just that much more ingenuity on the part of the so-called creative people who make this junk. They are a crafty bunch and will always find some way of getting to the kids with the most primitive jolt.

14   Take the much-discussed *Beavis and Butt-Head* show, which now leads the race for the lowest common denominator. When a 5-year-old in Ohio burned the family trailer to the ground, his mother blamed the show, her son's favorite, which had shown the two idiot characters setting fire to all sorts of objects. Hey, no problem, arson was taken out of the show in response to public outrage. There were the expected calls to ban *Beavis,* but no one stopped to ask the obvious question: Why had that mother let her 5-year-old watch endless hours of this repulsive show?

15   I asked the same question after reading a story in the *Los Angeles Times* about firefighters having to visit the schools of Orange County, California, to

warn the kids that setting fires at home is a no-no. In one class, almost all the 12-year-olds said they watched *Beavis and Butt-Head* regularly and then began chanting the call of the show's lead, "Burn, burn, burn." That was in the conservative white upper-middle-class community of Mission Viejo, one of those planned paradises. Again, why did all those parents allow their kids to watch the show? It is absurd to suggest that the government step in to censor viewing that parents have acquiesced in.

16   The more important question is, Why do the children of paradise delight in this and other stupidities? I don't really know the full answer but it can't be, as Dan Quayle charged in the last election, that the cultural elite of Hollywood has seized their minds. Orange County voted overwhelmingly for Quayle and his running mate, the parents have thrown up the strongest defenses against Satan and his permissiveness, and church, Little League and Boy Scout attendance is very high.

17   One answer provided by the creators of this stuff is that it doesn't mean a thing. Kids have always tuned in to cartoons and movies in which characters are splattered or blown away. They concede that things are a bit wilder now, with far more blood and gore and nastier images, but that's modern technology for you. The demand is there and the supply will follow, but no harm is done—it's just a picture.

18   I don't buy this argument, because the impact of television and movies is too pervasive to be so easily dismissed. For many kids the electronic picture is their world, the result of an ever more technically effective medium having drowned out all other avenues of learning and stimulation.

19   It does desensitize and, yes, I don't think young kids should be watching *Beavis and Butt-Head* scenes featuring a poke in the eye with a pencil with blood spurting out, or a dog thrown into a washing machine followed by an insane giggle of approval. I doubt very much that *Beavis* creator Mike Judge will allow his little girls to watch the show.

20   But "we," collectively, can't and should not do anything about it. We can't because we live in a market economy in which blood lust and other primitive needs of people will be met one way or another, and trying to ban something just makes it more attractive and marketable. We shouldn't because it is the adults' right to flick on whatever they want on the increasingly responsive cable smorgasbord. And it is parents' responsibility to monitor what kids watch. The "we" as represented by the state should do nothing.

21   The alternative is for the public, or rather some segment of it, to demand something better on at least a few of the many channels that are opening up. There are plenty of good television programs and movies that aim higher and do well at the box office. Since the market is master, people need not be passive about expressing their tastes. Where I live, for example, people have demanded successfully that the cable company carry the excellent Bravo channel, which it was threatening to drop.

22   "In the final analysis, it is still the law of supply and demand on all this stuff," says Norman Lear, whose *All in the Family* series first upped the ante for

thoughtful prime-time programing. "It goes back to the advertisers; they are the people who pay for this stuff. If they didn't want it, it wouldn't be there. They are just dealing with product. They know from experience that something hard and outrageous will sell faster than something soft.

23   "It's no secret that there's a lot of baseness to human nature, but we don't always pander to it, and reasonable people don't wish to pander to it. But there is nothing reasonable about the bottom line and about needing to please Wall Street by the quarter—to find the instant rating successes that satisfy the bottom line.

24   "The network goes to someone to make a pilot, then they take it to Madison Avenue, and people look at it and say, 'That's a fucking hit!' They're the first people to look at it and say, 'I want in. I will spend my millions of dollars here because I think it will rate.'"

25   He adds that because no single sponsor is identified with a show, as was the case in the "Golden Age" of the *Philco Playhouse* and the *Alcoa Hour,* "no sponsor is seriously associated with the quality of the show."

26   That's what happened with *Beavis and Butt-Head*—its creator, Judge, had originally prepared it as a one-time entry for a festival of "sick and twisted" cartoons. He had no intention of turning his one-liner into a series, but MTV execs saw it and ordered up thirty-five episodes, and soon it was a multinational operation with teams of animators in New York and Korea frantically turning the stuff out.

27   The MTV execs were right. The demand was there. It's MTV's hottest show, and sixty-five more episodes are on the way for 1994 and worldwide distribution. If you don't like that because you think it represents the dumbing-down of American and world culture, then vote—by just turning the damn thing off. Don't beg Big Brother to do it for you.

Topical Considerations

1. In paragraphs 3–8 Scheer describes his attitude toward violence in the media. On what points does Scheer's position match Cannon's? Where do the two writers disagree? What information does Scheer include about the issue not cited by Cannon?

2. Explain the purpose of Scheer's reference to the National Rifle Association (NRA) in paragraph 9.

3. Analyze the logic Scheer uses to support the claim that "we have all this mayhem in our art and our lives because we like violence" in paragraph 10. Are you persuaded by his reasoning here? Why or why not?

4. Describe Scheer's attitude toward television censorship. Consider the distinction Scheer makes between censoring material for children and for adults. Which approach to the question of censorship do you find more thoughtful, Cannon's or Scheer's?

5. What does Scheer find so troubling about the Orange County schoolchildren who are fans of *Beavis and Butt-Head*? Do you also find this anecdote disturbing? Why or why not?

6. Describe the solution Scheer proposes for the problem of television violence. Which solution do you find more persuasive, Cannon's or Scheer's? Why?

Rhetorical Considerations

1. Describe the tone of Scheer's opening. What language creates this tone? Did you find Scheer's tone offensive or appealing?

2. Characterize the organizational strategy of Scheer's essay. For example, indicate where Scheer refutes opposition; where he states his thesis; where he offers evidence supporting his claims. Evaluate the effectiveness of this organization.

3. Analyze Scheer's use of the MTV program *Beavis and Butt-Head* to illustrate his argument. What points does Scheer prove using this show? How effective do you find Scheer's use of this one example?

4. In paragraphs 22–25, Scheer quotes the television producer Norman Lear at length. Critique Scheer's use of this particular authority, considering what the choice of Lear adds to or detracts from the essay.

Writing Assignments

1. With two other students, write a group report assessing Scheer's claim that news programs "stress ambulance-chasing 'action news'" (paragraph 10). Before you begin to write, have each student watch both network and local news on one network for an entire week, assessing the coverage of violent events. Then put your observations together in order to support or attack Scheer's position, distinguishing, if possible, between network and local news and the treatment of violence on different network.

2. Since Scheer wrote in 1993, Congress has begun to take action on the problem of television violence. Do some research in order to discover what legislation is now pending on this issue. Then write a letter to your member of Congress supporting or attacking the legislation, supporting your position both with information from Scheer and Cannon and from your own experience.

In Praise of Gore
Andrew Klavan

Do you feel a dark and secret rush of pleasure, even joy, viewing a violent and blood-soaked scene from the latest slasher film? Well, according to Andrew Klavan, the answer is yes—whether you are willing to admit it or not. A basic premise of his view is that people get pleasure releasing their repressed violent impulses. That said, does Klavan think this delight in violence argues for censorship? Absolutely not, for " . . . [f]iction cannot make of people what life has not, good or evil." His fervently expressed conviction is that one should reserve art as a time and place to wrestle with and harmlessly release our darker side.

Andrew Klavan is a former newspaper and radio reporter. Klavan is a two-time winner of the Edgar Award for mystery fiction. Two recent novels include *Son of Man* (1988) and *Corruption* (1993).

BEFORE YOU READ

Can you think of recent violent acts (suicide, murder, beatings) reported in the news media and attributed to a film or recent record recording? Are you convinced there is a direct link between the event and the film or recording? Explain why or why not.

AS YOU READ

Klavan writes, "Pleasure that is unknowingly repressed is outwardly condemned." Find one or two examples of human behavior cited by Klavan to illustrate this point.

1   I love the sound of people screaming. Women screaming—with their clothes torn—as they run down endless hallways with some bogeyman in hot pursuit. Men, in their priapic cars, screaming as the road ends, as the fender plummets toward fiery oblivion under their wild eyes. Children? I'm a little squeamish about children, but okay, sure, I'll take screaming children too. And I get off on gunshots—machine gun shots goading a corpse into a posthumous jitter-bug; and the coital jerk and plunge of a butcher knife, and axes; even claws, if you happen to have them.

2   Yes, yes, yes, only in stories. Of course; in fictions only; novels, TV shows, films. I've loved the scary, gooey stuff since I was a child. I've loved monsters, shootouts, bluddy murther; women in jeopardy (as they say in Hollywood); the slasher in the closet; the intruder's shadow that spreads up the bedroom wall like a stain. And now, having grown to man's estate, I make a very good living writing these things: thriller novels like *Don't Say a Word,* which begins with a nice old lady getting dusted and ends with an assault on a child, and *The Animal Hour,* which features a woman's head being severed and stuffed into a commode.

3   Is it vicious? Disgusting? Sexist? Sick? Tough luck, it's my imagination—sometimes it is—and it's my readers' too—always, for all I know. And when they and I get together, when we dodge down that electric alleyway of the human skull where only murder is delight—well then, my friend, it's showtime.

4   But enough about me, let's talk about death. Cruel death, sexy death, exciting death: death, that is, on the page and on the screen. Because this is not a defense of violence in fiction; it's a celebration of it. And not a moment too soon either.

5   Hard as it is for a sane man to believe, fictional violence is under attack. Again. This year's list of would-be censors trying to shoulder their way to the trough of celebrity is hardly worth enumerating: Their 15 minutes might be up by the time I'm done. Film critic Michael Medved says cinematic violence is part of a pop culture "war on traditional values"; Congressman Edward Markey says television violence should be reduced or regulated; some of our less thoughtful feminists tried to quash the novel *American Psycho* because of its descriptions of violence toward women and even some of the more thoughtful, like Catharine MacKinnon, have fought for censorship in law, claiming that written descriptions of "penises slamming into vaginas" deprive actual human beings of their civil rights.

6   It's nonsense mostly, but it has the appeal of glamour, of flash. Instead of trying to understand the sad, banal, ignorant souls who generally pull the trigger in our society, we get to discuss the urbane cannibal Hannibal Lecter from *The Silence of the Lambs,* Ice-T, penises, vaginas. It makes for good sound bites, anyway—the all-American diet of 15-second thoughts.

7   But Britain—where I've come to live because I loathe real guns and political correctness—is far from exempt. Indeed, perhaps nowhere has there been a more telling or emblematic attack on fictional violence than is going on here right now. It is a textbook example of how easily pundits and politicians can channel honest grief and rage at a true crime into a senseless assault on the innocent tellers of tales.

8   It began here this time with the killing of a child by two other children. On February 12, Jamie Bulger, a 2-year-old toddler, was led out of a Merseyside shopping mall by two 10-year-olds—two little boys. The boys prodded and carried and tugged the increasingly distraught baby past dozens of witnesses who did not understand what they were seeing. When they reached a deserted railroad embankment, the two boys tortured, mutilated, and finally killed their captive for no reasons that anyone has been able to explain.

9   The nation's effort to understand, its grief and disgust, its sense of social despair, did not resolve themselves upon a single issue until the trial judge pronounced sentence. "It is not for me to pass judgment on their upbringing," Mr. Justice Morland said of the boys. "But I suspect exposure to violent video films may in part be an explanation."

10   No one knew why he said such a thing. There had been speculation in some of the papers that *Child's Play 3* (with its devil doll, Chucky), which had been rented by one of the killers' fathers, had given the son ideas. But there was no testimony at the trial, no evidence presented showing that the boy had seen it or that it had had a contributing effect. It didn't matter. As far as journalists were concerned, as far as public debate was concerned, "video nasties," as they are called here, became the central issue of the case.

11   We finally know what we are seeing when we look upon the rampaging fire of violence in our society: We are seeing the effects of fiction on us. Got it? Our moral verities are crumbling by the hour. Our families are shattering. Our gods are dead. The best lack all conviction while the worst are full of passionate intensity.

12   And it's all Chucky's fault.

13   The instinct to censor is the tragic flaw of utopian minds. "Our first job," said Plato in his classic attack on the democratic system, "is to oversee the work of the story writers, and to accept any good stories they write, but reject the others." Because the perfectibility of human society is a fiction itself, it comes under threat from other, more believable fictions, especially those that document and imply the cruel, the chaotic, the Dionysian for their thrills.

14   For me to engage the latter-day Platos on their own materialist, political terms would be to be sucked in to a form of dialogue that does not reflect the reality I know—and know I know. Because personally, I understand the world not through language but through an unfathomable spirit and an infinite mind. With language as a rude tool I try to convey a shadow of the world my imagination makes of the world at large. I do this for money and pleasure and to win the admiration of women. And when, in an uncertain hour, I crave the palliative of meaning, I remind myself that people's souls run opposite to their bodies and grow more childlike as they mature—and so I have built, in my work, little places where those souls can go to play.

15   The proper response to anyone who would shut these playgrounds down for any reason—to anyone who confuses these playgrounds with the real world—is not the specious language of theory or logic or even the law. It's the language of the spirit, of celebration and screed, of jeremiad and hallelujah. Of this.

16   Now, I would not say that my fictions—any fictions—have no effect on real life. Or that books, movies, and TV are mere regurgitations of what's going on in the society around them. These arguments strike me as disingenious and self-defeating. Rather, the relationship between fiction and humanity's unconscious is so complex, so resonant, that it is impossible to isolate one from the other in terms of cause and effect. Fiction and reality do interact, but we don't know how, not at all. And since we don't understand the effect of one upon the other—whence arises this magical certainty that violence in fiction begets violence in real life?

17   The answer seems to come straight out of Psychology 1A, but that doesn't negate the truth of it: Pleasure that is unknowingly repressed is outwardly condemned. The censor always attacks the images that secretly appeal to him or her the most. The assault on violent fiction is not really an attempt to root out the causes of violence—no one can seriously believe that. The attempt to censor fictional violence is a guilt-ridden slap at ourselves, in the guise of a mythical *them,* for taking such pleasure in make-believe acts that, in real life, would be reprehensible. How—we seem to be asking ourselves—how, in a

world in which Jamie Bulger dies so young, can we kick back with a beer at night and enjoy a couple of hours of *Child's Play 3?*

18   How can we enjoy this stuff so much? So very much.

19   Not all of us, perhaps. I'm forever being told that there are people who'd rather not take violence with their fiction—although I wonder how many would say so if you included the delicate violence of an Agatha Christie or the "literary" violence of, say, Hemingway and Faulkner. But even if we accept the exceptions, even if we limit the field to real gore, it does seem to me that the numbers are incredible, the attraction truly profound.

20   Once I picked out what looked like a cheap horror novel by an author I'd never heard of. For months afterward, I asked the readers I knew if they had heard of the book, *Salem's Lot,* or its author, Stephen King. None of them had. Later, the movie *Carrie* helped launch what has to be one of the most successful novelistic careers since Dickens. But even before that, readers were steadily discovering the nausea and mayhem and terror of the man's vision.

21   The moral, I mean, is this: To construct a bloodsoaked nightmare of unrelenting horror is not an easy thing. But if you build it, they will come. And so the maker of violent fiction—ho, ho—he walks among us in Nietzchean glee. He has bottled the Dionysian whirlwind and is selling it as a soft drink. Like deep-browed Homer, when he told of a spear protruding from a man's head with an eyeball fixed to the point, the violent storyteller knows that that gape of disgust on your respectable mug is really the look of love. You may denounce him, you may even censor him. You may just wrinkle your nose and walk away. But sooner or later, in one form or another, he knows you'll show up to see and listen to him. Fiction lives or dies not on its messages, but on the depth and power of the emotional experience it provides. An enormous amount of intellectual energy seems to have been expended in a failed attempt to suppress the central, disturbing, and irreducible fact of this experience: It's fun. Like sex: It's lots of fun. We watch fictional people love and die and screw and suffer and weep for our pleasure. It gives us joy.

22   And we watch them kill too. And this seems to give us as much joy as anything.

23   All right, I suppose you can talk about the catharsis of terror, or the harmless release of our violent impulses. Those are plausible excuses, I guess. It doesn't take a genius to notice how often—practically always—it's the villain of a successful piece of violent art who becomes its icon. Hannibal Lecter and Leatherface, Freddy Krueger and Dracula—these are the posters that go up on the wall, the characters that we remember.

24   So I suppose, if you must, you could say these creatures represent our buried feelings. Whether it's Medea or Jason (from *Friday the 13th*), the character who commits acts of savage violence always has the appeal of a Caliban: that thing of darkness that must be acknowledged as our own. Not that people are essentially violent, but that they are violent among other things and the violence has to be repressed. Some emotions must be repressed, and repressed emotions return via the imagination in distorted and inflated forms: That's the

law of benevolent hypocrisy, the law of civilized life. It is an unstated underpinning of utopian thought that the repressed can be eliminated completely or denied or happily freed or remolded with the proper education. It can't. Forget about it. Cross it off your list of things to do. The monsters are always there in their cages. As Stephen King says, with engaging simplicity, his job is to take them out for a walk every now and then.

25   But again, this business of violent fiction as therapy—it's a defense, isn't it, as if these stories needed a reason for being. In order to celebrate violent fiction—I mean, *celebrate* it—it's the joy you've got to talk about. The joy of cruelty, the thrill of terror, the adrenaline of the hunter, the heartbeat of the deer—all reproduced in the safe playground of art. A joy indeed.

26   When it comes to our messier, unseemly pleasures like fictional gore, we are downright embarrassed by our delight. But delight it is. Nubile teens caught out in flagrante by a nutcase in a hockey mask? You bet it's erotic. Whole families tortured to death by a madman who's traced them through their vacation photos? Ee-yewwww. Goblins who jump out of the toilet to devour you ass first? Delightful stuff.

27   And we've always been that way. The myths of our ancient gods, the lives of our medieval saints, the entertainments of our most civilized cultures have always included healthy doses of rape, cannibalism, evisceration, and general mayhem. Critics like Michael Medved complain that never before has it all been quite so graphic, especially on screen. We are becoming "desensitized" to bloodshed, he claims, and require more and more gore to excite our feelings. But when have human beings ever been particularly "sensitized" to fictional violence? The technology to create the illusion of bloodshed has certainly improved, but read *Titus Andronicus* with its wonderful stage direction, "Enter a messenger with two heads and a hand," read the orgasmic stalking of Lucy in *Dracula,* read de Sade, for crying out loud. There were always some pretty good indications of which way we'd go once we got our hands on the machinery.

28   Because we love it. It makes us do a little inner dance of excitement, tension, and release. Violent fiction with its graver purposes, if any, concealed—fiction unadorned with overt message or historical significance—rubs our noses in the fact that narratives of horror, murder, and gore are a blast, a gas. When knife-fingered Freddy Krueger of the *Nightmare on Elm Street* movies disembowels someone in a geyser of blood, when Hannibal Lecter washes down his victim with a nice Chianti—the only possible reason for this nonreal, nonmeaningful event to occur is that it's going to afford us pleasure. Which leaves that pleasure obvious, exposed. It's the exposure, not the thrill, the censors want to get rid of. Again: Celebration is the only defense.

29   And yet—I know—while I celebrate, the new not-very-much improved Rome is burning.

30   Last year sometime, I had a conversation with a highly intelligent Scottish filmmaker who had just returned from New York. Both of us had recently seen Sylvester Stallone's mountaineering action picture *Cliffhanger.* I'd seen it

in a placid upper-class London neighborhood; he'd seen it in a theater in Times Square. I had been thrilled by the movie's special effects and found the hilariously dopey script sweetly reminiscent of the comic books I'd read as a child. My friend had found the picture grimly disturbing. The Times Square theater had been filled with rowdy youths. Every time the bad guys killed someone, the youths cheered—and when a woman was murdered, they howled with delight.

31   I freely confess that I would have been unable to enjoy the movie under those circumstances. Too damned noisy, for one thing. And, all right, yes, as a repression fan, I could only get off on the cruelty of the villains insofar as it fired my anticipation of the moment when Sly would cut those suckers down. Another audience could just as easily have been cheering the murder of Jews in *Schindler's List* or of blacks in *Mississippi Burning.* I understand that, and it would be upsetting and frightening to be surrounded by a crowd that seemed to have abandoned the nonnegotiable values.

32   Michael Medved believes—not that one film produces one vicious act—but that a ceaseless barrage of anti-religion, anti-family, slap-happy-gore films and fictions has contributed to the erosion of values so evident on 42nd Street. I don't know whether this is true or not—neither does he—but, as with the judge's remarks in the Bulger case, it strikes me as a very suspicious place to start. Surely, the Scotsman's story illustrates that the problem lies not on the screen but in the seats, in the lives that have produced that audience. Fiction cannot make of people what life has not, good or evil.

33   But more to the point: Though the Times Square crowd's reaction was scary—rude, too—it was not necessarily harmful in itself, either to them or to me. For all I know, it was a beneficial release of energy and hostility, good for the mental health. And in any case, it took place in the context of their experience of a fiction and so (outside of the unmannerly noise they made) was beyond my right to judge, approve, or condemn. Nobody has to explain his private pleasures to me.

34   Because fiction and reality are different. It seems appalling that anyone should have to say it, but it does need to be said. Fiction is not subject to the same moral restrictions as real life. It should remain absolutely free because, at whatever level, it is, like sex, a deeply personal experience engaged in by consent in the hope of anything from momentary release to satori. Like sex, it is available to fools and creeps and monsters, and that's life; that's tough. Because fiction is, like sex, at the core of our individual humanity. Stories are the basic building blocks of spiritual maturity. No one has any business messing with them. No one at all.

35   Reality, on the other hand, needs its limits maintained by force if necessary, for the simple reason that there are actions that directly harm the safety and liberty of other people. They don't merely offend them; they don't just threaten their delicate sense of themselves; they *hurt* them—really, painfully, a lot. Again, it seems wildly improbable that this should be forgotten, but Americans' current cultural discussions show every evidence that it has been. Just as fictions are being discussed as if they were actions, actual crimes and atroci-

ties are being discussed as if they were cultural events, subject to aesthetic considerations. Trial lawyers won a lesser conviction for lady-killer Robert Chambers by claiming his victim was promiscuous; columnists defended dick-chopper Lorena Bobbitt, saying it might be all right to mutilate a man in his sleep, provided he was a really nasty guy. The fellows who savaged Reginald Denny during the Los Angeles riots claim they were just part of the psychology of the mob. And the Menendez brothers based much of their defense on a portrayal of themselves as victims, a portrayal of their victims as abusers. These are all arguments appropriate to fiction only. Only in fiction are crimes mitigated by symbolism and individuals judged not for what they've done but because of what they represent. To say that the reaction to fiction and the reaction to reality are on a continuum is moral nonsense.

36   Fiction and real life must be distinguished from one another. The radical presumption of fiction is play, the radical presumption of real life is what Martin Amis called "the gentleness of human flesh." If we have lost the will to defend that gentleness, then God help us, because consigning Chucky to the flames is not going to bring it back.

37   One of the very best works of violent fiction to come along in the past few years is Thomas Harris' novel *The Silence of the Lambs.* The story, inspired, like *Psycho,* by the real-life case of murderer Ed Gein, concerns the hunt for the serial killer Jame Gumb, a failed transsexual who strips his female victims' flesh in order to create a woman costume in which he can clothe himself.

38   When Harris introduces the killer's next victim—Catherine Martin—he presents us with a character we aren't meant to like very much. Rich, spoiled, arrogant, dissolute, Catherine is admirable only for the desperate cleverness she shows in her battle to stay alive. But for the rest of the novel—the attempt to rescue Catherine before it's too late—Harris depends on our fear for her, our identification with her, our deep desire to see her get out of this in one piece. He relies on our irrational—spiritual—conviction that Catherine, irritating though she may be, must not be killed because . . . for no good reason: because she Must Not. Harris knowingly taps in to the purely emotional imperative we share with the book's heroine, Clarice Starling, the FBI agent who's trying to crack the case: Like her, we won't be able to sleep until the screaming of innocent lambs is stopped. Harris makes pretty well sure of it.

39   At the end, in the only injection of auctorial opinion in the book, Harris wryly notes that the scholarly journals' articles on the Gumb case never use the words *crazy* or *evil* in their discussions of the killer. The intellectual world is uncomfortable with the inherent Must Not, the instinctive absolute, and the individual responsibility those words ultimately suggest. Harris, I think, is trying to argue that if we don't trust our mindless belief in the sanctity of human life, we produce monsters that the sleep of reason never dreamed of. *The Silence of the Lambs,* as the title suggests, is a dramatization of a world in which the spirit has lost its power to speak.

40   We live in that world, no question. With our culture atomizing, we think we can make up enough rules, impose enough restrictions, inject

enough emptiness into our language to replace the shared moral conviction that's plainly gone. I think all stories—along with being fun—have the potential to humanize precisely because the richest fun of them is dependent on our identification with their characters. But stories can't do for us what experience hasn't. They're just not that powerful. And if some people are living lives in our society that make them unfit for even the most shallow thrills of fiction, you can't solve that problem by eliminating the fiction. By allowing politicians and pundits to turn our attention to "the problem of fictional violence," we are really allowing them to make us turn our backs on the problems of reality.

41   After a crime like the Jamie Bulger murder, we should be asking ourselves a million questions: about our abandonment of family life, about our approach to poverty and unemployment, about the failures of our educational systems—about who and what we are and the ways we treat each other, the things we do and omit to do. These are hard, sometimes boring questions. But when instead we let our discussions devolve, as they have, into this glamour-rotten debate on whether people should be able to enjoy whatever fiction they please, then we make meaningless the taking of an individual's life. And that's no fun at all.

Topical Considerations

1. Summarize each of the seven sections into which Klavan divides his argument. If you are working with other students, assign each student (or group of students) one or two sections to summarize. After distilling the main point of each section into one complete sentence, put the sentences together in order to see the essay's overall construction. Discuss how effectively you think the different sections of the argument fit together.

2. Why does Klavan discuss the Jamie Bulger case at such length (in paragraphs 8–12)? Explain what point Klavan uses this case to prove.

3. Analyze Klavan's theory about the relationship between fiction, imagination and reality, described in paragraph 14. Do you agree with him about this relationship? Describe the importance of the theory to Klavan's argument.

4. Why, according to Klavan, does "the censor always attack . . . the images that secretly appeal to him or her the most" (paragraph 16)? Explain why you agree or disagree with Klavan's analysis of the motives of the censor.

5. Analyze Klavan's attitude toward the theory of "the catharsis of terror" (paragraph 23).

6. Why do you think Klavan relates his dispute with the unnamed Scottish filmmaker over the movie *Cliffhanger*? For you, did this anecdote prove or undercut Klavan's point, and why?

7. Restate Klavan's thesis in your own words. Explain the relationship between this thesis and other main points identified in your answer to Question 1.

8. Compare and contrast Scheer's attitude toward the appeal of violent fiction with Klavan's. Which position do you agree with, and why?

Rhetorical Considerations

1. Analyze the rhetorical strategy of Klavan's opening paragraph. What effect did this opening have on you as a reader? What are the benefits and drawbacks of beginning an argument in this manner?
2. Evaluate Klavan's credibility in this argument. How does the fact that Klavan himself is a writer in the horror genre contribute to the persuasiveness of his argument? In what ways does Klavan's profession detract from his credibility?
3. Where does Klavan successfully confront opposition to his position? What opposing argument does he **not** take into consideration?
4. Analyze Klavan's allusions to literary works in the fourth section of his essay (paragraphs 19–27). How do these allusions strengthen his argument? How might a reader critique Klavan's literary judgment here?

Writing Assignments

1. Klavan uses *The Silence of the Lambs* as an example of horror films in the final section of his essay. Write an analysis of this film which argues that it is not representative of the horror film genre.
2. U.S. Senate Majority Leader Robert Dole recently attacked the entertainment industry for its irresponsible attitude toward violence. Dole cited the film *Natural Born Killers* as socially irresponsible and praised *True Lies* as good family entertainment. Compare and contrast the way violence is treated in these two films. Support your essay with detailed examples from the movies.
3. Write a letter to Klavan arguing that he has grossly overestimated the appeal of violence in fiction. Support your position with personal observations and, if you can find them, statistics about the market share of violent or horror fiction in both books and movies.

RACIAL SLURS

Regulating Racist Speech on Campus
Charles R. Lawrence III

The last few years have seen a disturbing rise in racist and sexist language on college campuses. Some administrators have dealt with the problem by banning offensive language on the grounds that racial slurs are violent verbal assaults that interfere with students' rights to an education. Others fear that putting sanctions on racist speech violates the First Amendment guarantee of free expression. In the following essay, professor of law Charles R. Lawrence III argues for the restriction of free speech by appealing to the U.S. Supreme Court's landmark decision in *Brown v. Board of Education.*

Lawrence teaches law at Stanford University and the University of California at Los Angeles. He is the author of many articles on law and coauthor of the book *The Bakke Case: The Politics of Inequality* (1979). A longer version of this article appeared in the February 1990 issue of *Duke Law Review.*

BEFORE YOU READ

Does the saying "Sticks and stones may break my bones, but names will never hurt me" apply to racist speech—that is, insults or invectives directed at a person because of race or ethnic identity? Have you ever witnessed or experienced a verbal assault based on race? Was its impact slight or profound? When such incidents occur on college campuses, should they be ignored or dealt with formally?

AS YOU READ

As you read notice that the author cites and interprets the landmark case of *Brown v. Board of Education* to argue his point. How does he make this legal document accessible to the lay person? What does this demonstrate about the effective use of sources?

1   I have spent the better part of my life as a dissenter. As a high-school student, I was threatened with suspension for my refusal to participate in a civil-defense drill, and I have been a conspicuous consumer of my First Amendment liberties ever since. There are very strong reasons for protecting even racist speech. Perhaps the most important of these is that such protection reinforces our society's commitment to tolerance as a value, and that by protecting bad speech from government regulation, we will be forced to combat it as a community.

2   But I also have a deeply felt apprehension about the resurgence of racial violence and the corresponding rise in the incidence of verbal and symbolic assault and harassment to which blacks and other traditionally subjugated and excluded groups are subjected. I am troubled by the way the debate has been framed in response to the recent surge of racist incidents on college and university campuses and in response to some universities' attempts to regulate harassing speech. The problem has been framed as one in which the liberty of free speech is in conflict with the elimination of racism. I believe this has placed the bigot on the moral high ground and fanned the rising flames of racism.

3   Above all, I am troubled that we have not listened to the real victims, that we have shown so little understanding of their injury, and that we have abandoned those whose race, gender, or sexual preference continues to make

them second-class citizens. It seems to me a very sad irony that the first instinct of civil libertarians has been to challenge even the smallest, most narrowly framed efforts by universities to provide black and other minority students with the protection the Constitution guarantees them.

4   The landmark case of *Brown v. Board of Education* is not a case that we normally think of as a case about speech. But *Brown* can be broadly read as articulating the principle of equal citizenship. *Brown* held that segregated schools were inherently unequal because of the *message* that segregation conveyed—that black children were an untouchable caste, unfit to go to school with white children. If we understand the necessity of eliminating the system of signs and symbols that signify the inferiority of blacks, then we should hesitate before proclaiming that all racist speech that stops short of physical violence must be defended.

5   University officials who have formulated policies to respond to incidents of racial harassment have been characterized in the press as "thought police," but such policies generally do nothing more than impose sanctions against intentional face-to-face insults. When racist speech takes the form of face-to-face insults, catcalls, or other assaultive speech aimed at an individual or small group of persons, it falls directly within the "fighting words" exception to First Amendment protection. The Supreme Court has held that words which "by their very utterance inflict injury or tend to incite an immediate breach of the peace" are not protected by the First Amendment.

6   If the purpose of the First Amendment is to foster the greatest amount of speech, racial insults disserve that purpose. Assaultive racist speech functions as a preemptive strike. The invective is experienced as a blow, not as a proffered idea, and once the blow is struck, it is unlikely that a dialogue will follow. Racial insults are particularly undeserving of First Amendment protection because the perpetrator's intention is not to discover truth or initiate dialogue but to injure the victim. In most situations, members of minority groups realize that they are likely to lose if they respond to epithets by fighting and are forced to remain silent and submissive.

7   Courts have held that offensive speech may not be regulated in public forums such as streets where the listener may avoid the speech by moving on, but the regulation of otherwise protected speech has been permitted when the speech invades the privacy of the unwilling listener's home or when the unwilling listener cannot avoid the speech. Racist posters, fliers, and graffiti in dormitories, bathrooms, and other common living spaces would seem to clearly fall within the reasoning of these cases. Minority students should not be required to remain in their rooms in order to avoid racial assault. Minimally, they should find a safe haven in their dorms and in all other common rooms that are a part of their daily routine.

8   I would also argue that the university's responsibility for insuring that these students receive an equal educational opportunity provides a compelling justification for regulations that insure them safe passage in all common areas.

A minority student should not have to risk becoming the target of racially assaulting speech every time he or she chooses to walk across campus. Regulating vilifying speech that cannot be anticipated or avoided would not preclude announced speeches and rallies—situations that would give minority-group members and their allies the chance to organize counter-demonstrations or avoid the speech altogether.

9   The most commonly advanced argument against the regulation of racist speech proceeds something like this: we recognize that minority groups suffer pain and injury as the result of racist speech, but we must allow this hate mongering for the benefit of society as a whole. Freedom of speech is the lifeblood of our democratic system. It is especially important for minorities because often it is their only vehicle for rallying support for the redress of their grievances. It will be impossible to formulate a prohibition so precise that it will prevent the racist speech you want to suppress without catching in the same net all kinds of speech that it would be unconscionable for a democratic society to suppress.

10   Whenever we make such arguments, we are striking a balance on the one hand between our concern for the continued free flow of ideas and the democratic process dependent on that flow, and, on the other, our desire to further the cause of equality. There can be no meaningful discussion of how we should reconcile our commitment to equality and our commitment to free speech until it is acknowledged that there is real harm inflicted by racist speech and that this harm is far from trivial.

11   To engage in a debate about the First Amendment and racist speech without a full understanding of the nature and extent of that harm is to risk making the First Amendment an instrument of domination rather than a vehicle of liberation. We have not known the experience of victimization by racist, misogynist, and homophobic speech, nor do we equally share the burden of the societal harm it inflicts. We are often quick to say that we have heard the cry of the victims when we have not.

12   The *Brown* case is again instructive because it speaks directly to the psychic injury inflicted by racist speech by noting that the symbolic message of segregation affected "the hearts and minds" of Negro children "in a way unlikely ever to be undone." Racial epithets and harassment often cause deep emotional scarring and feelings of anxiety and fear that pervade every aspect of a victim's life.

13   *Brown* also recognized that black children did not have an equal opportunity to learn and participate in the school community if they bore the additional burden of being subjected to the humiliation and psychic assault contained in the message of segregation. University students bear an analogous burden when they are forced to live and work in an environment where at any moment they may be subjected to denigrating verbal harassment and assault. The same injury was addressed by the Supreme Court when it held that sexual harassment that creates a hostile or abusive work environment violates the ban

on sex discrimination in employment of Title VII of the Civil Rights Act of 1964.

14   Carefully drafted university regulations would bar the use of words as assault weapons and leave unregulated even the most heinous of ideas when those ideas are presented at times and places and in manners that provide an opportunity for reasoned rebuttal or escape from immediate injury. The history of the development of the right to free speech has been one of carefully evaluating the importance of free expression and its effects on other important societal interests. We have drawn the line between protected and unprotected speech before without dire results. (Courts have, for example, exempted from the protection of the First Amendment obscene speech and speech that disseminates official secrets, that defames or libels another person, or that is used to form a conspiracy or monopoly.)

15   Blacks and other people of color are skeptical about the argument that even the most injurious speech must remain unregulated because, in an unregulated marketplace of ideas, the best ones will rise to the top and gain acceptance. Our experience tells us quite the opposite. We have seen too many good liberal politicians shy away from the issues that might brand them as being too closely allied with us.

16   Whenever we decide that racist speech must be tolerated because of the importance of maintaining societal tolerance for all unpopular speech, we are asking blacks and other subordinated groups to bear the burden for the good of all. We must be careful that the ease with which we strike the balance against the regulation of racist speech is in no way influenced by the fact that the cost will be borne by others. We must be certain that those who will pay that price are fairly represented in our deliberations and that they are heard.

17   At the core of the argument that we should resist all government regulation of speech is the ideal that the best cure for bad speech is good, that ideas that affirm equality and the worth of all individuals will ultimately prevail. This is an empty ideal unless those of us who would fight racism are vigilant and unequivocal in that fight. We must look for ways to offer assistance and support to students whose speech and political participation are chilled in a climate of racial harassment.

18   Civil rights lawyers might consider suing on behalf of blacks whose right to an equal education is denied by a university's failure to insure a nondiscriminatory educational climate or conditions of employment. We must embark upon the development of a First Amendment jurisprudence grounded in the reality of our history an dour contemporary experience. We must think hard about how best to launch legal attacks against the most indefensible forms of hate speech. Good lawyers can create exceptions and narrow interpretations that limit the harm of hate speech without opening the floodgates of censorship.

19   Everyone concerned with these issues must find ways to engage actively in actions that resist and counter the racist ideas that we would have the

First Amendment protect. If we fail in this, the victims of hate speech must rightly assume that we are on the oppressors' side.

Topical Considerations

1. What reasons does Lawrence offer for protecting racist speech from governmental restrictions? Do you agree? How else can a community fight such speech?
2. According to the author, how in the debate over racist language does the fight against racism conflict with the fight for free speech? What fundamental problem does Lawrence have with this conflict? Are his reasons convincing? Why or why not?
3. According to the author, how can the case of *Brown v. Board of Education* be interpreted to cover protection of victims of racist speech?
4. Why, according to Lawrence, is racist speech "undeserving of First Amendment protection" (paragraph 6)? Do you agree? Why or why not? Can you think of any circumstances when racist speech should be protected?
5. What legal measures does Lawrence suggest for the protection of black students against hate speech?
6. Has this article affected your thinking on the subject of free speech and censorship? Has it changed your mind about the use of racially or sexually abusive language? Explain your answer.
7. Have you ever been the victim of abusive speech—speech that victimized you because of your race, gender, religion, ethnicity, or sexual preference? Do you agree with Lawrence's argument about the "psychic injury" such speech can cause? Did you ever experience such injury? Explain your answer.
8. Is there any racial tension on your campus? If so, do you see a link between racial tension and racist speech? What suggestions would you make to school officials to deal with such tension? Do you think that banning hate speech might lessen racial tension and violence? How about in society at large? Explain your reasoning.

Rhetorical Considerations

1. Where in this essay do you get a clear focus on Lawrence's line of argument? What are the first clues to the reader? Can you point to a thesis statement?
2. Lawrence opens his essay saying that he has a long history as a "dissenter." What is his strategy? What kinds of assumptions does he make about his audience? What does his refusal to participate in a civil defense drill have to do with the essay's central issues?

3. How convincingly does Lawrence argue that racist speech should not be protected by the First Amendment? What is the logic of his argument? What evidence does he offer as support?

4. Select one of Lawrence's arguments that you think is especially strong or especially weak, and explain why you think so.

5. Consider the author's voice in this essay. What sense do you get of Lawrence as an individual? In a paragraph, try to characterize him. Take into consideration his stand in the essay as well as the style and tone of his writing.

Writing Assignments

1. As Lawrence points out, many university officials—as well as legal scholars—view the outlawing of hate speech as contrary to the democratic spirit of pluralism and tolerance. Write a paper in which you argue that hate speech should be protected if we are to remain a legitimate democracy. In your discussion, explain where you would draw the line on the protection, if at all.

2. Taking the opposite stand from assignment 1, and using some of your own ideas, write a paper in which you argue that racist (and/or sexist) speech should be outlawed because it can only contribute to the victimization of people and the already-tense social conditions in America. In your discussion explain what kinds of hate speech you would want to see banned, and why. Also discuss why you think such speech could be controlled by regulation.

3. Suppose that a leader of a known hate group were invited to your campus—someone certain to speak in inflammatory racist language. Would you defend that person's right to address the student body? Why or why not? Should that person be protected under the First Amendment? Would you attend? Why or why not?

4. Imagine that a condition of acceptance to your school were signing an agreement that you would refrain from using racist, sexist, or otherwise abusive language on campus—an agreement that if broken could lead to suspension. Weighing the social benefits against the restrictions on freedom of expression, write a paper in which you explain why you would or would not sign such an agreement.

Free Speech on Campus
Nat Hentoff

In this essay, Nat Hentoff argues that instituting sanctions on hate speech seriously mocks the pluralistic nature of a university and academic freedom and inquiry. He warns that preventing or punishing offensive language could lead to Orwellian nightmares.

Nat Hentoff is a staff writer for *The New Yorker* and *The Village Voice* and a columnist for *The Washington Post*. Much of his writing, including his book *Free Speech for Me, But Not for Thee* (1993), focuses on the subject of freedom of expression. He is also the author of *American Heroes: In and Out of School* (1987) and *Boston Boy: A Memoir* (1988). This article first appeared in the May 1989 issue of the *Progressive*.

BEFORE YOU READ

If a member of the Ku Klux Klan, Louis Farrakhan, David Duke, or a member of a neo-Nazi group were invited to speak at your school, what would your reaction be? Would you hope that school authorities would act to rescind this invitation, or would you accept the presence of one of these speakers on your campus? Explain your thinking.

AS YOU READ

In his opening paragraphs Hentoff cites some particularly offensive examples of bigotry. Because his essay argues against sanctions on hate speech, what was his purpose in opening his essay with these remarks? Was it an effective technique?

1   A flier distributed at the University of Michigan some months ago proclaimed that blacks "don't belong in classrooms, they belong hanging from trees."

2   At other campuses around the country, manifestations of racism are becoming commonplace. At Yale, a swastika and the words WHITE POWER! were painted on the building housing the University's Afro-American Cultural Center. At Temple University, a White Students Union has been formed with some 130 members.

3   Swastikas are not directed only at black students. The Nazi symbol has been spray-painted on the Jewish Student Union at Memphis State University. And on a number of campuses, women have been singled out as targets of wounding and sometimes frightening speech. At the law school of the State University of New York at Buffalo, several women students have received anonymous letters characterized by one professor as venomously sexist.

4   These and many more such signs of the resurgence of bigotry and know-nothingism throughout the society—as well as on campus—have to do solely with speech, including symbolic speech. There have also been physical assaults on black students and on black, white, and Asian women students,

but the way to deal with physical attacks is clear: call the police and file a criminal complaint. What is to be done, however, about speech alone—however disgusting, inflammatory, and rawly divisive that speech may be?

5   At more and more colleges, administrators—with the enthusiastic support of black students, women students, and liberal students—have been answering that question by preventing or punishing speech. In public universities, this is a clear violation of the First Amendment. In private colleges and universities, suppression of speech mocks the secular religion of academic freedom and free inquiry.

6   The Student Press Law Center in Washington, D.C.—a vital source of legal support for student editors around the country—reports, for example, that at the University of Kansas, the student host and producer of a radio news program was forbidden by school officials from interviewing a leader of the Ku Klux Klan. So much for free inquiry on that campus.

7   In Madison, Wisconsin, the *Capital Times* ran a story in January about Chancellor Sheila Kaplan of the University of Wisconsin branch at Parkside, who ordered her campus to be scoured of "some anonymously placed white supremacist hate literature." Sounding like the legendary Mayor Frank ("I am the law") Hague of Jersey City, who booted "bad speech" out of town, Chancellor Kaplan said, "This institution is not a lamppost standing on the street corner. It doesn't belong to everyone."

8   Who decides what speech can be heard or read by everyone? Why, the Chancellor, of course. That's what George III used to say, too.

9   University of Wisconsin political science professor Carol Tebben thinks otherwise. She believes university administrators "are getting confused when they are acting as censors and trying to protect students from bad ideas. I don't think students need to be protected from bad ideas. I think they can determine for themselves what ideas are bad."

10   After all, if students are to be "protected" from bad ideas, how are they going to learn to identify and cope with them? Sending such ideas underground simply makes them stronger and more dangerous.

11   Professor Tebben's conviction that free speech means just that has become a decidedly minority view on many campuses. At the University of Buffalo Law School, the faculty unanimously adopted a "Statement Regarding Intellectual Freedom, Tolerance, and Political Harassment." Its title implies support of intellectual freedom, but the statement warned students that once they enter "this legal community," their right to free speech must become tempered "by the responsibility to promote equality and justice."

12   Accordingly, swift condemnation will befall anyone who engages in "remarks directed at another's race, sex, religion, national origin, age, or sex preference." Also forbidden are "other remarks based on prejudice and group stereotype."

13   This ukase is so broad that enforcement has to be alarmingly subjective. Yet the University of Buffalo Law School provides no due-process procedures

for a student booked for making any of these prohibited remarks. Conceivably, a student caught playing a Lenny Bruce, Richard Pryor, or Sam Kinison album in his room could be tried for aggravated insensitivity by association.

14   When I looked into this wholesale cleansing of bad speech at Buffalo, I found it had encountered scant opposition. One protestor was David Gerald Jay, a graduate of the law school and a cooperating attorney for the New York Civil Liberties Union. Said the appalled graduate: "Content-based prohibitions constitute prior restraint and should not be tolerated."

15   You would think that the law professors and administration at this public university might have known that. But hardly any professors dissented, and among the students only members of the conservative Federalist Society spoke up for free speech. The fifty-strong chapter of the National Lawyers Guild was on the other side. After all, it was more important to go on record as vigorously opposing racism and sexism than to expose oneself to charges of insensitivity to these malignancies.

16   The pressures to have the "right" attitude—as proved by having the "right" language in and out of class—can be stifling. A student who opposes affirmative action, for instance, can be branded a racist.

17   At the University of California at Los Angeles, the student newspaper ran an editorial cartoon satirizing affirmative action. (A student stops a rooster on campus and asks how the rooster got into UCLA. "Affirmative action," is the answer.) After outraged complaints from various minority groups, the editor was suspended for violating a publication policy against running "articles that perpetuate derogatory or cultural stereotypes." The art director was also suspended.

18   When the opinion editor of the student newspaper at California State University at Northridge wrote an article asserting that the sanctions against the editor and art director at UCLA amounted to censorship, he was suspended too.

19   At New York University Law School, a student was so disturbed by the pall of orthodoxy at that prestigious institution that he wrote to the school newspaper even though, as he said, he expected his letter to make him a pariah among his fellow students.

20   Barry Endick described the atmosphere at NYU created by "a host of watchdog committees and a generally hostile classroom reception regarding any student comment right of center." This "can be arguably viewed as symptomatic of a prevailing spirit of academic and social intolerance of . . . any idea which is not 'politically correct.'"

21   He went on to say something that might well be posted on campus bulletin boards around the country, though it would probably be torn down at many of them: "We ought to examine why students, so anxious to wield the Fourteenth Amendment, give short shrift to the First. Yes, Virginia, there are racist assholes. And you know what, the Constitution protects them, too."

22   Not when they engage in violence or vandalism. But when they speak or write, racist assholes fall right into this Oliver Wendell Holmes definition—

highly unpopular among bigots, liberals, radicals, feminists, sexists, and college administrators: "If there is any principle of the Constitution that more imperatively calls for attachment than any other, it is the principle of free thought—not free only for those who agree with us, but freedom for the thought we hate."

23   The language sounds like a pietistic Sunday sermon, but if it ever falls wholly into disuse, neither this publication nor any other journal of opinion—right or left—will survive.

24   Sometimes, college presidents and administrators sound as if they fully understand what Holmes was saying. Last year, for example, when the *Daily Pennsylvanian*—speaking for many at the University of Pennsylvania—urged that a speaking invitation to Louis Farrakhan be withdrawn, University President Sheldon Hackney disagreed.

25   "Open expression," said Hackney, "is the fundamental principle of a university." Yet consider what the same Sheldon Hackney did to the free-speech rights of a teacher at his own university. If any story distills the essence of the current decline of free speech on college campuses, it is the Ballad of Murray Dolfman.

26   For twenty-two years, Dolfman, a practicing lawyer in Philadelphia, had been a part-time lecturer in the Legal Studies Department of the University of Pennsylvania's Wharton School. For twenty-two years, no complaint had ever been made against him; indeed his student course evaluations had been outstanding. Each year students competed to get into his class.

27   On a November afternoon in 1984, Dolfman was lecturing about personal-service contracts. His style somewhat resembles that of Professor Charles Kingsfield in *The Paper Chase*.[1] Dolfman insists that students he calls on be prepared—or suffer the consequences. He treats all students this way—regardless of race, creed, or sex.

28   This day, Dolfman was pointing out that no one can be forced to work against his or her will—even if a contract has been signed. A court may prevent the resister from working for someone else so long as the contract is in effect but, Dolfman said, there can "be nothing that smacks of involuntary servitude."

29   Where does this concept come from? Dolfman looked around the room. Finally, a cautious hand was raised: "The Constitution?"

30   "Where in the Constitution?" No hands. "The Thirteenth Amendment," said the teacher. So, what does *it* say? The students were looking everywhere but at Dolfman.

31   "We will lose our liberties," Dolfman often told his classes. "If we don't know what they are."

32   On this occasion, he told them that he and other Jews, as ex-slaves, spoke at Passover of the time when they were slaves under the Pharaohs so that they would remember every year what it was like not to be free.

---

[1] A popular 1974 film starring John Houseman as a stern Harvard law professor.

33   "We have ex-slaves here," Dolfman continued, "who should know about the Thirteenth Amendment." He asked black students in the class if they could tell him what was in that amendment.

34   "I wanted them to really think about it," Dolfman told me recently, "and know its history. You're better equipped to fight racism if you know all about those post–Civil War amendments and civil rights laws."

35   The Thirteenth Amendment provides that "neither slavery nor involuntary servitude . . . shall exist within the United States."

36   The black students in his class did not know what was in that amendment, and Dolfman had them read it aloud. Later, they complained to university officials that they had been hurt and humiliated by having been referred to as ex-slaves. Moreover, they said, they had no reason to be grateful for a constitutional amendment which gave them rights which should never have been denied them—and gave them precious little else. They had not made these points in class, although Dolfman—unlike Professor Kingsfield—encourages rebuttal.

37   Informed of the complaint, Dolfman told the black students he had intended no offense, and he apologized if they had been offended.

38   That would not do—either for the black students or for the administration. Furthermore, there were mounting black-Jewish tensions on campus, and someone had to be sacrificed. Who better than a part-time Jewish teacher with no contract, and no union? He was sentenced by—George Orwell would have loved this—the Committee on Academic Freedom and Responsibility.

39   On his way to the stocks, Dolfman told President Sheldon Hackney that if a part-time instructor "can be punished on this kind of charge, a tenured professor can eventually be booted out, then a dean, and then a president."

40   Hackney was unmoved. Dolfman was banished from the campus for what came to be a year. But first he was forced to make a public apology to the entire university and then he was compelled to attend a "sensitivity and racial awareness" session. Sort of like a Vietnamese reeducation camp.

41   A few conservative professors objected to the stigmatization of Murray Dolfman. I know of no student dissent. Indeed, those students most concerned with making the campus more "sensitive" to diversity exulted in Dolfman's humiliation. So did most liberals on the faculty.

42   If my children were still of college age and wanted to attend the University of Pennsylvania, I would tell them this story. But where else could I encourage them to go?

Topical Considerations

1. In your own words, summarize the argument Nat Hentoff makes in his essay. What is his purpose?
2. How are college and university administrators dealing with the recent increase in incidents of verbal abuse on American campuses? What is Hentoff's reaction to their handling of such problems?

3. With regard to the First Amendment, Hentoff distinguishes between physical assaults and those that are verbal and/or symbolic. What distinctions does he make? How does Charles R. Lawrence III distinguish between the two in the previous essay? Explain the different interpretations between these authors.

4. If a leader of the Ku Klux Klan were barred from speaking at your school, would you protest? How about a member of the American Nazi party? The PLO? Louis Farrakhan? Explain your reasons.

5. Professor Carol Trebben does not think "students need to be protected from bad ideas" (paragraph 9). Do you agree? Do you feel that students can "determine for themselves what ideas are bad"? What constitutes a "bad idea"? Can you imagine any "bad ideas" that should be censored? What would they be, and under what circumstances?

6. Hentoff argues that may people who concur with sanctions on free speech do so to avoid being considered sexist or racist. Does this describe people you know? Do you think a person who opposes sexism and racism can still support freedom of speech? Or do you think it's racist and sexist to be opposed to sanctions on racist and sexist speech? Explain your answer.

7. What problems does Hentoff have with the University of Buffalo Law School's "Statement Regarding Intellectual Freedom, Tolerance, and Political Harassment"? What explanation does he offer for the wide acceptance of and "scant opposition" to that "ukase"? What are your feelings about such a statement?

8. Would Hentoff agree that "sticks and stones will break my bones, but names will never hurt me? What about Charles R. Lawrence III? What about you?

9. In paragraph 17, Hentoff cites the case of the UCLA student newspaper which ran an editorial cartoon satirizing affirmative action. From Hentoff's description, does the cartoon sound offensive to you? As described, how might it have been offensive to minority students? Do you think the administration was morally and legally justified in suspending the editor and art director? If this happened on your campus, explain how you would react?

10. What do you make of the Dolfman case that Hentoff discusses in the last half of the essay? From what we're told, do you think Dolfman was insensitive to the black students in his class? Do you think the black students were justified in their complaints? Do you think the administration was right in suspending Dolfman? Explain your answers.

Rhetorical Considerations

1. Consider the title of this essay. What different meanings can it have? How does it forecast Hentoff's position in the essay? Do you think it's an effective title?

2. Where in the essay does Hentoff's line of argument begin to take focus? Is his line of argument carried clearly throughout the essay? Where does he state his thesis?

458   PART TWO: CURRENT DEBATES

3. Consider the case of the editorial cartoon in the UCLA student newspaper (paragraphs 17 and 18). What does Hentoff want you to believe about the cartoon? Is his description satisfying to you? Would you prefer to actually see it before passing judgment on its offensiveness? Suppose you learned that Hentoff failed to mention some particularly offensive details in the cartoon—say, a racist caricature of the rooster. How would that affect the impact of his argument?

4. Find two or three of Hentoff's sentences that you find particularly effective as examples of persuasive writing, then explain why they are effective.

5. Explain the meaning of the aside to George Orwell in paragraph 38. How is it an appropriate remark?

6. What do you make of the essay's conclusion? What is the strategy of ending the essay with this question? What is Hentoff's message? Is his conclusion consistent with the development of his argument?

Writing Assignments

1. In paragraph 10, Hentoff claims, "Sending such [bad] ideas underground simply makes them stronger and more dangerous." Explore this claim in a paper in which you try to imagine how certain "bad ideas" could become stronger and more dangerous if they were censored.

2. Suppose your school had a statement such as the one at the University of Buffalo Law School. Weighing the social benefits against the restrictions to the freedom of speech, would you be willing to sign a pledge of allegiance to it? Write a paper in which you explain your decision.

3. Where does "offensive" language end and "racist" and "sexist" language begin. Write a paper in which you try to determine the distinctions. Give clear examples to support your arguments.

4. Take another look at Charles Lawrence's essay. Whose argument on the free speech issue is more persuasive—Lawrence's or Hentoff's? Explain. Support your answer with specific evidence from each of the essays.

5. Write a letter to Nat Hentoff arguing that hate speech—racist, sexist, and otherwise—should be regulated because it can only contribute to the already-tense social conditions in America.

In Praise of Censure
Garry Wills

When confronted with defamatory remarks, racial epithets, or offensive speech of any kind, what are our choices: censorship or tolerance? Are there any other choices between outright banning and First Amendment rights? Garry Wills thinks so. In this essay he argues that the open expression of moral disapproval—or censure—can be a powerful response to the objectionable. Censure does not repress ideas but holds them up for public scrutiny and examination. Such a mobilization of public opinion, he feels, is more likely than legislation or repression to bring about social change.

Garry Wills is the Henry R. Luce Professor of American Culture and Public Policy at Northwestern University and a syndicated columnist. His most recent books are *Under God: Religion and American Politics* (1990), *Lincoln at Gettysburg* (1992), and *Certain Trumpets: The Call of Leaders* (1994). This essay first appeared in *Time* magazine in July 1989.

BEFORE YOU READ

Do you think censure is an effective means of expressing disapproval of offensive material? Can you think of any recent examples of public censure that had an impact on the sale, promotion, or exhibition of something deemed offensive?

AS YOU READ

As you read determine what Wills means when he says, "It is a distortion to turn 'You can express any views' into the proposition 'I don't care what views you express.'"

1   Rarely have the denouncers of censorship been so eager to start practicing it. When a sense of moral disorientation overcomes a society, people from the least expected quarters begin to ask, "Is nothing sacred?" Feminists join reactionaries to denounce pornography as demeaning to women. Rock musician Frank Zappa declares that when Tipper Gore, the wife of Senator Albert Gore from Tennessee, asked music companies to label sexually explicit material, she launched an illegal "conspiracy to extort." A *Penthouse* editorialist says that housewife Terry Rakolta, who asked sponsors to withdraw support from a sitcom called *Married . . . With Children,* is "yelling fire in a crowded theater," a formula that says her speech is not protected by the First Amendment.

2   But the most interesting movement to limit speech is directed at defamatory utterances against blacks, homosexuals, Jews, women or other stigmatizable groups. It took no Terry Rakolta of the left to bring about the instant firing of Jimmy the Greek and Al Campanis from sports jobs when they made racially denigrating comments. Social pressure worked far more quickly on them than on *Married . . . With Children,* which is still on the air.

3   The rules being considered on college campuses to punish students for making racist and other defamatory remarks go beyond social and commercial pressure to actual legal muzzling. The rightwing *Dartmouth Review* and its imitators have understandably infuriated liberals who are beginning to take action against them and the racist expressions they have encouraged. The American Civil Liberties Union considered this movement important enough to

make it the principal topic at its biennial meeting last month in Madison, Wis. Ironically, the regents of the University of Wisconsin had passed their own rules against defamation just before the ACLU members convened on the university's campus. Nadine Strossen, of New York University School of Law, who was defending the ACLU's traditional position on free speech, said of Wisconsin's new rules, "You can tell how bad they are by the fact that the regents had to make an amendment at the last minute exempting classroom discussion! What is surprising is that Donna Shalala [chancellor of the university] went along with it." So did constitutional lawyers on the faculty.

4   If a similar code were drawn up with right-wing imperatives in mind—one banning unpatriotic, irreligious or sexually explicit expressions on campus—the people framing Wisconsin-type rules would revert to their libertarian pasts. In this competition to suppress, is regard for freedom of expression just a matter of whose ox is getting gored at the moment? Does the left just get nervous about the Christian cross when Klansmen burn it, while the right will react only when Madonna flirts crucifixes between her thighs?

5   The cries of "un-American" are as genuine and as frequent on either side. Everyone is protecting the country. Zappa accuses Gore of undermining the moral fiber of America with the "sexual neuroses of these vigilant ladies." He argues that she threatens our freedoms with "connubial insider trading" because her husband is a Senator. Apparently her marital status should deprive her of speaking privileges in public—an argument Westbrook Pegler used to make against Eleanor Roosevelt. *Penthouse* says Rakolta is taking us down the path toward fascism. It attacks her for living in a rich suburb—the old "radical chic" argument that rich people cannot support moral causes.

6   There is a basic distinction that cuts through this free-for-all over freedom. It is the distinction, too often neglected, between censorship and censure (the free expression of moral disapproval). What the campuses are trying to do (at least those with state money) is to use the force of government to contain freedom of speech. What Donald Wildmon, the free-lance moralist from Tupelo, Miss., does when he gets Pepsi to cancel its Madonna ad is censure the ad by calling for a boycott. Advocating boycotts is a form of speech protected by the First Amendment. As Nat Hentoff, journalistic-custodian of the First Amendment, says, "I would have to see boycotts outlawed. Think what that would do to Cesar Chavez." Or, for that matter, to Ralph Nader. If one disapproves of a social practice, whether it is racist speech or unjust hiring in lettuce fields, one is free to denounce that and to call on others to express their disapproval. Otherwise, there would be no form of persuasive speech except passing a law. This would make the law coterminous with morality.

7   Equating morality with legality is in effect what people do when they claim that anything tolerated by law must, in the name of freedom, be approved by citizens in all their dealings with one another. As Zappa says, "Masturbation is not illegal. If it is not illegal to do it, why should it be illegal to sing about it?" He thinks this proves that Gore, who is trying to make raunch in rock illegal, cannot even ask distributors to label it. Anything goes, as long as it's legal. The odd consequence of this argument would be a drastic narrowing

of the freedom of speech. One could not call into question anything that was not against the law—including, for instance, racist speech.

8   A false ideal of tolerance has not only outlawed censorship but discouraged censoriousness (another word for censure). Most civilizations have expressed their moral values by mobilization of social opprobrium. That, rather than specific legislation, is what changed the treatment of minorities in films and TV over recent years. One can now draw opprobrious attention by gay bashing, as the Beastie Boys rock group found when their distributor told them to cut out remarks about "fags" for business reasons. Or by anti-Semitism, as the just disbanded rap group Public Enemy has discovered.

9   It is said that only the narrow-minded are intolerant or opprobrious. Most of those who limited the distribution of Martin Scorsese's movie *The Last Temptation of Christ* had not even seen the movie. So do we guarantee freedom of speech only for the broad-minded or the better educated? Can one speak only after studying whatever one has reason, from one's beliefs, to denounce? Then most of us would be doing a great deal less speaking than we do. If one has never seen any snuff movies, is that a bar to criticizing them?

10   Others argue that asking people not to buy lettuce is different from asking them not to buy a rocker's artistic expression. Ideas (carefully disguised) lurk somewhere in the lyrics. All the more reason to keep criticism of them free. If ideas are too important to suppress, they are also too important to ignore. The whole point of free speech is not to make ideas exempt from criticism but to expose them to it.

11   One of the great mistakes of liberals in recent decades has been the ceding of moral concern to right-wingers. Just because one opposes censorship, one need not be seen as agreeing with pornographers. Why should liberals, of all people, oppose Gore when she asks that labels be put on products meant for the young, to inform those entrusted by law with the care of the young? Liberals were the first to promote "healthy" television shows like *Sesame Street* and *The Electric Company.* In the 1950s and 1960s they were the leading critics of television, of its mindless violence, of the way it ravaged the attention span needed for reading. Who was keeping kids away from TV sets then? How did promoters of Big Bird let themselves be cast as champions of the Beastie Boys—not just of their *right* to perform but of their performance itself? Why should it be left to Gore to express moral disapproval of a group calling itself Dead Kennedys (sample lyric: "I kill children, I love to see them die")?

12   For that matter, who has been more insistent that parents should "interfere" in what their children are doing, Tipper Gore or Jesse Jackson? All through the 1970s, Jackson was traveling the high schools, telling parents to turn off TVs, make the kids finish their homework, check with teachers on their performance, get to know what the children are doing. This kind of "interference" used to be called education.

13   Belief in the First Amendment does not pre-empt other beliefs, making one a eunuch to the interplay of opinions. It is a distortion to turn "You can express any views" into the proposition "I don't care what views you express." If

liberals keep equating equality with approval, they will be repeatedly forced into weak positions.

14   A case in point is the Corcoran Gallery's sudden cancellation of an exhibit of Robert Mapplethorpe's photographs. The whole matter was needlessly confused when the director, Christina Owr-Chall, claimed she was canceling the show to *protect* it from censorship. She meant that there might be pressure to remove certain pictures—the sadomasochistic ones or those verging on kiddie porn—if the show had gone on. But she had in mind, as well, the hope of future grants from the National Endowment for the Arts, which is under criticism for the Mapplethorpe show and for another show that contained Andres Serrano's *Piss Christ,* the photograph of a crucifix in what the title says is urine. Owr-Chall is said to be yielding to censorship, when she is clearly yielding to political and financial pressure, as Pepsi yielded to commercial pressure over the Madonna ad.

15   What is at issue here is not government suppression but government subsidy. Mapplethorpe's work is not banned, but showing it might have endangered federal grants to needy artists. The idea that what the government does not support it represses is nonsensical, as one can see by reversing the statement to read: "No one is allowed to create anything without the government's subvention." What pussycats our supposedly radical artists are. They not only want the government's permission to create their artifacts, they want federal authorities to supply the materials as well. Otherwise they feel "gagged." If they are not given governmental approval (and money), they want to remain an avant-garde while being bankrolled by the Old Guard.

16   What is easily forgotten in this argument is the right of citizen taxpayers. The send representatives to Washington who are answerable for the expenditure of funds exacted from them. In general these voters want to favor their own values if government is going to get into the culture-subsidizing area at all (a proposition many find objectionable in itself). Politicians, insofar as they support the arts, will tend to favor conventional art (certainly not masochistic art). Anybody who doubts that has no understanding of a politician's legitimate concern for his or her constituents' approval. Besides, it is quaint for those familiar with the politics of the art world to discover, with a shock, that there is politics in politics.

17   Luckily, cancellation of the Mapplethorpe show forced some artists back to the flair and cheekiness of unsubsidized art. Other results of pressure do not turn out as well. Unfortunately, people in certain regions were deprived of the chance to see *The Last Temptation of Christ* in the theater. Some, no doubt, considered it a loss that they could not buy lettuce or grapes during a Chavez boycott. Perhaps there was even a buyer perverse enough to miss driving the unsafe cars Nader helped pressure off the market. On the other hand, we do not get sports analysis made by racists. These mobilizations of social opprobrium are not examples of repression but of freedom of expression by committed people who censured without censoring, who expressed the kinds of belief the First Amendment guarantees. I do not, as a result, get whatever I approve of subsidized, either by Pepsi or the government. But neither does the

law come in to silence Tipper Gore or Frank Zappa or even that filthy rag, the *Dartmouth Review*.

Topical Considerations

1. What does Wills mean when he says "Everyone is protecting the country" (paragraph 5)?
2. How does Wills distinguish between censorship and censure? Which does he authorize in this essay? Cite specific examples from the essay to support your reasoning.
3. What does Wills think about "[e]quating morality with legality" (paragraph 7)? How does this statement function to support his thesis?
4. According to Wills, what is the point of freedom of speech?
5. What does Wills think of Christina Owr-Chall's claim that she canceled the Robert Mapplethorpe exhibit to protect it from censorship (paragraph 14)? Do you support Owr-Chall's decision? Why or why not?

Rhetorical Considerations

1. Wills presents two sides to nearly all of the arguments discussed in his essay. What effect does having both sides of an argument available to you simultaneously have on you as a reader? How does this tactic affect Wills' own argument?
2. Does the first paragraph let you know from which position Wills will be arguing? How effective is the lead paragraph in making you want to read on?
3. What assumptions do you think Wills is making about his audience? Does Wills assume that the reader is on his side of the censure issue?
4. What can you assume about Wills' political values? Would you say, from the evidence presented in the essay, that he is conservative or liberal? Point to specific parts of the text to support your reasoning.
5. In his conclusion, Wills recounts nearly all of the censorship issues discussed in his essay. Do you find this an effective strategy for emphasizing his stand, or is it unnecessarily repetitive? Why?

Writing Assignments

1. Try to reduce the whole of Wills' essay to a single paragraph, without directly quoting from it.
2. Write a letter to someone in another country explaining Wills' position in the freedom-of-expression debate. (Be sure to vividly describe the First

Amendment, Tipper Gore, Madonna, etc., to a person unfamiliar with American culture.)

OPPOSITIONS: PORNOGRAPHY

Let's Put Pornography Back in the Closet
Susan Brownmiller

To the solace of some and the discomfort of others, the First Amendment is widely applied to protect free speech of many sorts: political dissent, unpopular ideas, art of "questionable" taste, and pornography. Some feel that such freedom of expression protects the very fiber of our democratic society, whereas others feel it erodes the rights of democratic citizens. In this piece Susan Brownmiller argues that First Amendment protection should not extend to pornography. She further argues that obscene material depicts "hatred of women" and is intended "to humiliate, degrade and dehumanize the female body." Summoning the interpretations of revered authorities, she challenges the current application of First Amendment protection.

Susan Brownmiller is the author of *Against Our Will* (1976), a study of the history of rape. This essay originally appeared in *Newsday* in 1979.

BEFORE YOU READ

Think about the criteria by which materials can be judged obscene. What examples of books, videos, movies, and so on would you classify as obscene? Do you think your definition is a good one? What might be its strengths? Its weaknesses?

AS YOU READ

As you read notice how Brownmiller refers to previous statements of Supreme Court Justices to further her argument. How do these strengthen her case?

1   Free speech is one of the great foundations on which our democracy rests. I am old enough to remember the Hollywood Ten, the screenwriters who went to jail in the late 1940s because they refused to testify before a congressional committee about their political affiliations. They tried to use the First Amendment as a defense, but they went to jail because in those days there were few civil liberties lawyers around who cared to champion the First Amendment right to free speech, when the speech concerned the Communist Party.

2   The Hollywood Ten were correct in claiming the First Amendment. Its high purpose is the protection of unpopular ideas and political dissent. In the dark, cold days of the 1950s, few civil libertarians were willing to declare themselves First Amendment absolutists. But in the brighter, though frantic,

days of the 1960s, the principle of protecting unpopular political speech was gradually strengthened.

3   It is fair to say now that the battle has largely been won. Even the American Nazi Party has found itself the beneficiary of the dedicated, tireless work of the American Civil Liberties Union. But—and please notice the quotation marks coming up—"To equate the free and robust exchange of ideas and political debate with commercial exploitation of obscene material demeans the grand conception of the First Amendment and its high purposes in the historic struggle for freedom. It is a misuse of the great guarantees of free speech and free press."

4   I didn't say that, although I wish I had, for I think the words are thrilling. Chief Justice Warren Burger said it in 1973, in the United States Supreme Court's majority opinion in *Miller v. California.* During the same decades that the right to political free speech was being strengthened in the courts, the nation's obscenity laws also were undergoing extensive revision.

5   It's amazing to recall that in 1934 the question of whether James Joyce's *Ulysses* should be banned as pornographic actually went before the Court. The battle to protect *Ulysses* as a work of literature with redeeming social value was won. In later decades, Henry Miller's *Tropic* books, *Lady Chatterley's Lover* and the *Memoirs of Fanny Hill* also were adjudged not obscene. These decisions have been important to me. As the author of *Against Our Will,* a study of the history of rape that does contain explicit sexual material, I shudder to think how my book would have fared if James Joyce, D. H. Lawrence, and Henry Miller hadn't gone before me.

6   I am not a fan of *Chatterley* or the *Tropic* books, I should quickly mention. They are not to my literary taste, nor do I think they represent female sexuality with any degree of accuracy. But I would hardly suggest that we ban them. Such a suggestion wouldn't get very far anyway. The battle to protect these books is ancient history. Time does march on, quite methodically. What, then, is unlawfully obscene, and what does the First Amendment have to do with it?

7   In the Miller case of 1973 (not Henry Miller, by the way, but a porn distributor who sent unsolicited stuff through the mails), the Court came up with new guidelines that it hoped would strengthen obscenity laws by giving more power to the states. What it did in actuality was throw everything into confusion. It set up a three-part test by which materials can be adjudged obscene. The materials are obscene if they depict patently offensive, hard-core sexual conduct; lack serious scientific, literary, artistic or political value; and appeal to the prurient interest of an average person—as measured by contemporary community standards.

8   "Patently offensive," "prurient interest" and "hard-core" are indeed words to conjure with. "Contemporary community standards" are what we're trying to redefine. The feminist objection to pornography is not based on prurience, which the dictionary defines as lustful, itching desire. We are not opposed to sex and desire, with or without the itch, and we certainly believe that explicit sexual material has its place in literature, art, science and education.

Here we part company rather swiftly with old-line conservatives who don't want sex education in the high schools, for example.

9   No, the feminist objection to pornography is based on our belief that pornography represents hatred of women, that pornography's intent is to humiliate, degrade and dehumanize the female body for the purpose of erotic stimulation and pleasure. We are unalterably opposed to the presentation of the female body being stripped, bound, raped, tortured, mutilated and murdered in the name of commercial entertainment and free speech.

10   These images, which are standard pornographic fare, have nothing to do with the hallowed right of political dissent. They have everything to do with the creation of a cultural climate in which a rapist feels he is merely giving in to a normal urge and a woman is encouraged to believe that sexual masochism is healthy, liberated fun. Justice Potter Stewart once said about hard-core pornography "You know it when you see it," and that certainly used to be true. In the good old days, pornography looked awful. It was cheap and sleazy, and there was no mistaking it for art.

11   Nowadays, since the porn industry has become a multimillion dollar business, visual technology has been employed in its service. Pornographic movies are skillfully filmed and edited, pornographic still shots using the newest tenets of good design artfully grace the covers of *Hustler, Penthouse,* and *Playboy*, and the public—and the courts—are sadly confused.

12   The Supreme Court neglected to define "hard-core" in the Miller decision. This was a mistake. If "hard-core" refers only to explicit sexual intercourse, then that isn't good enough. When women or children or men—no matter how artfully—are shown tortured or terrorized in the service of sex, that's obscene. And "patently offensive," I would hope, to our "contemporary community standards."

13   Justice William O. Douglas wrote in his dissent to the Miller case that no one is "compelled to look." This is hardly true. To buy a paper at the corner newsstand is to subject oneself to a forcible immersion in pornography, to be demeaned by an array of dehumanized, chopped-up parts of the female anatomy, packaged like cuts of meat at the supermarket. I happen to like my body and I work hard at the gym to keep it in good shape, but I am embarrassed for my body and for the bodies of all women when I see the fragmented parts of us, so frivolously, and so flagrantly, displayed.

14   Some constitutional theorists (Justice Douglas was one) have maintained that any obscenity law is a serious abridgement of free speech. Others (and Justice Earl Warren was one) have maintained that the First Amendment was never intended to protect obscenity. We live quite compatibly with a host of free-speech abridgements. There are restraints against false and misleading advertising or statements—shouting "fire" without cause in a crowded movie theater, etc.—that do not threaten, but strengthen, our societal values. Restrictions on the public display of pornography belong in this category.

15   The distinction between permission to publish and permission to display publicly is an essential one and one which I think consonant with First Amendment principles. Justice Burger's words which I quoted above support

this without question. We are not saying "Smash the presses" or "Ban the bad ones," but simply "Get the stuff out of our sight." Let the legislatures decide—using realistic and humane contemporary community standards—what can be displayed and what cannot. The courts, after all, will be the final arbiters.

Topical Considerations

1. Has Brownmiller's article changed your opinion about free speech and pornography? If yes, in what ways? If no, where do you think Brownmiller's article failed?
2. Brownmiller is careful to furnish a definition of what she means by the term *pornography*. Do you think her definition is a clear one? A complete one? Why do you think she is so careful in defining her terms?
3. Brownmiller discusses a number of books that were nearly banned because they were considered "pornographic"—*Ulysses,* the *Tropic* books, *Lady Chatterley's Lover.* Why did people react negatively to these books? Can you think of other books (or movies, recordings, videos, etc.) that have caused a similar reaction in people?
4. Discuss Brownmiller's assertion that "[t]he distinction between permission to publish and permission to display publicly is an essential one" (paragraph 15). What does Brownmiller mean by this? Do you agree or disagree with this statement?
5. Brownmiller acknowledges the power that the courts have in the debate about pornography. Do you think that she trusts the courts to comply with her opinion? Support your reasoning with evidence from the text.

Rhetorical Considerations

1. "Free speech is one of the great foundations on which our democracy rests," opens Brownmiller. What is the effect of this introductory sentence on the reader? Does it point specifically to what the essay will discuss? If so, how? If not, why not?
2. Where does Brownmiller's argument begin? Do you think her thesis is in the most effective place in the essay?
3. What is the effect of paragraph 3, when Brownmiller says, "notice the quotation marks coming up"?
4. Why do you think that Brownmiller mentions *Lady Chatterley's Lover* and the *Tropic* books if she does not like them and does not find them accurate in depicting women's sexuality? Does this serve to strengthen or weaken her argument?
5. What is the effect of the last sentence in paragraph 12, when Brownmiller uses the language of the Supreme Court's obscenity standards to illustrate her viewpoint?

6. At the end of the essay, Brownmiller returns to Justice Burger's quotation and her admission that the courts "will be the final arbiters." Is this an effective conclusion to her argument? Why or why not?

Writing Assignments

1. Imagine that you are a parent, and write a letter in which you urge a teacher to remove certain books from the school curriculum. Be specific about which books you want banned and why. Try to use a calm, informed tone, like the one in Brownmiller's essay.
2. As a teacher, respond to the parent who has written the letter objecting to the choice of certain books on the school's reading list. Defend the books, making sure to cite useful parts of the First Amendment to support your argument, as well as excerpts from the books themselves, if necessary.
3. Lately, much controversy in the movie business has centered around the NC-17 rating given to certain "explicit" films. Write an essay in which you analyze the usefulness of this rating (and, perhaps, of the movie rating system in general). Do you think that an NC-17 rating is given for sexually explicit material more than it is for violent material? Is that how it should be? Why or why not? Cite specific films to support your opinion.

I Am a First Amendment Junkie
Susan Jacoby

Susan Jacoby is an absolutist when it comes to interpreting the First Amendment. As repugnant as various forms of free expression might be, from neo-Nazi rallies to pornographic material, Jacoby does not feel it is the place of the federal government to censor them. Resorting to censorship, she claims, is an abdication of democratic freedom. Jacoby further argues that instead of relying on government institutions to censor material, citizens should rely on their own powers of influence over the marketplace. A real victory would not be to cease publication of a pornographic magazine but, rather, to persuade people not to buy such publications.

Jacoby, with co-author Yelena Khanga, wrote *Soul to Soul: The Story of a Black Russian American Family,* published in 1992.

BEFORE YOU READ

Think of a controversial book, film, or photograph to which you and your friends had markedly different reactions: perhaps some thought it artistic and provocative while others found it disturbing or pornographic. What does such a wide variety of reactions to the same material suggest about the nature of taste and response? What does this suggest about the task of defining what is pornographic and what is not? About the relationship between censorship and individual taste?

AS YOU READ

Does Jacoby use quotations of Supreme Court Justices to support her argument as Brownmiller did in the previous essay? What does this demonstrate about the First Amendment and the ways it can be interpreted? Does this strengthen or weaken your confidence in the First Amendment?

1   It is no news that many women are defecting from the ranks of civil libertarians on the issue of obscenity. The conviction of Larry Flynt, publisher of *Hustler* magazine—before his metanorphosis into a born-again Christian—was greeted with unabashed feminist approval. Harry Reems, the unknown actor who was convicted by a Memphis jury for conspiring to distribute the movie *Deep Throat,* has carried on his legal battles with almost no support from women who ordinarily regard themselves as supporters of the First Amendment. Feminist writers and scholars have even discussed the possibility of making common cause against pornography with adversaries of the women's movement—including opponents of the equal rights amendment and "right-to-life" forces.

2   All of this is deeply disturbing to a woman writer who believes, as I always have and still do, in an absolute interpretation of the First Amendment. Nothing in Larry Flynt's garbage convinces me that the late Justice Hugo L. Black was wrong in this opinion that "the Federal Government is without any power whatsoever under the Constitution to put any type of burden on free speech and expression of ideas of any kind (as distinguished from conduct)." Many women I like and respect tell me I am wrong; I cannot remember having become involved in so many heated discussions of a public issue since the end of the Vietnam War. A feminist writer described my views as those of a "First Amendment junkie."

3   Many feminist arguments for controls on pornography carry the implicit conviction that porn books, magazines and movies pose a greater threat to women than similarly repulsive exercises of free speech pose to other offended groups. This conviction has, of course, been shared by everyone—regardless of race, creed, or sex—who has ever argued in favor of abridging the First Amendment. It is the argument used by some Jews who have withdrawn their support from the American Civil Liberties Union because it has defended the right of American Nazis to march through a community inhabited by survivors of Hitler's concentration camps.

4   If feminists want to argue that the protection of the Constitution should not be extended to *any* particularly odious or threatening form of speech, they have a reasonable argument (although I don't agree with it). But it is ridiculous to suggest that the porn shops on 42nd Street are more disgusting to women than a march of neo-Nazis is to survivors of the extermination camps.

5   The arguments over pornography also blur the vital distinction between expression of ideas and conduct. When I say I believe unreservedly in the First Amendment, someone always comes back at me with the issue of "kiddie

porn." But kiddie porn is not a First Amendment issue. It is an issue of the abuse of power—the power adults have over children—and not of obscenity. Parents and promoters have no more right to use their children to make porn movies than they do to send them to work in coal mines. The responsible adults should be prosecuted, just as adults who use children for back-breaking farm labor should be prosecuted.

6   Susan Brownmiller, in *Against Our Will: Men, Women and Rape*, has described pornography as "the undiluted essence of anti-female propaganda." I think this is a fair description of some types of pornography, especially of the brutish subspecies that equates sex with death and portrays women primarily as objects of violence.

7   The equation of sex and violence, personified by some glossy rock record album covers as well as by *Hustler*, has fed the illusion that censorship of pornography can be conducted on a more rational basis than other types of censorship. Are all pictures of naked women obscene? Clearly not, says a friend. A Renoir nude is art, she says, and *Hustler* is trash." Any reasonable person" knows that.

8   But what about something between art and trash—something, say, along the lines of *Playboy* or *Penthouse* magazines? I asked five women for their reactions to one picture in *Penthouse* and got responses that ranged from "lovely" and "sensuous" to "revolting" and "demeaning." Feminists, like everyone else, seldom have rational reasons for their preferences in erotica. Like members of juries, they tend to disagree when confronted with something that falls short of 100 percent vulgarity.

9   In any case, feminists will not be the arbiters of good taste if it becomes easier to harass, prosecute and convict people on obscenity charges. Most of the people who want to censor girlie magazines are equally opposed to open discussions of issues that are vital concern: rape, abortion, menstruation, contraception, lesbianism—in fact, the entire range of sexual experience from a woman's viewpoint.

10   Feminist writers and editors and film makers have limited financial resources: Confronted by a determined prosecutor, Hugh Hefner will fare better than Susan Brownmiller. Would the Memphis jurors who convicted Harry Reems for his role in *Deep Throat* be inclined to take a more positive view of paintings of the female genitalia done by sensitive feminist artists? *Ms* magazine has printed color reproductions of some of those art works. *Ms* is already banned from a number of high school libraries because someone considers it threatening and/or obscene.

11   Feminists who want to censor what they regard as harmful pornography have essentially the same motivation as other would-be censors: They want to use the power of the state to accomplish what they have been unable to achieve in the marketplace of ideas and images. The impulse to censor places no faith in the possibilities of democratic persuasion.

12   It isn't easy to persuade certain men that they have better uses for $1.95 each month than to spend it on a copy of *Hustler?* Well, then, give the men no choice in the matter.

13   I believe there is also a connection between the impulse toward censorship on the part of people who used to consider themselves civil libertarians and a more general desire to shift responsibility from individuals to institutions. When I saw the movie *Looking for Mr. Goodbar,* I was stunned by its series of visual images equating sex and violence, coupled with what seems to me the mindless message (a distortion of the fine Judith Rossner novel) that casual sex equals death. When I came out of the movie, I was even more shocked to see parents standing in line with children between the ages of 10 and 14.

14   I simply don't know why a parent would take a child to see such a movie, anymore than I understand why people feel they can't turn off a television set their child is watching. Whenever I say that, my friends tell me I don't know how it is because I don't have children. True, but I do have parents. When I was a child, they did turn off the TV. They didn't expect the Federal Communications Commission to do their job for them.

15   I am a First Amendment junkie. You can't OD on the First Amendment, because free speech is its own best antidote.

Topical Considerations

1. How does Jacoby use Brownmiller's definition of *pornography* to support her argument?
2. What does Jacoby mean when she calls herself a "First Amendment junkie"? Does this light-hearted nickname do justice to such a serious topic? Why or why not?
3. Who do you think are "[m]ost of the people" whom Jacoby describes in paragraph 9?
4. Do you think that Jacoby considers herself a feminist? Cite specific examples from the text to support your reasoning.
5. Is Jacoby clear about the difference between "art" and "trash" (paragraphs 7 and 8)? If not, why do you think that the distinction is vague?

Rhetorical Considerations

1. Jacoby presents explicit counterarguments to her position. What is the effect of her giving voice to her opposition? How does she counter her opposition?
2. How does the tone of this essay differ from Brownmiller's? Which essay, in your opinion, poses the stronger overall argument? Why, specifically?
3. How does Jacoby's use of a Supreme Court Justice's words (paragraph 2) differ from Brownmiller's? How does the quotation that Jacoby cites serve her argument?
4. In paragraph 8, Jacoby conducts a minisurvey and furnishes its results to discuss the difference between art and trash. Do you find this information reliable? Why or why not?

5. At the end of her essay, Jacoby switches from a discussion of pornography to a discussion of TV viewing by young people. What is the purpose of this shift? What point is Jacoby trying to make? Do you find this a persuasive conclusion?

Writing Assignments

1. Read a copy of the First Amendment, and use it as a basis for an argument either for or against censorship or freedom of speech. (Keep in mind this question: Are there ways that the First Amendment can be used to argue for both sides of this issue?)
2. Write an essay critiquing Brownmiller's and Jacoby's essays. Try to be as objective as possible in assessing each article's strengths and weaknesses.
3. Are you a "First Amendment junkie"? Why or why not? Do you believe in absolute freedom of speech at all times, or do you think that there are some magazines, movies, books, works of art that cross the line? Write an essay expressing your views, making sure to cite specific examples of what should and should not be protected under the First Amendment.

CHAPTER

14

EDUCATION

Education in 1990s America is at a turning point. Educators argue that students aren't learning the way they once did, while parents and students complain that teachers, professors, and curricula aren't measuring up to previous standards. Critics question the lecture format, a centuries-old conveyer of knowledge. University grading systems, more flexible and forgiving since the educational reforms of the 60s, face revamping by those who would return to more rigorous grading procedures. And the debate rages between those defending the traditional Western canon and those promoting multiculturalism. Everybody agrees that education faces the dilemma of incorporating rapid advances in knowledge while maintaining time-honored traditions and standards. The essays that follow reflect the clash of views regarding what's right and what's wrong with education as it adjusts to an American society influx.

Page Smith's "Killing the Spirit" looks critically at the pedagogical centerpiece of the college experience—the lecture. It has been estimated that almost 90 percent of all instruction at the university level uses the lecture method. Even if the lecturer is not dull, argues Professor Smith, without dialogue between student and instructor "there can be no genuine education." Continuing the critique of the contemporary university in "The College of the Future: Not a Pretty Picture," Patricia Nelson Limerick sketches the ideal collegial relationship between professor and student. The next piece, "A Liberating Curriculum," reflects not idealism but the weariness of a veteran professor. Exasperated by student complaints about grading, Professor Borkat offers a tongue-in-cheek solution to the problem: Automatic A's to all students. In "A War Against Grade Inflation," Jackson Toby defends the traditional approach to grading, including a defense of the "F" for failure.

Over the last few years higher education has undergone some fundamental revamping of course offerings. Traditional Western-World titles have been nudged aside to make room for minority and third-world authors. Not surprisingly, the movement has stirred up some vocal—even vicious—criticism. To conservatives, left-wing ideological pressures are fostering the disintegration of intellectual standards. To liberals, traditional curricula fail to mirror the growing cultural diversity of American society and must be purged of sexism, racism, and elitism. Because of its importance, we have devoted the next four pieces, including our two "Oppositions" pieces, to this "West-versus-the-rest" debate. We open with "The Debate Has Been Miscast from the Start" by black educator Henry Louis Gates. Gates takes the position that a pluralistic approach to education, one embracing many cultures, is the most reasonable, democratic step in creating mutual tolerance and respect. Not all educators agree. In "Too Many Have Let Enthusiasm Outrun Reason," history professor Kenneth T. Jackson contends that the whole multicultural approach to education has reduced history to a "feel-good" list of ethnic and racial "firsts" and created a dangerous us-versus-them mentality.

Our treatment of this issue culminates in our "Oppositions" section. One of the strongest voices of traditionalism is E. D. Hirsch, Jr., who in "Cultural Literacy" blames the deteriorating state of American education on educators. He argues that they have let standards slip by offering a smorgasbord education where students have almost no shared knowledge of their culture. Taking the offensive in "Cult-Lit," Barbara Herrnstein Smith responds directly to Hirsch, slashing his claim that our civilization is in decline, that the barbarians are at the gate. She argues that Hirsch's conservative ideal of a standardized, traditional education for all Americans is not only meaningless in our multi-ethnic society but also detrimental to the nation's schools.

THE CLASSROOM EXPERIENCE

Killing the Spirit
Page Smith

Drawing on some thirty years of college teaching, Page Smith scrutinizes the center-piece of the university experience: the lecture. Smith's contention is that "the lecture system is the most inefficient way of transmitting knowledge ever devised." Smith is the author of sixteen books, *Democracy on Trial: The Japanese-American Evacuation and Relocation in World War II* (1995) being his most recent. This essay was taken from *Killing the Spirit* (1990), a collection of essays on American education.

BEFORE YOU READ

Take a moment to evaluate the many lectures you've attended, making a list of strong and weak points. Ask yourself what makes a lecturer a success or a failure.

AS YOU READ

Would you maintain, abolish, or modify the lecture system? If you could eliminate the lecture, what would you recommend in its place? What strategies, formats, or classroom configurations would you design to better disseminate knowledge?

1   I came away from my years of teaching on the college and university level with a conviction that enactment, performance, dramatization are the most successful forms of teaching. Students must be incorporated, made, so far as possible, an integral part of the learning process. The notion that learning should have in it an element of inspired play would seem to the greater part of the academic establishment merely frivolous, but that is nonetheless the case. Of Ezekiel Cheever, the most famous schoolmaster of the Massachusetts Bay Colony, his onetime student Cotton Mather wrote that he so planned his lessons that his pupils "came to work as though they came to play," and Alfred North Whitehead, almost three hundred years later, noted that a teacher should make his/her students "glad they were there."

2   Since, we are told, 80 to 90 percent of all instruction in the typical university is by the lecture method, we should give close attention to this form of education. There is, I think, much truth in Patricia Nelson Limerick's observation that "lecturing is an unnatural act, an act for which providence did not design humans. It is perfectly all right, now and then, for a human to be possessed by the urge to speak, and to speak while others remain silent. But to do this regularly, one hour and 15 minutes at a time . . . for one person to drone on while others sit in silence? . . . I do not believe that this is what the Creator . . . designed humans to do."

3   The strange, almost incomprehensible fact is that many professors, just as they feel obliged to write dully, believe that they should lecture dully. To show enthusiasm is to risk appearing unscientific, unobjective; it is to appeal to the students' emotions rather than their intellect. Thus the ideal lecture is one crammed with facts and read in an uninflected monotone. Witness the testimony of the eminent sociologist Daniel Bell.

4   When Bell gave a talk to the faculty and staff and some graduate students at the Leningrad State University during a trip to Russia, he spoke extemporaneously (which professors seldom do) and with evident emotion, which clearly moved his listeners profoundly but which left Bell feeling "an odd turbulence. . . . For years," he writes, "I had fought within myself against giving emotional speeches. They were easy, cheap, sentimental, lachrymose. . . . In the lectures I usually give . . . I have tried to be expository, illustrative . . . resenting the cheap jibes to get a rise out of the audience." Here, to his discomfort, he had let emotion get the best of him and, plainly, of his audience. I would only note that the kind of austerity and lack of emotion that Bell normally strove for is the classic mode of the American professor lecturing to his class.

5   The cult of lecturing dully, like the cult of writing dully, goes back, of course, some years. Edward Shils, professor of sociology and social thought at the University of Chicago, recalls the professors he encountered at the University of Pennsylvania in his youth. They seemed "a priesthood, rather uneven in their merits but uniform in their bearing; they never referred to anything personal. Some read from old lecture notes—one of them used to unroll the dog-eared lower corners of his foolscap manuscript and then haltingly decipher the

thumb-worn last lines. Others lectured from cards that had served for years, to judge by the worn and furry edges. . . . The teachers began on time, ended on time, and left the room without saying a word more to their students, very seldom being detained by questioners. . . . Almost all male students wore suits, all wore neckties. . . . The classes were not large, yet there was no discussion. No questions were raised in class, and there were no office hours."

6   William Lyon Phelps described the Yale faculty in the 1890s thusly: "nearly all the members of the Faculty wore dark clothes, frock coats, high collars; in the classroom their manners had an icy formality. . . ." The clothes and manners have become informal, but the aloofness and impersonality, I fear, remain.

7   Karl Jaspers makes the point that the lecture, like research, must never become routine. It is the opportunity for the teacher to present in dramatic fashion, highlighted by his/her own insight and enthusiasm, material that cannot be conveyed with the same potency on the printed page. In the lecture the student must see *enacted* the power and excitement of ideas. The posture, gestures, and intonations of the lecturer carry as much force as the words themselves, words that, when reduced to notes, often lie quite inert on the page.

8   The lecture has a quasi-religious character about it, since exalted speech partakes of the sacred. Every lecture, listened to by dozens or hundreds of students, should partake of art (dramatic art being perhaps the closest). The lecturer who reads his notes dutifully is performing an act that the students can do better for themselves. Such an instructor gives up the very element of spontaneity which alone justifies the lecture as a form of teaching. The lecturer must *address* students. He/she is, after all, asking a good deal of them. If there are two hundred students in the class, the lecturer is saying to them, in effect: What I have to say is of such considerable consequence that I feel entitled to take up two hundred precious hours of your collective time in order to explain it to you, or, even better, in order to enlarge your sense of the possibilities of human existence in relation to this topic we are considering together. "Lectures which aim to sum up an entire subject are in a class by themselves," Jaspers writes. "Such lectures should be given only by the most mature professors drawing upon the sum total of their life's work. . . . Such lectures belong to what is irreplaceable in tradition. The memory of outstanding scholars lecturing, accompanies one throughout life. The printed lecture, perhaps even taken down word for word, is only a pale residue." The inspired lecture evokes, again in Jaspers' words, "something from the teacher which would remain hidden without it. . . . He allows us to take part in his innermost intellectual being." The great lecture is thus a demonstration of something precious and essential in the life of the spirit and the mind, and the dramatic power that inheres in that unity. Such lectures link us with the sermons and political addresses that have played central roles in the "great chain of being" that links classes and generations and nations together in "the unity of spirit." Thus the casual, the perfunctory, the oft-repeated, the read lecture, the *dead* lecture, is

a disservice both to the students and to the ideal of learning that presumably holds the whole venture together.

9   William Lyon Phelps at Yale was a "great teacher," in the class tradition. "If a teacher wishes success with pupils, he must inflame their imagination," he wrote. "The lesson should put the classroom under the spell of an illusion, like a great drama." The abstract should be avoided. "If a pupil feels the reality of any subject, feels it in relation to actual life, half the battle is gained. Terms must be clothed in flesh and blood . . . ," Phelps wrote. The modern professor often takes a contrary turn. The real things are the abstractions; the personal, the individual, the anecdotal are all distractions and indulgences. A professor may give the same course, covering the same material, year in and year out (it is, after all, his "field," and he is actively discouraged from stepping outside it). He/she may go so far as to incorporate in the lectures the latest "researchers," to the degree that they are relevant to undergraduate students, but unless he/she rethinks each lecture, reanimates it, *reappropriates* it, and thereby makes evident to his listeners why they should take their valuable time to listen, the lecturer is discrediting the lecture system and the process of learning that the lecture system represents. The lecturer is putting forward a "negative stereotype," as we say, not just of himself and of lectures in general, but of the whole edifice of higher education. If the lecturer is bored by the constant repetition of familiar material, he may be sure that his auditors are even more bored. The comedian Professor Irwin Corey had a popular routine in which he fell asleep while lecturing; it was invariably greeted with enthusiastic applause.

10   In his fourteen-week survey of the great universities in 1910, the journalist Edwin Slosson attended more than a hundred classes. His strongest impression was "the waste of time and energy in the ordinary collegiate instruction." There was "no lack of industry, devotion, and enthusiasm on the part of the teachers, but the educational results," Slosson wrote, "are not commensurate with the opportunities afforded and the efforts expended." One's strongest impression was of "lost motion." There was "no general appreciation of the fact that the printing press had been invented in the years since the rise of the Medieval university." Most of the professors lectured poorly, and many did not "even take pains to speak distinctly enough so that they can be heard in their small classrooms without strained attention." Conveying information by ear was a strikingly inefficient way of transmitting it, especially to passive, note-taking students who often showed little comprehension of what they were hearing. "The lecture," Slosson concluded, "is useful for inspiration and demonstration, but not for information." It was apparent to Slosson that, despite its obvious and, in the main, undisputed shortcomings, the lecture was persisted in because it was the quickest and easiest way for a professor to discharge his nominal obligations as a teacher of undergraduate students. One of the unfortunate consequences was that the professor commonly indulged himself in excessively detailed information in the field of his academic specialty,

often scanting or ignoring issues of the greatest importance and interest to his captive auditors.

11   I must confess that my own attitude toward lecturing was deeply influenced by my experience in teaching Dante's *Divine Comedy* in a seminar. When I suggested to my students that they devise some modern hells for modern sins, two students in the seminar offered interesting hells for professors-who-neglected-their-students. They proposed that the professors be required to listen to lectures for all eternity. The only point of dispute between them was whether it would be worse torment for professors to have to listen to their own lectures or to those of an especially dull colleague. I have never been able to feel the same way about lecturing since. Every time in the intervening years that I have undertaken to lecture, I have suffered from post-traumatic stress syndrome.

12   I think it is fair to say that the lecture system is the most inefficient way of transmitting knowledge ever devised. It would be much more effective, in most instances, simply to print up a lecturer's notes and distribute them to the students at the beginning of the course. Or students might be given reading lists of important books to pursue on their own initiative. In many instances it would be more useful to let the students give the lectures. All this is not to say, of course, that particularly inventive and enterprising professors can't overcome the most negative aspects of the lecture system, but only to point out that very few do. Indeed, it is the nature of things that there are only a few great lecturers. In the thirty-some years in which I had contact with the academic world, I knew only five or six. They were individuals who had passionately held views of life as well as deep knowledge of their subjects. They took every lecture with the greatest seriousness and spoke as though they realized that to speak was both a privilege and a responsibility. Eugene Rosenstock-Huessy, William Hitchcock, Mary Holmes, Norman O. Brown, Donald Nichol, and Paul Lee all fell into that category.

13   The most conclusive argument against the lecture system is that all true education must involve response. If there is no dialogue, written or spoken, there can be no genuine education. The student must be lured out of his or her instinctive passivity. This can only be done properly if an atmosphere of trust is built in the classroom or seminar. The professor cannot ask his students to expose their innermost hopes and feelings unless he is especially candid with them and allows them to see him as a fallable, searching individual.

14   The best discussion of the relationship between professors and their students (which, of course, is at the heart of all true teaching) is, I am pleased to say, by a former student of mine, Patricia Nelson Limerick, a professor of history at the University of Colorado. After describing a number of imaginative ways to involve students in classroom exercises designed to break down the barriers between "aloof professors" and "shy students," Limerick writes: "In all these exercises, my goals have been the same; to bump students out of passivity, and to bump myself out of self-consciousness and sometimes out of complacency. . . . By contrast, the more conventional tensions of the classroom

cause students and professors to fear making fools of themselves. . . . The underlying reason for holding class, whatever the subject or the course, has to involve the project of inviting students to think for themselves, to ask their own questions, and to pursue the answers with both freedom of thought and discipline of argument." If a professor tries to promote such a notion in the conventional classroom, "there is such a disjunction between the medium and the message," Limerick writes, "that the project will work for only a few. . . . The trial and burden of adventurous teaching is that it never feels safe—you never sign a contract with the universe guaranteeing success in all your experiments."

15   That, of course, is the essence of teaching—taking chances. And you can only do that if you are willing to come down from your perch as a professor of this or that and be as vulnerable (or almost as vulnerable) as your students. No professional vulnerability, no real teaching.

16   Karl Jaspers wrote, "The reverence and love rendered to the master's person have something of worship in them," but Jaspers goes on to point out that the master must turn this "reverence and love" into the channels of learning in a manner perhaps akin to the analytic "transference," wherein the scrupulous analyst directs the patient's instinctive attachment to the analyst back toward the process of healing. Jaspers' ideal in the teaching relationship is the Socratic method, whereby teacher and student "stand on the same level. . . . No hard and fast educational system exists here, rather endless questioning and ultimate ignorance in the face of the absolute."

17   The geologist Israel C. Russell wrote in the journal *Science* in 1904: "In the school of research . . . professor and student should be co-workers and mutually assist each other. From such comradeship, that intangible something which is transmitted from person to person by association and contact, but cannot be written or spoken—we may term it 'inspiration,' or personal magnetism, or perhaps the radium of the soul—is acquired by the student to a greater degree than at any previous time in his life after leaving the caressing arms of his mother."

18   Alfred North Whitehead's wife, Evelyn, told Lucien Price: "When we first came to Harvard, Altie's [Whitehead's] colleagues in the department said, '*Don't let the students interfere with your work!*' Ten or fifteen minutes is long enough for any conference with them." Instead of following his colleagues' advice, Whitehead, who lectured three times a week, would give his students "a whole afternoon or a whole evening. . . . The traffic was two-way, for Whitehead felt that he needed contact with young minds to keep his own springs flowing. 'It is all nonsense,' he said, 'to suppose that the old cannot learn from the young.'"

19   Contacts between professors and their students outside the classroom, ideally in walks or sports or social occasions, are as important as or perhaps more important than classroom contacts, because they reveal something to the student about reality that can, I suspect, be learned no other way. Such contacts demonstrate that ideas are "embodied." They do not exist apart from a

person, remote or near at hand, who enunciates, who takes responsibility for them by declaring them, by speaking about them. It is not only that ideas have consequences; they are held, passionately or perhaps frivolously, by individuals; otherwise they could not survive; they would die of inattention, and of course many do. We are all dependent, in the last analysis, on readers or listeners (and responders) who by responding remind us that we are talking to living souls.

20   In Woodrow Wilson's words: "The ideal college . . . should be a community, a place of close, natural, intimate association, not only of the young men who are its pupils and novices in various lines of study but also of young men with older men . . . of teachers with pupils, outside the classroom as well as inside. . . ."

21   When it became evident beyond question or cavil that professors were determined to ignore the "moral and spiritual" needs of their students, a new academic order called "counselors" was created. Counselors were in essence men and women employed to do what the traditional college education had professed to do (but which it had seldom done)—that is to say, care for what we would call today the psychological needs of the student, what, indeed, John Jay Chapman's ladies and bishops and teas had done at Harvard: provide some human contact, some counsel and advice. I suspect "ladies, Bishops and tea" were a sounder remedy for the distress of undergraduates not simply ignored but positively rebuffed by their instructors. The trouble was (and is) that most of the students who find their way to counselors are near the end of their rope. They have, as we say today, serious "problems." One can only speculate that there might be far fewer such "problems" if faculty members were willing to lend sympathetic ears to the trials and tribulations of the young men and women they are supposed to teach. Their defense, as one might suspect, is that they are not "experts" in matters pertaining to the psychological needs of students, they are only experts in Sanskrit, or economics or abnormal psychology or chemistry. I have long maintained that Ionesco's *The Lesson* should be performed each year for entering freshmen at our institutions of higher learning to prepare them for the years ahead. The reader may recall that in *The Lesson* the student arrives to interrupt the professor in his researches on the origin of ancient Spanish verbs. While he is lecturing on the subject, she experiences acute pain from a toothache. The professor ignores her cries until they become too obtrusive, at which point he strangles her. The play ends as another student arrives.

22   Testimony to the bad consciences of universities about the sorry state of the teaching function is the widespread practice of awarding, with much fanfare, cash prizes to the "teacher-of-the-year." This is supposed to demonstrate the institution's commitment to "excellence in teaching." What it does, in fact, is to distort and demean the true nature of teaching. It is also often the case that untenured winners of such awards soon disappear from the scene, victims of the publish-or-perish rule. So often has this been the case on some cam-

puses that there has been pressure from the administration to make the award only to faculty who have already attained tenure, thus sparing the university the embarrassment of firing someone who has just been recognized as an outstanding teacher. Moreover, although the awards doubtless go, in the main, to deserving individuals, the winners are often those lecturers whom the students simply find the most entertaining. William Arrowsmith, the classics scholar, has written: "At present the universities are as uncongenial to teaching as the Mojave Desert to a clutch of Druid priests. If you want to restore a Druid priesthood you cannot do it by offering prizes for Druid-of-the-year. If you want Druids, you must grow forests. There is no other way of setting about it." In other words, if you want good teaching, you have to create an academic atmosphere where good teaching is encouraged, recognized, and rewarded with something more substantial than "prizes."

23   It should also be said that one of the greatest obstacles to effective teaching is the grading system ("de-grading system" would be a better name for it). It treats the students as isolated individuals. It pits them against each other and, in a sense, against their teachers in a competitive struggle for survival. Only the fittest survive. I have heard not a few professors boast of the severity of their grading. How many students flunked a course was a measure of their tough-mindedness. In addition to discouraging cooperation among students, grades falsify the relation between teacher and student. The teacher's task is to win the student's confidence and to create an air of trust congenial to learning, but over this rather tender relationship there hovers the cloud of that grade. Professors often fall into the habit of thinking of students less as people in need of help and guidance than as A students or C students, a very bad frame of mind indeed.

Topical Considerations

1. Do you think the author prefers the classic style of William Lyon Phelps or the modern one? Explain your answer using specific details. Which do you prefer? Which style have you seen more of in your school?
2. Do you agree with Smith's notion that 80 to 90 percent of all university instruction is lecture? In your response, discuss your own experience in college classes.
3. Smith begins with the point that "Students must be . . . an integral part of the learning process." Has this been true for you during your experience as a high-school and college student? Explain your answer.
4. Many students have difficulty taking lecture notes, especially if the lecture is dull. Do you find it easy or difficult to record the important information from a lecture? Describe your note-taking process during a lecture.
5. Has Smith's view of teaching changed your views, reinforced your views, or had no effect on your views of teaching? Explain your reasoning.

6. Alfred North Whitehead said, "It is all nonsense to suppose that the old cannot learn from the young" (paragraph 18). Do you agree or disagree? Why or why not?

7. Why does Smith think entering freshmen should view Ionesco's *The Lesson?* Do you agree? Why or why not?

8. Have you experienced classrooms where there is a dialogue between teacher and student? Describe how the class works and whether that method is advantageous. If you have not had such an experience, describe how you think it might work and whether that method would be advantageous.

Rhetorical Considerations

1. At the beginning of the essay, Smith uses first-person point of view giving his opinion and backing it with several examples. After he gives a definition of lecturing, what change of tone does he use in the next three paragraphs? Is it effective? Explain why or why not.

2. The author interjects his personal feelings at several points. Give an example and explain whether you think it is effective or not.

3. When each of us writes an essay, we pull from our own experiences for examples. From where does Smith get his examples?

4. Is his use of past and present day examples effective? Use an example of each to agree or disagree.

5. Do you think this essay should end with paragraph 20, 21, or 22 rather than 23? Support your decision with valid reasoning.

6. Consider the voice of the author. Describe the author as a teacher based on his voice in this essay. Be sure to use specific examples.

Writing Assignments

1. Has this essay influenced your view of college professors? If so, write a paper describing the influence of Smith's essay on your own views, attitudes and/or behavior.

2. We have all sat through lectures that bored us miserably. Think of a teacher or professor whose classes habitually put you to sleep or nearly so. Write a paper analyzing just what made that instructor's classes so dull. Aside from the material, consider his or her style of talking (i.e., intonation, volume, variation, accent), personal deportment, attitude, and the use or lack of anecdotes, humor, abstractions, specific details, visual aids, physical movement, gestures, facial expression, and so forth.

3. Design your own dull-lecturer's hell. Write a paper describing what the experience should be like for outstandingly boring instructors. Try to come up with some original torments.

4. Write a paper, describing a professor or teacher you have had who was truly an exception to the rule—one who was, in Smith's words (paragraph 9), a "'great teacher' in the classic tradition." In your paper, try to explain just what it was that made that person such an outstanding teacher.

College of Future: Not a Pretty Picture
Patricia Nelson Limerick

According to the author of this piece, ". . . contact between teacher and learner is a university's heartbeat. When it stops education stops." In this argument, Limerick paints the ideal student/teacher relationship, one based on personal contact and exchange of ideas. She then goes on to explain why that relationship is imperiled on today's college campuses.

Patricia Nelson Limerick—former student of Page Smith who is the author of the previous essay—is a professor at the University of Colorado in Boulder where she is a historian specializing in the American West. In 1995 she was a recipient of a MacArthur Foundation "genius grant." This essay first appeared in *USA Today* in 1994.

BEFORE YOU READ

If you were asked to describe the ideal institution of higher education for you, what would be its five most important characteristics? Compare your list with those of other classmates. Do you find consensus or inconsistencies? Explain.

AS YOU READ

Are you convinced by Limerick that your actions can make a difference in the caliber of teacher/student relationships? Why or why not?

1   The company of a lively, motivated student is a pleasure of the highest order. But I fear for the future: When I see students in class, it will be several hundred of them in a lecture hall, and me in the distance, trapped at a podium. They will know my name; I will not know theirs.

2   And so, for the high school students and their parents reading this, I'm afraid we're in trouble: I'm afraid the colleges of your future are not going to do right by you.

3   The essence of higher education is a professor and a student meeting in a room where they can call each other by name and hear each other

speak. The other, often more expensive, things—computers, high-tech audiovisuals, administrators, even transcripts—can be useful but are not essential.

4   Professors and students who like and respect and want to listen to each other—that is the element without which colleges cannot live. That contact between teacher and learner is a university's heartbeat. When it stops, education stops.

5   The heartbeat now is faltering, and both students and professors have contributed to the problem. Understandably anxious about their careers in a depressed economy, many students have narrowed their horizons to grade-grubbing, doing the minimum amount of work for the maximum grade-point average. Under these terms, paying attention to their ideas can be about as interesting as reading pages and pages of classified ads.

6   Professors have yielded to their own version of career anxiety and grade-grubbing. College teachers are, with good reason, anxious about their futures in a system that defines merit in terms of publication and professional standing, not commitment to or talent for teaching.

7   This system has treated me well. But, on behalf of those treated less well, I must say that the emphasis on publication is a juggernaut that is running without guidance, without vision, without direction, without principle.

8   On top of (and partly because of) these internal afflictions, we now have a flood of public hostility to education and a universal crisis in funding. Money cannot guarantee quality in education. But the reduction of funding does, directly and tangibly, reduce essential services, facilities and, maybe most important, morale. When departments, programs, professors, graduate students and undergraduates are pitted against each other, tugging at scarce resources, a university comes apart at the seams.

9   Thus, I envision a future where my colleagues and I will be primarily processors of tests, grades, forms, names and numbers; I fear my future students will be a blur of faces in a crowded lecture hall; I mourn the erosion of my opportunities to be moved and instructed by the company of young people, opportunities that any teacher should cherish and fight to maintain.

10   My undergraduate college's motto was "The pursuit of truth in the company of friends." Many of my own teachers lived that motto. I know that the dream, the ideal, the myth of higher education is workable and practical, and I know as well that it is embattled and endangered.

11   If you are a teen-ager or the parent of a teen-ager, is there anything you can do individually to escape this dilemma? A few small liberal arts colleges may stay in the business of intense, personally engaged education. But even those places face a narrowing of resources and of access. The crisis of higher education is hitting every institution, and no private tutor or special cram course can buy an exemption for an individual student.

12   This is a dilemma we must respond to collectively. What we all—parents, students, alumni, professors, administrators and legislators—must do is clear:

13 • Keep funding for higher education at a level where scarcity does not poison the atmosphere of the campus.

14 • Reduce the pressure and pacing of demands for professorial publication.

15 • Remind students and professors that the point of the whole business is the pleasure they take in each other's company, the lessons they teach each other, the affection and memory tying a society's young to their elders.

16   Even in its tattered and vexed state, the university—unlike many other institutions—does far more good than harm. Even when the university is driving you crazy, you have to treasure the encounter between students and teachers made possible by its existence. This is an institution which could hold us together if we don't, in the next few years, tear it apart.

Topical Considerations

1. How does Limerick feel about her students? What kind of relationship with her students does she enjoy the most?
2. How does Limerick hope her students feel about her? What kinds of benefits does she believe students in an ideal situation can gain from close contact with professors?
3. What social and economic forces are encouraging universities and professors to stop offering the best kind of student-teacher relationships?
4. What social and economic forces are encouraging students to stop being part of the best kind of student-teacher relationships?
5. Do you agree that a depressed economy leads to "grade-grubbing," as Limerick says it does in paragraph 5? Are you a grade-grubber? Why or why not?
6. What recommendations does Limerick make for improving, or fostering the quality of relationships between professors and students? What real changes, specifically, will each of her recommendations make within a university?

Rhetorical Considerations

1. Limerick uses some vivid vocabulary in her article. Discuss the connotations of the following terms, and describe how they help her to build her argument: **grubbing** (paragraph 5); **juggernaut** (paragraph 7); **flood** (paragraph 8); **elders** (paragraph 15). Where else in the essay does she reinforce these connotations? (Look up terms you aren't familiar with in a good college-edition or unabridged dictionary.)
2. What groups of people does Limerick define as her primary audience? Where does she identify or appeal to specific groups? How effectively does

she reach these readers; what strategies does she use to get and hold their attention?

3. What groups of people does Limerick define as her secondary audience? Where does she identify or appeal to specific groups? How effectively does she reach her secondary audience without losing the primary audience?

4. What assumptions does Limerick make about her readers' class status or age—particularly, about their access to money? What evidence do you find that she has limited her target audience in specific ways?

5. Page Smith, in his essay "Killing the Spirit," seems to agree on many points with Limerick; he quotes from other works she has written extensively (in paragraphs 2 and 14). What is the difference in voice between Smith's article and Limerick's? How does original publication of each essay and the kinds of information each one uses to build an argument influence the voice?

6. Examine Limerick's paragraph structures carefully. Does she use topic sentences in each paragraph? Does she spend several sentences supplying evidence and elaboration? Can you find any sweeping generalizations? What do you think your own instructor would say about Limerick's paragraph structures and evidence, if this article were turned in as a response to a writing assignment?

7. Which writing style do you prefer, Smith's or Limerick's? Which would you most likely read to the end of your own free will (that is, rather than as assigned reading)? Why?

Writing Assignments

1. Find out what awards your university offers to professors for "outstanding teaching." Does your campus have a "teacher of the year" award? Several? What are the criteria for these awards? If your campus does have such an award system, interview some of the winners, and some of the professors you think are "good teachers" who have not won this recognition. Does everyone think the award system is fair? If your college doesn't have such an award system, find out why not; do your professors think it's a waste of time?

2. Write a letter to your college or university's president, enclosing this article. In your letter, explain what you do and do not like about the contact you have had with professors so far. In your opinion, do teachers spend enough time with you? Would you like to see more events at which you can get to know your professors? Can you make specific, realistic recommendations for ways your campus morale could be improved? You could also direct such a letter to the "reader opinion" section of your local campus newspaper.

3. Using this article, and Page Smith's "Killing the Spirit," prepare a list of Ten Commandments you would like all your college professors to follow. Make sure your list is simple enough that it could be posted on a bulletin board,

and that it applies to all subjects taught at your school (science, humanities, business, and so on). Your instructor may ask that you work in groups or individually on this project.

4. How well did your high school experience (and work experience, if you are an older student) prepare you for the kind of student-teacher relationships that Limerick promotes in her article? Were you encouraged to speak freely? to question and explore new ideas? Working as a group, prepare a set of survey questions to ask other students on your campus about their student-teacher relationships; try to get responses from students from a broad range of high schools and experiences. When you have compiled the results, discuss ways that your campus might help to make the transition into college easier.

A Liberating Curriculum
Roberta F. Borkat

Imagine taking courses in which you didn't have to worry about grades. Better still, imagine a curriculum whereby you get an automatic grade of A in each course you enroll in. No more anxiety, no more burden of competition as you breeze through four obstacle-free years to graduation. Isn't that what college is all about? Such is the plan that Roberta F. Borkat proposes after more than twenty years in the college classroom. Years, she says, of wasted efforts. Or were they?

Roberta F. Borkat is a professor of English and comparative literature at San Diego State University. Her essay first appeared in the "My Turn" column in *Newsweek* in April 1993.

BEFORE YOU READ

If you would automatically receive a grade of A in all your courses would that change the way you approach your academic work? Why or why not? What does your reaction to an automatic A say about your attitude toward learning? Your course work? Your professor? Your goals? The institution of learning you attend?

AS YOU READ

Would you rather be Borkat's student before or after she adopts her new grading policy? Explain your answer, referring to comments in her essay.

1   A blessed change has come over me. Events of recent months have revealed to me that I have been laboring as a university professor for more than 20 years under a misguided theory of teaching. I humbly regret that during all those years I have caused distress and inconvenience to thousands of students while providing some amusement to my more practical colleagues. Enlightenment

came to me in a sublime moment of clarity while I was being verbally attacked by a student whose paper I had just proved to have been plagiarized from "The Norton Anthology of English Literature." Suddenly, I understood the true purpose of my profession, and I devised a plan to embody that revelation. Every moment since then has been filled with delight about the advantages to students, professors and universities from my Plan to Increase Student Happiness.

2   The plan is simplicity itself: at the end of the second week of the semester, all students enrolled in each course will receive a final grade of A. Then their minds will be relieved of anxiety, and they will be free to do whatever they want for the rest of the term.

3   The benefits are immediately evident. Students will be assured of high grade-point averages and an absence of obstacles in their march toward graduation. Professors will be relieved of useless burdens and will have time to pursue their real interests. Universities will have achieved the long-desired goal of molding individual professors into interchangeable parts of a smoothly operating machine. Even the environment will be improved because education will no longer consume vast quantities of paper for books, compositions and examinations.

4   Although this scheme will instantly solve countless problems that have plagued education, a few people may raise trivial objections and even urge universities not to adopt it. Some of my colleagues may protest that we have an obligation to uphold the integrity of our profession. Poor fools, I understand their delusion, for I formerly shared it. To them, I say: "Hey, lighten up! Why make life difficult?"

5   Those who believe that we have a duty to increase the knowledge of our students may also object. I, too, used to think that knowledge was important and that we should encourage hard work and perseverance. Now I realize that the concept of rewards for merit is elitist and, therefore, wrong in a society that aims for equality in all things. We are a democracy. What could be more democratic than to give exactly the same grade to every single student?

6   One or two forlorn colleagues may even protest that we have a responsibility to significant works of the past because the writings of such authors as Chaucer, Shakespeare, Milton, and Swift are intrinsically valuable. I can empathize with these misguided souls, for I once labored under the illusion that I was giving my students a precious gift by introducing them to works by great poets, play-wrights and satirists. Now I recognize the error of my ways. The writings of such authors may have seemed meaningful to our ancestors, who had nothing better to do, but we are living in a time of wonderful improvements. The writers of bygone eras have been made irrelevant, replaced by MTV and People magazine. After all, their bodies are dead. Why shouldn't their ideas be dead, too?

7   If any colleagues persist in protesting that we should try to convey knowledge to students and preserve our cultural heritage, I offer this suggestion: honestly consider what students really want. As one young man graciously explained to me, he had no desire to take my course but had enrolled in it merely to fulfill a requirement that he resented. His job schedule made it

impossible for him to attend at least 30 percent of my class sessions, and he wouldn't have time to do much of the reading. Nevertheless, he wanted a good grade. Another student consulted me after the first exam, upset because she had not studied and had earned only 14 points out of a possible 100. I told her that, if she studied hard and attended class more regularly, she could do well enough on the remaining tests to pass the course. This encouragement did not satisfy her. What she wanted was an assurance that she would receive at least a B. Under my plan both students would be guaranteed an A. Why not? They have good looks and self-esteem. What more could anyone ever need in life?

8   I do not ask for thanks from the many people who will benefit. I'm grateful to my colleagues who for decades have tried to help me realize that seriousness about teaching is not the path to professorial prestige, rapid promotion and frequent sabbaticals. Alas, I was stubborn. Not until I heard the illuminating explanation of the student who had plagiarized from the anthology's introduction to Jonathan Swift did I fully grasp the wisdom that others had been generously offering to me for years—learning is just too hard. Now, with a light heart, I await the plan's adoption. In my mind's eye, I can see the happy faces of university administrators and professors, released at last from the irksome chore of dealing with students. I can imagine the joyous smiles of thousands of students, all with straight-A averages and plenty of free time.

9   My only regret is that I wasted so much time. For nearly 30 years, I threw away numerous hours annually on trivia: writing, grading and explaining examinations; grading hundreds of papers a semester; holding private conferences with students; reading countless books; buying extra materials to give students a feeling for the music, art and clothing of past centuries; endlessly worrying about how to improve my teaching. At last I see the folly of grubbing away in meaningless efforts. I wish that I had faced facts earlier and had not lost years because of old-fashioned notions. But such are the penalties for those who do not understand the true purpose of education.

Topical Considerations

1. Consider the main benefits Borkat says her "Plan to Increase Student Happiness" will have for students (paragraphs 2–3). Would you approve of such a plan? Why or why not?

2. In her last paragraph, Borkat describes how she wasted almost thirty years' time on teaching. Do you think this time was wasted or well spent? Why? Can you tell the difference between professors who put such effort into teaching, and those who do not? In general, do you believe you get a better education from harder-working teachers? Explain your answers.

3. Consider the students Borkat describes in her essay. What is their attitude toward school work? In what ways do the students in Borkat's essay accurately reflect today's college student? In what ways does Borkat misrepresent students?

4. Consider Borkat's attitude toward university administrators and her fellow professors. What, in Borkat's view, do these two groups believe is the goal of higher education? Does Borkat confirm your own observations, or do you have a different impression of university faculty and staff?

5. Borkat refers to the eighteenth century English writer Jonathan Swift twice. Why is Swift's work particularly relevant to this essay? If you know nothing about this writer, look him up in an encyclopedia or *The Norton Anthology of English Literature* mentioned in paragraph 1.

6. What do you think is Borkat's central point?

Rhetorical Considerations

1. Carefully analyze the words Borkat uses in paragraph 1. What, for example, is the connotation of a word like "blessed" (in the first sentence)? Do you find other such connotations in her language? How does Borkat's word choice in this paragraph signal her real attitude toward her Plan?

2. Consider the organization of Borkat's essay by identifying the purpose of each of the nine paragraphs. What argumentative strategy does Borkat spend most time on? Why?

3. Analyze the logic Borkat uses in paragraph 5 to refute the idea that "we should encourage hard work and perseverance." Do you agree with Borkat's definition of democracy?

4. Do you think this essay could result in educational reform? Why or why not? If this is not its purpose, then what is?

Writing Assignments

1. Using the same basic rhetorical strategy as Borkat, write an essay attacking some aspect of teacher belief or behavior.

2. Write a letter to Professor Borkat defending students against her criticism. Back up your argument with secondary research as well as personal interviews with other students, teachers, and members of the university administration.

3. Read Jonathan Swift's "A Modest Proposal" and write a paper in which you demonstrate how Borkat's own essay is similar in purpose, slant, tone, structure, and so forth.

A War Against Grade Inflation
Jackson Toby

Whether it's a semester transcript or a lengthy research paper, the eye invariably scans the material for that single telling letter—A, B, C, D, or F—scribbled by one's professor. That fateful cipher, collapsing a complex reaction into a stroke, can seal a student's fate for better or worse. It can mean an honors grade, a desirable job, the praise of parents, the respect of peers, or the approval of a professor. Thus, it is not difficult to appreciate the controversy surrounding grading systems at our colleges and universities. Fueled by the highly charged significance of grades and complicated by the subjective nature of the grading process, the debate is rancorous.

In this essay, Jackson Toby, a professor of sociology at Rutgers University, offers his view of grading, specifically the problem of grade inflation. He defends the grade, including the F, as a valuable tool of evaluation. This essay first appeared in the *The Wall Street Journal* in September 1994.

BEFORE YOU READ

How important are grades to you? What, in your opinion, do they reflect? Do you think the grading system at your college or university is fair? Are there abuses? What would you see as an ideal grading system?

AS YOU READ

In light of Professor Toby's comments on grades, would you want him grading your next English paper? Why or why not? Toby started university teaching 43 years ago. Would his experience enhance or hamper his ability to comment on grading systems today? Why or why not?

1   The anonymous note left under my office door in May 1991 was like a slap in the face: "How can you justify giving 13 A's in a class with over 200 people. You are just an old [expletive deleted]. I could have had a 4.0 for three straight semesters. You know you have a blow-off class. Burn in hell."

2   At the bottom of the note was a drawing of a hand in an obscene gesture. Uncivil? Certainly. What was more interesting, however, was that its author felt *entitled* to an A in my criminology course, one consequence of the grandiose expectations fed by grade inflation.

3   When I started teaching at Rutgers 43 years ago, A's constituted 13% of the grades awarded to our students, B's 29%, C's 34%, D's 12%, and F's 6%. In 1971 about a quarter of the Rutgers grades were A's and about a third were B's. By 1990–91, A's and B's were two-thirds of all grades. Grade inflation galloped even faster in the most highly selective—and expensive—private colleges. About 90% of the grades at Stanford and 73% at Harvard are A's and B's. Stanford, Brown, and Oberlin abolished the F, and Brown and Oberlin abolished the D for good measure.

4   Some faculty resistance to grade inflation has developed. This June the Stanford Faculty Senate voted 37 to 3 to bring back a failing grade in 1995–96—to be called NP for "not passed"—despite a poll of Stanford's un-

dergraduates showing that 48% of the sample opposed the return of the possibility of failure, compared with 40% who approved. A few professors also resisted failing grades. Ronald Rebholz of the English department accused the Faculty Senate of falling into a "punitive mode" that involved "branding students."

5   There is still much more to be done, at Stanford and at most other colleges. Grades cannot communicate clear meanings unless they are understood in the same way by the professor who assigns the grade, the student who receives it, and the other people who read the transcript. Stanford's NP decision does not attempt to deal with the confusion created by different professors with very different grading standards. This confusion drives grade inflation.

6   When some professors give everyone or nearly everyone an A, students who enroll in a course taught by a professor old-fashioned enough to give C's, D's and F's are at a competitive disadvantage. A "C" in that course can ruin their averages and jeopardize their chances of getting into law or medical school even though it does not mean what readers of the transcript think. This tempts many students to take courses with professors with the lowest grading standards, and tougher professors are tempted to sell out to the enrollment votes of student consumers.

7   A more pointed attack on grade inflation will begin this fall at Dartmouth. To reduce the incentive to give and to receive inflated grades, Dartmouth will start to include on the student's transcript not only the grade in each class but the size of the class and the median grade of all of its students. Predictably, some professors objected. Prof. Delo Mook of the physics department said this would "pit one student against another. I don't think it [competition] is something we want to encourage."

8   But one of the main reasons for going to schools and colleges instead of being educated by one's parents is to find out how one compares with agemates in the ability to learn what society thinks it is important to know. The grading system has to be consistent, however, for the competition to be fair. Without compelling professors to change their previous grading practices, the new Dartmouth policy, used also by a few other colleges and universities, seeks to return grading to a more honest evaluation of students, which is what grades are intended to be.

9   Students need to discover early whether they are wasting their time in college because they lack either the intellectual ability or the motivation to learn enough to justify taking four years out of their lives. An "A" should encourage the student to continue studying; he is learning what he is supposed to be learning; a "D" or an "F" should tell him that he may be in the wrong field or the wrong college. Or maybe a low grade tells him that he should stop fooling around and start studying.

10   Society—and society includes parents—also needs grades. Is the enormous expense of sending a student to college for four years—as much as $100,000—likely to pay off? It is now almost impossible for a student to

work his way through college without a subsidy from parents, government or the college itself. Shouldn't students justify the subsidy to their sponsors? Several high grades suggest that the investment has prospects of paying off. Several low grades suggest that the student may be better off quitting and taking a full-time job, or shifting his studies to a school or program where he will do better.

11   *Postscript:* I discovered the identity of the angry student. A computer check showed only one student with a B+ in criminology and two previous semesters with a straight A average: a graduating senior with a double major in economics and computer science. Had my evaluation of his work cost him an award at graduation? No, it hadn't. Although his cumulative average was very good, grade inflation had eroded the value of his achievements; many of his classmates had even higher averages.

Topical Considerations

1. Who was the student who left the note under Toby's door? What did the note say? What gestures and words does Toby not describe or print? How does Toby respond?

2. Graph the grade inflation Toby describes in his third paragraph. Do graphed numbers help you agree that grade inflation is a serious problem? For every 100 students enrolled, how many received As and Bs at Rutgers in 1951, the year Toby began teaching? How many in 1971? How many in 1990–1991? How many at Stanford? How many at Harvard?

3. Why do faculty and administrators allow grade inflation, or practices that encourage grade inflation?

4. Why does Toby offer to crack down on grade inflation? Why does he offer to return to "a more honest evaluation of students"?

5. If a student is studying hard, but earning poor grades, what do you think Toby would say about this student? Is this student just not very bright, or would Toby think about other possible reasons?

6. Do you think your grades are inflated? How do you respond to the grades you've earned in college classes so far, or (if this is your first semester) to grades you've received on papers and exams? Have you ever received a grade that you didn't think you had earned, either good or bad? What did you do about it—did it change your behavior?

Rhetorical Considerations

1. Why does Toby begin his article with an anecdote about a student's note slipped under his door? Do you think that this note was the only thing that

prompted Toby to write his article? If not, what function does it play in his argument?

2. Why does Toby wait until the end of the article to supply more information about the student's identity? What effect does this delay have on his argument?

3. How does Toby feel about comments by Ronald Rebholz at Stanford, about reinstating the failing grade? How does he feel about the comments of Dartmouth's Delo Mook, about the inclusion of class size and median grade on students' transcripts? How do you know what Toby thinks of his colleagues' objections?

4. Toby does not defend his argument against a possible objection: that students are actually doing better work than they were 43 years ago, and that the higher grades they earn are justified. If you were Toby, how would you disprove that students are not really doing better work—what sources could you use?

5. What is Toby's attitude toward students? What kind of an image does he project here—would you want to take a class from Professor Toby?

6. Given the choice of taking a class from any one of the four authors in this section (Smith, Limerick, Borkat, or Toby), which one would you choose? What would your criteria be for selecting one, rather than any of the other three?

Writing Assignments

1. Using the reasoning in this article, draft a letter from Professor Jackson Toby to the student who left the note under his door. Remember that although Toby may feel justifiably angry at the way the student expressed his views, he is also a professional who would respond with dignity.

2. Page Smith, in his final paragraph in "Killing the Spirit," says that grades "falsify the relation between teacher and student." Jackson Toby, in this article, and Roberta Borkat in "A Liberating Curriculum," argue for consistent, fairly tough grading standards. What do you think? Do grades help you do your best work, by providing good feedback? Do you feel like you are in competition with your peers? Do you feel that your relationship with professors is damaged by the presence of grades?

3. How important are grades in your ability to get a good job after graduation? Using your library's business news resources and your school's career counseling center, research the amount of importance placed on grade point averages by prospective employers. You'll probably want to limit your search to a career path you're already interested in. Did you find what you expected to find? Write an editorial to your school's newspaper about this project, telling your fellow students about your findings.

MULTICULTURALISM

The Debate Has Been Miscast
From the Start
Henry Louis Gates, Jr.

In response to the growing minority population and the cultural diversity of America, the curricula of secondary schools and colleges have undergone reshaping. History books, traditionally centered on the white Western World, have been rewritten to accommodate the experiences and contributions of ethnic and racial minorities. Likewise literary courses that had exclusively focused on Western Europeans have made room for authors of color. Such revamping of curricula, however, has been decried as a violation of tradition. Worse still, the new ethnic chauvinism threatens to further fragment society into hostile subgroups. In the following essay educator Henry Louis Gates, Jr., contends that while the multicultural approach may not be a cure-all for our social ills it can encourage social tolerance.

Gates is chairman of the Afro-American Studies Department and professor of English at Harvard University. He is the author of several award-winning books including *Signifying Monkey* (1989), *Loose Cannons* (1992), and *Colored People* (1993). This article appeared in *The Boston Globe Sunday Magazine* in October 1991.

BEFORE YOU READ

The face of America has changed and we live in a multicultural society. Should a college's curriculum reflect the ethnic diversity or should it reflect traditional Western culture?

AS YOU READ

Gates is an elegant essayist. As you read, find four or five sentences that crystalize Gates's major observations about the place of multiculturalism in school curriculum.

1   What is multiculturalism and why are they saying such terrible things about it?

2   We've been told that it threatens to fragment American culture into a warren of ethnic enclaves, each separate and inviolate. We've been told that it menaces the Western tradition of literature and the arts. We've been told that it aims to politicize the school curriculum, replacing honest historical scholarship with a "feel good" syllabus designed solely to bolster the self-esteem of minorities. The alarm has been sounded, and many scholars and educators—liberals as well as conservatives—have responded to it. After all, if multiculturalism is just a pretty name for ethnic chauvinism, who needs it?

3   But I don't think that's what multiculturalism is—at least, I don't think that's what it ought to be. And because the debate has been miscast from the beginning, it may be worth setting the main issues straight.

4   To both proponents and antagonists, multiculturalism represents—either refreshingly or frighteningly—a radical departure. Like most claims for cultural novelty, this one is more than a little exaggerated. For the challenges of cultural pluralism—and the varied forms of official resistance to it—go back to the very founding of our republic.

5   In the university today, it must be admitted, the challenge has taken on a peculiar inflection. But the underlying questions are time-tested. What does it mean to be an American? Must academic inquiry be subordinated to the requirements of national identity? Should scholarship and education reflect our actual diversity, or should they, rather, forge a communal identity that may not yet have been achieved?

6   For answers, you can, of course, turn to the latest jeremiad on the subject from, say, George Will, Dinesh D'Souza, or Roger Kimball. But in fact these questions have always occasioned lively disagreement among American educators. In 1917, William Henry Hulme decried "the insidious introduction into our scholarly relations of the political propaganda of a wholly narrow, selfish, and vicious nationalism and false patriotism." His opponents were equally emphatic in their beliefs. "More and more clearly," Fred Lewis Pattee ventured in 1919, "is it seen now that the American soul, the American conception of democracy, Americanism, should be made prominent in our school curriculums, as a guard against the rising spirit of experimental lawlessness." Sound familiar?

7   Given the political nature of the debate over education and the national interest, the conservative penchant for charging the multiculturalists with "politics" is a little perplexing. For conservative critics, to their credit, have never hesitated to provide a political defense of what they consider to be the "traditional" curriculum: The future of the republic, they argue, depends on the inculcation of proper civic virtues. What these virtues are is a matter of vehement dispute. But to imagine a curriculum untouched by political concerns is to imagine—as no one does—that education can take place in a vacuum.

8   So where's the beef? Granted, multiculturalism is no panacea for our social ills. We're worried when Johnny can't read. We're worried when Johnny can't add. But shouldn't we be worried, too, when Johnny tramples gravestones in a Jewish cemetery or scrawls racial epithets on a dormitory wall? And it's because we've entrusted our schools with the fashioning of a democratic polity that education has never been exempt from the kind of debate that marks every other aspect of American political life.

9   Perhaps this isn't altogether a bad thing. As the political theorist Amy Gutmann has argued: "In a democracy, political disagreement is not something that we should generally seek to avoid. Political controversies over our educational problems are a particularly important source of social progress because they have the potential for educating so many citizens."

10   And while I'm sympathetic to what Robert Nisbet once dubbed the "academic dogma"—the ideal of knowledge for its own sake—I also believe that truly humane learning, unblinkered by the constraints of narrow ethno-centrism, can't help but expand the limits of human understanding and social tolerance. Those who fear that "Balkanization" and social fragmentation lie this way have got it exactly backward. Ours is a world that already is fissured by nationality, ethnicity, race, and gender. And the only way to transcend those divisions—to forge, for once, a civic culture that respects both differences and commonalities—is through education that seeks to comprehend the diversity of human culture. Beyond the hype and the high-flown rhetoric is a pretty homely truth: There is no tolerance without respect—and no respect without knowledge.

11   The historical architects of the university always understood this. As Cardinal Newman wrote more than a century ago, the university should promote "the power of viewing many things at once as one whole, of referring them severally to their true place in the universal system, of understanding their respective values, and determining their mutual dependence." In just this vein, the critic Edward Said has recently suggested that "our model for academic freedom should therefore be the migrant or traveler: for if, in the real world outside the academy, we must need be ourselves and only ourselves, inside the academy we should be able to discover and travel among other selves, other identities, other varieties of the human adventure. But, most essentially, in this joint discovery of self and other, it is the role of the academy to transform what might be conflict, or context, or assertion into reconciliation, mutuality, recognition, creative interaction."

12   But if multiculturalism represents the culmination of an age-old ideal—the dream known, in the 17th century, as *mathesis universalis*—why has it been the target of such ferocious attacks? On this point, I'm often reminded of a wonderfully wicked piece of 19th-century student doggerel about Benjamin Jowett, the great Victorian classicist and master of Balliol College, Oxford:

Here stand I, my name is Jowett,
If there's knowledge, then I know it;
I am the master of this college,
What I know not, is not knowledge.

13   Of course, the question of how we determine what is worth knowing is now being raised with uncomfortable persistence. So that in the most spirited attacks on multiculturalism in the academy today, there's a nostalgic whiff of the old sentiment: We are the masters of this college; what we know not is not knowledge.

14   I think this explains the conservative desire to cast the debate in terms of the West vs. the Rest. And yet that's the very opposition that the pluralist wants to challenge. Pluralism sees cultures as porous, dynamic, and interactive, rather than the fixed property of particular ethnic groups. Thus the idea of a monolithic, homogeneous "West" itself comes into question (nothing new

here: Literary historians have pointed out that the very concept of "Western culture" may date back only to the 18th century). But rather than mourning the loss of some putative ancestral purity, we can recognize what's valuable, resilient, even cohesive, in the hybrid and variegated nature of our modernity.

15   Genuine multiculturalism is not, of course, everyone's cup of tea. Vulgar cultural nationalists—like Allan Bloom or Leonard Jeffries—correctly identify it as the enemy. These polemicists thrive on absolute partitions: between "civilization" and "barbarism," between "black" and "white," between a thousand versions of Us and Them. But they are whistling in the wind.

16   For whatever the outcome of the culture wars in the academy, the world we live in is multicultural already. Mixing and hybridity is the rule, not the exception. As a student of African-American culture, of course, I've come to take this kind of cultural palimpsest for granted. Duke Ellington, Miles Davis, John Coltrane have influenced popular musicians the world over. Wynton Marsalis is as comfortable with Mozart as he is with jazz; Anthony Davis writes operas in a musical idiom that combines Bartok with the blues.

17   In dance, Judith Jamison, Alvin Ailey, Katherine Dunham all excelled at "Western" cultural forms, melding these with African-American styles to produce performances that were neither, and both. In painting, Romare Bearden and Jacob Lawrence, Martin Puryear and Augusta Savage learned to paint and sculpt by studying Western masters, yet each has pioneered the construction of a distinctly African-American visual art.

18   And in literature, of course, the most formally complex and compelling black writers—such as Jean Toomer, Sterling Brown, Langston Hughes, Zora Hurston, Richard Wright, Ralph Ellison, James Baldwin, and Gwendolyn Brooks—have always blended forms of Western literature with African-American vernacular and written traditions. Then, again, even a vernacular form such as the spiritual took for its texts the King James version of the Old and New Testaments. Toni Morrison's master's thesis was on Virginia Woolf and Faulkner; Rita Dove is as comfortable with German literature as she is with the blues.

19   Indeed, the greatest African-American art can be thought of as an exploration of that hyphenated space between the African and the American. As James Baldwin once reflected during his long European sojourn, "I would have to appropriate these white centuries, I would have to make them mine. I would have to accept my special attitude, my special place in this scheme, otherwise I would have no place in any scheme."

20   "Pluralism," the American philosopher John Dewey insisted early in this century, "is the greatest philosophical idea of our times." But he recognized that it was also the greatest problem of our times: "How are we going to make the most of the new values we set on variety, difference, and individuality—how are we going to realize their possibilities in every field, and at the same time not sacrifice that plurality to the cooperation we need so much?" It has the feel of a scholastic conundrum: How can we negotiate between the one and the many?

21   Today, the mindless celebration of difference has proven as untenable as that bygone model of monochrome homogeneity. If there is an equilibrium to be struck, there's no guarantee we will ever arrive at it. The worst mistake we can make, however, is not to try.

Topical Considerations

1. What is the "ethnic chauvinism" that Gates mentions in paragraph 2? What does each word in that phrase mean? Does Gates believe that ethnic chauvinism is good? Is it the same as multiculturalism?
2. What is "multiculturalism"? Can you write a simple definition using Gates's discussion in paragraphs 4 and 5?
3. What is a "jeremiad" (paragraph 6)? Why does Gates equate the discussion about politics in education with the jeremiad, tracing it back to the early part of the century?
4. What is "politics," as Gates uses the term in paragraphs 7 through 9? What are "proper civic virtues"? What place do these elements have in discussions about education?
5. What is the "Balkanization" to which Gates refers in paragraph 10? Does he believe that Balkanization is a real problem for education?
6. In your own experience, is the United States already Balkanized? Do you often socialize with people of other races or classes? Do you ever feel uncomfortably different from other people in certain situations?
7. In paragraphs 11 and 12, Gates compares comments by Edward Said with a satirical poem written by a student about Benjamin Jowett. What are the two different assumptions about education to these sets of commentary?
8. What does Gates mean when he says that conservatives have misunderstood the debate as "the West vs. the Rest" (paragraph 14)? What is "pluralism"? What is the difference between these two terms?
9. What does Gates mean when he says he is comfortable with a "cultural palimpsest" (paragraph 16)? Are you aware of a cultural palimpsest in your daily life as well?

Rhetorical Considerations

1. What effect does Gates's opening rhetorical question have on this audience? Who are "they" and what are the "terrible things" being said? Do you see any other rhetorical questions in paragraph 8 that seem to reinforce or contrast with the tone he establishes with this one?
2. Who is "Johnny" in paragraph 8? What kinds of actions does Johnny take? Do you know anybody like this, or have you heard of incidents like the ones attributed to him? Why does Gates use a personal name here instead of a more abstract discussion of the benefits of multicultural education?

3. Are there any places where Gates sets up a "straw man" in this article—someone who disagrees and whose argument Gates portrays as ludicrous? Consider, for example, the statements Gates imputes to conservatives who don't agree with him in paragraph 2 and his "West vs. the Rest" catchphrase in paragraph 14.
4. Gates examines debates that are at least a century old as he makes his case for multiculturalism in the 1990s. What is the effect of his drawing on such old ideas? Does it effectively counter his opponents' claims that Gates wants to destroy "traditional " ideas of knowledge?
5. What kinds of fears does Gates assume his audience has about multiculturalism, and about education generally? Does he completely resolve those fears?
6. How effective an argument for multiculturalism does Gates make by providing a list of African-American artists and performers who use Western tradition to create something new?

Writing Assignments

1. Write an essay answering Gates's three questions in paragraph 5 about the relationship between American identity and education. What does it mean to be an American? Should teachers and scholars describe our diversity? Or should they prescribe what Americans should all strive to be—that is, "forge a communal identity" for all American citizens?
2. Select one of the artists Gates mentions at the end of his article. Using reference works such as the *Dictionary of Literary Biography* and the *Grove Encyclopedia of Music* and newspaper reviews (books reviews, performance reviews, and so on), research what critics have said about that individual's work. Do critics comment on the artist's mainstream influences? How does being able to synthesize several cultures enrich an artist's ability to express or create?
3. How might Gates respond to E. D. Hirsch's list of things that everyone should know? Would Gates's list be longer than Hirsch's? The same length, but including different elements? Or would Gates throw out the idea of a list entirely? Write your thoughts in an essay using specific examples to support your thesis.

Too Many Have Let Enthusiasm Outrun Reason
Kenneth T. Jackson

Historian and educator Kenneth T. Jackson agrees that there is nothing wrong with taking pride in our heritage or with wanting to treasure the traditions handed down by our parents. Our nation has grown rich from its "vibrant, vital, multi-ethnic and multi-racial culture." Yet, he argues, promotion of distinctive cultures should be the function of music festivals, churches, synagogues, and ethnic celebrations—and not the public schools. Jackson believes that what the "feel good" approach to multicultural education does is reduce history to a list of ethnic or racial "firsts."

Jackson is Barzun Professor of History at Columbia University. He is the author of *The Ku Klux Klan in the City* (1967) and *Crabgrass Frontier* (1985). He has also taught at Princeton, George Washington University, and UCLA. This article originally appeared in *The Boston Globe Sunday Magazine* in October 1991.

BEFORE YOU READ

If you were designing a high school social studies curriculum, what would be your reaction to the recommendation (made by the New York State Social Studies Syllabus Review Committee) that "Christopher Columbus be viewed from the perspective of the natives already resident in North America, that Thanksgiving be understood as a day of mourning as well as of celebration, and that slaves be referred to as 'enslaved persons.'"? Would you adopt these recommendations in whole, part, or not at all? What would be the reasons for your decision?

AS YOU READ

Jackson feels that four issues regarding multicultural education deserve more debate. Which issue do you think is the most important? Which is the least important?

1   In June, after almost a year of deliberation, the New York State Social Studies Syllabus Review Committee released its report "One Nation, Many Peoples: A Declaration of Cultural Interdependence." In July, the state Board of Regents adopted the document as a blueprint for educational change in the schools.

2   The report occasioned a firestorm of controversy, perhaps because the committee recommended, among other things, that Christopher Columbus be viewed from the perspective of the natives already resident in North America, that Thanksgiving be understood as a day of mourning as well as of celebration, and that slaves be referred to as "enslaved persons." Most important, however, was the realization that "One Nation, Many Peoples" is about the purpose of social studies, the nature of community, and the meaning of the United States itself.

3   Along with Arthur Schlesinger and Paul A. Gagnon, I was one of three dissenters to the report. I agonized over my decision, in part because I have spent most of the past three decades, almost my entire adult life, studying the very topics that the committee suggests should receive more attention—ethnicity, racism, discrimination, inequality, and civil rights—and in part because I do believe that we should celebrate the cultural diversity that has made the

United States unique among the world's nations. We should acknowledge the heterogeneity that has made this land rich and creative, and we should give our young people a varied and challenging multicultural education.

4   But too many of those who wave the flag for multiculturalism have let enthusiasm outrun reason. In particular, I believe four major issues deserve more debate and consideration before we embrace the brave new world of multicultural education.

5   First, we should not confuse moral judgment with historical judgment. To study a subject is not necessarily to endorse it. As William Shakespeare reminded us in a line in *Henry IV,* there is history in all men's lives. Because we cannot study all men's lives, however, the curriculum should emphasize those people, places, and events that have disproportionately influenced the world in which we live. Thus, Europe should be an academic focus not because it has been morally good or even because it is the ancestral home of most Americans, but because, for the last 500 years or so, it has been much more influential than any other place, and it has had a particularly heavy impact on the political, legal, and religious institutions of the United States.

6   This is a historical judgment, not a moral one. Quite simply, Europe has generated most of the political values which we hold dear, democracy and freedom prominent among them. It has also experienced more bloodletting, more intolerance, more terror, and more general nastiness than any other place. To analyze the Spanish Inquisition or the Thirty Years War or the Holocaust is not to wish we could have been there. Similarly, students need to know about Hitler because he may reasonably be held to account for 30 million or 40 million or 50 million deaths, not because anyone seeks to elevate the significance of Europe. Should the people of Africa, Asia, or South America feel historically slighted because they have not yet produced an approximation of Nazi Germany?

7   My second point is that in state after state across the country, a new social studies curriculum is already in place, and teachers have barely had time to familiarize themselves with the new guidelines. Why not give those revisions some time to percolate through the classrooms? In New York state, the focus of so much recent controversy, the entire social studies curriculum was revised just four years ago with the expressed purpose of making it more multicultural. The major consultants for the effort were Eric Foner, Hazel Hertzberg, and Christopher Lasch, three of the most respected historians in the United States. Their efforts to adjust classroom materials and objectives to the new social realities of our time were largely successful, and the current New York State curriculum in American history already reflects the latest social studies scholarship.

8   To hear multiculturalists talk, however, one would think that our teachers have changed not at all since the Eisenhower era. In fact, they are better prepared and more sophisticated than their critics allege, and most of them are already teaching a multicultural curriculum. In my quarter century of teaching, for example, I have encountered students who did not know whether Boston

was northeast or southwest of New York City, whether the Soviet Union fought Germany in World War II, or whether Tammany Hall was a billiard parlor. But I have never met a person, of any age or circumstance, who thought that Columbus discovered an uninhabited world, or that the natives he encountered ultimately received a fair shake from the white invaders.

9   Meanwhile, the "Eurocentric" curriculum is itself a myth, largely because European history, so much reviled by multiculturalists, has practically disappeared from the nation's classrooms. Before 1970, the history of Western civilization was a standard part of the American educational experience. Since that time, its decline has been precipitous. A general trend has been to substitute an introductory course in world history for the traditional course in Western civilization. An even greater trend has been to substitute other social studies courses for history.

10   In 1987, for example, fewer than half of all American high school graduates had taken a year of either European or world history. New York State again illustrates the trend. This year, under a curriculum presumed to be Eurocentric, students in New York spend no more time on Britain and Western Europe than they do on Africa, Asia, Latin America, or the Soviet Union. Equally important, they have little time to consider the history of any of the regions, whatever their location on the globe. Most students get around to Europe only in the last quarter of their sophomore year, and then the focus is on contemporary problems, not history. Only 1 percent of students take a yearlong course in European history, and those are the kids in advanced placement classes. Everyone else must make do with an historical concoction known as global studies.

11   My third reservation about multicultural education is the allegation of its supporters that a major purpose of the effort is to raise self-esteem, to make students feel good about themselves, and to make the curriculum reflect the demography of the classroom. These are questionable propositions that often lead to complications. One particularly dispiriting tendency is a willingness to teach controversial theories as facts. A favored theme of Afrocentrism at the moment is an insistence that ancient Egypt be regarded as a part of Africa, that many or most Egyptians were black or multiracial, and that residents of the Nile River Valley were largely responsible for the later glories of Greece and Rome in particular and of the West in general.

12   The specifics of the argument need not concern us here. The argument may indeed be correct. But this interpretation remains very much in dispute. Some distinguished scholars accept such claims; others ridicule them. Would it not be better to let the historians fight it out before we introduce such material in the classroom? Other, more generally accepted, examples could advance the argument that no one race, no one continent, and no one religion has a corner on human achievement. All students, for example, should know that Africa was once the home of many advanced civilizations, that Timbuktu, in what is now Mali, was a thriving center of learning and trade when Paris was a dump, and that Europe was a backwater for a thousand years while China was in its glory.

13   Another problem with the "feel good" approach is that it can reduce history to a list of "firsts" by each ethnic or racial group. This type of teaching strategy is the main reason that students habitually list the social studies as the most boring and irrelevant of all their courses. Alternatively, the feel-good approach might simply replace one myth, (e.g., slavery was a benign institution that actually benefited many of its victims) with another (slavery was a uniquely Western institution).

14   My final reservation is with the notion of cultural interdependence, the idea that all cultures are equal, and the proposition that no one tradition should have special status in the United States. I disagree. Every viable nation has to have a common culture to survive in peace. Precisely because we lack a common religion, a common race, and a common ethnicity, we need a common denominator of another sort. We can find it in our history, in our values, in our aspirations—in short, in our common culture. That common culture should be and has been ever changing. It began, in most Colonies, with the English language and with British legal and political institutions, but it has since metamorphosed over the centuries, and it is now an amalgam of every group that came here. Our food, our music, our holidays, our literature, our traditions, even our language, reflect this distinctive "American" culture.

15   This issue has special relevance in 1991, when ethnic, racial, religious, and nationality fault lines are creating earthquakes around the world. Canada, Yugoslavia, the Soviet Union, India, and a dozen other places are examples of a powerful sentiment, which I regard as pernicious, that suggests that a country is a country only if it is ethnically pure. Citizenship thus becomes less a function of residence than of blood. Thus, the Baltic countries may deny the vote to Russians who have lived there for decades because they lack the proper pedigree. As more and more people begin to regard loyalty to group as more important than loyalty to country, we get a chilling preview of what the United States might be like if each of us maintains our own culture, if we reject mainstreaming and assimilation, and if in fact there is no mainstream.

16   Fortunately, the United States does not have the massive cultural divides that are bringing other nations to separation and even to civil war. But we are not immune to the problem. Too often today there is an ugliness associated with feelings of pride, the development of an "us vs. them" mentality. Across the United States, the concept of community, the idea of the melting pot, the feeling that we are all Americans—all seem quaintly out of date. The consensus-building institutions that once held us together, especially the big-city public systems, are in decline. Increasingly, Americans are retreating into private realms.

17   Nothing is wrong with being proud of one's family, heritage, of wanting to remember and treasure the traditions handed down from parents. The United States has prospered and grown rich from its vibrant, vital, multi-ethnic and multiracial culture. But the maintenance of distinctive cultures should be the function of synagogues, churches, music festivals, ethnic celebrations, and, most especially, dinner tables. The public schools should emphasize common traditions and common values.

Topical Considerations

1. What is the report "One Nation, Many Peoples"? What kinds of changes did it recommend? How did educators respond to those changes? How did Jackson respond?

2. Why does Jackson believe that European history should be the focus of American social studies classes? What does he imply is the reason we teach history?

3. What does Jackson mean when he says that "we should not confuse moral judgment with historical judgment" (paragraph 5)? What examples does he provide for this statement?

4. How good, according to Jackson, was the New York State social studies curriculum before the report "One Nation, Many Peoples" was adopted? How much European history were students learning before the report?

5. Jackson complains that educators need to de-emphasize "mak[ing] students feel good about themselves" (paragraph 11). What does he mean by this statement? Does he want educators to make students feel bad about themselves?

6. What are the three main complications that the "feel good" approach creates, according to Jackson?

7. Why is Jackson distressed by educators who want to teach that all cultures within the United States are equal and should be given equal emphasis in history courses? How does he use current events in other countries to illustrate the danger of teaching such a notion?

8. Review Jackson's article and in your own words summarize in one sentence each of the four main reasons he disagrees with multicultural education.

9. How much non-European history did you study in your high school classes? Do you feel that your teachers and school policies focused enough, too much, or too little on Europe? On other countries? How valuable is European history to you personally?

Rhetorical Considerations

1. What does Jackson say about his own research and study interests in paragraph 3? How does that personal information affect your willingness to take his position seriously?

2. How might Jackson be "begging the question" by stating that European history is more important than African, Asian, or South American history, because Europe produced the Spanish Inquisition, the Thirty Years War, and the Holocaust? What does he assume his readers know about these three major events?

3. How convincing is Jackson's claim that the New York State social studies curriculum was already very multicultural, even before the report "One Na-

tion, Many Peoples" was adopted? What evidence does he provide? Are you satisfied with his evidence?

4. Look again at Jackson's defense of the social studies curriculum before "One Nation, Many People." Might there be additional unnamed reasons why he dislikes the new curriculum? What kind of a burden, for example, does this new curriculum place on teachers? Why might Jackson not want to talk about that burden?

Writing Assignments

1. Evaluate your own training in history and social studies against the four reservations Jackson has about multicultural education. Did your teachers "confuse moral judgment with historical judgment"? Did they seem to be switching programs too frequently in an effort to keep up with scholarly fashions? Did they seem to be working too hard to make students of all heritages feel good about themselves, thereby falling into the errors Jackson lists? Were you left with a sense that Americans have a common culture, or do you think you got bits and pieces without a whole, coherent framework?

2. Contact high school educators in your area, and obtain a copy of their curriculum materials. (You may need to limit yourself to a single subject within the academic year and to a single grade level.) Analyze the amount of multicultural material included. Are any of the shortcomings or problems that Jackson mentions present in these curricular materials?

OPPOSITIONS: CURRICULUM WARS

Cultural Literacy
E. D. Hirsch, Jr.

E. D. Hirsch opens this piece with jarring examples of a lack of cultural knowledge: high school students who don't know the dates of the Civil War, the location of Washington D.C., or the languages spoken in Latin America. Hirsch goes on to argue that this decline in shared knowledge rests with the failure of our schools to fulfill their acculturative responsibility. A lack of educational authority and cafeteria-style curricula combine to produce culturally illiterate students.

E. D. Hirsch is a professor of English at the University of Virginia. His famous book, *Cultural Literacy: What Every American Needs to Know,* from which this essay comes, was published in 1987.

BEFORE YOU READ

Think back on your high school curriculum. Would you describe it as systematically or loosely organized? How do you think its organization affected your level of cultural knowledge?

AS YOU READ

Consider the examples of cultural illiteracy Hirsch gives at the beginning of the essay. Do you find them difficult to believe? Or do they sound typical of the deficiencies you have seen among students? To what would you attribute this lack of cultural knowledge?

1   During the period 1970–1985, the amount of shared knowledge that we have been able to take for granted in communicating with our fellow citizens has also been declining. More and more of our young people don't know things we used to assume they knew.

2   A side effect of the diminution in shared information has been a noticeable increase in the number of articles in such publications as *Newsweek* and the *Wall Street Journal* about the surprising ignorance of the young. My son John, who recently taught Latin in high school and eighth grade, often told me of experiences which indicate that these articles are not exaggerated. In one of his classes he mentioned to his students that Latin, the language they were studying, is a dead language that is no longer spoken. After his pupils had struggled for several week with Latin grammar and vocabulary, this news was hard for some of them to accept. One girl raised her hand to challenge my son's claim. "What do they speak in Latin America?" she demanded.

3   At least she had heard of Latin America. Another day my son asked his Latin class if they knew the name of an epic poem by Homer. One pupil shot up his hand and eagerly said, "The Alamo!" Was it just a slip for *The Iliad?* No, he didn't know what the Alamo was, either. To judge from other stories about information gaps in the young, many American schoolchildren are less well informed than this pupil. The following, by Benjamin J. Stein, is an excerpt from one of the most evocative recent accounts of youthful ignorance.

> I spend a lot of time with teenagers. Besides employing three of them part-time, I frequently conduct focus groups at Los Angeles area high schools to learn about teenagers' attitudes toward movies or television shows or nuclear arms or politicians. . . .
>
> I have not yet found one single student in Los Angeles, in either college or high school, who could tell me the years when World War II was fought. Nor have I found one who could tell me the years when World War I was fought. Nor have I found one who knew when the American Civil War was fought. . . .
>
> A few have known how many U.S. senators California has, but none has known how many Nevada or Oregon has. ("Really? Even though

they're so small?") . . . Only two could tell me where Chicago is, even in the vaguest terms. (My particular favorite geography lesson was the junior at the University of California at Los Angeles who thought that Toronto must be in Italy. My second-favorite geography lesson is the junior at USC, a pre-law student, who thought that Washington, D.C. was in Washington State.) . . .

Only two could even approximately identify Thomas Jefferson. Only one could place the date of the Declaration of Independence. None could name even one of the first ten amendments to the Constitution or connect them with the Bill of Rights. . . .

On and on it went. On and on it goes. I have mixed up episodes of ignorance of facts with ignorance of concepts because it seems to me that there is a connection. . . . The kids I saw (and there may be lots of others who are different) are not mentally prepared to continue the society because they basically do not understand the society well enough to value it.

4   My son assures me that his pupils are not ignorant. They know a great deal. Like every other human group they share a tremendous amount of knowledge among themselves, much of it learned in school. The trouble is that, from the standpoint of their literacy and their ability to communicate with others in our culture, what they know is ephemeral and narrowly confined to their own generation. Many young people strikingly lack the information that writers of American books and newspapers have traditionally taken for granted among their readers from all generations. For reasons explained in this book, our children's lack of intergenerational information is a serious problem for the nation. The decline of literacy and the decline of shared knowledge are closely related, interdependent facts.

5   The evidence for the decline of shared knowledge is not just anecdotal. In 1978 NAEP [National Assessment of Educational Progress] issued a report which analyzed a large quantity of data showing that our children's knowledge of American civics had dropped significantly between 1969 and 1976. The performance of thirteen-year-olds had dropped an alarming 11 percentage points. That the drop has continued since 1976 was confirmed by preliminary results from a NAEP study conducted in late 1985. It was undertaken both because of concern about declining knowledge and because of the growing evidence of a causal connection between the drop in shared information and in literacy. The Foundations of Literacy project is measuring some of the specific information about history and literature that American seventeen-year-olds possess.

6   Although the full report will not be published until 1987, the preliminary field tests are disturbing. If these samplings hold up, and there is no reasons to think they will not, then the results we will be reading in 1987 will show that two thirds of our seventeen-year-olds do not know that the Civil War occurred between 1850 and 1900. Three quarters do not know what *reconstruction* means. Half do not know the meaning of the *Brown decision* and

cannot identify either Stalin or Churchill. Three quarters are unfamiliar with the names of standard American and British authors. Moreover, our seventeen-year-olds have little sense of geography or the relative chronology of major events. Reports of youthful ignorance can no longer be considered merely impressionistic.

7   My encounter in the seventies with this widening knowledge gap first caused me to recognize the connection between specific background knowledge and mature literacy. The research I was doing on the reading and writing abilities of college students made me realize two things. First, we cannot assume that young people today know things that were known in the past by almost every literate person in the culture. For instance, in one experiment conducted in Richmond, Virginia, our seventeen- and eighteen-year-old subjects did not know who Grant and Lee were. Second, our results caused me to realize that we cannot treat reading and writing as empty skills, independent of specific knowledge. The reading skill of a person may vary greatly from task to task. The level of literacy exhibited in each task depends on the relevant background information that the person possesses.

The Decline of Teaching Cultural Literacy

8   Why have our schools failed to fulfill their fundamental acculturative responsibility? In view of the immense importance of cultural literacy for speaking, listening, reading, and writing, why has the need for a definite, shared body of information been so rarely mentioned in discussions of education? In the educational writings of the past decade, I find almost nothing on this topic, which is not arcane. People who are introduced to the subject quickly understand why oral or written communication requires a lot of shared background knowledge. It's not the difficulty or novelty of the idea that has caused it to receive so little attention.

9   Let me hazard a guess about one reason for our neglect of the subject. We have ignored cultural literacy in thinking about education—certainly I as a researcher also ignored it until recently—precisely because it was something we have been able to take for granted. We ignore the air we breathe until it is thin or foul. Cultural literacy is the oxygen of social intercourse. Only when we run into cultural illiteracy are we shocked into recognizing the importance of the information that we had unconsciously assumed.

10   To be sure, a minimal level of information is possessed by any normal person who lives in the United States and speaks elementary English. Almost everybody knows what is meant by *dollar* and that cars must travel on the right-hand side of the road. But this elementary level of information is not sufficient for a modern democracy. It isn't sufficient to read newspapers (a sin against Jeffersonian democracy), and it isn't sufficient to achieve economic fairness and high productivity. Cultural literacy lies *above* the everyday levels of knowledge that everyone possesses and *below* the expert level known only to specialists. It is that middle ground of cultural knowledge possessed by the

"common reader." It includes information that we have traditionally expected our children to receive in school, but which they no longer do.

11   During recent decades Americans have hesitated to make a decision about the specific knowledge that children need to learn in school. Our elementary schools are not only dominated by the content-neutral ideas of Rousseau and Dewey, they are also governed by approximately sixteen thousand independent school districts. We have viewed this dispersion of educational authority as an insurmountable obstacle to altering the fragmentation of the school curriculum even when we have questioned that fragmentation. We have permitted school policies that have shrunk the body of information that Americans share, and these policies have caused our national literacy to decline.

12   At the same time we have searched with some eagerness for causes such as television that lie outside the schools. But we should direct our attention undeviatingly toward what the schools teach rather than toward family structure, social class, or TV programming. No doubt, reforms outside the schools are important, but they are harder to accomplish. Moreover, we have accumulated a great deal of evidence that faulty policy in the schools is the chief cause of deficient literacy. Researchers who have studied the factors influencing educational outcomes have found that the school curriculum is the most important controllable influence on what our children know and don't know about our literate culture.

13   It will not do to blame television for the state of our literacy. Television watching does reduce reading and often encroaches on homework. Much of it is admittedly the intellectual equivalent of junk food. But in some respects, such as its of standard written English, television watching is acculturative. Moreover, as Herbert Walberg points out, the schools themselves must be held partly responsible for excessive television watching, because they have not firmly insisted that students complete significant amounts of homework, an obvious way to increase time spent on reading and writing. Nor should our schools be excused by an appeal to the effects of the decline of the family or the vicious circle of poverty, important as these factors are. Schools have, or should have, children for six or seven hours a day, five days a week, nine months a year, for thirteen years or more. To assert that they are powerless to make a significant impact on what their students learn would be to make a claim about American education that few parents, teachers, or students would find it easy to accept.

14   Just how fragmented the American public school curriculum has become is described in *The Shopping Mall High School,* a report on five years of first-hand study inside public and private secondary schools. The authors report that our high schools offer courses of so many kinds that "the word 'curriculum' does not do justice to this astonishing variety." The offerings include not only academic courses of great diversity, but also courses in sports and hobbies and a "services curriculum" addressing emotional or social problems. All these courses are deemed "educationally valid" and carry

course credit. Moreover, among academic offerings are numerous versions of each subject, corresponding to different levels of student interest and ability. Needless to say, the material covered in these "content area" courses is highly varied.

15   Cafeteria-style education, combined with the unwillingness of our schools to place demands on students, has resulted in a steady diminishment of commonly shared information between generations and between young people themselves. Those who graduate from the same school have often studied different subjects, and those who graduate from different schools have often studied different material even when their courses have carried the same titles. The inevitable consequence of the shopping mall high school is a lack of shared knowledge across and within schools. It would be hard to invent a more effective recipe for cultural fragmentation.

16   The formalistic educational theory behind the shopping mall high school (the theory that any suitable content will inculcate reading, writing, and thinking skills) has had certain political advantages for school administrators. It has allowed them to stay scrupulously neutral with regard to content. Educational formalism enables them to regard the indiscriminate variety of school offerings as a positive virtue, on the grounds that such variety can accommodate the different interests and abilities of different students. Educational formalism has also conveniently allowed school administrators to meet objections to the traditional literate materials that used to be taught in the schools. Objectors have said that traditional materials are class-bound, white, Anglo-Saxon, and Protestant, not to mention racist, sexist, and excessively Western. Our schools have tried to offer enough diversity to meet these objections from liberals and enough Shakespeare to satisfy conservatives. Caught between ideological parties, the schools have been attracted irresistibly to a quantitative and formal approach to curriculum making rather than one based on sound judgments about what should be taught.

17   Some have objected that teaching the traditional literate culture means teaching conservative material. Orlando Patterson answered that objection when he pointed out that mainstream culture is not the province of any single social group and is constantly changing by assimilating new elements and expelling old ones. Although mainstream culture is tied to the written word and may therefore seem more formal and elitist than other elements of culture, that is an illusion. Literate culture is the most democratic culture in our land: it excludes nobody; it cuts across generations and social groups and classes; it is not usually one's first culture, but it should be everyone's second, existing as it does beyond the narrow spheres of family, neighborhood, and region.

The following list of items has been excerpted from "What Literate Americans Know: A Preliminary List," published in *Culture Literacy*. Compiled by Hirsch and his colleagues Dr. Joseph Kett and Dr. James Trefil, the full list of nearly 4500 entries was "intended to illustrate the character and range of the knowledge literate Americans tend to share."

Bunker Hill, Battle of
Bunyan, Paul
Burke, Edmund
Burma
Burns, Robert
burnt child fears the fire, The
burn the candle at both ends
burn the midnight oil
burn with a hard, gemlike flame
Burr, Aaron
Burr-Hamilton duel
bury the hatchet
business before pleasure
business cycle
bust (economic)
buy a pig in a poke
buyer's market
Byron, Lord
Byronic
byte
Byzantine (complexity)
Byzantine empire
cabinet (government)
cadre
Caesar, Julius
Caesar Augustus
Caesarean section
Cain and Abel
Cairo
calculus
Calcutta
Calder
fossil fuel
fossil record
Foster, Stephen
Founding Fathers
Four Freedoms
four-letter words
Fourteen Points
Fourteenth Amendment
fourth estate, the
Fourth of July
France
franchise (economics)
franchise (politics)

Francis Ferdinand, Archduke
Francis of Assisi, Saint
Franco
Frankenstein's monster
Frankfurt
Franklin, Benjamin
freedom of religion
freedom of speech
freedom of the press
Freedom Riders
free enterprises
free fall
free trade
free verse
free will
freezing point
French and Indian Wars
French château
French horn
French Impressionism
French Revolution
frequency modulation (FM)
fresco
Fresno, California
Freud, Sigmund
Mars (Ares)
Mars (planet)
Marseilles
Marshall, Chief Justice John
Marshall, General George C.
Marshall Plan
Martha's Vineyard, Massachusetts
Marx, Karl
Marx Brothers
Marxism
Marxism-Leninism
Mary
Mary had a little lamb (text)
Maryland
Mary Magdalene
Mary, Mary, Quite Contrary (text)
masochism
Mason-Dixon line
Masons, Fremasons
mass (physics)

Mass (religion)
Massachusetts
massive resistance
massive retaliation
mass media
mass production
Mata Hari
materialism
mathematical induction
Mather, Cotton
Matisse, Henri
matriarchy
matrilineal
Matterhorn
Matthew, Saint, Gospel
 according to
Maxwell, James Clark
Vinci, Leonardo da
viola
violin
VIP (very important person)
Virgil
Virginia
Virgin Islands
Virgin Mary
virtual image
vis-à-vis

visual aid
visual field
vital statistics
vitamin
vivisection
V-J Day
voilà
volcano
Volga River
Volstead Act
volt
voltage
Voltaire
Voting Rights Act of 1965
vowel
Vox populi vox Dei.
voyeurism
Vulcan
vulcanization
Vulgate Bible
wage scale
Wailing (Western) Wall
wake (Irish)
Walden (title)
walkie-talkie
walking papers
walk on water

Topical Considerations

1. In the first three paragraphs, Hirsch uses reports from his son and from a published author to demonstrate that American students are ignorant about cultural matters. What are the answers to the questions he asks? Do you know the answers? Do you agree these pieces of information are important?

2. According to paragraph 4, what are the major problems created by a lack of so-called cultural literacy? How does lack of shared information lead to a decline in literacy?

3. When did Hirsch first become aware of the decline in cultural literacy? What two conclusions did he draw from his research at that time?

4. What is the main reason Hirsch believes that educators no longer teach a common set of facts?

5. How does Hirsch define *cultural literacy* in paragraph 10? Can you supply some examples of facts about the United States that would not fit his definition?

6. According to Hirsch, what effect has the complexity of this country's school system had on cultural literacy? What effect has television had on cultural literacy?
7. Hirsch uses two metaphors for current educational policies: shopping mall and cafeteria. What qualities does he suggest by using these terms?
8. What is the "formalistic educational theory" that Hirsch mentions at the beginning of paragraph 16? Can you find a place in the first section of his article where he mentions this concept in different words? What advantages do educators believe it has? What problems does Hirsch believe this theory creates?

Rhetorical Considerations

1. At the beginning of his article, Hirsch uses three or four kinds of sources to substantiate his claim that the amount of shared knowledge is declining. What are the sources? How reliable is each source? Why does Hirsch use this many sources?
2. In paragraph 10 Hirsch defines *cultural literacy:* "Cultural literacy lies *above* the everyday levels of knowledge that everyone possesses, and *below* the expert level known only to specialists. It is that middle ground of cultural knowledge possessed by the 'common reader.'" Is this a satisfying definition? Can you predict what information will or will not fit this definition?
3. Hirsch believes that television watching has become excessive because schools do not assign enough homework. How much homework did you have to do in high school? If you're doing more homework in college, can you say you're learning more now than you learned in high school?
4. In his final paragraph, Hirsch cites Orlando Patterson in defense of his view that teaching traditional cultural literacy does not necessarily mean teaching conservative material. What does Hirsch mean by *conservative?* Why do you think he refers to Patterson, a well-respected black sociologist at Harvard?

Writing Assignments

1. Imagine that you are a high school principal who agrees with Hirsch's argument. Draft a memo to your school's teachers directing them to increase students' cultural literacy. Assume these teachers have read Hirsch's article, but that they are skeptical about the value of cultural literacy.
2. Examine the excerpted list from Hirsch's *Cultural Literacy.* How many items do you recognize? How many do you know in depth? How many are unfamiliar to you? How much knowledge does Hirsch expect people to have? Write a paper in which you discuss the idea of such a list.

3. Make a list of 10 terms, book or film titles, people, or places that have become important for members of your generation to know. Which terms do you think will be important 25 years from now? 100 years from now? Which do you think are part of what Hirsch calls "ephemeral and narrowly confined to [your] own generation" (paragraph 4)? Do you think you would agree with Hirsch's judgment on your terms? Explain your answers.

Cult-Lit
Barbara Herrnstein Smith

The notion of cultural literacy (the acquisition of shared cultural information, attitudes, and values) put forth by E. D. Hirsch, Jr., in the previous essay is straightforwardly rejected in the piece that follows. Barbara Herrnstein Smith challenges Hirsch's idea of a national culture arguing that there is "no single, comprehensive macroculture in which all or even most of the citizens of this nation actually participate." She then goes on to argue that the mastery of a common vocabulary will not solve society's ills.

Smith is a professor of English at Duke University. A longer form of this essay originally appeared in *South Atlantic Quarterly* in 1990.

BEFORE YOU READ

Reread E. D. Hirsch's essay. What, if any, specific objections did you have to his claims? What specific counterattacks do you anticipate Smith will make?

AS YOU READ

Do you find Smith's attack on Hirsch and other conservatives convincing? Which of her arguments and refutations are the most persuasive? Which the least?

1 It should be a matter of some concern, I think, that the current movement for educational reform duplicates so many of the perennial (indeed classic) themes of apocalyptic cultural criticism: most obviously, of course, the recurrent images of a civilization in decline (the young corrupted, the masses stupefied, barbarians at the gates of the *polis*), but also the nostalgic invocations of an allegedly once "whole" but now "fragmented" community (lost shared values, lost shared knowledge, lost shared attitudes, and so forth), where historical as well as contemporary diversities are, in one stroke, both forgotten and wishfully obliterated.

2 The force of this general concern will be apparent in my remarks, but I mean to focus specifically on E. D. Hirsch's book, *Cultural Literacy*, and I don't mean to mince words. I believe that the immediate objective it pro-

poses—that is, the acquisition, by every American child, of the alleged "common," "traditional," information, attitudes, and values shared by all literate Americans or, as Hirsch also refers to it, "*the* national culture"—is meaningless as stated and if not meaningless then, given what it evidently means to Hirsch, undesirable; that such an objective, if it were desirable, could not be achieved by the pedagogic methods it proposes; and that, if it were actually adopted on a national scale (as is clearly Hirsch's serious and now institutionalized intention), the pursuit of that objective by those methods—that is, the attempt to equip every child in the country with a putatively finite, determinate, measurable store of basic "American knowledge" in the form of standard definitions or "sets of associations" attached to disarticulated terms and phrases—would not only *not* alleviate the conditions it is supposedly designed to cure (among them, widespread illiteracy and a cycle of economic deprivation, social marginalization, and political ineffectuality), but would postpone even longer adequate analyses of, and appropriate responses to, those and other problems of the nation's schools.

3   I will amplify these points by examining several key passages in *Cultural Literacy,* beginning with the one, early in the book, in which Hirsch introduces the notion of a "national culture" and sets up his argument for a uniform national school curriculum based on his now-famous List.

4   The failure of our schools, Hirsch tells us, can be attributed to the educational theories of Rousseau, Dewey, and "their present-day disciples." In contrast to these, he writes, his own "anthropological" theory of education

> deems it neither wrong nor unnatural to teach young children adult information before they fully understand it. The anthropological view stresses the universal fact that a human group must have effective communications to function effectively, that effective communications require shared culture, and that shared culture requires transmission of specific information to children.

Each link in this argument bears scrutiny, as does also the nature of the logical/rhetorical syntax by which they are joined.

5   To begin with, the term "human group" is vague and, as Hirsch uses it here, slippery. The statement containing the phrase—that is, "a human group must have effective communications to function effectively"—makes sense when we think of a relatively small group of mutually interacting people, such as a family, a company of co-workers, or, given the quasi-anthropological auspices, a tribal community. A *nation,* however, and particularly what Hirsch refers to repeatedly as "a modern industrial nation," is not a "human group" in that sense; and, although his subsequent allusions to "our national community" manage to evoke, under the sign of scientific precision, a questionable (and, as will be seen, otherwise disturbing) nationalist communitarianism, the phrase is clearly question-begging here and the concept has no anthropological or other scientific credentials whatsoever.

6   The existence of an American "national culture" is by no means self-evident. Every citizen of this nation belongs to numerous communities (regional, ethnic, religious, occupational, etc.) and shares different sets of beliefs, interests, assumptions, attitudes, and practices—and, in that sense, cultures—with the other members of each of those communities. There is, however, no single, comprehensive macroculture in which all or even most of the citizens of this nation actually participate, no numerically preponderant majority culture in relation to which any or all of the others are "minority" cultures, and no culture that, in Hirsch's term, "transcends" any or all other cultures. Nor do these multiplicities describe a condition of cultural "fragmentation" except by implicit contrast to some presumed prior condition of cultural unity and uniformity—a condition that could obtain only among the members of a relatively isolated, demographically homogeneous and stable community, and has never obtained in this nation at any time in its history.

7   The invocation of *transcendence* noted above is justified in the book by an illegitimate analogy between language and culture: indeed, doubly illegitimate, for not only are cultures not like languages in the way Hirsch implies (that is, sets of discrete items of "information" analogous to "vocabulary" lists), but languages themselves are not the way he describes them and requires them to be for the analogies in question. Just as every national language, Hirsch writes, "*transcends* any particular dialect, region, or social class," so also does the "national culture." There is, however, no "national language," either in the United States or anywhere else, that all or most of the inhabitants of a nation speak *over and above* various regional and other (ethnic, class, etc.) dialects. There are only *particular* regional and other dialects, some—or one—of which may be privileged over and above all others in the state educational system and/or by various cultural agencies. An analogy from language to culture, then, would support a view of the latter quite different from that urged by Hirsch. Indeed, as his critics observe, what he refers to as "*the* national culture," and exemplifies by his List, is nothing but a *particular* (egregiously classbound and otherwise parochial) set of items of "knowledge" that Hirsch himself privileges and that he *wants* the state educational system to make "standard." (His recurrent reply to this observation is to dismiss it as "ideological," in presumed contrast to his own beliefs and proposals.)

8   Hirsch puts the culture/language analogy to other, remarkable uses. "[F]ixing the vocabulary of a national culture," he writes, "is analogous to fixing a standard grammar, spelling, and pronunciation"; and, he claims, Americans "need to learn not just the associations of such words as *to run* but also the associations of such terms as *Teddy Roosevelt, DNA,* and *Hamlet*" Indeed, he assures us, if children can all learn the associations of common words such as *to run,* there is no reason why they cannot all learn the associations of *Teddy Roosevelt, DNA,* and *Hamlet.* To speak of the "vocabulary" of a culture, however, is to presuppose the altogether Hirsch-generated culture/language analogy and thus, as usual, to beg the question. (It is because Hirsch characteristically presupposes the key points of his arguments—either as self-

evident or as already proved by his mere statement of them—that question-begging formulations are so recurrent in *Cultural Literacy.*). Moreover, the dubiousness—and, in fact, absurdity—of the analogy becomes increasingly apparent from the very use he makes of it. Can we really speak of *"the associations"* of *Teddy Roosevelt, DNA,* and *Hamlet* or, to choose some other items from Hirsch's List, of *Woodie Guthrie* or *Harlem?* Are there "standard associations" and, as he also claims, "traditional values" already in existence for such items, and are they really shared by all literate Americans? Or, if they are not already in existence (Hirsch is equivocal on the point), could associations and values for such items be "fixed" or "standardized" so that they really would be *independent,* as he implies, of the specific personal histories of whoever was doing the sharing and associating and valuing? And, if we really managed to teach children from Houston, Boston, Alaska, and Nebraska to memorize and recite standard associations and values for *Teddy Roosevelt, Woodie Guthrie, Hamlet, Harlem, DNA,* and five thousand other terms, do we really suppose that the "human group" constituted by the citizens of this country would have acquired a "shared culture," and would only then "have effective communications," and would only thereby and thereupon "function effectively"? What *are* we talking about?

9   Hirsch's claim that "effective communications require shared culture" is, in fact, false. For, given any sense of the term "culture" relevant to the passage under discussion—that is, either (a) as anthropologists would define it, the system of beliefs, skills, routine practices, and communal institutions shared by the members of some society as such, or (b) as Hirsch implies, familiarity with a list of academic set-phrases and vintage items of middle-class cultural lore—then it is a "universal fact" that people can communicate *without* a "shared culture" and that they do it all the time. Japanese suppliers, for example (a group whose presence hovers over the pages of *Cultural Literacy*), communicate with European and African buyers without sharing the latter's cultures in the anthropological sense; and, just to speak of other Americans, I communicate quite effectively with my eighty-five-year-old ex-mother-in-law from Altoona, Pennsylvania, my twenty-five-year-old hairdresser from Hillsborough, North Carolina, my five-year-old grandson from Brooklyn, New York, and my *cat,* without sharing much, if anything, of what Hirsch calls "the shared national culture" with any of them. The reason I can do so is that all the activities that Hirsch classifies as "communication" and sees as *duplicative transmissions* that presuppose *sameness*—"common" knowledge, "shared" culture, "standardized" associations—are, in fact, always *ad hoc,* context-specific, pragmatically adjusted negotiations of (and through) *difference.* We never have sameness; we cannot produce sameness; we do not need sameness. . . .

10   *What literate Americans know. What every American needs to know.* So Hirsch claims for his List, and so Americans in the hundreds of thousands may now be inclined to believe. The force of the claim is equivocal, however, and hedged throughout the book. Hirsch states, for example, that the appendix to *Cultural Literacy* is not meant to be "prescriptive" but is only "a *descriptive* list of the information actually possessed by literate Americans," forgetting the

book's subtitle and his recurrent imperatives concerning the centrality of the List to the educational reforms he is proposing. The continuous eliding of the prescriptive/descriptive distinction is significant because it permits Hirsch to evade the responsibilities of each kind of claim by moving to the other when criticisms are pressed. Thus, if the List's claims to descriptive adequacy and accuracy are questioned (is it really what literate Americans—*all* of them?— "actually" know?), Hirsch can claim to be offering only provisional recommendations and "guideposts"; conversely, when objections are raised to the manifestly patrician, self-privileging norms promoted by the List, Hirsch can claim that it has nothing to do with what *he* knows or thinks should be known, but simply describes the way things are among "literate Americans."

11   The method by which the List was generated is, in any case, exceedingly mysterious. According to Hirsch, it is not "a complete catalogue of American knowledge," but "is intended to illustrate the character and range of the knowledge literate Americans tend to share" and to "establish guideposts that can be of practical use to teachers, students, and all others who need to know our literate culture" (which is, of course, according to Hirsch, "every American"). But, one might ask (granting the double absurdity of a specifically "*American* knowledge" and a possible catalog of *any* actual human knowledge), what sorts of persons *are* the "literate Americans" whose knowledge is illustrated or represented by the List? How, for example, could one distinguish them from Americans who merely know how to read? And how does Hirsch himself know what "the literate reader" knows?

12   The answers to these questions cannot be determined from any explicit statements of procedure in the book. Indeed, the accounts of the List given by way of introduction and explanation could hardly be briefer or vaguer. Hirsch notes that "different literate Americans have slightly [sic] different conceptions of our shared knowledge," but assures his readers that "more than one hundred consultants reported agreement on over 90 percent of the items listed." Wonderful: more than one hundred, over 90 percent. But agreement on *what*? Was each "consultant" asked to compile an individual list and then all the lists compared for overlap? Or, quite differently, were the consultants asked, for each item on an already compiled list, to say whether they were themselves familiar with it? Or, again, and again quite differently, were the consultants asked, for each item, whether they agreed that every "literate American" (however defined for them—if at all) *knew* it—or, and also quite differently, whether they thought every literate American *should* know it? Nor does Hirsch indicate how the consultants themselves were chosen. At random from the Charlottesville telephone directory? From among his classiest friends, best students, and most congenial colleagues at the University of Virginia? Were they, by any chance, selected to be representative of various regions of the nation, and a range of ages, occupations, and degrees of formal education? Were they chosen, in fact, by any consistent and appropriate sampling principle?

13   The questions raised here are important because, depending on the specific procedures and selection criteria used, very different lists would have been produced. Moreover, without consistent and appropriate procedures and

criteria, the claims of representativeness (not to mention implications of unbiased, statistical authority) made for Hirsch's List—copies of which are now being delivered by the truckful to teachers and children across the nation—might seem, relative to the standards of responsible social science research, dubious. But never mind all that: like the old Ivory Soap ads, *99 and 44/100 percent pure—it floats!*

Topical Considerations

1. Smith uses the phrase "apocalyptic cultural criticism" (paragraph 1). To what does "apocalyptic" refer, and why and how does she apply this term to Hirsch's contentions about cultural literacy?
2. What are the three main problems Smith finds in Hirsch's book on cultural literacy (paragraph 2)?
3. Why, in her analysis of Hirsch's anthropological theory of education, does Smith object to his use of the term "human group" (paragraph 5)? Why does she call it "question-begging"? What is "national communitarianism" (paragraph 5)?
4. Think of some groups at your college or university. Which are small enough for Smith to accept as "human groups"? Which are too large? Do any of the groups intersect or overlap?
5. Why does Smith disagree with Hirsch's idea that cultural literacy transcends the various cross-cultural, regional, and class differences in the United States (paragraphs 6 and 7)?
6. What does the phrase "duplicative transmissions" (paragraph 9) mean? What does she mean in the concluding sentence, "We never have sameness; we cannot produce sameness; we do not need sameness"?
7. What does Smith mean when she charges Hirsch with "continuous eliding of the prescriptive/descriptive distinction" (paragraph 10)? What is Hirsch doing when he "prescribes"? What is he doing when he "describes"? Why is Smith bothered when she can't tell when he is doing one or the other?
8. How did Hirsch assemble his list? What questions does Smith still have about his methods?

Rhetorical Considerations

1. Examine Smith's choice of title: "Cult-Lit." Why do you suppose she abbreviates Hirsch's term "cultural literacy"?
2. Examine the second sentence in paragraph 2 of Smith's article. Is it "too long"? Can you rewrite it as two or more new sentences? Why do you think she uses such a long sentence here? What attitude might its length reflect?
3. In paragraph 9 the author lists several people with whom she can communicate effectively, despite those people's lack of what Hirsch might term "cul-

tural literacy." What does Smith mean by "communicate"? What does Hirsch mean by "communicate"? Are the two meanings the same, or is Smith equivocating here?

4. In paragraph 12 what is the effect of the questions Smith raises about Hirsch's methods for assembling his list? Does she ask different kinds of questions? Does she expect a specific answer to any or all of the questions she poses? If so, what is the effect of her knowing what the most likely answers will be?

5. Are there any points in the article where Smith seems to rely on her readers' own "cultural literacy" to make sense of what she says? Are there any points where you think you may have lost track of her argument because you sensed that you lacked some information?

Writing Assignments

1. Imagine that you are an irate parent involved in your child's high school PTA. Write a letter making the point that "our children do not know basic facts that we think they should be learning in school." Draw as needed on other articles in this chapter.

2. Using Smith and any other sources you find appropriate, write a response from the teacher who receives the letter from exercise 1. Explain in your letter that cultural literacy is impossible to teach.

3. Research the sample list of cultural literacy terms Smith provides in paragraph 8: Teddy Roosevelt, Woodie Guthrie, Hamlet, Harlem, DNA. (You may wish to consult dictionaries, encyclopedias, and specialized reference books.) Assemble a one-paragraph statement about what you think a high school graduate should be able to associate with each term. Then compare your set of "associations" with those of classmates. Did you arrive at the same set of conclusions? Did different sources provide different kinds of associations? Write a brief summary about what conclusions you can draw about cultural literacy from this exercise.

4. Write a brief description of all the activities you participated in yesterday (or during a typical day in your life). Assume that your reader has absolutely no cultural literacy—that he or she is about your age but has been living on a deserted island since age 5, with no human contact whatsoever. How successfully do you think you were able to communicate concepts and events in your day? Are there any activities you had to avoid describing because your reader would not have understood? Swap papers with a classmate and compare your sense of how well this reader would understand you.

CHAPTER 15

ADVERTISING

Advertising is the most pervasive form of persuasion in America. Over $135 billion every year is spent on commercials and print ads—more than the gross national product of many countries in the world. Advertising consumes nearly a quarter of each television hour; it accounts for the bulk of most popular magazines; it blazons the country coast-to-coast on billboards; it's printed on T-shirts, hot dogs, postage stamps, and even license plates. It's everywhere people are, and its appeal goes right to the quick of our fantasies: happiness, material wealth, eternal youth, social acceptance, sexual fulfillment, and power. And it does so in carefully selected images and words.

The essays in this chapter present some important debates about the impact of advertising in contemporary American society. We present different approaches—historical, economic, psychological, personal—as well as different views, including those who criticize advertising, those who defend it, and those who are some place in the middle. Although critics don't call for the elimination of ads, they do ask for honest, straightforward, and responsible advertising. And less of it. Proponents concede that advertising may occasionally manipulate and mislead consumers, but, they argue, it is hardly the insidious, mind-numbing craft which critics decry. On the contrary, much of it, they claim, is creative and entertaining. Besides, advertising feeds our natural urge to buy.

We open with a historical view of American consumerism. In "Work and Spend," economist Juliet B. Schor argues that consumerism is not a trait of human nature but a product of capitalism which, since the 1920s, has conditioned people to pursue an endless and giddy quest for material wealth. In "The Hard Sell," Deborah Baldwin laments the incessant roar of commerce that fills our day and narrows our worth to purchasing power alone. In defense of advertising is Michael Schudson whose "Delectable Materialism" argues that our abnormal craving to buy, buy, buy is not the result of advertising but, rather, our basic desire to own things.

The next four essays assess the persuasive appeal of advertising language. By nature it is a very special language, one that combines words cleverly and methodically for the sole purpose of separating consumers from their money. In "A Word

From Our Sponsor," ad writer Patricia Volk argues that there is only one rule in writing advertisements: "There are no rules." In the next essay, "With These Words I Can Sell You Anything," language-watcher William Lutz argues that advertisers tyrannically twist simple English words so that they appear to promise what the consumer desires. Taking a defense posture in "The Language of Advertising" is professional ad writer Charles A. O'Neill. He admits that the language of ads can be very appealing, but he makes a persuasive argument that no ad can force consumers to lay their money down. The last essay in this section, "Tapping the Youth Market" by Madeline Drexler, raises a provocative issue: What is the link between advertising by the liquor industry and the sometimes lethal drinking habits of the underage drinker? In its effort to promote brand awareness and cultivate future consumers, does the liquor industry deliberately manipulate the attitudes of underage drinkers?

Finally, our paired "Oppositions" go head-to-head on perhaps the oldest and most potent sales force in advertising: **sex.** Madison Avenue has always used sex appeal to pitch products. The results have been provocative and, on occasion, very successful. In "Sex in Advertising," adman Edward McCabe defends the fleshy come-on as an artful selling device. Fellow adman John Carroll could not disagree more. In "Sex Is Still Doing the Selling," Carroll accuses McCabe and others of practicing a trade that capitalizes on manipulation, bad taste, and the denigration of women.

CONSUMERISM

Work and Spend
Juliet B. Schor

Juliet B. Schor is a professor of economics at Harvard University and author of *The Overworked American: The Unexpected Decline of Leisure* (1992), from which this essay comes. In her book she argues that working hours in the United States have increased substantially over the last 20 years—by about 160 hours or one month per year. The result is less leisure time to enjoy ourselves and, thus, a decline in our standard of living. This is true of men and women, from corporate executives to hamburger flippers. As she explains in this excerpt, the prime culprit is the capitalist system, which has spawned a "consumerist treadmill and long-hour jobs" that have in turn created a cycle of work and spend.

BEFORE YOU READ

Do you believe, as Schor contends, that materialism has failed to make people happy? Can you think of examples of such discontent even among the affluent?

AS YOU READ

As you read her criticism of our "rat-race" society, try to determine Schor's solutions to consumer discontent. Do they strike you as reasonable recommendations? Could they make people happier while improving the quality of life?

1   [M]aterialism (and its attendant discontent) is taken for granted. It is widely believed that our unceasing quest for material goods is part of the basic makeup of human beings. According to the folklore, we may not like it, but there's little we can do about it.

2   Despite its popularity, this view of human nature is wrong. While human beings may have innate desires to strive toward something, there is nothing preordained about material goods. There are numerous examples of societies in which *things* have played a highly circumscribed role. In medieval Europe, there was relatively little acquisitiveness. The common people, whose lives were surely precarious by contemporary standards, showed strong preferences for leisure rather than money. In the nineteenth- and early twentieth-century United States, there is also considerable evidence that many working people exhibited a restricted appetite for material goods. Numerous examples of societies where consumption is relatively unimportant can be found in the anthropological and historical literature.[1]

3   Consumerism is not an historical trait of human nature, but a specific product of capitalism. With the development of the market system, consumerism "spilled over," for the first time, beyond the charmed circles of the rich. The growth of the middle class created a large group of potential buyers and the possibility that mass culture could be oriented around material goods. This process can be seen not only in historical experiences but is now going on in places such as Brazil and India, where the growth of large middle classes have contributed to rampant consumerism and the breakdown of longstanding values.[2]

4   In the United States, the watershed was the 1920s—the point at which the "psychology of scarcity" gave way to the "psychology of abundance." This was a crucial period for the development of modern materialist culture. Thrift and sobriety were out; waste and excess were in. The nation grew giddy with its exploding wealth. Consumerism blossomed—both as a social ideology and in terms of high rates of real spending. In the midst of all this buying, we can discern the origins of modern consumer discontent.

5   This was the decade during which the American dream, or what was then called "the American standard of living," captured the nation's imagination. But it was always something of a mirage. The historian Winifred Wandersee explains:

> It is doubtful that the average American could have described the precise meaning of the term "American standard of living," but nearly everyone

agreed that it was attainable, highly desirable, and far superior to that of any other nation. Its nature varied according to social class and regional differences, but no matter where a family stood socially and financially, it was certain to have aspirations set beyond that stance. This was the great paradox posed by the material prosperity of the twentieth century; prosperity was conspicuously present, but it was always just out of reach, for nearly every family defined its standard of living in terms of an income that it hoped to achieve rather than the reality of the paycheck.[3]

The phenomenon of yearning for more is evident in studies of household consumption. In a 1928 study of Yale University faculty members, the bottom category (childless couples with incomes of $2,000) reported that their situation was "life at the cheapest and barest with nothing left over for the emergencies of sickness and childbirth." Yet an income of $2,000 a year put them above 60 percent of all American families. Those at the $5,000 level (the top 10 percent of the income distribution) reported that they "achieve nothing better than 'hand to mouth living.'" At $6,000, "the family containing young children can barely break even." Yet these were the top few percent of all Americans. Even those making $12,000—a fantastic sum in 1928—complained about items they could not afford. A 1922 Berkeley study revealed similar sentiments of discontent—despite the facts that all the families studied had telephones, virtually all had purchased life insurance, two-thirds owned their own homes and took vacations, over half had motor cars, and nearly every family spent at least a little money on servants or housecleaning help.[4]

6   The discontent expressed by many Americans was fostered—and to a certain extent even created—by manufacturers. Business embarked on the path of the "hard sell." The explosion of consumer credit made the task easier, as automobiles, radios, electric refrigerators, washing machines—even jewelry and foreign travel—were bought on the installment plan. By the end of the 1920s, 60 percent of cards, radios, and furniture were being purchased on "time."[5] The ability to buy without actually having money helped foster a climate of instant gratification, expanding expectations, and, ultimately, materialism.

7   The 1920s was also the decade of advertising. The admen went wild: everything from walnuts to household coal was being individually branded and nationally advertised. Of course, ads had been around for a long time. But something new was afoot, in terms of both scale and strategy. For the first time, business began to use advertising as a psychological weapon against consumers. "Scare copy" was invented. Without Listerine, Postum, or a Buick, the consumer would be left a spinster, fall victim to a crippling disease, or be passed over for a promotion. Ads developed an association between the product and one's very identity. Eventually they came to promise everything and anything—from self-esteem, to status, friendship, and love.[6]

8   The psychological approach responded to the economic dilemma business faced. Americans in the middle classes and above (to whom virtually all advertising was targeted) were no longer buying to satisfy basic needs—such

as food, clothing and shelter. These had been met. Advertisers had to persuade consumers to acquire things they most certainly did not need. In the words of John Kenneth Galbraith, production would have to "create the wants it seeks to satisfy." This is exactly what manufacturers tried to do. The normally staid AT&T attempted to transform the utilitarian telephone into a luxury, urging families to buy "all the telephone facilities that they can conveniently use, rather than the smallest amount they can get along with." One ad campaign targeted fifteen phones as the style for an affluent home. In product after product, companies introduced designer colors, styles, even scents. The maid's uniform had to match the room decor, flatware was color-coordinated, and Kodak cameras came in five bird-inspired tints—Sea Gull, Cockatoo, Redbreast, Bluebird, and Jenny Wren.[7]

9   Business clearly understood the nature of the problem. It even had a name—"needs saturation." Would-be sellers complained of buyers' strike and organized a "Prosperity Bureau," urging people to "Buy Now." According to historian Frederick Lewis Allen: "Business had learned as never before the importance of the ultimate consumer. Unless he could be persuaded to buy and buy lavishly, the whole stream of six-cylinder cars, super helerodynes, cigarettes, rouge compacts, and electric ice boxes would be dammed up at its outlets."[8]

10   But would the consumer be equal to her task as "the savior of private enterprise"? The general director of General Motors' Research Labs, Charles Kettering, stated the matter baldly: business needs to create a "dissatisfied consumer"; its mission is "the organized creation of dissatisfaction." Kettering led the way by introducing annual model changes for GM cars—planned obsolescence designed to make the consumer discontented with what he or she already had. Other companies followed GM's lead. In the words of advertising historian Roland Marchand, success now depended on "the nurture of qualities like wastefulness, self-indulgence, and artificial obsolescence." The admen and the businessmen had to instill what Marchand has called the "consumption ethic," or what Benjamin Hunnicutt termed "the new economic gospel of consumption."[9]

11   The campaign to create new and unlimited wants did not go unchallenged. Trade unionists and social reformers understood the long-term consequences of consumerism for most Americans: it would keep them imprisoned in capitalism's "squirrel cage." The consumption of luxuries necessitated long hours. Materialism would provide no relief from the tedium, the stultification, the alienation, and the health hazards of modern work; its rewards came outside the workplace. There was no mystery about these choices: business was explicit in its hostility to increases in free time, preferring consumption as the *alternative* to taking economic progress in the form of leisure. In effect, business offered up the cycle of work-and-spend. In response, many trade unionists rejected what they regarded as a Faustian bargain of time for money: "Workers have declared that their lives are not to be bartered at any price, that no wage, no matter how high can induce

them to sell their birthright. [The worker] is not the slave of fifty years ago. . . . he [*sic*] reads . . . goes to the theater . . . [*and*] has established his own libraries, his own educational institutions. . . . And he wants time, time, time, for all these things."10

12   Progressive reformers raised ethical and religious objections to the cycle of work-and-spend. Monsignor John A. Ryan, a prominent Catholic spokesman, articulated a common view:

> One of the most baneful assumptions of our materialistic industrial society is that all men should spend at least one-third of the twenty-four hour day in some productive occupation. . . . If men still have leisure [after needs are satisfied], new luxuries must be invented to keep them busy and new wants must be stimulated . . . to take the luxuries off the market and keep the industries going. Of course, the true and rational doctrine is that when men have produced sufficient necessaries and reasonable comforts and conveniences to supply all the population, they should spend what time is left in the cultivation of their intellects and wills, in the pursuit of the higher life.11

       The debates of the 1920s clearly laid out the options available to the nation. On the one hand, the path advocated by labor and social reformers: take productivity growth in the form of increases in free time, rather than the expansion of output; limit private consumption, discourage luxuries, and emphasize public goods such as education and culture. On the other hand, the plan of business: maintain current working hours and aim for maximal economic growth. This implied the encouragement of "discretionary" consumption, the expansion of new industries, and a culture of unlimited desires. Production would come to "fill a void that it has itself created."12

13   It is not difficult to see which alternative was adopted. Between 1920 and the present, the bulk of productivity advance has been channeled into the growth of consumption. Economist John Owen has found that between 1920 and 1977, the amount of labor supplied over the average American's lifetime fell by only 10 percent; and since 1950, there has even been a slight increase.13 The attitude of businessmen was crucial to this outcome. As employers, they had strong reasons for preferring long hours, as I argued in chapter 3. As sellers, they craved vigorous consumption to create markets for their products. Labor proved to be no match for the economic and political power of business.

14   Finally, we should not underestimate the appeal of consumption itself. The working classes and the poor, particularly those migrating from Europe or the rural United States, grew up in conditions of material deprivation. The array of products available in urban America was profoundly alluring, at times mesmerizing. For the middle classes, consumption held its own satisfactions. Designer towels or the latest GM model created a sense of privilege, superiority, and well-being. A Steinway "made life worth living." Once the Depression

hit, it reinforced these tendencies. One of its legacies was a long-lasting emphasis on finding security in the form of material success.[14]

The Pitfalls of Consumerism

15 The consumerism that took root in the 1920s was premised on the idea of *dissatisfaction*. As much as one has, it is never enough. The implicit mentality is that the next purchase will yield happiness, and then the next. In the words of the baby-boom writer, Katy Butler, it was the new couch, the quieter street, and the vacation cottage. Yet happiness turned out to be elusive. Today's luxuries became tomorrow's necessities, no longer appreciated. When the Joneses also got a new couch or a second home, these acquisitions were no longer quite as satisfying. Consumerism turned out to be full of pitfalls—a vicious pattern of wanting and spending which failed to deliver on its promises.

16 The inability of the consumerist life style to create durable satisfaction can be seen in the syndrome of "keeping up with the Joneses." This competition is based on the fact that it is not the absolute level of consumption that matters, but how much one consumes relative to one's peers. The great English economist John Maynard Keynes made this distinction over fifty years ago: "[Needs] fall into two classes—those which are absolute in the sense that we feel them whatever the situation of our fellow human beings may be, and those which are relative only in that their satisfaction lifts us above, makes us feel superior to, our fellows." Since then, economists have invented a variety of terms for "keeping up with the Joneses": "relative income or consumption," "positional goods," or "local status." A brand-new Toyota Corolla may be a luxury and a status symbol in a lower-middle-class town, but it appears paltry next to the BMWs and Mercedes that fill the driveways of the fancy suburb. A 10-percent raise sounds great until you find that your co-workers all got 12 percent. The cellular phone, fur coat, or _____ (fill in the blank) gives a lot of satisfaction only before everyone else has one. In the words of one 1980s investment banker: "You tend to live up to your income level. You see it in relation to the people of your category. They're living in a certain way and you want to live in that way. You keep up with other people of your situation who have also leveraged themselves."[15]

17 Over time, keeping up with the Joneses becomes a real trap—because the Joneses also keep up with you. If everyone's income goes up by 10 percent, then relative positions don't change at all. No satisfaction is gained. The more of our happiness we derive from comparisons with others, the less additional welfare we get from general increases in income—which is probably why happiness has failed to keep pace with economic growth. This dynamic may be only partly conscious. We may not even be aware that we are competing with the Joneses, or experience it as a competition. It may be as simple as the fact that exposure to their latest "life-style upgrade" plants the seed in our own mind that we must have it, too—whether it be a European vacation, this year's fashion statement, or piano lessons for the children.

18   In the choice between income and leisure, the quest for relative standing has biased us toward income. That's because status comparisons have been mostly around commodities—cars, clothing, houses, even second houses. If Mrs. Jones works long hours, she will be able to buy the second home, the designer dresses, or the fancier car. If her neighbor Mrs. Smith opts for more free time instead, her two-car garage and walk-in closet will be half empty. As long as the competition is more oriented to visible commodities, the tendency will be for both women to prefer income to time off. But once they both spend the income, they're back to where they started. Neither is *relatively* better off. If free time is less of a "relative" good than other commodities, then true welfare could be gained by having more of it, and worrying less about what the Joneses are buying.

19   It's not easy to get off the income treadmill and into a new, more leisured life style. Mrs. Smith won't do it on her own, because it'll set her back in comparison to Mrs. Jones. And Mrs. Jones is just like Mrs. Smith. They are trapped in a classic Prisoner's Dilemma: both would be better off with more free time; but without cooperation, they will stick to the long hours, high consumption choice.[16] We also know their employers won't initiate a shift to more leisure, because they prefer employees to work long hours.

20   A second vicious cycle arises from the fact that the satisfactions gained from consumption are often short-lived. For many, consumption can be habit forming. Like drug addicts who develop a tolerance, consumers need additional hits to maintain any given level of satisfaction.[17] The switch from black and white to color television was a real improvement when it occurred. But soon viewers became habituated to color. Going back to black and white would have reduced well-being, but having color may not have yielded a permanently higher level of satisfaction. Telephones are another example. Rotary dialing was a major improvement. Then came touch-tone, which made us impatient with rotaries. Now numbers are preprogrammed and some people begin to find any dialing a chore.

21   Our lives are filled with goods to which we have become so habituated that we take them for granted. Indoor plumbing was once a great luxury—and still is in much of the world. Now it is so ingrained in our life style that we don't give it a second thought. The same holds true for all but the newest household appliances—stoves, refrigerators, and vacuum cleaners are just part of the landscape. We may pay great attention to the kind of automobile we drive, but the fact of having a car is something adults grew accustomed to long ago.

22   The process of habituation can be seen as people pass through life stages—for example, in the transition from student life to a first job. The graduate student makes $15,000 a year. He has hand-me-down furniture, eats at cheap restaurants, and, when traveling long distances, finds a place in someone else's car. After graduation, he gets a job and makes twice as much money. At first, everything seems luxurious. He rents a bigger apartment (with no roommates), buys his own car, and steps up a notch in restaurant quality.

His former restaurant haunts now seem unappetizing. Hitching a ride becomes too inconvenient. As he accumulates possessions, the large apartment starts to shrink. In not too many years, he has become habituated to twice as much income and is spending the entire $30,000. It was once a princely sum, which made him feel rich. Now he feels it just covers a basic standard of living, without much left over for luxuries. He may not even feel any better off. Yet to go back to $15,000 would be painful.

23   Over time, further increases in income set in motion another round of the same. He becomes dissatisfied with renting and "needs" to buy a home. Travel by car takes too long, so he switches to airplanes. His tastes become more discriminating, and the average price of a restaurant meal slowly creeps upward. Something like this process is why Americans making $70,000 a year end up feeling stretched and discontented.[18]

24   Of course, part of this is a life-cycle process. As our young man grows older, possessions like cars and houses become more important. But there's more to it than aging. Like millions of other American consumers, he is becoming addicted to the accoutrements of affluence. This may well be why the doubling of per-capita income has not made us twice as well off. In the words of psychologist Paul Wachtel, we have become an "asymptote culture . . . in which the contribution of material goods to life satisfaction has reached a point of diminishing returns. . . . Each individual item seems to us to bring an increase in happiness or satisfaction. But the individual increments melt like cotton candy when you try to add them up."[19]

25   These are not new ideas. Economists such as James Duesenberry, Edward Schumacher, Fred Hirsch, Tibor Scitovsky, Robert Frank, and Richard Easterlin have explored these themes. Psychologists have also addressed them, providing strong support for the kinds of conclusions I have drawn. My purpose is to add a dimension to this analysis of consumption which has heretofore been neglected—its connection to the incentive structures operating in labor markets. The consumption traps I have described are just the flip side of the bias toward long hours embedded in the production system. We are not merely caught in a pattern of spend-and-spend—the problem identified by many critics of consumer culture. The whole story is that we work, and spend, and work and spend some more.

Notes

1. On the United States, see Herbert Gutman, *Work, Culture and Society in Industrializing America* (New York: Vintage, 1977). See also the discussion of the 1925 Consumer League of New York study in Benjamin Hunnicutt, *Work Without End: Abandoning Shorter Hours for the Right to Work* (Philadelphia: Temple University Press, 1988), 68–69, where respondents displayed strong preferences for leisure.

On the anthropological evidence, see Marshall Sahlins, *Stone Age Economics* (New York: Aldine, 1972).

2. See Neil McKendrick, John Brewer, and J. H. Plumb, *The Birth of a Consumer Society: The Commercialization of Eighteenth-Century England* (London: Europa Publications, 1982); and Arjun Appadurai, "Technology and the Reproduction of Values in Rural Western India," in Frédérique Apffel-Marglin and Stephen A. Marglin, eds., *Dominating Knowledge: Development, Culture, and Resistance* (Oxford: Clarendon Press, 1990), 185–216.

3. Winifred D. Wandersee, *Women's Work and Family Values, 1920–1940* (Cambridge, Mass.: Harvard University Press, 1981), 7–8.

4. On the Yale study, see ibid., 10, table 1.1, and 21–22.

    On the Berkeley study, see Jessica Peixotto, *Getting and Spending at the Professional Standard of Living* (New York: Macmillan, 1927). Data from chapter 6.

5. Roland Marchand, *Advertising the American Dream: Making Way for Modernity* (Berkeley: University of California Press, 1985), 4, 5.

6. Ibid.

7. John Kenneth Galbraith, *The Affluent Society,* 4th ed. (Boston: Houghton Mifflin, 1984), 127. Marchand, *Advertising the American Dream,* chap. 5.

8. Hunnicutt, *Work Without End,* 38.

    Allen quoted in ibid., 45.

9. The "savior" phrase is Thomas Cochran's, cited in Hunnicutt, *Work Without End,* 44.

    Charles F. Kettering, "Keep the Consumer Dissatisfied," *Nation's Business,* January 1929; "organized creation," Marchand, *Advertising the American Dream,* 156.

    Marchand, *Advertising the American Dream,* 158, and Hunnicutt, *Work Without End,* chap. 2.

10. From an ILGWU pamphlet cited in Hunnicutt, *Work Without End,* 75.

11. Ibid., 94.

12. Galbraith, *Affluent Society,* 127.

13. This conclusion is from John Owen, *Working Lives: The American Work Force Since 1920* (Lexington, Mass.: Lexington Books, 1986), 23.

14. On "mesmerization," see Stuart Ewen and Elizabeth Ewen, *Channels of Desire: Mass Images and the Shaping of American Consciousness* (New York: McGraw-Hill, 1982).

    From a Steinway ad cited in Marchand, *Advertising the American Dream,* 142.

15. John Maynard Keynes, "Economic Possibilities for Our Grandchildren," in *Essays in Persuasion* (New York: Harcourt, Brace, 1932), 365.

    The classic statement of the importance of relative consumption was made in 1949 by Harvard economist James Duesenberry in *Income, Saving and the Theory of Consumer Behavior* (Cambridge, Mass.: Harvard University Press, 1949). Unfortunately, the ideas put forward in this pioneering work have not been adequately tested and pursued. For further discussion of these issues, in addition to Duesenberry, see the works of Tibor Scitovsky, Richard Easterlin, Fred Hirsch, and Robert Frank.

Investment banker from Brooke Kroeger, "Feeling Poor," p. 8.

16. In a Prisoner's Dilemma, both partners would be made better off if they co-operated, but failure to do so leads both to be worse off. This point has been made by Robert H. Frank in *Choosing the Right Pond* (New York: Oxford University Press, 1985), 133–35.

17. Galbraith calls this "the dependence effect"; Scitovsky, the difference be-tween "pleasure" (what one gets at first) and "comfort" (the sensation after habituation).

18. This passage from Jonathan Freedman, the author of a book on happiness, describes the syndrome: "As a student, I lived on what now seems no money at all, but I lived in a style which seemed perfectly fine . . . As my income has grown since then, I have spent more . . . but it has always seemed to be just about the same amount of money and bought just about the same things. The major change is that I have spent more on everything, and I consider buying more expensive items. None of this has had an appreciable effect on my life or on my feelings of happiness or satisfaction. I imagine that if I earned five times as much, the same would be true—at least it would once I got used to the extra money. This is not to say that I would turn down a raise—quite the contrary. But after a while everything would settle down, the extra money would no longer be 'extra,' and my life would be the same as before." From *Happy People* (New York: Harcourt, Brace, Jo-vanovich, 1978), 140.

19. Paul Wachtel, *The Poverty of Affluence: A Psychological Portrait of the Ameri-can Way of Life* (Philadelphia: New Society Publishers, 1989), 39.

Topical Considerations

1. In the first paragraph of this essay, Schor refutes the common belief that de-sire for material goods is a natural human urge. What influences you to want a new car, new clothes, and other material goods?

2. Does Schor's evidence, beginning in paragraph 2 and continuing through paragraph 11, convince you that consumerism has produced discontent in middle-class and lower-class Americans? Which of her examples are most convincing?

3. According to Schor which two groups challenged the rise of consumerism in the 1920s? Which side won the debate? Where do you think each of these groups would stand today on the conflict between consumerism and leisure time?

4. Schor argues throughout her essay that consumerism is based on the idea of dissatisfaction with what one has. If buying more things can make you happy, why are some rich people discontented with their lives, according to Schor? Would you be happier if you were rich? Why or why not?

5. In paragraph 16 the author quotes the great English economist John Maynard Keynes on the notion that there is a difference between absolute needs and relative needs. How does this thesis apply to "keeping up with the Joneses" (paragraph 17)? What relevance has Keynes's work to this essay?

6. Paragraphs 18 and 19 introduce two fictional women, Mrs. Jones and Mrs. Smith, who illustrate the problems of "keeping up with the Joneses." Describe people you know who fall into this category. Have you had the same experiences?

7. Would readers from other cultures and ethnic groups respond to this article any differently than middle-class Americans? How would Native Americans or New Age individuals view consumerism in contemporary culture?

Rhetorical Considerations

1. How does the author structure her argument in this essay? Is it an inductive or deductive argument? Where does her major claim appear?

2. How would you describe the tone of this essay? Do you find it difficult to follow? Why or why not?

3. Schor includes words such as "super heterodynes" in paragraph 9 and "asymptote" in paragraph 24, which she does not define in her footnotes. If you do not know the meanings of these words, look them up in an encyclopedia or dictionary and explain how they are used in this context. Did you wish the author had defined these terms?

4. Throughout this essay the author gives only her side of the argument that business has fostered unbridled consumerism over leisure time. She does not include any negative evidence from labor and religious groups—that labor is more interested in workers' rights than economic expansion, and that religious organizations try to keep people in their place. Could these omissions be considered the logical fallacy of stacking the deck? Do you think they weaken her argument? Why or why not?

5. In the first line of paragraph 10, Schor uses the pronoun *her* when referring to the general consumer, instead of the generic *him*. In paragraphs 18 and 19 she calls her characters, *Mrs.* Jones and *Mrs.* Smith, instead of the more usual title, *Mr.* How does this usage appeal to you? Have you noticed this trend toward gender balance in other publications?

Writing Assignments

1. In paragraphs 22–24 Schor gives an example of the "process of habituation" in the life of a graduate student. Write a story about this graduate student, or someone else going through this process of becoming "addicted to the accoutrements of affluence." Flesh out your character's life with descriptions of each stage in his or her life.

2. Write an essay on advertising in the 1990s, incorporating examples of "advertising as a psychological weapon against consumers." Find current ads from magazines, such as those mentioned in paragraph 7, that appeal to consumers' psychological needs. Discuss what the advertisers are trying to do in these ads.

3. If you disagree with specific sections of Schor's essay, write a rebuttal to these arguments, giving your own opinions. Back up your ideas with solid evidence.

The Hard Sell
Deborah Baldwin

Imagine our world without ads. If Deborah Baldwin's vision is accurate, it would be a world of reduced clutter, clamour, and anxiety. In this piece, Baldwin catalogues the innumerable ways advertising intrudes and, more dangerously, seamlessly blends into daily life through television, corporate sponsorships, sports events, museum exhibits, print media, and even school programs. What concerns her is not so much the "ad-saturation" per se, but how all the advertising has turned America into a consumption-crazy culture. She makes a strong argument that the line between citizen and consumer has nearly vanished.

Baldwin writes for *Common Cause Magazine,* in which this essay first appeared in longer form in 1991.

BEFORE YOU READ

Read only the first four paragraphs of this piece. Given this introduction, can you surmise what the key ideas in Baldwin's argument might be? Can you predict what value judgments she might make about our culture?

AS YOU READ

Ask yourself if the power of advertising as described accounts for your own behavior as a consumer.

1   Consider a day in the life of the semi-fictional American household—let's call them the Urbanes.

2   The Urbane family awakens to the strains of National Public Radio—"non-commercial" radio brought to us this morning by "REI, Recreational Equipment Inc., Providing Outdoor Gear and Clothing." Mom grabs her Liz Claiborne signature purse, stuffs her Fila sweats into a Bloomies shopping bag and heads downstairs. Let's eat! Pass the Teenage Mutant Ninja Turtle cereal to the kids. Front page of the newspaper looks grim, but not the ad for Petites

Week at Macy's or the article by the 15-Minute Gourmet on the back of the Safeway ad in yesterday's Food section.

3   Snatches of conversation about world affairs emanate from *Good Morning America* between plugs for Tylenol and Toyota. Dad reminds the kids to take their Flintstone vitamins. And for the third time, put on your Reeboks! They pile into the car with the She-Ra lunchboxes and Lands' End backpacks, drive past the bus-stop billboard advertising those bright Benetton clothes, turn on the oldies station and sing along with the Connie Francis remake that's now an ad for the local mall—"Where the Stores Are."

4   Five o'clock and time to go home! The country music station is playing a song from Barbara Mandrell's album "No Nonsense"—as in No Nonsense Pantyhose, which the singer is under contract to promote. Flipping through the mail, Mom finds three fund-raising appeals, a glossy from Hecht's department store announcing unbelievable sales, four catalogs, and a *New Yorker* with an attractive 10-page spread on the glories of the Caribbean, which turns out to be not colorized John McPhee but a paid "advertorial."

5   After the Urbanes wrest their kids away from the TV, they tuck them into their Little Mermaid sheets and catch the tail end of *Washington Week in Review,* made possible by a generous grant from Ford Motor Co., whose high-powered Crown Victoria sedan fills the screen. Checking the time on tomorrow's theater tickets, they notice a plug for USAir. Dad spends a few absorbing moments with the J. Crew catalog, then admires the way car ads during the 11 o'clock news are always photographed on empty mountaintops.

6   Bedtime already?

7   Welcome to Real Life, circa 1991. While our forefathers and mothers rose with the sun to labor in the fields, we rise with the radio and TV, immersed every waking hour in non-stop nudges from corporate America to Just Say Yes.

8   Round-the-clock commercialism has crept up on us, evolving from 19th-century pitches for products like Lydia Pinkham's medicinal pick-me-up into a sophisticated art form that pops up everywhere we are—from the brand-name labels that turn consumers into walking billboards to the corporate-sponsored informational posters that hang in classrooms.

9   Few things, it seems, are sacred: *Advertising Age* says there's a firm that sells space at the bottom of golf cups, reasoning that nothing concentrates the mind amid all that green like a word from a sponsor. Some advertisers have been known to put their messages in public restrooms—one of the few places most people think of as a commercial-free zone.

10   Despite such incursions, many people might nonetheless wonder: With all the problems besetting the world, why lie awake at night worrying about commercialism? Besides, what can one person do to beat back the media equivalent of a 20-foot snowstorm?

11   Enter the brave little Center for the Study of Commercialism. Just over a year old, it is headed by nutrition activist Michael Jacobson of the Center for Science in the Public Interest. Jacobson hopes to do the same thing to ad glut

that he has done to greasy food: make the public realize that too much of this stuff can make a person sick.

12   Armed with a board of advisers whose professional lives are dedicated to the study of the consumer culture, the Washington-based center wants to raise awareness of commercialism's costs and counteract the gimmees with a vision of a "less selfish, more civic-minded" lifestyle. As Jacobson and co-founder Ronald Collins wrote in one manifesto, "Omnipresent commercialism is wrecking America. Our cultural resources are dwindling. Value alternatives beyond those of the marketplace are disappearing. The very idea of *citizen* has become synonymous with *consumer.*"

13   Fighting commercialism, of course, is like wrestling your way out of a spider web. Indeed the commercial and non-commercial often blend together so seamlessly, says critic Mark Crispin Miller, an adviser to the center and author of *Boxed In: The Culture of TV,* that life can be lived as "a theme park experience."

14   He points to the way the war in the Persian Gulf was turned into a spectacle—partly thanks to the networks' presentation of this dramatic conflict in the best mini-series tradition. While advertisers initially were reluctant to sponsor war footage, before long they rushed to associate their products with patriotic good feelings, donating goods to the troops and incorporating the red white and blue in their ad campaigns.

15   Miller sees sharp parallels between the way the war was presented to the public and the way the 1988 presidential campaign unfolded on TV. Both involved simplistic plots, with beginnings, middles, and ends, and both made heavy use of emotional images and sound bites.

16   Sort of like ads.

17   Advertising has long oiled the machinery of our economy and probably always will. All told, corporations spent an unbelievable $130 billion on it last year—the equivalent of $6 a week for every man, woman, and child in the United States, according to the *Wall Street Journal.* That's 50 percent more per capita than is spent in any other nation. Essayist Pico Iyer once calculated that by age 40 we've seen one million ads, with incalculable effects on the way we view the world—never mind our capacity to absorb information of a more profound nature. And conventional ads are only the flotsam in the flood tide: Every day the average American is bombarded by hundreds of marketing messages, many of them adroitly woven into the content of the print and electronic media we depend on for information and entertainment.

18   The post office delivered 63 billion pieces of junk mail last year, much of it aimed at selling something. Product manufacturers stuck ads on videotapes and in movie theaters, and they spent millions to plant their products in Hollywood movies. Automatic dialing systems delivered canned messages at a rate of seven million a day, according to a congressional study, and that's nothing—coming soon to a store near you will be grocery carts outfitted with TV monitors that sense which aisle you're strolling down and advertise the relevant name-brand products.

19   The big brains on Madison Avenue are coming up with such innovations at a time when the public suffers, in the words of the *Wall Street Journal,* from "ad nauseam." The ads on TV come so thick that many advertisers overcompensate, stepping up the volume and intensity in order to be heard over the clutter. Or they act as seductively entertaining as the sitcoms and melodramas they make possible. Try zapping through the Taster's Choice campaign that basically consists of 45-second episodes from an ongoing soap opera, complete with romantic leads.

20   "It's no longer enough to show the product and tell what's good about it," says one marketing executive at a personal-care products company that is among the nation's top advertisers. "You have to be as entertaining as the regular programs."

21   Ads once celebrated the pleasures of society and the senses, says Miller, but today they're more likely to celebrate personal empowerment. Kids' candy ads, for example, used to suggest that having some would make you popular. Now such ads are more likely to revolve around the "story" of having it when someone else wants it.

22   Some of the most sophisticated ads—the so-called postmodernist genre—poke fun at the art form itself, which becomes a kind of shared joke. But this appealing self-parody doesn't mean audiences are so savvy that they know they're being manipulated. "Everybody's sophisticated," Miller says, "in a superficial kind of way. But a kind of knowingness, the fact of growing up with TV, does not imbue you with an understanding of how images work." And even when a specific ad fails to sell a certain product, adds Pat Aufderheide, a communications professor at American University who writes about popular culture for *In These Times,* it contributes to the ceaseless message that "you can solve life problems with commodities."

23   Corporations use various strategies to reach the various segments of the market. To move the consumer spirit of opinion leaders, they buy time on public broadcasting, where $250,000 will yield two mentions on National Public Radio six days a week for a year. Private art galleries and museums have become so dependent on corporate money in recent years they hardly mind when it comes with name-brand banners and posters attached.

24   To reach middle America, advertisers are turning to cable TV, which has greatly eroded the networks' hegemony because it divides the market into easily targeted segments. Low-cost time during sports events on cable, for example, is a big draw for the makers of shaving cream.

25   When companies aren't hawking their goods during halftime, they're hanging their logos everywhere the eye or camera can see, plugging beer and cigarettes to armchair athletes with no apparent irony. Sports sponsorship is a booming business, reports the *Wall Street Journal,* with 4,200 companies pouring nearly $3 billion into special events ranging from the Olympics to the Virginia Slims tennis tournament. Nike invested $7 million last year on basketball-related promotional efforts alone, including contracts with college coaches to put their teams in name-brand hightops, a *Washington Post* investigation revealed.

26   One of the fastest growing target audiences is America's youth. Companies spent about $500 million last year to reach children age 2 to 12—five times what they spent in the early '80s—according to James McNeal, a marketing professor at Texas A&M University.

27   As many beleaguered parents may suspect, advertisers are drawn to children because children have more influence over the household pocketbook than ever before. According to Consumers Union, children age 4 to 12 spend $8 billion annually and indirectly influence household expenditures of a $1 billion *a week.* Bombarded by slick ads for fast-food joints, junky breakfast cereals, and—a recent phenomenon—shoes and clothes, children have learned to speak up at the mall.

28   Corporations long ago infiltrated the schools, emblazoning their logos on educational materials and offering rewards like free computers and pizza in exchange for brand-name recognition among the next generation of consumers. Whittle Communications, which is credited with some of the most innovative marketing practices of the '80s, beams Channel One, a 12-minute TV news show that includes two minutes of ads, free to more than 8,900 high schools. To sweeten the deal, Whittle gives the schools satellite dishes, VCRs, and TVs as well; all the teachers have to do is round up the kids to watch the spots for Burger King, etc.

29   Unfortunately, many of us aren't even aware of the extent to which we are immersed in messages that say "buy, buy, buy," says George Gerbner, former dean of the Annenberg School for Communication and a member of the commercialism study center's board of advisers. "It's like saying, 'Is the average fish aware it's swimming in salt water?'" The average consumer literally can't imagine life without commercials, not to mention life without the many possessions commercials so effectively sell.

30   "My interest is the kind of culture we have created and in which our children are being raised," says Gerbner, a longtime critic of commercial TV who is trying to launch what he calls a cultural environment movement. "The mainstream of our culture is television, which is on an average of seven hours a day. It's not a product of the home, family, community, or even the native country for some, but transnational corporations with something to sell." He adds ominously, "Entertainment is the main source of information for most people . . . and whoever tells all the stories will guide what we think and do as a civilization."

31   If Gerbner seems most concerned about the impact of commercialism on the littlest consumers, it's because preschoolers spend more time watching TV than doing anything else except sleeping and are perceived as especially vulnerable to Madison Avenue's unsavory ways. As Neil Postman, an adviser to the center, argues in his book *The Disappearance of Childhood,* TV reduces literacy and distorts the learning process. Children also age quickly from exposure to violence, ineptitude, and other adult themes on TV.

32   If the ceaseless barrage of hyped-up, MTV-style plugs for toys and junk food during Saturday-morning cartoon shows strikes adults as manipulative and almost cynically deceptive, so are the ads targeted at the rest of society.

"The thing I hear most often is, 'I don't even look at ads, I don't pay any attention to them,'" Jean Kilbourne, a lecturer and adviser to the center, said in her film *Killing Us Softly: Advertising's Image of Women.* Yet "advertising is one of the most powerful socializing forces in the culture. And the effects are as inescapable as the effects of pollution in the air. . . . Ads sell more than products. They sell images, values, goals, concepts of who we are and who we should be. . . . They shape our attitudes, and our attitudes shape our behavior."

33   When we aren't buying self-images, we are "turning time into entertainment and connecting entertainment to buying," says Tom Engelhardt, who writes about advertising and children's TV. Tackling kidvid alone won't do much as long as kids keep getting the message that buying stuff is the ultimate fun. Adds Engelhardt, a father himself, "You can barely head into a museum without stumbling into seven gift shops. . . . Take the family on a visit to a historic site, and everything boils down to, yes or no, do we buy the Liberty Bell earrings?"

34   Once upon a time, Pat Aufderheide observes, children and adults alike could seek refuge from the commercial world at school—not to mention at home. Now the average busy household is itself a target of new products—such as kids' microwavable TV dinners—emanating from the outside world. The only sanctuary left, she says, is inside a church.

35   What's got the critics upset is not just marketing's encouragement of the human urge to own, which has done so much damage to the environment and eaten away so thoroughly at our sense of values. It's the changing nature of commercialism, its gradual intrusion into the privacy of our homes, the fabric of our cultural lives, and the sanctity of our public places.

36   The corporate invasion is taking place at a time when public institutions are particularly vulnerable to economic pressure—one legacy of the Reagan era, when taxes declined and so did the resources available for public libraries, schools, museums, and other institutions. Robbed of government support, these institutions "now have to appreciate the crumbs they get from corporations," says the Center for the Study of Commercialism's Michael Jacobson. "Instead of giving these companies tax deductions for their contributions," he adds, "the government ought to raise corporate income taxes."

37   That seems unlikely, given the tax-loathing politics of the '90s. Indeed, one element of President Bush's ballyhooed education initiative would be greater corporate involvement in the classroom, not less. This is the same administration, incidentally, that asked the Beer Institute to sponsor a safe-driving campaign for the National Highway Traffic Safety Administration.

38   Because corporate America feels strapped—thanks partly to the merger mania of the '80s—it is becoming more demanding of the media. In the magazine world, advertisers have become shameless in seeking special treatment from editors, a practice that has long plagued women's magazines. "It's not just a matter of individual advertisers influencing editorial content," says a former *Self* magazine editor. "The whole point of the magazine is to promote products, so the advertiser doesn't even have to ask." Once unique to beauty and fashion rags, this concept is spreading throughout the magazine world.

39   Moviemakers have long been open to the notion of incorporating paid ads into their works, but in the '80s the practice became institutionalized, says Mark Crispin Miller, as professional brokers set up business in Hollywood to negotiate ever more lucrative deals. According to one tally, the creative minds behind *Die Hard 2* found room for 19 paid ads. When one company, Black & Decker, discovered "its" scene on the cutting room floor, it sued for $150,000.

40   Feeding into the product placement phenomenon is the sheer cost of producing movie blockbusters, TV series, new magazines, and even books. While the practice is hardly commonplace—at least not yet—the *New York Times* uncovered one instance of literary encroachment in a novel featuring a Maserati whose "V-6 engine had two turbochargers, 185 horsepower, and got up to 60 in under seven seconds." Turns out the author had cut a deal with Maserati that landed her $15,000 worth of book promotion in exchange for the mention. The publisher meanwhile was thrilled to have the help.

41   So symbiotic are commercial and creative interests that well-known actors, producers, and filmmakers frequently "cross over," lending their talents to Madison Avenue and further blurring the line between merchandising and the arts.

42   In his book *Boxed In,* Miller quotes Bill Cosby as saying his popularity stems not from his role as the quintessential TV dad, but from his appealing ads for Jell-O and the like. Thirty-second commercials, he confided, "can cause people to love you and see more of you than in a full 30-minute show." Along with sheer entertainment, there's an intensity in these spots, a one-on-one connection that few can resist. Such intimacy helps explain why kids not only stick around when the commercials come on during those tiresome Saturday-morning cartoon shows, but pay special attention. "Don't turn it down!" my 9-year-old daughter exclaimed when I wandered by the TV during one particularly colorful, fast-cut spot. "This is the best part!"

Topical Considerations

1. In a single sentence summarize the message about advertising that Deborah Baldwin wants her readers to get from this essay. Who is the audience for whom she writes? Do you consider yourself part of that audience?

2. According to the author, what are the differences between today's ads and ads from earlier periods? How do these differences affect our roles as consumers and our self-image? Is it possible to solve the problems in our lives by buying products as ads suggest?

3. How do corporations advertise on public broadcasting networks and in private art galleries and museums? Do you think private companies should sponsor sporting events such as women's tennis tournaments and the Olympics? Do you think such sponsorship compromises the integrity of an art exhibit or a sporting event?

4. How do you feel about ad-saturation in your daily life? Do you enjoy ads, hate them, or simply ignore them? Do you agree with Jean Kilbourne that

"the effects [of ads] are as inescapable as the effects of pollution in the air" (paragraph 32)?

5. What is the Center for the Study of Commercialism? What key criticisms of the ad industry do the members of the center's advisory board make? Do you agree or disagree with their observations? Have their comments made you more aware of the high presence of advertising in your daily life?

6. What are some similarities between commercial ads and political ads? Analyze some of the political ads from the 1992 presidential campaign or more recent campaigns and show how these ads resemble product ads.

7. How, according to Baldwin, do advertisements influence the very young in our society? Do you see this as a problem? Do you agree or disagree with George Gerbner that children are very vulnerable to "Madison Avenue's unsavory ways" (paragraph 31)?

Rhetorical Considerations

1. Why does Baldwin begin her article with a description of a day in the life of the Urbane family? What does she mean by a "semi-fictional" American household? Do you find her description accurate and amusing, or do you find it offensive?

2. What does "advertorial" mean (paragraph 4)? Which two words are contained in this neologism, coined by *The New Yorker?* How does this word incorporate a basic message of the essay?

3. Where do you find the thesis statement in this essay? Which parts of the essay most strongly support the thesis? Were there sections of the essay that drifted from the main point? If so, where exactly were they?

4. Give two examples of words with negative connotations used to describe how the administrations of Presidents Reagan and Bush fostered greater corporate involvement in schools, libraries, and museums. How do these expressions project Baldwin's opinion of the administrations' treatment of these institutions?

5. How does the author use humor throughout the article to engage the reader? Point out specific examples, in addition to the opening six paragraphs, that a general audience would find amusing.

Writing Assignments

1. Listen to your local public radio station and/or watch your local public TV channel and identify the sponsors who fund various programs. How are these sponsors described on public broadcasting? Write an essay in which you argue that public broadcasting sponsorships are sneaky forms of advertisements.

2. In the periodical section of your library find editions of a popular magazine such as *Life* or *Time* published 20 and 10 years ago. Choose a product that

is still being advertised and compare the ads with current ads for the same product from the same publication if possible. Write an essay discussing how the ads have changed over the years. To which personal desires do the ads cater?

3. Rent a video of a current movie and watch it to see how many products are clearly identified during the movie. Write an essay in which you discuss the obvious commercialism in this movie.

4. Has reading this essay heightened your awareness about current marketing procedures? Write a paper discussing how you intend to respond to commercialism in your daily life if you have become sensitized to its insidiousness. Give examples from your own experiences.

5. Make a list of some of the ads you are exposed to in a single day. Then write your own funny account of your typical ad-saturated day.

Delectable Materialism
Michael Schudson

How big a role does advertising play in your life? Have ads really transformed you into an insatiable consumer as Deborah Baldwin claims—someone incapable of discriminating between mindless desire and legitimate needs? Michael Schudson thinks not. In this piece, he disputes those social critics who attribute near magical power to advertising. Instead, he challenges the reader to take the unusual view that it's not advertising that creates our acquisition frenzy but our natural love of material things that make life comfortable and convenient.

Schudson is a professor of sociology and chair of the communications department at the University of California, San Diego. He is the author of *Advertising, The Uneasy Persuasion* and numerous articles on advertising and the media. This piece originally appeared in *The American Prospect*, Spring 1991.

BEFORE YOU READ

Make a list of all the reasons that advertising is not a particularly strong force in the lives of most Americans. Arrange them from the strongest to the weakest. When you finish reading the essay, check to see if you had some of the same insights as the author.

AS YOU READ

As you read notice how Schudson builds his defense of advertising by rebutting one by one the various claims of its critics.

1   Contemporary social critics may imagine their ringing critiques of consumer culture to be deeply radical and subversive, but they are generally only new

versions of a critique that goes back a long way in American culture. And confused versions, at that. Take, for example, criticism of advertising, often attacked as the most egregious emblem of materialism, even as its cause. In fact, America was materialist, consumerist, and enterprising, as Alexis de Tocqueville observed in the 1830s, long before advertising held much visibility or importance in American cultural life. Yet advertising is looked on today as the chief symbol, if not the chief engine, of consumer culture.

2   As the chief symbol of consumer culture, advertising has also been a chief subject of analysis for social critics looking for the hidden springs of American life. David Potter, a widely respected American historian, got it wrong 40 years ago in his classic study of consumer culture, *People of Plenty* (1954), and much American thinking about advertising and culture has yet to recover from the error he expressed more directly and clearly than anyone else. Potter held that a society that moves from a producer orientation to a consumer orientation must develop a culture to correspond to it. Advertising responds to "the need to stimulate desire for the goods which an abundant economy has to offer and which a scarcity economy would never have produced."

3   For Potter, advertising was one of a very few institutions that could "properly be called instruments of social control." And what is an institution of social control? It is one that guides a person "by conceiving of him in a distinctive way and encouraging him to conform as far as possible to the concept." Potter used as examples the church, which conceives of a person as having an immortal soul; the schools, conceiving of the person as a reasonable creature; and the free-enterprise economy, conceiving of the person as a useful producer. Advertising, in contrast, "conceives of man as a consumer."

4   The trouble with Potter's argument is that advertising is not at all like church, school, and workplace, the institutions he listed as archetypal institutions of social control. Having recently watched my 5-year-old go off to kindergarten, I have no illusion that the kind of control advertising exercises is half as determinative, controlling, influential, or potentially as destructive as that exerted by the institution of schooling. Even if children were to spend as much time watching commercial television as they spend in school (and they do not—television is turned on in the average American household seven hours a day but no individual member of the family watches it for that length of time), they can exercise freedoms in front of the television that they instantly lose in the classroom. In front of the television, they can come and go as they like; they can choose to attend or not to attend without fear of the punishing glance, voice, or raised eyebrows of the advertiser responding immediately to their inattention. In short, the television advertisement can offer no social punishment, no social reward, no social reference group.

5   Potter, like many others, failed to distinguish the social control exercised by schools and churches from the cultural influence exercised by the mass media. A cultural or symbolic medium, like advertising, does not necessarily have a social dimension. Or, to put it another way, the social aspects of

consumption do not depend on advertising. For example, when we feel good and think we look smart wearing a cashmere coat, we may be reflecting some influence of advertising. But we are just as likely reflecting the practices of other people in the social set to which we belong or aspire. Owning a book rather than borrowing it, or owning a washer and dryer rather than using the neighborhood Laundromat, gives a pleasure of possession, convenience, and independence that ads for Stephen King blockbusters or laundry detergents have no part in. If the things we buy did not satisfy or seduce, the images conjured up by advertising would ordinarily fade. The consumer culture is sustained socially not by manufactured images but by the goods themselves as they are used.

6   Potter's analysis seems to suggest, as did other analyses of the 1950s that still guide our thought on this matter, that people need to be instructed in the emotions as well as the arts of consumption. People have to learn to desire more goods. That was the argument made by liberals like Potter and John Kenneth Galbraith and by social critic Vance Packard. It was the point argued by Marxists and taken up later by Stuart Ewen (see Ewen's "Our all-consuming quest for style," *Utne Reader,* Sept./Oct. 1989, p. 81). It is also a notion pushed by the people responsible for selling propaganda to business—that is, by advertising agencies themselves.

7   Curiously, both the critics of advertising and its advocates seem to share the peculiar premise that material goods require force feeding. But is consuming so unpleasant? Is wanting more so unnatural? Is aping the neighbors of seeking to be fashionable so unheard of that a multi-billion-dollar enterprise is required to coax us into it? Is desire for possessions so rare? Is pleasure in goods so unusual a joy?

8   I do not claim that wanting more is universal. But I do claim that in America no multi-billion-dollar industry was needed to make people want more and more or to breed in them a dissatisfaction that they could quell only in the marketplace.

9   Just as the longing for more has deep roots in American culture, so does criticism of consumer culture have deep roots in America. Indeed, criticism of what today we call consumer culture originated with the Quakers, the Puritans, and others before anything very closely resembling consumer culture had emerged—certainly before advertising as the central institution expression of abundance took root.

10   Advertising at times seems to be consumer culture materialism at its worst, the sizzle without the steak, the idolatry of goods divorced from the utility and enjoyment goods provide, but even this is too simple a view. It recognizes neither the aesthetic appeal of some advertising that touches us nor the plain wrapping, anti-magical character of most advertising. The most common advertising is, in a sense, Quaker itself—it points to price and so helps keep in mind economy as a chief criterion in buying. Or it is Puritan—recommending a product not because it provides moral or social or theological salvation but because it serves certain banal purposes well. It cleans your sink. It gets you to

New York in time for your business meeting. It provides high-fidelity sound recording.

11   True, advertising is rarely republican—it does not focus on the needs of public life. And it often takes a stance toward the public life that may not be healthy. If views of the person and the society can be ranged along a continuum between those that emphasize the moral embeddedness of the individual in a community and those that emphasize the isolation of the autonomous individual, then advertising typically falls near the latter end of the continuum.

12   Advertising offers and is expressive of an ideology of choice. It unifies us around a belief in difference, variety, abundance, pluralism, choice, democracy. Consumer culture and advertising, along with elections, are the most important institutions that promote the American ideology of choice.

13   In the past generation, people have listened to one set of voices from the East and have borrowed notions of a simple life, a life of self-discipline and self-denial, from Buddhist traditions of Asia. Now we are listening to a different set of voices from a different East—the voices of East Berlin, Hungary, and Russia, with their unashamed emulation of economic abundance. Eastern European nations, as symbol and substance of their legitimacy on a world stage, are seeking to partake in the kind of consumer affluence the West has enjoyed for two generations.

14   This should stir us to question our harsh criticisms of consumer culture. At the same time, we have growing concerns about environmental and ecological catastrophe and the distribution of consumption not only among rich and poor within a society but among rich and poor nations within a world system. We should not learn the lessons of Eastern Europe so well as to deny ourselves the right to criticize consumerism. But it must be a new critique. Freeing ourselves from biblical or Marxist moralisms and recognizing a certain dignity and rationality in the desire for material goods, we should seek to reconstruct an understanding of our moral and political view of consumption that we and others can live with.

Topical Considerations

1. In what ways does Michael Schudson disagree with Deborah Baldwin's contention that advertising invades all facets of our lives, including our institutions and homes? (See paragraphs 9, 23, and 28 of Baldwin's article.) Which author do you agree with regarding the influence of advertising on the American public?

2. Schudson argues that advertising is not as important an influence on children's lives as their schooling. What reasons does he give to support his viewpoint? Do you agree with him?

3. Schudson concurs with Baldwin's statement that the average American family has its TV running 7 hours a day. At what point does Schudson contradict Baldwin's comments about TV viewing? From your own TV-watching experience, who seems closer to the truth?

4. Do you buy products because you have seen them advertised? Because your friends have them? For other reasons? What are those other reasons? How would Baldwin respond to your reasons?

5. Do you think Schudson proves his contention that most advertising can be considered Puritan or Quaker? Give reasons from paragraph 10 to support your answer.

6. How would Eastern European refugees fleeing from ethnic wars react to Schudson's argument that the newly formed Eastern European nations should continue to emulate the West's consumerism? Would you give countries emerging from communist rule the same advice? Why or why not?

7. In paragraph 6 Schudson states the argument of liberals concerning consumerism: "People have to learn to desire more goods." This is the same point Juliet Schor makes throughout her essay, "Work and Spend." However, Schudson refutes this argument in the following paragraphs. Which author do you agree with and why?

Rhetorical Considerations

1. What argumentative technique or strategy does Schudson use to refute the arguments of John Kenneth Galbraith, Vance Packard, and Stuart Ewen? Is this an effective tactic?

2. What is the author's purpose in using so many questions in paragraph 7? How does he expect the reader to respond to these questions? Did you respond in the desired manner?

3. Does Schudson give enough evidence to support his criticism of the authorities he quotes? Which points are unsubstantiated? Can you find examples of logical fallacies (such as *ad populum* or hasty generalizations) in his article?

4. Schudson and Baldwin each offer a personal experience regarding the influence of ads in our lives. What is the personal experience in each piece? Do these anecdotes influence you to side with either of them?

5. What do the arguments presented by Schudson and Baldwin reveal about their political leanings? Would you label them "liberal" or "conservative"? What evidence do you have for your choices?

Writing Assignments

1. Take sides with either Deborah Baldwin or Michael Schudson and show how one author's argument is superior to the other's. Refer to the points that are contradictory in the articles. Resolve these contradictions according to the evidence in the essay you favor. Prove that one argument is more logical than the other by providing examples and evidence from your choice.

2. Make a one-week survey of your friends or family members to see how many hours a day their TV sets are on. Have them log the actual hours

watched. Write a paper determining the influence that TV has on its viewers. With which author's (Schudson or Baldwin) assessment do you tend to agree?

3. Write a paper agreeing or disagreeing with Schudson's contention in paragraph 12: "Consumer culture and advertising, along with elections, are the most important institutions that promote the American ideology of choice." Give examples from each institution to support your argument.

4. Write a letter to parents in which you try to persuade them that TV watching is harmless to children. If necessary, use evidence from Schudson's article for support.

The Language of Advertising

A Word from Our Sponsor
Patricia Volk

Although she worked as a professional advertising copywriter, Patricia Volk is anything but defensive about the practices of her profession. While demonstrating some of the jargon of ad writers, Volk confesses that the language of advertising is "without rules"—a language with "little to protect it." Ad people, she argues, will stop at nothing to make a product that the world neither wants nor needs sound wonderful.

In addition to being a copywriter, Volk is author of the award-winning short-story collection *The Yellow Banana and Other Stories* (1985), the novels *White Light* (1987), and *All It Takes* (1991). This article first appeared in the "On Language" column of the *New York Times Magazine* in August 1987.

BEFORE YOU READ

Try to think of how the language of advertising might be "without rules." Can you think of the claims of any recent ads that seem to stretch the truth? That exceed the truth? That downright lie?

AS YOU READ

Try to determine the different ways Volk projects her attitude toward the claims of advertising. Notice her choice of words, her tone of voice, the examples she offers. Putting these together, how would you characterize her attitude?

1   Linguistically speaking (and that's still the preferred way), there is only one rule in advertising: There are no rules. "We try harder," lacks parallelism. "No-

body doesn't like Sara Lee," is a double negative. And "Modess. Because . . ." Because . . . why? My friends didn't know. My mother wouldn't tell. My sister said, like Mount Everest, because it was there. The word "creme" on a product means there's no cream in it. "Virtually," as in "Virtually all our cars are tested," means in essence, not in fact. Even a casual "Let's have lunch," said in passing on Mad Ave. means "Definitely, let's not."

2   Language without rules has little to protect it. Some of the most familiar lines would disappear like ring-around-the-collar if you put a mere "Says who?" after them. "Coke is it." Says who? "Sony. The one and only." Oh, yeah?

3   Still, one word in advertising has virtually limitless power. It gives "permission to believe." It inspires hope. It is probably (disclaimer) the oldest word in advertising.

4   What "new" lacks in newness, it makes up for in motivation. Unfortunately, new gets old fast. Legally, it's usable for only six months after a product is introduced. As in, say, "Introducing New Grippies. The candy that sticks to 'the woof of your mouf.'"

5   Once Grippies are six months old, unlike newlyweds, who get a year, and the New Testament which has gotten away with it for who knows how long, Grippies are reduced to just plain Grippies. That's when you improve them and say "Introducing New Improved Grippies." Now they really stick like cwazy to that woof.

6   Had you named your product "New" to start with, as in "New Soap. The soap that cleans like new," you'd never have to worry about your product sounding old. Introduced as "New New Soap," six months down the road it segues into "New Improved New Soap." Or you could avoid the six-month thing entirely and just call it "The Revolutionary New Soap" from day one.

Pitching Glue

7 How do you get the Grippies account in the first place? You "pitch" it in a flurry of work called a "push." A creative team works weekends and sleeps in the office. It's intense.

8   A successful pitch winds up in a "win," and you've "landed" the account. By the end of the week, everyone in the agency has a free box of Grippies and work begins. This is the "honeymoon period."

9   Everybody loves everybody else. You take the factory tour. You eat Grippies till your molars roll. And you attend "focus groups," i.e., meetings between researchers and preselected members of your "target audience," the people you hope will love Grippies.

10   You sit behind a two-way mirror and watch people eat Grippies. You take notes. You start hating the man who scratches the exposed area of his leg between the top of his sock and the bottom of his pants. "Look! He's doing it! He's doing it *again!*" And what you learn in the focus group, you use to build

"share," which is the percentage of the population using your *kind* of product that buys yours in particular.

11   It gives you some idea of how large this country is when you realize that if you can raise Forever Glue's .01 share of market (one person per thousand) to .03, Forever Glue will be a dazzling success. So you do the "Nothing lasts like Forever" campaign, complete with "The Big Idea." You find a small town in a depressed area upstate and glue it back together. Brick by brick, clapboard by clapboard, you actually (favorite ad word) glue a town together and restore it in a classic "demo" with "product as hero." You get a corner office and a Tizio lamp.

12   Forever is stickier. Grippies are grippier. But what if your product is "parity," a "me-tooer"? What if it has no "unique selling point" or "exclusivity"? What if the world is not waiting for Mega-Bran, the cereal that tastes like Styrofoam pellets and gets soggy in the bowl?

13   Some folks "make it sing." It's what everybody thinks people in advertising do anyway, as in, "Oh, you're in advertising! You must write jingles!" So you write new words to Bon Jovi's "Never Say Good-bye," only the client doesn't want to spend $2 million for the rights. So you check out the P.D.'s, public domain songs, songs with lapsed copyrights that are at least 75 years old. You just have to hope the Mega-Bran lyrics work to the tune of "Ach, the Moon Climbs High," "Jim Crack Corn," or "Whoopee Ti Yi Yo—Git Along Little Dogies."

14   At last the new Mega-Bran campaign is ready to crawl through all the "loops" in the "approval cycle," from your client's kids to the network's lawyers. Everybody "signs off" on it.

15   In "pretest," you get "rich verbatims"—a lot of people who remember everything about your commercial. You go for it. You shoot a finished "spot." You spend $250,000 on production, "net net," and $3 million on network and uh-oh, nobody buys the bran. Your commercial has failed to generate "trial" and "brand awareness." It's the Edsel of brans.

16   Quick, you do another "execution," a celebrity endorsement using someone with a high "Q" (familiarity and popularity) score. (Bill Cosby has the highest.) You try "image advertising," which says almost nothing, but leaves the viewer feeling good about your product. (Soft drinks do it all the time.)

17   Still, no one remembers Mega-Bran. It's a case of "vampire video"— what people saw in your ad was so strong that it sucked the blood out of your message. The account becomes "shaky." "Doomers and gloomers" worry all over your carpet. They "bail." Bailers are people in a room who sniff out with whom the power lies; whatever that person says, the bailer agrees. The fastest bailer I ever knew was an account man who told me every time he was asked his opinion, he saw his mortgage float in front of his eyes.

18   The account goes from shaky to the ICU. Then it's "out the door." There is no funeral, no period of mourning because every loss presents an opportunity, a chance to roll up your sleeves, grease up your elbow and pitch again.

Body Parts

19 Clients like to find "niches" for their products. A niche is a special place no other product can fit. Sometimes you find the niche before you find the product and you have to find a product to fill the niche you found.

20 Body parts are always good, though by now almost everything has been spoken for. There are still the navel and the philtrum. If you can do "exploratories" and with a little prodding make consumers aware that their philtrums sweat too much, smell funny or have unwanted hair, you're in business. You create a new form of consumer anxiety and cure it in a single stroke. You launch "Creme de Philtrum," with no cream in it, and have "preemptiveness." You're hot.

21 You don't have to go to school to write great copy. The best writers I know wrap fish in the Elements of Style. Schools say they can teach it, but you either have it or you don't. It's like perfect pitch, good gums, or being able to sit on the floor with your ankles around your neck. They use language to convince, persuade, and, at its best, educate. They twist and twiddle words and understand their power. They make people do things they hadn't thought of doing before. They make them change.

22 One of the best writers ever had a great line: "The only thing we have to fear is fear itself." It led a whole country out of Depression. Imagine what he could have done with detergent.

Topical Considerations

1. How is the language of advertising a language "without rules?" Can you think of some current ads that illustrate this claim? What rules of grammar or meaning are being broken?

2. According to Volk, the advertiser's word "inspires hope" (paragraph 3). Do you agree? How do claims of "newness" appeal to the consumer? Have you ever been seduced into buying a product because it's "new" or "improved"? Can you think of any other potent "hope" words?

3. How does the author, who is an advertising copywriter, characterize her profession? Would you want to be an ad writer? Why or why not?

4. What strategies do ad writers resort to if their "product is 'parity,'" if it has no "unique selling point"?

5. What special power of advertising does Volk's hypothetical "Creme de Philtrum" illustrate (paragraph 20)? Can you think of any real products that this might describe?

6. Why does Volk say, "You don't have to go to school to write great copy" (paragraph 21)?

Rhetorical Considerations

1. Volk says that the language of advertising has no rules. How well does she illustrate this assertion in her essay? Can you think of other examples?

2. How would you characterize Volk's attitude toward advertising claims?

3. Throughout the essay, Volk resorts to ad industry jargon highlighted in quotation marks. What would you say her purpose is here? How do you evaluate her attitude toward the jargon? What do you think of some of the expressions? Do any strike you as particularly amusing?

4. Explain the effectiveness of the final paragraph. What point is being made? How does the paragraph summarize the theme of the essay? How consistent is her tone here with the rest of the piece?

Writing Assignments

1. Can you think of any ads whose claims particularly irritate you? Which ones? And what bothers you about them?

2. Volk says in paragraph 3 that there is "limitless power" in the words of advertising because what is being sold is hope. Select a familiar ad and write a paper analyzing how its language—verbal and visual—inspires hope.

3. Has this essay in any way changed your attitude toward advertising? Has it sensitized you to the power of advertising language? Has it made you more wary of the claims in ads? Discuss the article's effect on you in an essay.

4. Would you like to be a professional copywriter? Write an essay explaining why you would or would not want to write ad copy for a living.

With These Words I Can Sell You Anything
William Lutz

Words such as "help" and "virtually," phrases such as "new and improved" and "acts fast" seem like innocuous weaponry in the arsenal of advertising. But not to William Lutz who analyzes the way such words are used in ads—how they misrepresent, mislead, and deceive consumers. In this essay, he alerts us to the special power of "weasel words"—those familiar and sneaky little critters that "appear to say one thing when in fact they say the opposite, or nothing at all." The real danger, Lutz argues, is how such language debases reality and the values of the consumer.

Lutz has been called the George Orwell of the 1990s. Chair of the Committee on Public Doublespeak of the National Council of Teachers of English, Lutz edits the *Quarterly Review of Doublespeak,* a magazine dedicated to the eradication of misleading official statements. He also teaches in the English department at Rutgers University and is the author of *Beyond Nineteen Eighty-Four* (1984) and *Doublespeak* (1990), from which this essay was taken.

BEFORE YOU READ

Consider the phrase "like magic" as it might be used in an ad—for example, "Zappo dish detergent works like magic." What does the phrase mean at a quick glance? What does it mean upon detailed analysis? Make a list of other such "big promise" words or phrases you've heard in ads.

AS YOU READ

As you read the definition of "weasel words" (a word so hollow it has no meaning) you probably thought, "Now there is a gimmick I would never fall for." As you read Lutz's piece, list any ads using weasel words that have lured you into a purchase.

1   One problem advertisers have when they try to convince you that the product they are pushing is really different from other, similar products is that their claims are subject to some laws. Not a lot of laws, but there are some designed to prevent fraudulent or untruthful claims in advertising. Even during the happy years of nonregulation under President Ronald Reagan, the FTC did crack down on the more blatant abuses in advertising claims. Generally speaking, advertisers have to to be careful in what they say in their ads, in the claims they make for the products they advertise. Parity claims are safe because they are legal and supported by a number of court decisions. But beyond parity claims there are weasel words.

2   Advertisers use weasel words to appear to be making a claim for a product when in fact they are making no claim at all. Weasel words get their name from the way weasels eat the eggs they find in the nests of other animals. A weasel will make a small hole in the egg, suck out the insides, then place the egg back in the nest. Only when the egg is examined closely is it found to be hollow. That's the way it is with weasel words in advertising: Examine weasel words closely and you'll find that they're as hollow as any egg sucked by a weasel. Weasel words appear to say one thing when in fact they say the opposite, or nothing at all.

"Help"—The Number One Weasel Word

3   The biggest weasel word used in advertising doublespeak is "help." Now "help" only means to aid or assist, nothing more. It does not mean to conquer, stop, eliminate, end, solve, heal, cure or anything else. But once the ad says "help," it can say just about anything after that because "help" qualifies everything coming after it. The trick is that the claim that comes after the weasel word is usually so strong and so dramatic that you forget the word "help" and concentrate only on the dramatic claim. You read into the ad a message that the ad does not contain. More importantly, the advertiser is not responsible for the claim that you read into the ad, even though the advertiser wrote the ad so you would read that claim into it.

4   The next time you see an ad for a cold medicine that promises that it "helps relieve cold symptoms fast," don't rush out to buy it. Ask yourself what this claim is really saying. Remember, "helps" means only that the medicine

will aid or assist. What will it aid or assist in doing? Why, "relieve" your cold "symptoms." "Relieve" only means to ease, alleviate, or mitigate, not to stop, end, or cure. Nor does the claim say how much relieving this medicine will do. Nowhere does this ad claim it will cure anything. In fact, the ad doesn't even claim it will *do* anything at all. The ad only claims that it will aid in relieving (not curing) your cold symptoms, which are probably a runny nose, watery eyes, and a headache. In other words, this medicine probably contains a standard decongestant and some aspirin. By the way, what does "fast" mean? Ten minutes, one hour, one day? What is fast to one person can be very slow to another. Fast is another weasel word.

5   Ad claims using "help" are among the most popular ads. One says, "Helps keep you young looking," but then a lot of things will help keep you young looking, including exercise, rest, good nutrition, and a facelift. More importantly, this ad doesn't say the product will keep you young, only "young *looking."* Someone may look young to one person and old to another.

6   A toothpaste ad says, "Helps prevent cavities," but it doesn't say it will actually prevent cavities. Brushing your teeth regularly, avoiding sugars in food, and flossing daily will also help prevent cavities. A liquid cleaner ad says, "Helps keep your home germ free," but it doesn't say it actually kills germs, nor does it even specify which germs it might kill.

7   "Help" is such a useful weasel word that it is often combined with other action-verb weasel words such as "fight" and "control." Consider the claim, "Helps control dandruff symptoms with regular use." What does it really say? It will assist in controlling (not eliminating, stopping, ending, or curing) the *symptoms* of dandruff, not the cause of dandruff nor the dandruff itself. What are the symptoms of dandruff? The ad deliberately leaves that undefined, but assume that the symptoms referred to in the ad are the flaking and itching commonly associated with dandruff. But just shampooing with *any* shampoo will temporarily eliminate these symptoms, so this shampoo isn't any different from any other. Finally, in order to benefit from this product, you must use it regularly. What is "regular use"—daily, weekly, hourly? Using another shampoo "regularly" will have the same effect. Nowhere does this advertising claim say this particular shampoo stops, eliminates, or cures dandruff. In fact, this claim says nothing at all, thanks to all the weasel words.

8   Look at ads in magazines and newspapers, listen to ads on radio and television, and you'll find the word "help" in ads for all kinds of products. How often do you read or hear such phrases as "helps stop . . . ," "helps overcome . . . ," "helps eliminate . . . ," "helps you feel . . . ," or "helps you look . . . "? If you start looking for this weasel word in advertising, you'll be amazed at how often it occurs. Analyze the claims in the ads using "help," and you will discover that these ads are really saying nothing.

9   There are plenty of other weasel words used in advertising. In fact, there are so many that to list them all would fill the rest of this book. But, in order to identify the doublespeak of advertising and understand the real meaning of an ad, you have to be aware of the most popular weasel words in advertising today.

Virtually Spotless

10   One of the most powerful weasel words is "virtually," a word so innocent that most people don't pay any attention to it when it is used in an advertising claim. But watch out. "Virtually" is used in advertising claims that appear to make specific, definite promises when there is no promise. After all, what does "virtually" mean? It means "in essence or effect, although not in fact." Look at that definition again. "Virtually" means *not in fact.* It does *not* mean "almost" or "just about the same as," or anything else. And before you dismiss all this concern over such a small word, remember that small words can have big consequences.

11   In 1971 a federal court rendered its decision on a case brought by a woman who became pregnant while taking birth control pills. She sued the manufacturer, Eli Lilly and Company, for breach of warranty. The woman lost her case. Basing its ruling on a statement in the pamphlet accompanying the pills, which stated that, "When taken as directed, the tablets offer virtually 100% protection," the court ruled that there was no warranty, expressed or implied, that the pills were absolutely effective. In its ruling, the court pointed out that, according to *Webster's Third New International Dictionary,* "virtually" means "almost entirely" and clearly does not mean "absolute" (*Whittington v. Eli Lilly and Company,* 333 F. Supp. 98). In other words, the Eli Lilly company was really saying that its birth control pill, even when taken as directed, *did not in fact* provide 100 percent protection against pregnancy. But Eli Lilly didn't want to put it that way because then many women might not have bought Lilly's birth control pills.

12   The next time you see the ad that says that this dishwasher detergent "leaves dishes virtually spotless," just remember how advertisers twist the meaning of the weasel word "virtually." You can have lots of spots on your dishes after using this detergent and the ad claim will still be true, because what this claim really means is that this detergent does not *in fact* leave your dishes spotless. Whenever you see or hear an ad claim that uses the word "virtually," just translate that claim into its real meaning. So the television set that is "virtually trouble free" becomes the television set that is not in fact trouble free, the "virtually foolproof operation" of any appliance becomes an operation that is in fact not foolproof, and the product that "virtually never needs service" becomes the product that is not in fact service free.

New and Improved

13   If "new" is the most frequently used word on a product package, "improved" is the second most frequent. In fact, the two words are almost always used together. It seems just about everything sold these days is "new and improved." The next time you're in the supermarket, try counting the number of times you see these words on products. But you'd better do it while you're walking down just one aisle, otherwise you'll need a calculator to keep track of your counting.

14   Just what do these words mean? The use of the word "new" is restricted by regulations, so an advertiser can't just use the word on a product or in an ad without meeting certain requirements. For example, a product is considered new for about six months during a national advertising campaign. If the product is being advertised only in a limited test market area, the word can be used longer, and in some instances has been used for as long as two years.

15   What makes a product "new"? Some products have been around for a long time, yet every once in a while you discover that they are being advertised as "new." Well, an advertiser can call a product new if there has been "a material functional change" in the product. What is "a material functional change," you ask? Good question. In fact it's such a good question it's being asked all the time. It's up to the manufacturer to prove that the product has undergone such a change. And if the manufacturer isn't challenged on the claim, then there's no one to stop it. Moreover, the change does not have to be an improvement in the product. One manufacturer added an artificial lemon scent to a cleaning product and called it "new and improved," even though the product did not clean any better than without the lemon scent. The manufacturer defended the use of the word "new" on the grounds that the artificial scent changed the chemical formula of the product and therefore constituted "a material functional change."

16   Which brings up the word "improved." When used in advertising, "improved" does not mean "made better." It only means "changed" or "different from before." So, if the detergent maker puts a plastic pour spout on the box of detergent, the product has been "improved," and away we go with a whole new advertising campaign. Or, if the cereal maker adds more fruit or a different kind of fruit to the cereal, there's an improved product. Now you know why manufacturers are constantly making little changes in their products. Whole new advertising campaigns, designed to convince you that the product has been changed for the better, are based on small changes in superficial aspects of a product. The next time you see an ad for an "improved" product, ask yourself what was wrong with the old one. Ask yourself just how "improved" the product is. Finally, you might check to see whether the "improved" version costs more than the unimproved one. After all, someone has to pay for the millions of dollars spent advertising the improved product.

17   Of course, advertisers really like to run ads that claim a product is "new and improved." While what constitutes a "new" product may be subject to some regulation, "improved" is a subjective judgment. A manufacturer changes the shape of its stick deodorant, but the shape doesn't improve the function of the deodorant. That is, changing the shape doesn't affect the deodorizing ability of the deodorant, so the manufacturer calls it "improved." Another manufacturer adds ammonia to its liquid cleaner and calls it "new and improved." Since adding ammonia does affect the cleaning ability of the product, there has been a "material functional change" in the product, and the manufacturer can now call its cleaner "new," and "improved" as well. Now the weasel words "new and improved" are plastered all over the package and

are the basis for a multimillion-dollar ad campaign. But after six months the word "new" will have to go, until someone can dream up another change in the product. Perhaps it will be adding color to the liquid, or changing the shape of the package, or maybe adding a new dripless pour spout, or perhaps a _____. The "improvements" are endless, and so are the new advertising claims and campaigns.

18   "New" is just too useful and powerful a word in advertising for advertisers to pass it up easily. So they use weasel words that say "new" without really saying it. One of their favorites is "introducing," as in, "Introducing improved Tide," or "Introducing the stain remover." The first is simply saying, here's our improved soap; the second, here's our new advertising campaign for our detergent. Another favorite is "now," as in, "Now there's Sinex," which simply means that Sinex is available. Then there are phrases like "Today's Chevrolet," "Presenting Dristan," and "A fresh way to start the day." The list is really endless because advertisers are always finding new ways to say "new" without really saying it. If there is a second edition of this book, I'll just call it the "new and improved" edition. Wouldn't you really rather have a "new and improved" edition of this book rather than a "second" edition?

Acts Fast

19   "Acts" and "works" are two popular weasel words in advertising because they bring action to the product and to the advertising claim. When you see the ad for the cough syrup that "Acts on the cough control center," ask yourself what this cough syrup is claiming to do. Well, it's just claiming to "act," to do something, to perform an action. What is it that the cough syrup does? The ad doesn't say. It only claims to perform an action or do something on your "cough control center." By the way, what and where is your "cough control center"? I don't remember learning about that part of the body in human biology class.

20   Ads that use such phrases as "acts fast," "acts against," "acts to prevent," and the like are saying essentially nothing, because "act" is a word empty of any specific meaning. The ads are always careful not to specify exactly what "act" the product performs. Just because a brand of aspirin claims to "act fast" for headache relief doesn't mean this aspirin is any better than any other aspirin. What is the "act" that this aspirin performs? You're never told. Maybe it just dissolves quickly. Since aspirin is a parity product, all aspirin is the same and therefore functions the same.

Works Like Anything Else

21   If you don't find the word "acts" in an ad, you will probably find the weasel word "works." In fact, the two words are almost interchangeable in advertising. Watch out for ads that say a product "works against," "works like," "works for," or "works longer." As with "acts," "works" is the same meaningless verb

used to make you think that this product really does something, and maybe even something special or unique. But "works," like "acts," is basically a word empty of any specific meaning.

Like Magic

22 Whenever advertisers want you to stop thinking about the product and to start thinking about something bigger, better, or more attractive than the product, they use that very popular weasel word, "like." The word "like" is the advertiser's equivalent of a magician's use of misdirection. "Like" gets you to ignore the product and concentrate on the claim the advertiser is making about it. "For skin like peaches and cream" claims the ad for a skin cream. What is this ad really claiming? It doesn't say this cream will give you peaches-and-cream skin. There is no verb in this claim, so it doesn't even mention using the product. How is skin ever like "peaches and cream"? Remember, ads must be read literally and exactly, according to the dictionary definition of words. (Remember "virtually" in the Eli Lilly case.) The ad is making absolutely no promise or claim whatsoever for this skin cream. If you think this cream will give you soft, smooth, youthful-looking skin, you are the one who has read that meaning into the ad.

23 The wine that claims "It's like taking a trip to France" wants you to think about a romantic evening in Paris as you walk along the boulevard after a wonderful meal in an intimate little bistro. Of course, you don't really believe that a wine can take you to France, but the goal of the ad is to get you to think pleasant, romantic thoughts about France and not about how the wine tastes or how expensive it may be. That little word "like" has taken you away from crushed grapes into a world of your own imaginative making. Who knows, maybe the next time you buy wine, you'll think those pleasant thoughts when you see this brand of wine, and you'll buy it. Or, maybe you weren't even thinking about buying wine at all, but now you just might pick up a bottle the next time you're shopping. Ah, the power of "like" in advertising.

24 How about the most famous "like" claim of all, "Winston tastes good like a cigarette should"? Ignoring the grammatical error here, you might want to know what this claim is saying. Whether a cigarette tastes good or bad is a subjective judgment because what tastes good to one person may well taste horrible to another. Not everyone likes fried snails, even if they are called escargot. (*De gustibus non est disputandum,* which was probably the Roman rule for advertising as well as for defending the games in the Colosseum.) There are many people who say all cigarettes taste terrible, other people who say only some cigarettes taste right, and still others who say all cigarettes taste good. Who's right? Everyone, because taste is a matter of personal judgment.

25 Moreover, note the use of the conditional, "should." The complete claim is, "Winston tastes good like a cigarette should taste." But should cigarettes taste good? Again, this is a matter of personal judgment and probably depends most on one's experiences with smoking. So, the Winston ad is simply

saying that Winston cigarettes are just like any other cigarette: Some people like them and some people don't. On that statement R. J. Reynolds conducted a very successful multimillion-dollar advertising campaign that helped keep Winston the number-two-selling cigarette in the United States, close behind number one, Marlboro.

Can It Be Up to the Claim?

26   Analyzing ads for doublespeak requires that you pay attention to every word in the ad and determine what each word really means. Advertisers try to wrap their claims in language that sounds concrete, specific, and objective, when in fact the language of advertising is anything but. Your job is to read carefully and listen critically so that when the announcer says that "Crest can be of significant value . . ." you know immediately that this claim says absolutely nothing. Where is the doublespeak in this ad? Start with the second word.

27   Once again, you have to look at what words really mean, not what you think they mean or what the advertiser wants you to think they mean. The ad for Crest only says that using Crest "can be" of "significant value." What really throws you off in this ad is the brilliant use of "significant." It draws your attention to the word "value" and makes you forget that the ad only claims that Crest "can be." The ad doesn't say that Crest *is* of value, only that it is "able" or "possible" to be of value, because that's all that "can" means.

28   It's so easy to miss the importance of those little words, "can be." Almost as easy as missing the importance of the words "up to" in an ad. These words are very popular in sale ads. You know, the ones that say, "Up to 50% Off!" Now, what does that claim mean? Not much, because the store or manufacturer has to reduce the price of only a few items by 50 percent. Everything else can be reduced a lot less, or not even reduced. Moreover, don't you want to know 50 percent off of what? Is it 50 percent off the "manufacturer's suggested list price," which is the highest possible price? Was the price artificially inflated and then reduced? In other ads, "up to" expresses an ideal situation. The medicine that works "up to ten times faster," the battery that lasts "up to twice as long," and the soap that gets you "up to twice as clean" all are based on ideal situations for using those products, situations in which you can be sure you will never find yourself.

Unfinished Words

29   Unfinished words are a kind of "up to" claim in advertising. The claim that a battery lasts "up to twice as long" usually doesn't finish the comparison— twice as long as what? A birthday candle? A tank of gas? A cheap battery made in a country not noted for its technological achievements? The implication is that the battery lasts twice as long as batteries made by other battery makers, or twice as long as earlier model batteries made by the advertiser, but the ad

doesn't really make these claims. You read these claims into the ad, aided by the visual images the advertiser so carefully provides.

30   Unfinished words depend on you to finish them, to provide the words the advertisers so thoughtfully left out of the ad. Pall Mall cigarettes were once advertised as "A longer finer and milder smoke." The question is, longer, finer, and milder than what? The aspirin that claims it contains "Twice as much of the pain reliever doctors recommend most" doesn't tell you what pain reliever it contains twice as much of. (By the way, it's aspirin. That's right; it just contains twice the amount of aspirin. And how much is twice the amount? Twice of what amount?) Panadol boasts that "nobody reduces fever faster," but, since Panadol is a parity product, this claim simply means that Panadol isn't any better than any other product in its parity class. "You can be sure if it's Westinghouse," you're told, but just exactly what it is you can be sure of is never mentioned. "Magnavox gives you more" doesn't tell you what you get more of. More value? More television? More than they gave you before? It sounds nice, but it means nothing, until you fill in the claim with your own words, the words the advertiser didn't use. Since each of us fills in the claim differently, the ad and the product can become all things to all people, and not promise a single thing.

31   Unfinished words abound in advertising because they appear to promise so much. More importantly, they can be joined with powerful visual images on television to appear to be making significant promises about a product's effectiveness without really making any promises. In a television ad, the aspirin product that claims fast relief can show a person with a headache taking the product and then, in what appears to be a matter of minutes, claiming complete relief. This visual image is far more powerful than any claim made in unfinished words. Indeed, the visual image completes the unfinished words for you, filling in with pictures what the the words leave out. And you thought that ads didn't affect you. What brand of aspirin do you use?

32   Some years ago, Ford's advertisements proclaimed "Ford LTD—700% quieter." Now, what do you think Ford was claiming with these unfinished words? What was the Ford LTD quieter than? A Cadillac? A Mercedes Benz? A BMW? Well, when the FTC asked Ford to substantiate this unfinished claim, Ford replied that it meant that the inside of the LTD was 700% quieter than the outside. How did you finish those unfinished words when you first read them? Did you even come close to Ford's meaning?

Combining Weasel Words

33   A lot of ads don't fall neatly into one category or another because they use a variety of different devices and words. Different weasel words are often combined to make an ad claim. The claim, "Coffee-Mate gives coffee more body, more flavor," uses Unfinished Words ("more" than what?) and also uses words that have no specific meaning ("body" and "flavor"). Along with "taste" (remember the Winston ad and its claim to taste good), "body" and "flavor"

mean nothing because their meaning is entirely subjective. To you, "body" in coffee might mean thick, black, almost bitter coffee, while I might take it to mean a light brown, delicate coffee. Now, if you think you understood that last sentence, read it again, because it said nothing of objective value; it was filled with weasel words of no specific meaning: "thick," "black," "bitter," "light brown," and "delicate." Each of those words has no specific, objective meaning, because each of us can interpret them differently.

34   Try this slogan: "Looks, smells, tastes like ground-roast coffee." So, are you now going to buy Taster's Choice instant coffee because of this ad? "Looks," "smells," and "tastes" are all words with no specific meaning and depend on your interpretation of them for any meaning. Then there's that great weasel word "like," which simply suggests a comparison but does not make the actual connection between the product and the quality. Besides, do you know what "ground-roast" coffee is? I don't, but it sure sounds good. So, out of seven words in this ad, four are definite weasel words, two are quite meaningless, and only one has any clear meaning.

35   Remember the Anacin ad—"Twice as much of the pain reliever doctors recommend most"? There's a whole lot of weaseling going on this ad. First, what's the pain reliever they're talking about in this ad? Aspirin, of course. In fact, any time you see or hear an ad using those words "pain reliever," you can automatically substitute the word "aspirin" for them. (Makers of acetaminophen and ibuprofen pain relievers are careful in their advertising to identify their products as nonaspirin products.) So, now we know that Anacin has aspirin in it. Moreover, we know that Anacin has twice as much aspirin in it, but we don't know twice as much as what. Does it have twice as much aspirin as an ordinary aspirin tablet? If so, what is an ordinary aspirin tablet, and how much aspirin does it contain? Twice as much as Excedrin or Bufferin? Twice as much as a chocolate chip cookie? Remember those Unfinished Words and how they lead you on without saying anything.

36   Finally, what about those doctors who are doing all that recommending? Who are they? How many of them are there? What kind of doctors are they? What are their qualifications? Who asked them about recommending pain relievers? What other pain relievers did they recommend? And there are a whole lot more questions about this "poll" of doctors to which I'd like to know the answers, but you get the point. Sometimes, when I call my doctor, she tells me to take two aspirin and call her office in the morning. Is that where Anacin got this ad?

Read the Label, or the Brochure

37 Weasel words aren't just found on television, on the radio, or in newspaper and magazine ads. Just about any language associated with a product will contain the doublespeak of advertising. Remember the Eli Lilly case and the doublespeak on the information sheet that came with the birth control pills. Here's another example.

38   In 1983, the Estée Lauder cosmetics company announced a new product called "Night Repair." A small brochure distributed with the product stated that "Night Repair was scientifically formulated in Estée Lauder's U.S. laboratories as part of the Swiss Age-Controlling Skincare Program. Although only nature controls the aging process, this program helps control the signs of aging and encourages skin to look and feel younger." You might want to read these two sentences again, because they sound great but say nothing.

39   First, note that the product was "scientifically formulated" in the company's laboratories. What does that mean? What constitutes a scientific formulation? You wouldn't expect the company to say that the product was casually, mechanically, or carelessly formulated, or just thrown together one day when the people in the white coats didn't have anything better to do. But the word "scientifically" lends an air of precision and promise that just isn't there.

40   It is the second sentence, however, that's really weasely, both syntactically and semantically. The only factual part of this sentence is the introductory dependent clause—"only nature controls the aging process." Thus, the only fact in the ad is relegated to a dependent clause, a clause dependent on the main clause, which contains no factual or definite information at all and indeed purports to contradict the independent clause. The new "skincare program" (notice it's not a skin cream but a "program") does not claim to stop or even retard the aging process. What, then, does Night Repair, at a price of over $35 (in 1983 dollars) for a .87-ounce bottle do? According to this brochure, nothing. It only "helps," and the brochure does not say how much it helps. Moreover, it only "helps control," and then it only helps control the "*signs* of aging," not the aging itself. Also, it "encourages" skin not to *be* younger but only to "look and feel" younger. The brochure does not say younger than what. Of the sixteen words in the main clause of this second sentence, nine are weasel words. So, before you spend all that money for Night Repair, or any other cosmetic product, read the words carefully, and then decide if you're getting what you think you're paying for.

Other Tricks of the Trade

41   Advertisers' use of doublespeak is endless. Remember the explanation of advertising's function given by Rosser Reeves earlier in this chapter: to make something out of nothing. The best way advertisers can make something out of nothing is through words. Although there are a lot of visual images used on television and in magazines and newspapers, every advertiser wants to create that memorable line that will stick in the public consciousness. I am sure pure joy reigned in one advertising agency when a study found that children who were asked to spell the word "relief" promptly and proudly responded "r-o-l-a-i-d-s."

42   The variations, combinations, and permutations of doublespeak used in advertising go on and on, running from the use of rhetorical questions ("Wouldn't you rather have a Buick?" "If you can't trust Prestone, who can you

trust?") to flattering you with compliments ("The lady has taste." "We think a cigar smoker is someone special." "You've come a long way baby."). You know, of course, how you're *supposed* to answer those questions, and you know that those compliments are just leading up to the sales pitches for the products. Before you dismiss such tricks of the trade as obvious, however, just remember that all of these statements and questions were part of very success-ful advertising campaigns.

43   A more subtle approach is the ad that proclaims a supposedly unique quality for a product, a quality that really isn't unique. "If it doesn't say Goodyear, it can't be polyglas." Sounds good, doesn't it? Polyglas is available only from Goodyear because Goodyear copyrighted that trade name. Any other tire manufacturer could make exactly the same tire but could not call it "polyglas," because that would be copyright infringement. "Polyglas" is simply Goodyear's name for its fiberglass-reinforced tire.

44   Since we like to think of ourselves as living in a technologically ad-vanced country, science and technology have a great appeal in selling prod-ucts. Advertisers are quick to use scientific doublespeak to push their products. There are all kinds of elixirs, additives, scientific potions, and mysterious mix-tures added to all kinds of products. Gasoline contains "HTA," "F–310," "Plat-formate," and other chemical-sounding additives, but nowhere does an adver-tisement give any real information about the additive.

45   Shampoo, deodorant, mouthwash, cold medicine, sleeping pills, and any number of other products all seem to contain some special chemical in-gredient that allows them to work wonders. "Certs contains a sparkling drop of Retsyn." So what? What "Retsyn"? What's it do? What's so special about it? When they don't have a secret ingredient in their product, advertisers still find a way to claim scientific validity. There's "Sinarest. Created by a research sci-entist who actually gets sinus headaches." Sounds nice, but what kind of re-search does this scientist do? How do you know if she is any kind of expert on sinus medicine? Besides, this ad doesn't tell you a thing about the medicine it-self and what it does.

Advertising Doublespeak Quick Quiz

46 Now it's time to test your awareness of advertising doublespeak. (You didn't think I would just let you read this and forget it, did you?) The following is a list of statements from some recent ads. Your job is to figure out what each of these ads really says.

DOMINO'S PIZZA:	"Because nobody delivers better."
SINUTAB:	"It can stop the pain."
TUMS:	"The stronger acid neutralizer."
MAXIMUM STRENGTH DRISTAN:	"Strong medicine for tough sinus colds."
LISTERMINT:	"Making your mouth a cleaner place."

CASCADE:	"For virtually spotless dishes nothing beats Cascade."
NUPRIN:	"Little. Yellow. Different. Better."
ANACIN:	"Better relief."
SUDAFED:	"Fast sinus relief that won't put you fast asleep."
ADVIL:	"Advanced medicine for pain."
PONDS COLD CREAM:	"Ponds cleans like no soap can."
MILLER LITE BEER:	"Tastes great. Less filling."
PHILIPS MILK OF MAGNESIA:	"Nobody treats you better than MOM (Philips Milk of Magnesia)."
BAYER:	"The wonder drug that works wonders."
CRACKER BARREL:	"Judged to be the best."
KNORR:	"Where taste is everything."
ANUSOL:	"Anusol is the word to remember for relief."
DIMETAPP:	"It relieves kids as well as colds."
LIQUID DRĀNO:	"The liquid strong enough to be called Drāno."
JOHNSON & JOHNSON BABY POWDER:	"Like magic for your skin."
PURITAN:	"Make it your oil for life."
PAM:	"Pam, because how you cook is as important as what you cook."
IVORY SHAMPOO AND CONDITIONER:	"Leave your hair feeling Ivory clean."
TYLENOL GEL-CAPS:	"It's not a capsule. It's better."
ALKA-SELTZER:	"Fast, effective relief for winter colds."

The World of Advertising

47   In the world of advertising, people wear "dentures," not false teeth; they suffer from "occasional irregularity," not constipation; they need deodorants for their "nervous wetness," not for sweat; they use "bathroom tissue," not toilet paper; and they don't dye their hair, they "tint" or "rinse" it. Advertisements offer "real counterfeit diamonds" without the slightest hint of embarrassment, or boast of goods made out of "genuine imitation leather" or "virgin vinyl."

48   In the world of advertising, the girdle becomes a "body shaper," "form persuader," "control garment," "controller," "outwear enhancer," "body garment," or "anti-gravity panties," and is sold with such trade names as "The Instead," "The Free Spirit," and "The Body Briefer."

49   A study some years ago found the following words to be among the most popular used in U.S. television advertisements: "new," "improved," "bet-

ter," "extra," "fresh," "clean," "beautiful," "free," "good," "great," and "light."
At the same time, the following words were found to be among the most frequent on British television: "new," "good-better-best," "free," "fresh," "delicious," "full," "sure," "clean," "wonderful," and "special." While these words
may occur most frequently in ads, and while ads may be filled with weasel
words, you have to watch out for all the words used in advertising, not just the
words mentioned here.

50   Every word in an ad is there for a reason; no word is wasted. Your job is
to figure out exactly what each word is doing in an ad—what each word really
means, not what the advertiser wants you to think it means. Remember, the ad
is trying to get you to buy a product, so it will put the product in the best possible light, using any device, trick, or means legally allowed. Your only defense against advertising (besides taking up permanent residence on the moon)
is to develop and use a strong critical reading, listening, and looking ability.
Always ask yourself what the ad is *really* saying. When you see ads on television, don't be misled by the pictures, the visual images. What does the ad *say*
about the product? What does the ad *not* say? What information is missing
from the ad? Only by becoming an active, critical consumer of the doublespeak of advertising will you ever be able to cut through the doublespeak and
discover what the ad is really saying.

51   Professor Del Kehl of Arizona State University has updated the Twenty-
third Psalm to reflect the power of advertising to meet our needs and solve our
problems. It seems fitting that this chapter close with this new Psalm.

The Adman's 23rd

The Adman is my shepherd;
I shall ever want.
He maketh me to walk a mile for a Camel;
He leadeth me beside Crystal Waters
    in the High Country of Coors;
He restoreth my soul with Perrier.
He guideth me in Marlboro Country
For Mammon's sake.
Yea, though I walk through the Valley of the Jolly Green
    Giant,
In the shadow of B.O., halitosis, indigestion, headache pain,
    and hemorrhoidal tissue,
I will fear no evil,
For I am in Goods Hands with Allstate;
Thy Arid, Scope, Tums, Tylenol, and Preparation H—
They comfort me.
Stouffer's preparest a table before the TV
In the presence of all my appetites;
Thou anointest my head with Brylcream;
My Decaffeinated Cup runneth over.

Surely surfeit and security shall follow me
All the days of Metropolitan Life,
And I shall swell in a Continental Home
With a mortgage forever and ever.

Amen.

Topical Considerations

1. How would a copywriter for an advertising agency respond to this article? Would he or she agree with the way Lutz characterizes all advertisements as trying to trick consumers with false claims into buying the product?

2. How did "weasel words" get their name? Why, according to Lutz, do advertisers use them? Does his description of how weasel words got their meaning change your mind about truth in advertising?

3. What regulations restrict the use of the word "new"? How can manufacturers make a product "new" to sidestep these regulations? When you see the word "new" on a product, do you think twice about buying that product? Do these regulations serve the interests of the advertiser or the consumer?

4. What are the differences between regular weasel words and subjective weasel words (paragraph 33) according to Lutz? Give examples of both types of words and show how they are used in advertisements. Which kind of words do you find more difficult to interpret in ads?

5. Take another look at Lutz's "Doublespeak Quick Quiz." Choose five items and write a language analysis, using dictionary meanings, to explain what the ads really mean.

6. In paragraph 43 Lutz describes how manufacturers claim for their products unique properties that are not really unique. Could these claims be considered circular reasoning? Explain your answer.

7. According to the author, how can consumers protect themselves against weasel words?

Rhetorical Considerations

1. Lutz first mentions the terms "parity claims" in paragraph 1 and "advertising doublespeak" in paragraph 3, but he does not clearly define these phrases. Can you deduce their meanings from the information that appears later in the essay? Where are these references?

2. The author speaks to the reader throughout the article by using the second person *you*. Do you find this strategy effective? Why or why not?

3. What tone does the author use throughout the article? Is his writing style humorous, informal, or academic? What different strategies does he use to involve the reader in the piece?

4. What do you think about Lutz's ending has article with a parody of the Twenty-third Psalm? Do you find it appropriate and funny? Offensive? Does it suit the theme of the essay?

Writing Assignments

1. Rewrite five ads for the same type of product "literally and exactly, according to the dictionary definition." Write an essay discussing the weasel words, unfinished words, and subjective words that you have replaced. Pass in the ads with your essay. Heavily advertised products such as beer, laundry products, or aspirin would be good subjects for your discussion.

2. The essays in this section deal with advertising and its effects on consumers and their value systems. Describe how understanding the linguistic strategies of advertisers—as exemplified by Lutz—will or will not change your reaction to advertising.

3. As Lutz suggests, look at some ads in a magazine and newspaper (or television and radio commercials). Then make a list of all uses you find over a 24-hour period for one of the following weasel words: "help," "virtually," "new," "improved," "introducing," "now," "today's," "presenting," "acts," "works," "like," "can be," or "up to." Examine the ads to determine what is said and what the unwary consumer thinks is being said. Write a paper to report your finding.

4. Invent a product and have some fun writing an ad for it. Use as many weasel words as you can to make your product shine.

5. Imagine you are the disgruntled customer who bought the cosmetic product that promised it would "help stop the aging process." Write a letter to the manufacturer of the product demanding your money back and describing how the product failed to live up to its claims.

6. Imagine that you are the customer relations person for a popular cosmetic product that promised it would "help stop the aging process." Write an answer to a letter from a disgruntled customer who bought your product and found it was not satisfactory because it did not live up to its advertising claims.

The Language of Advertising
Charles A. O'Neill

Taking the minority opinion is marketing executive Charles A. O'Neill, who disputes the damning criticism by William Lutz and other critics of advertising. While admitting to some of the craftiness of his profession, O'Neill defends the huckster's language—both verbal and visual—against claims that it distorts reality. Examining some familiar television commercials and magazine ads, he explains why the language may be charming and seductive but far from brainwashing.

This essay, originally written for *Exploring Language,* edited by Gary Goshgarian, has been updated for this text. Charles O'Neill is Senior Vice President of Marketing for Colonial Investments Services in Boston.

BEFORE YOU READ

In this essay O'Neill makes several generalizations that characterize the language of advertising. Think about ads you've recently seen or read and make a list of your own generalizations about the language of advertising.

AS YOU READ

As you read remember that O'Neill is a professional advertiser. Does that fact color his motivations in this argument? Does it make his argument more or less persuasive?

1   The cosmopolitan figure on the billboard looks like a rock singer, perhaps photographed on a break in a music videotaping session. He is poised, confident, as he leans against a railing, a view of the night-time city behind him, the personal geometry is just right. He wears a white suit, dark shirt, no tie. He sports a small red flower in his lapel. He holds a cigarette in his left hand. His attitude is distinctly confident, urban: "I own this city." His wry smile and full lips are vaguely familiar.

2   Think. You've seen him before, carefully posed on the pages of magazines, on posters and matchbooks, sitting astride a motorcycle or playing in a band. Mick Jagger? Bill Wyman? No. He is truly a different sort of animal; more precisely, he is a camel, a cartoon camel, and his name is Old Joe. Next to him on the billboard is one sentence: "Smoke New Camel Lights."

3   At first glance, this combination of artwork and text does not appear to be unusual. What is different about Camel's ad campaign is that it has spawned debates on newspaper editorial pages and has triggered organized protest. Old Joe, imported to these shores in the late 1980s, after a successful test run in Europe, has been declared by some an unwelcome visitor—an intruder whose very charm and decidedly cool style is seducing the nation's youth into a deadly habit that results in 400,000 deaths by lung cancer every year. Those who want to eliminate Joe—send him back to obscurity amid the pyramids, as it were—have a simple argument: "Everyone knows smoking is bad for the health. You're using a cartoon to sell cigarettes to our children. The public interest is more important than your right to free speech. And it's in the public interest for us to protect our children from your unhealthy, dangerous product." Those who support Old Joe—principally his "colleagues" at R. J.

Reynolds—argue that their constitutionally affirmed right to free speech extends to advertisements about their product. Given the opportunity, they would likely add: "Is smoking unhealthy? Driving is dangerous, too. Where will the "advertising censors" draw the line? We feel people should make their own decisions about smoking. We've chosen to use a cartoon character in our ads only because it is noticeable and effective."

4   The obvious topic of the debate is cigarette advertising, but beneath the surface it signals something more interesting and broad based: the rather uncomfortable, tentative acceptance of advertising in our society. We recognize the value of advertising, but on some level we can't quite fully reconcile ourselves to it. At best, we view it as distracting, something wedged into 30- or 60-second spaces between scenes in a TV special. At worst, we view it as dangerous to our health and culture.

5   How does advertising work? Why is it so powerful? What thoughtful cases can be made for and against the advertising business, circa 1995? In order to begin to understand advertising, you must accept that it is not about truth, virtue, love, or positive social values. It is about money. Ads play a role in moving customers through the sales process. This process begins with an effort to build awareness of a product, typically achieved by tactics designed to break through the clutter of competitive messages. By presenting a description of product benefits, ads convince the customer to buy the product. Once prospects have become purchasers, advertising is used to sustain brand loyalty, reminding customers of all the good reasons for their original decision to buy.

6   But all of this detail does not sufficiently explain the ultimate, unique power of advertising. Whatever the product or creative strategy, advertisements derive their power from a purposeful, directed combination of images. Images can take the form of words, sounds, or visuals, used individually or together. The combination of images is the language of advertising, a language unlike any other.

7   Everyone who grows up in the Western World soon learns that advertising language is different from other languages. Most children would be unable to explain how such lines as "With Nice 'n Easy, it's color so natural, the closer he gets the better you look!" (the famous ad for Clairol's Nice 'n Easy hair coloring) differed from ordinary language, but they would be able to tell you, "It sounds like an ad." Whether printed on a page, blended with music on the radio, or whispered on the sound track of a television commercial, advertising language is "different."

8   Over the years, the texture of advertising language has frequently changed. Styles and creative concepts come and go. But there are at least four distinct, general characteristics of the language of advertising that make it different from other languages. Taken together, they lend advertising its persuasive power:

   1. The language of advertising is edited and purposeful.

2. The language of advertising is rich and arresting; it is specifically intended to attract and hold our attention.

3. The language of advertising involves us; in effect, *we* complete the message.

4. The language of advertising is a simple language; it holds no secrets from us.

Edited and Purposeful

9   In his book, *Future Shock,* Alvin Toffler describes various types of messages we receive from the world around us each day. As he sees it, there is a difference between normal "coded" messages and "engineered" messages. Much of normal, human experience is "uncoded"; it is merely sensory. For example, Toffler describes a man walking down a street. Toffler notes that the man's sensory perceptions of this experience may form a mental image, but the message is not "designed by anyone to communicate anything, and the man's understanding of it does not depend directly on a social code—a set of agreed-upon signs and definitions."[1] In contrast, Toffler describes a talk show conversation as "coded"; the speakers' ability to exchange information with their host, and our ability to understand it, depend upon social conventions.

10   The language of advertising is coded. It is also a language of finely engineered, ruthlessly purposeful messages. By Toffler's calculation, the average adult American is assaulted by at least 560 advertising messages a day.[2] Not one of these messages would reach us, to attract and hold our attention, if it were completely unstructured. Advertising messages have a clear purpose; they are intended to trigger a specific response.

Rich and Arresting

11   Advertisements—no matter how carefully "engineered" and packed with information—cannot succeed unless they capture our attention in the first place. Of the hundreds of advertising messages in store for us each day, very few (Toffler estimates seventy-six) will actually obtain our conscious attention.[3] The rest are screened out. The people who design and write ads know about this screening process; they anticipate and accept it as a basic premise of their business. They expend a great deal of energy to improve the odds that their ads will make it past the defenses and distractions that surround us.

12   The classic, all-time favorite device used to breach the barrier is sex. The desire to be sexually attractive to others is an ancient instinct, and few drives are more powerful. In a magazine ad for Ultima II, a line of cosmetics, retailer Jordan Marsh invites readers to "find everything you need for the sexxxxiest look around. . . ." The ad goes on to offer other "Sexxxy goodies," including "Lipsexxxxy lip color, naked eye color . . . Sunsexxxy liquid

bronzer." No one will accuse Ultima's marketing tacticians of subtlety. In fact, this ad is a current example of an approach that is as old as advertising.

13   After countless years of using images of women in various stages of undress to sell products, ads are now displaying men's bodies as well. A magazine ad for Brut, a men's cologne, declares in bold letters, "MEN ARE BACK," while in the background a muscular, shirtless young man is shown wrapping his hands in tape in preparation for boxing.

14   Whether it takes one approach or another, every successful advertisement uses a creative strategy based on an idea that will attract and hold the attention of the targeted consumer audience. The strategy may include strong creative execution, repetition for sheer impact, or a straightforward presentation of product features and customer benefits. Many ads use humor or simply a play on words:

"Reeboks let U B U"	(Reebok)
"My chickens eat better than you do."	(Perdue Chickens)
"Introducing the ultimate concept in air freight. Men that fly."	(Emery Air Freight)
"Look deep into our ryes."	(Wigler's bakery products)
"Me. 4 U."	(The State of Maine)
"If gas pains persist, try Volkswagen."	(Volkswagen)

Even if the text contains no incongruity and does not rely on a pun for its impact, every effective ad needs a creative strategy based on some striking concept or idea. In fact, the concept and execution are often so good that many successful ads entertain while they sell.

15   Consider, for example, the campaigns created for Federal Express. A campaign was developed to position Federal Express as the company that would deliver packages, not just "overnight," but "by 10:30 A.M." the next day. The plight of the junior executive in "Presentation," one TV ad in the campaign, is stretched for dramatic purposes, but it is, nonetheless, all too real: The young executive, who is presumably trying to climb his way up the corporate ladder, is shown calling another parcel delivery service and all but begging for assurance that he will have his slides in hand by 10:30 the next morning. "No slides, no presentation," he pleads. Only a viewer with a heart of stone can watch without feeling sympathetic as the next morning our junior executives struggles to make his presentation *sans* slides. He is so lost without them that he is reduced to using his hands to perform imitations of birds and animals in shadows on the movie screen. What does the junior executive *viewer* think when he or she sees the ad?

1. Federal Express guarantees to deliver packages "absolutely, positively overnight."

2. Federal Express packages arrive early in the day.
3. What happened to that fellow in the commercial will absolutely not happen to me, now that I know what package delivery service to call.

16   A sound, creative strategy supporting an innovative service idea sold Federal Express. But the quality and objective "value" of execution doesn't matter. A magazine ad for Merit Ultra Lights (August 1990) made use of one word in its headline: "Yo!"" This was, one hopes, not the single most powerful creative idea generated by the agency's creative team that particular month— but it probably sold cigarettes.

17   Soft-drink and fast-food companies often take another approach. "Slice of life" ads (so-called because they purport to show people in "real-life" situations) created to sell Coke or Pepsi have often placed their characters in Fourth-of-July parades or other family events. The archetypical version of this approach is filled-to-overflowing with babies frolicking with puppies in the sunlit foreground while their youthful parents play touch football. On the porch, Grandma and Pops are seen quietly smiling and apparently getting ready for all of this affection to transform itself into an astonishing climax of warmth, harmony, and joy. Beneath the veneer, these ads work through sheer repetition: How-many-times-can-you-spot-the-logo-in-this-commercial?

18   More subtly, these ads are designed to seduce us into feeling that if we drink the right combination of sugar, preservatives, caramel coloring, and a few secret ingredients—known only to a select group of the company's most trusted employees—we'll fulfill our yearning for a world where young folks and old folks live together in perfect bliss.

19   If you don't buy this version of the American Dream, search long enough and you are sure to find an ad designed to sell you what it takes to gain prestige within whatever posse you do happen to run with. As reported by the *Boston Globe* (March 1992), "the malt liquor industry relies heavily on rap stars in delivering its message to inner-city youths, while Black Death Vodka, which features a top-hatted skull and a coffin on its label, has been using Guns N' Roses guitarist Slash to endorse the product in magazine advertising." A malt liquor company reportedly promotes its 40-ounce size with rapper King T singing, "I usually drink it when I'm just out clowning, me and the home boys, you know, be like downing it . . . I grab me a 40 when I want to act a fool."

20   Ads do not emerge like Botticelli's Venus from the sea, flawless and fully grown. This happens, but rarely. Most often, the creative strategy is developed only after extensive research. "Who will be interested in our product? How old are they? Where do they live? How much money do they earn? What problem will our product solve?" Answers to these questions provide the foundation on which the creative strategy is built. The creative people in the advertising business are well aware that consumers do not watch television or read magazines in order to see ads. Ads have to earn the right to be seen, read, and heard.

Involving

21   We have seen that the language of advertising is carefully engineered; we have discovered a few of the devices it uses to get our attention. R. J. Reynolds has us identifying with Old Joe in one of his many uptown poses. Coke and Pepsi have caught our eye with visions of peace, love, or Ray Charles crooning, yes folks, "Uh Huh"—with the full and enthusiastic endorsement of the swaying female singers. Now that they have our attention, advertisers present information intended to show us that their product fills a need and differs from the competition. It is the copywriter's responsibility to express such product differences and to exploit and intensify them.

22   When product differences do not exist, the writer must glamorize the superficial differences—for example, differences in packaging. As long as the ad is trying to get our attention, the "action" is mostly in the ad itself, in the words and visual images. But as we read an ad or watch it on television, we become more deeply involved. The action starts to take place in us. Our imagination is set in motion, and our individual fears and aspirations, our little quirks and insecurities, superimpose themselves on that tightly engineered, attractively packaged message.

23   Consider, once again, the running battle among the low-calorie soft drinks. The cola wars have spawned many "look-alike" advertisements, because the product features and consumer benefits are generic, applying to all products in the category. Substitute one cola brand name for another, and the messages are often identical, right down to the way the cans are photographed in the closing sequence. This strategy relies upon mass saturation and exposure for impact.

24   In recent years, some companies have set themselves apart from their competitors by making use of bold, even disturbing, themes and images. In its controversial ad campaign, Benetton has tried to draw attention to its clothing line in unusual ways. One magazine ad displays a photograph of a father comforting his son who is dying of AIDS while other family members huddle nearby. The company's clothing may or may not be truly different from competitors' products, but the image surely is different—that of a company that focuses on social issues.

25   Is Benetton committing an outrageously immoral act by exploiting people who suffer from a horrible disease? Or is this company brilliantly drawing attention to itself while reminding a largely complacent consumer population that the scourge of AIDS needs to be arrested.

26   Benetton's campaign has made use of other, equally provocative images. Like the ad described above, other themes are intended to provoke controversy. But Benetton is far from the first company whose marketing efforts are subject to the charge of exploitation. In fact, on one level, all advertising is about exploitation: the systematic, deliberate identification of our needs and wants, followed by the delivery of a carefully constructed promise that we will find fulfillment or satisfaction by purchasing Brand X.

27   Symbols offer an important tool for involving consumers in advertisements. Symbols have become important elements in the language of advertising, not so much because they carry meanings of their own, but because we bring a meaning to them: We charge them with significance. Symbols are efficient, compact vehicles for the communication of an advertising message. One noteworthy example is provided by the campaign begun in 1978 by Somerset Importers for Johnnie Walker Red Scotch. Sales of Johnnie Walker Red has been trailing sales of Johnnie Walker Black, and Somerset Importers needed to position Red as a fine product in its own right. Their agency produced ads that made heavy use of the color red. One magazine ad, often printed as a two-page spread, is dominated by a close-up photo of red autumn leaves. At lower right, the copy reads, "When their work is done, even the leaves turn to Red." Another ad—also suitably dominated by a photograph in the appropriate color—reads: "When it's time to quiet down at the end of the day, even a fire turns to Red." Red. Warm. Experienced. Seductive. A perfect symbol to use in a liquor advertisement.

28   As we have seen, advertisers make use of a great variety of techniques and devices to engage us in the delivery of their messages. Some are subtle, making use of warm, entertaining, or comforting images or symbols. Others, like Black Death Vodka, are about as subtle as a recording of MTV's Generation X alter egos, "Beavis and Butt-head," played in fast-forward mode. Another common device used to engage our attention is old but still effective: the use of famous or notorious personalities as product spokespeople or models. Advertising writers did not invent the normal, human tendency to admire or otherwise identify ourselves with famous people. Once we have seen a famous person in an ad, we associate the product with the person. "Joe DiMagio is a good guy. He likes Mr. Coffee. Therefore, I'll add this to my shopping list." "Guns 'N Roses totally rule my world and Slash is the only reason I, like, live and all, so I will definitely make the scene with a bottle of Black Death stuck into the waistband of my four-sizes-too-large black sweat pants with 'Charlie Don't Surf' embroidered on the back pocket." The logic is faulty, but we fall for it just the same. The creators of testimonial ads did not create our interest in famous personalities; they merely recognize our inclinations and exploit them.

29   Advertising works, not because Joe DiMagio is a coffee expert or Slash has discriminating taste, but because we participate in it; in fact, we charge ads with most of their power.

A Simple Language

30   Advertising language differs from other types of language in another important respect; it is a simple language. To determine how the copy of a typical advertisement rates on a "simplicity index" in comparison with text in a magazine article, for example, try this exercise: Clip a typical story from the publication you read most frequently. Calculate the number of words in an average sentence. Count the number of words of three or more syllables in a typical 100-

word passage, omitting words that are capitalized, combinations of two simple words, or verb forms made into three-syllable words by the addition of *-ed* or *-es.* Add the two figures (the average number of words per sentence and the number of three-syllable words per 100 words), then multiply the result by .4. According to Robert Gunning, if the resulting number is seven, there is a good chance that you are reading *True Confessions.*[4] He developed this formula, the "Fog Index," to determine the comparative ease with which any given piece of written communication can be read. Here is the complex text of a typical cigarette endorsement:

> I demand two things from my cigarette. I want a cigarette with low tar and nicotine. But, I also want taste. That's why I smoke Winston Lights. I get a lighter cigarette, but I still get a real taste. And real pleasure. Only one cigarette gives me that: Winston Lights.

The average sentence in this ad runs seven words. *Cigarette* and *nicotine* are three-syllable words, with *cigarette* appearing four times; *nicotine,* once. Considering *that's* as two words, the ad is exactly fifty words long, so the average number of three-syllable words per 100 is ten.

$$
\begin{array}{rl}
7 & \text{words per sentence} \\
+10 & \text{three-syllable words/100} \\
\hline
17 & \\
\times\,.4 & \\
\hline
6.8 & \text{Fog Index}
\end{array}
$$

31   According to Gunning's scale, this particular ad is written at about the seventh grade level, comparable to most of the ads found in mass circulation magazines.[5] It's about as sophisticated as *True Confessions,* that is, harder to read than a comic book, but easier than *Ladies Home Journal.* Of course, the Fog Index cannot evaluate the visual aspect of an ad—another component of advertising language. The headline, "I demand two things from my cigarette," works with the picture (that of an attractive woman) to arouse consumer interest. The text reinforces the image. Old Joe's simple plea, "Try New Camel Lights," is too short to move the needle on the Fog Index meter, but in every respect it represents perhaps the simplest language possible, a not-distant cousin of Merit Ultra Lights' groundbreaking and succinct utterance, "Yo!"

32   Why do advertisers generally favor simple language? The answer lies with the consumer: Consider Toffler's speculation that the average American adult is subject to some 560 advertising or commercial messages each day. As a practical matter, we would not notice many of these messages if length—or even eloquence—were counted among their virtues. Today's consumer cannot, and does not, take the time to focus on anything for long, much less blatant advertising messages. With the advent of new media and an accelerating volume of product offerings, the message count today must be at least two to

three times greater than it was in 1970 when Toffler published the first edition of his seminal book. In effect, Toffler's "future" is here now, and it is perhaps more "shocking" than he could have foreseen at the time. Every aspect of modern life runs at an accelerated pace. Overnight mail has moved in less than ten years from a novelty to a common business necessity. Voice mail, cellular phones, E mail, Internet, Prodigy—the human world is always awake, always switched on, and hungry for more information, now. Time generally, and TV-commercial time in particular, is now dissected into increasingly smaller segments. Fifteen-second commercials are no longer unusual, and in that one-quarter minute, the advertiser is best advised to make every one-quarter second count.

33   Toffler views the evolution toward shorter language as a natural progression: three-syllable words are simply harder to read than one- or two-syllable words. Simple ideas are more readily transferred from one person to another than complex ideas. Therefore, advertising copy uses increasingly simpler language, as does society at large. In *Future Shock,* Toffler speculates:

> If the [English] language had the same number of words in Shakespeare's time as it does today, at least 200,000 words—perhaps several times that many—have dropped out and been replaced in the intervening four centuries. The high turnover rate reflects changes in things, processes, and qualities in the environment from the world of consumer products and technology.[6]

It is no accident that the first terms Toffler uses to illustrate his point ("fastback," "wash-and-wear," and "flashcube") were invented not by engineers, or journalists, but by advertising copywriters.

34   Advertising language is simple language; in the ad's engineering process, difficult words or images—which in other forms of communication may be used to lend color or fine shades of meaning—are edited out and replaced by simple words or images not open to misinterpretations. You don't have to ask whether Old Joe likes his Camels or whether King T likes to "grab a 40" when he wants to "act a fool."

Who Is Responsible?

35   Some critics view the advertising business as a cranky, unwelcomed child of the free enterprise system—a noisy, whining, brash kid who must somehow be kept in line, but can't just yet be thrown out of the house. In reality, advertising mirrors the fears, quirks, and aspirations of the society that creates it (and is, in turn, sold by it). This factor alone exposes advertising to parody and ridicule. The overall level of acceptance and respect for advertising is also influenced by the varied quality of the ads themselves. Some ads, including a few of the examples cited here, seem deliberately designed to provoke controversy. For example, it is easy—as some critics have charged—to conclude that Benetton's focus on social issues is merely a cynical effort to attract attention and

obtain editorial coverage. But critics miss the point. If an ad stimulates controversy, so what? This is smart marketing—a successful effort to make the advertising dollar work harder.

36   In his book, *Strictly Speaking,* journalist Edwin Newman poses the question, "Will America be the death of English?" Newman's "mature, well thought out judgment" is that it will. As evidence, he cites a number of examples of fuzzy thinking and careless use of the language, not just by advertisers, but by many people in public life, including politicians and journalists:

> The federal government has adopted the comic strip character Snoopy as a symbol and showed us Snoopy on top of his doghouse, flat on his back, with a balloon coming out of his mouth, containing the words, "I believe in conserving energy," while below there was this exhortation: savEnergy. An entire letter e at the end was saved. In addition, an entire space was saved.
>   . . . Spelling has been assaulted by Duz, E-Z Off, Fantastik, Kool, Kleen . . . and by products that make you briter, so that will not be left hi and dri at a parti, but made welkom. . . . Under this pressure, adjectives become adverbs; nouns become adjectives; prepositions disappear, compounds abound.[7]

In this passage, Newman represents three of the charges most often levied against advertising:

1. Advertising debases English.
2. Advertising downgrades the intelligence of the public.
3. Advertising warps our vision of reality, implanting in us groundless fears and insecurities. (He cites, as examples of these groundless fears, "tattletale gray," "denture breath," "morning mouth," "unsightly bulge," and "ring around the collar.")

Other charges have been made from time to time. They include:

1. Advertising sells daydreams—distracting, purposeless visions of lifestyles beyond the reach of most of the people who are most exposed to advertising.
2. Advertising feeds on human weaknesses and exaggerates the importance of material things, encouraging "impure" emotions and vanities.
3. Advertising encourages unhealthy habits.
4. Advertising perpetuates racial and sexual stereotypes.

37   What can be said in advertising's defense? Advertising is only a reflection of society; slaying the messenger would not alter the fact—if it is a fact—that "America will be the death of English." A case can be made for the concept that advertising language is an acceptable stimulus for the natural evolution of lan-

guage. Is "proper English" the language most Americans actually speak and write, or is it the language we are told we should speak and write?

38   What about the charge that advertising debases the intelligence of the public? Those who support this particular criticism would do well to ask themselves another question: Exactly how intelligent is the public? Sadly, evidence abounds that "the public" at large is not particularly intelligent, after all. Johnny can't read. Susie can't write. And the entire family spends the night in front of the television, channel surfing for the latest "SWAT Team Kicks Butt/Sexy Teen Transvestite Marries Own Half Brother" media fest.

39   Ads are effective because they sell products. They would not succeed if they did not reflect the values and motivations of the real world. Ads for Black Death Vodka, for example, may stimulate preference for this brand among certain buyers, but Slash can hardly be blamed for young men's interest in high-octane beverages.

40   Our discussion of advertising would not be complete without acknowledging that it both reflects and shapes our perception of reality. Consider several brand names and the impressions they create: Ivory Snow is pure; Edsel was a failure; Federal Express won't let you down. These attributes may well be correct, but our sense of what these brand names mean has as much to do with marketing communications as it does with objective "fact."

41   Advertising shapes our view of reality as surely as architecture shapes our impression of a city. Good, responsible advertising can serve as a positive influence for change while generating profits. Of course, the problem is that the obverse is also true: Advertising, like any form of mass communication, can be a force for both "good" and "bad." It can just as readily reinforce or encourage irresponsible sexual behavior, ageism, sexism, ethnocentrism, racism, homophobia, heterophobia—you name it—as it can encourage support for democracy, diversity, and important social causes. People living in society create advertising. Human society isn't perfect; neither is its image as reflected in advertising.

42   Perhaps much of the fault lies with the public for accepting advertising so readily. S. I. Hayakawa finds "the uncritical response to the incantations of advertising . . . a serious symptom of a widespread evaluation disorder." He does not find it "beyond the bounds of possibility" that "today's suckers for national advertising will be tomorrow's suckers for the master political propagandist who will, by playing up the 'Jewish menace,' in the same way as national advertisers play up the 'pink toothbrush menace,' and by promising us national glory and prosperity, sell fascism in America."[8]

43   Fascism in America is fortunately a far cry from Joe Camel, but the point is well taken. In the end, advertising simply attempts to change behavior. Like any form of communication, it can be used for positive social purposes, neutral commercial purposes, or for the most pernicious kind of paranoid propaganda. Do advertisements sell distracting, purposeless visions? Occasionally. But perhaps such visions are necessary components of the process through which our society changes and improves.

44   Old Joe's days as Camel's spokesman appear to be numbered. His very success in reaching new smokers may prove to be the source of his undoing. But standing nearby and waiting to take his place is another campaign; another character, real or imagined; another product for sale. Perhaps, by learning how advertising works, we can become better equipped to sort out content from hype, product values from emotions, and salesmanship from propaganda.

Notes

1. Alvin Toffler, *Future Shock* (New York: Random House, 1970), p. 146.
2. Ibid., p. 149.
3. Ibid.
4. Curtis D. MacDougall, *Interpretive Reporting* (New York: Macmillan, 1968), p. 94.
5. Ibid., p. 95.
6. Toffler, *Future Shock,* p. 151.
7. Edwin Newman, *Strictly Speaking* (Indianapolis: Bobs-Merrill, 1974), p. 13.
8. S. I. Hayakawa, *Language in Thought and Action* (New York: Harcourt, Brace, 1990), p. 235.

Topical Considerations

1. O'Neill opens his essay on a discussion of the controversial figure of Joe Camel. What are your views on the Joe Camel controversy? Do you think such ads target young people and, thus, should be outlawed? Why or why not?
2. Are you familiar with the Benetton AIDS patient ad O'Neill mentions here? If so, do you view it as an attempt to raise social awareness or as simple exploitation?
3. Do you think it is ethical for advertisers to create a sense of product difference when there really isn't any? Consider ads for gasoline, beer, and instant coffee.
4. In the last section of the essay, O'Neill anticipates potential objections to his defense of advertising. What are some of these objections? What does he say in defense of advertising? Which set of arguments do you find stronger?
5. O'Neill describes several ways in which the language of advertising differs from other kinds of language. Briefly list the ways he mentions. Can you think of any other characteristics of advertising language that set it apart?
6. What is "proper English," as contrasted with colloquial or substandard? Do you use proper English in your written course work and in your own correspondence? What do you think about using proper English in advertising?

7. O'Neill asserts that "symbols are efficient, compact vehicles for the communication of an advertising message" (paragraph 27). Can you think of some specific symbols from the advertising world that you associate with your own life? Are they effective symbols for selling?
8. In paragraph 28, O'Neill claims that celebrity endorsement of a product is "faulty" logic? Explain what he means. Why do people buy products sold by famous people?

Rhetorical Considerations

1. How effective do you think O'Neill's introductory paragraphs are? How well does he hook the reader? What particular audience might he be appealing to early on? What attitude toward advertising is established in the introduction?
2. O'Neill is an advertising professional. Does his writing style reflect the advertising techniques he describes? Cite examples to support your answer.
3. Describe the author's point of view about advertising. Does he ever tell us how he feels? Does his style indicate his attitude?

Writing Assignments

1. Obtain a current issue of each of the following publications: the *New Yorker, Time, GQ, Vogue,* and *People.* Choose one article from each periodical and calculate its Fog Index according to the technique described in paragraph 30. Choose one ad from each periodical and figure out its Fog Index. What different reading levels do you find among the publications? What do you know about the readers of these periodicals from your survey of the reading difficulty of the articles? Write a paper with your findings.
2. Clip three ads for products that use sex as a selling device, yet have no sexual connotations whatsoever. Explain how sex helps sell the products. Do you consider these ads demeaning to women or men?
3. The author believes that advertising language mirrors the fears, quirks, and aspirations of the society that creates it. Do you agree or disagree with this statement? Explain in a brief essay.
4. Choose a brand-name product you use regularly and one of its competitors—one whose differences are negligible, if they exist at all. Examine some advertisements for each brand. Write a short paper explaining what really makes you prefer your brand.
5. O'Neill says that advertising "can be used for positive social purposes, neutral commercial purposes, or for the most pernicious kind of paranoid propaganda" (paragraph 43). Write a research paper in which you undertake an analysis of actual propaganda. (Consulting your library, look at propaganda

from Nazi Germany or from this country during the Cold War.) How are they different? How are they the same?

Tapping the Youth Market
Madeline Drexler

Like any industry interested in increasing sales and attracting a new customer base, the liquor industry advertises aggressively. Two billion dollars fund this effort annually. But some critics question the ethics of liquor industry ad campaigns that clearly appeal to the "contemporary adult" market (ages 21–24) and possibly even target children in an effort to foster brand loyalty at a very early age. In this piece, Madeline Drexler splices images of collegiate drinking binges and their often tragic consequences with comments by spokespeople for the liquor industry explaining or defending their ad campaigns. This piece compels one to examine the rights and responsibilities of advertisers.

Madeline Drexler writes about issues of health for *The Boston Globe*. A longer version of this piece appeared in the *Globe Magazine* in 1994.

BEFORE YOU READ

List any current ads or ad campaigns for alcohol that stand out in your mind. Do any of these ads seem to be targeting a particular market? A young adult market? A child's market? Do these ads strike you as inappropriately targeting any group? Are these ads encouraging attitudes or behavior relevant to alcohol that you object to? If you object, how might ads be changed?

AS YOU READ

Do you find the alcohol industry's denial of charges that some advertisements appeal to children convincing? Why or why not?

1 Just before 2 A.M. on fraternity row, along Beacon Street and Bay State Road in [Boston's] Back Bay, the Saturday-night parties are fading into memory. Students stroll in small groups, talking and laughing. Strutting up to grand brownstones, a couple of young men relieve themselves in the bushes. Down the street, a fraternity brother, hoisted by three of his friends, climbs atop a traffic light and surveys his realm from a tottering perch before scrambling down.

2 Inside the once-resplendent residences that host tonight's parties, the scene is just as free-spirited. True, not everyone is drinking heavily, and no one looks falling-down drunk. But hundreds of beer cans and plastic cups litter the damp, sticky hardwood floors. People throng the bars that serve beer and mixed drinks, even if the drinker's don't sport hand stamps to prove their age.

On a sweeping staircase lined with partygoers, a funnel and tube are held aloft, appliances that will boost for a few the effects of the alcohol flowing tonight.

3   Americans may be sobering up, but heavy drinking among college and high school students is an enduring, often dangerous, rite of passage. It is also a key to the profits of an industry that has faced declining sales in recent years.

4   Despite the alcohol industry's embrace of such popular ideas as designated drivers and televised moderation messages, the industry needs the young revelers who congregate in Back Bay—and on state-college campuses, at auto races, and at major-league sporting events. Market analysts call this golden group of customers from 21 to 24 the "contemporary adult" market. Just as essential to continued sales are their replacements: 16- to 20-year-olds.

5   Employing sexy bar promotions, high-spirited TV ads, and appealing cartoon emblems, the alcohol industry is waging an aggressive campaign—backed by an annual media and promotion budget of about $2 billion—to woo young drinkers. With public and media attention focused on cigarette makers, the push by the alcohol industry has been largely overlooked. Beer ads urging moderation, which began airing in the early '80s in response to such influential voices as those of Mothers Against Drunk Driving, also may have helped forestall criticism.

6   But sooner or later, public-health advocates say, society will come to understand how saturated it is with the messages purveyed by beer, wine, and distilled-spirits producers, and how deeply advertising influences our tastes and norms.

7   To be sure, alcohol manufacturers spurn the idea that they target young drinkers. "This whole notion that we're preying on kids is absolutely false," says Jeff Becker, vice president of alcohol issues at the Beer Institute, which represents American brewers. "Kids have been drinking since long before we've been able to advertise or promote our products, and they will continue to do so whether we [advertise] or not."

8   It is true that young people as a whole are drinking less. But of the 11 million Americans designated as heavy drinkers by the 1993 National Household Survey on Drug Abuse, nearly one-third are 25 years old and under; more than 1.3 million are under 21. (Heavy drinking was defined by the survey as imbibing five or more drinks on five or more days in the past month, a definition that is generous in its leeway.) Other studies show that, on average, 18- to 21-year-olds drink more on each occasion than do their elders.

9   For the industry, those figures represent substantial income. Indeed, if every drinker in the United States drank moderately—no more than two drinks a day—alcohol sales would plummet by 40 percent, according to Bob Hammond, director of the Alcohol Research Information Service, a nonprofit organization in Lansing, Michigan.

10   "People who haven't played with heavy drinking by 21 probably drink heavily later," says Robin Room, vice president for research and development at the Alcohol Research Foundation, in Toronto. Or, as one unidentified mar-

keting executive was quoted in a 1983 report published by the Center for Science in the Public Interest: "Getting a freshman to choose a certain brand of beer may mean he will maintain his brand loyalty for the next 20 to 35 years. If he turns out to be a big drinker, the beer company has bought itself an annuity." . . .

11   College is a preeminent milieu for teenagers' rite of passage. College students, a captive audience for advertising and promotions, drink significantly more than their nonstudent peers. "College makes it so different," says Michael Leone, a 22-year-old patron of Dad's Diner, a gleaming, Art Deco-style watering hole on Boylston Street. "You don't have to drive. And you don't have to go home to your parents."

12   Freed of parental observation and community controls, excess becomes easy. "In a dorm room that normally holds maybe 12 or 20 people, there would be 100 people," recalls a recent Ivy League graduate. "Close to half an inch of beer on the floor from the keg spilling over. A constant line of people going in and out of the bathroom, either to throw up or relieve themselves."

13   Collegiate creativity knows no bounds in enhancing alcohol's psychoactive properties. Some aficionados "funnel" their beer, having a friend pour brew through a funnel attached to a plastic tube that leads directly into the gullet. Others "shotgun" their drink—make a tiny hole in the bottom of a can, then hold the can over the mouth and pop the tab, gulping to keep up with the beer shooting down. A good party might feature a "luge run," a block of ice with a sinuous course carved out, down which liqueur is poured and guzzled at the other end. Aspiring inebriates are held upside down, so that alcohol-spiked blood rushes to the brain. Jell-O shots, laced with vodka and molded in Dixie Cups, are potent forms of nostalgia (a few years ago, they killed a 15-year-old New Jersey girl who wasn't in on the recipe).

14   "We have drinking contests to see how much people can drink in an hour before throwing up," says one member of a fraternity at the Massachusetts Institute of Technology. Twelve cans of beer is usually the limit. Other competitions include the "hour of power," in which each participant downs a shot glass of beer every minute for an hour (the more ambitious MIT version is "centurion," which lasts for 100 minutes).

15   Admittedly, these ingenious improvisations may not be any different from what has always happened to young people on the verge of adulthood. Don't most people pull out the stops during this time and live to tell the tale? Doesn't this generation deserve its moment of inane self-obliteration? Why shouldn't alcohol producers be able to grab what market share they can?

16   "Because this product is the leading cause of death for teen-agers in America. So right there, we're not talking about selling soap," replies Larry Wallack, professor of public health at the University of California, Berkeley. Automobile accidents, most of which are alcohol-related, kill more 15- to 24-year-olds than any other cause. Describing a Coors beer commercial during a recent football game, Wallack recalls, "People were just flying all over the screen, rollerblading, jumping, skiing. To me, taking an audience that is more

likely to embrace risk and associating this product with it is a recipe for disaster. You've got youth, high-risk activities, and alcohol."

17   In 1993, the alcoholic-beverage industry spent nearly $1 billion on media advertising and perhaps close to the same amount on promotions, a category that has grown significantly in recent years. The companies insist that their target is responsible, legal-age customers. Asked if he takes into account the 16- to 20-year-olds who might make up his client base, Scott Barnum, franchise director of premium brands at Miller Brewing Company, says, "I'm not allowed to even consider that. We're not allowed to get data on them. That's by corporate policy at Miller."

18   But Lloyd Johnston, program director of the University of Michigan Institute for Social Research, in Ann Arbor, does gather data on underage drinkers. He found that in 1993, 26 percent of eighth graders, 41 percent of 10th graders, and 51 percent of 12th graders had had at least one drink in the past month, and that more than a quarter of the 12th graders had been drunk. Extrapolating from Johnston's data, it appears that 5 million people between the ages of 13 and 20 have had five or more drinks in a row in the past two weeks.

19   Are they drinking purely on their own, or are they responding to advertising—even if it's not directly aimed at them? "Drinking, for young people, is mostly a manifestation of other problems," such as stress, depression, and loneliness, says Jeff Becker. Wallack, at the University of California, disagrees. "It's foolish to think that younger people are not seeing these ads as role models of what young adulthood and the good life are all about," he says. "The values that are put forth in these ads are very attractive to adolescents: individuality, peer-group acceptance, being part of the crowd."

20   Consider Budweiser's Spuds MacKenzie, the poster dog of the 1980s, whose imperturbable mien captured the attention of those younger than 21. Or consider that companies are pushing an array of products aimed at young drinkers.

21   One of those products needs no introduction. Malt beverages have been popular in the United States since the late 1800s. Each year, more than 1.1 billion cans of beer are consumed by junior and senior high school students, according to the US Department of Health and Human Services, translating into $200 million in revenue for the beer industry. Ice beers, which debuted in 1993, pack a wallop, with upward of 5.6 percent alcohol by volume, compared to about 4.6 percent in regular beer. (The higher octane comes from freezing the brew, then removing the ice crystals.) "New. Hot. Different. Contemporary. Masculine. All that stuff rolled into one makes it a fairly attractive . . . proposition for these young guys," says Barnum. Coors makes Zima Clearmalt, a citruslike beverage that appeared last year and has made a college-crowd name as a "lady's beer."

22   Cordials, such as 70-proof Jagermeister and 107-proof Goldschlager, are consumed by college students as high-powered, rapid-fire shots. And because inexperienced drinkers prefer sweeter beverages, the industry has come

up with coolers and "refreshers" made by such established firms as Jack Daniels, Smirnoff, and Bacardi.

23   Alcohol companies gear promotions to youth. One recent showcase campaign has been for Jagermeister, a German cordial made from 56 herbs, with a taste somewhere between cough syrup and licorice. In 1974, 1,000 cases of Jagermeister were sold in the United States; this year, that figure will reach 400,000 cases, making it the third-most-popular imported liqueur behind Kahlua and Bailey's Irish Cream. Nine years ago, sales soared with the Jagerettes, a national corps of 900 young women who, in tight-fitting black dresses and high heels, roam bars handing out hats, shirts, and other prizes to customers who will shout the Jagermeister name or buy a "tooter"—a frozen test tube filled with a 5/8-ounce shot. "We try, not to get people drunk but to promote brand awareness," says Rebecca Lyttle, Jagermeister's Massachusetts state supervisor. "College students are our bread and butter."

24   Other promotions are just as canny. Distilled-spirits manufacturers have embarked on direct-mail-and-response campaigns, interactive diskettes, and online promotions. Such strategies are intended to appeal to what the makers of Black and White Scotch, in a recent trade ad, described as "passive-aggressive vidiots who grew up too fast and have no faith in the system and think holes in jeans are cool and that party is a verb." Twenty-somethings may be outraged by such labeling, but to the alcohol companies, demographic analysis, however misguided, means profit.

25   Southern Comfort, playing on the supposed cultural disaffection of the X generation, has put out a "Take it easy" line of ads, each of which shows young men at play. "Life is not work. It can't be. It better not be," says one ad. As the company explains in a trade ad: "Southern Comfort drinkers are not old folks rocking in their rocking chairs. It's time the world knew they are 21- to 29-year-old consumers."

26   Though many ad campaigns have shed or parodied their perennial babes-on-the-beach imagery, sponsorship of major-league sports and auto races remains a strong sales tool. "That's how brewers target entry-level drinkers, rather than doing anything that's obvious," says Bob Hammond, of the alcohol research service in Lansing, Michigan.

27   Sometimes, though, it is obvious. In California this summer, at the Marin County Fair, a local distributor of Coors sponsored a root-beer-chugging contest, with Coors mugs as prizes. "It's like training wheels on drinking games, a vivid example of how the conditioning starts for 8- and 9-year-olds," says Robin Wechsler, associate director of community programs and training at the Marin Institute for the Prevention of Alcohol and Other Drug Problems, in San Rafael.

28   Cartoonlike characters, animals, dinosaurs, and other fantasy imagery reminiscent of Joe Camel have also sprung up. Huge blowup dolls of the Bud Man, a plump antihero in cape and tights, often float over promotions. This past summer, Miller Draft launched a series of ads in California featuring 3-D dinosaurs appearing to emerge from billboards—images that captured the

fancy of preschool children riding down the freeway beside their parents. On TV, Miller Lite is airing a series about silly sporting events, like sumo diving and dachshund races—"juvenile humor" that has been shown to delight young children, according to Joel Grube, senior research scientist at the Prevention Research Center, in Berkeley. Other promotions, such as dancing Coors cans in silver lamé, are set up in groceries and convenience stores, where children often tag along with their parents.

29 The pursuit of youthful brand loyalty has even led to what one observer dubs "the alcoholization of Halloween." October had traditionally been a lackluster time of the year for alcohol sales. Then, in 1983, Coors ran a campaign declaring itself the "official beer of Halloween." Soon, other companies followed, with gift-laden displays.

30 Last year, the Miller Beer Company's promotion included trick-or-treat bags, Mylar balloons shaped like alien heads, glow-in-the-dark fangs, removable tattoos (they said "Genuine Draft" and "Lite"), bat earrings, Frankenstein bolts, glow buttons, and T-shirts—all emblazoned with company logos. "Halloween is the only holiday we have left that is a children's holiday," says Laurie Leiber, director of the Center on Alcohol Advertising, at the Trauma Foundation, which is part of San Francisco General Hospital. Soon, memories of candy bars may mingle with anticipation of devils' night binges.

31 So, is the alcohol industry winning over a new generation of drinkers? For many years, children have started trying alcoholic beverages at an average age of 12. In the usual progression, they get their supply of alcohol from parents' stocks or from older siblings and friends. By the kids' mid-teens, their parties feature beer. Soon after, adolescents buy alcohol at commercial outlets, especially convenience marts, despite legal restrictions.

32 But proving a link between particular ads and drinking behavior is one of the trickiest problems in public health. For one thing, people have a lifetime of memories of previous advertisements. For another, our culture is permeated with scenes of happy drinking—on TV, radio, films, billboards, sporting events, and elsewhere—and it's hard to separate society's saturation from any corporate campaign. The alcohol industry doesn't, by itself, build a drinking ethic; it builds on what's already there.

33 "How do you square the fact that advertising expenditures are continually going up and underage drinking is going down?" asks the Beer Institute's Becker. "As a practical matter, public-health advocates can't make a good case that advertising causes people to drink who otherwise would not, or initiates earlier drinking in young people than would normally be the case."

34 But in studies done in California of fifth and sixth graders, some links between advertising and attitudes have turned up. Those who are aware of television beer advertising have more favorable beliefs about drinking, greater knowledge of beer brands and slogans, and greater intentions to drink when they are adults, according to studies done in California by Grube, of the Prevention Research Center. Other studies by Charles Atkin, at Michigan State University, in East Lansing, have shown that adolescents more heavily ex-

posed to alcohol advertising were more likely to believe that drinkers were attractive, athletic, and successful, and they were themselves more likely to drink, drink heavily, and drink in hazardous situations such as when driving.

35   Though the alcohol producers disparage such reports, they have been quick to counterpunch. They have funded popular midnight-basketball and conflict-resolution programs that keep children and teen-agers off the street. They underwrite designated-driver programs (even though their effect on total consumption is debated, since nondesignated drivers are given license to indulge). They have supported so-called zero-tolerance laws, which revoke the licenses of underage drivers found to have alcohol in their blood. And they have set up voluntary server-training programs, teaching waiters and waitresses how to help those who have imbibed too much by offering soft drinks, solid food, and sometimes a cab ride home. . . .

36   Some argue that drinking is part of a bigger cycle that we can't control. Looking at long-term data, Robin Room has observed slow cycles of alcohol consumption, with 60 to 70 years between peaks. "There's partly a kind of generational forgetting," he says. "People react against the problems of heavy alcohol use with temperance sentiment, and then they forget why these silly rules came into effect in the first place"

37   Whatever the cycles, alcohol seems here to stay. "This is a product that's going to be legal and readily available," says the Trauma Foundation's Laurie Leiber. "What are we going to do about that?" She offers her own scenario: As with tobacco, research linking alcohol to health problems will seep into the public consciousness, prompting public action. Alcohol companies, sensitive to their image, will change where and how they sell their products. Ads will target adults, conveying qualities of the beverages themselves, not glamorizing drinkers. Public-health messages about alcohol will show up more often in the media. Wine, liquor, and, especially, beer will cost more. People will perceive alcohol (like tobacco) as part of a continuum of illegal drugs.

38   "We would probably be drinking infrequently and mostly lightly," says Leiber. "Which is how most people who avoid problems drink."

Topical Considerations

1. Summarize the argument Drexler makes about the relationship between advertising and alcohol consumption by teenagers? Do you agree with this argument? Why or why not?

2. What observations or generalizations would you make about alcohol consumption on your campus? In your opinion, is college-age drinking a serious problem? Explain your answer.

3. Throughout her essay, Drexler describes heavy drinking among college and high school students as a "rite of passage" (paragraphs 3 and 11). What does she mean by this? Based on your own experience or observations, is this an accurate assessment of why teenagers drink? Explain.

4. In paragraph 6, Drexler asserts that it is inevitable that society will come to understand "how deeply advertising influences our tastes and norms." Describe the role of ad images in shaping your opinions and tastes regarding alcohol. Cite specific ad campaigns. Do you believe that "society" is in denial about the power of advertising? Why or why not?

5. Re-read "The Language of Advertising" by Charles O'Neill. Would O'Neill find these alcohol ads unethical? Why or why not?

6. Do you agree with Drexler that the alcohol industry targets the youth market in its advertising, despite its support of anti-drinking groups such as Mothers Against Drunk Driving and sponsorship of midnight basketball games? In your opinion, is such targeting unethical? Should there be regulations against these marketing strategies? Explain.

7. In paragraphs 24–25, Drexler refers to the description of late teen, early twenties-aged consumers as generation x'ers, or more specifically, "passive-aggressive vidiots who grew up too fast and have no faith in the system and think holes in jeans are cool and that party is a verb." What is your evaluation of this description? As a member of this age group, do you feel that terms like "culturally disaffected" accurately capture your feelings and position?

8. Drexler concludes her essay with a "scenario" imagining an eventual increase in public consciousness about the harmfulness of drinking, and a perception of alcohol as "part of a continuum of illegal drugs" (paragraph 37). Do you agree with this view of alcohol? In your opinion, is it illogical that drugs like marijuana and cocaine are illegal and alcohol is not? Explain.

Rhetorical Considerations

1. How does Drexler capture the reader's attention in her opening paragraph? Where in the introduction does her tone shift, and what is the effect of this shift? Is her introductory material effective? Why or why not?

2. Who is the audience for Drexler's piece? Parents? Teenagers? Both? The advertising community? What signals does she give to direct her piece toward that certain audience? How do you feel as a reader of her piece?

3. In her thesis statement, Drexler makes two assertions: (1) that heavy drinking among college and high school students is a dangerous "rite of passage"; and (2) that advertisers in the alcohol industry manipulate this "rite of passage" to boost their sales. Does Drexler succeed in proving a connection between a teen rite of passage and advertising techniques over the course of her essay? Explain your answer.

4. Re-examine Drexler's article, making note of the different kinds of sources and authorities she uses to support her argument. Does her evidence seem carefully selected? Do you find that she has included any unnecessary facts or authorities? Why or why not?

5. What part of this essay did you find most interesting? What part was the least interesting? Why?

Writing Assignments

1. Drexler's essay seems to be directed at an adult readership. Write your own essay outlining the dangerous connections between alcohol industry ad campaigns and excessive drinking by 16- to 24-year-olds, targeting 16- to 24-year-olds as your intended audience. Start by thinking about what person you would want to speak from (first, second, or third), what voice or tone would be best suited to your audience, and how your voice and selection of facts might differ from Drexler's based on the shift in audience.

2. Write a paper in which you consider either the descriptions of advertising techniques offered by Drexler (see paragraphs 20–23, and 29–30) or the strategies of advertising campaigns with which you are familiar (from magazines, television, sporting events). Make an argument for the appropriateness—or exploitativeness—of such campaigns. You might use the essays by Patricia Volk, Charlie O'Neill, or William Lutz to support your arguments.

3. Using your own experience, write a response to Drexler's essay. If you disagree with her, try to formulate your own argument that there is not a substantive connection between advertising and drinking by the youth market. Include your feelings about the idea of drinking as a "rite of passage.": is it dangerous? Or is it "normal" coming of age behavior?

OPPOSITIONS: SEX IN ADVERTISING

Sex in Advertising
Edward A. McCabe

Critics and defenders of advertising agree on one thing: Sex sells. Whether pushing cologne, beer, or pickup trucks, advertisers will add a little flesh in the effort to make you prefer their product to the competition. But has the practice gone too far, as some critics claim? Have advertisers demeaned and stereotyped women especially in their campaigns? No, says Edward A. McCabe, who created some of the most successful campaigns in advertising history. In this article, which first appeared in *Playboy* magazine in August 1992, McCabe defends the oldest come-on in advertising against critics who claim that the sex in ads has become offensively explicit and widespread.

BEFORE YOU READ

Try to determine what line of persuasion or arguments a professional advertiser might use to defend sex in advertising. Consider the fact that this essay was written for *Playboy.*

AS YOU READ

Try to evaluate the support McCabe offers for his case. Does his evidence persuade you to his argument? If not, what objections do you have?

1   Even before I knew there was such a thing as an advertising business, I learned that sex was often an important attention-getting element.

2   As a teenager in Chicago, I worked in a Standard Oil service station. I remember being intoxicated by the smell of gasoline—the pink, cold and sweeter ethyl more than the pale, dry regular—transfixed, too, by the sound and feel of the pneumatic grease gun with its whooshes and pops as I snapped it from one silvery nipple to another beneath some chopped, channeled and lowered 1950 Merc.

3   Even more than the sounds and smells and work in the place, I loved the coming in early and the leaving late. It legitimized my loitering in the back among the tool benches and files and vises. That's where the changing lockers were. And where there were lockers, there were pictures of women.

4   It was dim and hushed and it smelled of oil back there. Every available surface was covered with ads torn out of magazines hawking some automotive product or another. The girls in them beckoned, ripe with the promise of much more than an oil additive or a more effective carburetor or wiper blade.

5   Where they got all those ads I knew not. But I lingered and leered and, though vaguely, recall them all. I remember the ad with the Jane Russell looka-like who had huge bosoms and wore a tight-fitting sweater, both hands wrapped suggestively around a shock absorber. And how could I forget the ad for the welding rods, the one with the girl in the low-cut bathing suit—her cleavage trying to climb off the page—juxtaposed with the words, "A good technique and the right rod for the job"? Dozens of these ads there were, pa-pered everywhere, some new, clean and freshly hung, others streaked, greasy and curling away from doors and walls, dangling hard and yellowed with strips of cellophane tape.

6   I knew even then that, as daring as they seemed, as involving and com-pelling as they were, most of these ads were more about chauvinism and cocksmanship than about salesmanship.

7   In our little service station, we neither owned nor sold any of the prod-ucts whose ads provided us with so much fascination. Not a one. Back then, advertising was the public's most accessible source of titillation. Today I sin-cerely doubt anyone looking for a sexual thrill grabs a magazine, races home and pants over the advertising. Unless we're talking about the Victoria's Secret

catalog—but even that doesn't seem as sexy today as it once did. And maybe someone is still clinging to a copy of *Vanity Fair* with Calvin Klein's sexually explicit 116-page "outsert" in its original condomlike wrapper. That, somehow, promised to rise above the mass of what we call "sex in advertising." But really, once you've slipped off the sensuous sleeve, how racy is a black-and-white photo of a guy groping himself with blue jeans under a shower? It all depends on what you're into, or used to, I guess. I once knew a guy who got off on a certain section of the Sears catalog. But that was in the Fifties.

8   Certainly any cursory look at today's advertising scene will reveal that sexual themes are more pervasive than ever. But how sexy are they? As we've all learned, a lot of sex is not the same as good sex.

9   In New York we have a thing called Channel 35. This is our cable TV sex channel. Many major cities have one now. Ours is sort of a blue version of the *New York Post* in that it's hard to find anyone who will admit to having anything to do with it. Nevertheless, it's there. And on any given night, that's where you'll find sex in advertising. Because on it, sex is being advertised.

10   Want an escort? Just call and she'll come a-knockin'. Channel 35 parades an assortment before you in all sizes and colors. Black, white, Asian. They even sort them according to class. You can get everything from a tall, svelte blonde in an evening gown to a jeans-wearing, leather-jacketed gumcracker. Gay sex? Lesbian sex? Group sex? It's got it all for you. S/M? Got that, too, you pathetic wimp.

11   If you're in the market for sexual apparatus, here's where you'll find it. There are stores pushing all the latest gimcracks, plus latex gizmos measured by the inch, foot and yard. They've even got a woman who'll come over and pee on you. Of course, they've also got people who will just talk dirty to you on the phone. But why get it only in the ear when you can get wet all over?

12   In such a world, what can poor Calvin Klein, Georges Marciano and the other national purveyors of sexually directed merchandise possibly do to keep up?

13   It's not easy. The mass media have codes and rule and guidelines designed to protect our puritanical sensibilities from prurience. The FCC or some such body grants greater latitude to—or doesn't even supervise—cable television. Needless to say, the boys over at Channel 35 play with a less-restrictive rule book.

14   Consider this. If you do a soap or shampoo commercial that is intended to run on one or more of the major networks, you can't show a man or woman who appears undressed in a shower. It's against the networks' code of decency to show so much of a person, even though that's the normal, natural, approved form of dress for taking showers. You are required to shoot close-ups, being careful to crop out or edit the sensitive areas.

15   In many newspapers, you can't run an ad that shows a belly button or more than an inch or so of cleavage.

16   Over in England and in other parts of Europe, pretty much anything goes. There they allow the public to see nudity in all its logical glory and no-

body gets particularly excited or upset about it. Right now, in Scandinavia there's a commercial running for a condom that uses an animated penis to get the point across, balls and all. I gather that one has raised a few eyebrows. But in a way, isn't that what advertising is supposed to do? Get folks to pay attention?

17   Now, I happen to believe most things in this world—in advertising or elsewhere—occur as a result of somebody trying to get away with something that's not supposed to be done. I call it the boomerang effect. Tell some people what they can't do and they'll generally come right back at you with a brilliant but sneaky way around the prohibition. (Look at Prohibition.)

18   Look at Victorian England. It was beneath the cloak of morality that the most deplorable sexual behavior flourished. When you have to be careful not to utter the word petticoat in public, what do you do to let off steam? You go home, strip, bind, gag, flog, rape and sodomize your maid, what else?

19   Anyway, a lot of the people who attempt to put sex into advertising are just trying to stretch the rules to capture your attention. And to a large extent, they're doing a damned fine job of pushing the edge of the envelope that contains the rule book. A rule book that, like all rule books, is hopelessly behind the times.

20   Even so, there is advertising out there that manages to flirt with some fairly dodgy and sensitive issues. Of course, the most artful and daring examples appear in magazines. Unlike other media, magazines issue little in the way of blanket prohibitions. They tend to accept advertising on the basis of its congruence with the publication's editorial policy and the appropriateness for its particular audience.

21   In all upscale fashion magazines, nudity has become almost commonplace, the controversial specifics masked by natural situational elements rather than by contrived editing or framing. There are perfume commercials and ads that clearly suggest putting it on means a ménage à trois is in the offing. Scan recent magazine and you'll be inundated with innuendo. There is fashion advertising with a sadomasochistic bent, jeans and sunglasses ads pushing the pairing of older men and very young girls, ads that clearly depict the idea of extramarital sex. In fact, today's ads touch on every area of sexual pleasure and perversion.

22   Critics of advertising will tell you that it has become too sexually explicit and that the use of sex in it too widespread. They might be right, but as is so often the case with zealots, when they're right, it's for the wrong reasons. Advertising is far less sexually explicit than much of what we can readily find elsewhere in our lives—in films, in magazine features, on cable TV, in literature. That advertising is as explicit as it is is not proof of the depravity of its creators and sponsors but is evidence that some of the outmoded restraints still in force are highly motivational. The irony is that in England, where advertising is allowed to deal with sex fairly openly, the advertising doesn't come across nearly as sexy as our advertising, which is less explicit.

23   Also, far from being demonic manipulators who slip subliminal sex images into ice cubes—a charge leveled at advertising people by those who have
nothing better to do in their lives than to imagine such nonsense—ad people
are too busy, too responsible and too scrutinized to waste a second thinking of
such crap. Besides, putting sexual images in ice cubes or drinks doesn't conjure up particularly appetizing imagery. Sexual excretions in your Scotch?
Yuck!

24   And how about those who swear the face of Old Joe Camel, the cigarette cartoon character, is really a drawing of male genitalia? I wish they'd
come off it. What company in its right mind wants consumers going around
calling its product symbol Old Scrotum Face?

25   Same with the new Pepsi can. Recently, it was brought to my attention that to some people the typography and graphic representation on the
front of the can might depict a man's penis and testicles. And, once
pointed out, darned if it doesn't look like that to me, too. But is such a
thing intentional? Are you kidding? You think the second-largest soft-drink
company in the country wants America's mothers thinking their daughters
are walking around publicly grasping, let alone placing their lips on, guys'
units?

26   Why would anybody knowingly do something like that? Do these people think every major company in America is as sex-crazed as they are?

27   That's not to say there are no abuses.

28   Sex in marketing is often unnecessary and even undesirable. In too
many instances, it's just a lazy cop-out. When you can't come up with an ad
that's truly distinctive or compelling, there's always that old fallback: Why not
put some pussy in it? There are still too many people concerned with selling
things like machine tools who simply must regress to the big-boobed babe.
That's boorish as well as as stupid. Unless a product is truly sexy—sexy to use,
look at or be seen in—using sex to market it just won't work. And trying to is
nothing more than gratuitous tastelessness.

29   Yes, on television, too many spots continue to demean women or insensitively threat them as sex objects. And yes, even some of today's magazine
advertisements may be going too far.

30   But that still leaves much that is smart and artful, charming or entertaining, and, certainly, the sheer volume of such ads reflects our continuing fascination with one of the more engaging aspects of life.

Topical Considerations

1. What difference does McCabe see in the pinup ads in the back of the service
    station where he worked as a teenager and today's sexy ads? Are you shocked
    by current advertising practices that promote sex to sell products, or do you
    think that almost anything can go in advertising?

2. In paragraph 29 McCabe writes, "Yes, on television, too many spots continue to demean women or insensitively treat them as sex objects." He also complains in paragraph 28 that "There are still too many people concerned with selling things like machine tools who simply must regress to the big-boobed babe." Would you say McCabe is consistent in his attitude toward using women in advertising? Would you consider him sexist? Explain your answer.

3. Why does McCabe bring Channel 35, New York's cable TV sex channel, into his argument? Is it necessary to describe the types of sex and equipment that are advertised on this channel? Explain your reasoning. Do you think Channel 35 and others like it should be allowed such freedom of expression when commercial advertisers on TV are restricted? What example does he give to illustrate the restrictive FCC code of decency?

4. How, according to McCabe, does advertising in England and Europe compare with American advertising?

5. Cite some examples of sexually charged magazine advertisements featuring "every area of sexual pleasure and perversion." Do you criticize or admire these ads for their content?

6. Do you believe that some advertisers deliberately use phallic symbols in their ads? What examples does McCabe give of such ads? Are you aware of any other ads making use of phallic symbols?

Rhetorical Considerations

1. How does McCabe's personal experience in the "little service station" that begins the essay help introduce his subject?

2. Where in the essay does he begin to discuss current American advertisements? What is his claim—the thesis statement of his argument?

3. McCabe uses at least one incomplete sentence and some slang expressions in this article—common advertising practices. Point out examples of colloquial language. Do these infractions of standard English bother you? Why or why not? How do they help establish the author's persona?

4. If you didn't know which magazine this essay was published in, could you guess? What clues give away the nature of the audience McCabe is addressing?

5. Notice the use of first person throughout the article—from the opening anecdote to paragraph 17 where McCabe states, "Now I happen to believe most things in this world. . . . " Do you get the impression that McCabe is an expert on sex in advertising from his statements? Does he quote any authorities on his subject?

6. Where in the article does McCabe begin to address opposing points of view regarding sex in advertising? Do you think his treatment of such anticipated opposition is sufficiently strong? In light of his concessions here, what can you assume about his overall view of sex in advertising?

Writing Assignments

1. Using the periodical room of your library, select two ads from a foreign magazine that are more sexually explicit than two American magazine ads for similar products. Describe the differences between these ads? What do these ads demonstrate about the social mores of the two countries?
2. Write an opposing argument to this essay in which you disagree with Mc-Cabe's fairly liberal point of view about sex in advertising.
3. Describe an event in your life when you became aware of the sexual appeal of advertising, using McCabe's service station experience as a model.
4. McCabe contends that even though "some of today's magazine advertisements may be going too far . . . [many ads are still] smart and artful, charming or entertaining" (paragraphs 29–30). Write an argument in which you take the contrary position—that is, how, in spite of the artfulness of some ads, women are demeaned when presented as sex objects to sell products.
5. Write a letter to a friend in a foreign country, possibly France or England, explaining why American advertising is so tame compared to the advertising in their country. Take a stand either defending or criticizing the tameness here.

Sex Is Still Doing the Selling
John Carroll

Like Edward A. McCabe, John Carroll is in the advertising business. Carroll is the head of his own advertising firm, Carroll Creative in Boston. Also like McCabe, Carroll is very much aware that sex sells. But unlike McCabe, Carroll deplores the practice of using women's sexuality to push products. Written in direct response to Edward McCabe, "Sex Is Still Doing the Selling," which first appeared in *The Boston Globe* in July 1992, attacks both McCabe and the ad industry for the cavalier perpetuation of what Carroll sees as demeaning and debasing sexist stereotypes.

BEFORE YOU READ

Ask yourself why a professional advertiser would criticize another practitioner of the craft. Try to anticipate Carroll's views. Try to second-guess his strategies. Would you expect Carroll to rely on logical, emotional, or ethical arguments?

AS YOU READ

Notice Carroll's technique of letting those he disagrees with indict themselves by quoting seemingly disingenuous defenses of their own practices. Do you think Carroll's characterizations of McCabe are fair? Do they strengthen or weaken Carroll's argument?

1   If capturing the consumer's attention is half the battle in advertising, sex is the industry's nuclear weapon. Ads for products from perfume to power tools routinely employ images of women in various states of relevance and undress. But in the wake of last year's Anita Hill/Clarence Thomas fiasco and the Navy's current Tailhook sex-abuse scandal, people inside and outside the advertising business have been taking a closer look at the way women are portrayed in ads. The chances that any significant change will occur, however, are slimmer than a high-fashion model.

2   Despite the tenor of the times—the back-to-basics, family values movement espoused by politicians and average Americans alike—the ad industry resolutely clings to its belief that sex sells at least as well as Bill Cosby does. The latest defense of sex in advertising appears in this month's issue of—no surprise here—Playboy magazine. Its author is longtime advertising bigfoot Ed McCabe, whose claim to fame mostly resides in recognizing Frank Perdue's uncanny resemblance to his product. McCabe's article attempts the seemingly impossible: to orchestrate a politically correct celebration of advertising's use of sex as a selling device. Sure, he says, some of it is unnecessary and tasteless, but in general we should become more like the Europeans, whose ads display "nudity in all its logical glory."

3   The entire article, in fact, relies on that same "yeah/but" foundation. Yes, there are abuses, and yes, too many television spots continue to demean women, and yes, even some of today's magazine advertisements may be going too far. But advertisers "are just trying to stretch the rules to attract your attention. And, to a large extent, they're doing a damned fine job of pushing the edge of the envelope that contains the rule book. A rule book that, like all rule books, is hopelessly behind the times."

4   What McCabe seems to be saying is that machine-tool manufacturers should avoid sexual imagery, but for perfume companies, anything goes. Dance as he might on this head of a pin, his argument is thoroughly undermined by the captions to the ads illustrating the text.

5   The reader is told that the offensive Swedish Bikini Team from the Old Milwaukee beer commercials has been "regrettably grounded." A man and a woman wearing nothing but ski boots represent "playful nudity." And then there's this beauty: "While some people see the use of gratuitous sexual imagery as a distraction, we view it as an unexpected bonus."

6   That attitude, of course, fits perfectly with the magazine's Velveeta brand of air-brushed sexuality. Ironically, the same issue also contains a pictorial "Salute to the All-American Housewife." A paean to motherhood? To community service? Nah, just the encyclopedia salesman's dream: naked women washing windows, ironing clothes, carrying bags of groceries. Processed cheesecake.

7   Ed McCabe certainly doesn't speak for the entire ad industry, but it's fair to say that his sentiments are shared by a majority of advertising professionals. And those sentiments aren't likely to change in the foreseeable future.

8   As advertising clutter grows, it becomes exponentially more difficult for any ad to attract attention. Not only that, many products are marketed solely to men, so even if certain ads do offend women, the impact on sales is minimal. Insensitivity to women is only part of the problem. Cold calculation plays an even bigger role.

9   Further complicating matters, it's not just unzipped flyboys like Mc-Cabe who create sexual stereotypes of women in advertising. Witness this opinion, voiced right after the Clarence Thomas confirmation hearings by Cathi Mooney, chairman of a San Francisco ad agency. "I'm sure most Americans are not even paying attention" to the Thomas controversy, she told a Boston Globe reporter. "The way I do advertising is: What's going to be a strong message to the consumer? I don't want to sit there and say, 'How are we treating women?'"

10   Andrew Dice Clay on line one, Ms. Mooney.

11   On another front of the women's libido movement, Linda Bartlett Keys, a Citrus Hills, Calif., graphic designer, created an ad for QuadCache software that featured the headline "Fast and Compatible" over a black-and-white snapshot of a young woman in low-slung jeans and a checked bustier. The subheadline read, "QuadCache Will Remind You Of Your First Date With Angela West."

12   A male executive at the company called it an effort "to inject a touch of sweet sexuality and humor into the adolescent, male-dominated computer industry. They don't call them nerds for nothing." Nothing, as it turned out, was exactly what they saw. In a highly unusual move, MacWeek magazine eliminated the snapshot and substituted the handwritten words "Photo removed by request of publisher," which roughly translates into "Your fantasy here." The censored ad was arguably more provocative than the original.

13   Although the software company agreed to the censored version, no one involved was particularly pleased with the solution. Keys expressed surprise at the negative reaction she received. "It's supposed to be funny," she said. "Every high school had a girl like that—you know, fast and compatible. People shouldn't take it so literally and seriously. It's just advertising."

Sex or Sexism?

14   "Just advertising" has a significant influence on all of us, though. Jean Kilbourne, a media critic and visiting scholar at Wellesley College, believes that advertising is one of the most powerful educational forces in our lives and a major way we learn our attitudes toward others and ourselves.

15   In "Still Killing Us Softly," a production of Cambridge Documentary Films, Kilbourne says, "What we learn [cumulatively from ads] is that woman's body is just another piece of merchandise. Not only is she a thing, she's a thing for sale. And women's bodies and products are completely interchangeable in the world of ads."

16   A typical example she cites is an ad that shows a woman straddling a man's out-stretched leg and pulling off his cowboy boot. "Treat 'em good and they'll treat you good," the headline promises. The copy begins, "Some men treat their boots better than their women. Not altogether admirable, but certainly understandable."

17   Kilbourne and other critics say this mix of sexuality and aggression doesn't necessarily cause violence, but does make us more callous to it. Much the same could be said of the advertising industry. Although protests over the depiction of women in ads have grown in recent years, the response has been tepid at best. Old Milwaukee, for one, replaced its bikini team with standard-issue footage of men hiking, camping and drinking in the great outdoors—classic malt-bonding stuff. Other advertisers have atoned for ads that offend women by employing reverse sexism and showing men as "himbos." That's nothing more than equality by subtraction, creating in the end the "double-ditz" couple.

18   Even the industry's efforts at self-enlightenment are prone to backfire. Bozell, a New York ad agency, recently held a seminar for its employees to try to eliminate sexism and exploitation from their advertising. According to The Wall Street Journal, "in announcing its seminar, Bozell put up in-house posters showing a grainy photograph of a woman's naked torso taken from a Calvin Klein Obsession ad. Between the woman's two erect nipples ran the line, 'Two of the points Ron Anderson will be covering at his next seminar.'"

19   Despite the Virginia Slims slogan, women still have a long way to go. But not as far as advertisers do—at least not as long as they continue to value a clever headline over good taste, and increased sales over basic decency.

Topical Considerations

1. In contrast to Edward McCabe, how does John Carroll view the use of sex in advertising? What current events focused attention on sex in advertising when the article was written?

2. What is Carroll's perception of *Playboy* magazine? What is your perception of this publication?

3. Carroll states in paragraph 12, "The censored ad was arguably more provocative than the original." To what is Carroll referring? Do you agree that something left to the imagination is more stimulating than "letting everything hang out"?

4. According to Carroll in the last paragraph, which are more important: clever headlines or good taste, increased sales or basic decency? Do you think that this is the usual view of advertising people?

Rhetorical Considerations

1. Contrast Carroll's use of authorities for supporting evidence with that of McCabe. Whose argument seems stronger and why?

2. Explain the following words and phrases used by Carroll in the context of his article.
   a. "Velveeta brand air-brushed sexuality" and "processed cheesecake" (paragraph 6)
   b. "Unzipped flyboy" (paragraph 17)
   c. "himbos" and "double-ditz" (paragraph 17)
3. What analogy does Carroll use to begin the article? How does it work in the context of the rest of the article?
4. Compare the tone of Carroll's essay with that of McCabe's. What do the articles have in common? Where do they differ? Which is more serious? Humorous? Personal? Sarcastic? Lively and engaging? Cite statements that amused you from both articles.

Writing Assignments

1. Write a letter to an advertising woman who creates ads using sexual stereotypes of other women. Express your opinion of her work, giving examples of the advertisements that offend you or amuse you.
2. Write an essay defending either McCabe's or Carroll's position on the use of sex in advertising. Use your own examples and authorities to support your side of the argument.
3. Find an ad from a magazine or newspaper that uses a man as a sexual stereotype—Carroll's "himbo." Describe how this ad is offensive and demeaning to men. Or take McCabe's view and discuss why you are not offended by the ad.
4. Find a copy of *Playboy* magazine and analyze two ads to see if they conform to McCabe's standards for sex in advertising. How would Carroll react to these ads?

ARGUMENTS THAT SHAPED HISTORY

The Allegory of the Cave
Plato

Much of the glory that was ancient Greece centered around Athens, and much of the renown belonging to Athens is attributed to three great philosophers who lived and taught there: Socrates, Plato, and Aristotle. The son of an aristocratic Athenian family, Plato (428–347 B.C.) was the friend and pupil of Socrates and the teacher of Aristotle. Although Plato had planned to enter politics, he turned instead to philosophy after an Athenian court unjustly condemned Socrates to death in 339 B.C. for impiety and the corruption of youth. Plato exiled himself from Athens until 387 B.C., when he founded his famous Academy, where he taught for the last 40 years of his life. Despite political turmoil, Plato's Athens flourished with philosophic debate as reflected in his legacy—some 24 dialogues that are regarded as one of the great cultural treasures of the western world. Purported to be conversations with Socrates and other Athenian followers, these dialogues cover a full range of topics: philosophy, logic, politics, science, aesthetics, education, law and justice, ethical codes, and religion. Although Socrates is considered one of the greatest thinkers in the Western world, he wrote nothing. His wisdom comes to us solely through Plato's writings. The very dialogue form itself, in fact, is a reflection of Socrates' own teaching method—a technique of asking questions that allows students to arrive at their own insights, their own wisdom. The best known dialogues include *The Symposium, Apology, Crito,* and *Timaeus.*

    "The Allegory of the Cave," taken from Plato's *Republic,* concerns the nature of truth and how we perceive it. (An *allegory* is a story in which the characters and circumstances have symbolic meanings that go beyond the story itself.) As Socrates explains, if all we have is our sensory perception, then our understanding of the truth is limited. And, yet, Plato believed that we are born with ideals or forms of the truth which, though dimly remembered, are made comprehensible by our senses, unreliable as they may be.

BEFORE YOU READ

Think of other allegories and parables (possibly Biblical) you have read. What do they have in common? What kinds of assumptions are made about the audience? What kinds of conclusions are usually drawn?

AS YOU READ

Try to determine the symbolic meaning of the following: life in the cave, the fire-light, the shadows on the wall, the sunlight outside, the task of the one who returns to those who remain in the cave. Also, try to determine the syllogistic line of reasoning Plato uses to explain human behavior in the allegory.

1   Next, said I, here is a parable to illustrate the degrees in which our nature may be enlightened or unenlightened. Imagine the condition of men living in a sort of cavernous chamber underground, with an entrance open to the light and a long passage all down the cave. Here they have been from childhood, chained by the leg and also by the neck, so that they cannot move and can see only what is in front of them, because the chains will not let them turn their heads. At some distance higher up is the light of a fire burning behind them; and between the prisoners and the fire is a track with a parapet built along it, like the screen at a puppet-show, which hides the performers while they show their puppets over the top.

2   I see, said he.

3   Now behind this parapet imagine persons carrying along various artificial objects, including figures of men and animals in wood or stone or other materials, which project above the parapet. Naturally, some of these persons will be talking, others silent.

4   It is a strange picture, he said, and a strange sort of prisoners.

5   Like ourselves, I replied; for in the first place prisoners so confined would have seen nothing of themselves or of one another, except the shadows thrown by the fire-light on the wall of the Cave facing them, would they?

6   Not if all their lives they have been prevented from moving their heads.

7   And they would have seen as little of the objects carried past.

8   Of course.

9   Now, if they could talk to one another, would they not suppose that their words referred only to those passing shadows which they saw?

10   Necessarily.

11   And suppose their prison had an echo from the wall facing them? When one of the people crossing behind them spoke, they could only suppose that the sound came from the shadow passing before their eyes.

12   No doubt.

13   In every way, then, such prisoners would recognize as reality nothing but the shadows of those artificial objects.

14   Inevitably.

15   Now consider what would happen if their release from the chains and the healing of their unwisdom should come about in this way. Suppose one of them were set free and forced suddenly to stand up, turn his head, and walk with eyes lifted to the light; all these movements would be painful, and he would be too dazzled to make out the objects whose shadows he had been used to see. What do you think he would say, if someone told him that what he had formerly seen was meaningless illusion, but now, being somewhat nearer to reality and turned towards more real objects, he was getting a truer view? Suppose further that he were shown the various objects being carried by and were made to say, in reply to questions, what each of them was. Would he not be perplexed and believe the objects now shown him to be not so real as what he formerly saw?

16   Yes, not nearly so real.

17   And if he were forced to look at the fire-light itself, would not his eyes ache, so that he would try to escape and turn back to the things which he could see distinctly, convinced that they really were clearer than these other objects now being shown to him?

18   Yes.

19   And suppose someone were to drag him away forcibly up the steep and rugged ascent and not let him go until he had hauled him out into the sun-light, would he not suffer pain and vexation at such treatment, and, when he had come out into the light, find his eyes so full of its radiance that he could not see a single one of the things that he was now told were real?

20   Certainly he would not see them all at once.

21   He would need, then, to grow accustomed before he could see things in that upper world. At first it would be easiest to make out shadows, and then the images of men and things reflected in water, and later on the things them-selves. After that, it would be easier to watch the heavenly bodies and the sky itself by night, looking at the light of the moon and stars rather than the Sun and the Sun's light in the day-time.

22   Yes, surely.

23   Last of all, he would be able to look at the Sun and contemplate its na-ture, not as it appears when reflected in water or any alien medium, but as it is in itself in its own domain.

24   No doubt.

25   And now he would begin to draw the conclusion that it is the Sun that produces the seasons and the course of the year and controls everything in the visible world, and moreover is in a way the cause of all that he and his com-panions used to see.

26   Clearly he would come at last to that conclusion.

27   Then if he called to mind his fellow prisoners and what passed for wis-dom in his former dwelling-place, he would surely think himself happy in the change and be sorry for them. They may have had a practice of honouring and commending one another, with prizes for the man who had the keenest eye

for the passing shadows and the best memory for the order in which they followed or accompanied one another, so that he could make a good guess as to
which was going to come next. Would our released prisoner be likely to covet
those prizes or to envy the men exalted to honour and power in the Cave?
Would he not feel like Homer's Achilles, that he would far sooner 'be on earth
as a hired servant in the house of a landless man' or endure anything rather
than go back to his old beliefs and live in the old way?

28   Yes, he would prefer any fate to such a life.

29   Now imagine what would happen if he went down again to take his
former seat in the Cave. Coming suddenly out of the sunlight, his eyes
would be filled with darkness. He might be required once more to deliver
his opinion on those shadows, in competition with the prisoners who had
never been released, while his eyesight was still dim and unsteady; and it
might take some time to become used to the darkness. They would laugh at
him and say that he had gone up only to come back with his sight ruined; it
was worth no one's while even to attempt the ascent. If they could lay
hands on the man who was trying to set them free and lead them up, they
would kill him.

30   Yes, they would.

31   Every feature in this parable, my dear Glaucon, is meant to fit our
earlier analysis. The prison dwelling corresponds to the region revealed to
us through the sense of sight, and the fire-light within it to the power of the
Sun. The ascent to see the things in the upper world you may take as standing for the upward journey of the soul into the region of the intelligible;
then you will be in possession of what I surmise, since that is what you
wish to be told. Heaven knows whether it is true; but this, at any rate, is
how it appears to me. In the world of knowledge, the last thing to be perceived and only with great difficulty is the essential Form of Goodness.
Once it is perceived, the conclusion must follow that, for all things, this is
the cause of whatever is right and good; in the visible world it gives birth to
light and to the lord of light, while it is itself sovereign in the intelligible
world and the parent of intelligence and truth. Without having had a vision
of this Form no one can act with wisdom, either in his own life or in matters of state.

32   So far as I can understand, I share your belief.

33   Then you may also agree that it is no wonder if those who have
reached this height are reluctant to manage the affairs of men. Their souls long
to spend all their time in that upper world—naturally enough, if here once
more our parable holds true. Nor, again, is it at all strange that one who comes
from the contemplation of divine things to the miseries of human life should
appear awkward and ridiculous when, with eyes still dazed and not yet accustomed to the darkness, he is compelled, in a law-court or elsewhere, to dispute
about the shadows of justice or the images that cast those shadows, and to
wrangle over the notions of what is right in the minds of men who have never
beheld Justice itself.

34   It is not at all strange.

35   No; a sensible man will remember that the eyes may be confused in two ways—by a change from light to darkness or from darkness to light; and he will recognize that the same thing happens to the soul. When he sees it troubled and unable to discern anything clearly, instead of laughing thoughtlessly, he will ask whether, coming from a brighter existence, its unaccustomed vision is obscured by the darkness, in which case he will think its condition enviable and its life a happy one; or whether, emerging from the depths of ignorance, it is dazzled by excess of light. If so, he will rather feel sorry for it; or, if he were inclined to laugh, that would be less ridiculous than to laugh at the soul which has come down from the light.

36   That is a fair statement.

37   If this is true, then, we must conclude that education is not what it is said to be by some, who profess to put knowledge into a soul which does not possess it, as if they could put sight into blind eyes. On the contrary, our own account signifies that the soul of every man does possess the power of learning the truth and the organ to see it with; and that, just as one might have to turn the whole body round in order that the eye should see light instead of darkness, so the entire soul must be turned away from this changing world, until its eye can bear to contemplate reality and that supreme splendour which we have called the Good. Hence there may well be an art whose aim would be to effect this very thing, the conversion of the soul, in the readiest way; not to put the power of sight into the soul's eye, which already has it, but to ensure that, instead of looking in the wrong direction, it is turned the way it ought to be.

38   Yes, it may well be so.

39   It looks, then, as though wisdom were different from those ordinary virtues, as they are called, which are not far removed from bodily qualities, in that they can be produced by habituation and exercise in a soul which has not possessed them from the first. Wisdom, it seems is certainly the virtue of some diviner faculty, which never loses its power, though its use for good or harm depends on the direction towards which it is turned. You must have noticed in dishonest men with a reputation for sagacity the shrewd glance of a narrow intelligence piercing the objects to which it is directed. There is nothing wrong with the power of vision, but it has been forced into the service of evil, so that the keener its sight, the more harm it works.

40   Quite true.

41   And yet if the growth of a nature like this had been pruned from earliest childhood, cleared of those clinging overgrowths which come of gluttony and all luxurious pleasure and, like leaden weights charged with affinity to this mortal world, hang upon the soul, bending its vision downwards; if, freed from these, the soul were turned round toward true reality, then this same power in these very men would see the truth as keenly as the objects it is turned to now.

42   Yes, very likely.

43   Is it not also likely, or indeed certain after what has been said, that a state can never be properly governed either by the uneducated who know

nothing of truth or by men who are allowed to spend all their days in the pursuit of culture? The ignorant have no single mark before their eyes at which they must aim in all the conduct of their own lives and of affairs of state; and the others will not engage in action if they can help it, dreaming that, while still alive, they have been translated to the Islands of the Blest.

44   Quite true.

45   It is for us, then, as founders of a commonwealth, to bring compulsion to bear on the noblest natures. They must be made to climb the ascent to the vision of Goodness, which we called the highest object of knowledge; and, when they have looked upon it long enough, they must not be allowed, as they now are, to remain on the heights, refusing to come down again to the prisoners or to take any part in their labours and rewards, however much or little these may be worth.

46   Shall we not be doing them an injustice, if we force on them a worse life than they might have?

47   You have forgotten again, my friend, that the law is not concerned to make any one class especially happy, but to ensure the welfare of the commonwealth as a whole. By persuasion or constraint it will unite the citizens in harmony, making them share whatever benefits each class can contribute to the common good; and its purpose in forming men of that spirit was not that each should be left to go his own way, but that they should be instrumental in binding the community into one.

48   True, I had forgotten.

49   You will see, then, Glaucon, that there will be no real injustice in compelling our philosophers to watch over and care for the other citizens. We can fairly tell them that their compeers in other states may quite reasonably refuse to collaborate: there they have sprung up, like a self-sown plant, in despite of their country's institutions; no one has fostered their growth, and they cannot be expected to show gratitude for a care they have never received. 'But,' we shall say, 'it is not so with you. We have brought you into existence for your country's sake as well as for your own, to be like leaders and king-bees in a hive; you have been better and more thoroughly educated than those others and hence are more capable of playing your part both as men of thought and as men of action. You must go down, then, each in his turn, to live with the rest and let your eyes grow accustomed to the darkness. You will then see a thousand times better than those who live there always; you will recognize every image for what it is and know what it represents, because you have seen justice, beauty, and goodness in their reality; and so you and we shall find life in our commonwealth no mere dream, as it is in most existing states, where men live fighting one another about shadows and quarreling for power, as if that were a great prize; whereas in truth government can be at its best and free from dissension only where the destined rulers are least desirous of holding office.'

50   Quite true.

51   Then will our pupils refuse to listen and to take their turns at sharing in the work of the community, though they may live together for most of their time in a purer air?

52   No; it is a fair demand, and they are fair-minded men. No doubt, unlike any ruler of the present day, they will think of holding power as an unavoidable necessity.

53   Yes, my friend; for the truth is that you can have a well-governed society only if you can discover for your future rulers a better way of life than being in office; then only will power be in the hands of men who are rich, not in gold, but in the wealth that brings happiness, a good and wise life. All goes wrong when, starved for lack of anything good in their own lives, men turn to public affairs hoping to snatch from thence the happiness they hunger for. They set about fighting for power, and this internecine conflict ruins them and their country. The life of true philosophy is the only one that looks down upon offices of state; and access to power must be confined to men who are not in love with it; otherwise rivals will start fighting. So whom else can you compel to undertake the guardianship of the commonwealth, if not those who, besides understanding best the principles of government, enjoy a nobler life than the politician's and look for rewards of a different kind?

54   There is indeed no other choice.

Topical Considerations

1. Plato's parable, written approximately 350 years before the birth of Christ, addresses the idea that people find it difficult to perceive truth. Do you think this parable is relevant today, given all the centuries of "progress" since it was originally written? In other words, do you feel that it is any easier now to perceive the truth than it was when Plato wrote this piece? Explain your answer.

2. Reread the allegory, attempting to assign meaning to the allegorical terms contained therein; the *underground den,* the *light,* the *chains,* the *fire,* and the *shadows.* How do these terms function within the parable?

3. In paragraph 35 Plato defines the allegorical nature of the "sun" as representing the "idea of good" which he equates with that which is reasonable, rational, and intellectual. Discuss the relationship, as you see it, between what you consider to be the highest "good" and Plato's terms. Do you agree that what is most good is that which is most rational? Explain.

4. What is the relationship between ideal images and reality, according to Plato? (See especially paragraph 39.)

5. Reread paragraphs 29–33, examining Plato's view of what happens to people who are able to develop a true idea of reality. How well do they compete with those who have not "seen the light?" Who is usually considered superior? Why? Do you find this a common situation in the present day?

Rhetorical Considerations

1. How does Plato use conversation to develop his argument? What is Glaucon's role in the conversation? Is this conversational or dialectic mode effective in conveying information or making an argument? Why or why not?
2. Plato relies strictly on logic in making his argument, without using any supporting evidence or proof. In light of this, do you find his argument convincing?
3. Plato uses syllogistic reasoning to derive human behavior from his allegory. Trace his line of reasoning in paragraphs 5–14. Can you reduce his argument to a syllogism?

Writing Assignments

1. Write an essay in which you explore the implications of varying perceptions of "truth" in the modern world. You might pick a particular issue in which you think that the truth is veiled or hidden in some way. What would happen if the truth were revealed? Would this revelation make for positive change?

A Modest Proposal
Jonathan Swift

Jonathan Swift (1667–1745) was born and educated in Dublin, Ireland, and was ordained as an Anglican priest. In his early twenties he became involved in current affairs and subsequently established himself as a writer with a talent for scathing political satires. True to his birthright and keen moral sense, Swift was particularly brutal in his protest against the injustices and oppressive poverty Ireland was made to suffer under English rule. Even though he had established himself as a pamphleteer and a poet, Swift is best known for *Gulliver's Travels* (1726), a book that is at once a fine children's fantasy as it is a brilliantly devastating satire of his age.

The following essay is perhaps the most famous example of irony in English. It was originally published under the title, "A Modest Proposal for Preventing the Children of Poor People in Ireland From Being a Burden to Their Parents or Country, and for Making Them Beneficial to the Public." Because it originally appeared as an anonymous pamphlet, many readers were shocked and horrified because they took the proposal at face value. No wonder, given its classic proposal features: the naming of the problem, the supporting facts and statistics, refutation of alternative solutions, the logically arrived at conclusion. Of course, it is a credit to Swift's masterful voice of irony that readers could have been duped into believing so monstrous a recommendation.

BEFORE YOU READ

If you are not aware of the subject matter of this essay, try to second-guess from its original title and other clues given in the introduction what the grand satirist's proposal was for easing the plight of poverty-stricken Ireland.

AS YOU READ

Try to determine when you begin to suspect that Swift is being ironic—that is, where he is no longer being serious in his proposal, that he means just the opposite of what he says. Are there places where Swift drops his satirical stance, where he reveals his true feelings beneath the adopted persona?

1   It is a melancholy object to those who walk through this great town, or travel in the country, when they see the streets, the roads and cabin-doors crowded with beggars of the female sex, followed by three, four, or six children, all in rags, and importuning every passenger for an alms. These mothers, instead of being able to work for their honest livelihood, are forced to employ all their time in strolling, to beg sustenance for their helpless infants, who, as they grow up, either turn thieves for want of work, or leave their dear native country to fight for the Pretender in Spain, or sell themselves to the Barbadoes.

2   I think it is agreed by all parties that this prodigious number of children, in the arms, or on the backs, or at the heels of their mothers, and frequently of their fathers, is in the present deplorable state of the kingdom a very great additional grievance; and therefore whoever could find out a fair, cheap, and easy method of making these children sound and useful members of the commonwealth would deserve so well of the public as to have his statue set up for a preserver of the nation.

3   But my intention is very far from being confined to provide only for the children of professed beggars; it is of a much greater extent, and shall take in the whole number of infants at a certain age who are born of parents in effect as little able to support them as those who demand our charity in the streets.

4   As to my own part, having turned my thoughts for many years upon this important subject, and maturely weighed the several schemes of other projectors, I have always found them grossly mistaken in their computation. It is true a child just dropped from its dam may be supported by her milk for a solar year with little other nourishment, at most not above the value of two shillings, which the mother may certainly get, or the value in scraps, by her lawful occupation of begging, and it is exactly at one year old that I propose to provide for them, in such a manner as, instead of being a charge upon their parents, or the parish, or wanting food and raiment for the rest of their lives, they shall, on the contrary, contribute to the feeding and partly to the clothing of many thousands.

5   There is likewise another great advantage in my scheme, that it will prevent those voluntary abortions, and that horrid practice of women murder-

ing their bastard children, alas, too frequent among us, sacrificing the poor innocent babes, I doubt, more to avoid the expense than the shame, which would move tears and pity in the most savage and inhuman breast.

6　　　　The number of souls in Ireland being usually reckoned one million and a half, of these I calculate there may be about two hundred thousand couples whose wives are breeders, from which number I subtract thirty thousand couples who are able to maintain their own children, although I apprehend there cannot be so many under the present distresses of the kingdom, but this being granted, there will remain an hundred and seventy thousand breeders. I again subtract fifty thousand for those women who miscarry, or whose children die by accident or disease within the year. There only remain an hundred and twenty thousand children of poor parents annually born: the question therefore is, how this number shall be reared, and provided for, which as I have already said, under the present situation of affairs is utterly impossible by all the methods hitherto proposed, for we can neither employ them in handicraft or agriculture; we neither build houses (I mean in the country), nor cultivate land: they can very seldom pick up a livelihood by stealing until they arrive at six years old, except where they are of towardly parts, although I confess they learn the rudiments much earlier, during which time they can however be properly looked upon only as probationers, as I have been informed by a principal gentleman in the County of Cavan, who protested to me that he never knew above one or two instances under the age of six, even in a part of the kingdom so renowned for the quickest proficiency in that art.

7　　　　I am assured by our merchants that a boy or girl before twelve years old, is no saleable commodity, and even when they come to this age, they will not yield above three pounds, or three pounds and half-a-crown at most on the Exchange, which cannot turn to account either to the parents or the kingdom, the charge of nutriment and rags having been at least four times that value.

8　　　　I shall now therefore humbly propose my own thoughts, which I hope will not be liable to the least objection.

9　　　　I have been assured by a very knowing American of my acquaintance in London, that a young healthy child well nursed is at a year old a most delicious, nourishing and wholesome food, whether stewed, roasted, baked, or boiled, and I make no doubt that it will equally serve in a fricassee, or a ragout.

10　　　　I do therefore humbly offer it to public consideration, that of the hundred and twenty thousand children already computed, twenty thousand may be reserved for breed, whereof only one fourth part to be males, which is more than we allow to sheep, black-cattle, or swine, and my reason is that these children are seldom the fruits of marriage, a circumstance not much regarded by our savages, therefore one male will be sufficient to serve four females. That the remaining hundred thousand may at a year old be offered in sale to the persons of quality, and fortune, through the kingdom, always advising the mother to let them suck plentifully in the last month, so as to render them plump, and fat for a good table. A child will make two dishes at an entertainment for friends, and when the family dines alone, the fore or hind quarter will make a reasonable dish, and seasoned with a little pepper or salt will be very good boiled on the fourth day, especially in winter.

11   I have reckoned upon a medium, that a child just born will weigh twelve pounds, and in a solar year if tolerably nursed increaseth to twenty-eight pounds.

12   I grant this food will be somewhat dear, and therefore very proper for landlords who, as they have already devoured most of the parents, seem to have the best title to the children.

13   Infant's flesh will be in season throughout the year, but more plentiful in March, and a little before and after, for we are told by a grave author, an eminent French physician, that fish being a prolific diet, there are more children born in Roman Catholic countries about nine months after Lent than at any other season; therefore reckoning a year after Lent, the markets will be more glutted than usual, because the number of Popish infants is at least three to one in this kingdom, and therefore it will have one other collateral advantage by lessening the number of Papists among us.

14   I have already computed the charge of nursing a beggar's child (in which list I reckon all cottagers, labourers, and four-fifths of the farmers) to be about two shillings *per annum,* rags included, and I believe no gentleman would repine to give ten shillings for the carcass of a good fat child, which, as I have said, will make four dishes of excellent nutritive meat, when he hath only some particular friend of his own family to dine with him. Thus the Squire will learn to be a good landlord and grow popular among his tenants, the mother will have eight shillings net profit, and be fit for work until she produces another child.

15   Those who are more thrifty (as I must confess the times require) may flay the carcass; the skin of which artificially dressed, will make admirable gloves for ladies, and summer boots for fine gentlemen.

16   As to our city of Dublin, shambles may be appointed for this purpose, in the most convenient parts of it, and butchers we may be assured will not be wanting, although I rather recommend buying the children alive, and dressing them hot from the knife, as we do roasting pigs.

17   A very worthy person, a true lover of his country, and whose virtues I highly esteem was lately pleased, in discoursing on this matter to offer a refinement upon my scheme. He said that many gentlemen of this kingdom, having of late destroyed their deer, he conceived that the want of venison might be well supplied by the bodies of young lads and maidens, not exceeding fourteen years of age, nor under twelve, so great a number of both sexes in every county being now ready to starve, for want of work and service; and these to be disposed of by their parents if alive, or otherwise by their nearest relations. But with due deference to so excellent a friend, and so deserving a patriot, I cannot be altogether in his sentiments. For as to the males, my American acquaintance assured me from frequent experience that their flesh was generally tough and lean, like that of our schoolboys, by continual exercise,

and their taste disagreeable, and to fatten them would not answer the charge. Then as to the females, it would, I think with humble submission, be a loss to the public, because they soon would become breeders themselves: and besides, it is not improbable that some scrupulous people might be apt to censure such a practice (although indeed very unjustly) as a little bordering upon cruelty, which I confess, hath always been with me the strongest objection against any project, howsoever well intended.

18   But in order to justify my friend, he confessed that this expedient was put into his head by the famous Psalmanazar, a native of the island Formosa, who came from thence to London, above twenty years ago, and in conversation told my friend that in his country when any young person happened to be put to death, the executioner sold the carcass to persons of quality, as a prime dainty, and that, in his time, the body of a plump girl of fifteen, who was crucified for an attempt to poison the emperor, was sold to his Imperial Majesty's Prime Minister of State, and other great Mandarins of the Court, in joints from the gibbet, at four hundred crowns. Neither indeed can I deny that if the same use were made of several plump young girls in this town who, without one single groat to their fortunes, cannot stir abroad without a chair, and appear at the playhouse and assemblies in foreign fineries, which they never will pay for, the kingdom would not be the worse.

19   Some persons of a desponding spirit are in great concern about that vast number of poor people, who are aged, diseased, or maimed, and I have been desired to employ my thoughts what course may be taken to ease the nation of so grievous an encumbrance. But I am not in the least pain upon that matter, because it is very well known that they are every day dying, and rotting, by cold, and famine, and filth, and vermin, as fast as can be reasonably expected. And as to the younger labourers they are now in almost as hopeful a condition. They cannot get work, and consequently pine away from want of nourishment, to a degree that if at any time they are accidentally hired to common labour, they have not strength to perform it; and thus the country and themselves are in a fair way of being soon delivered from the evils to come.

20   I have too long digressed, and therefore shall return to my subject. I think the advantages by the proposal which I have made are obvious and many, as well as of the highest importance.

21   For first, as I have already observed, it would greatly lessen the number of Papists, with whom we are yearly over-run, being the principal breeders of the nation, as well as our most dangerous enemies, and who stay at home on purpose with a design to deliver the kingdom to the Pretender, hoping to take their advantage by the absence of so many good Protestants, who have chosen rather to leave their country than stay at home and pay tithes against their conscience to an idolatrous Episcopal curate.

22   Secondly, the poorer tenants will have something valuable of their own, which by law may be made liable to distress, and help to pay their landlord's rent, their corn and cattle being already seized, and money a thing unknown.

23   Thirdly, whereas the maintenance of an hundred thousand children, from two years old, and upwards, cannot be computed at less than ten shillings a piece *per annum,* the nation's stock will be thereby increased fifty thousand pounds *per annum,* besides the profit of a new dish, introduced to the tables of all gentlemen of fortune in the kingdom, who have any refinement in taste, and the money will circulate among ourselves, the goods being entirely of our own growth and manufacture.

24   Fourthly, the constant breeders, besides the gain of eight shilling sterling *per annum,* by the sale of their children, will be rid of the charge of maintaining them after the first year.

25   Fifthly, this food would likewise bring great custom to taverns, where the vintners will certainly be so prudent as to procure the best receipts for dressing it to perfection, and consequently have their houses frequented by all the fine gentlemen, who justly value themselves upon their knowledge in good eating; and a skilful cook, who understands how to oblige his guests, will contrive to make it as expensive as they please.

26   Sixthly, this would be a great inducement to marriage, which all wise nations have either encouraged by rewards, or enforced by laws and penalties. It would increase the care and tenderness of mothers towards their children, when they were sure of a settlement for life, to the poor babes, provided in some sort by the public to their annual profit instead of expense. We should soon see an honest emulation among the married women, which of them could bring the fattest child to the market. Men would become as fond of their wives, during the time of their pregnancy, as they are now of their mares in foal, their cows in calf, or sows when they are ready to farrow, nor offer to beat or kick them (as it is too frequent a practice) for fear of a miscarriage.

27   Many other advantages might be enumerated. For instance, the addition of some thousand carcasses in our exportation of barrelled beef; the propagation of swine's flesh, and improvement in the art of making good bacon, so much wanted among us by the great destruction of pigs, too frequent at our tables, are no way comparable in taste or magnificence to a well-grown, fat yearling child, which roasted whole will make a considerable figure at a Lord Mayor's feast, or any other public entertainment. But this and many others I omit, being studious of brevity.

28   Supposing that one thousand families in this city would be constant customers for infants' flesh, besides others who might have it at merry meetings, particularly weddings and christenings; I compute that Dublin would take off annually about twenty thousand carcasses, and the rest of the kingdom (where probably they will be sold somewhat cheaper) the remaining eighty thousand.

29   I can think of no one objection that will possibly be raised against this proposal, unless it should be urged that the number of people will be thereby much lessened in the kingdom. This I freely own, and it was indeed one principal design in offering it to the world. I desire the reader will observe, that I

calculate my remedy *for this one individual Kingdom of* Ireland, *and for no other that ever was, is, or, I think, ever can be upon earth.* Therefore let no man talk to me of other expedients: *Of taxing our absentees at five shillings a pound: Of using neither clothes, nor household furniture except what is of our own growth and manufacture: Of utterly rejecting the materials and instruments that promote foreign luxury: Of curing the expensiveness of pride, vanity, idleness, and gaming in our women: Of introducing a vein of parsimony, prudence, and temperance: Of learning to love our country, wherein we differ even from* Laplanders, *and the inhabitants of* Topinamboo: *Of quitting our animosities and factions, nor act any longer like the* Jews, *who were murdering one another at the very moment their city was taken: Of being a little cautious not to sell our country and consciences for nothing: Of teaching landlords to have at least one degree of mercy towards their tenants.* Lastly, *of putting a spirit of honesty, industry, and skill into our shopkeepers, who, if a resolution could now be taken to buy only our native goods, would immediately unite to cheat and exact upon us in the price, the measure and the goodness, nor could ever yet be brought to make one fair proposal of just dealing, though often and earnestly invited to it.*

30   Therefore I repeat, let no man talk to me of these and the like expedients, till he hath at least a glimpse of hope that there will ever be some hearty and sincere attempt to put them in practice.

31   But as to myself, having been wearied out for many years with offering vain, idle, visionary thoughts, and at length utterly despairing of success, I fortunately fell upon this proposal, which as it is wholly new, so it hath something solid and real, of no expense and little trouble, full in our own power, and whereby we can incur no danger in disobliging England. For this kind of commodity will not bear exportation, the flesh being of too tender a consistence to admit a long continuance in salt, *although perhaps I could name a country which would be glad to eat up our whole nation*

32   *without it.*

        After all I am not so violently bent upon my own opinion as to reject any offer, proposed by wise men, which shall be found equally innocent, cheap, easy and effectual. But before some thing of that kind shall be advanced in contradiction to my scheme, and offering a better, I desire the author, or authors, will be pleased maturely to consider two points. First, as things now stand, how they will be able to find food and raiment for a hundred thousand useless mouths and backs? And secondly, there being a round million of creatures in human figure, throughout this kingdom, whose whole subsistence put into a common stock would leave them in debt two millions of pounds sterling; adding those who are beggars by profession, to the bulk of farmers, cottagers, and laborers with their wives and children, who are beggars in effect; I desire those politicians who dislike my overture, and may perhaps be so bold to attempt an answer, that they will first ask the parents of these mortals whether they would not at this day think it a great happiness to have been sold for food at a year old, in the manner I prescribe, and thereby have avoided such a perpetual scene of misfortunes as they have since gone through, by the oppression of landlords, the impossibility of paying rent without money or trade, the want of common sustenance, with neither house nor clothes to cover them from the inclemencies of weather, and the most inevitable prospect of entailing the like, or greater miseries upon their breed for ever.

33   I profess in the sincerity of my heart that I have not the least personal interest in endeavoring to promote this necessary work, having no other motive than the *public good of my country, by advancing our trade, providing for infants, relieving the poor, and giving some pleasure to the rich.* I have no children by which I can propose to get a single penny; the youngest being nine years old, and my wife past child-bearing.

Topical Considerations

1. Where in Jonathan Swift's proposal do you first begin to doubt that Swift is serious? What makes you suspect that he is writing ironically?
2. Describe the speaker's persona. How does the speaker differ from the author? Where in the proposal does Swift's own voice break through the mask of the speaker?
3. Swift's speaker refers to several authorities throughout the article. Who are these people? What purpose could Swift have for citing them?
4. In paragraph 31 the speaker says, "*I could name a country which would be glad to eat up our whole nation.*" To which country is he referring? In context of the proposal, what does the speaker mean here?
5. Where does the speaker list the real solutions to Ireland's problems? What are they? Had they been adopted at the time that Swift wrote this essay, how might the Irish-Anglo conflicts have been resolved?
6. From what you know, has the relationship between Ireland and England improved since Swift wrote this article? Discuss contemporary incidents in England and Ireland to illustrate your answer.

Rhetorical Considerations

1. Point out several examples of animal imagery that Swift employs throughout his proposal. Why does he describe humans in animalistic terms? What is Swift's purpose in making these comparisons?
2. Describe how Swift structures his proposal according to the classic argumentative form. In which paragraphs does he name his proposition? What are some of the supporting facts and statistics? Where is the refutation of the opposing argument? Where is the logical conclusion?

3. Beginning with the title, describe some of the different uses of irony that Swift makes throughout this essay.

4. In the original edition of Swift's proposal, and in ours as well, most of paragraph 29 is italicized. Why do you suppose Swift did this? How does the purpose of this paragraph differ from the rest of the essay?

5. Why does Swift's speaker give so many statistics to back up his argument? For the purpose of this essay, does it matter if these statistics are true?

6. What does Swift gain by inventing a sincere, self-effacing, serious speaker to put forth these monstrous suggestions? How does the speaker describe himself?

Writing Assignments

1. Do some research on Ireland's present and past economic conditions. In a paper compare Ireland today with Ireland in Swift's day. You could also discuss how the English absentee landowners' treatment of the Irish peasants contributed to the great potato famines of the nineteenth century, as well as today's "troubles" in Northern Ireland.

2. Write a biographical sketch of Jonathan Swift showing how he tried to help the Irish Catholic population even though he was the Dean of St. Patrick's, the Anglican cathedral in Dublin and part of the Church of England. Refer to Swift's many biographies for your sources.

3. Write a letter to a friend who is not a native English speaker, analyzing "A Modest Proposal." Describe Swift's use of satire and irony, and the problems between England and Ireland during Swift's day.

4. Think of a current social problem that has not been dealt with effectively, but which will ultimately cause even greater problems if not attended to. Write a satire that will arouse the public's awareness of that problem. Remember that satire suggests preposterous solutions to a serious issue. Also, to be effective, a satire must maintain a delicate balance between raising the readers' consciousness and alienating them altogether. (Some suggested problems: the rising crime rate, rush-hour traffic jams, disposal of big-city garbage, rising college costs, illegal immigration.)

The Declaration of Independence
Thomas Jefferson

Thomas Jefferson (1743–1826) was a lawyer, architect, scientist, musician, educator, and philosopher. In his impressive political life he served as a member of the Continental Congress (1769–1779), the governor of Virginia (1779–1781), the first Secretary of State (1789–1797), the second vice president (1797–1801), and the third President of the United States (1801–1809). He also founded the University of Virginia in 1809. Of all his extraordinary accomplishments, Jefferson is perhaps best known for writing the Declaration of Independence. While the Continental Congress had delegated that awesome responsibility to a committee of five, it was Jefferson who actually drafted the original document, being the most graceful stylist among them. It took Jefferson just 17 days to complete the task. In that time the document went through several revisions. Some of the changes required by the committee did not please Jefferson—in particular, the deletion of the clause calling for the abolition of slavery. Nonetheless, on July 4, 1776, the Continental Congress accepted the amended Declaration, which is today one of the most important documents in American history and one of the most revolutionary statements in world history.

Even though it underwent committee revisions, the Declaration of Independence reflects Jefferson's belief in the natural rights of the individual, his clarity of style, and his powers of logical argumentation. As a piece of writing, it is a classic example of deductive argumentation. Whereas most of the delegates to the Continental Congress would not have needed persuasion, there were some members who were reluctant to reject British colonial rule, oppressive as it was. In part the document was forged in an effort to persuade these reluctant few.

BEFORE YOU READ

In the second paragraph Jefferson says that each citizen has the "unalienable Rights" of "Life, Liberty and the pursuit of Happiness." What does "unalienable Rights" mean? Do you think that "Life, Liberty and the pursuit of Happiness" are in fact rights? Drawing from events in America today, do you think that Jefferson's goals have been achieved?

AS YOU READ

Jefferson lists his causes for declaring an end to British rule in paragraphs 3–29. Which strike you as most serious? Which are the least serious? Are any in and of themselves cause for a political revolution?

In Congress, July 4, 1776
The Unanimous Declaration of the Thirteen
United States of America

1   When in the Course of human events, it becomes necessary for one people to dissolve the political bands which have connected them with another, and to assume among the Powers of the earth, the separate and equal station to which the Laws of Nature and of Nature's God entitle them, a decent respect to the opinions of mankind requires that they should declare the causes which impel them to the separation.

2   We hold these truths to be self-evident, that all men are created equal, that they are endowed by their Creator with certain unalienable Rights, that among these are Life, Liberty and the pursuit of Happiness. That to secure these rights, Governments are instituted among Men, deriving their just powers from the consent of the governed. That whenever any Form of Government becomes destructive of these ends, it is the Right of the People to alter or to abolish it, and to institute a new Government, laying its foundation on such principles and organizing its powers in such form, as to them shall seem most likely to affect their Safety and Happiness. Prudence, indeed, will dictate that Governments long established should not be changed for light and transient causes; and accordingly all experience hath shown, that mankind are more disposed to suffer, while evils are sufferable, than to right themselves by abolishing the forms to which they are accustomed. But when a long train of abuses and usurpations, pursuing invariably the same Object evinces a design to reduce them under absolute Despotism, it is their right, it is their duty, to throw off such Government, and to provide new Guards for their future security.—Such has been the patient sufferance of these Colonies; and such is now the necessity which constrains them to alter their former Systems of Government. The history of the present King of Great Britain is a history of repeated injuries and usurpations, all having in direct object the establishment of an absolute Tyranny over these States. To prove this, let Facts be submitted to a candid world.

3   He has refused his Assent to Laws, the most wholesome and necessary for the public good.

4   He has forbidden his Governors to pass Laws of immediate and pressing importance, unless suspended in their operation till his Assent should be obtained; and when so suspended, he has utterly neglected to attend to them.

5   He has refused to pass other laws for the accommodation of large districts of people, unless those people would relinquish the right of Representation in the Legislature, a right inestimable to them and formidable to tyrants only.

6   He has called together legislative bodies at places unusual, uncomfortable, and distant from the depository of their Public Records, for the sole purpose of fatiguing them into compliance with his measures.

7   He has dissolved Representative Houses repeatedly, for opposing with manly firmness his invasions on the rights of the people.

8   He has refused for a long time, after such dissolutions, to cause others to be elected; whereby the Legislative Powers, incapable of Annihilation, have returned to the People at large for their exercise; the State remaining in the mean time exposed to all the dangers of invasion from without, and convulsions within.

9   He has endeavoured to prevent the population of these States; for that purpose obstructing the Laws of Naturalization of Foreigners; refusing to pass others to encourage their migration hither, and raising the conditions of new Appropriations of Lands.

10   He has obstructed the Administration of Justice, by refusing his Assent to Laws for establishing Judiciary Powers.

11   He has made Judges dependent on his Will alone, for the tenure of their offices, and the amount and payment of their salaries.

12   He has erected a multitude of New Offices, and sent hither swarms of Officers to harass our People, and eat out their substance.

13   He has kept among us, in times of peace, Standing Armies without the Consent of our legislature.

14   He has affected to render the Military independent of and superior to the Civil Power.

15   He has combined with others to subject us to a jurisdiction foreign to our constitution, and unacknowledged by our laws; giving his Assent to their acts of pretended Legislation:

16   For quartering large bodies of armed troops among us:

17   For protecting them, by a mock Trial, from Punishment for any Murders which they should commit on the Inhabitants of these States:

18   For cutting off our Trade with all parts of the world:

19   For imposing taxes on us without our Consent:

20   For depriving us in many cases, of the benefits of Trial by Jury:

21   For transporting us beyond Seas to be tried for pretended offences:

22   For abolishing the free System of English Laws in a neighbouring Province, establishing therein an Arbitrary government, and enlarging its Boundaries so as to render it at once an example and fit instrument for introducing the same absolute rule into these Colonies:

23   For taking away our Charters, abolishing our most valuable Laws, and altering fundamentally the Forms of our Governments:

24   For suspending our own Legislatures, and declaring themselves invested with Power to legislate for us in all cases whatsoever.

25   He has abdicated Government here, by declaring us out of his Protection and waging War against us.

26   He has plundered our seas, ravaged our Coasts, burnt our towns, and destroyed the lives of our people.

27   He is at this time transporting large armies of foreign mercenaries to compleat the works of death, desolation and tyranny, already begun with circumstances of Cruelty & perfidy scarcely paralleled in the most barbarous ages, and totally unworthy of the Head of a civilized nation.

28   He has constrained our fellow Citizens taken Captive on the High Seas to bear Arms against their Country, to become the executioners of their friends and Brethren, or to fall themselves by their Hands.

29   He has excited domestic insurrections amongst us, and has endeavoured to bring on the inhabitants of our frontiers, the merciless Indian Savages, whose Known rule of welfare, is an undistinguished destruction of all ages, sexes and conditions.

30   In every stage of these Oppressions We have Petitioned for Redress in the most humble terms: Our repeated Petitions have been answered only by

repeated injury. A Prince, whose character is thus marked by every act which may define a Tyrant, is unfit to be the ruler of a free People.

31   Nor have We been wanting in attention to our British brethren. We have warned them from time to time of attempts by their legislature to extend an unwarrantable jurisdiction over us. We have reminded them of the circumstances of our emigration and settlement here. We have appealed to their native justice and magnanimity, and we have conjured them by the ties of our common kindred to disavow these usurpations, which, would inevitably interrupt our connections and correspondence. They too have been deaf to the voice of justice and of consanguinity. We must, therefore, acquiesce in the necessity, which denounces our Separation, and hold them, as we hold the rest of mankind, Enemies in War, in Peace Friends.

32   We, therefore, the Representatives of the united States of America, in General Congress, Assembled, appealing to the Supreme Judge of the world for the rectitude of our intentions, do, in the Name, and by Authority of the good People of these Colonies, solemnly publish and declare, That these United Colonies are, and of Right ought to be Free and Independent States, that they are Absolved from all Allegiance to the British Crown, and that all political connection between them and the State of Great Britain, is and ought to be totally dissolved; and that as Free and Independent States, they have full Power to levy War, conclude Peace, contract Alliances, establish Commerce, and to do all other Acts and Things which Independent States may of right do. And for the support of this Declaration, with a firm reliance on the Protection of Divine Providence, we mutually pledge to each other our Lives, our Fortunes and our sacred Honor.

Topical Considerations

1. In your own words, why was the Declaration of Independence written? What were the stated purposes?
2. What does Jefferson mean in the first paragraph by "the Laws of Nature and of Nature's God"?
3. In making their case Jefferson and the other members of the committee based their appeal both on general principles and factual evidence. Which appeals to principle might still be made today by people wanting to win their independence?
4. What would you say is Jefferson's view of the relationship between government and the people? (See paragraph 2.)
5. The Declaration of Independence was written over 200 years ago. What are the unwritten assumptions its drafters make about gender and race? Could they be accused of sexism and racism?
6. Although Thomas Jefferson was opposed to slavery, he, like other drafters of the Declaration of Independence, owned slaves. Does this fact undermine

the validity of the document? Why do you suppose the anti-slavery passages were removed?

Rhetorical Considerations

1. The Declaration of Independence is a prime example of a deductive argument. Trace the deductive line of reasoning in the document. Try to reduce the logical structure to a syllogism with a clearly stated major premise, minor premise, and conclusion. Is the conclusion valid given the premises? Are the warrants underlying the major premise as convincing as the inductive evidence supporting the minor premise?
2. As we've said all along in this book, any good argument should anticipate objections. What objections, if any, did Jefferson anticipate in the Declaration of Independence?
3. If you were a supporter of King George III, how might you have reacted to the Declaration of Independence?
4. The Declaration of Independence was intended for various audiences. Which parts might have been addressed to reluctant loyalists? Which to the colonists eager for revolution? Which to the King of England? Which to the people of England? Which to the world at large? In other words, explain how the document was written with several audiences in mind.
5. Find examples of parallel structure. What repeated expressions help maintain that structure?
6. Consider the tone of the Declaration of Independence. What particular word choices create this tone? How might Jefferson have worded the document had he intended to use it solely to arouse people's enthusiasm for going to war against England?

Writing Assignments

1. After reviewing Jefferson's conception of government, try to formulate your own feelings about the function of government. Write a paper discussing the principles you think should guide the relationship between government and its people.
2. According to the Declaration of Independence, under what conditions do people have the right to abolish a government? Can you think of any groups in the world today who would be justified in abrogating their government under the principles outlined in the Declaration? Discuss your answer in a paper.
3. Paragraph 2 explicitly states that the Declaration will "prove" that the British government committed acts intended to establish "absolute tyranny" over the American colonies. Write a brief paper in which you argue that the given evidence proves or fails to prove the stated claim.

4. Write a declaration of your own, using this document as a model (as did Elizabeth Cady Stanton in her "Declaration of Sentiments and Resolutions" later in this chapter). You may wish to argue, for instance, that people who are terminally ill should be allowed to die with dignity, or that performing animals at Sea World should be set free, or that the national drinking age should be lowered to 18.

5. Write a rebuttal from King George III of England to Thomas Jefferson. You may want to point out flaws in Jefferson's reasoning, unconvincing evidence, or other reasons why it would not be a good idea for the colonies to begin a revolution.

Civil Disobedience
Henry David Thoreau

Henry David Thoreau (1817–1862) is one of the most important figures of literature and intellectual history in America. He was a philosopher, essayist, naturalist, and poet. His most famous work is *Walden* (1854), the classic meditation on Thoreau's two years of solitary cabin life on Walden Pond in Concord, Massachusetts. Deeply drawn to the natural world, Thoreau lamented America's obsession with materialism, technology, and nationalism. He was also a political activist who ardently opposed slavery. His famous speech "A Plea for Captain John Brown," now a classic piece of principled thinking, called on the government to spare the life of a man who led other abolitionists to storm a federal arsenal with the intention of arming the slaves for an uprising.

Originally published as "On the Duty of Civil Disobedience," this essay is an eloquent defense of Thoreau's refusal to pay his Massachusetts poll tax in protest of the Mexican War and of slavery. Central to this classic document is the argument that the individual is duty bound to oppose laws that violate higher natural and moral laws. It was such moral idealism that would later inspire two of this century's greatest advocates of nonviolent civil disobedience in the cause of human rights: Mahatma Gandhi and Martin Luther King, Jr.

BEFORE YOU READ

Thoreau believed individuals possess a high moral sense that transcends the limits of experience. Do you agree? Can an individual's moral conscience justify civil disobedience? Under what circumstances? How might such civil disobedience be wrong and dangerous?

AS YOU READ

Try to evaluate Thoreau's strategies of persuasion. Does he try to win over his audience primarily through logical appeals, emotional appeals, or ethical/moral appeals? Note an example of each, if possible.

1   I heartily accept the motto.—"That government is best which governs least"; and I should like to see it acted up to more rapidly and systematically. Carried out, it finally amounts to this, which I also believe,—"That government is best which governs not at all"; and when men are prepared for it, that will be the kind of government which they will have. Government is at best but an expedient; but most governments are usually, and all governments are sometimes, inexpedient. The objections which have been brought against a standing army, and they are many and weighty, and deserve to prevail, may also at last be brought against a standing government. The standing army is only an arm of the standing government. The government itself, which is only the mode which the people have chosen to execute their will, is equally liable to be abused and perverted before the people can act through it. Witness the present Mexican war, the work of comparatively a few individuals using the standing government as their tool; for, in the outset, the people would not have consented to this measure.

2   This American government,—what is it but a tradition, though a recent one, endeavoring to transmit itself unimpaired to posterity, but each instant losing some of its integrity? It has not the vitality and force of a single living man; for a single man can bend it to his will. It is a sort of wooden gun to the people themselves. But it is not the less necessary for this; for the people must have some complicated machinery or other, and hear its din, to satisfy that idea of government which they have. Governments show thus how successfully men can be imposed on, even impose on themselves, for their own advantage. It is excellent, we must all allow. Yet this government never of itself furthered any enterprise, but by the alacrity with which it got out of its way. *It* does not keep the country free. *It* does not settle the West. *It* does not educate. The character inherent in the American people has done all that has been accomplished; and it would have done somewhat more, if the government had not sometimes got in its way. For government is an expedient by which men would fain succeed in letting one another alone; and, as has been said, when it is most expedient, the governed are most let alone by it. Trade and commerce, if they were not made of India-rubber, would never manage to bounce over the obstacles which legislators are continually putting in their way; and, if one were to judge these men wholly by the effects of their actions and not partly by their intentions, they would deserve to be classed and punished with those mischievous persons who put obstructions on railroads.

3   But, to speak practically and as a citizen, unlike those who call themselves no-government men, I ask for, not at once no government, but *at once* a better government. Let every man make known what kind of government would command his respect, and that will be one step toward obtaining it.

4   After all, the practical reason why, when the power is once in the hands of the people, a majority are permitted, and for a long period continue, to rule, is not because they are most likely to be in the right, nor because this seems fairest to the minority, but because they are physically the strongest. But a government in which the majority rule in all cases cannot be

based on justice, even as far as men understand it. Can there not be a government in which majorities do not virtually decide right and wrong, but conscience?—in which majorities decide only those questions to which the rule of expediency is applicable? Must the citizen ever for a moment, or in the least degree, resign his conscience to the legislator? Why has every man a conscience, then? I think that we should be men first, and subjects afterward. It is not desirable to cultivate a respect for the law, so much as for the right. The only obligation which I have the right to assume, is to do at any time what I think right. It is truly enough said, that a corporation has no conscience; but a corporation of conscientious men is a corporation *with* a conscience. Law never made men a whit more just; and, by means of their respect for it, even the well-disposed are daily made the agents of injustice. A common and natural result of an undue respect for law is, that you may see a file of soldiers, colonel, captain, corporal, privates, powder-monkeys, and all, marching in admirable order over hill and dale to the wars, against their wills, ay, against their common sense and consciences, which makes it very steep marching indeed, and produces a palpitation of the heart. They have no doubt that it is a damnable business in which they are concerned; they are all peaceably inclined. Now, what are they? Men at all? or small movable forts and magazines, at the service of some unscrupulous man in power? Visit the Navy-Yard, and behold a marine, such a man as an American government can make, or such as it can make a man with its black arts,—a mere shadow and reminiscence of humanity, a man laid out alive and standing, and already, as one may say, buried under arms with funeral accompaniments, though it may be,—

> Not a drum was heard, not a funeral note,
> As his corse to the rampart we hurried;
> Not a soldier discharged his farewell shot
> O'er the grave where our hero we buried.

5   The mass of men serve the state thus, not as men mainly, but as machines, with their bodies. They are the standing army, and the militia, jailers, constables, posse comitatus, &c. In most cases there is no free exercise whatever of the judgment or of the moral sense; but they put themselves on a level with wood and earth and stones; and wooden men can perhaps be manufactured that will serve the purpose as well. Such command no more respect than men of straw or a lump of dirt. They have the same sort of worth only as horses and dogs. Yet such as these even are commonly esteemed good citizens. Others,—as most legislators, politicians, lawyers, ministers, and office-holders,—serve the state chiefly with their heads; and, as they rarely make any moral distinctions, they are as likely to serve the Devil, without *intending* it, as God. A very few, as heroes, patriots, martyrs, reformers in the great sense, and *men*, serve the state with their consciences also, and so necessarily resist it for the most part; and they are commonly treated as enemies by it. A wise man will

only be useful as a man, and will not submit to be "clay," and "stop a hole to keep the wind away," but leave that office to his dust at least:—

> I am too high-born to be propertied,
> To be a secondary at control,
> Or useful serving-man and instrument
> To any sovereign state throughout the world.

6　　He who gives himself entirely to his fellow-men appears to them useless and selfish; but he who gives himself partially to them is pronounced a benefactor and philanthropist.

7　　How does it become a man to behave toward this American government today? I answer, that he cannot without disgrace be associated with it. I cannot for an instant recognize that political organization as *my* government which is the *slave's* government also.

8　　All men recognize the right of revolution; that is, the right to refuse allegiance to, and to resist, the government, when its tyranny or its inefficiency are great and unendurable. But almost all say that such is not the case now. But such was the case, they think, in the Revolution of '75. If one were to tell me that this was a bad government because it taxed certain foreign commodities brought to its ports, it is most probable that I should not make an ado about it, for I can do without them. All machines have their friction; and possibly this does enough good to counterbalance the evil. At any rate, it is a great evil to make a stir about it. But when the friction comes to have its machine, and oppression and robbery are organized, I say, let us not have such a machine any longer. In other words, when a sixth of the population of a nation which has undertaken to be the refuge of liberty are slaves, and a whole country is unjustly overrun and conquered by a foreign army, and subjected to military law, I think that it is not too soon for honest men to rebel and revolutionize. What makes this duty the more urgent is the fact, that the country so overrun is not our own, but ours is the invading army.

9　　Paley, a common authority with many on moral questions, in his chapter on the "Duty of Submission to Civil Government," resolves all civil obligation into expediency; and he proceeds to say, "that so long as the interest of the whole society requires it, that is, so long as the established government cannot be resisted or changed without public inconveniency, it is the will of God that the established government be obeyed, and no longer. . . . This principle being admitted, the justice of every particular case of resistance is reduced to a computation of the quantity of the danger and grievance on the one side, and of the probability and expense of redressing it on the other." Of this, he says, every man shall judge for himself. But Paley appears never to have contemplated those cases to which the rule of expediency does not apply, in which a people, as well as an individual, must do justice, cost what it may. If I have unjustly wrested a plank from a drowning man, I must restore it to him though I drown myself. This, according to Paley, would be inconvenient. But he that would save his life, in such a case, shall lose it. This people must cease to hold slaves, and to make war on Mexico, though it cost them their existence as a people.

10   In their practice, nations agree with Paley; but does any one think that Massachusetts does exactly what is right at the present crisis?

> A drab of state, a cloth-'o-silver slut,
> To have her train borne up, and her soul trail in the dirt.

Practically speaking, the opponents to a reform in Massachusetts are not a hundred thousand politicians at the South, but a hundred thousand merchants and farmers here, who are more interested in commerce and agriculture than they are in humanity, and are not prepared to do justice to the slave and to Mexico, *cost what it may*. I quarrel not with far-off foes, but with those who, near at home, co-operate with, and do the bidding of, those far away, and without whom the latter would be harmless. We are accustomed to say, that the mass of men are unprepared; but improvement is slow, because the few are not materially wiser or better than the many. It is not so important that many should be as good as you, as that there be some absolute goodness somewhere; for that will leaven the whole lump. There are thousands who are *in opinion* opposed to slavery and to the war, who yet in effect do nothing to put an end to them; who, esteeming themselves children of Washington and Franklin, sit down with their hands in their pockets, and say that they know not what to do, and do nothing; who even postpone the question of freedom to the question of free-trade, and quietly read the prices-current along with the latest advices from Mexico, after dinner, and, it may be, fall asleep over them both. What is the price-current of an honest man and a patriot today? They hesitate, and they regret, and sometimes they petition; but they do nothing in earnest and with effect. They will wait, well disposed, for others to remedy the evil, that they may no longer have it to regret. At most, they give only a cheap vote, and a feeble countenance and God-speed, to the right, as it goes by them. There are nine hundred and ninety-nine patrons of virtue to one virtuous man. But it is easier to deal with the real possessor of a thing than with the temporary guardian of it.

11   All voting is a sort of gaming, like checkers or backgammon, with a slight moral tinge to it, a playing with right and wrong, with moral questions; and betting naturally accompanies it. The character of the voters is not staked. I cast my vote, perchance, as I think right; but I am not vitally concerned that that right should prevail. I am willing to leave it to the majority. Its obligation, therefore, never exceeds that of expediency. Even voting *for the right* is *doing* nothing for it. It is only expressing to men feebly your desire that it should prevail. A wise man will not leave the right to the mercy of chance, nor wish it to prevail through the power of the majority. There is but little virtue in the action of masses of men. When the majority shall at length vote for the abolition of slavery, it will be because they are indifferent to slavery, or because there is but little slavery left to be abolished by their vote. *They* will then be the only slaves. Only *his* vote can hasten the abolition of slavery who asserts his own freedom by his vote.

12   I hear of a convention to be held at Baltimore, or elsewhere, for the selection of a candidate for the Presidency, made up chiefly of editors, and men who are politicians by profession; but I think, what is it to any independent, intelligent, and respectable man what decision they may come to? Shall we not have the advantage of his wisdom and honesty, nevertheless? Can we not count upon some independent votes? Are there not many individuals in the country who do not attend conventions? But no: I find that the respectable man, so called, has immediately drifted from his position, and despairs of his country, when his country has more reason to despair of him. He forthwith adopts one of the candidates thus selected as the only *available* one, thus proving that he is himself *available* for any purposes of the demagogue. His vote is of no more worth than that of any unprincipled foreigner or hireling native, who may have been bought. O for a man who is a *man,* and, as my neighbor says, has a bone in his back which you cannot pass your hand through! Our statistics are at fault: the population has been returned too large. How many *men* are there to a square thousand miles in this country? Hardly one. Does not America offer any inducement for men to settle here? The American has dwindled into an Odd Fellow,—one who may be known by the development of his organ of gregariousness, and a manifest lack of intellect and cheerful self-reliance; whose first and chief concern, on coming into the world, is to see that the Almshouses are in good repair; and, before yet he has lawfully donned the virile garb, to collect a fund for the support of the widows and orphans that may be; who, in short, ventures to live only by the aid of the Mutual Insurance company, which has promised to bury him decently.

13   It is not a man's duty, as a matter of course, to devote himself to the eradication of any, even the most enormous wrong; he may still properly have other concerns to engage him; but it is his duty, at least, to wash his hands of it, and, if he gives it no thought longer, not to give it practically his support. If I devote myself to other pursuits and contemplations, I must first see, at least, that I do not pursue them sitting upon another man's shoulders. I must get off him first, that he may pursue his contemplations too. See what gross inconsistency is tolerated. I have heard some of my townsmen say, "I should like to have them order me out to help put down an insurrection of the slaves, or to march to Mexico;—see if I would go;" and yet these very men have each, directly by their allegiance, and so indirectly, at least, by their money, furnished a substitute. The soldier is applauded who refuses to serve in an unjust war by those who do not refuse to sustain the unjust government which makes the war; is applauded by those whose own act and authority he disregards and sets at naught; as if the state were penitent to that degree that it hired one to scourge it while it sinned, but not to that degree that it left off sinning for a moment. Thus, under the name of Order and Civil Government, we are all made at last to pay homage to and support our own meanness. After the first blush of sin comes its indifference; and from immoral it becomes, as it were, *un*moral, and not quite unnecessary to that life which we have made.

14   The broadest and most prevalent error requires the most disinterested virtue to sustain it. The slight reproach to which the virtue of patriotism is commonly liable, the noble are most likely to incur. Those who, while they disapprove

of the character and measures of a government, yield to it their allegiance and support are undoubtedly its most conscientious supporters, and so frequently the most serious obstacles to reform. Some are petitioning the state to dissolve the Union, to disregard the requisitions of the President. Why do they not dissolve it themselves,—the union between themselves and the state,—and refuse to pay their quota into its treasury? Do not they stand in the same relation to the state that the state does to the Union? And have not the same reasons prevented the state from resisting the Union which have prevented them from resisting the state?

15 How can a man be satisfied to entertain an opinion merely, and enjoy *it?* Is there any enjoyment in it, if his opinion is that he is aggrieved? If you are cheated out of a single dollar by your neighbor, you do not rest satisfied with knowing that you are cheated, or with saying that you are cheated, or even with petitioning him to pay you your due; but you take effectual steps at once to obtain the full amount, and see that you are never cheated again. Action from principle, the perception and the performance of right, changes things and relations; it is essentially revolutionary, and does not consist wholly with anything which was. It not only divides states and churches, it divides families; ay, it divides the *individual,* separating the diabolical in him from the divine.

16 Unjust laws exist: shall we be content to obey them, or shall we endeavor to amend them, and obey them until we have succeeded, or shall we transgress them at once? Men generally, under such a government as this, think that they ought to wait until they have persuaded the majority to alter them. They think that, if they should resist the remedy would be worse than the evil. But it is the fault of the government itself that the remedy *is* worse than the evil. *It* makes it worse. Why is it not more apt to anticipate and provide for reform? Why does it not cherish its wise minority? Why does it cry and resist before it is hurt? Why does it not encourage its citizens to be on the alert to point out its faults, and *do* better than it would have them? Why does it always crucify Christ, and excommunicate Copernicus and Luther, and pronounce Washington and Franklin rebels?

17 One would think, that a deliberate and practical denial of its authority was the only offense never contemplated by government; else, why has it not assigned its definite, its suitable and proportionate penalty? If a man who has no property refuses but once to earn nine shillings for the state, he is put in prison for a period unlimited by any law that I know, and determined only by the discretion of those who placed him there; but if he should steal ninety times nine shillings from the state, he is soon permitted to go at large again.

18 If the injustice is part of the necessary friction of the machine of government, let it go, let it go: perchance it will wear smooth,—certainly the machine will wear out. If the injustice has a spring, or a pulley, or a rope, or a crank, exclusively for itself, then perhaps you may consider whether the remedy will not be worse than the evil; but if it is of such a nature that it requires you to be the agent of injustice to another, then, I say break the law. Let your life be a counter friction to stop the machine. What I have to do is to see, at any rate, that I do not lend myself to the wrong which I condemn.

19   As for adopting the ways which the State has provided for remedying the evil, I know not of such ways. They take too much time, and a man's life will be gone. I have other affairs to attend to. I came into this world, not chiefly to make this a good place to live in, but to live in it, be it good or bad. A man has not everything to do, but something; and because he cannot do *everything,* it is not necessary that he should do *something* wrong. It is not my business to be petitioning the Governor or the Legislature any more than it is theirs to petition me, and, if they should not hear my petition, what should I do then? But in this case the State has provided no way: Its very Constitution is the evil. This may seem to be harsh and stubborn and unconciliatory; but it is to treat with the utmost kindness and consideration the only spirit that can appreciate or deserves it. So is all change for the better, like birth and death, which convulse the body.

20   I do not hesitate to say, that those who call themselves Abolitionists should at once effectually withdraw their support, both in person and property, from the government of Massachusetts, and not wait till they constitute a majority of one, before they suffer the right to prevail through them. I think that it is enough if they have God on their side, without waiting for that other one. Moreover, any man more right than his neighbors constitutes a majority of one already.

21   I meet this American government, or its representative, the State government, directly, and face to face, once a year—no more—in the person of its tax-gatherer; this is the only mode in which a man situated as I am necessarily meets it; and it then says distinctly, Recognize me; and the simplest, the most effectual, and, in the present posture of affairs, the indispensablest mode of treating with it on this head, of expressing your little satisfaction with and love for it, is to deny it then. My civil neighbor, the tax-gatherer, is the very man I have to deal with,—for it is, after all, with men and not with parchment that I quarrel,—and he has voluntarily chosen to be an agent of the government. How shall he ever know well what he is and does as an officer of the government, or as a man, until he is obliged to consider whether he shall treat me, his neighbor, for whom he has respect, as a neighbor and well-disposed man, or as a maniac and disturber of the peace, and see if can get over this obstruction to his neighborliness without a ruder and more impetuous thought or speech corresponding with his action. I know this well, that if one thousand, if one hundred, if ten men whom I could name,—if ten *honest* men only,—ay, if *one* HONEST man, in this State of Massachusetts, *ceasing to hold slaves,* were actually to withdraw from this copartnership, and be locked up in the county jail therefor, it would be the abolition of slavery in America. For it matters not how small the beginning may seem to be: What is once well done is done forever. But we love better to talk about it; That we say is our mission. Reform keeps many scores of newspapers in its service, but not one man. If my esteemed neighbor, the State's ambassador, who will devote his days to the settlement of the question of human rights in the Council Chamber, instead of being threatened with the prisons of Carolina, were to sit down the prisoner of Massachu-

setts, that State which is so anxious to foist the sin of slavery upon her sister,—though at present she can discover only an act of inhospitality to be the ground of a quarrel with her,—the Legislature would not wholly waive the subject the following winter.

22   Under a government which imprisons any unjustly, the true place for a just man is also a prison. The proper place today, the only place which Massachusetts has provided for her freer and less desponding spirits, is in her prisons, to be put out and locked out of the State by her own act, as they have already put themselves out by their principles. It is there that the fugitive slave, and the Mexican prisoner on parole, and the Indian come to plead the wrongs of his race, should find them; on that separate, but more free and honorable ground, where the State places those who are not *with* her, but *against* her—the only house in a slave State in which a free man can abide with honor. If any think that their influence would be lost there, and their voices no longer afflict the ear of the State, that they would not be as an enemy within its walls, they do not know by how much truth is stronger than error, nor how much more eloquently and effectively he can combat injustice who has experienced a little in his own person. Cast your whole vote, not a strip of paper merely, but your whole influence. A minority is powerless while it conforms to the majority; it is not even a minority then; but it is irresistible when it clogs by its whole weight. If the alternative is to keep all just men in prison, or give up war and slavery, the State will not hesitate which to choose. If a thousand men were not to pay their tax-bills this year, that would not be a violent and bloody measure, as it would be to pay them, and enable the State to commit violence and shed innocent blood. This is, in fact, the definition of a peaceable revolution, if any such is possible. If the tax-gatherer, or any other public officer, asks me, as one has done, "But what shall I do?" my answer is, "If you really wish to do anything, resign your office." When the subject has refused allegiance, and the officer has resigned his office, then the revolution is accomplished. But even suppose blood should flow. Is there not a sort of blood shed when the conscience is wounded? Through this wound a man's real manhood and immortality flow out, and he bleeds to an everlasting death. I see this blood flowing now.

23   I have contemplated the imprisonment of the offender, rather than the seizure of his goods,—though both will serve the same purpose,—because they who assert the purest right, and consequently are most dangerous to a corrupt State, commonly have not spent much time in accumulating property. To such the State renders comparatively small service, and a slight tax is wont to appear exorbitant, particularly if they are obliged to earn it by special labor with their hands. If there were one who lived wholly without the use of money, the State itself would hesitate to demand it of him. But the rich man,—not to make any invidious comparison,—is always sold to the institution which makes him rich. Absolutely speaking, the more money, the less virtue; for money comes between a man and his objects, and obtains them for him; and it was certainly no great virtue to obtain it. It puts to rest many questions

which he would otherwise be taxed to answer; while the only new question which it puts is the hard but superfluous one, how to spend it. Thus his moral ground is taken from under his feet. The opportunities of living are diminished in proportion as what are called the "means" are increased. The best thing a man can do for his culture when he is rich is to endeavor to carry out those schemes which he entertained when he was poor. Christ answered the Herodians according to their condition. "Show me the tribute-money," said he;— and one took a penny out of his pocket;—if you use money which has the image of Cæsar on it, and which he has made current and valuable, that is, *if you are men of the State,* and gladly enjoy the advantages of Cæsar's government, then pay him back some of his own when he demands it; "Render therefore to Cæsar that which is Cæsar's, and to God those things which are God's,"— leaving them no wiser than before as to which was which; for they did not wish to know.

24   When I converse with the freest of my neighbors, I perceive that, whatever they may say about the magnitude and seriousness of the question, and their regard for the public tranquility, the long and the short of the matter is, that they cannot spare the protection of the existing government, and they dread the consequences to their property and families of disobedience to it. For my own part, I should not like to think that I ever rely on the protection of the State. But, if I deny the authority of the State when it presents its tax-bill, it will soon take and waste all my property, and so harass me and my children without end. This is hard. This makes it impossible for a man to live honestly, and at the same time comfortably, in outward respects. It will not be worth the while to accumulate property; that would be sure to go again. You must hire or squat somewhere, and raise but a small crop, and eat that soon. You must live within yourself, and depend upon yourself always tucked up and ready for a start, and not have many affairs. A man may grow rich in Turkey even, if he will be in all respects a good subject of the Turkish government. Confucius said: "If a state is governed by the principles of reason, poverty and misery are subjects of shame; if a state is not governed by the principles of reason, riches and honors are the subjects of shame." No: Until I want the protection of Massachusetts to be extended to me in some distant Southern port, where my liberty is endangered, or until I am bent solely on building up an estate at home by peaceful enterprise, I can afford to refuse allegiance to Massachusetts, and her right to my property and life. It costs me less in every sense to incur the penalty of disobedience to the State, than it would to obey. I should feel as if I were worth less in that case.

25   Some years ago, the State met me in behalf of the Church, and commanded me to pay a certain sum toward the support of a clergyman whose preaching my father attended, but never I myself, "Pay," it said, "or be locked up in the jail." I declined to pay. But, unfortunately, another man saw fit to pay it. I did not see why the schoolmaster should be taxed to support the priest, and not the priest the schoolmaster; for I was not the State's schoolmaster, but I supported myself by voluntary subscription. I did not see why the lyceum

should not present its tax-bill, and have the State to back its demand, as well as the Church. However, at the request of the selectmen, I condescended to make some such statement as this in writing:—"Know all men by these presents, that I, Henry Thoreau, do not wish to be regarded as a member of any incorporated society which I have not joined." This I gave to the town clerk; and he has it. The State, having thus learned that I did not wish to be regarded as a member of that church, has never made a like demand on me since; though it said that it must adhere to its original presumption that time. If I had known how to name them, I should then have signed off in detail from all the societies which I never signed on to; but I did not know where to find a complete list.

26　　　I have paid no poll-tax for six years. I was put into jail once on this account, for one night; and, as I stood considering the walls of solid stone, two or three feet thick, the door of wood and iron, a foot thick and the iron grating which strained the light, I could not help being struck with the foolishness of that institution which treated me as if I were mere flesh and blood and bones, to be locked up. I wondered that it should have concluded at length that this was the best use it could put me to, and had never thought to avail itself of my services in some way. I saw that, if there was a wall of stone between me and my townsmen, there was a still more difficult one to climb or break through, before they could get to be as free as I was. I did not for a moment feel confined, and the walls seemed a great waste of stone and mortar. I felt as if I alone of all my townsmen had paid my tax. They plainly did not know how to treat me, but behaved like persons who are underbred. In every threat and in every compliment there was a blunder; for they thought that my chief desire was to stand the other side of that stone wall. I could not but smile to see how industriously they locked the door on my meditations, which followed them out again without let or hindrance, and *they* were really all that was dangerous. As they could not reach me, they had resolved to punish my body; just as boys, if they cannot come at some person against whom they have a spite, will abuse his dog. I saw that the State was half-witted, that it was timid as a lone woman with all her silver spoons, and that it did not know its friends from its foes, and I lost all my remaining respect for it, and pitied it.

27　　　Thus the State never intentionally confronts a man's sense, intellectual or moral, but only his body, his senses. It is not armed with superior wit or honesty, but with superior physical strength. I was not born to be forced. I will breathe after my own fashion. Let us see who is the strongest. What force has a multitude? They only can force me to obey a higher law than I. They force me to become like themselves. I do not hear of *men* being *forced* to live this way or that by masses of men. What sort of life were that to live? When I meet a government which says to me, "Your money or your life," why should I be in haste to give it my money? It may be in a great strait, and not know what to do: I cannot help that. It must help itself; do as I do. It is not worth the while to snivel about it. I am not responsible for the successful working of the machinery of society. I am not the son of the engineer. I perceive that, when an acorn and a chestnut fall side by side, the one does not remain inert to make way for the other, but both obey their own laws, and spring and grow and flourish as best they can, till one, perchance, overshadows and destroys the other. If a plant cannot live according to its nature, it dies; and so a man.

28   The night in prison was novel and interesting enough. The prisoners in their shirt-sleeves were enjoying a chat and the evening air in the doorway, when I entered. But the jailer said, "Come, boys, it is time to lock up"; and so they dispersed, and I heard the sound of their steps returning into the hollow apartments. My roommate was introduced to me by the jailer, as "a first-rate fellow and a clever man." When the door was locked, he showed me where to hang my hat, and how he managed matters there. The rooms were white-washed once a month; and this one, at least, was the whitest, most simply fur-nished, and probably the neatest apartment in town. He naturally wanted to know where I came from, and what brought me there; and, when I had told him, I asked him in my turn how he came there, presuming him to be an hon-est man, of course; and, as the world goes, I believe he was. "Why," said he, "they accuse me of burning a barn; but I never did it." As near as I could dis-cover, he had probably gone to bed in a barn when drunk, and smoked his pipe there; and so a barn was burnt. He had the reputation of being a clever man, had been there some three months waiting for his trial to come on, and would have to wait as much longer; but he was quite domesticated and con-tented, since he got his board for nothing, and thought that he was well-treated.

29   He occupied one window, and I the other; and I saw, that, if one stayed there long, his principal business would be to look out the window. I had soon read all the tracts that were left there, and examined where former prisoners had broken out, and where a grate had been sawed off, and heard the history of the various occupants of that room; for I found that even here there was a history and a gossip which never circulated beyond the walls of the jail. Prob-ably this is the only house in the town where verses are composed, which are afterward printed in a circular form, but not published. I was shown quite a long list of verses which were composed by some young men who had been detected in an attempt to escape, who avenged themselves by singing them.

30   I pumped my fellow-prisoner as dry as I could, for fear I should never see him again; but at length he showed me which was my bed, and left me to blow out the lamp.

31   It was like travelling into a far country, such as I had never expected to behold, to lie there for one night. It seemed to me that I never had heard the town-clock strike before, nor the evening sounds of the village; for we slept with the windows open, which were inside the grating. It was to see my native village in the light of the Middle Ages, and our Concord was turned into a Rhine stream, and visions of knights and castles passed before me. They were the voices of old burghers that I heard in the streets. I was an involuntary spec-tator and auditor of whatever was done and said in the kitchen of the adjacent

village-inn,—a wholly new and rare experience to me. It was a closer view of my native town. I was fairly inside of it. I never had seen its institutions before. This is one of its peculiar institutions; for it is a shire town. I began to comprehend what its inhabitants were about.

32 In the morning, our breakfasts were put through the hole in the door, in small oblong-square tin pans, made to fit, and holding a pint of chocolate, with brown bread, and an iron spoon. When they called for the vessels again, I was green enough to return what bread I had left; but my comrade seized it, and said that I should lay that up for lunch or dinner. Soon after he was let out to work at haying in a neighboring field, whither he went every day, and would not be back till noon; so he bade me good-day, saying that he doubted if he should see me again.

33 When I came out of prison,—for some one interfered, and paid that tax,—I did not perceive that great changes had taken place on the common, such as he observed who went in a youth, and emerged a tottering and gray-headed man; and yet a change had to my eyes come over the scene,—the town, and State, and country,—greater than any mere time could effect. I saw yet more distinctly the State in which I lived. I saw to what extent the people among whom I lived could be trusted as good neighbors and friends; that their friendship was for summer weather only; that they did not greatly propose to do right; that they were a distinct race from me by their prejudices and superstitions, as the Chinamen and Malays are; that, in their sacrifices to humanity, they ran no risks, not even to their property; that, after all, they were not so noble but they treated the thief as he had treated them, and hoped, by a certain outward observance and a few prayers, and by walking in a particular straight though useless path from time to time, to save their souls. This may be to judge my neighbors harshly; for I believe that many of them are not aware that they have such an institution as the jail in their village.

34 It was formerly the custom in our village, when a poor debtor came out of jail, for his acquaintances to salute him, looking through their fingers, which were crossed to represent the grating of a jail window, "How do ye do?" My neighbors did not thus salute me, but first looked at me, and then at one another, as if I had returned from a long journey. I was put into jail as I was going to the shoemaker's to get a shoe which was mended. When I was let out the next morning, I proceeded to finish my errand, and having put on my mended shoe, joined a huckleberry party, who were impatient to put themselves under my conduct; and in half an hour,—for the horse was soon tackled,—was in the midst of a huckleberry field, on one of our highest hills, two miles off, and then the State was nowhere to be seen.

35 This is the whole history of "My Prisons."

36 I have never declined paying the highway tax, because I am as desirous of being a good neighbor as I am of being a bad subject; and, as for supporting schools, I am doing my part to educate my fellow-countrymen now. It is for no

particular item in the tax-bill that I refuse to pay it. I simply wish to refuse allegiance to the State, to withdraw and stand aloof from it effectually. I do not care to trace the course of my dollar, if I could, till it buys a man or a musket to shoot one with,—the dollar is innocent,—but I am concerned to trace the effects of my allegiance. In fact, I quietly declare war with the State, after my fashion, though I will still make what use and get what advantage of her I can, as is usual in such cases.

37   If others pay the tax which is demanded of me, from a sympathy with the State, they do but what they have already done in their own case, or rather they abet injustice to a greater extent than the State requires. If they pay the tax from a mistaken interest in the individual taxed, to save his property, or prevent his going to jail, it is because they have not considered wisely how far they let their private feelings interfere with the public good.

38   This, then, is my position at present. But one cannot be too much on his guard in such a case, lest his action be biased by obstinacy, or an undue regard for the opinions of men. Let him see that he does only what belongs to himself and to the hour.

39   I think sometimes, Why, this people mean well; they are only ignorant; they would do better if they knew how: why give your neighbors this pain to treat you as they are not inclined to? But I think again, this is no reason why I should do as they do, or permit others to suffer much greater pain of a different kind. Again, I sometimes say to myself, When many millions of men, without heat, without ill will, without personal feeling of any kind, demand of you a few shillings only, without the possibility, such is their constitution, of retracting or altering their present demand, and without the possibility, on your side, of appeal to any other millions, why expose yourself to this overwhelming brute force? You do not resist cold and hunger, the winds and the waves, thus obstinately; you quietly submit to a thousand similar necessities. You do not put your head into the fire. But just in proportion as I regard this as not wholly a brute force, partly a human force, and consider that I have relations to those millions as to so many millions of men, and not of mere brute or inanimate things, I see that appeal is possible, first and instantaneously, from them to the Maker of them, and, secondly, from them to themselves. But, if I put my head deliberately into the fire, there is no appeal to fire or to the Maker of fire, and I have only myself to blame. If I could convince myself that I have any right to be satisfied with men as they are, and to treat them according, and not according, in some respects, to my requisitions and expectations of what they and I ought to be, then, like a good Mussulman and fatalist, I should endeavor to be satisfied with things as they are, and say it is the will of God. And, above all, there is this difference between resisting this and a purely brute or natural force, that I can resist this with some effect; but I cannot expect, like Orpheus, to change the nature of the rocks and trees and beasts.

40   I do not wish to quarrel with any man or nation. I do not wish to split hairs, to make fine distinctions, or set myself up as better than my neighbors. I

seek rather, I may say, even an excuse for conforming to the laws of the land. I am but too ready to conform to them. Indeed, I have reason to suspect myself on this head; and each year, as the tax-gatherer comes round, I find myself disposed to review the acts and position of the general and State governments, and the spirit of the people, to discover a pretext for conformity.

> We must affect our country as our parents;
> And if at any time we alienate
> Our love or industry from doing it honor,
> We must respect effects and teach the soul
> Matter of conscience and religion,
> And not desire of rule or benefit.

I believe that the State will soon be able to take all my work of this sort out of my hands, and then I shall be no better a patriot than my fellow-countrymen. Seen from a lower point of view, the Constitution, with all its faults, is very good; the law and the courts are very respectable; even this State and this American government are, in many respects, very admirable and rare things, to be thankful for, such as a great many have described them; but seen from a point of view a little higher, they are what I have described them; seen from a higher still, and the highest, who shall say what they are, or that they are worth looking at or thinking of at all?

41   However, the government does not concern me much, and I shall bestow the fewest possible thoughts on it. It is not many moments that I live under a government, even in this world. If a man is thought-free, fancy-free, imagination-free, that which *is not* never for a long time appearing *to be* to him, unwise rulers or reformers cannot fatally interrupt him.

42   I know that most men think differently from myself; but those whose lives are by profession devoted to the study of these or kindred subjects, content me as little as any. Statesmen and legislators, standing so completely within the institution, never distinctly and nakedly behold it. They speak of moving society, but have no resting-place without it. They may be men of a certain experience and discrimination, and have no doubt invented ingenious and even useful systems, for which we sincerely thank them; but all their wit and usefulness lie within certain not very wide limits. They are wont to forget that the world is not governed by policy and expediency. Webster never goes behind government, and so cannot speak with authority about it. His words are wisdom to those legislators who contemplate no essential reform in the existing government; but for thinkers, and those who legislate for all time, he never once glances at the subject. I know of those whose serene and wise speculations on this theme would soon reveal the limits of his mind's range and hospitality. Yet, compared with the cheap professions of most reformers, and the still cheaper wisdom and eloquence of politicians in general, his are almost the only sensible and valuable words, and we thank Heaven for him.

Comparatively, he is always strong, original, and above all, practical. Still his quality is not wisdom, but prudence. The lawyer's truth is not Truth, but consistency, or a consistent expediency. Truth is always in harmony with herself, and is not concerned chiefly to reveal the justice that may consist with wrongdoing. He well deserves to be called, as he has been called, the Defender of the Constitution. There are really no blows to be given by him but defensive ones. He is not a leader, but a follower. His leaders are the men of '87. "I have never made an effort," he says, "and never propose to make an effort; I have never countenanced an effort, and never mean to countenance an effort, to disturb the arrangement as originally made, by which the various States came into the Union." Still thinking of the sanction which the Constitution gives to slavery, he says, "Because it was a part of the original compact,—let it stand." Notwithstanding his special acuteness and ability, he is unable to take a fact out of its merely political relations, and behold it as it lies absolutely to be disposed of by the intellect,—what, for instance, it behooves a man to do here in America today with regard to slavery, but ventures, or is driven, to make some such desperate answer as the following, while professing to speak absolutely, and as a private man,—from which what new and singular code of social duties might be inferred? "The manner," says he, "in which the governments of those States where slavery exists are to regulate it, is for their own consideration, under their responsibility to their constituents, to the general laws of propriety, humanity, and justice, and to God. Associations formed elsewhere, spring from a feeling of humanity, or any other cause, have nothing whatever to do with it. They have never received any encouragement from me, and they never will."

43   They who know of no purer sources of truth, who have traced up its stream no higher, stand, and wisely stand, by the Bible and the Constitution, and drink at it there with reverence and humility; but they who behold where it comes trickling into this lake or that pool, gird up their loins once more, and continue their pilgrimage toward its fountain-head.

44   No man with a genius for legislation has appeared in America. They are rare in the history of the world. There are orators, politicians, and eloquent men, by the thousand; but the speaker has not yet opened his mouth to speak, who is capable of settling the much-vexed questions of the day. We love eloquence for its own sake, and not for any truth which it may utter, or any heroism it may inspire. Our legislators have not yet learned the comparative value of free-trade and of freedom, of union, and of rectitude, to a nation. They have no genius or talent for comparatively humble questions of taxation and finance, commerce and manufactures and agriculture. If we were left solely to the wordy wit of legislators in Congress for our guidance, uncorrected by the seasonable experience and the effectual complaints of the people, America would not long retain her rank among the nations. For eighteen hundred years, though perchance I have no right to say it, the New Testament has been written; yet where is the legislator who has wisdom and practical talent enough to avail himself of the light which it sheds on the science of legislation?

45   The authority of government, even such as I am willing to submit to,—
for I will cheerfully obey those who know and can do better than I, and in
many things even those who neither know nor can do so well,—is still an impure one: To be strictly just, it must have the sanction and consent of the governed. It can have no pure right over my person and property but what I concede to it. The progress from an absolute to a limited monarchy, from a limited
monarchy to a democracy, is a progress toward a true respect for the individual. Even the Chinese philosopher was wise enough to regard the individual as
the basis of the empire. Is a democracy, such as we know it, the last improvement possible in government? Is it not possible to take a step further towards
recognizing and organizing the rights of man? There will never be a really free
and enlightened State, until the State comes to recognize the individual as a
higher and independent power, from which all its own power and authority
are derived, and treats him accordingly. I please myself with imagining a State
at last which can afford to be just to all men, and to treat the individual with
respect as a neighbor; which even would not think it inconsistent with its own
repose, if a few were to live aloof from it, not meddling with it, nor embraced
by it, who fulfilled all the duties of neighbors and fellowmen. A State which
bore this kind of fruit, and suffered it to drop off as fast as it ripened, would
prepare the way for a still more perfect and glorious State, which also I have
imagined, but not yet anywhere seen.

Topical Considerations

1. Thoreau says that he refused to pay his poll tax in protest of the Mexican war
   and slavery. Can you think of any actions or inactions of the American government today that might compel Thoreau to withhold his taxes in protest?
   Any that could justify such civil disobedience by you or people you know?
   Explain.
2. What is Thoreau's opinion of majority rule? Under what circumstances
   should an individual protest against the majority? What kinds of protests
   does Thoreau condone?
3. Thoreau believes "That government is best which governs not at all" (paragraph 1). What is your opinion of this statement? Could we ever survive
   without an organized government? In your opinion, what might be the consequences of Thoreau's proposition?
4. In paragraph 10 Thoreau presents two lines of verse that compare the state of
   Massachusetts to a prostitute. What is your understanding of this comparison, within the context of Thoreau's essay? Is his comparison justified? Why
   or why not? Discuss the implications of the verse in terms of politics today.
5. What is Thoreau's opinion of the voting system? Do you agree with him?
   Why or why not?
6. In paragraph 16 Thoreau asks, "shall we be content to obey [unjust laws], or
   shall we endeavor to amend them, and obey them until we have succeeded,

or shall we transgress them at once?" What is your response to this question? How would Martin Luther King, Jr. answer this question?

7. Thoreau assesses the government from various perspectives in paragraph 40. What is your opinion of his assessment? What do you think Thoreau's idea of "truth" is? In your opinion, is there any such thing as real, undeniable truth?

8. Thoreau expresses a rather unusual view of the function of jail in society. What is paradoxical about this view? What is your opinion of his view? Explain.

Rhetorical Considerations

1. Thoreau is unabashed in his criticism of those he does not respect. Find two instances where his forthright criticism of a social or political group might be offensive to his readers. Explain why this works or does not work within the rhetorical strategy of his piece.

2. Why does Thoreau provide such a detailed account of his one day in prison? Is this account necessary to the function of the essay? Why or why not?

3. Thoreau uses a variety of persuasive strategies in his essay. Find one example each of logical, emotional, and moral/ethical arguments, examining which ones work best and why.

Writing Assignments

1. Write an essay outlining one issue about which you feel strongly enough to protest. What form would your protest take? Why is such a protest necessary, and why is that the most effective method? Be specific.

2. Write an essay in which you dispute Thoreau's contention that refusal to pay taxes is the most effective means of civil disobedience or protest. Think in terms of other methods of protest—for example, Martin Luther King, Jr.'s nonviolent campaign. Present a proposal for a more effective measure of civil disobedience.

3. Write an essay responding to Thoreau's statement that the "only obligation which I have the right to assume, is to do at any time what I think right" (paragraph 4). In your essay, consider the consequences of such a statement upon society as a whole.

Declaration of Sentiments and Resolutions
Elizabeth Cady Stanton

Elizabeth Cady Stanton (1815–1902) was one of the first activists for women's rights in America. Born in Johnstown, New York, she was educated at Johnstown

Academy, an all-male school to which she was admitted under special arrangement. After a few years of study at the Troy Female Seminary, she turned to law but was denied admission to the New York Bar because of her gender. Following her marriage to abolitionist Henry B. Stanton, she was denied recognition as a delegate at London's World Anti-Slavery Convention in 1840. Only men were recognized. Incensed by such prejudice, Stanton dedicated the rest of her life to the abolition of laws that restricted the freedom and denied the civil rights of women.

In 1848, Stanton helped organize the Seneca Falls Convention, which inaugurated the movement for women's suffrage. In 1869, she was elected the first president of the National Woman Suffrage Association, a post she held until 1890. Her writings include the three-volume *History of Woman's Suffrage* (1896), *A Woman's Bible* (1895), and her autobiographical *Eighty Years and More* (1898).

Stanton is probably best remembered for the Seneca Falls Convention and the following declaration which she read at that historic meeting. Modeled after Thomas Jefferson's Declaration of Independence, this piece enumerates women's grievances and calls for equal rights.

BEFORE YOU READ

Why do you think Stanton modeled her declaration at Seneca Falls on the Declaration of Independence? How might the association with that document have helped her cause?

AS YOU READ

Make a checklist of Stanton's grievances. Which ones seem to be given greater importance? Which ones might still be made today?

1   When, in the course of human events, it becomes necessary for one portion of the family of man to assume among the people of the earth a position different from that which they have hitherto occupied, but one to which the laws of nature and of nature's God entitle them, a decent respect to the opinions of mankind requires that they should declare the causes that impel them to such a course.

2   We hold these truths to be self-evident: that all men and women are created equal; that they are endowed by their Creator with certain inalienable rights; that among these are life, liberty, and the pursuit of happiness; that to secure these rights governments are instituted, deriving their just powers from the consent of the governed. Whenever any form of government becomes destructive of these ends, it is the right of those who suffer from it to refuse allegiance to it, and to insist upon the institution of a new government, laying its foundation on such principles, and organizing its powers in such form, as to them shall seem most likely to effect their safety and happiness. Prudence, indeed, will dictate that governments long established should not be changed for light and transient causes; and accordingly all experience hath shown that

mankind are more disposed to suffer, while evils are sufferable, then to right themselves by abolishing the forms to which they were accustomed. But when a long train of abuses and usurpations, pursuing invariably the same object evinces a design to reduce them under absolute despotism, it is their duty to throw off such government, and to provide new guards for their future security. Such has been the patient sufferance of the women under this government, and such is now the necessity which constrains them to demand the equal station to which they are entitled.

3   The history of mankind is a history of repeated injuries and usurpations on the part of man toward woman, having in direct object the establishment of an absolute tyranny over her. To prove this, let facts be submitted to a candid world.

4   He has never permitted her to exercise her inalienable right to the elective franchise.

5   He has compelled her to submit to laws, in the formation of which she had no voice.

6   He has withheld from her rights which are given to the most ignorant and degraded men—both natives and foreigners.

7   Having deprived her of this first right of a citizen, the elective franchise, thereby leaving her without representation in the halls of legislation, he has oppressed her on all sides.

8   He has made her, if married, in the eye of the law, civilly dead.

9   He has taken from her all right in property, even to the wages she earns.

10   He has made her, morally, an irresponsible being, as she can commit many crimes with impunity, provided they be done in the presence of her husband. In the covenant of marriage she is compelled to promise obedience to her husband, he becoming, to all intents and purposes, her master—the law giving him power to deprive her of her liberty, and to administer chastisement.

11   He has so framed the laws of divorce, as to what shall be the proper causes, and in case of separation, to whom the guardianship of the children shall be given, as to be wholly regardless of the happiness of women—the law, in all cases, going upon a false supposition of the supremacy of man, and giving all power into his hands.

12   After depriving her of all rights as a married woman, if single, and the owner of property, he has taxed her to support a government which recognizes her only when her property can be made profitable to it.

13   He has monopolized nearly all the profitable employments, and from those she is permitted to follow, she receives but a scanty remuneration. He closes against her all the avenues to wealth and distinction which he considers most honorable to himself. As a teacher of theology, medicine, or law, she is not known.

14   He has denied her the facilities for obtaining a thorough education, all colleges being closed against her.

15   He allows her in Church, as well as State, but a subordinate position, claiming Apostolic authority for her exclusion from the ministry, and, with some exceptions, from any public participation in the affairs of the Church.

16   He has created a false public sentiment by giving to the world a different code of morals for men and women, by which moral delinquencies which exclude women from society, are not only tolerated, but deemed of little account in man.

17   He has usurped the prerogative of Jehovah himself, claiming it as his right to assign for her a sphere of action, when that belongs to her conscience and to her God.

18   He has endeavored, in every way that he could, to destroy her confidence in her own powers, to lessen her self-respect, and to make her willing to lead a dependent and abject life.

19   Now, in view of this entire disfranchisement of one-half the people of this country, their social and religious degradation—in view of the unjust laws above mentioned, and because women do feel themselves aggrieved, oppressed, and fraudulently deprived of their most sacred rights, we insist that they have immediate admission to all the rights and privileges which belong to them as citizens of the United States.

20   In entering upon the great work before us, we anticipate no small amount of misconception, misrepresentation, and ridicule; but we shall use every instrumentality within our power to effect our object. We shall employ agents, circulate tracts, petition the State and National legislatures, and endeavor to enlist the pulpit and the press in our behalf. We hope this Convention will be followed by a series of Conventions embracing every part of the country.

Resolutions

21   WHEREAS, The great precept of nature is conceded to be, that "man shall pursue his own true and substantial happiness." Blackstone in his Commentaries remarks, that this law of Nature being coeval with mankind, and dictated by God himself, is of course superior in obligation to any other. It is binding over all the globe, in all countries and at all times; no human laws are of any validity if contrary to this, and such of them as are valid, derive all their force, and all their validity, and all their authority, mediately and immediately, from this original; therefore,

22   *Resolved,* That such laws as conflict, in any way, with the true and substantial happiness of woman, are contrary to the great precept of nature and of no validity, for this is "superior in obligation to any other."

23   *Resolved,* That all laws which prevent woman from occupying such a station in society as her conscience shall dictate, or which place her in a position inferior to that of man, are contrary to the great precept of nature, and therefore of no force or authority.

24   *Resolved,* That woman is man's equal—was intended to be so by the Creator, and the highest good of the race demands that she should be recognized as such.

25   *Resolved,* That the women of this country ought to be enlightened in regard to the laws under which they live, that they may no longer publish their

degradation by declaring themselves satisfied with their present position, nor their ignorance, by asserting that they have all the rights they want.

26   *Resolved,* That inasmuch as man, while claiming for himself intellectual superiority, does accord to woman moral superiority, it is preeminently his duty to encourage her to speak and teach, as she has an opportunity, in all religious assemblies.

27   *Resolved,* That the same amount of virtue, delicacy, and refinement of behavior that is required of woman in the social state, should also be required of man, and the same transgressions should be visited with equal severity on both man and woman.

28   *Resolved,* That the objection of indelicacy and impropriety, which is so often brought against woman when she addresses a public audience, comes with a very ill-grace from those who encourage, by their attendance, her appearance on the stage, in the concert, or in feats of the circus.

29   *Resolved,* That woman has too long rested satisfied in the circumscribed limits which corrupt customs and a perverted application of the Scriptures have marked out for her, and that it is time she should move in the enlarged sphere which her great Creator has assigned her.

30   *Resolved,* That it is the duty of the women of this country to secure to themselves their sacred right to the elective franchise.

31   *Resolved,* That the equality of human rights results necessarily from the fact of the identity of the race in capabilities and responsibilities.

32   *Resolved, therefore,* That, being invested by the Creator with the same capabilities, and the same consciousness of responsibility for their exercise, it is demonstrably the right and duty of woman, equally with man, to promote every righteous cause by every righteous means; and especially in regard to the great subjects of morals and religion, it is self-evidently her right to participate with her brother in teaching them, both in private and in public, by writing and by speaking, by any instrumentalities proper to be used, and in any assemblies proper to be held; and this being a self-evident truth growing out of the divinely implanted principles of human nature, any custom or authority adverse to it, whether modern or wearing the hoary sanction of antiquity, is to be regarded as a self-evident falsehood, and at war with mankind.

[At the last session Lucretia Mott offered and spoke to the following resolution:]

33   *Resolved,* That the speedy success of our cause depends upon the zealous and untiring efforts of both men and women, for the overthrow of the monopoly of the pulpit, and for the securing to woman an equal participation with men in the various trades, professions, and commerce.

Topical Considerations

1. Why did Elizabeth Cady Stanton model her "Declaration of Sentiments and Resolutions" after the United States' Declaration of Independence? Do you think her strategy was effective? Why or why not?

2. How does Stanton differentiate between the purpose of the original Declaration and the purpose of her declaration? Refer to the text of the Declaration of Independence (see earlier in this chapter) to compare and contrast the aims of the two documents.

3. Which of the "repeated injuries and usurpations on the part of man toward woman" are still going today?

4. According to paragraph 20, what measures will women take to "effect [their] object?" How successful were they in "enlist[ing] the pulpit and press in [their] behalf"?

5. What is the "great precept of nature" that Stanton refers to in paragraph 21? How does Stanton use this argument to provide a foundation for her resolutions? Where in the resolutions does she qualify her evidence from a higher authority when she refers to "a perverted application of the Scriptures"?

6. Why does Stanton urge women to be as responsible as men in "[promoting] every righteous cause by every righteous means" (paragraph 32)?

7. How much of Lucretia Mott's resolution, stated in paragraph 33, has been successfully fulfilled at this time?

8. Does Stanton state in her declaration that women are superior to men? What statements does she make concerning the equality of men and women?

9. What does Stanton mean by *the elective franchise* in paragraph 7 and the phrase *civilly dead* in paragraph 8?

Rhetorical Considerations

1. List some of the archaic words and phrases Stanton uses in paragraphs 1–2 in imitation of the Declaration of Independence. Why would Stanton duplicate these words and phrases as well as the overall structure of the original document?

2. In paragraphs 4–18 Stanton refers to "he" and "her." In the original Declaration "he" refers to the king of England. Who is Stanton referring to in these paragraphs, and why does she use the singular form?

3. How can you tell that the author expects to have her declaration received scornfully by many people? Where does the statement concerning the reception of her declaration appear?

4. Why does Stanton structure the last part of her argument, paragraphs 21–33, into individual resolutions unlike the original Declaration of Independence?

5. What parts of Stanton's argument would you rewrite in contemporary language to bring it up to date? Would anything be lost by modernization of the language?

6. The language used in this declaration is quite formal. Give some examples of words and phrases as well as sentence construction that demonstrate its formality.

Writing Assignments

1. Rewrite the particular resolutions of this declaration that you feel have not yet been achieved. Use the form that Stanton uses, but update the diction.
2. Research the reception that Stanton's "Declaration of Sentiments and Resolutions" got from both men and women of her time. Discuss the Seneca Falls Convention and the uproar that resulted from it.
3. Explore your own feelings about women's equality in contemporary issues such as military combat and the ministry. Why should or shouldn't women be accepted in these occupations?
4. Compare the general status of American women with that of women in other countries in order to demonstrate the wide range of women's rights and roles. Using library research and, if possible, personal testimony from people from or familiar with other countries, write up your findings in a paper.

On the Natural Superiority of the Aryan Race
Adolf Hitler

It was shortly after the bitter defeat of Germany in World War I that Adolf Hitler (1889–1945) discovered his political interests and powers of persuasion. Taking advantage of social and economic turmoil, Hitler took over the leadership of the National Socialist Party. In 1923 Hitler led his political party into a revolt in Munich—the so-called Beer Hall Putsch. But the putsch failed, and Hitler was sent to prison for 9 months for treason. It was during his incarceration that he wrote *Mein Kampf,* the distillation of his rage, racism, and psychopathic fantasies of world domination. Because of its softness on right-wing nationalists, the German government under von Hindenburg pardoned Hitler. Over the next decade Hitler's Nazi party gained considerable influence and power; and following von Hindenburg's death in 1934, Hitler became Germany's chancellor. Moments before the advancing Allied forces could capture him in April 1945, Hitler committed suicide outside his bunker among the smoke and rubble of Berlin.

Adolf Hitler's name is synonymous with fearsome political power, tyranny, and the worst human evil. It was his monomaniacal yearning for world rule that initiated World War II with Germany's invasion of Poland. It was his monstrous rage and racism that led to the slaughter of 6 million Jews and 2 million others in the Nazi death camps. It was the terrible power of his propaganda that persuaded a nation of people to destroy itself and much of Europe.

The following is an excerpt from *Mein Kampf* (the excerpt title is our own). In light of Hitler's legacy, his argument for the superiority of the Aryan race is a keen example of how logic and evidence can be darkly twisted to fit a conclusion already determined.

BEFORE YOU READ

Although there is no such ethnological group of people, Hitler used the term *Aryan* to designate individuals of non-Jewish Caucasian descent. Given Hitler's fanatical racism, attempt to second-guess the kinds of arguments he would offer in defense of his racial philosophy.

AS YOU READ

Try to find examples of faulty reasoning in Hitler's argument. What different kinds of logical fallacies can you locate?

1   There are some truths which are so obvious that for this very reason they are not seen or at least not recognized by ordinary people. They sometimes pass by such truisms as though blind and are most astonished when someone suddenly discovers what everyone really ought to know. Columbus's eggs lie around by the hundreds of thousands, but Columbuses are met with less frequency.

2   Thus men without exception wander about in the garden of Nature; they imagine that they know practically everything and yet with few exceptions pass blindly by one of the most patent principles of Nature's rule: the inner segregation of the species of all living beings on this earth.

3   Even the most superficial observation shows that Nature's restricted form of propagation and increase is an almost rigid basic law of all the innumerable forms of expression of her vital urge. Every animal mates only with a member of the same species. The titmouse seeks the titmouse, the finch the finch, the stork the stork, the field mouse the field mouse, the dormouse the dormouse, the wolf the she-wolf, etc.

4   Only unusual circumstances can change this, primarily the compulsion of captivity or any other cause that makes it impossible to mate within the same species. But then Nature begins to resist this with all possible means, and her most visible protest consists either in refusing further capacity for propagation to bastards or in limiting the fertility of later offspring; in most cases, however, she takes away the power of resistance to disease or hostile attacks.

5   This is only too natural.

6   Any crossing of two beings not at exactly the same level produces a medium between the level of the two parents. This means: The offspring will probably stand higher than the racially lower parent, but not as high as the higher one. Consequently, it will later succumb in the struggle against the higher level. Such mating is contrary to the will of Nature for a higher breeding of all life. The precondition for this does not lie in associating superior and inferior, but in the total victory of the former. The stronger must dominate and not blend with the weaker, thus sacrificing his own greatness. Only the born weakling can view this as cruel, but he after all is only a weak and limited

man; for if this law did not prevail, any conceivable higher development of organic living beings would be unthinkable.

7   The consequence of this racial purity, universally valid in Nature, is not only the sharp outward delimitation of the various races, but their uniform character in themselves. The fox is always a fox, the goose a goose, the tiger a tiger, etc., and the difference can lie at most in the varying measure of force, strength, intelligence, dexterity, endurance, etc., of the individual specimens. But you will never find a fox who in his inner attitude might, for example, show humanitarian tendencies toward geese, as similarly there is no cat with a friendly inclination toward mice.

8   Therefore, here, too, the struggle among themselves arises less from inner aversion than from hunger and love. In both cases, Nature looks on calmly, with satisfaction, in fact. In the struggle for daily bread all those who are weak and sickly or less determined succumb, while the struggle of the males for the female grants the right or opportunity to propagate only to the healthiest. And struggle is always a means for improving a species' health and power of resistance and, therefore, a cause of its higher development.

9   If the process were different, all further and higher development would cease and the opposite would occur. For, since the inferior always predominates numerically over the best, if both had the same possibility of preserving life and propagating, the inferior would multiply so much more rapidly that in the end the best would inevitably be driven into the background, unless a correction of this state of affairs were undertaken. Nature does just this by subjecting the weaker part to such severe living conditions that by them alone the number is limited, and by not permitting the remainder to increase promiscuously, but making a new and ruthless choice according to strength and health.

10   No more than Nature desires the mating of weaker with stronger individuals, even less does she desire the blending of a higher with a lower race, since, if she did, her whole work of higher breeding, over perhaps hundreds of thousands of years, might be ruined with one blow.

11   Historical experience offers countless proofs of this. It shows with terrifying clarity that in every mingling of Aryan blood with that of lower peoples the result was the end of the cultured people. North America, whose population consists in by far the largest part of Germanic elements who mixed but little with the lower colored peoples, shows a different humanity and culture from Central and South America, where the predominantly Latin immigrants often mixed with the aborigines on a large scale. By this one example, we can clearly and distinctly recognize the effect of racial mixture. The Germanic inhabitant of the American continent, who has remained racially pure and unmixed, rose to be master of the continent; he will remain the master as long as he does not fall a victim to defilement of the blood.

12   The result of all racial crossing is therefore in brief always the following:

13   (a) Lowering of the level of the higher race;

14   (b) Physical and intellectual regression and hence the beginning of a slowly but surely progressing sickness.

15   To bring about such a development is, then, nothing else but to sin against the will of the eternal creator.

16   And as a sin this act is rewarded.

17   When man attempts to rebel against the iron logic of Nature, he comes into struggle with the principles to which he himself owes his existence as a man. And this attack must lead to his own doom.

18   Here, of course, we encounter the objection of the modern pacifist, as truly Jewish in its effrontery as it is stupid! "Man's role is to overcome Nature!"

19   Millions thoughtlessly parrot this Jewish nonsense and end up by really imagining that they themselves represent a kind of conqueror of Nature; though in this they dispose of no other weapon than an idea, and at that such a miserable one, that if it were true no world at all would be conceivable.

20   But quite aside from the fact that man has never yet conquered Nature in anything, but at most has caught hold of and tried to lift one or another corner of her immense gigantic veil of eternal riddles and secrets, that in reality he invents nothing but only discovers everything, that he does not dominate Nature, but has only risen on the basis of his knowledge of various laws and secrets of Nature to be lord over those other living creatures who lack this knowledge—quite aside from all this, an idea cannot overcome the preconditions for the development and being of humanity, since the idea itself depends only on man. Without human beings there is no human idea in this world; therefore, the idea as such is always conditioned by the presence of human beings and hence of all the laws which created the precondition for their existence.

21   And not only that! Certain ideas are even tied up with certain men. This applies most of all to those ideas whose content originates, not in an exact scientific truth, but in the world of emotion, or, as it is so beautifully and clearly expressed today, reflects an "inner experience." All these ideas, which have nothing to do with cold logic as such, but represent only pure expressions of feeling, ethical conceptions, etc., are chained to the existence of men, to whose intellectual imagination and creative power they owe to their existence. Precisely in this case the preservation of these definite races and men is the precondition for the existence of these ideas. Anyone, for example, who really desired the victory of the pacifistic idea in this world with all his heart would have to fight with all the means at his disposal for the conquest of the world by the Germans; for, if the opposite should occur, the last pacifist would die out with the last German, since the rest of the world has never fallen so deeply as our own people, unfortunately, has for this nonsense so contrary to Nature and reason. Then, if we were serious, whether we liked it or not, we would have to wage wars in order to arrive at pacifism. This and nothing else was what Wilson, the America world savior, intended, or so at least our German visionaries believed—and thereby his purpose was fulfilled.

22   In actual fact the pacifistic-humane idea is perfectly all right perhaps when the highest type of man has previously conquered and subjected the world to an extent that makes him the sole ruler of this earth. Then this idea

lacks the power of producing evil effects in exact proportion as its practical application becomes rare and finally impossible. Therefore, first struggle and then we shall see what can be done. Otherwise mankind has passed the high point of its development and the end is not the domination of any ethical idea but barbarism and consequently chaos. At this point someone or other may laugh, but this planet once moved through the ether for millions of years without human beings and it can do so again some day if men forget that they owe their higher existence, not to the ideas of a few crazy ideologists, but to the knowledge and ruthless application of Nature's stern and rigid laws.

23   Everything we admire on this earth today—science and art, technology and inventions—is only the creative product of a few peoples and originally perhaps of *one* race. On them depends the existence of this whole culture. If they perish, the beauty of this earth will sink into the grave with them.

24   However much the soil, for example, can influence men, the result of the influence will always be different depending on the races in question. The low fertility of a living space may spur the one race to the highest achievements; in others it will only be the cause of bitterest poverty and final undernourishment with all its consequences. The inner nature of peoples is always determining for the manner in which outward influences will be effective. What leads the one to starvation trains the other to hard work.

25   All great cultures of the past perished only because the originally creative race died out from blood poisoning.

26   The ultimate cause of such a decline was their forgetting that all culture depends on men and conversely; hence that to preserve a certain culture the man who creates it must be preserved. This preservation is bound up with the rigid law of necessity and the right to victory of the best and stronger in this world.

27   Those who want to live, let them fight, and those who do not want to fight in this world of eternal struggle do not deserve to live.

28   Even if this were hard—that is how it is! Assuredly, however, by far the harder fate is that which strikes the man who thinks he can overcome Nature, but in the last analysis only mocks her. Distress, misfortune, and diseases are her answer.

29   The man who misjudges and disregards the racial laws actually forfeits the happiness that seems destined to be his. He thwarts the triumphal march of the best race and hence also the precondition for all human progress, and remains, in consequence, burdened with all the sensibility of man, in the animal realm of helpless misery.

30   It is idle to argue which race or races were the original representative of human culture and hence the real founders of all that we sum up under the word "humanity." It is simpler to raise the question with regard to the present, and here an easy, clear answer results. All the human culture, all the results of art, science and technology that we see before us today, are almost exclusively the creature product of the Aryan. This very fact admits of the not unfounded inference that he alone was the fonder of all higher humanity, therefore representing the prototype of all that we understand by the word "man." He is the Prometheus of

mankind from whose bright forehead the divine spark of genius has sprung at all times, forever kindling anew that fire of knowledge which illumined the night of silent mysteries and thus caused man to climb the path to mastery over the other beings of this earth. Exclude him—and perhaps after a few thousand years darkness will again descend on the earth, human culture will pass, and the world turn to a desert.

Topical Considerations

1. Hitler opens his essay with the statement, "There are some truths which are so obvious that for this very reason they are not seen or at least not recognized by ordinary people." After reading his article, discuss this opening statement in terms of Plato's "Allegory of the Cave." Does Hitler's statement support Plato's Allegory? Also, do you think that Plato would agree with Hitler's statement in the context of this essay? Explain your answer.

2. Discuss Hitler's term *racial purity*, especially in light of what we know about Hitler historically. Examine Hitler's idea that racial mixing leads to the destruction of the human race.

3. Hitler applies arguments about the nature of propagation of species to his conclusion about the mixing of races. How do you view the difference between an argument about animal species and an argument about human races? Is it a logical parallel? Why or why not?

4. In paragraph 15 Hitler claims that to reduce the purity of a race is to "sin against the will of the eternal creator." Discuss Hitler's reference here to God, especially in the context of the Darwinian arguments he has made throughout his essay, and also in view of the atrocities he committed during his leadership of Germany.

5. Reread paragraph 21. What is Hitler's view of pacifism? How does your own idea of peace relate to this view?

6. In paragraph 22 Hitler states, "[F]irst struggle and then we shall see what can be done. Otherwise mankind has passed the high point of its development and the end is not the domination of any ethical idea but barbarism and consequently chaos." Discuss the implications of this statement in terms of the means that Hitler uses to avoid "barbarism" and maintain "ethical idea[s]."

7. In paragraph 27 Hitler states, "Those who want to live, let them fight, and those who do not want to fight in this world of eternal struggle do not deserve to live." Would modern scientists agree that the laws of nature require unremitting struggle and conflict between human beings—until the master race conquers? Can you think of any groups which seriously endorse such an ideal today?

Rhetorical Considerations

1. What is the tone of Hitler's essay, especially as manifested in his opening paragraph? Do you find it effective? Why or why not?

2. How does your knowledge of Hitler's political life affect your reading of this essay? Do you find that knowledge presupposes your response to his argument? Explain your answer.

3. In paragraph 11 Hitler offers one example that in the "mingling of Aryan blood with that of lower peoples the result was the end of the cultured people." He then goes on in paragraph 12 to conclude that "[t]he result of all racial crossing is therefore in brief always . . . [the] [l]owering of the level of the higher race." What is missing from this argument? Why is it ineffective?

4. In paragraphs 23–30 Hitler tries to argue that all creative productivity on the earth today has been the result of the work of one "master" race. Examine those paragraphs, looking at his use of evidence, and analyze the effectiveness of his arguments. What kind of evidence does he provide for his statements?

5. Reread the essay, examining ways in which Hitler addresses his opposition. What is the effect of his references to his opposition? (See paragraph 28, for example.)

6. Describe the effect of the rhetoric that Hitler employs to conclude his essay (paragraph 30). Does it provide a logical, convincing conclusion to his argument? Why or why not?

Writing Assignments

1. Do some research in early human history to discover the degree of truth in Hitler's statement that "[a]ll human culture, all the results of art, science, and technology that we see before us today, are almost exclusively the creative product of the Aryan" (paragraph 30). What is, in fact, the Aryan race to which he refers? In your essay, focus upon one area of human culture.

2. Hitler makes the following claim: "When man attempts to rebel against the iron logic of Nature, he comes into struggle with the principles to which he himself owes his existence as a man. And this attack must lead to his own doom" (paragraph 17). In light of Hitler's attempted extinction of the Jews, Romani people ("Gypsies"), and other ethnic/racial groups, write an essay in which you try to demonstrate how Nazi Germany's own actions disprove the arguments behind Hitler's claim.

Warfare: An Invention—Not a Biological Necessity
Margaret Mead

Margaret Mead (1901–1979) was one of the most famous cultural anthropologists of our century. She was born in Philadelphia and educated at Barnard College and Columbia University, where she later served as professor of anthropology. Most of her field work focused on primitive societies in the South Pacific. Her particular interest was the influence of primitive cultures on the development of young people, especially adolescent girls. In 1928 her doctoral dissertation was published in book form as *Coming of Age in Samoa,* bringing her nationwide attention. She went on to publish hundreds of articles and some 45 books including among her most important works *Sex and Temperament in Three Primitive Societies* (1935), *Male and Female: A Study of the Sexes in a Changing World* (1949), *New Lives for Old* (1956), and *Culture and Commitment: A Study of the Generation Gap* (1970).

After retiring from academic life, Mead served as curator for the American Museum of Natural History. In addition to the various national and international commissions on which she served, Mead also wrote a monthly column for *Redbook* magazine for the last 17 years of her life. Although some of her early findings have recently come under question, Margaret Mead's contribution to cultural anthropology has been enormous.

Although she devoted her life to the study of different peoples of Pacific cultures, Mead's work was global in scope, addressing conditions experienced by all human beings everywhere—sexual development, education, nutrition, religion, family, community, environment, race, and war. The following article, written in 1940 for the journal *Asia,* boldly questions the universal assumption that war is an inevitable part of human experience. On the contrary, she argues that warfare is a "defective social institution" that needs to be replaced by a better invention.

BEFORE YOU READ

Try to second-guess the kind of evidence and logic people might use to argue that war is an inevitable part of human experience. Also try to think of ways that war might be considered "an invention—not a biological necessity."

AS YOU READ

As you read notice how Mead goes about challenging the views of her opponents. What aspects of her argument strike you as most convincing? Least convincing?

1 Is war a biological necessity, a sociological inevitability or just a bad invention? Those who argue for the first view endow man with such pugnacious instincts that some outlet in aggressive behavior is necessary if man is to reach full human stature. It was this point of view which lay back of William James's famous essay, "The Moral Equivalent of War," in which he tried to retain the warlike virtues and channel them in new directions. A similar point of view has lain back of the Soviet Union's attempt to make competition between groups rather than between individuals. A basic, competitive, aggressive, warring human nature is assumed, and those who wish to outlaw war or outlaw competitiveness merely try to find new and less socially destructive ways in which these biologically given aspects of man's nature can find expression. Then there are those who take the second view: warfare is the inevitable con-

comitant of the development of the state, the struggle for land and natural resources of class societies springing, not from the nature of man, but from the nature of history. War is nevertheless inevitable unless we change our social system and outlaw classes, the struggle for power, and possessions; and in the event of our success warfare would disappear, as a symptom vanishes when the disease is cured.

2   One may hold a compromise position between these two extremes; one may claim that all aggression springs from the frustration of man's biologically determined drives and that, since all forms of culture are frustrating, it is certain each new generation will be aggressive and the aggression will find its natural and inevitable expression in race war, class war, nationalistic war, and so on.

3   All three positions are very popular today among those who think seriously about the problems of war and its possible prevention, but I wish to urge another point of view, less defeatist perhaps than the first and third, and more accurate than the second: that is, that warfare, by which I mean organized conflict between two groups *as groups,* in which each group puts an army (even if the army is only fifteen Pygmies) into the field to fight and kill, if possible, some of the members of the army of the other group—that warfare of this sort is an invention like any other of the inventions in terms of which we order our lives, such as writing, marriage, cooking our food instead of eating it raw, trial by jury, or burial of the dead, and so on. Some of this list any one will grant are inventions: trial by jury is confined to very limited portions of the globe; we know that there are tribes that do not bury their dead but instead expose or cremate them; and we know that only part of the human race has had a knowledge of writing as its cultural inheritance. But, whenever a way of doing things is found universally, such as the use of fire or the practice of some form of marriage, we tend to think at once that it is not an invention at all but an attribute of humanity itself. And yet even such universals as marriage and the use of fire are inventions like the rest, very basic ones, inventions which were perhaps necessary if human history was to take the turn it has taken, but nevertheless inventions. At some point in his social development man was undoubtedly without the institution of marriage or the knowledge of the use of fire.

4   The case for warfare is much clearer because there are peoples even today who have no warfare. Of these the Eskimo are perhaps the most conspicuous example, but the Lepchas of Sikkim are an equally good one. Neither of these peoples understands war, not even the defensive warfare. The idea of warfare is lacking, and this lack is as essential to carrying on war as an alphabet or a syllabary is to writing. But whereas the Lepchas are a gentle, unquarrelsome people, and the advocates of other points of view might argue that they are not full human beings or that they had never been frustrated and so had no aggression to expend in warfare, the Eskimo case gives no such possibility of interpretation. The Eskimo are not a mild and meek people; many of them are turbulent and troublesome. Fights, theft of wives, murder, cannibal-

ism occur among them—all outbursts of passionate men goaded by desire or intolerable circumstance. Here are men faced with hunger, men faced with loss of their wives, men faced with the threat of extermination by other men, and here are orphan children, growing up miserably with no one to care for them, mocked and neglected by those about them. The personality necessary for war, the circumstances necessary to goad men to desperation are present, but there is no war. When a traveling Eskimo entered a settlement he might have to fight the strongest man in the settlement to establish his position among them, but this was a test of strength and bravery, not war. The idea of warfare, of one *group* organizing against another *group* to maim and wound and kill them, was absent. And without that idea passions might rage but there was no war.

5   But, it may be argued, isn't this because the Eskimo have such a low and undeveloped form of social organization? They own no land, they move from place to place, camping, it is true, season after season on the same site, but this is not something to fight for as the modern nations of the world fight for land and raw materials. They have no permanent possessions that can be looted, no towns that can be burned. They have no social classes to produce stress and strains within the society which might force it to go to war outside. Doesn't the absence of war among the Eskimo, while disproving the biological necessity of war, just go to confirm the point that it is the state of development of the society which accounts for war, and nothing else?

6   We find the answer among the Pygmy peoples of the Andaman Islands in the Bay of Bengal. The Andamans also represent an exceedingly low level of society: they are a hunting and food-gathering people; they live in tiny hordes without any class stratification; their houses are simpler than the snow houses of the Eskimo. But they knew about warfare. The army might contain only fifteen determined pygmies marching in a straight line, but it was the real thing none the less. Tiny army met tiny army in open battle, blows were exchanged, casualties suffered, and the state of warfare could only be concluded by a peacemaking ceremony.

7   Similarly, among the Australian aborigines, who built no permanent dwellings but wandered from water hole to water hole over their almost desert country, warfare—and rules of "international law"—were highly developed. The student of social evolution will seek in vain for his obvious causes of war, struggle for lands, struggle for power of one group over another, expansion of population, need to divert the minds of a populace restive under tyranny, or even the ambition of a successful leader to enhance his own prestige. All are absent, but warfare as a practice remained, and men engaged in it and killed one another in the course of a war because killing is what is done in wars.

8   From instances like these it becomes apparent that an inquiry into the causes of war misses the fundamental point as completely as does an insistence upon the biological necessity of war. If a people have an idea of going to war and the idea that war is the way in which certain situations, defined within their society, are to be handled, they will sometimes go to war. If they

are a mild and unaggressive people, like the Pueblo Indians, they may limit themselves to defensive warfare; but they will be forced to think in terms of war because there are peoples near them who have warfare as a pattern, and offensive, raiding, pillaging warfare at that. When the pattern of warfare is known, people like the Pueblo Indians will defend themselves, taking advantage of their natural defenses, the *mesa* village site, and people like the Lepchas, having no natural defenses and no idea of warfare, will merely submit to the invader. But the essential point remains the same. There is a way of behaving which is known to a given people and labeled as an appropriate form of behavior. A bold and warlike people like the Sioux or the Maori may label warfare as desirable as well as possible; a mild people like the Pueblo Indians may label warfare as undesirable; but to the minds of both peoples the possibility of warfare is present. Their thoughts, their hopes, their plans are oriented about this idea, that warfare may be selected as the way to meet some situation.

9   So simple peoples and civilized peoples, mild peoples and violent, assertive peoples, will all go to war if they have the invention, just as those peoples who have the custom of dueling will have duels and peoples who have the pattern of vendetta will indulge in vendetta. And, conversely, peoples who do not know of dueling will not fight duels, even though their wives are seduced and their daughters ravished; they may on occasion commit murder but they will not fight duels. Cultures which lack the idea of the vendetta will not meet every quarrel in this way. A people can use only the forms it has. So the Balinese have their special way of dealing with a quarrel between two individuals; if the two feel that the causes of quarrel are heavy they may go and register their quarrel in the temple before the gods, and, making offerings, they may swear never to have anything to do with each other again. Under the Dutch government they registered such mutual "not-speaking" with the Dutch government officials. But in other societies, although individuals might feel as full of animosity and as unwilling to have any further contact as do the Balinese, they cannot register their quarrel with the gods and go on quietly about their business because registering quarrels with the gods is not an invention of which they know.

10   Yet, if it be granted that warfare is after all an invention, it may nevertheless be an invention that lends itself to certain types of personality, to the exigent needs of autocrats, to the expansionist desires of crowded peoples, to the desire for plunder and rape and loot which is engendered by a dull and frustrating life. What, then, can we say of this congruence between warfare and its uses? If it is a form which fits so well, is not this congruence the essential point? But even here the primitive material causes us to wonder, because there are tribes who go to war merely for glory, having no quarrel with the enemy, suffering from no tyrant within their boundaries, anxious neither for land nor loot nor women, but merely anxious to win prestige which within that tribe has been declared obtainable only by war and without which no young man can hope to win his sweetheart's smile of approval. But if, as was the case

with the Bush Negroes of Dutch Guiana, it is artistic ability which is necessary to win a girl's approval, the same young man would have to be carving rather than going out on a war party.

11   In many parts of the world, war is a game in which the individual can win counters—counters which bring him prestige in the eyes of his own sex or of the opposite sex; he plays for these counters as he might, in our society, strive for a tennis championship. Warfare is a frame for such prestige-seeking merely because it calls for the display of certain skills and certain virtues; all of these skills—riding straight, shooting straight, dodging the missiles of the enemy and sending one's own straight to the mark—can be equally well exercised in some other framework and, equally, the virtues—endurance, bravery, loyalty, steadfastness—can be displayed in other contexts. The tie-up between proving oneself a man and proving this by a success in organized killing is due to a definition which many societies have made of manliness. And often, even in those societies which counted success in warfare a proof of human worth, strange turns were given to the idea, as when the Plains Indians gave their highest awards to the man who touched a live enemy rather than to the man who brought in a scalp—from a dead enemy—because killing a man was less risky. Warfare is just an invention known to the majority of human societies by which they permit their young men either to accumulate prestige or avenge their honor or acquire loot or wives or slaves or sago lands or cattle or appease the blood lust of their gods or the restless souls of the recently dead. It is just an invention, older and more widespread than the jury system, but none the less an invention.

12   But, once we have said this, have we said anything at all? Despite a few instances, dear to the hearts of controversialists, of the loss of the useful arts, once an invention is made which proves congruent with human needs or social forms, it tends to persist. Grant that war is an invention, that it is not a biological necessity nor the outcome of certain special types of social forms, still, once the invention is made, what are we to do about it? The Indian who had been subsisting on the buffalo for generations because with his primitive weapons he could slaughter only a limited number of buffalo did not return to his primitive weapons when he saw that the white man's more efficient weapons were exterminating the buffalo. A desire for the white man's cloth may mortgage the South Sea Islander to the white man's plantation, but he does not return to making bark cloth, which would have left him free. Once an invention is known and accepted, men do not easily relinquish it. The skilled workers may smash the first steam looms which they feel are to be their undoing, but they accept them in the end, and no movement which has insisted upon the mere abandonment of usable inventions has ever had much success. Warfare is here, as part of our thought; the deeds of warriors are immortalized in the words of our poets; the toys of our children are modeled upon the weapons of the soldier; the frame of reference within which our statesmen and our diplomats work always contains war. If we know that it is not inevitable, that it is due to historical accident that warfare is one of the ways in which we

think of behaving, are we given any hope by that? What hope is there of persuading nations to abandon war, nations so thoroughly imbued with the idea that resort to war is, if not actually desirable and noble, at least inevitable whenever certain defined circumstances arise?

13   In answer to this question I think we might turn to the history of other social inventions, inventions which must once have seemed as firmly entrenched as warfare. Take the methods of trial which preceded the jury system: ordeal and trial by combat. Unfair, capricious, alien as they are to our feeling today, they were once the only methods open to individuals accused of some offense. The invention of trial by jury gradually replaced these methods until only witches, and finally not even witches, had to resort to the ordeal. And for a long time the jury system seemed the one best and finest method of settling legal disputes, but today new inventions, trial before judges only or before commissions, are replacing the jury system. In each case the old method was replaced by a new social invention; the ordeal did not go out because people thought it unjust or wrong, it went out because a method more congruent with the institutions and feelings of the period was invented. And, if we despair over the way in which war seems such an ingrained habit of most of the human race, we can take comfort from the fact that a poor invention will usually give place to a better invention.

14   For this, two conditions at least are necessary. The people must recognize the defects of the old invention, and some one must make a new one. Propaganda against warfare, documentation of its terrible cost in human suffering and social waste, these prepare the ground by teaching people to feel that warfare is a defective social institution. There is further needed a belief that social invention is possible and the invention of new methods which will render warfare as out-of-date as the tractor is making the plow, or the motor car the horse and buggy. A form of behavior becomes out-of-date only when something else takes its place, and in order to invent forms of behavior which will make war obsolete, it is a first requirement to believe that an invention is possible.

Topical Considerations

1. Margaret Mead states that there are three ways to look at war. What are these three views? She also mentions a compromise between the two extremes? What is it? Which view do you favor?

2. How does Mead define war? How does she say war can be eliminated? Do you think such conditions could ever arise so as to put an end to war? Why or why not?

3. Explain what Mead means when she claims that warfare is an invention. How does she make use of certain primitive tribes to support her argument? Did you find her evidence convincing? Why or why not?

4. According to Mead how do those people who lack the invention of war settle their quarrels? Conversely, how do some people who participate in wars

treat war as a game? Can you think of any groups of people today who seem to view war as a game?

5. Even if Mead can prove her statement that war is an invention, she still wonders how we can stop it. In paragraph 12 she declares, "What hope is there of persuading nations to abandon war, nations so thoroughly imbued with the idea that resort to war is, if not actually desirable and noble, at least inevitable whenever certain defined circumstances arise?" How does she answer her own question? Is her answer complete?

6. Do you find Mead's argument logical? Is her evidence from primitive tribes relevant for a modern world? What are some of the basic reasons modern societies go to war? Are these the same reasons Mead refers to in her accounts of various primitive tribes?

Rhetorical Considerations

1. What is Mead's thesis? Take note of each time she repeats the thesis throughout the essay. Does she prove it for you?

2. Generally speaking, is this an inductive or deductive argument? How can you tell which type of argument it is?

3. Where does Mead refer to her opponents' arguments? Specifically, what are these arguments, and how does Mead refute them? Does she concede any points to her opponents? If so, does this strategy strengthen or weaken her argument?

4. Does Mead's example of the improvements in methods of trial (paragraph 13) demonstrate her contention that bad inventions usually give way to better? Is this one example enough to convince you? Why or why not?

Writing Assignments

1. Consider the conflicts between states in the former Soviet Union, the Israelis and Palestinians, the factions battling in the former Yugoslavia. In a paper explain how these conflicts fit into Mead's explanations for the causes of war.

2. In a paper evaluate how successfully Mead argues her case against war. Examine her claim, the evidence she presents, the soundness of her argument, her treatment of opposing views, and the logic of her conclusion. What do you see as the strengths of her essay? What are the weaknesses?

The Obligation to Endure
Rachel Carson

The following essay is the second chapter of Rachel Carson's *Silent Spring* (1962), a book that changed the course of history. It moved President John F. Kennedy to appoint a commission to investigate Carson's claims that poisonous chemicals were causing wholesale destruction of wildlife and its habitats and menacing the future of human life. In fact, with the publication of *Silent Spring,* "ecology became part of our national vocabulary, and the environmental movement as we know it was born. Although Rachel Carson (1907–1964) was a biologist by profession, it was her impassioned and eloquent writings about nature that distinguished her. A previous book, *The Sea Around Us* (1951), won her the highly coveted National Book Award. She also authored *The Edge of the Sea* (1955).

In "The Obligation to Endure" Carson demonstrates her skill at weaving scientific details with poetic sensitivity. Eloquently she warns that in a mere few decades the human race has drastically altered an ecological system that has taken nature some four billion years to evolve. Because we all have "the obligation to endure," she argues, it is our responsibility not just to protest all the destruction but to change the course of events for the sake of future life.

BEFORE YOU READ

This essay was composed over 30 years ago. Do you know of any major changes since 1962 that have been made in regulating the use of insecticides and herbicides? Can more changes be made? Have many recent health problems been traced to such chemicals?

AS YOU READ

Who do you think Rachel Carson was writing for here—a general audience? Professional scientists? Political leaders? People with some scientific training? Consider the vocabulary and technical concepts. Did you have any difficulty following her line of argument? Try to determine what Carson's purpose was in writing this text. Can you find a claim?

1   The history of life on earth has been a history of interaction between living things and their surroundings. To a large extent, the physical form and the habits of the earth's vegetation and its animal life have been molded by the environment. Considering the whole span of earthly time, the opposite effect, in which life actually modifies its surroundings, has been relatively slight. Only within the moment of time represented by the present century has one species—man—acquired significant power to alter the nature of his world.

2   During the past quarter century this power has not only increased to one of disturbing magnitude but it has changed in character. The most alarming of all man's assaults upon the environment is the contamination of air, earth, rivers, and sea with dangerous and even lethal materials. This pollution is for the most part irrecoverable; the chain of evil it initiates not only in the world that must support life but in living tissues is for the most part irreversible. In this now universal contamination of the environment, chemicals are the sin-

ister and little-recognized partners of radiation in changing the very nature of the world—the very nature of its life. Strontium 90, released through nuclear explosions into the air, comes to earth in rain or drifts down as fallout, lodges in soil, enters into the grass or corn or wheat grown there, and in time takes up its abode in the bones of a human being, there to remain until his death. Similarly, chemicals sprayed on croplands or forests or gardens lie long in soil, entering into living organisms, passing from one another in a chain of poisoning and death. Or they pass mysteriously by underground streams until they emerge and, through the alchemy of air and sunlight, combine into new forms that kill vegetation, sicken cattle, and work unknown harm on those who drive from once pure wells. As Albert Schweitzer has said, "Man can hardly even recognize the devils of his own creation."

3   It took hundreds of millions of years to produce the life that now inhabits the earth—eons of time in which that developing and evolving and diversifying life reached a state of adjustment and balance with its surroundings. The environment, rigorously shaping and directing the life it supported, contained elements that were hostile as well as supporting. Certain rocks gave out dangerous radiation; even within the light of the sun, from which all life draws its energy, there were short-wave radiations with power to injure. Given time— time not in years but in millennia—life adjusts, and a balance has been reached. For time is the essential ingredient; but in the modern world there is no time.

4   The rapidity of change and the speed with which new situations are created follow the impetuous and heedless pace of man rather than the deliberate pace of nature. Radiation is no longer merely the background radiation of rocks, the bombardment of cosmic rays, the ultraviolet of the sun that have existed before there was any life on earth; radiation is now the unnatural creation of man's tampering with the atom. The chemicals to which life is asked to make its adjustment are no longer merely the calcium and silica and copper and all the rest of the minerals washed out of the rocks and carried in rivers to the sea; they are the synthetic creations of man's inventive mind, brewed in his laboratories, and having no counterparts in nature.

5   To adjust to these chemicals would require time on the scale that is nature's; it would require not merely the years of a man's life but the life of generations. And even this, were it by some miracle possible, would be futile, for the new chemicals come from our laboratories in an endless stream; almost five hundred annually find their way into actual use in the United States alone. The figure is staggering and its implications are not easily grasped—500 new chemicals to which the bodies of men and animals are required somehow to adapt each year, chemicals totally outside the limits of biologic experience.[1]

6   Among them are many that are used in man's war against nature. Since the mid-1940's over 200 basic chemicals have been created for use in killing insects, weeds, rodents, and other organisms described in the modern vernacular as "pests"; and they are sold under several thousand different brand names.

7   These sprays, dusts, and aerosols are now applied almost universally to farms, gardens, forests, and homes—nonselective chemicals that have the power to kill every insect, the "good" and the "bad," to still the song of birds and the leaping of fish in the streams, to coat the leaves with a deadly film, and to linger on in soil—all this though the intended target may be only a few weeds or insects. Can anyone believe it is possible to lay down such a barrage of poisons on the surface of the earth without making it unfit for all life? They should not be called "insecticides," but "biocides."

8   The whole process of spraying seems caught up in an endless spiral. Since DDT was released for civilian use, a process of escalation has been going on in which ever more toxic materials must be found. This has happened because insects, in a triumphant vindication of Darwin's principle of the survival of the fittest, have evolved super races immune to the particular insecticide used, hence a deadlier one has always to be developed—and then a deadlier one than that. It has happened also because, for reasons to be described later, destructive insects often undergo a "flareback," or resurgence, after spraying, in numbers greater than before. Thus the chemical war is never won, and all life is caught in its violent crossfire.

9   Along with the possibility of the extinction of mankind by nuclear war, the central problem of our age has therefore become the contamination of man's total environment with such substances of incredible potential for harm—substances that accumulate in the tissues of plants and animals and even penetrate the germ cells to shatter or alter the very material of heredity upon which the shape of the future depends.

10   Some would-be architects of our future look toward a time when it will be possible to alter the human germ plasm by design. But we may easily be doing so now by inadvertence, for many chemicals, like radiation, bring about gene mutations. It is ironic to think that man might determine his own future by something so seemingly trivial as the choice of an insect spray.

11   All this has been risked—for what? Future historians may well be amazed by our distorted sense of proportion. How could intelligent beings seek to control a few unwanted species by a method that contaminated the entire environment and brought the threat of disease and death even to their own kind? Yet this is precisely what we have done. We have done it, moreover, for reasons that collapse the moment we examine them. We are told that the enormous and expanding use of pesticides is necessary to maintain farm production. Yet is our real problem not one of *overproduction?* Our farms, despite measures to remove acreages from production and to pay farmers *not* to produce, have yielded such a staggering excess of crops that the American taxpayer in 1962 is paying out more than one billion dollars a year as the total carrying cost of the surplus-food storage program. And is the situation helped when one branch of the Agriculture Department tries to reduce production while another states, as it did in 1958, "It is believed generally that reduction of crop acreages under provisions of the Soil Bank will stimulate interest in use of chemicals to obtain maximum production on the land retained in crops."[2]

12   All this is not to say there is no insect problem and no need of control. I am saying, rather, that control must be geared to realities, not to mythical situations, and that the methods employed must be such that they do not destroy us along with the insects.

13   The problem whose attempted solution has brought such a train of disaster in its wake is an accompaniment of our modern way of life. Long before the age of man, insects inhabited the earth—a group of extraordinarily varied and adaptable beings. Over the course of time since man's advent, a small percentage of the more than half a million species of insects have come into conflict with human welfare in two principal ways: as competitors for the food supply and as carriers of human disease.

14   Disease-carrying insects become important where human beings are crowded together, especially under conditions where sanitation is poor, as in time of natural disaster or war in situations of extreme poverty and deprivation. Then control of some sort becomes necessary. It is a sobering fact, however, as we shall presently see, that the method of massive chemical control has had only limited success, and also threatens to worsen the very conditions it is intended to curb.

15   Under primitive agricultural conditions the farmer had few insect problems. These arose with the intensification of agriculture—the devotion of immense acreages to a single crop. Such a system set the stage for explosive increases in specific insect populations. Single-crop farming does not take advantage of the principles by which nature works; it is agriculture as an engineer might conceive it to be. Nature has introduced great variety into the landscape, but man has displayed a passion for simplifying it. Thus he undoes the built-in checks and balances by which nature holds the species within bounds. One important natural check is a limit on the amount of suitable habitat for each species. Obviously then, an insect that lives on wheat can build up its population to much higher levels on a farm devoted to wheat than on one in which wheat is intermingled with other crops to which the insect is not adapted.

16   The same thing happens in other situations. A generation or more ago, the towns of large areas of the United States lined their streets with the noble elm tree. Now the beauty they hopefully created is threatened with complete destruction as disease sweeps through the elms, carried by a beetle that would have only limited chance to build up large populations and to spread from tree to tree if the elms were only occasional trees in a richly diversified planting.

17   Another factor in the modern insect problem is one that must be viewed against a background of geologic and human history: the spreading of thousands of different kinds of organisms from their native homes to invade new territories. This worldwide migration has been studied and graphically described by the British ecologist Charles Elton in his recent book *The Ecology of Invasions.* During the Cretaceous Period, some hundred million years ago, flooding seas cut many land bridges between continents and living things found themselves confined in what Elton calls "colossal separate nature re-

serves." There, isolated from others of their kind, they developed many new species. When some of the land masses were joined again, about 15 million years ago, these species began to move out into new territories—a movement that is not only still in progress but is now receiving considerable assistance from man.[3]

18   The importation of plants is the primary agent in the modern spread of species, for animals have almost invariably gone along with the plants, quarantine being a comparatively recent and not completely effective innovation. The United States Office of Plant Introduction alone has introduced almost 200,000 species and varieties of plants from all over the world. Nearly half of the 180 or so major insect enemies of plants in the United States are accidental imports from abroad, and most of them have come as hitchhikers on plants.

19   In new territory, out of reach of the restraining hand of the natural enemies that kept down its numbers in its native land, an invading plant or animal is able to become enormously abundant. Thus it is no accident that our most troublesome insects are introduced species.

20   These invasions, both the naturally occurring and those dependent on human assistance, are likely to continue indefinitely. Quarantine and massive chemical campaigns are only extremely expensive ways of buying time. We are faced, according to Dr. Elton, "with a life-and-death need not just to find new technological means of suppressing this plant or that animal"; instead we need the basic knowledge of animal populations and their relations to their surroundings that will "promote an even balance and damp down the explosive power of outbreaks and new invasions."

21   Much of the necessary knowledge is now available but we do not use it. We train ecologists in our universities and even employ them in our governmental agencies but we seldom take their advice. We allow the chemical death rain to fall as though there were no alternative, whereas in fact there are many, and our ingenuity could soon discover many more if given opportunity.

22   Have we fallen into a mesmerized state that makes us accept as inevitable that which is inferior or detrimental, as though having lost the will or the vision to demand that which is good? Such thinking, in the words of the ecologist Paul Shepard, "idealizes life with only its head out of water, inches above the limits of toleration of the corruption of its own environment . . . Why should we tolerate a diet of weak poisons, a home in insipid surroundings, a circle of acquaintances who are not quite our enemies, the noise of motors with just enough relief to prevent insanity? Who would want to live in a world which is just not quite fatal?"[4]

23   Yet such a world is pressed upon us. The crusade to create a chemically sterile, insect-free world seems to have engendered a fanatic zeal on the part of many specialists and most of the so-called control agencies. On every hand there is evidence that those engaged in spraying operations exercise a ruthless power. "The regulatory entomologists . . . function as prosecutor, judge and jury, tax assessor and collector and sheriff to enforce their own orders," said

Connecticut entomologist Neely Turner. The most flagrant abuses go unchecked in both state and federal agencies.

24   It is not my contention that chemical insecticides must never be used. I do contend that we have put poisonous and biologically potent chemicals indiscriminately into the hands of persons largely or wholly ignorant of their potentials for harm. We have subjected enormous numbers of people to contact with these poisons, without their consent and often without their knowledge. If the Bill of Rights contains no guarantee that a citizen shall be secure against lethal poisons distributed either by private individuals or by public officials, it is surely only because our forefathers, despite their considerable wisdom and foresight, could conceive of no such problem.

25   I contend, furthermore, that we have allowed these chemicals to be used with little or no advance investigation of their effect on soil, water, wildlife, and man himself. Future generations are unlikely to condone our lack of prudent concern for the integrity of the natural world that supports all life.

26   There is still very limited awareness of the nature of the threat. This is an era of specialists, each of whom sees his own problem and is unaware of or intolerant of the larger frame into which it fits. It is also an era dominated by industry, in which the right to make a dollar at whatever cost is seldom challenged. When the public protests, confronted with some obvious evidence of damaging results of pesticide applications, it is fed little tranquilizing pills of half truth. We urgently need an end to these false assurances, to the sugar coating of unpalatable facts. It is the public that is being asked to assume the risks that the insect controllers calculate. The public must decide whether it wishes to continue on the present road, and it can do so only when in full possession of the facts. In the words of Jean Rostand, "The obligation to endure gives us the right to know."

Notes

1. "Report on Environmental Health Problems," *Hearings,* 86th Congress, Subcom. of Com. on Appropriations, March 1960, p. 170.
2. *The Pesticide Situation for 1957–58,* U.S. Dept. of Agric., Commodity Stabilization Service, April 1958, p. 10.
3. Elton, Charles S., *The Ecology of Invasions by Animals and Plants.* New York: Wiley, 1958.
4. Shephard, Paul, "The Place of Nature in Man's World," *Atlantic Naturalist,* Vol. 13 (April–June 1958), pp. 85–89.

Topical Considerations

1. Primarily because of the arguments raised by Rachel Carson in *Silent Spring*—the source of this essay—the U.S. government decided to ban the

use of DDT. How did that chemical affect the chain of life that Carson discusses in paragraph 2?

2. What is the basis of Carson's claim that biological life lacks the time to adjust to the changes in the environment brought on by our technological society?

3. Who was Albert Schweitzer, and why would Carson quote him in paragraph 2: "Man can hardly even recognize the devils of his own creation"?

4. What were the two greatest problems of our age, according to Carson 30 years ago? Has either been resolved? What has happened to the Cold War, which has alleviated some of the threat? What new threats have arisen?

5. Explain the two major reasons why insects have come into conflict with humans. Why are the infestations worse in modern agriculture than in primitive farming methods?

6. In paragraph 22 Carson quotes ecologist Paul Shepard's description of an inferior life in a "world which is just not quite fatal." Do you think we are at that point yet? What has happened since Carson wrote this book to give us hope that we can "demand what is good"?

Rhetorical Considerations

1. What are Carson's main contentions in this essay? Where does she state them? Did you find them strong enough to support her proposal at the end of the essay?

2. Explain the meaning of the title Rachel Carson chose for this essay. Why does she leave this concept ("the obligation to endure") to the end of her essay? Does the title forecast the essay's contents?

3. Carson cites several authorities including Charles Elton. How do her quotations in paragraphs 17 and 20 from Elton's book, *The Ecology of Invasions,* support her statement concerning the movement of species into new territories?

4. Where does Carson refer to the opposition in the argument concerning chemical control of insects? Does she treat her opponents' cause fairly? How does she characterize those who favor the use of insecticides?

5. It has been said that Carson combines keen scientific observation with rich poetic description. Where in this essay can you find examples of this combination?

Writing Assignments

1. Find out what has happened to the use of DDT since Carson's book came out. Describe the effects of DDT on the food chain and explain why various countries have banned DDT's use. Which countries have not banned DDT?

2. Study Rachel Carson's life and works to see why she became such an important spokesperson for the environmental movement. Write a paper discussing her work and the opposition she faced when *Silent Spring* was first published.

3. Research a contemporary environmental group such as Green Peace or the Sierra Club. Write a paper on what the group is presently doing to ensure that no more chemicals find their way into our water, land, or air.

4. Write a rebuttal to Carson's case against pesticides, arguing that various chemicals have saved humans from diseases and have provided great increases in crops. Quote authorities for evidence to support your claims.

Letter from Birmingham Jail
Martin Luther King, Jr.

Martin Luther King, Jr. (1929–1968) was one of the most prominent and charismatic leaders for black civil rights in America. An ordained minister with a doctorate in theology, he organized the Southern Christian Leadership Conference in 1957 in order to promote justice and equality for black Americans. His sense of social responsibility, his moral vision, his ardent commitment to nonviolence, and the powerful eloquence of his voice distinguished King as a leader destined to transform America. Under his leadership, racist laws that prohibited blacks from using restaurants, public swimming pools, and seats in the forward sections of buses were eventually eliminated.

In 1963 King was arrested at a sit-in demonstration in a diner in Birmingham, Alabama. Written from a jail cell, the famous letter reprinted here was addressed to King's fellow clergy who were critical of his activities in the name of social justice. However, the letter also addresses the conscience of the American people or any people who care about human dignity and human rights. For his efforts King was awarded the Nobel Peace Prize in 1964. Four years later, while supporting striking sanitation workers in Memphis, King was assassinated.

BEFORE YOU READ

In many ways this letter is a defense of King's own civil disobedience. Before reading this letter, review the justifications offered by Thoreau in his essay, "Civil Disobedience." What principles guided Thoreau in calling for citizens to oppose unjust laws? To what higher moral laws do you anticipate King will appeal in his letter to other clergy?

AS YOU READ

Note King's handling of his critics. What different strategies does he use to win them over to his point of view? Also notice how King logically analyzes each point of their criticism.

April 16, 1963

My Dear Fellow Clergymen:*

1   While confined here in the Birmingham city jail, I came across your recent statement calling my present activities "unwise and untimely." Seldom do I pause to answer criticism of my work and ideas. If I sought to answer all the criticisms that cross my desk, my secretaries would have little time for anything other than such correspondence in the course of the day, and I would have no time for constructive work. But since I feel that you are men of genuine good will and that your criticisms are sincerely set forth, I want to try to answer your statement in what I hope will be patient and reasonable terms.

2   I think I should indicate why I am here in Birmingham, since you have been influenced by the view which argues against "outsiders coming in." I have the honor of serving as president of the Southern Christian Leadership Conference, an organization operating in every southern state, with headquarters in Atlanta, Georgia. We have some eighty-five affiliated organizations across the South, and one of them is the Alabama Christian Movement for Human Rights. Frequently we share staff, educational, and financial resources with our affiliates. Several months ago the affiliate here in Birmingham asked us to be on call to engage in a nonviolent direct-action program if such were deemed necessary. We readily consented, and when the hour came we lived up to our promise. So I, along with several members of my staff, am here because I was invited here. I am here because I have organizational ties here.

3   But more basically, I am in Birmingham because injustice is here. Just as the prophets of the eighth century B.C. left their villages and carried their "thus saith the Lord" far beyond the boundaries of their home towns, and just as the Apostle Paul left his village of Tarsus and carried the gospel of Jesus Christ to the far corners of the Greco-Roman world, so am I compelled to carry the gospel of freedom beyond my own home town. Like Paul, I must constantly respond to the Macedonian call for aid.

4   Moreover, I am cognizant of the interrelatedness of all communities and states. I cannot sit idly by in Atlanta and not be concerned about what happens in Birmingham. Injustice anywhere is a threat to justice everywhere. We are caught in an inescapable network of mutuality, tied in a single garment of destiny. Whatever affects one directly, affects all indirectly.

---

*This response to a published statement by eight fellow clergymen from Alabama (Bishop C. C. J. Carpenter, Bishop Joseph A. Durick, Rabbi Hilton L. Grafman, Bishop Paul Hardin, Bishop Holan B. Harmon, the Reverend George M. Murray, the Reverend Edward V. Ramage and the Reverend Earl Stallings) was composed under somewhat constricting circumstances. Begun on the margins of the newspaper in which the statement appeared while I was in jail, the letter was continued on scraps of writing paper supplied by a friendly Negro trusty, and concluded on a pad my attorneys were eventually permitted to leave me. Although the text remains in substance unaltered, I have indulged in the author's prerogative of polishing it for publication. [King's note]

Never again can we afford to live with the narrow, provincial, "outside agitator" idea. Anyone who lives inside the United States can never be considered an outsider anywhere within its bounds.

5   You deplore the demonstrations taking place in Birmingham. But your statement, I am sorry to say, fails to express a similar concern for the conditions that brought about the demonstrations. I am sure that none of you would want to rest content with the superficial kind of social analysis that deals merely with effects and does not grapple with underlying causes. It is unfortunate that demonstrations are taking place in Birmingham, but it is even more unfortunate that the city's white power structure left the Negro community with no alternative.

6   In any nonviolent campaign there are four basic steps: collection of the facts to determine whether injustices exist; negotiation; self-purification; and direct action. We have gone through all these steps in Birmingham. There can be no gainsaying the fact that racial injustice engulfs this community. Birmingham is probably the most thoroughly segregated city in the United States. Its ugly record of brutality is widely known. Negroes have experienced grossly unjust treatment in the courts. There have been more unsolved bombings of Negro homes and churches in Birmingham than in any other city in the nation. These are the hard brutal facts of the case. On the basis of these conditions, Negro leaders sought to negotiate with the city fathers. But the latter consistently refused to engage in good-faith negotiation.

7   Then, last September, came the opportunity to talk with leaders of Birmingham's economic community. In the course of the negotiations, certain promises were made by the merchants—for example, to remove the stores' humiliating racial signs. On the basis of these promises, the Reverend Fred Shuttlesworth and the leaders of the Alabama Christian Movement for Human Rights agreed to a moratorium on all demonstrations. As the weeks and months went by, we realized that we were the victims of a broken promise. A few signs, briefly removed, returned; the others remained.

8   As in so many past experiences, our hopes had been blasted, and the shadow of deep disappointment settled upon us. We had no alternative except to prepare for direct action, whereby we would present our very bodies as a means of laying our case before the conscience of the local and the national community. Mindful of the difficulties involved, we decided to undertake a process of self-purification. We began a series of workshops on nonviolence, and we repeatedly asked ourselves: "Are you able to accept blows without retaliating?" "Are you able to endure the ordeal of jail?" We decided to schedule our direct-action program for the Easter season, realizing that except for Christmas, this is the main shopping period of the year. Knowing that a strong economic-withdrawal program would be the by-product of direct action, we felt that this would be the best time to bring pressure to bear on the merchants for the needed change.

9   Then it occurred to us that Birmingham's mayoral election was coming up in March, and we speedily decided to postpone action until after election

day. When we discovered that the Commissioner of Public Safety, Eugene "Bull" Connor, had piled up enough votes to be in the run-off, we decided again to postpone action until the day after the run-off so that the demonstrations could not be used to cloud the issues. Like many others, we waited to see Mr. Connor defeated, and to this end we endured postponement after postponement. Having aided in this community need, we felt that our direct-action program could be delayed no longer.

10   You may well ask, "Why direct action? Why sit-ins, marches, and so forth? Isn't negotiation a better path?" You are quite right in calling for negotiation. Indeed, this is the very purpose of direct action. Nonviolent direct action seeks to create such a crisis and foster such a tension that a community which has constantly refused to negotiate is forced to confront the issue. It seeks to dramatize the issue that it can no longer be ignored. My citing the creation of tension as part of the work of the nonviolent resister may sound rather shocking. But I must confess that I am not afraid of the word "tension." I have earnestly opposed violent tension, but there is a type of constructive, nonviolent tension which is necessary for growth. Just as Socrates felt that it was necessary to create a tension in the mind so that individuals could rise from the bondage of myths and half truths to the unfettered realm of creative analysis and objective appraisal, so must we see the need for nonviolent gadflies to create the kind of tension in society that will help men rise from the dark depths of prejudice and racism to the majestic heights of understanding and brotherhood.

11   The purpose of our direct-action program is to create a situation so crisis-packed that it will inevitably open the door to negotiation. I therefore concur with you in your call for negotiation. Too long has our beloved Southland been bogged down in a tragic effort to live in monologue rather than dialogue.

12   One of the basic points in your statement is that the action that I and my associates have taken in Birmingham is untimely. Some have asked: "Why didn't you give the new city administration time to act?" The only answer that I can give to this query is that the new Birmingham administration must be prodded about as much as the outgoing one, before it will act. We are sadly mistaken if we feel that the election of Albert Boutwell as mayor will bring the millennium to Birmingham. While Mr. Boutwell is a much more gentle person than Mr. Connor, they are both segregationists, dedicated to maintenance of the status quo. I have hoped that Mr. Boutwell will be reasonable enough to see the futility of massive resistance to desegregation. But he will not see this without pressure from devotees of civil rights. My friends, I must say to you that we have not made a single gain in civil rights without determined legal and nonviolent pressure. Lamentably, it is an historical fact that privileged groups seldom give up their privileges voluntarily. Individuals may see the moral light and voluntarily give up their unjust posture; but, as Reinhold Niebuhr has reminded us, groups tend to be more immoral than individuals.

13   We know through painful experience that freedom is never voluntarily given by the oppressor; it must be demanded by the oppressed. Frankly, I have

yet to engage in a direct-action campaign that was "well timed" in the view of those who have not suffered unduly from the disease of segregation. For years now I have heard the word "Wait!" It rings in the ear of every Negro with piercing familiarity. This "Wait" has almost always meant "Never." We must come to see, with one of our distinguished jurists, that "justice too long delayed is justice denied."

14   We have waited for more than 340 years for our constitutional and God-given rights. The nations of Asia and Africa are moving with jetlike speed toward gaining political independence, but we still creep at horse-and-buggy pace toward gaining a cup of coffee at a lunch counter. Perhaps it is easy for those who have never felt the stinging darts of segregation to say, "Wait." But when you have seen vicious mobs lynch your mothers and fathers at will and drown your sisters and brothers at whim; when you have seen hate-filled policemen curse, kick, and even kill your black brothers and sisters; when you see the vast majority of your twenty million Negro brothers smothering in an airtight cage of poverty in the midst of an affluent society; when you suddenly find your tongue twisted and your speech stammering as you seek to explain to your six-year-old daughter why she can't go to the public amusement park that has just been advertised on television, and see tears welling up in her eyes when she is told that Funtown is closed to colored children, and see ominous clouds of inferiority beginning to form in her little mental sky, and see her beginning to distort her personality by developing an unconscious bitterness toward white people; when you have to concoct an answer for a five-year-old son who is asking, "Daddy, why do white people treat colored people so mean?"; when you take a cross-country drive and find it necessary to sleep night after night in the uncomfortable corners of your automobile because no motel will accept you; when you are humiliated day in and day out by nagging signs reading "white" and "colored"; when your first name becomes "nigger," your middle name becomes "boy" (however old you are) and your last name becomes "John," and your wife and mother are never given the respected title "Mrs"; when you are harried by day and haunted by night by the fact that you are a Negro, living constantly at tiptoe stance, never quite knowing what to expect next, and are plagued with inner fears and outer resentments; when you are forever fighting a degenerating sense of "nobodiness"— then you will understand why we find it difficult to wait. There comes a time when the cup of endurance runs over, and men are no longer willing to be plunged into the abyss of despair. I hope, sirs, you can understand our legitimate and unavoidable impatience.

15   You express a great deal of anxiety over our willingness to break laws. This is certainly a legitimate concern. Since we so diligently urge people to obey the Supreme Court's decision of 1954 outlawing segregation in the public schools, at first glance it may seem rather paradoxical for us consciously to break laws. One may well ask: "How can you advocate breaking some laws and obeying others?" The answer lies in the fact that there are two types of laws: just and unjust. I would be the first to advocate obeying just laws. One

has not only a legal but a moral responsibility to obey just laws. Conversely, one has a moral responsibility to disobey unjust laws. I would agree with St. Augustine that "an unjust law is no law at all."

16   Now, what is the difference between the two? How does one determine whether a law is just or unjust? A just law is a man-made code that squares with the moral law or the law of God. An unjust law is a code that is out of harmony with the moral law. To put it in the terms of St. Thomas Aquinas: An unjust law is a human law that is not rooted in eternal law and natural law. Any law that uplifts human personality is just. Any law that degrades human personality is unjust. All segregation statutes are unjust because segregation distorts the soul and damages the personality. It gives the segregator a false sense of superiority and the segregated a false sense of inferiority. Segregation, to use the terminology of the Jewish philosopher Martin Buber, substitutes an "I-it" relationship for an "I-thou" relationship and ends up relegating persons to the status of things. Hence segregation is not only politically, economically, and sociologically unsound, it is morally wrong and sinful. Paul Tillich has said that sin is separation. Is not segregation an existential expression of man's tragic separation, his awful estrangement, his terrible sinfulness? Thus it is that I can urge men to obey the 1954 decision of the Supreme Court, for it is morally right; and I can urge them to disobey segregation ordinances, for they are morally wrong.

17   Let us consider a more concrete example of just and unjust laws. An unjust law is a code that a numerical or power majority group compels a minority group to obey but does not make binding on itself. This is *difference* made legal. By the same token, a just law is a code that a majority compels a minority to follow and that it is willing to follow itself. This is *sameness* made legal.

18   Let me give another explanation. A law is unjust if it is inflicted on a minority that, as a result of being denied the right to vote, had no part in enacting or devising the law. Who can say that the legislature of Alabama which set up that state's segregation laws was democratically elected? Throughout Alabama all sorts of devious methods are used to prevent Negroes from becoming registered voters, and there are some counties in which, even though Negroes constitute a majority of the population, not a single Negro is registered. Can any law enacted under such circumstances be considered democratically structured?

19   Sometimes a law is just on its face and unjust in its application. For instance, I have been arrested on a charge of parading without a permit. Now, there is nothing wrong in having an ordinance which requires a permit for a parade. But such an ordinance becomes unjust when it is used to maintain segregation and to deny citizens the First Amendment privilege of peaceful assembly and protest.

20   I hope you are able to see the distinction I am trying to point out. In no sense do I advocate evading or defying the law, as would the rabid segregationist. That would lead to anarchy. One who breaks an unjust law must do so

openly, lovingly, and with a willingness to accept the penalty. I submit that an individual who breaks a law that conscience tells him is unjust, and who willingly accepts the penalty of imprisonment in order to arouse the conscience of the community over its injustice, is in reality expressing the highest respect for law.

21   Of course, there is nothing new about this kind of civil disobedience. It was evidenced sublimely in the refusal of Shadrach, Meshach, and Abednego to obey the laws of Nebuchadnezzar, on the ground that a higher moral law was at stake. It was practiced superbly by the early Christians, who were willing to face hungry lions and the excruciating pain of chopping blocks rather than submit to certain unjust laws of the Roman Empire. To a degree, academic freedom is a reality today because Socrates practiced civil disobedience. In our own nation, the Boston Tea Party represented a massive act of civil disobedience.

22   We should never forget that everything Adolf Hitler did in Germany was "legal" and everything the Hungarian freedom fighters did in Hungary was "illegal." It was "illegal" to aid and comfort a Jew in Hitler's Germany. Even so, I am sure that, had I lived in Germany at the time, I would have aided and comforted my Jewish brothers. If today I lived in a Communist country where certain principles dear to the Christian faith are suppressed, I would openly advocate disobeying that country's antireligious laws.

23   I must make two honest confessions to you, my Christian and Jewish brothers. First, I must confess that over the past few years I have been gravely disappointed with the white moderate. I have almost reached the regrettable conclusion that the Negro's great stumbling block in his stride toward freedom is not the White Citizen's Counciler or the Ku Klux Klanner, but the white moderate, who is more devoted to "order" than to justice; who prefers a negative peace which is the absence of tension to a positive peace which is the presence of justice; who constantly says, "I agree with you in the goal you seek, but I cannot agree with your methods of direct action"; who paternalistically believes he can set the timetable for another man's freedom; who lives by a mythical concept of time and who constantly advises the Negro to wait for a "more convenient season." Shallow understanding from people of good will is more frustrating than absolute misunderstanding from people of ill will. Lukewarm acceptance is much more bewildering than outright rejection.

24   I had hoped that the white moderate would understand that law and order exist for the purpose of establishing justice and that when they fail in this purpose they become the dangerously structured dams that block the flow of social progress. I had hoped that the white moderate would understand that the present tension in the South is a necessary phase of the transition from an obnoxious negative peace, in which the Negro passively accepted his unjust plight, to a substantive and positive peace, in which all men will respect the dignity and worth of human personality. Actually, we who engage in nonviolent direct action are not the creators of tension. We merely bring to the surface the hidden tension that is already alive. We bring it out in the open,

where it can be seen and dealt with. Like a boil that can never be cured so long as it is covered up but must be opened with all its ugliness to the natural medicines of air and light, injustice must be exposed, with all the tension its exposure creates, to the light of human conscience and the air of national opinion, before it can be cured.

25   In your statement you assert that our actions, even though peaceful, must be condemned because they precipitate violence. But is this a logical assertion? Isn't this like condemning a robbed man because his possession of money precipitated the evil act of robbery? Isn't this like condemning Socrates because his unswerving commitment to truth and his philosophical inquiries precipitated the act by the misguided populace in which they made him drink hemlock? Isn't this like condemning Jesus because his unique God-consciousness and never-ceasing devotion to God's will precipitated the evil act of crucifixion? We must come to see that, as the federal courts have consistently affirmed, it is wrong to urge an individual to cease his efforts to gain his basic constitutional rights because the quest may precipitate violence. Society must protect the robbed and punish the robber.

26   I had also hoped that the white moderate would reject the myth concerning time in relation to the struggle for freedom. I have just received a letter from a white brother in Texas. He writes: "All Christians know that the colored people will receive equal rights eventually, but it is possible that you are in too great a religious hurry. It has taken Christianity almost two thousand years to accomplish what it has. The teachings of Christ take time to come to earth." Such an attitude stems from a tragic misconception of time, from the strangely irrational notion that there is something in the very flow of time that will inevitably cure all ills. Actually, time itself is neutral; it can be used either destructively or constructively. More and more I feel that the people of ill will have used time much more effectively than have the people of good will. We will have to repent in this generation not merely for the hateful words and actions of the bad people, but for the appalling silence of the good people. Human progress never rolls in on wheels of inevitability; it comes through the tireless efforts of men willing to be co-workers with God, and without this hard work, time itself becomes an ally of the forces of social stagnation. We must use time creatively, in the knowledge that the time is always ripe to do right. Now is the time to make real the promise of democracy and transform our pending national elegy into a creative psalm of brotherhood. Now is the time to lift our national policy from the quicksand of racial injustice to the solid rock of human dignity.

27   You speak of our activity in Birmingham as extreme. At first I was rather disappointed that fellow clergymen would see my nonviolent efforts as those of an extremist. I began thinking about the fact that I stand in the middle of two opposing forces in the Negro community. One is a force of complacency, made up in part of Negroes who, as a result of long years of oppression, are so drained of self-respect and a sense of "somebodiness" that they have adjusted to segregation; and in part of a few middle-class Negroes who, because of a

degree of academic and economic security and because in some ways they profit by segregation, have become insensitive to the problems of the masses. The other force is one of bitterness and hatred, and it comes perilously close to advocating violence. It is expressed in the various black nationalist groups that are springing up across the nation, the largest and best known being Elijah Muhammad's Muslim movement. Nourished by the Negro's frustration over the continued existence of racial discrimination, this movement is made up of people who have lost faith in America, who have absolutely repudiated Christianity, and who have concluded that the white man is an incorrigible "devil."

28   I have tried to stand between these two forces, saying that we need emulate neither the "do-nothingism" of the complacent nor the hatred and despair of the black nationalist. For there is the more excellent way of love and nonviolent protest. I am grateful to God that, through the influence of the Negro church, the way of nonviolence became an integral part of our struggle.

29   If this philosophy had not emerged, by now many streets of the South would, I am convinced, be flowing with blood. And I am further convinced that if our white brothers dismiss as "rabble-rousers" and "outside agitators" those of us who employ nonviolent direct action, and if they refuse to support our nonviolent efforts, millions of Negroes will, out of frustration and despair, seek solace and security in black nationalist ideologies—a development that would inevitably lead to a frightening racial nightmare.

30   Oppressed people cannot remain oppressed forever. The yearning for freedom eventually manifests itself, and that is what has happened to the American Negro. Something within has reminded him of his birthright of freedom, and something without has reminded him that it can be gained. Consciously or unconsciously, he has been caught up by the *Zeitgeist,* and with his black brothers of Africa and his brown and yellow brothers of Asia, South America, and the Caribbean, the United States Negro is moving with a sense of great urgency toward the promised land of racial justice. If one recognizes this vital urge that has engulfed the Negro community, one should readily understand why public demonstrations are taking place. The Negro has many pent-up resentments and latent frustrations, and he must release them. So let him march; let him make prayer pilgrimages to the city hall; let him go on freedom rides—and try to understand why he must do so. If his repressed emotions are not released in nonviolent ways, they will seek expression through violence; this is not a threat but a fact of history. So I have not said to my people, "Get rid of your discontent." Rather, I have tried to say that this normal and healthy discontent can be channeled into the creative outlet of nonviolent direct action. And now this approach is being termed extremist.

31   But though I was initially disappointed at being categorized as an extremist, as I continued to think about the matter I gradually gained a measure of satisfaction from the label. Was not Jesus an extremist for love: "Love your enemies, bless them that curse you, do good to them that hate you, and pray for them which despitefully use you, and persecute you." Was not Amos an extremist for justice: "Let justice roll down like waters and righteousness like

an ever-flowing stream." Was not Paul an extremist for the Christian gospel: "I bear in my body the marks of the Lord Jesus." Was not Martin Luther an extremist: "Here I stand; I cannot do otherwise, so help me God." And John Bunyan: "I will stay in jail to the end of my days before I make a butchery of my conscience." And Abraham Lincoln: "This nation cannot survive half slave and half free." And Thomas Jefferson: "We hold these truths to be self-evident, that all men are created equal. . . ." So the question is not whether we will be extremists, but what kind of extremists we will be. Will we be extremists for hate or for love? Will we be extremists for the preservation of injustice or for the extension of justice? In that dramatic scene on Calvary's hill three men were crucified. We must never forget that all three were crucified for the same crime—the crime of extremism. Two were extremists for immorality, and thus fell below their environment. The other, Jesus Christ, was an extremist for love, truth, and goodness, and thereby rose above his environment. Perhaps the South, the nation, and the world are in dire need of creative extremists.

32   I had hoped that the white moderate would see this need. Perhaps I was too optimistic; perhaps I expected too much. I suppose I should have realized that few members of the oppressor race can understand the deep groans and passionate yearnings of the oppressed race, and still fewer have the vision to see that injustice must be rooted out by strong, persistent, and determined action. I am thankful, however, that some of our white brothers in the South have grasped the meaning of this social revolution and committed themselves to it. They are still all too few in quantity, but they are big in quality. Some—such as Ralph McGill, Lillian Smith, Harry Golden, James McBride Dabbs, Ann Braden, and Sarah Patton Boyle—have written about our struggle in eloquent and prophetic terms. Others have marched with us down nameless streets of the South. They have languished in filthy, roach-infested jails, suffering the abuse and brutality of policemen who view them as "dirty nigger-lovers." Unlike so many of their moderate brothers and sisters, they have recognized the urgency of the moment and sensed the need for powerful "action" antidotes to combat the disease of segregation.

33   Let me take note of my other major disappointment. I have been so greatly disappointed with the white church and its leadership. Of course, there are some notable exceptions. I am not unmindful of the fact that each of you has taken some significant stands on this issue. I commend you, Reverend Stallings, for your Christian stand on this past Sunday, in welcoming Negroes to your worship service on a nonsegregated basis. I commend the Catholic leaders of this state for integrating Spring Hill College several years ago.

34   But despite these notable exceptions, I must honestly reiterate that I have been disappointed with the church. I do not say this as one of those negative critics who can always find something wrong with the church. I say this as a minister of the gospel, who loves the church; who was nurtured in its bosom; who has been sustained by its spiritual blessings and who will remain true to it as long as the cord of life shall lengthen.

35   When I was suddenly catapulted into the leadership of the bus protest in Montgomery, Alabama, a few years ago, I felt we would be supported by the white church. I felt that the white ministers, priests, and rabbis of the South would be among our strongest allies. Instead, some have been outright opponents, refusing to understand the freedom movement and misrepresenting its leaders; all too many others have been more cautious than courageous and have remained silent behind the anesthetizing security of stained-glass windows.

36   In spite of my shattered dreams, I came to Birmingham with the hope that the white religious leadership of this community would see the justice of our cause and, with deep moral concern, would serve as the channel through which our just grievances could reach the power structure. I had hoped that each of you would understand. But again I have been disappointed. . . .

37   There was a time when the church was very powerful—in the time when the early Christians rejoiced at being deemed worthy to suffer for what they believed. In those days the church was not merely a thermometer that recorded the ideas and principles of popular opinion; it was a thermostat that transformed the mores of society. Whenever the early Christians entered a town, the people in power became disturbed and immediately sought to convict the Christians for being "disturbers of the peace" and "outside agitators." But the Christians pressed on, in the conviction that they were "a colony of heaven," called to obey God rather than man. Small in number, they were big in commitment. They were too God intoxicated to be "astronomically intimidated." By their effort and example they brought an end to such ancient evils as infanticide and gladiatorial contests.

38   Things are different now. So often the contemporary church is a weak, ineffectual voice with an uncertain sound. So often it is an arch-defender of the status quo. Far from being disturbed by the presence of the church, the power structure of the average community is consoled by the church's silent—and often even vocal—sanction of things as they are.

39   But the judgment of God is upon the church as never before. If today's church does not recapture the sacrificial spirit of the early church, it will lose its authenticity, forfeit the loyalty of millions, and be dismissed as an irrelevant social club with no meaning for the twentieth century. Every day I meet young people whose disappointment with the church has turned into outright disgust.

40   Perhaps I have once again been too optimistic. Is organized religion too inextricably bound to the status quo to save our nation and the world? Perhaps I must turn my faith to the inner spiritual church, the church within the church, as the true *ekklesia* and the hope of the world. But again I am thankful to God that some noble souls from the ranks of organized religion have broken loose from the paralyzing chains of conformity and joined us as active partners in the struggle for freedom. They have left their secure congregations and walked the streets of Albany, Georgia, with us. They have gone down the highways of the South on torturous rides for freedom. Yes, they have gone to jail with us. Some have been dismissed from their churches, have lost the sup-

port of their bishops and fellow ministers. But they have acted in the faith that right defeated is stronger than evil triumphant. Their witness has been the spiritual salt that has preserved the true meaning of the gospel in these troubled times. They have carved a tunnel of hope through the dark mountain of disappointment.

41   I hope the church as a whole will meet the challenge of this decisive hour. But even if the church does not come to the aid of justice, I have no despair about the future. I have no fear about the outcome of our struggle in Birmingham, even if our motives are at present misunderstood. We will reach the goal of freedom in Birmingham and all over the nation, because the goal of America is freedom. Abused and scorned though we may be, our destiny is tied up with America's destiny. Before the pilgrims landed at Plymouth, we were here. Before the pen of Jefferson etched the majestic words of the Declaration of Independence across the pages of history, we were here. For more than two centuries our forebears labored in this country without wages; they made cotton king; they built the homes of their masters while suffering gross injustice and shameful humiliation—and yet out of a bottomless vitality they continued to thrive and develop. If the inexpressible cruelties of slavery could not stop us, the opposition we now face will surely fail. We will win our freedom because the sacred heritage of our nation and the eternal will of God are embodied in our echoing demands.

42   Before closing I feel impelled to mention one other point in your statement that has troubled me profoundly. You warmly commended the Birmingham police force for keeping "order" and "preventing violence." I doubt that you would have so warmly commended the police force if you had seen its dogs sinking their teeth into unarmed, nonviolent Negroes. I doubt that you would so quickly commend the policemen if you were to observe their ugly and inhumane treatment of Negroes here in the city jail; if you were to watch them push and curse old Negro women and young Negro girls; if you were to see them slap and kick old Negro men and young boys; if you were to observe them, as they did on two occasions, refuse to give us food because we wanted to sing our grace together. I cannot join you in your praise of the Birmingham police department.

43   It is true that the police have exercised a degree of discipline in handling the demonstrators. In this sense they have conducted themselves rather "nonviolently" in public. But for what purpose? To preserve the evil system of segregation. Over the past few years I have consistently preached that nonviolence demands that the means we use must be as pure as the ends we seek. I have tried to make clear that it is wrong to use immoral means to attain moral ends. But now I must affirm that it is just as wrong, or perhaps even more so, to use moral means to preserve immoral ends. Perhaps Mr. Connor and his policemen have been rather nonviolent in public, as was Chief Pritchett in Albany, Georgia, but they have used the moral means of nonviolence to maintain the immoral end of racial injustice. As

T. S. Eliot has said, "The last temptation is the greatest treason: To do the right deed for the wrong reason."

44   I wish you had commended the Negro sit-inners and demonstrators of Birmingham for their sublime courage, their willingness to suffer, and their amazing discipline in the midst of great provocation. One day the South will recognize its real heroes. They will be the James Merediths, with the noble sense of purpose that enables them to face jeering and hostile mobs, and with the agonizing loneliness that characterizes the life of the pioneer. They will be old, oppressed, battered Negro women, symbolized in a seventy-two-year-old woman in Montgomery, Alabama, who rose up with a sense of dignity and with her people decided not to ride segregated buses, and who responded with ungrammatical profundity to one who inquired about her weariness: "My feets is tired, but my soul is at rest." They will be the young high school and college students, the young ministers of the gospel and a host of their elders, courageously and nonviolently sitting in at lunch counters and willingly going to jail for conscience' sake. One day the South will know that when these disinherited children of God sat down at lunch counters, they were in reality standing up for what is best in the American dream and for the most sacred values in our Judaeo-Christian heritage, thereby bringing our nation back to those great wells of democracy which were dug deep by the founding fathers in their formulation of the Constitution and the Declaration of Independence.

45   Never before have I written so long a letter. I'm afraid it is much too long to take your precious time. I can assure you that it would have been much shorter if I had been writing from a comfortable desk, but what else can one do when he is alone in a narrow jail cell, other than write long letters, think long thoughts, and pray long prayers?

46   If I have said anything in this letter that overstates the truth and indicates an unreasonable impatience, I beg you to forgive me. If I have said anything that understates the truth and indicates my having a patience that allows me to settle for anything less than brotherhood, I beg God to forgive me.

47   I hope this letter finds you strong in the faith. I also hope that circumstances will soon make it possible for me to meet each of you, not as an integrationist or a civil rights leader but as a fellow clergyman and a Christian brother. Let us all hope that the dark clouds of racial prejudice will soon pass away and the deep fog of misunderstanding will be lifted from our fear-drenched communities, and in some not too distant tomorrow the radiant stars of love and brotherhood will shine over our great nation with all their scintillating beauty.

Yours in the cause of
Peace and Brotherhood,
MARTIN LUTHER KING, JR.

Topical Considerations

1. After reading King's essay, what is your understanding of "nonviolent" action? What kinds of measures does it constitute? What is your opinion of the effectiveness of this policy on nonviolence? Explain.

2. In paragraph 8, King discusses his workshops on nonviolence, stating that "we repeatedly asked ourselves: 'Are you able to accept blows without retaliating?'" In terms of the goal of King's movement, how would you answer this question? Explain your answer.

3. King says that Birmingham government officials were at the time "dedicated to maintenance of the status quo" (paragraph 12). What does he mean? In your estimation, do today's politicians still practice this? In what ways? What might be done to rechannel such "dedication" in a more useful direction?

4. King states, "We will have to repent in this generation not merely for the hateful words and actions of the bad people, but for the appalling silence of the good people" (paragraph 26). What does this statement mean to you? Do you agree with it? In what situations might silence be "appalling"? Explain.

5. In your own words, what is the relationship between Martin Luther King's nonviolent anti-racism campaign and Christianity? How does one complement the other? How might his civil rights movement been affected without the underlying tenets of Christianity?

6. King refers to both racial and economic injustice. In your opinion, how are race and class connected to one another? How does one affect the other?

7. In paragraph 27 King refers to Elijah Muhammad's Muslim movement, the movement for which Malcolm X acted as a spokesperson for quite some time. Discuss your understanding of the similarities and differences between King's and Malcolm X's movements and the two leaders. In your opinion, is one method more useful in the struggle for civil rights? Is neither movement very effective? Explain.

Rhetorical Considerations

1. Early in his essay (paragraph 3), King establishes himself as a Christian among a long line of eminent Christians. In terms of the argument he makes in this letter, what might be King's strategy here? Did you find it effective?

2. Reread paragraph 10, paying attention to King's strategy in addressing his opposition. What is King's argumentation strategy, and how effective is his technique?

3. In paragraph 14 King provides a sort of "catalogue" of reasons why the civil rights movement could not "wait" any longer. Analyze this technique in terms of King's argument. What effect does such "cataloguing" have on the reader?

4. In paragraphs 15–20 King provides logic and proof regarding the difference between just and unjust laws. Examine this section and determine whether or not his logic is effective.

5. What is your opinion of King's voice in this letter? What does this voice reveal about King's personality, and what role does it play in his argument? In other words, how does King establish credibility, authority, and personality in his letter?

6. Analyze the oratorical nature of this letter, keeping in mind that King was a Christian preacher. How effective would this letter be if delivered as a speech? Explain. Is it as effective in letter form?

Writing Assignments

1. Using King's techniques, write a letter protesting an injustice that you feel may not be entirely understood by people you respect. Take care to explain the nature of the injustice, your idea as to the reason for the injustice, and the reasons why your argument should be accepted.

2. Write a paper in which you focus on some aspect of civil rights today. In this paper, outline your own plan of protest or action, providing, as King does, logic and proof as to the effectiveness of your plan.

GLOSSARY OF RHETORICAL TERMS

abstract language   Words that refer to ideas, qualities, attitudes, and conditions that can not be perceived with the senses—for example, *freedom, beauty, joy*. Opposite of *concrete language*.

ad hominem   From the Latin meaning "against the man"—that is, making an attack on the person rather than on the person's argument or the particular issue.

ad misericordiam   An argument that is an appeal to the emotions of the audience.

ad populum   From the Latin meaning "to the people"—an argument that plays on the prejudices of the *audience*.

analogy   A comparison between something familiar and something unfamiliar. The things being compared are similar in some ways but not in others, although the reasoning process infers likeness in most ways. For instance, the analogy of discrimination against gays in the military to past discrimination against racial minorities is such a comparison.

anticipating the opposition . The process of trying to determine what objections an opponent will make in an argument.

argument   The reasoning process and presentation of evidence about controversial issues. Also writing of which the primary purpose is to convince readers to adopt a particular idea or position, or to persuade them to take a particular course of action.

assertion   A statement of belief. An assertion is the backbone of any argument.

audience   The intended readers of a piece of writing. Knowledge of the audience's needs and expectations helps a writer shape the writing so that it is clear, interesting, and convincing. A *general audience* consists of people of diverse backgrounds and interests.

authority   An expert in a particular field; a reliable and respectable source of information used to support an argument.

backing   The assurance upon which an assumption or *warrant* is based.

bandwagon   The tactic of inviting an audience to accept an assertion because everybody else does.

begging the question   In an argument, making an assumption that what's being argued has already been proven or confirmed.

cause-and-effect analysis   The explanation of why something has happened or what its consequences were or will be.

circular reasoning   Reasoning where the conclusion is hidden in the premise of the argument.

claim   What the writer of an argument is trying to prove; the conclusion of an argument.

cliché   A worn-out or stale expression that dulls the writing and suggests that the writer is lazy or careless.

colloquial language   Words and expressions from everyday speech. Colloquial language can enliven informal writing but is generally inappropriate in formal academic or business writing.

comparison and contrast The identification of similarities (comparison) and differences (contrast) between two or more subjects.

concession In an argument, an acknowledgment of the merits of the opposition's position.

concrete language Words that refer to objects, persons, places, or conditions that can be perceived with the senses: *St. Louis, tree, sharp*. Opposite of *abstract language*.

connotation An association called upon by a word that is beyond its dictionary definition.

credibility The reliability or trustworthiness of the writer or sources. The audience's belief in such.

data Factual information used to support one's reasoning or argument.

definition The clarification or explanation of the meaning of a word or phrase. Specifying the characteristics of something to establish what it is and is not.

denotation The dictionary definition or literal meaning of a word. Contrast *connotation*.

diction The choice and use of words.

ethical appeal An attempt to engage and persuade readers by presenting the writer as a competent, sincere, and fair person.

evidence The facts, statistics, examples, expert opinions, personal testimony, and other information used to support a claim or a thesis.

fact Something that is believed to have objective reality; a piece of information that is regarded as verifiable.

factual evidence Supporting data that an audience considers objectively verifiable.

fallacy See *logical fallacies*.

false analogy The fallacy of comparing two thing that are not sufficiently alike to be compared. Such a comparison erroneously concentrates on a single similarity while ignoring all differences.

false dilemma Reducing a complex problem into an either/or choice.

freewriting A technique for generating ideas. It usually takes place during a fixed amount of time (say, 15 minutes) and you write continuously without stopping to reread.

generalization An assertion inferred from evidence.

grounds The minor premise supporting evidence.

hasty generalization An assertion or conclusion drawn on insufficient evidence.

logical fallacies Errors in reasoning. Some evade the issue of the argument; others oversimplify the argument. See Chapter 7 for a checklist and discussion of logical fallacies.

narration The telling of a story; the recounting of a sequence of events, usually in the order of their occurrence.

neologism From the greek "neo" (new) and "logos" (words). A word coined recently and not in established use.

non sequitur From the Latin meaning "it does not follow." The fallacy of claiming a conclusion that does not follow logically from the premise. Irrelevant "proof" used to support a claim.

opinion A conclusion based on facts or judgments; an arguable, potentially changeable assertion. Assertions of opinion form the backbone of an argument.

post hoc, ergo propter hoc Argument from the Latin meaning "after this, therefore, because of this." The false claim that one event is the cause of another from the mere fact that the first occurs earlier than the second.

process analysis The step-by-step explanation of how something works or how something is done.

proposition The claim or the point to be discussed or proven in an argument.

purpose   What the writer hopes to accomplish in a piece of writing. The chief reason for communicating something about a topic to one's audience.

qualifier   A restriction placed on the *claim* to indicate that it may not always be true as so stated.

racist language   Slurs or derogatory terms that discriminate against or denigrate members of certain races or ethnicity.

reason   A statement that explains or justifies a *claim*.

rebuttal   Exception to a *claim*.

refutation   An attack on an opposing point of view in order to lessen its credibility or to invalidate it.

rhetorical question   A question asked for affect, with no answer expected. The person asking the question either intends to provide the answer or assumes it is obvious; for example, *If we don't put restrictions on the violent language in popular music, what is the message we're sending to the young people.*

sexist language   Language expressing narrow ideas about men's and women's roles, positions, capabilities, or values.

slang   Expressions used by members of a group to create bonds and sometimes exclude others. Most slang is too vague, short-lived, and narrowly understood to be used in any but informal writing.

slanted language   Words or expressions whose connotations favor a particular bias of the arguer and which distort the opposition.

slippery slope   The fallacious claim that one step will inevitabley lead to an undesireable second step.

stacking the deck   To give evidence supporting a premise while disregarding or withholding contrary evidence.

statistics   Information that is expressed in numerical form; quantitative data.

strategy   The rhetorical choices writers make in order to achieve their purposes.

straw man   Setting up an unduly exaggerated version of an opponent's argument for refutation.

syllogism   A form of deductive reasoning in which two premises (major and minor) stating generalizations or assumptions together lead to a conclusion.

> *Major premise:* All Freshmen must take English.
> *Minor premise*: I am a Freshman.
> *Conclusion:* Therefore, I must take English.

thesis   The central controlling idea of an essay to which all assertions and details relate.

thesis sentence   A sentence that asserts the central controlling idea of an essay. It conveys the writer's purpose and attitude and perhaps previews the essay's organization.

tone   The sense of a writer's attitude (serious, playful, angry, cynical, etc.) toward self, subject, and readers revealed by words and sentence structures as well as by content.

transitions   Words or phrases such as *thus* or *similarly* or *by comparison* that link sentences and paragraphs for the sake of enhancing coherence.

unity   The quality of an effective essay or paragraph in which all parts relate to the central idea and to each other.

values   Principles or ideas that are used as standards for determining the worth of something—that is, good or bad, ugly or beautiful, useful or worthless, right or wrong.

warrant   An assumption or general principle that establishes a connection between the evidence and the *claim*.

CREDITS

Pages 9–11, Elizabeth M. Whelan. "Perils of Prohibition." *Newsweek.* 5/29/95. Copyright © 1995, Newsweek, Inc. all rights reserved, reprinted with permission.

Pages 38–39, Clara Spotted Elk. "Skeletons in the Attic." *The New York Times,* March 8, 1989. Copyright © 1989 by The New York Times Company. Reprinted by permission.

Pages 49–50, Michele T. Fields. "The Bottomless Cup." Reprinted by permission.

Pages 54–56, John O'Sullivan. "Simply Killing." *National Review,* March 2, 1992. Copyright © 1992, by National Review Inc., 150 East 35th Street, New York, NY 10016. Reprinted by permission.

Pages 95–102, Meg Kelley. "RU486: The French Abortion Pill and Its Benefits." Reprinted by permission.

Pages 110–112, Michael Levin. "The Case for Torture." *Newsweek,* 1982. Reprinted by permission of the author.

Pages 116–120, Melissa Spokas. "For the Love of the Game." Reprinted by permission.

Pages 184–187, Scott Russel Sanders. "The Men We Carry in Our Minds." Copyright © 1984 by Scott Russel Sanders; first appeared in *Milkweed Chronicle;* reprinted by permission of the author and Virginia Kidd, Literary agent.

Pages 190–193, Warren Farrel. "Men as Success Objects." *Family Therapy Network,* November–December 1988. Reprinted by permission.

Pages 194–195, Bill Persky. "Conan and Me." From *Esquire* Magazine, Copyright © 1989. Reprinted with permission.

Pages 199–203, Susan Brownmiller. *Femininity.* Copyright © 1993 by Susan Brownmiller. Reprinted by permission of Simon & Schuster Inc.

Pages 205–209, Deborah Tannen. "Wears Jumpsuit. Sensible Shoes. Uses Husband's Last Name." *The New York Times.* Copyright © 1993 by the New York Times Company. Reprinted with permission.

Pages 211–218, Katherine Dunn. "Just as Fierce." *Mother Jones,* Reprinted by permission from *Mother Jones* magazine, Copyright © 1993, Foundation for National Progress.

Pages 221–222, Anna Quindlan. "Life in the Thirties: Feminist." *The New York Times,* April 24, 1988. Copyright © 1988 The New York Times Company. Reprinted by permission.

Pages 224–226, Kay Ebeling. "The Failure of Feminism." From *Newsweek,* November 1990. Copyright © 1990 Newsweek Inc. All rights reserved. Reprinted by permission.

Pages 230–232, Barbara Ehrenreich. "Hers: Cultural Baggage." *The New York Times Magazine,* April 5, 1992. Copyright © 1992 The New York Times Company. Reprinted by permission.

Pages 234–237, Amoja Three Rivers. "Cultural Etiquette, A Guide." *Market Wimmin,* page 206. Reprinted by permission.

INDEX OF AUTHORS AND TITLES

Instructor's Manual

Instructor's Manual
to Accompany

Crossfire
An Argument Rhetoric and Reader

Second Edition

Gary Goshgarian
Northeastern University

Kathleen Krueger

with assistance from

Jeanne Phoenix Laurel
Niagara University

Phebe Jensen
Utah State University

Elizabeth Swanson Goldberg
Miami University of Ohio

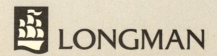
LONGMAN

An imprint of Addison Wesley Longman, Inc.
New York • Reading, Massachusetts • Menlo Park, California • Harlow, England
Don Mills, Ontario • Sydney • Mexico City • Madrid • Amsterdam

CONTENTS

PREFACE

This instructor's manual provides answers to the questions asked after each selection in *Crossfire: An Argument Rhetoric and Reader,* Second Edition. Such answers do not presume to do the work for the instructor. They are just meant to help. Certainly these answers are not exhaustive nor the only ones appropriate, and we hope the students and instructors will conspire to provide others.

   Note: The following table of contents begins with Chapter 9 in correspondence with the reading chapters in the text.

Gary Goshgarian
Kathleen Krueger

Gender Identity

Being Male

The Men We Carry in Our Minds
Scott Russell Sanders

Topical Considerations
1. Students' answers will vary.
2. Sanders probably feels this confusion toward women because he grew up in an environment where men endured lives of labor and physical hardship. Women, due to involvement in school and community, had lives encompassing the social and intellectual: time at libraries and church. To Sanders women's lives appeared more expansive and free than those of men. He finds it easy to identify the injustice inflicted on minorities such as Native Americans but difficult, in a sense, to understand the deprivation women have suffered.
3. Sanders wants readers to become more sympathetic toward men, particularly those of lower-income. The many descriptions of failing physical health and early deaths (paragraphs 10–12), as well as the differences he cites between power division in different socioeconomic classes (paragraph 13) illustrate this.
4. Students' answers may vary, but they might point out that each group discussed (men, women, lower-class, upper-class) might have experiences that do not support Sanders' stereotypes.
5. Sanders' ability to comprehend the complexity of life for women is clear in paragraphs 16 and 19. He sympathizes with the hard work of mothering and the frustration of job limitations due to gender.
6. Students' answers will vary.

Rhetorical Considerations
1. By using the dialogue with Anneke, Sanders sets up the issue of gender relations as a complicated one especially when Anneke, who is female, asserts that she thinks men have a harder time coping in today's world.
2. The essay would read more like a factual report on the relationship between men and women. In fact, the argument would not be nearly as effective; the personal anecdotes are what make the reader sympathetic. Statistics (if those supporting this argument even exist) would not help the reader to relate to the situation.

3. The descriptions that Sanders uses help to illustrate his perspective on gender relations, as he recalls them from childhood, very clearly. However, they do not help to clarify general stereotypes.

4. Men and women would be equally sympathetic to the essay: men, because they could relate to Sanders' description of watching their fathers work themselves nearly to death; and women, because of Sanders' admitted confusion about male-female relations, as well as his setting himself up as an ally to women at the end of his essay.

5. Although he makes it sound factual, Sanders' statement is based more on conjecture and stereotypes of the upper-class than it is on fact. Still, the strength of the statement makes it effective in furthering Sanders' argument.

6. Since Sanders began his essay by describing his confusion, ending with a question does fit with the overall searching tone of the piece.

Men As Success Objects
Warren Farrell

Topical Considerations
1. Farrell's argument is one not frequently made; as such, he may not win over many opponents of his cause to his side. In fact, with some of his supporting details (male-female options, his prom senario, and calling women models "quasi-anorexic"), he might drive away some female supporters. Men would probably be his most sympathetic readers.

2. Students' answers will vary.

3. Farrell states in paragraphs 9 and 10 that men must work full-time, while women have the choice to work full-time, to have children, or to do both. Students' experiences and reaction to Farrell's options will vary.

4. Students' answers will vary.

5. Although Farrell's strong argument might actually strengthen students' feelings about and beliefs in opposing arguments, answers may vary.

Rhetorical Considerations
1. Farrell's opening discussion of divorce might not help to strengthen his overall argument that men are success objects, but it does frame his discussion nicely by setting up a reason for the changing relationships between men and women.

2. Although the analogy is clear, it might actually serve to weaken Farrell's argument because it paints feminists as unaware of how men and women relate in reality.

3. For the most part, Farrell uses statistics extremely well; consider, for example, his discussion in paragraph 4 about researcher Fred Hayward's study, as well as Farrell's own research of greeting cards and book titles. However, when he describes the relationship between adolescent boys and girls in paragraph 13 and uses percentages that are hypothetical at best, the credibility of his support is weakened.

4. Farrell's voice is authoritative throughout the article. At times, though, he tends to sound, if not angry, then perhaps dismissive toward or weary of women's issues.

5. Although Farrell uses more objective information to get his point across, and although at times he seems to write in a calm, authoritative manner, this piece has a definite attitude regarding women and feminism and toward sexism against men. See paragraph 13, where Farrell renders factual a situation that is mostly hypothetical.

Conan and Me
Bill Persky

Topical Considerations

1. Persky's essay has to do with the reality of one's "self," and how to shed cultural affectations in order to get to that reality. In his opening, Persky cites "feelings of inadequacy" as the reason for adopting an affected accent—that is, if one speaks with a cultured British accent, one is assumed to be *cultured,* leaving those around him feeling less so. Some students might concede that a crisp British accent makes them feel inferior; yet the inverse also might be true: that they feel superior to people speaking with a dialect considered less cultured than their own. Ask students if they have ever taken on affectations—in dress, accent, or social or economic position—and how societal expectations contributed to the need for such.

2. Persky sets up a standard for a heroic male response to crisis earlier in the paragraph by describing an *ideal* male reaction. His actual confrontation with the intruder juxtaposes the desire to play that ideal with his actual reaction to real-life fear and terror. This says something about gender stereotypes and their effect on the behavior and attitudes of people in everyday life, as well as the reinforcement of these stereotypes in the media. Discussion might expose the difficulty of living up to such expectations—and the resultant need for hiding traits that do not jive with gender stereotypes.

3. Persky attributes his fear and hysteria (screaming in a high-pitched voice, hitting the intruder with a pillow) to his mother, while claiming to resemble Schwarzenegger when he barks his macho command and engages in "hand to hand combat" (paragraph 5). This dichotomy illustrates archetypal feminine and masculine traits found in most people. At the same time, however, such models of behavior serve to perpetuate those stereotypes.

Rhetorical Considerations

1. Persky's introduction is an apt way of getting at the complicated issue of cultural affectation and concealed identities. The anecdote is also a good way to set the tone for the piece, which is informal, chatty, occasionally bemused, and written as a first-person narrative. Persky makes himself accessible to his reader as just a guy telling a story, and he starts off with another guy telling a story in order to set the chummy mood.

2. Persky's narrator consistently makes himself vulnerable to his reader, encouraging empathy and identification. This strategy is particularly suitable to the piece. In paragraph 2, Persky surprises the reader with a particularly revealing statement: "I have some images of myself that I'd like to think are real." It's a courageous confession identifying the author as an uncertain individual striving to know his "self" despite the pervasive cultural forces that insist he act like a film hero. Similarly, the author's admitted fear of fighting (paragraph 9) has the same effect. Perskey continues with this honest—at times self-deprecating—tone throughout the piece.

3. Again, these clues serve to improve reader identification: Persky uses them to position himself as a man, just like any other, an active participant in pop culture, vulnerable to the pains and triumphs of cultural sex-role conditioning. The first clues are the most obvious: his comparison with a combination of Arnold Schwarzenegger and his mother. Next, Persky says that he is currently reading *The Bonfire of the Vanities*, a popular book representing the lives of hard-hitting lawyers and businessmen ("Masters of the Universe," Wolfe calls them) in the Big Apple. Next, he considers drawing upon the "new, upper-body strength" developed at the "Vertical Club," implying a kind of artificiality in the current mania for health clubs. Each of these clues is familiar enough to allow for reader recognition and identification.

4. In paragraphs 11 and 12, Persky shifts gears into the issue of right and wrong. Persky uses the anecdote of the intruder to illustrate a moment of purity in self-knowledge. Some might feel that this equation of a morally clear-cut situation with a person's ability to "be himself" is somewhat unclear, and introduced too late in the argument to be effective.

Being Female
Femininity
Susan Brownmiller

Topical Considerations
1. Children's social roles are definitely influenced and shaped by fairy tales, movies, and advertisements, no matter the gender. Even parents are influenced by the media depictions of gender stereotypes illustrated by the belief that there are masculine toys and feminine toys. Students' examples will vary.

2. Brownmiller's essay concludes that the origin of femininity can be found in "borrowed affectations of upper-class status, and in the historic subjugation of women through sexual violence, religion and law, where certain myths about the nature of women were put forward as biological fact", (paragraph 13). Given, then, the lack of an inherently female nature, Brownmiller would most likely concur with Perrin's idea of the androgenous male and support Barkalow's views of women in combat.

3. Brownmiller's "exquisite esthetic" refers to the fact that femininity (and beauty) can be cultivated for its (their) own sakes to some degree, and that,

while precious attributes which can give pleasure, they are also "practical"; they can be used to define a woman, to assure her success, to help her "survive." This concept is actually not explained very clearly by Brownmiller and, yet, it does seem a central tenet to her argument. Defining this term more clearly would, perhaps, serve her argument in a more constructive way.

4. Brownmiller defines traditional notions of masculinity and femininity in paragraph 8. She calls masculinity and femininity "polar ends of the human continuum . . . sun and moon, yin and yang, soft and hard, active and passive." She says that, traditionally, men have an "ethos of superiority", which drives them on to success, while women are more vulnerable. Students' opinions on these definitions will vary, though most will probably mention that such absolute opposites are unrealistic.

5. As society becomes more accepting of different kinds of people, and as men and women negotiate their ways through different kinds of relationships, ideas of sexuality change; oftentimes they change too quickly to be explained or defined, but media (TV, movies) are good sources for depicting (and sometimes explaining) the changing attitudes towards gender and towards sexuality. Students' examples will vary.

Rhetorical Considerations

1. Brownmiller's introduction is effective in that it sets up male-female stereotypes right from the start, while illustrating how "mythological" they are and how they arbitrarily become part of a child's view of men and women. The analogies are helpful to depict the silly ways men and women are often described ("formidable" vs. "softly curved").

2. Students' opinions on which author uses the biological argument best will vary.

3. When Brownmiller philosophizes on beauty, her writing tends to be oblique, making her argument a bit difficult to pin down or summarize. Students will probably respond better to her personal anecdotes because these describe situations closer to students' experience.

4. Students' responses will vary, though the essay tends to be more general than specific.

Wears Jump Suit. Sensible Shoes. Uses Husband's Last Name.
Deborah Tannen

Topical Considerations

1. The styles Tannen describes are coherent in that all aspects of each woman's appearance—from hair to clothing to makeup to shoes—are aligned to provide a unified overall effect. The woman in sensible shoes, for instance, does not have wild, sexy, frosted hair. Tannen's descriptions serve to illustrate the danger of stereotyping, the human tendency to associate certain *styles* with certain *personality types*. Based on Tannen's observations, each woman fits a common stereotype: the sensible no-frills woman, the sophisticate, the slut.

Discussion calls for critical thought about the validity of unconscious judgments based solely on the messages sent by appearances.

2. According to Tannen, women's fashion choices make statements about them—"marking" them—while men have the option of remaining "unmarked" by wearing standard attire such as a suit or shirt and slacks. Men who choose unmarked clothes are not subject to judgments based on their appearances; women, on the other hand, are always subject to character inferences drawn from their appearance.

3. In paragraph 17, Tannen writes, "The range of women's hairstyles is staggering, but a woman whose hair has no particular style is perceived as not caring about how she looks, which can disqualify her for many positions, and will subtly diminish her as a person in the eyes of some." Class discussion might touch on job requirements of airline stewardesses, who must maintain a certain weight, or TV journalists who are let go because of their appearance, or hiring decisions based upon a woman's appearance. Documented cases of such discrimination are fewer for men for whom age and even weight are often culturally seen as signs of wisdom and authority rather than of physical deterioration.

4. In biological terms, women are "unmarked" while men are "marked"—for example, males have nonfunctional nipples. The point illustrates that the construct of male as the neutral, unmarked term and female as the marked is cultural and political rather than biological.

5. As Tannen points out in paragraph 28, "the female was declared by grammarians to be the marked case." This was a decision with specific motivations and consequences. Tannen uses the notion of marking to move from the topic of appearance, to language, and back again. The relationship she builds between the two illustrates her argument about how widespread gender marking is for women, and how relatively absent it is for men. Discussion might focus on student experience with gender marking.

6. Marking women who discuss gender issues as feminist is further evidence of the phenomenon. In Tannen's experience, male colleagues conducting similar kinds of research are not labeled feminist. Tannen has problems with being marked feminist by virtue of her research since her work is not slanted toward a specific political position on gender. It simply records her observations and draws conclusions from those observations, which, according to Tannen, are strictly objective and undeserving of markings.

Rhetorical Considerations

1. This introduction might seem inordinately long and detailed to students at first. However the descriptions in these paragraphs provide an explicit visual foundation for Tannen's argument about marked and unmarked dress—which, in turn, lead to her argument about gender marking in our culture.

2. Paragraph 9 marks the first change in focus from the style markings to linguistic markings. The transition is marked by additional space between the

lines; the same device is used in paragraph 24 to mark a similar shift. Tannen deftly relates the two issues, emphasizing the illogic of gendered marking. Her argument moves from describing contemporary gender marking in paragraphs 1–8, making the link with linguistic theory in paragraph 9, and providing biological evidence to refute the logic of the female as a marked case in paragraph 24. Ultimately she proves that the marking of the female originates in decisions reflecting the historical power imbalance between men and women rather than from some essential or biological "fact." This method of argument might be used as a model for students writing persuasive essays.

3. Tannen's essay is largely written in the first person, which allows her to personalize the gender marking phenomenon and, thus, establish reader identification. The first-person perspective also establishes her own position on the subject, rather than writing from behind the screen of the third person, or "objective," voice. She shifts into a third-person voice when providing background information to her argument—for example, in paragraphs 9–11 where, in an informative, impersonal tone, she explains the marking in linguistic theory. Similarly, Tannen assumes the third-person voice in paragraphs 24–28 when summarizing Ralph Fasold's arguments on biological gender differences in language. Note that in both cases this shift of tone into the third person is followed by a reversion to the first person, which allows Tannen to relate the third-person "evidence" to her first hand experience, each "voice" supplementing the other while strengthening the overall argument. Again, this technique might be useful as a model for students experimenting with voice and point-of-view in narrative or persuasive essays.

4. Tannen has provided three different types of evidence: information based on topical experience (paragraphs 1–8), information based on "common knowledge" (paragraphs 17–23), and information derived from the findings of outside sources (paragraphs 9, 10, 24–28). These different kinds of evidence provide layers of support to her argument. Personal experience alone might leave readers feeling a lack of credibility. An argument based on common knowledge might likewise seem thin or obvious, while an article whose authority was derived solely from the words of experts might lack vitality and appear boring or removed from the practicality of real life.

Just as Fierce
Katherine Dunn

Topical Considerations
1. Dunn's argument is that prevailing cultural assumptions about gender present women as inherently less aggressive than men—especially with regard to the use of physical force or violence as a response to conflict—and that such notions are false. She argues that the "myth" of women as caring nurturers who are incapable of brutality has stripped them of an empowering

aspect of their identities. As Dunn grounds her argument in the context of women's equal rights, instructors might ask students to think about their responses to her arguments in that context: is the acknowledgment of women's capacity for violence an important part of attaining gender equality in this country? And on a more basic level, do students agree, given the evidence Dunn provides as well as their own experiences, that women have the same capacity for violence that men have?

2. Instructors might begin this discussion by asking students to list the characteristics that they believe are typically "assigned" to each gender—whether or not they agree with those attributions. Students will often assert that—even though they are well-versed in ideologies that place women in the home as nurturers and men in the workplace as aggressive earners—these perceptions no longer reflect the real, that "things have changed." Discussion might then examine the division between the realm of cultural representations and the realm of "real life," emphasizing the constraints on real behavior that such representations impose. Students should consider how they believe things have changed, if gender ideologies really have changed substantially, and what work is left to be done on gender equality (and if that work includes revising cultural representations of women to include their capacity for violence).

3. The "nature" side of this debate takes the position that there are inherent biological, genetic, or physiological reasons that women are different from men. The "nurture" argument asserts that gender differences are constructed by learned behaviors and cultural factors as opposed to resulting from biological or genetic differences. This debate is fundamental to the way scholars and researchers think about basic identity characteristics such as race and gender. Dunn clearly comes down on the side of "nurture": for Dunn, if we change the pervasive thinking about and behavior toward women that denies their ability to physically protect themselves or to inflict physical harm on others, we will be able to restore that ability. She does not believe that women are inherently less inclined to violent responses than men, or that they are physiologically "weaker" or less able to inflict harm.

4. Open for discussion. Instructors might place discussion in the context of other civil rights debates about the exclusion of certain groups from certain spaces or activities, considering the moral and ethical aspects of these issues. These debates might include the segregation of African American soldiers in the military in the mid-twentieth century; the debate about exclusion of gay or lesbian people from the military in the 1990s; and controversies around opening certain military training schools to women in the 1990s.

5. Dunn's position is that not only are women denied an aspect of their identities by being considered incapable of brutality, but they are also reduced to the status of children, unable to claim responsibility for their actions. She calls this a deeply patronizing attitude, and invokes the case of Lorena Bobbitt, quoting a columnist who described the decision that Bobbitt was not responsible for actions "a decision that infantilizes and imperils all women."

Dunn also believes that because women are considered to be physically passive, when they do actually commit a violent crime, they are "branded monster[s] far more frightening than a male perpetrating the same acts." Denying women's responsibility for their own acts means not taking women seriously. In the scheme of her argument as a whole, this issue is inseparable from her basic argument that women's capacity for violence be taken seriously.

6. The double standard to which Dunn refers is that women's aggression is not taken seriously, while men's is. Women's aggression is always constructed in terms of men, as a response to a man's violence. When a woman is seen as responsible for her own violence, she is represented as a "monster," an "unnatural" woman, while men who are violent are understood on some levels to be living out their natural genetic code (consider boxing). Dunn locates the origin of this mythology of women as nonviolent in the mythologies surrounding women's roles as mothers—she calls it "a sort of gender version of the non-combatant status of medics and Red Cross workers." Dunn's solution is to recognize—and produce appropriate cultural representations of—women's capacity for physical aggression. This means letting women into the boxing ring and the military, as well as allowing women to take full responsibility for their actions.

7. In her concluding paragraph, Dunn claims that "[women] don't just deserve power, we have it." Certainly this essay is about women's power, in a physical context. However, in the conclusion, Dunn relocates this issue in terms of the larger scope of women's social power, including their power in the workplace and in the home. Dunn's use of the word power shifts here from referring specifically to the physical to including all the different kinds of power that would be necessary for gender equality.

Rhetorical Considerations

1. Dunn's first paragraph is effective because it functions as the first line of an anecdote that she goes on to tell and also provides subtle clues to the purpose of the essay as a whole. The details given about the girl who "wanted to fight" are revealing, and each evokes certain cultural mythologies: she is blonde (unintelligent, unserious, eroticized); young (inexperienced, unserious); and spoke good English (upper-class, perhaps intelligent, not "tough" or "rough" enough to fight). We know from the verb "wanted" in the first sentence that there was a problem with her desire to fight. We know that the problem is rooted in gender difference by the fact that the guys in the boxing gym laughed. In her next paragraph Dunn argues that this young woman who wanted to fight was fighting a larger battle than the one in the ring, she was fighting a battle against the "ancient and powerful tradition of what it is to be female." That first line with its descriptions has already given the reader clues to the tradition that the girl—and Dunn herself, in this essay—must fight.

2. Dunn makes a smooth transition from her introductory remarks about Dallas Malloy into the two anecdotes about her mother and her Aunt Myrtle. Dunn startles the reader by describing her mother as adept with a rifle. She then locates these shooting skills in a series of other activities not traditionally considered appropriate for women, followed without pause by traditionally "female" activities like embroidering and child-raising. Without calling attention to her statement, Dunn has just revised the tradition that has relegated women to certain arenas. The reader will undoubtedly register the seeming contradictions that Dunn is attempting to undo. She employs the same strategy in the following anecdote about Aunt Myrtle, who fearlessly shoots a pack of wolves and then stitches wolfskin mittens for the kids in her family. The ability to "show" without "telling" is good writing in any genre, but particularly in a provocative essay which readers might otherwise find too sharply didactic.

3. Dunn uses her introductory anecdotes to identify herself as a strong woman coming from a line of strong women, and as a woman who has entered the male arena of boxing as a professional reporter. She also positions herself as a certain kind of feminist, unapologetic for her criticism of other kinds of feminism, which she believes weaken women's status in the world by denying their capacity for aggression (she names names in paragraph 17). Her attitudes strengthen her essay in that readers know she is personally invested in her arguments, and that she is familiar with her subject, both through her family experiences and as a female reporter covering boxing. However, some readers might perceive her position as an alienating factor. Feminists from other "camps" might be turned off by her critiques, and she also might find that male readers are resistant to her insistence that women be allowed into certain traditionally "male" spaces such as athletics and the military. Open for discussion.

4. Although Dunn does site specific "authorities," she often does not document the sources she is using. For example, in paragraph 17 she cites three feminist writers without referring to their work; in paragraph 15 she makes a statistical claim about rape in the United States without citing any source or numerical figure; in paragraph 20 she refers to the work of Anne Fausto-Sterling without identifying it; and in paragraph 39 she refers to "other more widely publicized studies" of domestic violence without providing names or sources, though she has given extensive source information for studies supporting her own argument. Students should consider her use of documentation and source information, noting when she does and does not provide such information, why she makes those choices, and how that affects their reception of her argument.

5. Dunn's claims here are questionable in light of her manipulation of source materials. She suggests that the vast majority of information given to "the public" about domestic violence is inaccurate, and presents specific examples of studies and information counteracting this information. Not only does she provide source information in more detail than she has anywhere

else in the essay, she also devotes three paragraphs to describing the results of these studies. She then goes on to note the discrepancy between these studies and "more widely publicized studies." She neither identifies these studies, nor does she describe their findings, except in an attempt to refute them by claiming that the studies are "based on small, self-selected 'treatment group' samples or police records." The discrepancies in *Dunn's* presentation of materials is deeply slanted, weighted in favor of her own argument, thereby negatively affecting reader acceptance of her arguments.

6. Dunn's tone in this piece is provocative and demanding: she uses active present tense subject/verb constructions like "we do," "we are," "we live," "we must," and so on. Her tactic is an absolute refutation of opposition views, rather than a negotiation with them. This tone is certainly in keeping with her subject: had she presented this information in a format that made concessions to opposition viewpoints, she might be accused of falling into the "traditionally female" stereotype of nonaggression, which she is attempting to counter. However, some readers might find the tone off-putting, feeling an angry response which is as adamantly committed to defending an opposing view without concession as she seems to be. Open for discussion.

Oppositions: Feminism
Feminist
Anna Quindlen

Topical Considerations
1. Although Quindlen considers herself a liberal feminist (especially when she first came to feminism), she now believes that practicing a more radical brand of feminism would have instituted greater changes for women.
2. Quindlen is saying that women still live by the laws set by men, and that they still depend on men, to some degree, to support them, be it financially or emotionally or otherwise. Her reference to Supreme Court Justices alludes most likely, to rulings on abortion and reproductive rights. Students' experiences and examples will vary.
3. Quindlen may respect individualists, though she does not explicitly state that. She does acknowledge gratitude that she had her "sisters" to support her during the early years of feminism; and since she begins her last sentence with "luckily," we can guess that she truly admires and respects groups of people working together for a cause. Her language, though, does not exclude individualists from her argument.
4. Women without college educations might agree with certain points in Quindlen's essay, and they might support her as a feminist, but they might have a hard time sympathizing with her discussion of her lack of choices, since she at least had the choice (and the ability) to further her education.
5. Responses will vary.

Rhetorical Considerations

1. Quindlen's first sentence makes her seem "human," down-to-earth, and honest because she admits that her initial allegiance to feminism grew out of "self-centeredness." Since the sentence does establish a conspiratorial tone, people will most likely read on.

2. Quindlen's piece maintains an informal, believable tone throughout, relying more on a sense of honest and clear narrative than on jargon.

3. Were the piece written from a third-person omniscient point-of-view, readers might regard it more as a description of feminism (which they might already be familiar with) and less as a person's experiences, both positive and negative, with the feminist movement.

4. Quindlen's analogy is very effective in that it is clear and in that it does not exclude many readers (except perhaps those without a college education). In general, analogies are used to draw a relationship between two objects, which will ideally clarify whatever relationship you are highlighting in your argument.

5. Quindlen uses emotional appeals to help make her readers sympathetic towards and understanding of her cause. Paragraphs 2 and 9 illustrate the use of emotional appeal.

6. Although the title suggests that the essay will be about feminism, it does not hint at what particular slant the argument will take in the essay. Students will create their own titles, but one might be "An Early Feminist Looks Back" or "Looking Ahead and Behind on Feminism."

The Failure of Feminism
Kay Ebeling

Topical Considerations

1. Ebeling's argument can be accurately summarized by the title of the essay: that feminism has failed. Specifically, she sees feminism as failing women who have left their husbands and cannot support themselves financially. Students' answers will vary as to which of Ebeling's points they found most and least useful.

2. Quindlen would probably agree that feminism has not yet succeeded in correcting all unfairness to women, but she might dispute the fact that it has failed entirely, or that women must be dependent on men for financial support. Students' responses will vary.

3. Ebeling says that men are the only winners in the feminist cause because they remain able to support themselves without being tied down to a wife and children. She also depicts men as always seeking the youngest, most attractive women. Most students will probably seen this as an unfair generalization; there are many fathers who share custody of their children. Also, not all men are so financially successful as to drive BMWs, nor do they chase women with 20-inch waists. This over-simplification might weaken the force of her argument for some readers.

4. Ebeling argues that since women are biologically destined to bear children, the only way for them to keep up with men is to deny this part of their life. She uses examples of married mothers who must work, raise a family, and exist on 5 hours of sleep a night to illustrate the difficulty of "having it all."

5. Ebeling's statement in paragraph 9 works to exclude (or will be refuted by) successful professional women who also have families.

6. Students' answers will vary, but one point that might arise is that men are more willing than Ebeling lets on to help women with the responsibility of raising a family.

Rhetorical Considerations

1. The first paragraph lets the reader know that the discussion will, in some way, focus on relationships between men and women. It also serves to establish the tone of the essay as slightly sarcastic, while giving the reader a hint about the author's experience with, and subsequent attitude toward, men.

2. Since it is a clear and forceful statement, it might be fairly persuasive to a general reader. However, if the reader has a strong feminist background or is familiar at all with feminist ideaology, this statement will come across as a gross over-simplification of feminism's means and its ends.

3. By bold-facing "Biological thing," Ebeling highlights it as key support for her argument.

4. Ebeling's conclusion is humorous, which fits in well with the overall tone of the essay. Still, the scene it describes is almost too pathetic, making readers doubt her sincerity and weakening the force of her closing point, often the part of the argument that stays with the reader the longest.

5. Using short sentences can be a very effective stylistic tool in a persuasive paper, as long as they are interspersed with longer, more complex sentences. When they are used only occasionally, short sentences call attention to themselves as a verbal punctuation for whatever point the author is arguing.

10
Race and Ethnicity

Identity and Stereotypes
Cultural Baggage
Barbara Ehrenreich

Topical Considerations

1. Attempting to be more ethnic, Ehrenreich describes how she prepared a seder "of her own design" for her children; but instead of displaying "ethnic genes," her children proceeded to "[butter] their matzohs." Eschewing ethnicity, she explains her children's ancestors' "shaking off their Orthodox Judaism" as proof that her heritage is rooted in people "who do not do things just because someone has done them before." Such views of Jewish customs as ("cultural freight") might be offensive to some Jews. Also, the implication that Orthodox Jews practice their customs only because "someone else has done it before them."

2. Ehrenreich suggests that an Anglo-Celtic background is equivalent to no ethnic culture. Nonetheless, she suggests that its lack of ethnic distinction constitutes the American standard—that is, the traditional White Anglo-Saxon norm. The source of her "ethnic chauvinism" might be the only "cultural freight" she boasts: "skepticism, curiosity, and wide-eyed ecumenical tolerance" which she lauds as "worthy elements of the human tradition." In other words, the democratic ideals of America.

3. For the student.

4. Some might find Ehrenreich more incendiary than insightful. Her tone is subtly condescending when discussing those who do celebrate their cultural identity. The woman in paragraph 1 has "eyes gleaming with enthusiasm"; in paragraph 3, Ehrenreich refers to other groups' cultural awareness as "all this excitement over ethnicity"; and paragraph 12 refers to celebrants of ancient traditions as "newly enthusiastic." Students will raise other points.

5. Ehrenreich wants to make space for the possibility of the "race of none." She traces her Anglo-Celtic heritage and finds its traditions lacking, particularly when compared to the rise of other groups' cultural awareness during the sixties and seventies. She then seeks to acquire cultural identity for her future children through marriage to a man of Eastern-European Jewish heritage. When this fails, she realizes her culture is rooted in the rejection of tradition and belief in skepticism, curiosity, and tolerance. She claims

that this replaces and perhaps supersedes a traditional definition of cultural identity.

Ehrenreich's argument makes a false analogy between a part of a culture (skepticism, curiosity) and an entire culture (Croatian, Serbian, Jewish). Her examples of Anglo-Celtic history and traditions refute her claim that her ethnic background is "none." While it is her choice not to acknowledge her Anglo-Celtic heritage, replacing her entire cultural identity with broad philosophical underpinnings could be construed as substituting a part for the whole. Her insistence that her race is "none" does not support her argument, nor does her pleasure in her children's rejection of cultural identity. Instead these reveal Ehrenreich's unease with the emergence of multiculturalism and cultural awareness.

Rhetorical Considerations

1. The terse two-word title announces that the author has made her mind up about her culture, that she does not romanticize her heritage. Paragraph 2 begins with the author's response to a friend who has found the "joys of rediscovering her ethnic and religious heritage" and who inquires about the author's: "'None,' I said, that being the first word in line to get out of my mouth." The author spends the rest of the essay convincing the reader that no culture is better than any culture.

2. Ehrenreich addresses a "neutral" audience. Her somewhat condescending tone (e.g., "newly enthusiastic celebrants of Purim and Kwanzaa and Solstice" [paragraph 12]) and her pride in her children's comment that the "world would be a better place" if no one else celebrated their roots (paragraph 13) suggest that she is writing to those who "sank ever deeper" in their seats watching "African-Americans, Latinos, Native Americans stand up and proudly reclaim their roots" (paragraph 3). Because she never slips into the inclusive "we" mode, Ehrenreich seems to address the "Britannically derived."

3. Ehrenreich begins diminishing those who celebrate their heritage with reference to her friend who knows "exactly what my ancestors were doing 2,000 years ago" (paragraph 1). She implies that celebrating one's heritage means looking backwards. She also implies that there was no cultural awareness before the sixties and seventies—i.e., that African Americans, Native Americans, etc. discovered their heritage only lately. Her concluding reference to the "newly enthusiastic celebrants" of ancient traditions suggests this recent enthusiasm is but a tentative thing. On the other hand, hers is a culture rooted in a people "whose whole world was inverted every thirty years," a people who can adapt. She doesn't know what her ancestors did 2,000 years ago, only that "they remained loyal" to values such as "Try new things" (paragraph 12). Because Ehrenreich has held onto values and not specific traditions or events, hers will "march on."

Cultural Etiquette: A Guide
Amoja Three Rivers

Topical Consideration

1. Students might mention the fact that "at least four-fifths of the world's population consists of people of color" (paragraph 4); "locking is the natural tendency of African hair to knot and bond to itself" (paragraph 9); that "concentration camp" and "Gestapo" are "only appropriate when used in reference to the Holocaust" (paragraph 25), etc. It is interesting to note that each of these rules applies to different realms within a culture—population statistics, appearance, language. Students not familiar with the political correctness movement may disagree with some of Three Rivers' rules.

2. Along with specific examples there is the pervasive anger in the piece that may make a reader uncomfortable. A "well-meaning liberal" may be taken aback when told that it is offensive to want racial balance at an event; that use of "Gestapo" for hyperbole's sake may offend.

3. Because Three Rivers specifically mentions race and cultural background, ["People are attacked, abused . . . because of racism and anti-Semitism," (paragraph 12)] she seems to mean people of color and Jews. That Three Rivers doesn't consider poverty, domestic violence, and drugs as factors of oppression and abuse is further proof that hers is selective "people." She says that "People" will include everybody after presumably non-Jewish white Americas 1) "accept responsibility when it is appropriate" and 2) "actively work for change" (paragraph 37). Three Rivers writes that racism has caused "a big horrible Mess" (paragraph 37); therefore, it is unclear whether she believes her claim that "All people are people" (paragraph 2).

4. Some people who are physically challenged understand what it means to be ostracized by society and the American political system. Three Rivers might write: "Yes. It is ok to smile at people in wheelchairs. We're aware that we're in our chairs; so you don't have to look away."

Rhetorical Considerations

1. The "We" is African American, Native American, Latin people, (all people of color) and Jewish people. She abandons first person and switches to the imperative voice when addressing whites: "If you are white, don't neglect your ancient traditions" (paragraph 34). The fact that she accurately deflates the stereotypes of many different cultures lends credibility to her "we." However, she may be presumptuous in her assumptions of how people of cultures outside her own might react. Students may disagree.

2. Three Rivers has written her guide for everyone, but for different reasons. She probably aims her do's-and-don'ts lecture at whites to both teach and chastise them, at people of color and Jews to elicit approval of her frank, cutting and pointed address. She covers her bases with the caveat that "no

one living in Western society is exempt from the influences of racism, racial stereotypes, race and cultural prejudices, and anti-Semitism" (paragraph 1).

3. While there is room for subjective interpretations, what is clear is that Three Rivers is passionate in her attempt to dispel cultural myths and stereotypes. She is assertive, at times abrasive, but clearly sincere. Her short, emphatic statements and use of the imperative imply a strong, opinionated speaker. The text seems closed, leaving little room for multiple interpretations. At times, Three Rivers is so opinionated that the reader may feel left out.

4. Three Rivers addresses both her white and "ethnic" audience with a blend of colloquial and academic language. For any reader, the author adds validity to her point with academic language that states facts; after she mentions that "four-fifths of the world's population consists of people of color," she concludes that "it is statistically incorrect as well as ethnocentric to refer to us as minorities" (paragraph 4). Colloquial language such as "natty dreads" can exclude readers who have no knowledge of Jamaican or African-American culture, while language such as "Well, how many [people of color] do you need?" is caustic, sharp, and an effective balance to academic language.

5. Three Rivers mocks the Emily Post/Miss Manners genre with her title. Etiquette books usually make much ado about folding your napkin, while Three Rivers is using this predominantly frivolous genre to address a serious topic. The quick do's-and-don'ts format works well because hers is a comprehensive guide covering many races and religions.

6. Some might consider her argument *ad populum*. Three Rivers assumes her audience is either white and in need of cultural education or non-white and already in total agreement with her teaching.

What's Behind the 'Asian Mask'?
Alexandra Tantranon-Saur

Topical Considerations

1. Tantranon-Saur avoids stereotyping because she can offer valid reasons for cultural habits that are misunderstood. She explains that Asian/Pacific people seem quiet because they are taught speech habits from a "purely technical point of view" (paragraph 7) and from a social view that demands that they be "constantly aware of the attention level" of their listener. In paragraph 13 she affirms that Asian/Pacific people seem "to pay better attention to the feelings of our oppressors than vice versa." She also states that "Exchange is an important cultural principle" (paragraph 20) because the "historical lack of natural resources required cooperation and discouraged individualism" (paragraph 31). She explains that cultural traits or habits are largely determined by unavoidable circumstances shaped by a people's need to survive and are, therefore, on a higher level that stereotyping.

2. Behind the "Asian Mask" are the faces of Asian/Pacific people whose "sorrow" and "mask" have been created by "ordinary white people blinded by stereotypes" (paragraph 1). According to the author, Asian/Pacific people

are "not quiet" (paragraph 3); are considerate (paragraph 8); are "gracious and hospitable" (paragraph 18); are emotional—"our feelings are written all over our faces and bodies" (paragraph 19); are believers in "cooperation and exchange" (paragraph 20). In paragraph 19 she notes that behind the mask Asian/Pacific people are "just like anyone else."

3. Tantranon-Saur uses the expression "bumper-car social interactions" three times in the essay to depict her view of "ordinary white American" social practice. This description of the callous, hurried Ameerican is slightly derogatory and inconsistent with the rest of the essay. Tantranon-Saur is careful to credit "Some" Americans with "beginning to know the violence and sorrow visited upon the Asian and Pacific peoples." She also adopts a light tone that enables her to poke fun at the reader while still driving home her message: "non-Asian people will talk on and on, marveling that they have found such a good listener who claims to have nothing to say" (paragraph 7). However, because the phrase "bumper car social interactions" is not clichéd, it jumps at the reader and is a label that contradicts the author's message.

4. The term "model minority" is derogatory simply because it is a stereotype that does not allow for differences within Asian cultures. It implies that Asians are the "best" minority, but not a level of "dominant" Anglo culture. Other seemingly innocuous stereotypes include categorizing Jews as "too successful" or "too ambitious." Stereotypes of African-Americans' athletic and musical prowess often falsely presupposes that these are innate talents of the race. These preclude other abilities of blacks. Another seemingly complimentary stereotype is that gay men are "fastidious." This is offensive because it implies that gay men cannot be "masculine" as defined by the dominant heterosexual culture.

5. "Nice and polite" has a condescending tone. Such trite empty phrases diminished even "seemingly" positive attributes. More thoughtful, less clichéd terms such as "gracious and hospitable" eliminate the potential for an individual to construe the tone as patronizing. It makes more sense to avoid trying to characterize a whole race with a term.

Rhetorical Considerations

1. "We" are all Asian-Pacific peoples. It is the "you" or reader that makes the author's relationship with her audience interesting. She writes in the first paragraph: "Most of you know enough to scoff at these racist stereotypes." Those not included in "most" are the "ordinary white people blinded by stereotypes" (paragraph 1). Therefore, she is appealing to people who are ready to learn; those not blind, but with clouded vision. Students' opinions will differ on this question. However, this strategy seems effective because she has faith that the reader can unlearn these assumptions and begin to recognize them for the derogatory images they area. Also, the fact that Tantranon-Saur does not hesitate to take a few jabs at her audience ("we see you

imagining we should prefer your cultures to ours!") suggests her willingness to share some truths about her culture.

2. Most students have had part-time jobs and can relate to "talking about the boss" (paragraph 13) and how "the boss is unlikely to know" (or be interested in) anything about his employees' personal lives. Students can also use this analogy to discuss how ignorance is at the root of misunderstanding.

3. Tantranon-Saur invites those unfamiliar with the Asian/Pacific culture to experience it: "Get together with people who talk like this, hold your tongue, and you'll see how comfortably a conversation goes" (paragraph 7). She also admits that her culture is not perfect: "It sure never stopped us from making war on each other, exploiting each other . . . " (paragraph 18). In paragraph 19, she writes, "And, just like anyone else, our feelings are written all over our faces and bodies." The author reaches out to the audience and likens her culture to the readers', thereby creating a non-threatening realm to explore.

   Three Rivers takes the opposite tack and risks alienating her readership. She writes in the imperative, speaking to her audience as if it were a naughty child. Students' reactions to the two styles will probably differ.

4. The author's "What's-a-friend-to-do" guide does two things: it recaps her essay and it shows that she intended to educate her readers. All seven of the approaches can be applied when talking with people from different cultures. However, numbers 3 and 5 may differ from different cultures. For example, people from the Middle East may have a different style of conversation than those of Asia. However, Tantranon-Saur's overall message *to see behind the mask* is applicable to all cultures.

5. The author may be stereotyping when she says, "For the Chinese, as for many cultures, the issue of people speaking loudly versus quietly is a class issue" (paragraph 3). Because she does not specify the other cultures, it is difficult to know whether this is true. However, by mentioning the "Chinese working-class women" in Chinatown "waiting tables and shouting to each other," Tantranon-Saur is most likely appealing to a middle- to upper-class audience that will agree that working class people are louder. Some students may find this both offensive and short-sighted.

The Revolt of the Black Bourgeoisie
Leonce Gaiter

Topical Considerations

1. The anecdote graphically introduces Gaiter's main point: that exactly those programs designed twenty years ago to help blacks advance professionally are now in danger of actually impeding their progress. Gaiter is almost not hired by the network, despite excellent qualifications, because he does not fit the stereotypical image of the black person—a stereotype that, as he later argues, was itself initially constructed in order to implement such programs. Analyzing the hiring program's title will alert students to the way even well

intentioned efforts to promote racial equality can produce opposite results: the word "advancement" implies inferior status and makes the department head reluctant to hire this articulate, Harvard-educated black applicant.

2. Gaiter tells his stories backward, starting with an apparently early job experience, moving to his college years, then on to junior high school, revealing the persistence of such ideas through his own lifetime. All three anecdotes raise the "question of black authenticity" because the network executive, the white Harvard classmate, and the black junior high student all share a sense of what a "'real'" black person is—a person who bears little resemblance to Gaiter. If a "'real' black person" is, as Gaiter's department head suggests, a "semiliterate, hoop-shooting former prison inmate" (paragraph 2), then Gaiter's college classmate is right that Gaiter is "'not a real black person,'" (paragraph 3), and his junior high schoolmate is right that he "couldn't exist" (paragraph 4).

   One of the perhaps unintentional effects of these three anecdotes is that together they illustrate the fact that Gaiter has himself moved in a largely white world. Some students might note that what's missing from his essay is any sense of how blacks in predominantly African American institutions think of themselves.

3. Students should quickly see that the "black political agenda" of paragraph 6 is founded on the assumption that "'real'" black people are comprised of a single monolithic cultural unit. Although Gaiter seems to accept the historical necessity of focusing political attention on the lowest economic strata during the early stages of black activism, now that twenty years have passed, he thinks that the emphasis on uniformity is misplaced. Moreover, Gaiter apparently only supported part of the strategies of this agenda. Affirmative action policies, Gaiter asserts, "have forced an otherwise unwilling majority to open some doors for the black middle class" (paragraph 6); on the other hand, "social welfare and Great Society-style programs aimed at the black lower class have shown few positive results" (paragraph 6). Here Gaiter demonstrates again that he speaks for the middle class: he does not endorse those programs most often championed by people who speak for the poor.

4. Gaiter clearly has a lot of animosity for the white liberals whose attitude to black Americans he believes is "just as informed by racism as white conservatism" (paragraph 8). White liberals, Gaiter suggests in this paragraph, adopted a "picture of black downtrodden masses in need of their help." This image of African-Americans has proved so persistent only because it "maintained the lifeline of white superiority." In other words, instead of being motivated by idealism, liberals, like their ideological counterparts on the right, were also invested in a certain image of black Americans because it enabled them to feel superior. The persistence of this myth means that even blacks who have advanced professionally and materially can still be seen as "inferiors, victims, cases, and not as equals, individuals or, heaven forbid, competitors" (paragraph 8).

Such bitter language suggests that Gaiter holds a special revulsion for these particular perpetuators of stereotypes about black people. Gaiter believes it is the political momentum of the white liberal's image of black Americans as "downtrodden masses" that ultimately made Gaiter feel those "questions of black authenticity", which are at the heart of his essay. For any attempt "to be recognized and recognize oneself as middle upper class was to threaten the political progress of black people" (paragraph 9) by giving the lie to the image that legitimized supposedly "progressive" social programs.

5. Much of Gaiter's essay suggests that the stereotypes that make the myth of a black underclass possible are deliberate fictions. By starting with an examination of the nationally televised Reginald Denny trial (paragraph 10), Gaiter is able to show how biased even supposedly "objective" news coverage is, graphically demonstrating how "fiction" can be packaged as fact. Gaiter uses statistics for further support, here to undermine the public perception that the vast majority of participants in the Los Angeles riots were black. Once he has established the racist slant of news programs, he can quickly move from network melodramas like "Laurel Avenue" (paragraph 12) to the public humiliation of black America he sees taking place in the "blue humor" comedy series, "Martin."

Rhetorical Considerations

1. "Bourgeois" is a term used with derision by the socialist writers who coined and popularized it. By enthusiastically embracing the term, Gaiter makes a deliberate point of championing the middle class so despised by Marxism. In doing so, Gaiter suggests his enthusiastic acceptance of capitalist ideology. Small wonder he rejects federal programs that are redolent of socialism, those "social welfare and Great Society-style programs" that Gaiter claims "have shown few positive results" (paragraph 6). The title of Gaiter's essay in this way identifies a capitalist, economically and perhaps politically conservative bias, though his discussion is generally balanced.

2. With the first reference, Gaiter seemed simply to record a personal anecdote relevant to his own questions of "black authenticity" (paragraph 3). But in the second context, by re-analyzing the girl's comment as a subtle accusation "of political sins—of thwarting the progress of our race," Gaiter makes it appear that the child was in fact being exploited by self-serving politicians, "media-appointed black leaders and the white media" (paragraph 9). Now, the girl seems less an ignorant young classmate, feeling alienated and alone in a largely white suburban school, and more the pawn in the carefully engineered dissemination of a political ideology.

3. Gaiter places great emphasis on the black male positions related in paragraph 5. These views from an Ivy League academic, an author quoted in Newsweek, and perhaps the best known black Rhodes scholar, Bill Cosby, are introduced as reasoned reflections of Gaiter's own thoughts. It is this company, the intellectual and cultural elite of black America, with which Gaiter identifies most clearly. By referring to these men by name—while the

network executive, the Harvard student, and the junior high student all remained anonymous—Gaiter makes these men the opposite of the faceless, downtrodden, indistinguishable masses defined by white liberals and black activists as African American culture.

4. The statistics of paragraph 7 support Gaiter's contention that the fastest growing segment of the black population is composed of individuals whose incomes are rising. The statistics are rhetorically remarkable as an effort to introduce hard facts into an argument that up to this point has been built largely on anecdote and personal opinion. These data make it appear that Gaiter is in touch with trends that will shape the future; he lets the math speak for itself as a way of establishing the self-evident logic of his position. Students will probably see that these numbers come at the center of the essay and function as a sort of objective fulcrum that gains Gaiter the rhetorical authority to advance his argument about the manipulation of black culture by politicians and the media.

5. Throughout the essay, Gaiter has argued against monolithic images of "'real'" African Americans. As part of this strategy, he has rhetorically distanced himself from many segments of the black American population, identifying himself only with the "black bourgeoisie and intelligentsia" (paragraph 10), including those prominent cultural figures mentioned in paragraph 5. Now, Gaiter creates a much larger "we," one that conceptualizes African Americans as a collection of individuals, "not as shards of a degraded monolith" (paragraph 17). The creation of this larger "we" coincides with an implicit suggestion that the African heritage denoted in the "African" half of the term "African American" benefits from increased respect for the individualism so important to the "American" half. By insisting on a "we" made up of individuals, Gaiter is simply claiming for blacks the "American ideal [which] places primacy on the rights of the individual" (paragraph 17). At this point in his essay, then, Gaiter replaces the monolithic myth of racial difference with a pluralistic vision of richness in diversity. He urges his readers black and white to see race as a feature of personal identity that benefits from breadth of "opinions, idiosyncrasies and talents" the same way that national identity does (paragraph 17). In the essay's last sentence Gaiter simultaneously creates the broader African American "we" while stressing that in doing so, he is only participating fully in the great American national project: "We blacks can effectively demand those rights . . . accorded any other American."

Presumed Guilty
Anton Shammas

Topical Considerations

1. This question should provoke a list of the most offensive stereotypes attached to Arab Americans, a list that will help clarify Shammas' point about the difficulty many Americans have seeing people of Arab descent as individuals. The tendency to stereotype Arabs as secretive is suggested directly here by the spurious

"evidence" news sources presented in support of Arab involvement, the sighting of a "pickup truck with tinted windows" (paragraph 4). Another stereotype is the idea of the rich Arab. The most powerful generalization about Islamic peoples, of course, is the idea that they are all religious and political fanatics.

The class should consider why Detroit may be especially prone to such stereotyping. A city like this, with a faltering economy and a large Arab American population, may be especially vulnerable to the belief that America is being invaded rather than strengthened by the introduction of new racial and ethnic traditions. Who better to blame for social and economic woes than the newest immigrants?

2. Responses to this question should clarify Shammas' presentation of Arab Americans as a people who suffer throughout the world for the radical acts of a small minority. If Ibrahim Ahmad was wearing a jogging suit, as opposed to flowing robes or other distinctively Arab dress, then he had been singled out for interrogation purely on the basis of race. The clothes he was wearing can be considered distinctively American; they perhaps indicate he was proud, or at least supremely comfortable, with his American identity. These details promote the conclusion that Americans who unthinkingly subscribe to racial stereotypes undermine the belief in justice and equality for all that has always attracted people to the United States.

3. Students will quickly see that Shammas is positioning himself in one of the greatest publicly funded institutions of learning in America. This sends the message that racial stereotypes have penetrated not just the heartland of the midwest but the institutions the nation depends on to provide intellectual leadership. By contrasting Ann Arbor with Jerusalem, he forces readers to recognize that America is not the safe place they like to think it is. When Shammas states that Ann Arbor "seemed the perfect refuge," he states a belief that many readers share with him.

4. This question should provoke thought about the economic and social basis of racial fear. The fact that Mark Koernke is a "custodian on the Ann Arbor campus" places him in the center of the institution, but it also suggests that he has relatively little influence over what goes on there. Students may want to argue that Shammas undermines his position by making too much of Koernke's limited influence. They may see the Koernke reference as evidence supporting the claim that racism is predominantly a working class problem where employment is least secure and most easily threatened by alien peoples. Others may argue that even a lowly custodian can influence the course of national history, as the case would be if it were proven that Timothy McVeigh was guilty and Koernke was indeed one of his "ideological mentors." Shammas wants readers to see that no place in American is truly safe as long as racism is allowed to grow unchecked.

5. A Palestinian novelist, Shammas was living in Jerusalem when he decided to "take time off from the danger zone and leave the unsettled dust of the Israeli-Palestinian conflict behind me for a while" (paragraph 6). By indicating that he lived in Israel, not the West Bank, and that he was fleeing not

terrorism per se but the "Israeli-Palestinian conflict," Shammas implies that the terror of the Middle East results as much from the actions of Israel, America's ally, as from the depraved actions of "Islamic militants." Since the article was published in the *New York Times,* in a city with a large Jewish and pro-Israeli population, it is understandable that Shammas and his editors might press lightly on the implication that the "danger-zone" of the Middle East is created not only by Arabs but by Israel. At any rate, Shammas subtly indicates here that the stereotype of Arabs as "the world's only fanatic extremists" (paragraph 8) is a political as well as an ethnic slur.

6. What Shammas is "taken in" by is not entirely clear. Given the last sentence of the previous paragraph, where Shammas says that he "had foolishly thought [Ann Arbor] was the most peaceful place on earth" (paragraph 7), Shammas may feel taken in by his sanguine belief that in Michigan he would find "a perfect refuge" (paragraph 6). But he also seems to have felt "taken in" by the media, which has refused to issue an apology even though, had "Islamic militants" turned out to be truly to blame for the bombing, he would have had to endure the "self-appointed experts" pontificating on the offensive belief "that Muslims are the world's only fanatic extremists" (paragraph 8).

Rhetorical Considerations

1. Members of the class will point out that the first three paragraphs, as well as paragraph 7, are all single sentences. This sort of writing suggests urgency, as if the author were a messenger gasping for breath while delivering staggering news. The lengthy syntactic units pile pieces of information on top of one another so quickly that the details are hard to follow; what does stand out though is a pronounced sense of injustice and betrayal.

2. The word "absolved" denotes both legal and religious innocence. In this way the word covers both aspects of the injustice perpetrated by the news media against Arab Americans: they have been unfairly indicted on both legal grounds, for "a crime they did not commit" (paragraph 1), and on religious grounds, stereotyped for being part of a religious culture that makes them different from mainstream America.

3. The essay is less a reasoned presentation than a passionate cry. This impression is created in a variety of ways: by the series of breathless, one word paragraphs; the repeated references to a "sense of injury" (paragraph 2), hurt, and betrayal; by the dramatic final two paragraphs, where Shammas describes how "[h]ome has become an uncertain, uncharted, shifting ground" (paragraph 9). Students may debate the appropriateness of this tone; some may find it conveys a sense of sincerity and earnestness; others may find it nasty, bitter, and self-defeating. Those holding the latter opinion may see the tone undercutting the strength of the argument by allowing readers to stereotype Shammas himself as a passionate Arab; it could be argued that Shammas enforces the stereotype of "Islamic militants" by delivering his own terrorist attack in print.

Ultimately, the class will probably agree that Shammas attempts to bridge the cultural divide by emphasizing shared values. Even his shrillest denunciations convey something like the prophet's call to action, not flat condemnation. Coming to terms with the high emotional pitch of his presentation, however, can be difficult for students who are accustomed to greater objectivity. Working through the question of tone can awaken the class to their own prejudices about print decorum.

4. "Home" is a loaded word used to magnify Shammas' point that no place is safe from the corrupting influence of racist stereotypes. The short sentences present a winding down from the emotional intensity of the longer single-sentence paragraphs; he wants to communicate a sense of clear-headedness here. These are the sad but unavoidable facts of modern life in America.

Affirmative Action
Harping on Racism
Roger Wilkins

Topical Considerations

1. Wilkins feels it is the responsibility of whites to make attempts to redress past racial injustices through measures such as affirmative action. Wilkins would probably argue that those who reject affirmative action, while not considering themselves racist, are denying the historic realities of the black experiences in America (paragraphs 12–14).

2. Students may have different opinions. Reasons for whites' reticence to talk about racism could range from guilt to denial, or the feeling that only blacks as the targets of racism can adequately discuss its ramifications.

3. In paragraph 11 Wilkins writes, "Like it or not, slavery, the damage from legalized oppression during the century that followed emancipation and the racism that still infects the entire nation follow a direct line to ghetto life." Wilkins believes the purpose of revealing past racial injustices is to erase centuries of denial and begin to solve the problem by first admitting it exists (paragraph 14).

4. Wilkins feels that Rasberry's criticisms are much more important to address, because Rasberry, and others like him, is much more influential in the black community. As perceived by Wilkins, black denial of racism is also more damaging to the black community.

5. In paragraph 10, Wilkins paints a very bleak picture of the racial climate, calling it the "war on blacks." Students may agree or disagree with this assessment.

Rhetorical Considerations

1. Wilkins believes the significance of documenting past instances of racial injustice is being attacked, and that prominent black leaders such as William Rasberry are engaging in the attacks.

2. This is not an *ad hominem* attack because even though Rasberry is mentioned by name, Wilkins focuses on his position, rather than on personal traits. To the extent he adequately portrays Rasberry's position, the attack is justified.

3. Students may differ in their response. Their answers should include several of Wilkins' key points.

4. The title suggests an ironic tone that is not fully revealed until the third paragraph of the essay. He underscores the word "harping" to reveal what he considers inadequate arguments against his position.

Affirmative Action: The Price of Preference
Shelby Steele

Topical Considerations

1. The Faustian bargain refers to the legendary medieval alchemist who makes a pact with the devil. As dramatized in Goethe's *Faustus,* Faust sells his soul for power and fame. The Faustian dilemma Steele confronts is whether to allow his children college preference by virtue of their race even though they are middle-class. He feels that this initial benefit may actually be a burden in disguise. The remainder of his essay explains why he feels affirmative action is actually a burden for blacks.

2. Steele would answer "no" to both these questions. In paragraph 16 he asserts, ". . . it is impossible to repay blacks living today for the historic suffering of the race. If all blacks were given a million dollars tomorrow morning it would not amount to a dime on the dollar of three centuries of oppression, nor would it obviate the residues of that oppression that we still carry today." In addition he states, "suffering can be endured and overcome, it cannot be repaid." He feels that society's feeble attempts to repay blacks for their suffering are ineffective, and possibly corrupting of blacks.

3. To Steel affirmative action is like social engineering: It emphasizes numerical and statistically correct ratios, offering "remediation of preference on the basis of mere color rather than actual injury" (paragraph 7). In its haste to create proportionate representation, it neglects the business of developing oppressed peoples' skills.

4. Although Steele sees a place for affirmative action in society by guarding constitutional rather than racial rights, he feels the keys to black advancement are social policies that are "committed to two goals: the educational and economic development of disadvantaged peoples, regardless of race, and the eradication from our society—through monitoring and severe sanctions—of racial, ethnic, or gender discrimination" (paragraph 26).

5. Steele enumerates many problems associated with affirmative action: (1) they distort our understanding of racial discrimination by allowing us to believe remediation can occur on the basis of color rather than actual injury; (2) it leaps over the development of an oppressed group directly to proportionate representation; (3) it creates demoralization and self-doubt; (4) it encourages blacks to exploit their past victimization as a source of power;

(5) it adds to the belief that historical suffering can be repaid; (6) it can create suspiciousness in white employers and co-workers thus hindering blacks from advancing beyond a certain organizational level.

6. Students may have different opinions. Although Steele makes an allusion to the "Princess and the Pea" fairy tale, the likelihood of affirmative action creating a class of "super-victims" is remote. Steele does not offer evidence for this supposition.

7. In emotional terms suffering can never be "repaid." However, some individuals experience psychic healing in others' attempts to "repay" them for their suffering. This is probably as much a part of human nature as the fact that suffering must be overcome. Steele discounts the symbolic importance of reparation attempts for both the victims and the oppressors.

Rhetorical Considerations

1. Steele's use of "true stories" from his life lends an authenticity and credibility to his argument. It proves he is actively struggling with the issues he writes about and not merely observing the fray from the sidelines. This anecdote is a strong reminder that these issues affect him and his children personally. It indicates that he is emotionally invested in this argument and not merely posing it as an academic exercise.

2. Steele uses statistical data in paragraph 9 to bolster his argument when he writes, ". . . a full six years after admission, only about 26 percent of black students graduate from college." Although this statistic is no doubt true, Steele cannot, as he attempts, link this directly to the failure of affirmative action. This statistic is blurred by past admission rates of black students.

3. Steele makes a persuasive argument against the benefit of affirmative action by piling up various negative aspects of it. Without ever having to damn it outright, which is clearly a position Steele does not want to take, he builds a very effective argument against it.

4. Steele is careful to qualify every statement. He makes neither rash nor sweeping comments. He frequently begins with "I believe" (instead of presenting it as indisputable); in paragraph 17 he notes, "I don't think the mandates in themselves were wrong." In paragraph 8, he writes "some blacks" and "some whites."

5. In paragraph 2 Steele states the opposition's argument by offering the following statements: "Many blacks and a considerable number of whites . . . would say that this small business is the meagerest recompense for centuries of unrelieved oppression. In America, many competent or incompetent whites are hired everyday—some because of their white skinned suits, the conscious or unconscious preference of your employer. The white children of alumni are often grandfathered into elite universities in what can only be seen as a residual benefit of historic white privilege." These statements strengthen Steele's argument for the very fact that he is confident enough in his own views to print the oppositions. By presenting both sides he will alienate only the most radical, closed-minded reader.

6. Wilkins would perceive Steele as denying the full effects of racism and the responsibility of whites in solving the racial problem as the main flaw in his argument. Steele would perceive Wilkins as glorifying a "victim mentality" with his cataloguing of past racial injustices and his belief that blacks need the assistance of whites in solving this problem.

It's Past Time to Speak Out
Charles G. Adams

Topical Considerations

1. In paragraph 7 Adams says that civil rights laws require that institutions do not segregate or discriminate against blacks. He believes these laws are necessary but "are not sufficient measures to correct long-entrenched wrongs against blacks." Steele believes civil rights laws alone are adequate to ensure justice for blacks (paragraphs 23–25).
2. Students may have different opinions. The strengths of affirmative action lie in its promise to give blacks a truly equal stance by providing them with opportunities that whites have always had. Its weaknesses lie in its appearance of giving preferential treatment to people who are not qualified.
3. Steele would agree with the first part of this statement. However, unlike Adams, Steele does not believe affirmative action is "that something special." What is: blacks' abilities to focus on their own problems and to seize opportunities as they arise.
4. President Ronald Reagan was against affirmative action and initiated the repeal of many affirmative action mandates. Reagan and his supporters believed that a person should be professionally judged only on his or her own merit, with no consideration of race. Hence, "Reagonistically color-blind." Students may agree or disagree with the premise underlying the phrase.
5. Students may have different responses.

Rhetorical Consideration

1. The author uses the late Whitney Young to add credibility to his argument. Not only is it his argument but that of a deceased, respected figure in the black community as well. Using well-respected authorities to bolster one's own argument is an effective rhetorical device.
2. Adams is guilty of applying "slippery slope" reasoning in these paragraphs— e.g. "Either it will be vigorously defended or it will be totally destroyed." He might be using this to emotionally draw his readers into his argument as well as to signify the seriousness of the problem.
3. Parables "personalize" abstract concepts; and their simple narrative format makes them easy to follow and remember. Students may have different opinions on the effectiveness of this particular parable.
4. Quoting the Bible lends significance to his essay in its sacredness and importance. The church figures prominently in the lives of many blacks, and biblical reference would resonate strongly.

Oppositions: Immigration Policy
A Statue With Limitations
B. Meredith Burke

Topical Considerations

1. Most readers, through work or school, will have met immigrants. Students might also know of Russian immigrants who have benefitted from an open door policy. They may also remember the image of the Haitian boat people refused entrance into the United States and forced to turn back to face possible death in their country. To some the U.S. immigration policy seems arbitrary at best, deliberate at worst—giving preference to those from one country over those from another. Although Burke uses effective tactics to persuade people that enough is enough, some readers may still feel it is America's duty to take in the tired and poor.

2. Readers can choose any of the facts from the California of 50 million people to an American population of 611 million people who have consumed the Everglades. However, these are all projections of which there is no certainty. What is perhaps more convincing is Burke's summation: "In short, demographic reality will not permit us to evade hard choices" (paragraph 10). Her honesty and commitment to keeping America from ruin are most evident when phrased in her own words.

3. The demographic future is in the hands of American voters. Burke is subtly hinting at the power of the vote (which the new immigrant doesn't possess) to ensure that "states most affected by growth . . . have a decisive vote in changing immigration policy" (paragraph 10). Burke faults the executive and legislative branches (whom voters elect) for designing immigration policies "with barely a nod to the resultant American demographic future" (paragraph 4).

4. While it does seem odd that, according to Burke, there have historically been no provisions made for increasing waves of immigrants, this lack of foresight seems to prove that America and the federal government, like Governor Wilson, consider immigration a fundamental right.

5. The statistics that are included in the essay support Burke's call for limitations. However, the one set of figures that is missing but alluded to (those of the Census Bureau) tends to weaken her essay. The Census Bureau provides *the* standard population figures. Because Burke has somewhat overburdened the essay with statistics, she owes her readers the chance to determine if the Census Bureau assumptions are realistic.

Rhetorical Consideration

1. Burke's analogy to smoking is the most effective section of the essay. The author is suggesting that if it is possible to stop a problem, do it. A person should not continue a life-threatening habit. Substituting the first paragraph with overpopulation it reads as follows: If someone had identified

"over-population" as a major problem, had pinpointed "immigration" as a contributory factor . . . and then had assumed that "immigration was a timeless 'given'" . . . Burke proves that with respect to immigration, more direct, tough questions have to be asked, and solutions found.

2. After mentioning that the future is in "our" hands, the author turns a bit autocratic, stating that if her alternatives ("one-child families and moderate immigration; or two children families and no immigration") "seem unappealing, we can go with unchanging policies and end up with 550 million Americans . . . " (paragraph 9). In effect she asks the reader to accept only her alternatives or suffer the consequences.

3. Burke's description of the California population spread includes the phrases "urban sprawl," "environmental degradation," "paving over of prime agricultural land," (paragraph 4). In paragraph 7 she mentions a state that will be "congested with 10 million people" who will try to keep the Everglades "free from further encroachment." In paragraph 6 she warns that either "all growth stops or the size expands until our natural resources run out." Her words reinforce her anxiety over America's future. Whether or not her fears are legitimate, she tries to move her readership to action.

4. Burke "stacks the deck" unfairly because she makes no mention of how American has successfully managed population growth to date. She also neglects to include the Census Bureau figures which may not have been the doomsayers her demographers were. It seems hard to believe that a bill increasing immigration quotas by more than 25 percent left no one questioning the impact. Yet Burke states that "No one asked then: by how much will immigration increase?" (paragraph 4). Some readers might feel that she does not have a sufficient balance of information to make her argument completely sound or convincing.

5. "A Statue With Limitations" could be a play on "statute of limitations," suggesting there be fixed quotas. It could also mean that the Statue of Liberty needs to become a statue with limitations that will only allow a fixed number of people into the country. A third meaning could be that America cannot afford shelter to the world anymore.

6. Students may agree or disagree with the effectiveness of statistics.

The Big New Mix
Renee Loth

Topical Considerations

1. In paragraph 24 writer Thomas O'Connor explains that at the turn of the century politics could provide "wealth and power" for successful politicians who then provided assistance to immigrants in the form of "food, eyeglasses, pardons, jobs" (paragraph 24). Politics is not as accessible to today's immigrants; Asian immigrants who have no experience/understanding of democracy also feel "cultural resistance to political activism" (paragraph 25). Also, many Vietnamese and Cambodian immigrants have not been here the

seven years prerequisite to vote. Professor Andrew Buni notes that because of the different languages and cultural traditions that make up Asian peoples, there isn't a common political base among them (paragraph 27). As a result there have been few immigrant politicians.

2. Burke herself is a demographer; her essay is based on demographic facts whose assumptions she considers "much more realistic about future mortality, fertility, immigration" than even the U.S. Census (paragraph 7). She even scraps personal anecdotes to free up more space for demographic facts. Loth, on the other hand, criticizes "the dry terminology of demographic science" (paragraph 3) and its practitioners "who limit their study to just the stratistics" (paragraph 2). Loth believes demographics must "come with the caveat that demography is an inexact science, its predictive purity corrupted by politics, human behavior, and other imponderables" (paragraph 9); their "defintions are quirky and ever changing" (paragraph 10).

   Loth's piece is convincing. Her ability to dismiss actual numbers reveals confidence in her own research.

3. Today, some contend that "the current flood of immigrants . . . will be easier to absorb than the so-called European migration" because it is a "fraction of the European migration when taken as a percentage of the US population" (paragraph 7). However, according to Loth, there is only "One key difference between the European migration and the current waves" (paragraph 14). Loth writes that the "migrations were interrupted by restrictive legislation, then by the Great Depression and World War II" (paragraph 14). Immigrants over the past few years have been streaming into the country, "keeping the old-country customs, and language, alive" (paragraph 14). The essay concludes with the assertion that this wave of immigrants is quite similar to those of sixty years ago. Notes Loth, "Most of our demographers agree that our nativist fears about the 'wretched refuse' at our shores could be cooled significantly by a quick course in American history" (paragraph 31).

4. Paragraph 4 begins, "The overwhelming number of people who emigrate want an American passport, not just the green card"; "They want to play baseball, not pachinko." Loth writes that immgrants tend to "intermarry, become fluent in English, and have smaller families with each succeeding generation" (paragraph 3). It is evident that the capitalist system appeals to immigrants. However, some immigrants are realizing that with the popularity of multiculturalism, they will "realize there is a benefit to retaining their ethnic distinctions" (paragraph 6).

5. "The Big New Mix" not only leaves room for different cultures but for cultures within a culture. When Asians include (among others) Cambodians, Vietnamese, Koreans, Hmong, and Laotians and their respective languages, it is clear that we have surpassed the traditional melting pot ideal. The author also offers a stew, a parfait, and a salad. "The Big New Mix" seems appropriate to tackle the political agendas associated with multiculturalism, as well as our newest immigrants from Russia.

6. Elevating the special interest might occur because "some believe that the trend toward multiculturalism could itself retard assimilation" while others "realize there is a benefit to retaining ethnic distinctions" (paragraph 6). If the special interest becomes more important than the national interest, the whole philosophy of the "Big New Mix" will disappear and the core of the nation will be divided into segments of special interests. Most of the essays in this chapter recommend shedding ignorance and learning about each other's differences for the purpose of putting the national interest first.

Rhetorical Considerations

1. Yes. Loth writes an effective essay by writing in the third person, illustrating her points with facts, consulting numerous experts, and demographers. Some readers might feel that she is getting at the truth because she has no vested interest.

2. The argument in this essay revolves around whether or not demographers are correct in their assumption that "immigrants adjust to America more than the country adjusts to them" (paragraph 2). The counterstatement is that America adjusts to immigrants better than they adjust to America. Loth argues that because the country survived the skepticism over European migration sixty years ago, it will do so again. She "proves" this statement with many examples including one economist's belief that immigrants "are a nearly-unalloyed good: They'll stimulate the economy, improve the American standard of living, reverse the birth dearth and provide for baby boomers in their old age" (paragraph 18). Less effusive, but equally sincere, is Loth's statement that "Most of our demographers agree that nativist fears about the 'wretched refuse' at our shores could be cooled by a quick course in American history" (paragraph 31).

3. Loth's essay is completely inductive because she pieces together facts to prove that America can and will adjust to the wave of immigrants. She uses demographers, economists, historians, the U.S. Immigration Service, the U.S. Census, etc. to go from the particulars to the general. There are no personal anecdotes or human interest stories from which to make an emotional appeal.

4. Because the author has chosen to fight on behalf of the immigrant, she seems liberal in philosophy. In the first paragraph she writes of "the ascendancy of English-only movements, the backlash against political correctness, and the dismantling of hiring quotas" that are "the symptom of a growing anxiety" of some "natives." She uses the safe past to quell the fears of the natives. She has been careful to present "redistricting" not as a solution for immigrants to get into the political realm but as a problem.

5. Loth bolsters her argument by citing experts in various fields. Her own voice may be muffled among the statements of others.

11
Social Issues

Gun Control
The Right to Bear Arms
Warren E. Burger

Topical Considerations
1. Open for discussion. However, the point may be made that most of these incidents involve unregistered guns, so that Burger's suggestions of tougher regulation of handgun registration would not be effective. Reform in these instances would need to take place on the level of the suppliers of illegal weapons—involving law enforcement authorities rather than lawmakers.
2. Burger does a good job of pointing out how the concerns that necessitated the Second Amendment in the eighteenth century have long since changed; therefore, the Amendment itself may need some revision. The issue comes down to how flexible the Constitution was intended to be: should such a document "change with the times"?
3. According to Burger, at the time of the Constitution, Americans were afraid of oppression by a standing army, based on their ancestors' experiences in Europe. Instead, they opted for the more democratic concept of a "militia" (our modern-day National Guard), which would hand the power of national security over to the people. Burger states in paragraph 13 that in the two centuries since the Constitution was ratified, after two world wars, "we have no choice but to maintain a standing national army," thereby changing the premise upon which the Constitutional right to bear arms was based.
4. Open for discussion.
5. Open for discussion, although there is a point where "taking the law into one's own hands" does not constitute a viable defense in court.
6. Some students may object to the idea of government control of handgun registration and ownership, while others may feel that even more regulation is necessary. Still others might feel that Burger does not address the more relevant and urgent question of illegally obtained handguns, which is more a criminal than a legislative issue.

Rhetorical Considerations
1. Using such shocking statistics to open an essay is effective in getting the attention of the reader; it also serves to validate the need for the essay. By emphasizing the urgent nature of the problem with such statistics, Burger pro-

vides a compelling reason for readers not only to continue reading, but also to accept his arguments.

2. Some students may find the extent of this historical information daunting or distracting to the main argument; however, such thorough documentation of historical and social changes since the writing of the Constitution sets a solid foundation for Burger's argument that it is time for a change in legislation.

3. The analogy is effective in that, as Burger states in paragraph 15, "the right to keep and own an automobile is beyond question; equally beyond question is the power of the state to regulate the purchase of the transfer of such a vehicle and the right to license the vehicle and the driver with reasonable standards." However, as Burger also states, the Constitution does not mention automobiles; therefore, the argument about the right to bear arms will always "stick" on the issue of Constitutional rights. It might be helpful in discussion to focus on a comparison of the reasons for regulation of guns and the regulation of automobiles.

4. Using the form of questions for his proposals, Burger asks whether it is "unreasonable," in the light of the "mindless homicidal carnage" associated with handgun misuse, to require his new regulatory plans. This strategy implies that if the reader's answer to whether these proposals are unreasonable is yes, then the reader will somehow be advocating or at least permitting "mindless homicidal carnage."

5. Open for discussion. His contextualization of the Second Amendment is very helpful; however, times have also changed significantly enough that most guns now owned and carried are unregistered. Some may argue that by not addressing this large aspect of the issue, his argument is essentially inapplicable.

A Case Against Firearms
Sarah Brady

Topical Considerations
1. Brady argues that too many Americans are dying by handguns—in the 1980s more than the number who died in the Vietnam War. It is certainly a sobering argument given the numbers.

2. Students will see the attempt on Ronald Reagan in 1981 as a grim reminder of other political assassinations: John Kennedy, Robert Kennedy, Martin Luther King, Jr., and Malcolm X. Whether or not banning handguns would have prevented these killings is up to the students to argue. You might ask students to consider what other means might be available to potential assassins and if these assassins would be as likely to use those. Probably so.

3. Brady is asking for two specific pieces of federal legislation: (1) a national waiting period for the purchase of handguns; (2) the end to the sale and domestic production of semiautomatic assault weapons. She offers the example of New Jersey; this state has required the background check of gun purchasers—a measure, she reports, that has successfully stopped more than ten

thousand convicted felons from buying handguns. As for assult weapons, she cites three separate massacres of people in paragraph 5.

4. The NRA is, perhaps, Washington's most effective lobbying organization. Many of its millions of members are wealthy sportsmen who have resources to contribute to an organization that promotes their interests.

5. Being the wife of Jim Brady makes the author's arguments very compelling.

Rhetorical Considerations

1. She first mentions the quarter million victims—four times as many as were killed in the Vietnam War. In the next three paragraphs she cites examples of how "we are killing our future."

2. Open for discussion.

3. Reasoned and objective.

4. This is a sarcastic slam at the lack of will in Congress to pass legislation against assault rifles.

Gun Owners Are Not Bad People
Warren Cassidy

Topical Considerations

1. Open for discussion.

2. Cassidy says that gun control proponents want to waive constitutional rights to bear arms for the sake of social reform. The word "peculiar" does undercut the motives.

3. Cassidy, like other opponents of gun control, argues that the Second Amendment to the Constitution protects the right of the individual to bear arms. Although citation of this amendment is valid, Cassidy does not mention that the amendment refers to a state militia and was originally intended to allow the states to defend themselves against unjust encroachment by the federal government and not necessarily to grant free license to anyone and everyone who wanted to own a gun.

4. As an alternative to gun control, Cassidy offers tough NRA-supported laws that punish "the incorrigible minority" who commit gun-related violent crimes. He claims that such measures have shown a leveling off and even a decline of violent crimes with firearms. He does not, however, specify the level of such laws—that is, municipal, state, or national—or where exactly in America this leveling off and decline is taking place. Certainly not in big cities where, he even admits, violent crimes continue to rise regardless of tough gun control statutes and punishment.

5. Cassidy argues that criminals don't buy guns the way law-abiding citizens do. No gangster is going to register or allow for a background check. If they want guns they buy them on the streets from other criminals. The only effect of a waiting period is inconvenience for the "honest citizen." Cassidy's point is a good one, and, yet, it can be argued that a waiting period might allow a cooling-off period for someone waiting to get a gun on an impulse

to even a score or hold up a gas station. Also, background checks will screen for people with criminal records or histories of mental problems.

6. Cassiday would defend the gun-owner's right to an assault weapon. Although such weapons are used for the sole purpose of killing people, he would argue for the rights of responsible collectors of military weaponry

7. Open for discussion.

Rhetorical Considerations

1. Cassidy's tone is quite controlled and reasonable. He does a little flag waving in the opening paragraphs, though it does not become obtrusive.

2. Students might argue all three. There seems to be an equal balance between a case for guns and case against prohibitionists' arguments. Paragraph 3 cites the political strength of the NRA, but it is not until the last two paragraphs that he makes an obvious pitch for the organization with an invitation in the last line. Some students might be turned off by this. Others might want to write for applications.

3. Cassidy does not convincingly debunk gun prohibitionists. Nor does he show their obvious flaws and failures. His strongest point is that waiting periods will not stop criminals from getting guns.

Handguns in Our Homes Put Children at Risk
Derrick Z. Jackson

Topical Considerations

1. Jackson blames the epidemic primarily on two things: what Chicago Police Superintendent Matt Rodriguez calls "the proliferation of firearms" (paragraph 2), and the immaturity of children, who do not understand "'mortality'" (paragraph 3). Though he admits that an attraction to guns can be exacerbated "by hopelessness or boredom in the streets and by child abuse" (paragraph 5), Jackson specifically denies that only disadvantaged children are at risk from this scourge: "Young, low-income African American males are doing the a [sic] lot of the dying, but the carnage this year defies any stereotype" (paragraph 10).

2. Jackson's opposition to the death penalty is implied in paragraph 6. There he claims that the prevalence of "children killing children exposes [the death penalty] as a cheap thrill" (paragraph 6). Jackson's point seems to be that when children kill it puts the death penalty in a new, more lurid light, because it is hard to imagine a child being put to death no matter what the offense—especially given mitigating factors such as child abuse.

   Jackson apparently includes this brief reference to the death penalty in order to refute a common argument, expressed in fact by Warren Cassidy, that "tough, NRA-supported measures that punish the incorrigible" will reduce crime as gun control never could ("Gun Owners are Not Bad People," paragraph 6). Jackson attempts to undercut the logic of people like Cassidy by demonstrating how horrific the punishment of the death penalty can seem when applied to child murderers.

3. To Jackson, both guns and cigarettes present a serious public health risk. But whereas cigarettes have been regulated, taxed, and denounced with public dollars, guns remain relatively untouched for reasons of political expediency Jackson finds deplorable. "[T]here is no tax proposed on handguns, as there is on cigarettes, to help fund health care reform," even though politicians have "proclaimed guns a public health disaster" (paragraph 8). There is no comparable "massive public education campaign" against guns as there is against cigarettes (paragraph 9). In the final paragraph, Jackson appropriates the language of cigarette regulation to insist on handgun regulation: "We have banned smoking from most public indoor spaces because of secondhand smoke. We must now get handguns out of our homes so our children stop becoming victims of secondhand possession" (paragraph 12).

   Students can debate the effectiveness of the parallel. A possible weakness in the analogy is the apparent constitutional protection of the right to bear arms. For Cassidy, for example, a more fitting parallel to gun control than antismoking regulations would be attempts to control free speech (see "Gun Owners," paragraph 1).

4. Open for discussion. Students might note some of the cases cited by Jackson of accidental shootings by children, tragedies apparently encouraged (if not caused) by wide availability of firearms. Also, Jackson's statistics about the number of firearms—100 million in 1970; 216 in 1994—coupled with the facts that "100,000 teen-agers bring guns to school every day" and "[t]he US teen-age murder rate is seven times higher than any nation in Western Europe" (paragraph 5) at least imply a connection between the availability of firearms and childhood violence. But NRA advocates could still argue, as Cassidy does, that none of these statistics directly proves that guns themselves, and not something nefarious in American culture, cause such appalling violence.

Rhetorical Considerations

1. Open for discussion. On the positive side, Jackson's statistics are, in and of themselves, appalling: the fact that the number of firearms in America more than doubled from 1970 until 1994 (paragraph 4); the number of teenagers killed by gunfire in the United States each year (paragraph 5); the years of "potential life" lost since 1991 because of guns; the claim that "[a]t the current pace of destruction, guns will replace cars as the nation's most deadly product within 10 years" (paragraph 12). On the other hand, the logical connection between the statistic and the argumentative point they are invoked to support is not always clear. The number of firearms, for instance, surely supports Jackson's claim that we live in a gun culture aptly titled the "United States of Arms," but it does not necessarily prove that guns cause crime.

2. The emotional power of Jackson's argument results largely from the piling-up of tales of young lives tragically cut off by guns. Students may note, how-

ever, that although such examples are powerful, he only gives one statistic indicating the breadth of the problem—"5,356 children and teen-agers were killed by gunfire" in 1991 (paragraph 5). Alert students will notice that even this figure is not broken down to indicate how many of these children were killed by other children, how many by adults, how many as the result of involvement with gangs or drugs which might have claimed their lives eventually with or without guns. In other words, the proliferation of anecdotes constitutes a powerful emotional appeal, but Jackson does not precisely describe the frequency of such occurrences. As always with anecdotes, they are effective more because in their specificity they provoke the reader emotionally than because they logically support the writer's claim.

Students can be led to discuss a central political and philosophical question raised by this article: how many dead children is too many? Some students might claim that one tragic incident justifies gun control; others, for whom owning a gun is an important American liberty, that the risk of such tragedy is the price we all pay for freedom.

3. Jackson is angry, primarily at those he feels have done nothing in the face of mounting evidence that "Handguns in our homes put children at risk." Jackson's anger is clear from the first sentence, "Nothing will come of last week's killings of children by children unless the grownups have had enough of guns." The phrase "nothing will come of [it]" itself conveys disappointment and anger; the use of "grownups" here, a word usually used by children, is in this context derisive, since Jackson clearly implies here that the adults, in playing with their guns, have abnegated their responsibility to protect society's children. Jackson's anger is soon focused on politicians who "agonize over a crime bill that bans only the most hideous of assault weapons, while children pop away with the pistols owned by their parents" (paragraph 5). The angry tone here is created by Jackson's ironic use of the word "agonize." Again, when Jackson refers to "[s]ome relatively bold politicians" who have discussed taxes on bullets, the irony is palpable: these politicians, anything but bold, will not risk strong legislative action against guns "since fear and the image of being tough on crime wins elections" (paragraph 9). Finally, the essay ends on a drippingly ironic note: "What are we waiting for? A newborn to come firing out if its mother's womb?" (paragraph 12).

4. Jackson states his thesis directly in the opening sentence of the essay, then spends the rest of the article supporting it. He does this first with two anecdotes, in paragraphs 2 and 3, both accompanied by the comments of officials who believe that too many guns, and the psychological immaturity of children, are the cause of the present crisis. After almost seven paragraphs denouncing current policy on guns and offering statistics to support these claims, Jackson ends his essay with four other examples of children killing and being killed because of the ready availability of firearms. In this way, Jackson alternates logical arguments with emotionally powerful anecdotes, which appeal to the reader's emotions.

Poverty and Homelessness
Helping and Hating the Homeless
Peter Marin

Topical Considerations

1. When Marin was younger he felt a personal affinity to the homeless. He enjoyed the same anonymity and absence of constraint. Like many homeless, he felt at home on the road and had many homeless friends. As he grew older, his first reaction to the homeless was fear for his family and annoyance—what he refers to as "bourgeois fears." Students may have differing responses on whether their views of the homeless have changed as they've gotten older.

2. According to Marin "homeless" contains so many different groups of individuals with different circumstances that it is a meaningless term. It is also the final stage for a variety of problems, and, therefore, tells us nothing about the root causes or circumstances of those problems. One alternative to this "catch basin" label is to refer to individuals by the specific circumstances of their lives, rather than focusing on their home status.

3. Marin believes that liberals and conservatives are equally responsible for the problem of the homeless. He believes the problem of the homeless is "the sum total of our dreams, policies, intentions, errors, omissions, cruelties, kindness, . . . " According to Peter Marin, we are all to blame for homelessness.

4. The "margins" of society are places where people without homes, jobs, and mental and/or physical health can gather. Street people, rebels, recalcitrants, Vietnam vets, mentally ill, physically disabled, elderly, jobless, single parents, runaway children, alcoholics, immigrants, and traditional tramps, hobos and transients are individuals who may exist in the margins of society. They contribute a sense of "breathing space" in our culture. They represent a necessary flexibility and elasticity. They demonstrate that there is a place for the darker, less organized, and controllable recesses of our souls, similar to that which artists provide a culture. Students may agree or disagree with Marin's vision of a society without margins and should explain their answers.

5. Selma, Alabama was the site of the first civil rights march led by Dr. Martin Luther King, Jr. Just as policymakers during the civil rights movement were pressured into enacting legislation that would integrate the South, the council in Santa Barbara that Marin writes about was repealing the sleeping ordinance, not out of any sense of "compassion or justice," but because of pressure brought by the threat of massive demonstrations by the homeless.

6. He perceives these shelters as covertly or overtly proselytizing to their inhabitants. All are run by strict rules and rigid controls. Marin refers to the mandatory evaluation and counseling by social workers at the shelters as

"therapeutic bullying." He seems to be biased against these shelters. One could argue that any institution that handles that many people must have rules and regulations. Many would perceive what he labels "therapeutic bullying" as a necessary and helpful service. Similarly, religious overtures and instructions might be seen as caring and helpful, rather than as intrusive and manipulative.

7. Marin believes that the Victorians fostered the intertwining of social obligation with self-protection, the strategy of masking self-interest by calling it "moral duty." Hygiene was the core component of the Victorian medical, aesthetic, and moral systems. Their attitudes toward the poor were shaped by this focus, not by a sense of justice or empathy. According to Marin, this is still the motivating force for reform in America today. To illustrate his theory, Marin utilizes a part of a student's paper on her first visit to a Rescue Mission on skid row. Marin feels that many programs for the homeless are geared as much to the needs of those giving help as to the needs of those receiving it. Students may not agree that hygiene is the sole motivating force for reform in this country, though they may feel it plays a significant part.

Rhetorical Considerations

1. The essay explores personal and societal attitudes that help and hinder the homeless. Marin says that he felt differently about the homeless when he was younger than he does today. He also discusses their contribution to our society, and our responsibility to them. He divides the homeless into two categories: those who do not want to be there and those who do. He criticizes both those opposed to helping the homeless and those helpers who attach demands to their help. Marin points out the dichotomies of sympathizing and criticizing the homeless, our zeal for reform and the homeless individual's desire to be left alone. Through personal narration he demonstrates the human tendency to feel affinity and fear toward the homeless. Students should be able to empathize with these conflicting emotional responses.

2. The three different dramas that Marin describes: those struggling to survive by regaining their place in the social order; those struggling to survive outside the social order; and the tension and contention all humans experience between the magnanimity of life and the darker tendencies of the human psyche, including fear of strangeness, hatred of deviance, and love of order and control. Marin believes that the resolution of the first two dramas will depend to a large extent on how society resolves the third drama. It's up to the student whether the metaphor is accurate or far-fetched.

3. Clearly, Marin's use of the term "visited on" implies he does not believe the homeless are responsible for their plight. He also does not name who is responsible here. It is unclear whether Marin believes the "active" homeless are totally responsible for their own plight, although he does believe that some have chosen it to an extent. Marin would probably believe that both types

of homeless are victims, though "active" homeless are less victimized than those who did not choose their circumstances.

4. Marin gains credibility with three different examples. He displays a breadth of personal knowledge and experience. Furthermore, he personalizes his analysis by depicting real people and places instead of rendering abstract information. These anecdotes are relevant because they represent the two cultures of homeless people—those who have chosen it and those who are victims of it.

5. Marin's experiences help create a cohesion to his argument. Affinity and fear support the metaphor he develops in paragraphs 41 and 42 that illustrate the contrary forces in this problem. In paragraph 22 he explains that historically it has been our annoyance, even disgust, with the homeless that has led to our zeal to reform them. Likewise, it is confusion and fear that motivates the individuals in paragraph 4 to repeal a "sleeping ordinance" that benefits the homeless. Marin echoes the tensions at work in society in his recollection of conflicting responses to the homeless at different times in his life (1 and 20).

Brother, Don't Spare a Dime
Christopher Awalt

Topical Considerations

1. Awalt's extensive work with the homeless has led him to several conclusions about them. He believes some homeless people are truly victims of tragic circumstances and are working hard to return to jobs and "normal" lives. Many, however, are chronically homeless, content to remain as they are. Whatever policy we enact to assist the homeless must include a notion of self-reliance and individual responsibility. All programs to help must require some effort and accountability on the part of the individuals targeted. Otherwise, the problem of the homeless will not be solved. Students may agree and disagree with this reasoning.

2. He puts the blame on the homeless themselves because his experience has convinced him that many have chosen their "lifestyle." They enjoy the freedom and the lack of responsibility. Students may debate this assessment; however, they should note how Awalt lumps together conditions such as mental illness, alcoholism, poor education, drug addiction, and "simple laziness" without distinguishing them or their causes. This lack of insight (or examination) may make his assessment of "root" causes of the problem suspect to some readers.

3. Awalt defines people who lead "normal lives" as "responsible citizens, working in the shelters and applying for jobs" . . . "eager to reorganize their lives" (paragraph 5). Implied in this definition is the notion of belonging to mainstream culture. Marin discusses the "marginal world" of

the homeless in his essay, as well. According to Marin, this is a world "parallel to our own world" . . . "but always separate." A world inhabited by people who have chosen not to be a part of mainstream culture for various reasons. Awalt sees no place for people who choose homelessness. Through policy and discipline, he is anxious to see them returned to the fold of "normalcy." Marin, on the other hand, feels that these individuals serve a necessary purpose in our culture, and should be allowed to live as they please.

4. Awalt casts a wide net over those he considers the "chronically homeless": people who are homeless because of "mental illness, alcoholism, poor education, drug addiction, or simple laziness" (paragraph 6). They are "content" to remain as they are, he says, enjoying the freedom and lack of responsibility prohibited in "normal life." Students may agree or disagree with this assumption, but they should acknowledge some of the logical inconsistencies in his position—i.e., the assumption that those who suffer from drug addiction, alcoholism, poor education, or mental illness are "content" and consciously choose their lifestyle.

5. Basically, Awalt's experience has taught him that many homeless people have actively chosen their condition to avoid the responsibilities of work and "normal life." Students may dispute whether this is a unique or typical view of those who work with the homeless. Obviously, Peter Marin who has spent time with the homeless has learned quite a different "lesson" about them. Much depends on the individual's perspective, philosophy toward life, direct experiences.

6. Awalt's solution to homelessness would involve some policy change that includes a notion of self-reliance and individual responsibility. We cannot allow them to take over our public spaces, nor can we provide rehabilitative social programs without requiring some form of personal accountability from them, he says. Ultimately, he believes that unless the homeless "are willing to help themselves," there is nothing the rest of us can do (paragraph 10).

Rhetorical Considerations

1. Words and phrases such as "haggard character," "constant symbols of wasted lives and failed social programs," and "danger to public safety" convey a negative perception of the homeless. Students may agree or disagree as to whether this is a persuasive rhetorical device, although they should mention that this subjective, opinionated opening may lead readers to question how objective or balanced the essay will be.

2. In the last paragraph Awalt's constant use of the pronoun "we" and "our" as well as "taxpayer" conveys an "us-versus-them" mentality. Our money and public spaces are in danger of being wasted, according to Awalt. This is an *ad populum* attempt at persuasion. He is clearly not writing to a homeless audience or to an audience sympathetic to their plight.

3. The "brother" Awalt refers to is any non-homeless reader. His use of personal pronouns conveys a familiar, persuasive tone. In paragraph 9 he implores his readers directly to take action: "Please don't take my word for it. The next time you see someone advertising that he'll work for food, take him up on it."

4. As stated above, Awalt writes from a personal perspective. He has worked with the homeless in various capacities (chaplain, food server, counselor, etc.) for two years. He has been intimately involved in trying to help one homeless individual, buying him clothing, placing him in a detox center, and attempting to get him a job (paragraph 7). These experiences, Awalt believes, allow him to speak authoritatively on the subject and make him a credible voice. However, the very personal nature of his experiences, in particular that of failing to return a homeless man to "normal" life, may also make his account more slanted. Ironically, that which renders him more credible may also render him prejudiced, in the eyes of some readers. Someone who has worked with the homeless longer than two years might question Awalt's authority on the subject, as might a homeless person.

5. Although he sees the homeless issue in terms of choice or necessity, Awalk does acknowledge that "not everyone who finds himself out of a job and in the street is there because he wants to be. Some are victims of tragic circumstances." He also admits that he has met dignified, capable people during this time working with the homeless. However, he feels that these people are not part of the "real" homeless problem, since they usually resume "normal" lives within a period of weeks. The rest of the homeless—"chronically homeless"—are the real problem. His conflating of various conditions—drug addiction, alcoholism, and mental illness—doesn't address the vast set of circumstances that have led individuals to homelessness (paragraph 6). Awalt provides only one example of a man who could not adjust to "normal" life, and from that he generalizes to the experience of all.

Yes, Something Will Work: Work
Mickey Kaus

Topical Considerations

1. Kaus proposes to "de-enable" the underclass by radically reforming welfare. He believes that replacing welfare with a "neo-WPA" program that paid below the minimum wage and expanding the Earned Income Tax Credit would transform "the underclass." Students may agree or disagree with Kaus' proposal.

2. Kaus seems to suggest that the "restraints" placed on inner city blacks are the staples of middleclass life: a job, a "traditional" family, and role models. Kaus' choice of the phrase "freed from the restraints" is sarcastic and mocks the "poorest elements of black society" who live "in broken homes with no workers." Kaus implies that unemployed single mothers are unemployed and single by choice. It is likely that the majority of the inner city poor would consider these "restraints" to be privileges.

3. According to Kaus, welfare helped the underclass to form because it enabled people to stay in the "ghetto," remain jobless, and raise children in single parent families. Kaus' is an interesting theory; however, the issue seems more complex than the author suggests.

4. Kaus probably defines "working families" as two-parent households that are economically independent of government assistance. "Forming working families" is a euphemism that seems to advise single mothers to marry a man with a job. This might be an unrealistic recommendation.

5. Some might complain that Kaus has singled out and attacked black single mothers, thus lessening his credibility by failing to describe any other segment of the "underclass."

6. This question is up to the student. However, economics is only one factor that has driven the tradition of the two-parent family. Other factors that play a part in the two-parent American nuclear family include love, culture, formal education, knowledge of birth control, a two-parent upbringing.

Rhetorical Considerations

1. By writing "does anybody really think . . . ," Kaus gives Kemp's initiative no credibility and therefore intends his question to be rhetorical. However, as Republican Jack Kemp, President Clinton, and a Democratic Congress have all backed enterprise zones as a viable source to boost economic development in the inner cities, Kaus should have attempted to answer his question.

2. Kaus cites Kasarda and Fitzwater to show that he is not alone in his view of the welfare system. Kasarda provides a neutral source of factual information. Fitzwater, associated with the Bush administration, lends support to Kaus' belief that ghetto poverty was caused by welfare programs.

3. When Kaus writes that Marlin Fitzwater "blamed ghetto poverty on welfare programs, he creates a *post hoc* fallacy. Fitzwater's assumption is inconclusive: Because ghetto poverty increased after welfare began does not necessarily mean that welfare was the cause of it. Without any definitive proof, Kaus also implies that there is a direct connection between the "explosion" of welfare recipients and the increase in the number of children born to black single mothers.

The Culture of Cruelty
Ruth Conniff

Topical Considerations

1. Because, as Conniff states in paragraph 7, "The people on welfare whom I know have nothing wrong with them." She, unlike Kaus and Jencks, does not judge people's character by their circumstances.

2. Conniff writes that many poor people are caught in an "endless cycle." They "live in bad neighborhoods. They can't find safe, affordable child care . . . In short, they are poor." The author's argument reduces the complexity of the

welfare problem, drawing on what have become the clichés of the welfare issue. Her explanation is not informative enough to adequately dispel criticisms of the system.

3. Welfare families and former mental patients are not breaking the law and would probably be offended by being grouped with street hustlers and drug addicts. The latter two have historically been considered the "underclass." Grouping the four reflects the "rhetoric about lazy welfare bums . . . taking the country by storm" (paragraph 8).

4. More useful, Conniff believes, is "understanding the roots of the culture of cruelty and trying to determine how through the adoption of decent social values, we might overcome it" (paragraph 16).

5. Conniff does not quote Jencks and Kaus very much. Consequently, readers must rely on Conniff's interpretation of their theories. Because the reader gets second-hand, subjective information (noting their work is "based on prejudice rather than fact"), there is room for misinterpretration.

Rhetorical Considerations

1. This line, reminiscent of Ebenezer Scrooge, is a hyperbolic example of the wrath of taxpayers over the welfare system. Obviously, this statement illustrates the "culture of cruelty" that Conniff claims has crept into our public consciousness.

2. Each paragraph is effective in different ways. This is a good question to spark discussion over which is more persuasive, quantitative or anecdotal information. Students may also find that they enhance each other.

3. One problem with Conniff's pervasive criticism of opponents to the welfare system is that readers cannot evaluate her own position very well. Another is that the reader sees only Conniff's interpretration of her opponents' positions; and her generalizations might not render a balanced assessment of welfare opposition.

4. When Conniff claims, "They lend legitimacy to the racist and misogynist stereotypes so popular with conservative politicians and disgruntled taxpayers . . . ," she displays a bias against conservatives and taxpayers who may not hold these stereotypes. She risks alienating part of her audience with these assumptions.

5. Conniff makes an *ad hominem* argument when she calls opponents "precocious sophomores, dominating the class discussion, eager to sound off about the lives and motivations of people they have never met" (paragraph 18).

6. The account strengthens Conniff's argument because by directly quoting Kaus and providing a less interpretive, more analytic explanation of his idea, she gains the reader's confidence, appearing more objective and authoritative. By directly responding to his work, she is able to provide a more persuasive response.

7. Kaus would believe that welfare advocates such as Conniff believe that "throwing money at the problem" is still a viable solution to the problem.

Because she neither discounts this or provides other options to solving the problem, welfare opponents may interpret this as a failure to reform the current welfare system in any significant manner.

Teenage Pregnancy
Countering the Culture of Sex
Ellen Goodman

Topical Considerations

1. Though not adopted by Congress, the welfare reform policy proposed, among other things, to make teenage mothers ineligible for welfare for life. Goodman attempts to shift the focus of these debates from the transgressions of the teenagers to the culpability of the culture at large. Offering "'tough love,'" the nickname of the proposed congressional policy, is inappropriate in a world where the culture has always offered free love—"[s]ex without consequences." Though she does not actually say so, Goodman seems opposed to the congressional policy; a clue to this attitude is the use of the word "concoct" to describe Congress's actions.

2. Goodman endorses Kathleen Sylvester's claim that "'[i]t's wrong to bring a child into the world that you can't take care of'" (paragraph 14). Goodman specifically does not claim, as some students and certainly some of their parents might believe, that sex outside of marriage is inherently wrong, or that there is something shameful in having an illegitimate child: "we can't preach," she suggests, with a glance at Madonna, "however much papa (and mama) may want to" (paragraph 14). For Goodman, the issue is not one of sexual morality but of personal responsibility.

   Students should be encouraged here to discuss, and perhaps dispute, their own attitudes toward teenage pregnancy, examining what (if anything) they think is morally wrong about it.

3. Open for discussion. In analyzing both Madonna and other pop culture figures, students should realize that there are exceptions to the rule Goodman asserts.

4. Goodman argues that because sex is depicted without consequences in the popular culture so influential on teenagers, "any national campaign that goes to the heart and hard core of the problem is going to have to engage these cultural message makers" (paragraph 8). Goodman wants "parents and other responsible adults" to "campaign against unwed parenthood" (paragraph 13) by encouraging popular culture to say "unequivocally in rhythm, rap or reel" that teenage parenthood is wrong (paragraph 14).

   The strength of this proposal is that it seems accurately to assess the power popular culture has had in fostering sexual irresponsibility. One weakness of the proposal lies in its feasibility. How exactly might popular message makers be "engaged"?

5. Noting that media executives tend to "wave furious charges of censorship at any critic," Goodman claims that her plan to "engage cultural message makers" as "allies" in the fight against irresponsible sexual behavior is not a call for censorship, but rather for "more reality" (paragraph 17): "one part passion to two parts diapers" (paragraph 20). But how, really, is Goodman's proposal different from other calls for controlling media content—that is, from censorship? If Goodman wants "responsible adults" such as herself to dictate to artists the content of their work, isn't she veering dangerously close to censorship, though refusing to own the term? Artists are notoriously wary of turning their work into "successful pitch[es]" (paragraph 11) about anything, no matter how noble the cause. Students should acknowledge that the censorship issue provides a major unresolved point of opposition to Goodman's argument.

Rhetorical Considerations

1. Goodman claims here that "[s]ex without consequences" is now celebrated in "mainstream films, music, television" (paragraph 8). "[C]ounter-culture," usually thought of as the place where traditional taboos against sexual behavior are transgressed, is now made up of "parents and reasonable adults who are left to literally counter the culture" (paragraph 8). The centrality of Goodman's redefinition is indicated in the title, "Countering the Culture of Sex."

   By redefining counter-culture, Goodman rhetorically appropriates some of the powerful appeal of being unconventional to "parents and reasonable adults"; she defuses the romantic appeal of cultural messages celebrating sexual freedom by labeling them "mainstream" (paragraph 8). Students can see in Goodman's strategy a canny argumentative use of definition.

2. Goodman uses Madonna to open her essay with an anecdote, reported by researcher Kathleen Sylvester, about a school principal's two-word response to the question of how to reduce teen-age pregnancies: "Shoot Madonna" (paragraph 2). The use of Madonna here gives the opening of Goodman's essay a humorous touch, apparently designed to draw readers in to her argument. However, Goodman soon indicates that she is not interested in simply scapegoating Madonna, who is for her not the cause but a central symbol of the problem: she represents "a culture that sells kids sex as successfully as it sells them sneakers" (paragraph 5). Goodman suggests that her own proposal "goes beyond using Madonna for target practice" (paragraph 15).

   In addition to using Madonna as a rhetorical device (to enliven the opening of the essay) and symbol (of popular culture's attitude toward sexuality), Goodman also indirectly alludes to the words of Madonna's "paean to teen-age motherhood" (paragraph 4): "we can't preach, however much papa (and mama) may want to" (paragraph 14). This quotation suggests Goodman is aware of the need to speak to teenagers using their own idiom; it enacts Goodman's claim that we should "engage . . . cultural message-makers" (paragraph 9) when discussing teenage sexuality. The allusion also indicates Goodman's willingness to take seriously youth's often strong resistance to the moralizing of their elders.

3. These three paragraphs precede Goodman's statement of a major point: that it's flatly "wrong" for teenagers to have a child they cannot support. In these paragraphs, Goodman attempts to counter one source of potential opposition: that convincing film-makers, musicians, and television producers to represent "[s]ex with consequences" (paragraph 20) is a hopeless task. The passage marks a central concession to opposition. Here, in three paragraphs that begin with parallel construction ("It will . . . "), Goodman admits the difficulties confronting such a project, difficulties even greater than the more successful recent campaigns against smoking, drugs (the "Just say no" campaign) and drunken driving. The parallelism creates a repeating pattern which serves as a kind of drum-roll preparing the reader for the most direct statement of thesis in the essay, in paragraph 14: "'It's wrong to bring a child into the world that you can't take care of.' It's not cool, it's not manly, it's not womanly. It's wrong."

The Name of the Game Is Shame
Jonathan Alter

Topical Considerations

1. Both Goodman and Alter are worried about teenage pregnancy, but the similarity ends there. Whereas Goodman says only that it is "wrong to bring a child into the world that you can't take care of" (paragraph 14), Alter, very differently, endorses "'the notion that it is dishonorable for a man to father a child he does not support"; he also claims that "single motherhood" is a "selfish act" and that "it is 'morally wrong'" for unmarried teens to bear children" (paragraph 1).

2. "Reactionary" is a word usually applied to political conservatives who "re-act" against change by insisting on the higher good of supposedly traditional values. But Alter uses this label here to describe people who are usually termed liberals: those spokesmen for "moral relativism" (paragraph 2) who, according to Alter, are wary of "blaming the victim" (paragraph 2) in social policies. Since "reactionary" (as opposed to conservative) has negative connotations, suggesting knee-jerk, tired, often nostalgic responses to social problems, Alter effectively brands his opponents with this label when he himself might be vulnerable to it. In this way, Alter rhetorically creates himself as the radical, or at least forward-looking, risk-taking innovator, especially as he ends his essay: "Risk ridicule. Think anew" (paragraph 8).

3. Alter claims that "every threat to the fabric of this country—from poverty to crime to homelessness—is connected to out-of-wedlock pregnancy" (paragraph 3). Since Alter offers no support for this claim, students might well find it hyperbolic and unconvincing.

4. Clearly, Alter means shame in the old-fashioned, sense: awareness of having transgressed a moral rule. Alter wants to see "the moral judgment of society

. . . restored—in law and in everyday life" (paragraph 3), even though this means potentially hurting the "'self-esteem' of the young mother and fathers" (paragraph 3). On the other hand, shame does not mean labeling illegitimate children bastards (paragraph 6). And when Alter gives examples of what actions can illicit shame, they are both economic. Shame means "being forced to live with your parents instead of using welfare to get your own apartment" and making sure that "every birth certificate contain the social-security number of the father" so that all fathers will suffer the indignity of having their pay check docked for child support. Students may wonder whether these legal actions will really result in ashamed teenage parents; they might also discuss whether shame is something that can actually be taught to grown human beings.

5. Alter is supporting what he claims is a general "comeback" of "the notion of shame" (paragraph 1) as a prophylactic against teen pregnancy. Responses to this project will vary. Students may voice concerns both about its feasibility—how exactly could the culture accomplish this major attitude shift—and its effect on both the stigmatized illegitimate children and their parents.

Rhetorical Considerations

1. Tupac Shakur is a practitioner of "gansta rap," a genre of music characterized by lyrics celebrating brutality, misogyny, and homicide, among other things. Alter uses Shakur here as a representative of his opposition. The rhetorical strategy here is to characterize the opposition by its most radical, and unappealing, fringe. In other words, to disagree with Alter is to identify oneself with Shakur. Students should recognize this strategy as rhetorically clever, but not necessarily justified, since there is plenty of middle ground between Alter and Shakur, including many law-abiding citizens of a more liberal stripe than Alter.

    For different reasons, Hester Prynne is also problematic as a representative of Alter's opposition, as any student familiar with *The Scarlet Letter* will know, since Hawthorne's book is a denunciation of the use of shame in a hypocritical, repressive society.

2. Without arguing the point, Alter assumes, in the first paragraph, that his readers will share his belief that teenage pregnancy is "'morally wrong'": "This might sound to many Americans like saying the sky is blue. Of course that behavior is wrong."

    The strength of this approach is that, like the use of Tupac Shakur to characterize the opposition, it leaves little room for a reader who disagrees with Alter to stand. By assuming most Americans hold Alter's own truths to be self-evident, Alter might make readers inclined to disagree feel somewhat ashamed of their (apparently) morally aberrant position. The weakness of Alter's approach in this opening paragraph is that it makes no effort to create a common ground with opposition; the essay's first paragraph may well spark animosity, and resistance, in readers not already convinced of Alter's position.

3. In this paragraph, Alter takes on an almost apocalyptic tone, using words and phrases evocative of fire and brimstone oratory. Biblical language creeps into Alter's argument when he describes teen mothers as "sinners" and teen pregnancy as "sin," as when he characterizes unwed pregnancy as a "scourge." Students may also find the reference to "the fabric of our country" to be a bit of patriotic bombast. Together, this dramatic, hyperbolic language adds to the sense Alter seems to want to create of himself as a moral arbiter. Students should be encouraged to dispute the effectiveness of this strategy.

4. Alter appeals to authorities from across the political spectrum, ranging from conservative spokesman David Blankenhorn (paragraph 4); Kathleen Sylvester, a researcher with the Progressive Policy Institute (paragraph 3); an unnamed "moderate Democrat" (paragraph 1); White House aide Bruce Reed (paragraph 5); and the distinguished philosopher Amitai Etzioni (paragraph 7). Generally, the breadth of experts effectively suggests consensus on Alter's major assumption: that the problem of teenage pregnancy is largely the result of relaxed moral standards.

5. Alter does not provide any evidence, in the sense of statistics, facts, controlled studies or case studies to support his argument that shame would be effective in battle against teenage pregnancy. In fact, in the course of his argument Alter makes some rather dubious claims of fact: most astonishingly, that "every threat to the fabric of this country—from poverty to crime to homelessness—is connected to out-of-wedlock teen pregnancy" (paragraph 3).

   This lack of evidence does not necessarily destroy Alter's essay, since his argument is largely based on values —a kind of argument that often relies on appeals to the morality and emotions of readers. Alter supports his argument by adopting a tone of moral conviction; by canny definition (of New Reactionaries); and by the use of authoritative opinions from across the political spectrum.

In Defense: Teenaged Mothers
Mike Males

Topical Considerations

1. Males focuses first on the claim, expressed by Alter, that the current welfare system rewards teen pregnancy by enabling young mothers to move out of their homes and set up independent housekeeping with the help of federal tax dollars. On the contrary, Males points out that "[m]ore than 60 per cent" of teenage mothers live at home, according to a 1992 study (paragraph 6). Of those who leave, many "cannot return home" because they are fleeing sexual abuse or physical violence by parents, guardians, or other relatives (paragraph 5). Also being ignored, in Males' estimation, is the fact that the majority of children born to teenage mothers are fathered by "adult men over the age of twenty" (paragraph 7). This statistic proves that the problem

is not only teenage sex, but teen-adult sex—a possibility not considered by either Goodman or Alter.

2. Males suggests that many teenagers become pregnant as "'a way out,'" in the words of one young mother (paragraph 2). Pregnancy can be perceived as a way to leave abusive homes (paragraph 4); more broadly, according to a 1990 study cited in paragraph 16, "teenaged mothers show significantly lower rates of substance abuse, stress, depression, and suicide than their peers" (paragraph 16). Students can debate the persuasiveness of this claim, using their own understanding of teenage sexual practices. Even on a sub-conscious level, is sexual activity, and the attendant risk of pregnancy, really undertaken with such clearly defined motives?

3. Males believes the poster campaign inaccurately depicts both the typical pregnant teen and problems that cause teenage pregnancy. Teenage mothers are not "naughty airheads," as one of the posters suggests. Further, both posters—of the "airheads" and of the "callous varsity jock" do not acknowl-edge that many teen pregnancies are caused by adult males. Students can discuss whether these posters, which imply teen pregnancy happens largely to infatuated, unthinking young women, are consistent with their own ex-perience. They might note that the "callous varsity jock" could himself eas-ily be an "adult [man] over the age of twenty" (paragraph 7).

4. Males claims that "[p]overty causes early childbearing" (paragraph 12); Al-ter makes the opposite claim that "every threat to the fabric of this coun-try—from poverty to crime to homelessness—is connected to out-of-wed-lock teen pregnancy" (paragraph 3). Where Alter insists that teen pregnancy is "not caused by economics," Males cites figures that show that a "rapid in-crease in child and youth poverty, from 14 per cent in 1973 to 21 per cent in 1991, was followed—after a ten-year lag—by today's rise in teenaged childbearing" (paragraph 12).

   As students will already have noticed, Alter offers no support, apart from strongly moralistic language, for his claim on this issue; Males, on the other hand, refers to several studies that support his position, though they are not fully cited. Students should recognize the need to do further research to adjudicate between the claims of Alter and Males.

5. Open for discussion.

Rhetorical Considerations

1. Analyzing the quotations Males uses should alert students to the fact that his major claim—that getting pregnant may be an effective way for teenagers to raise themselves out of destructive home situations—relies almost exclusively on the opinion of a single source, Yale Gancherov, the supervising social worker at the Crittenton Center. Gancherov believes that "troubled, abused girls become more centered emotionally" (paragraph 14), and that these girls "are more likely to stay in school with a baby than without" (paragraph 15).

   Students can dispute whether Gancherov's conclusions are sufficient to support this broad argument. On one hand, she is in a position to know about teenage pregnancy, and Males does find support for her opinion in one "1990 study of 2,000 youths" (paragraph 16). On the other hand, Gancherov's opinions are just that: they are apparently based on anecdote and personal observance, rather than statistical studies done with a controlled sample. And without more details about the 1990 study, it is difficult to assess its credibility.

2. Males opens his essay with a series of anecdotes designed to appeal to the reader's emotions. In one breath in the essay's first sentence, Males mentions LaSalla Jackson's "tiny infant" and the "scars on her calves where her drug-addicted mother beat her with an extension cord." Similarly, the description of Almonica's murderous mother in paragraph 2 would appall any reader. The anecdotes are certainly effective in gaining the reader's attention and making them sympathetic to the plight of these young women. But students should also note that no claim is made that these anecdotes are representative.

3. In these paragraphs Males makes explicit what he has been implying throughout his essay: that current attacks on teenage mothers are a shameless bullying of the poor and weak by the strong and powerful. Characterizing teenage mothers as "reckless" and "guilty of abusing adult moral values and welfare generosity" (paragraph 19) is not only inaccurate, as the essay has argued throughout, but morally wrong. The strength of this appeal is that it appeals to a widely held moral belief: that it is wrong for the strong to attack the weak. The strategy is also useful because it attempts to appropriate, in defense of welfare mothers, the kind of moral high ground almost exclusively inhabited by writers with Alter's point of view. Students should discuss whether they find themselves vulnerable to this appeal or not.

Menaces to Society?
Stephanie Coontz

Topical Considerations

1. Coontz is angry about recent efforts to characterize single mothers as "menace[s]" to society (1). Such sentiments are emanating from "pundits and politicians of every stripe" (paragraph 1). Coontz names part of her opposition explicitly in paragraph 3; it includes the writer of a *Newsweek* column, Democratic Senator Daniel Patrick Moynihan, conservative columnist David Broder, and President Clinton.

   The focus of Coontz' essay is single motherhood; both Alter and Goodman's essays are concerned more specifically with teenage single mothers. Nevertheless, Alter could clearly be included in the group of "pundits" who have provoked Coontz, for he believes we should see "single motherhood as a selfish act" (paragraph 1) and that we "'must resurrect the notion that it is dishonorable for a man to father a child he does not support'" (paragraph 1). Goodman, on the other hand, though she deplores teen pregnancy, does not characterize single motherhood more generally as wrong. Since Goodman only claims that "'[i]t's wrong to bring a child into the world that you can't take care of'" (paragraph 14), she does not necessarily think poorly of women like Coontz who are able to care for their children.

2. In paragraph 10, Coontz describes the stories of "three . . . never-married mothers" who differ in class, educational status, and age. Students can dispute whether these three stories are enough to prove Coontz' point: that it is unfair to generalize about the morality of all single mothers as have many recent commentators.

  The point that "there are hundreds of paths leading to single motherhood" (paragraph 9) is central to Coontz's essay because she wants to argue that the morality of any individual unwed mother's case is much more complicated than people like Alter will admit. Given that some stories "would seem irresponsible to even the most ardent proponent of women's rights," and "others stem from complicated accidents or miscalculations that even the most radical right-winger would probably forgive" (paragraph 9), Coontz believes no one can condemn all single mothers collectively: "What government agency or morals committee should decide which of us single mothers to stigmatize and which to excuse?" (paragraph 11). Goodman can only convince her readers of this point if she first persuades them to see that there are many different reasons why single women become mothers.

3. Aside from the moral claim that no one person should pass judgment on single mothers collectively, the major claim of this essay is that innocent children will suffer from recent attempts to stigmatize illegitimacy. One of the most important strategies Coontz uses to make this point is by creating a vivid picture of her son Kristopher. Far from being a pariah, Kristopher emerges as a typical American adolescent. By practicing "his electric guitar" at apparently astonishing volume, Kristopher is behaving like middle-class American teenagers everywhere; because he seems so typical, readers can well imagine that, like most adolescents, he "takes labels very seriously" (paragraph 4) and is sensitive to being branded as illegitimate.

  Both this sensitivity, as well as a certain principled self-confidence, is conveyed when Coontz describes Kristopher standing up to a teacher who made a "particularly cruel remark . . . about single mothers" (paragraph 5). Coontz evokes Kris's self-confidence again when she worries that it "might lead him to do risky things or to question authority once too often" (paragraph 15). Kristopher emerges, then, as a child who seems to have suffered little in self-confidence from being the son of a never-wed mother; as a typical American adolescent; and as someone who could be potentially devastated by current "mean-spirited" invective (paragraph 1) about children like him.

4. Coontz characterizes herself as an engaged, loving, and affectionate parent in several ways. First, the brief anecdote recounted in paragraph 4 suggests she and her son have an affectionately joking relationship—especially when Coontz kids Kris that although he "didn't inherit a normal set of eardrums"

she doubts he is truly "a new species." Secondly, readers can infer that mother and son are quite close, not only because Coontz tells us so (paragraph 14) but because Kris tells his mother about the episode with the health teacher (paragraph 5).

Perhaps the most effective way in which Coontz conveys her strengths as a mother is in having the confidence to describe her weaknesses, in paragraphs 12–15. Coontz reveals that, like many single parents, she is "consumed with guilt and fear" (paragraph 12) that her life choices might mean "an inevitable sentence of doom" for her son. She admits that, like most single parents, she tends to "spend less time supervising [my] child's schoolwork or talking to teachers than do adults in two-parent families" (14); that "the adolescent years can be particularly trying" in a single parent home (paragraph 15), and that "setting firm limits" can be especially difficult for a single parent (paragraph 15). But even while admitting these drawbacks, Coontz suggests some of the advantages of parenting alone: she, again like most single parents, spends more time talking to her child; she tends to "praise good grades more than adults in two-parent families"; her son is "more candid with [her] about what's happening at school than most of his friends" (paragraph 14). Further, the self-analysis itself suggests important parenting skills, since it indicates Coontz thinks hard and critically about her strengths and weakness as a parent.

5. In paragraph 8, Coontz offers several examples of how attacks on illegitimacy seem motivated by a desire to return women to traditional roles. She describes the following:

> ". . . family-values crusaders [who] . . . begin by castigating welfare mothers but move easily to 'careerist' mothers; divorced women who put 'individual self-actualization' before their kids' needs; women who remarry and expose their daughters to the 'severe risk' of sexual abuse by men who lack a biological 'investment' in the child.

Coontz also cites an article that suggests that social problems would be solved if women allowed themselves once again to be "'cared for' by men" (paragraph 8). Later in her essay, Coontz argues that "[t]he new family-values crusade also appeals to those uncomfortable with the changing role of women by emphatically reestablishing men as the 'heads of households'" (paragraph 17). She describes with derision President Clinton's remark that children of unwed mothers "aren't sure they're the most important person in the world to anybody'" (paragraph 18), a comment Coontz claims reflects centuries-old attitudes denigrated women's role in childbearing and child-rearing.

6. Both Males and Coontz are responding to moralistic attacks on single motherhood. But they take very different approaches in their response, perhaps because they focus on different constituencies. Males is specifically defending low-income, inner city teenagers, claiming that in the context of deprived, abusive home lives pregnancy can actually be a way out. Males is

angry at the "blame-the-victim" tendency of attacks on these women. Instead of focusing on teenage mothers, Coontz takes a broader look at the problem, arguing that it is impossible to make moral generalizations about single mothers because they come in all ages, colors, and class backgrounds.

Rhetorical Considerations

1. Clearly fed up with current attacks on single motherhood, Coontz expresses this attitude by using ironic, sometimes sharply connotative language to describe her opposition in the opening paragraph. When she describes politicians and pundits as "going on about the dire consequences of single parenthood," she uses the derogatory phrase "going on about" to suggest the talk is so much meaningless, repetitive drivel. The ominous adjective "dire," usually reserved for describing the truly horrific things, is so extreme in this instance as to seem ironic; a similar ironic effect is created by her use of the word "menace" in the title of her essay and its first paragraph. Describing the attackers as "politicians and columnists of every stripe" who are "trumpeting" their arguments, Coontz conveys her derision of writers by subtly comparing them with pack animals ("of every stripe"). Coontz ends the paragraph with language that insists on her own humanity, in comparison with these pack-like creatures: such "mean-spirited and cynical" invective "takes my breath away" (paragraph 1).

2. Coontz' credibility, one of the major strengths of the essay, is enhanced by the fact that she is both personally and professionally concerned with single motherhood. As a "family historian," Coontz knows from research "that unwed motherhood is not the major cause of our society's problems" (paragraph 7). Moreover, because she is a "white, middle class, older, well-established professional" (paragraph 5), her own life story serves as an example of the dangers of generalizing about unwed motherhood.

3. Coontz' long analysis of the drawbacks and benefits of single motherhood offers some concessions to readers who would want to point out the inescapable problems of raising a child alone. The opposition that Coontz does not attempt to refute is the idea that out-of-wedlock childbearing is morally wrong—a position taken by Alter.

4. In a canny response to conservatives who claim to be speaking for traditional values, Coontz here hearkens back 300 years to the "family values" of a Native American tradition (paragraph 19). In response to European Jesuit missionaries who encourage the Montagnais-Naskapi Indians to "take control of women's sexuality" and "discipline their children more harshly, the Native Americans respond with what sounds like a magnanimous sense of community and parenthood: "You French people love only your own children . . . but we love all the children of the tribe" (paragraph 19). By identifying her point of view as the oldest one within a multicultural understanding of the word "American," Coontz establishes herself as the traditionalist, a position almost always taken by those who attack illegitimacy.

Oppositions: Capital Punishment

Capital Punishment is Justice

Edward Koch

Topical Considerations

1. Some of Edward Koch's refutations of the seven arguments against the death penalty appeal to reason and some to emotions. Koch views life as precious and the taking of life as the most heinous act. Therefore, for such a crime, justice can only be death—a moral stand at least as ancient as the Old Testament's code: "an eye for an eye, a tooth for a tooth." Although he does not make much of this argument, he does point to execution as being a deterrent to murder. His arguments are convincing if one accepts the biblical premise.

2. Most of Koch's own arguments are rooted in justice rather than deterrence. Only in his discussion of the third argument against capital punishment does Koch directly address the subject of deterrence: ". . . one of the best ways to guarantee that protection is to assure that convicted murderers do not kill again" (paragraph 8).

3. Koch enlists the support of death-penalty foe, Hugh Adam Bedau, whose research has not demonstrated that innocent defendants have been put to death. Koch quotes Bedau's figures—some 7000 executions from 1893 to 1972. Then Koch goes on to talk about multiple murders. This is Koch's thinnest and least convincing argument. As Bruck points out in the next essay, Bedau did not say the innocent defendants had not been executed, but that this fact is very difficult to establish. Koch also changes the subject matter very quickly deflecting attention—and doubt—to ugly details of multiple murderers.

4. It is not clear that Koch is saying some murders are more "heinous" than others. However, the implication is there. He does cite in the essay cases of brutal or multiple killings when he is building his argument. One would presume that Koch would consider "heinous" premeditated murder, multiple murder, and murder that was particularly grisly (mutilation and dismemberment). One would assume that Koch would consider "heinous" drug kingpins who order killings, as well as those who commit the killings. He would also support the death penalty, one assumes, for those who kill law-enforcement officers.

5. For the student.

Rhetorical Considerations

1. The opening sentence of paragraph 3 serves as Koch's thesis statement: "Life is indeed precious, and I believe the death penalty helps to affirm this fact."

2. It is an apt analogy and one what would muster support for his view. Cancer is a pathological equivalent to evil, and one we all fear.

3. ETHICAL: arguments 1, 4, 6
   LOGICAL: arguments 2, 5, 7
   EMOTIONAL: arguments 3,7

4. Edward Koch is known as a feisty, hard-fisted, no-nonsense kind of man who enjoys the outrage he can create. Yet, little of that offensiveness is visible here, for the essay is composed in a voice of reason and moral purpose. The reader may not agree with Koch's stand on capital punishment, but he or she must respect the measured tone in Koch's presentation. Where necessary, Koch is direct and forceful, never shrill. In paragraph 13 for instance, Koch dismisses "a popular argument among opponents of capital punishment" as "transparently false." Yet, he does show some tooth as when he accuses Jimmy Breslin of "sophistic nonsense."

No Death Penalty
David Bruck

Topical Considerations

1. Two aspects of the J.C. Shaw case are omitted by Koch: (1) that Shaw was suffering mental illness and the effects of PCP; and (2) that he made his statement about the wrongness of killing moments before his execution. These are important omissions that may not sway opinion, but in the right court of law could render a different verdict than that which Shaw suffered. The circumstances of mental illness and drug influence may not lessen the awfulness of the crime for readers as much as it might convince them to consider a lighter sentence for cases of mental incompetency. In the next paragraph, Bruck brings up litigation against Alvin Ford by the Florida Supreme Court, which in 1986 lost its case because he was too insane to know he was to be put to death and for what reasons. Should Ford eventually be deemed sane, he can be executed. Koch's omission of the circumstances of the Shaw crime weakens his argument somewhat. So does his railing against Shaw for his lecture on morality. Shaw was, according to Bruck, not condemning the state in the name of clemency, but of killing itself.

2. The heart of Bruck's argument is that capital punishment is reckless in practice and "irreverent" in its view of human life. The system, he argues, is inherently faulty even if one innocent defendant has been executed. And it is a fact that the death penalty has been applied prejudicially for decades.

3. The Jeter case is convincing.

4. Koch's own use of Bedau is very selective as he carefully quotes just what he needs for support. However, Bruck makes the point that Bedau was simply saying that questions of guilt can never be completely resolved in some cases. Bruck goes on to say that Bedau is currently working on a compilation of "wrongful deaths," a fact that undermines Koch's argument as it does Bedau's own in the Koch essay.

5. Probably Bruck would call for life sentences without parole for the most "heinous" crimes.

6. Koch says in paragraph 11 of his essay that discriminatory use of the death penalty "no longer seems to be the problem it once was." About the Knighton case, Koch might admit that a life sentence should have been in order and that any sign of prejudice should have been caught in the appeal process.

7. Some might agree that the public, so frustrated with crime and the seeming inability to stem it, views the death penalty as a compensation.

Rhetorical Considerations

1. The opening line of paragraph 15 serves as Bruck's thesis statement.

2. This detail about the death-house crowds illustrates just what Bruck is complaining about when he says in paragraph 15 that the death penalty "encourages an attitude toward human life that is not relevant, but reckless." The cry for blood is ugly, a nasty reminder of the kind of rage that kills. When death is a spectacle, something is lost.

3. Bruck effectively dismisses Koch's Old Testament code of justice with extrapolations from other crimes. In paragraph 16, he says that following the same logic of a-death-for-a-death, perhaps rapists should be sodomized. Also effective and persuasive is Bruck's claim that "neither justice nor self-preservation demands that we kill men whom we have already imprisoned."

12

Ethical and Moral Issues

Euthanasia
Scared to Death of Dying
Herbert Hendin

Topical Considerations

1. Patients in the Netherlands need not seek a second, unbiased opinion on the appropriateness of their decision; the only second doctor they must see is the one who will assist the suicide. In paragraph 13, Hendin observes that assisted suicide has eroded to euthanasia (implying the doctor's volition has become stronger than the patient's), for increasingly more trivial reasons, and even without the patient's consent. In the next paragraph, Hendin outlines two cases in which patients' immediate response to crisis—death of a son, asymptomatic HIV diagnosis—might well have changed within a year, or even weeks, with proper counseling. In concluding that new statutes protect only doctors, Hendin implies that patients are being murdered.

2. For student discussion. Students probably won't admit to having had suicidal impulses in the public forum of the classroom; but if they do, or discuss someone they know who committed suicide, it may be necessary to make the distinction that this is not really the issue at hand. Rather, Hendin wants public thought and policy to address suicide as an option for the terminally ill, or perhaps those in chronic and excruciating physical pain. Most traditional-age college students are more likely to think themselves immortal, and thus immune to this kind of exigency.

3. From information in paragraph 5, a patient must either be in pain or "imminently about to die"—or more likely, both, to meet Hendin's approval for assisted suicide. For Hendin, "imminent" clearly doesn't mean six months; even six days might be pushing it. From his case studies and comments about law, students can infer that the following are bad reasons or conditions: (1) poor chance of surviving a medically risky procedure; (2) anxiety about death; (3) single physician's approval—lack of second or third disinterested opinion; (4) psychological distress; (5) non-lethal bodily pain. Since he makes a distinction (albeit not fully explored) between assisted suicide and euthanasia in paragraph 13, the patient's own volition, rather than someone else's urging (or perhaps even prompting), must be the primary force setting an assisted suicide in motion.

4. Hendin's case studies supply good sketches of the severe emotional trauma which may lead a patient to request assisted suicide inappropriately. These

can be summarized broadly as fear of the unknown and quality of life concerns. Death, of course, is the biggest unknown, especially for an increasingly secular or agnostic society. A patient could also develop anxiety about high-risk medical procedures, preferring the certainty of immediate death rather than waiting for an unlikely cure—or, as with the HIV case, for the other shoe to drop with full-blown AIDS symptoms liable to strike at any time. Patients also fear that the quality of their continued lives may be poor; Hendin provides a good list in paragraph 8, including "pain, dependence, loss of dignity." The grieving mother example also suggests that emotional suffering, including depression, should be considered part of the trauma. (Although he does not say so, Hendin must surely consider the murky, fuzzy legal and moral tangles of this debate as contributing to an individual's distress.) Even if students haven't considered suicide, assisted or not, they've probably had some brush with these feelings: grief over a grandparent's death, the itchy immobilization of a broken arm or leg in a cast, fear of assorted small unknowns (such as their grade on the next paper for you!)

5. Patients must receive adequate counseling so they can make informed decisions. Neither they nor their doctors should allow the fear of unpleasant unknowns to mask the real fear of death—a topic we refuse to discuss openly, and thus fumble and sublimate. To that end, doctors must receive adequate training (paragraph 18); and they must defer to some kind of systematic federal network or oversight group in agreeing to assisting an individual's suicide (implied in paragraphs 9 and 10). Doctors and social policy makers must also provide better care for terminally ill patients. Although Hendin doesn't offer much discussion on what this might mean, he seems to have sweeping changes in mind. These might range from ameliorating the individual's physical, psychological, social, and economic discomforts, to social institutions such as hospices and counseling groups, which not only address the terminal patient's needs, but make death a more visible, normal part of the fabric of our lives.

Rhetorical Considerations

1. Hendin does not express his feelings about Kevorkian explicitly, but labels him as the "only champion of the terminally ill." The term is overblown, as if to suggest that he stands as a shorthand reference for a broader range of hyperbole, media antics, and individuals with a warped conscience. Yet paradoxically, Kevorkian plays an effective role in Hendin's argument against Kevorkian-like actions. The "Doctor of Death" is the logical outcome of our failure as a society to formulate an adequate and humane public policy about terminally ill patients. If Kevorkian hadn't existed, we would have invented him.

2. The leukemia patient humanizes the consequences of right and wrong decisions in requests for assisted suicide. The patient fervently wishes to die, and has a pretty good set of reasons to make his request. However, Hendin's

counseling not only convinces him of the folly of his earlier request, but allows him the time to live long enough to validate Hendin's wisdom in dissuading him. He was grateful for the chance to have a leisurely leave-taking from his loved ones. Hendin then speculates that in Oregon, this same patient would easily have found a doctor to provide assisted suicide, depriving him of the benefits that the patient himself agrees he has received. The detailed cameo portrait, then, allows us to develop enough empathy for the patient to wish him "all the best," and to shudder at the thought that his death was a good one only by the happenstance that he didn't live in Oregon. Finally, the leukemia patient allows Hendin to establish his own credentials. Rather than pompously declaring his medical degree, Hendin creates a miniature portrait of his professional life as sage and compassionate counselor, rather than mere wielder of scalpel. Further, he's no backwoods general practitioner, but one to whom patients get referred when they have exhausted their own doctor's expertise. Hence he's fairly high up on the pecking order of specialization, and has earned enough respect from his colleagues to get referrals. (Or, in a nutshell, Marcus Welby on the set of "Love Story.")

3. Student responses will vary. The first question uses the abstract word "euthanasia" and makes no personal references; it's easy to favor a broad concept. But the other two questions ask the respondent to consider her or his own death. Further, by offering only one of two polarized options, Hendin makes us long for the power to equivocate, to add conditions: "Yes, but only if . . ." By turning directly to his readers with such sharply limited "either/or choices," Hendin humanizes his argument more effectively than case studies. First, we've all been in situations where we've had to choose between the devil and the deep blue sea, and have yearned for an alternative. Case studies, however, are about "other people," not ourselves. Posing the question for readers to think about as applicable to themselves drives home the point that whatever we decide as personal or public policy may well govern the specifics of our own deaths some day.

4. Hendin's use of Scandinavian policies as counterexample is weak for at least four reasons. First, he lumps together several countries without distinguishing them or their policies. Second, he waffles in phrasing; what exactly do "excessive measures," "virtually dead," or "choose death prematurely" mean? Third, he introduces a new variable which he doesn't discuss completely elsewhere with much specificity, the quality of care for the terminally ill (thus building an analogy on his own say-so; care is either "good" or "bad," but what does that mean?) Finally, he approves of Scandinavian policy because of the doctors' attitudes, but not because of the results of the laws or the specific features of those laws.

5. Possibly he fears that U.S. statistics would be skewed by inaccurate data collected over too short a period of time (since doctors have probably been doing assisted suicide without recording it as such for some time—else why the flap about changing the laws?) But Hendin seems to want to avoid sen-

sationalizing the issue with grisly cases or eye-popping numbers. Making Kevorkian his fall-guy specifically as "champion" for the underdog terminally ill, Hendin tries to keep the debate on the high ground of sober, intelligent consensus rather than letting it drift to the low ground of sound bites and manipulated statistics.

When Is It Right to Die?
Ronald Dworkin

Topical Considerations

1. Dworkin's brief outline of ballot initiatives, statutes, and case law in four states in paragraph 2 suggests that the issue is too important to basic human freedoms to be left to a state-by-state hodge-podge. Although all states are bound to follow the Constitution, some national consensus, especially interpreting the 14th amendment, is necessary. Such national consensus can only be attained in a federal jurisdiction.

2. Dworkin cites a portion of Judge Rothstein's decision referring to this amendment in paragraph 4. All citizens are acknowledged to have certain rights that accrue not as the result of privilege, but simply because they are human. The government must uphold and protect those rights. Liberty here means not only freedom from constraint, but the ability to make choices that affect one's life, as long as those choices do not impinge on the rights of others and do not damage the commonweal. Dworkin agrees with Rothstein's assessment that the ability to choose a dignified, comfortable death must be included.

3. The term "slippery slope" refers to moral decisions in which we are unable to draw a firm line between permissible and impermissible behaviors, in a way that accounts adequately for all possible permutations and individual cases. In other words, we cannot define qualities that are both necessary and sufficient to categorize an act as one or the other, and at the same time defend against our logic being used in ways that our gut reaction cannot countenance. One instance is the fear that doctors may execute "sick, old, unwanted people"; that is, doctors will be more ready to persuade or even act on behalf of a patient for reasons that benefit others, rather than benefiting the patient. Dworkin believes that doctors have more compassion and common sense than to slip on this slope. They know, without having to unsnarl the logic, when they are benefiting the patient, and when they are abetting gold-digging relatives. Students may select other examples from paragraphs 5–11.

4. Matthew Habiger argues that contraception, abortion, and euthanasia all fail to value life as "a sacred gift from God." Even if sympathy for an individual request would make euthanasia seem attractive, the symbolic value of all life would be irreparably eroded by just one instance. But Dworkin believes that it is possible to disagree about how to act in ways that respect

life—and, by implication, that one set of interpretations must not be imposed on others. Habiger sees a slippery slope because he believes the only way to respect life is to preserve it. Dworkin does not see a slippery slope because he believes that life may, under some circumstances, be more respected by ending it.

5. We've all experienced shame: it is a basic tool to socialize children. A comment like "Aren't you ashamed of whacking your little brother over the head," helps children learn to empathize, and to avoid actions that others experience as painful or disgusting. But Dworkin wants to exclude at least two kinds of shame as a basis either for or against euthanasia. The first is explicitly stated: the shame of an individual who feels obliged to compensate, to a self-denying extent, for unalterable facts of his or her existence. Dworkin mentions this kind of shame in paragraphs 8 and 10, with patients who accept death rather than inconvenience or gross out their loved ones. The second is implied in Dworkin's article: the shame in which an individual sets aside deeply held convictions to satisfy a persuasive or powerful majority (or even an outspoken minority). A student example might be the shame of a devout Catholic student who does not challenge the instructor of a composition class who is adamantly pro-choice, and who grades on his or her convictions.

Rhetorical Considerations

1. Dworkin does not carefully qualify the timeframe for imminence of death, and hence leaves a weak point in his argument. Since none of us is immortal, we could all be technically described as "dying." Or, taken to a less strained extreme, what about people who have just tested HIV-positive, but are asymptomatic, like the Dutch patient in Hendin's article? He may well have lived 10 years or more in good health. Dworkin leaves an even bigger gap in his argument when he does not defend against suicide for someone who may be miserable—depressed or in chronic pain, for example—but not dying. Nothing in his or Rothstein's attempt to argue for suicide as a liberty would expressly rule out such an application. However, it is hardly likely that he would endorse suicide as a legal option for just anyone who asks three times without expressing ambivalence.

2. Student responses may vary, especially if they already have strong anti-abortion sentiments. But it's still worth pointing out Dworkin's sparklingly deft strategy here as a model for students' own writing. He begins with a fairly full accounting of Habiger's position, in Habiger's own words rather than paraphrasing. He does not attack Habiger *ad hominem,* nor belittle his opponent's logic. Rather, Dworkin praises the principle on which his opponent's views are based, even if he cannot agree with the application of that principle in practice. On a sticky issue where Dworkin knows he cannot convert all readers to his stance in a single sitting, he nevertheless leaves the door open for further discussion, rather than slamming it shut with insults or rigid intransigence.

3. Dworkin takes a risk by setting down this detail about lethal doses of painkillers. However, he uses several strategies to minimize the risk. First, he is only setting down a practice that readers must surely suspect has been going on for a long time. Second, Dworkin makes this information part of unpleasant alternatives to legalize euthanasia, along with "assembly-line suicides" and death accompanied by "great pain or . . . drugged stupor." Finally, he makes this information part of a slippery-slope argument about painkillers, not about life. How much pain (not to mention how do we measure pain) qualifies a patient for painkillers such as heroin, which may eventually cause deterioration and death even in "nonlethal" doses?

4. Dworkin can hardly sidestep abortion, since both Judge Rothstein, with whom he agrees, and Matthew Habiger, with whom he disagrees, have made it an inextricable part of their cases. Rothstein presents the basic similarity: that both abortion and euthanasia are "the most intimate and personal choices," and hence fall under 14th Amendment protection. Dworkin returns to this theme at the end of the article, pointing out that individual beliefs cannot be subjected to majority consensus rule. Habiger suggests another similarity: both involve decisions made by someone other than the individual whose life is affected. (I'm assuming that he regards the fetus as "life." But Dworkin defends against this similarity by distinguishing that the euthanasia he advocates is specifically voluntary, at the patient's explicit request. A second difference is that Dworkin limits his appeal for euthanasia to those who are near death, and have no expectation of joyful, fulfilling life. Except for abortions on deformed fetuses, the potential for individual enjoyment is unknowable, if not entirely unlimited.

5. Student responses to the tangents on abortion may vary, depending on their prior stances and knowledge about the issue. Some may simply find it "information overload" and have a hard time telling when Dworkin is talking about which issue. Those who have given abortion little thought may also find some of Dworkin's language difficult. He relies heavily on lingo developed in the abortion-debate trenches, such as Roe V. Wade and "slippery slope." It may be helpful to chart differences and similarities between euthanasia and abortion on the chalkboard. Who takes the action? Whom does the action affect?

Dead Complicated
Elizabeth Rosenthal

Topical Considerations

1. In the early 1980s, if a person's heart and lungs worked on their own, the person was alive. If those organs did not function, the person was dead. But 10 years later, medical advances had dramatically undermined that simple definition. Machines could keep blood and breath circulating. In paragraph 9, Rosenthal cites the example of a woman who read, knitted,

and socialized although she would have been "dead" by 1982 standards. Because such patients were clearly "alive," legal definitions changed to avoid macabre, ludicrous error. By 1992, a patient could be declared legally dead only if the whole brain—not just selected portions—had ceased functioning.

2. The answer to this question depends in part on the healthcare providers' specialties and experience. A group of doctors and nurses undifferentiated by speciality, tested in 1989, could spit back the textbook definition of whole-brain death. But they floundered when asked about cases described on paper (paragraph 6). Further, even among those who have thought through the issues more carefully, there exists disagreement: "society's conservatives" and "some doctors" who disagree (paragraph 11). Finally, doctors rely on specialized neurologists to perform a battery of arcane, counterintuitive tests to determine whether a patient is dead or alive (paragraph 12). In other words, the specialists must call in their own specialists.

3. The first is the eye movement test. Cold water is squirted into a patient's ear; if any brain stem activity remains, the eyes will move toward the stimulus. The second is the apnea, or breathing test. After doctors take preventive measures to avoid oxygen loss, the patient's respirator is turned off. He or she must take at least one unassisted breath within 10 minutes, a reflex to rising carbon dioxide levels, to be declared alive. Rosenthal finds both tests unpleasant. The first would cause dizziness and vomiting in a conscious patient; and anyone who has stayed underwater too long can readily imagine the pain of 10 minutes without breathing.

4. The tests are "devious" because they seem so unrelated to what's being tested for. Students might call a test for a literature course that asks more history questions than literary questions devious, in this sense—or perhaps a French test on which unfamiliar vocabulary is liberally sprinkled, without explanation or sufficient contextual clues. The eye movement and apnea tests call for mundane movements (or lack of movements) that don't satisfy our intuitive wish or expectation of a more grand, dramatic gesture declaring life.

5. The slippery slope constructed by Rosenthal is a good example for students who were unable to fully grasp it in earlier articles in this section. Rosenthal is concerned that defining death as the inability to feel, to experience sensation, may lead us to unacceptably lenient definitions involving "quality of life" as a criterion. Earlier, she has noted that even she cannot tell on visual inspection which patients are "alive" and which are "dead." They don't seem to have any sensation or awareness. But that doesn't mean they lack cognition—only that Rosenthal cannot discern it. Likewise, she wouldn't be able to discern much (if any) cognition in a severely retarded person, or one who has suffered a stroke or paralysis. Thus, applying the physician's ability to communicate with the patient, or the non-neurologist's eyeball-assessment of "death," opens a slippery slope. Were we to admit this kind of observation as an acceptable determination of death, we could not formulate a rea-

sonable defense against declaring a retarded person "dead," simply on the say-so of a physician who says "well, the lights are on but nobody's home—better to end the suffering."

6. The case of baby Theresa illustrates how painful it can be to err on the side of caution. As she moves toward this conclusion, Rosenthal says she must "balk" at declaring the child dead because it seems like far too much power for her to have. While she is a physician, and therefore someone with great expertise, she does not pretend to have all the moral issues of life and death sorted out, much less the sense that imposing her own set of answers on other people could ever be appropriate. Rosenthal certainly regrets this painful paradox, but finds it an unavoidable side effect of a definition of death that leaves no margin for unintentional murder.

Rhetorical Considerations

1. Rosenthal uses a strongly charged vocabulary. While she begins with the technical term anencephalic, the extent of her brain is only a "tiny stump"—deformed, truncated, and unquestionably too small to be effective. Rosenthal focuses not on the amount of brain present, but the amount missing: "virtually all." And her heart and lungs are "faltering"—valiantly trying to perform the functions of life, but increasingly weakened, fatigued, and miserable.

2. Rosenthal's sequence of contiguous states traces the route of a hypothetical patient from one high-tech hospital to another. As the patient's train-ride passes through five states, he or she could be declared dead or alive depending solely on geographic boundary, rather than on changes in health. The lack of consistency is meant to be jarring, especially if (as Rosenthal later quotes a lawyer) "being buried alive is the ultimate fear." This patient could legally have been buried alive, if two contiguous states' definitions of life and death were used. This hypothetical journey supports the argument for using the whole-brain definition of death, because, although it is intuitively more satisfying than heart-lung definitions, it is also less dependent on the medical technology that happens to be familiar to inexpert lawmakers.

3. At the end of paragraph 3, Rosenthal uses the phrase "we doctors." It's an easy reference to miss because she doesn't speak to us as an arrogant professional, but as a compassionate individual who has coincidentally seen more life-and-death borderline cases than most of us ever will. She is able to relate real cases, rather than abstractions or composite hypotheticals, which helps make her case believable. For example, she was probably in on the decision to pull the plug on the patient described in paragraph 18, who failed her brain-stem test the fourth time.

4. Information on respirators, carbon dioxide, and oxygen at first seem irrelevant, perhaps a red herring. Student paraphrases may vary, of course; here's one possibility: "Doctors prevent damage to the patient by making sure that he or she has received extra oxygen before turning off the respi-

rator." In contrast to this bland phrasing, Rosenthal's two paragraphs seem gruesomely vivid. The patient's life is entrusted to the physicians running these machines; far be it from them to make a hasty decision to declare the patient dead. We can at least be assured that we have pursued the patient to the very end of his or her life and beyond before we've given up.

5. In the first instance, mention of donating Theresa's organs seems a little strange. While the first paragraph stresses that her organs might help other infants—and thus prevent the horrible suffering Theresa herself is experiencing—the second paragraph vaguely hints at another possibility. With all the experts jumping on the bandwagon to argue that this baby is legally dead, it's conceivable that there could be a well-motivated doctor who has just such a donor recipient in mind, and who therefore has hastily jumped the gun. The effect is perhaps to shift our sympathy ever so slightly toward declaring Theresa is "alive."

In the second instance, the reference seems almost incidental, but raises the same fear a little more pointedly. One condition of organ transplantation is that "hearts, livers, and lungs . . . must be removed from bodies with blood and oxygen still coursing through their veins." Have we changed our definition of "death" simply to accommodate transplant technology? Are we bumping off patients prematurely to alleviate the shortage of donor organs?

The third set of references offers more reassurance. Speaking of both a large number of cases and of baby Theresa, Rosenthal assures us that the new definition of death has "limited the supply of donor organs." She admits that there is some dissent from this limiting definition, but indicates that their views are a numerical minority that does not govern the structure of present-day laws. Collectively, these mentions of organ donation serve to reinforce the stringently conservative definition of death that Rosenthal has advanced.

Abortion
Some Thoughts About Abortion
Anna Quindlen

Topical Considerations

1. Students may have come to the article with a black-and-white attitude on abortion. It is possible that Quindlen's thoughtful discussion may have muted some vehemence, lent a sense of balance.

2. In paragraph 7 Quindlen writes, "I believe that in a contest between the living and the almost living, the latter must, if necessary, give way to the will of

the former. That is what the fetus is to me, the almost living." Her own pregnancies as well as those of young people she has counseled led her to this conclusion.

3. In paragraph 10, Quindlen questions the moral right to choose abortion when a pregnancy is inconvenient, when one can support a child financially and emotionally. Legally she always wants the right, but she wonders about the morality of her decision.

4. Student responses will vary.

5. Paragraph 8 seems to be the turning point in the essay. Although she stated her position in paragraph 4—"reality is something in the middle. And that is where I find myself now, in the middle, hating the idea of abortions, hating the idea of having them outlawed"—she develops this idea further by questioning the idea of abortion for convenience. Her husband's comment and her description of the potential baby's characteristics (blue eyes, red hair, athletic ability) all reinforce her view that abortion may not always be morally defensible though it should be legally available.

6. These descriptions underscore the potential humanity of the fetus. Coming at the end of the essay, the discussion of the fetus's behavior seems to reflect Quindlen's changing attitude toward abortion.

Rhetorical Considerations

1. The form of this argument is closer to an inductive argument than a deductive one because Quindlen begins the article with examples that lead up to her conclusions.

2. Quindlen starts the article with a vivid description of the incidents that make her pro-choice. Then she startles the reader by abruptly changing her tone in a description of her first look at her newborn son. This ambivalence forecasts her view in the rest of the essay—one that supports the legality of abortion but questions its morality in some cases.

3. No, the essay would lose much of its power if Quindlen simply used factual examples, quoted from other people's experiences, or referred to authorities from both sides of the abortion issue.

4. The author calls the antiabortionists "so-called pro-lifers" because she is against "the people who hand out those execrable little pictures of dismembered fetuses at abortion clinics [and who] seem to forget the extraordinary pain children may endure after they are born when they are unwanted, even hated or simply tolerated." But she also condemns pro-choicers who espouse a monolithic position—i.e., that abortion is right in every case.

5. Quindlen's claim comes at the end of the paragraph 4: "And that is where I find myself now, in the middle, hating the idea of abortion, hating the idea of having them outlawed." Refinement of this claim occurs when Quindlen questions an abortion simply for convenience.

6. For the student.

Which Way Black America? Pro-Choice
Faye Wattleton

Topical Considerations
1. Wattleton links the two to foreground the importance of women's reproductive health care.
2. The information Wattleton provides in paragraph 4 shows the difficulty that poor black women have in accessing health care in this country.
3. The "tragedy" is how our failure to provide children with "the ways and means of preventing pregnancy" (paragraph 5) has led to a pregnancy rate for black women that is twice that for white women. Wattleton's word choice may lead to a discussion of persuasive language.
4. Student answers will vary.
5. Wattleton links poor women and black women. Poor women, she suggests, have less access to "contraceptive and abortion services."
6. Student answers will vary.

Rhetorical Considerations
1. Point students to the importance of choosing persuasive language. "Pro-choice" is a much more "attractive" word than "anti-life" or "pro-abortion."
2. To Wattleton, abortion is a "personal" right, and the erosion of this right undermines others rights.
3. Wattleton sees a link between race and class, perhaps, even gender.
4. This is Wattleton's way of including her readers. Students' reactions to this strategy will vary. Lead students to link this strategy with the inclusion of personal experience in Carr's opposing essay, which is next.

Which Way Black America? Anti-Abortion
Pamela Carr

Topical Considerations
1. Students may have common assumptions that women who have abortions are certain "types" of women. Carr's comment shows abortion as a global issue—affecting many different "types" of women. Depending on students' own cultural assumptions, many will be sympathetic to Carr's experience; others may not be swayed by her personal appeal. It might be a good idea to have students write about the abortion issue before reading either piece.
2. Carr addresses the black community in her initial paragraph. Wattleton begins her essay on the topic of abortion, but it is not until paragraph 4 that she specifically names the black community. She may do this to start with a larger audience.
3. Both statements point to assumptions in each author's argument. Wattleton claims that lack of access to information and services raises abortion numbers in the black community. By claiming that abortion is not linked to lack

of sex education, Carr, on the other hand, makes her personal experience a universal "truth."

4. Carr implies that abortion, as a method of "genocide," erodes the rights that African-American leaders fought and won for the black community. Students may also call on examples of political or religious leaders.

5. Genocide is the systematic killing of a race, religion, or nation, among others. Carr emphasizes "silent" because the "genocide" occurs on unborn children. Student answers will vary on the effectiveness or accuracy of Carr's analysis, but most will note Carr's attempt to draw a parallel to the genocide of World War II. Encourage students to think of other examples.

6. According to Carr, "the lie" is "that we can improve the quality of our lives by terminating the lives of our children" (paragraph 17). In other words, the African American community wrongly believes that abortion is a solution to the problems of poverty, drugs, and pregnancy. Try to get students to see the logic or lack of logic in Carr's equation.

7. Answers to this question will vary, but encourage students to go back to the text. Carr does say that abortion is "deeply wrong and unjust" (paragraph 20), but she never says anything about outlawing abortions or prohibiting women from having them. In fact, her opinion hardly reaches beyond the black community, though it is a global issue.

8. Students' responses will vary, but encourage them to speak from their own subject position. Although Carr focuses only on race, issues of gender, class, religion, age, and ethnicity are also crucial to any analysis of this issue.

Rhetorical Considerations

1. Carr's introduction draws readers into her personal experience. Discuss the importance of audience and the benefits or drawbacks of anecdotal writing. Carr makes her audience part of her essay. Wattleton, on the other hand, begins her essay more objectively. Ask students to employ each method in a writing exercise.

2. The subtleties of *pro* and *con* here are useful in discussing persuasive language. Carr uses quotation marks around such phrases as "procedure" (paragraph 12), "blob of tissue" (paragraph 11), and "the products of conception" (paragraph 11) to foreground the statement, "I had killed my baby." Encourage students to discuss the way euphemisms work in our language.

3. Carr's invocation of these leaders acts as an endorsement. See if students can make connections between these leaders and the abortion issue. Students will likely raise the issue of advertising and the use of names and faces to sell a product.

4. Carr makes the assumption that abortion is an "injustice" that threatens to erode the strides made by the African American community.

5. Most students will probably point to Carr's use of personal example and emotional appeal.

An Abortionist's Credo
Elizabeth Karlin

Topical Considerations

1. In paragraph 2, Karlin lists reasons that make raising a child impossible for some women: "rape, incest, alcohol, youth, poverty or an abusive relationship." Materials in paragraphs 6–8 suggest that many patients either come from religious or family backgrounds that have led them to feel extreme personal guilt for having "let" their lives come to such a state of affairs that they must seek an abortion. Finally, many women have been kept ignorant by their own doctors' inability to offer sound advice about birth control. The portrait of "things" that emerges is a set of social conditions and expectations that assign women all of the responsibility for family planning, but little of the authority to make choices or use resources to make morally sound choices.

2. "The punishers" is Karlin's own phrase for individuals and groups involved in public demonstrations against abortion. Although the term might be appropriate for individuals who oppose abortion in forums within their own families or churches, Karlin applies it here only to the boisterous, annoying, or lethal contingents that make front-page news. They punish both abortion-seekers and abortion-providers. They frighten abortion-seeking women with the fear of hell in the afterlife, and violence in this life, even resorting to lies that abortion causes sterility and breast cancer. The punishers also attack doctors like Karlin by frightening her (grisly pictures, ambushes, the Jericho march); denouncing her to family and business associates, or harassing them too; vandalizing her office; and killing doctors who provide abortions. (Although Karlin apparently hasn't been shot at yet, she fears that her harassers may eventually try to kill her.)

3. When confronted with a steady stream of telephone calls, Karlin's 86-year-old mother stuck her tongue firmly in cheek and expressed gratitude for the opportunity to chat. The calls stopped. Most traditional-age college students are still trying to peel themselves out from under parental scrutiny and would be appalled if someone were to report their behavior—even the legal parts. Student examples of what they might not want their parents to hear will vary, although to fit this analogy, the behavior would have to be something legal. (President of the gay and lesbian student union? Blotto drinking spree on 21st birthday? Protesting—or joining—ROTC classes on campus?)

4. Karlin isn't surprised that Clinton would speak out of both sides of his mouth, or that Foster would try to minimize and rationalize abortions he had performed. After all, abortion protesters' strategies have made "these people . . . very frightening." But Karlin seems to scoff at the same time at the spineless political waffling when she corrects Foster in the first sentence of the next paragraph: "His reasons are between him and his patients." Karlin would never equivocate. In the first sentence of her article, she explicitly refuses to equivocate or apologize that "it's a filthy job and somebody has to

do it." She emphasizes pride and integrity in her work, and refuses to make ambivalent, cowardly disclaimers.

5. Karlin's analogy is that allowing a religious minority to prohibit abortion access for a general population of women is like consulting Christian Scientists about treatment of coronary disease. Religious "punishers" hold views that prohibit abortion; Christian Scientists hold views that prohibit many forms of human medical intervention, including both balloon angioplasty and drugs. If consulted, then, people in these groups would not approve the treatment, because they neither "believe in nor understand the medicine involved." Karlin tends to violate the grounds on which she bases the rest of her article here by presenting abortion primarily as a medical procedure.

6. Karlin believes that the only reason women seek abortions is to enable themselves to be better mothers—to bear and raise a child only when they know they can offer material and emotional resources sufficient for a healthy, joyful life. Karlin begins citing different kinds of bravery in paragraph 6; women must be brave to change their minds on such a hot-potato issue. In paragraph 7, she describes the sources of internal and external shame many of her patients are struggling to overcome: church teachings; family pressure; and unrealistic, gender-specific standards of chaste behavior. In paragraph 8, she lists the personal consequences these women fear, including eschatological damnation and medical complications.

Rhetorical Considerations

1. Throughout most of the article, Karlin sees the physical procedure of abortion as only part of the work she does. Instead she focuses on the positive changes through education she hopes to create in her clients' lives. She counsels women on the psychological consequences of choosing abortion; on using birth control to avoid repeat abortions; and (suggested by the wording in paragraph 12) on ways to create healthier, happier patterns of choices in their lives, including but not limited to reproductive choices. This perspective helps her argument by demonstrating that she has her patients' best interests very much at heart.

2. Karlin says relatively little directly about her own moral beliefs. She does provide abortions on request, provided the patient will take responsibility for her own action (rather than making Karlin responsible). She also describes herself as "feisty" and "increasingly radical" in her refusal to cede to the sometimes lethal threats of anti-abortion protesters. Hence she believes in access to abortion strongly enough to risk her own life. Finally, she tells us she is "an honors medical graduate, a respected doctor in the community," rather than a stereotypical back-alley butcher; she feels she has earned both institutional and social approbation. But she doesn't tell us much about her own moral beliefs. Whether Karlin has had, or would consider having, an abortion herself remains unclear, as does the exact moral reasoning of her choice to provide abortion. However, this lack paradoxically strengthens her argument. In her refusal to allow punishers, government agencies, or even family members

to have a right to prohibit abortion, she defines the choice as belonging solely to the provider and the seeker of abortion.

3. That Karlin has adult children supports her argument in at least two ways. First, if she's old enough to have children the age of medical school students, she is a mature woman—not a young intern who's never had time to test her professional ethics against extensive practical experience and reflection. Second, she's also an experienced mother who has nurtured her children. In this latter connection, she helps support her case that the only reason for abortion is "the desire to be a good mother." Whether this is a jarring note is for students to decide. It's a rather sketchy *ad hominum* kind of support; after all, her kids could just as easily be warped products of a "Mommie Dearest" parenting style, rather than having had all the love and attention she implies she's given them. The reference also seems gratuitous due to the brevity of her article, and the lack of much other personal detail.

4. Karlin's term "punishers" stacks the deck heavily in her favor. She doesn't use "pro-life," which emphasizes positive values, or even the negative "anti-abortion." Rather, she focuses on vindictive and violent qualities of a faceless, emotionally inflamed mob marching under the banner of the Old Testament. (This imagery is specifically reinforced by reference to the Jericho march; see the sixth chapter of Joshua for the biblical correlate.) By using this term, Karlin lumps all opponents into a monolithic clump of lunatics—and this collapsing of categories substantially weakens her argument by allowing anyone whose beliefs and actions are not so extreme to say "hey, wait a minute, that's not what I said (or did or meant) at all!"

5. A credo (or creed) is a brief statement of beliefs or principles, usually about a religious faith. It's a serious word, referring to conviction that is firm, about a matter that is bedrock for a group's sense of its own and its individual members' existential purpose. By comparison, titling this article "An Abortionist's Beliefs," while it could be construed as meaning roughly the same thing, could also suggest doubt with the word "beliefs." The word "credo" may imply as much of a leap of faith as "beliefs," but insists that this belief is unassailable. Using the third person helps reinforce the sense already implicit in the word "credo" that she speaks as a member of a group, rather than as a solitary voice.

Animals in Research
Animal Liberation
Peter Singer

Topical Considerations

1. "Speciesism," as defined in Singer's essay, is discrimination on the basis of species, in this context, used as a justification for cruelty to animals in the form of laboratory research and experimentation. Open to discussion.

2. Open for discussion.

3. The example of dissection of the frog in biology class is good because many students most likely felt squeamish or uncomfortable with it, but were compelled to participate as a class requirement. The term *indoctrinate* means simply "to instruct in a doctrine or ideology"; however, the term carries negative overtones of brainwashing. Students may feel that the pressures of a classroom setting combined with the authority figure of the professor or lab reseacher do indeed contribute to a negative sense of "indoctrination" or at least forced participation.

4. Open for discussion.

5. The laws as presented by Singer do not cover anything occurring in the laboratory, but simply transportation to and from laboratories. As such, the laws do appear to be less than adequate. Open for discussion.

6. Most students will find this statement quite controversial. However, Singer's logic is difficult to refute. Open for discussion.

7. There is a problem with this comparison in that a scientific distinction may be made between humans and animals, whereas discrimination based on race involves humans among whom no real scientific distribution may be made outside of those involving physical attributes.

8. Open for discussion. Some students may not be aware of the existence of such products.

9. Open for discussion.

10. Singer does not take a position on these related issues, but the implications of his argument would certainly change if it were discovered that he has no problem with eating meat or wearing fur or leather.

Rhetorical Considerations

1. Singer argues very effectively in this essay. He makes extensive use of documented case studies, statistics, and quotations.

2. Using specific accounts of experiments, taken directly from the journals that publish them, evokes a much more empathic response from the reader than simply stating that such cruel experiments exist. This strategy also makes the opposition look hard and insensitive in that it apparently studies such documentation routinely without finding anything offensive.

3. See paragraphs 22, 3, 8, and 20–22. Particularly in paragraph 8 and paragraphs 20–22, Singer brilliantly appropriates "unofficial" or "offhand" comments made by the opposition in order to implicate itself. The reader cannot help but notice opposition condemning its own practices.

4. Singer uses a deductive logic to prove his point in these paragraphs, beginning with the general statement, "If the experimenter would not be prepared to use a human infant then his readiness to use nonhuman animals reveals an unjustifiable form of discrimination on the basis of species. . . ." In the next two paragraphs he gives specific proof for his thesis.

5. Singer produces a catalogue of proposed measures to stop animal testing in the last three paragraphs of his essay. This list may be less than effective in

that the measures he calls for are sometimes quite drastic, and he does not address the consequences of such measures—for example, student demonstrations, public failure to pay taxes, etc.

6. Singer addresses the general public in his essay, providing all necessary definitions, support and information for the understanding of his argument. He does not assume that his reader comes equipped with specific background knowledge of the subject, nor does he assume that the reader is on his side; instead, he uses his evidence in a strong attempt to sway the reader's opinion in his favor.

I Am the Enemy
Ron Karpati

Topical Considerations

1. Open for discussion.
2. Students may feel that this is an effective method of campaigning, or they may find it manipulative. Proponents of other issues who use this graphic poster method (abortion or pornography, for example) might be brought up in discussion to get a sense of student opinions—that is, whether in certain instances the technique is useful or even necessary, while harmful or counter productive in others.
3. Open to discussion. Many students may feel that this is a flimsy argument, a cliché used as evidence or proof, and, as such, is invalid.
4. This statement implies that we as a society have begun to take medical "miracles" for granted, and that we push the idea of suffering and death farther away each day, relying on doctors and technology to cure our ills. Consequences may be that people are less prepared to deal with the trauma of sickness and death when it happens. On the other hand, modern medicine has made it possible to prolong life in so many instances. It would be difficult to argue that this sort of progress should be stopped or modified. A discussion of medical ethics might be appropriate here.
5. Students might discuss the idea of speciesism as a springboard to this discussion.
6. The term "animal fraud" is unexplained and ambiguous in the text. It most likely means that animal rights activists frame their arguments with the idea that animals and the rights of animals are being misrepresented by those responsible for them—lab technicians, researchers, professors, and doctors. Open for discussion.

Rhetorical Considerations

1. By referring to himself as the "enemy," Karpati immediately takes the opportunity to establish himself as the exact opposite: a benevolent man who became a pediatrician because of his love for children and his desire to keep them healthy. The strategy of referring to himself from the opposition's viewpoint allows him to address that viewpoint and refute it in a manner that would not be possible otherwise.

2. Karpati's essay is very lean on real proof and full of personal experiences and opinions. Paragraph 4 is exemplary of that problem—he offers three choices for research physicians but does not explain any of them in any depth, nor does he explain why each one is useful or not. One of the choices, to experiment on human beings, contains a disclaimer ("some experiments will succeed, most will fail") without ever explaining that disclaimer or giving proof for the statement. The essay would be strengthened by inclusion of facts, statistics, or other evidence.

3. Because Karpati's method of proof in the essay rests so heavily on personal experience and opinion, it is logical that he would write in the first person. Students may find that this choice allows for easy identification with Karpati and thus that his position is strengthened.

4. While this article is largely a statement of position—Karpati is defending his stance on the animal rights issue—the last paragraph does make a proposal for a solution to the problem: that the "apathetic majority . . . be aroused to protect its future against a vocal, but misdirected, minority."

5. Karpati's use of the term "apathetic public" obviously includes the reader (paragraph 2), and his suggestion in paragraphs 7 and 8 that society has become "unappreciative of the health we enjoy" and "isolated" from the real fact of death also points to the reader, who is necessarily a part of that society. In his final paragraph he returns to the idea of that "apathetic majority" that does not respond to the need for animals in research. Students may view this as a call to action, or at least a call to re-examine their views on the subject; or they may feel defensive and see the strategy as negatively altering reader response.

6. The essay needs more research, statistics, and overall proof of generalized statements. See paragraphs 2, 4, 5, 8 and 9.

Why Worry About the Animals?
Jean Bethke Elshtain

Topical Considerations

1. Open for discussion. Advocacy of violence might seem incongruous or hypocritical for those fighting violence against animals.

2. Open for discussion. Many people believe, as does Elshtain, that humans, being capable of reasoning and logic, have a responsibility to treat animals with respect and care.

3. In paragraph 8 Elshtain describes the link between women's suffrage and animal rights in the nineteenth and early twentieth century. In paragraph 11 she says that in the Western rationalist tradition "women were often located on a scale somewhere between 'man' and 'beast,' being deemed human but not quite rational," thereby connecting women and animals in the need for liberation. In paragraph 36 the author makes a case that men who abuse women are often likely to abuse animals. In all of these examples, the point is that women have historically been the objects of abuse and violence, as

have animals, thus forming a natural relationship between the two "liberation" movements, feminism and animal rights.

4. Open for discussion.

5. Many students will feel that the use of animals for medical research is valid because of the benefits of that research for humans, while the same reasoning cannot be applied to war research. This may come down to a question of whether or not the end justifies the means.

6. Elshtain makes the argument that some harmful tests of cosmetics or household products are not required by law, but rather, "they continue in use because manufacturers want to avoid alarming consumers by placing warning labels on products." In this case, it seems that corporations are being downright negligent, seeking profit rather than available alternatives such as computer simulations. Such motives might not, to some students, justify the painful nature of the tests.

7. Open for discussion. This "thirst for violence" might be fed by television and film, the media, domestic violence, and even violence in the lyrics of rock and rap songs. See the opposition essays (Michael Kinsley vs. Barbara Ehrenreich) on Ice-T at the end of readings Chapter 12.

Rhetorical Considerations

1. Elshtain takes an almost journalistic approach to her introduction, stating that "these things are happening or have happened recently . . ." and then listing, quite graphically and bluntly, examples of seven painful animal experiments. For some students, this tactic may seem manipulative, or may actually turn off the reader. Others, however, may feel that such "shock value" is needed to make readers aware of the problem.

2. Elshtain beings with a broad overview of the history of various animal rights movements as well as the ways in which animals are oppressed or violated. She then moves to a statement of her own position, finishing up with a series of possible solutions. While this strategy provides a great deal of information, the reader might feel overwhelmed by the sheer amount, which might actually cause lessened comprehension.

3. The essay might be restructured by narrowing the topic to one or two aspects of the animal rights debate. Or, it might be more effective were it either an informative history, or a statement of position, or a statement of proposal, rather than all three at once. In any case, reader comprehension might be aided by a clearer, narrower focus.

4. At the end of paragraph 37, Elshtain moves from providing information to offering her statements of position and proposal, with no transition. She simply says "Reasonable people should be able to agree on . . ." and then goes on to list her position and proposals. Again at the end of paragraph 47, she jumps into a section on meat-eating which may seem "stuck on," like an afterthought. Students might try coming up with stronger transitions to ease the flow between sections.

5. Elshtain's article ends rather abruptly, with an isolated anecdote and her reactions to it. A more effective conclusion might provide some reference to the issues raised throughout the piece.
6. This appeal implies that those who do not agree with Elshtain's proposals are not reasonable. This may work as a sort of "guilt" tactic, or it may serve to alienate readers who view themselves as reasonable yet who oppose Elshtain's views.

Oppositions: Legalization of Drugs
The American Nightmare
William J. Bennett

Topical Considerations
1. Public opinion seemed to be in favor of legalizing drugs at the time Bennett appeared on Larry King's television news talk show, but this was illusory. In fact, 88 percent of Americans polled (by whom? Bennett doesn't say) rejected the idea. Yet a number of well-known public intellectuals, from conservative (if not staid) institutions, endorsed legalization. Further, while calls for legalization have most often come from liberals and lefties, now conservative right-wingers were on record favoring legalization as well.
2. The initial "beheading" comment was a half-jest with one caller whom King thought was an extremist. Bennett seems to have endorsed this solution to rattle King and his listeners out of complacency as much as anything else. However, Bennett qualifies his response immediately. Drug abuse is a horrible enough crime that he personally has no moral qualms about literally beheading dealers who sell to children. But he's also aware that this punishment will not meet either constitutional or public-opinion endorsement; it would probably be defeated as cruel and unusual. Nevertheless, he stands by beheading as a metaphor, stating that the punishment must fit the crime.
3. Washington newspapers, political cartoonists, and liberal politicians misrepresented Bennett's original statement, at least in the screeching headlines. However, Bennett claims that public sentiment was squarely behind him, quoting as evidence Lee Atwater, acting as a sort of spy behind media-drawn lines (the beltway surrounding Washington, D.C.) Bennett confirms this opinion with a composite of responses drawn from audience feedback at speeches he has given.
4. Bennett discusses marijuana directly only in paragraphs 16 and 17, although it's included by implication in the category "drugs" thereafter. Gorman would be appalled at Bennett's images, probably calling them cheap *ad hominum* pot-shots. Bennett does indeed make an unfounded leap, based

on one incident, when he concludes that "marijuana makes people inattentive and stupid."

5. (1) Drug use would soar. As evidence, Bennett mentions the crack epidemic. Crack was never legal, of course, but it was extremely cheap and available. (2) Crime and catastrophe would soar. People with drug-impaired judgment would have accidents involving themselves and others at work and at home. (3) Child abuse would soar. Children would be born ill from the effects of their mothers' drug consumption; they would be abused and possibly killed by drug-impaired parents; and they would have access to drugs despite any nominal restrictions on purchase age.

6. In paragraph 19, Bennett states that drug legalization is immoral because it sends the wrong message to the polity: that drug usage is acceptable. In paragraph 28, he points out that legalization would be especially confusing to children, who would continue to receive anti-drug training in schools. Bennett would argue that even if virtually everyone used drugs, we must keep laws against drug use on the books. (He also wants enforcement of these laws, but that's a separate issue.) Laws are not only rules that restrict or compel certain behavior, but are symbolic codifications of a society's value system.

7. As Bennett is at some pains to observe in paragraph 23, drug users inevitably harm others by subjecting them to accidents, productivity losses, clogged hospital services, and social or physical co-addiction. In his conclusion, paragraphs 34 to the end, Bennett casts the debate in even stronger terms. Drugs undermine the kind of personal judgment and responsibility necessary to sustain a democracy

Rhetorical Considerations

1. The media is demonized at several points in the first 14 paragraphs. In paragraph 1, Bennett contrasts the impression a foreigner would pick up about public sentiment ("evenly divided") and actual public opinion (an "overwhelming majority" reject legalization). In relating the Larry King anecdote, Bennett provides extensive discussion of media misrepresentation and lampooning of his comments in paragraph 13. Finally, in relating his own and Lee Atwater's more impressionistic evidence of public opinion, he implies without directly stating that the media is deliberately obscuring true public opinion.

2. Student responses may vary. Some students may have used this strategy in their own papers, with resulting teacher comments about "anecdote too long"—these students may slam Bennett's material as too rambling, or irrelevant. Yet Bennett's work originally appeared in a book, allowing him to develop ideas at length; and this anecdote helps suggest what an explosive issue drugs are at present.

3. Bennett uses humor to show the "dangers" of marijuana, which here seem to hinge mostly on the danger of looking foolish (the misprinted flyer date) or anachronistic ("bedraggled sixties types"). He probably isn't convincing

to anybody who has strong feelings about marijuana legalization one way or
the other. However, he does accomplish one rhetorical goal; the inclusion of
marijuana on the list of drugs that must be kept illegal. Humor allows him
to sidestep questions such as marijuana's leading to harder drugs, or the conflicting scientific discussion about whether it actually causes physical change
and harm to the body.

4. Some parts of this analogy are flawed. As Bennett observes, crack became
"cheap and widely available" in the mid 1980s. It does not follow, however,
that legalized drugs would be either cheap or widely available. Further, crack
is highly addictive. It does not follow that the drugs that are legalized would
be as highly addictive or physically addictive at all. The analogy does not
work perfectly; only those who accept Bennett's blanket categorization of all
drugs being cheap, addictive, and available will be able to agree with his
predictions.

5. The kind of progress Bennett seems to promise in paragraph 29 is statistical—that drug use is falling. But in fact, the only progress he relates in the
material that follows is rhetorical. That is, more people are speaking out
against drugs, their bad effects, and their legalization. But even if rhetorical
progress satisfies readers, there's something fishy about the rhetorical
progress Bennett cites— most of it is his own. Of four quoted passages in
paragraphs 30–33, two are lengthy extracts from Bennett's own speeches.

6. Student discussion may vary. Bennett makes several bandwagon appeals.
The first seems to be to readers who consider themselves good, decent people. Drug use is too dangerous for personal consideration because it can
erode moral sense, overpowering even one's sense of obligation to "God,
family, children, friends, and jobs." In a social structure based on an inter-
locking set of obligations, drug use can destroy the very fabric of society,
making self-government impossible. Hence the second bandwagon appeal is
to patriotism, possibly harking back to the McCarthyist threat of a hostile
takeover by outside forces while all the drug-impaired liberals are asleep at
their switches.

It's Time to Legalize
Peter Gorman

Topical Considerations

1. In 1894, a commission set up by British colonial officials, then ruling India,
decided not to prohibit the use of marijuana, although it did recommend
taxation and regulation. The commission based these recommendations on
observations that showed no ill effects to the individual or society, except in
rare cases. (Note: If your students are not familiar with world history, they
may be unable to recognize the implications about colonial rulership provided by the year and the commission's title.)

2. The United States should follow recommendations of the British commission: legalize, tax, and regulate, and otherwise butt out. Gorman believes

that the U.S. hesitation to legalize marijuana is simply treading over the same ground as the British decision to legalize it in India. In the process, the U.S. government is trampling citizens' rights, wasting tax money, and denying itself substantial industrial and medical benefits.

3. In paragraph 5, Gorman cites a U.S. Department of Health and Human Services poll showing that 9 million people (roughly 4 percent of the population) had smoked marijuana in the past month. A poll conducted by *PARADE* (a magazine insert in many Sunday newspapers) showed that 90 percent of respondents approve of medical uses for marijuana, and 75 percent approve of its recreational use. In paragraph 14, he cites (and debunks) National Institute of Drug Abuse claims that marijuana does not lead to harder drugs; and the National Institute of Health statistics showing that today's marijuana is no stronger than it was in 1980. He also cites an item in a small California newspaper in paragraph 10 about damage caused by smoking marijuana, but does so only to debunk it.

4. Gorman relies on his own expertise, or claims "expert" status on the subject, in a number of places. Following are some references—your students may find others. Paragraph 4: numbers of Americans arrested. Paragraph 8–9: industrial and medical uses for hemp, as well as its industrial use in other countries. Paragraph 10: the lack of medical complications caused by smoking marijuana. Paragraph 16: the benefits that would ensue from legalizing marijuana.

5. Gorman uses the term "alcohol prohibition" only once, toward the end of paragraph 15. He says that the results of legalizing marijuana would probably be similar to the results of legalizing alcohol—more people would use it for a short period of time, but that spike in usage would drop as the novelty of open marijuana use wore off. Gorman also uses the term prohibition as a generic noun in paragraphs 3, 10, and 14.

6. Gorman hints at conspiracy and scandal, and most likely profitable kickbacks. First, he names Partnership for a Drug Free America as "the single loudest voice against legalization." That sounds suspicious, as if other sensible people believe it's a non-issue. He states that PDFA is financed by drug companies, expanded to "cigarette, alcohol and pharmaceutical companies" in paragraph 10; and that it has run inaccurate public service advertisements. PDFA is painted as so desperate to promote its aims that it will lie. Its efforts are not in the public interest at all, but serve to protect pharmaceutical companies from competition by a cheap, easily grown, more effective substance, and to protect alcohol and tobacco industries from competition by a safer recreational drug.

Rhetorical Considerations

1. Student responses may vary. However, if nothing else, they should question the wisdom of applying science that is over 100 years out of date. Psychopharmacology is in its stone age now. It didn't exist in 1894. The United States of today is also far different from the India of 1894. British govern-

ment officials in India considered their subjects an inferior race and did not always act in the Indians' best interests. Further, our high-tech toys (forklifts, insecticides, even automobiles) can kill if mishandled by someone under the influence—even the influence of too many chips or cookies. The British commission didn't have to consider potheads around such a lethal arsenal.

2. If students have responded thoughtfully to questions 3 and 4 in the section above, they will begin to notice a pattern. Gorman refers to national scientific organizations, gaining plausibility for his argument by name-dropping. But he does not use any of these big-name agencies to refute claims that marijuana is medically harmless—rather, he does this on his own authority.

3. Gorman spends little time discussing marijuana's potential industrial or medical benefits because these are not primarily the reasons it is illegal. Aside from the possibility of monopolistic conspiracy, nobody would want to forego the environmental and medical benefits Gorman describes in paragraphs 8 and 9. The question is whether we can have these benefits at the same time we avoid the purported harm of marijuana as a recreational drug. Thus Gorman must focus here, an effective strategy because this is where most of his arguments come from.

4. An argument for one kind of use is not necessarily an argument for the others. However, Gorman does not at any point suggest divorcing this menage-a-trois of uses to see whether one may stand without the other two. This strategy may work to his detriment, if readers believe that the industrial and medical uses he cites are mere enticements, or red herrings, to get them to stop thinking about how much pleasure Gorman takes in savoring recreational marijuana use, and how near and dear this argument is to his heart.

5. Gorman uses humor to defuse the silly things the newspaper in California printed. First, he mentions an obscure paper, without mentioning that it probably picked up a wire service story, rather than sending its own reporters into the field. Next, he uses slapstick: "waiting for the millions of breasted men and bearded women to appear." Finally, he contrasts the effects most marijuana smokers have probably experienced (short-term anxiety, or none of the above) to uglier medical problems such as cancer, emphysema, clogged arteries, obesity, and heart failure. These are the really serious diseases—anything pot produces is lighthearted by comparison.

6. Prohibition was widely regarded as a farce while it was in effect, from 1920 to 1933. Most people could find alcohol easily; whether or not Prohibition fueled organized crime (Bennett, in the companion article in this section of the textbook, believes it did not), it did promote scofflaw behavior. Students who aren't familiar with the details may recognize names like Al Capone, and the Chicago gangster mystique embedded in popular culture icons like the film *Dick Tracy.* Gorman uses the connotations to present marijuana prohibition as a foolish effort to impose meaningless restrictions, which create more harm than good; we'll all breathe a sigh of relief when it's over.

13

Freedom of Expression

Movie and Television Violence
Honey, I Warped the Kids
Carl M. Cannon

Topical Considerations

1. Cannon cites an impressive array of studies that seem irrefutably to prove an association between media violence and aggressive behavior. Perhaps most convincing is Professor Aletha C. Huston's claim before a congressional committee in 1988 that "'Virtually all independent scholars agree that there is evidence that television can cause aggressive behavior'" (paragraph 22). Also impressive is Cannon's claim that out of three thousand studies "the only one that failed to find a causal relationship between television violence and actual violence was paid for by NBC" (paragraph 23). The listing of "highlights from the history of TV violence research" (paragraphs 25–36) suggests a wealth of scientific research supporting the link.

2. The scenes from the movie *Grand Canyon* dramatize two separate points central to Cannon's essay: that any sane person knows the entertainment industry "glorifies violence and bloodshed and brutality" (paragraph 5); and that, motivated primarily by greed, industry executives defend themselves against this charge with predictably specious arguments. Not only does the scene graphically convey these ideas; rhetorically, inserting a piece of vivid narrative action—complete with readily visualized movie stars—increases the liveliness of this crucial opening section of his argument. On the other hand, students might protest that this film, with its ironic look at the entertainment industry, suggests that Hollywood is capable of thoughtful self-analysis, even self-critique—a possibility that Cannon's argument does not allow.

3. According to Cannon, programming has in fact changed very little: "a study of television programming from 1967 to 1989 showed only small ups and downs in violence, with the violent acts moving from one time slot to another but the overall violence rate remaining pretty steady—and pretty similar from network to network" (paragraph 48). The arguments of network executives in their own defense have changed, however. In the 1950s, the television industry defended television violence by arguing that "[w]atching violence is cathartic. A violent person might be sated by watching a murder" (paragraph 18). However, "[b]y 1989, network executives were arguing that [media] violence was part of a larger context in which bad guys get their just desserts" (paragraph 51). And of course, Cannon also has found a standard

contemporary media response in the words of Steve Allen in *Grand Canyon:* "My movies reflect what's going on; they don't make what's going on" (paragraph 8).

4. Although Cannon effectively proves the link between televised and real violence, students may find his solution both obliquely stated and, to the extent it is identifiable, problematic. Cannon never directly suggests what action he endorses. Clearly, he is pessimistic about Hollywood's ability to police itself voluntarily, a sense conveyed not only by his article-long derision of the entertainment industry, but also by his account of Senator Paul Simon's ultimately ineffectual attempts to work with the industry on this issue (paragraphs 60–66). Cannon quickly undercuts Simon's optimistic prediction that the industry's stated willingness to address media violence is "more than a bunch of talk" (paragraph 69) when, at the end of his article, he says with apparent doubt, "Maybe Simon is right. Maybe Hollywood executives will get together and make a difference" (paragraph 72). And by returning to the earlier-cited *Grand Canyon* scene to end the essay, he clearly expresses skepticism about the degree of industry commitment to this project. At the same time, although he does not directly endorse regulation of broadcast media by congressional legislation, Cannon hints at the appeal of this route by reminding readers that "[t]he federal government, of course, possesses the power to regulate the airwaves through the FCC" (paragraph 30).

5. Instead of addressing the problem head on, Cannon uses the comments of Dr. Frank M. Palumbo (in paragraph 56) and PTA spokesman Arnold Fege (paragraph 57) to address the fear of censorship. This strategy is significant in and of itself: using the words of Palumbo and Fege at this crucial moment suggests Cannon wants to tread lightly on the issue. He lets these two argue for him that censorship, in the form of congressional regulation of the airwaves, is justified by the nature and extent of the problem.

Significantly, both Palumbo and Fege argue against censorship by making analogies that are emotionally powerful, though logically somewhat dubious. Palumbo compares television violence to a "toxic substance in the environment" (paragraph 56). This analogy begs the question of how television violence should be best regulated: if these media messages are like toxic fumes, then they must indisputably be controlled at the point of emission—to follow the logic of the metaphor, by regulating television. Similarly, Fege's comparison of television to teachers similarly assumes that government's point of intervention should be the creation and initial transmission of the "message." But the analogy is dubious, since television is arguably part of a free market system, and in this way is not comparable to a government employee hired to shape young minds.

Rhetorical Issues

1. Students can discuss the relative value of the scientific studies, which mostly appeal to reason, and the more emotional appeal of the anecdotes, which describe individual tragedies allegedly linked to media violence. They

should be encouraged to notice a somewhat startling problem with Cannon's anecdotal evidence: though his major argument is about televised violence, almost all the anecdotal evidence concerns movies: *Friday the 13th, The Deer Hunter, The Believers, Nightmare on Elm Street,* and *Rambo.* Since film and television raise somewhat different issues in terms of regulation, Cannon's failure to draw distinctions between the two could be seen as a weakness in his argument.

2. Cannon compares Hollywood liberals to the National Rifle Association in an attempt to discredit the former's laissez-faire attitude toward violence in the media. With this analogy, as with the opening description of the political activities of certain Hollywood stars, Cannon suggests the hypocrisy of the entertainment industry, which is willing to speak to "noble causes far removed from their lives" (paragraph 2) but abandons progressive political positions when their own economic (or artistic) welfare is at stake. Students from various sides of the political spectrum can dispute whether the comparison is apt: is the question of the relationship between fiction and reality the same as the question of the relationship between hardware (guns) and reality?

3. For one thing, the proliferation of short paragraphs keeps the pace of reading fast and furious. By firing out short blasts of information and commentary, Cannon increases his argument's dramatic effect. The briefness of the paragraphs should also alert students to the fact that, although there is an enormous amount of information in this essay, there is very little thoughtfulness or philosophical complexity. Cannon does not think through any deeper issues related to the issue of media violence, such as the true relationship between life and art or the implications of controlling the media in a free society. Instead, he is trying to rouse his audience to the same height of moral outrage that he himself has reached, and to incite his readership to quick action.

4. Alert students will have noticed that the article first appeared in *Mother Jones,* a left-wing publication that prides itself on political activism. Such an audience may be expected to despise both the NRA and any infringements on freedom of speech. Cannon's tendency to press only lightly on the problem of censorship may well indicate an awareness of this audience, as does his use of the NRA to taint Hollywood liberals by association.

5. The tone is one of moral outrage. Cannon creates this tone primarily with the derisive language directed against the Hollywood industry who has, by his analysis, refused to act responsibly despite decades of studies linking media to actual violence. In the opening paragraphs, for example, Cannon describes the hypocrisy of Hollywood stars who are "constantly speaking out for noble causes far removed from their lives" while refusing to speak out about "excessive violence in the entertainment industry" (paragraph 2). Students might also note that Cannon creates the tone of moral outrage partially by constructing that Hollywood establishment as the villain in the piece, and by depicting the issue as a black-and-white struggle between

those forces of evil and the forces of good—the "legion of writers, researchers, and parents who have tried to force Hollywood to confront the . . . disturbing truth" (paragraph 10).

6. By returning to Steve Martin's words at this point in his essay, Cannon highlights an aspect of the *Grand Canyon* scene not of primary importance in the initial description: the tendency of Hollywood to quickly forget any high-minded commitments to social improvement. In this sense, the scene comments ironically on the entertainment industry's recent lip service to the idea of reducing television violence. The anecdote is rhetorically effective because it creates a sense of closure by connecting the end to the beginning of the essay. Finally, Cannon's use of the anecdote enacts what he claims: we learn lessons from Hollywood that we apply to our lives. With *Grand Canyon,* the message is instructive; with films like *Friday the 13th* and *Nightmare on Elm Street,* the messages are potentially destructive to our society.

Violence Is Us
Robert Scheer

Topical Considerations

1. Scheer clearly agrees with Cannon that a link exists between media and actual violence; they disagree heartily on what should be done about that fact. Scheer believes that "violence and base stupidity on TV and in the movies is excessive and getting worse" (paragraph 3); he does not dispute "the claims of most experts that viewing violence desensitizes people, particularly children, to the actual effects of violence, leaving them more likely to act out in anti-social ways" (paragraph 5). But in describing the problem Scheer also reveals his liberal bias; he is pro–gun control, sensitive to the role of class in social problems, and, most importantly for his argument, anti-censorship. In paragraph 6, Scheer gets in a dig at "pro-censorship prudes" who won't admit that violence, not sex, is what provokes some male viewers violent sexual behavior. Scheer also points out that poor families, who often use TV "as the only available babysitter" (paragraph 7) are most vulnerable to the effects of televised violence. Finally, Cannon cites "the ease with which children can get guns in this society" as a factor in the connection between televised and real-life violence (paragraph 8). Also important for the argument that follows is Scheer's belief, introduced here, that the problem of media violence stems not only from fiction, but from fact: from the "cleaner assassinations" presented on both network news and "[s]o-called news show featuring real-life crime" (paragraph 4).

2. Scheer uses Wayne LaPierre, NRA spokesman, to highlight a dichotomy between the high moral tone of the some news programs and the gratuitous violence of entertainment programming. Scheer endorses LaPierre's claim that the networks are hypocritical when they lecture the NRA on the nightly news "and then . . . go to their entertainment programming and

show all kinds of gratuitous violence" (paragraph 9). Students may have noticed that Cannon also mentioned the NRA as a way to indicate the hypocrisy of liberal-leaning media executives.

3. Scheer supports this claim by pointing out the great appeal held, not only by fictionalized violence, but by real violence on local and foreign news. As "endless focus groups conducted by news organizations report," news is watched most often "when death and destruction are at hand" (paragraph 10). Quoting Steven Bochco—one of those media executives so vilified by Cannon—Scheer endorses the view that "'there's more violence on the 5 o'clock news than anything you'll see on the networks during prime time'" (paragraph 10).

   With this paragraph, Scheer suggests a more complicated relationship between real and media violence than Cannon. Whereas Cannon believed simply that media violence caused real violence, Scheer here points out that the two are mutually dependent: we are drawn to real life violence, which perhaps spawns the popularity of fictionalized violence, which in turn leads to higher crime rates. Such circularity is indicated graphically in paragraph 8: youngsters watching media violence may be more inclined to "real life" violence, "[a]nd when they do it in real life they can be assured of their fifteen minutes of fame with top billing on the nightly local news" (paragraph 8).

4. Scheer is an active opponent of censorship, an attitude students will have already noticed in his reference to "pro-censorship prudes" (paragraph 6). When he starts to consider how to address the acknowledged problem of excessive media violence, Scheer looks for a solution that will preclude "putting decision-making into the hands of small-minded censors" (paragraph 11). Even the "reasonable" solutions suggested by University of Michigan professor Leonard Eron are too extreme for Scheer's dislike of censorship. Eron suggested that "'Perpetrators of violence should not be rewarded for their violent acts,' and that 'those who act aggressively should be punished'"—two guidelines which Scheer believes will "distort a reality in which many criminals get away with their crimes" (paragraph 11).

   But while Scheer clearly believes film and television producers need the freedom to tell the truth about how "crime is out of control" (paragraph 11), and that adults need the freedom to "watch what they want" (paragraph 12), he does think children's fare needs to be controlled. Even for children, censorship is not Scheer's answer—mainly because it simply doesn't work: "every regulation produces just that much more ingenuity on the part of the so-called creative people who make this junk" (paragraph 13).

   To summarize, Scheer's attitude toward censorship is fourfold: (1) most censors are "small-minded" or "prudes"; (2) adults should not have their access to programs censored in any way; (3) children do need to have their access to violent programming controlled; but (4) censoring children's television simply does not work. Students should note that Scheer's treatment of the issue of censorship, even if they do not agree with it, is much more thoughtful and complex than Cannon's.

5. Scheer finds two things troubling about the *Beavis and Butthead* anecdote: first, why parents in this "conservative white upper-middle-class community" allowed their children to watch this idiotic show; and second—and more importantly—why "the children of paradise" (paragraph 16), recipients of all the privileges American culture has to offer, find so much "delight in this and other stupidities" (paragraph 16). Scheer rejects both the explanation offered by Dan Quayle—"that the cultural elite of Hollywood has seized their minds" (paragraph 16)—and the dismissive claim that "it doesn't mean a thing" (paragraph 17). The question of the show's appeal remains, for Scheer, a troubling symptom of something wrong with American culture.

   Students who may themselves have been fans of the *Beavis and Butthead* show may have a different take on the show's appeal.

   Scheer believes that "[t]he 'we' as represented by the state should do nothing. . . ." Rather, "it is parents' responsibility to monitor what kids watch" (paragraph 20). Instead of asking "Big Brother," the Orwellian symbol of cultural censorship, to begin controlling what is transmitted over the television airwaves, Scheer encourages his readers to exercise constitutional liberties in their own homes. In language evocative of the central mechanism of democracy, Scheer suggests the correct response to an offensive program is to "vote—by just turning the damn thing off" (paragraph 29.

Rhetorical Considerations

1. In the opening paragraph Scheer sneeringly describes those "network executives, sincere visages firmly in place, [who] are promising to clean up their act." The use of the somewhat old-fashioned formal word "visages" signals irony: these are clearly masks put on to suggest an artificial sense of concern. The irony is further suggested by the contrast between this formal language and the informal phrase, "clean up their act." In the next paragraph Scheer brands the words of everyone attacking TV violence as "hand-wringing," expressing in this single word the insincerity and inefficacy of these people. In these first paragraphs, Scheer sets the tone of the essay: informal, ironic, exasperated—some might say superior. Certainly this is the impression created by Scheer's comment that "There is something so beside the point" about the controversy, as if only he can see the true significance of an important contemporary debate.

2. Scheer's organizational strategy could be called conversational. Instead of proposing a thesis at the opening of the essay, Scheer leads his readers into the argument first by attacking those who would call for television censorship. Instead of denying the problem exists, however, Scheer spends several paragraphs creating a common ground with potential opposition, admitting that he believes in the connection between violent media and violence in American society. Only after this section of his argument, in paragraph 10, does Scheer state his thesis, in the process of accounting for the prevalence of violence in both "art" and "life": that perhaps "we like violence"—or, as Scheer's title puts it, "Violence is Us." At this point, between paragraphs 10

and 11, Scheer turns to a second question: not whether media violence has deleterious effects, but what to do about the problem? It is this question that Scheer spends the rest of the essay answering.

3. Scheer refers to *Beavis and Butthead* three different times: in the story of the five-year-old boy who set fire to his family trailer; in the story of the privileged 12-year-old fans in Orange County who responded to visiting fire fighters by "chanting the call of the show's lead, 'Burn, burn, burn'" (paragraph 15); and at the very end of the article, when he describes how the show became a "multi-national operation" (paragraph 26) with "world-wide distribution" (paragraph 27). Each example proves another facet of Scheer's argument. Scheer first uses the show to raise a reasonable question that few people apparently asked in the rush to censor the show: "Why had that mother let her 5-year-old watch endless hours of this repulsive show?" (paragraph 14). The show suggests the importance of parental responsibility in issues of censorship. The anecdote of the Orange County students further illustrates the need for parental responsibility and suggests that indeed "Violence Is Us," since even the "children of paradise" are drawn to this sort of violent trash. The final reference to the show illustrates Norman Lear's claim that "the bottom line" determines what gets put on television, and the bottom line is often best served by mindless shows such as *Beavis and Butthead.* Scheer certainly gets a lot of argumentative use out of this one show; his use of a single example, analyzed in depth, gives the second half of his argument unity. Students could also critique Scheer for relying too heavily on one incident: is this single example truly representative of the problem of media violence and children?

4. Lear is a particularly appropriate spokesman for the position that television violence results from the imperatives of the bottom line. Lear himself creates not violent trash but "thoughtful prime-time programming" such as *All in the Family;* he has credibility as a serious, responsible producer who clearly feels he swims against the tide in his profession. Without endorsing exploitative programming, Lear acknowledges that the prime reason for its existence is advertisers who "know from experience that something hard and outrageous will sell faster than something soft" (paragraph 22). Students might consider whether Lear, who is himself living proof that good television can be made, and made profitably, gives the lie to advertiser's obsession with bad television.

In Praise of Gore
Andrew Klavan

Topical Considerations
1. Breaking the argument into sections may help students grasp the overall shape of this relatively long and complex essay.
   The essay summarizes as follows:
   (a). The author, and his fans, love horror and violence in fiction.

(b). Fictional violence is again under attack, in Britain as well as America.

(c). The Jamie Bulger murder was irresponsibly blamed on "'video nasties'" as a way of making sense of an otherwise incomprehensible tragedy (paragraph 10).

(d). Because language represents not reality, but "unfathomable spirit and . . . infinite mind" (paragraph 14), violence in fiction is socially harmless.

(e). The reason we want so desperately to censor fictionalized violence is because we secretly find it so thrilling.

(f). Violence has a universal appeal, as represented by its centrality to great literature from all ages and most countries of the world.

(g). The contemporary world has many problems, but they cannot be blamed on fiction because "[f]iction and real life must be distinguished from one another" (paragraph 36).

2. Klavan describes the Bulger case as a "textbook example of how easily pundits and politicians can channel honest grief and rage at a true crime into a senseless assault on the innocent tellers of tales" (paragraph 7). As Klavan describes it, the judge in the case irresponsibly, and without any evidence, expressed his suspicion that "exposure to violent video films may in part have been an explanation" of why two 10-year-olds senselessly and brutally murdered a 2-year-old toddler. Fiction—in this case, the horror film *Child's Play 3*—becomes a scapegoat, a way to satisfy the culture's need to find some explanation for what is a horrifically inexplicable crime.

3. This theory provides the philosophical underpinnings for Klavan's political point. Klavan uses the example of Plato to suggest that "[t]he instinct to censor is the tragic flaw of utopian minds" (paragraph 13). He takes on "latter-day Platos" by arguing that language and literature do not represent material reality; instead, writers simply body forth the form of things unknown—specifically, his "unfathomable spirit and . . . infinite mind" (paragraph 14). Klavan believes his role as an artist is to represent precisely those things that are not part of our daily lives. Because, for Klavan, fiction represents "people's souls," he plans to defend violence in literature not with "the specious language of theory or logic or even the law"—the language used by most attacks on censorship, including Scheer's—but "the language of the spirit, of celebration and screed, of jeremiad and hallelujah" (paragraph 15). Klavan concedes that there is some relationship between reality and fiction, but argues that it is "so complex, so resonant, that it is impossible to isolate one from the other, in terms of cause and effect" (paragraph 16).

Students should be encouraged to notice that this is only one possible theory of the relationship between literature and reality. Others, including representational theories of language and literature, would increase the relationship between life and art. At any rate, Klavan at least acknowledges the complexity of the relationship between fiction and reality, as Cannon does not, and effectively proves here that the dispute over censorship has long roots in western civilization.

4. Admitting that "[t]he answer seems to come straight out of Psychology 1A" (paragraph 17) Klavan accepts, somewhat half-heartedly, the theory that censorship repeats the repression routinely practiced by our superegos on the perverse desires of our ids: censorship is "a guilt-ridden slap at ourselves . . . for taking such pleasure in make-believe acts that, in real life, would be reprehensible" (paragraph 17). By relying on a psychoanalytic model, Klavan downplays the social motives of censorship represented by Plato.

5. Klavan admits that it may be true that fictional violence allows a harmless outlet for our violent tendencies. But although he finds the cathartic defense reasonable, he is not really interested in defending violence; he wants instead to celebrate it. The theory of catharsis—"this business of violent fiction as therapy"—implies that "these stories needed a reason for being" (paragraph 25). Because Klavan wants to celebrate fictional violence, he wants instead to talk about its "joy": "the joy of cruelty, the thrill of terror, the adrenaline of the hunter, the heartbeat of the deer" (paragraph 25).

6. Klavan's claims that calls for censorship are misguided because violence in fiction is not only socially harmless, but good for our souls. The first three sections of the essay analyze the current debate, arguing that fiction has become a scapegoat for social problems. Section 4 provides the philosophical underpinning for Klavan's claim that fictional violence is harmless; section 5 attacks the opposition by seeing it as the result of misplaced guilt; section 6 supports the claim that fictional violence is good for us by describing its universal appeal. In the final section, Klavan argues that fictional violence is socially harmless.

7. With this anecdote, Klavan takes on the opposition's claim that media violence causes aggressive behavior. The opposition is represented here by a Scottish filmmaker who relates an experience in a Times Square theater. In response to the film *Cliffhanger,* "[e]very time the bad guys killed someone, the youths cheered—and when a woman was murdered, they howled with delight" (paragraph 30). Klavan claims that "the Scotsman's story illustrates that the problem lies not on the screen but in the seats, in the lives that have produced that audience" (paragraph 32). He also suggests that, disturbing though the audience's response might be, "it was not necessarily harmful in itself " (paragraph 33).

   Students who have read the arguments of Cannon and Scheer should be able to see that the scientific audience gives the lie to Klavan's claim: that in fact, viewing such films can incite people to real-life violence. Also, given Klavan's reasonable prior claim that the relationship between fiction and life is deeply complex, isn't it true that the "lives that have produced" this horrific audience include the constant onslaught of films like *Cliffhanger?* Students may well find themselves siding with the "highly intelligent Scottish filmmaker" who found his experience in the theater "grimly disturbing" (paragraph 30).

8. Whereas Scheer asks his readers to "face" the inherently unpleasant fact that "we like violence," Klavan's strategy is not to defend the appeal of violence in fiction but to celebrate it. Again and again in his essay, Klavan refuses the

temptation to simply defend the right to produce violent fiction. Rather, having argued that there is no clear relationship between violence in life and art, Klavan's essay sets out to "celebrate" gore: "[t]he joy of cruelty, the thrill of terror, the adrenaline of the hunter, the heartbeat of the deer—all reproduced in the safe playground of art" (paragraph 25). Students can discuss which approach they find most palatable.

Rhetorical Considerations

1. Klavan's essay begins with the best defense: a good offense. The first paragraph is designed to shock. Here, Klavan lists the horrific things he loves—"the sound of people screaming. . . . machine gun shots goading a corpse into a posthumous jitterbug; and the coital jerk and plunge of a butcher knife." Only at the start of the second paragraph does Klavan tell us he loves these things "only in stories." The opening of the essay dramatically enacts Klavan's determination not to apologize for fictional violence, but to celebrate it. Students can dispute whether they found this approach refreshing or offensive.

2. On one hand, as a professional writer, Klavan's voice is important in the debate over fictional violence. And partly because he brings a writer's sensibilities, Klavan is able to cogitate about philosophical and aesthetic issues as well as social and legal ones. Students who are more critical of Klavan could argue that, because he makes his living as a writer of horror literature, he is inherently biased since he stands to suffer financially, as well as artistically, from censorship.

3. Klavan makes several gestures to his opposition throughout his essay. He allows, for example, that "[n]ot all of us" may enjoy violent television as much as he and his readers (paragraph 19); he admits he himself might have found it "upsetting and frightening" to be in the Times Square theater with his Scottish friend, listening to the crowd "howl . . . with delight" when a woman was murdered on the screen (paragraph 30). But Klavan does not take into account any of the evidence, cited by both Scheer and Cannon, that watching violence actually causes aggressive behavior. Having read these other two essays, students should be able to recognize this as a major weakness in his argument.

4. In this section, in order to argue that human beings crave violence in literature, Klavan refers to a plethora of characters and works from world literature. By comparing contemporary horror books and films to some of the most enduring works of literature and philosophy in western history, Klavan rhetorically increases the value of the work he is defending; he also ratchets up his own prestige by indicating his own wide-reading and erudition. Klavan claims that "the maker of violent fiction . . . walks among us in Nietzschean glee"; that "[h]e has bottled the Dionysian whirlwind and is selling it as a soft drink"; that horror writers resembles "deep-browed Homer." Such comparisons invest the writers of pulp fiction with a seriousness not often accorded them. Similarly, in paragraph 24 Klavan draws no distinction between "Medea or Jason (from *Friday the 13th*), both of whom have

"the appeal of a Caliban: that thing of darkness that must be acknowledged as our own." Are *Friday the 13th* and *Nightmare on Elm Street* really similar in depth and complexity to *The Tempest* and *Medea?*

Racial Slurs
Regulating Racist Speech on Campus
Charles R. Lawrence III

Topical Considerations

1. Lawrence says that the protection of racist speech from government regulation "reinforces our society's commitment to tolerance as a value, and that . . . we will be forced to combat it as a community." An alternative means of combating racist speech might be public protests and demonstrations.

2. Lawrence says that by so framing the issue, the racial bigot ends up being morally elevating while "the rising flames of racism" are fanned. Lawrence says that racist language is an assault on its victim, not an invitation to dialogue. Also, by allowing unrestricted rights to those who practice hate language, we allow both psychic injury and racial victimization of minority people to continue.

3. Any "system of signs and symbols" that suggests the inferiority of blacks would fall under the legislation of the *Brown v. Board of Education* case, says Lawrence, since that case articulates "the principle of equal citizenship" (paragraph 4).

4. Lawrence argues that racist speech functions as a "preemptive strike" against its victim. "The invective is experienced as a blow" (paragraph 6) that is intended to hurt not to "discover truth or initiate dialogue."

5. Lawrence suggests that civil rights lawyers might sue on behalf of black students "whose rights to an equal education is denied by a university's failure to insure a non-discriminatory education climate or conditions of employment." Such threats would move many academic administrations to take action.

6. Open for discussion.
7. Open for discussion.
8. Open for discussion.

Rhetorical Considerations

1. In paragraph 2 Lawrence's line of argument begins to take focus as he explains his apprehension about the rise in racial incidents and racist speech. The first clue to his opposition is the opening word, "But," which has been clearly prepared for by the whole first paragraph. Probably the clearest thesis statement is the last sentence of paragraph 4.

2. Right off Lawrence establishes himself as one who questions authority and who ardently defends individual rights, including his refusal to participate

in a civil-defense drill in high school. His strategy is to set himself up as seemingly inflexible on such issues to underscore the dangerous consequences of unrestricted racist speech to which, in the next paragraph, he concedes strong opposition.

3. Lawrence's argument is clearly syllogistic: The First Amendment does not protect utterances that "inflict injury or tend to incite an immediate breach of peace"; racist speech injures and incites violence; thus, the First Amendment does not protect racist speech.

4. Open for discussion.

5. For the students.

Free Speech on Campus
Nat Hentoff

Topical Considerations

1. Hentoff is arguing that instituting sanctions on speech poses a serious threat to the very idea of the university and the spirit of academic freedom and free inquiry.

2. According to the author, more colleges are handling the problem by "preventing or punishing speech." Hentoff is strongly opposed to such measures.

3. Hentoff makes a clear distinction between racially motivated physical attack and racist or sexist speech, "however disgusting, inflammatory, and rawly divisive." Lawrence, on the other hand, argues that verbal abuse "functions as a preemptive strike" that is "experienced as a blow" and that causes "psychic injury." By categorizing it as such, Lawrence makes a case that racist speech falls within the "fighting words" exception to First Amendment protection.

4. Open for discussion.

5. Open for discussion.

6. Open for discussion.

7. Hentoff is troubled by a few things: first, the ironic deception of the very title of the Statement; second, he is appalled at the "scant opposition" by faculty and students who would prefer to "go on record as vigorously insensitive to these malignances." Hentoff finds such "politically correct" silence frightening. He also finds frightening the implications of the Statement— that a student who opposes affirmative action could be "branded a racist." Or somebody caught playing a Lenny Bruce album could be "tried for aggravated insensitivity by association."

8. Open for discussion.

9. Open for discussion.

10. Open for discussion.

Rhetorical Considerations

1. The title has two possible meanings: (1) the state of free speech on campus; and (2) the imperative, "You must free speech on campus!" It's a clever and apt choice.

2. Hentoff's argument does not begin to take focus until paragraph 5 where he also gives his thesis statement in the last line. Up to this point, he establishes the background—that is, the recent surge in racist incidents on college campuses.

3. Hentoff wants the reader to believe that the cartoon was not particularly offensive. Some students might not want to pass judgment without having seen the cartoon. Though there is no way to tell from the essay, it is quite possible that Hentoff leaves out details which would weaken his argument.

4. For the student.

5. The Orwell reference is aptly ironic. You might remind students that Orwell was a novelist, essayist, and one of the most important social critics of this century. In 1949 he published the novel *1984,* which painted a nightmare vision of a totalitarian state in which free speech and free thought were capital crimes.

6. The concluding line is ominously appropriate; it brings to a head the fear underlying Hentoff's argument that the trend toward sanctioning free speech may be universal. Whether or not students buy his arguments, they must recognize the implications and impact of the closing question.

In Praise of Censure
Garry Wills

Topical Considerations

1. Wills means that people on both sides of the free speech debate believe that they are doing the "right thing." Those who seek to ban certain products of the media are doing so to protect the moral fiber of the country, while those who seek to uphold the First Amendment at any cost are doing so to protect Constitutional Rights.

2. Wills sees censorship as the outright refusal to make public any offensive media. Censure, on the other hand, has more to do with boycotting a certain product (or entertainer, etc.) to make an active political statement against it, while still allowing others to decide for themselves whether the particular situation is offensive or not. Wills authorizes censure in this essay.

3. Wills believes that "equating morality with legality" would (and does) have a negative impact on society, because it assumes (and perhaps requires) that all people think about and react to certain situations in the same way. This leaves no room for individuality or for personal freedom of expression.

4. The point of freedom of speech, to Wills, is explained in paragraph 10: It's not to make ideas exempt from criticism but to expose them to it. Wills

wants people to actively form their own opinions rather than have opinions thrust blindly upon them.

5. Wills does not agree with her decision. He asserts that she was indeed protecting her institution so that it may benefit from NEA grants in the future. Students' opinions on this matter will vary.

Rhetorical Considerations

1. Giving both sides of an argument can have both positive and negative effects on the reader. If the author seems to be sympathetic to the opposition readers might feel that he or she is confused on the issue and not authoritative enough. On the other hand, presenting both sides makes the author seem well-informed about the topic and, therefore, more credible. Since Wills is calling for censure so that people can make up their own minds, presenting both sides is an excellent rhetorical strategy.

2. Since Wills presents some of the pros and cons of the censorship debate in the first paragraph without stating his opinion directly, the reader is drawn into the argument, if only to find out where the author stands.

3. Wills assumes his audience is fairly well-educated and well-informed on the issue. He feels no need to explain many of his examples. He simply pits Frank Zappa against Tipper Gore, assuming audience familiarity with these opponents. Since he also does not go into depth about how censure can work, Wills assumes his audience will be aware of the matter, perhaps even sympathetic to his cause.

4. Wills' political values are difficult to pin down since he seems to take issue with both sides of each debate. However, he does single out "liberals" as often failing to make strong arguments on their behalf. As such, it might be safe to say that Wills leans more towards the conservative camp. Still, an argument could also be made that he would not want to align himself with either side, being a person distrustful of labels.

5. This essay presents a fairly difficult concept. Thus, the repetition in the conclusion serves to reiterate his point, rather than obscure it. Again, censure asks people to take an active role in the shaping of media and culture. By representing opposing slants, Wills emphasizes the individual's power to control his or her intake of the media.

Oppositions: Pornography
Let's Put Pornography Back in the Closet
Susan Brownmiller

Topical Considerations

1. Students' answers will vary.
2. Yes, Brownmiller's definition (which occurs mainly in paragraph 9) is clear and easily understood. She is careful to define her terms so that what she is

saying has less of a chance of being misconstrued. It's very important when writing, and especially when writing persuasive discourse, to stipulate exactly what you mean by certain "key" terms (especially those that do have multiple shades of meaning). This way, opponents cannot base counterattacks on semantics alone.

3. Students' opinions will vary, though most will probably have a hard time thinking of literature (and especially literature now valorized by the academy) as potentially pornographic.

4. Brownmiller means that people can publish or print whatever kinds of work they want to, but that putting that work on a shelf (in a drug store, in magazine or book store, or in a grocery store, for example) where the general public has ready and easy access to it should be controlled. Students' opinions on this will vary.

5. Since Brownmiller argues with an extremely assured voice, and since she does invoke the Supreme Court so often (in a manner that suggests she agrees with certain decisions), she most likely does trust the court to agree with her stance on this issue.

Rhetorical Considerations

1. This is a very forceful opening statement because it seems absolute and confidently put forth. However, it does not necessarily concur with the rest of Brownmiller's argument, which focuses on the "fact" that free speech can indeed go too far. (She says it does as far as pornography is concerned.)

2. The slant of Brownmiller's argument is apparent in paragraph 3; and her thesis is in that same paragraph—at the end. What is interesting, however, is that fact that Brownmiller's thesis is not stated in her own words; rather, the words of Chief Justice Warren Burger supply her thesis. This is an effective maneuver, because she lends authority to her own voice (and to her argument) by quoting from a respected source.

3. By telling the reader to notice the quotation marks around a sentence, Brownmiller calls attention to (or highlights) the statement, while also letting the reader know that she is borrowing from another authority on the matter of free speech and pornography. She is also letting us know that she already has supporters for her argument.

4. She mentions these books as evidence of a time when claims of "pornography" went too far—and to explain that, had these works been deemed pornographic, some of her writing might have been. This does not necessarily function to help her argument because, first of all, she shows how time changes the notion of what is and what isn't acceptable. (We can assume that her argument, too, might weaken with time.) Also, this passage serves to show exactly how subjective these kinds of judgements can be.

5. As she does throughout this essay, Brownmiller uses quotation marks to highlight certain parts of her argument (to give these ideas emphasis), as well as to invoke an authority within her writing, which illustrates the "powerful" support that her position has.

6. This is a safe and fair way to end her argument, although it tends to lack punch. By the end of her essay, Brownmiller seems to have given up all rights to her opinions to the court, which some readers might find off-putting—"If the courts just decide anyway, why the argument?"

I Am a First Amendment Junkie
Susan Jacoby

Topical Considerations
1. Jacoby quotes Brownmiller in paragraph 6 to present a strong feminist definition of pornography. Taken out of context as it is, this definition lacks a particular slant making it effective in Jacoby's essay. It is interesting to note, though, that Jacoby does not give in whole-heartedly to Brownmiller's description of what constitutes pornography. Indeed, she qualifies the definition by saying that it applies to "some types of pornography."
2. Jacoby means that she does more than just support the First Amendment; she is nearly "obsessed" by it, and wishes to see it enacted wherever possible. The term is appropriate because it clearly conveys where Jacoby stands on the issue. It is also unique and, therefore, memorable.
3. Jacoby seems to be talking about people who are not concerned with women's issues, or who are embarrassed to discuss other issues related to female sexuality. It is difficult to discern, however, whether she is referring to men or women, though it might be safe to say that "conservative" could modify "most of the people" whom she points to.
4. Jacoby does seem concerned about women's rights, which might lead readers to believe that she is a feminist. However, it might be more accurate to say that Jacoby is sympathetic to the feminist cause, rather than definitely being a feminist. As evidence, she continually says "feminists do this," "feminists do that," which creates a me-versus-them dichotomy—i.e., Jacoby vs. feminists.
5. Jacoby doesn't use the terms "art" and "trash" well. She does not set up a clear distinction between the two. She mentions *Playboy* and *Penthouse* to illustrate her point; but she does not clearly distinguish for her audience which is art and which is trash.

Rhetorical Considerations
1. By giving a voice to her opposition, Jacoby shows that she has considered more than just her side of the argument. She directly counters the opposition arguments within the same paragraphs they appear (see paragraphs 3 and 4) so as to immediately establish control over her opposition.
2. Though students' opinions on which essay is more effective will vary, Jacoby's tends to be a bit more informal than Brownmiller's, while it is just as well informed. For some these factors may make the essay appear more effective than Brownmiller's.

3. Jacoby's use of a justice's quote differs from Brownmiller's simply in that it represents an opposing side of the issue. The quotation that Jacoby uses does work in favor of her argument, but it is interesting to note how often published authors invoke an "outside," authoritative voice to back up their opinions.

4. Although the anecdote that Jacoby provides works in the sense that it is well-written and amusing, it does not pack the punch of a more empirical, statistical survey, and, as such, might serve to weaken her argument.

5. Jacoby makes this switch to discuss the subjectivity inherent in deciding if something is "appropriate." She gives the example of TV because it is a readily understandable one. Also, she parallels parents' right and responsibility to control what their children watch to the individual's right and responsibility to decide what to watch, read, listen to, etc.—and not the FCC's.

14
Education

The Classroom Experience
Killing the Spirit
Page Smith

Topical Considerations
1. Smith would prefer the classic tradition of the great lecturer because that style encourages the lecturer to avoid the abstract, inflame the imagination of the pupils, and relate the subject matter to real life. The modern lecturer presents the "negative stereotype" by repeating the same lecture merely by adding the latest research without considering his or her listeners.
2. Students will agree or disagree. The examples they use from their own experiences will vary.
3. Answers will vary depending on the students' individual expereinces.
4. Students will describe a variety of note-taking methods, which may lead to an interesting classroom discussion.
5. Again the answers will vary, but this question may lead to an active classroom discussion.
6. Students will agree or disagree. Their specific reasons will vary.
7. The play would prepare students for the way most of their professors will treat them, in Smith's view. In the play the professor refuses to stop lecturing when the student suffers a toothache. When she interrupts his lecture by crying out in pain, he strangles her. Another student arrives as the curtain comes down.
8. Students will either describe an experience that they have had or they will describe how they think a student-teacher dialogue might work. All students should explain whether they think the experience would be advantageous.

Rhetorical Considerations
1. Smith gives the professional point of view of lecturers with a tongue-in-cheek tone mocking seriousness. The first paragraph is statement, followed by an example, then he extends this tone with further examples.
2. In paragraph 2, he interjects, "we are told," as if this may or may not be true. He also inserts an "I think" for emphasis. In the last sentence of paragraph 5, Smith adds "I fear," indicating his displeasure that professors are still aloof and impersonal. In the opening sentence of paragraph 14, Smith says, "I am pleased to say" to reinforce his pride in a former student.

3. Smith's examples come from the history of education, contemporary works on education, television comedians, his own experience as an educator for over thirty years, and his former students.

4. Use of historical and contemporary examples help to reinforce Smith's points and add credibility.

5. Answers will vary. Students may feel that the essay should end with paragraph 20 because it has closure with the relationship between professors and students, and because it reinforces the ideas of the first paragraph. Students may choose paragraph 21 because it ends with good information and with a powerful example. Some may choose 22 because of the reinforcement with another example and the use of a strong ending.

6. Some students may consider Smith a braggart using his own success stories—that is, teaching Dante and using Limerick's words. They may also see Smith as a realistic teacher who practices what he preaches (i.e., the same examples compared with examples from historical and contemporary educators).

College of Future: Not a Pretty Picture
Patricia Nelson Limerick

Topical Considerations

1. Limerick's first sentence announces that she enjoys the company of her students. The alternative seems stultifying: publishing for its own sake, probably with little publishable to say; and automaton-like processing of grades after holograph-like appearances in massive lecture halls. Both alternatives involve almost no human contact. Interaction needs to be a two-way street; her endorsement of her own alma mater's motto indicates that she sees students as potential friends, not as bodies filling up a classroom, or as adversaries in a battle for grades.

2. Limerick hopes students will genuinely want to listen to her and talk to her—that students will take pleasure in an ongoing dialogue. She hopes they will enjoy intellectual activity for its own sake, rather than for vocational rewards. Finally, her comment in paragraph 15 about "the affection and memory tying a society's young to their elders," suggests that benefits to students will last a lifetime. Students can gain an increased capacity to savor, contribute to, and pass on a cultural and intellectual heritage in this dialogue.

3. Professors are caught up with expectations that they publish and acquire high "professional standing." But publishing, grantsmanship, fellowships, and travel take them out of the classroom, away from students. Limerick also mentions "public hostility to education" and the "crisis in funding." The public believes that professors aren't "doing enough." They are urged to teach more students in each section, to cut budgets, and to reduce faculties. Universities pay scant attention to excellence in teaching, and pit "departments, programs, professors, graduate students and undergraduates" against each other for a shrinking pool of resources.

4. Students are "understandably anxious" about earning high grades so they will stand the best chance of landing a first job in their chosen career. They are "grade-grubbing," doing only as much as they have to for a grade; and they are signing up either for "gut" courses, in which the professor is an easy grader, or for courses limited to a vocational track. Under these conditions, students are not interested in ideas. Limerick suggests that they are both preoccupied with the economy, and too depressed (perhaps drinking away their troubles) to care.

5. For student discussion. The connection between the depressed economy and grade-grubbing seems tenuous, at best. Unless they're stunningly high or low, grade-point averages don't affect employment—internships, extracurricular activities, and summer jobs are more important, as any academic or career counselor should have told students.

6. In paragraphs 13–15, Limerick offers three specific recommendations. Most of the tangible benefits can be had from a careful review of the rest of the article. First, she recommends funding. Expensive electronic doo-dads and a fatly padded bureaucracy aren't necessary; rather, she is concerned with facilities (comfortable classrooms); services (counseling, student activities, awards programs); and hiring and retaining personable faculty. Second, she recommends revised expectations of professors, specifically in publishing. Making academic survival contingent on library-burrowing removes professors from circulation with students. Limerick's final recommendation is harder to codify; you can't legislate "pleasure . . . in each other's company." But she wants a sea-change in priorities, attitudes, and expectations to be reinforced on many different fronts.

Rhetorical Considerations

1. **Grubbing** suggests "grub," a maggot; or as the gerund, someone digging tediously through dirt. Students whose professors don't respect them may feel grub-like, halfway through metamorphosis into adulthood, or dirty and tired. A **juggernaut** is a terrible object of adoration, from an incarnation of the Hindu god Vishnu, whose followers would fling themselves beneath the wheels of his idol pulled in religious procession. Limerick uses it to describe the publish-or-perish ethos, which sacrifices the life of the university to an idolatrous page count. **Flood** has apocalyptic connotations; Limerick applies it to public hostility to education. Wise foresight and planning may mitigate its effects, but once you see it coming, it's too late. **Elders** have attained great wisdom with advanced age, creating generational continuity by passing on that wisdom. The term resonates with Limerick's final sentence, calling the university "the institution which could hold us together."

2. In paragraphs 2 and 11, Limerick identifies her primary audience as "you": high school students and their parents. Parents and students must worry that colleges will not "do right" by them; education is increasingly expensive, but their dollars buy less contact with professors. Even parents who can afford "small liberal arts colleges" can't be assured of a quality education for

their children. They may be gypped and swindled. This threat is an appeal to parents, who control the pocketbooks, rather than to children. Whether Limerick appeals to pre-college teens is for your students to discuss; she seems to write off this audience as already caught up in "grade-grubbing," needing to be woken up to the pleasurable pursuit of ideas.

3. Limerick uses the inclusive "we" in paragraph 12, including "alumni, professors, administrators and legislators." Of these four, she appeals most directly to other professors: contact with students is something "that any teacher should cherish and fight to maintain." Junior faculty may respond enthusiastically. But there's little to convince a senior fellow at a prestigious research institute to change. Nor are alumni, administrators, or legislators offered incentives beyond working for "a better tomorrow." What's in it for them? However, Limerick doesn't really have enough room in this piece (originally published in *USA Today*) to actively court and persuade everyone.

4. Limerick assumes that all of her readers are at least middle class. Her secondary audience (professors, administrators, legislators) will be middle class, as will most alumni. Her primary audience will too, with all parents expecting their children to go to college. Scraping together the money to send them isn't at issue. But Limerick is not addressing people for whom the main crisis in budgeting is the cutbacks in grants and scholarships, and for whom any college degree has become impossible. Nor is she addressing the older student, for whom budget cuts have meant deferral and part-time enrollment. She uses the terms "high school student" and "teenager" interchangeably to mean "person soon to be enrolled in college."

5. Page Smith's article was first published in a book; Limerick's article was a one-column op-ed piece in a national newspaper. The format greatly influences each author's voice and material. Smith has much more space; he quotes extensive passages and supplies examples and elaborations. In paragraph 11 he can afford to tell us, for instance, not only about the hell his students designed for their dull professors, but the dispute between the two students, and the effect of their exercise upon his own composure during lectures. He can luxuriate in sonorous, well-balanced sentences, with lengthy qualifiers nestled into complex grammatical structures. On the other hand, Limerick must zap. Readers want quick news. That's why they're reading a national newspaper. Vocabulary and sentences are simpler. Each word must be weighed, fat pared. With less clutter, her vivid terms stand out more sharply.

6. Many of Limerick's paragraphs would be judged deficient by an academic writing structure; they are frequently only one or two sentences long. She does not always use topic sentences; many of her paragraphs could be combined to satisfy the conventions of academic writing. Further, some of her ideas ("crisis in funding," "hostility to education") seem to be sweeping generalizations. But the point is that she isn't writing in an academic mode— she's writing a column for a newspaper. The conventions are different. Paragraph breaks come quickly to keep the pacing and rhythm speedy. Some

ideas assume that readers have prior knowledge, and have been following news media debates about education for some time. For student discussion. If students have thought through questions 5 and 6 above, they should be able to forego the simplistic pleasure of pronouncing Limerick "good" and Smith "bad."

A Liberating Curriculum
Roberta F. Borkat

Topical Considerations

1. Borkat says her plan to award the grade of A to all students in the second week of the semester will relieve anxiety, free students up "to do whatever they want," and assure them of "high grade-point averages and an absence of obstacles in their march toward graduation" (paragraph 3). Students may find this amusingly appealing, though they will also notice that the absurd plan would make a mockery of education and render their degrees useless.

2. This question should provoke an interesting discussion; responses will vary.

3. Students will probably have noticed Borkat's deeply cynical opinion of students; they may or may not think this opinion is justified. The student in paragraph 1 (who returns in paragraph 8) is a plagiarizer; the young man in paragraph 7 wants the assurance of a good grade even though he plans neither to do the reading nor attend class regularly; another student wants to be guaranteed a B after failing the first exam. All want good grades without working for them.

4. In paragraph 3, Borkat suggests her plan will relieve professors of "useless burdens," enabling them time to "pursue their real interests"; universities "will have achieved the long-desired goal of molding individual professors into interchangeable parts of a smoothly operating machine." In paragraph 8, Borkat imagines the "happy faces of university administrators and professors, released at last from the irksome chore of dealing with students." These passages suggest that university administrators want simply to create an efficient bureaucracy, and that professors are more interested in their personal and professional development than in teaching. Students should also note the "one or two forlorn colleagues" who have more idealistic aims. By and large, Borkat is as cynical about these groups as she is about students.

5. Some students will probably know the essay that provides the model for this one: Swift's "A Modest Proposal." There, Swift attacks contemporary social practices by making a shockingly outlandish proposal with an absolutely straight face. Students familiar with Swift's work can describe the similarity between Swift's satire and Borkat's: In both, the author consistently states the exact opposite of what he or she actually believes.

6. Students may still not find Borkat's main point absolutely clear—and with good reason, since satire almost always works obliquely. Though never directly stated, Borkat clearly believes that some people involved in higher education—students, faculty, and university administrators—have no real

commitment to learning. Instead, education has become merely a trouble-some obstacle blocking the path to what these people really want: graduation; "professorial prestige, rapid promotion and frequent sabbaticals" (paragraph 8); and a "smoothly operating" bureaucratic machine (paragraph 3).

Rhetorical Considerations

1. Borkat sardonically relates her new belief in her "Plan" to a kind of religious conversion; the diction is so patently inappropriate to the topic at hand that it helps signal her ironic intent. Once students have seen the pseudoreligious connotations of the word "blessed" in the first sentence they should be able to identify its appearance in subsequent words and phrases: the suggestion that knowledge has been "revealed" to her; that "Enlightenment came to me in a sublime moment of clarity"; that her conversion was effected by a "revelation."

2. After introducing her plan in paragraphs 1 and 2, Borkat suggests potential benefits in paragraph 3. She then spends four paragraphs (4–7) addressing the opposition to her argument. Paragraph 8 suggests that her plan will satisfy not only students, but university administrators; paragraph 9 facetiously regrets she wasted almost thirty years trying to help students learn. Borkat spends most of her time presenting—and facetiously addressing—opposition to her proposal. This strategy allows Borkat to express her real view at some length, since she actually concurs with her opposition.

3. Here Borkat uses faulty reasoning to promote a point with which she actually disagrees. Borkat falsely defines democracy as a system "that aims for equality in all things"; students should see a conflict between this notion of democracy and the concept as they know it. The inaccuracy of the definition debilitates this part of Borkat's argument.

4. Borkat's purpose does not seem to be educational reform, primarily because she makes little or no effort to achieve common ground with the villains in the story—the students, teachers, and university administrators whose ideas need reforming. This is, of course, a central characteristic of satire, which is almost by definition critical rather than constructive. Borkat's satire, like Swift's, identifies and attacks a problem with withering wit but makes little or no effort to win over the people who might reform the abuse in question. Since the essay first appeared in *Newsweek,* a general interest periodical, Borkat's audience is not necessarily academic; rather, the piece seems designed for the public at large, whom it invites to scorn academic folly.

A War Against Grade Inflation
Jackson Toby

Topical Considerations

1. The student who left the rude note under Toby's door was, by a process of elimination, a graduating senior with a double major in economics and computer science. The note berated Toby in foul language and signs for not having given a higher percentage of A's—and specifically, for not having

given him an A. Toby responds first with dismay ("slap in the face"), then by smoothing his ruffled feathers ("Uncivil? Certainly"), and finally by getting even: discovering the student's identity and publishing the details which indict him as a rude brat.

2. Toby supplies only A and B grades consistently. In 1951, 42 of each 100 students enrolled at Rutgers received As and Bs. In 1971, roughly 58 of each 100 students at Rutgers received an A or a B. In 1990–1991, the number of A or B students was 66 in 100. Comparable grades at Harvard are 73 in 100 students, and at Stanford, 90 in 100 students. (Toby doesn't give a year for the Harvard and Stanford grades, but he uses the present tense "are.")

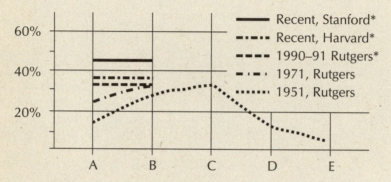

*Assumes that equal numbers of students receive A's and B's.

3. Grade inflation has been institutionalized for three reasons. First, discussion of changing the F to to NP ("not passed"), and abolition of Fs and even Ds suggests a molly-coddling effort to make students feel good about themselves by awarding them higher grades than they deserve. Second, there is no consensus about what grades mean. Few people really believe that C means "satisfactory," or even "average" anymore. Third, grade inflation is driven by students exercising consumer pressure on professors (what if you gave a class and nobody came . . . would you still get paid?)

4. Toby offers three reasons to curb grade inflation. First, students need and deserve honest feedback about how they stack up against their peers. College is a buffer zone between parental insulation (with high schools part of this insulation) and the cold, harsh realities of the Real World. Paychecks are, after all, a kind of grading system. Second, students need the feedback of honest grades to make decisions about immediate behavior and long-range goals. Good grades signal good study habits and aptitude matches to both college and career choice. Poor grades signal a need to rethink study habits, choice of college, or discipline. The third reason is that good grades signal to financial benefactors that their investment is paying off. Parents, loan grantors, and fellowship or scholarship agencies need a fair way of tracking how well their investment is paying off.

5. Poor grades do not always mean lack of intellectual ability. Putting a student who is verbally gifted into advanced calculus doesn't always yield good

grades. A sports analogy might work for students who don't understand: asking a shot-put champion to perform well at gymnastics will probably yield poor results. Motivational problems (parents shoving a career choice down their offspring's throats) may also damage grades with subconscious self-sabotaging, like keg-partying the night before exams.

6. Most questions are a litmus test for students to test their personal experiences with grades against Toby's reasons for wanting to curb grade inflation. Do students really "stop fooling around and start studying" or rethink their decisions about a major when they receive poor grades? Has high school grade inflation damaged their perceptions? What do students really think when two professors award them widely disparate grades?

Rhetorical Considerations

1. This anecdote is a classic example of a "hook" to catch readers' attention: brief, to the point, and shocking without being gratuitous. (Note that Toby leaves out the obvious shocking word and gesture.) This incident may have catalyzed Toby into researching statistics, and into paying more attention to news articles about a long-standing trend. But then, his discipline is sociology, so this would be within his bailiwick as a professional.

2. Toby's splitting the anecdote into two parts helps create sympathy for his case, and highlights the student's unreasonableness. At the article's start, we're left to wonder, gee, what grade did Toby assign this nasty student? Who's to say he didn't deserve the "slap in the face"? But the student received a B+. He lost only the symbolic value of a straight-A average, and then not even in his major. These details provide a satisfying punch line to the anecdote, turning it into a joke.

3. Toby doesn't approve of either professor's comments. Toby places Rebholz's words into scattershot quotation marks: ". . . accused the Faculty Senate of falling into a 'punitive mode' that involved 'branding students.'" Toby doesn't dignify these comments with a direct refutation, but his later comments suggest that accurate grading is fair, not punitive. To grade accurately isn't to "brand" (the scarlet letter F?), but to provide useful feedback. Similarly, in debates about notations on Dartmouth transcripts, Toby doesn't debunk Mook's disapproval of competition. But he assumes in the next paragraph that competition is an appropriate part of college experience.

4. For student discussion. Toby might compare SAT or GRE scores then and now. He might also compare exams or papers written by students then and now. However, all possible grounds for defending the proposition that "students are doing poorer work than they were 43 years ago" are themselves subject to measurement problems. Standardized tests have also become inflated; exams and essays may have been subject to different criteria; and knowledge itself has changed.

5. Since he's been teaching at Rutgers 43 years, Toby is not a neophyte who could be bamboozled into leniency. His treatment of Rebholz and Mook suggests that, while he's not the type to go for the jugular in advancing his

own ideas, Toby also isn't going to hesitate to point out that the emperor lacks appropriate attire. Students can expect tough grading—but then, he attracted over 200 people to the course that rankled the angry student. He seems to draw a crowd without selling out to "enrollment votes of student consumers." He believes his students should learn about their own abilities, as well as about criminology. A student who visits his office hours can expect a straight-shooting response about his or her performance in the course, rather than misleading platitudes.

6. For student discussion. This question can help students think about ways to backtrack and structure their reasons for making a speedy, intuitive decision. It might be worth charting their criteria on the board, especially if your students respond to entreaties for reasoning with a shrug, and the claim "well, that's just the way I feel about it."

Multiculturalism
The Debate Has Been Miscast from the Start
Henry Louis Gates, Jr.

Topical Considerations

1. Ethnic chauvinism, according to Gates, is often mistaken for multiculturalism, although he views the two as decidedly different. "Ethnic" refers to distinctive cultural styles—be they derived from so-called white ethnic groups—e.g., Italian, Polish, and Swedish—or from racial groups—e.g., African Americans, West Indians, and Asians "Chauvinism" broadly means fanatical patriotism, or overzealous promotion of one's own narrowly defined group culture as superior to others. According to Gates it is a narrow mindset that isolates cultural groups from one another; it promotes wrongheaded educational practices, which focus on ego stroking rather than on intellectual rigor; and it brings divisive political arguments into the classroom. Gates doesn't think that ethnic chauvinism is good.

2. Gates never really settles on a solid definition for multiculturalism. However, students should appreciate that Gates wants to use the term to expunge the cast of fanaticism from the alternative phrase, ethnic chauvinism. He views multiculturalism as a communal American identify composing diverse elements.

3. A jeremiad is a blustering, angry speech, which errs on the side of passion in denouncing or lamenting a sorry state of affairs. Hulme and Pattee, whom Gates quotes to 1917 and 1919, are satisfactorily impassioned, although just what they are complaining about—propaganda for Hulme, and experimental lawlessness for Pattee—is mysterious. Their vagueness, of course, is exactly what Gates wants; he finds the complaint that multiculturalists introduce politics just as silly. Gates uses examples from the beginning of the

century to substantiate his claim that discussions of multiculturalism are not as radically new as some people think.

4. Gates is hazy on what he means by "politics"—although he might mean laws and policies that regulate individual and sub-group behavior within a larger national entity. One goal of education, he agrees, is the "inculcation of proper civic virtues"—presumably a set of attitudes and behaviors that promote obedience to laws and policies in deference to a greater common good, and a willingness to compromise about what the laws and policies ought to be. Gates cannot imagine a system of education that does not involve politics, or political concerns, precisely because civic virtues involve compromise. In fact, he agrees with political theorist Amy Gutman that discussion, even controversy, must be aired publicly. Public discussion itself can educate citizens. The implied alternative, perhaps, is blind obedience to authority for its own sake, rather than equitable negotiation.

5. "Balkanization" was a word coined in the aftermath of World War I when larger states were broken up into hostile smaller nations. It took on added specificity in the early 1990s following the breakup of the Soviet Union and the formation of numerous small nations in the Balkan region. Gates rejects the claim of his adversaries that teaching about different cultures will disrupt the United States social or political structure. He points out that our cultural or natural identity is already fragmented; Balkanization is not a real threat, because the large, unified common culture that his adversaries envision simply does not exist. Rather, Gates believes that educators must work to build such a unified common culture.

6. For student discussion. Much of the outcome of this discussion will depend on student variables—whether they come from a largely homogenized part of the country, whether they are honest with themselves, or willing to be honest in a classroom situation, and on your campus's racial-ethnic climate. Students of all ethnic groups—not just white students—may feel angry, guilty, or confused.

7. Critic Edward Said (pron. "Sigh-EED") says that students and scholars should be most like wide-ranging travelers, discovering different cultures, and in the process discovering what their own culture contains. In Said's view, schools should not inhibit or even necessarily direct that broad travel itinerary, but should serve as a catalyst for respectful mutual understanding. The student's verse pokes fun at a stodgy old schoolmaster in England who takes only the confines of his own experience as a measure for what is and is not knowledge—and thus what is worth teaching, and what is beneath notice. Ironically, this solipsistic old man is also the gatekeeper for students aspiring to a degree. Said's view might be described as dynamic and dialectic, whereas Jowett's is static and monologic.

8. By "the West vs. the Rest," Gates pinpoints how he thinks the debate has been misunderstood. Those who disagree with multiculturalism, he says, can only see antagonism and competition on a "win-lose" model, such as a

courtroom drama in which one party must lose in order for the other one to win. He shifts slightly when defining pluralism as "porous, dynamic, and interactive." That is, cultures may still have different, even antithetical approaches and assumptions, just as in a "win-lose" situation. With pluralism, however, no culture wins, and no culture loses; rather, they engage in synthesis, presumably resulting in a hybrid that is in some way better than either original.

9. A palimpsest is a parchment or vellum upon which documents have been written, erased, and written over several times, with traces of the original writing still slightly visible underneath the most recent layer of writing. Thus, a cultural palimpsest is one in which a single culture predominates, but in which traces of other cultures are visible. Student awareness of the phenomenon will vary. Rock & roll began as rhythm & blues, an African American musical style. Modigliani, Picasso and other modernist painters were heavily influenced by African art forms. Silk and spaghetti both hail from China. Students may be able to generate other examples.

Rhetorical Considerations

1. Gates begins on a light, engaging tone with his rhetorical question. "They" seem to be a vaguely menacing figment of a paranoid's imagination—as in, "they are out to get me." The "terrible things" are somewhat dismissively rehearsed in paragraph 2, relabeled as "ethnic chauvinism." The question is patterned on a stock question from light reading or gossipy situations—such as a teen-audience romance serial novel. The overall effect is open to student discussion. It's a "hook" to get readers interested. Some might see it as flippant—the equivalent of a shoulder shrug signifying, "okay, I'll talk about this, but you don't really expect me to take it seriously, do you?" He begins paragraph 8 with an allusion to a 1980s campaign by a hamburger chain, "where's the beef?" This question too seems to trivialize his antagonists' views.

2. Johnny is an archetypical figure for any student. He is illiterate and innumerate, thus illustrating the failure of American schools to teach basic skills. Johnny is also a bigot. That he tramples gravestones in specifically Jewish cemeteries demonstrates his vicious anti-Semitism; his racial epithets on dormitory walls, a more generalized racism. By using a name for this character, Gates humanizes the problems; and the name, of course, is not randomly chosen. It refers to a series of books about the failures of education using this eponymous name, beginning with *Why Johnny Can't Read* (Rudolph Franz Flesh, 1955). As with his quotations from earlier jeremiads, he illustrates that complaints about schools' competency have been with us for some time.

3. In paragraph 2, Gates' language is alarmist, casting his opponents as extremists. Critics claim that multiculturalism "menaces the Western tradition of

literature"; that it "replac[es] honest historical scholarship"; that it "bolster[s] the self-esteem of minorities" (rather than teaching minority students real skills or useful knowledge). He makes critics sound rather like the lone hero in "Invasion of the Body Snatchers," witnessing the replacement of real scholarship with a deadly substitute that will cause the collapse of life on the planet as we know it. When he accuses critics of multiculturalism of using a "West vs. the Rest" model (paragraph 14), he perhaps draws the alternatives too sharply. If cultures clash, conquer, and replace each other as cleanly as this catchy phrase suggests, then we would end up with an Orwellian "newspeak" set of history books—constantly under revision as prevailing trends reinterpret history and contemporary life.

4. Gates is almost surprisingly dependent on old debates as he makes his case for future educational policy. He says that the central questions of multiculturalism "go back to the very founding of our republic," and that the "underlying questions are time-tested." He refers to Cardinal Newman's thoughts in support of his own views; and he peppers his discussion with a 17th, 18th, and 19th century commentary and intellectual history. He accomplishes at least two objectives by his historical references. First, he establishes the breadth of his own erudition while adding lustre to his authority. Second, his references counter those opponents who claim that multiculturalism is just a passing fad, an *ignus fatuus* educators are stampeding after during a dark period when American education is universally acknowledged to be in decline. Gates is not completely successful here because he never really defines contempory multiculturalism (or, for that matter, any of the historical precedents). His analogies are incomplete and somewhat intuitive—although the article does not seem intended as a piece of rigorous scholarship.

5. Gates implicitly raises a number of fears about both the problem and its solution. First, he assumes readers are concerned about the state of education today. He does not dispute that "Johnny" in paragraph 8 is an appalling ignoramus, nor that Johnny got that way because schools have failed to do their jobs. Further, he assumes that readers are worried about the rise in incidents of racial bigotry of the crudest kind; Johnny's actions are gratuitously vicious, rather than tragedies born of misunderstanding. Readers also probably worry that the crisis in basic skills education isn't going to be solved by quick-fix answers. Further, if schools are demonstrably negligent in teaching reading and writing skills, then adding on yet another task or area of knowledge (the promotion of tolerance through knowledge) is going to overburden those schools still more. Gates does not really put to rest any of these fears.

6. There's something counterproductive about this list. If these musicians, dancers, artists, and authors had not been trained in precisely the traditional, mainstream, western culture that Gates is trying to undermine as central to American education, then they would not have had the raw materials with which to create their brilliant syntheses.

Too Many Have Let Enthusiasm Outrun Reason
Kenneth T. Jackson

Topical Considerations

1. The report "One Nation, Many Peoples" was prepared by the New York State Social Studies Syllabus Review Committee, presumably a group of concerned experts charged with overhauling the nuts and bolts of social studies teaching—i.e., syllabi, lesson plans and activities. Their disciplinary scope was social studies—history, anthropology, political science, sociology, psychology, and other related areas. The document was adopted; it became New York State's official policy on how primary and secondary schools must teach social studies. The report "occasioned a firestorm of controversy"; some people were delighted, others disgusted, but apparently one could not read the report without some kind of violent emotional response. Jackson was among those who disliked the report's recommendations.

2. Jackson believes that Europe has been a far more influential force in world politics in the last 500 years than any other continent. He names specific events to substantiate his claim: the Spanish Inquisition, the Thirty Years War, and the Holocaust. His implication is that we learn history in order to learn about social, political and intellectual currents that have shaped our lives today.

3. Jackson is not blind to the scourge of racism, discrimination, and bigotry. However, he says, we cannot afford to shift our emphasis in teaching history simply because we would like to redress historical slights and contemporary disadvantages of maligned minorities. Historical judgment, then, concerns how much of an effect a nation or ethnic group's actions has actually had on contemporary life. To teach about the real effect is not to endorse or approve of those actions. Moral judgment, on the other hand, concerns how morally a nation or ethnic group has acted—or, how poorly an ethnic group has fared, and how responsible a larger community should be about remedying past wrongful action against that group. To endorse or approve the position of a wronged ethnic group does not necessarily make it a good candidate for extensive treatment as historically significant. As evidence, he uses the Holocuast. Hitler's Third Reich did have an extremely large impact on contemporary life, but to teach about that sequence of events is not to endorse Hitler's position.

4. According to Jackson, New York State schools had just revised their curriculum four years ago with exactly the same goal in mind: increased multiculturalism. This revision, he says, was highly successful because it used the latest scholarship and because it drew upon the talents of teachers dedicated to multicultural goals. In fact, the curriculum immediately prior to the report was so insistently multicultural that studnets were being shortchanged on European history. Since 1970, European history has either been displaced by larger omnibus courses with a breadth so large that it seemingly cannot

cover any continent's history except in the most shallow terms; or it has been shunted into a tiny fragment of most students' overall social studies training.

5. Jackson doesn't want educators to make students feel bad about themselves. But he does warn that educators should not distort facts or misrepresent the relative importance of an ethnic or racial group in an effort to make all students feel that their ancestors had an important role in shaping America. That is, educators should not immediately revise their lesson plans and begin teaching that Group X had an important impact just because a student from Group X enrolled in the school yesterday.

6. The three main complications with the "feel good" approach, says Jackson, are:
   * Educators are too willing to teach controversial theories as facts. Students should not be subjected to untested theories or hypotheses until experts have come to some agreement among themselves about the truth. Otherwise, each new class full of students will learn different "facts," and the result will be a lack of a common body of knowledge.
   * History becomes a dry exercise in rote memorization of ethnic or racial group "firsts," which students justifiably find boring and irrelevant. Presumably, Jackson's view of history involves discussion of cause-and-effect chains, rather than isolated events.
   * History becomes a sequence of myths, one replacing the other, as a new group of people wishes to feel good about itself.

7. Jackson is concerned that the citizens of the United States have no single common bond—no religion, no race or ethnicity. Thus we are in special need of a common history, which, for Jackson, means a heavy emphasis on British legal and political institutions. He refers to disputes in several countries that have led to bloody conflicts as a warning of how important such a common understanding is. In each case, he finds, heightened emphasis on inter-group loyalties, rather than allegiance to the nation as a whole, has led to divisions that have the power to tear a country apart.

8. Student responses will vary somewhat. Model sentences might include:
   * Social studies should teach about those events and peoples that have had an important influence on American life today, rather than about peoples whose role in history, we feel, could or should have been more important.
   * Social studies teachers are already including multicultural material in their classrooms, almost to the exclusion of European history.
   * Social studies should not be taught simply to make students feel good about themselves, because it leads to several unsound educational practices.
   * Schools should teach a common American history, because Americans hold so few of the usual bases for national unity in common.

9. For student discussion. This question asks for subjective judgments; it may lead to further discussion about the purpose of each history. That

is, students who are willing to provide a quantitative value on their history classes might be asked, "What good do you think such history does you?"

Rhetorical Considerations

1. Jackson says that he has spent the best part of 30 years studying "ethnicity, racism, discrimination, inequality, and civil rights," which are important focal points for the report "One Nation, Many Peoples." He also says that he understands the United States as a country comprised of a large variety of cultures, and that he would like to see education teach young people more about this diversity than it does at present. When he critiques the ways educators want to implement these ideas, he makes clear that he is not a bigoted, crusty curmudgeon who has been stuck on a desert island since sometime before the Civil Rights movement. However, he believes that schools have a much more important job, which (as he will state in the final paragraph) is the teaching of a common culture that will make intercultural harmony more possible, rather than less.

2. Jackson could be begging the question by naming these events because he assumes they are more important than, say, the Chinese Opium Wars, or the Boer settlement of South Africa. As Jackson's own sense of urgency in teaching history would suggest, just because we don't know of a specific historical event's occurrence does not mean it has no impact on contemporary American life. Likewise, just because we have singled out a sequence of events in Europe does not mean that events in other locations are not presently having repercussions that we do not perceive.

3. Jackson offers little satisfactory evidence about the quality of the curriculum immediately preceding the "One Nation, Many Peoples" report. He offers the names of three noted authorities, but the success of their efforts depends largely on Jackson's say-so. He alleges that teachers are "better prepared and more sophisticated than their critics allege," but he offers no proof of that statement; indeed, that there are critics suggests that teacher preparation is a matter of some controversy. His claim that students do not need additional multicultural preparation is substantiated only by an informal poll of his young acquaintances about a limited historical incident.

4. One of the real problems Jackson seems to hint at with a rather impatient tone is that teachers have to shift gears yet again. Two major curriculum revisions within four years means that teachers must once again spend extensive time outside of the classroom reading the new directives, rewriting lessons plans, and perhaps filling out forms and gaining administrative approval for the results. If, as Jackson claims, the previous curriculum was already multicultural enough, then this new set of directives wastes time that could better be spent working with students or strengthening teacher effectiveness.

Oppositions: Curriculum Wars
Cultural Literacy
E. D. Hirsch, Jr.

Topical Considerations

1. Most people in Latin America speak Spanish. Homer's epic poems were *The Odyssey* and *The Iliad*. The Alamo, a mission in San Antonio, was the site of a bloody massacre in 1836 in the United States' annexation of Texas from Mexico. The years for official American involvement in World War II are 1941–1945; in World War I, 1917–1918; and the American Civil War lasted 1861–1865. Each state has two senators (the number of representatives differs by population). Chicago is in Illinois (on the southern tip of Lake Michigan); Toronto in Canada (north of Buffalo across Lake Ontario); and Washington D.C., along the borders of Maryland and Virginia (south of Baltimore). Thomas Jefferson was the 3rd President of the United States and the primary drafter of the Declaration of Independence adopted by Congress on July 4, 1776. The first ten amendments to the U.S. Constitution comprise the Bill of Rights; they include the following: 1, freedom of speech and religion; 2, militia and the right to bear arms; 3, no soldiers to be quartered in private homes; 4, no unreasonable search and seizure; 5, judicial due process (no double jeopardy; no witness against himself; no unreimbursed taking of property); 6, speedy and public trial; 7, trial by jury; 8, no excessive bail, fines, or cruel and unusual punishment; 9, constitutional rights do not deny other rights retained by the people; 10, powers not delegated are reserved to the states or the people.

   Students may debate the relevance of this information. It might be interesting (or embarrassing) to have students respond to the questions and compare notes, However, it might still be worth asking those who assert that "the knowledge isn't important, it's knowing where to look it up," where they would actually turn in the library.

   For classes with a high proportion of foreign students, it might be interesting to compare their knowledge with that of U.S. citizens.

2. First, Hirsch concedes that the students he criticizes "know a great deal." However, the knowledge they possess is "ephemeral and narrowly confined to their own generation." That is, they are immersed in a popular culture, the signs and symbols of which will leave no lasting impression on generations to come. Their lack of knowledge, says Hirsch, makes them unable to understand books and newspapers, because they lack references for many of the terms beyond their own solipsistic sphere. The full implications of his argument are indeed frightening. The lack of references in turn makes reading a confusing, difficult activity; and the difficulty makes students shun reading all the more. Consequently, they share less and less of the pool of information Hirsch believes they need; also, they are cut off from sources of information about their own lives and times. And cut off from information

about current events, they have no hopes of controlling their own environment, whether by voting in a participatory democracy, actively working to promote change, or persuading others to vote or act through written and oral communication.

3. Hirsch says in paragraph 7 that he first became aware of the problem in the 1970s when he was doing research on college students' reading comprehension and writing skills. Hirsch drew one minor conclusion and one major conclusion. Respectively, that he could not make any assumptions about what students understood. Apparently, his students were unable to perform simple writing tasks not for lack of grammatical, syntactic, or structural skills, but because they did not understand the subject matter. Secondly, that reading and writing are not "empty skills," divorced from content or relevant background information.

4. Hirsch believes that educators have taken common knowledge for granted. They expect students to have acquired such knowledge in a previous grade; or they have become lazy; or their expectations are naive; or perhaps they have been misled. It's difficult to tell from Hirsch's comments here.

5. "Cultural literacy lies above the everyday levels of knowledge that everyone possesses, and below the expert level known only to specialists. It is that middle ground of cultural knowledge possessed by the 'common reader.'" The examples he provides are much clearer than his attempts at a concise definition. If working strictly from the definition, students may have some difficulty producing terms. They might proceed from the two examples: a penny is worth 1/100th of a dollar; marijuana is an illegal drug but alcohol is not; the weather in Florida is, on average, warmer than the weather in Maine.

6. Hirsch believes that the decentralization of school governance has had a very large impact on cultural literacy. He points out that the United States has 16,000 independent school districts (not to mention private schools), each making decisions about what factual information students should learn. However, Hirsh implies, there is no effort among these school districts to achieve a consensus about even the most important facts. He discounts the importance (or perhaps the responsibility) of television in reducing cultural literacy. Students have indeed been substituting television for reading; but some broadcasts have "acculturative" value—a fancy way of saying that TV can sometimes teach cultural literacy. However, schools are completely responsible for excessive television-watching because they do not insist on "significant" amounts of homework or hold students to high standards.

7. Hirsch's "shopping mall" metaphor has decidedly negative connotations. Shopping malls are showcases of conspicuous consumption in which stores compete to convince potential buyers that they have the best selection and prices, when in reality goods are mass-produced, often shoddy, and prices homogenized. Malls depend on cloyingly artificial environments for their allure. They have also become a major social source for suburban high school students seeking escape and diversion from schoolwork. A school

that offers a shopping mall selection of courses, then, offers frivolous subjects that appear enticing but have little lasting value, that are easily "learned" by a student who invests minimal effort, and that are all more or less clones of other courses covering the same material.

His term "cafeteria" is somewhat less damning, but it carries the same sense: an excess of offerings, blandly homogenized in taste, prepared in mass quantities, and served on dinnerware that is either thick ceramic or plastic. It might be interesting to point out the difference between "cafeteria" and "smorgasbord," Sikes and Murray's term. The smorgasbord is by far a more appetizing proposition, carrying connotations of indulgence in especially well-prepared food and elegant atmosphere.

8. For Hirsch, "formalistic educational theory" means that any subject can be plugged into a student's schedule as long as it teaches reading, writing and thinking skills. It is "formalistic" in that it concentrates on form only and ignores content. Hirsch first mentions this approach to education when he recalls his first observation in the 1970s, that students didn't know the facts he expected them to know. Administrators, says Hirsch, have embraced this theory because it allows them "political advantages"—i.e., to make massive substitutions in the curriculum in response to allegations that traditional fare is too narrowly defined by a dominant race, class, gender, religious, or hermispheric perspective. For Hirsch, these substitutions seem to be the rough, "grown-up" equivalent to students' limited perspectives, which are "ephemeral and narrowly confined to their own generation." That is, the inclusion of diversifying material in the curriculum caters to passing trends generated by ideological factions, rather than focusing on material which is timeless and enduring. The result of this endless sequence of substitutions is fragmentation.

Rhetorical Considerations

1. The four sources are popular news journals, such as *Newsweek* and the *Wall Street Journal*; his son's observations teaching secondary school Latin classes; published comments by Benjamin J. Stein (which closely resemble the son's anecdotal evidence); and a pair of extensive reports conducted in 1978 and 1985 with the impressive-sounding title "National Assessment of Educational Progress." The audiences, reliability of these sources, and scope of their data-gathering activities differ greatly. The most informal set of evidence comes from Hirsch's son. The son's reports are hearsay. The comments by Stein in the long quoted paragraph are also hearsay, although they have an aura of greater credibility because they have appeared in print.

News journals are more credible. However, while news writers may draw on a broader base of information, they rarely have time to assemble large compilations of raw data about national trends. Their findings may be slanted by editorial bias, or by incomplete research. The NAEP reports are perhaps most credible. The audience for these reports, however, is highly specialized: educational policy-planners and top-level school administrators.

Hirsch uses these varied sources to reinforce each other. His readers could discredit his complaints if his evidence were drawn from one, or even two of these sources. It is difficult, however, to quibble with the similar judgment drawn by all of them.

2. Hirsch's definition leaves much to be desired. First, his spatial references, "above," "below," and "middle ground," are metaphoric, and do not refer clearly to anything. Second, he does not clearly explain how or why his "common reader" should have more than "everyday levels of knowledge." Another problem is relativity. Hirsch does not account for changes in common knowledge over time, nor does he account for cultural differences. One example of chronological relativity is computers: Most students will probably recognize the term "floppy disk" even if they can't discourse at length about RAM, bytes, baud rates, or coprocessing chips. A decade or so ago, only specialists would have known what a floppy disk was. Similarly, many African-American students will know something about the Black National Anthem "Lift Ev'ry Voice and Sing," even if they can't remember all the words; most white students would probably deny that such an anthem exists.

3. For student discussion.

4. By "conservative" Hirsch seems to mean hegemonic, restricted to reflecting the views and values of a comparatively small group of upper-class Anglo-Saxon Protestant men. Patterson points out that mainstream culture, and by extension the elements citizens are expected to know as part of their cultural literacy, is constantly changing. Although Hirsch mentions Patterson only in passing, as if he expects this name to be part of his readers' own cultural literacy baggage, he seems to be strengthening his claim that his proposition is not racist. Hirsch is indeed treading on thin ice, since the preceding paragraph suggests that much of the new curricula incorporating African-American studies, women's studies, and other "multicultural" fields of inquiry are irrelevant. His appeal to Patterson doesn't necessarily resolve Hirsch's problems. Patterson may indeed agree with the idea of cultural literacy; but that doesn't necessarily mean all Black people, or even all Black educators, would agree.

Cult-Lit
Barbara Herrnstein Smith

Topical Considerations
1. Smith alludes to the book of *Revelations* in which the apocalypse is a set of terrifying events signaling the end of the world. Hirsch, she implies, is broadcasting exaggerted warnings that if we don't agree on a standard set of information, we will suffer cultural doom.

2. Roughly paraphrased, Smith believes that acquisition of cultural literacy (1) is meaningless or undesirable; (2) is impossible to teach as Hirsch proposes; (3) if adopted, would lead to more problems rather than fewer.

3. Smith finds the term "human group" to be vague. A group, she says, is small
and tightly-knit; in her examples (a family, a company, a tribe) every individual might expect to know every other individual with a fair degree of intimacy. However, the term "group" does not make sense when applied to the
United States. Even if sheer numbers and geographical distance were not lo-
gistical barriers to a cohesive set of goals, individuals' ethnic, regional, occupational and other differences prevent all but the most vague consensus
about values and information.

   "National communitarianism" basically refers to the nation as a political unit in which goals and values, economic networks, language and educational criteria are homogenized and standardized. Hirsch implies that
such homogenization can be achieved by negotiation, compromise, and
friendly agreement, where Smith recognizes that only centralized authoritarian experts, imposing standards from a rigidly hierarchal perspective, could
achieve the consensus Hirsch advocates. To call the United States a "human
group," then, is to get the question by asserting that human-group intimacy
exists, while militating for a solution to the problem that human-group intimacy does not exist.

4. For student discussion. Answers will vary, depending on the size of the campus. At medium-size institutions, for example, the freshman class might reasonably be said to form a human group, but not the entire undergraduate
population. At larger institutions, only a dormitory, or a floor of the dormitory, or a wing of a floor might quality. Some undergraduates might want to
include graduate students, professors and administrators in that group; others, even at very small colleges, might want to exclude all but their own narrowly defined peer group. Some may change their minds about the campus
as a whole constituting a "human group" if asked to reflect on "town-gown"
relations.

   Instructors might also broach concerns of fragmentation and campus unrest: do special-interest groups, such as minority support units, gay
and lesbian groups, or women's studies programs constitute separate "human groups"? Is Smith's term "human group" adequate for the overlapping
or concentric circles of relationships these groups represent?

5. Smith finds that every individual is a member of various human groups,
each with its own set of important information, values, and so on. However,
no single group, nor even any synthesis of several groups, can be said to
form a "macroculture." In other words, while Smith admits to some overlap
among groups, no single area of concern is common to all those groups so as
to promote a single standard of American cultural literarcy.

6. "Duplicative transmissions" are those instances of communication in which
a speaker restates exactly the same information he or she received in the first
place. Smith criticizes Hirsch's list as useless because it leads to a closed pool
of knowledge and information. Genuine communication, for Smith, is always "ad hoc," arising from the moment or the context, rather than existing
in a fixed, static, contextless field. In repudiating "sameness," she presup-

poses that the impetus to all communication is difference. People who repeat only what everyone else already knows are not really communicating; they are "droning on." Students who complain that an instructor is merely reading from the last night's textbook assignment are complaining about sameness; they are not hearing anything new. Similarly, composition instructors who complain that their students merely restate what a reading has already covered, rather than analyzing it, are also complaining about sameness. The students have not communicated anything about that reading.

7. To "prescribe" implies that Hirsch is using the verb "should." This formulation assumes that his list is authoritative because he says it is—or, since he dubs it a preliminary list, that once enough people have contributed to the list it will be authoritative because they say it is. Prescription also implies deficiency, just as a doctor might presribe a drug for a patient whose body chemistry needs to be "fixed": people who do not know this information are lacking or deprived. To "describe" implies that Hirsch is using the verb "is." This formulation assumes that Hirsch has distilled his list from the knowledge of people who are already educated. Description does not imply deficiency: it is simply an accurate rendering or representation of what is actually there. Smith is bothered that she can't tell exactly what he is doing because the two activities are very different. In the former he's offering his own opinions as authoritative; in the latter, he's deauthorizing himself and claiming that he has merely represented the status quo.

8. Smith finds Hirsch's methods somewhat mysterious. He apparently asked more than 100 people, 100 of whom agreed on 90 percent of the items. She wants to know what they agreed on; whether Hirsch began with a predrafted list, or with a group of consultants who assembled the list; whether the consultants were asked to prescribe or describe; and how the consultants were chosen. Even more problematic, his wording could mean the Hirsch asked 1,000 people, and then selected carefully the 100 who were in agreement 90 percent of the time. She would also want to know why one group's prescribed list is better than another group's list; or, just who they used as models or an "educated" person.

Rhetorical Considerations

1. Her abbreviations are intended to invoke a negative response even before the reader goes beyond the title. The abbereviation "cult," a word in its own right, refers to fanatic religious groups whose beliefs and practices are extreme, rigid and dogmatic and sometimes infringing on the civil rights of members. "Lit" doesn't have quite this cachet, except perhaps among literary professionals who use it to trivialize areas of inquiry they don't take seriously—for example, "kiddie lit" for "children's literature." Furthermore, compared to the long and convoluted nature of academic paper titles, this one conveys impatience, as if the author finds Hirsch's proposal too absurd for words.

2. Most students might find this sentence excessive. Yet it does serve as an omnibus (almost filibuster) thesis sentence for her attack on Hirsch's ideas about cultural literacy. That Smith can wedge so many complaints into a single sentence, along with her refusal to "mince words," suggests her exasperation.

3. Smith says that she can communicate with her 85-year-old ex-mother-in-law in Altoona, her 5-year-old grandon in Brooklyn, her 25-year-old Hillsboro hairdresser and her cat. She means transmission of information about situations both parties find to be of mutual interest—perhaps knitting, Batman movies and canned tuna, respectively. Hirsch on the other hand would likely omit all of these subjects as significant to what he styles "communication." This is another instance of begging the question as he has predefined what will count as significant communication. Hirsch, she adds, only counts "duplicative transmissions" as important: dialogues that replicate what the speakers already know.

4. Eight of 13 sentences (more than half) in that paragraph are phrased as questions. Further, none of these questions can be answered from Smith's article; and, if we trust her thoroughness in reading the full text of the book neither does Hirsch offer any answers within his own work.

   Smith asks at least two kinds of questions. She begins with questions for which she has no answers: about whether Hirsch began checking for agreement with a prepared list in hand, or by asking the consultants to assemble a list. The more questions she asks, however, the more she seems to anticipate a specific answer. On his selection of consultants, she seems certain that Hirsch consulted only his colleagues, people presumably of similar views. Her final two questions point to negative answers, implying the list was made with no recognizable standards—i.e., the fabrication of a single individual. She effectively undermines Hirsch's credibility here because he can only answer with one of two responses: that he does not know, or that he did not see fit to reveal this information to the reader. Since it's unlikely he does not know, we're left to surmise that he withheld the information. If so, his list takes on a rather sinister cast, for he seems to have deliberately obscured sloppy scholarship in a bid to advance his own, unsubstantiated views.

5. Smith assumes the highly specific degree of cultural literacy that she disparages. For example, discussion in paragraph 1 is heavily dependent on reader's knowledge of the Bible, antiquarians' explanation of the decline and fall of the Roman empire, and contemporary developments in anthropology. Both she and Hirsch situate "transcendence" in the American Romantic transcendentalism of Emerson and, thus, in German phenomonology, and even further back in Plato's notion of forms as she quibbles with his notion of a transcendent culture in paragraphs 6 and 7. Her question about children in Houston, Boston, Alaska, and Nebraska toward the end of paragraph 8 makes sense only if the reader knows where these places are and that each locale has cultural perspectives distinct from the other three. Her reference to Japanese suppliers in paragraph 9 assumes readers know something

of Japan's role in the global economy. Her sneer at Hirsch's list-compilers in paragraph 12 requires readers to agree that Charlottesville and the University of Virginia are provincial or at least far from a normative slice of the United States' intelligensia. In fact, any time Smith gives a concrete example, or leavens a theoretical discussion with metaphor, she assumes cultural literacy. When she leaves out specific examples, she again assumes cultural literacy by assuming that readers have the training to follow an abstract discussion. Further, even her absractions are bounded (albeit invisibly, for most students) by assumptions of knowledge about prior philosophical debates.

15
Advertising

Consumerism
Work and Spend
Juliet B. Schor

Topical Considerations

1. Schor says that the view of human nature as naturally acquisitive is wrong, since many societies, such as the common people in medieval Europe and in nineteenth- and early twentieth-century United States, "exhibited a restricted appetite for material goods." Consumerism, according to her, is a "specific product of capitalism." Students will decide for themselves which view of human nature is true.

2. Again, students will have to make up their own minds about modern consumer discontent. Schor gives evidence that the "American dream" of improving each generation's standard of living was always a mirage. She cites statistics from a 1928 Yale faculty study and a 1922 Berkeley faculty study. She also includes examples from advertising in the 1920s when ads were first used as psychological warfare or scare techniques.

    Agreeing with Galbraith, she finds that manufacturers did attempt to "create the wants [they] attempt[ed] to satisfy," and succeeded in creating a dissatisfied customer. Business made this customer "discontented with what he or she already had," and led to the "consumption ethic."

3. Trade unions and social reformers, including religious groups, attempted to stop this "consumption ethic," which led to working long hours by offering the enticement of leisure time instead. However, labor and reformers lost the battle for increases in free time and decreases in consumption to business, which prefers long working hours and vigorous consumption.

    Consumerism still is the victor over leisure time in the 1990s. Labor groups seem more interested in health care and retirement benefits than in working shorter hours. Social reformers and religious groups spend more energy in trying to get people jobs and decent housing tha in worrying about the length of the working day.

4. Students' answers will vary.

5. The authority is John Maynard Keyes (1883–1946), whose chief work is *The General Theory of Employment, Interest, and Money* (1936). Instead of a free economy, Keyes advocated active government intervention in the market, and influenced nations to adopt spending programs such as the New Deal in the United States in the 1930s. In spite of Keyes' favoring a govern-

mental planned economy and wide control of economic life by democratic public-service corporations, his faith in the capitalistic system led him to accept business' domination over labor and social groups, therefore accepting the consumer ethic.

6. For the students.

7. Native American cultures originally placed little value on material goods and practiced public disposal of wealth in ceremonies such as the potlatch, a ceremonial feast in which the host gives away articles of value to his guests. This communal culture would not place much value on "keeping up with the Joneses."

       Those who practice alternative cultures, such as the New Age individuals, strive for greater leisure and fewer material goods. This group scorns the consumer mentality and considers consumers spoilers of the environment.

Rhetorical Considerations

1. Schor's main purpose is stated in paragraph 27. "My purpose is to add a dimension to this analysis of consumption which has heretofore been neglected—its connection to the incentive structure operating in labor markets. The consumer traps I have described are just the flip side of the bias toward long hours embedded in the production system." Even though the claim appears in the final paragraph, the argument is an inductive one. All preceding material leads up to this conclusion.

2. The tone of this essay (or chapter) is formal, structured, and serious. It seems to be written for an academic audience, with all the scholarly paraphernalia such as lengthy quotations and footnotes this audience requires. Presumably the audience is made up of scholars knowledgeable in economics, because most of the references to people well-known in that field are unknown to the general reader.

3. "Super heterodynes" simply means radios. "Asymptote" refers to a straight line, always approaching, but never meeting a curve. Although Schor does not clarify an "asymptotic culture," its consumers assume that they will reach a state of complete satisfaction with purchase of the newest luxury, but they never get there, just as the straight line never meets the curve. Students may wish the terms were defined.

4. Schor is trying to prove her side of the argument by painting a black picture of business and a white picture of labor and social reformers. The focus of her book is after all, the overworked American. In this excerpt she blames the advertising industry for creating dissatisfied consumers who must work more in order to buy things they really don't need. To show the weaknesses of the labor unions and social reformers would be counterproductive to her contentions, so she stacks the deck by quoting only those economic authorities who agree with her. She also quotes a ILGWU pamphlet in paragraph 12 and a prominent Catholic spokesman in paragraph 13, but no one from the business world.

5. Many students find the use of the feminine pronoun somewhat disconcerting at first, since they are used to the universal "he." However, many authors of textbooks and magazine articles now use "she" and female names instead of male. Students can look in their textbooks for examples.

The Hard Sell
Deborah Baldwin

Topical Considerations

1. Baldwin wants to sensitize her readers to "round-the-clock commercialism" (paragraph 8). She quotes Michael Jacobson and Ronald Collins of the Center for Science in the Public Interest, "Omnipresent commercialism is wrecking America . . . " (paragraph 12). Her audience is comprised of the kind of people she describes as the Urbane family—middle-class liberal urbanites. Although students may not include themselves in this audience, they probably will agree with some of Baldwin's points.

2. Today's ads, the author argues, are more about personal empowerment than the pleasures of society and the senses—ideas that sold products in previous eras, according to Baldwin in paragraph 21. Also, current TV ads must be as entertaining as regular programs to get consumers' attention. Some advertisers on TV increase the volume and intensity of their ads to steal attention from other ads. Other ads satirize advertising itself, such as those that brag that their announcer is the worst, even if their product is the best. Advertisers want us to think we *can* solve all of our problems in life by buying their products, even if this is not possible. Death and taxes continue inexorably, in spite of advertising.

3. Corporations buy time on public broadcasting where they are mentioned twice a day, six days a week, for a year—for $250,000. Corporations donate money to art galleries and museums and get, in addition to good public relations, their names emblazoned on banners and posters. Students may argue that in a recession corporate sponsors make possible a special museum exhibit or sporting event. Or they may argue that when art and sports become commercialized, freedom of expression is threatened.

4. Since the average consumer is unaware of how his or her life is filled with commercials, most students will become aware of this saturation only after reading about it. As Kilbourne continues in paragraph 32, ads "sell images, values, goals, concepts of who we are and who we should be. . . ."

5. The Center for the Study of Commercialism is a Washington-based group that "wants to raise awareness of commercialism's costs" and to change single-minded consumers into civic-minded individuals. Michael Jacobson, a nutrition activist, founder and head of the center, wants to make the public aware of the glut of advertising. Cofounder Ronald Collins joins Jacobson in warning how cosumerism is destroying America. The members of the board include critic Mark Crispin Miller who states that life today can be lived as a theme park because of the blend of commercial and noncommer-

cial in our existence. Another board member George Gerbner, former dean of a communication school, worries about TV commercials' effect on children, as does Neil Postman who also is concerned about TV's influence on the learning process. Jean Kilbourne studies the power of advertising as a socializing force. Students should agree with some of these warnings.

6. Some parallels between political advertising and commercial advertising are found in paragraph 15. "Both involved simplistic plots, with beginnings, middles, and ends, and both made heavy use of emotional images and sound bites." Students could discuss political ads for the 1996 election campaign.

7. Gerbner is afraid that our children are being brought up in a culture dictated, not by the child's home, family, community, or country, but by a "transnational corporation with something to sell." Students may agree that children are very vulnerable to the advertisers' ploys.

Rhetorical Considerations

1. Baldwin begins her article with a day in the life of the Urbanes to show how advertising has become an integral part of our existence. She gives many examples of his phenomenon, such as corporations mentioned on "non-commercial" radio, clothing displaying manufacturers' names, and popular singers who turn their songs into commercials.

2. "Advertorial," in paragraph 4, means an advertising section in *The New Yorker* that looks like part of the magazine's regular content but is really one long commercial travelogue devised to lure tourists and business people. The neologism "advertorial" is made up of "advertisement" and "editorial," and sounds better than "ad."

3. In paragraph 7 Baldwin states her thesis: "While our forefathers and mothers rose with the sun to labor in the fields, we rise with the radio and TV, immersed every waking hour in non-stop nudges from corporate America to Just Say Yes." The entire essay supports this statements, enlarging it with specific examples from various authorities and published sources. The essay does not drift from the main point.

4. In paragraph 36 Baldwin refers to the Reagan administration's actions towards institutions that were "robbed of government support." In paragraph 37 she discusses President Bush's ballyhooed education initiative." Both "robbed" and "ballyhooed" have very negative connotations, which show Baldwin's feelings towards these presidents' treatments of institutions.

5. Baldwin's humor can be seen in her examples of ads placed in places—that is, at the bottom of golf cups and in public restrooms, the plugging of beer and cigarettes to armchair athletes; teachers rounding up students to watch Burger King ads on classroom Channel One; and Liberty Bell earrings sold at national historic sites. The "ad nauseums" are the funniest sections. The final irony of the essay is Baldwin's statement that her daughter prefers the vibrant Saturday morning ads to the insipid children's cartoons.

Delectable Materialism
Michael Schudson

Topical Considerations

1. Schudson does not find that advertising has the strong influence on our lives that Baldwin claims. In spite of the fact that advertising is pervasive in our society, Schudson says that consumers buy because they desire the convenience and pleasure conferred by products, not because of the irresistible allure of advertising. In paragraph 5 he says, "The consumer culture is sustained socially not by manufactured images but by the goods themselves as they are used." In order words, people purchase items for practical purposes (mowing the lawn and washing dishes) and sometimes for simple pleasure as in the purchase of a cashmere coat. He also disagrees with Baldwin regarding the influence TV has on children, saying that school is much more influential than TV because children are a captive audience when they attend school.

2. As stated above, he does not agree that TV influences children to the extent maintained by George Gerbner and Neil Postman in Baldwin's article. Schudson says that children have the choice of watching TV or leaving the room and of paying attention to the ads or letting their minds wander, without being caught by a teacher.

3. In paragraph 4 Schudson first agrees with then contradicts Baldwin in the parenthetical statement, "television is turned on in the average American household seven hours a day but no individual member of the family watches it for that length of time." Since Schudson gives no evidence for this statement, students may disagree with him, citing their own experiences.

4. Schudson finds nothing wrong with "wanting more," "aping the neighbors," and "seeking to be fashionable." He maintains that consuming is so pleasant that material goods do not have to be "force fed" to customers by advertisers. Students will give their own reasons for buying products.

5. Schudson claims that advertising has a Quaker quality; some ads emphasize price and, thus, "keep in mind economy as a chief criterion in buying." Advertising has a Puritan quality in that many ads stress simple function and practicality—for example, ads for detergents and other cleaning products.

6. Eastern European refugees probably want stable governments more than consumer goods. They need the basic necessities of life, beginning with an end to the ethnic wars in their countries, and continuing with food and shelter. Only when these necessities have been taken care of, will the Eastern Europeans be able to emulate the Western consumer societies.

7. Schor begins her essay by declaring that humans are not naturally acquisitive of material goods; that consumerism is "a specific product of capitalism." In paragraph 9 she contents that "advertisers had to persuade consumers to acquire things they most certainly did not need." She agrees with

Galbraith's quotation, in contrast to Schudson's denial of this liberal line. Students should be encouraged to weigh the authors' evidence before making up their own minds about the contradictory opinions.

Rhetorical Considerations

1. Throughout the article Schudson states opinions of authorities, then corrects them according to his own beliefs. He begins by contradicting contemporary social critics and calling them "confused." Then he refutes the finding of historian David Potter, stating that Potter "got it wrong 40 years ago"—that is, that advertising cannot be considered an institution of social control. Schudson also disagrees with advertising critics Galbraith, Packard, and Ewen in their belief that "people have to learn to desire more and more," because, as he says, in a materialistic society, Americans want more and more naturally. At the end of the article he agrees that advertising has some negative qualities such as its not being republican, but refutes these qualities by saying that advertising "unifies us around a belief in difference, variety, abundance, pluralism, choice, democracy." The tactic is particularly effective because Schudson contradicts the idea of well-established if not eminent authorities in the field of economics and social science.

2. In paragraph 7 all of Schudson's rhetorical questions require affirmative answers. He expects his reader to agree with him that material goods do not require force feeding, that consumerism is pleasant, that aping the neighbors or seeking to be fashionable is not unheard of, that we don't need a multi-billion-dollar enterprise to coax us into buying, that desire for possessions is not rare, and that pleasure in goods is not so unusual. The structure of this paragraph carries out the same overall structure of the entire article, that is, he contradicts statements to affirm his own argument.

3. Although Schudson quotes many authorities in this article, he only quotes them to refute their arguments. His arguments are not backed up by any evidence except his own experience and contentions. He may be guilty of several fallacies. For instance, he cites only his own son to support his argument that children are not influenced as much by television as by school. This is an example of a "hasty generalization." He also may be making an *ad populum* argument by assuming that his audience are inveterate consumers who would applaud his insights.

4. In the last paragraph of her article, Baldwin describes how her young daughter would rather watch ads on the Saturday children's programs because they are more vivid and immediate than the regular cartoons. Schudson's persona experience is watching his son go to kindergarten in paragraph 4 of his article. Their first-hand experiences help to illustrate their points, but, as mentioned above, this is Schudson's only positive example to back up his case, while Baldwin's entire article is filled with evidence to prove her case.

5. Baldwin is probably liberal, and Schudson is probably conservative. Baldwin's authorities, particularly the Center for Science in the Public Interest,

seem liberal and she agrees with them. Schudson disagrees with all of his authorities, some of whom are known liberals (David Potter and John Kenneth Galbraith).

Language of Advertising
A Word from Our Sponsor
Patricia Volk

Topical Considerations
1. As Volk illustrates, the language of advertising violates rules of grammar in, for example, its use of double negatives and its lack of parallelism. But more serious is the fact that advertising also violates "rules" of truth. Big, simple claims such as "Coke Is It" are made without question, without substantiation, without clear meaning. And that is Volk's major point, that the message of advertising has little to do with truth. Even legal protection of the truth can be gotten around, as she illustrates in the way *new* becomes *improved* after six months.
2. As Charles O'Neill says in the essay: "The Language of Advertising" one of the familiar charges against advertising is that it sells daydreams. Volk is making a similar claim. The power of the ad writer's word is "virtually limitless." *New* is a powerful buzzword and always has been, simply because it appeals to our desire to have the latest thing, to be *au courant*. What is interesting is that although O'Neill deflects the blame away from adverisers to the uncritical consumer, Volk seems to express some guilt at bending the truth.
3. Much of the effectiveness of the essay is in the cynical humor. One might even feel some of Volk's regret at being part of an industry that best succeeds where it best deceives (as in paragraph 12, where the author exclaims, "What if the world is not waiting for Mega-Bran, the cereal that tastes like Styro-foam pellets and gets a soggy in the bowl?").
4. There are only a couple of options, according to Volk, open to ad writers whose product has no unique selling point. They can "make it sing"—that is, come up with catch jingles as songs—or buy celebrity endorsement.
5. It illustrates how advertisers can create consumer anxiety—as well as the products to cure it.
6. Volk says that the talent to write great ad copy is almost genetic. One has to have an instinct to "twist and twiddle words." Her point is consistent with her initial claim that the language of advertising has no rules. And "rulelessness" can't be taught.

Rhetorical Considerations
1. She gives several good examples in the first two paragraphs: lack of parallelism, double negatives, and outright deceptions (*creme* and *virtually*).
2. She's cynical.

3. Her use of industry jargon does several things. First, it introduces us to advertising lingo—the "inside" argot that identifies the copywriting profession while it excludes nonmembers. Second, it creates some of the humorous tension in the piece, some of the cynicism, since Volk wants to distance herself from the silliness of expressions. Third, it illustrates how professional jargon serves as a kind of linguistic fig leaf—for example, making a bad product "sing" its way into the consumer's life.

4. The suggestion that Franklin Roosevelt would have made a great adman for detergent is very amusing and effective—and is also cynically consistent with her attitude throughout. As she says early on, hope is what advertising sells best. And such was the message of Roosevelt's mighty line.

With These Words I Can Sell You Anything
William Lutz

Topical Considerations

1. Most copywriters would not agree with Lutz's contention that advertisements are written to trick the customers. They would instead argue that the words used in the ads are those that most people are familiar with and respond to positively. The connotations of these words are universally understood, according to those who write the copy for the ads.

2. Like the eggs sucked dry by weasels, weasel words are hollow. They appear to contain lexical meaning and value, yet on closer inspection they say "just the opposite, or nothing at all." Advertisers use weasel words to create the illusion of making a claim for a product when, in fact, little or nothing truthful is being communicated.

3. A product is considered new for a period of six months during a national advertising campaign, and for as long as two years if a product is being advertised in a limited test market. A product is also considered new if it has undergone "a material functional change." This does not have to be an actual improvement in the product; just a simple alteration will qualify it. Thus, it is easy to side-step the regulatory intention by creating a "new" product by adding lemon scent, for instance. Product performance does not have to be improved, in other words. These regulations seem to assist efforts of advertisers to mislead the consumer. Consumers should identify exactly what is "new" before buying a product.

4. Weasel words are words without any meaning, while subjective words are words that mean different things to different people. In paragraph 33 examples of subjective words are "body," "flavor," and "taste." The author qualifies his definition of weasel words when used subjectively to mean those words of "no specific, objective meaning, because each of us can interpret them differently." These subjective words are used in advertisements such as coffee ads ("thick," "black," "bitter," "light brown," and "delicate.") Beer ads also use subjective weasel words ("lighter," "more taste," and "body").

5. For the student.

6. If a manufacturer makes up a trade name for its product, then advertises that only this particular manufacturer has the product, the technique could be considered circular reasoning. For instance, the Goodyear ad, "If it doesn't say Goodyear, it can't be polyglas," is really saying "If it doesn't say Goodyear, it can't be Goodyear's (polyglas) fiberglass-reinforced tire."

7. The entire article instructs us in ways to avoid being duped by weasel words. In his concluding remarks, Lutz summarizes his advance (the penultimate paragraph) reminding us that one's only defense against advertising is "to develop and use a strong critical reading, listening, and looking ability."

Rhetorical Considerations

1. "Parity claims," according to information found later in the essay, are claims that one product is just as good as the other products in its category; an example is aspirin. The term "doublespeak" appears in the information given in the introduction to the article, but is not defined. It comes from Orwell's book, *1984,* and is a term for language that is deliberately misleading.

2. The second person address engages readers, drawing them into the argument. Although students may have been taught that the use of "you" is taboo, in this essay the second person suits the tone, which is conversational, informal, and instructive.

3. The author uses an informal, chatty, humorous tone throughout the article. Many comments are not only informative and instructive, but quite entertaining. See the end of paragraphs 18 and 19, for example. He ends the article with a humorous update of the Twenty-third Psalm to reflect the power of advertising. He also engages the reader very directly in the process of analyzing weasel words, giving his reader instructions if not commands in order to get them involved. For instance: "Ask yourself what this claim is really saying. Remember, 'help' means only that the medicine will aid or assist" (paragraph 4).

4. Some would prefer that the essay ended at paragraph 50. The parody seems an odd and awkward tack on. First, the theme of the poem, "the power of advertising to meet our needs and solve our problems," is not directly relevant to the preceding discussion of weasel words. Why end with a poem about advertising in general when the essay deals with a very specific subject—weasel words? In straining to be funny and entertaining, Lutz made a poor choice for a conclusion.

The Language of Advertising
Charles A. O'Neill

Topical Considerations

1. Open for discussion. Many students will recall the efforts of many to have Joe Camel banned from advertising.
2. Open for discussion.
3. O'Neill says that writers "must glamorize the superficial differences" when product differences do not exist, or they must create differences by getting

the audience involved in the action in the ad, not the product itself. For discussion, consider the recent Taster's Choice instant coffee series of ads that presents a courting sequence between two neighbors who meet as strangers on an elevator then several commercials later go flying off to Paris in a still-evolving story.

4. O'Neill cites six charges that have been made against advertising. He quotes critics who think that advertising debases English; that it downgrades or underestimates the intelligence of the public; that it warps our vision of reality; that is sells us daydreams—distracting, purposeless visions of lifestyles beyond our reach; that it feeds on human weaknesses; and that it encourages unhealthy habits. In support of advertising, O'Neill's primary argument is simply that advertising language is only a reflection of the society around it, and that "slaying the messenger would not alter the fact—if it is a fact—that 'America will be the death of English.'" On the positive side, he also offers the thought that advertising is an acceptable stimulus for the natural evolution of language. Furthermore, he says that advertising does not *force* us to buy anything, but rather stimulates the development of new products in the marketplace and conveys useful information.

5. According to O'Neill, the language used in advertising has special characteristics that separate it from other languages; it is edited and purposeful, rich and arresting, calculated to involve those exposed to the advertising message, and usually simple in structure. In addition to these general characteristics, which O'Neill examines in some detail, he suggests that advertising language is different from other languages because it often carries its own special rules of grammar. For example, most of the statements in the Winston Lights ad cited in paragraph 30, are incomplete thoughts and, therefore, do not meet the requirements of a formal English sentence.

6. Proper English—that is, English that follows the rules from Strunk and White's *Elements of Style* and consists of word meanings from the gargantuan *Oxford English Dictionary*—prescribes the correct grammar, usage, and spelling. Colloquial or substandard English describes what most people, particularly college students, use in their own correspondence and in general conversation, even if they write their papers in standard English. Students will decide for themselves which usage they prefer for advertisements.

7. Any number of symbols may be suggested. O'Neill refers to the use of the color red in the depiction of autumn and fire to suggest warmth, experience, and wisdom. Other symbols could include the strong-armed man on the Mr. Clean detergent bottle, the giant of Jolly-Green fame, or BMWs. Are symbols effective? O'Neill believes they are, because with repeated exposure they acquire the power to call up in the consumer's mind a host of ideas and images that could not be communicated as effectively in any other way.

8. Even if a famous person endorses a product, he or she is not an expert in that particular field, so it does not follow that the product is especially good or even any better than the competition's product. That boxing champ Marvin Haggler has recently pushed Oscar Mayer franks doesn't make for a better hot dog, since he is not an expert on processed meats. But we might

think that if Oscar Mayer is good enough for Mr. Haggler, it's good enough for us.

Rhetorical Considerations

1. O'Neill hooks the reader's interest immediately with a kind of guessing game, teasing us with descriptions of a nameless celebrity who turns out to be Old Joe, the cartoon camel. O'Neill likening Old Joe's image to that of a rock star reveals the author's awareness of his college audience—which is also that of R. J. Reynolds. His use of Old Joe also reveals the author's attitude toward advertising—one that is neither damning nor naive. He makes the point in paragraph 4 that the clamor over Old Joe underscores America's ambivalence about advertising. The reference to the ad campaign serves as a springboard to the rest of the discussion about how advertising mirrors society's values and expectations. He does not commit himself to either side of the Joe Camel debate.

2. O'Neill's style could be described as "advertising" style. In his own writing, he makes use of some of the techniques he describes. First, he personalized his writing, involving the reader in the communication process. Several times, especially up front, he addresses the reader as *you*. To emphasize his point about the simplicity of ad language, he supports his narrative with the most effective kind of testimonial available, an invitation for the reader to conduct fog index calculations on ads. A second feature of advertising language found in O'Neill's essay is the simplicity of language. O'Neill's own language is direct and simple. In a sense, he is selling the language of advertising in his discussion, without raising his vocabulary or voice. Finally, he carefully engineers his own language as do ad writers, selecting the words. You can see this in his discussion of Joe Camel at the beginning and the very end.

3. Open for discussion.

Tapping the Youth Market
Madeline Drexler

Topical Considerations

1. Drexler argues that, despite the alcohol industry's protests to the contrary, advertisers for alcoholic beverages directly target the "youth market" (21- to 24-year-olds and 16- to 20-year-olds.) Drexler believes that even if it is difficult to prove a concrete cause-and-effect connection, there is a definite link between advertising campaigns (which make drinking look appealing to youths) and heavy drinking on the part of young people. Drexler's implicit point is that the alcohol industry is in part responsible for the consequences—often tragic—of heavy alcohol consumption by young people. She also asserts that alcohol is part of a continuum of illegal drugs, and that the public must eventually develop a greater consciousness about its harmful effects.

2. Drexler presents detailed testimony from college-aged people about the often extreme "games" played in order to enhance the effects of drinking. Most students will probably have had some experience—vicarious or otherwise—with such drinking games; all will certainly be aware of alcohol-related deaths, either from alcohol poisoning or from driving while intoxicated.

3. Discussion might begin with an attempt to define *rites of passage*: what are they, who creates/follows them, are they positive cultural phenomena, how are they culturally specific, etc. Students also might be asked to consider such rites in their own lives, including religious/familial traditions such as confirmation, bar mitzvah, or "sweet sixteen" parties, and to compare them with other, less formal or tangible moments such as first drinks, first dates, etc. Finally, discussion should attempt to understand whether or not the *motivations* for drinking by young people can be understood in such terms, or whether other explanations, such as teen stress or depression (offered by Drexler in paragraph 19), are more plausible.

4. Instructors might focus discussion by asking students to consider passages in Drexler's essay describing specific ad campaigns (paragraphs 17, 20–23, and 27–30). Are these campaigns influential? Are they exploitative? This discussion will provide preliminary work for Writing Assignment 2.

5. Given O'Neill's position as a defender of advertising techniques and language, clearly he would be in disagreement with Drexler's implication that advertisers who target the youth market are unethical. In paragraph 38, O'Neill states that "advertising attempts to convince us to buy products; we are not forced to buy something because it is heavily advertised." O'Neill advocates consumer responsibility for consumer habits; that is, individuals are to be held accountable, responsible for their own choices and behaviors in spite of the influence of advertising. O'Neill also claims that advertising is a mirror (paragraph 41), and that negative responses to it are responses to what we don't like in ourselves, as opposed to pernicious messages sent by advertisers. There is much to be debated in these two claims: in the first, O'Neill's claim does not take into account the role of visual/verbal images and messages in shaping opinions and behaviors; in the second, he does not begin to deal with the issue of who is looking at whom in this advertising "mirror." Do ad images really accurately reflect the "truth" of society? Or do they help to shape it?

6. One way to approach this discussion would be to consider recent governmental regulation of the tobacco industry for the purpose of keeping young people from being a targeted market for cigarette sales. Students might consider the fine line between such regulations and censorship, as well as the fact that the tobacco industry is suing the federal government for violating their right to free speech. Should advertising be protected by the First Amendment?

7. Generation X images might be compared with other, earlier manifestations of the "lost youth" phenomenon; in particular, the "flower children" of the 1960s. However, the term *generation X* carries a connotation specific to the 1990s; that

is, alienation from a rabidly consumer, high-tech culture. Studnets might take apart the term *vidiot*. What is the relationship between generation X'rs and the growth of video as a form of entertainment? Criticism of video as an "art" form often focuses on the flashy, disjointed nature of its images, and the fact that kids who grow up on MTV, for instance, never cultivate a mature attention span— or the ability to think critically. Why are generation X'ers described as "passive aggressive?" Students might unpack some 1990s cultural events that could lead to a "lack of faith in the system": culture wars, the discrepancy between rich and poor in the United States,a problems with drugs and violence, etc.

8. This discussion might be placed in the historical context of the failure of 1920s prohibition—could alcohol ever effectively be made illegal, and is that a desirable goal? Strong arguments have been made for the legalization of all drugs, in the hopes that legalization will enable regulation of drug traffic in addition to deflating the economic profits of black market drug trade. Students might be asked to consider how much "consciousness" about alcohol might be developed, a point that Drexler does not elaborate.

Rhetorical Considerations

1. Drexler begins her piece by describing a scene, telling a story. This descriptive rhetoric continues until paragraph 3, when Drexler states her thesis: first that heavy drinking continues to play a large role in college life, and second, that the alcohol industry is preying on this market as a means of bolstering its "declining sales." Drexler uses this strategy later in the piece when she again paints a descriptive portrait of college drinking life (paragraphs 13 and 14), followed by deductive arguments connecting such portraits with facts about alcohol industry advertising campaigns. This is an effective technique, especially in the introductory paragraphs, in that it provides an engaging "window" through which readers may enter the piece—the scene we see through that window leads directly into her statements regarding drinking and the youth market.

2. Clearly Drexler's intended audience is "adults," and, more specifically, adults who are raising children or teens. This essay is *not* directed toward its subject, the "youth market." The most obvious signal that this essay is directed toward an adult/parent population is the way in which it talks *about* 16- to 24-year-old people, rather than *to* them (consider paragraphs 24–25, which describe young people as "vidiots," also consider Drexler's use of quotations from young people themselves about their drinking habits—these quotes simply provide information about *how* young people consume alcohol, information that young people themselves would not need to read about in an essay). The only problem with Drexler's strategies of targeting her audience is that she does not, ultimately, provide any concrete suggestions/solutions to coping with the onslaught of alcohol ads targeting kids, which might leave even her intended audience dissatisfied.

3. Throughout her essay Drexler presents facts about excessive alcohol consumption by young people and alcohol industry ads promoting excessive

drinking habits; however, she also continuously makes concessions to the "other side." These moments include paragraphs 7, 8, 19, and 22–32, wherein Drexler herself concedes the difficulty in establishing a connection between particular advertisements and increased alcohol consumption by the youth market. Indeed, the quotes she provides from the opposition (usually alcohol industry spokespeople) are often quite persuasive—of the opposing viewpoint to her own. One might argue that presenting "both sides" of the issue in such a fair way is an effective technique; hwoever, Drexler neither refutes the opposition quotes she uses strongly enough nor provides a solid enough argument against or solution to teenage drinking to offset the concessions she makes. In the end, it seems that the reader is left wondering if there is indeed any real connection between teenage drinking and alcohol industry marketing techniques.

4. Drexler cites a great many "authorities" on both sides of the issue. Her evidence falls into four categories: quotations from experts both within and without the alcohol industry; the results of professional studies and surveys conducted on the subject of alcohol consumption and advertising; quotations from college-age drinkers themselves; and descriptions of drinking scenarios and alcohol ad campaigns. One criticism might be that Drexler includes too many quotations from the opposition, which weakens her argument. Another might be that the force of her argument is diluted by the large amounts of (often contradictory) evidence and statistics presented. However, a reader looking less for a persuasive argument and more for an "unbiased" presentation of facts for consideration would feel that Drexler had provided a complete picture of the issue to contemplate.

5. This last question should help students to combine their feelings about the appropriateness of the material for the intended audience of the essay, Drexler's use of sources and evidence, and the overall tone and mood of the piece. It should also help lead them into the Writing Assignments.

Oppositions: Sex in Advertising

Sex in Advertising
Ed McCabe

Topical Considerations

1. McCabe says that the women in the service station ads "beckoned, ripe with the promise of much more than an oil additive . . ." One ad featured a "Jane Russell look-alike who had huge bosoms and wore a tight-fitting sweater, both hands wrapped suggestively around a shock absorber." Another ad for welding rods showed a girl in a low-cut bathing suit, exposing her cleavage, with the caption, "A good technique and the right rod for the job." Current advertising has become much more explicit and says McCabe, "the sexual themes are more pervasive than ever." Even though advertising today has to

compete with sex channels on cable TV and restrictions from the FCC, up-scale magazine advertising is "inundated with innuendo," from such taboos as a *ménage à trois,* sadomasochism, pairing of older men and young girls, extramarital sex, and "every area of sexual pleasure and perversion." A good example are the Calvin Klein ads for Obsession cologne.

2. His descriptions of "big-boobed babes" in paragraph 28 he says may strike some as sexist. Yet he might also be mocking the practice of using flesh to sell machine tools. Those who do so regress to boorish and stupid behavior. He seems to want to come across as liberated yet not desexualized.

3. McCabe compares the explicit sexual content of New York's Channel 35 with advertising that is comparatively restrained. He differentiates between sex that is being advertised and sex in advertising. His description of the prostitutes and the varieties of sex and sexual equipment offered on Channel 35 contrast vividly with the FCC's ruling that soap or shampoo commercials cannot show an undressed man or woman in a shower and newspaper ads that are restricted from showing more than an inch of cleavage or a belly button.

4. European and English advertising allows the "public to see nudity in all its logical glory" and Scandinavia even runs condom ads featuring an animated penis. But the ads in the United States, which leave something to the imagination, are more sexy than the more permissive English, just because they don't show everything.

5. Obsession perfume shows *menage a trois* and also group nudity ads. Calvin Klein jeans, and Guess clothing ads feature tough-looking men somewhat sadomasochistic looking in their beatup trucks or standing beside mean-looking motorcycles. Very young girls (in their early teens) with much older men (with distinguished-looking grey hair) adorn many Ralph Lauren ads. Their relationship is usually ambiguous. Various liquor ads, for examples Johnnie Walker ads in which the model says, "My new number is 259–0370," could be said to promote extramarital sex.

6. Advertisers who research every aspect of their ads certainly are aware of the power of phallic symbols and, therefore, include them consciously. McCabe refers to Old Joe Camel in the cigarette ads and the new Pepsi logo as possible examples of these symbols. Many designs of men's toiletries are phallic or come in phallic containers. Some critics would even include cars and guns, especially those assuming suggestive positions.

Rhetorical Considerations

1. McCabe begins his articles by describing the thrills he got from "pink, old, and sweeter ethyl" and the "sound and feel of the pneumatic grease gun with its whooshes and pops as I snapped it from one silvery nipple to another . . ." These sexual charged images lead into the content of his article, as do his descriptions of the girly pinup ads.

2. He doesn't discuss current American advertising until paragraph 20, well beyond halfway into his argument. Up to this point he has discussed sex

that sells products, TV programs that sell sex, European uncensored commercials, and what happens when sex is inhibited. The last sentence of the article might serve as his claim—a conclusion he inductively builds up to throughout.

3. Paragraph 19 ends with an incomplete sentence. "A rule book that, like all rule books, is hopelessly behind the times." Some of the slang words are "a-knockin'" in paragraph 10, "yuck" in paragraph 23, "guys' units" in paragraph 25, and "pussy" in paragraph 28. These lapses in standard English fit the tone of the entire piece, which reflects the editorial policies of *Playboy* magazine. They also reflect the persona McCabe is trying to project—a with-it adman who knows the business and who can "talk straight."

4. (See answer above.) In addition to occasionally colloquial style, *Playboy* also is famous for the sexual nature of its articles and ads. McCabe could not have placed this article in a family periodical.

5. McCabe sets himself up as an authority on ethics as well as on sex in advertising. All of McCabe's supporting evidence are either first-hand experiences or examples from advertising. He does not quote any authorities (except himself) on sex in advertising.

6. The anticipated criticism of sex in advertising does not appear until paragraph 28, and continues only through the next paragraph. Out of 30 paragraphs, McCabe devotes only these two where he discusses why "in too many instances, it's just a lazy copout." One can assume that in his heart of hearts, McCabe approves of the use of sex in advertising. He says, "Trying [to market a product that is not inherently sexy] is nothing more than gratuitous tastelessness."

Sex is Still Doing the Selling
John Carroll

Topical Considerations
1. In contrast to McCabe, who sees little wrong with sex in advertising, Carroll strongly criticizes gratitutious usage (in ads "from perfume to power tools"). Carroll says that in the wake of the 1991 Hill/Thomas Senate hearings and the 1992 Tailhook scandal, people both inside and outside the advertising industry are reassessing how women are portrayed in ads. Yet he doubts that any change will be forthcoming.

2. Carroll portrays *Playboy* as a mildly titillating publication with his humorous descriptions of the magazine's "Velveeta brand of airbrushed sexuality" and "processed cheesecake." He also refers to a recent article, "the encyclopedia salesman's dream," which features naked housewives going about their daily routines.

3. Carroll's statement is similar to McCabe's comment in paragraph 22 of McCabe's article, which compares American advertising with more forthright English advertising, which "doesn't come across nearly as sexy as our advertising, which is much less explicit." Carroll refers to the QuadCache software ad which was not published in its entirety in *MacWeek*. The magazine

eliminated entirely the photo of a provocatively dressed girl and part of the offending caption.

4. Although Carroll does not specify his choices, the reader understands that Carroll chooses good taste over a clever headline and basic decency over increased sales. He also infers that McCabe makes the opposite choices. The two women in advertising referred to in the article, Ms. Mooney and Ms. Keys, have the same values as McCabe, while other advertisers "have atoned for ads that offend women by employing reverse sexism and showing men as 'himbos.'" You can deduce that Carroll feels his ethical claims separate him from other advertisers' crassness.

Rhetorical Considerations

1. The only authority McCabe refers to is himself. Carroll, on the other hand, quotes two women in advertising. Jean Kilbourne, whom Carroll identifies as a visiting scholar at Wellesley College and a media critic, appears in a documentary film, "Still Killing Us Softly," denouncing ads and by extension the advertising industry. She criticizes the industry for promoting the idea in its ads that "a woman's body is just another piece of merchandise." Carroll also cites a *Wall Street Journal* quotation from a New York ad agency's ludicrous seminar poster showing a naked woman from a Calvin Klein Obsession ad. Carroll strengthens his argument with solid evidence and examples, as well as statements from authorities and well-known publications.

2. Carroll uses "Velveeta brand air-brushed sexuality" and processed cheesecake" to describe the editorial slant of *Playboy* magazine, which is not as crude or heavy handed as the sexuality of such publications as *Hustler* or *Penthouse*. Velveeta cheese is processed yellow cheese, not sharp or flavorful, but bland, soft and easy to digest. Processed cheesecake (pinup photos of naked or seminaked women) contrasts with regular cheesecake, as *Playboy's* airbrushed nudes contrast with those in the other publications mentioned above.

   "Unzipped flyboy" describes Ed McCabe and others who "create sexual stereotypes of women in advertising. "The condition of their undress could refer to their readiness for sexual adventure, an allusion to Erica Jong's famous phrase.

   "Himbos" is a word play on the term "bimbo" used to describe a dumb blonde woman, especially a comparison of a famous politician or other celebrity. A "double-ditz" couple consists of a bimbo and a himbo.

3. The analogy compares the world of advertising to a battlefield where the advertisers are combatants who attempt to capture the consumer's attention by using various weapons. The nuclear bomb of sex is the ultimate weapon. Using sex to sell products in this advertising war wins. But Carroll does not go along with this view and spends the rest of the article telling why he disagrees, even though he realizes that the chances of changing the way advertising uses women are "slimmer than a high-fashion model."

4. Both McCabe and Carroll use humorous, satiric tones in their articles. However, Carroll is on the attack and, therefore, is more serious in his annoyance. McCabe, on the other hand, is more personal in his style—for example, his slang, interjections, and exclamations such as "I wish they'd come off it" and "Sexual excretions in your Scotch? Yuck!" both articles are lively and engaging.

16

Arguments That Shaped History

The Allegory of the Cave
Plato

Topical Considerations

1. Open for discussion; however, many students may feel that with the rise of science and technology in the past two centuries, "truth" accompanies such empirical data as scientific proofs, experiments and numbers. It might be helpful here to talk about how perspective still affects many ideas of truth; that is, different people at the same crime or accident scene are likely to have very different ideas of the facts.

2. The underground den represents the environment of people in their still unenlightened state, before they have perceived the light of truth; the light represents the ideal truth itself; the chains are representative of the forces that keep people from reaching that ideal; the fire is the light of sun, which presides over the world of truth; and the shadows represent the distorted reflections of perceptions of truth received by the people in the cave.

3. This too is open for discussion; however, if the ideal good is what is true and it has been determined that truth may change with perception, then it does not necessarily follow that what is most good is that which is most rational. It would be interesting here to discuss concepts of rationality and reasonability; most likely they will be as difficult to define as truth itself, giving students a sense of the importance of perspective and experience, and of the difficulty of imposing fixed meaning upon abstract concepts.

4. For Plato, ideal images are largely out of the reach of society, making social "reality" more comparable to his allegorical shadows than his allegorical sun. In other words, he criticizes society for being so often blind to real truths. Students might discuss Plato's criticism of Socrates' death in this context.

5. The irony that Plato illustrates here is that, in its brilliance, the truth (while in every way superior and more desirable than the shadows of the cave) will temporarily blind one who has looked upon it. Therefore, if someone competes with others engaged in measuring the shadows, he or she would appear handicapped, weakened, incapable, thereby providing evidence that the source of the brilliance was dangerous. Thus, as those unenlightened would perceive the ideal truth as undesirable, their darkness would be perpetuated.

Rhetorical Considerations

1. The conversational (or dialogic) mode used by Plato develops his argument while appearing to allow Glaucon to arrive at his own conclusions. Glaucon's role, however, is simply to provide pointed questions or statements that will expedite Plato's argument. Some students may feel that this form is ineffective in that Glaucon's role seems largely predetermined and therefore unconvincing.

2. Plato's argument works without "evidence" in the modern sense of the word for two reasons: it is a philosophical argument and, therefore, needs logic, rather than "facts" or "proofs" to be convincing. Also, it is an allegory and, therefore, relies on the symbolic power of its terms to carry its meaning and ensure its effectiveness.

3. The ideal truth is found in ideal images. People in the cave see ideal images only in the form of shadows on the wall. Therefore, people in the cave perceive the ideal truth as shadows on the wall. (If truth = images, and images = shadow, then truth = shadow).

A Modest Proposal
Jonathan Swift

Topical Considerations

1. The persona's harsh descriptions of the Irish beggars at the beginning of the essay might signal to some that Swift is setting up the reader for drastic solutions to the problem. However, now until paragraph 4 does Swift give us evidence that he's up to something—"a child just dropped from its dam . . ." Also in paragraph 6 his reference to "breeders" should alert readers to be on guard. Most students, however, are not convinced of the monstrosity of Swift's proposal until paragraph 9 when the cooking methods are discussed. By paragraph 17 even the most obtuse reader should be suspicious of Swift's intentions: ". . . it is not probable that some scrupulous people might be apt to censure such a practice . . . [eating the flesh of young lads and maidens] as a little bordering upon cruelty; which, I confess, hath always been with me the strongest objection against any project, how wellsoever intended." Swift's irony peaks in paragraph 29: "I can think of no one objection that will possibly be raised against this proposal, unless it should be urged that the number will be thereby much lessened in the kingdom. This I freely own, and it was indeed one principal design in offering it to the world."

2. The speaker is a serious, self-effacing, conscientious citizen, one who is educated in the art of argumentation. He is married and has children. His sole intention is to alleviate the suffering of the poor Irish Catholic, brought on by absentee English landlords, rather than to gain anything for himself. Swift was an Anglo-Irishman, born and raised in Ireland, but who spent many years in England in literary pursuits before he returned to become Dean of St. Patrick's Cathedral in Dublin. His satirical writings, especially *Tale of a Tub,* did not endear him to the English nobility or government. He was never married, nor did he have any children. Swift's real message comes through in paragraph 12 when he states, "I grant this food will be somewhat dear, and therefore very proper for landlords, who, as they have already devoured most of the parents, seem to have the best title to the children."

3. None of Swift's authorities are named or credible. The first three are: a "principal gentleman in the county of Cavan," who informed the speaker

about young thieves; "a very knowing American," who gave the speaker ways to cook the babies; and "a very worthy person, a true lover of his country, and whose virtues I highly esteem," who suggested adolescents were too tough for the table. The "famous Psalmanazar" who told the speaker about executionary practices in Formosa, was a literary fake. The "grave author, an eminent French physician," who instructed the speaker about the attributes of a fish diet, was Rabelais, the famous satirist who wrote *Gargantua*.

4. In this paragraph Swift is referring to England. During the reign of Henry VIII, England seized Irish land formerly owned by the Catholic church and gave it to upper-class Englishmen. Their descendents, in many cases, were absentee landlords who owned the land the Irish peasants farmed. These landlords gouged their tenants, making them pay high rents for their small holdings, while ignoring them in time of famine. Swift refers to these English landlords who would be glad "to eat up our whole country."

5. In paragraph 29 beginning with the phrase "Therefore let no man talk to me of other expedients . . ." and continuing to the end of the paragraph, Swift lists the real solutions to the problems that the Irish themselves as well as the English must undertake to solve the problems of the poor. These solutions, particularly the expedient of "taxing the absentees at five shillings a pound," would have given Ireland income instead of draining it of resources and keeping it the poor country it is today. "Teaching landlords to have at least one degree of mercy toward their tenants," might have avoided some of the terrible deprivations of the potato famine and the burning hatred the Irish still feel toward the English today.

6. The relationship between Ireland and England, specifically Northern Ireland, is as bad, if not worse, than when Swift wrote this article. The killings and bombings by the IRA have destroyed targets in London, as well as areas around Belfast and the border between Northern Ireland and the Irish Free State.

Rhetorical Considerations

1. The first animal image is the "child just dropped from its dam" in paragraph 4, which sets the tone for the rest of the references. The terms, "dropped" and "dam," are usually reserved for breeding animals; also referring to the child as "it" removes its humanity. Since his proposition is to use infants as food, he must desensitize his readers and he does this by referring to infants and their mothers in animal terms. Other animal images include "breeders" in paragraph 6, the discussion of the one male serving four females in paragraph 10, and the comparison of the treatment of pregnant wives with pregnant mares, cows, or sows in paragraph 26.

2. Swift structures his argument by first introducing his subject, in paragraphs 1–8, then offering his proposal in paragraphs 9 and 10. He gives his calculations of the numbers of children available for sale in paragraph 10, the weight of the chid ready for table in paragraph 11, when the meat will be most available in paragraph 13, and the benefits to the landlord and mother

in paragraph 14, as well as suggestions for the use of the skin in paragraph 15, and methods and places of butchering in paragraph 16. After a few paragraphs of diversion, the writer continues with facts supporting the moral and financial benefits of his proposal (paragraphs 21–28).

Swift put forth the real solutions in paragraph 29, "let no man talk to me of other expedients . . . ," but immediately refutes them in paragraph 30 with these words: "Therefore I reepeat, let no man talk to me of these and the like expedients, till he hath at least some glimpse of hope that there will ever be some hearty and sincere attempt to put them in practice." In paragraph 32 he also refers to other possible solutions, "After all, I am not so violently bent upon my own opinion as to reject any offer proposed by wise men, which shall be found equally innocent, cheap, easy, and effectual."

3. Swift's irony begins with the title, when he calls his horrible suggestion of killing babies and selling them for food, "modest." Throughout the essay Swift's irony overwhelms the reader, especially when he refers to the practice of raising young lads and maidens for food: "It is not improbable that some scrupulous people might be apt to censure such a practice (although indeed very unjustly).. . . " In paragraph 19 he replies to "some persons of a desponding spirit" who worry about "poor people who are aged, diseased, or maimed." "I am not in the least pain upon that matter, because it is very well known that they are every day dying and rotting by cold and famine, and filth and vermin, as fast can be reasonably expected." The final paragraph, a masterprice of irony, states the speaker's moral and patriotic reasons for making this proposal.

4. Swift may not have trusted his audience to understand the real expedients which he mock-negates. Thus, the italics. He states, "Let no man talk to me of other expedients"; yet, it is in this paragraph alone that he offfrs real proposals that could save Ireland: taxing absentee landlords, using clothes and furniture manufactured in Ireland, rejecting luxurious goods, curing women of various vices, introducing frugality, learning to love their country, stopping factionalism, not selling "country and conscience for nothing," teaching landlords to have a little mercy towards tenants, and "putting a spirit of honesty, industry, and skill into our shopkeepers."

5. Swift's speaker includes so many statistics in order to convince his reader of the workability of his plan. It also reflects the proper and classical structure of an argument. Since this is an ironic proposal not an actual one, Swift could have made up the numbers.

6. The reader must decode Swift's real intention behind the irony and satire. Swift's unstated principal purpose is to alert the world to the terrible situation in Ireland where the poor are dying of starvation and deprivation, due in great measure to the English landlords' cruelty and avariciousness. The chilled rationalistic persona satirizes British indifference toward Ireland's plight. The irony throughout resides in contradition between the cold tone and the meaning of the words. For instance, the speaker's matter-of-fact calculations of the number of infants to be offered for sale; his suggestion that the sale be nine months after Lent; his estimation of mothers' profits from the sale of her

child; his discussion of using adolescent children in place of game for the table; and, climactically, his claim that "the advantages by the proposal which I have made are obvious and many, as well as of the highest importance."

The speaker describes himself in the final paragraph, "I profess, in the sincerity of my heart, that I have not the least personal interest in endeavoring to promote this necessary work, having no other motive than the public good of my country . . . [since] I have not children by which I can propose to get a single penny; the youngest being nine years old, and my wife past childbearing." He is a "good" man who has "been wearied out for many years with offering vain, idle, visionary thoughts, and at length utterly despairing of success . . . fortunately fell upon this proposal, which . . . hath something solid and real, of no expense and little trouble, full in our own power, and whereby we can incur no danger in disobliging England." The ultimate irony is that this decent man should make such a monstrous suggestion and believe it is good. Ultimately it is this caricature that is most damning of the English soul.

The Declaration of Independence
Thomas Jefferson

Topical Considerations

1. The Declaration was intended to present the reasons and evidence for the thirteen colonies to unanimously declare their independence from Great Britain. The opening paragraph is an explanation of why a formal declaration is being made. With "a decent respect to the opinions of mankind" and while working within "the Laws of Nature and of Nature's God," Jefferson proclaims in so many words that when one body of people finds it necessary to sever its political ties to another body of people, it is expected that they explain their reasons. While this introduction presents the philosophical framework, the actual argument and support begin in the second. The whole of Jefferson's argument was based upon the belief that "all men were created equal" and that they had "certain unalienable Rights" including "Life, Liberty, and the pursuit of Happiness." Guided by these principles, he constructed his argument on rigid syllogistic logic, presenting in 26 paragraphs (3–28) specific evidence of human rights grievances against the British King and British rule.

2. By "the Laws of Nature and of Nature's God," Jefferson says that he is arguing from a rationalistic world view common among educated people of his time. In other words, it will be a rationalistic argument ("Laws of Nature") based on moral principles ("Nature's God").

3. Given the political turmoil in parts of Africa and states of the former Soviet Union and the former Yugoslavia, one might seen any of the Declaration's principles justifiable for revolution today.

4. Jefferson's political philosophy regarding human rights and the role of government was essentially derived from British philosopher John Locke, who a

century earlier justified the "Glorious Revolution", which removed James II from the throne and established William and Mary—a revolution that ironically made possible the enthronement of George III during the American Revolution. According to this Lockean view, government exists to serve and protect those governed, and that when that government fails in those duties, all rights return to the people. In the syllogistic reasoning of the Declaration's argument, this is the minor premise—that is, that the British government failed to serve and protect the citizens of the American colonies.

5. Today the falsely generic "men" and "mankind" for all people is considered outright sexist in its exclusion of one half of the human race—females. However, the eighteenth century men who championed human freedom and civil liberties were not just subsuming all people; in reality they were not seriously concerned with the opinions of women regarding political governance. In short, they were concerned with the rights of men, not women. Sexist exclusion of women is intrinsic to history—America's and most of the world's. Yes, the framers of the Declaration might be considered male chauvinists. They also owned slaves and were, thus, racists. However, it would be dubious to condemn them from enlightened attitudes of the present time. While we may not want to let them off the hook, we should accept the fact that they were working from a tradition still only half-liberated.

6. Open for discussion.

Rhetorical Considerations

1. The major premise is stated in the third sentence of paragraph 2: "that whenever any Form of Government becomes destructive of these ends it is the Right of the People to alter or to abolish it, and to institute new Government, laying its foundation on such principles and organizing its powers in such form, as to them shall seem most likely to effect their Safetry and Happiness." In a deductive argument, the support for the premises may differ depending on the audience being addressed. The audience of the Declaration of Independence was primarily the populace of the colonies for whom Jefferson's major premise was "self-evident." However, Jefferson also had to convince reluctant loyalist statesmen, lawyers, British ministers, and the British King himself that this revolutionary abrogation was moral, legal, and justifiable in terms of the political philosophy of the day. Without the support of important colonial citizens and other countries, especially France, the revolution would risk failure. Thus, the Declaration had to make the strongest legal case in the most logical form.

   Because the minor premise is anything but self-evident, Jefferson offers 26 paragraphs of support. With so much evidence weighed against the minor premise, the conclusion naturally follows. Essentially, the whole of the argument can be reduced to the following pattern of logic:

   Major premise: Whenever any form of government becomes destructive of the basic human rights they were meant to secure, then the people have the right to abolish that government and institute a new one.

Minor premise: The British government has a long history of destroying human rights they were meant to secure in the colonies.

Conclusion: Therefore, the people of the colonies have the right to declare themseves free and independent of the government imposed on them by the British Crown.

While readers today might not find that sufficient enough evidence, the colonists apparently did.

2. Any good argument should anticipate possible objections. The Declaration is no different. Following the long list of Crown abuses, Jefferson raises two potential counterpoints. In paragraph 30 he makes clear that the colonists did not let their grievances go unheard; on the contrary, he says that for each of the "Oppressions" the colonists had petitioned for rightful compensation ("Redress") only to be "answered . . . by repeated injury." In paragraph 31, Jefferson then addresses the possible objection that the colonists were rebelling not just against the Kind of England but also the English people. "Nor have we been wanting in attention to our British brethren," declares Jefferson. And in defense he explains how they had "warned," "reminded," "appealed to" the British people who also played "deaf to the voice of justice and of consanguinity." The conclusion is, thus, inevitable: that colonies are left with no other recourse than to declare their independence from England.

3. Open for discussion.

4. The opening two paragraphs might be addressed to the world of reasonable people. Here Jefferson is his most abstract and philosophical. Here he sets forth the guiding moral and legal principles. Justifying a revolution meant convincing a good number of colonial lawyers, bankers, merchants, and farmers who had prospered under British rule and who would risk the greatest loss should the revolution fail. Therefore, the second paragraph also sets up not just a moral right but a legal right of the people to "throw off such a government" that fails in its duty to protect and serve the governed. In particular this paragraph is aimed at those highly influential colonialists who may not have entertained the abrogation of British rule. The specific charges that make up the body of the document have particular appeal to the colonial citizens who would be most familiar with the offenses. Paragraph 28 seems to be addressed to British citizenry who may not be aware of the ongoing conflicts the colonies had with native Americans ("merciless Indian Savages"). Paragraph 29 seems to be directed at the King himself. Paragraph 30 refers by name to "our British brethren." And, yet, this paragraph might also be an appeal to France and other countries for arms and other aid.

5. There are several examples of parallel structure. In paragraph 2: ". . . that all men are created equal, that they are endowed . . . , that among these are life, liberty, and the pursuit of happiness." Paragraphs 3–14 each begins with "He has . . ." past participle + predicate (offensive act); likewise 15–23 each begins with "For" + present participle (offensive act); 24–28 (with the ex-

ception of paragraph 26) each begins with "He has" + past participle (offensive act) + direct object. Paragraph 30 uses the construction "We have . . ." four consecutive times. The final paragraph includes four consecutive "that" + noun + to-be verb phrases culminating in the final pledge. In terms of structure, it is a masterpiece of unity, coherence, and persuasion.

6. Jefferson wanted to make the strongest possible case to the widest audience. Therefore, he strove to create a tone of reasonableness. He succeeded since the Declaration is formal without being overly intricate, bombastic, or verbose. The style is direct, open, and logical. The enumerated emotional appeals are well controlled, projecting the colonists as a reasonable citizenry unjustly wronged by the crown.

Civil Disobedience
Henry David Thoreau

Topical Considerations

1. Open for discussion.
2. For Thoreau, ethical acts turn on the idea of conscience. For him, a "majority" does not have a conscience and, thus, does not do what is right or necessarily moral. An individual, on the other hand, should be guided by his or her conscience (see paragraphs 4, 5, 11, and 20). Individuals have the power to act according to their consciences through nonviolent protest and civil disobedience.
3. Discussion of this question might focus on theories of government evident in the current party system—that is, Republican laissez-faire philosophies versus Democratic involvement policies. Some students may feel that a government that governs "not at all" could only mean chaos and anarchy.
4. Thoreau uses this verse to indicate the appropriateness of the economic aspect of his protest. His argument is that the government continues such unethical practices as slavery and the Mexican war for economic reasons, thereby making the state a sort of "prostitute." Thus, his protest of refusing to aid and abet the state economically is logical. Open for discussion.
5. In paragraph 11, Thoreau states that "All voting is a sort of gaming, like checkers or backgammon"—in other words, when an individual votes, he or she still leaves to chance the outcome of the majority's decision. This leads the reader back to Thoreau's argument that the majority is without conscience, and only an individual acting with conscience can enact change.
6. King sees no other option than transgressing unjust laws, while Thoreau sees the possibility of working to amend them. In both cases, the means of transgression is civil disobedience, always nonviolent. Open for discussion.
7. This passage indicates that for Thoreau there is no inalienable "truth"; rather, truth varies depending on how you look at it. Seen from the perspective of "high" moral ideals, Thoreau believes that the Constitution is not

"worth thinking about at all." Students might compare this idea of truth with Plato's parable of the Cave.

8. For Thoreau, the civil protester, the only true freedom is in the prison; for this is where the individual enjoys freedom from moral complicity in actions that he or she protests. Thoreau also emphasizes that the state can only lock up the body, never the senses, intellect, or morals.

Rhetorical Considerations

1. In paragraph 5, Thoreau refers to soldiers or members of the standing army as "wooden men" who can command no more respect than "men of straw or a lump of dirt." In paragraph 10, he describes the mass of men who are opposed to slavery but who hypocritically do nothing about it. Such statements probably offended some readers so implicated, thereby weakning the persuasiveness of the argument for them. However, Thoreau's main appeal is to courageous individuals not afraid to stand up for what they believe. As such, he leads by example.

2. Thoreau's account of his one day in prison serves to illustrate the ineffectiveness of imprisonment as a means of punishment of those who are civil protesters. He emerges triumphant and more free, perhaps, than when he first entered.

3. Paragraph 10 provides an example of a moral argument, discussing as it does the concept of real virtue and honesty. Paragraphs 16–18 provide logical arguments around the idea of unjust laws. The lengthy exposition of the night in prison provides examples of emotional arguments regarding the treatment of prisoners. Open for discussion.

Declaration of Sentiments and Resolutions
Elizabeth Cady Stanton

Topical Considerations

1. Stanton modeled her declaration after the historical Declaration of Independence because she wanted to give her own work the prestige of the universally-admired American document of freedom from tyranny. She felt that the oppression of women was equal to the oppression of the American colonies by King George III of Great Britain. Although her strategy of imitating the famous document aroused anger and scorn among her contemporaries, modern day feminists praise this document, which began the fight for women's independence. Many of the statements of injustice and the resolutions are still valid.

2. The purpose of the "Declaration of Independence" was to offer reasons for "one people to dissolve the political bands which have connected them with another, and to assume among the powers of the earth, the separate and equal stations to which the Laws of Nature and of Nature's God entitle them. . . ." Stanton's declaration states, not "one people," but "one portion of the family of man to assume among the people of the earth a position dif-

ferent from that which they have hitherto occupied, but one to which the laws of nature and of nature's God entitle them. . . ."

Stanton is referring to the inferior position of women, while the founding fathers of the United States were referring to the rights of the citizens of the American colonies. Since women had no vote during the colonial era, they were simply not recognized as citizens. However, Abigail Adams, wife of John Adams, admonished her husband to "Remember the ladies" in the writing of the Declaration. But, as patriarchial tradition would have it, he and the rest of the Continental Congress forgot the women as they intentionally left out blacks because of the prodding of Southern delegations.

3. "She receives but a scanty remuneration." "He closes against her all the avenue to wealth and distinction which he considers most honorable to himself" (paragraph 13). At present women still do not make the same salaries as men. The most powerful and best paid positions are still held by men, who are usually white and middle-aged.

"He allows her in Church, as well as State, but a subordinate position, claiming apostolic authority. . . ." (paragraph 15). It is still true that some religions, most notably the Catholic church, referring to the Bible's authority, do not allow women to become priests, bishops, or take other high positions. The United States governing bodies, including the Senate and the House of Representatives, currently contain very few women.

"He has created a false public sentiment by giving to the world a different code of morals for men and women. . . ." (paragraph 16). There is still a double standard of conduct for men and women. Students can cite several contexts, especially sexual behavior. A woman known to have more than one sexual partner is condemned. Such a man would be praised for his conquests. Also, in English there are no male equivalents to *slut, whore,* or *strumpet.*

4. The women of the Seneca Falls Convention who endorsed this declaration pledged to "employ agents, circulate tracts, petition the State and National legislature, and endeavor to enlist the pulpit and press in our behalf." However, in spite of their zeal, or perhaps because of it, American women had to wait until the passage of the 19th Amendment in 1920 to win the vote. As was stated in answer 3, many other inequalities still remain.

5. This "great precept of nature" means that "man shall pursue his own true and substantial happiness." Of course, Stanton also includes women's happiness in this precept and uses it as a foundation for all of the resolutions that follow, since women have the same right to "true and substantial happiness" as men. Stanton states in paragraph 22 any laws that "conflict in any way, with the true and substantial happiness of woman, are contrary to the great precept of nature and of no validity, for this is "superior in obligation to any other [laws]." In paragraph 29 she refers to a "perverted application of the Scriptures," presumably those that state that the apostolic succession is limited to men. Her evidence of God's word, evidently, does not include those parts of the Bible she disagrees with.

6. Stanton urges women to "promote every righteous cause by every righteous means; especially ... morals and religion. ..." She equates the rights of women to participate in this teaching with men because it is "a self-evident truth growing out of the divinely implanted principles of human nature." In other words, Stanton uses evidence for this resolution based on God's laws, similar to the "great precept of nature" in paragraph 21.

7. Women still do not have access to the pulpit in many churches of various conservative Protestant sects and in the Catholic church. Women have not been able to break through the "glass ceiling," which is the monopoly men hold in many higher executive positions in the "various trades, professions, and commerce," as well as state and national government.

8. In paragraph 2 Stanton declares that "all men and women are created equal." In paragraph 24 she says, "woman is man's equal—[she] was intended to be so by the Creator. ..." In paragraph 26 she adds that man claims himself to be superior in intellect and gives woman moral superiority, but she does not mention that women agree with this ranking. In paragraph 27 she equates this need for "virtue, delicacy, and refinement of behavior" for both sexes. Nowhere in this declaration does Stanton state that women are superior to men.

9. The "elective franchise" is the vote, which American women were denied until 1920. By "civilly dead" Stanton means that married women have no rights of property or in law as she shows in paragraphs 9–12.

Rhetorical Considerations

1. Words such as "hath shown" ("shewn" in the original Declaration) and phrases such as "hitherto occupied" and "evinces a design to reduce them under absolute despotism" come directly from the model. Even though this was archaic diction for Stanton's time, she was attempting to emulate the Declaration of Independence by using the same words all Americans recognized from this document. The closer her own declaration is to the original model, the more it is equated with Jefferson's august and revolutionary purpose.

2. In paragraph 3 Stanton states "the history of mankind is a history of repeated injuries and usurpations on the part of man toward woman. ..." The same phrase in the Declaration of Independence is "The history of the present king of Great Britain is a history of repeated injuries and usurpations. ..." Stanton follows her model by beginning her list of these "injuries and usurpations" in paragraphs 4–18 with the singular pronoun "he" to suggest that the generalized American man is just as reprehensible toward woman as George III was toward the colonists.

3. In paragraph 20 Stanton declares presciently, "in entering upon the great work before us, we anticipate no small amount of misconception, misrepresentation, and ridicule. ..." In fact, the entire women's equal rights movement has aroused the same feelings throughout its history.

4. Since Stanton calls her work a "Declaration of Sentiments and Resolutions," it is not surprising that she lists these resolutions separately, after she has established her format from the Declaration of Independence. Presumably by this time her readers would have accepted the borrowed sanctity of her declaration and would be ready for Stanton's original format.

5. Although students may suggest that the argument could be improved by updating the language, most of the declaration is still valid and comprehensible, even after almost 150 years. If the language is updated and the format is modernized, the document loses its ties to the Declaration of Independence.

6. The language is formal, which is fitting for an important social manifesto. Paragraphs 4–18 contain parallel sentence structure beginning with the phrase, "He has," a sign of formality. The resolutions found in paragraphs 21–33, are parallel also. Sentence length also indicates formality, as does the serious tone of the essay. Inverted sentence structure, such as "As a teacher of theology, medicine, or law, she is not known," found in paragraph 13 indicates formal structure as well. In paragraph 32 the phrase "the hoary sanction of antiquity" could also be considered formal.

On the Natural Superiority of the Aryan Race
Adolf Hitler

Topical Considerations

1. Hitler's opening statement is the inverse of Plato's allegory in that Plato compares the truth to the sun, asserting that it is too brilliant to be seen by the "naked" eye. Hitler, on the other hand, states that truths are too obvious and familiar to be recognized. The kind of truths that are too obvious to be seen would most certainly be represented by Plato in terms of the shadows in the cave: not truths at all, but only false representations or perceptions of truth. Plato would not agree with Hitler's use of the term "truth" in this context because for Plato the truth represented an "ideal," unalterable and brilliant. In Hitler's essay the "truth" of racial purity or the consequences of racial "impurity" is manipulated for the political ends of a madman.

2. Open for discussion. A discussion of the term "Aryan" might be useful here meaning "a non-Jewish Caucasian," or, in Hitler's mind, a member of the "master" race. It might also be useful to cover the relationship between Darwinism and Hitler's racial theory, as well as the historical atrocities of his extermination of the Jewish race.

3. The main fallacy of Hitler's argument is the lack of parallel between human and animal survival motives: that animals act purely on instinct in the interest of survival (especially in terms of instinctive activities like mating), while humans have the ability to reason, think, speak, and love (capabilities that preclude us from acting on survival instinct alone).

4. Darwin's belief in God and creation has long been debated. While it is known that he did indeed have a strong faith in God, it is also true that his theory of evolution undermines religious theories of creation. For that reason alone, Hitler's assertion that to "impurify a race is a sin against the eternal creator" is an ineffective mixing of opposing terms and theories. It becomes even more problematic for Hitler to call upon a morality that he so completely eschewed in his murderous acts against Jews and other non-Aryans during the Nazi reign.

5. Hitler calls "pacifism" contrary to Nature and reason. In his view the human precondition is one of eternal struggle, and any other view is seen by him as weak and "Jewish." Open for discussion.

6. Hitler's statement is absolutely paradoxical in that his prescription for the avoidance of "barbarism" and the maintenance of "ethical ideas" (fascism, war, and the extermination of Jews and other "non–Aryan" races) is infintely barbaric and contrary to any moral or ethical code.

7. Open for discussion.

Rhetorical Considerations

1. Hitler's tone is one of bombast and self-righteousness. He also structures his arguments in the form of strict logic, a form that attempts to veil the frequent fallacies in his arguments. Open for discussion.

2. Open for discussion.

3. Hitler's first mistake is the fact that he bases a positivistic assertion for all races on "data" gleaned about one race. Second, his "data" is completely subjective, based on wrongly conceived racist stereotypes, and therefore carries the reliability and "logic" of an opinion.

4. Hitler makes outrageous statements in these passages, replacing hard evidence or fact with absurd racist rhetoric.

5. Hitler "addresses" his opposition by dismissing them: "Even if this were hard—that's how it is!"

6. In his closing paragraph Hitler calls up all sorts of hyperbolical racist rhetoric, employing the myth of Prometheus to represent his Aryan race and evoking the threat of "darkness" descending on the earth, the passage of human culture and the transformation of the world into a desert as a warning of what will happen if the races are allowed to become "impure." Open for discussion.

Warfare: An Invention—Not a Biological Necessity
Margaret Mead

Topical Considerations

1. Mead says the three views of war are: (1) "a biological necessity"; (2) "a sociological inevitability"; and (3) "just a bad invention." The compromise position between the extremes of biological necessity and sociological inevitabil-

ity is this: "all aggression springs from the frustration of man's biologically determined drives and that, since all forms of culture are frustrating, it is certain each new generation will be aggressive in race war, class war, nationalistic war, and so on." Students will have their own views on war—views that may change after reading Mead's article.

2. Mead defines warfare in paragraph 3 as "organized conflict between two groups *as groups,* in which each group puts an army . . . into the field to fight and kill, if possible, some of the members of the army of the other group. . . ." According to those who take the position that war is a sociological inevitability, war cannot be eliminated "unless we change our social system and outlaw classes, the struggle for power, and possessions. . . ." Students might feel that these conditions will never come about and can point to any of the dozens of wars taking place at any one time in the world.

3. Mead states that war is an invention "like any other of the inventions in terms of which we order our lives, such as writing, marriage, cooking our food instead of eating it raw, trial by jury, or burial of the dead. . . ." Even those inventions that we think of as universal attributes of humanity—for example, marriage or the use of fire—had to be invented "if human history was to take the turn it has taken," according to Mead. In paragraph 8 she restates her contention, "If a people have an idea of going to war and the idea that war is the way in which certain situations . . . are to be handled, they will sometimes go to war."

   Mead offers the Eskimos and Lepchas of Sikkim as examples of people who, even today, have no warfare. It may seem natural that the Lepchas, a "gentle, unquarrelsome people" do not have war; but the Eskimos, who are "turbulent and troublesome," also have no war. However, other relatively "uncivilized" peoples who hunt and gather do practice war. For instance, some tribes in Papua New Guinea, the Pygmy peoples of the Andaman Islands, and some Australian aborigines.

4. People such as the Balinese deal with quarrels between individuals by registering their complaints with the gods in the temple and swearing never to speak to each other again. Other people go to war "merely for glory" of winning "prestige which within that tribe has been declared obtainable only by war and without which that no young man can hope to win his sweetheart's smile of approval." They treat war as a game to prove manliness. Students might point to the bands of snipers in some of the populated though ruined cities of former Yugoslavia as men who take war as a game—each kill adding to their scorecard. In fact, one might generalize that to some men war is fun since it is a chance to play soldiers for real, to use real weapons, to bond with other men, to get their aggressions out, to kill with minimal moral conflict, to get paid for doing it, to live dangerously.

5. For a new invention to take place of the old warfare, Mead says that two conditions are necessary. First, people "must recognize the defects of the old invention"; second, "someone must make a new one." Although Mead says

it is possible to teach people to feel that warfare is a "defective social institution" and to make them believe there are new methods to make war obsolete, she does not describe these new inventions. Therefore, her answer leaves her reader unsatisfied.

6. Students will formulate their own responses to the question whether Mead's argument is logical or not. They may find her examples of primitive tribes convincing that warfare is an invention is true. Modern people go to war to protect their territory from those who would take it over, such as the ongoing conflict between Israelis and Palestinians. People also make war on those who would usurp their power, such as the warlords in Somalia. But the most frequent reason people to go war today seems to be rooted in ethnic or religious intolerance—for example, India and Pakistan, Northern Ireland, Serbs and Bosnians, Iraq and the Kurds, Armenians and Azeris, etc. Of course, Mead may not agree that the limited conflicts between these modern tribes constitute war, according to her limited definition of war. But for the most part they are. The root conflicts are not cited by Mead in her accounts of primitive tribal warfare.

Rhetorical Considerations

1. Mead's thesis is that war is a bad invention of the human race. She begins the essay questioning this statement, and repeats her thesis in various forms in paragraphs 3, 8 and 10–14. She attempts to demonstrate her thesis with examples of primitive peoples, but she doesn't "prove" that other good inventions can and will replace warfare.

2. This is an inductive argument since Mead starts out with her thesis and attempts to prove it with supporting evidence.

3. Mead begins the essay by referring to William James' essay that puts forth the biological necessity of warfare. His thesis is that this human aggression must be channeled into other outlets. This is the only instance in the essay where Mead names an opponent. She does refer to other questions about her thesis, such as in paragraph 10 when she writes about the congruence between warfare and warlike people. In paragraph 12 she again questions herself and asks what we are to do about war, granting that "war is an invention, that it is not a biological necessity nor the outcome of certain special types of social forms." Obviously Mead does not concede any points about her thesis to her opponents, although she does acknowledge how difficult it is to change this invention. Students may find Mead's tactics weaken her argument.

4. Mead needs more evidence to prove that good inventions can and will replace bad ones, such as trial by jury replacing trial by ordeal and by combat. One example is not enough to convince most people, even though they would like to believe that sometimes war can be replaced by some other invention.

The Obligation to Endure
Rachel Carson

Topical Considerations

1. Banned in the United States and other countries, DDT (2,2-bis-1,1,1,-trichloroethane, chlorinated hydrocarbon compound) was first used in the 1940s to kill insects that feed on crops and spread diseases such as malaria. DDT enters the food chain in the lower forms of life and passes on to higher organisms, resulting in widespread calamities as the well-publicized near-destruction of such birds as eagles. When the DDT invades the life cycle of eagles and other birds, the eggs they lay have shells so fragile that they break before the new birds are born.

2. Because scientists introduce more than 500 new chemicals a year into the atmosphere, humans and animals cannot adjust or adapt to these chemicals; nor could they even if they had eons of time, which they don't.

3. Albert Schweitzer was the famous theologian, musician, and medical missionary who established and managed a hospital at Lambarene, Gabon from 1913 until his death in 1965. His concept, "Reverence for Life" demanded a respect for the lives of all beings. Carson alludes to Schweitzer's reputation and his philosophy when she mentions him. The quotation points to the many problems created by our use of chemicals—problems beyond those ever dreamed of by the creators.

4. According to Carson in paragraph 9, the two greatest probems we face are the "extinction of mankind by nuclear war" and the "contamination of man's total environment with . . . substances of incredible potential for harm. . . ." Although neither problem has been resolved, the dissolution of the Soviet Union has lessened the possibility of nuclear war. Of course, many smaller and unstable countries either have or will have nuclear bombs, such as Pakistan and communist North Korea, and the various republics of the former Soviet Union. In spite of the banning of the use of DDT, other toxic chemicals continue to be used to control pests in large agricultural areas—for example, the insecticides used on table grapes in California, which are reported to be highly toxic to the pickers. Another current problem is the difficulty of cleaning up dumping sites of various chemicals, such as the notorious Love Canal site.

5. Carson says that insects come into conflict with humans because of our crowded cities where sanitation is poor. The other major reason is single-crop farming, as opposed to crop diversification, which inhibits the growth of pests afflicting only one variety. To demonstrate the problems brought on by single-species planting, she points to the sorry fate of elm trees, which once lined Main Streets of rural America but were ravaged by the Dutch elm beetle. Had a variety of trees interspersed the elms, the beetles would have been kept in check, she argues.

6. Students' answers will vary. Optimists can discuss various citizen groups dedicated to protecting the environment—for example, the Audubon Soci-

ety. They can point to recent administrations sympathetic to ecological problems. Pessimists, on the other hand, will remind us that the United States is the most wasteful and consumptive nation in the world. Furthermore, they can point to Brazil's destruction of the rain-forest habitats of thousands of flora and fauna all for the sake of increasing subsistence crop farmland and grazing pastures for cattle.

Rhetorical Considerations

1. This essay is divided into two parts (paragraphs 1–12, and 13–end). Carson's claim for the first part appears in paragraph 12. After stating that there is an insect problem and a need of control, she writes: "I am saying, rather, that control [of insect infestation] must be geared to realities . . . and that the methods employed must be such that they do not destroy us along with the insects." In the second part of the essay she sums up her previous argument by stressing that it is not her "contention that chemical insecticides must never be used," but that "we have put poisonous and biologically potent chemical indiscriminately into the hands of persons largely or wholly ignorant of their potential for harm." She further contends that "enormous numbers of people" have been subjected to these chemicals without their knowledge, and that little or no "advance investigation of their effect on soil, water, wildlife, and man himself" has been done. These contentions are powerful support for her recommendations to do something about the indiscriminate use of insecticides.

2. The concept is that humankind has a right if not an obligation to endure as a species and, therefore, a right to know just exactly what chemicals are being used indiscriminately by people ignorant of their potential for long term destruction. Carson argues that it is the public that must decide what course to take, and the public can do this only "in full possession of the facts." While the title does not predict all the points of Carson's argument, it does prepare the reader for the urgency regarding the threat to life by wanton use of chemicals. The title serves as Carson's call to arms.

3. These quotations from Elton's book, *The Ecology of Invasions,* are intended to prove Carson's statements about the recent importation of new species into new territories. The original species, which were confined into "colossal, separate nature reserves" with the floods of the Cretaceous Period, began their movement to new territories when the land masses rejoined. This situation has been repeated on a much grander, immediate scale with the introduction of new species into the United States. Most of these new insect enemies have come as plant hitchhikers.

4. Except in the statements (framed in double negatives) in paragraphs 12 and 24, Carson has little positive to say about her opponents' arguments. She refers to "the crusade to create a chemically sterile, insect-free world [which] seems to have engendered a fanatic zeal on the part of many specialists and most of the so-called control agencies. On every hand there is evidence that

those engaged in spraying operations exercise a ruthless power." Here, as well as elsewhere, she may be guilty of bad-mouthing her opponents. It can be urged that the urgency of her case, nonetheless, warrants such strong language.

5. See the poetic descriptions in paragraph 4, especially: "the calcium and silica and copper and all the rest of the minerals washed out of the rocks and carried in rivers to the sea. . . ." Also in paragraph 7: ". . . nonselective chemicals that have the power to kill every insect, the 'good' and the 'bad,' to still the song of the birds and the leaping of fish in the streams, to coat the leaves with a deadly film, and to linger on in soil."

Letter from Birmingham Jail
Martin Luther King, Jr.

Topical Considerations

1. In paragraph 6 King spells out the four basic steps of nonviolent campaigning: collection of acts; negotiation; self-purification; and direct action. It may be helpful also to refer to the Christian notion that King advocates of "turning the other cheek." Also, the nonviolent movement might be contrasted with other protest movements that are not based upon nonviolence. You might bring up the vocal appeals to nonviolence following the Los Angeles riots of 1992. Open for discussion.

2. Open for discussion.

3. It may be helpful for this discussion to provide a definition of "status quo," not only as the existing condition or state of things, but also in its somewhat pejorative sense of the maintenance of systems that are entrenched but no longer useful, held in place by reactionaries and power seekers.

4. It is a Christian tenet that sins stem both from what is done and what is left undone. In that context, those who maintain silence in the face of the terrible injustice shown to blacks in the civil rights movement are committing the sin of leaving undone necessary deeds. This problem is felt today in terms of the seemingly pervasive social and political apathy in America.

5. King bases his civil rights campaign upon the moral tenets of the Christian church. As is evident in his letter, the two are inextricable. Without Christianity as his working philosophy, King might not have advocated nonviolence or "turning the other cheek," thereby changing drastically the face of the movement itself. Open for discussion.

6. Racial oppression and economic oppression are virtually inseparable. One cannot be examined without the other: The cycle of poverty and lack of opportunity are major contributing factors to the concentration of certain races and ethnic groups in "ghetto" areas. These areas are rife with problems of drugs, crime and disease, conditions that, in turn, perpetuate the marginalization and oppression of such groups. This oppression, then, takes place on the level of race and ethnicity but is manifested through class.

7. King is most commonly remembered for his Christian campaign of nonviolent protest, while Malcolm X is more controversially linked with the Muslim Movement, perceived as a Black nationalist, separatist movement that advocated violence. Attention may be drawn to current renewed interest in Malcolm X as a man who did not, in fact, preach separatism and violence but who did claim that civil rights should be achieved "by any means necessary." Open for discussion.

Rhetorical Considerations

1. King's strategy is effective in that he is addressing fellow clergymen of the Christian church. By establishing himself as a Christian, and, further, by setting up a comparison between his work and that of the Apostle Paul, he successfully legitimizes his position and authority.

2. In his letter, King consistently addresses his opposition by anticipating their questions, which he then answers in terms of his own philosophy. In this instance, he acknowledges the correctness of the position of his opposition and then shows why his method is the best means of maintaining that position. This techniques leaves very little room for further argument from his opposition.

3. In this passage King uses an emotional appeal in the form of a long list of injustices committed against the black community. The effect of placing such a catalogue of emotionally moving facts one after another is to raise the reader's consciousness as to the seriousness and extent of injustice, a tactic that also leaves the reader nearly incapable to rebut his argument.

4. King calls upon two Christian theological and philosophical authorities (St. Thomas Aquinas and St. Augustine) as foundation for his logical position that segregation cannot be considered a just law because it is a human law unrooted in eternal and natural law. Therefore, as he has established that segregation is not a just law, it follows that "one has a moral responsibility to disobey unjust laws."

5. Open for discussion. The rationality and firmness of King's voice in this letter is often remarked on as is the seamless logic of his arguments. He establishes credibility by aligning himself with a particular moral position and alluding to authorites of that position in his arguments.

6. King is known for his speaking ability. This letter, which follows the tradition of Christian sermons, would be highly effective if delivered orally. It might be useful to show a videotape of King's "I Have a Dream" speech to give students a sense of his acclaimed oratorical style.